D0181159

OREGON

REVISED BY JUDY JEWELL & BILL MCRAE

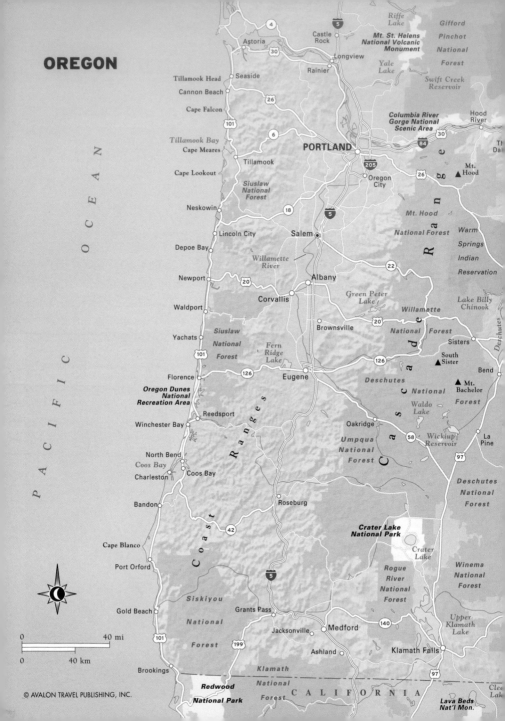

DISCOVER OREGON

Within the boundaries of Oregon are some of
the nation's most diverse landscapes. To the west, the state's rugged
coastline is pounded by the waves of the Pacific Ocean. Much of
this coastline – remarkably undeveloped for such a dramatic piece
of real estate – is preserved in state parks (Oregon has over 200).
A number of towns – Astoria, Cannon Beach, Newport, Florence,
Bandon, and Port Orford – are charming coastal destinations and
provide easy-going lodgings and tourist facilities.

The Pacific's moist air and moderate temperatures flow inland to
create forests and farmlands of legendary fertility: this was the Eden
sought by the Oregon Trail pioneers from the 1830s to the 1860s. The
Willamette Valley, capped by the state's largest city, Portland, is home
to two-thirds of the state's population, as well as farms, orchards,
vineyards, and captivating smaller cities, such as the university center
of Eugene. The spine of Oregon is the towering Cascade Range, a
string of glacier-capped volcanic peaks that rise above the state like

Downtown Portland, as viewed from the Eastbank Esplanade

© BILL MCRAE

a row of incisors. The eastern two-thirds of Oregon is high desert, with miles and miles of rangeland cut by deep river canyons and spiked with arid mountain ranges. Here, where cattle ranches and golf resorts dot the countryside beneath year-round blue skies, the major destination is Bend, a haven for hikers, skiers, mountain bikers, and golfers. On Oregon's southern border is Ashland, home to the superlative Oregon Shakespeare Festival and a bevy of enchanting bed-and-breakfast inns, while along the northern border flows the mighty Columbia River. The river, over a mile wide, winds through the 3,000-foot-deep Columbia Gorge, flanked by volcanic peaks and laced with delicate waterfalls that plunge over brooding basalt cliffs.

The land is truly epic in its breadth and drama, but Oregon is much more than a scenic abstraction. In few places has human civilization meshed so agreeably with the environment. A history of progressive land-use policies, which have preserved vast tracts of irreplaceable land and helped curb the blight of suburban sprawl,

Columbia River from Rowena Crest

© BILL MCRAE

attest to Oregonians' appreciation of their gemlike coastline, productive farmland, mountain ranges, and other unspoiled landscapes.

In other words, what helps make Oregon unique is the attitude of its citizens, who are fiercely proud of their state, its culture and its open spaces. To a remarkable degree, Oregon remains a community that is still environmentally, socially, and culturally intact. Equal to the great outdoors, the arts are cherished here; music, dance, theater, and a myriad of visual arts enrich the lives of residents and draw visitors by the multitude. The state also celebrates its historical heritage, ethnic makeup, and straightforward high spirits in a thousand festivals. And the food? With the same latitude and a similar climate to France, much of Oregon is quite simply a huge garden where the finest vegetables, fruit, wine grapes, and farm and ranch products reach perfection. Mighty rivers and 360 miles of Pacific coast provide succulent shellfish, plus salmon, tuna, and halibut of high distinction. Visit a farmers market during your visit – nearly 70 Oregon cities and towns have community markets that bring local produce, cheese, meats, baked goods, seafood, and wine directly

Peterson's Rock Garden is a monument to one man's obsession.

from producers to consumers – to marvel at Oregon's incredible natural bounty.

The rewards of the good life didn't come easily, though. It took Oregon Trail pioneers many months to cross 2,000 miles of treacherous deserts and forbidding mountain passes to reach this promised land during the mid-19th century. This pioneer determination was born of something more than the desire for wealth. It is significant that Oregon was settled not by single-minded prospectors who came west looking for gold, but by young idealistic farmers seeking an agrarian utopia. This focused purposefulness still informs Oregon's attitudes to its civic culture, environment, and quality of daily life in ways that make Oregon sometimes seem old-fashioned or out of the mainstream. It's this slight skewing of the average that leads one of our Canadian friends to note that Oregon is the most Canadian state in the United States, and is perhaps what the *New York Times* had in mind when it claimed that Portland was this country's most European city. Whether it's "three-days-and-four-plays" at the Oregon Shakespeare Festival in Ashland or shopping for wild morel

Hosmer Lake with Mount Bachelor in the background

mushrooms at the Sisters farmers market; dueling pinot noir tastings in Carlton or kite boarding on the Columbia River near Hood River, you'll find that Oregonians engage with everyday life with a verve and spirit that's at once intensely local yet tied to a larger, more universal perspective.

Oregonians like to tell a fable about a crossroads on the old Oregon Trail. Pointing south toward the California gold fields was a sign with a drawing of a bag of gold. Pointing north was another sign with the words "To Oregon." The punch line? Only those pioneers who could read continued to Oregon.

Of course, the Oregon Trail is history now, but that doesn't mean that the movement to Oregon is over. The same vaguely agrarian and utopian ideals that drew the pioneers still works its magic on a new crop of young immigrants eager to move to the Beaver State to open a restaurant, start a software company, or simply seek the good life and a pint of microbrewed beer at the end of the Oregon Trail.

Crater Lake is the deepest and clearest lake in the United States.

© BILL MCRAE

Contents

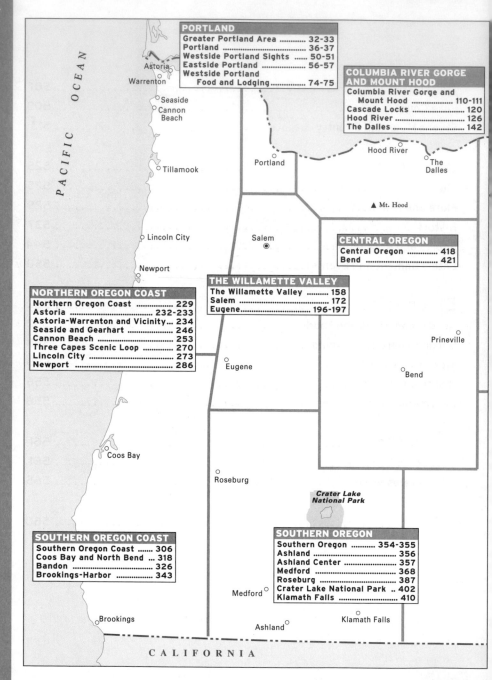

OCEAN

PACIFIC OCEAN

Astoria
Warrenton
Seaside
Cannon Beach
Tillamook
Portland
Hood River
The Dalles
▲ Mt. Hood
Lincoln City
Salem
Newport

Prineville
Eugene
Bend
Coos Bay
Roseburg

Crater Lake National Park

Medford
Brookings
Ashland
Klamath Falls

CALIFORNIA

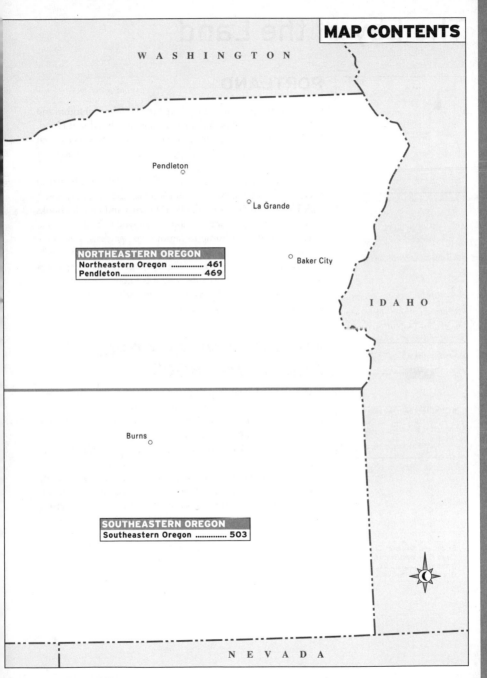

MAP CONTENTS

W A S H I N G T O N

Pendleton

La Grande

Baker City

I D A H O

Burns

N E V A D A

The Lay of the Land

PORTLAND

Graced by the presence of two large rivers—the Columbia and the Willamette—a huge urban forest, and nearby Mount Hood, Portland is the state's green, urban core. It's equal parts cultural center, marketplace, and working metropolis, and it's known as one of the nation's most livable cities.

Downtown's culture district with the Oregon Historical Society and Portland Art Museum is centered on the leafy South Park Blocks. To the north, the Pearl District and Powell's Books are each worth hours of exploration. Just west from downtown, Washington Park is home to famous rose gardens; trails here connect to Forest Park, the nation's largest urban forested park, with over 70 miles of trails. The Willamette River separates downtown from the east side, which is known for its thriving neighborhoods, each with a distinct personality and streets lined with locally owned shops and restaurants.

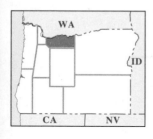

COLUMBIA RIVER GORGE AND MOUNT HOOD

This is the Northwest's primal landscape and weekend wilderness: towering waterfalls, moss-draped rainforests, snowcapped volcanoes soaring above cherry orchards—all in a sweeping chasm 5 miles wide, 80 miles long, and 4,000 feet deep.

Just as it has since it was built in the days of Model T Fords, the Historic Columbia Gorge Highway ushers travelers to Multnomah Falls and a plethora of other waterfalls and hiking trails. The gorge town of Hood River gained fame as a prime windsurfing spot; many others have discovered its lovely setting at the foot of Mount Hood. From Hood River, drive up the mountain to the landmark Timberline Lodge to more hiking trails and nearly year-round skiing.

THE WILLAMETTE VALLEY

The historic end of the Oregon Trail, the Willamette Valley is still agriculturally rich, with the emphasis now on wine grapes. Even though three-quarters of the state's population lives in the Valley, it is still largely rural, with many of the historic areas little changed. Visit Champoeg State Park, a riverside park where Oregon statehood got its start, and Salem, the state capitol. Nearly the entire west side of the valley is a wine-lovers pilgrimage route. Cycling wine country adds an active dimension to such a tour. Hike past some of the state's prettiest waterfalls at Silver Falls State Park and explore the Willamette's main tributaries, especially the wild McKenzie River. For a dose of youthful culture, visit the university towns Eugene and Corvallis.

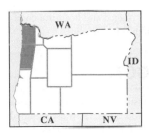

NORTHERN OREGON COAST

Sandy beaches along the northern coastline are separated by headlands, most traced by a hiking trail. Lots of beach towns, ranging from quirky spots that are lost in time to sophisticated full-service resorts, and everything in between, mean that everyone can find a place to adopt as their own.

Astoria has a rich history and is newly vibrant; Cannon Beach is an upscale Portlanders' getaway with a beautiful beach; the Three Capes Loop west of Tillamook skims through a few small towns and provides access to some spectacularly scenic beaches, including the one at Cape Kiwanda; Lincoln City's sophisticated side shows up a few miles south of town at Salishan, one of the state's finest resorts. Head out on a whale-watching tour from Depoe Bay and visit Newport's bay front and aquarium and then spend the night in the Nye Beach neighborhood. South of Yachats are the astounding tide pools and coastal old-growth forests of Cape Perpetua.

SOUTHERN OREGON COAST

Rugged rock formations jut out of the ocean along this wild stretch of coastline, where powerful rivers and broad, lazy estuaries meet the sea. The beaches here are beautiful and surprisingly uncrowded; the towns are mostly small, with struggling economies.

South of Florence you'll find the Oregon Dunes, mountains of sand that call out for exploration. West of the rather working-class port city of Coos Bay, find places to fish, surf, swim, camp, hike through an estuarine preserve, or view gardens. To the south, the charming town of Bandon is home to a world-class golf resort. At Port Orford, the coast is truly wild and rugged. Twenty-seven miles to the south, the Rogue River meets the Pacific at Gold Beach; from here, buzz upstream on a jet-boat tour. Between Gold Beach and Brookings, at the state's southern border, stretches some of the most rugged and beautiful coastline, with rocky outcroppings and hidden beaches.

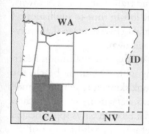

SOUTHERN OREGON

Southern Oregon is a land of opposites, ranging from Oregon's premier arts town, Ashland, to some the state's most secluded backcountry. Here you'll find well-off California retirees as well as backwoods escapees from modern urban life.

Explore the valleys of the North Umpqua and Rogue Rivers; both of these are attractive to hikers and anglers, and the raft trip down the Rogue is one of the top whitewater trips in the country. Crater Lake is the other highlight of the natural world in Southern Oregon; south of the national park, the Klamath Falls area has excellent bird-watching. Finally, no trip to Southern Oregon is complete without a stay in Ashland, known for its Shakespeare Festival, fine dining, and wealth of B&Bs.

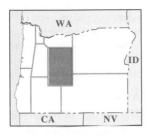

CENTRAL OREGON

The high desert of central Oregon is blanketed with lava, cut through by the Deschutes and Crooked Rivers, and dotted with volcanic peaks.

It's also a place of growth and transformation, with much of the traditional rangeland now replaced by resorts and golf courses. The energetic hub of the region is Bend, where visitors can be assured of finding good food and a comfortable place to spend the night.

For most visitors, central Oregon is above all else a recreation mecca, with many trails for hiking, mountain biking, and cross-country skiing. Mount Bachelor is the Northwest's largest ski resort, with snow often lasting into June. Raft trips vary from tame floats in downtown Bend to the rip-roaring rapids outside Maupin. Anglers dream of casting into the Crooked or Deschutes Rivers. Visit the Warm Springs Reservation to get a sense of how Native Americans lived—and still live—here.

NORTHEASTERN OREGON

You'll hear echoes of the Old West in northeastern Oregon, whether you're touring Chief Joseph's homeland, tracing the steps of the Oregon Trail's eager pioneers, or cheering the cowboys at the Pendleton Round-Up. Go even further into Oregon's past at the John Day Fossil Beds, or explore the geology of Hell's Canyon with a boat ride down the Snake River. A gondola ride to the top of Mount Howard, on the edge of Wallowa Lake, is about as fast as life gets in this region.

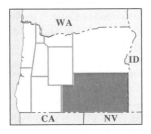

SOUTHEASTERN OREGON

This high-desert region boasts deep blue skies, geologic marvels, and plenty of elbow room. Soak in natural hot springs, view migrating birds at the vast Malheur Wildlife Refuge, and get to know your fellow travelers at the Frenchglen Hotel. A visit to this corner of Oregon will reconnect you with nature, and give you plenty of time and space for reflection.

Planning Your Trip

WHEN TO GO

Most travelers plan their Oregon trips as summer vacations, when the weather is most reliably sunny and the days are long, with daylight lasting until nearly 10 P.M. around the time of the solstice. Even in the summer season, it's worth considering a few subtle nuances, most notably the fact that June is often quite cloudy and cool in the Willamette Valley—in fact, locals will tell you that summer starts in Portland on July 5.

However, by June eastern and southern parts of the state are already getting pretty hot. Springtime is ideal for touring southeastern Oregon, unless you want to make it all the way to the top of Steens Mountain, which is usually closed by snow until early July.

Don't plan to do much hiking in the Cascades until mid-July—instead, find springtime hikes at lower elevations in the Columbia Gorge, or take a late-spring backpacking trip along the Rogue River Trail.

When the Willamette Valley heats up in the summer, the coast usually remains cool, with morning (or all-day) fog. There's much to be said for travel in the early fall, especially on the Oregon coast, when the crowds thin out and the skies are mostly clear.

Autumn's first big rains usually soak Portland in September, but October's weather often starts off clear and beautiful. Even after the rains start, remember that cloudy days with scattered rain are the norm, and that "sunbreaks" are common.

Although the mountainous parts of the state accumulate huge amounts of snow during the winter (think 13 feet at Mount Hood's ski areas), snowfall is rare on the coast and in the western valleys. Wintertime temperatures are usually above freezing, though the dampness can make it seem colder. Most Oregonians don't let the weather bother them; in Portland, you'll see bicycle commuters crossing the bridges into downtown every morning of the year, and Forest Park runners stage an informal winter solstice "Mud Grand Prix." An added bonus to winter travel is that locals have less "tourist fatigue" and are even more welcoming than usual.

WHAT TO TAKE

Oregon is notoriously casual, and it's hard to underdress here. Even Portland's finest restaurants demand no more than clean jeans and a nice shirt. That said, if it's more your style to dress up, you won't be out of place in the larger cities or resort areas.

Even in the summer, evenings (and mornings, especially on the coast) can be cool, so bring a sweater and a jacket. At any time of year, it's a good idea to pack rain gear, although you probably won't need it in the summer. In the fall, winter, and spring, it is essential; if you plan to do much hiking, biking, or skiing, breathable waterproof gear is worth the extra cost, and rainpants are a vital part of the outfit.

Aside from that, let your packing list be determined by your own inclinations. If you're camping in the mountains, it's best to have a warm sleeping bag, a fleece jacket, a tent with a rain fly, and a ground cloth. If you're not car camping, bring a rope and a stuff bag to hang your food from a tree.

If you're a birder, you won't forget to pack binoculars and a field guide, but other travelers should also consider bringing these along. No matter where you travel in Oregon, you're likely to see some sort of wildlife, and it will make your trip a richer experience if you take some time to look at it.

Finally, if you are traveling into the mountains in the winter, make sure your car has tire chains in the trunk. During snowstorms, many mountain passes are closed to vehicles without chains, and the state patrol takes the task of enforcing this requirement very seriously.

Explore Oregon

THE BEST OF OREGON

It's almost impossible to cover all of Oregon in a week, so we've crafted a 10-day tour that hits most of the highlights. Don't take this itinerary too seriously—although we think it would be a great trip, don't hesitate to stay longer at one site, or discover your own favorite places along this route. Also, since this is a "best of" tour, we haven't gone the budget route; feel free to find less expensive lodging options in the travel chapters of this book.

With a mere ten days to explore the entire state in this itinerary, we couldn't quite get you into the heart of eastern Oregon, but that doesn't mean we don't highly recommend this part of the state. In fact, we like it so much we've devoted an entire itinerary to it (see *Eastern Oregon Ramble*, below).

Day 1

Fly into **Portland** and either pick up a rental car at the airport or take the MAX light rail train into town and arrange to get a rental car in downtown Portland. Spend the afternoon strolling around downtown, visiting **Powell's Books** and the **Pearl District**. Spend the night at the Heathman Hotel and dine at nearby Higgins.

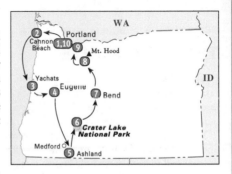

Day 2

Head northwest out of Portland on U.S. 30 to **Astoria**. Explore this historic town at the mouth of the Columbia River, including a visit to the replica of Fort Clatsop, which served as Lewis and Clark's winter home in 1805–1806. Then continue south and spend night in Cannon Beach at the Stephanie Inn.

Day 3

Head south out of town on U.S. 101, and stop for a walk at **Oswald West State Park**, where you can follow the trail to Short Sands Beach to watch surfers. Continue down the coast as far as **Yachats** and spend the night at Overleaf Lodge. Eat dinner at the Drift Inn.

Day 4

Spend the morning exploring the tide pools and old-growth forest around **Cape Perpetua**.

Take a tour of **Sea Lion Caves** (or just peer down from the road with your binos). From the seaside town of Florence, cut east on Route 126 to **Eugene**, with a detour south to Lorane for a visit to the King Estate Winery tasting room. Spend the night near Eugene's riverside trails at the Campbell House B&B.

Day 5

Drive south along I-5 to **Ashland** and a play. Dine at New Sammy's Cowboy Bistro (reserve well in advance) or Amuse and spend the night at the Ashland Springs Hotel.

Day 6

From Medford, just north of Ashland, drive up the Rogue River on ORE 62 through the tiny towns of Prospect and Union Creek to **Crater Lake**

National Park, where you'll spend the night at the Crater Lake Lodge.

Day 7

Head north on Route 97 to **Bend,** visiting the Lava Lands Visitor Center and High Desert Museum on the way. Stay at McMenamin's Old St. Francis School.

Day 8

Continue north to **Maupin** to meet your raft guide for a day-long float down the Deschutes. At the end of the day, drive up **Mount Hood** and spend the night at Timberline Lodge.

Day 9

Hike along the **Timberline Trail** (or spend the morning skiing-even in August) and then drive to Hood River. Take a hike to Upper Horsetail Falls and then continue west to **Troutdale,** where you'll spend your final night at the old county poorfarm, now McMenamin's Edgefield Lodge.

Day 10

It doesn't take long to get from Edgefield to the Portland airport, about 20 minutes. If you have a late flight, spend the day in **Portland,** visiting Washington and Forest Parks.

THE WINE ROUTE

Oregon wines have been in the news ever since the 1980s when a Willamette Valley pinot noir came in second in a blind tasting in France—defeating a field of more expensive and highly esteemed French burgundies. Today there are around 350 wineries in the state, producing more than a million cases per year and contributing about $1.4 billion to the state's economy.

Wine grape production now takes place across the state, everywhere except the dry rangelands of eastern Oregon. Planning a trip through Oregon's many wine regions is a good way to explore the state and to track down little-known vintages that don't make it across state lines.

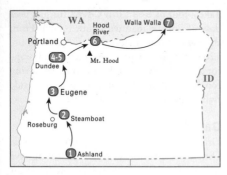

Day 1

Start your wine odyssey in Ashland, where Shakespeare and fine restaurants make good companions for wine exploration. Near town is **Ashland Vineyards,** famous for the white wine Shakespeare's Love, and **Weisinger's Vineyard,** which produces fine gewürztraminer and cabernet sauvignon. The area's best wines, and the greatest concentration of wineries, are over the ridge in the Applegate Valley. Here high summer heat enables the production of red wines such as cabernet and syrah, and some California–style chardonnays; check out the wines at **Valley View Winery** or **Troon Vineyard.** Spend the night at the Ashland Creek Inn, a luxury inn right on the water, and dine at Peerless Restaurant, known for its wine cellar and dedication to regional foods.

Day 2

Travel north toward Roseburg, central for the wines of the **Umpqua Valley. Abacela**

Vineyards and Winery is noted for the many variety of wine grapes it grows, offering unusual-for-Oregon Italian varietals such as tempranillo, dolcetto, and sangiovese. Henry Estate Winery is one of the state's oldest, and has lovely gardens that make an excellent picnic destination. The wines here range from full-bodied pinot noir and merlot to refreshing riesling. Girardet Wine Cellars produces a range of wines, such as chardonnay, cabernet sauvignon, and pinot noir, and also makes wine from more unusual grapes such as Baco Noir and Marechal Foch. Drive 38 miles up the North Umpqua for the region's best dining and lodging choice, the historic Steamboat Inn.

Day 3

Continue north to Eugene, at the southern edge of the Willamette Valley, Oregon's primary wine growing region. Here the weather is cooler than the Umpqua and Applegate valleys, favoring the production of pinot noir and chardonnay, the grapes of France's Burgundy valley, as well as pinot gris, from northern Italy and the French Alsace region. Near Eugene be sure to stop at King Estate Winery, with a hilltop tasting and wine-making facility near Lorane that's (literally) palatial. Territorial Vineyards & Wine Company has vineyards near the Coast Range but a wine-making facility and tasting room in downtown Eugene. From their estate-grown pinot noir grapes, Territorial makes a series of regular pinot noir bottlings and a fantastic rosé. Make dinner reservations at Marche restaurant, and spend the night at the Campbell House B&B, an 1892 mansion.

Days 4 and 5

Between Rickreal and Carlton, on the west side of the Willamette Valley, is the greatest concentration of wineries in the state. Here are the pinot noir vineyards that have put Oregon on the world wine map. With over 200 wineries in a relatively compact area, there's no single route

to recommend, so pick up a copy of the widely available Willamette Valley Winery Association's winery map, and follow your instincts. Not to miss, however, is Sokol Blosser vineyards perched on a hill just above Dundee. Domaine Drouhin, also near Dundee, is the Oregon outpost of France's famed Drouhin family and makes excellent pinot noirs in the Burgundy style. Anne Amie Vineyards makes fine pinots and has a beautiful facility with one of the most panoramic views in the valley. The Rex Hill Vineyards is just east of Newberg, and is one of the closest vineyards to Portland, with premium pinot and a lovely garden setting.

If it seems like there are just too many wineries to choose from, consider a stop at the Oregon Wine Tasting Room, on Route 18 southwest of McMinnville, a tasting room and wine shop with wines from over 80 Oregon winerie. Also try The Tasting Room in downtown Carlton, in the lobby of a century-old bank, which offers a selection of wines from many smaller wineries that don't have their own tasting facilities. Also in Carlton is the Carlton Winemakers Studio, a cooperative where small winemakers share a wine-making facility and tasting room. Stay at the Wine Country Farm bed-and-breakfast, at the same location as Wine Country Farm Cellars in Dayton, and plan to dine at Joel Palmer House, one of Oregon's top restaurants.

Day 6

Drive north through Portland on I-5 then out to the Columbia River Gorge on I-84. Here, microclimates create niches where cool-climate grapes like pinot noir thrive, while just up the road syrah and merlot vineyards may be planted, which require intense summer heat to ripen. There are wineries on both sides the Oregon and Washington sides of the Gorge, so don't hesitate to cross bridges to taste wine. Across the Columbia in Bingen is Gorge Wine Merchants, which carries wines from most Gorge wineries, including such notable producers as Syncline and Cor Cellars, and offers about 20 different bottles for tasting. Also in Bingen is a tasting room for **Bad Seed Cider House,** which produces boutique apple and pear hard cider. Stay at the grand and historic Columbia Gorge Hotel in Hood River and dine at Celilo Restaurant and Bar, for sophisticated fine dining and a wine list rich in local vintages.

Day 7

Continue up the Columbia Gorge to Pendleton, where you can book a room then continue north toward Walla Walla, Washington, on Highway 11. About a third of the official Walla Walla wine growing area is in Oregon, and several tasting rooms here merit serious attention from lovers of cabernet and merlot.

NATURAL HISTORY ROAD TRIP

On this tour, be prepared to camp or stay in more rustic lodgings. Apart from the price of gas, this is a pretty low-cost tour. If you are serious about watching wildlife, recognize that sitting and waiting is the key element to successful viewing, and plan to spend more than a day at each location.

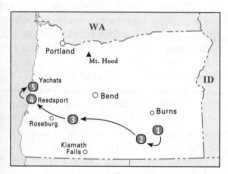

Day 1

From Bend, it's roughly 130 miles along Route 20 to Burns. Head to the big lakes and irrigation canals south of Burns at the **Malheur Wildlife Refuge.** Here you'll find a wide variety of migratory birds, especially waterfowl. If you have time, spend a day driving up **Steens Mountain,** where wild mustangs live in the Kiger Gorge. Even if the horses elude you, you're sure to see raptors. Camp at Page Springs or stay in a trailer at the Malheur Field Station.

Day 2

From the town of **Frenchglen** near the refuge's southern border, head west across

the **Hart Mountain National Antelope Refuge,** known for its pronghorn. Camp at the refuge campground (and soak in the adjacent hot springs) or spend the night in Lakeview at Hunter's Hot Springs motel.

Day 3

From Lakeview, head west across Highway 140 to **Klamath Falls,** with birding on Klamath Lake. From Klamath Falls, take U.S. 97 north to **Diamond Lake** and stay at a campground or in a cabin at Diamond Lake Resort. If by now your credit card is burning a hole in your pocket, air it out by staying at the Steamboat Inn, west of Diamond Lake along the North Umpqua River.

Day 4

From Diamond Lake, go west on Highway 138 and along the **North Umpqua River** for an immersion in west side forests and fish. From the I-5 town of Roseburg, continue west to **Reedsport** to see the Oregon Dunes. Camp at the dunes and explore the unique coastal ecosystem here.

Day 5

Finally, head north to **Sea Lion Caves** and

the tidepools of **Cape Perpetua**. There's a campground at Cape Perpetua and the reasonably priced beachfront Yachats Inn in Yachats. The streams that flow into the ocean at Cape Perpetua are surrounded by protected coastal old-growth forest.

FOLLOWING THE OREGON TRAIL

Follow the wagon tire ruts from desert landscapes near the Snake River Crossing near Ontario all the way west to the verdant end of the trail in the Willamette Valley.

Day 1

Cross the Snake River from Idaho into Oregon on I-84, but leave the freeway at Ontario and take U.S. 26 west 17 miles to Vale, where you can still see the deep ruts from pioneer wagons at the **Keeney Pass Oregon Trail Historic Site.** Then head back to I-84 and continue to **Farewell Bend State Park,** which marks the spot where the pioneers rested before leaving the Snake River heading toward the Blue Mountains. If you're feeling like resting here also, the state park has nice cabins. Otherwise, head on to Baker City and bed down there.

Day 2

In **Baker City,** visit the **National Historic Oregon Trail Visitor Center,** walk down the hill from the museum to see more ruts, then continue north to spend the night in **La Grande.** If you'd rather not drive the freeway, take the North Powder exit from I-84 and go to La Grande via County Road 237.

Day 3

In La Grande, the wagon trains paused before crossing the Blue Mountains. When you leave La Grande, you, like the Oregon Trail pioneers who preceded you, will have to cross the Blues. In fair weather, this isn't a problem, but the pass can get hairy when storms come through. At the top, take exit 284 off I-84 to visit the **Oregon Trail Interpretive Park,** an especially interesting rut site where actors in period dress will talk with you as you hike the trails. Head north on I-84 to Pendleton, and follow Old Pendleton Road along the Umatilla River to an interpretive site that marks the spot where the Oregon Trail crossed the Umatilla. Continue west on I-84 to **The Dalles** and spend the night here.

Day 4

At **The Dalles,** the wagon train parties had to decide whether to travel down the Columbia River with wagons packed onto boats—a risky and expensive venture—or make the agonizing trip over Mount Hood via the Barlow Road. Visit some sites on the Barlow Road by taking I-84 to Hood River, then turning south and following Highway 35 up Mount Hood to its junction with U.S. 26, which follows the route of Barlow Road as it comes down off the mountain. Turn west off 26 at Boring, and follow Highway 212 to I-205; take I-205 south to **Oregon City** and the **End of the Trail Interpretive Center.**

CAMPING THE BEAVER STATE

This itinerary showcases ten of our favorite campgrounds. Although it involves a lot of driving, and might be better done as a series of shorter trips by region, we invite you to share our ideal camping tour of Oregon.

SOUTHERN OREGON COAST

Start this tour on the southern Oregon coast, where, just north of Port Orford and Humbug Mountain, you'll find the beautiful and often-blustery **Cape Blanco State Park** campground at the state's westernmost point. Campground trails lead down to the beach and to the nearby lighthouse.

North on U.S. 101, between Florence and Yachats, **Carl G. Washburne Memorial State Park** is another coastal classic. Pile your gear into a wheelbarrow (provided) and trundle it to one of the great walk-in campsites. After pitching the tent, take a hike along the Hobbit Trail.

THE WILLAMETTE VALLEY

From Florence, head east, passing through Eugene and up the McKenzie River on Route 126 until you find Paradise. **Paradise Campground** is just about 50 miles east of Eugene on the McKenzie River, with access to the 26.5-mile McKenzie River National Recreation Trail and the nearby commercially developed but still appealing Belknap Lodge and Hot Springs.

Follow Route 126 as it turns north. When it hits U.S. 20, drive east for a few miles, then north on Route 22 to Detroit Lake. From the crossroads town of Detroit, turn up Forest Service Road 46 toward Breitenbush. Camp at **Cleator Bend Campground,** nine miles north of Detroit on the Breitenbush River just a short distance from Breitenbush Hot Springs.

If you're obsessed with the quest for a truly top-notch campground with great lakeside views of Mount Jefferson, and you've got a sturdy car with decent clearance, continue along Forest Service Road 46, turn right onto Road 4690, and follow it 13 slow miles to the shores of Olallie Lake, where you'll find a fine campground and a little resort.

CENTRAL OREGON

Head back to Detroit and turn east on Route 22. Follow this road 30 miles east and south, and when it intersects U.S. 20, turn east. From here it's about 15 miles to the turnoff for the **Metolius River recreation area.** Any of the many campgrounds here, especially those downstream from **Camp Sherman,** would be a great place to spend the night.

From the Metolius, head back to Route 20 and follow this road through the town of Sisters to U.S. 97, which you'll take south to Bend. From 97, take the turnoff for the Cascade Lakes Highway, and follow the signs out of town and up Century Drive toward Mount Bachelor. **Devils Lake** is 29 miles from Bend. The prime lakeside campsites are set away from the parking area, so you'll have to schlep your gear. Across the highway is the climber's trail for South Sister.

SOUTHEASTERN OREGON

Here's another pretty long drive. From Devils Lake, backtrack a few miles to Mount Bachelor and take Forest Road 45 about 20 miles, passing the Sunriver turnoff and continuing to U.S. 97. Turn south on 97, and follow it 17 miles to Route 31, just past La Pine. Take Route 31 about 120 miles to U.S. 395. (Actually, when we've done this segment, we've gone a couple of extra miles on Route 31 to gas up in Lakeview.) Head south on 395 18 miles to the turnoff for Route 140. Take Route 140 east 16 miles to the Plush cut-off, and take that road 19 miles to Plush. From Plush, head north and east through the Warner wetlands, following signs for the final 23 miles to **Hart Mountain National Antelope Refuge.** The hot springs campground is four miles south of the refuge headquarters. Hey! It's worth it! Soak the drive away in the hot springs, and explore the area on foot or mountain bike.

It's a relatively short but bumpy drive across the refuge to Route 205 and the tiny town of Frenchglen. From Frenchglen, go four miles up the Steens Mountain Loop Road to **Page Springs Campground,** where you can hike along the Donner und Blitzen River.

NORTHEASTERN OREGON

Backtrack to Frenchglen, turn north on Route 205, and follow it about 60 miles to Burns. Head north from town on U.S. 395 to John Day (70 miles), then east on U.S. 26 to Prairie City (13 miles). From Prairie City, head south 11 miles to the **Strawberry Campground,** which is actually a 1.25-mile hike from the campground to the lake.

Drive back to Prairie City and continue east 16 miles on U.S. 26 to the turn-off for County Road 7. Turn north onto County Road 7 and follow it about 55 miles to I-84 and Baker City. Hop on I-84 westbound for about 17 miles to the North Powder exit. Follow the road 20 miles to **Grande Ronde Lake Campground,** which is about a mile past Anthony Lakes Ski Area. Grande Ronde Lake, a small lake in a meadow of tiny streams, is the headwaters of the Grande Ronde River; hiking trails into the Elkhorn Mountains start nearby.

EASTERN OREGON RAMBLE

Jettison your notions of Oregon as a cloud-enshrouded dark-green spot on the map and get set for expansive views, lots of wildlife, and a dose of the West in this tour of an area sometimes referred to as "Oregon's outback."

If you're flying in for this trip, consider using the Boise, Idaho, airport. It's much closer to Baker City, where this itinerary begins and ends, than the Portland airport.

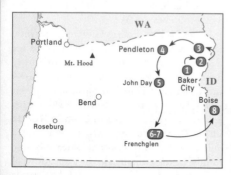

Day 1

Start your tour of eastern Oregon in **Baker City,** but don't linger in town for too long; head west to near ghost town of **Sumpter** (30 miles) and then up a ways into the Elkhorns for more gold-era history and mining ghost towns. North of Sumpter, follow the **Elkhorn Drive National Scenic Byway,** to the near-ghost town of **Granite.** If you're enjoying the drive, continue north and east to Anthony Lakes; from there, continue east back to I-84 and Baker City.

Day 2

Visit the **National Historic Oregon Trail Interpretive Center** near Baker City, then head about 70 miles east on Route 86 to **Hell's Canyon** at Oxbow, where you can take a look at the Snake River's gorge by car, jet boat, or on foot. Backtrack and stay the night in **Halfway,** just beneath the southern edge of the Wallowa Mountains.

Day 3

From Halfway, head about 15 miles east on Route 86, then turn north on Forest Road 39. This 54-mile summer-only road will take you up the eastern edge of the Wallowas past the area's most accessible viewpoint onto **Hells Canyon,** to lodgings in the artsy town of **Joseph** or at nearby **Wallowa Lake.**

Day 4

Take the **Wallowa Lake Tramway** from Wallowa Lake. The tram lets you off at the top of Mount Howard, where there is a network of hiking trails. Then head west to I-84 at La Grande and follow the interstate to Pendleton. Tour the **Pendleton Underground** and spend the night in town.

Day 5

Hop back onto I-84 and take it west to Arlington. From Arlington, drive south on Highway 19 to the **John Day Fossil Beds.** Just south of the Thomas Condon Paleontology Center, turn west onto U.S. 26 and take it to your night's lodging in John Day.

Day 6

It's a pretty drive south from John Day on U.S. 395 through Burns to the **Malheur Wildlife Refuge.** Visit the refuge headquarters, a few miles east of Route 205, then continue south on 205 to lodgings in **Frenchglen.**

Day 7

If the snows have melted, drive the 59-mile **Steens Mountain Byway.** Spend another night in Frenchglen or head 60 miles north to Burns.

Day 8

Drive "back" to Boise (about 150 miles) to fly home.

TRACING OREGON'S VOLCANIC PAST

Most of Oregon was born of fire, and in many parts of the state a variety of volcanic features are still easily seen.

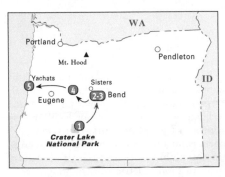

Day 1

Start your trip at **Crater Lake,** which is actually the caldera of the erstwhile Mount Mazama, once the largest of the Cascade peaks. Spend the night at Crater Lake Lodge.

Days 2 and 3

Head north on U.S. 97, with stops at **Newberry Crater, Lava River Caves, Lava Lands Visitor Center,** and **Benham Falls.** Here you'll see glossy black obsidian, more lakes nestled into a caldera, lots of lava rocks—both exposed on the ground and

forming streambeds—and a perfect cinder cone. It'll take a while to explore all of these places, so plan to spend two nights in **Sunriver** or **Bend.**

Day 4

Turn off U.S. 97 onto U.S. 20 and head through **Sisters.** Take summer-only Route 242 over lava-strewn **McKenzie Pass.** Stop at the **Dee Wright Observatory** to walk on the flows and look at the Cascade peaks—all former volcanoes—looming to the north and south. Drop down the west side of the pass to explore the upper reaches of the McKenzie River; in places here, the river plays peek-a-boo under lava flows. Spend the night at Belknap Lodge and Hot Springs or at a campground along the McKenzie.

Day 5

Head west on Route 126 and pass through Eugene on your way to the coast. Turn north on U.S. 101 at Florence and go about 25 miles to **Cape Perpetua,** where the tide pools that extend out into the ocean were formed by lava flows. Spend your final night in **Yachats.**

PORTLAND

Oregon's largest city, Portland is at the confluence to two great rivers; it is shadowed by towering trees and dominated by ancient volcanoes. This epic natural setting sets the stage for a cosmopolitan city with a metro area population of 2.1 million, though the city's easygoing and quirky spirit make Portland feel like a much smaller town. In fact, even as the city grows, its reputation as a center of alternative and populist politics and unconventional lifestyles increases—Portland is currently the top West Coast destination for "young creatives," that is, college educated 25- to 34-year-olds, and "Keep Portland Weird" has gone from bumper sticker to manifesto as many of the city's inner neighborhoods positively heave with youthful energy reminiscent of the "hippie" movement heyday in the late 1960s.

But there's more to Portland than youthful tattoos and indolent coffee shops. Amid lush greenery rare in an urban environment, high-tech business ventures, top-notch cultural institutions (including a first-rate symphony, opera company, and art museum) and a distinctive architecture lend the air of worldly sophistication. A latticework of bridges spanning the Willamette River adds a distinctive profile, while parks, malls, and other public spaces give Portland a heart and a soul. The overall effect is more European than American—a *New York Times* article in 2006 pronounced that Portland was the most European city in the United States—where the urban core is equal parts marketplace, cultural forum, and working metropolis.

Such a happy medium is the result of

HIGHLIGHTS

◖ Portland Art Museum: Portland's green, shady South Park Blocks are home to this excellent collection of art and artifacts, and just across the park are the Oregon History Center and the stages of the Portland Center for Performing Arts (page 43).

◖ International Rose Test Garden: The most spectacular sight in Washington Park are these tamed gardens containing 10,000 rose plants. You can't beat the postcard-perfect views or Mount Hood and downtown, either (page 45).

◖ Pearl District: Oregon's most densely populated neighborhood is this upscale shopping, dining and condo district, where 20 years ago abandoned warehouses and rail yards once slumbered. Many of the city's top galleries and restaurants are now here (page 52).

◖ Powell's City of Books: Long before the Pearl District was developed, book lovers ventured to the edge of the neighborhood to visit Powell's. As the surrounding neighborhood has flourished, so has this huge bookstore, known for its mix of new and used titles (page 53).

◖ Hawthorne District: Hop on bus #14 and ride across the Hawthorne Bridge to explore one of Portland's eastside neighborhoods. Hawthorne, with its kicked-back hippie vibe, is a good place to sip coffee and people-watch. The corner of S.E. 37th and Hawthorne is the heart of the district (page 58).

◖ Forest Park and the West Hills: Hit the trails of Forest Park, the nation's largest forested urban park. Mountain bike or walk on Leif Erikson Drive, or explore part of the 30-plus-mile-long Wildwood Trail (page 59).

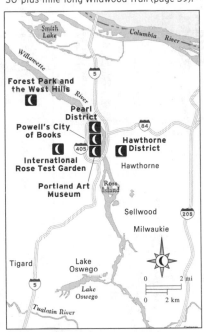

LOOK FOR ◖ TO FIND RECOMMENDED SIGHTS, ACTIVITIES, DINING, AND LODGING.

progressive planning and a fortunate birthright. Patterns of growth in this one-time Native American encampment at the confluence of the Willamette and Columbia Rivers were initially shaped by the practical Midwestern values of Oregon Trail pioneers, as well as by the sophistication of New England merchants. Rather than the boom-bust development that characterized Seattle and gold-rush San Francisco, Portland was designed to be user-friendly over the long haul.

During the modern era, planners added such progressive refinements as extensive mass-transit systems and strict limits on building height and spacing. In this vein, Portland's decades of growth have thankfully preserved the city's aesthetically pleasing and historic architecture. Over time, the place once called "Stumptown" has become the poster child for cities that work.

Another blessing is Portland's auspicious location. Even though it sits 110 miles from the

PORTLAND

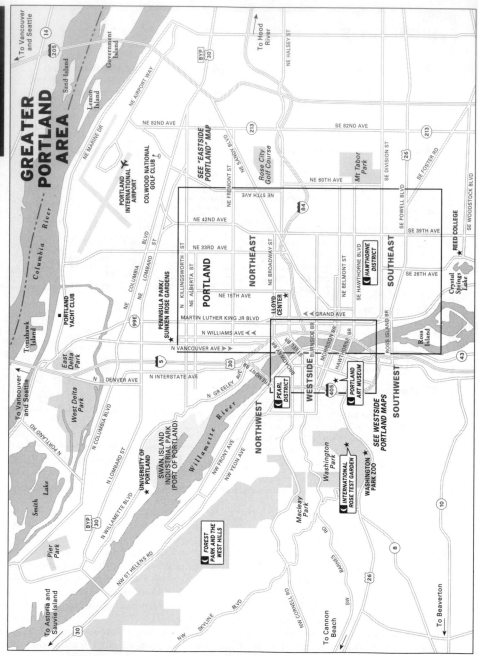

GREATER PORTLAND AREA

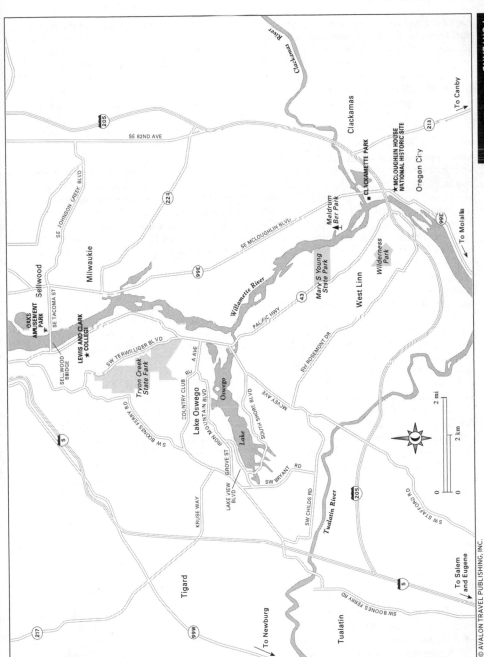

Clackamas River

To Canby

205

SE 82ND AVE

Clackamas

213

MCLOUGHLIN HOUSE
NATIONAL HISTORIC SITE

★ CLACKAMETTE PARK

Oregon City

SE JOHNSON CREEK BLVD

224

99E

To Molalla

SE MCLOUGHLIN BLVD

Maldrum
Ber Park

Milwaukie

99E

Wilderness
Park

Sellwood

Willamette River

Mary S Young
State Park

West Linn

SE TACOMA ST

OAKS
AMUSEMENT
PARK

LEWIS AND CLARK
★ COLLEGE

PACIFIC HWY

43

SW ROSEMONT DR

SELLWOOD
BRIDGE

SW TERWILLIGER BLVD

A AVE

RD

Tryon Creek
State Park

COUNTRY CLUB RD

Oswego

SOUTH SHORE BLVD

MCVEY AVE

SW BOONES FERRY RD

Lake Oswego

IRON MOUNTAIN BLVD

Lake

2 mi

2 km

5

KRUSE WAY

LAKE VIEW
BLVD

GROVE ST

SW BRYANT

RD

SW CHILDS RD

Tualatin River

205

SW STAFFORD RD

0

0

Tigard

To Newburg

99W

217

Tualatin

SW BOONES FERRY RD

5

To Salem
and Eugene

Pacific Ocean on the Columbia River, the city's port is one of the West Coast leaders in overall tonnage of foreign waterborne cargo and is recognized as the second-leading grain export site in the world. In addition to this commerce on the Columbia, battleships, ocean liners, and other vessels go into dry dock here for repair and renovation.

Portland's waterways are its lifeblood in other ways. Mount Hood's Bull Run watershed supplies some of the purest drinking water anywhere in the United States. The printing, textile, papermaking, and high-tech industries also place a premium on Portland's clean-running aqueous arteries. Cheap and abundant power from the Willamette and Columbia Rivers' hydro projects has enticed other industries to locate here as well.

The traveler will appreciate Portland's proximity to rural retreats, outdoor recreation, and natural beauty. With scenic Columbia Gorge and year-round skiing on Mount Hood to the east, and the Pacific coastline to the west, relief from urban stress is little more than an hour away. Other nearby getaways include the Willamette Valley wine country and the historic sites of Champoeg and Oregon City. Closer to home, Portland's Forest Park is the largest urban wilderness in the country, and after a visit to Washington Park, you'll know why Portland is nicknamed the "Rose City."

Portland's cultural offerings are noteworthy for their scope and excellence. Whether it's the wine, cheese, and camaraderie on first-Thursday-of-the-month gallery walks or the smorgasbord of live theater and state-of-the-art concert halls, Portland's music mavens and culture vultures enjoy a full table. In like measure, bibliophiles revel in one of the world's largest bookstores, Powell's, as well as many other outlets for specialty titles and rare editions. The literary set enjoys a full calendar of lectures and readings by prominent visiting authors and local literati such as Ursula Le Guin and Jean Auel. For music lovers, top rock acts regularly hit Portland, while the local pub scene—liberally irrigated with fine microbrewed ales (Portland has more independent breweries than any

other city in the nation)—showcases many fine blues and jazz players. The alternative music scene in the Rose City is currently one of the hottest on the West Coast. The flames of art and knowledge are kept burning at such fine institutions as the Portland Art Museum and the Oregon Museum of Science and Industry. Rounding out this array of cultural offerings are more movie screens, radio stations, bookstores, and dining spots than in any American city of comparable size.

However, all is not rosy in the City of Roses. In recent years, Portland has suffered its share of such urban challenges as gang violence, escalating real estate prices, and a growing homeless population. Locals will tell you that rush-hour traffic jams on the Banfield Expressway (I-84), the Sunset Highway (U.S. 26), and the "Terwilliger Curves" portion of I-5 get worse each year. Despite these problems, Portland's quality of life is still frequently touted by surveys and media as unsurpassed by few, if any, major American cities. In 2000, *Money* magazine selected Portland the best place to live in the United States. Come now and see Portland in its Golden Age.

PLANNING YOUR TIME

Portland isn't like London or San Francisco, cities filled with loads of top-notch destinations that serve as pilgrimage sights for every visitor. Aside from a handful of unique institutions and sights, Portland is more a city that you explore for its way of life. You won't understand Portland if you come expecting to appreciate the city after a pleasant if disengaged connect-the-dots tour of all the top sights. To capture Portland's potent allure—to "get it"— you need to do some serious hanging out.

Don't, however, miss a walking tour of downtown's top sights, including the South Park Blocks—now deemed the Culture District by city boosters—with the newly expanded Portland Art Museum, Oregon Historical Society, the Portland Center for the Performing Arts, and the opulent Arlene Schnitzer Concert Hall, home of the Oregon Symphony. If you really want to see what Portland's like, though, come on a summer Wednesday or Saturday when this same series of shady park blocks are transformed into the Portland Farmers Market, a cornucopia of local produce, cheese, meats, seafood, and baked goods—and some of the best street food you'll find. Into this crowded, three-block area throng farmers, students, restaurateurs, downtown professionals, housewives, and back-to-the-earth activists of all stripes, all seeking the wondrous bounty of Oregon's fields, rivers, and coastlines. But what makes the city unusual is that an average Portlander may visit the culture district by day to buy local artisan cheese, then return later in the day to check out the exhibit of Russian icons at the art museum and perhaps return again in the evening to attend a performance of Elvis Costello. The city supports many communities equally, and these overlapping and interlocked communities in turn are fiercely proud of their city.

The point is that it's the fabric of life in Portland that makes it such a unique city. Portlanders are actively engaged with their city, and

there's not a big distinction made between high and low art, lesser or greater lifestyles. As a visitor with a few days to spend in Portland, pick out a local coffeehouse to frequent—you'll soon be chatting with new friends and hearing about hot new bands or private dining clubs that are by invitation only. Go to a reading at Powell's Books, and find yourself amidst the local literati. Spend an afternoon on Alberta Street, or Mississippi Avenue, the trendy gallery and restaurant areas, and you'll hear the stories of entrepreneurial young idealists who have come to Portland—like so many before them to pursue their dream at the end of the Oregon Trail.

There aren't six degrees of separation here everyone knows everyone else. To make your own entrée into the grid, get just a little bit involved and you'll be surprised how quickly the doors open. Chat with your waiter about art galleries, ask for dining advice from an art-gallery owner, get to know someone at a brewpub, and soon you'll find yourself holding the keys to unlock the city's doors.

PORTLAND'S ECONOMY

With the world's second-most-active grain export port, I-84 and three transcontinental railroads linking the city to the east, and I-5 providing connections north and south, Portland is perfectly located to take advantage of Pacific Rim trade as well as stateside business opportunities. As such, Portland is the second-most-active freight hauling and distribution center on the West Coast.

Portland's early stages of revival picked up steam in the 1970s, turning a city mostly known for rain, roses, and run-down buildings into a showplace of eye-catching art and architecture. In the 1990s, the town made a graceful shift from old-tech timber burg to high-tech metropolis; Portland's economic prosperity over the last several decades seemed to be limitless. In 2000, with more than 1,000 technology companies, from Intel – the largest private-sector employer – to Hewlett-Packard, Epson, NEC, and scores of small software

firms, onlookers predicted it would be the best-poised U.S. city to make the transition to the new millennium. But with the decline of high tech, Oregon's jobless rate soared to one of the highest in the nation. The slump hit Portland's social services and public schools particularly hard. In 2003, its wounded public schools became the subject of national ridicule in Doonesbury's running comic strip.

City planners are optimistic about the future, so much so that plans are underway for what the *Oregonian* calls the "boldest, riskiest venture the city has undertaken": a $1.9 billion plan to develop a 31-acre area south of the Ross Island Bridge. The South Waterfront District, as it has been named, aims for a new high in neighborhood design, complete with aerial tram and urban waterfront. It may be a decade in the making, but the city expects that the development will bring 5,000 jobs and provide 2,700 housing units for starters.

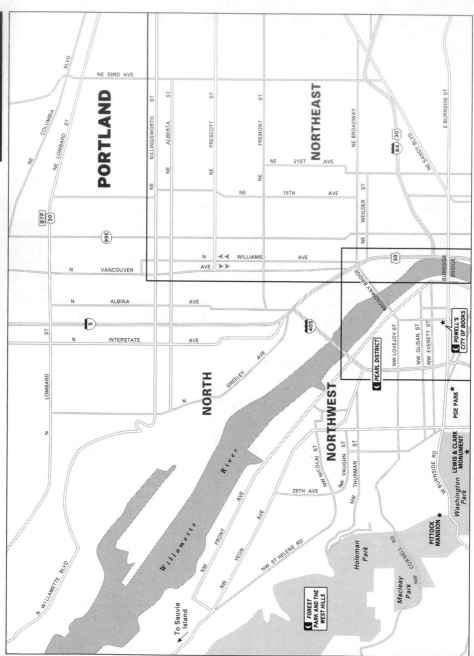

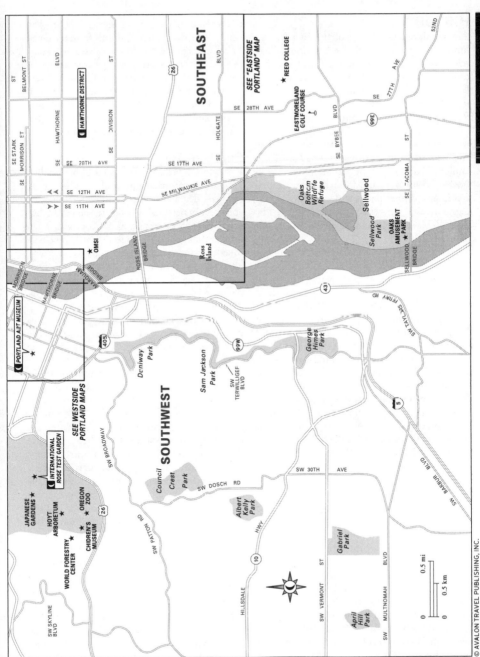

HISTORY

Sauvie Island, northwest of the current city limits, was the site of a Native American village whose name inspired William Clark to christen the nearby river the Willamette in 1805. In 1825, the Hudson's Bay Company established Fort Vancouver across the Columbia River, bringing French and Scottish trappers into the area, some of whom retired around what would eventually become Portland. The city was officially born when two New Englanders, Pettygrove from Portland, Maine, and Lovejoy from Boston, Massachusetts, flipped a coin at a dinner party to decide who would name the 640-acre claim they co-owned. The state-of-Mainer won and decided in the winter of 1844–1845 to name it after his birthplace. The original claim is located in the vicinity of Southwest Naito Parkway.

The trade that grew up along the Willamette River and the Tualatin Plank Road south of the city allowed Willamette Valley lumber and produce an outlet to sea trade through Portland's Columbia River port. This was especially important in the mid-19th century, during the California gold rush, when San Francisco needed resources to feed its housing boom. Portland thus transitioned from a sleepy village called Stumptown to the major trade and population center in the state, incorporating in 1851. Another defining event was Portland's selection as the terminus of the Northern Pacific Railroad in 1883, linking city to the eastern United States.

The single greatest boost to the emergence of Portland as Oregon's leading city, however, was the Lewis and Clark Exposition in 1905. An estimated three million people attended this centennial celebration of the famed expedition, establishing the city as the gateway to the Orient for the American business community and paving the way for the dramatic growth that followed. By 1910, Portland had grown to a metropolis of 250,000 people, nearly tripling its population in just five years.

The years between 1905 and 1912 saw the substantial expansion of railroads, farming, and livestock-raising east of the Cascades, due in part to Portland's growth as a commercial hub. The shift of America's timber industry from the Great Lakes states to the Northwest also occurred during this period. In response to this deluge of commodities, new wharves and factories were built at the northern end of the Willamette Valley. On the grounds of the original Lewis and Clark exposition site, northwestern Portland became a center of housing and commerce.

Portland Today

Portland is a little city with a lot of personality. From the town's inception, civic leaders have made visionary decisions dedicated to maintaining livability and a rich quality of life. In the 1850s, during Portland's first blush of development, town fathers thought to set aside the Park Blocks, a mile-long stretch of greenery, sculpture, and towering trees in the heart of downtown. Throughout its history, the city's desire to be more than just a commercial center has been expressed by the creation of numerous parks and gardens.

In the modern era, measures designed to prevent the blight of its urban core by the automobile have resulted in what is likely the best mass transit system in America. Other progressive planning initiatives from the 1970s have become part of the fabric of life here. The elimination of a freeway to give way to Waterfront Park and the creation of Pioneer Square, a European-style piazza in the city center, are two such outgrowths. On the heels of these developments, the "1 percent for art" provision dedicating a portion of any new construction costs to public art became a prototype for similar programs in other cities. A more recent statement of Portland's priorities came in 1998 with the central library's multimillion-dollar restoration to turn-of-the-century elegance. The integration of these decisions provides structure for a town whose character is rural yet urbane, artistic, and green.

Recently, Portland's growth-related stresses have been eased by other innovative decisions such as the extension of the light-rail transit system (MAX) into distant suburbs, citywide recycling, the creation of an inner city street car, and implementation of an urban growth boundary. The idea of the urban growth boundary is to stop leapfrog development across the open countryside by confining the new subdivisions and commercial enterprise to agreed-upon areas. In so doing, it also keeps Willamette Valley farmland from being exploited by real estate interests for quick profit. In the late 1990s, the *New York Times* selected Portland as the only large population center with a chance of weathering the transition into the next century gracefully, thanks to visionary urban planning.

On the downside, limited acreage for expansion created by the urban growth boundary has led to escalating land prices. And in a city whose inhabitants savor public green spaces and the immediacy of the great outdoors, increased urban density is not to everyone's liking.

However history will judge Portland's land use planning legacy, travelers will immediately recognize that this is a place to live as well as to sightsee. Visitors come here not for a glimpse of a Golden Gate Bridge or a Space Needle, but rather to enjoy a clean, compact city in the midst of spectacular natural surroundings with enough cultural attractions, dining spots, and shopping opportunities to merit an extended stay.

Sights

Before you arrive, contact **Travel Portland** (26 S.W. Salmon St., Portland 97204-3299 or 877/678-5263, www.travelportland.com) for free maps and their informative magazine-like publication *Travel Portland*. In addition to in-depth Portland coverage, coastal and Columbia Gorge highlights are briefly detailed.

Second, familiarizing yourself with directional reference points will help you smoothly navigate the city. The line of demarcation between north and south in addresses is Burnside Street; between east and west it's the Willamette River. These give reference points for the address prefixes southwest, southeast, north, northwest, and northeast. Avenues run north–south and streets run east–west. Almost every downtown address carries a southwest or northwest prefix. For more tips on orienting yourself, see *Getting There* and *Getting Around* later in this chapter.

DOWNTOWN PORTLAND

The best introduction to Portland is a walking tour that also takes advantage of the city's excellent mass transit. Despite the convenience of car travel, the flavor of the tree-shaded downtown is better appreciated on foot supplemented by bus or bike. Otherwise, Portland's mix of people, parks, and public art is too easy to miss. Also, the compact beauty of the city center invites strolling—the main downtown business and retail area is only some 13 by 26 blocks, and the blocks are half the length (200 feet) of those in most other cities. What's more, downtown is basically flat, letting you log miles on foot relatively painlessly. So for the downtown area, ditch the car, put on your walking shoes, and get a mass transit schedule at the TriMet office at Pioneer Courthouse Square. You should also ask for a free "Walking Tour Map" of Portland published by Powell's Books, and available from the bookstore or from various other tourist offices throughout the city. No matter how fast you move, it's not possible to do all of the different portions of this tour in one day, so slow down and savor each part.

Portland Building, Ira's Fountain, and Public Art

We'll begin our tour below a statue that is said to symbolize the city: Raymond Kaskey's *Portlandia,* which ranks right behind the Statue of Liberty as the world's largest hammered copper sculpture. Located outside Michael Graves's postmodern Portland Building, S.W. 5th Avenue between S.W. Main and S.W. Madison, the golden-hued female figure holding a trident re-creates the Lady of Commerce on the city seal. Locals refer to it as "Queen

PORTLAND

PORTLAND BRIDGES

Of all the metro areas in the United States, Portland is arguably *the* City of Bridges. With a dozen bridges on the Willamette and two on the Columbia, the spans are both numerous and diverse. The three oldest were built prior to World War I. Bridge-ophiles can also revel in the broad array of bridge types presented here that were designed by the preeminent engineers of their day. Many of the Willamette River crossings are illuminated at night by strategically placed floodlights, adding yet another pleasing visual dimension. The **Steel Bridge**'s (1912) two spans can be raised and lowered independently. The **St. John's Bridge** (1931) is the only steel suspension bridge in Portland and one of only three major suspension bridges in Oregon (the other two are across the Crooked River/Lake Billy Chinook).

From the newest bridge, the **Fremont** (1973) to the oldest, the **Hawthorne Bridge** (1910), downtown bridges are located a third of a mile from each other and are, for the most part, safe and accessible for bicyclists and pedestrians (only the I-5 Marquam and I-405 Fremont Bridges are off-limits to non-motorized vehicles and pedestrians).

Kong," and practical jokers from Portland State University sometimes dangle a giant yo-yo from her outstretched finger. Inside the Portland Building on the second floor is the **Metropolitan Center for Public Art** (1120 S.W. 5th Ave.), where you can pick up a brochure annotating a walking tour of the city's murals, fountains, sculptures, statues, and other public art pieces. This profusion of public art comes from the "1 percent for art" program, founded in the early 1980s.

More graphic evocations of the region are rendered by the simulated cascades at **Ira's Fountain,** also known as Forecourt Fountain. To get to the fountain, walk down S.W. 4th Avenue to Clay Street. Walk down the hill (east)

to Portland's **Civic Auditorium** (also known as Keller Auditorium; see the theater listing in the "Entertainment" section) at S.W. 3rd and Clay for a full-frontal view of the fountain. At the southern end of the Civic Auditorium is Main Street, where a left turn and a two-block stroll takes you to the waterfront.

Tom McCall Waterfront Park

Your introduction to mile-long Tom McCall Waterfront Park begins at **RiverPlace,** an attractive area of restaurants, specialty shops, and boating facilities. The boutiques, brewpubs, and an ornate piazza on the southern edge of this complex overlook the Willamette in the shadow of the Marquam Bridge. It's hard to imagine that 1894 floodwaters were high enough here to totally submerge many of RiverPlace's present-day storefronts. It's equally difficult to conjure hundreds of citizens volunteering to pile sandbags along this part of the waterfront in 1996 to prevent a reprise of the earlier disaster. In any case, you can follow the paved riverside walkway north to a more benign encounter with water at the **Salmon Street Springs Fountain,** in the park a few minutes north of RiverPlace near where Salmon Street abuts Naito Parkway. This is often the centerpiece of Portland's many festivals and provides a refreshing shower on a hot day. The fountain water's ebb and flow is meant to evoke the rhythms of the city.

Tom McCall Waterfront Park is named for the governor credited with helping to reclaim Oregon's rivers. In the early 1970s the park's grassy shore replaced Harbor Drive, a freeway that impeded access to the scenic Willamette River. Today, the park is frequently the scene of summer festivals, while the wide paved riverside esplanade is a favorite for joggers, bikers, and strolling families.

To go back to the time when the town's destiny was entwined with shipping on the Willamette and the Columbia, walk north along the waterfront until you are just south of the Burnside Bridge. Across Naito Parkway at the Ash Street stoplight is the oldest part of the city.

When the weather heats up, kids can't resist a run through Salmon Street Springs, located in Waterfront Park.

The Skidmore Historical District

A block south of the corner of Ash Street and Naito Parkway, the **Oregon Maritime Museum** (113 S.W. Naito Pkwy., 503/224-7724, open 11 A.M.–4 P.M. Fri.–Sun., $4 adults) has photos of the era when sternwheelers plied the rapids of the Columbia River Gorge that are worth the admission price alone. Also, don't miss the USS *Portland,* the last steam-operated tug on the West Coast, moored in the harbor across from the museum. After the museum go back to Ash Street (look for the historic firehouse) and head west a block. Make a right on S.W. 1st and Ash, and walk along the cobblestones through the Skidmore Historic District. Along with the neighborhood's classic architecture, heritage markers help inspire historical reverie.

A little south of the Burnside Bridge, you'll read that the **Skidmore Fountain** (S.W. 1st Ave. and S.W. Ankeny St.) is named for a man who intended that the fountain provide refreshment for "horses, men, and dogs." Local brewery owner Henry Weinhard offered to fill the fountain with beer for its grand opening,

but the city leaders declined, fearing the horses would get drunk. Just south of the fountain, read the Ankeny Block placard on the wall for a good, concise description of Portland's architectural evolution. Despite the spouts and animal troughs, the 1888 bronze-and-granite fountain is still purely decorative. It does serve, however, as a portal to the largest continuously operating open-air handicrafts market in the United States.

Saturday Market (www.saturdaymarket .org) is an outdoor potlatch of homegrown edibles, arts, crafts, and excellent street performers. The market takes place every Saturday and Sunday from March through Christmas Eve in the shadow of the Burnside Bridge. On Saturday the hours are 10 A.M.–5 P.M.; on Sunday the market operates 11 A.M.–4:30 P.M.

The food booths here are a street-food lover's delight. The handicrafts range from exquisite woodwork (at reasonable prices), pottery, and jewelry to more uniquely Portland items like homemade fire-starter kits and juggling toys. What's astonishing is the high quality that's been maintained here for decades. Travelers on a budget should note that prices at food booths drop as closing time approaches.

Across S.W. 1st Avenue and cobblestoned **Ankeny Square** from the Skidmore Fountain is the **New Market Theater,** constructed in 1872 as a theater and a produce market.

The Burnside Bridge cuts through an enclave of historic buildings that form the heart of Old Town, the Victorian-era city center when Portland was a busy harbor and its primary commercial district faced the Willamette River. Prior to Portland's era of expressways and bridge building, this whole neighborhood was filled with cast-iron facades and Italianate architecture. More information on the Old Town area follows later in this chapter. Meanwhile, the current downtown tour is heading back to the heart of modern Portland. At 1st Avenue beneath the Burnside Bridge catch the MAX light rail (which is free downtown) heading south then west on Morrison Street. Exit the train at Pioneer Courthouse Square.

Pioneer Courthouse Square is a red brick plaza in the core of downtown.

Pioneer Courthouse Square

If you follow Morrison across 5th Avenue you'll be on the north side of Pioneer Courthouse (555 S.W. Yamhill), the oldest public building in the state, constructed between 1869 and 1873. The classic contours of this gray granite structure contrast with the blue-tiled, mauve-and-beige tuxedo-patterned facade you saw at the Portland Building. This landmark is surrounded by statuary with small bronzed beavers, ducks, and sea lions congregating near a series of pools on the north side of the Pioneer Courthouse. On the south side of the courthouse on Yamhill Street, a bear with a fish in its mouth may be seen.

One block west, across from the courthouse front door, is **Pioneer Courthouse Square,** bordered by Yamhill, Morrison, 6th Avenue, and Broadway, a block-square, red-brick plaza that's the cultural vortex of downtown. Pioneer Courthouse Square is important to visitors for a number of reasons. If you have any questions about Portland at this point, stop off at **Portland Information Center,** a visitors center for Travel Portland (503/275-9750

or 877/678-5263, www.travelportland.com) located through the doors between the waterfalls (this will make sense when you are there). Free maps and sightseeing literature are available and attendants are on hand to answer questions. Sharing the same lobby are the **TriMet** offices (503/238-7433, www.trimet.org), where mass-transit information can be procured, tickets bought, and questions answered 9 A.M.–5 P.M. weekdays.

Pioneer Courthouse Square is also a showcase for public art. On the south side of the square is **Allow Me,** a life-sized—and lifelike— statue of a businessman with an umbrella hailing a cab. Diagonally across the square is a 25-foot column known as the **weather machine.** Every day at noon the forecast is delivered by one of three creatures: a dragon in stormy weather, a blue heron if it's overcast, or a sun figure. As if that's not enough, the machine also emits a small cloud accompanied by a fanfare while colored lights display temperature and air quality.

The square in summer hosts a variety of free

concerts; typically at noon on weekdays during the summer when jazz, folk, and other types of musicians come to entertain crowds of lunchtime diners (this is a great spot to hang out while eating a sandwich or street food from one of the many food carts here). The rest of the day, there's usually something going on in the square, whether its buskers, hack-sack contests, or intense games of chess.

Should you tire of people-watching, inspect the bricks on the square, each of which bears the name of one of the 50,000 donors who paid $15–30 for the privilege. From the northeast corner of the square gaze up at the white-brick and terra-cotta clock tower of the Jackson Tower on S.W. Yamhill and Broadway—a Queen Anne beauty from 1912—and at the cruise-ship-fronted Fox Tower, a handsome addition to the Portland skyline from 2001, which represent the span of architectural styles found in central Portland.

Another part of the Pioneer Courthouse Square experience can be had in the middle of the amphitheater located on the northwest corner of the square. Here you might notice people talking to themselves. If you follow suit, you'll be treated to a perfect echo bouncing back at you.

Pioneer Place is also at ground zero for downtown shopping. Immediately west, across Broadway, is indigenous-to-the-Northwest clothier Nordstrom, across the corner at Morrison and 6th Avenue is Macy's (formerly Meier & Frank), and one block east along Morrison or Yamhill is Pioneer Place. Pioneer Place is an upscale shopping development that features a number of national merchandisers, including Eddie Bauer, Ann Taylor, J.Crew, and Coach, and other retailers found in Rouse developments. The lower level features a vast food court with dozens of quality concession stands purveying an array of cuisines. On the third (topmost) floor is **Todai,** an all-you-can-eat Japanese seafood buffet.

The South Park Blocks Cultural District

South of the square, paralleling Broadway, is the South Park Blocks Cultural District, which contains a number of Portland's showcase museums, performance spaces, and historic churches. These institutions line the South Park Blocks, part of 25-block-long set of parks set aside in 1852, during the city's infancy. Come to the South Park Blocks in the fall and you can sense Portland's New England heritage as century-old, monumental American elm trees (elsewhere very rare) with their bright yellow leaves tower above cast-iron benches, heroic bronze statues, and neatly trimmed lawns. On this part of the park blocks (and elsewhere downtown) note the bronze drinking fountains put in by early-20th-century lumber magnate Simon Benson to promote a teetotaling mindset among his workers. Close by is the Italianate Shemanski Fountain with its **Rebecca at the Well** statue. Be sure to check out the clever tromp l'oeil murals portraying Lewis and Clark, Sacajawea, fur traders, and Oregon Trail pioneers on the south and west walls of the Oregon Historical Center on Main Street. **Portland State University** is at the end of the South Park Blocks.

The **Oregon History Center** (1230 S.W. Park Ave., 503/222-1741, 10 A.M.–5 P.M. Tues.–Sat., noon–5 P.M. Sun., closed Mon., $6 adults, $3 students, and $1.50 ages 6–18), which holds the collection of the Oregon Historical Society, unfurls a pageant of Oregon's patrimony with interactive exhibits, artifacts, paintings, and historical documents relating to early explorers and pioneers as well as vintage photos of native tribes. The extensive collection of photographs, maps, documents, and artifacts from the center's second-floor library is catalogued onto an electronic database linked to the Internet and accessible via research terminals within the exhibit galleries and library. The museum's admission allows patrons to use the photo archives (the best collection of historic Oregon photos in existence) and library. Call or consult local media to check on revolving exhibits here.

Portland Art Museum

Across the park, the Portland Art Museum (1219 S.W. Park Ave., 503/226-2811, open 10 A.M.–5 P.M. Tues.–Sun., until 9 P.M. the first Thurs. of each month, $7.50 adults with discounts for seniors and students), was designed by famed architect Pietro Belluschi. The museum's collections are varied, and some are impressive indeed. The Grand Ronde Center for Native American Art can broaden your perspective on Northwest Native American art. The masks and baskets displayed here are not merely ornamental but are intimate parts of tribal ritual. The totem animals, rendered with loving detail, represent archetypes in native belief systems. Eons-old basalt carvings and 19th-century beaded bags and reed baskets by Columbia River Gorge natives are on the third floor while the second floor highlights Alaskan and western Canadian coastal art. It also displays plateau tribe and Mesoamerican pieces. The Native American art exhibits make a nice lead-in to the pioneering generations of the Portland art scene displayed on the third floor. The fourth floor houses work from the last 40 years of Oregon art. Northwest themes are also breathtakingly displayed in Albert Bierstadt's historic painting of Mount Hood (European and American Collection) and in the century-old photos of Oregon on the basement level.

The Asian art wing is also noteworthy. Four galleries illuminate different eras of Chinese, Japanese, and Korean art. The museum's collection of European masterworks includes Picasso, Monet, Degas, Calder, Brancusi, Stella, and Renoir. Perhaps the museum's most touted acquisitions are Monet's *Water Lilies* and Brancusi's sculpture *The Muse.*

In recent years, blockbuster exhibits such as *The Imperial Tombs of China,* Wyeth's Helga pictures, a Monet retrospective, and *The Splendors of Ancient Egypt* have put this place on the map for art aficionados. Add a recent 60,000-square-foot addition to gallery space, and its clear that the West Coast's oldest art museum has come into its own.

Each Memorial Day weekend the median mall of the South Park Blocks in front of the museum hosts the only annual art festival in the country organized by Native Americans. With more than 250 Native American artists exhibiting and selling everything from ceramics to beadwork to basketry and weaving, this is a Northwest regional take on the famed Santa Fe Indian Market in New Mexico. Music, arts demonstrations, ceremonial dances, and a food court featuring fry-bread tacos, alder-smoked salmon, and other indigenous dishes also make this a worthwhile event. The outdoor marketplace runs 10 A.M.–6 P.M. Saturday and Sunday; there is a $2–5 suggested donation and some cultural events charge admission. For more information call 503/224-8650.

Another institution of high art backs onto the South Park Blocks. At Broadway and Main, the Portland Center for the Performing Arts has three performance stages in two different buildings, including the ornate Arlene Schnitzer Concert Hall, home to the Oregon Symphony. This jewel-box concert venue was once a 1920s vaudeville hall, but you'd never know it after a 1980s makeover turned this neglected theater into the city's premier classical music concert space. Directly across Main Street is the Performing Arts Center, with two theatres and a soaring lobby topped by a confetti-like glass dome. Schnitzer Concert Hall isn't usually open for casual visits, so you'll need a concert ticket to see its glittering interior, but the Performing Arts Center is open all day and during the evening when performances are scheduled.

Portland Public Library

Portland is a city of readers, with the busiest library system in the United States. A landmark for bibliophiles, The **Central Library** (801 S.W. 10th Ave., 503/223-7201, www .multcolib.org, open 10 A.M.–6 P.M. Mon., Thurs.–Sat.; 10 A.M.–8 P.M. Tues. and Wed.; noon–5 P.M. Sun.) is an architecturally stunning renovation of a 1913 building designed by Alfred Doyle (architect of the Benson Hotel and downtown U.S. Bank) that houses an accessible (60 percent open stacks) collection of books, CDs, videos, and periodicals. Climb the sweeping staircases to the top floor to get a sense of the scale of this building—three stories have never seemed so monumental. There's even a Starbucks coffee shop on-site. This is the most-used central branch of a public library per capita in the nation. Call for hours.

WASHINGTON PARK

From downtown, you can get to Washington Park via TriMet bus #63 (from Washington St.) or by westbound MAX light rail. Once there you'll find that the hillside is home to the International Rose Test Garden, the Japanese Gardens, and the Oregon Zoo. In addition, you'll find the Portland Children's Museum, the Forest Discovery Center and Museum, the Hoyt Arboretum, the Vietnam Memorial, and nearby, the Pittock Mansion.

◖ International Rose Test Garden

The Rose City's welcome mat is out at this four-acre garden overlooking downtown. With more than 400 species and 10,000 rose plants it's the largest rose test garden in the country, containing 4.5 acres of roses, mani-

cured lawns and other formal gardens (free admission). "Rose test" refers to the fact that the garden is one of 24 official testing sites for the All American Rose selections, a group of leading commercial rose growers and hybridizers in the United States. The blossoms are at their peak in June, commemorated by the Rose Festival, but even if you're down to the last rose of summer, there's always the view of the city framed (if you're lucky) by Mount Hood. Photographers, this is the classic view of Portland: The best vantage point for the latter is the east end of the garden along the Queen's Walk, where the names of the festival beauty-contest winners are enshrined (since 1907).

By car from downtown, you can begin your tour of Washington Park by going west on Burnside about a mile past N.W. 23rd and hang a fishhook left at the light onto Tichener. Follow the hill up to Kingston and make a right. Follow Kingston 0.25 mile into Washington Park and park at the tennis courts. Just below

The classic shot from the International Rose Test Garden in Washington Park is best taken on a clear day.

© BILL MCRAE

PORTLAND

ESCAPE TO WASHINGTON COUNTY

For early settlers, getting the crops to market and to Columbia River ports via Portland necessitated a frontier thoroughfare, the Tualatin Plank Road. Today, a different sort of promised land has grown up around the Plank Road: Washington County. Given the million-dollar deals cut in high-tech boardrooms (Intel, headquartered in Hillsboro, is Oregon's largest employer with 10,000 employees) and the Nike headquarters here, the region between Portland and the Coast Range summit may be more aptly termed "Oregon's tomorrow country."

Equally prominent is Washington County's identity as a retreat from Portland's urban stress. Thanks to Portland's urban growth boundary, you can enjoy a bacchanal 10 minutes from downtown Beaverton at places like **Ponzi Vineyards** (Vandermost Rd., Beaverton, 503/628-1227, www.ponzivineyards. com); hike Coast Range trails a half hour away (contact the **Tillamook State Forest Office** in Forest Grove, 503/357-2191, www.odf.state. or.us); or follow a primrose path through botanical displays and U-pick farms (contact the **Washington County Visitor's Association** in Beaverton, 503/644-5555 or 800/537-3149, www.wcva.org).

Other Washington County escapes include the 10-mile bike trail around man-made Hagg Lake, seven miles southwest of Forest Grove

(503/359-5732), and **Pumpkin Ridge golf course** (N. Plains Exit on U.S. 26, 15 miles west of Portland, 503/647-4747, www.pumpkinridge.com), one of *Golf Digest's* top choices for the best public course in the country. After 18 holes, cool down with microbrews in the homey confines of a 142-year-old estate at McMenamins **Cornelius Pass Roadhouse** (4045 N.W. Cornelius Rd., 503/640-6174) or at one of the world-class wineries in the county. Two tasting rooms of note around Forest Grove are **Montinore** (3663 S.W. Dilley Rd., 503/359-5012, www.montinore .com), whose red and white wines have scored gold medals at the Oregon State Fair, and **Momokawa** (820 Elm St., Forest Grove, 503/357-7056, ext. 233, www .sakeone.com), the Northwest's only producer of premium sake. Brochures annotating vineyard and scenic loops are available at tasting rooms and from the visitors association.

To avoid rush-hour traffic on the Sunset Highway (U.S. 26), follow Burnside Street and Barnes Road out of downtown along a beautiful winding route through the West Hills across the county line. Paradoxically, this itinerary parallels the old Tualatin Plank Road, one of Oregon's preeminent pathways to economic opportunity in the old Oregon Territory 150 years ago.

the tennis courts is the Rose Garden, and the Japanese Gardens sign and access road should be visible up the hill from where you parked. Another way to reach Washington Park is by taking U.S. 26 to the zoo exit. Drive past the zoo and Forest Discovery Center. Make a right and follow the road over the hill and through the woods down to the Rose Garden.

Japanese Gardens

The five-acre Portland Japanese Gardens so moved the Japanese ambassador in 1988 that he pronounced them the most beautiful and authentic landscape of its kind outside Japan. Ponds and bridges, sand and stone, April

cherry blossoms, and a snowcapped Fujiyama-like peak in the distance help East meet West here. This is always an island of tranquility, but connoisseurs will tell you to come during the fall-foliage peak in October; many people in Japan feel gardens such as these are at their best when it's raining (good news to visitors in the winter and spring!).

To reach the Japanese Gardens from the Rose Garden, head west up the steps that go past the parking lot and tennis courts on the way to the Japanese Gardens (off Kingston Ave. in Washington Park, 503/223-9233, www.japanesegarden.com, open every day except Thanksgiving, Christmas, and New

After a visit to Washington Park, you'll know why Portland is called the Rose City.

Year's Day, with daily guided tours are offered at 10:45 A.M. and 2:30 P.M. April 15–October 31, $6.50 for adults). You can walk up the short but steep road that leads to the Japanese Gardens, or hop the free open-air shuttle that climbs up the hill every 10 minutes or so.

Oregon Zoo

The Oregon Zoo (4001 S.W. Canyon Rd., 503/226-1561, www.oregonzoo.org, open 9:30 A.M.–5:30 P.M. April–Memorial Day, 9:30 A.M.–6 P.M. June–Labor Day, and 9:30 A.M.–4 P.M. the rest of the year, $8.50 for adults) predates the Rose Garden (1887 versus 1917), and it exerts almost as ubiquitous a presence within the city. The city is justly proud of the zoo's award-winning elephant-breeding program and the nation's largest chimpanzee exhibit. Also noteworthy is a colony of Humboldt penguins from Peru. Whenever possible, animals are kept in enclosures that re-create their natural habitats. An example is the African Grasslands exhibit, a savannalike expanse housing impalas, zebras, giraffes, and a black

rhinoceros. Steller Cove showcases gargantuan sea lions, sea otters, tidepools, and other creatures evocative of the state's shoreline. Because many of the animals are nocturnal, it's usually best to get to the zoo early in the morning.

The zoo features several trains, one of which, the Zooliner, runs the four miles to/from the Japanese Gardens. Passengers must pay for zoo admission before boarding the train, which runs at 40-minute intervals. Figure on 35 minutes for a round-trip. The ride itself is worth your time if only because the Zooliner is a circa-1958 steam engine. But that's not all. The forested ridge defining the route features 112 species of birds, 62 kinds of mammals, and hundreds of plants. During a brief stopover, you may see some peaks of the Cascade Range. The train does not run during the rainy season or when zoo attendance is low. Call the zoo for schedule.

There are several food service outlets at the zoo. The major restaurant is the **Cascade Grill Restaurant,** which opened recently as part of a redesign of the zoo's entry plaza. It's open 9 A.M.–4 P.M. in summer, and 9 A.M.–3P.M. in winter. There's also **AfriCafe,** which offers a good selection of moderately priced cafeteria food. The chance to dine overlooking a glassed-in aviary is the big attraction, however.

Compounding the impression that it's all happenin' at the zoo are the concerts in the amphitheater (see *Festivals and Events* later in this chapter).

Children's Museum 2nd Generation (CM2)

Adjacent to the zoo is the Children's Museum (4015 S.W. Canyon Rd., 503/223-6500, www.portlandcm.org, open daily March 1–August 31, Mon.–Sat. 9 A.M. to 5 P.M., Sun. 11 A.M. to 5 P.M.; Sept. 1–Feb. 28 closed Mon.), which moved to this location in 2001. Activities here are designed for children 6 months old–10 years old. The bulk of visitors tend to be preschoolers with parents exploring places like the clay studio or a re-creation of "Mister Rogers Neighborhood" with props and look-alike sweaters and sneakers.

© BILL MCRAE

Forest Discovery Center and Museum

Up the hill from the MAX elevator in the zoo parking lot, you'll see the Forest Discovery Center (4033 S.W. Canyon Rd., 503/228-1367, www.worldforestry.org, open 9 A.M.–6 P.M. daily in summer, 10 A.M.–5 P.M. in winter, closed Christmas, $3.50–4.50 adults, discounts for children and seniors), which has exhibits on the natural processes of trees, the types of forests in the world, fighting forest fires, silviculture, and timber industry activities. Also featured is the Jessup Wood collection, which displays examples from the 505 trees native to North America. Dioramas, films, and mechanized exhibits are complemented by lectures, shows, and special events. The center's best-known (and after five minutes, most boring) attraction is the 70-foot talking tree. Worth more of your time is the second-floor rainforest exhibit. Perhaps the best way to understand the mixed conifer forests of the region is by taking in *The Old Growth Forest: Treasures in Transition.* Outside the museum are an old-growth stump of impressive girth and a steam engine that began hauling logs in the Coast Range in 1909. Also, don't miss the unique wooden items in the gift shop.

Hoyt Arboretum

Linked to Washington Park by hiking trails, the Hoyt Arboretum straddles the crest of the West Hills, and preserves 1,100 species of trees in 185 acres. Marking the start of the 30-plus-mile Wildwood Trail, the Hoyt Arboretum covers 214 acres and seven miles of trails, including a one-mile tour through one of the country's largest collections of conifers. At 2 P.M. on Saturdays and Sundays October through April, guided tours highlight foliage season. Prize species include the endangered Brewer's weeping spruce and the dawn redwood. This tree had been considered extinct for five million years until a remote stand was found in China. Hoyt's dawn redwood bore the first cones produced in this hemisphere in 50 million years.

Pittock Mansion

Built in 1914 by Henry Pittock, then editor of the daily *Oregonian,* Pittock Mansion (3229 N.W. Pittock Dr., 503/823-3624, www.pittockmansion,com, open daily) stands as showcase of pioneer opulence. Built in an eclectic style that encompasses French Chateau and Queen Anne vernacular, the 22-room mansion can be visited on tours that highlight the structure's exquisite handcraftsmanship and the "modern" conveniences of past generations. The gatehouse doubles as a teahouse. It's worth the trip up to this coign of vantage simply to take in the fabulous views of Portland and the Cascade peaks rising to the east (free admittance to the grounds and gardens)

NORTHWEST PORTLAND
Old Town/Chinatown

The tile-roofed clock of **Union Station** on N.W. 6th Avenue has been a beacon since the 1890s, when passenger trains first rolled into the red-brick terminal. This is the second-oldest operating major passenger terminal in the United States, and the oldest city depot west of St. Louis. Inside, check out the ornate high ceilings, marble floors, and vintage photographs. While Portland has always had a rep as a port city, much of the shipboard cargo arrived or departed behind a locomotive. By the late 19th century Portland was served by no fewer than three major rail lines.

If you walk south from Union Station along S.W. 3rd, you pass through Chinatown and Old Town, a compact area of restaurants, galleries, and the remnants of Portland's historic Asian community. In 1890 Portland had the largest Chinatown on the West Coast. The Chinese came to work on the railroad and in eastern Oregon gold mines. Back then, opium and gambling dens and houses of negotiable affection proliferated in the neighborhood. Perhaps the most notorious corner of Old Town/Chinatown was S.W. 2nd and Couch, the location of Erickson's Saloon. Here sailors would partake at a bar that stretched a length of 684 feet. In the Bad Old Days, bartenders sometimes conspired with work contractors to

BIRD'S-EYE VIEWS

These eye-popping excursions to stunning vistas are best undertaken by car as mass transit is problematic in the West Hills behind the city and at Sauvie Island.

PITTOCK MANSION

This mansion is frequently featured as the first stop on many bus tour itineraries because of its history, architecture, and all-encompassing view of the city. Situated at nearly the highest point in the West Hills, 1,000 feet above sea level, this French Renaissance mansion completed in 1914 also stands above the rest of the grand edifices in the city for other reasons. *Oregonian* founder Henry Pittock spared little expense in furnishing his 22-room manor house with such accoutrements as modern showers with multiple shower heads, a central cleaning system, room-to-room telephones, and a Turkish smoking room. The "whorl-pattern" wooden floors in some of the public rooms here are a must-see as are the views of the city from the bedrooms upstairs. The antique furniture, access to Forest Park trails, and fair-weather views of the Cascades (Mounts Hood, St. Helens, and Rainier are potentially visible) from the lavishly landscaped back yard also make this place a fixture on many itineraries.

Regular tours are conducted daily (503/823-3624), except for dates in mid-November when the house is decorated for Christmas. The grounds are open to the public until dark. The mansion is especially nice to visit when it's bedecked in Christmas finery. Be that as it may, the summer flowers surrounding the structure and the vistas in back of the mansion may well offer the most compelling reasons to come up here. Lunch and afternoon tea are available in the Gate Lodge, the former caretaker's cottage behind the mansion. In the north corner of the Pittock parking lot, a trail leads two miles down to Cornell Road through an old-growth forest.

Mass-transit access from downtown is provided by bus #77 to N.W. Barnes and Burnside Street, at which point you'll have to walk the steep 0.5 mile up Pittock Avenue. To get there by car, head west up Burnside past the turn-off to Washington Park. Turn right at the sign for Pittock Mansion onto Pittock Avenue and follow the signs. From here, it's a 0.25-mile drive up steep and curving switchbacks.

COUNCIL CREST

Considered to be among Portland's preeminent vistas, Council Crest can be enjoyed from atop a butte in a ridge-top neighborhood in the posh West Hills. At 1,073 feet above sea level, this is the highest point within the city limits. Purportedly named during an 1898 National Council of Congregational Churches conference that met here, Council Crest later gained notoriety in its early decades as an amusement park at the end of a streetcar line. The bluff looks out on snowcapped volcanoes and 3,000 square miles of territory. As you circle the summit, out to the west the panorama of the Tualatin Valley and Washington County is worth a gander, particularly at sunset. On the eastern side, steps lead up to an observation platform with arrows indicating locations of five Cascades peaks (check out the echo here). Even if the peaks are not visible, the view of downtown and the rest of the city to the east is breathtaking.

From here, you'll note the two tallest buildings in the Portland skyline. In case you're wondering which of the two bank towers is the highest, consider the following, then decide upon your frame of reference. The Wells Fargo tower, the whitish building in the center of the city, has 40 stories. Sitting to the north is a big pink structure, the 42-story U.S. Bank tower. Number crunchers might take interest in the fact that the top of the Wells Fargo tower is still a tad higher (despite a shortfall of two stories) when the slope of downtown Portland is taken into account.

To get to Council Crest from Burnside, turn left (south) on Vista (N.W. 23rd), turn left on Greenway, then take the right fork, Council Crest Way, into the park.

PORTLAND

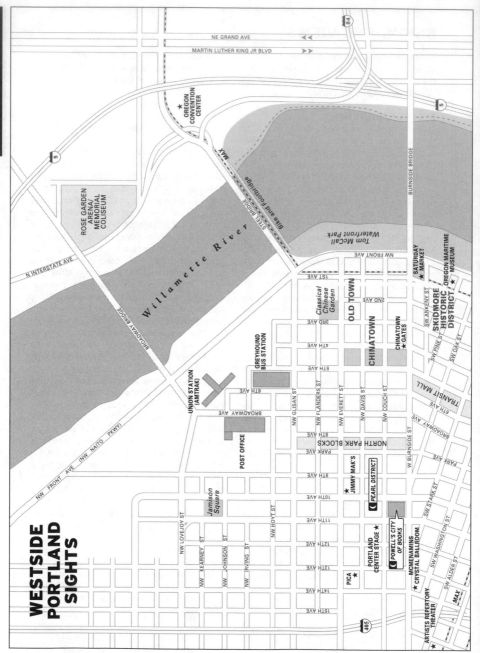

WESTSIDE PORTLAND SIGHTS

NE GRAND AVE

MARTIN LUTHER KING JR BLVD

84

5

OREGON CONVENTION CENTER

ROSE GARDEN ARENA/ MEMORIAL COLISEUM

MAX

STEEL BRIDGE

Bike and Footbridge

Willamette River

N INTERSTATE AVE

BROADWAY BRIDGE

NW FRONT AVE (NW NAITO PKWY)

Tom McCall Waterfront Park

NW FRONT AVE

5

BURNSIDE BRIDGE

SATURDAY MARKET

Classical Chinese Garden

1ST AVE

2ND AVE

OLD TOWN

CHINATOWN

CHINATOWN GATES

OREGON MARITIME MUSEUM

SKIDMORE HISTORIC DISTRICT

SW ANKENY ST

SW PINE ST

SW OAK ST

GREYHOUND BUS STATION

3RD AVE

4TH AVE

5TH AVE

6TH AVE

NW GLISAN ST

NW FLANDERS ST

NW EVERETT ST

NW DAVIS ST

NW COUCH ST

TRANSIT MALL

6TH AVE

BROADWAY AVE

W BURNSIDE ST

UNION STATION (AMTRAK)

BROADWAY AVE

POST OFFICE

7TH AVE

8TH AVE

9TH AVE

10TH AVE

11TH AVE

12TH AVE

13TH AVE

14TH AVE

15TH AVE

NORTH PARK BLOCKS

PARK AVE

JIMMY MAK'S

PEARL DISTRICT

POWELL'S CITY OF BOOKS

PORTLAND CENTER STAGE

PICA

MCMENAMINS CRYSTAL BALLROOM

ARTISTS REPERTORY THEATER

SW STARK ST

SW WASHINGTON ST

SW ALDER ST

MAX

Jamison Square

NW LOVEJOY ST

NW KEARNEY ST

NW JOHNSON ST

NW IRVING ST

NW HOYT ST

405

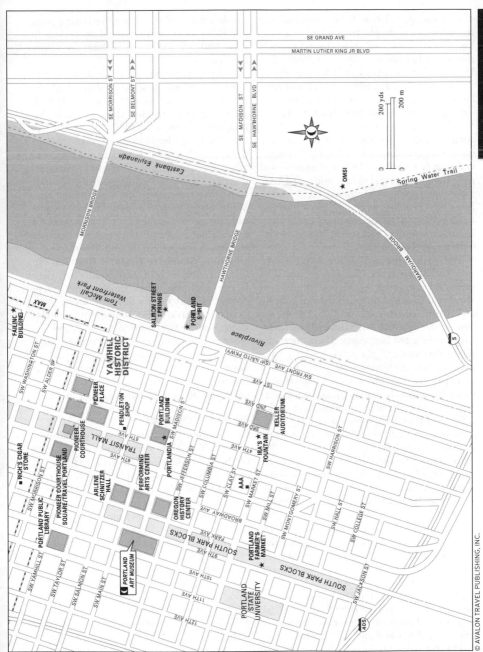

SE GRAND AVE

MARTIN LUTHER KING JR BLVD

SE MORRISON ST

SE BELMONT ST

SE MADISON ST

SE HAWTHORNE BLVD

Eastbank Esplanade

200 yds

200 m

★ OMSI

Spring Water Trail

MORRISON BRIDGE

HAWTHORNE BRIDGE

MARQUAM BRIDGE

I-5

Tom McCall Waterfront Park

SALMON STREET SPRINGS ★

PORTLAND SPIRIT ★

Riverplace

SW FRONT AVE (SW NAITO PKWY)

FAILING BUILDING ★

MAX

YAMHILL HISTORIC DISTRICT

SW WASHINGTON ST

SW ALDER ST

PIONEER PLACE

PENDLETON SHOP

PORTLAND BUILDING

SW MADISON ST

KELLER AUDITORIUM

1ST AVE

2ND AVE

3RD AVE

4TH AVE

5TH AVE

6TH AVE

SW HARRISON ST

RICH'S CIGAR STORE ■

PIONEER COURTHOUSE

TRANSIT MALL

PORTLANDIA ★

PERFORMING ARTS CENTER

SW JEFFERSON ST

IRA'S FOUNTAIN ★

AAA ▲

SW MARKET ST

SW COLUMBIA ST

SW CLAY ST

SW MILL ST

SW MONTGOMERY ST

SW HALL ST

SW COLLEGE ST

ARLENE SCHNITZER HALL

OREGON HISTORY CENTER

BROADWAY AVE

PIONEER COURTHOUSE SQUARE/TRAVEL PORTLAND

PORTLAND PUBLIC LIBRARY

PARK AVE

SOUTH PARK BLOCKS

PORTLAND FARMER'S MARKET ★

9TH AVE

10TH AVE

11TH AVE

12TH AVE

PORTLAND ART MUSEUM

SW YAMHILL ST

SW TAYLOR ST

SW SALMON ST

SW MAIN ST

SW MORRISON ST

PORTLAND STATE UNIVERSITY

SW JACKSON ST

SOUTH PARK BLOCKS

I-405

drug a seaman's drink. When unconscious, the sailor would then be transported to a waiting ship by means of underground tunnels that extended down to the waterfront. The "Shanghaied" seaman would later awake to find himself "hired" and at sea. (Tours of Portland's "Underground" and a Shanghai tunnel are offered by **Portland Walking Tours,** 503/774-4522, www.portlandwalkingtours. com.) Shanghaied seamen were not the only ones down on their luck in Portland's rough-and-tumble waterfront. In fact, the term "skid row" is sometimes said to have originated here. This expression came from the "skid roads," paths on which logs were slid downhill to waterfront mills. After logging booms went bust, folks down on their luck would "hit the skids" in these parts of town.

Today, the area puts its best foot forward two blocks west at the Chinatown gates. The gargoyled gate at 4th Avenue and Burnside is always good for a photograph. Notice that the male statue is on the right with a ball under his foot, while the female has a cub under her paw. Also note the red lampposts. These are traditional Portland gaslight posts, but they have street names on them written in Chinese. In other parts of Chinatown and Old Town, acupuncture houses, herbal shops, and traditional groceries keep the old ways alive next to the galleries of Portland's contemporary art scene. A number of traditional Chinese restaurants are found along S.W. 3rd Avenue.

In spring, the cherry blossoms on 5th and Davis become the highlight of Chinatown along with the contemplative repose found at the **Portland Classical Chinese Garden,** (at N.W. 2nd Ave. and Everett St., 503/228-8131, www.portlandchinesegarden.org, open 9 A.M.–6 P.M. in spring, summer, and fall. After Halloween, winter hours are 10 A.M.–5 P.M., $7 for adults, $6 for seniors, $5.50 for students, free for children under 5). Three hundred tons of cloud-shaped rock and elaborate carvings were imported from China—along with a small army of Chinese workmen—to help shape the largest and most authentic garden of this type outside of China. Decorative

pavilions, a teahouse, a large reflecting pool, and other motifs were inspired by gardens in the 2,500-year-old city of Suzhou, the Venice of China.

Overlapping this neighborhood are the museums, galleries, restaurants, shops, and signature architecture of Old Town (along with many homeless people). Many of the buildings here date from the 1880s, despite the fact that Portland's beginnings stretch back four decades earlier. This is because an 1872 fire razed much of what was then the commercial district. Cast-iron buildings with Italianate flourishes went up in the wake of the fire. While a large number of these foundry facades were torn down in the 1940s to make way for a Willamette River bridge and a waterfront freeway, a few survive in Old Town and the adjoining **Skidmore Historic District.** (In fact, there are more of these facades here than in any other place in the United States except New York City's Soho district.) While these neighborhoods are adorned with antique street signs, newly touched-up "old brick," and lots of iron and brass to evoke old Portland, such accoutrements aren't always necessary to induce historical reverie. There are enough early 20th-century white terra-cotta building facades and other period architecture for that.

🄫 Pearl District

For long-time Portlanders, few urban transformations have been more incredible than that of the Pearl District. This area, roughly between N.W. Broadway and N.W. 14th, between Burnside and Marshal Streets, was until very recently a wasteland of moldering warehouses, abandoned rail yards, and moribund light industry. In a short 15 years, the area has been utterly transformed into one of the city's most exclusive residential neighborhoods, with newly paved streets (until the gentrification, this antique area of town still boasted some paving-stone streets) lined with upscale furniture and home decor boutiques, fine restaurants, and art galleries. First-Thursday-of-the-month gallery walks feature hors d'oeuvres and 8 P.M. closing time at neighborhood galleries. Now that nearly

©PAUL LEVY

The Portland Streetcar runs past Jamison Park, in the Pearl District.

all the original warehouses have been converted to loft apartments, brand-new warehouse-like buildings and high-rise apartments are being constructed to house the affluent masses.

Even though the boundaries of the Pearl District are seemingly ever-expanding, a good place to begin your exploration is along N.W. 10th Avenue. At the corner of West Burnside Street and 10th Avenue is the mothership **Powell's Books** store, one of the nation's largest bookstores. Nearby is the **Portland Institute for Contemporary Art,** with an impressive calendar of cutting-edge art exhibitions/installations/performances. If you're looking to decorate your home, the myriad art galleries and furniture and decor stores along N.W. Glisan Street between 10th and 14th Avenues ought to provide inspiration. Further north, at 13th and Johnson, the **Pacific Northwest College of Art** is one of the West Coast's top art schools. The lobby of this converted warehouse contains two art galleries for contemporary art. Student art is usually on display in the central atrium. If all this arty

exploration has made you thirsty, consider a stop at the **Bridgeport Brew Pub,** one of Portland's first and still one of its finest.

The Portland Streetcar runs through the Pearl District along 10th and 11th Avenues.

Powell's City of Books

Portlanders buy more books per capita than people in most other parts of the country; in bookstore sales per household Portland ranks ahead of New York City. Powell's Books (1005 W. Burnside, 503/228-4651, 9 A.M.–11 P.M. Mon.–Sat., 9 A.M.–9 P.M. Sun.) is not only a Portland institution, it is the largest independent bookstore in the world. Add such accolades as author Susan Sontag calling it "the best bookstore in the English-speaking world" and you can believe tales of shoppers finding books here that were impossible to find elsewhere. Over a million new and used books are housed in a labyrinth of hallways that take up a city block. A helpful staff and maps of the stacks help locate whatever you might be looking for in 50 sections ranging from automobiles to Zen. The Coffee Room, on the west side of the store, sells gourmet coffee drinks, pastries, salads, soups, and snacks. It's a favorite place for singles to make connections. Free parking in the store garage and frequent readings by renowned authors enhance the store's appeal. Browse www.powells.com to get a sense of what the *Wall Street Journal* called "one of the most innovative and creative enterprises in the country."

N.W. 21st and 23rd Avenues

Sometimes referred to as Nob Hill, the lovely Victorian neighborhoods around N.W. 21st and N.W. 23rd Avenues, represent an island of upscale dining and retail. Victorian homes have been remodeled into boutiques to join stylish shopping arcades, bookstores, restaurants, and theaters. Generally speaking, N.W. 21st Avenue has the greater number of restaurants, while N.W. 23rd Avenue has more shops—mostly locally owned boutiques dedicated to women's clothing and home decor. The neighborhood's artsy shops and café society attract strollers en masse, creating a people-watcher's paradise. Looming over this part of Northwest Portland are the West Hills, a range of extinct volcanoes now capped by

SAUVIE ISLAND

Ten miles northwest of Portland at the confluence of the Willamette and Columbia Rivers is the rural enclave of Sauvie Island, a scant 20 minutes from downtown. On clear days here, views of the snowcapped Cascades Range backdrop oceangoing freighters and cruise ships. Visitors enjoy horseback riding, swimming, and U-pick farms plying apples, berries, peaches, pears, nectarines, melons, green beans, corn, zucchini, tomatoes, and pumpkins. A favorite spot for bird-watching, the area sees eagles, great blue herons, geese, and sandhill cranes among the 250 species that pass through on the Pacific Flyway. Wildlife aficionados see red foxes and black-tailed deer on the island's northern half. In addition, anglers come to Sauvie's lakes and sloughs for panfish and bass, and to the Columbia side for sturgeon, salmon, and steelhead. Bikers come for the 12-mile "hill-less" biking loop. Nearby is **Collins Beach,** a nudist hangout.

Other seasonal highlights here include watching the Christmas ships (whose colored lights and yule-time decor resemble the most elaborate parade floats imaginable) and swimming at **Walton Beach** at the end of N.W. Reeder Road. Mid-January offers a rare chance to see bald eagles feeding here.

This is Oregon as it was, before Starbucks, gas stations, and souvenir shops. Described by the British Navy and Lewis and Clark as a major outpost of Chinook culture, in the early 19th century Sauvie drew Euro-American settlers, who came to engage in the extensive trade along the Columbia River and to till the fertile soil.

History buffs and nature lovers can enjoy fall foliage at the **James Y. Bybee House** (Howell Park Rd., 503/222-1741). This 1858 farm, built by Oregon Trail pioneers, is furnished with pieces from that period. If you're not edified by reading Sauvie Island's history dating back to Lewis and Clark, the Bybee House also features a collection of old farming implements and an orchard with 115 species of apples brought by the pioneers. The house is open noon–5 P.M. Saturday–Sunday, June–Labor Day.

In late September, the Bybee House is open for the **Wintering-In Festival.** Combining this event with a bike ride through the island's pumpkin patches, yellow-leafed cottonwoods, and river views is a wonderful way to herald the coming season.

Be aware that if you park at one of Sauvie Island's public beaches or wildlife viewing areas, you'll need a parking certificate, available for $3.50 per vehicle at Sam's Cracker Barrel Grocery on Sauvie Island Road; turn left after coming off the bridge. Also remember to gas up and hit the ATM beforehand heading to the island; neither are here.

To reach Sauvie Island, take U.S. 30 northwest to St. Helens, Linnton, and Sauvie Island.

Forest Park, the largest urban wilderness in the United States.

NORTHEAST PORTLAND
Lloyd Center and Inner Northeast

The world's largest shopping center in 1960 (also one of the world's first), today Lloyd Center mall boasts more than 100 retail outlets; a domed ice-skating rink, **Lloyd Ice Pavilion;** and one of the largest theaters in the city, **Lloyd Cinemas** (4510 N.E. Multnomah, 503/248-6938), with 10 screens and a futuristic neon interior. Lloyd Center is increasingly an adjunct to downtown, joined by frequent MAX light-rail trains (which are free as far east as Lloyd Center).

Inner Northeast Portland—the neighborhoods between Lloyd Center and the Willamette River—contain a number of major public buildings. The **Oregon Convention Center** is easy to spot with its twin glass steeples. The **Portland Rose Garden Arena** is home to the NBA's Portland Trail Blazers, while the adjacent **Memorial Coliseum** hosts the Portland Winter Hawks ice hockey franchise and other sporting and cultural events.

On the north edge of Lloyd Center is N.E. Broadway, a major arterial that links the northeast residential neighborhoods with downtown Portland. Between N.E. 21st Avenue and N.E. 8th, N.E. Broadway offers a wide variety of casual and ethnic dining options. The historic Irvington neighborhood north of Broadway offers a number of fine bed-and-breakfast inns with easy public transportation to downtown.

North Mississippi Avenue

A travel guide written in the late 1990s wouldn't even have mentioned North Mississippi Avenue as a destination, as it was a decrepit, early 20th-century trolley-stop neighborhood that had become a haven for drug use and itinerancy. In the years since, Portland's influx of "young creatives" discovered this historic community center and found it an inexpensive place to start restaurants, art galleries, bars, brewpubs, coffeehouses, bakeries, and other one-of-a-kind enterprises. Fast forward a few years, and Mississippi Avenue is one of the hubs of Portland's most creative cooking, and a hotbed of youthful nightlife. A testament to progressive politics and entrepreneurial instincts, Mississippi Avenue is six blocks of Portland's renowned neighborhood-oriented lifestyle, with enough nightlife and dining choices to justify a trip for travelers staying in not-far-distant downtown.

Any trip to North Mississippi Avenue should include a stop at **The Rebuilding Center** (3625 N. Mississippi Ave., 503/331-1877, 9 A.M.–6 P.M. Mon.–Sat., 10 A.M.–5 P.M. Sun.), the largest non-profit used-building-materials resource in North America. Building salvage of all sorts finds its way to this 64,000-square-foot warehouse and lumberyard. If you're a homeowner and looking for a cheap sink, a period match for picture moulding, or cheap used-once two-by-fours, this labyrinth of old house stuff is fascinating.

Alberta Street

Another East Side neighborhood that's the focus of youthful artists and chefs, Alberta Street is a somewhat attenuated destination for travelers who want to explore the cutting edge of the Portland art scene, particularly on the last Friday of the month, when the length of the street (from around N.E. 10th Ave. to N.E. 39th Ave.) erupts in a street fair. It's also an excellent destination for diners: Inexpensive rents provide a haven for young chefs whose restaurants push the boundaries of Northwest cuisine.

The Grotto

The Grotto (N.E. 85th and N.E. Sandy Blvd., 503/254-7371, open 9 A.M.–dusk daily, free) is a Catholic shrine whose hand-hewn cavern surrounded by lushly landscaped grounds can induce a profound sense of peace, no matter your religion. Within the ivy-covered, fern-lined grotto is an impressive marble pietà. Outside the 30- by 50-foot enclosure, old-growth firs tower over the 110-foot cliff housing the shrine. Roses, camellias, rhododendrons, azaleas, and a cliffside view of the Columbia River also make this worth the 20-minute pilgrimage from downtown Portland (take TriMet bus #12).

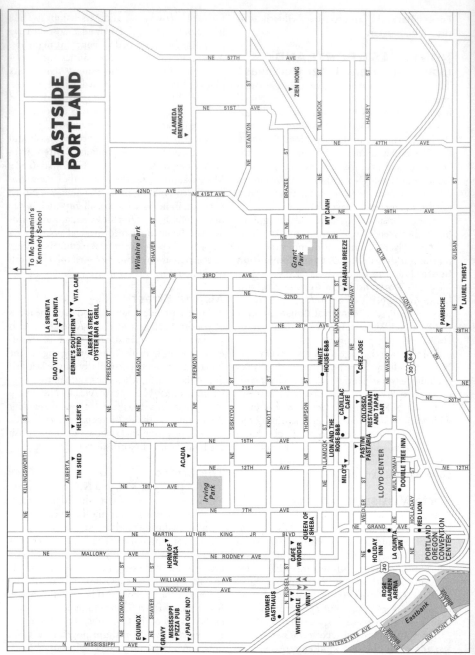

EASTSIDE PORTLAND

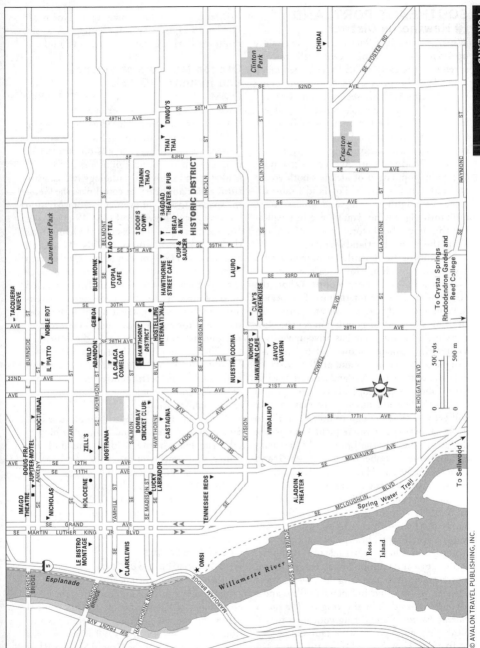

ICHIDAI

Clinton
Park

SE FOSTER RD

SE 52ND AVE

SE 50TH AVE

DINGO'S

SE 49TH AVE

CLINTON ST

Creston
Park

THAI
THAI

43RD ST

SE 42ND AVE

THANH
THAO

HISTORIC DISTRICT

LINCOLN

SE 39TH AVE

BAGDAD
THEATER & PUB

3 DOOFS
DOWN

BREAD
& INK

GLADSTONE

BELMONT ST

TAO OF TEA

SE 35TH AVE

SE 35TH PL

CUP &
SAUCER

HAWTHORNE
STREET CAFE

LAURO

SE 33RD AVE

Laurelhurst Park

BLUE MONK

UTOPIA
CAFE

SE 30TH AVE

CLAY'S
SMOKEHOUSE

TACQUERIA
NUEVE

NOBLE ROT

GENOA

HOSTELLING
INTERNATIONAL

HARRISON ST

SE 28TH AVE

BURNSIDE ST

IL PIATTO

WILD
ABANDON

SE 26TH AVE

HAWTHORNE
DISTRICT

LA CALACA
COMELOA

NUESTRA COCINA

SE 24TH AVE

NOHO'S
HAWAIIAN CAFE

SAVOY
TAVERN

POWELL BLVD

22ND
AVE

MORRISON ST

SE 20TH AVE

SE 21ST AVE

VINDALHO

SE 17TH AVE

SEHOLGATE BLVD

NOCTURNAL

STARK ST

NOSTRANA

SALMON ST

BOMBAY
CRICKET CLUB

CASTAGNA

HAWTHORNE

SE LADD AVE

SE ELLIOT

DIVISION

MILWAUKIE AVE

To Sellwood

ZELL'S

DOUG FIR/
JUPITER MOTEL

ANKENY

HOLOCENE

SE 12TH AVE

SE 11TH AVE

LUCKY
LABRADOR

TENNESSEE REDS

YAMHILL ST

SE MADISON ST

ALADDIN
THEATER ★

Spring Water Trail

MCLOUGHLIN BLVD

IMAGO
THEATRE

NICHOLAS

SE GRAND AVE

SE MARTIN LUTHER KING JR BLVD

CLARKLEWIS

LE BISTRO
MONTAGE

OMSI

ROSS ISLAND BRIDGE

Ross
Island

Esplanade

Willamette River

MARQUAM BRIDGE

BURNSIDE
BRIDGE

MORRISON BRIDGE

HAWTHORNE BRIDGE

SW FRONT AVE

To Crysta Springs
Rhododendron Garden and
Reed College

0   50C yds
0   500 m

SOUTHEAST PORTLAND
◖ Hawthorne District

When you think of Portland, do you conjure up images of the hippie era? Well, rest assured that the early 1970s haven't aged much along Hawthorne Avenue. Stores purveying records, fine coffees, secondhand clothing, antiques, crafts, and books join cafés and galleries recalling the hip enclaves of Berkeley, California, and Cambridge, Massachusetts. A dense concentration of these establishments between 32nd and 46th Avenues is catnip for a friendly population of idealists both young and old. This is one of Portland's most alternative neighborhoods, and unless you're militantly right-wing, you'll have fun exploring the shops, bookstores, and coffee shops along this iconic Portland avenue.

Hawthorne Boulevard was named after a psychiatrist and long-time area resident who oversaw an asylum near **Mount Tabor,** the neighborhood's eastern terminus. This peak is the country's only extinct volcano within the city limits of a major population center. Now a city park, Mount Tabor has drive-up views of Mount Hood and downtown Valley. There are also old-growth conifers and brilliant vistas of fall color dotting the Portland cityscape visible from Tabor's upper slopes. If you don't have a car, a #15 Belmont bus (or #14 Hawthorne) will get you close enough to hike the trails to these panoramas. If you're picnicking on the slopes, try Hawthorne Boulevard's best bakery (also voted number one in Seattle), **Grand Central** (2230 S.E. Hawthorne Blvd.), for baguettes, scones, pies, and cakes.

North of Hawthorne is N.E. Belmont, and south of Hawthorne is S.E. Clinton. Both are heirs-apparent to hip-strip status. Belmont features restaurants, brewpubs, a theater, and espresso bars. On the other side of Hawthorne, at S.E. 26th and Clinton Street, is a nucleus of hipster enterprises, including the Clinton Street Theater, which offers independent films and a Saturday-at-midnight showing of *The Rocky Horror Picture Show* (bring your own toast). Nearby are good pubs and restaurants.

To get to Hawthorne Boulevard, hop a #14

TriMet bus from downtown. From Northeast Portland's Halsey Transit Center (a.k.a. the Hollywood MAX Station) catch a #75 bus.

Oregon Museum of Science and Industry (OMSI)

OMSI (1945 S.E. Water Ave., 503/797-4000, www.omsi.edu, in summer open 9:30 A.M.–7 P.M. daily; in winter, closed Mondays, open 9:30 A.M.–5:30 P.M. Tues.–Sun., $9 adults, $7 seniors and kids) is a hands-on, interactive museum where you can pilot a ship from its bridge, gain insight on cardiology from a walk through a giant heart, or coordinate the Gemini space capsule's movements from Mission Control. The showcase of OMSI's riverfront 18.5-acre campus, however, is the Omnimax theater ($8.50–12 adults, $6.50–10 children and seniors). Here you can be transported into such exotic locales as a volcano or deep space through the medium of 70-mm film projected onto a four-story-high domed screen. Incredibly vivid acoustics make it possibly the most intense audiovisual experience ever created. Astronomy and laser shows at the Murdock Sky Theater (additional admission) and six exhibit halls containing interactive displays make OMSI the perfect entrée into the world of science and technology for all ages and levels of sophistication.

To get here from I-5 northbound, take Exit 300-B onto Water Avenue. From downtown, take the Hawthorne Bridge, and look for brown signs once you reach the east bank of the Willamette. TriMet's #6 bus picks people up downtown on S.W. Salmon and 5th Avenue and drops them off in front of OMSI. This bus can also be caught at the Oregon Convention Center MAX station.

Crystal Springs Rhododendron Garden

Southeast of downtown near the Reed College campus, distinguished for producing the highest number of Rhodes Scholars in the United States and ranked the finest academic institution in the country in a 1999 *U.S. News and World Report* survey, is the Crystal Springs Rhododendron Garden (S.E. 28th Ave. at Woodstock Blvd., 503/823-3640). Come in April and May to see 600 varieties of rhodies and azaleas on seven acres, including an island on a spring-fed lake. Even without the 2,500 individual broad-leaf evergreens here, bird-watching and fall foliage encourage a visit. From March through Labor Day, a $3 admission fee is charged every day except Tuesday and Wednesday, when it's free.

Sellwood Antique Row

Antique hunters will be drawn from downtown to Sellwood in the southeast of Portland. Once a separate city, it annexed itself to Portland in 1890. More than 30 antique stores—with names like Den of Antiquity and Gilt—are spread along 13 blocks. This shopper's paradise is clustered around S.E. 13th Avenue be-

tween Tacoma and Bybee Streets. Don't come early, as many of the stores open after 11 A.M. Take the #70 bus from the Rose Quarter, which stops every two blocks on 13th.

After antiquing, head over to **Sellwood Park** (S.E. 7th Ave. and Sellwood Blvd.). The western extremity of this park sits on a tree-lined bluff above the Willamette. Tennis courts, a pool, picnic tables, and access to Oak Bottoms Wildlife Refuge make this park a delight in spring and summer. Below the bluff is **Oaks Park,** where a vintage carousel and roller rink on the Willamette's eastern shore add to the recreational menu. To drive to Oaks Park from downtown, take McLoughlin Boulevard south to the Tacoma Street Exit. Follow Tacoma Street west to S.E. 7th Avenue, turn right on 7th, and then take the first left onto Spokane. Follow the signs to Oaks Park.

Sports and Recreation

SPECTATOR SPORTS

Portland is a town more for athletes than devotees of spectator sports. Nonetheless, the two stadiums in the Rose City draw huge crowds.

The **Rose Garden Arena** (located at the east end of the Broadway Bridge, 503/235-8771, www.rosequarter.com) is home to the National Basketball Association's **Portland Trail Blazers.** (If you MAX out to the complex, exit the train at the Rose Quarter transit center.)

The Rose Garden's high seating capacity (20,339) and enhanced views have given Portland an exciting arena for basketball and concerts.

While most Trail Blazers' seats are reserved for season ticket-holders, some are available at Ticketmaster outlets or through the arena box office. Then, of course, there are always the overpriced offerings of ticket brokers advertised in the *Oregonian* or scalpers who may be found beyond a four-block radius of the Rose Garden. It's best to call the Blazers' ticket line (503/231-8000 or 503/797-9600), or write their corporate offices (700 N.E. Multnomah, Ste. 600, Portland, OR 97232) well in advance. You can

also log on to www.nba.com/blazers to check ticket prices or buy tickets.

The Blazers' former home, the **Memorial Coliseum** (1401 N. Wheeler, 503/235-8771) now hosts the **Winter Hawks,** a minor-league hockey team of the Western Hockey League.

HIKING

Portland is famous for more park acreage per capita than any other major American city—Portland has over 37,000 acres preserved as parkland—with one-twelfth of the city's area devoted to public recreational venues. Within these holdings, the city has more urban wilderness than any other municipality in the country.

(Forest Park and the West Hills

Without doubt, the part of Portland most conducive to a walk on the wild side is up in the hills behind the Northwest neighborhood. The largest urban wilderness in the country, Forest Park stretches along the crest of Portland's West Hills, and is 8.5 miles long and 1.5 miles wide. What other city has a park in which bear, elk, deer, and cougar have been sighted? What other city park has old-growth trees and wild scenic areas? To explore Forest Park's trails beyond the basic introduction given here, pick up a copy of the excellent pocket-sized maps put out by Friends of Forest Park (www.friendsof forestpark.org), available at the local REI and Patagonia stores and at Powell's Books.

To reach Forest Park from I-5, take the Fremont Bridge into Northwest Portland and head west on Vaughn Street. Turn left onto 26th Avenue and follow it to Thurman Street. Make a right on Thurman and follow it to its end to reach the portal of Forest Park. From N.W. 23rd Avenue, just head north to Thurman Street, turn left (west) and head about 1.5 miles uphill to the top of Thurman. Also, the #15 Thurman Street bus from downtown stops about a quarter-mile downhill from the entrance to the park.

A scenic adjunct is **MacLeay Park,** which can be reached via the Fremont Bridge–Vaughn

© JUDY JEWELL

Deer ferns and oxalis grow in Forest Park and around western Oregon.

Street route, and turning left onto N.W. 28th Avenue, then right onto Upshur Street, following it to its end. The gentle uphill trail here follows a deep gully paralleling a creek.

Another way to reach MacLeay and Forest Parks is via the 14-mile **Wildwood Trail,** which heads north through the Hoyt Arboretum and near Pittock Mansion before plunging downhill into the parklands below. The trail begins on Canyon Road near the zoo and Forestry Center. Or you can drive to the **Arboretum Visitor Center** (4000 S.W. Fairview Blvd., 503/288-8733, www.hoytarboretum.org, open 10 A.M.–4 P.M. daily) or the Pittock Mansion to begin your descent into MacLeay and Forest Parks. The park itself is open 6 A.M.–10 P.M. daily.

Wildwood Trail is part of a proposed larger network of trails to loop the city. This was originally the brainchild of the Olmsted brothers (of Yosemite Valley and Central Park fame) at the turn of the 20th century. Their proposed 40-mile loop concept has expanded to a 140-mile matrix. Now the goal is to complete a hiking/biking path connecting parks along the Columbia, Sandy, and Willamette Rivers. To find out more, contact the **Portland Parks and Recreation Department** (503/823-2223, www.portlandparks.org).

Oaks Bottom

On the other end of town, another potential component of the loop beckons urban walkers in search of rural pleasures. Snaking along the east bank of the Willamette River between the Sellwood and Ross Island Bridges, the **Oaks Bottom Wildlife Refuge** is a bird-watcher's paradise. Great blue and green herons find this wetland a prime habitat. In winter, a dozen species of waterfowl can be sighted. Summertime residents include warblers, orioles, swallows, and woodpeckers. Whenever you go, look for wood ducks joining such permanent denizens as beavers and muskrats.

A ridge along Sellwood Boulevard frames Oaks Bottom and offers good views. You can hike into it at the north end of Sellwood Park at S.W. 7th Avenue and Sellwood Boulevard. A parking lot at the 5000 block of S.E. Milwaukie Avenue also offers access. After you descend, a loop trail encircles the wetlands, paralleling the bluff on the east side and following the railroad tracks to the west.

PADDLING

If you're tempted to get out onto the Willamette River, take a tour or rent a sea kayak from **Portland River Company** (0315 S.W. Montgomery St., 503/229-0551, www.portlandriver company.com), located on the west side of the Willamette River at RiverPlace. The three-hour tour around Ross Island ($43) is suitable for beginners and gives paddlers a chance to see great blue herons and, oftentimes, osprey and eagles.

On the east side of the river, **Alder Creek Kayak** (49 S.E. Clay St., 503/285-1819, www .aldercreek.com) has a boathouse located on the Eastside Esplanade immediately south of the Hawthorne Bridge. Kayak rentals start at $10 per hour, $30 per day. From the boathouse, it's easy to launch into the Willamette River.

CAMPING

Portland isn't particularly convenient for campers. If you are planning to use a campground as your base for visiting downtown Portland, you'll be facing a lengthy commute. The good news is that within 30 miles of so of downtown you'll find some lovely state parks. But with today's traffic, be prepared to spend up to an hour to get in and out of the city center. South of Portland, with easy access off I-5 is **Champoeg State Park** (503/678-1251, www .oregonstateparks.org), a lovely park along the Willamette River that's also a major sight in Northwest history. Campsites are in shaded groves alongside the river, and bike and hiking paths and museums make this park a worthy recreational destination. In addition to year-round tenting ($12) and RV ($16) sites, there are also yurts ($27) and rustic cabins ($35). Champoeg State Park is about 30 miles south of downtown Portland, off I-5 Exit 278. Reserve campsites at 800/452-5687 or www .reserveamerica.com.

For those who enjoy rural serenity within commuting distance of downtown, there's camping in **Milo McIver State Park** (503/630-7150 or 800/551-6949, www.oregonstateparks .org). This retreat, set on the banks of the Collowash River (five miles northwest of Estacada), is 25 miles from downtown Portland, but in spirit it seems farther away, particularly when you're gazing at the knockout sunset view of Mount Hood. To get to the park, take I-84 east to I-205 south and follow the exit to Route 224/Estacada. The road forks right at the town of Carver to go 10 miles (look for Springwater Road) to the campground. There are 44 hookup sites, flush toilets, showers, firewood, and a laundry here, as well as fishing for winter steelhead and late-fall salmon. Other recreation includes hiking, horse trails, and a boat ramp. Campground fees are $17 per night with no reservations, and it's open March–October.

Another camping option about 35 miles east of Portland off I-84 is **Ainsworth State Park** (503/695-2301 or 800/551-6949, www.oregon stateparks.org). Picnic tables, fire rings, flush toilets, and an RV camp enhance a prime location near the trails and waterfalls of the Columbia River Gorge. Nightly rates are $10–16 on a first-come, first-served basis. You can get there via the Columbia River Highway or by taking Exit 35 off I-84 West. Bring earplugs here if you're a light sleeper as freeway noise tends to echo between the Gorge walls.

East of Portland, a few miles north of I-84 on the Sandy River is **Oxbow Park** (503/797-1850), operated by the Portland regional government, Metro. Oxbow Park is right on a bend of the river in a quiet woodsy setting, and offers flush toilets but no showers. There's also a strict no-dog policy. To reach Oxbow Park, take I-84 exit 17, and follow 257th Avenue to Division Street and turn east (right) and follow signs to the river. Campsites are $15.

TENNIS, GOLF, AND WATER RECREATION

Tennis courts, golf courses, public pools, and lakes offering swimming and sailing abound in the Portland area.

Portland Parks and Recreation (503/823-3189, www.portlandparks.org) oversees the city's

115 tennis courts. The best public courts in terms of surface and surrounding environment are located up the hill from the Rose Garden in Washington Park. Use of them is free of charge. To get there from downtown, take Burnside west up the hill. About a mile past N.W. 23rd, hang a sharp left (feels almost like a U-turn) at the light onto Tichner. Take the next right onto Kingston, and proceed for a minute or so to the parking lot adjacent to the tennis courts.

For golfers, Portland has more publicly owned golf courses per capita than any other U.S. city. Two of these, Heron Lakes and Eastmoreland, are ranked by *Golf Digest* as among the top 75 public courses in the U.S. Portland public course fees average around $25–30 for 18 holes.

Heron Lakes (3500 N. Victory Blvd., 503/289-1818, www.heronlakesgolf.com) is 15 minutes from downtown. Heron Lakes is the premier public golf facility in Portland, with 36 holes (the Greenback and Great Blue courses), a grass driving range, and good short-game practice areas. The two courses offer varying challenges at different green fee rates. The easier and shorter Greenback is good for beginners and moderate players, though it doesn't drain as well. The more challenging—and costlier—Great Blue, designed by Robert Trent Jones II, is better manicured and drains better in wet weather. To get there, take Exit 307 off I-5, head south of the Expo Center, and look for signs. The route here included the floodplain of the Vanport flood that obliterated a whole town in the late 1940s.

Eastmoreland Golf Course (2425 S.E. Bybee Blvd., 503/775-2900, www.portland parks.org/parks/eastmorelandgolf.htm), located near the Crystal Springs Rhododendron Garden. Eastmoreland is Oregon's second-oldest course, and one of the most beautiful. Located near Reed College in southeast Portland, the mature and lengthy 18-hole course is lined with beautiful mature trees and gardens. Ranked in the nation's top 25 courses by *Golf Digest,* Eastmoreland is operated by the Portland Parks Bureau and features a two-tier driving range, pro shop, and full bar and restaurant facilities. De-

signed by former U.S. Amateur champion H. Chandler Egan, who later helped redesign Pebble Beach Golf Links in the early 1900s.

The 36-hole **Pumpkin Ridge Golf Club** (U.S. 26, N. Plains Exit, 503/647-4747, www .pumpkinridge.com) contains perhaps the finest golf course accessible to the public in the immediate Portland area. It's located about 30 minutes west of Portland off Highway 26. The public Ghost Creek course is exquisitely manicured and challenging. The private Witch Hollow course, for members only, is a two-time host of the U.S. Women's Open and is not accessible to the public—without some pull on the inside.

For information on area lakes and public swimming pools, contact **Portland Parks** (1120 S.W. 5th Ave., Room 502, 503/823-2223, www.portlandparks.org).

ICE-SKATING

Skaters can follow in the tracks of Portland personality Tonya Harding and hit the ice at **Lloyd Center** (between Weidler St. and Multnomah Blvd. and N.E. 13th and N.E. 15th Sts., 503/282-2511, www.lloydcenter.com) and **Clackamas Town Center** (12000 S.E. 82nd Ave., 503/786-6000, www.clackamastown center.com). For a couple bucks' skate rental, you too can cut double axles in these practice venues. Call ahead for hours.

RUNNING AND WALKING

Named the "best running town" in the country in 2003 by *Runner's World* magazine, Portland hosts numerous running and walking events. The well-regarded **Portland Marathon** (503/226-111, www.portlandmarathon.org) and the **Cascade Classic** are two of them. To find out about these and other events, contact the **Oregon Road Runner's Club** (P.O. Box 2115, Gresham, OR 97030, 503/646-7867); they'll be glad to recommend the best places to run.

For both runners and walkers, one top downtown route connects the Waterfront Park promenade with the Eastbank Esplanade, a floating 1,200-foot-long walkway at eye-level with the Willamette River. Connect these two riverside routes into a 2.8-mile loop by using the Steel Bridge's pedestrian crossing and the broad walkway on the Hawthorne Bridge.

For a quieter and more secluded hiking or jogging experience, go to **Tryon Creek State Park** (503/636-9886 or 800/551-6949, www.oregonstateparks.org), the only Oregon state park within the Portland metro area. The 645-acre park offers eight miles of trails in a vernal woodland setting. Streamside wildlife includes beavers and songbirds. In late March there are wondrous displays of trillium, a wild marsh lily. To reach the park, take I-5 Exit 297 south of Portland, following S.W. Terwilliger Boulevard for 2.5 miles past Lewis and Clark College, watching for signs for the park.

Another top choice for joggers and walkers is the West Hills' **Forest Park,** with 70 miles of trails amid mature Northwest forest. For information, see *Hiking.*

CYCLING

Portland has twice been selected by *Bicycling* magazine as the most bike-friendly city in the nation. The website of the City of Portland's Office of Transportation (www.portland online.com/transportation) lists up-to-date information for cyclists. A handy map called *Getting There by Bike,* published by the government agency Metro, is sold at bike shops and bookstores across town. Bikers should know that Portland is a city of bridges but not all bridges are recommended for cyclists. A river-level foot/bike bridge forms the lower level of the Steel Bridge and connects the Eastbank Esplanade to Waterfront Park and downtown; otherwise, the Hawthorne, Broadway, and Burnside Bridges are best, although bikes must share sidewalks with pedestrians. Bikes are allowed on TriMet buses (bike racks are mounted on the front of every bus), the

MAX, and the Portland Streetcar, which can be handy to get out of the congested city center and to more suitable biking destinations. For more information, see TriMet's website (www.trimet.org/guide/bikes.htm) or call their bike hotline, 503/962-7644.

Although there are many worthy bike routes throughout the Portland area, there are several standouts. For further information on the following, contact **Portland Parks and Recreation** (1120 S.W. 5th Ave., Room 1302, Portland 97204, 503/823-2223). The 16.8-mile **Springwater Corridor** is a bike thoroughfare built on reclaimed rail line from S.E. Portland through Gresham to Boring. Views of Mount Hood abound throughout much of the route. Along the way, easy access to Leach Botanical Gardens, Powell Butte, and other worthy detours are available. A top choice for mountain bikers is **Leif Erikson Trail** in Forest Park. From the park gate at the end of N.W. Thurman to the junction at Salzman Road is a steady but easy six-mile climb through mature forest. It's 12 miles to the trail's end at Germantown Road, but signposts provide directions to shorter loops.

North of Portland, at the confluence of the Columbia and Willamette Rivers is Sauvie Island, a perfectly flat island where farms and truck gardens share space with wildlife refuges. The island's 12-mile loop road is a scenic delight reminiscent of rural France. Sauvie Island is 10 miles north of Portland off Highway 30. Rent bikes from **Fat Tire Farm** (2714 N.W. Thurman St., 503/222-3276). Repair bikes at the **Bicycle Repair Collective** (4438 S.E. Belmont, 503/233-0564).

Hardened cyclists looking for organized 30- to 100-mile rides at a touring pace should hook up with the **Portland Wheelmen Touring Club** (503/257-7982, www.pwtc.com).

PORTLAND

Entertainment and Events

Portland's concentration of first-rate theater as well as opera, dance, and other kinds of stage productions is fast becoming one of the West Coast's worst-kept secrets. In addition to the more formal music and theater listings below, there's a very active summer festival itinerary that ranges from the superb Chamber Music Northwest series to blues and jazz festivals (see *Festivals and Events,* later in the chapter).

Headquarters for much of this activity is the **Portland Center for the Performing Arts** (1111 S.W. Broadway, 503/248-4335, www.pcpa.com). Four stages grace this facility: 3,000-seat **Keller Auditorium,** 2,776-seat **Arlene Schnitzer Concert Hall,** 900-seat **Newmark Theater,** and 350-seat **Dolores Winningstad Theater.** Each theater has features suited to different kinds of productions. Schnitzer Hall is a sumptuously restored 1928 vaudeville and movie house. The Winningstad is a high-tech Shakespearean courtyard theater with wraparound balconies. The Intermediate is the crown jewel here, with elegant cherry paneling and a stage as large as the seating area. Keller Auditorium at 3rd and Clay is designed to accommodate larger audiences. On the way to the stage, the aisles are pitched at such an incline that women should think twice about wearing high heels. While lacking the aesthetic flair of the other theaters, the acoustics and vantages of the stage here are top-notch.

MUSIC AND DANCE PERFORMANCE

The **Oregon Symphony** (503/228-1353 or 800/228-1353, www.orsympony.org) is the oldest orchestra west of the Mississippi, and it performs in the historic jewel-box of an auditorium, Arlene Schnitzer Concert Hall. The baton has recently passed from long-time maestro James dePriest to Austrian Carlos Kalmar, promising a fresh perspective for the century-old institution. **Portland Opera** (503/241-1802 or 866/739-6737, www.portlandopera.

org) stages four operas a year, and hosts traveling Broadway shows. Shows are mounted at the 3,000-seat Keller Auditorium. **Oregon Ballet Theatre** (503/222-5538 or 888/922-5538, www.obt.org) is the city's classical dance troupe, usually performing at Keller Auditorium; **White Bird Dance** (503/245-1600, www.whitebird.org) brings an impressive number of world-class modern dance troupes to Portland. White Bird sponsors two different series each year, one at Arlene Schnitzer Concert Hall that features established troupes such as Paul Taylor or Mark Morris. The other series features edgier and more intimate dance pieces and is held at Portland State University's Lincoln Hall.

THEATER

More than a dozen theatrical troupes make up a significant presence on Portland's cultural scene. **Imago Theatre** (27 S.E. 8th Ave., 503/231-9581, www.imagotheatre.com) is an internationally acclaimed troupe that employs multimedia visuals, masks, puppets, dance, and animation to achieve dramatic resonance. Imago performs in an old Masonic hall that's at once intimate and spacious enough for the ambitious visual effects and movement of this cutting-edge troupe. **Do Jump Extremely Physical Theater** (Echo Theater, S.E. 37th and Hawthorne, 503/231-1232, www.dojump.org), like Imago, wowed New York critics while touring recent innovative productions. Trapeze and other circus arts combine with whimsical choreography here to make social commentary or aesthetic statements that can be appreciated by everyone from children to urban sophisticates.

For more traditional theater, **Portland Center Stage** (128 N.W. 11th Ave., 503/274-6588, www.pcs.org) operates out of the newly renovated Portland Armory Building in the Pearl District. PCS produces innovative and sometimes daring productions in an annual series that blends classical, contemporary, and premiere works in addition to an annual summer playwrights festival. Portland's other major theater group, **Artists Repertory Theater** (1516 S.W. Alder St., 503/241-1278, www.artistsrep.org), produces intimate, often edgier productions from its "black box" theater just west of downtown.

GALLERIES

Portland has a dynamic fine art scene, with over 130 galleries listed in the Yellow Pages. Many of the top galleries are in the Pearl District and other neighborhoods in Northwest Portland. Another gallery row is along N.E. Alberta. To preview some of Portland's leading galleries, the **Portland Art Dealers Association** website (www.padaoregon.org) has details of monthly shows at a dozen of the city's top galleries.

One of the best times to explore Portland's galleries is on the first Thursday of every month during the **First Thursday Gallery Walk.** More than 30 gallery owners coordinate show openings the first Thursday of every month, many offering complimentary refreshments. Visit the conflagration of galleries in the Pearl District around N.W. 11th and 12th at Glisan, which draws the biggest crowds. In this neighborhood, **Elizabeth Leach Gallery** (417 N.W. 9th Ave., 503/224-0521) is one of Portland's most successful and long-established galleries, and presents challenging and inventive art pieces from top regional and national artists.

The Portland Art Museum offers free admission on First Thursdays.

For something completely different, plan to attend **Last Thursdays,** a similar event at month's end highlighting the dynamic gallery and independent designer district on N.E. Alberta Street. A mix of street fair, performance art, and gallery tour, Last Thursday is a much more raucous and youthful than First Thursday, with live bands, fire-eaters, and other hijinks adding an almost circus atmosphere to the Alberta Street art scene.

Portland Institute for Contemporary Art, or PICA (224 N.W. 13th, 503/242-1419, www.pica.org), is Portland's leader in cutting-edge performances, experimental theater, new music, and dance. Throughout the year PICA offers lectures, performances, and exhibitions at many venues throughout the city, but the organization's top event, the Time-Based Art Festival (TBA), is a contemporary art festival of regional, national, and international artists presenting theatre, dance, music, film, and visual exhibition and installation. During TBA, which spans two weeks in mid-September, PICA presents movement and imagery across Portland—under bridges, over rivers, on stages, and throughout the city. TBA bridges disciplines and geography with morning workshops, afternoon lectures, evening performances, outdoor happenings, and late-night music parties.

Art in The Pearl (503/722-9017, www.artinthepearl.com) is an outdoor arts and crafts fair held over Labor Day weekend in the North Park Blocks, along the eastern edge of the Pearl District, between N.W. Park and 8th Avenues and Burnside and Glisan Streets. This street fair provides a showcase for the creations of the local artistic community, and also features food booths and music.

COMEDY

Music and laughs, they're all here in the Rose City, but in varying degrees. To put it more bluntly, jazz is hot, comedy is usually not. Portland's major comedy club, **Harvey's** (436 N.W. 6th Ave., 503/241-0338, www.harveyscomedyclub.com) might suffer from poor acoustics and a lack of intimacy if you sit in the back, but the talent is there; besides, it's just about the only game in town. The cover charge is normally $12. A reasonably priced menu and a full bar are available at this club.

DANCE CLUBS

In Portland, there's not a hard line between bars that have live music and bars that have DJs and qualify as dance clubs or discos. It mostly depends what night of the week it is. Check *Willamette Week* or the *Portland Mercury,* both available free throughout central Portland, to find out what's on during your visit.

The 1970s never died at **Embers** (110 N.W. Broadway, 503/222-3082, open nightly), a disco that's ostensibly a gay club but is usually filled with plenty of straight couples dancing beneath the mirrored ball. Another downtown dance venue is **Betty Ford's Lounge** (S.W. 12th & Washington, 503/445-8331) part intimate lounge and part far-out dance club with DJs from Wednesday through Sunday evenings.

Jubitz Ponderosa Lounge (10205 N. Vancouver Way, 503/345-0300, www.jubitztravelcenter.com) is a place to do your boot-scootin' boogie and Texas two-step to live bands. Just take I-5 north to Exit 307 and veer right on the frontage road onto Vancouver Way.

Fernando's Hideaway (824 S.W. 1st Ave., 503/248-4709, www.fernandoshideaway.com), a tapas bar (the food here is good, too) near Yamhill Market, offers Latin dancing upstairs in very tight confines. There's usually a small cover ($3–5) and women very often get in free. There are free salsa-dancing lessons Thursday through Saturday evenings.

Tango and country swing dance are very popular in Portland; one of the best places for both is **Nocturnal** (1800 E. Burnside, 503/232-7323, www.nocturnalpdx.com), with Wednesday evening tango lessons and dancing, and swing dancing usually Thursday through Saturday evenings.

CINEMA

Portland has plenty of new, multi-screen movie theaters that show the latest Hollywood releases. Thankfully, it also has a rich selection of alternative and repertory cinemas that feature independent, foreign, and vintage movies as well. Almost 85 percent of the city's first-run movie theaters are controlled by the Regal Cinemas chain (www.regalcinemas.com). Mainstream first-run cinemas convenient to central Portland include the Fox Tower Stadium 10 (846 S.W. Park Ave., 503/221-3280), the Broadway Metroplex 4 (1000 S.W. Broadway, 503/243-1404), Pioneer Square Stadium 6 (340 S.W. Morrison, 503/295-0909), the Lloyd Mall 8 Cinema (2320 Lloyd Center Mall, 503/335-3760) and the Lloyd Center 10 Cinema (1510 N.E. Multnomah St., 503/287-0338). Adults can expect to pay $9 for a movie

after 5 p.m. at most Regal theaters. Prior to that, half-price matinees are in effect. At some theaters, seniors and students enjoy discounts for evening shows.

Portland offers an array of genre movie houses, such as **Cinema 21** (616 N.W. 21st Ave., 503/223-4515, www.cinema21.com), which is the city's principal independent art house movie theater. Another independent theater that shows offbeat, foreign, and cult movies is **Hollywood Theatre** (N.E. 41th and Sandy, 503/281-4215, www.hollywoodtheatre.org), housed in a vintage movie palace. The **Clinton Street Theater** (2522 S.E. Clinton, 503/238-8899, www.clintonsttheatre.com) is an art house cinema featuring films that generally would not have a market in most other theaters. This might mean the *The Rocky Horror Picture Show* every Saturday night or dated propaganda films such as *Reefer Madness*. The Clinton Street Theater also hosts the Longbaugh Film Festival in early April, with feature-length and short independent films.

Courtesy of brewpub-meisters the brothers McMenamin, Portland also features several restored vintage theaters (among other screening facilities) featuring just-past-first-run flicks (tickets $2–5) along with pub grub and beer. The most convenient to central Portland neighborhoods are the **Mission Theater** (1624 N.W. Glisan St., 503/223-4031) and the neo-Moorish **Bagdad Theater & Pub** (3710 S.E. Hawthorne Blvd., 503/230-0895). For info on what's playing at McMenamins establishments, check out www.mcmenamins.com. It's not a McMenamins operation, but the budget-priced **Laurelhurst Theater** (N.E. 28th and Burnside, 503/232-5511, www.laurelhursttheater.com) also serves beer along with a mix of vintage and slightly dated first-run films.

The February **Portland International Film Festival** (503/221-1156, www.nwfilm.org), held at Portland Art Museum's Northwest Film Center, showcases foreign and art flicks that serious film-lovers will especially appreciate.

TOURS

Portland Walking Tours (503/774-4522, www.portlandwalkingtours.com) offers a variety of art, architecture, and history tours of the downtown area. Most depart from the visitors center at Pioneer Courthouse Square. The 2.5-hour "Best of Portland" tour visits public art, downtown parks, and the waterfront ($15 adult); for the same price the "Underground Portland" tour captures the spirit of the city's historic Old Town and Chinatown, culminating in a visit to an underground business district and a Shanghai tunnel. Food lovers will enjoy the 3.5-hour "Epicurean Excursion" with opportunities to sample food and drinks at nearly 30 Pearl District restaurants and food vendors ($59 adult).

Get out on the Willamette to see the river side of Portland. The **Portland Spirit** (503/224-3900 or 800/224-3901, www.portlandspirit.com) offers a variety of sightseeing and dining cruises aboard a 150-foot yacht with three public decks. The usual tour routing travels between downtown and Lake Oswego, south (upstream) from the Portland. Two-hour lunch ($34 adult) and 2.5-hour dinner ($62 adult) cruises are available Monday through Saturday, and there are also two-hour Saturday and Sunday brunch cruises ($40). Sightseeing passengers may also accompany any dining cruise ($18 adult for lunch and brunch sailings, $32 for dinner sailings) with drinks and snacks available on board. Most cruises depart from the dock at Salmon Street Springs Fountain (the base of S.W. Salmon St at Waterfront Park). Call or check the website for departure times, and to learn about other cruise options.

Willamette Jetboat Excursions (503/231-1532 or 888/538-2628, www.willamettejet.com) offers two jet-boat tours of the Willamette. A two-hour cruise available daily from late April through September travels up to Oregon City's historic Willamette Falls ($30 adult, $19 for children 4–11) while a one-hour "Bridges Tour" explores the waterfront and all ten of Portland's bridges (operates late June through Labor Day, $20 adult, $14 children 4–11). Tours depart from the OMSI dock at 1945 S.E. Water Avenue.

Ecotours of Oregon (3127 S.E. 23rd Ave., Portland 97202, 503/245-1428 or 888/868-7733, www.ecotours-of-oregon.com) runs tours blending ecological understanding with having a good time. Door-to-door van transport from anywhere in the Portland area, lunch, and commentary are included in itineraries that run $45–73 per person per day (Portland microbrewery tours to whale-watching, respectively). Packages focusing on whale-watching, Native American culture, Mount St. Helens, and the Columbia Gorge typify the refreshing focus of this small company. Trips are usually confined to vans of six with a professional naturalist-historian guide.

Finally, there is **Gray Line of Portland** (Pioneer Courthouse Square, 888/684-3322). Gray Line in most cities runs competent tours with experienced drivers; Portland's outfit is no exception. In addition to day trips to such locales as Mount Hood, the Oregon Coast, and the Columbia River Gorge, three-hour city tours depart all year long from Union Station. Half-day trips such as the Multnomah Falls/Columbia Gorge tour (about $47 per person) and full-day trips such as the Mount Hood Loop (about $65 per person) are highly recommended. Gray Line offers free hotel pick-ups in conjunction with their tours in the downtown area.

FESTIVALS AND EVENTS

The **Cinco de Mayo Fiesta** (www.cincodemayo.org) celebrates the Mexican victory over the French army in the Battle of Puebla in 1862 at Tom McCall Waterfront Park the first weekend (including Thursday and Friday) in May. This has become one of the largest celebrations of its kind in the country. Mariachis, folk dance exhibitions, a large selection of Mexican food, and fireworks displays are included in the festivities. Admission is $6 for adults, $5 youths and seniors, free for children 10 and under.

The **Waterfront Blues Festival** (503/282-0555, www.waterfrontbluesfest.com) is the largest festival of its kind on the West Coast. It takes place the first weekend in July at Tom McCall Waterfront Park, and many famous artists attend. The $8 admission and

© PAUL LEVY

Portland loves a festival, and the Waterfront Blues Festival, held over the Fourth of July weekend, is one of the biggest.

donations (two canned-good items) go to the Oregon Food Bank.

During the same period, end of June through mid-July, **Chamber Music Northwest** (503/294-6400, www.cmnw.org) presents concerts for five weeks nightly except Sunday. Music begins at 8 P.M. with many people picnicking beforehand. Tickets to this nationally acclaimed series range $21–40 for adults. Concerts are held in two locations: Reed College in Southeast Portland and at Catlin Gabel School in Northwest Portland.

In July, check out the **Multnomah County Fair** (Oaks Park in Sellwood, 503/761-7577, www.oregonfairs.org). The prize bulls, cowpokes, and carnival midway remain, but the fair has ventured into the great beyond of multicultural diversity. In the fair's present incarnation you're likely to find an authentic Native American powwow, Mexican folk ballet, and a photo exhibit featuring well-known professionals. In addition, you can enjoy Latin combos and jazz groups as well as an array of international cuisines alongside the expected country music and cotton candy. (Usual hours noon–11 P.M. Wed.–Sat., noon–9 P.M. Sun. Admission $5–7, discounts for ages 6–12.)

The **Mount Hood Jazz Festival** (P.O. Box 696, Gresham 97030, 503/665-2837, www.mthoodjazz.com) is *the* event for jazz and blues connoisseurs. World-renowned jazz artists converge the first weekend of August at Mount Hood Community College in Gresham 20 minutes east of downtown Portland. Buying tickets in advance (about $15 per day and up) through Ticketmaster is advisable due to frequent sell-outs. If lawn chairs or picnic-style blankets are not your perch of preference, the covered west grandstand provides protection from the sun as well as views of Mount Hood.

For summer outdoor concerts, it's all happening at the **Oregon Zoo** (503/280-2493, www.oregonzoo.org/Concerts/index.htm). Crowds spread out on the lawn below the stage to hear first-rate, often big-name talent such as Etta James and Pink Martini (ticket prices vary, but are usually upwards of $18). In addition, Wednesday "Plus" concerts feature world

PORTLAND ROSE FESTIVAL

The Portland Rose Festival (503/227-2681, www.rosefestival.org) has been Portland's major summer event for nine decades. The Rose Queen and her court (chosen from local high school entrants), sailors and prostitutes, and floats from several parades clog Portland's traffic arteries during this 18-day citywide celebration each June. Air shows, a hot-air balloon classic, the Indy World Series car race, and a traditional rose show round out the main attractions. Check out the website for a schedule of what is essentially a small town festival done with big town flair. Even if parades and crowds are not your thing, the civic pride here is genuine and appealing. Portlanders camp out along the parade route in the same places year after year, sometimes several days in advance just to catch a coveted glimpse at the floats passing by.

The key to enjoying festival events is avoiding traffic and parking hassles. A $4.25 TriMet (503/238-7433) day ticket entitles the passholder to unlimited rides on MAX, the Portland Streetcar or the bus all day long. As for traffic, be especially wary of the waterfront. Such festival features as food booths and carnival rides in Tom McCall Park, as well as military ship displays on the Willamette, draw crowds reminiscent of lemmings to the sea.

Another good reason to come to the waterfront is the chance to see the dragon boat races. These brightly painted ceremonial canoes from China have been taken up in earnest here. With 16 paddlers and a coxswain, teams compete on the Willamette River.

Two of the more colorful events of the June fete are the **Grand Floral Parade** and the **Festival of Flowers** at Pioneer Courthouse Square. In the latter, all manner of colorful blossoms fill the square to overflowing. This bouquet is on display during the first week of the several-week celebration. As for the Grand Floral Parade, this usually begins the Saturday following the opening of the festival. The floats combine the beauty of flowers with high-tech wizardry in aesthetically whimsical creations. You can reserve seats in the Coliseum ahead of time, but save your money and station yourself on an upper floor along the parade route or visit the floats at Oregon Square between Lloyd Center and the Convention Center during the week following the parade. Any lofty perch is sufficient for taking in all the hoopla, drill teams, Rose Queen, and equestrian demonstrations. This procession is the second largest all floral parade in the United States.

---

beat bands from around the world with ticket prices less than $10. The concerts take place between late June and late August. Check the website for current listings and dates.

Taking place the last full weekend in July in Portland's Tom McCall Waterfront Park, **Oregon Brewers Festival** (www.oregon brewfest.com) is North America's largest gathering of independent brewers. The four-day event showcases the wares of more than 70 breweries, and attracts more than 50,000 beer lovers. Admission is free but to sample the product of dozens of brewers, you must buy a 14-ounce souvenir mug for $4 and then purchase tokens for $1 apiece. It takes four tokens to fill the mug, or one token for a taster. Live

musical entertainment is offered throughout the weekend.

An August festival, **The Bite of Oregon** (Tom McCall Waterfront Park, 503/657-5382, www.biteoforegon.com) lets you sample local culinary specialties of Portland restaurants, with the proceeds going to the Special Olympics. Live music is also featured.

In October, watch the salmon spawn at Oxbow Park in the Sandy River Gorge outside Gresham. Old-growth walks, an eight-kilometer run, a barbecue, and arts and crafts round out this fête. To get there from downtown, take I-84 east to the Wood Village Exit. Turn south on Division and east on Oxbow Parkway, then follow the signs to Oxbow Park. Or, take I-84 to Exit 17, drive east a mile, then make a right on 257th Street and follow it to Division, where the previous directions take effect. There's a vehicle fee and an additional charge for lunch and activities. Festival-goers will tell you that a rainy day seems to encourage salmon-spawning activity. Call 503/248-5050 for more information. Hours are 10:30 A.M.–5 P.M. Saturday and Sunday.

HOLIDAY EVENTS

The day after Thanksgiving, a Christmas tree is lit in Pioneer Square and a skating rink installed. Skate rentals are available and a small admission is charged. The best Christmas lights display is on Peacock Lane in southeast Portland near beautiful Laurelhurst Park, 29th and Stark; check at Travel Portland for more details (503/275-9750 or 800/962-3700).

The Christmastime **Grotto's Festival of Lights** (N.E. 85th and Sandy Blvd., 503/254-7371, www.thegrotto.org) includes animated lighting displays, narrated fiber-optic displays, and other illuminated depictions of the holiday. Set amid gorgeous surroundings, this is the largest choral event in the Pacific Northwest and a very special holiday event. Admission is $7.

Finally, a Portland event that's sure to please is the annual parade of **Christmas ships** (www.christmasships.org). Boats with lights creating images of a fire engine, Santa's sleigh, angels, and other fanciful designs parade on the Columbia and the Willamette. Portlanders line waterfront parks and restaurants to enjoy this spectacle, which usually runs for about a week and ends on December 23.

LIVE MUSIC CLUBS

Portland is fortunate to have a critical mass of talented musicians. Notable among the tuneful offerings from this community is one of the West Coast's most vibrant jazz and blues scenes, and plenty of places to suit fans of country, rock, and folk music. Portland is especially notable for indie rock and a new generation of folk music singers.

Many nationally known jazz players (such as bassist Ben Wolf and drummer Mel Brown) and blues men (Robert Cray, Paul DeLay, and Curtis Salgado, to name a few) were spawned from Portland's jazz milieu. In addition to fostering homegrown talent, Portland has become a prime stop for touring practitioners of this quintessentially American art forms.

There are *a lot* of music clubs in Portland, and anyone coming to Portland wanting to check out the scene should definitely spend some time checking upcoming events at the *Oregonian* website (www.oregonlive.com/events), or at the *Willamette Week* event calendar (www.wweek.com). First-time visitors will be surprised at the breadth of live music available in Portland. The suggestions here are just the beginnings of what's available.

Cover charges vary quite a bit from club to club, and from night to night. Expect to pay $5–10 most evenings to hear live music in Portland clubs.

Jazz and Blues

The hottest jazz club in Portland is **Jimmy Mak's** (221 N.W. 10th Ave., 503/295-6542, www.jimmymaks.com). Monday through Thursday evenings you'll hear renowned local artists Dan Balmer and Mel Brown, and on the weekend the best of regional and national jazz acts. Closed Sundays. **Blue Monk,** (3341 S.E. Belmont St., 503/595-0575, www.the bluemonk.com) is a basement-level jazz club in one of southeast Portland's hippest neighborhoods. Not only is there great live jazz Tuesday through Saturday, the club offers good Italian food till 1 A.M.

The **Heathman Hotel Lounge** (1009 S.W. Broadway, 503/790-7752, www.heathman hotel.com) is another quality jazz spot with small plates from a five-star kitchen and prices to match. Nightly jazz with Frenchified Northwest cuisine, at moderate prices, is also a focal point in the art-filled Euro bistro **Brasserie Montmartre** (626 S.W. Park Ave., 503/224-5552; open daily). Drinks and great hors d'oeuvres with live jazz several nights a week can be enjoyed at the Lobby Court at the **Benson Hotel** (309 S.W. Broadway, 503/228-2000, www.bensonhotel.com)

in wood-paneled elegance that harks back to 1913. Blues aficionados will appreciate the array of talent showcased nightly at both **The Candlelight** (2032 S.W. 5th, 503/222-3378, www.candlelightcafebar.com), a gritty, smoky bar near Portland State University, and **The White Eagle** (836 N. Russell St., 503/282-6810, www.mcmenamins.com). The White Eagle is one of Portland's oldest bars (from 1905) with a long reputation as a blues club (plus country folk in its current manifestation as a McMenamins brewpub).

Rock

Rock fans enjoy **Berbati's Pan** (231 S.W. Ankeny St., 503/248-4579), where great Greek food and music of all genres have made it Portland's leading late-night live music club. A block from Berbati's is **Dante's** (S.W. 3rd Ave and Burnside, 503/226-6630, www.danteslive.com), where in addition to live alternative bands you'll find often outrageous cabaret and burlesque shows.

One of downtown's most intriguing clubs is **McMenamins Crystal Ballroom** (1332 W. Burnside, 503/225-0047, www.danceonair.com/crystal). This majestic 1914 restored dance hall hosts some of Portland's best bands, though its history predates rock and roll. Imagine a dance floor on ball bearings in a Roaring '20s–era dance hall bedecked with artwork and ornate chandeliers, with a legacy going back to Tommy Dorsey and Glen Miller and continues up through Aretha Franklin and the Grateful Dead. In the 1960s Marvin Gaye, James Brown, Etta James, Ike and Tina Turner, the Allman Brothers, and others gave this vintage moveable dance floor a workout.

The Crystal Ballroom is the nucleus for a set of other noteworthy clubs (many of them also McMenamins offshoots). Sharing a building with the Crystal Ballroom is **Lola's Club** noted for its "Shut Up And Dance" '80s-era

disco nights. On the same building's ground floor, **Ringler's Pub** is by day a straightforward brewpub by day, but has live music and DJs on weekend evenings. There's another great little refuge just kitty-corner across Stark from Ringler's: **Ringler's Annex,** a subterranean nook where savvy nightclubbers rendezvous with friends. This neighborhood is party central for downtown Portland, with the gay bar district stretching down Stark Street immediately to the east.

Portland's East Side has developed a lively music scene. A major destination in any tour of Portland music hotbeds would include **Doug Fir** (830 E. Burnside, 503/231-9663, www.dougfirlounge.com). The Doug Fir attracts some of Portland's most interesting acts, and is part of a hip development that includes a vintage motorcourt motel and late-night restaurant. Another hot spot is **Holocene** (1001 S.E. Morrison, 503/239-7639, www.holocene.org), where the nightly entertainment can range from live music, DJs, performance art, and regularly scheduled evening events like the twice-monthly Tart, a "swank soiree where the queer girls play."

If you came to Portland to find the remnant of its hippie, Grateful Dead roots, then the **Laurelthirst Public House** (2958 N.E. Glisan St., 503/232-1504) is where you need to be. This old and funky tavern has excellent local folk and country swing bands, and a feel-good vibe that takes you back to the Summer of Love.

Before you hit town, check out the performers scheduled at the **Aladdin Theater** (3017 S.E. Milwaukie Ave., 503/233-1994, www.aladdin-theater.com). This 1920s burlesque house has been gussied up to host an eclectic array of performers such as Laurie Anderson, Buena Vista Social Club, Rufus Wainwright, and Arlo Guthrie. Many folk, world beat, and indie rock bands play here, and it's a wonderful small theater for taking in a concert.

Shopping

Don't forget that Oregon has no sales tax, so you'll find Portland shopping very satisfying.

DOWNTOWN PORTLAND

In the heart of the downtown shopping district, **Pioneer Place** (S.W. 5th Ave and Morrison, 503/228-5800) is an upscale shopping development that features a number of national merchandisers, including Eddie Bauer, Ann Taylor, J.Crew, and Coach, and other retailers found in Rouse developments. The lower level features a vast food court.

Indigenous to the Northwest, **Nordstrom** (701 S.W. Broadway, 503/224-6666) offers downtown shoppers quality clothing and shoes from its location just west of Pioneer Courthouse Square. Founded in 1854, Meier & Frank was Portland's home-grown downtown department store; it's now a **Macy's** (621 S.W. 5th Ave., 503/223-0512).

Real Mother Goose (901 S.W. Yamhill St., 503/223-9510 or 800/968-1070) is a quality crafts gallery that presents jewelry, pottery, woodcrafts, and other design goods from hundreds of Northwest artists and craftspeople. It's an excellent place to buy one-of-a-kind gifts. Another excellent local crafts gallery with particularly cool jewelry is **Twist,** found both in Pioneer Place (700 S.W. 5th Ave., 503/222-3137) and in Northwest (30 N.W. 23rd Place, 503/224-0334).

If you don't have time to make a trip to Oregon's wine country, stop by **Oregon Wines on Broadway** (515 S.W. Broadway, 503/228-4655 or 800/943-8858), a wine shop devoted to Northwest wines. Wine-tastings and wine-maker events are often held on Thursday nights.

Saks Fifth Avenue (850 S.W. 5th Ave, 503/221-3200), the New York–based clothing has a Portland outlet that offers designer clothing and upscale accessories. It's linked to Pioneer Place via walkways.

Based in the Portland metro area, **Columbia Sportswear** has its flagship store downtown (911 S.W. Broadway, 503/226-6800) and an outlet in Sellwood (1323 S.E. Tacoma St., 503/238-0118).

This is the place to go for fashionable, hard-working outerwear for recreation and heavy weather.

NORTHWEST PORTLAND
Pearl District

At **Pendleton Home** (210 N.W. Broadway, 503/535-5584), woolen goods from Pendleton Woolen Mills are an Oregon tradition. This store showcases the beloved plaid shirts typical of Pendleton along with more unusual housewares and blankets.

For many visitors, **Powell's Books** (1005 W. Burnside St., 503/228-0540 or 800/878-7323) is one of Portland's primary attractions. A block square and three stories tall, Powell's combines new, used, and out-of-print books, and is usually absolutely thronged with bibliophiles. In addition to miles of bookshelves, Powell's offers a coffee shop and free author events and book signings. There are a total of six Powell's Books stores in metro Portland, including Powell's Books for Cooks and Gardeners.

Whether you're a professional chef or an enthusiastic home cook, you'll find every culinary device known to humankind, plus handsome china and pottery, at **Sur La Table** (1102 N.W. Couch St., 503/295-9679). Cooking classes and wine-tasting courses are held in the adjacent display kitchen.

Synonymous with earth-friendly and socially responsible manufacturing, **Patagonia** (907 N.W. Irving St., 503/525-2552) shares a large and strikingly handsome historical storefront with Ecotrust Foundation in the Pearl District. Patagonia offers serious gear and clothing for the serious outdoorsperson.

The Pearl has become an excellent place to shop for sporty women's clothing. In addition to Patagonia, try **Title 9 Sports** (1335 N.W. Kearney St., 503/243-2220), **Signal Sports** (1327 N.W. Kearney St., 503/546-9905), **Physical Element** (1124 N.W. Lovejoy St., 503/224-5425), **Lucy** (1015 N.W. Couch St., 503/226-0220), or **Lululemon** (1231 N.W. Couch St., 503/274-0007). If you still can't find the perfect yoga top, head over to **REI** (1405 N.W. Johnson St., 503/221-1938).

NORTHEAST PORTLAND

The first shopping center in North America, **Lloyd Center** (N.E. 12th and Weidler Ave., 503/282-2511) got its start in the 1950s, back when its location in inner Northeast Portland made it an alternative to downtown for neighborhood shopping. Nowadays, Lloyd Center is best thought of as an extension of downtown. After a major face-lift in the 1990s, Lloyd Center is one of Portland's major shopping destinations, with over 160 stores and businesses under one roof, including Nordstrom, Sears, Macy's, and Marshalls. Lloyd Center also boasts an indoor ice-skating rink and two muliplex cinemas. The MAX light-rail train between Lloyd Center and downtown is free; however, buses between the two retail centers are not.

SOUTHEAST PORTLAND

Acres of upholstery fabric from around the world make the **Whole Nine Yards** (1820 E. Burnside St., 503/223-2880) a must-stop for home decorators. Portland has a wealth of historic homes from the Arts and Crafts period at the turn of the 20th century, so perhaps its no surprise to find **Rejuvenation** (1100 S.E. Grand Ave., 503/238-1900) in the city. A vast enterprise dedicated to modeling and decorating period homes, Rejuvenation is filled with everything you need to replace or restore historic homes, from brass hinges and push-button light switches, to period lighting, to Victorian furniture. Within a few blocks of Rejuvenation are a number of other tile, lighting, stone, and decor stores. A must-stop for anyone who loves period homes.

A quintessential Portland business, **Music Millennium** (3158 E. Burnside, 503/248-0163) is a vast and funky CD and music store of the sort that once typified the 1970s. However, In Portland, the chain stores haven't yet managed to drive this much-loved institution out of business. You'll find almost every kind of music, old, new, rare, foreign—you name it, it's probably here. Next door is Classical Millennium, which offers the same expansive selection to opera and classical music fans. A one-of-a-kind store and as close to the still-beating subversive heart of Portland as you'll come on a casual visit.

Portland is famed for its parks and gardens, and no wonder—the climate here is so mild and nurturing that gardeners can grow almost anything. As if to prove the point, there's **Portland Nursery** (5050 S.E. Stark St., 503/231-5050). If you've got a green thumb, or just enjoy plant life, consider a trip to this block-square nursery, the city's largest and most comprehensive. Portland gardeners are a demanding and experimental lot, and chances are you'll see plants here that you've only ever seen in catalogs or magazines.

Accommodations

Portland has a broad range of lodging choices, many of which represent good value—but few are particularly cheap. The good news is that many of the best lodging options are in the central city, close to arts, restaurants, and nightlife. In general, downtown presents the most lodging options, while Northeast Portland, near Lloyd Center and the Convention Center, offers another wide selection at somewhat lower price points that are linked to downtown by MAX light rail. Travelers of all descriptions need to reserve well in advance for June, July, and August.

The rates quoted below are for summer high-season double rooms. Off-seasons rates drop dramatically, with savings of 25–50 percent. Also, shopping for rooms on Internet discount lodging sites such as www.hotels.com can yield unexpected discounts even in high season.

DOWNTOWN PORTLAND

Unless otherwise noted, you'll pay to park at the following downtown hotels. The parking fee ranges $12–24 a night, so be sure to ask when booking a room, as these fees add up fast.

PORTLAND

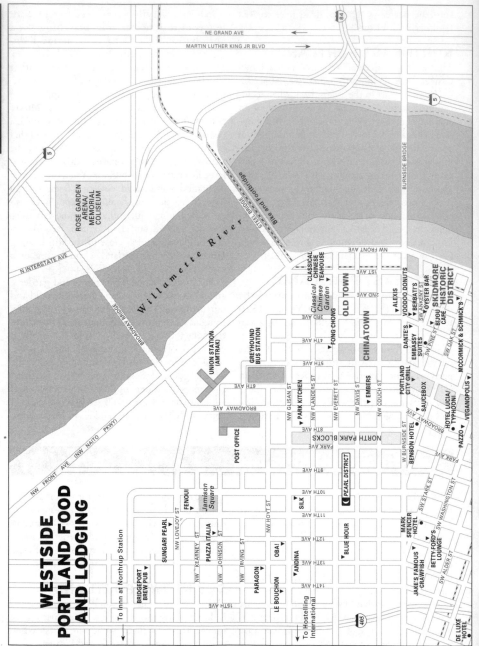

WESTSIDE PORTLAND FOOD AND LODGING

Willamette River

ROSE GARDEN ARENA/ MEMORIAL COLISEUM

N INTERSTATE AVE

NE GRAND AVE

MARTIN LUTHER KING JR BLVD

BURNSIDE BRIDGE

STEEL BRIDGE

Bike and Footbridge

BROADWAY BRIDGE

NW FRONT AVE

CLASSICAL CHINESE TEAHOUSE

Classical Chinese Garden

OLD TOWN

CHINATOWN

1ST AVE
2ND AVE
3RD AVE
4TH AVE
5TH AVE

FONG CHONG

UNION STATION (AMTRAK)

GREYHOUND BUS STATION

VOODOO DONUTS

ALEXIS

BERBATI'S

BIJOU CAFE

SW ANKENY ST

SW PINE ST

DANTE'S

EMBASSY SUITES

SAUCEBOX

PORTLAND CITY GRILL

EMBERS

SKIDMORE/HISTORIC DISTRICT

OYSTER BAR

SW OAK ST

McCORMICK & SCHMICK'S

NW GLISAN ST

NW FLANDERS ST

NW EVERETT ST

NW DAVIS ST

NW COUCH ST

PARK KITCHEN

6TH AVE
7TH AVE
8TH AVE

BROADWAY AVE

POST OFFICE

PARK AVE

NORTH PARK BLOCKS

W BURNSIDE ST

BENSON HOTEL

BROADWAY AVE

PAZZO

HOTEL LUCIA/ TYPHOON!

VEGANOPOLIS

PARK AVE

9TH AVE
10TH AVE
11TH AVE
12TH AVE
13TH AVE
14TH AVE
15TH AVE

PEARL DISTRICT

SILK

BLUE HOUR

FENOUI

JAMISON Square

To Inn at Northrup Station

BRIDGEPORT BREW PUB

SUNGARI PEARL

NW LOVEJOY ST

NW KEARNEY ST

PIAZZA ITALIA

NW JOHNSON ST

NW IRVING ST

NW HOYT ST

OBA!

PARAGON

ANDINA

LE BOUCHON

To Hostelling International

MARK SPENCER HOTEL

SW STARK ST

SW WASHINGTON ST

SW ALDER ST

JAKE'S FAMOUS CRAWFISH

BETTY FORD'S LOUNGE

DE LUXE HOTEL

NW FRONT AVE / NW NAITO PKWY

To Ihnn at Northrup Station

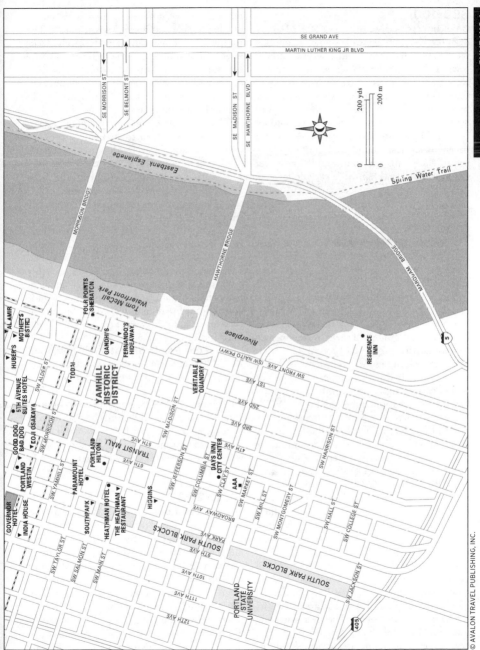

$50-100

Days Inn (1414 S.W. 6th Ave., 503/221-1611 or 800/899-0248, www.daysinn.com, doubles from $60) is centrally located between downtown and Portland State University. You can walk from here to almost anywhere in downtown Portland, and since it's on the free bus mall, you can catch a bus for the rest of your travels. Amenities range from a heated outdoor pool to free covered parking. There is also a decent on-site restaurant. While nothing glamorous, the rooms are comfortable and cover the basics well making this a very dollar-wise downtown lodging choice, particularly with free parking.

$100-150

The **MacMaster House B&B** (1041 S.W. Vista Ave., 503/223-7362 or 800/774-9523, www.macmaster.com, doubles with shared bath from $95, doubles with en suite bath $169) is behind downtown in the West Hills, in a residential neighborhood close to Washington Park. In one of the city's ritziest neighborhoods, the eight rooms in this mansion include two units with private bathroom. The other rooms share facilities. All guestrooms are handsomely appointed with European antiques or period furnishings, down comforters, quality bed linens, luxurious robes, and a TV/VCR. Some rooms have fireplaces or interesting murals and one has a claw-foot tub. The public rooms also have objets d'art and decor that are the essence of Victoriana. Free parking.

The **Hotel deLuxe** (729 S.W. 15th Ave., 503/219-2094 or 866/895-2094, www.hoteldeluxeportland.com, doubles from $139) is the newly updated and long-beloved Mallory Hotel, a comfortable older hotel just west of city center that's served for generations as a refuge for value-conscious travelers. The bad news is that with its transformation to Hotel deLuxe, the prices have gone up a bit, but the good news is that the entire hotel has had a good scrubbing and looks just great with its period movie-poster decor. The always-striking interior, with a lobby boasting ornate plaster, crystal chandeliers, and an elegant, sky-lit interior, seems even more evocative with images of Clark Gable and Bette Davis as motifs. The rooms aren't huge, but they are nicely decorated and comfortable—all you'll need if you're here for an active Portland getaway. A location on the MAX line not far from the boutiques of the Northwest district and South Park Blocks cultural attractions also recommend it.

Thank goodness not every vintage downtown hotel has been turned into a modern luxury Xanadu. Travelers looking for a great value will like the **Mark Spencer Hotel** (409 S.W. 11th Ave., 503/224-3293 or 800/548-3934, doubles from $129) a former residential hotel that's now a comfortable, completely ship-shape lodging that's just a few blocks from shopping and dining in the Pearl District. The rooms once rented as apartments, so even the standard rooms are spacious and have complete kitchens. The suites are truly large and apartment-like, with a separate bedroom, living room, and kitchen. Rates include continental breakfast. The Mark Spencer is the closest hotel to Stark Street nightlife and Portland's top theaters.

The **Four Points Sheraton** (50 S.W. Morrison, 503/221-0711 or 888/627-8263, www.fourpoints.com, doubles from $120) overlooks Waterfront Park and the Willamette River. The guest rooms and lobby are stylish and comfortable, with high-speed Internet and access to a fitness center. The Four Points Sheraton is ideally located for morning joggers, and for folks who want to visit Saturday Market or shop in Pioneer Place.

$150-200

The **Hotel Lucia** (400 S.W. Broadway, 503/228-7221 or 800/225-1717, www.hotellucia.com, doubles from $165) is another older hotel that received a major face-lift in the early 2000s, emerging as one of the most stylish downtown hotels. Rooms, while not large, are decorated with a striking modern élan, and the location couldn't be more central to downtown shopping, dining, and nightlife. Typhoon!, Portland's top Thai restaurant, is on-site, and Powell's Books is a five-minute walk away. Book rooms on upper floors to diminish the noise of downtown.

If you're staying in Portland for a while, or are traveling with a family, consider **Residence Inn Portland Downtown/RiverPlace** (2115 S.W. River Pkwy., 503/552-2115 or 800/331-3131, www.marriott.com/pdxri, doubles from $179), a new hotel on the waterfront with one-and two-bedroom suites all with fully furnished kitchens. Rates include a complimentary breakfast buffet. Facilities include indoor pool and spa, plus complimentary high-speed Internet access. While the Residence is not exactly at the center of Portland's shopping and arts scene (though half the rooms have great river views), the Portland Streetcar stops just outside the hotel doors.

The **Paramount Hotel** (808 S.W. Taylor St., 503/223-9900, www.portlandparamount.com, doubles from $169) is one of Portland's newest European-style boutique hotels. Within just a few blocks of MAX, Pioneer Square, department stores, and fine dining, its city center location can't be beat. Each of the 154 oversized guest rooms and suites feature granite-finished bathrooms. For those who want to splurge, the Paramount Class rooms feature large terraces and jetted tubs; Grand Suites offer fireplace, wet bar, whirlpool bath, and sweeping views of downtown Portland. The on-site Dragonfish restaurant serves pan-Asian cuisine, and Café Appassionato provides coffee and light fare for guests.

The **Portland Hilton** (921 S.W. 6th Ave., 503/226-1611, www.portland.hilton.com, doubles from $169) is a full-service business hotel that offers lots of extras and advantages to leisure travelers. With newly remodeled rooms, full fitness and pool facilities, three restaurants (including Alexander's, an exceptional rooftop restaurant), and a miracle-working concierge, the Portland Hilton is too nice to waste on business travelers. A location in the heart of the theater district across the street from Niketown and the Schnitzer Concert Hall are other extras that rate thumbs up the savvy traveler.

The **5th Avenue Suites Hotel** (506 S.W. Washington, 888/861-9514, www.5thavenue suites.com, doubles from $159) is rather unusual—this structure was once one of Portland's major department stores until the original 1910s structure was totally redesigned as a boutique hotel in the 1990s. Rooms were created to fit modern standards of size and comfort, while retaining the sense of venerable charm. A mix of classical and contemporary art and indoor greenery decorate the public rooms, but the plush furnishings in the guest units are what captures most travelers' attention. It occupies an absolutely central location in downtown and has an affordable restaurant, the Red Star Grill, emphasizing gourmet interpretations of American food.

The interior of the **Heathman Hotel** (1009 S.W. Broadway, 800/551-0011, www.heathmanhotel.com, doubles from $169) exudes understated Old World elegance with generous use of teak paneling and marble. The public rooms feature art ranging from Andy Warhol to turn of the 20th century prints. The location amid theaters and museums has attracted everyone from John Updike, Alice Walker, and Luciano Pavarotti to presidents and foreign dignitaries. While standard queen rooms are usually a little smaller than similarly priced accommodations at Portland's other top hotels, the antiques and quality room appointments here set the Heathman apart. A first-class restaurant, a 400-film video collection, a library, and afternoon tea are appreciated extras. At night the Heathman bar has jazz, and you'd be hard-pressed to find better mixed drinks, appetizers, and atmosphere anywhere else in Oregon.

Although you wouldn't know it from the name, **Embassy Suites** (319 S.W. Pine St., 503/279-9000, doubles from $189) is in fact the historic Multnomah Hotel, one of Portland's grandest and largest hotels from 1912. Each of the suites has a large living area and separate bedroom, and has the look and feel of a private apartment. The grand lobby looks like something out of a suave Carey Grant film, and the Portland Steak and Chophouse is one of the city's best. Priding itself on guest loyalty due to exceptional personalized service, Embassy guests have access to an indoor pool, fitness room, cocktail reception, and complimentary cooked-to-order breakfast.

$200-250

History buffs and downtown explorers will all find something to appreciate at the lovingly renovated **Governor Hotel** (S.W. 10th at Alder, 503/224-3400 or 800/554-3456, www.govhotel.com, doubles from $200). Built in 1909 during one of the city's exponential growth spurts, the vintage Governor had a complete 1990 makeover followed by a 2006 facelift, emerging with its sparkling terra-cotta facade and old-style charm intact. Inside, high ceilings, Arts and Crafts–style furnishings, and the lobby's sepia-toned mural depicting scenes from the Lewis and Clark Expedition all contribute to the turn-of-the 20th century sense of taste and proportion. In addition to high-quality modern amenities and a central location in a classic setting, you'll appreciate Jake's Grill, one of Portland's top steak and seafood restaurants, with a lively bar that's hung with buffalo and moose heads.

One of Portland's newest and finest hotels, the **Portland Westin** (750 Southwest Alder St., 503/294-9000 or 888/625-5144, www.starwoodhotels.com, doubles from $239) is in the center of the city's business, retail, and cultural districts. Rooms are stylish and large, and feature the trademark Westin beds and bathroom gear—truly luxury-level furnishings. If you're here for business you'll approve of the business desk and workstation and ergonomic leather desk chair. The hotel also features a complimentary health and fitness suite, plus The Daily Grill bar and restaurant.

NORTHWEST PORTLAND
Under $50

Hostelling International–Portland, Northwest (425 N.W. 18th Ave., 503/241-2783 or 888/777-0067, www.nwportlandhostel.com, bunks $20 for HI members, $23 for non-members) has a great location right between the shopping and dining of N.W. 21st and 23rd Avenues and the artsy Pearl District—in other words, within walking distance of Portland's most exciting neighborhoods. The hostel is in a restored turn-of-the 20th century building and features dorms with 2–4 beds per room, private rooms, a fully equipped kitchen, and a coffee bar.

$100-$150

Easily one of Portland's most unique lodging choices, the **Inn @ Northrup Station** (2025 N.W. Northrup St., 503/224-0543 or 800/224-1180, www.northrupstation.com, doubles from $119) is an older motel in now-trendy Northwest Portland that's been totally, and we mean totally, renovated into a retro-hip showcase with a wild color palate—sort of George Jetson meets the Summer of Love. Each of the rooms has full kitchens, boldly designed furniture, and lots of room to make yourself at home (if your home's a design showcase). There's a rooftop garden, high-speed Internet access, free parking, plus lots of curious and outrageous art everywhere. Plus, the inn is right on the Portland Streetcar line, so you can get to the Pearl District or downtown in minutes, without having to worry about parking.

Convenient to both the I-405 freeway and the sights of Northwest Portland, the **Silver Cloud Inn** (2426 N.W. Vaughn St., 503/242-2400 or 800/205-6939, www.silvercloud.com, doubles from $119) is a comfortable hotel with fitness center, guest laundry, and wireless Internet access. Rooms come with microwaves, refrigerators, and premium cable. Free parking is another plus.

The top B&B in Northwest Portland is **Heron Haus Bed & Breakfast Inn** (2545 N.W. Westover Rd., 503/274-1846, www.heronhaus.com, doubles from $145). This ivy-covered 10,000-square-foot 1904 English Tudor home offers six guest rooms, all with air-conditioning, private bath, cable TV, phone, and computer jacks for modem and DSL. The Heron Haus was built back when a quality house featured sunrooms, morning room, mahogany-paneled library, and a study in addition to a dining rooms and formal living room. The stylish decor is warm and understated, blending historical authenticity with casual elegance. Heron Haus is just a few minutes stroll from the shops and cafes of N.W. 23rd Avenue.

SOUTHEAST PORTLAND
Under $50

Hostelling International (3031 S.E. Hawthorne Blvd., 503/236-3380 or 866/447-3031, www.portlandhostel.org, bunks $17 for HI members, $20 for non-members) offers easy access to some of Portland's most vibrant and youthful neighborhoods—within walking distance of Clinton, Belmont, and Hawthorne "hip strips" as well as area eateries and bars. It's also an easy bus ride to downtown. Most accommodations are in bunk-style rooms, though at least two private rooms are available. A spacious screened-in back porch provides a cool place to sleep in July and August. A full kitchen, large common areas (including a shady front porch), and laundry machines are available to all guests. In summer, the hostel sometimes organizes van trips to the wine country, Columbia Gorge, the coast, and other getaways. Make reservations well in advance for this large, rambling white hostelry in summer due to the influx of folks from other countries; this hostel is deservedly popular. To reach here from downtown take TriMet bus #14 up Hawthorne Boulevard.

$50-100

At the east side of the Burnside Bridge, as Burnside Street mounts the hill, there are a number of older motor-court motels, some of dubious quality. However, one of these older properties has an interesting tale to tell. The **Jupiter Hotel** (800 E. Burnside St., 503/230-9200 or 877/800-0004, www.jupiterhotel.com, doubles from $89) is what you might call a boutique motel, an older motel that's been totally updated with a chic, modern look and such stylish accoutrements as fine linens, eye-grabbing art, and high-end toiletries. Though the standard rooms aren't large, they are certainly chic; some larger rooms have kitchens. Best of all, the Jupiter Hotel is also home to the Doug Fir Restaurant and Lounge, one of Portland's top music clubs with a popular dining room open till 4 A.M. daily. Weekends can get pretty noisy here, so bring earplugs or just dance till dawn. Since you're likely to stay up late at the Doug Fir, you might want to consider waiting until after midnight to rent your room, when all rooms are just $59.

NORTHEAST PORTLAND

Between downtown Portland and Lloyd Center are the Portland Oregon Convention Center and the Rose Garden sports arena, along with a number of good-value hotels. There are often deep discounts on these hotels at Internet hotel reservation sites. Note that some of these hotels have free parking, while others do not. This neighborhood offers easy access to downtown and the airport on the MAX light-rail train—in fact, the train is free between Lloyd Center and downtown. None of the hotels below are more than five minutes walk from the MAX line.

$50-100

Just across the street from the Oregon Convention Center and immediately on the MAX line, the **Red Lion Hotel Portland Convention Center** (1021 N.E. Grand Ave., 503/235-2100 800/343-1822, www.redlion.com, doubles from $89) has newly redecorated rooms with free wireless Internet access, voicemail phones, refrigerators, and coffeemakers. Facilities include two restaurants, with the rooftop Windows Lounge a popular spot for drinks and appetizers overlooking Portland. Parking is $8.

Another good choice in this neighborhood is **La Quinta Inn Portland Convention Center** (431 N.E. Multnomah, 503/233-7933 or 800/531-5900, www.lq.com, doubles from $95). This hotel offers a 24-hour indoor pool, a fitness center, and complimentary continental breakfast. Parking is free. All rooms come with a coffeemaker, hair dryer, and free high-speed Internet access.

$100-150

Holiday Inn Portland Downtown (1441 N.E. 2nd Ave., 503/233-2401 or 888/465 4329, www.ichotelsgroup.com, doubles from $129) is in a quiet corner of this busy neighborhood, and the upper floors have good views. Newly renovated guestrooms are large, have microwaves, mini-fridges, and irons, while suites have full kitchens. Facilities include a beautiful indoor pool, spa, and state-of-the-art fitness center, plus a restaurant and bar. Add in free on-site parking you've got one of the best deals in inner Portland.

For something completely different, **(Kennedy School** (5736 N.E. 33rd, 503/249-3983 or 888/249-3983, www.kennedyschool.com, doubles from $100) is an unusual McMenamins hotel in the Concordia neighborhood, about six miles northeast of downtown. The hotel is set in an old elementary school that has been transformed into a complex with a brewpub, movie theater, restaurant, three small bars (including the Detention Lounge), and concert venue. Madcap mosaics, carvings, and paintings festoon the hallways along with historic photos from the days the building was a citadel of learning. The rooms are lavishly decorated with art as well as antique furniture. Add a phone and private bath to such perks as admission to the movie theater, and use of the pool, and you can understand why this place is more than just a chance to sleep soundly in a classroom. Be sure to inquire about lodging/dining packages that feature discounts and or extra amenities. Free parking.

Three blocks north of the MAX line is **Courtyard by Marriott Lloyd Center** (435 Wasco St., 503/234-3200 or 800/321-2211, doubles from $134), with an indoor pool and fitness area, restaurant, and rooms with coffeemaker, refrigerator, premium cable, and iron. You'll pay for $9 for parking.

The historic Irvington neighborhood north of Lloyd Center has several fine B&Bs. The opulent **(White House Bed and Breakfast** (1914 N.E. 22nd, 503/287-7131 or 800/287-7131, www.portlandswhitehouse.com, dou-

bles from $125) gives you the presidential treatment. Located just off Broadway near an avenue of shops and restaurants, only 5–10 minutes from Lloyd Center and downtown, this lovingly restored 1912 lumber baron's mansion with Greek columns evocative of its namesake in D.C. is one of the city's top B&Bs. Beyond the tall mahogany front doors here, hand-painted murals in the huge foyer usher guests into the crystal-chandeliered dining room. Antique guest room furnishings and claw-foot tubs may sustain the illusion that you're staying in the Lincoln Bedroom, but the innkeeper's baked scones and other goodies at breakfast (sautéed apple French toast) and tea, together with complimentary sherry nightcaps, impart the touch of home.

The landmark **Lion and the Rose Victorian Bed and Breakfast Inn** (1810 N.E. 15th Ave., 503/287-9245 or 800/955-1647, www.lionrose.com, doubles from $119) is a 1906 Queen Anne mansion, listed on the National Register of Historic Places. The six guest rooms (all with private baths) are each unique and although charming in an authentically Victorian way, they're also up to date, with air-conditioning, telephones, cable TV, and high-speed wireless Internet access. The parlors and dining room are comfortable, spacious, and decorated in period furnishings.

$150-200

Across form Lloyd Center shopping mall and right on the MAX line is one of Portland's largest hotels, **Doubletree Hotel Lloyd Center** (1000 N.E. Multnomah St., 503/281-6111 or 800/996-0510, www.doubletree.com, doubles from $179). The Doubletree is a full-service hotel, with two restaurants, lounge, fitness room and indoor pool, room service, and convention facilities. The large, well-decorated guest rooms have balconies, high-speed Internet access, coffeemakers, and irons. Parking is $18.

AIRPORT

The expansion of PDX airport has been paralleled by the growth of nearby lodging alternatives, most with free shuttle to and from the airport. There are a lot of new hotels at I-205 Exit 23. Except on holiday weekends you probably won't need reservations, but here are a few options from all price categories if you want to call ahead.

$50-100

A 12-minute ride from the airport (by free shuttle) is **Quality Inn** (8247 N.E. Sandy Blvd., 503/256-4111 or 800/424-6423, www .choicehotel.com, doubles from $75). Located near The Grotto (old-growth trees and contemplative surroundings) and the Cameo Cafe (see listing later in this chapter), it's a world away from terminal traffic snarls. Better yet, it's halfway between the airport and downtown with easy access via city bus. While the rooms are typical of moderately priced chains, the free breakfast and other amenities make it a good choice.

The **Country Inn and Suites** (7025 N.E. Alderwood Rd., 503/255-2700 or 888/987-2700, www.countryinns.com, doubles from $90) is a 150-room hotel with a pool, spa,

fitness center, and well-appointed rooms. A free airport shuttle and breakfast are also available.

$100-150

Courtyard by Marriott (11550 N.E. Airport Way, 503/252-3200 or 800/321-2211, www .marriott.com, doubles from $119), offers rooms with microwaves, wet bars, and other appreciated extras. A restaurant, pool, and spa facilities are also on-site. It's three miles east of the airport, with 24-hour free shuttle service to the terminal.

$150-200

The closest hotel to the airport, **Sheraton Portland Airport Hotel** (8253 N.E. Airport Way, 503/281-2500 or 800/325-3535, www.sheraton.com/portland, doubles from $154) is pretty classy, with oversized, well-furnished rooms, indoor pool, fitness center, room service, restaurant, and a small conference center. Free shuttles run to the airport terminal 24/7.

Food

Portland is second only to San Francisco in the highest number of restaurants per capita in the country. Bring your appetite.

A few peculiarities are worth mentioning: Many dinner places listed here are closed on Mondays; Portland restaurant coffee will probably be stronger than what you're used to if you aren't from Seattle or San Francisco; You can get away with virtually any mode of dress here in even the most upscale establishments; The recent proliferation of pan-Asian restaurants and Mexican taquerias reflects recent immigration trends. What also might surprise newcomers to Portland dining is the large number of places that focus on breakfast.

Portland is a very neighborhood-oriented city and restaurants too have strong associations with their locale. Restaurants tend to be located near other restaurants, creating mini-enclaves

within dining neighborhoods that each offer distinctively different atmospheres. The restaurant scene—and dining experience—will be very different in the Pearl District than in the Mississippi Avenue neighborhood, for instance, though both offer top quality and selection. The following dining selections are broken down into broad quadrants, along with a brief overview of that neighborhood's dining hotbeds. You may find it as tempting to choose a neighborhood in which to dine as to choose a specific restaurant or cuisine type, because many of the dining neighborhoods have a strong and appealing character of their own.

DOWNTOWN PORTLAND

If you're on a budget, or looking for downtown al fresco dining, join the bus commuters, cyclists, and pedestrians on the go who eat at

street food carts. Food carts are scattered all over the city center, purveying all sorts of street food (including burritos, bento, stir-fry, barbecue, and the like) but the greatest concentration is in the heart of the bus mall around S.W. 5th and Stark. There's also a large food court in the lower level of **Pioneer Place Shopping Center,** most directly reached by the escalators at S.W. Salmon and 5th Avenue.

Breakfast and Light Meals

Downtown Portland's most famous breakfast spot is 🄲 **Bijou Café** (132 S.W. 3rd Ave., 503/222-3187, breakfast and lunch daily, $5–13), the epitome of the breakfast café. While fried cinnamon bread and red snapper or roast beef hash are morning mainstays in this cheery café, ordinary breakfast foods are done perfectly here with the freshest and most nutritious ingredients.

Just when you thought Portland was a health-food kind of place, you find **VooDoo Doughnut** (22 S.W. 3rd Ave., 503/241-4704, www.voodoodoughnut.com, 1 P.M.–11 A.M. Mon.–Fri.—yes, that's 22 hours a day, 1 P.M.–4 A.M. and 6 A.M.–11 A.M. Sat., closed Sun.). This famed donut shop is in the thick of the Old Town bar zone, and offers all-night donuts to club kids and anyone else who stumbles by. You'll be amazed at the selection, and the devotion that mighty fine donuts can induce—try the maple bars with bacon (reported a fave of Brad Pitt) or the vegan donuts (!). Just in case you're in the mood, the Triple Chocolate Penetration, a combo of chocolate donut, chocolate glaze, and cocoa-puffs—is legal in Portland.

For a great meal for less than $7, try **Good Dog, Bad Dog** (708 S.W. Alder, 503/222-3410, 11 A.M.–7 P.M.Mon.–Sat., noon–5 P.M. Sun.). The Oregon Smokey is a spicy introduction to the flavors of the Northwest. Choose from 10 meaty sausages at this budget diner's dream and treat yourself to a microbrew.

Downtown's top vegetarian choice is **Veganopolis** (412 S.W. 4th Ave., 9 A.M.–6 P.M. Mon.–Sat.) a cafeteria with all-vegan foods such as flavorful and nutritious soups, salads, sandwiches, and baked goods.

American

Nothing says upscale comfort food like **Mother's Bistro and Bar** (212 S.W. Stark St., 503/464-1122, breakfast and lunch Tues.–Sun., dinner Tues.–Sat., main courses $9–18). This handsome Victorian storefront is a cozy spot to enjoy perfectly crafted meatloaf, mashed potatoes, and chicken and dumplings, made the way mom did—if mom were Julia Child.

Huber's (411 S.W. 3rd, 503/228-5686, open for lunch and dinner Mon.– Fri., dinner only Sat. and Sun.) bills itself as the oldest restaurant in town, dating back to 1879. Spanish coffee served with a flame-juggling flourish and the best turkey dinner in town are claims to fame here, but the draw for many patrons is the chance to dine surrounded by tropical hardwoods, stained glass, and the glory that was 19th century. Turkey remains the specialty (the menu offer six different preparations, including a fantastic Thanksgiving-style roast tom), but the dining room also features up-to-date preparations of Northwest fish and meats. Many come for late-night coffee and desserts in the impressive stained-glass-lit bar.

Steak and Seafood

Dan and Louis Oyster Bar (208 S.W. Ankeny, 503/227-5906, lunch and dinner daily, dinner main courses $10–20) is a 1907 treasure trove of maritime memorabilia and antiques as well as oyster stew made with prized Yaquina Bay oysters. Over a century ago the owners' ancestors helped start an oyster farm on the coast that made these bivalves famous. You can enjoy this legacy today along with other fresh Oregon seafood. While it ain't exactly cutting-edge cuisine, this restaurant's affordability and decor make it a good choice for family seafood dining.

Atop the U.S. Bancorp Tower, **Portland City Grill** (111 S.W. Fifth Ave., 30th floor, 503/450-0030, lunch Mon.–Fri., dinner daily, main courses $10–25) offers fine views of Portland from its 30-story perch. Popular with corporate business diners, it's also a fine spot for romantic dinner, or a light supper of appetizers in the busy jazz piano bar. Steaks and seafood are the best bet on the rather unadventurous menu—but then you came here for the view.

PORTLAND BY THE SLICE

Pizza styles from Chicago, New York, and other locales are represented in the Pacific Northwest. Expect to pay $2.50 a slice on the average and enjoy a great variety of toppings.

Pizza in Portland means **Escape From New York** (622 N.W. 23rd Ave., 503/227-5423) if you're an East Coast purist who likes foldable crust, copious cheese, and conventional toppings. Open 11:30 A.M.-11 P.M. daily.

If you're not averse to paying a little more for your pizza, head to one of **Pizzicato's** half-dozen outlets around town (two of them at 705 N.W. Alder, 503/226-1007, and 2811 N.E. Burnside, 503/236-6045, 11 A.M.-9 P.M. daily). Exotic toppings such as lamb, sausage, chanterelle and shitake mushrooms, and rock shrimp make a meal out of a slice. For price, selection, an array of organic toppings, and a stimulating campus ambience, **Hot Lips Pizza** (1909 S.W. 6th, 503/224-0311), near Portland State University, is a good choice. Open 11 A.M.-10 P.M. Monday-Saturday and noon-8 P.M. Sunday. Another outlet is open in the Pearl District at N.W. 10th

and Irving (503/595-2342) and at S.E. Hawthorne and 22nd Avenue (503/234-9999).

The **Oasis Café** (37th and Hawthorne, 503/231-0901) may be bare bones in terms of decor, but a seat at the ample window front counter allows you to enjoy not only some of the best pizza in town, but also the best people-watching. Open 11 A.M.-11 P.M. daily.

Up on N. Mississippi Avenue, the **Mississippi Pizza Pub** (3552 N. Mississippi Ave., 503/288-3231) offers wondrous thin crust pizza in a funky DIY storefront that's totally Portland and totally delicious. The staff at **Apizza Scholls** (4741 S.E. Hawthorne Blvd., 503/233-1286) have earned the reputation as the "pizza Nazis" for their formidable resistance to allowing patrons to choose their own toppings or to make enough pizza dough to stay open through their posted hours. But the cracker-like crusts and pleasant deck seating in summer keep the crowds lined up. Open 5 P.M.-9:30 P.M. Wednesday-Saturday and 5 P.M.-8:30 P.M. Sunday.

Jake's Famous Crawfish (901 S.W. 12th St., 503/226-1419, lunch and dinner Mon.–Fri., dinner only Sat. and Sun., dinner main courses $12–30) is not known for just crawfish. Easily Portland's most famous restaurant, Jake's is also renowned for one of the widest-ranging seafood menus in the Northwest and one of the most extensive Oregon wine lists. The largest privately owned fine art collection in the region also graces the mahogany-paneled confines of Jake's. Other specialties include clam chowder, smoked salmon and sturgeon, fresh oysters, steamed butter clams, spring chinook salmon, bouillabaisse, and the best Irish coffee in town. Getting reserved seating in this 100-plus-year-old landmark is often difficult, but not enough to deter dozens of reservationless people who might wait more than an hour for a table.

McCormick and Schmick's Seafood Restaurant (235 S.W. 1st Ave., 503/224-7522, lunch and dinner Mon.–Sat., dinner only on Sun., dinner main courses $12–30) has ven-

erable roots—it's the offspring of century-old Jake's Famous Crawfish restaurant and enjoys a location in the historic Failing Building on the edge of Old Town. Also like Jake's, it offers an extensive list of fresh fish plus prime steaks and chops. Despite its bloodline and Victorian digs, this place is inclined to experiment with such avant-garde combinations as Cajun seared rockfish with lime cilantro butter sauce or seafood stir-fry with lemon-ginger glaze. The fresh sheet often features more than a dozen kinds of oysters and more than 25 varieties of fish.

For dinner in a classic setting, try **Jake's Grill** (Governor Hotel, S.W. 10th and Alder, 503/220-1850 or 800/554-3456, three meals daily, dinner main courses $8–30), another offspring of the famous Jake's seafood restaurant but with a different emphasis than its patrimony might suggest. Jake's Grill offers a selection of classic American comfort food in addition to steaks, chops, and seafood. Expect expertly prepared chicken potpie as well as filet mignon with cabernet mushroom sauce.

Middle Eastern

Portland has many quality Lebanese restaurants, but one long-time favorite is **Al Amir** (233 S.W. Stark, 503/274-0010, lunch and dinner Mon.–Fri., dinner only Sat. and Sun., main courses $12–17), located downtown in the dark paneled Gothic elegance of a home once belonging to Portland's archbishop (circa 1879). The menu emphasizes Lebanese specialties, and there's a belly dancer on Friday and Saturday evenings. The lentil soup with plenty of cumin, babaghanoush (an eggplant dip), lamb kebabs, and rich, garlicky hummus are standouts. A mezza plate lets you sample a variety of items including falafel, hummus, babaghanoush, and tabouleh. Another downtown favorite for Middle Eastern cooking is **Karam Lebanese Cuisine** (316 S.W. Stark St., 503/223-0830, lunch and dinner Mon.– Sat., dinner main courses $8–19) where the menu goes far beyond standard shish kabobs. The menu features delicious Lebanese-style home cooking with such dishes as braised goat, a complex and satisfying artichoke-heart stew, and *batenjan mekle,* a grilled stuffed eggplant roll.

Japanese

Sushi is very popular in Portland and right downtown you'll find good sushi and a boisterous bar scene at **Dragonfish** (in the Panorama Hotel at 909 S.W. Park Ave., 503/243-5991, lunch and dinner daily, main courses $11–17). Dragonfish has an intriguing pan-Asian menu that includes sushi, but the real deal here is happy hour, 4–6 P.M. and 10 P.M.–1 A.M. every day, when sushi rolls are $1.95.

Koji Osakaya (606 S.W. Broadway, 503/294-1169, lunch and dinner daily, dinner main dishes $5–15) is a reliable choice for Japanese food. Don't come looking for quaint—Koji's is a standard-looking dining room with a full service bar but its sushi, soba, and teriyaki can accommodate everyone from hard-core devotees of fresh raw fish to the most demanding vegetarian. There are also Koji locations

in Northeast Portland at 1502 N.E. Weidler, 503/280-0992 and in Southwest Portland at 10100 S.W. Barbur Boulevard, 503/977-3100.

East Indian

If you're downtown, you'll find a number of Indian street food carts with very tasty and inexpensive food. Another option is **Gandhi's** (827 S.W. 2nd Ave., 503/219-9224, lunch Mon.– Fri.) a little hole-in-the-wall joint with very tasty cooked-to-order food—the excellent chicken vindaloo is just $5. If you prefer all-you-can-eat buffet-style Indian food, the **India House** (1038 S.W. Morrison St., 503/274-1017, lunch and dinner daily) may be to your liking. Here, for $7 you can load up a plate with a variety of vegetable curries, samosas (triangular potato pastries with flaky crust), tandoori chicken, basmati rice, and salads. At night, India House offers a large menu of northern Indian favorites a la carte.

Portland's most upscale Indian restaurant is **Plainfield's Mayur** (852 S.W. 21st Ave., 503/223-2995, dinner nightly, main courses $12–30), located in a Victorian house in the West Hills behind downtown. The food is extremely well prepared and subtly nuanced by rich spices, and the wine cellar features 4,000 bottles. Lobster simmered in onions, ginger and cream, duck breast in almond Korma sauce and tamarind-coconut-coated halibut are highlights at Plainfield's, which regularly receives accolades from the national food press.

Thai

Typhoon! (400 S.W. Broadway at Hotel Lucia, 503/224-8285, or 2310 N.W. Everett St., 503/243-7557, plus two suburban locations, www.typhoonrestaurants.com, lunch and dinner Mon.–Sat, dinner only Sun., dinner main courses $9–18) has graced the pages of national gourmet magazines and other high-profile media. What all the fuss is about is Thai food reflecting the culinary and aesthetic sensibilities of the chef/owner Bo Kline. This is as evident in the boldly colorful decor of its Northwest Everett location and ornate presentation on each plate as it is from one bite of *miang kum*. Inspired by Thai street food, this build-it-yourself dish consists of fresh spinach leaves wrapped around toasted coconut, dried shrimp, shallots, ginger, and Thai chilies, topped with plum sauce. Seafood dishes such as Fish on Fire (halibut flambé with curry sauce) and Bags of Gold (shrimp wontons tied up with chives) also might make you forget pad Thai noodles (though the version here is excellent).

A Tiki island of cocktails and pan-Asian synergy, **Saucebox** (214 S.W. Broadway, 503/241-3393; dinner and late night menu Tues.–Sat, main courses $8–16) isn't sure whether it's a high-style restaurant or an atmospheric dance club. One thing's for certain: The cutting-edge, small-plates-style Asian cooking is great. Come early to enjoy zippy Thai curries, grilled lamb satay, spicy meatballs, crisp-fried noodles, and Korean pork ribs, or come late to dance and snack. Be sure to check out the cocktails, as this is one of the city's top spots for inventive libations.

Northwest Cuisine

Perhaps no other downtown restaurant better exemplifies Northwest cuisine more than **Higgins** (1239 S.W. Broadway, 503/222-9070, lunch Mon.–Fri., dinner daily, main dishes $12–30). Housed in a comfortably informal old storefront, the restaurant is devoted to serving the fresh produce of local organic farmers, meats from area farms and ranches, and fresh fish and seafood from local rivers and seaports in uncluttered preparations that let the natural flavors sing. The back bar is a favorite of downtown office workers and after-theater thespians.

At the **Heathman Restaurant** (1001 S.W. Broadway, 503/790-7752 or 800/551-0011, three meals daily, main courses $25 and above), French meets Northwest in a constantly changing menu featuring the best of organically raised and foraged ingredients. Fare ranges from a marinated sea bass salad for lunch to a pistachio-stuffed leg of rabbit for dinner. The creative use of local ingredients can be seen with salmon, which may be served smoked in

a hash for breakfast or seared with wasabi bearnaise sauce later in the day.

The **Veritable Quandary** (1220 S.W. 1st Ave., 503/227-7342, lunch and dinner daily, brunch on Sat. and Sun.) is a downtown Portland institution. This quirky spot right beside the Hawthorne Bridge is known as one of the city's best spots for an after-work drink (the leafy patio is second to none in downtown). But it's more of an insider's secret just how good the food is at the VQ. This venerable wood-paneled bar and dining room offers Northwest cuisine to match any in the city. Try petrale sole with Dungeness crab and blood oranges, wild mushroom and brie ravioli—or go comfort food with delectable fried chicken and mashed potatoes. The VQ is also one of downtown's best spots for late-night drinks.

Italian

Downtown Portland's finest Italian restaurant, **Pazzo** (627 S.W. Washington, 503/228-1515, lunch and dinner daily, dinner main courses $12–28), has charm to burn, and a broad menu of well-prepared pasta and grilled meats. Located in the exquisitely renovated Hotel Vintage Plaza, this is a wonderful spot for a lively, sophisticated meal with friends. Pazzo's insistence on local fresh produce, meats, and fish has resulted in such creative dishes as smoked salmon ravioli in lemon cream with asparagus. Great desserts, designer pizzas, and low-priced gourmet takeout items can be found at **Pazzoria Bakery** next door.

The large, comfortably informal dining room at **SouthPark** (901 S.W. Salmon, 503/326-1300, lunch and dinner daily, main courses from $11–22) is, as its name suggests, just a block from the South Park Blocks and the busy cultural venues at the Portland Center for the Performing Arts. The focus is on sunny foods of the Mediterranean, with especially noteworthy seafood stew. The adjacent wine bar is a favorite for a pre-symphony quaff, and it's a good spot to savor a hamburger, one of the city's best.

SOUTHWEST PORTLAND
Breakfast and Light Meals

South of downtown off Barbur Boulevard, one of Portland's most famous breakfast haunts is the **Original Pancake House** (8601 S.W. 24th St., 503/246-9007, 7 A.M.–3 P.M. Wed.–Sun.). This operation has spawned many imitations, but the Original is still the greatest. Get there early on weekends because waits for seating can be excruciatingly long. Once at the table, the famous apple pancake is a Frisbee-sized cinnamon-laced delight for the growing boy or girl. The menu also features four gourmet omelettes. Despite the 1950s knotty pine walls, expect to pay around $8 for breakfast—not bad for a place James Beard and Art Buchwald once ranked as among the top 10 restaurants in the nation.

Another suburban favorite, moderately priced **Marco's** (7910 S.W. 35th, 503/245-0199, three meals daily) is in a cluster of antique shops, boutiques, and cafés known as Multnomah Village. At breakfast, intriguing omelette combinations (try Italian sausage, sweet peppers, tomatoes, onions, herbs, and asiago cheese), wonderful home fries, and a culinary approach that keeps nutritional concerns foremost makes this worth the 12-minute trip from downtown by car. (Take Exit 296 off southbound I-5.) Later on, come back to Marco's for lunch or dinner, saving room for a multi-ethnic menu that's partial to vegetarians as well as carnivores who prefer their beef from naturally grazed cattle. There are also nightly fresh fish specials, Marco's legendary mulligatawny soup each Thursday, imaginative desserts such as coconut mango cheesecake, and an assortment of newspapers and magazines to help you pass time till you're hungry again.

Italian

Alba Osteria & Enoteca (6440 S.W. Capitol Hwy., 503/977-3045, lunch Wed.– Fri., dinner Tues.–Sun., main courses $12–20) features the sophisticated cooking of northwest Italy's Piedmont region, which combines French esprit and the Italian dedication to purity of flavor. House-made pastas—such as tajarin, a ribbon noodle rich in egg yolk—are featured in dishes that are simultaneously lighter and richer than

the standard. The wine list is notable for its depth and fair prices. For a neighborhood-style restaurant, this is seriously good cooking.

NORTHWEST PORTLAND

Northwest Portland begins just north of downtown, across Burnside Street. Two of the city's most vibrant dining districts are here, within minutes of downtown hotels. The **Pearl District** and **Old Town** offer the best of Portland's old and the new. Old Town, which also encapsulates historic Chinatown, is the heart of the city's Victorian-era commercial district. In addition to stylish restaurants, Old Town is also a hotbed of music clubs and late-night bars - and homeless shelters. Although it's rough around the edges, there's no particular danger here. You may choose to ferry in and out by cab, particularly if you're walking alone.

The Pearl District is just west of Old Town, and started out as the city's old rail warehouse area. It's blossomed into a high-rise loft residential and retail district, with some of the city's top restaurants. The Portland Street Car travels through the Pearl District, linking it with downtown. Another restaurant hotbed is along **N.W. 21st and 23st Avenues,** two pedestrian-friendly streets that are at the heart of an attractive 19th century neighborhood. Parking is very limited in this neighborhood, so if you're downtown consider taking a cab or the Portland Street Car to this popular dining mecca.

Breakfast and Light Meals

For in-the-know early risers, breakfast in Northwest Portland means a trip to the **Stepping Stone Cafe** (N.W. 24th and Quimby, 503/222-1132), a retro formica-styled hash house that serves up traditional breakfasts in a quiet and leafy neighborhood. Breakfast served every day until 2 P.M.

Founded by French-Canadian loggers, **Besaw's** (N.W. 23rd and Savier, 503/228-2619, www.besaws.com, open for breakfast, lunch, and dinner Tues.–Sun., dinner main courses $8–20) is a meat-and-potatoes-meets-brie-and-chablis kind of place, where comfort

THE MCMENAMIN'S BREWPUB EMPIRE

If you drink beer and if you go out at night, you're likely to run into a MeMenamins brewpub during a trip to Portland. This highly successful local enterprise now has over 50 pubs and related businesses in Washington and Oregon, and whenever a historic venue goes on sale, there's at least a large minority of Northwesterners who hope that it will become a McMenimans brewpub. The McMenimans are in fact brothers Brian and Mike, who are equally devoted to brewing quality beer, designing fun spaces to drink it in, and preserving distinctive buildings.

The typical McMenamins pub features imaginative antiques, art, and architecture on a grand scale. In fact, the decor can be rather silly but the desired effect is to create a space that doesn't take itself too seriously. According to the McMenimans: "Be wary of things too formal, too complicated and too orthodox. Ultimately, the most important realization has been that the essence of a pub is its people. Trendy decor doesn't attract a lasting clientele. It's the other way around: The neighborhood clientele is the atmosphere – and that never goes in and out of style."

Portland has the most microbreweries of any city in the U.S., and any short-list of pub destinations should include several McMenimans outlets because of their dedication to preserving historic structures. The **Ringler's/Crystal Ballroom complex** in downtown (at 14th and Burnside) combines a funky pub atmosphere (there are four venues here) with a floating-floor dance hall from 1914. The ballroom hosts some of Portland's top bands and musical events. Just across the Willamette from downtown, the **White Eagle Saloon** (836 N. Russell St., 503/282-6810) is one of Portland's oldest still-operating bars (from 1905) with a lively late-night live music scene. The **Kennedy School** (5736 N.E. 33rd Ave., 503/249-3983 or 888/249-3983) is an unusual enterprise – a block-square 1915 grade school that's been converted into a brewpub, restaurant, and hotel, plus movie theater (think couches in the auditorium). In the suburbs of Portland are two of the grandest extensions of the McMenamins' dream. On the way to the Columbia Gorge, **Edgefield** (2126 S.W. Halsey St., Troutdale, 503/669-8610 or 800/669-8610) began its existence as the Multnomah County Poor Farm. This vast 25-acre operation now contains multiple restaurants and drinking establishments, plus a delightful period hotel, movie theater, and winery. On the way to the coast, just south of Highway 26, is the **Grand Lodge** (3505 Pacific Ave., Forest Grove, 503/992-9533 or 877/992-9533), completed in 1922 as a retirement home for Masons and Eastern Star adherents. This 13-acre property offers dining, drinking, hotel rooms, movies, and a 10-hole disc golf course.

Lest we forget, McMenimans pioneered the notion of cinema brewpubs, where you can buy a microbrew, chow down on a burger, and watch a recent movie. Closest to downtown Portland are the **Mission Theatre** (1624 N.W. Glisan, 503/223-4527) and the **Bagdad Theatre & Pub** (3702 S.E. Hawthorne Blvd., 503/236-9234) in the thick of the trendy Hawthorne neighborhood.

No one would claim that the food at McMenimans is cutting edge or that they produce the most sophisticated ales in Portland. But overall the quality is just fine and a fine deal and chances are that you'll enjoy your pint and burger in a truly unique setting. Try the raspberry-flavored Ruby, Strawberry Fields, or the seasonal Kris Kringle (spiked with ginger, cinnamon, and allspice), along with more traditional brews such as Hammerhead Ale or Terminator Stout.

For more info on locations and music and movie offerings within the McMenamins empire, visit www.mcmenamins.com or call 503/249-3983.

food shares the menu with dishes prepared with house-smoked salmon, wild mushrooms, and other locally sourced ingredients. This orientation is in evidence at breakfast—the preferred meal here—with the prosciutto and egg scramble, breakfast burritos, and banana-pecan buttermilk pancakes. The lunch menu includes grilled salmon sandwiches, and dinner offers pepper-glazed pork with apple chutney and coq au vin. Made-from-scratch desserts such as apple-raspberry bread pudding and berry brown Betty can conclude your meal of high-class comfort food. Drinks at Besaw's century-old mahogany bar can make waiting for a table here eminently bearable.

Famous for its desserts—towering, many-layered concoctions that defy gravity and description—**Papa Haydn** (701 N.W. 23rd, 503/228-7317, lunch and dinner Mon.–Sat., lunch/brunch only Sun., also at 5829 Milwaukie Ave., 503/232-9440) is Portland's doyenne of desserts, in a decadent league of its own. This restaurant also is also an excellent place for light lunches and suppers. Sandwiches and salads are as carefully fashioned as the marjolaine. But it's the refrigerated case filled with 30 or more eye-popping desserts that will form your permanent memory of this Portland landmark.

American

Imagine flavorful, all-American comfort food like pot roast, baked chicken, and pan-fried fish, and then imagine them raised to the level of fine dining. **Paragon** (1309 N.W. Hoyt St., 503/833-5060, lunch and dinner daily, main courses $13–25) calls it American bistro cuisine, and that just about captures it. The dining room is bright and pleasant, but on weekend nights the bar's live music and singles scene detract from dining pleasure.

Greek

At the edge of Old Town is a Portland institution. High spirits are in the air when you step into **Alexis** (215 W. Burnside, 503/224-8577, lunch and dinner Mon.–Fri., dinner Sat., main courses from $9–16), but it's not just the retsina. This is the best traditional Greek food

in Oregon. Appetizers such as calamari or saganaki (fried cheese) might start your meal here. You can spend an evening just ordering appetizers and enjoying the crusty bread, but it would be a shame to forgo such entrées as the moussaka and oregano chicken. On weekends this moderately priced taverna features belly dancing and an atmosphere that'll bring out the Zorba in anyone.

Chinese

While Portland's long-time Chinatown is in the Old Town district, the business and culinary center for today's Chinese immigrants has long ago shifted to the area around S.E. 82nd Avenue and Division Street. While there's perfectly acceptable Americanized Chinese food in Chinatown, head out to Wong's King (see *Southeast Portland*) for Portland's best Chinese food. However, if you're hankering for dim sum while in Chinatown, go to **Fong Chong** (301 N.W. 4th, 503/228-6868, lunch and dinner daily, dinner main dishes $8–15) for an exotic and low-cost dining adventure. It all begins at 11 A.M. every day, when carts of steaming Cantonese delicacies come whooshing down the aisles. Even if the mumbled explanations of the barely bilingual staff don't translate, the array of crepes and buns stuffed with chicken, shrimp, pork, and other fillings are so varied and cost so little (averaging $3–5) that you can't miss. After 3 P.M. the restaurant reverts to standard Cantonese fare.

Quiet and sophisticated, **Sungari Pearl** (1105 N.W. Lovejoy St., 971/222-7327, lunch Mon.–Sat., dinner nightly, main courses $11–18) is central Portland's best Chinese restaurant, featuring Szechwan cuisine in a stylishly modern dining room. Sungari has consistently been awarded the honor of top Chinese restaurant by the local food press.

Italian

The Pearl District is home to some of Portland's most expensive loft real estate and to some of its most ambitious restaurants. However, tucked in amid the high-rises are a few less expensive restaurants where you can enjoy the neighborhoods high-quality food without too much pain to the wallet. **Piazza Italia** (1129 N.W. Johnson St., 503/478-0619, lunch and dinner daily, main courses $10–20) is an authentic Italian pasta joint where dishes like rigatoni alla Bolognese and lasagna will transport you to an idealized Roman trattoria.

One of Northwest Portland's favorites, **Caffé Mingo** (807 N.W. 21st Ave., 503/226-4646, lunch and dinner Mon.– Fri., dinner Sat and Sun, dinner main courses $12–24) Is a small neighborhood trattoria that offers honest full-flavored Italian fare such as rigatoni with spicy Italian sausage or a perfectly roasted chicken with braised endive. This pocket-sized restaurant doesn't take reservations so come early or late to avoid standing on the street.

French

It doesn't get much more Left Bank than **St. Honoré Boulangerie** (2335 N.W. Thurman St., 503/445-4342, 7 A.M.–8 P.M. daily, panini, soup, and salads from $4–9) a little bit of France that's drifted fully intact to 23rd Ave in Northwest Portland. Of course, St. Honoré is foremost a bakery—filled with fragrant baguettes, *épis* and *pains complètes* to say nothing of wonderful pastries like *mille feuilles*. But the reason that this chic restaurant is so packed from morning till night is the selection of truly French-style salads, sandwiches, and light entrées.

A classic French bistro down to the miniature tables and mirrored specials board, **Le Bouchon** (517 N.W. 14th Ave., 503/248-2193, lunch and dinner Tues.– Fri., dinner Sat., main courses $14–22) doesn't venture far from the traditional standards of French cooking. Duck breast, roast chicken, wine-braised beef, mussels, and housemade pâtés can't really be improved on when they're done right, as they are here.

Simultaneously flamboyant and studied, **Fenouil** (900 N.W. 11th Ave., 503/525-2225, lunch and dinner daily, brunch on Sun., main courses $12–26) is visually one of the most impressive restaurants in Portland. The vast two-story Euro-sleek dining room opens out onto the Pearl District's Jamison Square, pulsing with fountains. This opulent setting demands equally stylish food, and for the most part the kitchen delivers. The menu offers a mix of traditional French classics and up-to-date dishes honed with Gallic savoir faire. Seared duck breast and a confit duck leg are served with perfectly cooked citrus-y lentils, while seared fois gras comes with delicate brioche toasts. If you like to dress up and pretend you're a VIP once in a while, then here's the place to enjoy yourself.

Paley's (1204 N.W. 21st Ave., 503/243-2403, dinner nightly, main dishes $19–40) is the quintessential French-by-Northwest bistro and, according to many Portlanders, one of the most enjoyable dining experience in town. This intimate restaurant (16 tables seating maybe 50 people) has a few stalwart dishes backing up the seasonally rotating menu. The latter might include fennel-pollen-dusted pork tenderloin or peppered sweetbreads with grilled romaine and mushroom caper relish. The front porch of Paley's 20th century Victorian makes outdoor dining on a summer night a delight.

Northwest Cuisine

It's a lovely spot, directly across from the shady North Park Blocks where the locals toss balls in a game of boules. But **Park Kitchen** (422 N.W. 8th Ave., 503/223-7275, lunch Mon.–Fri., dinner Mon.–Sat., main courses $13–22) has a lot more going for it than location. Chef Scott Dolich, named one of the nation's top chefs by *Food & Wine* magazine, relies on seasonal and regional ingredients to ensure heights of freshness and flavor, but injects an eclectic touch of genius that makes even ordinary ingredients shimmer. The menu, divided into small and large plates, offers such diversions as gin-cured mussels and root-beer-spiced duck breast.

Bluehour (250 N.W. 13th Ave., 503/226-3394, lunch Mon.–Sat, dinner daily, brunch Sun., main courses $22–45) has been Portland's restaurant of the moment for several years now, garnering raves from the national press, and with good reason. Though the prices pack a wallop, the Italian-by-Northwest cuisine here is equal parts inventive and traditional, which suits the tastes of the local Beautiful People who haunt this Pearl District ex-warehouse. On busy nights, the artfully spare dining room doubles as an echo chamber.

Wildwood (1221 N.W. 21st Ave., 503/248-9663, lunch and dinner daily, main courses $12–32) was Portland's first "celebrity chef" restaurant, created when local-boy-made-good Cory Schreiber returned from San Francisco to open his own restaurant. Wildwood has done as much as any other local restaurant to make Northwest cuisine a reality, with seasonal dishes focusing on local ingredients and simple, often old-fashioned preparations that let fresh flavors sing. Local lamb, rabbit, and salmon are usually excellent choices. The hard-edged dining room is attractive but loud—this is no place for a quiet romantic dinner.

Vietnamese

For artfully prepared Vietnamese cuisine served in the trendy Pearl District, try **Silk** (1012 N.W. Glisan, 503/248-2172, lunch and dinner Mon.–Sat., main courses $8–22), which takes already very refined Vietnamese to gourmet heights. Expect such temptations as lotus and banana blossom salad and barbecued shrimp and crisp lentil-flour pancakes. Choose from the typical fare (such as *pho*, a beef noodle soup) or the more unusual (sea bass steamed in banana leaves, for example).

Japanese

Sinju (1022 N.W. Johnson St., 503/223-6535, lunch and dinner Mon.–Fri., dinner only Sat. and Sun., sushi from $7–13) offers some of Portland's freshest sushi in a handsomely decorated dining room. Call ahead to reserve the tatami rooms.

Latin American

You may be forgiven if you don't immediately think of Peruvian cooking when you think of a scintillating night out with outstanding indigenous cuisine. And in Portland? However, put these preconceptions aside and join the crowds at **Andina** (1314 N.W. Glisan St., 503/228-9535, lunch Mon.–Sat, dinner daily, main courses $14–30). The restaurant's take on South American cooking

is unexpectedly delicious. The many small plates are rich in vegetarian choices—like quinoa-stuffed piquillo peppers—and can make a meal, or go for one of traditional Peruvian main courses, like lamb shanks braised in black beer, or a new cuisine hybrid like seared yellowfin tuna crusted with black pepper and orange zest.

A popular drinks and dinner spot in the Pearl District is **Oba!** (555 N.W. 12th Ave., 503/228-6161, dinner nightly, main courses $8–19), where the vibrant flavors of Latin America come alive. Stop by for a mango margaritas and zesty appetizers such as crispy coconut prawns with jalapeno citrus marinade and seared rare ahi tuna with mango tomatillo salsa. Whether it's spicy sausages with cheese from Spain, arepa corncakes from Colombia, Brazilian black bean pork feijoada, or yuca, the starchy tuber ubiquitous throughout equatorial South America, the focus is on Latino cuisine, albeit with New World interpretations.

East Indian

Swagat (2074 N.W. Lovejoy St., 503/227-4300 and 4325 S.W. 109th Ave., Beaverton, 503/626-3000, open daily for lunch and dinner, lunch buffet $8, main courses $9–18) features southern Indian food with its crepe-like dosas filled with a spicy vegetable curry, crispy tempura-like spinach pakoras, and tasty breads. Vegetarians will appreciate the meatless entrées on the dinner menu here.

Spanish

Just when you thought that the tapas trend was over, along comes **Patanegra** (1818 N.W. 23rd Place, 503/227-7282, dinner Mon.–Sat., tapas $5–14) a true Spanish-style tapas bar that takes you back to the time when small plates was an exciting way to experience mini explosions of flavor and texture—and just not an expensive form of appetizers. The standout dishes at Patenegra are grilled squid stuffed with chorizo sausage and scallops wrapped in envelopes of tangy Serrano ham.

Steaks and Seafood

For more than 60 years, the **RingSide** (2165 W. Burnside, 503/223-1513, dinner nightly, main courses $14–30) has been Portland's top local steakhouse, and today with competition from national steakhouse chains, it's still the preferred place for succulent steaks, chops, and prime rib. Lighter dishes are also available: Caesar salad (with a seafood option) as well as grilled salmon and halibut (also consider the lamb chops and chicken livers) are highly recommended. Many come here simply for the onion rings; the traditional red leatherette and dim lighting add to the lost-in-the-1950s appeal.

NORTHEAST PORTLAND

Twenty years ago, a guide to Portland dining wouldn't have even included a section on Northeast Portland. However, the influx of Portland's DIY youth culture has turned once sleepy Northeast neighborhoods into hotbeds of cuisine. Linked to downtown by MAX light rail and near the Lloyd Center shopping mall, the area along **N.E. Broadway** is the hub of close-in Northeast Portland, with many dining choices just minutes from downtown hotels.

Radiating through the rapidly gentrifying neighborhoods are other streets with restaurants enclaves. A Northeast Portland destination for diners looking for inexpensive yet cutting edge food is **North Mississippi Avenue.** A century ago this area was a major commercial crossroads, but it slowly fell into decline until young chefs and entrepreneurs came looking for inexpensive real estate for new restaurants, coffee shops, and other businesses aimed at Portland's burgeoning "young creative" class. Lots of restaurants now line the streets.

Northeast Alberta Street is one of Portland's newest alternative neighborhoods, where youthful newcomers came looking for inexpensive real estate, and in the process created a land-rush of its own. Amid the galleries and coffee shops are a number of good dining choices. Out past the Hollywood neighborhood along **Sandy Boulevard** is the heart of today's Vietnamese community, where you'll find inexpensive and delicious *pho* and other Indochinese specialties.

Breakfast and Light Meals

Northeast Portland's breakfast hot spot is the **Cadillac Cafe** (1801 N.E. Broadway, 503/287-4750, 6 A.M.–2:30 P.M. Mon.–Fri., 7 A.M.–3 P.M. Sat.–Sun), an always jammed café with a '61 pink Caddy fixation. Simple, honest American fare with lots of flavor is what draws the crowds. Even food as simple as French toast is noteworthy here—just imagine how the breakfast burrito will rock your world. Be prepared for long waits on weekends.

One of Northeast Portland's best kept secrets is **Milo's City Cafe** (1325 N.E. Broadway, 503/288-6456, three meals daily, main courses $8–17) a popular breakfast and lunch spot that recently added a dinner menu to bolster its reputation as *the* local café for casual dining. At breakfast and lunch, Milo's has made something of a name for itself as a purveyor of eggs Benedict—the menu rings six different changes on the classic recipe. At dinner, pasta and grilled chicken dishes offer good value.

With a name like **Gravy** (3957 N. Mississippi Ave., 503/287-8800, breakfast, lunch, dinner Tues.–Sat., breakfast and lunch only Sun., main courses $6–17), you'd rightly expect home cooking. And you'd be right. This is the place for biscuits and gravy for breakfast, "double wide" slices of bacon, or a massive chicken fried steak for dinner. The decor is Portland thrift store, but all the meats, eggs, and veggies are organic and the crowd is young, tattooed, and artistic.

Alberta Street is especially blessed with friendly and informal places for breakfast and lunch. The **Tin Shed** (1438 N.E. Alberta St., 503/288-6966, open Mon.–Tues. 7 A.M.–3 P.M., Wed.–Sunday 7 A.M.–10 P.M.) has a comfortable and pet-friendly dining room that opens out to a large outdoor patio with a fireplace and herb garden. Come here for breakfast, where creative egg scrambles—combinations of veggies and sausage, ham or tofu, with a buttermilk biscuit and potato pancakes or cheese grits—are legendary. Breakfast is also the star at **Helsers** (1538 N.E. Alberta, 503/281-1477, breakfast and lunch Tues.–Sun.), where you can get egg and homemade crumpet sandwiches, Scotch eggs, potato pancake torta, or spinach, tomato, and mushroom eggs Benedict in a sunny and bustling dining room. For both these restaurants, expect an hour wait for tables on weekend mornings.

In far Northeast Portland, near The Grotto and not too far from the airport, the **Cameo Cafe** (8111 N.E. Sandy, 503/284-0401, breakfast and lunch daily) is a homey café always busy satisfying devotees of its "acre" pancakes and waffles, "real" home fries, and home-baked multigrain bread.

Italian

Moderately priced **Pastini Pastaria** (1426 N.E. Broadway, 503/288-4300, lunch and dinner Mon.–Sat., dinner Sun., dinner main courses $6–14) features almost two dozen pasta dishes inspired by the friendliness of neighborhood pasterias in Italy. This is a good choice when you don't feel like fine dining but want good, prepared-from-scratch food that doesn't cost a fortune. New outlets are at 1506 N.W. 23rd Avenue and 2027 S.E. Division.

Northeast Portland's top Italian restaurant is **Ciao Vito** (2203 N.E. Alberta, 503/282-5522, dinner nightly, main courses $13–28) where robust flavors meld perfectly with a sunny, handsomely decorated dining room. Dishes like pork sugo—like a pulled pork sandwich only with a tangy-sweet tomoto sauce—is served over polenta and perfectly represents the chef's affinity for full-flavored, well-crafted Italian comfort food.

Tapas and Cocktails

Is **Colosso** (1932 N.E. Broadway, 503/288-3333, open nightly, tapas from $3–14) a cocktail bar or a small-plates restaurant? It probably depends which side of the 30-year-old age divide you fall on. Portland's young and trendy gather in this busy fish-bowl of a hot spot to drink cocktails, while more mature customers wander in from the adjoining neighborhoods to make a meal of the excellent tapas. Either way, Colosso is a great showcase of good food and strong drinks.

Under the soaring Fremont Bridge ramps along North Russell Street, in a gritty though up-and-coming neighborhood that was a major commercial center in late 19th-century Portland, is a cocktail maven's nirvana. **Mint** (816 N. Russell St., 503/284-5518, dinner Mon.–Sat., main courses $8–18) is where owner Lucy Brennan stirs up delicious and elaborate cocktails (earning her a dubbing from *Food & Wine* magazine as one of the top five mixologists in the country). The food in this swank, moodily lit dining room derives from Latino and Caribbean roots, and is perfectly paired with such libations as an avocado daiquiri or a fresh tangerine Sidecar.

Café Wonder (128 N.E. Russell, 503/284-8686, dinner Tues.–Sat., main courses $5–12) is in the basement level of the Wonder Ballroom, a newly renovated club and event space that was originally a 1914 meeting hall of the Ancient Order of Hibernians. Café Wonder offers cocktails plus sophisticated comfort food like mac 'n' cheese, burgers, meat loaf, and killer chicken croquettes, plus outside seating when weather permits.

Northwest Cuisine

Somewhere between a cocktail bar and a regionally focused bistro, **Echo Restaurant** (2225 N.E. M. L. King Blvd., 503/460-3246, open nightly, main courses $8–18) is a friendly, neighborhood joint in inner Northeast Portland that serves food worthy of uptown palates. Echo offers sandwiches and "half plates" for lighter appetites, though the weekly-changing menu also features a handful of main courses ("full plates") that are full-on cuisine. Seared Pacific cod is served with cranberry beans, artichokes, and mint-ginger broth. Grilled lamb loin comes with wilted arugula and chanterelle mushroom jus. The high-ceilinged red-brick dining room is cozy, and in good weather there's al fresco seating in a side garden.

International

For something a bit more upscale in the Mississippi neighborhood, there's **Equinox** (830 N.

Shaver St., 503/460-3333, dinner Wed.–Sun., brunch Sat. and Sun, main courses $7–19) with an international and eclectic menu and one of the city's nicest al fresco dining spaces, in a quiet courtyard just off Mississippi Avenue. You'll face choices like sweet corn risotto with smoked mozzarella, a spinach salad with roast Bing cherries and apples, or the Horns of Diablo, roast peppers stuffed with shitake mushrooms.

Middle Eastern

The owners of the wildly successful Nicholas Lebanese restaurant on S.E. Grand Avenue have recently opened a more attractive and refined Middle Eastern restaurant called **Arabian Breeze** (3223 N.E. Broadway, 503/445-4700, lunch and dinner Mon–Fri., dinner Sat.) with the same excellent homemade pita and standard Lebanese favorites as the original, plus less commonly tasted dishes like *laghna,* a yogurt cheese, mint and tomato salad, and *sambousik,* a kind of fried turnover available with a variety of fillings (try the spinach with pine nuts and almonds). No credit cards.

Cajun and Creole

A few blocks north of Northeast Broadway restaurant row, **Acadia** (1303 N.E. Fremont St., 503/249-5001, dinner Mon.–Sat, lunch Wed., main courses $13–17) is a cozy and elegant outpost of New Orleans–style fine dining. Come here for fantastic "barbecue" shrimp, one of the city's best filet mignon and an original pasta jambalaya. A good deal here is the $25 three-course menu, available weeknights and after 9 P.M. on weekends.

Ten minutes north of the Mississippi Avenue scene is another notable restaurant. **Roux** (1700 N. Killingsworth St., 503/285-1200, dinner daily, brunch Sat. and Sun.) is one of Portland's most authentic New Orleans–style restaurants, with an avid following of Portland's artsy night owls (call for reservations). Hoist a Sazarac cocktail and order perfectly prepared shrimp Creole or the spicy-cornmeal-stuffed loin of rabbit. The restaurant cures its own meats and prepares all the condiments from scratch.

Bernie's Southern Bistro (2904 N.E. Alberta, 503/282-9864, dinner nightly, main courses $11–20) offers a complex medley of Southern cooking (such as boneless buttermilk fried chicken) and award-winning service. It just doesn't get any better than peach bourbon barbecued ribs accompanied by sweet-potato salad, unless it's the crispy fried okra. The bar menu can't be beat for bargain eats.

African

Portland has a number of popular Ethiopian restaurants, and one favorite is the **Queen of Sheba** (2413 N.E. M. L. King Blvd., 503/287-6302, lunch Thurs.–Sat., dinner nightly, dinner main dishes $8–15). Meals are served family style, and typically feature platters of highly spiced, stewed or grilled meats and vegetables, which are scooped up with house-made *injera,* the slightly sour-tasting bread. Vegetarian dishes are among the most tempting, including braised lentils with mustard greens and okra.

While Ethiopian restaurants aren't a rarity, it's more unusual to chance across Somali food. The **Horn of Africa** (3939 N.E. M. L. King Blvd., 503/331-9844, lunch and dinner Mon.–Fri., dinner Sat., dinner main courses $8–13) offers more flavorful and less fiery stewed meats and vegetables than is typical of Ethiopian cooking, all meant for sopping up with your fingers using pancake-like breads. The lunch buffet is a great way to sample this unusual cuisine.

Mexican

¿Por Que No? (3524 N. Mississippi Ave., 503/467-4149, lunch and dinner daily) is a little hole-in-the-wall taqueria (literally a converted garage) that serves up seven kinds of tacos (none over $3.50) plus seviche and other inexpensive Mexican favorites. The house-made sangria is dandy.

Northeast Alberta Street is also home to a number of excellent traditional taquerias. Favorites include **La Sirenita** (2817 N.E. Alberta St., 503/335-8283, 10 A.M.–10 P.M. daily) and **La Bonita** (2839 N.E. Alberta St., 503/281-3662, 11 A.M.– 9 P.M. Tues.–Sat, closed Monday).

Vegetarian

Leading the resurgence in the Albina neighborhood is a bright, quirky, veggie-friendly place known as the **Vita Cafe** (3024 N.E. Alberta, 503/235-8233, lunch and dinner daily, breakfast Sat. and Sun., main courses $7–14). With an easy-on-the-wallet menu that pleases vegans as well as burger-lovers (serving free-range and hormone-free beef), and a clientele running the gamut from eastside matrons to spike-haired students, this place embodies the changing character of the neighborhood. Local artists' creations adorn the walls and all kinds of meat substitutes fill the plates here.

Seafood

The owners of **Alberta Street Oyster Bar and Grill** (2926 N.E. Alberta St., 503/284-9600, dinner Wed.– Mon., main courses $8–25) set out to create an old fashioned oyster bar atmosphere, and they succeeded admirably at this Alberta Street hot spot. By focusing on oysters, this restaurant does service to the wonderful bivalves available on the West Coast—there are usually eight varieties of oysters to choose from (though be aware that the quality and price are both high). The good eating doesn't end at the oyster bar, however: Save room for house specialties like chilled English pea soup with Dungeness crab and morel mushroom cream and crispy veal sweetbreads with escargots, hazelnuts, grapes, and Pernod cream.

Vietnamese

Portland's large Vietnamese community has graced the Rose City with some of the best purveyors of this cuisine outside Saigon, according to *New Yorker* food philosopher Calvin Trillin. The neighborhood along Northeast Sandy Boulevard east of Northeast 50th to Northeast 82nd Avenue is the vortex of Portland's Southeast Asian business community. Several restaurants here are dedicated to *pho*, or Vietnamese noodle soup, while others offer Vietnamese, Malaysian, Chinese, and Thai cooking. Vietnamese restaurants to try include **Zien Hong** (5314 N.E. Sandy Blvd., 503/288-4743) and **Yen Ha** (6820 N.E. Sandy Blvd., 503/287-3698). In Portland's Hollywood District, **My Canh** (1801 N.E. 39th Ave, 503/281-0594, lunch and dinner Mon.– Sat., dinner only Sun.) offers both Vietnamese and Chinese cooking. The curried chow mein noodles are a revelation and the *pho* soups are excellent. Perhaps because the chefs are Vietnamese, the Chinese food here is lighter and less greasy than is typical.

SOUTHEAST PORTLAND

Southeast Portland is filled with restaurant enclaves where it's a good idea to just park the car and wander the streets before making a dining choice. While some of Portland's most popular and acclaimed restaurants are in the industrial warehouses of **Inner Southeast Portland,** just across the Willamette from downtown, other neighborhoods are almost totally devoted to dining. There are so many restaurants along a six-block stretch of **28th Avenue and East Burnside Street** that the area is referred to not as 28th East but as 28th Feast. A casual diners' utopia, this area has over a dozen restaurants, most of them chef-owned independents that consistently serve up some of the city's most inventive, but reasonably priced, meals. Menus change frequently, so the best way to check out the exciting dining scene here is to drive up (or take the #16 or #20 bus from downtown to 28th and Burnside) to see what's cooking. Dining here is casual—most of the restaurants are either wine bars or small-plates outfits, so you'll be able to sample several restaurants if you're up to the challenge.

The heart of Portland's evergreen, seemingly unaging hippie community is **S.E. Belmont Street and S.E. Hawthorne Avenue,** and you can expect to find lots of moderately priced cafés, pubs, and restaurants along these streets—along with boutique shopping and superlative people-watching.

Further south are more streets lined with restaurants. In the last five years, **S.E. Division Street and S.E. Clinton Street** have blossomed as dining destinations. **Sellwood,** at one time a separate town south of Portland, offers a real neighborhood atmosphere and a handful of excellent dining choices.

SOUTHEAST COFFEEHOUSES

Portland's coffeehouses are a regional take on the European tradition of café society – homes away from home to spend an idle hour reading a paper, gabbing with the "regulars," or writing the great American novel while sipping rich European-style brewed drinks made from whole-bean coffee. While chain establishments like Starbucks, Coffee People, and Peet's pour quality brew throughout Portland, independent coffeehouses have the kind of ambience that better evokes the Beat era, when these establishments were incubators to a nascent counterculture. And while there are myriad coffeehouses throughout Portland, Southeast Portland, with its overlay of old hippies and young trendoids each seeking a dilatory and indolent nirvana through caffeine, is the perfect spot to capture the essence of Portland coffee culture.

The **Pied Cow** (3244 S.E. Belmont, 503/230-4866) is a coffeehouse set in a striking old Victorian home. Outside, a tree-shaded yard with tables fills up during warm weather. Most of the year, however, the tastefully garish interior with multiple alcoves provides shelter from the storm. Add the Pied Cow selection of espresso drinks and baked treats and you have the perfect setting to revive the grand old art of conversation. Open 4 P.M.-midnight Tuesday-Friday, noon-midnight Saturday and Sunday.

The **Fresh Pot Cafe** (3723 S.E. Hawthorne, 503/232-8928) is set inside Powell's Books on Hawthorne, so you can peruse prospective purchases while enjoying house-roasted java. Open 9 A.M.- 10 P.M. Monday-Thursday, 9 A.M.-11 P.M. Friday and Saturday, and 9 A.M.-9 P.M. Sunday.

As you approach **Rimsky-Korsakoffee House** (707 S.E. 12th Ave., 503/232-2640), the old red house gives no indication (not even a hand-lettered sign bearing its name!) that this is Portland's favorite artsy hangout. Only the lines extending out the door on a crowded weekend convey that the place is something special. Folks come for mocha fudge cake washed down by espresso drinks, live classical music, and people and ideas in creative ferment. You'll shell out around $6 a person to indulge in dessert (try the raspberry fool) and a cappuccino. The atmosphere of a refined house party reigns here 7 P.M.-midnight weekdays and 7 P.M.-1 A.M. weekends.

The coffee lover's holy grail, the perfect cup, could well be found at **Stumptown Roasters** (4525 Division St., 503/230-7797). Fresh-roasted just-ground beans are made into a gourmet elixir with the addition of pure water and the French press. While the decor is nothing fancy, it's a comfy place where couches, a well-stocked magazine rack, and a good sound system compel a diverse clientele to linger. They have a second location at 3352 S.E. Belmont St.

The latter combination is also in evidence at **Common Grounds** (4321 S.E. Hawthorne, 503/236-4835). Add a reasonably priced menu of light meals and tasty dessert fare washed down by Italian roast Torrefazione coffee and you can understand why this is the Hawthorne neighborhood's most popular coffeehouse. Open 6:30 A.M.-10 P.M. Monday-Friday, 7 A.M.-10 P.M. Saturday and Sunday.

Portland's most aesthetic kaffee klatsch takes place at **Palio** (1996 S.E. Ladd Ave., 503/232-9412), a big-windowed, tiled dessert house located in a tree-lined neighborhood of public gardens and Craftsman bungalows. Come in June to see the nearby Ladd's Addition rose gardens bloom and sip a cup on the outdoor patio. During Portland's dreary winter, the books, board games, and intimate corners complement the rich cakes and espresso here to combat seasonal affective disorder. Open 7 A.M.-11 P.M. Monday-Friday, 9 A.M.-11 P.M. Saturday and Sunday. The #10 TriMet bus stops in front of this hard-to-find retreat.

Breakfast and Light Meals

Laid-back Southeast Portland is perfect habitat for breakfast joints, and one of the favorites is **Cup and Saucer Cafe** (3566 S.E. Hawthorne Blvd, 503/236-6001) at the heart of the funky Hawthorne neighborhood. The decor is Formica Chic, but the hearty breakfasts—mostly organic and many vegetarian are served all day. Get there early on weekends. The tofu scramble is worth the wait.

The **Bread and Ink** (3610 S.E. Hawthorne, 503/239-4756, three meals daily, dinner main courses $12–22) is known as *the* gathering place in the Hawthorne neighborhood. For breakfast, an assortment of homemade breads and imaginative omelettes will sustain you. Lunchtime diners line up for a massive burger topped with Gruyere cheese and Bermuda onion and locally esteemed salmon sandwiches. Dinner is a primer on local cuisine—whatever's in season, the freshest ingredients, creatively prepared.

The **Utopia Cafe** (3308 S.E. Belmont, 503/235-7606, breakfast and lunch Wed.–Mon.) began as an espresso shop but now is known as a place to enjoy breakfast and lunch. Start the day with brioche French toast, blue-corn pancakes, or such scrambled egg fantasies as the Little Italian, made with basil, sun-dried tomatoes, and sour cream. Across the street, all-night gourmet market **Zupans** (open daily) has reasonably priced takeout options.

Step into tradition at **Zell's** (1300 S.E. Morrison, 503/239-0196, breakfast and lunch daily), a longtime eastside favorite. A late Sunday repast of German pancakes washed down by Zell's excellent Irish coffee is guaranteed to put a spring in your step. Also recommended are the salmon Benedict and any of the blackboard specials. Otherwise, their locally famous Fisherman's Stew can sate the hungriest hiker.

Middle Eastern

For house-baked Middle Eastern flatbreads and excellent Lebanese street food, go to **Nicolas Restaurant** (318 S.E. Grand Ave., 503/235-5123, lunch and dinner daily, main dishes from $4–12), which must have the most unprepossessing exterior in the Portland restaurant firmament. A bright red and yellow storefront on a busy thoroughfare, Nicholas nonetheless has lines out the door for its excellent Lebanese cooking (no credit cards or alcohol).

Cajun and Creole

Le Bistro Montage (301 S.E. Morrison, 503/234-1324, lunch Mon.–Sat., dinner nightly, open Sunday through Thursday till 2 A.M. and Friday and Saturday till 4 P.M., main courses $6–14) is the salvation of Portland night owls in search of quality cheap eats after midnight. In addition to such bayou classics as jambalaya (try it with smoked mussels or Andouille sausage), étouffée, and blackened catfish, intriguing variations on macaroni-and-cheese redefine the meaning of budget gourmet. This is a place that charmingly flaunts its view "that the customer is not always right" in everything from its refusal to serve decaf coffee (and only Rainier beer) to the way the Chopin nocturne dinner soundtrack might give way to Nine Inch Nails and Bob Marley late into the night.

Northwest Cuisine

No single restaurant captures the spirit of Portland's recent food renaissance better than **C clarklewis** (1001 S.E. Water Ave., 503/493-9500, dinner Mon.–Sat., main courses $10–30). Intensely focused on regional and seasonal ingredients, the cooks at clarklewis excel at drawing every iota of flavor out of even the most basic of foods. You'll have green beans and carrots to make you swoon. For $38 submit yourself to the will of the kitchen and have Chef's Choice—three or four courses that sample what the chef considers the best food of the day. The industrial setting and high-decibel dining room won't be to everyone's taste but there's no denying that the food here can be superlative.

Proof that good things come in small packages, the frescoed jewel-box of a restaurant called **Wild Abandon** (2411 S.E. Belmont St., 503/232-4458, dinner Wed.–Mon., main courses $9–20) belies its tiny size and funky decor to offer up some of the most satisfying dining in Southeast Portland. The menu features a changing array of seasonal dishes, though pastas are usually outstanding (the daily ravioli special usually deserves consideration), and the chef has a deft touch with fish and seafood—if on the menu, the seafood stew is sublime.

Coolly elegant, **Castagna** (1752 S.E. Hawthorne Blvd., 503/231-7373, dinner Wed.– Sat., main courses $20–28) is probably Portland's finest restaurant outside the downtown core—though you normally wouldn't come looking for sophisticated cooking at a Hawthorne Boulevard address. The austere formality of the dining room is at odds with full-flavored and inventive cuisine that's difficult to characterize except as Northwest-by-Mediterranean. The small menu usually features a number of standout fish and seafood dishes; meats are local and organic. A knockout lamb shoulder is braised with salsify, cardoon, artichoke, while scallops are sautéed with blood oranges and fennel. Save room for desserts. Next door, the same kitchen prepares simple and hearty dishes for **Café Castagna,** (503/231-9959, open nightly) a relaxed and moderately priced version of the mothership.

Caprial's Bistro (7015 S.E. Milwaukie Ave., 503/236-6457, www.caprialandjohnskitchen. com, lunch and dinner Tues.–Sat., dinner main courses $19–26) turns out a changing chalkboard menu of visually stunning, complex, creative dishes inspired by Caprial Pence, who oversees this restaurant with the same geniality that characterizes her cooking shows on the Learning Channel and public TV. What you're paying for can best be appreciated by Caprial's treatment of salmon. Instead of the tired preparations of this regional staple, you might get it here baked in a chive-breadcrumb crust with sorrel stuffing, topped by a pinch of melted butter and lemon. The nominal corkage fee charged for wine purchased at retail prices is also noteworthy. And if cleaned your plate, you can buy one of Caprial's cookbooks on your way out of this spacious yet cozy restaurant.

Wine Bars

Along 28th Avenue, **(Noble Rot** (2724 S.E. Ankeny St., 503/233-1999, lunch Mon.–Fri., dinner Mon.–Sat., main courses $9–16) offers flights of wines and really delicious small plates. **Navarre** (10 N.E. 28th Ave., 503/232-3555, main courses from $6–$18, dinner daily) is another tapas-style eatery and wine bar, anchored in the food of northern Spain, though the chef here is a leader in the local organic food movement so the food is completely fresh and of the moment.

Mexican and Caribbean

In the Sellwood neighborhood, **Cha-Cha-Cha's** (1605 S.E. Bybee Blvd., 503/232-0437, with two other locations at 1208 N.W. Glisan St. and 2635 N.E. Broadway, lunch and dinner daily, main courses $6–12) is a brightly colored Grandma's house serving Mexican dishes at reasonable prices. A great place to take the kids.

Taqueria Nueve (28 N.E. 28th Ave, 503/236-6195, open nightly, main courses $8–18) is the place for zesty, updated Mexican food. Forget tortilla chips and salsa (in fact, don't ask for them unless you want to see your waiter sneer)—instead, you'll be eating upscale cuisine like beer-braised wild boar or duck confit tacos.

Just off N.E 28th at Glisan Street is **Pambiche** (2811 N.E. Glisan St., 503/233-0511, lunch and dinner daily, main courses $8–19) a small and colorful restaurant that serves Portland's top Cuban cooking.

Even though **Esparza's Tex-Mex Café** (2725 S.E. Ankeny St., 503/234-7909, lunch and dinner Mon.– Sat., main courses $9–20) offers, hands down, the best border Mexican food in Portland, people come here as much for the decor as the dining. A veritable museum of Texas and Mexican kitsch, this shoe-box-sized restaurant turns out fantastic Tex Mex cooking, and doesn't blanch at offering the real stuff, like scrambled calf brains or beef tongue tacos. The squeamish can stick to the excellent tacos or the superlative beef brisket.

Dingo's (4612 S.E. Hawthorne, 503/233-3996, lunch and dinner Mon.–Fri.) is what happens when you cross the hip Hawthorne ghetto with the fish taco stands so popular in Baja. This place gets salmon, tuna, and halibut trimmings from a supplier who purveys the filets to gourmet restaurants.

Another hot spot for Mexican food is **La Calaca Comelona** (2304 S.E. Belmont, 503/239-9675, lunch and dinner Mon.–Sat., main courses $6–13). Frida Kahlo–style murals and Day of the Dead puppets festoon the walls here. Instead of just the usual tacos and tostadas, this place includes combination taco platters consisting of several kinds of cooked meats and vegetables served with homemade tortillas. To ease the fire, fresh-squeezed tropical juices are worth a few extra bucks, if you can forgo a bottle of Negra Modelo, any true Mexican beer connoisseur's choice. By the time you leave, you should understand that the restaurant's name ("the hungry skeleton") refers only to the decor.

Forget American-style Mexican food. Step up to the plate to try **Nuestra Cocina** (2135 S.E. Division St., 503/232-2135, dinner Tues.–Sat., main courses $13–16) a truly sophisticated South of the Border cuisine in a lively and elegant Eastside dining room. Here, the flavors of Oaxaca, Yucatan, Vera Cruz, and tropical Mexico jump off the plate. The mole sauces contain labyrinths of flavor, and you'll love the Cochinito Pibil, spice-braised pork with pickled red onion and black beans. This spot is deservedly popular and doesn't take reservations, so come early or late.

Italian

A few blocks off 28th Avenue, **Il Piatto** (2348 S.E. Ankeny, 503/236-4997, lunch Tues.–Fri., dinner nightly, dinner main courses $12–24) is an intimate and popular neighborhood place with charming faux Tuscan decor. Culinary flights of fancy include dishes such as house-made white bean salad with prosciutto-wrapped prawns. While some entrées may seem overly rich to American palates, you can box up the always-flavorful leftovers for tomorrow's lunch.

For decades, **Genoa** (2832 S.E. Belmont, 503/238-1464, dinner nightly, four-course dinner $60, seven-course dinner $75) has been Portland's special-occasion restaurant, rated the top Italian restaurant in the Northwest according to Zagat and *Gourmet* magazine. This is the kind of place that Mick Jagger stops by when he's in town. The menus for its seven- and four-course dinners change monthly—diners get a choice of main course, and the rest is left up to the imagination and considerable skills of the chef. For a full-on feast of excellent handcrafted Italian food, you can't go wrong, although the plain-jane dining room looks pretty lame compared to upscale venues elsewhere in town. A three-course dinner for $30 is available Sunday through Thursday evenings.

One of the most anticipated restaurant openings in recent years was for (**Nostrana** (1401 S.E. Morrison St., 503/234-2427, lunch Mon.–Fri., dinner nightly, main courses $8–16). At the helm is Cathy Whims, who led the much-revered Genoa kitchen for many years. Her new enterprise takes her a ways from Italian high cuisine—Nostrana is part wood-fired pizza joint and part rustic Italian home cooking. Order one of the excellent pizzas—perhaps proscuitto and arugula—and augment it with a selection of wonderful salads, soups, house-cured meats, and wood-oven cooked meats. The menu changes nightly to ensure that everything here is absolutely fresh and seasonal.

3 Doors Down (1429 S.E. 37th Ave., 503/236-6886, dinner Tues.–Sat., main courses $15–24), as its name implies, is a few doors away from Hawthorne Boulevard. Dishes are Italian influenced but inspired by the Northwest's bounty. The most requested dish here is vodka penne with spicy Italian sausage and plum tomato cream sauce, followed closely by tender roasted chicken draped with truffle oil and cream atop velvety mashed potatoes. The restaurant doesn't take reservations so get here early or late.

Gino's Restaurant and Bar (8057 S.E. 13th Ave., 503/233-4613, dinner nightly, main courses $8–22) serves standout pasta dishes in a charming 100-year-old building. The red-checked tablecloths and the Italian-accented dinner menu say trattoria, but lunch-time sandwiches, homemade soups and bread, and salads can satisfy anyone looking for a light midday repast. For dinner, the steamed mussels and clams is the best version of this dish you'll find in Portland. To find Gino's, just look for the sign indicating the Leipzig Tavern, the defunct historic watering hole that previously occupied this building, on the corner of 13th and Spokane.

For dinner, take the Neapolitan night train to **Assaggio** (7742 S.E. 13th, 503/232-6151, lunch Mon.–Fri., dinner nightly), where the adventurous, moderately priced fare (most of the 20 pastas on the menu are under $10) is conducive to sampling multiple dishes. A great deal for dinner is the choice of three pasta dishes for $13 per person. The charmingly rustic decor, pastas prepared with wild mushrooms, fresh pesto, and the like, and affordable high quality Italian wines by the glass pull in the crowds here, so arrive early or call for reservations.

East Indian

The Eastside's best Indian food comes from **Bombay Cricket Club** (1925 S.E. Hawthorne Blvd., 503/231-0740, dinner nightly). This always packed two-tiered restaurant offers superbly cooked traditional Indian dishes (and a few from the Middle East) with plenty of options for vegetarians.

Don't come to **Vindalho** (2038 S.E. Clinton St., 503/467-4550, dinner Tues.–Sat.) looking for "authentic" Indian cooking. Instead, the chef at Vindalho has refined the sauces and spices of traditional Indian cooking and uses them to create a sophisticated hybrid cuisine that's a delicious adjunct to Northwest-style cooking. The upscale dining room is stylish and full of energetic colors—the outdoor courtyard is a great place for cocktails and samosas on a warm evening.

Thai

Thanh Thao (4005 S.E. Hawthorne, 503/238-6232, lunch and dinner Mon.–Sat., dinner main courses $8–16) is the favorite of devotees of southeast Asian food. In a vast menu of Vietnamese and Thai specialties, peanut chicken, eggplant in garlic sauce, and barbecue pork rice noodle typify the well-prepared, moderately priced entrées.

One of the most exciting Thai restaurants is not the fanciest. In fact, **Pok Pok Thai** (3226 S.E. Division, 503/232-1387, lunch and dinner Mon.–Sat., main courses $5–9) barely has indoor seating and the kitchen is more a shed than a restaurant. Nonetheless, the Thai food produced here—specializing in the foods of the Chaing Mai region—is incredible. The roast game hen with dipping sauces is delicious and *Muu Sateh,* charcoal grilled pork loin skewers marinated in coconut milk and turmeric and served with cucumber relish, tastes exactly like freshly prepared Thai street food. You may prefer to order take-out, or in summer there's patio seating at picnic tables.

Mediterranean

One of Southeast Portland's leading restaurants is **Lauro Mediterranean Kitchen** (3377 S.E. Division St., 503/239-7000, dinner daily, main courses $10–19), which started out as a Portuguese restaurant but now has a more general "cuisines of the sun" mandate. The mussels with chorizo sausage appetizer, swimming in tomato garlic broth, is outstanding, as are the small and zippy pizzas from Lauro's open hearth wood oven. Our favorite main courses are the savory chicken tangine, rich with the flavors of Tangiers, and the paella, studded with clams, crab, and sausage.

Barbecue

Clay's Smokehouse (2932 S.E. Division, 503/235-4755, lunch and dinner Wed.–Sun, main courses $8–15) serves up slow-smoked, Oklahoma-style barbecue meats and fish with aromas of hickory, mesquite, and alderwood. We recommend the cold-smoked seafood platter featuring smoked oysters, salmon, and catfish. And, as you might expect, there's a selection of microbrews to accompany your repast.

Tennessee Red's (2133 S.E. 11th Ave., 503/231-1710, lunch and dinner Mon.–Sat., dinner only Sun.) is the place for barbecue, whether you like Texas-style beef brisket or North Carolina pork loin. This small ribs joint operated by an hombre who has cooked for heads of state won't fail to please. The house ribs are brine-marinated, spice-rubbed, and then wood-smoked the way Red learned to do it in Memphis. Red's moderate prices make it easy to savor it all and still have enough left over for a takeout order. Outdoor seating in summer here is a pleasure and on weekends occasionally feature live blues music.

Chinese

Portland's contemporary Chinese community is centered in the S.E. 82nd and Division neighborhood, and Portland's best Chinese food is also found here at **Wong's King** (8733 S.E. Division St., 503/788-8883, dim sum, lunch, and dinner daily, main courses $8–15). The chef here has won prestigious cooking awards in China, and the huge dining room is always thronged with Chinese families, but the staff is very solicitous to non-Chinese diners who may be confounded by the extensive menu. Dim sum is terrific (try the shrimp or pork dumplings) and, like many Portland restaurants, it's known for its excellent seafood.

Vietnamese

A few blocks north of S.E. Division Street on 82nd Avenue is one of the Portland's top purveyors of excellent Vietnamese food. **Pho Van** (1919 S.E. 82nd Ave., 503/788-5244, lunch and dinner daily, dinner main courses $8–18), offers a broad selection of the namesake soup, plus the popular family-style feast Seven Courses of Beef and myriad other Indochinese specialties.

More convenient to downtown is the new **Pho Van Hawthorne** (3404 S.E. Hawthorne Blvd., 503/230-1474, lunch and dinner daily, main courses $8–18), an offshoot of the original.

American

Heartland American comfort food has never tasted so good as at **Savoy Tavern + Bistro** (2500 S.E. Clinton St., 503/808-9999, dinner Tues.–Sun., main courses $8–18). Chef Alton Garcia doesn't seek to update or transform classics of home-cooking as much as to replicate them gloriously with top-notch ingredients and the savvy of modern cooking techniques.

Pickles are homemade, and so is the "boiled dressing" for the delectable coleslaw. Unless you're from Wisconsin, you probably didn't know that fried cheese curds existed. Start you're meal with these molten dairy product wonders, and move on to excellent meatloaf, smoked trout, or grilled hanger steak. On Sundays, come for the fried chicken dinner.

Hawaiian

Large portions of ribs, Hawaiian stir-fry, and a blast of hot-sweet flavors served in a bustling friendly atmosphere have made **Noho's Hawaiian Cafe** (S.E. Clinton and 26th, 503/233-5301, lunch and dinner daily, main courses $8–15) the dining hub of an up-and-coming "hip strip" of antique shops, quirky restaurants, and an avant-garde theater. Huge servings of sweet barbecued ribs and macaroni salad and occasional live music explain the lines of wait-listed diners that extend out the door on weekend nights.

Japanese

Probably the city's best sushi is at **Ichidai** (5714 S.E. Powell Blvd., 503/771-4648, lunch and dinner daily, sushi from $5–16), an unprepossessing little restaurant in a strip mall. The fish is incredibly fresh and favorites like lobster and scallop rolls, and catch-of-the-day nigiri brings in a steady stream of regulars. The rest of the Japanese menu here is also top-notch. When Portland's Japanese consulate hosts a reception, Ichidai does the catering, that's how good the food is.

WATERING HOLES
Brewpubs

Brewpubs are built around microbrews and pub grub with personality. These bastions of beer and ale helped create Portland's identity as "Munich on the Willamette." While excellent establishments abound, Portland's preeminent brewpub meisters are the McMenamin brothers. With dozens of establishments throughout western Oregon, this chain has been a major catalyst to the current popularity of craft beers (see sidebar *The McMenamin's Brewpub Empire*).

The **Widmer Brewery and Gasthaus** (929 N. Russell St., 503/281-3333) is revered by beer lovers throughout the country as the birthplace of Oregon's most popular microbrew, Widmer Hefeweizen, distributed nationally in bottles. The Gasthaus is the place to enjoy this wheat beer straight from the tap, still cloudy with sediment. The elegant back bar and a mix of wood and brick throughout the restaurant impart a feeling of warmth here complementing home-style German cooking with Northwest ingredients. To get here, follow N.E. Interstate near the Broadway Bridge and Rose Garden Arena 0.5 mile down to the corner of Russell Street. Open daily for lunch and dinner.

Portland's first microbrewery started out in a warehouse in the then-derelict Pearl District that became the **Bridgeport Brew Pub** (1313 N.W. Marshall St., 503/241-3612, lunch and dinner daily). The company then opened another operation, the **Bridgeport Ale House** (3632 S.E. Hawthorne, 503/233-6540, lunch and dinner daily) across the river on trendy Hawthorne Boulevard. The original brewpub, a sprawling, red-brick warehouse with a shipping dock, was wildly popular for its funky, kid-friendly atmosphere, laid-back attitude, and wonderful pizza. Oh, and for Blue Heron Ale, one of the marvels of local brewing. In 2006, the brewpub reopened after a 14-month remodel to reveal itself as a high concept, corporatized restaurant with three sleek dining rooms. While purists are aghast, at least the beer hasn't changed. Given these changes, just go to the Hawthorne location—it's cozy, the food (pizza, salads, light entrées) is really good, and there's still a real pub feeling to the crowded beer hall.

A favorite of the Southeast Portland crowds is **Lucky Labrador Brewing Company,** whose original brewpub is at 915 S.E. Hawthorne (503/236-3555). This previous sheet-metal warehouse is a very comfortable and unpretentious place—slip on your flip-flops, bring your dog, and head down to the large, shady patio for some very tasty brews. A Northwest Portland location, the **Lucky Labrador Beer Hall** (1945 N.W. Quimby St., 503/517-4352) opened in 2006. **Roots Organic Brewing** is Oregon's first all-organic brewery, with a brewpub at 1520 S.E. 7th Avenue (503/235-7668). The Island Red is a fearsomely rich and delicious red stout, while Burghead Heather Ale is brewed with heather instead of hops. The Woody Indian Pale Ale (IPA) is the most fun to order: "Give me a Woody!" Pub fare at roots is mostly deli sandwiches and individual pizzas.

If a pub named **New Old Lompoc** (1616 N.W. 23rd Ave., 503/255-1855) seems like a mental tongue twister, just imagine how it will seem after a couple pints of fine LSD! That's Lompoc Strong Draft in these parts, a delicious ale with smoked malt and plenty of hops. The food—salads, sandwiches, burgers, and light entrées—is notably good for a pub. Other locations are in southeast Portland at 3412 S.E Division (503/235-2215) and in northeast Portland at 3901 N. Williams Avenue (503/288-3996).

If your local pub has a children's play area, you know you must be in Portland. **Laurelwood Public House & Brewery** (1728 N.E. 40th Ave., 503/282-0622) is a family-friendly brewpub with restaurant-quality food in the heart of Northeast Portland's Hollywood District. While the Space Stout (say that twice quickly) may look like a pint of pure, opaque chocolate, it's not for the children. Instead, it's an award-winning stout that's Portland's version of Guinness. A second location, **Laurelwood NW Public House,** is in northwest Portland at 2327 N.W. Kearney Street (503/228-5553).

In the Pearl District is **The Rogue Public House** (1339 N.W. Flanders, 503/222-5910), a Portland outlet of Rogue Brewing in Newport. This is some of Oregon's best beer: Most of the elixirs here are wonderful, but check out the Maibock-style Dead Guy Ale and St. Rogue Red. The burgers here tend to be an afterthought, but with ale as good as this, who needs solid food?

Up in far Northeast Portland is **Alameda Brewhouse** (4765 N.E. Fremont, 503/460-9025), with an ambitious menu, a sleekly stylish dining room, and appreciative crowds for both food and ales. Klickitat Pale Ale is the highlight here, though some prefer the Juniper Porter, a darker beer brewed with eastern Oregon juniper berries.

Unfortunately, one of Portland's most famous breweries—**Hair of the Dog Brewing Company**—doesn't have a brewpub. This outfit—famous for its commitment to unusual and high-alcohol beers that are meant to be aged and drunk like fine wines—makes most of its beer for bottling, as they require time in the cellar to reach their full flavor. However, most pubs carry the properly aged bottles and a few pubs carry the limited production of brewery's draft beer. The best place to sample Hair of the Dog brews on tap is at the **Horse Brass Pub** (4534 S.E. Belmont, 503/232-2202), one of the most authentic British-style pubs in the city, and with over 50 brews on tap it's a great place to sample the rest of the local talent.

Teahouses

Although known for its coffee and beer joints, Portland boasts several character-laden teahouses. The rainy clime seems to be conducive to sipping tea while contemplating the nature of life.

The **Tao of Tea** (3430 S.E. Belmont, 503/736-0119, 11 A.M.–11 P.M. Wed.–Mon. and 5–11 P.M. Tues.) is a feat of architecture and design. Bamboo, reclaimed wood, low tables, and Asian artifacts unite to create an ambience that is immaculately Zen. The teahouse proffers over 100 teas from around the world. Among their most popular are the oolong teas, served in traditional Chinese gung fu earthenware. A diverse food menu complements the tea selections. Our favorites are chana chaval (chickpea curry with rice) and stuffed flatbreads (cauliflower, miso, or potato) served with a side salad and dahl. The Tao of Tea also operates the **Classical Chinese Teahouse** at Portland's Chinese Gardens (N.W. 2nd and Everett, 503/224-8455, 10 A.M.–5 P.M. daily). Lauded as the most authentic Chinese teahouse in the United States, the 16th-century style teahouse serves over 30 Chinese teas. Sitting in the teahouse, sipping tea amidst the gardens while gazing upon the reflection of the sky in the opposing pond, it's easy to understand why the teahouse is called the "Tower of Cosmic Reflections."

Located in the Pearl District, the **Tea Zone** (50 N.W. 11th, 503/221-2130, 8 A.M.–6 P.M. Mon.–Wed., 8 A.M.–8 P.M. Thurs.–Fri., 10 A.M.–8 P.M. Sat., and 10 A.M.–6 P.M. Sun.) offers over 60 loose-leaf teas (many organic) and boasts the largest selection of teapots and accessories in the city.

U-PICK AND FARMERS MARKETS

The free *Tri-County Farm Fresh Produce Guide* (503/725-2101, www.tricountyfarm.org) lists dozens of U-pick outlets and farm-fresh fruit stands in the Clackamas (Washington) and Multnomah County areas. The guide supplies addresses, phone numbers, hours, maps, and the best months to find produce items. The **Ripe and Ready Hotline** (503/226-4112, operates April 15—November) can further help you locate outlets.

U-pick concessions, roadside stands, and farmers markets are often the best and sometimes the only places to find Oregon strawberries, whose ripened-on-the-vine sweetness comes with a fragility that precludes a shelf life in supermarket chains.

Farmers markets have become a major part of life for many Portland households. In high summer, there's an open-air market somewhere in town almost every day, but for most visitors the most convenient and compelling is the **Portland Farmers Market** downtown in the South Park Blocks near Portland State University and Montgomery Streets (503/241-0032, www.portlandfarmersmarket.org, 8:30 A.M.–2 P.M. Sat., Apr.–mid-Dec.). The market attracts throngs of people, and not just for shopping. The market features famous local chefs giving cooking demonstrations, great street food carts, and musical entertainment. People-watching is of the highest caliber here as are the breads and baked goods, locally grown fruits and vegetables, artisan cheeses, wild mushrooms, organic meat and poultry, and nursery stock. On Wednesdays

Our favorite weekend outlet for fresh produce, spring through fall, is the **Hollywood Farmers Market** (N.E. Hancock between 44th and 45th Aves., 503/233-3313, www.hollywoodfarmersmarket.org), just north of Sandy Boulevard and minutes from downtown. It's a smaller affair, but you can still find homemade goat cheese, live music, gourmet wild mushrooms, fresh berries, master gardener consultations, and children's activities. Hours are 8 A.M.–1 P.M. Saturdays and may change seasonally (the market runs early May–October).

U-pick aficionados flock to **Sauvie Island** on the Columbia for peaches, apples, pumpkins, raspberries, and strawberries. This rural retreat is about eight miles from downtown via I-5 north to the Fremont Bridge. After crossing the bridge, go west on Nicolai, looking for U.S. 30 signs to St. Helens, Linnton, and Sauvie Island. If the pickings are slim, superlative bird-watching and a nudist beach are the island's other claims to fame. A long-time truck farm here is the **Pumpkin Patch** (16511 N.W. Gillihan Rd., 503/621-3874), with abundant vegetables in season, plus horse-drawn tours of the pumpkins near Halloween for the tots, plus a corn maze for the older kids.

© JUDY JEWELL

Portland's finest chefs stop by the farmers market, both to shop and to give cooking demonstrations.

10 A.M.–2 P.M. there's a smaller version of this farmers market a few blocks to the north, at S.W. Salmon and Park.

Practicalities

INFORMATION AND SERVICES

Portland's visitors-information resources are far-reaching and extensive. Begin at **Travel Portland** (701 S.W. 6th Ave., Portland 97204, 503/275-8355 or 877/678-5263, www.travelportland.com, 8:30 A.M.–5:30 P.M. Mon.–Fri., 10 A.M.–4 P.M. Sat.), located in Pioneer Courthouse Square. In addition to knowledgeable personnel, Travel Portland has the most complete collection of travel-information pamphlets in the state. While Portland is naturally the focus of most of these publications, materials about every part of the state fill the racks here. Sharing the space with the visitors in-

formation center is TriMet's customer service center, where you can buy bus tickets and pick up schedules.

Media

The *Oregonian* (www.oregonlive.com), Portland's only daily, is joined by a host of alternative or community papers that circulate around the city. The *Oregonian*'s "Arts and Entertainment" section comes out each Friday.

Of all the free weeklies, most useful to the traveler is *Willamette Week*. This publication's excellent cultural listings and restaurant reviews make it a valuable resource. It comes out every Wednesday and can be found at cafés, bookstores, and restaurants in the greater Portland area.

Portland's nearly three dozen radio stations have something for everybody. The AM band features a preponderance of call-in talk shows. The FM band concentrates more on music, though several listener-subscriber stations do their part to revive the grand old art of conversation with interviews and news commentary. KBOO (90.7 FM) features eclectic community-based programming. KOPB (91.5 FM) offers classical music and National Public Radio news shows.

Internet fans will find the Citysearch Portland website (www.portland.citysearch.com) to be an easy-to-use directory to the community. Restaurants, hotels, and cultural attractions are continually updated and supplemented by graphics and maps. The listings go beyond the usual electronic Yellow Pages format with content-laden blurbs written by savvy locals.

It's easy to find wireless Internet access in Portland, and it will only become easier—city government has taken steps to "unwire" Portland, providing free or low-cost Internet access throughout the city.

GETTING THERE
By Air
Portland International Airport (877/739-4636, www.flypdx.com) is among America's fastest-growing airports, setting traffic records each month. PDX is served by more than a dozen major airlines, all of which can be accessed from the airport website's list of airlines.

If you're heading in the other direction, the Portland Airport is situated a mere 20-minute drive from the western portal of the Columbia River Gorge in Troutdale. With car rental facilities and limo services to Gorge resorts such as Skamania Lodge, you can be out of the airport and off on an adventure within an hour of landing.

Airport MAX (www.trimet.org) enables arriving and departing travelers to take light rail. This Red Line runs from Beaverton Transit Center through downtown Portland to the Portland International Airport (PDX), every

15 minutes during the day. For $1.65, the trip from/to the airport and City Center takes just 38 minutes. MAX's low-floor cars enable passenger to easily roll luggage on board.

Several cab companies and shuttle services serve the airport (look for them at the center section of the airport terminal's lower roadway—out the doors from the baggage claim). Expect to pay about $30 from the airport to downtown in a cab or about $15 in a shuttle bus.

To drive to the city from PDX, follow the signs to downtown. This takes you first to I-205 South which then flows into I-84 East. About 10 minutes later, you'll flirt briefly with I-5 South before quickly exiting onto the Morrison Street Bridge. This takes you across the river where the first cross street encountered is S.W. 2nd Avenue.

By Car
Portland sits on or near the routes of Interstates 5, 405, 205, and 84. I-5 runs from Seattle to San Diego and I-84 goes east to Salt Lake City. I-405 circles downtown Portland to the west and south. I-205 bypasses the city to the east. U.S. 26 heads west to Cannon Beach on the coast and east to the Cascades.

For parking information, see *By Car* under *Getting Around.*

GETTING AROUND
In Portland, streets are named and run east and west, avenues are numbered and run north and south, and boulevards exist in the netherworld of thoroughfares that go in many directions. Newcomers should note that the Willamette River delineates east–west address prefixes and Burnside Street, north–south ones. Also, Northwest Portland streets proceed in alphabetical order from Burnside moving north with streets keyed to names of early settlers. Back in midtown, Naito Parkway runs alongside the Willamette and is, in effect, "Zero Avenue," with numbers going up as you move west away from the river. These avenues are all one-way. Traffic along 5th and 6th Avenues is largely restricted to mass tran-

sit. Broadway (in the downtown corridor, the equivalent of 7th Avenue) is Portland's only undefined arterial, having an east-west orientation when it has the prefix N.E.; with the prefix S.W. or when it's just plain Broadway, it runs north–south.

Finally, addresses increase by 100 each block, beginning at the Willamette River for streets and Burnside for avenues. Despite idiosyncrasies, Portland is, for the most part, easily navigable, although no rules of logic seem to apply in the West Hills when it comes to finding your way.

By Car

The parking situation in Portland has its good news and bad news. Even though parking meters and day parking proliferate in the city, it's often hard to find an empty spot. Even so, the parking sticker kiosks on every block throughout downtown make it easy to pay for parking (credit and debit cards are accepted); the stickers are placed on the sidewalk-side windows. Valid stickers (those with time left on them) can be used at more than one parking place. In addition, many of the parking garages accept merchant validation stamps (on the garage receipt) for free parking. Street parking is free 7 P.M.– 8 A.M. on weekdays and all day Sunday.

Two reliable cab companies are **Broadway Cab Company** (503/227-1234) and **Radio Cab** (503/227-1212). Cabs charge about $2 upon pick-up and each additional mile is $1.50. It can be difficult to hail a cab here, so it's best to give them a call or catch one in front of a hotel.

Public Transportation

Portland's excellent public transportation system has three components: TriMet buses, the MAX light-rail trains, and the Portland Streetcar. Buses reach out into every neighborhood, the Max runs along a few well-traveled lines, and the sleek streetcar connects downtown with the Pearl District and Northwest Portland (downtown and in the Pearl, the streetcar travels on 10th and 11th Avenues). Thankfully, each part of the system uses the same tickets

or fare structure, and bus transfers or cancelled streetcar or MAX tickets can be used on any part of the system.

The first step in setting up your own personalized mass-transit tour is picking up a schedule at one of the TriMet service centers or bus-information racks scattered around town. TriMet's website is excellent, with good map, schedule, and trip-planning information, and the TriMet office at Pioneer Square (701 S.W. 6th Ave., 503/238-7433, www.trimet.org) is open weekdays 9 A.M.–5 P.M. Information can also be obtained from TriMet drivers or hotel front-desk clerks and concierges. Adult fares range from $1.65 (basic fare) to $1.95 (long trips); senior fares are discounted. Buy tickets from machines at MAX stations before boarding. Streetcars are equipped with fare boxes that dispense tickets and change. TriMet buses require exact change deposited in the fare box or tickets purchased in advance at the TriMet office. When you pay your fare, the driver will give you a transfer, which is good for a couple of hours and can also be used on MAX trains and the streetcar.

Passengers in the downtown area can ride free anywhere in "Fareless Square." This 300 square-block area is defined by I-405 to the south, N.W. Hoyt Street to the north, and the Willamette River to the east (on the MAX, Fareless Square extends east to the Lloyd Center). Thirty-one shelters (color-coded by their region) make up Transit Mall. Southbound buses pick up passengers on S.W. 5th Avenue; northbound travelers board on S.W. 6th Avenue.

Gorge-bound travelers can bypass 17 miles of suburbs by taking MAX light rail from downtown to the Gresham stop. Here catch a #80, #24, or #81 TriMet bus to Troutdale and the western portal of the Historic Highway.

By Bike

Portland has long been known as a bicycle-friendly city. Its nationally recognized bicycle program provides a comprehensive, safe bikeway network to increase the number of residents who bicycle to work, on errands, and for exercise or pleasure. To accomplish this, the city has created close to 262 miles of bikeways (bicycle lanes, boulevards, and multi-use trails). Cyclists even have their own special directional signs along some routes, pointing the way to potential destinations and estimating the riding time. Because it's so easy to cycle in Portland, many more folks are riding bicycles. In 1975 about 200 cyclists crossed the Hawthorne Bridge daily by bike; today, it's over 2,400.

TriMet buses, which are all equipped with bike racks, can accommodate cyclists, as can all MAX trains. For more information check the TriMet website (www.trimet.org/guide/bikes) or contact their 24-hour hotline (503/962-7644). For more general biking info contact the **Office of Transportation Bicycle Program** (503/823-7082, www.trans.ci.portland.or.us/bicycles).

COLUMBIA RIVER GORGE AND MOUNT HOOD

To native tribes, the Gorge was the great gathering place. To Lewis and Clark and Oregon Trail pioneers, it was the gateway to the Pacific. To first-time visitors today, the Columbia River's enormous canyon carved through the Cascade Mountains is one of the Pacific Northwest's most dramatic and scenic destinations. The river, over a mile wide, winds through a 3,000-foot-deep gorge flanked by volcanic peaks and austere bands of basalt. Waterfalls tumble from the mountain's edge and fall hundreds of feet to the river. Clinging to the cliff walls are deep green forests, filled with ferns and moss. It's the living rendition of a Northwest postcard.

While most visitors confine themselves to the cliffs and dense woodlands at the western end of the Gorge, a surprise awaits the newcomer venturing farther east. Halfway through this cleft in the Cascades, the greenery parts to reveal tawny grasslands and sage-covered deserts under an endless sky. This 80-mile long, five-mile wide chasm has as much variety in climate, topography, and vegetation as terra firma can muster.

Visitors can revel in a cornucopia of attractions: the world's largest concentration of high waterfalls, one of the planet's most diverse botanical communities, and a wide spectrum of recreational opportunities that includes skiing, fishing, hiking, rock climbing, windsurfing, and much more—all in the same day.

Immediately south of the Columbia River Gorge rises 11,240-foot Mount Hood, Oregon's highest peak. Mount Hood is an all-season, outdoor playground for all of northern Oregon. Besides skiing at five ski areas, the mountain is popular with hikers, mountain

© PAUL LEVY

COLUMBIA RIVER GORGE

HIGHLIGHTS

◖ **Crown Point and Vista House:** At the Gorge's western entrance, this viewpoint provides the classic vista of the Columbia River and its mountain canyon (page 113).

◖ **Multnomah Falls:** Plunging 620 feet, the second-highest drop in the nation, this is one waterfall you can't miss (page 115).

◖ **Elowah Falls/McCord Creek Trails:** Leading to two fantastic overviews of the same beautiful waterfall, these trails comprise one of the Gorge's lesser-known hiking routes (page 117).

◖ **Eagle Creek Trail:** The one trail you must hike in the Gorge, it leads to numerous waterfalls along a steep-sided valley (page 123).

◖ **Rowena Crest and Tom McCall Nature Preserve:** One of the few drive-to vistas in the Gorge, this promontory is famed for its spring wildflower displays (page 139).

◖ **Columbia Gorge Discovery Center and Wasco County Historical Museum:** The best museum in the Gorge, relating the complex and fascinating history of the region (page 143).

◖ **Ramona Falls Trail:** An easy hike leads to a dramatic weeping wall falls, one of the most beautiful near Mount Hood (page 148).

◖ **Timberline Lodge:** A fantastic log lodge built by hand in the 1930s, Timberline Lodge is an icon for the Northwest (page 153).

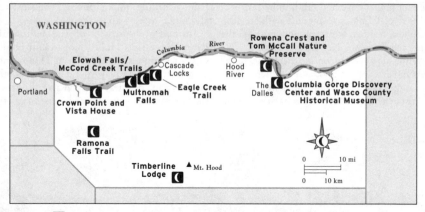

LOOK FOR ◖ TO FIND RECOMMENDED SIGHTS, ACTIVITIES, DINING, AND LODGING.

climbers, and those who come to marvel at the extravagant WPA-era Timberline Lodge.

If there's one word to describe the forces that created the Columbia River Gorge, it's *cataclysmic.* Volcanic activity, flooding, and landslides have sculpted the present-day contours of this fjord-like border between Oregon and Washington. While eons-old mud and lava flows are visible throughout the Gorge, and ancient avalanche scars still mar the land, what's sculpted

the Gorge more than these forces are recent floods of biblical proportions.

During the last Ice Age, a 2,000-foot ice dam formed Lake Missoula, a vast inland sea in what's now northern Idaho and western Montana. The collapse of the ice dam some 15,000 years ago released a wall of water that steamrolled westward at 60 miles an hour. These torrents entered the eastern Gorge at depths exceeding 1,000 feet. The floodwaters submerged what is now Portland and then surged 120 miles south, depositing rich alluvial sediments in the Willamette Valley. Scientists estimate there were at least 40 such inundations between 12,000 and 19,000 years ago.

The Columbia River

The 1,243-mile Columbia River has its primary headwaters at Lake Columbia in British Columbia, from where it flows north and west from Canada's Kootenay Range. Glacial runoff, snowmelt, and such impressive tributaries as the Kootenay and Snake Rivers guarantee a fairly consistent flow year-round. At peak flows, the river pumps a quarter-million cubic feet of water per second into the Pacific Ocean after draining 259,000 square miles, an area larger than France.

Flow peaks in spring and early summer, coinciding with the region's irrigation needs. Another leading use of the river is hydropower. The Columbia River Basin is the most hydroelectrically developed river system in the world, with more than 400 dams in place throughout the mainstem and tributaries. As a result, the current incarnation of the Columbia is a stark contrast to the white water that filled its channel before the dams were built. Back in that era, spawning salmon had to jump over several sets of roiling cascades, and shipping was a hazardous enterprise. Floods were commonplace; the flood of 1894, for example, inundated Hood River and The Dalles. Though the Columbia no longer exerts so pervasive an influence on the topography here, it still is more powerful than any river in North America except the Mississippi.

PLANNING YOUR TIME

The heart of the Columbia Gorge is just an hour from Portland, making this a major getaway for residents and travelers alike. Any trip to the Gorge should include a drive along the Historic Columbia River Highway with hikes to waterfalls, and a drive up the "Fruit Loop" (Rte. 35) from Hood River to Mount Hood. Even though the Gorge is very popular, it's also vast, so it's easy to lose the crowds if you hike a lesser-known trail or get off the main routes.

While most people visit the Gorge as a day

trip from Portland, consider spending a night in Hood River or at Mount Hood to make this a more relaxing trip—and to get a feel for the youthful culture of windsurfers and bikers that use this stunning landscape as their playground. In addition to excellent hotels and restaurants, you'll find wine-tasting rooms aplenty.

Also, if you're based in Portland and plan to drive out I-84 to visit the Gorge as a day trip, consider driving back to the Portland metro area along the Washington side of the Columbia. Two-lane Highway 14 along the north side of the river offers a different perspective on the river and its mighty canyon and provides a break from the relentless truck traffic along I-84. Highway 14 joins I-205 east of Portland for an easy detour back to the Oregon side of the Columbia.

Weather can be capricious in the Gorge, making for dangerous driving conditions any time of the year. The Cascade summits can wring more than 200 inches of rain yearly from eastward-moving cloud masses, yet at The Dalles the annual rainfall is just six inches annually.

Given these contrasts, it's not surprising that the convergence of weather systems at mid-Gorge often results in meteorological bedlam. In fact, Bonneville Dam recorded the state's one-day record for snowfall, 39 inches, in January 1980. Strong, reliable westerlies make the Gorge a windsurfing paradise but can also make driving RVs a real challenge.

West of the Cascades, winter lows seldom dip below freezing. A notable exception to this happens when frigid winds originating in the Rockies blow through the Gorge in winter, resulting in ice storms that can make for freezing rain and black ice, with the weather sometimes closing the freeway.

The **Columbia River Gorge National Scenic Area** (902 Wasco St., Hood River, OR 97031, 541/308-1700, www.fs.fed.us/r6/columbia/forest) is the federal entity that oversees the Columbia River Gorge in both Oregon and Washington. From its website you can print out a handy guide to the Gorge and learn more about recreational options.

COLUMBIA RIVER GORGE

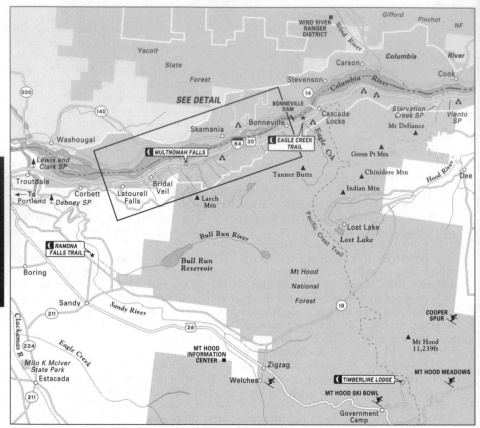

Historic Columbia River Highway (U.S. 30)

In 1911, Samuel Hill, a wealthy, eccentric railroad lawyer, began promoting an idea for an automobile route through the Columbia River Gorge. Hill found supporters in the Portland business community who were swept up in the fervor stirred up by the national Good Roads campaign of the time. This movement supported the construction of paved highways with scenic qualities to foster tourism.

As the first Model T rolled off Henry Ford's assembly line in 1913, Hill's dream began to take form. Timber magnate and hotelier Simon Benson coordinated the project's fiscal man-agement and promotion, and mill-owner John Yeon volunteered as roadmaster of the work crews. Samuel Lancaster, a visionary Tennessee engineer recruited by Hill, added the artistic inspiration for what came to be known as "a poem in stone." Together Hill and Lancaster journeyed to Italy, Switzerland, and Germany to view European mountain roads.

Hill and Lancaster were able to convince the Oregon government to finance the Columbia River Highway, the first road linking The Dalles to Portland through the Gorge. To these idealists, the highway was not meant to be an

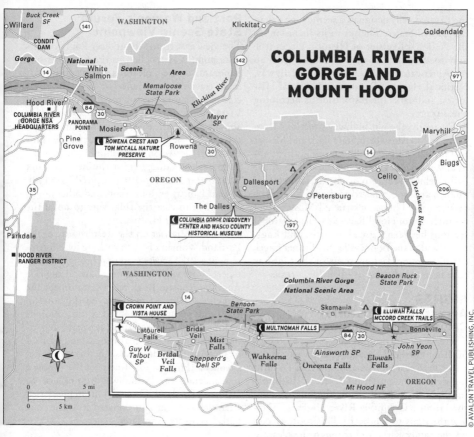

intrusion on the wilderness; instead, the road was designed to be a part of the landscape.

This would not only be the Northwest's first paved public road but one of the defining events in the growth of modern American tourism. Scores of middle-class Portland families in their Model Ts took to the hills above the Columbia on this architecturally aesthetic thoroughfare following the 1915 completion of this highway's first section, from Troutdale to Hood River. After the stretch between Hood River and The Dalles was completed in 1922, it was dubbed "king of roads" by the *Illustrated London News*.

Service stations, roadside rest stops, motor courts (later called "motels"), and resort hotels that catered to the motorized carriage trade developed here, contributing to the Gorge's economic growth. Of the several dozen road-houses that lined this highway 1915–1960, only a few structures remain today. A new interstate was constructed in the 1950s and 1960s that made Gorge travel faster but the charm of the earlier era was lost. Some sections of the old highway became part of the freeway; two sections remained open to car travel as U.S. 30.

Fortunately, the "king of roads" experienced a renaissance in the 1980s. Political activists, volunteers, government agencies, and federal legislation provided the spadework for the creation of the Historic Columbia River Highway, the first federally designated scenic highway in the United States. Thanks to its inclusion on the National Register of Historic Places (the only road on the list) as well as listings as an All-American Road, National Scenic Byway, National Heritage Road, and National Historic Landmark, the restoration is becoming a reality.

Currently, the old highway's sections from Troutdale to Ainsworth State Park and Mosier to The Dalles attract millions of motorists annually. Other segments of the old road are being rebuilt with attention to architectural nuance and potential recreational and interpretive uses. The reconstructed Mosier Twin Tunnels east of Hood River as well as restored sections between Cascades Locks and Eagle Creek and in the Bonneville–to–Tanner Creek corridor exemplify how parts of the highway have been rededicated as hiker/biker trails.

SIGHTS
Access to the Historic Columbia River Highway (U.S.30)
There are several options for getting onto U.S. 30 from Portland. If you're in no particular hurry, head east on I-84 and take Exit 17, turning right at the outlet mall, left at the blinking light up the hill from the outlets onto the Historic Columbia River Highway. (Follow the signs to Corbett.) This route snakes up the Sandy River and through the pleasant small towns of Troutdale and Corbett before reaching the Gorge's big attractions. The next 20 miles traverse historic bridges and stonework, lush orchard country, rainforested slot canyons, more than a half-dozen large waterfalls, and cliff-side views of the Columbia River Gorge. The attractions between Corbett and Horsetail Falls explain why both the American Automobile Association and Rand McNally rate the Historic Highway as one of the top 10 scenic roads in the country.

For quicker access to waterfalls and hikes, take Exit 22 at Corbett, which joins U.S. 30 just before the first major viewpoints. To reach this section of U.S. 30 from the east, take Exit 35 at Ainsworth State Park.

Portland Women's Forum State Scenic Viewpoint
The view east from Chanticleer Point, as this vista point is also called, is the first cliff-side panorama of the Columbia and its gorge that most travelers experience on U.S. 30. This classic tableau features Crown Point's domed Vista House jutting out on an escarpment about a mile to the east, giving human scale to the cleft in the Cascades 725 feet below. This same perspective on the Columbia (minus the domed observatory) from the now-defunct Chanticleer Hotel in 1913 inspired Sam Hill, Samuel Lancaster, John Yeon, and other prominent men to cast the final vote to build the Columbia River Highway.

Behind a barrier on the western side of the Portland Women's Forum parking lot is a remnant of a 1912 access road that brought Chanticleer Hotel visitors here on a hair-raising ride from the Rooster Rock train station near the shoreline. After a fire destroyed the hotel in 1930, the point was annexed to the holdings of Julius Meier, a prominent Portland department store owner who also became governor of Oregon. Travelers pass his former estate, Menucha (Hebrew for "waters of life"), now a retreat center, on the highway west of here. In 1956, the Portland Women's Forum purchased Chanticleer Point and donated it to the state park system six years later.

Larch Mountain Turnoff
If you veer right on the road marked "Larch Mountain" at the Y intersection with the highway, you'll go 14 miles to an overlook featuring views of the snowcapped Cascades as well as of the Columbia all the way west to Portland. There are also picnic tables and trailheads to the Gorge below, with gorgeous beargrass blossoms in June. Later, huckleberries in August and mushrooms after the first rains await foragers. Also of interest are old-growth firs. Despite this botanical bounty, there's not a larch tree in sight—this species grows east of the Cascades.

To enjoy one of Oregon's classic sunsets, head to the northeast corner of the Larch Mountain parking lot around dusk and follow a gently rolling quarter-mile paved path through forests of old-growth noble fir. The trail's last 100 yards involve a steep climb up to an outcropping. This is **Sherrard Point,** with preeminent alpine views on a clear day. To the east, across miles of treetops, is Mount Hood. To the south is Mount Jefferson's symmetrical cone. To the north, Mounts St. Helens, Rainier, and Adams are visible. To the west, the Columbia River becomes bathed in reddish glow during sunset. With the coming of nightfall, the lights of Portland blink in the darkness.

An ambitious hike involving a car shuttle between trailheads lets you trek from Larch Mountain down to Multnomah Falls Lodge. This trail drops 4,000 feet in 6.8 miles. To reach the descent route from Larch Mountain viewpoint, retrace your steps along the path back toward the parking lot. At about halfway, veer right up the spur trail that crests on a hill. From this hilltop head west a short distance toward a picnic area where the trail down to the Gorge begins.

C Crown Point and Vista House

Driving the interstate, you might notice the distinctive outline of an octagonal structure on a high bluff in the western Gorge. This is the **Vista House Visitors Center at Crown Point** (503/695-2230, www.vistahouse.com, 9 A.M.–6 P.M. daily, Apr.–Oct.), 733 feet above the Columbia. Construction began in 1916 when the Columbia River Highway was formally dedicated. The occasion was marked when Woodrow Wilson pressed a button in the White House, which electronically unfurled "Old Glory" at the flat circular dirt area that was to become the visitors center. In deference to Prohibition, the event was toasted with loganberry juice.

Vista House was completed two years after the highway's official dedication. The outside observation deck up the steps from the main rotunda showcases 30 miles of the Columbia River Gorge. A plaque outside pays homage to Samuel Lancaster for the "poetry and drama" the highway embodies. Photos of the various stages of the road's construction are displayed in the main rotunda, as are wildflower cuttings of the region's endemic plants. In the gallery of Vista House, volunteers run an information desk while educational exhibits and displays relate the history of the building and highway.

Crown Point was originally called Thor's Crown by Edgar Lazarus, architect of Vista House. This promontory began as a basalt flow 14.5 million years ago when lava filled a canyon of the ancestral Columbia River.

Figure Eight Loops

The highway between Crown Point and Latourell Falls drops 600 feet in elevation in several miles. As you wend your way downhill from Vista House, it becomes apparent that Lancaster softened the grade of the road here by means of switchbacks. With a grade never exceeding 5 percent and a curve radii of not less than 100 feet, this section presents little problem for modern vehicles, but it challenged period cars and trucks during the highway's first decades. During construction, Scottish stonecutters and Italian masons sometimes hung suspended on ropes, singing while they worked on the precipitous, circuitous roadbed.

Latourell Falls

Latourell Falls is the first of a half-dozen roadside falls seen by motorists. When the highway was built, special care was taken to ensure the bridge crossing Latourell Creek provided a good view of the falls. Nonetheless, be sure to take the paved 150-yard trail from the parking lot to the base of this 249-foot cataract. Here, the shade and cooling spray create a microclimate for fleabane, a delicate bluish member of the aster family, and other flowers normally common to alpine biomes. The filmy tendrils of water against the columnar basalt formations on the cliffs make Latourell a favorite with photographers. Foragers appreciate maidenhair fern and thimbleberries but not enough to denude the slope.

Another trailhead begins in the middle of the parking lot and climbs around and above the falls, though bushes obscure the overhang from which the water descends when you're looking down from the top. You'll probably be more inclined to stop after 50 yards and take in the distant perspective of Latourell from across the canyon. Latourell Creek flows from the falls underneath the highway bridge toward Guy Talbot State Park with picnic tables shaded by an ancient forest.

Shepperd's Dell

Shepperd's Dell is named for a settler who retreated here for spiritual renewal because of the lack of good roads to a nearby church. This lush forested canyon cut by a waterfall is one of the visual highlights of the Gorge despite the fact that little of this splendor is apparent from the road. An 80-yard paved sloping walkway descends from a bridge (and a parking lot east of it) whose intricate architecture can be appreciated with a glance over your shoulder. Chances are, however, your gaze will be riveted on Shepperd's Dell Falls coursing down out of the forest to plummet sharply over a precipice.

Bishop's Cap

Bishop's Cap embodies the highway engineering genius of Samuel Lancaster. Here, the base of a basalt outcropping was undercut as little as possible to accommodate traffic. Locals call this altered formation "mushroom rock" due to the simulation of a stem connecting to a mushroom cap. The same motif is repeated around the bend. More highway architecture is visible here with dry masonry walls and stone guardrails.

Bridal Veil Falls State Park

Another legacy from the past can be experienced at the 1926-era Bridal Veil Lodge across from the state park. This establishment, along with the Columbia Gorge Hotel west of Hood River, is the only operating lodging from the heyday of the Columbia River Highway.

Across from Bridal Veil Lodge are the falls for which the state park is named, reached by a trailhead at the east end of the parking lot. A short two-thirds of a mile round-trip hike takes

you to the observation platform at the base of this voluminously gushing bi-level cascade.

Bridal Veil Falls State Park is also the western trailhead for the 33.5-mile **Gorge Trail 400.** Between here and Wyeth, this largely level trail takes in the Gorge's highest waterfalls as well as newly opened sections of the old Columbia River Highway that are closed to vehicular traffic.

In addition to tree-shaded picnic tables and restrooms open all year, the park features the largest camas patch in the Columbia River Gorge. Blue-flowering camas and wapato once were the leading food staples for local Native Americans. The camas bulb looks like an onion and tastes very sweet after it is slowly baked. Please leave the camas alone, out of respect for a traditional food source as well as for your own safety—camas with white flowers are poisonous, a fact that is not always established when the bulb is being harvested.

If you're here in April, look for patches of camas along the short **Overlook Trail** to the Pillars of Hercules, a pair of giant basalt monoliths with I-84 and the Columbia River in the background. These formations are also called Spilyai's children, after the Native American coyote demi-god. According to legend, Spilyai transformed his wife into Latourell Falls and his children into these volcanic formations to keep them from leaving him. Overlook Trail is about 20 yards west of the Bridal Veil Falls trailhead.

Wahkeena Falls

The name means "most beautiful," and this 242-foot series of cascades that descends in staircase fashion to the parking lot is certainly a contender. To the right of the small footbridge abutting the road is a 0.6-mile trailhead to upper Wahkeenah Falls. Follow this largely paved trail to a bench just beyond the falls that affords views of both upper and lower cascades. Higher up are panoramic vistas of the Columbia River and Gorge and the ridgeline pathway connecting Wahkeenah to Multnomah. This trail is especially striking in October, when the cottonwoods and the bigleaf and vine maples

NATIVE PEOPLES OF THE GORGE

Archaeological findings date native presence in the Gorge to some 10,000 years ago. When Lewis and Clark first came through the Columbia River Gorge in 1805, they found a gathering of the tribes near present-day Wishram, Washington, whose numbers and variety surpassed any other native trading center on the continent.

The region hosted indigenous peoples from as far away as Alaska and the Great Lakes, who would come for barter fairs during salmon fishing season. Gambling, races, and potlatches (parties where individuals gave away possessions to gain status) supplemented trade and fishing.

Lewis and Clark encountered evidence of foreign contact on the Columbia from such disparate sources as a Chinook tribal chieftain with red hair and Gorge natives with swords, coins, Hudson's Bay blankets, and other European and Asian goods. Certain artifacts suggest trade with natives from as far away as present-day Missouri and the southwestern United States. The currency of trade consisted of shells from Vancouver Island and blankets crafted by the English Hudson's Bay Company rather than indigenous articles.

When Lewis and Clark passed through, an estimated 13,500 native people lived in the Columbia River region. However, with the waves of white settlers and traders in the early 19th century came diseases to which the local tribes had no resistance. Measles and smallpox epidemics killed up to three-quarters of the region's native population, greatly reducing their ability to resist the influence of European and American colonists. While the arrival of settlers on the Oregon Trail brought about some isolated conflicts with Gorge tribes, far more damaging to the long-term survival of native culture here was the destruction of their dietary staples, such as the camas root and salmon. Tribes were moved to reservations outside the Gorge as a result of treaties enacted in 1855 and or the flooding of ceremonial fishing sites at Celilo by The Dalles Dam in 1957.

The complex and sophisticated culture of Gorge tribes can be appreciated today at a number of Gorge interpretive centers, where you'll find artifacts, oral histories, photos, and other exhibits. Most petroglyphs, pictographs, cemeteries, and other indigenous cultural landmarks have been largely destroyed by construction or buried beneath reservoirs.

COLUMBIA RIVER GORGE

sport colorful fall foliage. A picnic area is north of the Historic Highway across from the falls.

🄲 Multnomah Falls

At 620 feet, Multnomah is the second-highest continuously running waterfall in the country. This huge cascade pours down from the heights with an authority worthy of the prominent Native American chief for whom it is named. The falls drop twice: once over 560 feet from a notch in an amphitheater of vertical rock, and then another 70 feet over a ledge of basalt. A short trail leads to an arch bridge directly over the second falls.

The 0.5-mile-long uphill trail to the bridge should be attempted by anyone capable of a small amount of exertion. Here you can bathe in the cool mists of the upper falls and appreciate the power of Multnomah's billowy flumes.

The more intrepid can reach the top of the falls and beyond, but even the view from the base of the falls is edifying. Placards detailing forest canopies and their understories at different elevations and other aspects of the ecosystem are on display in the first 100 yards of the trail. On the way up keep an eye out for such indigenous species as the Larch Mountain salamander and Howell's daisy. If you hear a whistle at higher elevations, it might be a pika.

While some of the falls in the surrounding area emanate from creeks fed by melting snows on Larch Mountain, Multnomah is primarily spring-fed, enabling it to run year-round. Between one and two million visitors yearly make Multnomah Falls the most-visited natural attraction in the state.

The falls area also has a snack bar as well as **Multnomah Falls Lodge** (503/695-2376, www.multnomahfallslodge.com). A magnificent structure, the lodge was built in 1925 and is today operated by a private concessionaire under license from the National Forest Service. The day lodge is open 8 A.M.–9 P.M. daily and has an on-site restaurant but no overnight accommodations. There's also a Forest Service visitors center.

Oneonta Gorge

Just east of Multnomah Falls, Oneonta Gorge is a narrow chasm cut into a thick basalt flow by Oneonta Creek. Walls over 100 feet high arch over the stream. This peculiar ecosystem, preserved as **Oneonta Gorge Botanical Area,** is home to a number of rare, cliff-dwelling plants that thrive in this moist, shadowy chasm. There's no room along the sheer walls of Oneonta Gorge for a trail. However, for those unperturbed by the thought of wet sneakers, the shallow stream can be waded for about a half mile to Oneonta Falls, where Oneonta Creek drops 75 feet into its gorge.

Horsetail Falls

Only a few hundred feet east of Oneonta Gorge is Horsetail Falls, which drops out of a notch in the rock to fall 176 feet. While the waterfall is easily seen from the turnout along U.S. 30, hikers should consider the three-mile **Horsetail-Oneonta Loop Trail.** Starting at Horsetail Falls, the trail quickly climbs up the side of the gorge wall and along the edge of a lava flow. The trail continues *behind* Ponytail Falls (also called Upper Horsetail Falls) which pours out of a tiny crack into a mossy cirque. The trail then drops onto Oneonta Creek, with great views over its narrow gorge and waterfalls. The trail returns to U.S. 30 about a half mile west of the Horsetail Falls trailhead.

HIKING

There are many wonderful hikes along the Historic Highway. In addition to those described below, check out the National Forest Service's *Short Hiking Loops* map, available free at the Multnomah Falls Lodge.

Up from the Ashes– Angel's Rest Trail

In early October 1991, massive fires engulfed portions of the Mount Hood National Forest off the Historic Highway. At the time, it was feared that massive erosion from the devastation of the trees and the understory would do in the network of trails in and around the route of the waterfalls. But, as you will see, this cloud had a silver lining.

For a good perspective on the fire as well as a great view of the gorge, Angel's Rest Trail #415 is recommended. To get there off I-84 take eastbound Exit 28 and follow the exit road 0.25 mile to its junction with the Historic Highway. At this point hang a sharp right as if you were going to head up the hill toward Crown Point, but pull over into the parking area on the north side of the highway instead. The trailhead is on the south side of the road.

The steep 2.3-mile path to the top of this rocky outcropping gains 1,600 feet and takes you from an unburned forest through vigorous

© BILL MCRAE

Multnomah Falls Lodge and its namesake waterfall

© BILL MCRAE

Wade upstream to explore Oneonta Gorge.

new brush growth beneath live evergreens with singed bark. The latter gives way to charred conifers as you near the summit. Scientists hope these snags and new openings in the forest can breed more biodiversity in the ecosystem. At any rate, the lack of foliage on the branches of burnt trees has opened new vistas of the Columbia Gorge below.

From the top you can enjoy a balcony-seat view overlooking the action. The stage in this case juts out over the Columbia River with sweeping views toward Portland; to the northeast the snowcapped carapace of the Washington Cascades plays peekaboo behind a series of smaller ridges.

Wahkeena-Multnomah Loop

This is a hike of about five miles with panoramic river views, perspectives on four waterfalls, and ancient forests.

To get to Wahkeena Falls, drive I-84 to Exit 28, Bridal Veil Falls. Several miles later you'll come to the falls parking area and trailhead. If you take the trail to the right of the bridge,

in about a mile you'll come to Fairy Falls, so named for its ethereal quality. Just past Fairy Falls leave trail #420 for Vista Point Trail #419 to see panoramas from 1,600 feet above the river. There's also a revealing look at the singed trunks left over from the fires of October 1991. Old-growth Douglas fir ushers you through higher elevations on this trail.

Rejoin trail #420 a mile east of where #419 began. Once you get past the first 1.5 miles of this trail's initial steep ascent, the rest of the route is of moderate difficulty. As you begin your descent, you might become confused by a lack of signs at the junction of #420 and the Larch Mountain Trail. Hang a sharp left on #441 to head west and down along Multnomah Creek. At the rear of this gorge is pretty Ecola Falls. There are several other cascades along the route.

When you hit the blacktopped section of #441, you hang a left to enjoy views from the top of Multnomah Falls, and then descend, crossing the bridge and dropping onto the parking area.

◖ Elowah Falls/McCord Creek Trails

To avoid the crowds while taking in spectacularly varied gorge landscapes, try Elowah Falls/Upper McCord Creek Trails.

From Portland, take I-84 past Multnomah Falls east to Exit 35, Ainsworth State Park. As you come off the access road you'll have a choice of left turns. Take Frontage Road with signs for Dodson. The latter may also be accessed by the Historic Highway after driving five miles east of Multnomah Falls. Drive about two miles to the small parking lot of John Yeon State Park, named for one of the major benefactors of the Columbia River Highway. In the western corner of the lot is the trailhead. Follow it a half mile up the hill. When you reach a junction of two trails, turn right for Upper McCord Creek and left for Elowah Falls.

The Upper McCord Creek trail leads to a mossy glade framing a creek at the top of a waterfall just under a mile from the junction.

COLUMBIA RIVER GORGE

En route, the trail narrows to a ledge carved out of a cliff. From behind a railing, gaze hundreds of feet down at the Columbia in the foreground of 12,306-foot Mount Adams. Across the gully, layered basalt strata indicate successive lava flows. This is a good place to look for osprey riding the thermals before they dive down to the Columbia for a fish. The trail continues to a view of dual cascades descending the rock face.

Retrace your steps to where the trail forks and descend 0.5 mile from the junction to Elowah Falls. This several-hundred-foot-high feathery cascade is set in a steep rock amphitheater amid hues of green that conjure the verdant lushness of Hawaii.

SWIMMING

Swimming at **Glen Otto Park** on the west side of the Sandy River Bridge can be precarious due to cold water and swift currents. In the last decade, more than a half-dozen drownings have occurred here. Look for lifeguards here in late spring through summer before diving in. The city government is contemplating requiring swimmers to wear lifejackets here.

Swimming is safe at historic and scenic **Rooster Rock State Park,** Exit 25 off of I-84 near Troutdale. A $3 parking charge is levied on each car. West of the parking area is the monolith for which the park is named. According to some sources, Lewis and Clark labeled the cucumber-shaped promontory on November 2, 1805. Playing fields and a gazebo front a sandy beach on the banks of the Columbia here. The water in the roped-in swimming area is shallow but refreshing. A mile or so east is one of the only nude beaches officially sanctioned by the state (the other one is Collins Beach on Sauvie Island).

ACCOMMODATIONS

None of the sites in this chapter is more than 30 miles from Portland or from Hood River, so most travelers will visit the waterfalls of the Columbia Gorge from the comfort of these cities. For a special escape, however, there are two

© BILL MCRAE

You'll need to hike to see Elowah Falls, one of our favorite Columbia Gorge waterfalls.

wonderful accommodations in this area that deserve special consideration.

Imagine a 38-acre estate featuring a restaurant, hotel, brewery, winery and tasting room, movie theater, and golf course amid lavish gardens and artwork at every turn. That's McMenamins **(Edgefield** (2126 S.W. Halsey, Troutdale, 503/669-8610 or 800/669-8610, www.mcmenamins.com). Oregon's preeminent brewpub-meisters have transformed what had been the County Poor Farm and later a convalescent home into a good base from which to explore the Gorge or Portland. This is truly the best of the country near the best of the city. This range extends to lodging styles. You can choose between hotel rooms charmingly decorated with artwork and antiques from $50 (with shared bath) or for $80 (with private bath).

Also unique is **Bridal Veil Lodge Bed & Breakfast** (P.O. Box 10, Bridal Veil, 503/695-2333, www.bridalveillodge.com, $90 double). The lodge, across the road from Bridal Veil Falls State Park, is the last surviving accommodations from the 1920s "roadhouse" era on this part of the Historic Columbia River Highway; the knotty pine walls, antique quilts, and historic photos set the mood. Hospitality is second nature to the innkeepers, as their family has served travelers since 1926. You can stay in the main lodge where you share a bath down the hall or in the cottage rooms. The guest cottage boasts open-beam ceilings, sky windows, and private baths. This is a great place to stay with kids if you are visiting Portland because you're only a half-hour drive from the city but surrounded by the grandeur of the Gorge.

FOOD

In addition to the seven dining options at Edgefield (see *Accommodations*), **Tad's Chicken 'n' Dumplins** (1325 E. Historic Columbia River Hwy., 503/666-5337, open Mon.–Thurs. 5 – 10 P.M., Fri.–Sat 4–P.M., Sun. 2–10 P.M., main courses $11–22) is a Portland-area original. Located right on the Sandy River, its classic weather-beaten roadhouse facade has graced this highway since the 1930s. If you decide to forego the restaurant's namesake dish, try the decent fried oysters, fried chicken, steak, or salmon. It's good ol' American food that'll taste even better with drinks on the deck overlooking the Sandy River.

Service can be uneven at the dining room at **Multnomah Falls Lodge** (503/695-2376, www.multnomahfallslodge.com, open daily 8 A.M.– 9 P.M., main courses $16–22), but the food is surprisingly good when the kitchen isn't overwhelmed. A cheery solarium adjacent to the wood-and-stone dining room makes a casually elegant setting to begin or end a day of hiking. If it's cold, however, stay in the main dining room near the fireplace to enjoy the paintings and vintage photos of Columbia Gorge scenes. On warm days the outside patio is delightful and if you crane your neck you can see the falls. Particularly recommended is the mini loaf of home-baked wheat bread and soup for lunch and the steak, seafood, and chicken main courses for dinner. To get there, take I-84 to Exit 28 (Bridal Veil exit) and continue east for three more miles on Historic Columbia River Highway.

INFORMATION

The **Multnomah Falls Information Center** (at the Multnomah Falls Lodge, 503/695-2372) has a ranger and volunteers on duty year-round to recommend campgrounds and hikes. Ask here about such nearby jaunts as Horsetail Falls, Triple Falls, and Oneonta Gorge. Be sure to request the *Short Hiking Loops Near Multnomah Falls* map for a visual depiction of this network of trails. The center is open 9 P.M.–5 P.M. daily.

Cascade Locks

The sleepy appearance of modern-day Cascade Locks belies its historical significance. The town is perched on a small bluff between the river and I-84, and its services and creature comforts are mostly confined to its main drag, Wa-Na-Pa Street. Below the town were rapids—called the Cascades—that blocked steamboat traffic between Portland and The Dalles, and caused hardship to raft-bound Oregon Trail pioneers. Before the shipping locks that inspired the burg's utilitarian name were constructed in 1896 to help steamboats navi-

gate around hazardous rapids, most boats had to be portaged overland.

The Bridge of the Gods, a steel cantilever bridge spanning the Columbia River at Cascade Locks, was built in 1926, thus replacing a legendary bridge that, according to Native American myth, spanned this same channel.

The construction of the Bonneville Dam in the late 1930s inaugurated boom times in the area. The dam created 48-mile Lake Bonneville, which submerged the shipping locks. Today you can see Native American dip-net fishermen by the 1896 locks site in the town's riverfront Marine Park. Look for tribespeople selling whole fresh salmon and other species late August into September, weekends 10 A.M.– dusk. Bring waxed paper and or a cooler with ice to help the fish keep till you're back in camp. Call 888/289-1855 for more information. Sales are cash only.

Reasonably priced food and lodging, a historical museum, the Bonneville Dam, and sternwheeler tours together with superlative hiking trails nearby make Cascade Locks a nice stopover, as long as you don't come during winter. Most of the 75-inch annual precipitation falls at that time, along with ice storms and gale-force winds.

SIGHTS
Bonneville Dam
The Bonneville Dam (541/374-8820, www .nwp.usace.army.mil/op/b/home.asp) can be reached via Exit 40 off I-84. The signs lead you under the interstate through a tunnel to the site of the complex, Bradford Island. En route to the visitors center you drive over a retractable bridge above the modern shipping locks. On the other side are the powerhouse and turbine room. Downriver on the Washington side is the second-largest exposed monolith in the world (Gibraltar is first). This 848-foot lava promontory abutting the shoreline is known as

Beacon Rock, a moniker bestowed by Lewis and Clark.

Beyond the generating facilities is a bridge, underneath which is the fish-diversion canal. These fish-ways cause back eddies and guide the salmon, shad, steelhead, and other species past turbine blades. You'll want to stop for a brief look at the spillways of the 500-foot-wide Bonneville Dam, especially if they're open.

While Bonneville isn't anywhere near the largest or the most powerful dam on the river, Bonneville Dam was one of the largest and most ambitious of the Depression-era New Deal projects. Completed in 1937, it was the first major dam on the Columbia River. The building of the dam brought Oregon thousands of jobs on construction crews, and the cheap electricity that it produced promised future industrial employment. President Franklin Roosevelt officiated at the dam's opening in 1938, attended by cheering throngs of thousands. The two hydroelectric powerhouses together produce over a million kilowatts of power, and back up the Columbia River for 15 miles.

The **visitors center** (503/374-8820) is open daily 9 A.M.–5 P.M. year-round. Ask the Army Corps of Engineers personnel at the reception desk about tours of the power-generating facilities and about public campgrounds, boat ramps, swimming, and picnic areas. Be aware

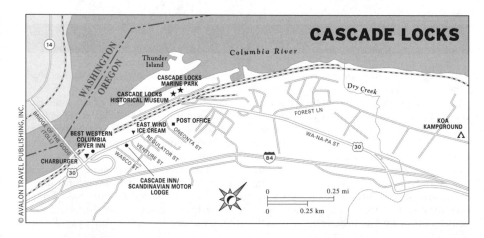

CASCADE LOCKS

that the dam may be closed to visits without warning due to security alerts.

The reception area has exhibits on dam operations, pioneer and navigation history on the Columbia, and fish migration. A long elevator ride takes you down to the fish-viewing windows, where the sight of lamprey eels—which accompany the mid-May and mid-September salmon runs— are particularly fascinating. Outside the facility there's access to an overlook above the fish ladders. A walkway back to the parking lot is decorated with gorgeous roses from spring into fall.

Retrace your route back to the mainland from Bradford Island and turn right, following the signs to the **fish hatchery.** This facility is open 7:30 A.M.–5 P.M. daily. Visit during spawning season (May and September) to see the salmon make their way upriver. At this time, head to the west end of the hatchery, where steps lead down to a series of canals and holding pens. So great is the zeal of these fish to spawn that they occasionally leap more than a foot out of the water.

Inside the building you can see the beginnings of a process that produces the largest number of salmon fry in the state. Here fish culturists sort the fish and extract the bright red salmon roe from the females. These eggs are taken to the windowed incubation building, where you can view trays holding millions of eggs that will eventually hatch into salmon. Once these fry grow into fingerlings, they are moved to outdoor pools where they live until being released into the Columbia River by way of the Tanner Creek canal. The whole process is annotated by placards above the windows inside the incubation building.

The salmon and trout ponds and the floral displays are worth your attention at certain times of the year, but the sturgeon pools to the rear of the visitors center are always something to see. Bonneville is the nation's only white sturgeon hatchery and the government has made this facility user-friendly. Biologists claim the Columbia River white sturgeon, with bony plates instead of scales, has remained unchanged for 200 million years. Despite being the largest freshwater species in North America, this river-bottom scavenger was largely ignored until the gourmet feeding frenzy of the last two decades put a premium on domestic sources of caviar. When *New York Times* food columnist Craig Claiborne pronounced the Columbia's product superior to that of the Caspian Sea several decades ago, its notoriety was established and catch limits were brought back. The Bonneville Dam visitors center and fish hatchery are both free of charge.

Cascade Locks Marine Park

Down by the river is the Cascade Locks Marine Park (Exit 44 off I 84 East). Look for it on your left going east on Wa-Na-Pa Street; just follow the signs. Here the sternwheeler **Columbia Gorge** (reservations: 541/374-8427 or 800/643-1354, www.sternwheeler.com) makes it possible to ride up the river in the style of a century ago. This 145-foot, 330-ton replica carries 599 passengers on three decks. There are several interesting packages of varying themes and duration. The two-hour sightseeing cruise times vary; ask the sales department for schedules. The fare is $25 for adults and seniors, $15 for children. Dinner and weekend brunch cruises are also available.

Port of Cascade Locks (541/374-8619, www.portofcascadelocks.org) houses the ticket office as well as an information center and gift shop, which sells an excellent local hiking trails map.

About a quarter mile west of the visitors center, **Cascade Locks Historical Museum** (503/374-8535) is housed in an old lockkeeper's residence and exhibits Native American artifacts and pioneer memorabilia. Information about the fish wheel, a paddlewheel-like contraption that conveyor-belted salmon out of the river and into a pen, is especially fascinating. This diabolical device was perfected in Oregon in the early 20th century and was so successful at denuding the Columbia of fish that it was outlawed. The museum is open daily May–September, 10 A.M.–4 P.M. Outside the museum is the diminutive Oregon Pony, the first steam locomotive on the Pacific coast. Its

CRUISING THE COLUMBIA RIVER

Thanks to a revival of interest in Lewis and Clark's journey, Columbia River cruises are more popular than ever. Most of these small cruise ships carry 150–180 people and offer weeklong trips that hub out of Portland. These are rather pricey packages but offer a highly scenic and relaxing alternative to a lengthy road trip. The well-appointed ships boast gourmet meals and ideal sightlines on the shipping locks and dam facilities. Add expert commentary by qualified interpreters and you have a trip to remember.

Cruise West (800/888-9378, www .cruisewest.com) has a seven-day, 1,000-mile itinerary along the Columbia and Snake Rivers on three small cruise ships that depart Portland in April, May, September, and October. The tour passes through the Gorge, continues up the Snake River to Clarkston, Washington, and includes a jet-boat trip up Hells Canyon. On the return, the tour visits the Walla Walla wine region and continues to Astoria before doubling back to Portland. Per person prices start at $1,800 based on double occupancy, and include all meals and lodging.

Linblad Expeditions (800/762-0003, www .expeditions.com) packages trips on state-of-the-art craft with groups small enough to guarantee individualized attention from an attentive crew. In addition to luxury, these cruises offer an in-depth experience into the human and natural history of the region thanks to visiting authors, historians, and professors. There are frequent trips ashore, plus Zodiac explorations to remote side canyons. The ship is equipped with kayaks, which allow guests the freedom to explore on their own. The seven-day itinerary is similar to the one noted above; cruises run May and September, October and November, with prices starting at $2,900 per person based on double occupancy.

American West Steamboat (800/234-1232, www.americanweststeamboat.com) offers two different Columbia River itineraries, but covers the same river territory as those above. Their paddlewheelers generally don't go faster than 10–15 miles an hour, a pace more conducive to appreciating the scenery. In addition, the *Queen of the West* also has the most extensive on-board entertainment and longest season. Weeklong cruises start at $2,100.

For day trips on a sternwheeler, June–October, contact **Sternwheeler Columbia Gorge,** in Cascade Locks (541/374-8427, www.sternwheeler.com). Each two-hour cruise concentrates on a different aspect of Gorge heritage (Lewis and Clark, Oregon Trail, etc.), with the option of dinner cruises nightly and brunch sailings on weekends. The basic sightseeing cruise starts at $25 adult.

---

maiden voyage dates back to 1862 when it replaced the 4.5-mile portage with a rail route around the Cascades.

Take a walk over to the old locks. Begun in 1878 to circumnavigate the steep gradient of the river, they were completed in 1896. By the time the Cascade shipping locks were completed, however, river traffic had unfortunately decreased due to cargo being sent by train, so the effects of altering the river flow here were negligible.

HIKING

The following hikes require a $30 annual Northwest Forest Pass or $5 per vehicle day pass. (See *User Fees and Passes* in the *Background* chapter for more information.)

Wahclella Falls and Old Columbia River Highway Hiker-Biker Trail

The best short hike in the Gorge that doesn't involve significant elevation gain is the walk along Tanner Creek to Wahclella Falls. After a mile of walking you've reached the terminus of the canyon framing the creek. En route, the gently hilly pathway shows off this pretty steep-walled arroyo to great advantage, but the destination is better than the journey.

In a scene evocative of a Japanese brush-stroke painting, a waterfall pours down dramatically at canyon's end, seen to best advantage from a bridge over the creek. While the trail on the other side of the stream is worthwhile, it doesn't loop all the way back to the parking lot so you'll have to retrace your steps. From I-84 eastbound, reach the trailhead by taking the Bonneville Dam Exit (Exit 40) and making a right at the bottom of the exit ramp into a small parking lot (instead of a left under the tunnel to Bonneville Dam).

From this same parking lot you may access a resuscitated portion of the Columbia River Highway by heading east. However, with lanes barely wide enough to accommodate a golf cart you'll have to leave the car behind. The state decided to re-pave this section of the old road for hikers and bikers, recreating the arched guardrails, bridges, viaducts, and tunnels between here and Cascades Locks to join the surviving ones. In addition to the ornate stonework, the curving, undulating roadbed blasted out of the mountainside before 1920 offers unsurpassed views.

While the Historic Highway parallels the interstate, its elevated perspective on the river and surrounding architectural artistry are a refreshing change of pace from the modern thoroughfare. The highlight of the route is a reproduction of the Toothrock Viaduct annotated by plaques and heritage markers. After exiting this section of the highway via a stairway into the parking lot of the Eagle Creek Fish Hatchery, head east a short distance to the second leg of this hiker-biker trail. The Eagle Creek–to–Cascades Lock section is highlighted by a pretty waterfall at the beginning and a well-rendered tunnel near the end. The distance between Bonneville and Cascades Locks is around four miles.

◖ Eagle Creek Trail

Hikes up a spectacular side canyon of the Gorge are the highlight of this popular recreational area. The Eagle Creek Trail #440, constructed in 1915, was a kind of engineering feat. Volunteers blasted ledges for trails along vertical cliffs, spanned a deep chasm with a suspension bridge, and burrowed a 120-foot tunnel behind a waterfall. If you have time for only one-day hike in the Gorge, this should be it.

The classic day hike into Eagle Creek leads up along the face of a cliff to a viewpoint over Met-

lano Falls. Part of the trail then drops back to a streamside near Punchbowl Falls, a good spot to break for lunch and to splash in pools of cool water. Casual day hikers can return at this point; the hike is an easy 4.5-mile roundtrip stroll.

More ambitious hikers can continue along to High Bridge, a suspension bridge spanning a deep crevice, and Tunnel Falls, so named because of the 120-foot tunnel blasted into the rock behind the falls. Work your way through the tunnel for great views up and down Eagle Creek's canyon. The round-trip hike from the trailhead to High Bridge is 6.5 miles; to Tunnel Falls and back, a strenuous 12 miles.

Be warned that the Eagle Creek Trail is very popular. Try to avoid summer weekends when the trail throngs with hikers. Some sections of the trail inch along vertical cliffs, with cable handrails drilled into the cliff-side for safety. This isn't a good trail for unsupervised children or unleashed pets.

Wildflowers spring up in April and linger on into August in the higher elevations. Many one-of-a-kinds are species left over from a previous glacial period that have adapted because of the shade and moisture on the south side of the Gorge. Almost two dozen varieties of fern, trillium, beargrass, yellow arnica, penstemon, monkeyflower, and devil's club are among the more common species here.

As a prelude to hiking Eagle Creek or one of several other trails in the area, you might want to wander an informative interpretive loop of less than a mile. Just cross the footbridge on the approach road to the Eagle Creek Trailhead over to the other side of the river. After crossing the bridge, follow the markers that describe the region's mixed-conifer forest at various elevations. At trail's end, you might want to take on the steep two-mile trail to Wauna Point. While this trail isn't as visually arresting as other area jaunts, the view of the Columbia River and Gorge at the summit makes the effort worthwhile.

CAMPING

There's no shortage of options for campers in this area. Keep in mind the western Gorge is

Portland's backyard and can be very crowded, so avoid peak times when possible. In addition to first-come, first-served Ainsworth State Park (see *Camping* in the *Portland* chapter) several other sites are worth considering. These have been chosen on the basis of location (e.g., near attractions or a prime trailhead) or for special amenities.

While the **Eagle Creek Campground** (541/386-2333) can be noisy and crowded, it's an ideal base camp for hiking as it's close to several trailheads. Reservations are accepted only for groups at this, the first campground ever created by the National Forest Service, in the 1930s. There are sites for tents and RVs up to 22 feet long, with picnic tables, fire grills, flush toilets, and sanitary services available. It's located between Bonneville Dam and Cascade Locks off I-84 and is open mid-May–October. The fee is $10. At the seven-mile point of the Eagle Creek Trail (see *Hiking*, earlier in this chapter), there's a primitive free campground, but it fills up on summer weekends.

Herman Horse Camp (541/386-2333) is a half mile east of Cascade Locks, near the Pacific Crest Trail, and a half mile from Herman Creek. A full array of services including a laundry, a store, a café, and showers are within two miles, supplementing the seven tent and RV sites. Piped water, fire grills, picnic tables, and stock-handling facilities are also welcome additions here. It's open mid-May–October, with no reservations and a fee of $8. There are trails here for hiking and horse-packing. Other attractions include the historic Forest Work Center and nearby rock walls, where visitors can admire the handiwork of the Civilian Conservation Corps.

At I-84 Exit 51 is the **Wyeth Campground,** a beautiful and secluded Forest Service site that was used as a CCC camp in the 1930s. Today's it's popular as a wind-surfing spot, with piped water and flush toilets. Sites are $10.

Cascade Locks Marine Park (P.O. Box 307, Cascade Locks 97014, 541/374-8619, www.sternwheeler.com) has campsites close to the center of town. The museum and the stern-wheeler are housed in the complex. Whatever amenities are not available on site are within walking distance. It's open all year and the fee is $15. No reservations.

Finally, two miles east of town near the banks of the Columbia is the Cascade Locks **KOA Kampground** (841 N.W. Forest Ln., Cascade Locks 97014, information 541/374-8668, reservations 800/562-8698). Open February–November 30, this private campground features the basics plus a spa (hot tub/sauna), hot showers, and a heated swimming pool for $22 per tent site, $26–28 for RVs, and $3 each extra person. Kamping Kabins—one room (queen bed and a bunk bed) or two room (queen bed and two sets of bunks)—rent for $45 and $53 per night, respectively (bring your own linens, pillows, towels, sleeping bag, etc.). Kabins fill up quickly, especially on weekends, so reserve well in advance. To get there, take U.S. 30 east from town, and turn left onto Forest Lane. Proceed 1.2 miles down and you'll see the Kampground on the left.

ACCOMMODATIONS AND FOOD

If the best view of the Columbia from a hotel room is important to you, then make reservations at Cascade Locks' **Best Western Columbia River Inn** (735 Wa-Na-Pa St., 541/374-8777 or 800/595-7108, www.best western.com/columbiariverinn, doubles from $89). Some rooms have hot tubs and all rooms have microwaves and refrigerators. Many rooms also have balconies. In addition to views, there's a health club with a whirlpool, pool, and exercise facilities. With the Char-burger restaurant next door and the Marine Park down the street, this property has an excellent location.

Forget health food and haute cuisine until you get to Hood River. In Cascade Locks, you get down-home country cookin'—and lots of it—at a decent price.

The **Charburger** (745 Wa-Na-Pa St., 541/374-8477) is near the Bridge of the Gods at the beginning of town. This is a great place if you're on the go and don't want to spend a fortune for a quick bite. In addition to an extensive salad bar and a bakery, there is a cafeteria line specializing in "home-baked" (and it tastes that way) chicken, omelettes cooked to order, and other wholesome but unexotic dishes at low prices.

East Wind Ice Cream (located between the Charburger and Marine Park) is a traditional stop for families on a Columbia River Gorge Sunday drive.

The **Salmon Row Pub** (corner of Wa-Na-Pa and Regulator Streets, 541/374-8511) is a small dark brewpub whose smoked salmon chowder, pizza, and sandwiches fill you up on the cheap.

INFORMATION

In addition to the Marine Park Visitors Center, the **Port of Cascade Locks Tourism Committee** (P.O. Box 355, Cascade Locks 97014, 541/374-8619) can provide help.

Hood River

In the past, Hood River was known to the traveling public primarily as the start of a scenic drive through the orchard country beneath the snowcapped backdrop of Mount Hood, Oregon's highest peak. Since the early 1980s, however, well-heeled adherents of windsurfing have transformed this town into an outdoor recreation mecca. Instead of just the traditional dependence on cherry, apple, peach, and pear production, Hood River now rakes in tens of millions of dollars annually from the presence of "boardheads."

The fury of the winds derives from the heat of the eastern desert drawing in the Pacific westerlies. The confining contours of the Gorge dam up these air masses and precipitate their gusty release. Many local business owners are familiar with the "20-knot clause," permitting their workers time off to "catch a blow" when the winds are "nukin'" at this speed.

Bounded by picturesque orchard country and the Columbia River with the snowcapped volcanoes serving as distant backdrops, this town of 6,000 enjoys a magnificent setting. The main thoroughfare, Oak Street (which becomes Cascade Street as you head west) is set on a plateau between the riverfront marine park to the north and streets running up the Cascade foothills to the south. New brick facades dress up old storefronts, and casual attire and sandals predominate.

History

Dr. Herbert Krieger, curator of the Smithsonian Institution, came here in 1934 to excavate alongside a stream that once ran between 13th, Oak, and State Streets. Arrowheads and artifacts told of native presence here, but the discovery of 30 ash pits of the type found in Chinook tepees indicated that at one time there had been a village in the area of present-day downtown Hood River. Another dig in Mosier a few miles east of Hood River unearthed an ancient cemetery. Many coins of diverse origin were found here, probably taken by the natives in trade. These included Chinese coins, possibly from Warrendale salmon cannery workers. There were also Roman coins and a token from the Northwest Fur Trading Company predating this enterprise's early 19th-century presence in Astoria. Finally, Russian flag standards also pointed to a rich legacy of Columbia River barter.

Pioneers began to build farms in the Hood River Valley after the land giveaways of the Donation Land Act of 1850. The rich volcanic soil, glacier water, and mild climate here provided an impetus for agriculture. In 1855 the Coe family came to establish the first post office and planted orchards in the area of present-day 11th and State Streets. Five years later a sawmill was built in the Hood River Valley. At that time, the first census showed that only 70 people lived in the area. The region's first large-scale commercial orchard was established in 1876 specializing in Newtown pippin apples.

In the next decade, rail lines enabled strawberries from the area to gain renown in New

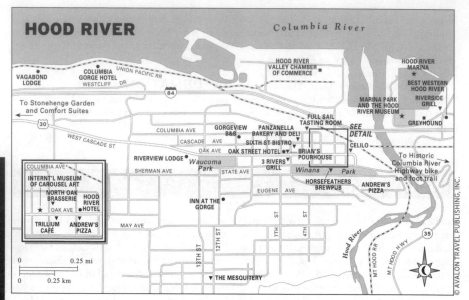

York. Similar prominence was soon accorded Hood River pears and apples in other large cities. Pears took over the produce business when a killer frost devastated local apple orchards here in 1919 and the commercial strawberry crop here was wiped out forever by a fungus in the 1930s. Today, the valley is considered the U.S. leader in winter pears and ranks first in production of Anjou pears. Today 75 percent of the crop is devoted to pears, with apples, cherries, and peaches marketed in smaller quantities.

While the completion of the Columbia River Highway and the Columbia Gorge Hotel in the 1920s gave birth to tourism here, it wasn't until the early 1980s, when windsurfing became popular, that the leisure economy became a focal point of the local identity. On days when sailboarders can't "rig up," many take to the hills on mountain bikes or hit the slopes at nearby Mount Hood, enlarging the appeal of the town as a magnet for outdoor recreationists.

SIGHTS

Downtown Hood River is a lively place, with many shops and restaurants along Oak Street.

A sense of fun and youthfulness pervades the town, the result of the many tanned, buff visitors who come here for the world-famous windsurfing and kite boarding. A good spot to catch the spirit of the windsurfing scene is at Marina Park, just past the Hood River Museum, at the mouth of the Hood River. From here, lots of river athletes set sail and trade stories.

Hood River Museum

At the Hood River Museum (300 E. Port Marina Dr., 541/386-6772, 10 A.M.– 4 P.M. Mon.– Sat., noon–4 P.M. Sun. Apr.–Aug., noon–4 P.M. daily Sept.–Oct., admission by donation), exhibits trace life in the Hood River Valley from prehistoric times to the founding of the first pioneer settlement in 1854. Native American stone artifacts, beadwork and basketry, pioneer quilts, and a Victorian parlor set the time machine in motion. Thereafter, the area's development as a renowned fruit-growing center is emphasized. The contributions of the local Finnish and Japanese communities, along with World War I memorabilia, introduce the first half of the 20th century. Photos and implements related to fruit harvesting and packing methods round out the historical collections on the first floor. Antique logging equipment, dolls, and remnants of a presentation by local schoolchildren for the Lewis and Clark Exposition in 1905 are also on display.

International Museum of Carousel Art

The International Museum of Carousel Art (304 Oak St., 541/387-4622, www.carousel museum.com, 11 A.M.–3 P.M. Mon.–Sat., noon–4 P.M. Sun., $5 adults, $4 seniors, $2 children) boasts the world's largest and most complete collection of antique carousel art. This collection, which was formerly on display in the Portland Carousel Museum, represents the passion of the Perron family, which has for over 30 years gathered hundreds of carousel animals, rare artifacts, and more than a dozen complete carousels from around the world. A major portion of the Perron family collection is on permanent loan at this museum. Although most examples of this turn-of-20th-century genre have been lost, taken out of circulation, or broken, the museum boasts more than 110 carved animals on display as well as an operational Wurlitzer band organ, chariots, carving exhibits, and many other artifacts from the golden age of carousels. Also included in the museum are exhibits on major American carvers and the restoration process.

Panorama Point

If you don't have time to drive up the Hood River Valley to enjoy the fantastic vistas of Mount Hood above the orchards, here's an close-to-town alternative. Drive to the east end of town and turn south on Route 35. Head south till you see the sign for Panorama Point. After a left turn, head south about a mile on East Side Road and make a left on a road that'll take you to the top of a knoll with views south and west that do justice to the name. Panoramic vistas here afford a distant perspective on the orchards below Mount Hood that have for decades served as a visual archetype of the Pacific Northwest.

The Hood River Valley

South of Hood River, the river of the same name drains a wide valley filled with orchards. During the spring, nearly the entire region is filled with the scent and color of pink and white blossoms. Later on, fruit stands spring up along roadsides, selling apples, pears, cherries, berries, and vegetables. Watch for wineries as wine grapes are the most recent crop to find a home in this famously fruitful valley. Route 35, which traverses the valley, leads up the south and east flanks of Mount Hood, only 25 miles south. On a clear day, this is one of the most scenic drives in Oregon, and one leg of the popular "Mount Hood Loop" that is for many Portland visitors their first glimpse of rural Oregon.

Driving south on Route 35 to Parkdale, be sure to visit the **Hutson Museum** (541/352-6808). Native American artifacts, pioneer hand tools, and one of the better rock collections in the Northwest make it worthwhile. A nominal admission is charged.

Also near Parkdale is a series of **lava beds.** From Route 35 south, go right at the Mount Hood Country Store on Baseline Road en route to Parkdale, then right on Lava Bed Drive. The beds are located a mile west of town. Surprisingly, this lava did not emanate from the slopes

Mount Hood rises above Hood River.

CCLUMBIA RIVER GORGE

THE OTHER SIDE OF THE GORGE

Though this guide focuses on the sights of Oregon, it's clear that the Columbia River has two shores and only one is in Oregon. Cross a bridge and you're on Washington side of the Gorge, which offers a number of excellent destinations.

Across the Columbia from Hood River, the **White Salmon River** cuts a narrow canyon down through the gorge walls as it rushes to meet the Columbia. A number of white-water rafting guides offer half-day trips on the White Salmon, which bounces down through near-constant Class IV rapids. It's a short but exhilarating rafting trip and easily added to a Gorge itinerary. Guided trips are roughly $60 per person and available from **River Drifters** (800/972-0430, www.riverdrifters.net) and **All Star Rafting and Kayaking** (800/909-7238, www.white-salmon-river.com).

The area around Bingen and Lyle is transforming into a wine-producing mecca. The hot summer weather is perfect for growing Syrah, Grenache, Roussane, Viognier, and other wine grapes from France's Rhone Valley. Two notable wineries here are **Syncline Wine Cellars** (509/493-4705) with a tasting room in Lyle, and **Cor Cellars,** on Old Highway 8 between Lyle and Bingen (509/365-2744). Both operations are open for tasting on summer weekends, or call ahead to set up a time for a private tasting during the week. Or just stop by **Gorge Wine Merchants** (218 W. Stueben, 509/493-5333, www.gorge winemerchants.com), a wine shop that offers a selection of many Gorge wines, with many open for tasting. Just across the street at **Bad Seed Cider House** (221 W. Stueben,

509/493-3881) you can taste local hard apple and pear cider.

There's also a winery at Maryhill, 25 miles east of Lyle and directly across the Columbia from Biggs, Oregon, and the **Maryhill Museum** (509/773-3733, www.maryhillmuseum.org, open daily Mar. 15–Nov. 15, $7 adults), an idiosyncratic collection of art and artifacts in a grand country estate. You'd be right to think that a 20,000-square-foot manor house is rather unusual in the Columbia Gorge. Maryhill was built by Sam Hill, an early-20th-century mogul whose family controlled the Great Northern Railroad and who was instrumental in the building of the Columbia River Highway in the 1910s. Atop an 800-foot cliff above the Columbia, Maryhill was designed to resemble a French chateau and to serve both as home for Hill and his wife and as the center of a utopian Quaker community. Although construction began on Maryhill in 1913, it wasn't completed until 1926, as Hill lost interest in the project after it became clear that his wife was unwilling to live in this god-forsaken country and the imported Belgian Quakers found the arid cliffs unsuitable for agriculture. Maryhill opened as a museum in 1940, and has a very good collection of Native American artifacts, an impressive set of 19th-century landscape and portrait paintings, sculpture and drawings by Auguste Rodin, and French fashion mannequins from the early 20th century. The museum also offers classes, lectures, and concerts.

Just east of Maryhill is another of Hill's eccentric constructions. Dedicated to the area's fallen soldiers from World War I, a full-scale replica of **Stonehenge** looms above the Gorge.

of the mountain. Instead it came from a vent more than three miles south and west of town. This flow is thought to be several thousand years old, a fraction of the 30-million-year-old volcanic legacy of the Gorge.

Mount Hood Railroad

Train buffs will be delighted to ride the Mount Hood Railroad (541/386-3556 or 800/872-4661, www.mthoodrr.com), which goes from the old Hood River railroad depot just off I-84 Exit 63 up the scenic Hood River Valley to its terminus in Parkdale, seemingly at the very base of Mount Hood, due to the volcano's immensity and proximity. Riders sit in a lovingly restored enclosed Pullman coach. Also featured are an antique concession car and, of course, the obligatory red caboose. The standard ride takes about four hours round-trip, including a stop in Parkdale. The railroad also features dinner and brunch trains, and many special event rides, such as the Fruit Blossom Special in April and Christmas Tree Trains, bedecked with carolers and other holiday trimmings. The main season is April–October. Fares for the regular excursion train are $23 for adults, $21 for seniors, and $15 for kids under 12.

Wine-Tasting

The moderate climate in the Hood River Valley favors production of cool weather grapes such as pinot noir and pinot gris, while just across the Columbia River near Bingen and Lyle in Washington the microclimate makes possible heavier red wines such as syrah and whites such as viognier. There are five wineries on the Oregon side (and roughly twice that number across the river in Washington), all open daily for tasting May–October (call to confirm opening times during the winter) and all easily found by using the readily available Columbia Gorge Wine map (www.columbiagorgewine.com). In the Hood River area, **Quenett Winery** (111 Oak St., 541/386-2229, 10 A.M.–6 P.M. daily) has a tasting room right in Hood River. **Cathedral Ridge Winery** (4200 Post Canyon Rd., 541/386-2882, open 11 A.M.–5 P.M. daily) is just west of town near the golf course. The valley's oldest winery (since 1981) is **Hood River Vineyard** (4693 Westwood Dr., Hood River, 541/386-7772, open 11 A.M.–5 P.M. daily Mar.–Oct.). The microclimate at this winery is similar to that which produces Germany's Rhine wines. In addition to the rieslings, chardonnays, gewürztraminers, and other white-wine varietals produced here, the area is famous for fruit wines and award-winning pinot noir. Sweet wines, such as Anjou pear, marionberry, and zinfandel are done with great flair.

Cross the Columbia River on the Hood River Bridge (with a $0.75 toll) to Bingen, where the **Gorge Wine Merchants** (218 W. Steuben, 509/493-5333, www.gorgewinemerchants.com) offer a selection of many Gorge wines, with many open for tasting. Just up the street at **Bad Seed Cider House** (221 W. Steuben, 509/493-3881) you can taste local hard apple and pear cider.

Lost Lake

The postcard photo of Mount Hood from Lost Lake, with the white mountain peak rising above a deep-blue lake reflecting pool amid a thick green forest, is probably the most famous image of Oregon's most famous volcano. The lake, about 25 miles southwest of Hood River, is a popular getaway when Hood River temperatures spike.

The 25-mile drive to Lost Lake from Hood River begins on 13th Street, which changes names (Hwy. 281, Tucker Road, and Dee Highway) on its way up the flanks of Mount

---

THE FRUIT LOOP

When in the Hood River area, pick up a map to the Fruit Loop, a 45-mile stretch of meandering highway and back roads that directs area visitors to some of the richest farmland and most breathtaking scenery in the state – along the Hood River with Mount Hood the backdrop to it all. Vineyards, orchards, farm stands, and country stores dot the decade-old route that crisscrosses over the river, beckoning visitors to picnic, tour, or taste-test the fresh produce.

The route is popular year-round, but folks can sample some of the season's ripest pears, apples, pumpkins, and gourds September–November; tomatoes, corn, peaches, and herbs abound in August and September; and farm-fresh berries and apricots ripen June–August. Bike trails follow the routes in some places. Contact the Hood River Chamber of Commerce (www.hoodriver.org) or consult www.hoodriverfruitloop.com for the Fruit Loop map and a list of participating farms and country stores.

A few precautions: Parking can be a problem, so farmers ask that you not block other visitors' egress, driveways, or farm vehicles. Fortunately, parking lots usually afford ample space, as they can accommodate larger vehicles, buses, and RVs. Farmers and concessionaires also ask that you leave the family pooch at home as he or she may disturb resident pets or farm animals.

Hood. About 12 miles from downtown, take a right at the Dee Lumber Mill, where a green Lost Lake sign points the way. From here, bear left and follow the signs.

The lake offers hiking trails, fishing, rowboat rentals, and a small store. There are also campsites and cabins. The cabins range $45–100, with the high-end unit sleeping 6–8. Call 503/386-6366 at least two weeks in advance to reserve campsites and cabins. Come prepared; the closest fuel is in Parkdale.

Late August huckleberry season is a highlight here, but the weather and diminished crowds in September are preferable. In July and August, the rangers have campfire programs on Saturday night. The Lakeshore Trail features a 0.5-mile long boardwalk through an old-growth cedar grove. You'll enter the old-growth grove two miles into the trail, passing eight-foot thick cedars. Pick up a map with natural history captions that correspond to numbered posts along the route.

SPORTS AND RECREATION

Windsurfing

Hood River is recognized around the world as a major center for windsurfing and related sports, equally in terms of gusty sailing sites, related businesses, and the sport's unique subculture. In fact, the meteoric rise of windsurfing in the early and mid-1980s transformed this formerly sleepy rural community into a vibrant, hipster-jock haven. It catapulted Hood River onto the international scene, as evidenced by the whimsical bumper stickers around town bearing the legend "Paris, Tokyo, Rome, Hood River." Blessed by a propitious mix of geography, climate, and river currents, the Gorge was discovered as a place with strong, very reliable summer westerlies (winds going west to east), countered by the strong, westbound Columbia River current.

Three of the top-rated sites for advanced sailors (and for fans) are accessed from the Washington side of the river. Doug's Beach, the Hatchery, and Swell City are just across the Hood River Bridge.

Three distinct windsurf beaches are within

Windsurfing put Hood River on the recreational map.

© BILL MCRAE

the Hood River city limits. The **Hood River Marina Sailpark** is the largest and most developed of the three, including bathrooms with showers, food concessions, picnic area, grassy lawn for rigging, an exercise course, and a great family swimming beach area with sheltered, shallow water for tykes. And, as the name implies, you'll find the largest marina with boat launches here. Beware of shallow sandbars off the shore, and the boats entering and exiting the marina. Due to the offerings here (including ample, close-by parking), this can be one of the most crowded sites around.

The **Event Site,** a newer and somewhat smaller site, is located to the west of the Hood River's confluence with the Columbia. Major events, including well-known competitions, occur here. It has a lawn for rigging and a small bleacher for spectators. These factors, plus a location convenient to downtown, make this an ideal spot for spectators. It provides quicker access to deeper water than the Marina, but it can also be quite crowded at times. Chemical toilets and water are available on site. The

Event Site is located off Exit 63, or at the north end of Second Street.

Several windsurfing schools located in The Hook, named for the shape of the artificial berm built some years back to create a protected harbor, provide instruction in the gentle basin, an ideal location for beginners; once you're out in the main channel, winds can be strong. Other than chemical toilets, amenities are scarce in this area. Instead of a beach, the shore is largely steep and rocky, and the dirt road can get a bit dusty in late summer. Conditions are quite variable, particularly as some places are in a wind shadow caused by nearby Wells Island, a sensitive wildlife area vulnerable to prolonged human exposure. The views to the west (and hence, the sunsets) are just grand.

Access to the Hook is at the west end of Portway, the paved road that first takes you to the Event Site. All three in-town sites charge a $4 per vehicle day-use fee. Call the Port of Hood River (541/386-1645) for more info.

About eight miles west of town, **Viento State Park** offers good river access for sailing in a beautiful, natural setting. The park has a campground, picnic area, restrooms, and water. Spectators won't have a lot of room, but the wind and wave action can get spicy here. Viento is served by Exit 56 off I-84.

In the opposite direction, six miles east of Hood River, you'll find the **Rock Creek** launch site in Mosier. Amenities are sparse, but include chemical toilets. The river is wide here, and the chop can get high. You can reach Rock Creek off I-84, Exit 69. At the top of the ramp, hang a right, then your first left on Rock Creek Road. The site's on your right just past the dry creek bed.

In business since 1986 **Big Winds** (207 Front St., 541/386-6086, www.bigwinds.com) offers board and full rig rentals starting at $55 a day, and $320 per week, depending on the equipment. Big Winds also offers three levels of beginner lessons, which cost $60 each, or choose the "Learn to Windsurf" package that includes all three lessons for only $165. The price includes a wetsuit, booties, and all the necessary windsurfing equipment. There are many other windsurf lessons and rental operations in Hood River, with similar prices and options as those above.

Adepts will tell you that fall windsurfing is best. It's less crowded, the water's warm, and winds are lighter at school sites. It easier to find parking and rigging space at launching areas, and there's a quality of light upon the water with enough clear days to add aesthetic appeal. Best of all for beginners is the availability of individualized instruction during fall. While conditions are generally good at most locations along the river during the season, the best places are in the east end of the gorge, notably around Three Mile Canyon and other launch sites in the Arlington, Oregon, and Roosevelt, Washington, areas.

Other Water Sports

The **Hood River Marina** offers an excellent family swim area and boat marina, and also has personal watercraft rentals. **The Hook** offers a nice area (when the winds and windsurfers are absent) for some gentle canoeing or kayaking. (For information on both, see *Windsurfing*).

Koberg Beach State Park, one mile east of town off I-84, but accessible from westbound lanes only, offers a sandy swim beach in a pretty setting. Be warned, however, the drop-off is steep and not safe for little kids or weak swimmers.

Fishing

The area offers two different types of fishing. You can go for trout in several beautiful small mountain lakes, most of which are west and south of the Hood River Valley. Notable among the latter are Wahtum, Rainy, and North Lakes, all about 45 minutes west of town on good gravel roads. Then, too, there is Lost Lake, whose heavy visitation might detract from its desirability during some seasons. Pick up licenses in any Hood River sport shop.

The other option is fishing the Hood River itself, or the Columbia. The former has good trout fishing and both of them have good seasonal steelhead/salmon fishing. The Hood

DAMS AND SALMON

Beginning with Bonneville in 1938, the construction of the great dams on the Columbia changed the course of one the world's mightiest rivers and the way of life in the Gorge forever. Bonneville and Grand Coulee dams supplied power for the World War II shipyards in Portland and Vancouver, Washington, and Boeing in Seattle. Besides billions of dollars worth of pollution-free renewable energy at the lowest cost in the western United States, other Bonneville byproducts include 370 miles of lucrative inland shipping, irrigation water for agriculture, and perfect windsurfing conditions.

Today, Northwest businesses and residents still benefit from the cheap hydropower but at the possible cost of the greatest salmon runs ever known. Salmon are anadromous fish, meaning they live most of their lives in the ocean, but they breed in fresh water. They are hatched in rivers, then swim to the ocean where they mature. They then swim back up the same rivers they were born in, spawning in exactly the same spot where they were hatched, after which effort the fish die. The great salmon migrations up the Columbia were once so vast and strong that in the 1850s it was considered dangerous to row across the Columbia near Portland – the size and the number of salmon were so great that they could inadvertently capsize small boats as they struggled upriver.

However, this massive population of salmon in the Columbia basin was not immune to the actions of humans. During the 1880s, 55 canneries operated on the Columbia, employing such then-new technologies as the salmon wheel, a Ferris wheel-like scooping device that extracted salmon from the river in such large numbers that the wheels were banned in the first decades of the 20th century. Starting with Bonneville Dam, the hydroelectric dams on the Columbia served as enormous barricades to the natural migrations of these fish, resulting in drastically smaller salmon populations. While hundreds of millions of dollars have been spent on research and efforts to mitigate the ill effects posed by the dams, salmon populations in the Pacific Northwest generally continue to decline. Not all the news is bad: The Columbia Basin chinook salmon run consisted of less than a million fish for much of the 1990s, though the numbers have been trending upwards since 2000. By contrast, an estimated 10-16 million Columbia River salmon were caught annually by Native Americans in the 1800s.

Polls continually confirm that a large majority of Pacific Northwest residents want to restore the salmon runs, even if financial and other sacrifices are involved. It's as if there is a shared realization echoing the traditional Native American belief – after the salmon, we're next.

River can be accessed from the county parks covered under *Camping* later in this chapter. Call the **Gorge Fly Shop** (541/386-6977) for information. For a guide, call **Gorge Flyfishing Expeditions** (541/354-2286). **Phoenix Pharms** (just off Rte. 35, 10 miles south of town, 541/386-7770) is a stocked rainbow trout pond where the kids are guaranteed to reel in a big one.

Golf

Offering great views of Mount Hood is the relatively new and popular **Indian Creek Country Club** (3605 Brookside Dr., 541/386-

3009). A little farther from town is **Hood River Golf** (1850 Country Club Rd., Hood River, 541/386-3009). It has nine holes (a bit hillier than Indian Creek) and beautiful views of Mount Hood, Mount Adams, elk, and geese. It's open daylight to dark. Come in fall if only to see the spectacular foliage.

Hiking

While the most famous Gorge hikes tend to cluster around the west end waterfall area, the Hood River environs has its fair share of great trails for two feet. Three of these trails are right on the Gorge, eight miles west of town on the south side of the highway, accessible via the Viento Park Exit (Exit 56) off I-84.

The **Starvation Creek to Viento Trail** is the shortest and by far the easiest of the three. Actually a restored segment of the Historic Columbia River Highway, this mostly paved path runs a little over a mile each way. It offers some decent Gorge views but will be of more interest to history buffs who want to retrace extant remnants of the old highway. This trail also provides access to the other two trails in the area.

Both the **Mount Defiance Trail** (Trail 413) and **Starvation Ridge Trail** (Trail 414) used to be accessible through the Starvation Creek rest stop exit of the highway, which is now closed. So walk the Starvation Creek to Viento Trail, then look for signs for either of the other trails once you get to the west side of the rest stop. Both trails eventually head for the same place, converging high above the Gorge just below the top of Mount Defiance. Being the highest point on the Gorge proper at 4,960 feet, Mount Defiance presents a strenuous workout for anyone up for the challenge.

Either route rewards you with spectacular views of the Gorge, as well as old-growth woods and pristine Warren Lake. The Starvation Ridge is somewhat steeper than the Mount Defiance Trail. This long loop is about 12 miles round-trip. A short, two-mile loop is also possible, by following Trail 413 for a mile, then heading east (left) onto Trail 414. This eventually takes you back to the highway where you started. These trails are really best for hikers only, due to steepness and narrowness.

The **Wygant Trail** is reached off the eastbound-only Exit 58 off I-84, at Mitchell Point. Go right (west) at the top of the ramp, then follow the road heading west. This eventually becomes the trail and follows the old route of the Historic Highway for a stretch. The trail eventually winds its way for almost four miles to the top of Wygant Peak, at 2,214 feet. Along the way, you'll pass through some native Oregon white oak groves, mixed conifer forests, and some openings with lovely views.

There are many beautiful trails south of Hood River off Route 35 in Mount Hood National Forest. The **East Fork Trail** offers an easy, but very scenic amble along the swift, glacial-fed East Fork of the Hood River. Accessed from either the Robin Hood or Sherwood Campgrounds (24 miles south of Hood River) along Route 35, this trail is great on foot or mountain bike. It's about four miles between the two campgrounds, and the trail continues beyond (north) of the Sherwood Campground into the Mount Hood Wilderness.

Tamanawas Falls Trail takes off from the East Fork Trail, just about a half mile north of that campground. A short but steeper hike, this trail is uphill all the way to the reward: beautiful Tamanawas Falls.

Perhaps the best place to experience the transition from western alpine conifer forest to interior high desert is **Lookout Mountain** in the Badger Creek Wilderness. This aptly named 6,525-foot peak is the second highest in the Mount Hood National Forest. To get there, drive 25 miles south of Hood River on Route 35 to Forest Road 44 (the Dufur cutoff). Follow it east for five miles up a steep hill to Forest Service Road 4410, marked for High Prairie. This route takes you six miles to a parking area opposite the trailhead to High Prairie Trail (Trail 493).

The 20-minute walk to the top of Lookout Mountain on Trail 493 takes you through wildflower meadows to the former site of an old fire spotter's cabin. Directly west looms Mount Hood. Turn 180 degrees and you face the sagebrush and wheat fields of eastern Oregon. To the south, there's the Three Sisters and Broken Top. West and north of those peaks, Mount Jefferson's tricorn hat rises up. The body of water to the southwest is Badger Lake. To the north, views of Mounts Adams, St. Helens, and Rainier (on a clear day) will have you reeling with visual intoxication.

Mountain Biking

Just west of town there's a network of old gravel and dirt roads that local mountain bikers love. **Post Canyon Road** starts out as a typical paved rural road, with houses scattered along each side. Shortly after its start at Country Club Road, the pavement ends and the fat tire fun begins. Several side roads branch off from Post Canyon into the Cascade foothills. You can ride for a long time without seeing any buildings, but you will, no doubt, encounter some clear-cuts and other logged areas, so don't expect pristine forests. Also, be forewarned: The road is at times used by groups of motorbikers, so stay alert.

To get there, take Exit 62 off I-84, turn right at the top of the ramp, then take an immediate right onto Country Club Road. Follow this road about a mile as it bends to the south, then head right into the well-signed Post Canyon.

Surveyor's Ridge Trail (Trail 688) traverses the ridgeline on the east side of the upper Hood River Valley for 17 miles. It offers some great Mount Hood and valley views and is especially fun for mountain bikers. The trailhead is off of Forest Service Road 17, which intersects Route 35 about 11 miles south of Hood River and just past the big lumber mill to the left of the highway.

© BILL MCRAE

Camp at Lost Lake and enjoy the view of Mount Hood.

Camping

Hood River County runs three parks with campgrounds in the Hood River Valley.

Tucker Park (2440 Dee Hwy,, 541/386-4477) is only four miles from town, in a lovely spot along the banks of the gurgling, boulder-strewn Hood River. It's the most developed of the three county parks, with a store, restaurant, laundry, and ice machine just four miles away in town. It has 14 RV sites with water and electricity ($19), and 80 tent sites ($18).

Tollbridge Park (Rte. 35, 541/387-6888) is also set along the Hood River but in the upper valley. It's 17 miles south of Hood River. It offers showers and two grocery stores a short distance away. Full hookup sites are $20, $19 for water/electric, and $18 for tent sites.

Routson Park (off Rte. 35, 541/387-6888) sits along a roaring stretch of the Hood River's East Fork, at the gateway to the Mount Hood National Forest. It provides a more rustic setting higher in the mountains, only 25 minutes from town. For the 20 campsites, amenities are

more sparse (flush toilets and drinking water available), and trailers are not recommended. Only $10 per site.

Oregon State Parks offers two full-service campgrounds right on the Columbia River. **Viento State Park** is eight miles west of Hood River on the river side of I-84 (800/551-6949 or 800/452-5687). From mid-April to late October, you'll pay $14–16 for one of the 57 sites with water and electric, or $14 to pitch your tent at the other 18 sites. Viento also offers direct recreational access to the mighty Columbia.

Memaloose State Park (11 miles east of Hood River on I-84, 800/452-5687) is accessible from westbound lanes of I-84 only. On the Columbia with limited river access, the park offers 43 full hookup sites and 67 tent spaces, showers, and an RV dump station. Sites are $16–20. It's only fair to mention that both of these campgrounds are not far from a main freight train line; in other words, expect to hear the trains go by, even at night.

The private **Sunset RV Park and Campground** (in town at 2300 West Cascade,

541/386-6098), with a laundry on the premises, has hookup sites for 21 RVs.

There are several nice but semiprimitive forest service campgrounds in the Mount Hood National Forest, which surrounds the valley on three sides. All are in pleasant settings. Call the Hood River Ranger Station for information (6780 Rte. 35, 541/352-6002). Some of the Forest Service campgrounds south of town are Sherwood and Robin Hood, both on Route 35, Laurence Lake (off Forest Rd. 2840), and Lost Lake.

EVENTS

The third weekend in April, **Hood River Blossom Festival** (Hood River Chamber of Commerce, 541/386-2000 or 800/366-3530, www.hoodriver.org) celebrates breathtaking views of the valley's orchards in bloom. Arts and crafts, dinners, and the seasonal opening of the Mount Hood Railroad are some of the highlights.

The fall counterpart to the spring Blossom Festival is the **Hood River Valley Harvest Fest** (541/386-2000 or 800/366-3530). On the second or third weekend in October, the valley welcomes visitors for two days of entertainment, crafts, fresh locally grown produce, and colorful foliage. The apples and pears are ripe, and admission is free. Hood River is the winter pear (Anjou) capital of the world and produces Bartlett, comice, bosc, and other varieties at different times of the year. Cherries, peaches, and apples round out this horn of plenty. Newton pippin apples are another renowned Hood River product. The 15,000 acres of orchards are still the leading economic factor in the county, with Diamond Packing the leading pear-shipper in the United States.

ACCOMMODATIONS

Finding a room in Hood River in the summer isn't easy, and the rates reflect the area's popularity. Nevertheless, the area has a surprising variety of good, relatively reasonable places to stay. All prices listed here are summer rates; remember to add a 9 percent room tax within the city of Hood River.

The ◖ **Vagabond Lodge** (4070 Westcliff Dr., 541/386-2992, www.vagabondlodge.com, doubles from $59) has lovely landscaped grounds with a playground for kids, and is set back from the highway. Three rooms have full kitchens, and a number have large stone fireplaces. The best are the view rooms (extra charge), which take in an eye-popping vista of the Gorge. Vagabond Lodge is also right next to the Charburger, a basic family-fare type restaurant, with cheap but filling breakfasts.

On the west end of Hood River, about a mile from downtown, **Comfort Suites** (2625 W. Cascade, 541/308-1000, doubles from $119) is the newest hotel in the area. It offers immaculate rooms and amenities such as a pool/spa and some suites with kitchens. **Riverview Lodge** (1505 Oak St., 541/386-8719, www.riverviewforyou.com, doubles from $65) has some suites with kitchens, plus a pool. Both these hotels are within easy walking distance of Cascade Commons, Hood River's new shopping center, with several grocery stores and eating options.

Summer brings crowds to downtown Hood River.

In the heart of downtown is the **Hood River Hotel** (102 Oak St., 541/386-1900 or 800/386-1859, www.hoodriverhotel.com, doubles from $69), an impeccably restored turn-of-the-century hotel with a first-rate restaurant (Cornerstone Cuisine, see *Food*). Special vacation packages are also featured. The oak-paneled, high-ceilinged lobby, with cozy fireplace and adjoining lounge/restaurant, is particularly inviting. The river-view rooms also face onto the rail lines, so if you're light sleeper you may want to opt for a lesser-price town-view room. All in all, "the Hotel" (as locals call it) is a nexus of activity and the most charming in-town digs to be found.

A large 1909 home right on the edge of downtown is now the **Oak Street Hotel** (610 Oak St., 541/386-3845 or 866/386-3845, www.oakstreethotel.com, doubles from $129), a small boutique hotel with just nine rooms, all stylishly furnished.

If being on the river is essential to you, **Best Western's Hood River Inn** (1108 E. Marina Way, 541/386-2200 or 800/828-7873, www.hoodriverinn.com, doubles from $89) is the only place in town to boast direct river frontage and even a small private beach. Its location, however, next to fast food places off Exit 64 and isolated from downtown, is less than ideal. Nonetheless, the rooms provide great opportunities to watch sailboarders, and there's a lounge and decent restaurant on the premises (Riverside Grill, see Food). Best of all, however, are the heated outdoor pool and spa. There's a complex formula for determining room rates, so it's worth getting on the website before calling to make reservations.

The ⟨ **Columbia Gorge Hotel** (4000 Westcliff Dr., 541/386-5566 or 800/345-1921, www.columbiagorgehotel.com, doubles from $159) is a lovingly rendered homage to the Jazz Age of the Roaring Twenties, when it was graced by visits from Presidents Coolidge and Roosevelt, Rudolph Valentino, Clara Bow, and the big bands. Built in 1921 by lumber magnate Simon Benson, the hotel has been called the "Waldorf of the West" for its neo-Moorish facade, glittering chandeliers, and 207-foot

waterfall on the grounds. Large wing chairs around the fireplace and fresh-cut bouquets in the dining room also bespeak the hotel's enduring refinement. To get there, take Exit 62 off I-84 and drive over the bridge to the north side of the highway and follow Westcliff Drive west.

Spacious rooms with heavy wooden beams, brass beds, fluffed-up pillows, and period furniture clearly demonstrate what was meant by the "good ol' days." The readers of *Condé Nast Traveler* agree, ranking the inn among the top 500 hotels in the world. Rates are high, but a more romantic retreat would be hard to come by.

Bed-and-Breakfasts

Two quaint B&Bs are located in the leafy old neighborhood near the historic center. **The Inn at the Gorge** (1113 Eugene St., 541/386-4429, www.innatthegorge.com, doubles from $100) is a nicely refurbished 1908 Victorian that offers the informality of a sailboarder hangout but in a classy B&B. Three of the five guestrooms are suites, very large rooms with full kitchens. All rooms have private baths. Even if you're not a "boardhead," the large and tasty breakfast included in the rate is reason enough to stay here.

Also catering to sailboarders, the **Gorgeview Bed and Breakfast** (1009 Columbia, 541/386-5770, www.gorgeview.com, doubles from $89, open May–Oct.) is located in a historic house with a great porch view and a hot tub. You'll have a choice of regular private rooms or hostel-style bunk rooms.

Up at Parkdale, near Mount Hood, the **Old Parkdale Inn** (4932 Baseline Rd., Parkdale, 541/352-5551, www.hoodriverlodging.com, doubles from $115) has three rooms, two of which are spacious suites. All have private baths, TVs, VCRs, microwaves, coffeemakers, and refrigerators. The breakfast is gourmet-quality and the peaceful village will satisfy those looking for an escape from the rat race. The gardens, full kitchens, mountain views, and rural setting will get you in relaxation mode.

The **Mount Hood Hamlet Bed & Breakfast** (6741 Rte. 35, 541/352-3574 or 800/407-0570, www.mthoodhamlet.com, doubles from $125) is a purpose-built B&B with the look of a historic home. The large and nicely decorated rooms have all the features you'd expect at an upscale hotel, but with fantastic Mount Hood views and full breakfasts. The B&B is south of Hood River off Route 35, near the little village of Mount Hood.

FOOD

Hood River's status as the premier windsurfing town in North America has brought sophisticated tastes to the Gorge with a resulting spike in restaurant quality. No other small town in the Gorge (or the Pacific Northwest, for that matter) can boast such a roster of fine restaurants, not to mention gourmet coffee and options for vegetarians.

In the parking lot between 5th and 6th Streets and Cascade and Columbia is the **Saturday Farmers Market** featuring local craft and food booths along with live music. Just up the street on 5th is **Panzanella's Bakery and Deli,** serving delicious bread, baked daily, and scrumptious pre-made deli sandwiches (on fresh bread).

A cluster of informal but good deli/lunch/coffee places is located along Oak Street in the downtown area. **Andrew's Pizza and Bakery** (104 Oak St., 541/386-1448) easily wins our vote for best pizza in the Gorge. East Coast transplants will especially appreciate the thin-crusted triangles, so reminiscent of the Big Apple's. Lots of extravagant toppings are available, as well as microbrews and great coffee.

Although the name sounds like a brew pub, **Brian's Pourhouse** (606 Oak St., 541/387-4344, www.brianspourhouse.com, dinner daily, main courses $15–22) is in fact a notable restaurant for locally sourced seasonal cuisine. Few places in town can match the Pourhouse for sheer culinary creativity, and Brian's has become a local hangout for the under-40, outdoor-sports-oriented crowd. The chef offers inventive dishes that combine the best of traditional Asian, European, and nouvelle elements, always with a fresh flair. Chile-crusted calamari is served with lemon

aioli and bison osso buco comes with crispy Nicoise olive polenta.

Another great addition to the Hood River dining scene is **Celilo Restaurant and Bar** (16 Oak St., 541/386-5710, dinner daily, main courses $14–24) with a daily changing menu and an updated lodge look that features hefty wood beams and splashes of soothing color. The food is very well executed, with up-to-the-minute preparations, such as seared scallops with truffle oil and fresh porcini mushroom salad.

Cornerstone Cuisine (in the Hood River Hotel at 102 Oak St., 541/386-1900 or 800/386-1859, three meals daily, main courses $9–19) offers a mix of sandwiches, light entrées, seafood, and Northwest cuisine, with some outdoor seating. This is a fun and always bustling place to eat, with a lovely historic dining room and bar. You'll enjoy such eclectic dishes as pomegranate-glazed salmon with parsnip fries and grilled pear. **North Oak Brasserie** (113 3rd St., 541/387-2310, open daily for dinner, main courses $8–18) is downtown's top Italian choice. Besides a solid repertoire of regional Italian entrées, the Brasserie features delectable appetizers, such as grilled goat cheese and roasted garlic. The roasted garlic and brie soup is the house specialty, and serious oenophiles will be drawn here to sample the wine collection. The **Sixth Street Bistro** (6th and Cascade, 541/386-5737, lunch and dinner daily, main courses $8–16) has a good selection of microbrews on tap and an eclectic menu featuring fresh locally grown organic ingredients.

For great views of the Gorge, climb the steps up to **3 Rivers Grill** (601 Oak St., 541/386-8883, lunch and dinner daily, main courses $12–24) with expansive decks overlooking downtown and the Columbia. The selection of Northwest seafood and steaks is large and well prepared.

On "The Heights" (the plateau forming the start of the lower Hood River Valley, a few hundred feet above downtown) you'll find **The Mesquitery** (1219 12th St., 541/386-2002, lunch Wed.–Fri., and dinner nightly, main courses $8–19), where wood-smoke and barbecue flavors issue a wake-up call to your taste buds. You'll find the best ribs in town here, not to mention steaks, fish, and many other dishes.

The **Columbia Gorge Hotel Dining Room** (4000 Westcliff Dr., 541/386-5566 or 800/345-1921, www.columbiagorgehotel.com, main courses $18–39) looks east at the Columbia rolling toward the hotel from out of the mountains and west toward sunset alpenglow. Local mushrooms, fruits, and wild game as well as Columbia River salmon and sturgeon are featured prominently here. The "world-famous farm breakfast" can't be beat. Imagine four courses running the gamut of American breakfast food served with such theatrical flourishes as "honey from the sky"—Hood River Valley apple blossom honey poured from a height of several feet above the table onto hot, fresh-baked biscuits. This symbolizes the 207-foot-high Wah Gwin Gwin ("Rushing Water") Falls that descend the precipice in back of the hotel. As they say at the hotel, "You don't just get a choice—you get it all."

Two other highly recommended restaurants are ensconced at opposite ends of town. For a special occasion, try **Stonehedge Garden** (3405 W. Cascade, 541/386-3940, dinner nightly, main courses $18–25), located in a historic house in a romantic wooded setting on the west end of town. Stonehedge specializes in classic renditions of aged beef and fresh seafood, served with fine wines.

East of downtown, in the Best Western Hood River Inn, is the **Riverside Grill** (1108 E. Marina Way, 541/386-2200, three meals daily, main courses $8–19) with the best riverfront views in town. The menu features fresh seafood and steaks.

Brewpubs

Hood River and environs has spawned its own mini-microbrew scene, with three establishments brewing and selling their own suds. The most famous is the **Full Sail Tasting Room** (506 Columbia, 541/386-2247), offering beautiful river views with its renowned ales. Hours are noon–9 P.M. daily. The **Horsefeathers Brew**

Pub (115 State St., 541/386-4411), in addition to selling several varieties of its Big Horse–brand ales (the India Pale Ale is recommended), also serves up a full menu of lunch and dinner items at pub prices. Tucked away in the upper valley, in the heart of tiny Parkdale, is the charming **Elliot Glacier Public House** (4945 Baseline Rd., 541/352-1022). They make great beers, such as a Scottish ale and ample-bodied porter, and also serve some dinner items, with nightly specials. It's the perfect place to stare at the awesome view of nearby Mount Hood while you wet your whistle.

INFORMATION

The **Hood River County Chamber of Commerce** (at the Hood River Expo Center, Portway Ave., 541/386-2000 or 800/366-3530, www.hoodriver.org) has an extensive array of maps, pamphlets, and other information about the area. They also have a huge, 3-D model of the Gorge terrain that is an excellent way to get oriented to local geography. Take Exit 63 off I-84 and head north (toward the river), following the signs to the Expo Center. Another source of local visitor information, although limited to outdoor recreation, is the **National Forest Service Scenic Area Office** (902 Wasco Ave., 541/386-2333). To get there, head down 7th Street until it winds around to the left, becoming Wasco Avenue, then follow the signs.

GETTING THERE AND AROUND

Greyhound serves Hood River with three buses daily in each direction, stopping at the Port of Hood River office (600 E. Marina Way, 541/386-1212). Also at the same location is **Columbia Area Transit** (541/386-4202), providing van and special bus service, but not offering regularly scheduled routes in town. **Hood River Taxi and Transportation** (1107 Wilson St., 541/386-2255) provides taxi service in and around the city, using just one cab, around the clock except 3 A.M.–7 A.M. on Saturday. **Blue Star Columbia Gorge Airporter** (800/247-2272) offers airport shuttle service between

Hood River and Portland International Airport. **Gorge Central Reservation Service** (220 Eugene St., 541/386-6109) is a one-stop travel agency that can line you up with home rentals, airline reservations, windsurfing rentals/lessons, and bed-and-breakfasts.

HISTORIC COLUMBIA RIVER HIGHWAY AND ROWENA CREST

East of Hood River, the highly scenic route up and over Rowena Crest is a segment of the Historic Columbia River Highway that remains open to motorists. Another section, between Hood River and Mosier (the western gateway to Rowena Crest) was closed in the 1950s. However, in the 1990s public officials re-opened a five-mile stretch of this route, containing a number of tunnels, to hikers and bikers, making it possible to view the amazing engineering and craftsmanship of the original 1920s highway.

Historic Columbia River Highway Trail

This five-mile long segment of the Historic Columbia River Highway is worth a visit. It provides a great walking and biking experience (car traffic is verboten), with the spectacular engineering feat of the re-opened **Mosier Twin Tunnels** in the middle. Carved out of solid basalt and adorned with artful masonry work, the highway has become famous for the tunnels. They are about a mile from the trail's east end and 600 feet above the river. To start on the east end, take Exit 69 off I-84, turn right off the ramp, then take your first left on Rock Creek Road. Go under the railroad and continue for less than a mile. The parking area is on your left; the highway segment begins across the road.

This segment of the old road was closed in 1953, after years of serious rockfall problems at the tunnel's west portal and the construction of the river grade highway. The State of Oregon has constructed a special rockfall shelter to protect recreationists from the hazard. The trail also features restored original stone masonry work in several places, besides the tunnels. The trailhead parking areas on either end are both called the Mark O. Hatfield Trailhead, just east and west versions. This reflects the instrumental role the influential ex-Senator had in securing federal funding to make this dream a reality.

Access to the west-side parking area is gained from downtown Hood River by going to the State Street and Route 35 junction, then heading up the hill on Old Columbia River Drive. This road actually is the Historic Columbia River Highway (officially numbered as U.S. 30). The west end has a small visitors center with restrooms.

Going west to east lets a hiker, in a mere five miles, witness a rapid climate/vegetation transition zone rarely encountered in such a short distance. Starting on the Hood River side, the highway winds its way through lush, towering Douglas fir groves. By the time you reach the east side of the tunnels by Mosier, you're in a dry oak savannah-grassland ecosystem.

About halfway down the trail, a short interpretive loop trail has been developed, rewarding hikers with stunning views of this varied and beautiful piece of the Gorge. Also, rockhounds will marvel at the dramatic precipice located across the river in Washington, visible from the east end. Locally called "Coyote Wall" it's technically part of a big syncline/anticline system in the area.

◖ Rowena Crest and Tom McCall Nature Preserve

East of Mosier, a section of the Historic Columbia River Highway begins again for automobile traffic, climbing up over a spectacular volcanic promontory called Rowena Crest. For eastbound traffic, this route begins at Mosier, at I-84 Exit 69, while westbound traffic can pick up the route at I-84 Exit 76.

Almost nowhere else can you see both the dry eastern and wetter western faces of the Columbia River Gorge with such clarity and distinction than at Rowena Crest. The dark Columbia River basalt cliffs are derived from massive lava flows 15 million years ago. The terracing of the region was due to the action of the Missoula Floods upon Columbia Plateau fault scarps. More information on the geology and ecosystem is available from a free pamphlet in the drop box on the north side of the highway, courtesy of the Tom McCall Nature Preserve. This 2,300-acre sanctuary on part of Rowena Crest was created by the Nature Conservancy and has trails on the hillsides that are open to the public.

These cliffs represented the beginning of the last hurdle facing Willamette Valley–bound Oregon Trail pioneers. After Rowena, the Gorge cliffs rose up so high that the pioneers were forced to either build rafts and float the then-hazardous rapids on the river, or to follow the Barlow Trail around the south flank of Mount Hood.

Today, Tom McCall Nature Preserve is the site of a mid-May pilgrimage by wildflower lovers. Because the preserve lies in the transition zone between the wet west and the dry east, several hundred species flourish here, including four that occur nowhere else in the world. Included in the spring display are yellow wild sunflowers, purple blooms of shooting stars, scarlet Indian paintbrush, and blue-flowered camas. While the flowers are enticing, be careful of ticks and poison oak. And of course, as with any nature preserve or public park, love the flowers but leave them behind for the next person to enjoy.

© BILL MCRAE

Balsamroot is one many wildflowers at the Tom McCall Nature Preserve at Rowena Plateau.

Accommodations

Mosier, a dramatically situated town of just 400 people, doesn't offer much in the way of tourist facilities, but there is the charming **Mosier House Bed and Breakfast** (704 3rd Ave., 541/478-3640 or 877/328-0351, doubles from $69), an ornate Queen Anne Victorian home with five guest rooms.

The Dalles

It hits you shortly after leaving Hood River. Verdant forests give way to scrub oak, which transitions to sage and the grasslands of eastern Oregon. You've come to The Dalles, a place Lewis and Clark in 1805 called the "Trading Mart of the Northwest." Instead of seeing a Native American potlatch on the Columbia, however, the modern visitor will see 10,000 souls living in the industrial hub of the Gorge. One also sees now-defunct aluminum plants and Google's new multi-million-dollar processor farm, both by the river.

These days, The Dalles focuses on historical tourism as well as an emerging red-wine grape industry and already thriving cherry-growing agriculture. The new Google facility is reckoned to provide about 200 new jobs for the community.

However, for a traveler interested in Northwest history, a complete perspective on Oregon's past is impossible without a day trip here. The Dalles downtown is awash in bits of Oregon's past—the Oregon Trail Marker, the stunning 1897 old St. Peters Landmark, and the historic Baldwin Saloon. Explore the old Fort Dalles grounds and the Fort Dalles Museum, housed in the original surgeon's quarters from the days when the fort was active. Another early landmark, Pulpit Rock, still stands in the middle of 12th Street, just as it did in the 1800s when the Methodist ministers preached to the native populations and settlers. Enjoy the work of local artists at The Dalles Art Center located in the historic Carnegie Library.

The Dalles played a preeminent role in Oregon's early history. Five hundred years ago, nowhere in the Northwest boasted such a cosmopolitan mix of peoples as the area around The Dalles. During the great fall and spring migrations of salmon, the Columbia shores—and particularly those near Celilo Falls, just upstream and now smothered by The Dalles Dam—were lined with many Native American tribes trading, fishing, performing ceremonies, gambling, and socializing. Lewis and Clark floated passed The Dalles in 1905, and later the land route of the Oregon Trail terminated at The Dalles, as the Gorge's high cliffs and rapids precluded further wagon travel along the Columbia.

The first white settlement at this transport hub was a Methodist mission, established in 1838. In 1854 the town of The Dalles was platted, and a town charter granted in 1857. Then as now, the Gorge was the principal corridor between eastern and western Oregon, and almost all freight bound in either direction passed through The Dalles. Steamboats docked at the riverfront; stagecoaches rattled off to far-flung desert communities. The streets were crowded with miners, ranchers, and traders.

The completion of first the railroad and then barge lines through Columbia River reservoirs served to increase freight transport through The Dalles. The area is also the nation's largest producer of sweet cherries, and orchard workers from Latin America impart the community with cultural influences from their countries of origin. Despite the recreational boom of the

last decade, The Dalles remains largely hard-working and practical.

Self-Guided Walking Tours

Shortly after you enter town on Exit 82 (City Center exit), stop off at the **Chamber of Commerce** (corner of 2nd and Portland Sts., 404 W. 2nd St., 800/255-3385) and pick up its pamphlets, *The Dalles: Historic Gateway to the Columbia Gorge* and *Walking Tours to Historic Homes and Buildings.* Take a gander at the restored Wasco County Courthouse next door, which was moved from its original location. This court presided over much of the country west of the Rockies in the mid-1800s. At the time, Wasco County comprised 130,000 square miles, and included parts of Idaho and Wyoming.

SIGHTS

Note that due to homeland security directives, tours of The Dalles Dam are not currently offered, though the dam's visitors center in Seufert Park (I-84 Exit 87, 541/296-9778) remains open.

Fort Dalles

Established in 1850, Fort Dalles (15th and Garrison Sts., 541/296-4547, 10 A.M.–5 P.M. daily Apr.–Oct. $3 adult) was meant to protect the incoming settlers along the Oregon Trail from the large Native American presence in the area. At the time it was built, Fort Dalles was the only U.S. Army garrison between the Pacific Coast and Wyoming.

Of the original 10-square-mile encampment, only a grassy park with the Surgeon's Quarters, dating back to 1856, remains. The wooden structure serves as a museum for armaments, period furniture, and other pioneer items, as well as Native American artifacts. This is Oregon's oldest historic museum, dating back to 1905.

Just down the hill, **Pulpit Rock,** a curious thumb of rock near the corner of 12th and Court Streets, combines geology and theology. From this natural pulpit, early Methodist missionaries preached to the Native Americans. The rock still serves as a pulpit for local Easter services.

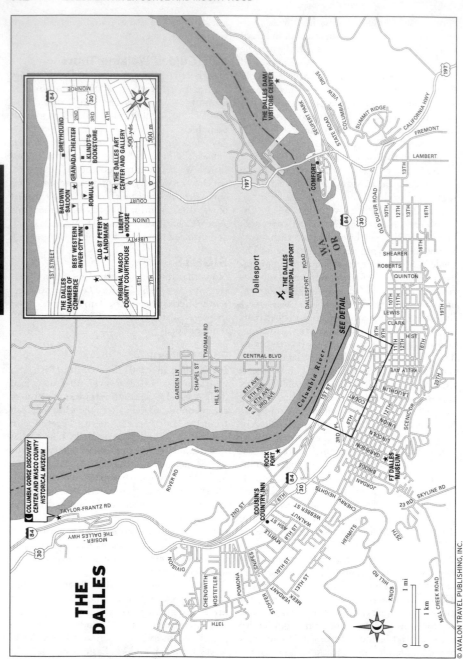

THE DALLES

© BILL MCRAE

the surgeon's quarters at Fort Dalles

Columbia Gorge Discovery Center and Wasco County Historical Museum

The Columbia Gorge Discovery Center and Wasco County Historical Museum (5000 Discovery Dr. N., Crates Point, three miles west of The Dalles, U.S. 30, 541/296-8600, 9 A.M.–5 P.M. daily, $8 adults, $7 seniors, $4 ages 6–16) coalesce the rich historical, geological, biological, and cultural legacies of this region. The Discovery Center addresses the region as a whole, articulating a 40-million-year time line with scale models and videos (as well as simulated "hands-on" experiences) that begins with the cataclysms that created the Gorge on through its Native American occupation, to the coming of the pioneers and subsequent domination by Euro-Americans. Along the way, native plants and animals are given attention along with such diverse activities as road building, orchards, and windsurfing. A decent cafeteria is located on-site. A short walk away, the Wasco County Historical Museum reviews 10,000 years of Native American life, early ex-

plorers, and industry. A single fee admits you to both venues

ACCOMMODATIONS AND FOOD

Conveniently located off I-84 Exit 87, the **Comfort Inn** (351 Lone Pine Dr., 541/298-2800, www.dalleshotels.com, doubles from $100) has a pool, fitness facility, and free continental breakfast. Rooms come equipped with microwaves and coffeemakers. **Cousins Country Inn** (2114 West 6th, 541/298-5161 or 800/848-9378, www.cousinscountryinn.com, doubles from $88) is a high-quality new motel with indoor hot tub, outdoor pool, as well as complimentary passes to The Dalles Fitness Club. Guest rooms have microwaves, refrigerators, and coffeemakers; some have fireplaces. The on-site restaurant and lounge is one of The Dalles' most popular.

At the west end of the old downtown is **Best Western River City Inn** (112 2nd St., 541/296-9107 or 888/935-2378, doubles from $88), with a pool, restaurant, bar, and guestrooms with refrigerators.

Baldwin Saloon (1st and Court Sts., 541/296-5666, lunch and dinner Mon.–Sat., main courses $8–18) is in an 1876 building that's seen a bit of history—it was built as the dining hall for the local railway crews. The red-brick interior houses a repository of early 20th century oil paintings and the 18-foot mahogany bar and the pendulum clock also ensure a historical reverie. Fresh oysters are the house specialty, but sandwiches, salads, steaks, and burgers are also good here

Romul's (312 Court St., 541/296-9771, lunch and dinner Mon.–Sat., main courses $10–24) is a good Italian restaurant with a decor that's meant to recall Imperial Rome. Fortunately, the food is more reminiscent of Tuscany. There is a selection of excellent pasta dishes, and a number of chicken and seafood dishes that provide a bit of variety in an otherwise pretty meat-and-potatoes town; try the seafood Romesco. Romul's makes an excellent Caesar salad and the wine list has an impressive selection of both Italian and local bottles.

THE COLUMBIA GORGE IN THE JOURNALS OF LEWIS AND CLARK

The dramatic topography the explorers described in *The Journals of Lewis and Clark*, as well as accounts of their own undaunted courage, remain to inspire modern-day Gorge travelers. In the course of a day, you can visit all the landmarks noted by the Corps of Discovery during 17 days in the winter of 1805 and 12 days in the spring of 1806.

On November 3, 1805, the Corps of Discovery's journey to the Pacific temporarily halted at the mouth of the **Sandy River** at present-day Lewis and Clark State Park in Troutdale. It was in this approximate location that Meriwether Lewis noted the river's current threw out "emence quantities of sand and is very shallow. Clark attempted to wade across but found the bed was a very bad quicksand." The incident inspired the name "Sandy River," but in actuality there is no quicksand here.

The expedition traveled upstream 1.5 miles on the Sandy before returning to make camp on Diamond Island in the Columbia River, now known as Government Island. This island is now crossed by the present-day I-205 bridge, northeast of Portland. Noting the presence of more game and timber for fuel in the western Gorge than east of the Cascades, Lewis and Clark considered this region a "good wintering place" before their eventual choice of Fort Clatsop on the coast.

Besides the availability of resources for survival, the Gorge's western portal had special significance for the expedition. Their arrival here in early November 1805 marked the first time in thousands of miles the Corps of Discovery had reached an area documented by previous explorers, the 1792 Vancouver Expedition. By combining the routes charted by the British navy west of the Sandy River with the transcontinental route followed by the Corps of Discovery east of this waterway, the United States could be mapped for the first time from sea to shining sea.

An observation on November 3, 1805, by Private Joseph Whitehouse suggests that this juncture of the expedition's journey was auspicious for other reasons:

> Towards evening we met Several Indians in a canoe who were going up the River. They Signed to us that in two Sleeps we Should See the Ocean vessels and white people.

Heading east on their homeward journey in April 1806 the expedition camped the better part of a week on a "handsome prairie" opposite the Sandy to make some "selestial observations, to examine the Quicksand River and kill some meat."

During this time, three men canoed about six miles up the Sandy. Meanwhile, the captains had determined from local natives that they had bypassed a major Columbia tributary en route to their present location at the western portal of the Gorge. According to the *Journals*, the natives also communicated to the explorers that the river drained an "open plain of great extent." Accompanied by seven men and a Native American guide, Clark backtracked to explore the lower Willamette River, making landfall in the northern part of present-day Portland. The discovery of this tributary, called the Multnomah River by Clark, planted seeds for future exploration and settlement in the Willamette Valley, Oregon's current center of population, agriculture, and commerce.

Beacon Rock, the 848-foot core of an ancient volcano, is another prominent topographic feature described by Lewis and Clark. It first becomes visible to eastbound Historic Highway travelers at Portland Women's Forum State Park in Corbett, Oregon. This bell jar-shaped mound of basalt appears on the distant Washington shoreline across a 20-mile sweep of river. It is the world's second-highest freestanding monolith behind Gibraltar. Beacon Rock's name is commonly thought to have derived from its visibility, but on October 31, 1805, Clark noted:

a remarkable high detached rock stands in a bottom on the starboard side near the lower part of this island about 800 feet high and 400 paces around we call the Beaten rock.

Not until the homeward journey in April 1806 did the *Journals* refer to it by its current name. On April 6, Lewis observed that:

it is only in the fall of the year when the river is low that the tides are persceptable as high at the beacon rock.

The superlatives Lewis and Clark used to describe Multnomah Falls echo the adjectives in guidebooks today:

we passed several beautifull casscades which fell from a great height over the Stupendous rocks which closes the river on both sides nearly, except for a small bottom on the South side in which our hunters were encamped. The most remarkable of these casscades falls about 300 feet perpendicularly over a solid rock into a narrow bottom of the river on the south side. it is a large creek situated about 5 miles above our encampment of the last evening. Several smaller streams fall from a much greater hight, and in their decent become a perfect mist which collecting on the rocks below again become visible and decend a second time in the same manner before they reach the base of the rocks.

At The Dalles, Rock Fort, a naturally fortified indentation in the rocky riverbank, was Lewis and Clark's favored local campsite both to and from the Pacific. The corps must have presented a curious spectacle to the native people who gathered around them for here the explorers had become infested with fleas. Lewis wrote in his journal:

[The fleas] are very troublesom and dificuelt to get rid of, perticularly as the men have not a Change of Clothes to put on, they strip off their Clothes and kill the flees, dureing which time they remain nakid.

INFORMATION

Additional information on this area can be had by contacting **The Dalles Area Chamber of Commerce** (404 W. 2nd St., 541/296-2231, www.thedalleschamber. com). **Klindt's Booksellers** (315 E. 2nd St., 541/296-3355, www.klindtsbooks.com) represents another bit of history in The Dalles. Established in 1870, it is the oldest bookstore in Oregon, complete with original wood floors, a high ceiling, and oak and plate-glass display cases.

GETTING THERE

Greyhound provides bus service from The Dalles to Portland in the west and to Spokane and Boise to the east. The terminal is at 201 Federal Street (541/296-2421).

Mount Hood

Oregon's highest and best-known mountain, Mount Hood (or "Wy'East," as the region's Native Americans knew it) rises 11,239 feet above sea level less than an hour's drive from Portland, and dominates the city's eastern horizon in clear weather. Like Japan's Mount Fuji, California's Shasta, and Washington's Rainier, Adams, and St. Helens, Hood is a composite volcano (or stratovolcano), a steep-sided conical mountain built up of layers of lava and ash over the millennia.

Mount Hood was formed about 500,000 years ago, and has since erupted repeatedly, most recently during two periods over the last 1,500 years. Centuries before the first white explorers entered the region, native tribes of the Pacific Northwest witnessed the mountain's eruptions, and the retelling of the events became tribal lore handed down over generations. According to one legend, Wy'East and Pahto were sons of the Great Spirit, Sahale, who both fell in love with a beautiful maiden named Loowit. She was unable to choose between the two of them, and the braves fought bitterly to win her affection, laying waste to forests and villages in the process. In his anger at the destruction, Sahale tranformed the three into mighty mountains: Loowit became Mount St. Helens, Pahto Mount Adams, and to the south, Wy'East became Mount Hood.

The first white men reported seeing the mountain in 1792, when British Navy Lt. William E. Broughton viewed it from the Columbia River near the mouth of the Willamette River. Broughton named the peak after the British Navy's Admiral Samuel Hood (who would never see the mountain himself).

Hood's latest volcanic episode ended in the 1790s, just prior to the arrival of Lewis and Clark in 1805. On October 18, 1805, William Clark sighted Mount Hood, and made this laconic entry in his journal: "Saw a mountain bearing S.W. conocal form Covered with Snow." They named the peak "Timm Mountain" (after the Native American name for the falls area near The Dalles), before they learned that it had already been named by the British. As the Corps of Discovery passed farther down the Columbia, they encountered a wide, shallow river still clogged with sediment from the recent eruptions, and named it the Quicksand River. Today, it's the Sandy River, which flows some 50 miles from the flanks of Mount Hood. About 40 years later, Oregon Trail pioneers opened the Barlow Road on the south side of Hood, the first wagon trail over the Cascades, leading down to the Willamette Valley.

Since recordkeeping began in the 1820s, no significant volcanic activity has been noted, though in 1859, 1865, and 1903 observers noted the venting of steam, accompanied by red glows or "flames." Though the mountain is quiet, volcanologists keep a careful watch on Hood.

Today, the mountain is the breathtaking centerpiece of the Mount Hood National Forest, which embraces 1,067,043 acres of natural beauty and recreational opportunities right in Portland's backyard. Five downhill ski resorts and numerous cross-country trail systems,

1,200 miles of hiking trails, dozens of jewel-like alpine lakes, and more than 80 campgrounds are just the beginning.

SIGHTS

Pull off U.S. 26 on the way up the mountain to visit the **Cascade Streamwatch,** the 0.75-mile gently rolling and accessible Wildwood Wetland Trail. It goes through a beautiful second-growth mixed conifer forest along the Salmon River to several viewing windows built into the shoreline embankment, giving visitors a great opportunity to view fish in a natural river. Trailside fish carvings and sculptures and information placards on forest ecology and salmon spawning enhance the experience, and you may see such species as the giant Pacific salamander, red-legged frog, and coho salmon. While spring and fall spawning seasons are optimum to see the coho, it's possible to see fish at most times of the year. The trail is located 39 miles east of Portland on the south side of the highway in the BLM's Wildwood Recreation corridor (503/375-5646) near the town of Zigzag. A nearby pullout shares info about the Barlow Road, the final leg of the Oregon Trail, which went through these woods.

Farther down the slopes of Mount Hood, the **Philip Foster Farm and Homestead** (29912 S.E. Rte. 211, Eagle Creek, 503/637-6324, 11 A.M.–4 P.M. Fri.–Sun. mid-June–Sept., donations appreciated) is the end of the historic Barlow Road, the place that greeted the emigrants after crossing Mount Hood en route to the Willamette Valley. This working historical farm features a home, an antique barn, a blacksmith shop filled with period artifacts, and pioneer gardens of flowers, herbs, and vegetables. There is also an apple orchard containing varieties from the pioneer era. Visitors can have hands-on experience grinding corn, building log cabins, and partaking of other chores typical of the pioneers. The Pioneer Store features Northwest food, crafts, and history-oriented items. A lilac dating back to 1843 is also of interest here. Shady picnic tables make this site ideal for a family outing. Just pick up Route 211 off U.S. 26 in Sandy and head south for six miles to Eagle Creek.

HIKING

Hikes in the **Zigzag Ranger District** (70220 U.S. 26 E., Zigzag, 541/666-0704 or 503/622-3191 from Portland) are an excellent introduction to the wealth of recreation options in the Mount Hood National Forest off U.S. 26. Whether you're driving the whole Mount Hood Loop (U.S. 26 to Rte. 35 to I-84) or just looking for a nice day trip from the Portland area, the Zigzag District's relatively low elevation and spectacular views of the state's highest mountain can be enjoyed by neophyte hikers or trailwise veterans.

Coming from Portland, take I-84 to the Wood Village Exit and follow the Mount Hood Loop signs to U.S. 26. En route to the trailheads, U.S. 26 is often lined with vehicles during winter ski weekends and summer vacation, with less traffic during the best hiking seasons, spring and fall.

The first stop you'll want to make is at the **Mount Hood Information Center** (65000 U.S. 26 E., Welches, 541/622-4822 or 888/622-4822, www.mthood.info), located in Mount Hood Village Resort on the south side of the highway. This facility will help you get your bearings, with a wealth of pamphlets and an information desk. Pick up the free Forest Service flier "Mount Hood Hikes" here.

Salmon River Trail

Here's a trail that's pretty, easy, and low-elevation, meaning that there's no excuse not to hike it. The 33-mile **Salmon River** is one of the very few protected as a National Wild and Scenic River for its entire length—from its headwaters on Mount Hood to its confluence with the Sandy River near Brightwood. This trail, which goes for 14 miles in the Salmon-Huckleberry Wilderness Area but is most often hiked in much smaller chunks, runs right alongside the river; hikers can expect to see wildflowers, old-growth Douglas firs, and a number of campgrounds. In fall, enjoy red and gold maples; year-round, giant cedars and firs dominate. Access, especially to the lower portion of the trail, is easy. From Sandy, follow U.S. 26 east for 17.9 miles and turn right

BIGFOOT

One of the secrets the Columbia Gorge might share if it could talk would be the whereabouts of Bigfoot, or Sasquatch.

Whether it exists outside the mind or not, the King Kong of the Northwest forests has attracted to the region everyone from hunters and academics to curiosity seekers and *National Enquirer* reporters. Although the notion of a half-man, half-ape eluding human capture seems implausible at first, a brief look at some of the evidence might convince you otherwise.

Native American tribes of the region regarded this creature as a fact of life and celebrated its presence in art and ritual. As recently as the winter of 1991, reports from a remote area of eastern Oregon's Blue Mountains told of more than 60 miles of tracks left in the snow by a large five-toed creature. Scientists on the scene were of the opinion that the pattern of the prints and the gait could not have been faked. A similar conclusion was reached in 1982 about a plaster cast of footprints taken from the same mountain range. A Washington State University professor detected human-like whorls on the toe portions of the prints, which he said showed that the tracks had to have been made by a large hominid.

Reports and evidence of actual encounters abound in Northwest annals, compelling the U.S. Army Corps of Engineers to list the animal as an indigenous species, accompanied by a detailed anatomical description. Skamania County, Washington, whose southern border is the Columbia River shoreline, declared the harming of these creatures a gross misdemeanor punishable by a year in jail and a $1,000 fine.

The unwavering belief in Bigfoot and the native insistence that it's a living entity have naturally met with skepticism. But considering that stories about black-and-white bears roaming the alpine hinterlands of China persisted for centuries until the 1936 discovery of pandas, there could be something new under the sun in the 21st century.

(south) onto the Salmon River Road. Follow this road five miles to the trailhead.

(Ramona Falls Trail

This 4.5-mile loop trail to a stunning falls is one of the most popular on Mount Hood. From the trailhead, it initially parallels the Sandy River. In a little more than a mile you'll come to a seasonal bridge over the river with a pretty view of Mount Hood. On the other side of the river, Trail 797 will get you to Ramona Falls in about two miles. The grade of the slope is gentle throughout, and while much of the trail isn't especially scenic (except for the bridge over the Sandy River, June rhododendrons, and views of Mount Hood), Ramona Falls itself makes it all worthwhile.

Here a multitude of cascades course over a 100-foot-high, 50-foot-wide series of basalt outcroppings. This weeping wall is set in a grove of gargantuan Douglas firs. The spray beneath this canopy of trees can drop the temperature 20°F, making the place a popular retreat on hot summer days.

This trail connects with the Pacific Crest Trail, and backpackers often use it as a part of a longer trip.

To reach Ramona Falls, drive 18 miles east of Sandy on U.S. 26 to Lolo Pass Road, close by the ranger station. Turn left (north) and go five miles up Lolo Pass Road; stay right onto Forest Service Road 1825. From here, you'll take the road about four miles to its end.

McNeil Point Shelter

Though this hike is gorgeous and culminates at a cool old stone shelter, it has some tricky trail nuances and requires a map and consultation, both available at the Mount Hood Information Center. Its trailhead is not far from Ramona Falls, making this is a nice follow-up to that hike. (Between the two hikes, you can camp at the McNeil Campground.)

Start at the Top Spur Trailhead. A half-mile

up the hiking trail, take a right on the Pacific Crest Trail and keep right continuing up the trail to a four-way intersection. Views of Mount Hood and, in the month of June, a spectacular wildflower display—will greet you.

The remaining three miles contain some twists and turns (essentially, you're skirting Bald Mountain) that need cartographic clarification from the Forest Service. Your reward will be breathtaking above-timberline views of the Mount Hood National Forest. This excursion is four miles each way and tame enough for weekend warriors. Just start early enough to give yourself sufficient daylight.

To reach the McNeil Point trailhead from U.S. 26, turn north onto Lolo Pass Road at Zigzag and follow it four miles. Veer right onto Forest Service Road 1828 and proceed 13 miles until you reach the Top Spur Trailhead #785.

Mirror Lake Trail

It's easy to find the trailhead for this popular trail—it's right on U.S. 26 and is usually marked by a flock of parked cars. There's good reason for the crowd. The 1.5 mile trail gains 700 feet in elevation and passes wild rhododendrons and a passel of other wildflowers on the way up to the lake which, as its name suggests, forms a perfect reflecting mirror for Mount Hood. A trail circumnavigates the lake, and ambitious hikers can continue another two miles to the top of Tom, Dick, and Harry Mountain.

Find the trailhead at the footbridge one mile west of Government Camp on U.S. 26. Because of its popularity, try to do this hike on a weekday.

Timberline Trail

More ambitious trekkers will take on the 40-mile Timberline Trail, a three- to five-day backpack usually begun at Timberline Lodge. If you undertake this loop, you'll finish up back at the lodge to cool off in the showers or swimming pool. While the alpine meadows on the Timberline Trail are beautiful, consult the rangers to see if water in the half-dozen creeks

passed en route is too high during the June and July snowmelt seasons.

With almost two dozen trails branching off the Timberline, opportunities for shorter day-trip loop hikes abound. Most of the main trail follows the base of the mountain near timberline at elevations of 5,000 to 7,000 feet. On the northwest side, however, it drops to 3,000 feet and merges with the Pacific Crest Trail. This means that there's snow on the trail for most of the year. Make the trip in the early fall to avoid the crowds; in July and August the mountain meadows are ablaze with wildflowers.

Backpackers must camp at least 200 feet from water and 100 feet from any trail, mountain meadow, or obvious viewpoint.

Buried Forest Overlook

An easy one-mile round trip leads to this overlook, which provides a dramatic view of the White River Canyon, where a thick forest was buried during one of the mountain's major eruptive periods about 200–250 years ago. Superheated gases blew down giant trees like matchsticks, and in the next instant, all was buried underneath a mixture of water, ash, and mud. The erosional forces of wind and water have since exposed the remains of the Buried Forest. To get here, follow one of the trails behind Timberline Lodge up the mountain about a quarter mile until you reach the Pacific Crest National Scenic Trail. Turn east (right) onto the Pacific Crest Trail and follow it another quarter mile or so to the overlook.

Cloud Cap

The best way to get up close and personal with Mount Hood is with a visit to Cloud Cap. There is a beautiful old lodge up here (which is closed) and the entrance to the Mount Hood Wilderness on the north side of the volcano. To get there take Route 35 twenty-four miles south of Hood River to Cooper Spur Road. Drive past the ski area until you come to Cloud Cap at the end of a 10-mile twisting gravel road. The road is passable only in summer months due to snow at that altitude. From here, hardy adventurers can rub elbows with glaciers, walking up Cooper Spur (a side ridge of Mount Hood) without climbing gear in late summer, to almost 8,600 feet above sea level.

SKIING

Wherever you ski here, be sure to purchase and display a **Sno-Park permit.** Most ski shops near the slopes sell them for $15/season, $7/ three days, $3/day.

From Portland you can hear road- and ski-condition reports on KINK 102 FM at 6:30 A.M., 7:30 A.M., and 12:15 P.M. Monday–Friday, December–March. Log on to www.tripcheck. com or call 800/977-6368 for road conditions and traveler advisory information.

Mount Hood Meadows

In addition to being the state's highest mountain, Mount Hood also boasts the most ski areas, five in all.

The mountain's largest and most varied ski area is Mount Hood Meadows (503/287-5438, ext. 182, or 800/754-4663, www.skihood.com, $48 adult full-day, $41 adult afternoon, $27 junior), with hundreds of acres of groomed slopes, terrain parks, five high-speed quads, and half a dozen slower lifts. Even with all the lifts, this place is so popular at times you might have to wait. Night skiing is also popular here.

Meadows is located 10 miles from Government Camp on Route 35. It's often sunny here on the east slope of the mountain when on the west side it's snowing and raining (call 503/227-7669 for snow report and hours of operation). Check the ski area's website for current information about bus transportation from Portland.

Cooper Spur

A popular destination for families and beginners is Cooper Spur (541/352-7803, www.cooper spur.com, $18). Located on the northeastern flank of the mountain, 24 miles south of Hood River on Route 35, it occasionally offers protection from storms and prevailing westerlies, yet has more than enough snow for a good time

cross-country skiing on Mount Hood

© PAUL LEVY

and is affordable. (Depending on weather conditions, it may not be open.) However, its trails are only served by a slow double chairlift and a rope tow. Nordic skiers appreciate the Tilly Jane Trail here.

Mount Hood SkiBowl

SkiBowl (503/658-4385, www.skibowl.com, $36 adults, $22 night, $20 junior or senior) is only 53 miles away from metropolitan Portland on U.S. 26 and features the most extensive night skiing in the country. The upper bowl has some of the most challenging skiing and snowboarding to be found on the mountain. Within the complex are summer venues for bungee jumping, an alpine slide, and mountain biking and much more.

Timberline Ski Area

Timberline Ski Area (503/231-7979 information, 503/222-2211 snow report, www.timber linelodge.com, $43 adult full-day, $36 afternoon, $26 junior full-day, $23 junior afternoon) is known for its high-elevation Palmer lift and its nearly year-round season.

With the highest vertical drop of any ski area in Oregon (3,600 feet) as well as the highest elevation accessible by chairlift (8,600 feet), 60 percent of Timberline's ski runs are in the intermediate-level category. Timberline has the longest ski season in the nation.

Although you'll rarely find powder conditions at Timberline, the 31 runs are so well groomed that Timberline snow is easily navigable. The chairlifts (six in winter, two in summer) are mostly obscured by trees or topography, so you get a feeling of intimacy with the natural surroundings when you're schussing downhill. You can go up two lifts, enjoying a nearly two mile long run that drops 2,500 feet vertically.

The upper Palmer lift, highest on the mountain, is open late spring through fall, when conditions are safe for skiing on the Palmer glacier. The Magic Mile chair, directly below the Palmer, is open to the 7,000-foot level for sightseers as well as skiers ($12).

Located 60 miles east of Portland on U.S. 26, the skiing starts where the trees end. To get here, go east of Government Camp on U.S. 26 and take Forest Service Road 50 for six miles. Check the resort's website for information about bus transportation.

Summit Ski Area

A mile south of the Timberline turnoff on U.S. 26 is Summit Ski Area (503/272-0256, www.summitskiarea.com, $25 adults, $20 under 12 or over 60), the place for families, beginners, and people who just like to play in the snow. You can ski on beginners' slopes or rent an inner tube to barrel down the gently sloping surrounding hills. Several other good sliding hills are close by. To get to Summit, drive through the town of Government Camp off U.S. 26. Beyond the stores and concessions you'll see a large parking lot on the left side of the road with a structure housing a burger joint and equipment rental.

Cross-Country Skiing

Across Route 35 from the Mount Hood Meadows turnoff, **Teacup Lake** offers a great network of cross-country skiing trails, maintained by a club that requests a small donation. Another popular trail that's easy after you get past the first long downhill goes to **Trillium Lake.** Find the Sno-Park for this trail about three miles east of Government Camp on U.S. 26.

Rent cross-country skis and get info about current conditions in the town of Sandy at **Otto's** (38716 Pioneer Blvd., 503/668-5947).

CLIMBING

Mount Hood (11,239 feet), the highest mountain in Oregon, has the additional distinction of being the second-most-climbed glacier-covered peak in the world. Nicknamed the Fujiyama of America, Mount Hood offers hikes that cater to everyone, from beginners to advanced climbers. Another similarity to its Japanese counterpart is that only a short part of the year is safe for climbing, from May to mid- or late July.

Since the summer heat brings on the threat of avalanche danger and falling rock hazards, the time of day of your departure is just as important as the time of year. Most expeditions depart in the wee hours of the morning when the snow is firm and rock danger is lessened. Though you won't get as much sleep, you will be able to enjoy beautiful sunrise scenery as you venture to the top.

Unless climbers are very experienced, it is best to go with a guide. All climbers should register at the kiosk by Timberline Lodge before climbing and check out after the climb. While the climb looks like only a few miles on the map, it takes 10–15 hours to make the trip from Timberline Lodge to the top and back. The four primary routes up Mount Hood—Hogsback, Mazama, Wyeast, and Castle Crags—are all technical climbs; there is no hiking trail to the summit. Having the right equipment means little if you don't know how to use it. (That said, all climbers should rent a Mount Hood Locator Unit, or MLU, available at local climbing shops and at the Mt. Hood Inn off of U.S. 26 in Government Camp.)

Guided climbs are offered by **Timberline Mountain Guides** (541/312-9242, www.timberlinemtguides.com, $390). **The Mazamas**

(503/227-2345, www.mazamas.org), a Portland hiking and climbing club formed on the summit of Mount Hood in 1894, also leads climbs.

CAMPING

Set along the banks of the Salmon River is **Green Canyon** (Zigzag Ranger District, 65000 U.S. 26 E., Welches, 503/622-3191). Here you'll find 15 campsites for tents and RVs (22 feet maximum), with picnic tables and fire grills, piped water, pit toilets, and firewood available seasonally. Green Canyon is open May–mid- to late-September, and the fee is $14–16 per night, depending upon the site. No reservations, so arrive early. The Salmon River Trail is nearby. A store and a café are about five miles away. To get there, go to Zigzag on U.S. 26 and take Salmon River Road (2618) four miles to the campground.

Near the replica of the Barlow Road Tollgate is **Tollgate Campground.** Set along the banks of the Zigzag River, this campground has 15 tent sites (16 ft. maximum RV length). Open from late May to mid-September, the campground costs $16 per night. Because it's close to the Mount Hood Wilderness and many hiking trails, it's so popular that finding a campsite here without a reservation (877/444-6777, www.reserveusa.com) on a summer weekend is next to impossible. Take U.S. 26 one mile past Rhododendron to get here.

Situated on the Clear Fork of the Sandy River, **McNeil Campground** has a good view of Mount Hood. The campground has 34 sites for tents and RVs (22 feet maximum) with picnic tables and fire grills, vault toilets, and firewood are also available. Open May–late September, McNeil charges $12 per night. (First come, first served; no reservations.) To reach the campground, turn onto Lolo Pass Road (County Route 18) at Zigzag and follow it for four miles. Turn right onto Forest Service Road 1825 and follow signs to the campground, about a mile farther.

For a beautiful drive from this campground, go back to Lolo Pass Road and make a right, heading over the pass 25 miles to Dee. It takes about an hour if you drive straight there, but

allow another 15 minutes for photo stops from Lost Lake, located on a spur road. Lolo Pass Road's gravel surface sees a fair number of log trucks during the week, so be careful. From Dee it takes 25 minutes to reach I-84 to loop back to Portland. No reservations accepted.

A popular place for a night out in the woods is **Camp Creek.** This campground has 25 sites for tents and RVs (22 feet maximum), with piped water, picnic tables, and fire grills. Vault toilets and firewood are also available. Open from late May to late September, Camp Creek charges $16 and up per night. Situated along Camp Creek not far from the Zigzag River, the campground has double campsites that two parties can share. To get here, go three miles east of Rhododendron on U.S. 26 and turn south to the campground. Reserve at 877/444-6777 or www.reserveusa.com.

About a mile down the road from Timberline Lodge is **Alpine.** The high-elevation setting here lives up to its name, with snow remaining on the ground until late in the summer during heavy snow years. There are 16 campsites for tents plus piped water, picnic tables, and fire grills. Alpine is open July to late September, and the fee is $14 per night. In addition to summer skiing up at Mount Hood, the Pacific Crest Trail passes by very close to the camp. No reservations accepted.

Near the junction of U.S. 26 and Route 35 is **Still Creek.** Here you'll find 27 sites for tents and RVs (16 feet maximum), with picnic tables and fire grills. Piped water, pit toilets, and firewood are also available. Open from mid-June to late September, Still Creek costs $16 per night, reservations accepted at 877/444-6777 or www.reserveusa.com. The campground has many large trees and good fishing and is close to a pioneer cemetery and Trillium Lake. To reach this spot, drive past Government Camp to Forest Service Road 2650.

A good place for a base camp for those who like to canoe is at **Trillium Lake.** At only 60 miles from Portland, the lake is a great place for city kids. If they're 13 years and under, they don't need a fishing license and may keep up to 10 fish per day. Crayfish also prowl the lake bottom awaiting capture. Families also appreciate the opportunity to cruise the lake in a canoe or some other non-motorized craft. At night, a new amphitheater hosts campfire programs and nature talks. There are 57 sites for tents and RVs (40 feet maximum), with picnic tables and fire grills. Piped water and flush toilets were installed recently; boat docking and launching facilities are nearby, but no motorized craft are permitted on the lake. The campground is open from late May to late September and costs $16–32 per night, depending upon the site. To get here, take U.S. 26 two miles southeast of Government Camp, then turn right onto Forest Service Road 2656. Proceed one mile to the campground. Reserve at 877/444-6777 or www.reserveusa.com.

A spot that offers good fishing, swimming, and windsurfing is **Clear Lake** (Hood River Ranger District, 541/328-6211 or 877/444-6777 reservations, www.mthood.info). Here you'll find 28 tent and RV sites (32 feet maximum) with picnic tables and fire grills. Piped water, vault toilets, and firewood are also available. Clear Lake is open late May to early September, and the fee is $16 per night. Boat docking and launching facilities are nearby, and motorized craft are allowed on the lake. To get there, go 11 miles southeast of Government Camp on U.S. 26, then one mile south on Forest Service Road 2630 to the campground.

A midsized county park called **Toll Bridge** (7360 Toll Bridge, Parkdale, 541/352-6300) is located 18 miles south of Hood River on Route 35. This campground has 18 tent and 20 RV (20 feet maximum) sites with electricity, piped water, sewer hookups, and picnic tables. Flush toilets, showers, firewood, a recreation hall, and a playground are also featured. Open April–November (and weekends during the off-season, weather permitting); $18–20 per night. Set along the banks of the Hood River, this campground includes bike trails, hiking trails, and tennis courts.

Nottingham and Sherwood (15 and 11 miles south of Parkdale, respectively, Hood River Ranger District, 541/352-6002, www.mthood.info, no reservations accepted) are both open from Memorial Day to Labor Day and include basic amenities. Fees for each are $10 per night. Both are located on the east fork of the Hood River and offer good hiking.

If you're taking the back road to Breitenbush, you can bed down at one of the several campgrounds on the shores of **Timothy Lake** (reservations 877/444-6777 or information 800/622-3360). Although this version of the forest primeval doesn't have RV hookups, you'll find 1,270 sites with water, picnic tables, vault toilets, and fire rings. Leashed pets are permitted, as are mountain bikes. We prefer Timothy Lakes to Trillium Lake because it can support more campsites, imparting a sense of seclusion. Of the five campgrounds here, **Hoodview** is the most scenic ($16). To get there, take U.S. 26 about 39 miles past Sandy. Turn south onto Forest Service Road 42 and proceed for nine miles until you reach Forest Service Road 57. Go west on 57 for a couple of miles and you'll see signs for the campground.

ACCOMMODATIONS

Since Mount Hood is only an hour away from Portland, most people return to the city instead of staying at one of the commercial properties on the loop.

◖ Timberline Lodge

Of all the lodgings on Mount Hood, one is nearly as archetypal as the mountain itself: Timberline Lodge (27500 E. Timberline Rd., Government Camp, 503/622-7979 or 800/547-1406, www.timberlinelodge.com, $95–250). This massive log lodge, built during the Depression by craftspeople put to work by the Works Progress Administration, is one of the best examples of the rustic Craftsman style (the style that you'll see mimicked in just about every millionaire's slopeside McMansion) and gained widespread fame when it was used as the setting for the 1983 film *The Shining.* One of many charms of Timberline is the individuality of each room, which range from bunkbed-equipped "chalet rooms," with bath down the hall, to large fireplace suites. No matter how humble the room, it will have the lodge's signature hand-loomed curtains and handcrafted furniture. Guests also have access to a sauna and the year-round outdoor pool.

The lodge's lobby is a good place to visit even if you aren't a guest. Take a moment to admire the hand-carved newel posts, sit beside the huge lobby fireplace, or check out the historical displays. The upstairs bar is a classic place for a aprés-ski or post-hike drink, and the dining room serves outstanding dinners.

$100-150

Adventuresome groups of travelers should check out the **Silcox Hut** (503/622-7979 or 800/547-1406, www.timberlinelodge.com, $100–130 per person includes dinner and breakfast), a spacious but cozy one-time skiers' warming hut perched up the mountain from the main lodge, at 7,000 feet. The hut does have electricity, running water, and toilets, but, with its stone walls and big timbers, has a sense of rusticity. Guests reach the hut either by a snow-traversing vehicle or the ski area's Magic Mile chairlift and have the option of skiing back down to the base area in the morning. The hut's host prepares a family-style dinner (typically, something like lasagna) and breakfast. A minimum of 12 people (16 on weekends and holidays) is required to rent the hut, and it is a popular spot for weddings.

$150 and Up

More conventional lodgings are available in Government Camp. The **Mt. Hood Inn** (87450 E. Government Camp Loop, 503/272-3205 or 800/443-7777, www.mthoodinn.com, $149–169) is a good bet here. If that's too expensive, the venerable **Huckleberry Inn** (Government Camp Loop, 503/272-3325, www.huckleberry-inn.com, $80 and up) has both standard rooms and a slightly funky bunkroom that you can rent for a group of up to 14 people ($175).

Speaking of housing large groups, cabins are a cost-effective way for groups of three or more to stay in beautiful surroundings near hiking trails, ski slopes, and other outdoor recreation. Some of the most popular and most well-situated cabins on the mountain are those

at **Summit Meadow** (503/272-3494, www.summitmeadow.com, $140–200). The five cabins here range from a cozy one-bedroom with a sleeping loft to a large 2-bedroom cabin with a loft that'll sleep you and nine of your closest friends. These cabins are located 1.5 miles south of Government Camp in a secluded setting surrounded by national forest. The cabins are open year-round, and in the winter are accessible only by cross-country ski or snowshoe (about 1.5 miles from the Sno-Park).

Mount Hood Village (65000 E. U.S. 26, Welches, 800/255-3069, $129–200) is another good value. Although it is primarily an RV park, it also includes a cluster of wooden cabins near the Salmon River. Close by the Forest Service information center and bookstore as well as the Ramona Falls trailhead, Cascade Streamwatch, and the Rendezvous Grill and Tap Room, the resort includes a fitness room, and the Courtyard Cafe serving breakfast and lunch. Choose between basic "cabins in the woods" sleeping four and large "vacation cottages" with features like hot tubs and saunas. While this complex does not have the seclusion and feeling of privacy found in the offerings by Cascade Property Management, Mount Hood Village is a good choice for families.

Cascade Property Management (24403 E. Welches Rd., Suite 104, 503/622-5688 or 800/635-5417, www.mthoodrentals.com) posts dozens of enticing offerings on their website, most located down the mountain around the Sandy River. These cabins come with all the amenities you'd find in a hotel room and then some (firewood and kitchen implements included). Rates vary with the season and the size of the unit. A typical summer rate for a 1,500-square-foot unit with several bedrooms sleeping six might be $280 per night. Rates go as low as $160 for small units and to over $500 for larger cabins sleeping more than a dozen people. Many of these cabins enjoy secluded locations and the rental office provides discounted lift tickets to several Mount Hood ski areas. Look for the rental office just west of the Hoodland shopping center.

For more listings of cabins and property management companies, see www.mthood.info.

FOOD

It doesn't really matter what you've been up to on the mountain. Whether you've been skiing, hiking, climbing, or biking, the end result is usually the same by the time you get down the hill. You're hungry. The Mount Hood corridor is endowed with a selection of eateries that fit most any mood and pocketbook. From fast food on the fly to leisurely dining, it's all here.

Far and away, the top dining choice is the █ **Cascade Dining Room** at Timberline Lodge (503/622-0700, breakfast, lunch, and dinner daily, dinner main courses $16–30, dinner reservations recommended). Like most of the top Oregon chefs, Leif Benson of Timberline prepares meals to showcase regional foods—in this case often wild mushrooms from Mount Hood's forested slopes and huckleberries from its meadows. Even if a full dinner doesn't fit into your plans or your budget, lunch in this huge timbered dining room is a hearty treat—take a break from skiing for some polenta served with roasted vegetables or a salmon BLT.

Down the hill at the west end of Government Camp, find the **Mount Hood Brewing Company** (503/272 0102, $8 12). Sandwiches, pasta, chili, and design-your-own pizza can be washed down by microbrews (try their own oatmeal stout), espresso drinks, and local wines. Also in town the **Huckleberry Inn** (Government Camp, Oregon Business Loop, 503/272-3325) deserves mention if only for its 24-hour, seven-days-a-week restaurant and, you guessed it, wild huckleberry pie.

One mile west of Zigzag on U.S. 26 in Welches is **The Inn Between** (503/622-5400), open for lunch and dinner. Here you can tour the taps (a dozen draft beers are available) and enjoy a steak cooked just the way you like it (because you can supervise how it's cooked). If you've got a beef against red meat, the inn can prepare a feast to suit even the most discriminating of vegetarian palates. Seafood specialties, teriyaki chicken, and gourmet sandwiches are also among the many offerings. For lighter appetites, a variety of salads and delicious homemade soups are available.

The Resort at the Mountain has two din-ing choices: The main restaurant **Tartan's** (503/622-3101, breakfast, lunch, and dinner daily May–Oct., dinner entrees $13–29) on the east side of the property closes at end of October, when they shift from high to low season. At the Resort at the Mountain's **Highlands Restaurant** (68010 E. Fairway Ave., Welches, 503/622-3101), the salads, seafood items, and meat dishes (especially the pepper bacon) for Sunday brunch ($20), served year-round at the main resort building, alone would justify mention of this local favorite. Add reasonable prices and a lush setting in the foothills of Mount Hood, and you have the ingredients for one of the state's best Sunday repasts. To get there, turn right off U.S. 26 just west of the Hoodland Shopping Center and follow the signs.

Despite its location abutting U.S. 26, the **Rendezvous Grill and Tap Room** (67149 E. U.S. 26, Welches, 503/622-6837, lunch and dinner daily, dinner main courses $15–20) is easy for eastbound travelers to miss in the heavy tree cover on the north (left) side of the highway. Once inside, the alpine motif and friendly hosts set a mood appropriate to the surroundings. As for the menu, the chef imbues the ever-changing bill-of-fare with seasonal flourishes showcasing fresh regional produce and seafood. Whatever the season, expect to see such signature dishes as rigatoni topped with alder-smoked chicken, toasted hazelnuts, dried cranberries, and fresh spinach, all in a champagne cream sauce. And if you're just in for a burger, fries, and a micro-brew, count on a good, honest meal with such optional dipping sauces as red-pepper pesto. The chanterelles might come from the surrounding forests, and the pasta and bread might come from Portland's Grand Central Bakery, but the desserts are straight from heaven.

INFORMATION

The **Mount Hood Information Center** (P.O. Box 819, 65000 E. U.S. 26, Welches, 503/622-4822, www.mthood.info) is staffed by Forest Service rangers who can provide information about local places of interest. This is really an excellent stop, even for people who travel up to the mountain quite often.

THE WILLAMETTE VALLEY

The Willamette Valley, which was the main destination of Oregon Trail pioneers, is one of the most productive agricultural areas in the world. This is something that is meaningful not only to long-ago pioneers or present-day residents, but to nearly every visitor. Wineries abound, as do plant nurseries and U-pick berry fields. During the spring, the tulip and iris fields are beautiful, especially when (as is not uncommon) they're backed up by a rainbow. Superb green beans, the highest-yielding sweet corn in the United States, and domination of world markets in grass seed and hazelnuts compound the impression of pastures of plenty.

The Willamette Valley is also the population center of Oregon, supporting 100 cities and 70 percent of the state's population. (Geographically speaking, Portland is part of the Willamette Valley, but it has its own chapter in this book.) Nonetheless, once you get south of Portland's suburbs, you'll seldom have the feeling of being in a big metropolis, which is partly thanks to the state's land-use regulations, which have historically sought to preserve agricultural land.

This mix of environmental conservation, excellent growing conditions, and culture is probably best exemplified by the phenomenal success of the winemaking industry here. Best known for the cool-climate wine grapes, Oregon's handcrafted wines are produced in small lots rather than corporate quantities.

PLANNING YOUR TIME

Although it's only about 100 miles from Portland to Eugene, it's worth taking some time to

HIGHLIGHTS

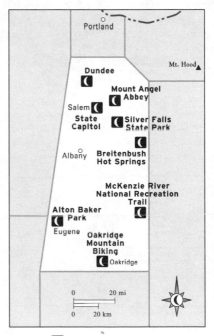

Dundee: Although wine grapes are now grown all over the state, the area around Dundee in Yamhill County remains the best place to tour some of the nation's top pinot noir and pinot gris wineries (page 162).

State Capitol: If a visit to the capitol seems like something that you should've gotten out of the way in grade school, think again. The art alone in the Oregon capitol building is worth the trip (page 171).

Mount Angel Abbey: The hilltop abbey is a good place for both quiet reflection and architectural tourism; the splendid abbey library was designed by famed Finnish architect Alvar Aalto (page 180).

Silver Falls State Park: Aren't waterfalls what Oregon is all about? Here a seven-mile trail passes 10 waterfalls (page 181).

Breitenbush Hot Springs: The rest of the world will slip away as you ease yourself into one of the lovely natural hot pools here. Come for an organized yoga or spiritual retreat, a weekend of personal reflection, or simply an afternoon soak. Clothing, however, is a seldom-used option in the hot springs (page 184).

Alton Baker Park: This sprawling park, just across the Willamette River from downtown and the university, is home to Pre's Trail, a four-mile trail commemorating the late great runner, Steve Prefontaine. The park's trail network hooks up with other running, walking, and biking trails — these trails along the Willamette and up into the nearby hills are a large part of what makes Eugene such a pleasant, livable place (page 201).

McKenzie River National Recreation Trail: Ride the city bus (or drive your car) up the McKenzie River to the start of this 26-mile trail. The McKenzie is a magical river, with falls cascading over lava rocks and lush green streamside vegetation (page 219).

Oakridge Mountain Biking: In the hills just outside this working-class mill town you'll find some of the state's best mountain biking (page 225).

LOOK FOR **(** TO FIND RECOMMENDED SIGHTS, ACTIVITIES, DINING, AND LODGING.

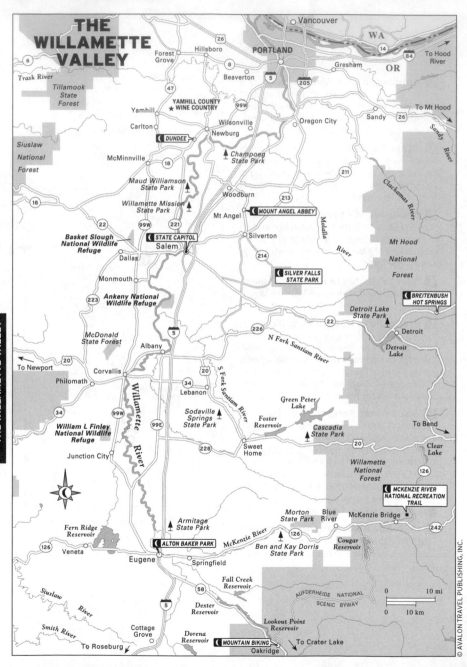

THE WILLAMETTE VALLEY

© AVALON TRAVEL PUBLISHING, INC.

explore the back roads and smaller towns off I-5. For starters, plan to spend at least one day and a night in the north Willamette Valley's **wine country.** By spending the night you'll get to really relax and enjoy a dinner at one of several excellent restaurants in the area. From there, head over to **Champoeg State Park** to take in some of Oregon's early history and a walk along the Willamette River.

Head south and east from Champoeg to the town of **Mount Angel,** where a trip to the local abbey is a highlight. From Mount Angel, it's a short hop to the town of Silverton, which is a good place to stay for your second night on the road. In fact, you can chose to stay either in a local B&B or motel, or head up to **Silver Falls State Park** to camp or stay in a cabin. The park's hiking trails can take a full day to explore, so you might want to spend an extra night in this area.

From Silver Falls, head west to Salem and tour the **state capitol.** This probably won't take all day, leaving plenty of time to explore up the North Santiam River, perhaps as far as **Breitenbush Hot Springs** or the lower slopes **Mount Jefferson.** Spend a night up the Santiam in one of the many local campgrounds or in a rustic cabin at Breitenbush.

Continue up the North Santiam (the road will turn south), turn west onto U.S. 20 then, after a few miles, turn south onto Route 126. Stop to visit Clear Lake, then continue along the McKenzie River. **McKenzie Bridge** is another good place to spend the night; while in the area, hike a bit of the **McKenzie River National Recreation Trail.**

Drive west along the McKenzie to **Eugene,** where there are more trails to explore, a couple of good museums, lots of good eating, and plenty of accommodations. If you still have some time, and especially if you have a mountain bike in tow, be sure to visit the trails around **Oakridge,** up the Middle Fork of the Willamette River, east of Eugene.

THE LAND

Within 50 miles of the fertile Willamette Valley are the Pacific Ocean to the west and the Cascade Mountain Range to the east. At the north, or downstream, end of the Willamette is Portland, and to the south (beyond Eugene) are the Rogue and Umpqua Valleys. East of Eugene, up the McKenzie River and the Middle Fork of the Willamette, the land rises toward the western slopes of the Cascades.

The Native Americans who first lived in the area never cultivated the soil or logged, save for burning to provide browse for deer and soils for grasses, roots, and berries. But centuries of fire in the valley had cleared the land of trees and set the stage for the current agricultural colossus. This practice exposed rich alluvial soils deposited by floods thousands of years ago, earth that is ideal for farming.

The first Europeans who came here in the second decade of the 1800s declined to take advantage of the prime farmland, preferring instead to reap easy money from the fur trade. It fell to the Oregon Trail influx in the mid-19th century to break ground for the present-day agricultural success story.

HISTORY

Before the white settlers arrived, the Kalapuya tribe lived in this fertile area for centuries, supplied with endless amounts of game, berries, camas (a lilylike perennial with a sweet bulbous root) and wapato tubers, and fish. All the evidence suggests that the Willamette Valley people had achieved a remarkably stable equilibrium with their environment. The ancestors of these people were most likely the first settlers in the valley.

They lived seasonally, wintering in the area for more than 5,000 years. Although an estimated 80,000 Kalapuyas once dwelled here, their numbers decreased in the early 19th century due to exposure to diseases brought in by non–Native American explorers and traders.

The first European-Americans arrived in 1812, and numbers swelled in the middle part of the century as Oregon Trail pioneers settled here. To early white settlers, this place offered a second chance and a stage upon which to play out their most cherished economic, civic, educational, and cultural impulses.

The progressive orientation of the 1960s and '70s arose from the Willamette River area's history. Once the river became the transport route for valley produce to Portland en route to gold rush–era San Francisco, prosperity and people coalesced around its shores. A century later, 20 municipalities and more than 600 industrial plants along the river had so befouled the waters that Governor Tom McCall described it as an "open sewer." The next decade's Willamette Greenway legislation put $50 million and the efforts of industry toward a cleanup. The results were the first significant salmon spawning runs in 40 years and a spate of riverfront parks and recreation areas. Although this environmental legacy has not escaped untrammeled, it is still an almost entirely pleasant experience to tour the Willamette via canoe.

Wine Country

Although there's an increasing amount of excellent wine made in southern Oregon and in the Columbia Gorge, Oregon's "wine country" is generally thought to include those vineyards west and southwest of Portland in Yamhill County. This is where the rich soil and long, gentle growing season have created conditions that sustain the largest concentration of vineyards in the Northwest. The slow-cooling fall days engender a complexity in the regional product by inhibiting high sugar concentrations while maintaining the natural acidity of the grape. In summer, Oregon's northern latitude makes for long sunny days without excessive heat, a condition that bodes well for the harvest. These factors combine to produce wines delicate in flavor, low in alcohol, and crisp in finish, despite a tendency toward fruitiness.

A good website focuses on Willamette Valley wines (www.willamettewines.com). Tasting rooms in Oregon range from no-frills, makeshift back rooms to relatively grand affairs. Some of the best wineries don't even maintain regular tasting rooms, but just about every place opens its doors during Thanksgiving and Memorial Day weekends, the two best (though most crowded) times to sample a really wide range of excellent wines.

The only better opportunity to taste pinot noirs is at the annual **International Pinot Noir Celebration** (503/472-8964 or 800/775-4762, www.ipnc.org). More than 60 American and international pinot noir producers are on hand for symposiums, tastings, and winery tours.

Meals prepared by internationally known chefs are also a highlight. The three-day event takes place at the end of July on the Linfield College campus in McMinnville. While the cost of registration, $795, is prohibitive for all but the most serious oenophiles, tickets to the final tasting can be purchased separately for $125. Registration forms go out in February, and the event sells out pretty quickly.

Tasting and Touring

Willamette Valley wineries and tasting rooms are generally open 11 A.M.–5 P.M. daily, but if you have your heart set on visiting a particular winery, it's always a good idea to call in advance to confirm hours and other details. Blue-and-white signs on Route 99W and its offshoots help point the way to such pantheons of pinot as Erath, Sokol Blosser, Yamhill Valley, and Amity.

Good wine and good food go together, which explains the creation of some surprisingly sophisticated restaurants and bed-and-breakfasts in this very rural area. Of late, a profusion of espresso shops, art galleries, and other outgrowths of "big city" culture have sprung up alongside the wine country's grange halls and feed stores. Wine touring has also become popular because downtown Portland sits a mere 30–40 miles away from the state's greatest concentration of wineries. Just take I-5 south of the city and go west on Route 99W, and within 45 minutes you'll find yourself in the midst of filbert orchards and grapevines.

In terms of distance, this might evoke wine-touring routes from San Francisco to the Napa and Sonoma Valleys, but the similarity ends there. Don't expect extensive tours of Oregon wineries and on-site restaurants. Nevertheless, as the Oregon wine country grows in popularity, weekend traffic gets worse every year. Hiring a car and driver or a tour company is becoming an increasingly appealing (and safer) alternative for many wine enthusiasts. See *Information and Services* later in this chapter for details on these providers.

YAMHILL COUNTY WINE COUNTRY

Yamhill County and, to a somewhat lesser extent, adjoining Washington County, are thick with wineries. Although this is known as one of the major pinot noir–producing regions in the world, the area's local wineries also produce pinot gris, pinot blanc, chardonnay, riesling, gewürztraminer, sparkling wine, sauvignon blanc, cabernet, and merlot.

You'll note that this tour starts west of Port-

land in Forest Grove and heads south from there. As much as we love exploring the wine country, we hate driving Route 99W. This route largely avoids it. To return to Portland without driving 99W traffic, get a good road map and from Amity make your way east to the little town of Hopewell and the Wheatland Ferry. Ride the tiny car ferry across the Willamette (and notice here that you're in hop-growing territory) and continue east, following signs to I-5.

Forest Grove

The northernmost reach of the Willamette Valley's wine country is in Forest Grove, about 20 minutes west of Portland. Here you'll find **Shafer Vineyard Cellars** (6200 N.W. Gales Creek Rd., 503/357-6604) on a pretty oak-shaded hillside. In addition to its standard pinot noir, Shafer makes an excellent pinot noir blanc and a sparkling pinot noir.

Don't leave Forest Grove without stopping in at **Sake One** (820 Elm St., 503/357-7056) to taste the local sake and tour the sakery. The sakes, made from California rice, range from the delicate Noma sake, a fresh, unpasteurized wine that's available only at the tasting room to a milky, coconut-scented Pearl or a clean-tasting, very slightly fruity Asian pear sake.

Montinore Estate (3663 Dilley Rd., 503/359-5012) is just south and west of downtown Forest Grove. As is the practice at many Willamette Valley vineyards, the grapes are grown sustainably, using biodynamic practices.

Gaston

South of Forest Grove on Route 47, Gaston is home to **Elk Cove Vineyard** (27751 N.W. Olson Rd., 503/985-7760), one of the oldest and most respected operations in the area. Elk Cove's tasting room is especially lovely, and their pinot gris here is, year-in and year-out, one of the region's best.

Yamhill

At Yamhill, head east of Route 47 on Route 240 to find, in a beautiful rural setting, the hillside vineyards of **Willakenzie Estate** (19143 N.E.

THE WILLAMETTE VALLEY

© BILL MCRAE

Yamhill County vineyards dusted with snow

Laughlin Rd., 503/662-3280). The three-level, gravity-fed design of the winery (a tradition in Burgundy) allows gentle handling of the wine. Along with several different estate-grown pinot noirs, the tasting room pours a lush pinot gris and a crisp pinot blanc. Don't miss this place—even though it's off the main highways, it's a real treat to visit!

East of Willakenzie, in the area known as Ribbon Ridge, are a number of mostly small wineries. These back roads (which lie north and west of Newberg) are home to some of Oregon's finest wineries. **Beaux Frères** (15155 N.E. North Valley Rd., 503/537-1137, open only Thanksgiving and Memorial Day weekends), an old pig farm that has been transformed into a top-notch winery, is partially owned by *Wine Advocate* author and publisher Robert Parker (no, he doesn't rate his own wines). **Patricia Green Cellars** (15225 N.E. North Valley Rd., 503/554-0821, open Memorial and Thanksgiving weekends, at other times call ahead for an appointment) is another small, very well respected winery specializing in pinot noir and sauvignon blanc.

Newberg

Adelsheim (16800 N.E. Calkins Ln., 503/538-3652), founded in 1971, was one of the first Willamette Valley wineries. From their lovely setting on the slopes of the Chehalem Mountains, the Adelsheims have continued to produce good wine.

Another family-owned winery, **Penner-Ash Wine Cellars** (15771 N.E. Ribbon Ridge Rd., 503/554-5545, Fri.–Sun.), is typical of the small, quality-driven pinot wineries.

Two miles east of Newberg, **Rex Hill Vineyards** (30835 Rte. 99W, 800/739-4455) highlights pinot noir, pinot gris, chardonnay, and riesling. Persian rugs, antiques, an ornately carved front door, and a lit fireplace extend a warm welcome to visitors. In warm weather, the garden beckons. Try the winery's excellent pinot gris.

◖ Dundee

At one time, Dundee was known mostly for its filberts (known to most of the world as hazelnuts) and the roadside Dundee Nut House. Now the town has several good restaurants, and a plethora of wineries in the hills above town. But drive around and you'll still see filbert orchards!

One of Oregon's largest and oldest (dating from 1967) wineries is **Erath** (9409 N.E. Worden Hill Rd., 503/538-3318), which in 2006 was purchased by Washington's largest winery, Chateau Ste. Michelle. Erath's wood-paneled tasting room sits high in the Red Hills of Dundee, where beautiful picnic sites command an imposing view of local vineyards and the Willamette Valley. To get there, go two miles north from the center of Dundee until you see a blue state highway sign marking the turnoff near the junction of Route 99W and 9th Street. Ninth Street turns into Worden Hill Road, a thoroughfare that's more or less the glory road of Oregon wine. Appropriately, the road looks out over vistas dominated by grapevines.

Close by is **Lange Estate Winery and Vineyards** (18380 N.E. Buena Vista Dr., Dundee, 503/538-6476), a good place to try pinot noir, chardonnay, or pinot gris. Oregon-style pinot gris is medium-bodied, bright, and acidic, with citrusy overtone—really good with grilled salmon.

An easy stop on 99W east of Dundee is **Duck Pond Cellars** (23145 Route 99W, 503/538-3199), which produces wines from both Oregon- and Washington-grown grapes. If you're a price-driven wine shopper, note that this is the place to pick up some less-expensive (but still quite drinkable) wine.

The intersection of Sokol Blosser Lane and Route 99W sits about two miles west of Dundee. Sokol Blosser Lane leads to a winery of the same name. In addition to its pinot noir, the **Sokol Blosser** (5000 Sokol Blosser Ln., 800/582-6688) chardonnay is especially recommended at the tasting room. Robert Parker in *Wine Spectator* raved about the latter varietal here. Also good, and somewhat unusual, is the rosé of pinot noir—don't turn up your nose at this pink wine; it's fruity and floral, but not overly sweet.

HISTORY OF OREGON PINOT NOIR

If you look at a globe, you'll notice that Route 99 west of Portland shares a latitude in common with many of the great winemaking regions of the world. Nonetheless, it may well be America's coldest, wettest wine-growing region. While Oregon's Yamhill County (located on the northern cusp of the Willamette Valley) is not yet Burgundy or the Loire Valley of France, its early-ripening grapes, notably the pinot noir and chardonnay, regularly vie with the world's best in international competitions. In 1983 Oregon pinot noir beat out dozens of French pinot noir burgundies in a blind tasting, astonishing the French winemaking community. In the competition, Yamhill Valley

Vineyards came in first, Sokol Blosser second, and Adelsheim third. The French vineyard Domaine Drouhin took fourth place, thereafter buying a vineyard in Yamhill County.

Oregon also gained attention from the wine world for its truth-in-labeling law, which mandates that the varietal grape named on the bottle must be 90 percent of the pulp used to make the wine in question (many other states require just 75 percent).

As time passes, maturity of both the vine and the vintner will continue the popularity of Oregon pinot noir. As the vineyards have aged, so too have the winemakers who have learned how to create better and better wine.

Located in an old farmhouse in downtown Dundee, the **Argyle Winery** (691 Rte. 99W, 503/538-8520) tasting room is the place to come to sample sparkling wine good enough to have graced the Clintons' White House table (and a certain travel writer's wedding reception). It is the state's leading producer of sparkling wine in the tradition of French champagne.

Domaine Drouhin (6750 Breyman Orchards Rd., 503/864-2700, 11 A.M.–4 P.M. Wed.–Sun.), also near Dundee, is the Oregon outpost of France's famed Drouhin family, and makes excellent pinot noirs in the Burgundy style.

While cruising the wine country, antique collectors can pull off Route 99 into the town of Lafayette to visit **Lafayette Schoolhouse Antiques** (748 Rte. 99W, 503/864-2720, 10 A.M.–5 P.M. daily) where Oregon's largest antique display can be found in the old schoolhouse, mill, and auditorium. Imagine 10,000 square feet of antiques spread over three floors in a 1910 building. The mall promises it won't sell reproductions.

Carlton

From Route 99W, jog north on Route 47 to the small town of Carlton, where the **Carlton**

Winemaker's Studio (801 N. Scott St., 503/852-6100, www.winemakersstudio.com, closed Jan.) houses several boutique wineries, including Andrew Rich, Hamacher, and Domaine Meriwether. Right in the heart of tiny downtown Carlton, **The Tasting Room** (105 W. Main St., 503/852-6733, closed Tues. and Wed.) pours from the bottles of a wide variety of local producers, many of whom run small wineries without formal tasting rooms. Another good place to stop in Carlton is **Ken Wright Cellars** (236 N. Kutch St., 503/852-7070, www.kenwrightcellars.com), another high-quality winery with chardonnay and pinot blanc in addition to the pinot noir.

Anne Amie Vineyards (6580 N.E. Mineral Springs Rd., 503/864-2991) makes fine pinots and has a beautiful facility with one of the most panoramic views in the valley.

McMinnville

The tasting room of **Yamhill Valley Vineyards** (16250 Oldsville Rd., off Route 18, 503/843-3100 or 800/825-4845, closed winters, open daily Memorial weekend–Thanksgiving weekend, weekends during spring) is set amid an oak grove on a 200-acre estate and features a balcony overlooking the vineyard. This winery's first release,

THE WILLAMETTE VALLEY

an '83 pinot noir, first distinguished itself at a 1985 tasting of French and Oregon vintages held in New York City. Since the 1980s, the winery has maintained this standard.

More than almost any other winemaker, David Lett of **The Eyrie Vineyards** (935 E. 10th St., 503/472-6315, open only Memorial and Thanksgiving weekends) is responsible for shepherding Oregon's fledgling wine industry. Eyrie started up in 1966, and produced the Willamette Valley's first pinot noir and chardonnay as well as the first pinot gris in the United States. The winery, in an unmarked building on the edge of downtown McMinnville, is usually closed to visitors, but you can taste their wine at The Tasting Room in Carlton, or at most area restaurants.

Southwest of McMinnville, on the road to the coast, the **Oregon Wine Tasting Room** (19690 S.W. Rte. 18, 503/843-3787) pours wines from over 80 Oregon wineries. Here you'll find good wines from the Umpqua and Applegate Valleys, as well as those from all over the Willamette Valley.

Step away from the tasting room and into the giant hangar of the **Evergreen Aviation Museum** (500 N.E. Captain Michael King Smith Way, McMinnville, 503/434-4180, www.sprucegoose.org, 9 A.M.–5 P.M. daily, $11 adults, $10 seniors and veterans, $7 students, $6 active military), just off Route 18 south of McMinnville. There's a good reason for the vast size of the museum: It houses the Spruce Goose, the giant wooden seaplane built for billionaire Howard Hughes in the 1940s. The plane (which Hughes called a "flying boat") flew only once, for approximately one minute. In addition to the Goose, the museum houses many other aircraft, ranging from really funky little hand-built planes to bombers to large cargo planes.

Amity

A classic Yamhill County winery is **Amity Vineyards** (18150 Amity Vineyards Rd. S.E., 503/835-2362 or 888/264-8966, closed Jan.). The tasting room is located in a huge old barn on a 500-foot hill looking out over southern Yamhill County to the Coast Range, making for some beautiful sunset views. Amity, which was founded in 1974, is one of Oregon's oldest wineries, and still has a homespun feel that belies its excellent wines.

The nearby **Kristin Hill Winery** (3330 S.E. Amity Dayton Hwy., 503/835-0850, closed Feb.) specializes in a traditional "Methode Champenoise" (sparkling wine). Picnickers welcome.

Amity wines are also featured at the **Lawrence Gallery** (503/843-3633) in Sheridan, nine miles southwest of McMinnville on Route 18. Several dozen other Oregon wines are featured here, as well as the work of a multitude of Oregon artists and craftspeople. Five acres of sweeping lawns and gardens surrounding this renovated century-old building make it even more of a reason to stop. Outdoor art pieces proliferate in these elegant landscapes at every turn. The Fresh Palate Cafe is also on-site, open daily for wine-friendly lunches and Sunday brunch.

Not far from Amity is the monastery of the **Brigittine monks** (23300 Walker Lane, Amity 97101, 503/835-8080). Their chocolate truffles and fudge are highly regarded, and rooms are rented for spiritual retreats.

ACCOMMODATIONS

Given the proximity of Portland, most folks do the wine country as a day trip. Should you care to extend your stay, there are plenty of bed-and-breakfasts and a smattering of hotels to accommodate you.

McMenamins **(Hotel Oregon** (310 N.E. Evans St., McMinnville, 800/472-8427, www .mcmenamins.com, $60–121) has the spirit of fun, good food and drink, and art of the other outposts of the Brothers M empire. A rooftop outdoor bar, comfy (but not exactly posh) rooms (some with private bath, some with bath down the hall), and a sumptuous included breakfast make this a winner. For a good dollar value, ask about wine country packages including a tour of vineyards and meals along with bed and board.

Situated off of Route 18, close to Route

99W, the **Red Lion Suites McMinnville** (2535 N.E. Cumulus Ave., McMinnville, 503/472-1500, www.westcoasthotels.com, $85 and up) provides standard accommodations. If you're traveling with a dog, this is your best bet.

The **Mattey House** (10221 N.E. Mattey Ln., McMinnville, 503/434-5058, www.mattey house.com, $105 and up) combines Old World charm and proximity to wineries. Set in the middle of vineyards and orchards, this 1892 Victorian mansion looks inviting at the end of a day of wine touring. While some of the rooms may be small or lack phones or TVs, you can't beat the Mattey House for coziness and refinement. All rooms have private bathrooms. A homemade breakfast gets your bacchanal off to a great start. To get there, turn off Route 99W between McMinnville and Lafayette onto Mattey Lane and drive until you get to a large oak tree near the house.

In downtown Carlton, it's a short walk from the **Carlton Inn** (648 W. Main St., 503/852-7506, www.thecarltoninn.com, $75–100) to tasting rooms and restaurants. There's a touch of Scandinavian cheery colors at this friendly place. Three of the four rooms share a bath; one has private bath.

Just east of Carlton, the **Lobenhaus B&B** (6975 N.E. Abbey Rd., Carlton,, 503/864-9173 or 888/339-3375, www.lobenhaus.com, $135–155 includes breakfast) is a tri-level lodge on 27 acres, with comfortable accommodations and a peaceful atmosphere. Each guestroom has a private bath and a deck overlooking a spring-fed pond. Guests can take advantage of two common living rooms, each with TV and fireplace.

Nearby, the **Abbey Road Farm B&B** (10501 N.E. Abbey Rd., Carlton, 503/852-6278, www .abbeyroadfarm.com, $195) has elegant rooms located in (no joke) converted grain silos. This upscale B&B is very nicely appointed; the 82-acre Abbey Road Farm has cherry orchards, goats, llamas, donkeys, and gardens; guests can ask about helping out with farm chores.

Just up the road from Sokol Blosser, **Wine Country Farm Cellars** (6855 Breyman Orchards Rd., Dayton, 503/864-3446 or 800/261-3446, www.winecountryfarm.com, $125–185) combines wine growing with bed-and-breakfast accommodations. Watch the pinot noir grow, take a hike, get a massage, or take a trail ride on the resident horses. Rooms all have private baths and Wi-Fi.

The **Flying M Ranch** (23029 N.W. Flying M Rd., Yamhill, 503/662-3222, www.flying-m -ranch.com, $60 and up) is more "Western" than wine-snob. Here you can stay in a cabin or a bunkhouse motel. The accommodations are fairly rustic (only a few cabins have telephones or TVs, so ask if that's important to you) and are nestled into the woods, many with decks overlooking the Yamhill River. Explore the area either on foot or horseback; the ranch's horses head out on the trails several times a day (no rides Tuesdays or Wednesdays).

FOOD

As the wine industry has flourished in the northern Willamette Valley, the restaurant scene has developed to keep pace. There used to be one clearly excellent restaurant in the area: Nick's. Now wine-country residents and travelers can pick from a number of good places to eat.

Make reservations well in advance to dine at one of the best Italian restaurants in the state, **Nick's Italian Cafe** (521 3rd St., McMinnville, 503/434-4471, dinner Tues.–Sun.). The low-key atmosphere of McMinnville's downtown and the 1950s feel of this one-time soda fountain might at first make you wonder about such an assessment, but any trepidation will be quickly dispelled by the aroma of Nick's hearty fare and a wine list that is both extensive and distinctive. As a host to many wine-country functions, Nick is privy to special releases found nowhere else. The latter are fitting accompaniments to such culinary interpretations as lasagna with Dungeness crab and pine nuts or rabbit braised in Oregon pinot gris and rosemary with gorgonzola polenta. A five-course, fixed-price dinner goes for $42 and is highly recommended, although a la carte ordering is available.

Another gem of a restaurant, **Tina's** (760

Rte. 99W, Dundee, 503/538-8880, lunch Tues.–Fri., $9–14, dinner nightly, $20–30) is located a bit closer to Portland. As you're heading west on Route 99 look for a small red box-like structure on the right-hand side of the road across from the Dundee fire station. Tina's uses the freshest Oregon ingredients to create simple yet elegant fare. This place is a gem, as one bite of the pan-fried oysters will tell you. Unlike many of the other great restaurants in the area, Tina's is open for lunch and, though it's not cheap, it's a justifiable splurge. In what can only be interpreted as a good sign, it's not uncommon to see local winemakers hanging out at the tiny bar here.

Just east, where Route 99 meets 7th Street, **Your Northwest** (110 S.W. 7th St., 503/554-8101) is a complex selling a good selection of indigenous Northwest food and crafts. The venerated **Ponzi Vineyards** has a tasting room here (its main tasting room is in Beaverton) and the **Dundee Bistro** (503/554-1650, lunch about $10) is a decent spot for lunch or dinner; it's a good place to stop for lunch when Tina's is closed or booked up.

Red Hills Provincial Dining (276 Rte. 99W, Dundee, 503/538-8224, dinner nightly, entrées about $25) is a cozy, charm-filled restaurant, using only the freshest local ingredients to create awarding-winning French- and Italian-inspired food.

In Carlton, a good place to sit down to a dinner of country-style French food is **Cuvée** (214 W. Main St., 503/852-6555, dinner Wed.–Sun., lunch Sat.–Sun. during the summer, dinner entrées $10–13). Not only is the food in this small restaurant prepared with great care, but it is very reasonably priced.

The ◖ **Joel Palmer House** (600 Ferry St., Dayton, 503/864-2995, www.joelpalmer house.com, dinner Tues.–Sat., reservations recommended) is considered one of Oregon's finest historic homes, on both the Oregon and the National Historic Registers. It was origi-

nally owned by the aforementioned, who was speaker of the Oregon house of representatives in 1862, and Oregon state senator 1864–1866. Jack and Heidi Czarnecki have turned the Joel Palmer House into a one-of-a-kind restaurant that combines their love of mushroom hunting with fine wine. Many dishes include wild mushrooms, and unless you're a really phobic about fungi, they're highly recommended. Located at the junction of Highways 221 and 223 (off of Highway 18).

INFORMATION AND SERVICES

Willamette Valley Wineries (P.O. Box 25162, Portland 97298, 503/646-2985, www.willa mettewines.com) maintains an excellent website. Contact the **McMinnville Chamber of Commerce** (417 N. Adams St., McMinnville 97128, 503/538-2014, www.mcminnville.org) or the **Yamhill Valley Visitors Association** (503/883-7770, www.yamhillvalley.org) for winery and accommodations information.

If you prefer to leave the driving and commentary to someone else, several companies offer tours by bus or car (particularly for parties of four or more). Prices vary widely depending on the number of people, the amount of customization, and whether or not meals are provided: a full-day tour can range $55–125 per person; half-day tours are also available. One particularly well-established company is **Grape Escape Winery Tours** (503/283-3380, www.grapeescapetours.com); tours are also provided by **Adventures in Wine** (503/256-5673, www.adventuresinwine.us); **Eco Tours of Oregon** (503/245-1428, www. ecotours-of-oregon.com); and **Wine Tours Northwest** (503/439-8687 or 800/359-1034, www.winetoursnorthwest.com).

Want to see the valley from a hot-air balloon? Get in touch with the folks at **Vista Balloons** (503/625-7385 or 800/622-2309, Apr.–Oct., $179).

Northeastern Willamette Valley

Much of Oregon's early history played out near the banks of the Willamette River between present-day Portland and Salem. Here settlers made a break from the British Hudson's Bay Company and established a pro-American provisional government. The fertile land here was also the destination of Oregon Trail pioneers. Over 150 years later, these Willamette Valley towns are still mostly small and the surrounding countryside lush, inviting a ramble through history.

CHAMPOEG STATE PARK

Below Yamhill County, just southeast of Newberg on Route 219, is Champoeg (pronounced "sham-poo-ee" or "cham-poo-ee-eck"), often touted as the birthplace of Oregon. The name means "field of roots" in Chinook, referring to the camas coveted by Native Americans, who boiled it to accompany the traditional salmon feast.

Champoeg State Heritage Area (503/678-1251, visitors center open 9 A.M.– 5 P.M. daily, $3 day-use fee) commemorates the site of the 1843 vote to break free from British and Hudson's Bay Company rule and establish a pro-American provisional government in the Oregon country. To get there from Portland, drive south on I-5 until you see signs for Exit 278. This exit directs you to a rural route that goes five miles to the park visitors center. The 568-acre park is equidistant from Portland and Salem along the Willamette River.

The visitors center has exhibits detailing how the Kalapuyas, explorers, French Canadian fur traders, and American settlers lived in the Willamette Valley. The grounds also contain several historic buildings. Adjacent to the visitors center is the Manson Barn, built in 1862. The Old Butteville jail (1850) and one-room schoolhouse have also been

© JUDY JEWELL

the Willamette River through Champoeg State Park

THE WILLAMETTE VALLEY

moved to Champoeg to help evoke frontier life. Just west of the park entrance is a replica of the 1852 house of pioneer Robert Newell (503/678-5537, noon–5 P.M. Wed.–Sun. Feb.–Nov.). Particularly interesting is the second floor, which showcases Native American artifacts and a collection of inaugural gowns worn by the wives of Oregon governors. The **Pioneer Mother's Museum** replicates the dwellings in the Willamette Valley circa 1850. A collection of guns and muskets 1775–1850 is also on display. Besides the historical exhibits, Champoeg features a botanical garden of native plants and hiking and biking trails.

If you want to extend your stay, Champoeg State Park offers six tent sites and 48 sites with RV hookups ($16–20). There are also six yurts for rent ($27). Call 800/452-5687 for reservations ($6 reservation fee). This year-round facility is one of the few out-of-town campgrounds within easy driving distance (25 miles) of Portland. Add beautiful Willamette River frontage, and prime bike-riding on the nearby country roads and you might consider this the consummate budget alternative to a night in the city or a pricey wine-country B&B.

Willamette Mission State Park is also in this area (just look for signs). It is home to one of the world's largest cottonwoods and the charming Wheatland car ferry across the Willamette River.

FRENCH PRAIRIE LOOP

Before leaving Champoeg State Park, pick up a brochure at the visitors center outlining the French Prairie Loop, a 40-mile byway for car and bicycle touring. History buffs, thrift shoppers, and antique aficionados will enjoy the chance to indulge their passions on this drive. French-Canadian trappers settled here in the 1820s and '30s to help the Hudson's Bay Company establish a presence in the Willamette Valley. During the 1849 California gold rush, wheat and produce from this area were shipped to granaries and warehouses in the area of present-day Portland and on to San Francisco.

Churches and buildings dating back to the 19th century have earned **St. Paul,** one of the towns on the loop (Rte. 219), National Historic District status. The Northwest's oldest Catholic church, St. Paul's (circa 1846—some parishioners claim ancestral links with the French-Canadian trappers who were Oregon's first permanent white settlers), underwent a million-dollar reconstruction after being damaged by an earthquake in 1993. The church was rebuilt with its original bricks and was reinforced with concrete. Each July 4 weekend, an Oregon tradition takes place here with the flat-out fun **St. Paul Rodeo** (800/237-5920, www. stpaulrodeo.com), which includes a fireworks display, a barbecue, and an art auction. The prize money is good here, so you'll see many top riders and ropers competing.

On the east side of the loop, **Aurora,** at the junction of Route 219 and Route 99, also enjoys National Historic District status. Oregon's legacy as a haven for utopian communities began here with a Prussian immigrant, Dr. William Keil. He started up a communal colony for Oregon Trail pioneers, naming the town that grew out of it after his daughter. The Aurora colony fused Christian fundamentalism with collectivist principles, garnering distinction for its thriving farms and the excellence of its handicrafts. Despite Aurora's early success, a smallpox epidemic in 1862 and the coming of the railroad (which undermined Willamette River trade in the next decade) provided the catalysts for the town's demise. Keil himself died in 1877, and the struggling colony disbanded a few years later.

The **Old Aurora Colony Museum** (212 2nd St., Aurora, 503/678-5754, 11 A.M.– 4 P.M. Tues.–Sat., noon–4 P.M. Sun. Feb.–Dec. (closed Jan.), $4.50 adults, $3.50 seniors, $2 children under 18) consists of five buildings, including two of the colony's homesteads, the communal wash house, and the farm equipment shed. Items of interest include old tools, a musical instrument collection, and a recording left over from the colony band, as well as quilts and an herb garden.

The museum is easily located by turning east as you enter town. After one block, you'll see the museum, housed in a former ox barn. Sometimes colony descendants are on-hand to answer questions or demonstrate historical objects such as an ingenious spinning wheel devised by William Keil. After visiting the museum, you can take an Aurora walking tour (ask for the free pamphlet) of 33 nearby structures such as clapboard and Victorian houses, and antique shops, all clustered along Route 99E.

OREGON CITY

North of Canby, Route 99E attractively parallels the Willamette River. Jagged rock bluffs on one side of the highway contrast with the smooth-flowing river framed by stately cottonwood and poplar trees. More variety is added by islands in the channel and the broad expanse of 40-foot **Willamette Falls** in Oregon City. As the terminus of the Oregon Trail and the only seat of American power in the territory until 1852, this town is the site of many firsts. Leading off the list is Oregon City's status as the first incorporated city west of the Rockies. Other claims to fame include the West's first mint, paper mill, and newspaper, and the world's first long-distance electric power transmission system. The Oregon territorial capital also was the site of the state's first Protestant church and Masonic lodge.

Ironically, a representative of British interests in Oregon country is credited with starting Oregon City. John McLoughlin, the Canadian-born chief factor of the Hudson's Bay Company, encouraged French-Canadian trappers to cross the Columbia River from Fort Vancouver and settle here in the northern Willamette Valley, inspiring the name French Prairie. To further the development of this British beachhead, McLoughlin built a flour mill near Willamette Falls in 1832. He moved down to Oregon City himself in the 1840s and became an ardent supporter of American settlers who wanted Oregon to be independent of England and part of the United States.

McLoughlin's flour mill set the precedent for other uses of water power here. It also helped attract pioneers who came over the Cascades via the Barlow Road extension of the Oregon Trail. As a result, Oregon City became a manufacturing center. Its river port thrived due to Willamette Falls impeding the movement of merchant ships farther south on the river. Although the development of the railroad and the city of Portland diminished Oregon City's importance, its glory days live on today thanks to National Historic District status. Buildings that date back to the mid-19th century exemplify Queen Anne, Federal, and Italianate architectural styles.

Basalt terraces divide the city into three levels. Downtown is wedged between the river and a 100-foot bluff. A municipal elevator provides transportation between the commercial traffic in the lower part of town and the historic building on the bluff. Years ago, the McLoughlin House was originally situated on the river but later was moved to the heights to make room for "progress."

Museum of the Oregon Territory

Heading north on Route 99E from Willamette Falls, look for the Tumwater turnoff on the east side of the highway for the Museum of the Oregon Territory (211 Tumwater Dr., Oregon City, 503/655-5574, 11 A.M.–4 P.M. daily, $7 adults, $5 children). From the elevated perspective of the museum parking lot you'll have a great bird's-eye view of Willamette Falls. Prior to perusing the diaries, artifacts, and historic photos on the second floor, you'll encounter a timeline that correlates world events over thousands of years to the geologic, political, and social growth of Oregon. This imparts a larger perspective to what you'll see in the exhibit hall. Signposts for your journey through the ages include Native American baskets and arrowheads, a horse-drawn carriage, and the world's first kidney dialysis machine (invented locally). The county collection serves as a valuable complement to the End of the Trail Interpretive Center and historic homes just north of here, and one admission fee gets you into most of these places.

THE WILLAMETTE VALLEY

McLoughlin House

For a glimpse of the glory that was 19th-century Oregon City, take a right turn (east) off Route 99E (McLoughlin Boulevard) onto 7th Street and follow it to the base of the cliff. At 7th and Railroad Streets, you'll see an immense gray elevator scaling the 90-foot escarpment (operates 7 A.M.– 7 P.M. Mon.–Sat. free of charge) backdropping the lower section of town. Take a left turn when you exit the elevator, and a few minutes' stroll northeast along the cliff top will have you peering across a street at the back yard of an Oregon City landmark.

The McLoughlin House (713 Center St., 503/656-5146, between 7th and 8th Streets, 10 A.M.–4 P.M. Wed.–Sat., 1–4 P.M. Sun., closed mid-Dec.–Jan. 31, free, subject to change) is an impressive clapboard-style home of the "Father of Oregon." To spare it flood damage, the building was moved from its original site near the river to this location. Behind it are steps leading back to the lower section of town. The collection of original and period furnishings may not be terribly exciting, but the ranger's ghost stories and historical insights can make it all come alive. In addition, the grounds are lovingly landscaped with rhododendrons, azaleas, and roses. The McLoughlin House is actually a national park site that's part of Fort Vancouver, just across the Columbia River in Washington.

End of the Trail Interpretive Center

The End of the Trail Interpretive Center (1726 Washington St., 503/657-0988, www.end oftheoregontrail.org, 11 A.M.–5 P.M. Mon.–Sat., noon–4 P.M. Sun., $7 adults, $5 children includes admission to Museum of the Oregon Territory) showcases Oregon City's claim as the terminus of the Oregon Trail. This status is also claimed by The Dalles (a city in the Columbia River Gorge). Without belaboring the merits of each claim, it suffices to say that Oregon City was at the end of the Barlow Trail, a spur route over Mount Hood from The Dalles for pioneers understandably leery of the raft trip down the Columbia River.

This large interpretive center was built to commemorate the 150th anniversary of the

The huge outdoor wagons at the End of the Trail Interpretive Center used to be covered with canvas, but like the settlers' wagons, they were hit hard by stormy weather.

© PAUL LEVY

Great Migration of 1843. To get there coming from Portland, take I-205 south to the Park Place Exit, turn south on Route 213 and follow the signs to Abernethy Green. Organizers have selected an area often identified as the end of the Barlow Road section of the trail to set up these facilities. To find them, just follow Washington Street north to its intersection with Abernethy Road or ask one of the locals for directions to Kelly Field. From I-205, you should be able to see three connected buildings in the shape of giant covered wagons.

Another way to take in the history of Oregon City and the Oregon Trail is at the pageant held at 8 P.M. Tuesday–Saturday at the Interpretive Center's outdoor amphitheater, mid-July through the beginning of August. Tickets are $10 with discounts for seniors, students, children, and families. Call 503/657-0988 or 503/656-1619 for more information.

John Inskeep Environmental Learning Center

The John Inskeep Environmental Learning Center (Clackamas Community College, 19600 South Molalla Ave., Oregon City 97045, 503/657-6958, ext. 2351, dawn–dusk daily, $2), three miles north of Kelly Field on Route 213, is pioneering efforts of a different sort. The 80-acre environmental-study area showcases alternative technologies and recycling against a backdrop of ponds, trails, and wildlife. Exhibits on aquaculture, birds of prey, and wetlands are included in this environmental education center's portrayal of Oregon's ecosystems. The exhibits are supplemented by one of the largest telescopes in the Northwest (Sat. after sunset, $3). Adjacent to the Inskeep Environmental Learning Center is the **Home Orchard Society Arboretum,** displaying Oregon's array of fruit-bearing plants.

Information

If you're exploring Oregon City and need a map, you can get one in the municipal elevator. There's also a **I-205 State Welcome Center** at 1726 Washington Street (503/657-9336, ext. 114 or 800/424-3002).

Salem

The used-car lots and fast-food outlets encountered on the way into Salem off I-5 contrast with the inspiring murals and displays in the capitol, where it's comforting to be reminded of Oregon's pioneer tradition and proud legacy of progressive legislation. Close by, the tranquil beauty and stimulating museums of historic Willamette University also provide a break from the carbon-copy drabness of a town dominated by gray buildings housing the state's bureaucracies.

The Kalapuyan name for the locality of Salem was Chemeketa, or "Place of Rest." Connotations of repose were also captured by the Methodist missionary appellation "Salem," an anglicized form of the Arabic *salaam* and the Hebrew *shalom* meaning "peace." The surrounding croplands along with Willamette River transport and waterpower quickly enabled Salem to become the New Jerusalem envisioned by Oregon Trail pioneers. Over the years, the city forged an economic destiny in government, food processing, light manufacturing, and wood products. Today, it has a population of about 145,000 people.

SIGHTS
❰ State Capitol

If visiting the State Capitol (900 N.E. Court St., 503/986-1388, 9 A.M.–4 P.M. Mon.–Fri., 9 A.M.–3 P.M. Sat., free) strikes you as the kind of saccharine excursion best reserved for a first-grade class trip, you're in for a pleasant surprise. The marble halls of Oregon government are adorned with attractive murals, paintings, and sculptures of the seminal events in this state's history. The capitol is located on Court Street between West Summer and East Summer Streets, just north of Willamette University.

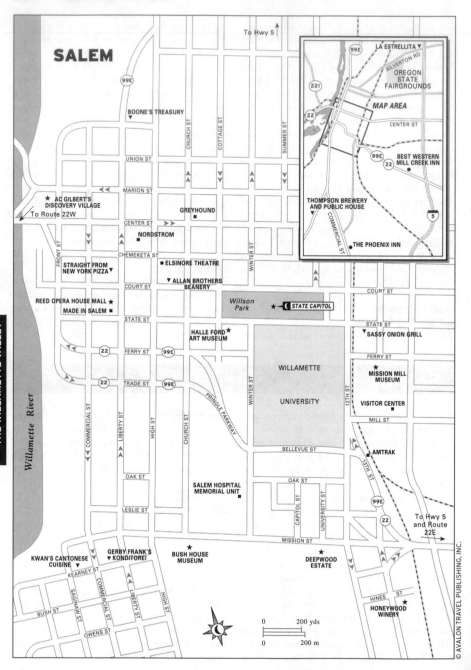

ENCHANTED FOREST

Seven miles south of Salem off I-5 on Exit 248 is the Enchanted Forest (8462 Enchanted Way, Turner 97392, 503/363-3060, www.enchanted forest.com), one man's answer to Walt Disney. An enterprising Oregonian has single-handedly built a false-front western town, a haunted house, and many more attractions.

In the 1960s Roger Tofte, the father of four young children, realized there was very little for a family to see and do together in Salem. He formulated the idea for a theme park where he could use his creative talents. Though he had very little time or money to make his dream a reality, he was able to purchase the original 20 acres of land off I-5 for $4,000, in monthly payments of $50. In 1964, he began construction.

Finally, in 1971, Tofte officially opened the park. Over the years, Tofte has successfully incorporated three of his children into the business: Susan (co-operations officer and artistic director), Mary (co-operations officer and chief financial officer), and Ken (head of attractions development and ride maintenance).

Whether it's the old woman who lived in the shoe, the seven dwarves' cottage, or Alice in Wonderland's rabbit hole, these and other nursery-rhyme and fairy-tale re-creations will get thumbs up from anyone under 99 years of age. One of the most inventive attractions is an old English village, which features a life-sized Geppetto and Pinocchio telling stories punctuated by animated characters popping their heads out of windows.

The park has a few schedule quirks; it's best to check the website if you are going to be visiting between 5 and 6 P.M. Basically, it is open daily 9:30 A.M.-5 or 6 P.M. March 15-March 31; weekends only April; daily May-Labor Day; weekends only September; closed October-March 15th. Admission is $8.95 for adults, $7.95 for ages 3-12, $0.75 extra for some rides.

Atop the capitol dome is a gold-leafed bronze statue of a bearded, axe-wielding pioneer. Massive marble sculptures flank the main entrance—*Covered Wagons* on the west side and *Lewis and Clark by Sacajawea* on the east. Maps of the Oregon Trail and the route of Lewis and Clark are visible on the backs of the statues. The symbolism is sustained after you enter the double glass doors to the rotunda. Your eyes will immediately be drawn to an eight-foot-diameter bronze state seal, set into the floor, which juxtaposes an eagle in flight, a sailing ship, a covered wagon, and forests. The 33 marble steps beyond the cordoned-off emblem lead up to the House and Senate chambers, and symbolize Oregon's place as the 33rd state to enter the Union. Four large murals adorning the rose travertine walls of the rotunda illustrate the settlement and growth of Oregon: Robert Gray sailing into the Columbia estuary in 1792; Lewis and Clark at Celilo Falls in 1805; the first white women to cross the continent being welcomed by Dr. John McLoughlin in 1836;

and the first wagon train on the Oregon Trail in 1843. Bronze reliefs and smaller murals symbolic of Oregon's industries also are here. The best part of the capitol is the legislative chambers, up the sweeping marble staircases.

Near the ceiling in the Senate and House chambers are friezes depicting an honor roll of people who influenced the growth and settlement of Oregon. Included are Thomas Jefferson, who sanctioned the Lewis and Clark expedition, and Thomas Condon, native son and naturalist extraordinaire. Also among the names are those of six women, headed by Lewis and Clark's interpreter-guide Sacajawea. The biggest surprise in the array might be John Quincy Adams, who determined the southern boundary of Oregon when he was secretary of state. In both legislative chambers look for forestry, agricultural, and fishing symbols woven into the carpets; murals about the coming of statehood are behind the speakers' rostrums.

Among the many architecturally eye-catching features to be found in the capitol are the rotunda's black marble, the House chamber walls and furnishings of golden oak, black walnut room appointments in the Senate, a walnut-paneled governor's office, and bronze doorknobs inlaid with the state seal throughout the building. There is also a carved myrtlewood table inlaid with a mosaic of the capitol in the reception area outside the governor's suite between the House and the Senate. All this was paid for with part of the $2 million it took to build the capitol in 1938.

If you don't want to roam independently, free half-hour building tours are given on the hour 9 A.M.–4 P.M. weekdays and 9 A.M.–3 P.M. Saturday, with a lunch break on all days noon–1 P.M.

A tower at the top of the capitol dome gives a superlative view of the valley and surrounding Cascade peaks, worth the 121-step climb from the fourth floor. It's open Memorial Day–September (but closes when the temperature reaches 90°F) and other times of the year by appointment; call 541/986-1388 for tour information. Also worth a look is the ongoing exhibit of outstanding Oregon artists in the governor's ceremonial office upstairs. Downstairs is a fine gift shop and a café. On the west side of the building (Court Street entrance) is an indoor visitors information kiosk.

To get to the Oregon State Capitol from I-5, take Exit 253 to Route 22 West. Take the Willamette University/State Offices Exit and follow the signs for 12th Street/State Offices. Turn left onto Court Street.

State Archives Building

At the entrance to the Capitol Mall on North Summer Street, another softly arched marble building has become a popular destination, but not just for the purposes of soaking in Oregon's pioneer and political traditions. The luxurious interior decor of the state archives building is viewed by Oregonians as a symbol of bureaucratic extravagance in an era of belt-tightening for everyone else. They come here and glare at $127-a-square-yard carpet covering $180-a-square-yard travertine limestone floors, all illuminated by light fixtures costing $5,000 apiece.

Overpriced adornments notwithstanding, the quilt of Oregon historical scenes on the second floor and other thematic objets d'art are both aesthetically pleasing and inspiring. In this vein, anyone who goes to look at the archives themselves will come away with a special perspective on pioneer history. It's hard not to get chills as you read the scrawled accounts of a meeting of early state leaders, or first-hand descriptions of settler life. Original documents relating to the Oregon Territory as well as the first copy of the state constitution also highlight this paper trail. It's all summed up quite well by the words below a glass mural of the pioneers in the reception area: "To think we came all that way, risked everything, used our bodies as plows, and arrived here with our lives."

Capitol Grounds

At each end of the capitol are parks featuring giant sequoias, magnolias, and camperdown elms. Between the capitol and the state executive building on the corner of Court and Cottage Streets is **Willson Park.** Lush lawns, a gazebo for concerts, and a wide variety of trees, including sequoia, Port Orford cedar, Asian cedar, blue spruce, mountain ash, dogwood, and incense cedar, invite a picnic. Two large multicolored rose gardens bloom through much of the year to garnish your spread, and a trio of bronze beavers make the perfect lunch companions. Also to the west of the building are the beautiful E. M. Waite Memorial Fountain and a replica of the Liberty Bell. To the east is **Capitol Park,** where you can admire Corinthian columns salvaged from the old capitol (destroyed by fire in 1935) and statues of Dr. John McLoughlin, Reverend Jason Lee, and the circuit rider, honoring horseback evangelists to the pioneers during the era of missionary zeal.

The oldest government building in Salem is the **Supreme Court building** (1147 State St.) dating back to 1914. It's located to the east of the capitol on the southern half of the block across Waverly Street, facing State Street and bounded by 12th Street. The building's facade is white terra-cotta, and the marble interior has tile flooring. Visual highlights include an ornate stairwell and a stained-glass skylight in the third-floor courtroom framing a replica of the Oregon state seal. Above all, don't miss the public restrooms. Tastefully appointed in marble, oak, and tile, these facilities were described in *Oregon* magazine as "doing justice to public needs."

Willamette University

Just south of the capitol mall is Willamette University (900 State St., 503/370-6300), the oldest institution of higher learning west of the Mississippi. It began as the Oregon Institute in 1842, a school that Methodist missionary Jason Lee founded to instill Christian values among the settlers. Over the years, Willamette University has turned out its share of Oregon politicos, including longtime senators Mark Hatfield and Bob Packwood. It also has to be one of the prettier campuses in the nation.

The campus is one of Salem's many oases of greenery that soften the hard edge of a city dominated by government buildings and nondescript downtown thoroughfares. Campus landscape architecture features a Japanese garden (the Martha Springer Garden, at the southeast corner of campus, also boasts roses, a rock garden, and an English perennial garden), ornate fountains, and a grove of five sequoias six feet in diameter. When you stand in the middle of these redwoods, you should be able to discern a star pattern formed by their canopies, giving rise to the name "star trees." This grove, which sits between the state capitol and Collins Hall (home of the science departments), has beside it an Oregon rock of ages. Found atop Ankeny Hill in Salem, the granite boulder floated down from northeastern Washington on an ice raft during the same Missoula Floods that shaped the Columbia River Gorge eons ago. This glacial erratic stands as a reminder that the Willamette Valley is largely composed of Lake Missoula sediments. In Collins Hall, crystals and exhibits on Oregon glacial activity join an impressive taxidermic array of Oregon wildlife. There's no admission charge and it's open during university hours. Finally, if you're hungry, the food court at the student union, Goudy Commons, is exceptional, reasonably priced, and with enough variety to suit all tastes.

Hallie Ford Museum of Art

Also part of Willamette University, the Hallie Ford Museum (700 State St., 503/370-6875, 10 A.M.–5 P.M. Tues.–Sat., $3, $2 students and seniors) features Native American baskets and a third-century Buddhist bas-relief from Pakistan. Asian pieces are also prominent here. Contemporary work is exhibited on a rotating basis.

Mission Mill Museum

In 1840–1841 the site of the Jason Lee House and Parsonage moved from the Willamette River upstream to Mill Creek, laying the foundations for the present-day cityscape. These structures along with the Boon Home were part of a Methodist mission to the Native Americans. The reconstructed Thomas Kay Woolen Mill (take Exit 253 off I-5), dating back to 1889, is also on the four-acre site of what is now called Mission Mill Museum, (1313 S.E. Mill St., 503/585-7012, 10 A.M.–5 P.M. Mon.–Sat., $7 adults, $6 seniors, $4 youth 6–18). Tours led by guides in period costumes begin at 10 A.M., noon, and 2 and 4 P.M. The oldest frame house in the Northwest and water turbines converting fleece into wool fabric are interesting, but those with limited time might prefer to come here just to obtain brochures about the Salem area at the reception area in front.

To get to the museum from I-5, exit at Route 22, go west on Mission Street for two miles to the 13th Street overpass, turn north onto 12th Street, and go west on Mill Street. If you arrive by Amtrak, Mission Mill is within walking distance.

Deepwood Estate

The historic Deepwood Estate (1116 S.E. Mission St., 503/363-1825, gardens dawn–dusk daily, house tours, noon–5 P.M. Sun.–Fri. May–Sept., noon–4 P.M. Tues.–Sat. Oct.–Apr., $4 adults, $3 students and seniors, $2 children) features tours of an elegant 1894 Queen Anne–style home with hand-carved woodwork, gorgeous stained-glass windows, and a well-marked nature trail. English formal gardens here evoke a more genteel era, and the Pringle Creek Trail's native flora and the public greenhouse's tropical plants have a timeless appeal. Parking is at 12th and Lee Streets near the greenhouse. Sit in Deepwood's pagoda-like gazebo with the scent of boxwood heavy in the air on a spring afternoon and you'll soon forget the hue and cry of political proceedings at the capitol.

Bush House and Park

Bush House Museum (600 Mission St., 503/363-4714, noon–5 P.M. Tues.–Sun. May–Sept., 2–5 P.M. Tues.–Sun. Oct.–Apr., last tour 4:30 P.M., $4 adults, $3 students and seniors, $2 children 6–12) is located in Bush Pasture Park off Mission, High, and Bush Streets. This 1877 Victorian, with many original furnishings, is the former home of pioneer banker and newspaper publisher Asahel Bush, who once wrote about his competitor, "There's not a brothel in the land that would not have been disgraced by the presence of the *Oregonian*." Even if you're not big on house tours, the Italian marble fireplaces and elegant walnut-and-mahogany staircase are worth a look. The house is part of the 80-acre Bush Pasture Park. Besides being a sylvan retreat for picnickers and sports enthusiasts, the park is home to the **Bush Barn Art Center** (541/581-2228, 10 A.M.–5 P.M. Tues.–Fri., noon–5 P.M. Sat.–Sun.). Located next to the Bush House, this center features two galleries with monthly exhibits. On the grounds you'll also find the Bush Conservatory Greenhouse and rose gardens (8 A.M.–4 P.M. Mon.–Fri., 2–4:30 P.M. Sat.). Both have free admission. To get there from I-5 take Exit 253 and drive two miles west on Route 22 (Mission Street). Turn south on High Street and enter the park on Bush Street, one block south of Madison.

A. C. Gilbert's Discovery Village

If you liked Portland's OMSI and Eugene's Science Center, A. C. Gilbert's Discovery Village (116 N.E. Marion St., 503/371-3631, 10 A.M.–5 P.M. Tues.–Sat., noon–5 P.M. Sun., $5.50, $4 seniors) should sate your inquiring mind or those of your kids. Also housed in this cheerful cluster of restored Victorians by the Willamette River is the national Toy Hall of Fame. Inspired by A. C. Gilbert, a Salem native whose many inventions included the Gilbert Chemistry Set and the Erector Set, Discovery Village's hands-on expositions incorporate art, music, drama, science, and nature. Whether you're designing a card or bookmark in the craft room, putting on a puppet show, or disassembling a parking meter, the outlets for creativity here are adaptable to any mood or mindset. If you don't have participatory inclinations, you can still enjoy fascinating exhibits like the one dedicated to A. C. Gilbert, whose Olympian athletic exploits and proficiency as a world-class magician were overshadowed by his inventions. As you might expect, even the gift shop here is a winner.

Honeywood Winery

Of the half-dozen local vintners, Honeywood Winery (1350 S.E. Hines St., 503/362-4111, 9 A.M.–5 P.M. Mon.–Fri., 10 A.M.–5 P.M. Sat., 1–5 P.M. Sun.) is the oldest and the most easily reached. It also bills itself as Oregon's oldest winery, having opened in 1933. Honeywood produces a full line of fruit and varietal wines. Salem's wine country is largely clustered along Route 22 (north of the highway) in a region known as the Eola Hills. Ask the folks at the Honeywood tasting room for information.

Reed Opera House Mall

At the corner of Court and Liberty is the Reed Opera House Mall. This one-time venue of minstrel shows and other pioneer cultural activities still retains a brick facade and long windows but has new tenants—the boutiques and restaurants of a tastefully rendered shopping mall.

Gardens

Both **Schreiner's Iris Gardens** (3625 N.E. Quinaby Rd., Salem, 503/393-3232) and

Cooley's Gardens (11553 N.E. Silverton Rd., Silverton, 503/873-5463) bill themselves as the world's largest iris growers. Both claims are correct based on different criteria, but the important thing to remember is that from mid-May through the first week of June these are the places to visit to take in the peak blossom seasons. Schreiner's is seven miles north of Salem next to I-5, and Cooley's is on the way to Silver Falls State Park. Both places can be visited 8 A.M.–dusk.

ENTERTAINMENT AND EVENTS

Salem's recreational mix belies its reputation for being a town dedicated to legislation and little else. Cultural life revolves around the **Pentacle Theatre** (324 52nd Ave. N.W., 503/364-7121, www.pentacletheatre.org), located five miles west of downtown Salem. From the government buildings, follow the signs marked "ocean beaches" and "Dallas." Signs on the right hand side of the highway, at N.W. 52nd Avenue, direct you up the hill and to the theater. This large, attractive wooden building hosts an award-winning eight-play season.

The **Elsinore Theatre** (170 High St. S.E., 503/375-3574, www.elsinoretheatre.com) is a vintage theater and emerging downtown cultural venue, featuring music performances and classic films as well as live theater. Check the *Statesman Journal* for what's scheduled. Along with the L. B. Day amphitheater at the fairgrounds hosting big-name acts and brewpubs featuring live music, there are summer concerts at Salem Riverfront Park.

Salem is full of studio tours, downtown art tours, and art galleries, as well as theater and musical events (Salem is the Oregon Symphony's home away from home). The Friday *Statesman Journal*'s "Weekend" section gives complete cultural listings.

The Salem Art Association (600 Mission St., 503/581-2228) puts on the **Salem Art Fair and Festival** the third week of July. This multiday event includes 200 artists, performing arts, food, children's activities, a five-kilometer run, an Oregon authors' table, wine and cheese tasting, and art-technique demonstrations.

The **Oregon State Fair** (2330 N.E. 17th St., 503/947-3247 or 800/833-0011, www.oregonstatefair.org) is an annual celebration held in Salem during the 12 days prior to Labor Day. The fair showcases Oregon agriculture, industries, tourist attractions, natural resources, government, and cultural activities. Big-name entertainment (well, it's actually often big-name has-beens), amusement-park rides, an international photography show, and a horticultural exhibit are also included in this blend of carnival and commerce. The best way to get there off I-5 is via Exit 253 or 258. Admission is $9 for ages 13 and up, $5 for seniors, $4 children 6–12, children under 5 get in free; save a couple of bucks by buying tickets in advance at Safeway. Parking is $5. Entertainment tickets for musical events will run you an extra $5–25. This is the largest agricultural fair on the West Coast. It is also host to one of the 10 largest horse shows in the nation. While there's no shortage of worthwhile events, family fun can come with a hefty price tag.

SPORTS AND RECREATION
Golf

The **Salem Golf Club** (2025 Golf Course Rd., 503/363-6652) is one of the best public courses in the state. Another option is **Santiam Golf Course** (8724 Golf Club Rd., Aumsville, 503/769-3485). If you drive 15 minutes east on Route 22 (at Exit 12), you can look forward to combining a round of golf with a walk in the country. Low greens fees and a full-service restaurant and bar add to the pleasure. Greens fees are $18–29.

ACCOMMODATIONS

Salem has a handful of B&Bs, but its lodgings are largely mid-priced chain hotels clustered east of I-5, at Exit 252 south of downtown. The "high-end" choice here is the **Phoenix Inn** (4370 Commercial St., 503/588-9220, www.phoenixinnsuites.com, $80–131). Here you'll get a "mini-suite" with microwave and refrigerator as well as access to exercise and spa facilities. (Note that if you're booking online, this is the "Salem-South" Phoenix Inn.) Not far behind is the **Best Western Mill Creek**

Inn (3125 Ryan Dr. S.E., 503/585-3332 or 800/346-9659, www.bestwestern.com/mill creekinn, $95–112). In addition to large rooms and a range of amenities comparable to those found at the Phoenix Inn, such extras as a free shuttle service to the Salem Airport and Amtrak and an included breakfast at a nearby Denny's are noteworthy.

If you're looking for more modestly priced accommodations, try the **Travelodge** (1555 State St., 503/581-2466, $46–55). It's nothing fancy, but it is very clean and convenient.

For more choices, log on to www.salem lodging.com.

FOOD
Salem is blessed with an unusually large number of small Mexican restaurants for a Northwest city this size. Many of these establishments boast regional specialties from the state of Jalisco that cater to the large influx of agricultural workers who've come to the Willamette Valley from northwestern Mexico. Ubiquitous entrées in these places include *carne asada* and *camarones al mojo de ajo*. *Carne asada* is grilled beefsteak, often tough but flavorful. *Camarones al mojo de ajo* is shrimp coated with garlic and butter. These eateries include **Los Arcos Mexican Restaurant** (3969 Commercial St. S.E., 503/581-2740) and **Taquería El Padrino** (3545 Portland Rd. N.E., 503/581-4964).

The **Sassy Onion Grill** (1244 State St., 503/378-9180, breakfast and lunch daily, dinner Fri.–Sat., lunch $6–8) is the kind place that caters to state employees by covering the traditional bases with enough forays into ethnic cuisine to keep things interesting. Fresh fruit smoothies, delicious oatmeal, a portobello pesto wrap, and a sesame chicken salad demonstrate a range that is very "today."

Coffee-lovers will take note that the top three leading coffee purveyors in Salem (according to a *Statesman Journal* reader poll) are within a couple of blocks of each other on Court Street. The poll-winning **Allan Brothers Beanery** (545 Court St., 503/399-7220) has light breakfasts, homemade pastries (cheesecake is recommended), soups, salads,

quiche, spanakopita, and lasagna. All are high quality and less than $5.

Another hangout conducive to conversation is **Boon's Treasury** (888 N.E. Liberty, 503/399-9062), which is a McMenamins enterprise. You can down microbrews and enjoy live blues and jazz amid the brick confines of the old treasury building. **Straight from New York Pizza** (233 Liberty St. N.E., 503/581-5863) sells delicious thin-crusted East Coast–style slices for about $3.

The other Salem branch of the McMenamins brewpub empire, the **Thompson Brewery and Public House** (3575 S. Liberty Rd., 503/363-7286, 11 A.M.–1 A.M. Mon.–Sat., noon–midnight Sun.) offers a casual brewpub meal. The restaurant's pizza, appetizers, burgers, sandwiches, or salads (all less than $10), washed down by McMenamins ales, beers, or their own Edgefield wines, are guaranteed to please. Best of all, it's set in a charming old house that'll make you forget south Salem's commercial sprawl.

Everyone knows that a half-hour after you've eaten a large Chinese meal, you're hungry enough for dessert. Perhaps this inspired the location of **Gerry Frank's Konditorei** (310 S.E. Kearney St., 503/585-7070, open daily for three meals) across from **Kwan's Cantonese Cuisine** (835 S.E. Commercial, 503/362-7711). These restaurants flank two sides of Commercial Street near its intersection with Kearney, so it's a good bet that many diners have enjoyed Kwan's delicacies, such as steamed salmon or Dungeness crab in black bean sauce, then topped it off with a slice of baklava or Black Forest cake at the Konditorei. In any case, it was Gerry Frank who brought Chef Kwan from Hong Kong to Salem, blessing this corner of Commercial Street with a delicious union of opposites. And while you're downing a second piece of torte at the Konditorei (open till midnight Fri.–Sat.), you can console yourself that the meal you just finished at Kwan's had no MSG and was prepared with organic vegetables (when available) and purified water. Kwan's also has dishes prepared with low-cholesterol emu. Dinner checks at Kwan's seldom exceed $15 per person; lunch is usually less than $6.

One of the most popular fancy restaurants in town is **Alessandro's 120** (120 Commercial St. N.E., 503/370-9951, lunch and dinner Mon.–Fri., dinner Sat., $12–25), with Salem's best Italian food served in a classy old downtown building.

U-pick farms are a delight from spring through fall in and around Salem. Cherries, strawberries, apples, peaches, plums, and blackberries are some of the bounty available. Early in June, the *Statesman Journal* puts out a list of local outlets in the area (what's available where and when) titled "Oregon Direct Market Association." Fruit stands are listed in this guide as well. Many concessionaires, such as **Bauman Farms** (12989 Howell Prairie Rd., 503/792-3524) offer both self-service harvest and over-the-counter sales. Several dozen agricultural products are available here, ranging from 10 berry varieties to pumpkins. Items such as fresh home-pressed apple cider and holiday gift packs round out the array. To get to Bauman's take Route 99E one mile south of Woodburn to Howell Prairie Road. Following the signs, go about a half mile to reach the stand.

INFORMATION

The **visitors center** (1313 Mill St., 503/581-4325 or 800/874-7012, www.salemvisitor center.com), located in the first building of the Mission Mill complex, has pamphlets and brochures covering Salem and the entire state. It's open 8 A.M.–5 P.M. Monday–Friday.

The Salem *Statesman Journal* (503/399-6622) is sold throughout the Willamette Valley, central coast, and central Oregon. The newspaper's "Weekend" section features entertainment listings and reviews every Friday that cover the week to come. Although these listings focus on Salem, considerable attention is also given to events throughout the Willamette Valley, central Oregon, and the coast.

GETTING THERE AND AROUND

Salem's State and Center Streets run east–west, while Commercial and Liberty Streets run north–south. East and West Nob Hill Streets run southeast. With a profusion of one-way streets and thoroughfares that end abruptly, it's important to keep your bearings. One helpful frame of reference is supplied by remembering that Commercial Street runs north–south along the Willamette River on the western edge of town.

Salem provides a lot of ways to get in and out of town. The **Greyhound** station (450 N.E. Church St., 503/362-2428) is open 6:45 A.M.–8:45 P.M. daily. **Amtrak** (13th and Oak Streets, 503/588-1551 or 800/872-7245) sits across from Willamette University and is close to Mission Mill Museum. The Salem **airport** (503/588-6314) is a few miles east of downtown. A Salem-to-Portland airport shuttle is run by **Hut Limousine Service** (503/364-4444). For short hops to town, there's Salem **A-Cab Taxi Company** (503/763-6969). Or rent a car at **Enterprise Rent-a-Car** (355 Pine St. N.E., 800/325-8007).

Mass-transit bus service in town means **Salem Area Mass Transit (Cherriots)** (216 High St., 503/588-2877 or 503/588-2424, $0.85). Terminals are in front of the courthouse.

SILVERTON
Oregon Garden

The Oregon Garden (879 W. Main St., Silverton, 503/874-8100 or 877/674-2733, www.oregon garden.org, 10 A.M.–6 P.M. daily May–Sept., 10 A.M.–4 P.M. daily Oct.–Apr., $10 adults, $9 seniors, $8 students, half price in off-season), while pleasant, has never become the world-class attraction originally envisioned. The botanical display was projected to grow to 250 acres—five times the size of the famous Butchart Gardens in Victoria, British Columbia—and was designed by a dream team of landscape architects with the backing of the state's dynamic nursery industry. Unfortunately, the garden was slow to develop, and the tourists even slower to arrive. The financially beleaguered garden was purchased by Moonstone Hotel Properties in spring 2006; the new owners plan to build a garden-themed hotel here.

In spite of its problems, there are some lovely and even innovative parts of the gardens.

Especially intriguing is the wetlands section, which uses treated wastewater from Silverton to create a wetland. The water travels through a series of terraced ponds and wetland plants to a holding tank; from here it is used to irrigate the entire garden.

One attraction that makes the trip the gardens worthwhile for architecture buffs is the **Gordon House** (879 W. Main St., Silverton, 10 A.M.–5 P.M. daily, $5 for guided tour), a Frank Lloyd Wright–designed home located within Oregon Garden complex. The house, originally located in Wilsonville, was moved to its current location in 2000, when the original property was sold and the new owners planned to demolish the house and rebuild to suit their own tastes. The modestly sized house is an example of Wright's populist "Usonian" style, and has beautiful western red cedar trim, many built-in drawers and cabinets, and lots of natural light. Terraces bring the outdoors in, and low ceilings in the bedrooms create a sense of retreat. Docents lead tours on the hour; this is the only way to see the upstairs of the house.

Accommodations and Food

At the top-drawer **(Silver Grille** (206 E. Main, 503/873-4035, 5–9 P.M. Mon.–Sat., entrées $16–24), the world travels of the deft restaurateurs meet the agricultural bounty of the region.

A couple of places serve good Thai food. Of the two, the **Red Thai Room** (211 Oak St., 503/873-1122, www.redthai.com) is a bit more elegantly hip, with many vegan choices; **Thai Dish** (209A N. Water St., 503/873-8963, lunch and dinner daily, $8–13) has a comfy small-town feel and surprisingly good food. Just down the block, **Macs Place** (201 N. Water St., 503/273-8441) is a hoppin' blues joint.

After a hike at Silver Falls or a walk around the Oregon Garden, stop in for tea at the **Oregon Tea Garden** (202 N. 1st St., 503/873-1230), where you can go with a really lavish high tea ($25) or stick with tea and a scone ($6). The slightly old-fashioned atmosphere is definitely girly, though men have been known to enjoy the scones.

Should you decide to stay in town rather than camp at the park, a convenient and recently remodeled option is the **Nordic Hotel** (310 N. Water St., 503/873-5058, doubles $110). Or you might upgrade a bit and stay at the **Water Street Inn** (421 N. Water St., 503/873-3344, www.thewaterstreetinn.com, $125–165), a renovated 1890s hotel that now operates as a quite lovely B&B.

The big annual "do" in Silverton is **Homer Davenport Days** (503/873-5211, www.davenportdays.com), usually held the first weekend in August, when locals enjoy crafts, food, music, and the spectacle of neighbors racing furniture down Main Street. Davenport was a nationally famous cartoonist in the 1930s and a Silverton favorite son. Most of the action takes place at Coolidge-McClain Park Friday evening and 10 A.M.–8 P.M. Saturday.

MOUNT ANGEL
(Mount Angel Abbey

Four miles northwest of Silverton off Route 214 is a rather special. High above the rest of the Willamette Valley is Mount Angel Abbey. From miles away, the neo-Gothic outline of St. Mary's steeple beckons the outside world to this monastery; on the way up to the abbey, stop in to enjoy the serenity of the church, established by Father Odematt after his arrival from Europe in 1883 to start a colony of German Catholics.

The Benedictine abbey sits on a 300-foot hill overlooking cropland and Cascade vistas. From the bluff, look northward to Mount Hood, Mount St. Helens, Mount Adams, and, according to locals, Mount Rainier on exceptionally clear days. The abbey **library,** designed by the famous Finnish architect Alvar Aalto, is an architectural highlight. The beautiful light and modern lines of the interior are nearly as inspiring as the texts on the shelves. But the texts are also pretty amazing, especially those housed in the Rare Book Room. Also worth checking out are the display cases in the lobby; the exhibits are invariably interesting.

The other Mount Angel Abbey building

that's nearly mandatory to visit is the delightfully old-fashioned and non-interpretive museum (10 A.M.–4 P.M., free), which is tucked in a basement to the side of the main church. (Get a map from the librarian and ask to have the museum pointed out.) Displays include religious artifacts such as a crown of thorns, crystals, and a huge collection of taxidermy, including an eight-legged calf.

The abbey's late July Bach Festival features professional musicians in an idyllic setting; call for tickets months in advance (503/845-3321).

Guided tours of the abbey are offered by appointment. Meditative retreats can be arranged at the abbey's **retreat house** (503/845-3025, www.mtangel.edu, $60 includes all meals). Although the accommodations are ascetic, the peace of the surroundings and the beauty of the monks' rituals will deepen your personal reflections no matter your spiritual orientation.

Other Sights

The town of Mount Angel's other claim to fame is its **Oktoberfest** (541/845-9440), which takes place in mid-September, when thousands of folks flock here to enjoy the *Weingarten,* the beer garden, and the oompah-pah of traditional German music. The biggest ethnic folk festival in the Northwest offers stage shows, art displays, yodeling, and street dancing amid beautiful surroundings. The biggest attraction of all, however, is the food. Stuffed cabbage leaves, strudels, and an array of sausages are the stuff of legend in the Willamette Valley. In this vein, don't miss the Benedictine sisters' coffeecake and the Old World–style farmers market.

Bicyclists relish the foothills and farmland around Mount Angel, which are nearly devoid of traffic. Fall color is exceptional here, and a varied topography ensures an eventful ride whatever the season. Lowland hop fields and filbert orchards give way to Christmas tree farms in the hills. On the way up, pumpkin and berry patches also break up the predominantly grassy terrain. This region is known as well for its crop of red fescue, a type of grass

seed grown almost nowhere outside the northern Willamette Valley.

Another kind of ride is even more popular just up the road in Woodburn. Here, the **Woodburn Dragstrip** (7730 Rte. 219, Woodburn, 503/982-4461, www.woodburn dragstrip.com, $10 adults for most events) is an incredibly popular car-racing area.

For those who'd rather avoid the roar of the car engines, nurseries abound in the area as well. If you were to visit the **Wooden Shoe Bulb Company** (33814 S. Meridian Rd., Woodburn, 541/634-2243, www.woodenshoe.com, $5 per car during tulip festival) in late March and early April, it would colorfully illustrate Oregon's rites of spring. The 17-acre tulip farm is located near Woodburn; take Exit 271 off I-5 and follow Route 214 east… it will become Route 211 to Molalla, turn right at the flashing yellow light onto Meridian Road, and go 2 miles to the tulip fields. Afterward you can head south through the town of Monitor and reach Mount Angel via a delightful rural route.

Mount Angel's location an hour south of Portland makes it an excellent day trip. Just take the Woodburn Exit 272 off I-5 and follow the blue Silver Falls tour route signs. If you're approaching the Mount Angel Abbey from Salem off I-5, take the Chemawa Exit and follow the signs.

◖ SILVER FALLS STATE PARK

If this state park (22024 Silver Falls Hwy., Sublimity, 503/873-3495, www.oregonstateparks. org, $3 day use, $16–20 campsites, $35 cabins) were in California instead of the remote foothills east of the Willamette Valley, it would probably be designated a national park and be flooded with visitor facilities and people year-round. Instead, one of Oregon's largest and most spectacular state parks remains relatively quiet except during the summer. At that time, hordes seeking relief from the valley heat head up to this cool enclave of waterfalls, 26 miles northeast of Salem. They come to see 10 major waterfalls 30–178 feet in height cascading off canyon walls in a forest filled with gargantuan

A classic Oregon campsite at Silver Falls State Park.

Douglas fir, ferns, and bigleaf and vine maple. There are also yew, chinquapin, and hemlock trees. The best time to come is during fall foliage season when there are few visitors, just before icy roads and trail closures inhibit travel. Freezing east winds of autumn sometimes make the falls here appear like ice sculptures. In spring, the mid-April blooming of trilliums and yellow wood violets on the canyon bottom is another highlight.

The park's campground has 46 tent sites, 47 sites for trailers or motor homes up to 35 feet long, and several log cabins. Large groups can rent larger dormitory-style bunkhouses for $100 a night. From mid-April to early October this facility operates with electricity, piped water, and picnic tables. Showers, firewood, and a laundry are available. In addition to hiking, swimming, and biking, there are stables near the park's entrance.

Serious hikers will want to take on the seven-mile **Silver Creek Canyon Trail,** which heads down into a fern-lined basalt gully going past all the falls. The profusion of trees and mois-

ture gives the air a special freshness, and when the sun hits some of the 10 falls just right you can see rainbows. A two-car shuttle is recommended if you plan to hike the whole loop. The highlights of this 1930s-vintage Civilian Conservation Corps trail are 177-foot **South Falls** and 136-foot **North Falls.** The opportunity to walk behind these waterfalls attracts a lot of visitors, who follow the trail through a basalt overhang in the cleft of each cliff. Bikers and horseback riders also enjoy specially designated trails in this 8,300-acre paradise.

North Falls and South Falls are easily reached from the North Falls parking lot and the day-use area, respectively, so you don't have to hike the whole loop to see both. To get to the day-use area from North Falls parking lot, drive several miles south up the hill (on Rte. 214), stopping after a mile or two to look back at a spectacular view of North Falls.

A museum near the day-use parking area features vintage photos from the area's incarnation as a logging site founded by land speculator James "Silver" Smith (so named for his penchant for carrying around a sack of silver dollars) and wildlife exhibits provide a nice introduction. A short distance from the museum is a viewpoint and the trailhead to South Falls. Like the North Falls trail, this is a steep ascent of about a quarter mile.

If you plan to visit the park from Portland, leave I-5 at Woodburn and follow rural Route 214 south through Mount Angel and Silverton. From Salem, either drive east on Route 213 to Silverton or approach the park farther south by taking Route 22 east out of Salem and following the signs northeast to the park from Sublimity. Although longer, the latter route enables you to do a Salem-to-Silver Creek Falls loop on different roads, taking in more varied landscapes in the process.

The main drag in Silverton, Water Street (a.k.a. Route 214 , the Silver Creek Falls Highway) heads south out of town toward the park. En route, stop at the chamber of commerce outdoor information kiosk (421 S. Water St., 503/873-5615) to pick up a Silverton directory/ map and a park folder. Traveling south and eventually east en route to the park on Route 214, the road climbs up into gently undulating hills past Christmas tree farms and nursery stock. A dearth of signs and a distance that seems longer than the posted 15 miles from town will have you second-guessing these directions until you come to the North Falls parking lot. While North Falls is a few miles north of the visitor services and facilities of Silver Creek Falls State Park headquarters at the day-use area, you can park your car at the trailhead here and skip the admission kiosk and shopping-mall-sized parking lot down the road.

OPAL CREEK

The old-growth forests and emerald pools of Opal Creek were an environmental battleground for years until a land swap with a timber company who owned logging rights here. Opal Creek's 31,000-acre watershed, which includes a grove of thousand-year-old, 250-foot red cedar, has been called the most intact old-growth ecosystem on the West Coast.

To get here from Salem, take Route 22 for 19 miles east to Mehama. At the second flashing yellow light (at the corner with Swiss Village), turn left off Route 22 onto Little North Fork Santiam River Road past the State Forestry office and go about 15 miles toward the Elkhorn Recreation Area. Stay on this route until Forest Service Road 2209 (mostly gravel) and be sure to veer left, uphill, at the Y intersection. About six miles past the Willamette National Forest sign, a locked gate will bar your car from proceeding farther down Road 2209. Park and follow the trail to a large wooden map displaying various hiking options. Sometimes a box with leaflets also has routing information.

While old-growth trees abound not far from the parking lot, be sure to cross over to the south side of the North Fork of the Little Santiam River (indicated by trailside signs). Here you can take in the placid Opal Pool, a small circular translucent aquamarine catch-basin at the base of a cascade that cuts through limestone. Located several miles from the parking lot over gently rolling terrain, Opal Pool is the perfect day-hike destination.

DETROIT LAKE

It's a Salem tradition to take to the hills via Route 22 along the North Santiam River to enjoy the fishing and camping at Detroit Lake. This large and busy 400-foot-deep reservoir is known for its boating, waterskiing, swimming, and fishing for rainbow trout, land-locked Chinook, and kokanee. Boat rentals are available at the marina. Because the reservoir was built for water storage, during drought years it can be drawn down enough to make recreation unappealing.

Although most Detroit Lake recreationists camp at the **Detroit Lake State Recreation Area** (503/854-3346, reservations at 800/452-5687, www.oregonstateparks.org, $16–20) on the lake's north shore, the more remote south-shore **Cove Creek** (Blowout Road, 503/854-3366, www.fs.fed.us/r6/Willamette, $16) is much more peaceful. With 63 sites, flush toilets, pay showers ($0.25 per minute in quarters only), a boat launch, and other amenities, it's

THE WILLAMETTE VALLEY

still not exactly a wilderness experience, but it's quite pleasant. Campsites are located in a lush second-growth Douglas fir forest against a slope. Because there are no individual RV hookups, dump sites, or phones, Cove Creek is designed more for car campers, backpackers, and outdoor recreationists than people looking for a place to park a rig long-term. The campground is located east of Detroit off Blowout Road. With no reservations, a sign on the highway will announce if the site has reached capacity.

BREITENBUSH
(Breitenbush Hot Springs

Breitenbush Hot Springs Retreat and Conference Center (503/854-3314, www.breitenbush. com) offers mineral-springs baths, trails forested with old growth, as well as a wide variety of programs aimed at healing body, mind, and spirit. Set in the Cascade foothills, this one-time Native American encampment's artesian-flow hot springs have attracted people for healing throughout the ages. The pools, set variously in forest and meadow, contain 30 freely occurring minerals, including lithium. Music, storytelling, yoga, and superb vegetarian cuisine are also part of the Breitenbush experience. Although many visitors come to Breitenbush to take part in an organized workshop (such as yoga, meditation, or spirituality), it's also possible to come on your own for a personal retreat. Please know before you go that most hot-springs bathers forgo the option of clothing.

The retreat cabins are spartan but sufficient. All have electricity and heat, and some have indoor plumbing. Rates are about $90 per person for a cabin without a bathroom (there are a couple of bath houses) or about $105 for a cabin with a bath (bring your own bedding or pay $15 extra), including three sumptuous vegetarian meals and use of the facilities and waters. Single visitors may sometimes be assigned a cabin-mate unless they specify otherwise (and pay extra). Large tents on platforms are also available June–October for $60–66 per person, or you can camp in your own tent for $49–55.

Day-use fees for hot springs and other facilities are $12–25. Individual all-you-can-eat meals for daytime visitors cost $10. Be sure to bring your own caffeine if that's something that you require. Do not bring alcoholic beverages.

Near Breitenbush are such remarkable natural areas as Breitenbush Gorge, Opal Creek, Bull of the Woods, and Jefferson Park; for more information contact the Detroit Ranger Station at 503/854-3366.

On-site you'll find the Spotted Owl Trail near the entrance of Breitenbush parking lot. In addition to this and other trails (get maps at the reception desk), sacred sweat-lodge ceremonies conducted by Native Americans are offered free of charge. Pre-registration is required, however, and participants are financially responsible for all other Breitenbush services and facilities used (hot springs and cabins).

To get to Breitenbush from Salem, take Route 22 to the town of Detroit. Turn at the gas station—the only one in town—onto Forest Service Road 46. Drive 10 miles to Cleator Bend Campground. Go 100 feet past the campground and take a right over the bridge across Breitenbush River. Follow the signs, taking every left turn after the bridge, to the Breitenbush parking lot.

If Breitenbush is full, the nearby **All Seasons Motel** (Rte. 22 and Forest Service Road 46, 503/854-3421) is clean and comfy ($55/double). The ecumenical spirit is on display in the rooms with Eastern holy books alongside Gideon's Bibles. It's not at all inconvenient to drive 15 minutes from here to the retreat center.

Cleator Bend

On the way up Route 22 to Breitenbush Hot Springs, Cleator Bend (Willamette National Forest, Route 22, Detroit, 503/854-3366, www.fs.fed.us/r6/willamette) offers a campground close enough to the Breitenbush Hot Springs Retreat Center and facilities to permit day use there. Nearby, the Breitenbush River has good fishing. There are nine sites for trailers or motor homes up to 16 feet long, as well as picnic tables and fire grills. Fees are $10 a night from mid-May to late September. On Forest Service Road 46, you'll pass several other campgrounds between Route 22 and the retreat center.

OLALLIE LAKE

To the east of Breitenbush, and almost directly north of Mount Jefferson, Olallie Lake is one of the nicest camping and hiking getaways in the area. The lake, which has a small resort with cabins and yurts (503/557-1010, www. olallielake.com, late June–Oct., $30–110) and a campground ($14), is along the Pacific Crest Trail, and there are hiking trails galore, many leading to other small lakes. In the early summer, wildflowers are an attraction; late in summer, this is a great place to pick wild huckleberries. The lakeside resort rents rowboats and canoes, and the views of Mount Jefferson from the lake are superb.

From the Detroit area, head north and east on Forest Service Road 46, then turn right on Forest Service Road 4220 (a rough gravel road) and follow it 13 miles to the lake.

MOUNT JEFFERSON

After a soak in the pools at Breitenbush, your muscles will be primed to hike up Mount Jefferson, Oregon's second-highest peak, 10,495 feet above sea level. This snowcapped symmetrical volcanic cone dominates the Oregon Cascades horizon between Mount Hood to the north and the Three Sisters to the south. Unlike Mount Hood, Mount Jefferson is rarely visible to motorists approaching from the west.

Twelve miles east of Detroit on Route 22 turn left; follow Forest Service Road 2243 (Whitewater Creek Road) 7.5 miles to the Whitewater Creek trailhead. Then it's an easy 4.5-mile hike to Jefferson Park. This is the northern base of the mountain and features a plethora of lakes and wildflowers. The alpine meadows here are full of purple and yellow lupine and red Indian paintbrush in July. On the way up, wild strawberries and red huckleberries can provide a delectable snack. For a special experience during the summer, start the walk after 5 P.M. when there's a full moon and the trail is bathed in soft lunar light.

Above Jefferson Park, the ascent of the dormant volcano's cone is a precarious endeavor and should only be attempted by the best in the business. You'll reach the bottom of Whitewater Glacier at 7,000 feet. Thereafter, climbing routes steepen to 45 degrees and snow and rock ridges destruct upon touch. Near the top, the rocks aren't solid enough to allow the use of ropes or other forms of climbing protection. Climbers must resort to "death moves," particularly because going down is even more dangerous than going up. Even if you head up the more sedate south face, you can expect difficulties due to the instability of the final 400 feet of rock on the pinnacle. It must be emphasized that almost every year a climber dies on Jefferson.

Those who elect not to make the ascent may also run into problems. Sometimes the mosquitoes in Jefferson Park are bloodthirsty enough to pierce thick clothing. On occasion the area is so crowded with day-use visitors and folks trekking the nearby Pacific Crest Trail, this place seems more like a city park than a mountain wilderness. No matter. The sight of Mount Jefferson in alpenglow at sunset or shrouded in moonlight will make you forget the intrusions of humankind or the elements.

Corvallis

The name "Corvallis" refers to the city's pastoral setting in the "Heart of the Valley." But this appellation tells just part of the story. The influence of Oregon State University looms so large here that it might as well be called "College Town, U.S.A." In fact, Cascadia, the quintessential college town in the novel *A New Life,* by the late Oregon State University professor Bernard Malamud, was modeled on Corvallis. Everything from the coffeehouses and used bookstores to the pizza joints and network of biking trails seems to owe its existence to the ivy-covered walls of academe here.

Beauty, tranquility, and Corvallis's central location in the heart of the valley recommend it as a base from which to explore the bird sanctuaries, the Coast Range, and nearby historic communities. In town, you'll be struck by the abundance of stately old trees, some dating back to the first pioneers, who arrived in 1847. Streets with wide bike lanes and scenic routes for cyclists that parallel the Willamette and Mary's Rivers also contribute to the idyllic time warp feeling here. This is especially the case in summer, when many students leave town.

SIGHTS
Campus and Downtown
In springtime, the daffodil-lined approach to Corvallis on Route 99W is made even more glorious by the Coast Range and its highest mountain, 4,097-foot **Mary's Peak,** to the west over the hay meadows. During much of the winter, rain and fog obscure the summit from view.

Your first stop in town should be the 500-acre campus of **Oregon State University** (OSU), home to 15,200 students (follow the signs to Jefferson or Monroe Streets, 541/737-0123, www.oregonstate.edu). The parklike campus of this 1868 land-grant institution is the hub of activity in town, with a slew of eateries, bookstores, and craft boutiques on its periphery. Cultural activities on campus include lectures, concerts, theater productions, films,

and art exhibits. Many are free and open to the public.

Visit Corvallis from the end of February through mid-March and you can watch ewes giving birth in the lambing barns at the university's **Sheep Center** (7565 N.W. Oak Creek Dr., 541/737-4854, 9 A.M.– 3 P.M. daily). To get to the center from downtown Corvallis, head west on Harrison Boulevard to the 53rd Street intersection. Continue west through the intersection on N.W. Oak Creek Drive (a.k.a. Walnut St.). A sign after 1.8 miles will indicate the road to the center; this one-lane road has turnouts allowing you to yield to oncoming traffic.

While the notion of one of these fleecy specimens on a dinner plate might seem akin to eating Bambi, this facility's research has helped establish Oregon lamb as a gourmet product. Thanks to a diet of nutritious grasses indigenous to Northwest soils, Oregon lambs are larger and richer in flavor than their better-publicized New Zealand counterparts. The barns are open every day during daylight hours. While there are no formal guides, student staffers and informational fliers will help answer questions. The sight of a newborn standing and walking a few minutes after birth is amazing to first-time visitors.

The university also maintains 11,500 acres of woodlands, notably **McDonald Experimental Forest** and **Peavy Arboretum,** entrance eight miles north of Corvallis on Route 99W, which feature hiking trails as well as the chance to see the rare Fender's blue butterfly. The species had been thought extinct for 50 years until a habitat was discovered here in 1990. This ecosystem serves primarily as a living laboratory for the university's Forestry Department.

Benton County Courthouse, near 4th, 5th, and Monroe, is the oldest functioning courthouse in the lower Willamette Valley. You can't miss its large white clock tower. Also downtown is the **Corvallis Art Center** (7th and Madison Streets, 541/754-1551, noon–5 P.M. Tues.– Sun.), located in the renovated 1889 Episcopal

In the spring, the Oregon State University Sheep Center is full of activity.

church near Central Park. It sells local crafts and hosts weekly lunchtime concerts.

Houses, Heritage, and Hospitality

A large concentration of historic homes and covered bridges can be found around Corvallis. In addition to the surrounding heritage-conscious communities, artifact collections and pageantry also liven up the historical landscape of Linn and Benton Counties.

Six miles west of Corvallis on Route 34 is the town of **Philomath,** home to the **Benton County Historical Society** (1101 Main St., Philomath 97370, 541/929-6230, Tues.–Sat. 10 A.M.–4:30 P.M. free). Looms, carriages, printing presses, and other pioneer-history exhibits are mildly diverting here, but the real star is the 1867 Georgian-style brick structure housing the collection. Just look for the imposing building on the right side of the highway as you head toward the coast.

Tyee Winery

Located 10 miles off Route 99W south of Cor-

vallis on the way up into the Coast Range is Tyee Wine Cellars (26335 Greenberry Rd., Corvallis, 541/753-8754). It's easy to incorporate a stop here into trips to nearby destinations such as Finley Wildlife Refuge, Mary's Peak, or Alsea Falls. Pinot gris, pinot noir, chardonnay, and gewürztraminer are featured here. After wine-tasting, you can enjoy a picnic on the grounds of this historic farm site or a 1.5-mile loop to beaver ponds. Open noon–5 P.M. weekends April–December, noon–5 P.M. daily mid-June–Labor Day, closed January–March.

Natural Attractions

The pastures of Lebanon and Brownsville east of Corvallis are good places to spot bald eagles. Venture out to the fields (beginning in February) when sheep are lambing to see eagles soaring above the newborn lambs. In the winter, grass seed farms outside Albany, Coburg, and Junction City attract tundra swans.

West of Corvallis, two spots have drawn seekers of natural beauty and solitude for many years. Mary's Peak and Alsea Falls are

THE WILLAMETTE VALLEY

WILLAMETTE BIRD SANCTUARIES

The federal government established several bird sanctuaries between Salem and Eugene in the mid-1960s because of the encroachment of urbanization and agriculture on the winter habitat of the dusky Canada goose. This species now comes to **Baskett Slough National Wildlife Refuge** (NWR), west of Salem, **Ankeny NWR,** southwest of the capital, and **Finley NWR,** south of Corvallis, each October after summering in Alaska's Copper River Delta. Refuge ecosystems mesh forest, cropland, and riparian environments to attract humming-birds, swans, geese, sandhill cranes, ducks, egrets, herons, plovers, sandpipers, hawks and other raptors, wrens, woodpeckers, and dozens of other avian ambassadors. Migrating waterfowl begin showing up in the Willamette Valley in mid-October. By mid-March, large numbers of Canada geese, tundra swans, and a variety of ducks descend on the refuge.

The pamphlet *Birds of Willamette Valley Refuges* details the best months to bird-watch, frequency of sightings, and locations of hundreds of kinds of birds (available from Refuge Manager, Western Oregon Refuges, 26208 Finley Refuge Rd., Corvallis 97337, 541/757-7236, www.fws.gov/willamettevalley/finley/).

To maintain the sanctity of the birds' habitat, the refuges restrict birders by closing some trails in winter; other trails farther from feeding grounds are kept open year-round. A hike that can be enjoyed any time of year is Finley NWR's one-mile **Woodpecker Loop.** A variety of plant communities exists here, due to Kalapuyan field burning followed by pioneer logging and cattle grazing. Its location on the border between the Coast Range and the Willamette Valley also contributes to the diversity. Forests of oak and Douglas fir, and a mixed-deciduous grove, combine with marshes to provide a wide range of habitats. Look for the rare pileated woodpecker in the deciduous forest. The loop's trailhead is reached by taking Route 99W (from Corvallis) to Refuge Road. Look for the footpath on the right after driving three miles. A drop box has a pamphlet with pictures and information on the birds, wildlife, and plant communities here.

Ankeny NWR is located 12 miles south of Salem off I-5 at Exit 243, and Baskett Slough NWR lies northwest of Rickreall on Route 22. Visit fall through spring for the best chance to see ducks, geese, swans, and raptors.

In recent years, the proliferation of Canada geese in the lower Willamette Valley has compelled people to question if the refuges have been too successful. Farmers complain that the birds interfere with crops. Currently, state wildlife managers are rethinking the protections accorded to the migratory fowl. After seeing the dwindling numbers of the state bird, the western meadowlark, in the Willamette Valley due to human encroachment, let's hope the powers that be can reach a healthy balance.

each a short drive from Route 34, a scenic route to Waldport, which branches off of U.S. 20 southwest of Philomath.

Mary's Peak sits about 12 miles southwest of Corvallis. From I-5, take U.S. 20 into Corvallis, then Route 34 to Philomath. From here it's nine miles west to the road's Coast Range Summit (1,230 feet). A sign north of the highway points the way to a 10-mile drive to the top of the Coast Range's highest peak (4,097 feet) on Forest Service Road 30, the only road on the peak's south side. Along the way, pretty cascades, interesting rock outcroppings, and over-the-shoulder views of the Cascades on the eastern horizon intensify your anticipation of this mountaintop Kalapuyan vision-quest site.

When you get to the parking lot at the end of the road, the view is impressive—but don't stop there. If it's a clear day, take the short walk across the meadows to either of the two summit lookouts for perspectives on Mounts Hood and Jefferson, the Three Sisters to the east (reportedly eight Cascades peaks in total are potentially visible from here), and the Pacific Ocean at the base of the Coast Range to the west. For information contact **Siuslaw National Forest Supervisor's Office** (4077 Research Way, P.O. Box 1148, Corvallis 97333, 541/750-7000).

The summit, thanks to its status as a federally designated botanical area, remains untouched by clearcuts that speckle the forests nearby. A biome unique to the Coast Range exists up here, with such flora as alpine phlox, beargrass, iris, tiger lily, Indian paintbrush, purple lupine, and the blue-green noble fir. Exceptionally large species of this fragrant tree grow on the Meadows Edge Trail. This trail connects to a primitive car-camping area with 16 sites (open March 21–Oct. 31, $4 per night) two miles below the summit. It's part of a nine-mile network of trails around the upper slopes of the mountain.

You'll also find hemlock, fir, and grand fir here. Local creeks are home to the unique Mary's Peak salamander, and the surrounding woods host bald eagles, red-tailed hawks, spotted owls, and Clark's nutcrackers—seldom seen west of the Cascades. There are also, very occasionally, black bears. Mary's Peak is a prime viewing spot (when it's clear) in western Oregon for the Perseid meteor shower in August.

Snow, an infrequent visitor to most Coast Range slopes, can often be found here in winter, even at lower elevations. In fact, the road is sometimes impassable without chains from late fall till early spring. A Sno-Park permit is required for day use, November 15–April 15. Contact the Waldport Ranger Station (541/563-3211) for more information.

Farther down Route 34 is the town of **Alsea.** The adjoining Lobster Valley area drew many countercultural refugees here in the 1970s, a portion of whom have remained to become farmers and craftspeople. The greenness of the valley surrounded by Coast Range foothills recalled the lower alpine regions of Europe enough to inspire the nickname "Little Scotland."

South of here, a paved-over logging road through the tall timbers of the Coast Range can take you back to the Willamette Valley on a remote scenic byway. Look for a sign that says "Alsea Falls, South Fork Road/Monroe." There's also a campground with 16 sites, piped water, pit toilets, picnic tables, and fire rings for $14 per night. You'll follow the Alsea River much of the way until you come to the sloping parking lot near Alsea Falls on the east side of the road. A short trail leads you to a picturesque cascade, ideal for a picnic. The road continues through once-active logging towns into farming country and the Finley Wildlife Refuge south of Corvallis (see the *Willamette Bird Sanctuaries* sidebar). From here, Route 99W goes north to Corvallis or south to Junction City and Eugene.

Camping

Camping in this part of the Willamette Valley can be delightful, especially in late spring and early autumn.

About 14 miles east of Sweet Home off U.S. 20 is **Cascadia State Park,** near the banks of the South Santiam River (for reservations, call 800/452-5687, Mar.–late Oct., $14, plus $6 reservation fee). Rocks here form great swimming holes. A nearby waterfall, a cave with petroglyphs, an old-growth Douglas fir, and a hand pump to draw up mineral water are other appeals. Also along U.S. 20 are superlative boating and fishing on Green Peter and Foster Lake reservoirs. Such amenities as piped water, flush toilets, and firewood are available, and a store is located within a mile.

In Corvallis, your best bet April–late October is **Willamette Park** (Corvallis City Parks & Recreation Department, 541/757-6918, www.ci.corvallis.or.us). To get here drive a mile south of the city on Route 99W, then go 0.5 mile east on S.E. Goodnight Road to the park. For $9 a night, you can enjoy one of the 25 sites for tents and RVs serviced by vault toilets, piped water, and a small outdoor kitchen. If you need supplies, a store, café, and laundry are a mile away. Trails to the nearby Willamette River yield bird-watching and fishing opportunities in this 40-acre park.

ENTERTAINMENT AND EVENTS

The **Peacock Tavern** (125 S.W. 2nd, 541/754-8522) is where Corvallis rocks out to live music

Wednesday–Sunday. Oregon blues stars such as Lloyd Jones, Paul De Lay, and Curtis Salgado perform here. Another good place to dance to live music or DJs is **Platinum** (126 S.W. 4th St., 541/738-6996).

The Corvallis drama scene coalesces around the **Majestic Theater** (115 S.W. 2nd, 541/766-6976), a 1913 restored vaudeville house. Close by is the excellent **Grassroots Books and Music** (227 S.W. 2nd, 541/754-7558).

Aside from OSU Beavers football games, the biggest event in Corvallis is **Da Vinci Days** (541/757-6363, www.davinci-days.org) held the third weekend in July to on the creative spirit embodied by the genius for whom the festival is named. Sculpt, play chess on a computer, take part in a drama, or just sit and listen to music, as Corvallis's vibrant artistic and scientific community shares its inspirational bounty. New vaudeville acts and food booths also showcase the region's creativity. Kinetic sculpture races—these must be seen to be believed—lectures by scientists, and interactive exhibits impart an intellectual air to the proceedings. The festival takes place on the Oregon State University campus and in Central Park, between 9th and 11th Streets, beginning 6 P.M. Friday and continuing 10 A.M.–11 P.M. Saturday and 10 A.M.–6 P.M. Sunday. One-day admission is $10 for adults, $5 for kids; full weekend tickets are $15 adults, $10 kids. Because festival events are spread out all over town, a car or a bike is necessary to take full advantage of it all.

Another big Corvallis celebration is the **Corvallis Fall Festival** (541/752-9655, www.corvallisfallfestival.com). This gathering of artists and craftspeople is now in its second decade. Nonstop varied entertainment and a block of food concessions, including an Oregon wine garden, provide a backdrop for this hotbed of creative ferment 10 A.M.–6 P.M. the fourth weekend in September in Central Park, between 6th and 8th, Monroe and Madison.

The Oregon State University **basketball** season at Gill Coliseum (26th and Washington, 541/754-2951) is a favorite wintertime activity. Football is played at nearby Reser Stadium; it's the hottest ticket in town.

The first full weekend of June, the town of **Lebanon** celebrates its **Strawberry Festival** (541/258-4444, www.ci.lebanon.or.us/festival hist). Southeast of Albany off U.S. 20, Lebanon has become famous for its annual *Guinness World Record*–sized strawberry shortcake, the 17,000 pieces of which are dished out at the climax of the event.

Two area musical events held each summer are the **Memorial Day Bluegrass Festival** at Airlie Winery about 20 miles northwest of Corvallis (15305 Dunn Forest Rd., Monmouth 97361, 503/838-6013, www.airliewinery.com) and Sweet Home's **Oregon Jamboree** (541/367-8800, www.oregonjamboree.com), Oregon's largest country music event. In years past, Merle Haggard, Wynonna Judd, Dwight Yoakam, LeAnn Rimes, and other big names have appeared for this early August event, organized to help timber-dependent communities cope economically with the era of limits in Oregon forests.

ACCOMMODATIONS

Of the two dozen or so lodging options (mostly chain motels) in Corvallis, the following are best in their respective price ranges. The **Super 8 Motel** (407 N.W. 2nd St., 541/758-8088, $54–80), a few blocks from downtown and on the Willamette River, is nothing fancy, but there's a spa and pool.

With a sister location in Reedsport, **Salbasgeon Suites** (1730 N.W. 9th St., 541/753-4320 or 800/965-8808, www.salbasgeon.com, $74–176) is situated in the heart of Corvallis's business district, just a jaunt from dining and shops. Guests have access to the large indoor heated swimming pool, sauna, and a gym as well as in-room high-speed Internet access. There's also a good restaurant on-site.

The **Hilton Garden Inn** (2500 S.W. Western Blvd., 541/752-5000 or 800-445-8667, $79–189) has rooms that range from simple to suite. At the corner of 26th and Western, this is one of Corvallis' finest accommodations for the business traveler, featuring rooms with large desks, ergonomic chairs, high-speed Internet access, and two dual-line speakerphones with voicemail and data ports.

The **Hanson Country Inn** (795 S.W. Hanson St., 541/752-2919, www.hcinn.com, $95–145) gives you the feeling you're way out of town though it's actually within walking distance of campus. Antiques, canopy beds, 1920s woodwork, and a book-lined library warm up the interior. On the outside, a hillside overlooking the Hanson farm offers a feeling of tranquility. A two-bedroom cottage, ideal for families, sits behind the main house.

FOOD

Bombs Away Cafe (2527 Monroe St., 541/757-7221, lunch and dinner Mon.–Fri., dinner Sat.) is an always-filled-to-capacity 65-seat restaurant with colorful murals on the walls, frequent live music, and lines of waiting-list hopefuls anxious to sample finger food made with the freshest ingredients and organic produce. Another reason for the queue are the prices, $3–13. Try the duck chimichangas, jalapeno fries, green chili, or chicken tamales. On the same block you'll find a coffee shop, a pizza place, and a Thai restaurant.

Evergreen Indian Restaurant (136 S.W. 3rd St., 541/754-7944, lunch and dinner daily, lunch $8, dinner $10–15) has surprisingly good Indian food. Along with good standards such as chicken makani, saag paneer, and garlic naan, a variety southern Indian dishes such as dosas (sort of like Indian crepes) are served. The lunch buffet gives you a chance to try a wide variety of dishes.

Perhaps the best place to provision a picnic is **First Alternative Co-op** (1007 S.E. 3rd, 541/753-3115), which you'll encounter as you come into town via Route 99W from the south. The organic produce section is a marvel, and the largely volunteer staff can give excellent leads on what's happening in the area.

Another spot for those who place a premium on wholesome fare is **Nearly Normal's** (109 N.W. 15th, 541/753-0791, breakfast, lunch, and dinner Mon.–Sat., $6–9), whose jungle of greenery and mismatched kitschy decor does justice to its name (inspired by a character in a

Tom Robbins novel). Low prices and huge helpings reflect the predominantly student clientele, who savor egg and stir-fry dishes, burritos (Mex dishes are big here), and falafel. Patio dining on sunny days is a highlight. Closed Sundays.

The **Gables** (1121 N.W. 9th, 541/752-3364) is full of students and parents on graduation day enjoying prime rib, fresh seafood, rack of lamb, and other traditional standbys. Before the arrival of the heavy artillery, try the elegant chicken bisque as an appetizer. This is the most expensive place in town (entrées $12–30, 25 percent off at the early-bird special), but the understated elegance and venerable cuisine make it perfect for an occasion. To get here, follow Harrison to 9th; the restaurant is located 0.5 mile west of Route 99W.

Thanks to its riverside setting in an old railroad depot and a varied menu at once upscale and affordable, **Michael's Landing** (603 N.W. 2nd, 541/754-6141, lunch and dinner Mon.–Sat., brunch and dinner Sun., $8–14 lunch, $11–21 dinner) is one of Corvallis's most popular restaurants. While Italian, Cajun, and Asian flavors occasionally assert themselves here, the menu seldom strays from beef, chicken, and seafood. What does stand out is the finesse of the experienced chef.

Corvallis also has a farmers market that takes place 9 A.M.–1 P.M. Saturday late May–late October in the City Hall parking lot, at 6th and Monroe. There is also a market held 8 A.M.–1 P.M. Wednesday at the Benton County Fairgrounds (110 S.W. 53rd St.). Look for excellent Alsea Acre Alpine's goat cheese and The Co-op's calzones here along with other regional staples.

INFORMATION

The **Corvallis Visitor's Information Center** (553 N.W. Harrison Blvd., 541/757-1544, www.visitcorvallis.com) maintains a good website.

To catch up on local events, read the *Corvallis Gazette Times* (www.gtconnect.com). KOAC (550 AM) is an excellent public radio station with a top-notch news team and classical music offerings. Serving much of western Oregon, KOAC can be picked up in remote coastal and mountain communities.

THE WILLAMETTE VALLEY

GETTING THERE AND AROUND

Greyhound and **Valley Retriever** (153 N.W. 4th, 541/757-1797) operate every day, with routes north, south, and west to the coastal town of Newport.

Corvallis Transit (501 Madison, 541/757-6988, Mon.–Sat., $0.75) operates city buses. To get back and forth between Corvallis and Albany, catch the **Linn Benton Loop System** buses (541/917-7667, Mon.–Fri., $1) by the university at the corner of 15th Street and Jefferson Avenue. Buses stop outside Albany's City Hall on Broadway and 2nd.

Corvallis is laid out logically, and it's easy to get anywhere within 15 minutes. With 47 miles of bike trails and 13 miles of paved bike paths, it's not surprising the city has garnered kudos from national media for its commuter-friendly traffic arteries. Recreational bikers sing the praises of the Corvallis-to-Philomath bike path. It begins along the Willamette River in downtown Corvallis and continues eight miles through rural Benton County before ending in Philomath.

ALBANY

Twelve miles east of Corvallis on U.S. 20 is Albany, which has more historic homes than any other city in Oregon. More than 350 Victorian houses bespeak Albany's golden age, 1849 to the early 20th century, when wheat was the primary crop and steamships and railroads exported Willamette Valley produce and flour. In 1910, 28 trains departed this commercial hub daily. The **Albany Visitors Association** (Two Rivers Mall, 300 S.W. 2nd Ave., 800/526-2256, daily mid-May–Dec. 31, Mon.–Sat. Jan.–mid-May) and an information gazebo at the corner of 8th and Ellsworth Streets have maps and pamphlets about the three historic districts covering 100 blocks here. While you're here, be sure to get directions to the **Monteith House** (518 W. 2nd Ave., 800/526-2256), the oldest pioneer frame building in Albany, dating to 1849. Also inquire about the **Albany Regional Museum,** whose exhibits on the Kalapuya tribe and Albany's pioneer and Victorian eras provide a good introduction.

In their heyday, two Albany residential districts were rivals. The **Hackleman District,** Ellsworth to Madison Streets and 2nd to 8th Avenues, was a working-class neighborhood that at one time featured a furniture factory and a railroad station. These houses are practical but rich in Victorian nuance. The adjoining **Monteith District,** Elm to Ellsworth Street and 2nd to 12th Avenues, was home to wealthy merchants and businessmen; the houses here are grand and opulent.

Also imbued with Willamette Valley history are the area's charming **covered bridges.** These canopied crossings protected the wooden trusses from rain, extending the life of the bridges by several decades. By the late '30s, many of the 300 or so covered bridges in the state had fallen into disrepair or were replaced by modern steel and concrete spans. Statewide, 48 remain, with 30 in the Willamette Valley. A pamphlet available from the Albany Visitors Association lays out a self-guided tour of eight bridges within a 20- to 30-minute drive from the Albany-Corvallis area. All of these fall within an eight-mile radius of Scio, a town 13 miles northeast of Albany on Route 226.

To get to Scio, head north on I-5 for about 10 or 15 minutes, then take Exit 233 and follow the signs east to Route 226. Of all the bridges in this loop, don't miss the bright red paint job of the Shimanek Bridge and the creekside splendor of the Larwood Bridge. In Scio itself a small **pioneer museum** (contact the Albany Visitors Association, 800/526-2256, for hours, location, and information) survives on donations. The hodgepodge of Oregon Trail memorabilia, wood carvings, 19th-century newspapers, and family heirlooms in this oddly curated assemblage can be more affecting than the slicker, high-tech displays you'll encounter elsewhere in the state. Visitor services in this area are minimal, so take advantage of state rest areas on the interstate and the A&W Root Beer Stand in Scio.

Prime time for a stroll down Albany's memory lane is during the Christmas holiday season. In December (usually the second Sunday), annual old-fashioned **parlor tours** (800/526-5526, $10 adults, $8 seniors, free for children

12 and under) let you revel in eggnog, snapping fires, and frontier hospitality as a guest at a number of Victorian homes. Visitors are welcomed by hostesses at each home and are permitted to walk through the parlor and other open rooms. Entertainment and homemade refreshments are part of the festivities. Historical district hay-wagon and trolley caroling tours are part of the package and can get you in the holiday spirit.

Interior tours of historic houses are available during the last weekend in July ($10 adults, $8 seniors). Visitors are invited to walk through the gardens and entire interiors of several homes; background anecdotes are supplied by guides. Old-fashioned quilts and dolls complement the tour, as do many people in turn-of-the-century dress strolling the avenues. At all times of the year, more than a dozen antique shops also lure visitors here. A list of these stores is available at the information gazebo. **Flinn's Parlor** (222 1st Ave. W., downtown Historical District, 541/928-5008) also provides tours with costumed guides.

Albany's **World Championship Timber Carnival** (541/928-2391) takes place July 1–4. While such events as speed-climbing, springboard-chopping, and log-rolling have little place in the increasingly mechanized world of modern timber management, they're still fun to watch.

Check www.albanyvisitors.com for more information about Albany events.

Accommodations and Food

Both Eugene and Corvallis are more lively places to stay, but if you're going to spend the night in Albany, it should be in an 1856 Victorian. The **Trainhouse Inn B&B** (206 7th Ave., 541/794-5281, www.trainhouseinn.com, $100–110), located in the center of the historic district, fits the bill precisely. Don't worry that you'll be kept awake by railroad noise; the inn takes its name from Samuel Train, an early newspaper publisher.

The **Albany Farmer's Market** (Water and Broadalbin Sts., Albany, open 9 A.M.–noon Sat., June–Thanksgiving) is a short drive from Corvallis. Enjoy the Willamette Valley's bountiful harvests of corn, fruit, garlic, peppers, or whatever else happens to be in season. Cut flowers are on sale as well as such regional specialties as the mild-tasting, large-cloved elephant garlic, marionberries (a tart hybrid blackberry developed by OSU), and dried jumbo Brooks prunes. Best of all, you're buying direct from the grower at a fraction of supermarket cost.

Another Albany tradition is **Novak's Hungarian Restaurant** (2306 Heritage Way S.E., 541/967-9488, breakfast, lunch, and dinner daily, dinner $10–19). Authentic *kolbasz* (a spicy sausage), stuffed cabbage, and chicken paprika exemplify the earthy Eastern European fare served in a family-friendly atmosphere.

Albany's **Greyhound** (108 4th Ave. S.E., 541/926-2711) has service to Klamath Falls and Bend as well as Willamette Valley locations. Albany also hosts an **Amtrak** station (110 W. 10th St., 541/928-0885).

BROWNSVILLE

A down-home version of the pioneer experience awaits in Brownsville. Drive south on Route 99E (or I-5) and take Exit 216; Route 228 will take you five miles east into this small town located between the Calapooia River and the Cascade foothills. This 1846 settlement began to prosper in 1862 with a woolen mill and, shortly thereafter, the coming of the railroad. Today, the **Linn County Historical Museum** (101 Park Ave., 541/466-3390, 11 A.M.–4 P.M. Mon.–Sat., 1–5 P.M. Sun., donations suggested) is located in a turn-of-the-century train depot flanked by freight cars and a circus train. Inside these structures are displays (a barbershop, kitchen, post office, etc.) illustrating the lifestyle of the area's first settlers, the Kalapuya tribe, and local natural history. Kids will especially relish the vintage covered wagon and 50 miniature horse-drawn wagons, sleighs, carriages, and carts.

The museum also coordinates wagon-ride interludes into the past. Known as **Carriage Me Back Days,** these excursions reenact daily life from days of old. This historical festival takes place the first weekend of May. Check here too about tours of the **Moyer House** (204 N. Main St.), the elegant 1881 Italianate home of a successful mill owner/door manufacturer. The home's high-ceilinged interior features a Carrera marble fireplace, ornate wood trim, hand-painted floral patterns, stencils on the ceilings, and oil-painted outdoor scenes on the upper panels of the bay windows. The 1881 grand piano in the south parlor is another must-see. The distinctive cupola perched atop the roof housing a glass observatory will catch your eye from a distance. Come in June to see the strangely twisted wisteria tree on the front lawn in full bloom.

The Brownsville area has other worthwhile attractions. A **pioneer cemetery** on the east end of Kirk Street shelters the grave of the last known member of the Kalapuya tribe; some headstones here date to 1846, when Brownsville was established. What ended up being Oregon's third-oldest continuously operating settlement began as a ferry stop on the Calapooia River. A collection of rocks, tribal arrowheads, and woodcarvings is housed in an interesting stone structure at the **Living Rock Studio** (911 W. Bishop Way, 541/466-5814, 10 A.M.–5 P.M. Tues.–Sat., $2 suggested donation). The highlight is the series of colorful Biblical scenes made from thin slabs of rock, but don't miss out on the second-floor logging exhibit.

Northeast of Brownsville between Sweet Home and Lebanon is the **Council Tree,** a huge Douglas fir that served as the site of the annual gathering of the Kalapuyas. This 400-year-old tree can be reached by taking Route 228 to Sweet Home and heading north a few miles on U.S. 20 to Liberty Road, which goes a mile to the turnout.

Northeast of town, the **Quartzville Creek** recreational corridor has gold-panning opportunities. Follow U.S. 20 seven miles and turn left to the access road that goes 27 miles to Quartz Creek. A week's panning here is not likely to produce a quantity large enough to fill a tooth, but the pleasant surroundings and primal thrill of finding "color" in your pan is sure to get you hooked. The Sweet Home area is famous among rockhounds for petrified wood and agates. Finally, Brownsville might evoke a feeling of déjà vu, having provided big-screen backdrops for a number of films, including *Stand By Me.*

The third weekend in June, the 100-year-old **Brownsville Pioneer Picnic** features an old-time fiddlers jamboree and a tug-of-war involving large local teams. Also on the agenda are a parade, carnival, crafts fair, foot race, and tour of historical homes. The three-day celebration is held near the spot where a ferry plied the Calapooia in 1846, now part of 10-acre Pioneer Park, located off Main Street at the end of Park Avenue. Each day of the event begins with a wagon-train breakfast.

Another event of interest is the **Antique Fair** on the first weekend of August, where food, entertainment, and treasures from old farmsteads are featured.

Should you decide to overnight in the Brownsville area, you can get a room for at **Pioneer Best Western Lodge** (intersection of I-5 and Rte. 228, 800/359-4827, $65–75).

Eugene

Eugene's location confers many blessings. The Willamette River curves around the northwest quarter of the community (pop. about 140,000), and abundant trees and flowers dot the cityscape. From an elevated perch you can see the Coast and Cascade Ranges beckoning you to beach and mountain playgrounds little more than an hour away.

In town, a world-renowned Bach Festival and other big-time cultural events are showcased in the Hult Center, praised by the *Los Angeles Times* as having the best acoustics on the West Coast. The University of Oregon campus provides another forum for the best in art and academe, while its Hayward Field track has been the site of the U.S. Olympic Trials several times.

Outdoor gatherings such as Saturday Market and the Oregon Country Fair (see sidebar) bring the community together in a potlatch of homegrown edibles, arts, and crafts. But it doesn't take an organized festival to draw the townsfolk outside. Even during persistent winter rains, locals can be seen jogging, bicycling, and gardening.

For residents of the sparsely populated hamlets east, west, and south of town, Eugene is a hub for health care and shopping. Visitors from rural Lane County flock to the Eugene/Springfield area on weekends to shop at Valley River Center, see a movie, attend a convention, or simply go "garage saling."

Eugene's labor, environmental, and human services organizations (more per capita than any city of comparable size) have labored with quiet effectiveness for several decades, giving the town a distinct lefty touch with worker-owned collectives, a wheelchair-friendly cityscape, preserved ancient forests, and wetland protection against industrial pollution.

As lovely as Eugene is, it might pose some problems for those with sensitive respiratory systems. Because of sporadic temperature inversions over the southern Willamette Valley, which is framed by mountain ranges that narrow like a funnel near the town, wintertime air stagnation is not uncommon. And the Eugene area, like most of the Willamette Valley is notorious for its springtime pollens from ornamentals, trees, and grass-seed fields, making this season a challenge for the allergy sufferer. August field burning occasionally causes air quality emergencies as well.

Be that as it may, Eugene belongs on the itinerary of anyone who wants to experience urban sophistication and active pursuits in a beautiful natural setting.

SIGHTS

Two major areas of interest to visitors are immediately south of the Willamette River. The campus, in Eugene's southeast quadrant, and the downtown (bounded by 5th and 10th Aves. and Charnelton and High Sts.) are only a five-minute drive from each other. Serious walkers can

© PAUL LEVY

Downtown Eugene is full of good restaurants and shopping.

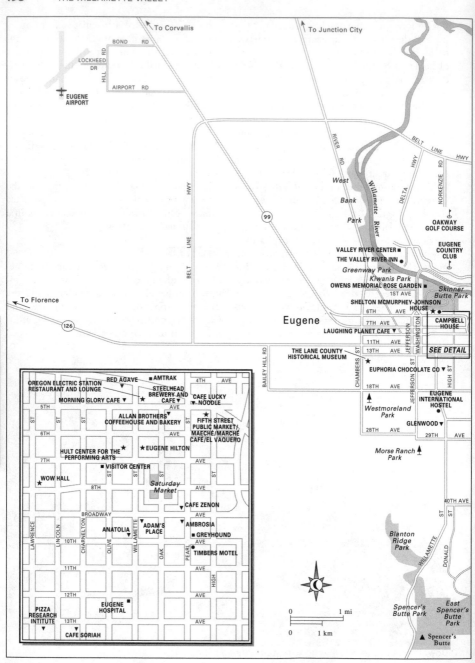

To Corvallis

To Junction City

BOND   RD

LOCKHEED
DR

HILL RD

AIRPORT   RD

EUGENE
AIRPORT

RIVER RD

Willamette River

BELT   LINE   HWY

DELTA

NORKENZIE RD

West

Bank

Park

99

BELT   LINE

HWY

OAKWAY
GOLF COURSE

EUGENE
COUNTRY
CLUB

VALLEY RIVER CENTER ■
THE VALLEY RIVER INN ●

Greenway Park

Kiwanis Park

OWENS MEMORIAL ROSE GARDEN ■

1ST AVE

Skinner
Butte Park

SHELTON MCMURPHEY-JOHNSON
HOUSE ★

6TH   AVE

CAMPBELL
HOUSE

To Florence

126

Eugene

7TH   AVE

LAUGHING PLANET CAFE ▼

11TH   AVE

13TH   AVE

JEFFERSON

WASHINGTON

SEE DETAIL

THE LANE COUNTY
HISTORICAL MUSEUM

BAILEY HILL RD

CHAMBERS   ST

EUPHORIA CHOCOLATE CO ▼

HIGH ST

18TH   AVE

EUGENE
INTERNATIONAL
HOSTEL

Westmoreland
Park

GLENWOOD ▼

28TH   AVE

JEFFERSON

29TH   AVE

Morse Ranch
Park

40TH AVE

ST

ST

Blanton
Ridge
Park

WILLAMETTE

DONALD

Spencer's
Butte Park

East
Spencer's
Butte
Park

▲ Spencer's
Butte

0   1 mi

0   1 km

RED AGAVE ■ AMTRAK

4TH   AVE

OREGON ELECTRIC STATION
RESTAURANT AND LOUNGE

STEELHEAD
BREWERY AND
CAFE ▼

MORNING GLORY CAFE ▼

CAFE LUCKY
NOODLE ▼

AVE

5TH

ST

ST

ST

ALLAN BROTHERS
COFFEEHOUSE AND BAKERY ★

FIFTH STREET
PUBLIC MARKET/
MAECHE/MARCHÉ
CAFE/EL VAQUERO

6TH

AVE

HULT CENTER FOR THE
PERFORMING ARTS ★

★ EUGENE HILTON

7TH

ST

ST

ST

AVE

■ VISITOR CENTER

ST

WOW HALL ★

Saturday
Market

AVE

8TH

AVE

BROADWAY

▼ CAFE ZENON

AVE

LAWRENCE

LINCOLN

CHARNELTON

ANATOLIA
▼

WILLAMETTE

ADAM'S
PLACE ★

OLIVE

▼ AMBROSIA

■ GREYHOUND

AVE

10TH

OAK

PEARL

TIMBERS MOTEL

11TH

AVE

HIGH

12TH

AVE

PIZZA
RESEARCH
INTITUTE
▼

13TH

EUGENE
HOSPITAL

AVE

CAFE SORIAH ▼

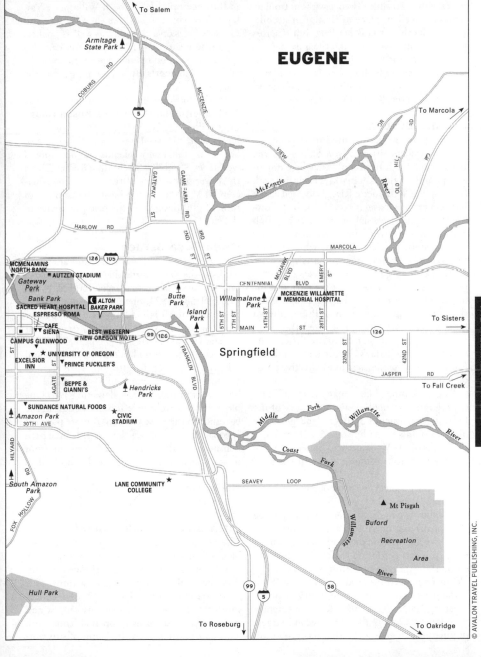

EUGENE

To Salem

Armitage
State Park

To Marcola

COBURG   RD

MCKENZIE

GATEWAY   ST

GAME-ARM   RD

VIEW

McKenzie

OR

RD

OLD   HILL   7TH

River

ST

HARLOW   RD

2ND   ST

3RD   ST

MARCOLA

126   105

MCMENAMINS
NORTH BANK

AUTZEN STADIUM

CENTENNIAL   BLVD

MCHAWK   BLVD

EMERY   S

Gateway
Park

Bank Park

ALTON
BAKER PARK

Butte
Park

Willamalane
Park

MCKENZIE WILLAMETTE
MEMORIAL HOSPITAL

SACRED HEART HOSPITAL
ESPRESSO ROMA

Island
Park

5TH ST   7TH ST   14TH ST   28TH ST

To Sisters

126

CAFE
SIENA

MAIN   ST

CAMPUS GLENWOOD

BEST WESTERN
NEW OREGON MOTEL

99   126

32ND ST   42ND ST

EXCELSIOR
INN

ST

UNIVERSITY OF OREGON

PRINCE PUCKLER'S

FRANKLIN   BLVD

Springfield

JASPER   RD

To Fall Creek

AGATE   ST

BEPPE &
GIANNI'S

Hendricks
Park

SUNDANCE NATURAL FOODS

Amazon Park

30TH   AVE

CIVIC
STADIUM

Middle   Fork

Willamette

River

Coast   Fork

HILYARD

OLD

FOX   HOLLOW

South Amazon
Park

LANE COMMUNITY
COLLEGE

SEAVEY   LOOP

Mt Pisgah

Buford

Recreation

Area

Willamette   River

Hull Park

99

5

58

To Roseburg

To Oakridge

THE WILLAMETTE VALLEY

manage the two-mile distance without trouble. Another excellent place to stroll, run, or bike with the locals, Alton Baker Park, is just across the river from downtown and the university.

The major north–south thoroughfare is Willamette Street, which can be followed from downtown five miles south to Eugene's favorite hiking haunt, Spencer's Butte.

Skinner Butte

A good place to get oriented in Eugene, visually as well as historically, is Skinner Butte. If you look north from most anywhere downtown you'll see this landmark. A beautiful park fronting the Willamette River is located at the butte's northern base. It's reachable by following the Scenic Drive signs to the river via High Street. This riverfront site served as a dock for pioneer sternwheelers and was where founding father Eugene Skinner ran a ferry service for farmers living north of the river. The town tried to become a major shipping port, but the upper Willamette was uncharted, as well as too shallow and meandering. In addition, sunken logs, gravel bars, and submerged trees and rocks made steamboat navigation difficult. As a result, Ben Holladay's Oregon and California Railroad became Eugene's most effective mode of transport in 1871.

Eugene Skinner, like so many Oregon Trail–era migrants, wanted to take advantage of the federal government's 320-acre land giveaway offer to pioneers, so he staked a claim from the banks of the Willamette to present-day 8th Avenue and from Monroe Street to the river on Hilyard Street. He built his shelter on 2nd and Lincoln Streets and later opened up Lane County's first trading post.

By following the Scenic Drive signs from the park or driving north on Lincoln Street (you can also walk up from the south side in 15 minutes), you can get to the top of the butte and enjoy the vantage point from which Eugene Skinner surveyed the landscape in June 1846. Kalapuyas called this promontory Yapoah, meaning "High Place," and used it for ceremonial dances. Despite the state's second-largest population concentration that has grown up

in the once-pristine southern Willamette Valley below, you can still see the Cascade and Coast Ranges on a clear day, as well as pockets of greenery throughout the city. You can also spot another good reference point in your orientation, **Spencer's Butte,** looming above the southern hills four miles away.

In the Skinner Butte area don't miss the 1888 **Shelton McMurphey-Johnson House** (303 Willamette St., 541/484-0808, www.smj-house.com, 10 A.M.–1 P.M. Tues.–Fri., 1–4 P.M. Sat.–Sun., tours on weekends and occassional weekdays, $5 adults, $2 children under 12), on the lower south slope of the butte. The aqua-colored Victorian is the most eye-catching of some 2,000 designated historic properties in the city.

Owen Rose Garden

Near the base of Skinner Butte and along the banks of the Willamette, the thirty varieties of roses at the Owen Rose Garden (300 N. Jefferson, 541/682-4824, open daily) peak in June and bloom until fall. Along with 4,500 roses and magnolia blossoms in spring, tremendous old cherry and oak trees also command attention. To get here from I-5, take I-105 West and take the West Eugene offramp. Turn right at the bottom of the ramp onto Madison and follow it north toward the Willamette River. One block to your right is Jefferson Street and the entrance to the Rose Garden. A more pleasant approach is on foot, via the riverside bike path behind the Valley River Inn (ask at the front desk to clarify) until you get to the footbridge. On the other side of the river, loop back in the direction of the hotel for about a half mile till you arrive at the rose garden.

Fifth Street Public Market

The past and the present happily coexist a few blocks from the butte's south flank at the Fifth Street Public Market (296 E. 5th Ave.), an old-time feed mill converted into an atrium. This rustic structure houses an impressive collection of craft boutiques, specialty stores, and restaurants surrounding an open-air courtyard. This courtyard is a favorite haunt of sun worshippers, people-watchers, and street performers. Note: Though the market bears the word "street" in its name, it is actually located on East 5th Avenue and High Street.

Eugene Saturday Market

For a more down-home version of the public market, explore the crafts, food, and street performances at the Saturday Market (8th Ave. and Oak St., 541/686 8885, www.eugene saturdaymarket.org, 10 A.M.–5 P.M. Sat. Apr.–mid-Nov.), the good vibes and creative spirit of the community are in ample evidence. The market moves indoors to the Lane County Fairgrounds (13th and Jefferson) to become the Holiday Market from the weekend before Thanksgiving to Christmas Eve (open Sat. and Sun., some weekdays).

The small farmers market set up across 8th Avenue from the crafts area (9 A.M.–5 P.M. Sat. Apr.–Nov. and 10 A.M.–4 P.M. Tues. Apr.–mid-Oct.) is a good place to get fresh, inexpensive produce.

Hult Center for the Performing Arts

While you're walking between the two markets, you might look west past the Eugene Hilton and notice another imposing building close by. This is the Hult Center for the Performing Arts (1 Eugene Center, Willamette St. between 6th and 7th Aves., 541/687-5000, www.hult center.org). In addition to its status as a top-flight performance venue, this place is worth a look for aesthetics alone. From the frog and troll statues that greet you at the 6th Avenue entrance to the high-ceilinged interior bedecked with masks, artistic touches abound.

Hult Center talent (with nine resident companies) is showcased beneath interlocking acoustic panels on the domed ceiling and walls of the 2,500-seat **Silva Concert Hall** (which resembles a giant upside-down pastel-colored Easter basket). The **Jacobs Gallery** exhibits local artwork, providing another feast for the eyes. Even the bathroom tile here is done up in a visually pleasing theatrical motif. Free one-hour guided tours are offered every Thursday and Saturday at 1 P.M. or by special arrangement. Call for reservations or make arrangements at the front desk.

University of Oregon Campus

From downtown head a few blocks south to 13th Avenue then east to the University of Oregon campus (visitor information available at Oregon Hall, Agate and 13th, 541/346-3111, www.uoregon.edu), bounded by Franklin Boulevard, 11th and 18th Avenues, and Alder and Moss Streets. With an enrollment around 20,000 students, you might be expecting a bureaucratic, impersonal feeling here. Instead, the grounds of the campus are graced by architecturally inviting buildings dating back to the school's creation in the 1870s, as well as 400 varieties of trees.

Deady Hall, the oldest building on campus, was built in 1876. Also noteworthy are two museums on campus: the Jordan Schnitzer Museum of Art and the Natural History Museum (see *Museums*). The quiet and tranquility of the campus are sustained by a ban on vehicular traffic beyond 13th Avenue and Kincaid Street. A free **campus tour** leaves from the Schnitzer Museum of Art weekdays at 10:30 A.M. and 2 P.M. and from Oregon Hall Saturdays at 10:30 A.M. But unless you're a prospective student, you're better off just picking up the map and setting your own pace.

Across from the Schnitzer Museum of Art is the **University of Oregon Library.** On the second floor, the **Oregon Collection** (541/346-3468) has books and periodicals about the state in open stacks—a great place to plan trips or learn about the region. The nationally famous map library on the first floor can also augment the trip-planning process with its extensive collection of all sorts of maps, its helpful staff, and its well-tuned photocopying machines.

This campus has often been selected by Hollywood to portray the ivy-covered halls of academe, most notably in the comedy *Animal House.*

If you wander the north part of the University of Oregon complex toward Franklin Boulevard, you'll see majestic and rare trees (including a Chinese dawn redwood) dotting the landscape between the law and journalism schools. Interesting outdoor sculptures also liven up a stroll of the campus.

Museums

A must on any campus tour is the recently renovated and expanded **Jordan Schnitzer Museum of Art** (next to the main library, 1430 Johnson Ln., 541/346-3027, http://uoma.uoregon.edu, 11 A.M. –5 P.M. Thurs.–Sun., 11 A.M. –8 P.M. Wed. year-round, $5 adults, $3 students and seniors). This museum is a real gem, with a surprisingly good collection of contemporary art, including works by Chuck Close, Mark Tobey, Morris Graves, and many Northwest artists. Another major highlight is a nationally renowned Asian collection (don't miss the jade); the revolving paintings and photography exhibits on the first floor are also usually worthwhile.

The university's other quite wonderful museum is entirely different: the **Natural History Museum** (1680 E. 15th Ave., 541/346-3024, www.uoregon.edu/~mnh, 11 A.M.–5 P.M. Tues.–Sun., $3, $2 students and seniors), showcases Oregon's prehistory and includes artifacts from digs in eastern Oregon and bird and mammal fossils from around the state. A portion of Thomas Condon's fossil collection displays the curiosities culled from the earth by the man known as Oregon's first geologist and the discoverer of the John Day Fossil Beds (see the *Northeastern Oregon* chapter). There's also a set of sagebrush sandals dated at 9,350 years of age (from the collection of those found by Dr. Luther Cressman), 15-million-year-old shell fossils, and a whale vertebra and mammoth tusks. To get there from Hayward Field on Agate Street, go east on 15th and look for a fish sculpture on your right (in front of an attractive wooden building) across the street from the dorms. Pick up the *Trees of Eugene* tour pamphlet at the information desk to annotate a scenic and historic jaunt through Eugene's leafy glades.

Maude Kerns Art Center (1910 E. 15th

© PAUL LEVY

Eugene's riverside trails are great, and the Peter DeFazio Footbridge connects Alton Baker Park with downtown.

Ave., 541/345-1571, www.mkartcenter.org, 10 A.M.–5:30 P.M. Mon.–Fri., noon–4 P.M. Sat., free.) is just east of the University of Oregon campus. Set in an old church, this gallery is dedicated to contemporary art of nationally known as well as regionally prominent artists. This gallery and others downtown are the focal points of a first Friday of the month gallery walk 5:30–8:30 P.M. (contact Lane Arts Council for details, 541/485-2278). These galleries have open houses with food and drink, combining art appreciation with conviviality. Exhibiting artists are on hand to talk about their work.

Just across the river, in Alton Baker Park **Science Factory** (2300 Leo Harris Pkwy., 541/682-7888, www.sciencefactory.org, noon–5 P.M. Wed.–Sun., closed on the days of U. of O. home football games, $7 exhibits and planetarium, $4 either exhibits or planetarium alone) is designed to stimulate scientific understanding and curiosity in everyday life. Permanent exhibits here are similar to those at Portland's OMSI, and are complemented by a new set of scientifically thematic expositions every three months. The Science Factory's hands-on orientation reaches its apex during the summer thanks to these traveling exhibits.

The museum's excellent **planetarium** is highly recommended (shows at 1 P.M. and 2 P.M. Sat., 2 P.M. Sun., $4). The Science Factory/Planetarium complex is reached from I-5 by taking I-105 West to the Coburg Road Exit and following the signs to Autzen Stadium (look for Centennial Boulevard and the Leo Harris Parkway).

The **Lane County Historical Museum** (740 W. 13th Ave., 541/682-4242, www.lchmuseum.org, 10 A.M.–4 P.M. Wed.–Fri., noon–4 P.M. Sat.–Sun., $2 adults, $1 seniors, $0.75 for youth) can be found next to the fairgrounds. Just look for the steam donkey on the front lawn. There are other 19th-century logging vehicles and period rooms on display. The Oregon Trail exhibits are among the most interesting.

Close to the Eugene Airport, the **Oregon Air and Space Museum** (90377 Boeing Dr.,

541/461-1101, noon–4 P.M. Wed.–Sun., $5) has vintage aircraft, artifacts, and displays depicting the history of aviation space.

PARKS AND TRAILS

If you're looking for what makes Eugene Eugene, you'll get some pretty big clues by visiting the city's parks. Especially appealing and easy to get to is the **Willamette River Bike Trail,** a six-mile pathway running east–west on both sides of the river, which takes in parts of Skinner Butte Park and Alton Baker Park.

◖ Alton Baker Park

Just across the Willamette River from downtown, the 400-acre Alton Baker Park is home to a world-class running trail, the Science Factory/Planetarium complex, gardens, ponds, picnic areas, a canoe canal, and part of a very cool scale model of the solar system (the sun and inner planets are here; Pluto (though it's no longer a planet) is 3.66 miles to the northwest, along the bike path). The western part of the park is more developed; to the east it includes the 237-acre Whilamut Natural Area.

The four-mile **Pre's Trail** runs along the Willamette River east of Alton Baker Park. Named after Steve Prefontaine, whose world-record times and finishing kicks used to rock the Hayward Field grandstands before his untimely death from a car accident in 1975, this soft path meanders along the river and connects to the network of trails along the Willamette.

Reach Alton Baker Park from downtown by taking the Ferry Street Bridge and turning right just after crossing the river; if you're on foot, the Peter DeFazio footbridge is right by the Ferry Street Bridge, and is an easy walk from the Fifth Street Market area. From the U. of O. area, walk or bike across the Autzen Bike Bridge to the park.

Hendricks Park

About two miles east of the campus on a forested ridgeline is Hendricks Park (541/682-5324), home to 850 naturally occurring rhododendrons and azaleas and about 10,000 hybrids. There are several ways to get to the park, the easiest being to turn

OFF THE BEATEN PATH

Along with the well-known hiking areas described in this chapter, the nearby Cascade and Coast Ranges also have some recently developed hidden gems, thanks, paradoxically, to such extractive industries as logging and gravel. The industrial "cat" trails that once cut swaths through these forests are today maintained (and sometimes paved over) by the Forest Service for access to natural wonders. Two such places are Kentucky Falls and a grove of the tallest trees in the Northwest.

Picturesque **Kentucky Falls** is set in an old-growth forest on the upper slopes of the Coast Range. To get here from downtown Eugene, drive 35 miles west on Route 126 to the Whiteaker Creek Recreation Area on the south side of the road, approximately six miles west of the Walton Store and post office. The route to Kentucky Falls winds through the clear-cut lower slopes of 3,700-foot-high **Roman Nose Mountain.**

From Whiteaker Creek Recreation Area drive one mile south and make a right turn. Then after one mile bear left on Dunn Ridge Road (Forest Service Road 18-8-28). After about seven miles the pavement ends and you'll turn left on Knowles Creek Road; go 2.7 miles. Make a right onto Forest Service Road 23 (gravel) and proceed 1.6 miles until you make a right onto Forest Service Road 919. Continue for 2.6 miles to the Kentucky Falls trailhead, marked by a sign on the left side of the road. An old-growth Douglas fir forest on gently rolling hills for the first 0.5 mile gives way to a steep descent into a lush canyon. The upper falls is visible a little more than a mile down the trail. You'll hear the water before you actually get a full cross section of a broad cascade pouring out from over the rim of this green canyon. On your drive back to Route 126, retrace your route carefully to avoid veering off on a hair-raising spur route to Mapleton.

A chance to see what may be the **Northwest's tallest trees** is possible northeast of Lowell. This recently discovered grove's 500-year-old Douglas firs average nearly 300 feet in height. The tallest tree has been measured at 322 feet, which places it in the rarefied atmosphere of the giant sequoia. Be sure to take along a forest map from the Lowell Ranger Station (541/937-2129) or the Forest Service headquarters in Eugene (211 E. 7th Ave., 541/465-6517).

To get here from Eugene, take Route 58 to Lowell. From Lowell, follow Jasper-Lowell Road two miles to the Unity Covered Bridge and turn right onto Big Fall Creek Road. Proceed down Big Fall Creek Road for 11 miles to where it becomes Forest Service Road 18. Turn left onto Forest Service Road 1817 and continue for 10 miles until you reach Forest Service Road 1806, at which point you will turn left. Go down 1806 for three miles and then turn left onto Forest Service Road 427. The trailhead is 0.5 mile down the road on the left side, but park on the right.

---

from Fairmount Boulevard onto Summit Drive. Or take Lane Transit bus #27/Fairmount, disembark at Summit Drive, and hike on up the hill a quarter mile. Two parking lots accommodate cars—one near the picnic area of stoves and tables, the other at the upper entrance on Sunset Boulevard. The rhododendron gardens are in their glory during May, with 15- to 20-foot specimens in shades of pink, red, yellow, and purple. Even though the display declines by late June, it's always a great place to stroll. Gorgeous views of the city can be enjoyed

from the west end of the garden, and tree-shaded footpaths lead to benches located in secluded cul-de-sacs on the hillside.

Ridgeline Trail

The South Hills Ridgeline Trail is only minutes from downtown Eugene and offers wildlife-watching opportunities (look for deer, tree frogs, garter snakes, and all kinds of birds) and more species of fern than perhaps any other single spot in Oregon. In addition, old-growth Douglas fir and the lovely and increasingly hard-to-find calypso orchid grow here. The trail is seldom steep and has some spectacular views of the city through clearings. A spur route leads up to the highest point in Eugene, 2,052-foot Spencer's Butte, via a steep and often muddy trail. The Ridgeline Trail can be reached from several points, including Dillard Road; near the corner of Fox Hollow and Christenson Roads; near Willamette and 52nd; off Blanton Road near 40th; and the Spencer's Butte parking area.

Spencer's Butte

According to one legend, the butte was named after a 19th-century English trapper killed by Native American arrows. The Kalapuyans called it Chamate, meaning "Rattlesnake Mountain." An 1848 account (from Batterns DeGuerre's *Ten Years in Oregon*) of the view from the summit reads as follows:

> On one hand was the vast chain of Cascade Mountains, Mount Hood looming in solitary grandeur far above its fellows; on the other hand was the Umpqua Mountains, and a little farther on, the coast ridge. Between these lay the whole magnificent panorama of the Willamette Valley, with its ribbon streams and carpetlike verdure.

The view today has all of the above, but there are some differences. Below the north summit you look down on Eugene/Springfield, with Fern Ridge Reservoir in the northwest toward Junction City. Beyond the reservoir you can sometimes see Mary's Peak. Other Cascade Mountains not noted in the previous account but sometimes visible from the butte include Mount Jefferson, Mount Washington, the Three Sisters, and Mount Bachelor. To the southeast, Creswell and the hills around Cottage Grove are visible.

The two main trails to the top vary in difficulty. If you bear left immediately after leaving the parking lot, you'll come to the route known among the locals as The Face. This trail is shorter in distance than its saddleback counterpart but much steeper and littered with boulders and, sometimes, muddy spots.

It can be scaled in 40 minutes by reasonably fit hikers.

The main trail is a straight shot from the parking lot, looping up and around the steep hills. These inclines are broken up by flat stretches. Allow about an hour for the ascent. Signs caution against rattlesnakes, falling limbs, and poison oak, the last being the most likely problem. A mixed-conifer forest featuring old-growth Douglas fir with an understory of numerous ferns and wildflowers will usher you along. Die-hard hikers will enjoy "shooting the butte" in the snow. A "snow shoot" leads you up into a winter wonderland with trails wreathed by old-growth fir dusted with snowflakes.

The main parking lot for Spencer's Butte is on Willamette Street. Just drive south on Willamette Street until you see the signs on the left side of the road. There's also parking on Fox Hollow Road.

Mount Pisgah Arboretum

The Mount Pisgah Arboretum (Buford Park, 34901 Frank Parrish Rd., 541/747-3817, www. efn.org/~mtpisgah/) features seven miles of trails that pass through a number of different habitats. The arboretum at the end of Seavey Loop Road (plant and bird lists are often available at the visitors center, open weekends) sponsors such events as a fall fair dedicated to area mushrooms and a spring wildflower show and plant sale (dates vary; call ahead). Mount Pisgah can be reached by following E. 30th Avenue from Eugene past Lane Community College to the I-5 interchange. Cross the bridge over the freeway, turn left, and take the next right onto Seavey Loop Road. You'll cross the Coast Fork of the Willamette River and then turn left onto a gravel road (look for the Mount Pisgah signs) that leads to the trailhead; the arboretum is just beyond the parking lot.

The path to the 1,514-foot summit has few trees, enabling hikers to enjoy vistas of the Willamette Valley on the way up. At the top an unforgettable perspective of the valley in the foreground and the Three Sisters and other Cascade peaks in the distance awaits.

THE WILLAMETTE VALLEY

A monument is on the summit, honoring author Ken Kesey's son and other members of the University of Oregon wrestling team who perished in a van accident (Oregon's most celebrated author lived two miles to the east in Pleasant Hill). This memorial consists of a sculpture with a relief map depicting the mountains, rivers, towns, and other landmarks in the Eugene area. Supporting the map are three five-sided bronze columns upon which the geologic history of Oregon over the past 200 million years is portrayed, using images of more than 300 fossil specimens.

Those making the climb in August will find blackberry bushes for browsing along the way. If you're perspiring from the climb, when you're back on the valley floor head south of the trailhead to the adjoining **Buford Recreation Area** for a dip in the cool waters of the Willamette River. The banks of the Coast Fork here also have a great profusion of white oak, blackberry bushes, and poison oak.

AROUND TOWN
Wineries
Right in town, you can visit the **Territorial Vineyards & Wine Company** winery (907 W. 3rd Ave., 541/684-9463, www.territorialvineyards.com, 2–7 P.M. Fri.–Sat.) to taste pinot noir, pinot gris, and riesling.

LaVelle Vineyards (89697 Sheffler Rd., Elmira, 541/935-9406, www.lavellevineyards.com) makes a wonderful stop on the way out to the coast with a location just off Route 126 near Elmira. In addition to secluded tables with umbrellas at which to enjoy LaVelle's pinots and rieslings with your picnic lunch, the works of local artists are on display in the winery itself. A trail to a hillside on the grounds lets you see the snowcapped Three Sisters on a clear day. The winery is also represented by a wine bar in the Fifth Street Market.

Also west of town off Route 126 is **Secret House Winery** (88324 Vineyard Lane, Veneta, 541/935-3774, www.secrethousewinery.com) is known for its relatively reasonably priced and high-quality pinot noir.

Silvan Ridge/Hinman Vineyards (27012 Briggs Hill Rd., 541/345-1945, www.silvanridge.com, noon–5 P.M. daily), 15 miles southwest of downtown near Crow, is a perfect place to spend a summer afternoon. Drive west on 11th Avenue, turn left on Bertelson Road, then right on Spencer Creek Road. A left down Briggs Hill Road takes you to the tasting room, located on a hillside overlooking a valley. The ride out here is a favorite of the local bicycling community, many of whom typically continue on into the Coast Range via Vaughan Road (ask for directions at the winery for the Crow Valley Store that sits opposite Vaughan Road). While at the vineyard, ask to sample Hinman's award-winning gewürztraminer; the pinot gris is also delightful.

The lavish **King Estate Winery** (80854 Territorial Rd., 541/942-9874 or 800/884-4441, www.kingestate.com, noon–5 P.M. daily) is set on 820 acres with a state-of-art winery resembling a European chateau. Production focuses on organically grown pinot gris and pinot noir. In addition to wine, you can also buy sandwiches and salads at a market here. To reach the winery from Eugene, take I-5 South to Exit 182 (Creswell), turn west on Oregon Ave. (which becomes Camas Swale Rd. and then Ham Rd.) to Territorial Highway. Turn left onto Territorial Highway and follow it about 2.5 miles to King Estate.

Cottage Grove
The town of Cottage Grove, some 20 miles south of Eugene, is known for its covered bridges (there are six in the area, find excellent details at www.oregon.gov/odot/hwy/bridge/covered_bridges.shtml) and as being the gateway to the **Bohemia mining district** (see *Events* later in this chapter), site of old abandoned mines. Check the **Cottage Grove Pioneer Museum** (Birch and H Sts., 541/942-3963) for more information on these attractions, or contact the **Cottage Grove Chamber of Commerce** (710 E. Gibbs, 541/942-2411, www.cgchamber.com). The chamber of commerce is located two miles east of the ranger station in Cottage Grove, which has a map of a 70-mile Bohemia driving loop ("Tours of the

Golden Past"), as well as updates on snow conditions. Ask also about the 14.1-mile **"rails to trails" loop** that follows the paved-over tracks of an old mining train from Cottage Grove to Culp Creek—perfect for mountain biking, birding, and mushroom hunting (especially after the first fall rains). For more information on this route, contact the Bureau of Land Management, Eugene District (2890 Chad Dr., 541/683-6600).

While you're in the area, the **Cottage Restaurant** (2915 Row River Rd., 541/942-3091) is recommended for homemade soups, vegetarian dishes, fudge pie, and cheesecake. For lunch, their large salads and sandwiches are the best in the area. In town, the **Book Mine** (702 Main St., Cottage Grove, 541/942-7414) is one of the best bookstores between Eugene and Ashland.

SPORTS AND RECREATION

Eugene's identity is rooted in its reputation as "Tracktown, U.S.A.," and also in its superlative Parks and Recreation Department, miles of bike paths and on-street bike lanes, and backcountry cycling minutes from downtown.

Water Recreation

Alton Baker Park, along the Willamette, and the **Millrace Canal,** which parallels the river for three or four miles, provide escapes from Eugene's main downtown thoroughfares. The canal is easily accessed from the University of Oregon campus by crossing Franklin Boulevard. Farther west on the Willamette, near Skinner Butte and the Owen Rose Garden, is the **Riverhouse Outdoor Program** office (301 N. Adams St., 541/682-5329), headquarters of the Parks Department outdoor program and a roped-off swimming area. This is the place to rent river craft.

Reservoirs beyond downtown Eugene provide a wide range of recreation. The one closest to town is **Fern Ridge Lake.** Camp, picnic, swim, water-ski, sail, or watch wildlife here. In addition, fishing for crappie, cutthroat trout, largemouth black bass, and catfish is excellent in early spring. This lake was formed when

the Long Tom River was dammed in 1941. Its southeast shore was designated a wildlife refuge in 1979.

To reach the lake drive 10 miles west of downtown on W. 11th Avenue (Rte. 126) toward Veneta, or take Clear Lake Road off of Route 99W. Sailboaters and sailboarders launch from marinas on north and south shores. The lake is drained in winter to allow for flood control, but the resulting marsh and wildlife refuge host tree frogs, newts, ospreys, rare purple martins (in spring), black-tailed deer, red foxes, beavers, muskrats, minks, pond turtles, and great blue herons. The wildlife area is closed to the public January–March 15 for the protection of wintering birds. There are 250 species of birds found here, including tundra swans, northern harriers, Canada geese, mergansers, peregrine falcons, and egrets, which, with their white plumage, long legs, and large size are spectacularly easy to identify. To get here, make a right off Route 126 onto Territorial Road and look for a sign on the right. This section of Territorial Road is also part of the Old Applegate Trail, the southern counterpart to the Oregon Trail. This trail ended in the Salem area after coming up through Northern California into Oregon.

Dorena Reservoir, 50 minutes south of Eugene, has camping, fishing, and boating. The Army Corps dammed the Row River to create the reservoir, which can be reached by driving south on I-5 or Route 99 for 20 miles to Cottage Grove. Then head under the bridge below I-5's Cottage Grove Exit (Exit 174) and pick up Row River Road (this goes up into the mountains, so check snow conditions), which goes eight miles east to Dorena Lake. Several miles up Row River Road, pick up Layng Road and go 1.5 miles to Currin Bridge, one of the area's six covered bridges. Another 1.2 miles south down Layng Road is Mosby Creek Bridge.

A popular retreat for locals is **Cougar Reservoir and Hot Springs.** From Eugene go 42 miles on Route 126 to the town of Blue River, then four miles down Forest Service Road 19 (the paved Aufderheide Drive) up to the west side of Cougar Reservoir. The springs

THE WILLAMETTE VALLEY

can be reached by hiking to the end of a short trail; thanks to user fees, they have remained a splendidly kept site. This trail overlooks a steep drop-off, so be careful. The several pools in this tranquil forest setting can be crowded on weekends. Purchase a Forest Service Recreation Pass at the ranger station or risk a fine.

Sports Facilities and Programs

Go for a swim in the indoor pools at **Echo Hollow** (1560 Echo Hollow Rd., 541/682-5525) or **Sheldon** (2445 Willakenzie Rd., 541/682-5314). Drop-in visitors pay a few bucks. If you're staying at the Hilton or the Valley River Inn, you can pay slightly more and get a pass to visit the **Downtown Athletic Club** (999 Willamette St., 541/484-4011,), a fairly swanky club with a 25-yard pool, fitness equipment, and classes.

Lane County Ice (Lane County Fairgrounds, 13th and Monroe, Eugene, 541/687-3615) offers ice-skating lessons and open public skating.

If you're more interested in taking to the trails on horseback, head to **C-Bow Arrow Ranch** (33435 Van Duyn Rd., 541/345-5643), located off I-5 at Exit 199, four miles north of Beltline Highway. Trail rides and lessons are also available east of town up the McKenzie at **Triangle S Ranch** (39841 McKenzie Highway, 541/747-7039).

It must be said that sometimes Eugene's weather makes indoor activities more appealing than scampering up wet rocks. On those days, or after a day of running and biking, drop in for some yoga at **Four Winds Center** (in the Tamarack Wellness Center, 3575 Donald St., 541/484-6100, www.fourwindsyoga.org), which offers a wide variety of classes with some very good teachers.

Of the many public **tennis** courts throughout Eugene, the best-lit facilities are at the University of Oregon and at 24th and Amazon Parkway near Roosevelt Middle School.

Hiking and Biking

Near the Amazon courts, runners will enjoy the bark-o-mulch trail that follows Amazon Creek in a one-mile loop. Of course, the best

jogging is along **Pre's Trail** along the Willamette River east of Alton Baker Park. Another good route is the road behind 24-Hour Fitness (1475 Franklin Blvd.), which is closed off to motorized traffic. This leads to a footbridge that takes bikers, hikers, and joggers to Pre's Trail, the Willamette River Bike Trail, Autzen Stadium, and other facilities found along the Willamette River Greenway.

Eugene and Springfield together boast 120 miles of on-street bike lanes, limited-access streets, and off-street bikeways. The two cities collaborate to publish a free bicycle map; find it online by going to the Eugene city website (www.eugene-or.gov) and searching for "bicycle map." **Collins Cycle Shop** (60 E. 11th, 541/342-4878) is centrally located. Here and elsewhere, look for the high-quality bikes, bike equipment, backpacks, and raingear made by the local **Burley Designs** co-op. Another innovative local bike business is **Bike Friday** (541/687-0487 or 888/777-0258, www.bikefriday.com), known for their extra-cool custom-made folding bicycles.

Spectator Sports

Each spring, the University of Oregon track team, a perennial contender for the status of best team in the nation, holds meets at **Hayward Field** (Agate and 15th Ave.). This site has also hosted such world-class events as the NCAA Finals and the United States Olympic Trials.

Fall means Duck football at **Autzen Stadium** (Martin Luther King Blvd. on Day Island). To get there, head north on Ferry Street. Just after crossing the Willamette River, take a hard right on Martin Luther King Boulevard. In winter, the townsfolk cram into **MacArthur Court,** a funky anachronism from the 1920s located just south of the physical education building on University Street. Even if you're not a fan, you're bound to get caught up in the frenzied decibels of "quacker backers" who support a team known for its never-say-die attitude.

In summer, the **Eugene Emeralds** play ball at Civic Stadium (2077 Willamette St., 541/342-5367), for honor, glory, and a chance to break into the big leagues. Even if you don't catch a future hall-of-famer on the way up, enjoy the best concession food you'll ever taste at a ballpark.

Golf

Laurelwood Golf Course (2700 Columbia St., 541/484-4653 for tee times) is a city-owned golf course with a 250-yard driving range. Greens fees ($14 weekdays) and rentals are reasonable.

Of the many courses in Lane County, **Tokatee** (54947 Rte. 126, Blue River, 541/822-3220 or 800/452-6376, $40 for 18 holes) is the best. In fact, on several occasions *Golf Digest* rated it among the top 25 courses in the nation, and *Back Nine* rated it the best public course in the Pacific Northwest. To get here, drive 47 miles east of Eugene on the McKenzie Highway (Rte. 126). The 18 holes here are set in a mountainous landscape patrolled by elk and other forest creatures in the shadow of the Three Sisters.

Climbing

Some of the best urban **climbing** to be found anywhere is at The Columns, a basalt cliff located on public land against the west side of Skinner Butte in downtown Eugene. Limited parking is available at The Columns, but it's more enjoyable to ride a bike here by following the road rimming the butte. Climbing is free.

Camping

If you're looking for campsites in the covered-bridge country above Cottage Grove try **Baker Bay** (52 tent sites, $16/night, 541/942-7669). Located about 18 miles from Eugene, Baker Bay offers sail- and motorboats for rent. Take I-5 South to Mosby Creek Road (take the Cottage Grove Exit), turn left, then left again on Row River Road, and then take the right fork.

If you just need a parking-lot–style RV campground with a few tent sites, **Eugene Kamping World RV Park** (541/343-4832) is just north of Eugene near the quaint town of Coburg. Take the Coburg Exit off I-5, head west, and you'll find the RV park a mile or so down the road.

Between the coast and the Oregon Country Fair grounds, **Triangle Lake Park** (541/927-6189) has 18 sites for $10 a night. Proceed 25 miles northwest from the fairgrounds on Route 126. Take a right onto Territorial Highway, then a left on Route 36 to Triangle Lake. You'll find the campsites just after the lake.

Fern Ridge Shores (541/935-2335) is located in a quiet family park 12 miles west of Eugene. Take Jeans Road off Route 126 near Veneta. Unlike the other previously mentioned sites, Fern Ridge Shores does not accept reservations. Campsites go for $25 per night; hookups are $25.

RVers, Oregon Country Fair–goers, rock concert attendees, and Scandinavian Fair visitors have been taking advantage of **Richardson County Park** (25950 Richardson Park Rd., Junction City, 541/935-2005) on the shores of Fern Ridge Reservoir six miles northwest of Eugene. The 88 sites with hookups and water can be accessed by taking Clear Lake Road off of Route 99 to its intersection with Territorial Road. Space availability is on a first-come first-served basis in this shaded campground rich in amenities and recreation. It's open April 15–October 15 and costs $20 per night.

ENTERTAINMENT

Keeping up with Eugene's multifaceted entertainment offerings involves previewing the listings put out by two local newspapers, *Eugene Weekly* (http://eugeneweekly.com) and the daily *Eugene Register Guard* (www.registerguard.com); both have good online events listings, with the *Weekly* being a little more alternative. Call the University of Oregon ticket office (541/346-4461) for athletic event information. For more information on what's happening around town, peruse the community bulletin boards at Fifth Street Public Market and Sundance Natural Foods.

Dancing and Music

If you tire of watching other folks in action, the best spot for frenetic dancing in town is the **W.O.W. Hall** (291 W. 8th Ave., 541/687-2746, www.wowhall.org). This old Wobblie (International Workers of the World) meeting hall has remained a monument to Oregon's activist past in labor history (well, sort of anyway: its motto is now "Fighting to save rock & roll since 1975"). Despite having all the ambience of a junior-high-school gym, it hosts some surprisingly famous rock and blues performers. The W.O.W. bills itself as having the best hardwood dance floor in the Pacific Northwest. In any case, it's probably the most crowded and features an interesting cross section of Eugenians. Beer and wine are served downstairs.

Dancing to live bands at the **Erb Memorial Union Ballroom** (13th and University, 541/346-6000) is a Eugene tradition. Local-guy-who-made-good Robert Cray and other nationally known performers have played here. The dance floor is more spacious than the W.O.W. Hall's but can actually exceed its downtown counterpart in BTUs generated by the mass of writhing bodies.

Concerts frequently take place within the cavernous enclaves of Autzen Stadium, the home field to the Oregon Ducks football team. A good sound system has made it possible for tens of thousands of concert attendees to enjoy such artists as Bob Dylan and U2.

The **Eugene Hilton Ballroom** (66 E. 6th Ave., 541/342-2000, www.hiltoneugene.com) also hosts big names running the gamut of popular music. For more sedate listening, the **Hult Center** is next door to the Hilton. The Eugene Symphony and other estimable local groups like the Eugene Concert Choir perform here along with a wide-ranging array of headliners from the world of music and comedy. This is also where the Bach Festival concerts occur. At Christmastime, the Eugene Ballet's *Nutcracker* is always a treat.

Live jazz in the basement of **Jo Federigo's** (259 E. 5th Ave., 541/343-8488) is made more enjoyable by crayons, paper, and one of their famous Long Island iced teas. Decent Italian food is served upstairs.

Down the block, the **Oregon Electric Station Restaurant and Lounge** (27 E. 5th, 541/485-4444) hosts live jazz and rhythm-and-blues acts. This historic landmark fea-

tures excellent dinner ($15–45) and lunch ($8–16) entrées, a full bar, a back room with wing chairs, and the ambience of an English club. But you never forget you're in Tracktown, U.S.A. thanks to a wall festooned with photos of Alberto Salazar and Steve Prefontaine. Open nightly.

In the same neighborhood, **The Beanery** (152 W. 5th Ave., 541/342-3378) has live folk and blues at night and the same excellent coffee as its Corvallis outlets. This spacious coffeehouse, located in a charming old building across from the Lane County Jail, attracts everyone from off-duty cops to madmen playing speed chess. Home-baked goodies and breakfast, lunch, and dinner entrées (under $10) can be ordered at the counter. Open daily.

Several clubs are clustered within about a two-block area around West Broadway. **John Henry's** (77 W. Broadway, 541/342-3358) is a music-oriented bar, with a bit of a punky touch. **Jameson's** (115 W. Broadway, 541/485-9913) has a good atmosphere; it's classy but not overly fussy. **SNAFU** (64 W. 8th Alley) is a gay-oriented dance bar with fancied-up disco-ball lighting.

At **Good Times Cafe and Bar** (375 E. 7th Ave., 541/484-7181), you can hang out and play pool or catch Tuesday night blues acts. Out in the Whiteaker neighborhood, **Sam Bond's Garage** (407 Blair Blvd., 541/343-2635) serves live music, microbrews and a menu of vegetarian pub grub till dawn; open every day.

Theaters

While there's no shortage of movie houses in this town, the real screen gems are usually found at the university (consult the *Oregon Daily Emerald,* the U. of O. student newspaper, available free on and near campus) and the **Bijou Theatre** (492 E. 13th Ave., 541/686-2458, www.bijou-cinemas.com). The university series favors cult films and classics (*Yellow Submarine, The Last Wave, The Bicycle Thief, King of Hearts,* etc.) and the inexpensive ticket price helps you forget the oppressiveness of the lecture halls that serve as theaters. For about twice the price, the Bijou is the place to see foreign films, art flicks, and

OREGON COUNTRY FAIR

Just after the Bach Festival in mid-July, the Oregon Country Fair takes place as the second major cultural event of the summer. If you've been too busy to follow the growth of the '60s counterculture, put on your paisley and follow an eclectic caravan of hand-painted school-buses, Volkswagen Beetles, Volvos, and BMWs to the Oregon County Fair.

After buying your ticket at the gatehouse, join the crowds of tie-dyed, fringed, and love-beaded fair-goers. Entering, you wander through a kaleidoscope of natural fabrics, graceful ceramics, stained glass, rainbow candles, and thousands of other variously sculpted wares. Machine-manufactured items are simply unavailable. Every aspect of the fair — its 350-plus booths and its participants — is, in a sense, art.

What? Two hours gone by already? You need a cup of espresso and a piece of torte if you're going to make it through this day. Or perhaps you want a **Ritta's** burrito bulging with avocado, salsa, and sprouts. The choices are mouthwatering: Get fried rice, sushi, blazing salads, or even a tofuless tofu burger (100 percent ground beef), and more.

Overwhelmed by the constant parade of costumed stilt walkers, strolling musicians, winged "country fairies," children in face paint, bare-breasted men and women, and other ambient wonders? Not far from any burnout point is a stage.

Shady Grove is a quiet venue for acoustic folk, classical, new age, and other music. The **Daredevil, W. C. Fields,** and **Energy Park** stages host contemporary New Vaudeville stars and other rollicking performers. See the **Royale Famille du Canniveaux** debut a unique musical comedy. Marvel as the **Reduced Shakespeare Company** performs *Romeo and Juliet* backward in one minute flat. Shake your head and mutter as **Up For Grabs** juggles circular-saw blades and/or small children.

But wait, there's more. Try **The Circus** with its parade, orchestra, and veteran virtuosos. Ogle snake charmers and belly dancers at the **Gypsy Stage.** Or dance to the national and international stars of rock 'n' roll, reggae, and alternative music on the **Main Stage.**

Starting to sound less like a hippie fair and more like a well-catered and -established art convention? Don't worry; there's always a sojourn into geo-socio-political-eco-conscious-ness at **Community Village.** Several booths here and in **Energy Park** teach and demonstrate the latest in new and matured '60s activism and environmental awareness.

Tired already? So are we, but there's a whole year to rest up and reminisce before the next Oregon Country Fair.

This annual fantasyland is staged among the trees east of Noti on Route 126. The best way to get there without much traffic is to take the free shuttle from Eugene's downtown bus station near 11th and Willamette. It goes directly to the wooded fair site near the Long Tom River, 13 miles from Eugene. Another shuttle departs from Civic Stadium on Pearl across from South Eugene High School. Bus service usually begins at about 10:30 A.M., with the last departure from the fair site at 7 P.M. Due to the popularity of this event, which attracts more than 50,000 attendees, mandatory advance ticket purchase prior to arrival on-site has been instituted for those taking mass transit. Car access to the fair is open 10 A.M.-6 P.M., but on-site parking is limited. Parking costs $5 at the gate, a couple of bucks less when reserved in advance.

For more information, contact the Oregon Country Fair (P.O. Box 2972, Eugene 97402, 541/343-4298, www.oregoncountryfair.org). Admission is $10-15 (kids 12 and under free, 55 and above half price). Purchase tickets in advance through **Fastixx** (800/992-8499) at the Hult Center, or at the U. of O. Erb Memorial Union. Gates open at 11 A.M. and close at 7 P.M. Dogs, drugs, and video recorders are prohibited.

less commercial mainstream movies. Located in an intimate Moorish-style converted church, the Bijou offers great munchies and late-night presentations.

Cutting-edge theater can be enjoyed at **Lord Leebrick** (540 Charnelton, 541/684-6988).

EVENTS

There is a lot happening in this south Willamette Valley hub of culture and athletics. Several events, however, best impart the flavor of the area.

Oregon Bach Festival

Of all the kulturfests in the Willamette Valley, only one enjoys international acclaim. The Oregon Bach Festival (541/346-5666 and 800/457-1486, www.oregonbachfestival. com) takes place over two weeks late June–early July under the baton of famed Bach interpreter Helmuth Rilling from Germany. The *New York Times* once rated the festival the best of its kind in the country, and an influx of renowned visiting opera and symphonic virtuosi guarantees that this will remain the case. More than two dozen separate concerts are featured, with musical styles ranging from the baroque era to the 20th century. The centerpieces of the festival, however, are Bach works such as the *St. Matthew Passion,* numerous cantatas, and the Brandenburg Concertos.

Performances take place in the Hult Center and at the Beall Concert Hall at the University of Oregon Music School. Free events, including "Let's talk with the conductor," miniconcerts, and children's activities also take place at these venues during the festival. Particularly recommended is the festival's Discovery Series: six concertos preceded by a short lecture-demo by Helmuth Rilling. Each 5 P.M. concert features a different Bach church cantata. Free noon concerts in the Hult lobby are also popular. A scheduled series of brunches, lunches, and dinners with the musicians also adds a special touch to the event.

Art and the Vineyard

Appealing to lowbrow and highbrow alike is Art and the Vineyard, which generally takes place over the July 4 weekend in Alton Baker Park. This event brings together art, music, and wine in a tranquil park near the Willamette River. One hundred artists' booths and the offerings of a dozen vineyards frequently grace the affair, along with live music (jazz, country, blues, and folk) and food concessions. An admission is charged to this outdoor celebration of Eugene's cultural richness. Contact the Maud Kerns Art Center (541/345-1571) for details and tickets.

Other Events

A gallery walk the first Friday of every month lets culture vultures enjoy open house exhibitions all over town. Consult the preceding Sunday *Register Guard* for a complete listing of participating venues.

The university sponsors the **Willamette Valley Folk Festival** (541/686-INFO) in May, which has attracted loosely defined folkies ranging from Tom Paxton to Doc Watson to Ani DiFranco. Call for a schedule of upcoming concerts. The free event is held in Alton Baker Park at the Cuthbert Amphitheatre; bring some cash to enjoy Eugene's amazing array of food vendors.

Music lovers also revel in the city's summer **Concerts in the Parks** festival. A series of free concerts is also held in Alton Baker Park's Cuthbert Amphitheatre mid-July to late August. Nancy Griffith, David Grisman, and Robert Cray typify the national names appearing here. Call 541/687-5000 for tickets and information. Lower profile groups grace Amazon and Westmoreland Parks as well as several other venues throughout the city. Contact CVALCO (800/547-5445) for a schedule and more information.

Bohemia Mining Days (541/942-5064, www.bohemiaminingdays.org) convenes in mid-July; many of the events take place at re-created Bohemia City south of Eugene on Route 99 in Cottage Grove. Highlights of the four-day event include the Miner's Dinner and street dance, gold-panning demonstrations, and a carnival. Don't miss the Grand Miner's

Parade, which happens on Saturday morning. Floats, horse teams, drill teams, and color guards make their way from Harrison Avenue to Row River Road with colorful costumes and the kind of enthusiasm last seen around here after turn-of-the-century lucky strikes.

Also outside of Eugene, the annual **Junction City Scandinavian Festival** (Greenwood Street, between 5th and 7th, Junction City, www.scandinavianfestival.com) celebrates the town's Danish founders the second weekend in August. Swedish, Finnish, Norwegian, and Icelandic heritage also exert a presence at the festival. Folk dancing, traditional crafts, and food make up the bulk of the activities. Skits of Hans Christian Andersen folktales are enacted during the four-day event, along with guided hour-long bus tours that take you by Scandinavian pioneer farmsteads. Tour tickets are available at the information windmill for $2.50. Junction City is 12 miles northwest of Eugene off Route 99. Another Junction City–area event is the mid-March Daffodil Drive, west of town at the Long Tom Grange.

Another summer event outside Eugene is Springfield's **Filbert Festival** (541/746-6750, www.filbertfestival.com, mid-August). Held at Island Park by the river, this assemblage of food and crafts booths and music acts is augmented by a filbert (a.k.a. hazelnut) cook-off and other events.

Autumn is ushered in with the **Eugene Celebration** (541/681-4108, www.eugene celebration.com, $6 day pass, $10 three-day pass). This three-day fete in late September includes such events as two parades (one is a pet parade), an art show, a jazz festival, and the coronation of the Slug Queen. Street performers all over town and food booths in the parking lot at 8th Avenue and Willamette also help the community put its best foot forward.

ACCOMMODATIONS

A few bed-and-breakfasts and a youth hostel provide the best values for the dollar in town, and there are plenty of inexpensive motels on East Broadway and moderately priced ones on Franklin Boulevard. (Before you check into one of these places, walk or drive a couple of blocks behind the motel toward the river just to make sure that the train tracks aren't too close—at 3 A.M. it can sound like trains are driving right through some of these budget motels!) Discounts are often available at the more upscale Valley River Inn, which is a very pleasant place to stay. Campsites and rustic digs are east of town on the McKenzie River Highway (see *The McKenzie River Highway*). As with many Oregon towns, an 8 percent room tax is added to the tariff.

Under $50

Budget travelers with a hippie bent will appreciate the **Eugene International Hostel** (2352 Willamette St., 541/349-0589, $19 dorm bed), a spacious historic home with a comfortable living room, large dining area, and patio. With some of Eugene's best food shopping close by, it's possible to take full advantage of excellent kitchen facilities (the kitchen is vegetarian and there's an organic garden out back, which is available for guests' use in season), assuming you can resist the equally compelling area dining. The hostel is an easy walk from downtown or the university, and the #24 or #25 city buses go from downtown to the corner of 24th and Willamette, stopping a few blocks from the hostel.

Of the budget hotels near downtown, the **Timbers Motel** (1015 Pearl St., 541-343-3345, 800/643-4167, www.timbersmotel.net, $49 and up, lower in winter) is a good bet, with clean and relatively attractive rooms. Note that it's just down the block from the Greyhound station, which unfortunately means there can be some pretty scruffy-looking folks on the sidewalks. But it's also practically across the street from the Cafe Zenon and the Palace Bakery, two great places to eat.

Downtown Motel (361 W. 7th Ave., www. downtownmotel.com, about $50) is another conveniently located bargain. Don't expect luxury, and enjoy the 1950s ambiance of this classic court motel.

$50-100

The **Best Western New Oregon Motel** (1655

Franklin Blvd., 541/683-3669, $89–99) is a good choice for visiting parents of U. of O. students or for folks in town to attend a sporting or cultural event. It's located right across the street from the Registration Office and dormitories. Like all Best Westerns, this place offers many amenities (spa, pool, fitness room, racquetball court) and well-appointed rooms. Behind the hotel lie Alton Baker Park and a walking and jogging trail along the river.

$100 and Up

The **Campbell House** (252 Pearl St., 541/343-1119, www.campbellhouse.com, $119 and up, including breakfast) is a 19-room Victorian in the historic east Skinner Butte neighborhood. Proximity to the Fifth Street Market and the river, as well as the sophistication of a European-style pension, makes this antique-filled 1892 gem a good lodging choice.

The upstairs of a popular eatery just a block from campus, the **Excelsior Inn,** (754 E. 13th Ave., 541/485-1206, www.excelsiorinn.com, $99–225 includes breakfast, less in winter) offers 14 elegant bed-and-breakfast rooms featuring antiques, cherry furniture, marble tile, and fresh-cut flowers. An elevator makes the rooms wheelchair accessible; computer ports are in every room.

The best standard motel in town is **Valley River Inn** (1000 Valley River Way, Valley River Center, 541/687-0123, www.valley riverinn.com, $150 and up, lower in winter, Web specials often available). Don't be deterred by its location away from downtown in back of a giant shopping mall; the inn backs up to the Willamette River, and provides easy access to the riverside trail network. In fact, it's easier to get downtown along the bike path than it is to drive. It's also a good place to stay if you're traveling with a dog; the inn is pet friendly, and the riverside path makes for delightful dog walks. A decent restaurant, a crackling fire in the lobby, and pool and spa facilities add to the allure. If it's in the budget, pony up for a riverside room—the view is worth it.

In the downtown area, the **Eugene Hilton** (66 E. 6th Ave., 541/342-2000 or 800/445-8667, www.hilton.com, $154 and up) is the top high-end hotel, and host to many conferences. It has a great location right across the street from the Hult Center and within easy walking distance to the city's best restaurants. One caveat: if you plan to stay here during Eugene Celebration, bring earplugs if you want to get to sleep before the street party winds down for the night.

FOOD

Eating out in Eugene has long been a delight, thanks to such restaurants as long-standing Cafe Zenon and the highly regared Marché. You may also be impressed by the staggering array of locally made gourmet products and natural foods available at markets here. As you might have guessed, many of these delectables are foremost organically grown and nutritionally sound. And, although perhaps not as nutritionally sound as, say, Toby's Tofu Pate (the spicy version is quite good), be sure to treat yourself to some **Prince Puckler's** ice cream (1605 E 19th Ave., 541/344-4418).

Fifth Street Market Area

Since it opened in 1997, **Marché** (296 E. 5th Ave., 541/342-3612, lunch and dinner daily, dinner entrees $16–32) has set the standard for fine dining in Eugene. The restaurant, in the ground-floor southwest corner of the Fifth Street Market, is as close to a French bistro as you're going to find in this town, and the food is decidedly French-inflected, with an emphasis on fresh local produce and meat. Don't feel like you have to dress up or take out a second mortgage to eat here. The atmosphere is crisp but not fussy, and if you sit in the bar, you can while away an enjoyable but not particularly expensive evening with drinks and small plates.

For a more casual take on Marché's food, head upstairs in the Fifth Street Market to the **Marché Café** (296 E. 5th Ave., 541/342-3612, 8:30 A.M.–7 P.M. Mon.–Fri., 9 A.M.–7 P.M.Sat., 9 A.M.–6 P.M. Sun., $6–8 for a light meal), where the food spans the hours from late breakfast to early dinner with quiche, tasty open-faced sandwiches, soups, and salads.

Just around the corner in the Fifth Street Market, █ **El Vaquero** (296 E. 5th Ave., 541/434-8272, lunch and dinner daily, tapas $5–8) has one of Eugene's most stylish and liveliest restaurant bars, serving excellent and sometimes untraditional tapas, including a "roll your own" skirt steak served with guacamole and tortillas. For those who want to sit down at a quiet table and tuck into a steak dinner, that's also an option here.

The two young women who own El Vaquero have another casual and appealing Nuevo Latino restaurant just a couple of blocks away. **Red Agave** (454 Willamette St., 541/683-2206, small plates $6–10, large plates around $20) can also be bustling and loud, but the bright colors, pomegranate daiquiris, and friendly staff can quickly put you in a mellow Latin groove. The menu has lots of fish on it, and it's all more sophisticated and alluring than your standard Baja fish taco.

You'll find vegan food and lefty politics at **Morning Glory Café** (450 Willamette St., 541/687-0709, 7:30 A.M.–3:30 P.M. daily). Some menu items do contain dairy, but this is the place to come for a very tasty tempeh sandwich.

In a complex across the street from the Fifth Street Market, **Café Lucky Noodle** (205 E. 5th Ave., 541/484-4777, breakfast, lunch, and dinner daily, entrées $9–18) serves both Asian and Italian noodle dishes as well as breakfast, espresso, and gelato in a airy, stylish space. Somehow, this works… although the prices are a bit on the steep side (pad Thai is over $10), the food is flavorful and the portions generous. Lucky Noodle's sister restaurant, **Ring of Fire** (1099 Chambers St., 541/344-6475, lunch and dinner daily, main courses around $12) is also recommended.

One block west of the Fifth Street Market, the **Steelhead Brewery and Cafe** (199 E. 5th Ave., 541/686-2739, entrées $5–9) gives suds connoisseurs a place to quaff the city's best local brew. The paneled walls, comfortable seating, and quality pub fare are other enticements to pass an hour or two here. The varied menu can include calzones, pizza, burgers,

sandwiches, pastas, soups, vegetarian entrées, and calamari plates.

Central Downtown Area

In the heart of downtown, **Anatolia** (992 Willamette, 541/343-9661, lunch Mon.–Sat. and dinner daily) features Greek and Indian food par excellence. Spicy curries and vindaloo chicken are complemented by *saganaki* (fried cheese), spanakopita (spinach cheese pie), and gyro sandwiches. The best baklava in town with a shot of ouzo or retsina can finish off a richly flavored and moderately priced repast (most expensive dinner entrée, $14)

A few blocks east is downtown's gourmet gulch. █ **Cafe Zenon** (898 Pearl St., 541/343-3005, all meals daily, dinner $12–22) has an incredibly wide-ranging, constantly changing international menu. Despite this challenge, the Zenon manages to pull off dishes ranging from Italian to Thai in fine style. The only problems you'll run into are getting in—reservations aren't taken and there's often a wait—and getting out without stopping at the eye-popping dessert display. Breakfast and lunch can be enjoyed here at half the price of dinner. When there's a wait at Cafe Zenon, **Full City Coffee** (842 Pearl St., 541/344-0475), several doors down, can be counted on to sustain you with the best coffee in a town. Famous for its daily grind, this is one of several locations in town. If a light breakfast will do, have a scone at the adjacent **Palace Bakery** (844 Pearl St., 541/484-2435).

Across the street from Cafe Zenon is a spacious two-story Italian restaurant, **Ambrosia** (174 Broadway, 541/342-4141, lunch and dinner, dinner entrées $13–22). Antique furnishings and stained glass set the stage for Old World cuisine prepared to suit contemporary tastes. The individual-size gourmet pizzas (cooked in an extra-hot wood-burning oven), a wonderful squid-in-batter appetizer, a great wine list, and northern Italian specialties will make spaghetti and meatballs seem like old hat here.

For sheer romantic indulgence, **Adam's Place** (30 E. Broadway, 541/344-6948, dinner Tues.–Sat., over $20) has an elegance that

THE WILLAMETTE VALLEY

Eugene's other restaurants can't touch. As is expected in fine Northwestern restaurants, the ingredients are largely local, and simply prepared in ways that enhance, rather than obscure, their flavors.

At the southwestern edge of downtown, **Cafe Soriah** (384 W. 13th Ave., 541/342-4410, dinner entreés $14–25) is a popular choice for a romantic dinner or weekday business lunch. Both its patio for summer outdoor dining and its bar topped a local restaurant poll for ambience, but the Mediterranean/Middle Eastern cuisine is the real attraction. Moussaka and various dishes featuring chicken and lamb with vegetables sautéed in olive oil stand out here.

Just around the corner, the **Pizza Research Institute** (1328 Lawrence St., 541/343-1307, lunch and dinner daily) has the most innovative pizza in town. In this case, innovation equals excellence—try the chef's choice, which is invariably tasty. PRI, which serves only veggie pies, has a friendly, spunky feel that's thoroughly Eugenian.

Newman's (1545 Willamette St., 541/344-2371, lunch and early dinner Mon.–Sat.) is a walk-up fish-n-chips window. Here you can get gourmet renditions of salmon, halibut, and cod with chips for about $6. A block south from the Vets Club on the corner of Willamette is **Euphoria Chocolate Co.** (6 W. 17th Ave., 541/343-9223), a chocolatier of national repute. Their Grand Marnier truffle and other confections are sold around town. Come here after holidays and buy the bite-size Santas, hearts, and bunnies at reduced price.

If you want to just grab a bagel and some tofu paté, stop by the **Kiva** (125 W. 11th, 541/342-8666), a funky but well-stocked natural foods store.

Near Campus

The eateries on the campus periphery are a cut above those found in most college towns. Start the day at **Campus Glenwood** (1340 Alder, 541/687-0355) or at the southside **Glenwood** (2588 Willamette St., 541/687-8201), both open daily. The menus offer standard American breakfast fare, with a few entrées deferring to eclectic college-town tastes. What these establishments have in common are large portions in the $5 range.

If your tummy can just handle coffee and a croissant in the morning and your wallet can yield no more than several dollars, head to **Espresso Roma** (825 E. 13th Ave., 541/484-0878, daily). There is also a delightful outside courtyard that fills up when the rain stops. A few doors down, tasty, inexpensive breakfasts and lunches can be had at **Cafe Siena** (853 E. 13th Ave., 541/344-0300, 8 A.M.–7 P.M. Mon.–Fri., 9 A.M.–4 P.M. Sat.–Sun.). With menu choices in the $3–6 range, this place is popular with the campus crowd. Homemade soup seems to be a lunchtime staple for regulars here.

In the shadow of the campus is one of the best restaurants in town, the **Excelsior Cafe** (754 E. 13th Ave., 541/485-1206, lunch and dinner daily, Sunday brunch, $10–26), located in a charming old colonial home. The Italian menu changes with the seasons, but you can always find gourmet pizzas and dinner main courses garnished with such Willamette Valley signature ingredients as goat cheese, elephant garlic, filberts, and Oregon blue cheese. Despite a reputation for fine food, it's the desserts and cozy bar that are the biggest draws here on weeknights.

Not too far from the campus, McMenamins **High Street Brewery & Cafe** (1243 High St., 541/345-4905, 11 A.M.–1 A.M. Mon–Sat., noon–midnight Sun.) is in a comfy converted old house, with a tree-shaded brickwork back patio that makes the perfect hangout on a hot afternoon.

Rennie's Landing (1214 Kincaid, 541/687-0600, all meals daily) serves breakfast, gourmet burgers, homemade soups, beer, and wine. Late-night and predawn hours, an outside deck, and a location right across from the U. of O. campus make this a favorite with the campus crowd—particularly after Ducks games.

South of Downtown

Sundance Natural Foods (748 E. 24th, 541/345-6153) features excellent selections of wine and organic produce. Sundance's fresh salad bar and hot buffet is a good deal. Just around the corner from Sundance, find

Humble Bagels (2435 Hilyard, 541/484-4497), a landmark Eugene eatery, and the excellent **Iraila** (2435 Hilyard, 541/684-8400, dinner Wed.–Sun., about $15), with food influenced by a wide range of Mediterranean cuisines, including North African, served in a down-to-earth atmosphere.

Dinner on the outside deck at **(Beppe & Gianni's Trattoria** (1646 E. 19th Ave., 541/683-6661, dinner nightly, $13–19) is one of Eugene's coveted summertime dining experiences. The menu features homemade pastas with light northern Italian cream or olive oil based sauces, graced by fresh vegetables, meats, or fish.

Whitaker Neighborhood

A quarter mile west of center city is Blair Boulevard and the Whitaker neighborhood. In recent years, a budget restaurant row has been developing in what had been a strip of fast-food places and greasy spoons in previous decades. These places are, for the most part, easy on the pocketbook while offering an interesting variety of cuisines.

A few blocks south across 7th Street is a concentration of eateries including **La Tiendita/ Taco Loco** (900 Blair Blvd., 541/683-9171, closed Sun.), serving up locally renowned tamales and other south-of-the-border specialties adjacent to a store devoted to Latino foodstuffs. Low prices ($7–9), huge portions, and down-home Mexican and El Salvadoran specialties (try the *pupusas*) draw a large takeout clientele at lunch. Close by, **Los Jarritos** (764 Blair Blvd., 541/344-0650), operated by a member of the same family, offers similar fare. The **Jade Palace** (906 W. 7th Ave., 541/344-9523, closed Mon.) is noteworthy for seafood and vegetarian fare, with buffets offering good dollar value.

Vegetarians can get a good, inexpensive meal at **Laughing Planet Café** (760 Blair Blvd., 541/868-0668). A bean burrito will fill you up, but daring diners will order the dish called soylent green.

On the east side of Blair Boulevard on 7th Street is **Full Boat Cafe** (830 W. 7th Ave., 541/484-2722, open daily), a fish market with an attached café. The array of fish-n-chips (about $6) is noteworthy for its freshness and tartar sauces. The attached fish market sells the freshest Dungeness crab in town, excellent smoked salmon, and microbrews.

North of the Willamette

Although **Sweetwaters** (1000 Valley River Way, 541/687-0123, $12–20) is basically a fancy hotel restaurant, it is an easy and pretty tasty bet for those staying at the Valley River Inn, and it boasts a riverside outdoor deck that might offer Eugene's most delightful dining experience on a warm summer night. Be sure to take a sweater—it cools down fast at night.

Vying with Sweetwaters for Eugene's most scenic restaurant river frontage is McMenamins' **North Bank** (22 Club Rd., 541/343-5622, 11 A.M.–11 P.M. Mon–Thurs., 11 A.M.–midnight Fri.–Sat., noon–11 P.M. Sun.). With an outdoor deck, picturesque windows overlooking the Willamette, and a moderately priced menu ($7–12 for sandwiches and pasta dishes) of quality pub grub featuring everything from eggplant sandwiches to the Communication Breakdown Burger, this is the best place to experience how Oregon's preeminent brewpub-meisters have made dining fun. Should wintertime mist obscure river views, you'll appreciate the penchant of the Brothers M for eccentric woodwork and wistful murals.

Shiki (81 Coburg Rd., 541/343-1936, 11 A.M.–2 P.M. Tues–Fri, 5–10 P.M. Tues.–Sun., $15 and up) is located across the Ferry Street Bridge, a few miles north of downtown shortly before the exit for I-105 to Springfield. The classic decor of the restaurant's tatami rooms, 53 kinds of sushi, a varied selection of sake, and such traditional dishes as *shabu shabu* belie the symmetrical western contours of the restaurant's facade, a former Sizzler, located in the Goodwill parking lot.

INFORMATION

Find info about Oregon's second-most-populated town at the Convention and Visitors Association of Lane County, **CVALCO** (115 W.

8th Ave., Suite 190, Eugene 97401, 800/547-5445, www.visitlanecounty.org). The entrance is on Olive Street. Also useful is the Planet Eugene website (www.planeteugene.com). The **Smith Family Bookstore** (768 E. 13th, 541/345-1651, and 525 Willamette St., 541/343-4717) purveys an excellent collection of used books. The **University of Oregon Bookstore** (13th and Kincaid, 541/346-4331) has a good selection of new titles and periodicals.

KLCC (89.7 FM) the public-radio dominant presence. The station's programming ranges from new-wave jazz to blues. It also has a dynamic news department. The University of Oregon station KWAX (90.1 FM), broadcast in eastern Oregon and on the coast, provides continuous classical music. Perhaps the most popular AM station in the area is talk radio KUGN (590 AM).

Eugene Weekly (1251 Lincoln St., 541/484-0519) has the best entertainment listings in Eugene. At the beginning of each season, the magazine's *Chow* edition will point you in the direction of Eugene gourmet restaurants. This publication is available free at commercial establishments all over town.

GETTING THERE AND AROUND

If you're in your own car or on a bike, remember (1) the campus is in the southeastern part of town; (2) 1st Avenue parallels the Willamette River; and (3) Willamette Street divides the city east and west. Navigation is complicated by many one-way roads and dead-ends. Look for alleyways that allow through traffic to avoid getting stuck.

Amtrak (4th and Willamette, 541/344-6265, www.amtrak.com) offers once-daily service both north to Portland and Seattle and south to Sacramento, Oakland, and Los Angeles on the *Coast Starlight*. There are also high-speed trains heading north to Portland daily. In addition, Amtrak runs several express buses each day between Portland and Eugene.

Greyhound (9th and Pearl, 800/231-2222) is the other major mode of long-distance public transport, heading south to San Francisco or north to Portland (two daily) from Eugene. Sample fares from Eugene to Portland are $15 one-way, $25 round-trip.

Around town, **Lane Transit District** (541/687-5555, www.ltd.org, $1.25) has canopied pavilions displaying the bus timetables downtown. All buses are equipped with bike racks. The **ride board** on the bottom floor of the Erb Memorial Union at the University of Oregon has a list of rides available for those willing to share gas and driving. **Emerald City Taxi** (541/686-2010) is fast, reliable, and reasonably priced.

The **Eugene Airport** (541/682-5430, www.ci.eugene.or.us) is a 20-minute drive northwest from downtown. Just get on the Delta Highway off Washington Street and follow the signs. United and United Express (800/241-6522) and Horizon (800/547-9308) all operate flights in and out of Eugene. There is no city bus service to the airport. **OmniShuttle** (541/461-7959, www.omnishuttle.com) provides door-to-door shuttle service to and from Eugene Airport to six geographic zones in Lane County. **Rental car companies** Avis, Budget, Hertz, and Enterprise also have kiosks at the airport.

The McKenzie River Highway

From I-5 near Eugene, reach this scenic road by taking I-105 east. Take a left at the end of the interstate near the outskirts of Springfield and you will be on the McKenzie River Highway. There are four lanes for a couple of miles, and this is one of your best chances to ease by any slow-moving vehicles. However, beware of the highway patrol on the road here—it's easy to end up with a ticket!

Just past where the four lanes merge into two, the McKenzie River Recreation Area begins. For the next 60 miles, you will not see any major population centers, as most of the towns consist of little more than a post office. However, you will see beautiful views of the blue-green McKenzie River with heavily forested mountains, frothy waterfalls, jet-black lava beds, and snowcapped peaks as a backdrop. The river was named for Donald McKenzie, a member of Astor Pacific Company, who explored the region in 1812.

The first 15 miles of the McKenzie River Highway pass through many fruit and nut orchards (primarily apples, cherries, and filberts), Christmas-tree farms, and berry patches. McKenzie River farmers enjoy plentiful water supplies from the McKenzie diversion canal, as well as fertile soils and a mild climate.

The Leaburg Dam signals your entry into the middle section of the McKenzie, where there are many vacation homes. A total of six dams on the McKenzie provide power, irrigation, and what the Army Corps of Engineers calls "fish enhancement." A favorite haunt of fishing enthusiasts, the mellow waters of the middle McKenzie teem with trout, steelhead, and salmon. You'll notice many driftboats parked in driveways. These boats have bows at both ends to prevent water inundation from either front or back. Mild white-water rafting and driftboat fishing are popular here, and there are many local guides and outfitters ready to help you float your expeditions.

The Willamette National Forest boundary is near Blue River. Huge, old-growth Douglas firs usher the clear blue waters of the McKenzie through the mountains. The McKenzie River National Recreation Trail and many of its counterparts also feature waterfalls, mountain lakes, or lava formations a short trek from the road. In addition to the myriad recreational opportunities, hot springs, quality accommodations, and a dearth of crowds give you the western slopes of the Cascades at their finest.

SIGHTS
Aufderheide National Scenic Byway

One of the nation's first 50 National Scenic Byways, the 58-mile Aufderheide Drive links Route 126 to Route 58 near Oakridge. You'll find the Auferheide turnoff (Forest Service Road 19) at mile marker 45.9 about five miles east of Blue River. The road winds along the south fork of the McKenzie River, crests the pass, and then follows the north fork of the

The upper McKenzie River is a magical place.

© BILL MCRAE

THE WILLAMETTE VALLEY

middle fork of Willamette River down to Oakridge and Route 58. Sights along the way include the Delta Old-Growth Grove Nature Trail, Terwilliger (a.k.a. Cougar) hot springs, the spectacular Willamette River Gorge, and the Westfir covered bridge.

Terwilliger (Cougar) Hot Springs

If you'd like to try a hot springs in a natural setting, head for Terwilliger Hot Springs, located in a forested canyon at the end of a quarter-mile trail. Hot water bubbles up out of the earth at 116°F and flows down through a series of log and stone pools, each one a few degrees cooler than the previous one. A series of access steps and railings have also been built to help you get to the various soaking ponds. The local custom is to forgo the option of clothing.

To get there, take the Aufderheide Drive from Route 126 south toward Cougar Reservoir. The trailhead for the hot springs on the west (right) side of the road is marked by a sign just past Mile Marker 7. You can park in a large lot on the east side of the road about a tenth of a mile past the trailhead (alongside the reservoir). Parking alongside the road is prohibited (and enforced) from sunset to sunrise one mile from the trailhead. A $5-per-person day-use fee is required, which has enabled this place to be well maintained.

The several pools in this tranquil forest setting can be overcrowded on weekends. Although this hot spring offers an exceptionally nice soaking experience, it can occasionally attract an unsavory crowd. As with all of the more remote and wild hot springs, take a friend.

Proxy Falls

To get to Proxy Falls, follow the old McKenzie Pass road (Rte. 242) from the new McKenzie Pass highway (Rte. 126) for 10 miles. Look for a small hiker-symbol sign on the south side of the road. This is the only marker for the trail to a spectacular pair of waterfalls, Upper and Lower Proxy Falls.

It's an easy 0.5-mile walk to Upper Proxy, an A-plus trail. The trail goes through a lava field and lush forest that changes with the season.

There are giant rhododendrons that bloom in late spring, tart huckleberries in summer, and brilliant red foliage from the vine maples in the fall. Take a left at the first fork in the trail. This will take you to Upper Proxy Falls. A particularly good view of the falls can be found near the giant Douglas fir at the base of the pool.

Now that you've seen Upper Proxy Falls from the bottom up, check out Lower Proxy Falls from the top down. Go back to the fork in the trail and take a left. In less than a half mile, you will suddenly be on a ridge looking across a valley at Lower Proxy Falls. A good time to photograph both of these falls is around midday, when the sun's angle best illuminates the water.

Dee Wright Observatory

The Dee Wright Observatory (57600 McKenzie River Hwy., 541/822-3381, on Rte. 242), closed in winter, at the first sign on snow, is at McKenzie Pass, about halfway between Route 126 and Sisters. Built in the early 1930s as a Civilian Conservation Corps project, it was named for the building's supervisor, who died prior to its completion. The tower windows line up with views of Mount Jefferson, Mount Washington, and two of the Three Sisters, as well as the eight-mile-long, half-mile-wide lava flow that bubbled out of nearby Yapoah a little less than 3,000 years ago. On a clear day, you can even see the tip of Mount Hood.

The 0.5-mile Lava River Trail next to the observatory offers a fine foray into the surrounding hills of rolling black rock. In addition to helpfully placed and concise interpretive placards explaining the lava formations, the trail is wheelchair-accessible. But while the walk is easy enough, the 5,300-foot elevation can sometimes make it seem a little more difficult. Note that on Route 242, the vehicle length is restricted to a 35-foot maximum.

Koosah Falls

This cascade is about 20 miles from McKenzie Bridge on Route 126. The visitor facilities here provide wheelchair access and excellent views of this impressive 70-foot-high falls on the McKenzie. The blue water bounces and bubbles over and through a basalt formation that flowed into the McKenzie thousands of years ago. If you look carefully, you can see many small springs flowing from crevices at the base of the falls. The blue water may have inspired the name Koosah, which comes from the Chinook word for sky.

Sahalie Falls

Another beautiful waterfall is only 0.5 mile farther east on Route 126 from Koosah Falls. (From McKenzie Bridge, travel east on Route 126 to Road 2672. Follow Road 2672 to Forest Service Road 655. Follow Forest Service Road 655 to Sahalie Falls Day Use Area.) On the trail from Koosah Falls, giant cedar and fir trees line the path. It is only a few yards from the parking lot to the viewpoints of the falls. Also the result of a lava dam from the Cascade Range's not-so-distant volcanic past, here the river tumbles 100 feet into a green canyon. These are the highest falls on the McKenzie River—*sahalie* means "high" in the Chinook dialect. It's said that this waterfall churns out the highest volume of water of any falls in the state.

Clear Lake

Just north of Sahalie and Koosah Falls and east of Route 126 is Clear Lake, which forms the headwaters of the McKenzie River. The best way to appreciate this lake, which is indeed remarkably clear, is in a canoe, so that you can paddle out to the northern end of the lake and look down to see the 3,000-year-old underwater forest that was submerged when lava flows dammed the flow of water and created Clear Lake. A campground and a resort are at the lake; the resort rents canoes.

Sawyer's Cave

This ice cave is on the right just past the junction of Route 126 and U.S. 20, near Mile Marker 72. You'll need a flashlight and a sweater to explore Sawyer's Cave; watch your head and watch your step. Classified as a lava tube, it's the result of a lava flow that cooled faster on the top and sides, forming a crust. Underneath, the hotter lava continued to drain

downhill, leaving the lava tube behind. There are also small stalactites hanging down from the ceilings, formed from lava drippings. The basalt rock is a poor heat conductor, and like a natural refrigerator it keeps the coolness of winter and night inside the cave. Ice can be found on the floor of the cave during the hottest summer months.

HIKING
Delta Old-Growth Grove Nature Trail

Find this 0.5-mile loop trail through an old-growth ecosystem on the west side of the Aufderheide Byway not far from Route 126. In addition to 650-year-old conifers, you'll see other layers of life from shrubs and ground-cover plants to fish, mammals, birds, and amphibians. Many plant species are clearly marked along the trail.

❰ McKenzie River National Recreation Trail

The McKenzie River National Recreation Trail (3507) runs for 26.5 miles. It starts just east of the small town of McKenzie Bridge and goes to the Old Santiam Wagon Road, about three miles south of the junction of Route 126 and U.S. 20. But don't let the long distance scare you. There are enough access points to let you design treks of three, five, eight, or more miles along this beautiful trail. It is hard to say which section of the footpath is the best, as each portion has its own charms; the following highlights give you a sample of what to expect.

Start at the top of the McKenzie River Trail at the Old Santiam Wagon Road. Completed in the early 1860s, this was the first link of the route from the mid–Willamette Valley to central and eastern Oregon. Way stations were established a day's journey apart to assist the pioneers along their weary way. Although most of these primitive establishments are no more, some of the historic buildings have survived and are still used today by packers. There isn't much left of the Old Santiam Wagon Road either, as much of it was destroyed with the construction of Route 126. However, a seven-mile stretch remains from Route 126 through the rugged lava country to the Pacific Crest Trail. A short walk on this former road to the promised land helps you to appreciate both the hardiness of the pioneers and the comforts of modern travel.

From the Old Santiam Wagon Road, the McKenzie River Trail surveys many remarkable volcanic formations. Lava flows over the last few thousand years have built dams, created waterfalls, and even buried the river altogether. Koosah and Sahalie Falls were also created by lava dams, and the view of these white-water cascades from the McKenzie River Trail is much different than the version accessible from the highway. Another interesting sight is the Tamolitch Valley, where the McKenzie gradually sinks beneath the porous lava, disappearing altogether until it reemerges three miles later at cobalt-colored Tamolitch Pool. This area is accessible only on the National Recreation Trail.

If possible, arrange your McKenzie outing with friends and run a two-car shuttle. Also keep in mind that hikes starting at the upper end of the trail take advantage of the descending elevation. Mountain bikes are allowed on all sections of the McKenzie River Trail.

Robinson Lake Trail

The 0.25-mile Robinson Lake Trail takes you to a heart-shaped lake with some fishing and swimming. To get here, take Route 126 about 16 miles east of McKenzie Bridge and turn right onto Robinson Lake Road. Be on the lookout for logging trucks and rocks on the gravel road. Follow the signs marked Forest Service Road 2664. At the unmarked junction, drive straight onto the red pumice road (Forest Service Road 2664), and continue until you reach the parking lot. It takes about 10 minutes to drive the four miles in. The easy hiking trail is in good condition; the left fork takes you to the center shore of Robinson Lake. The shallow lake warms up considerably during the summer, making a swim all the more inviting.

RAFTING

The McKenzie River becomes navigable at the Olallie campground, about 11 miles east of McKenzie Bridge. Between the Olallie campground and the town of Blue River, there are seven public boat launches, including at Paradise and McKenzie Bridge campgrounds. Expect to encounter Class II and III rapids along the Upper McKenzie. Many local outfitters can guide you down the river.

McKenzie River Adventures (541/822-3806 or 800/832-5858, www.mckenzieriver adventure.com) has half-, full-, and two-day white-water rafting trips May–September. The half-day (four-hour) trip (lunch included) is $80 per person, $60 per child; the full-day (seven-hour) trip (lunch included) is $100 per person, $80 per child. The cruises range from seven to 18 miles and take in some Class II and III rapids. Reservations are recommended.

Destination Wilderness (541/549-1336 or 800/423-8868, www.wildernesstrips.com) floats the McKenzie March–October. Half-day trips are $65 adults, $55 kids; full-day $95 adults, $75 kids; and two-day $290 adults, and $240 kids.

Larger parties interested in a mellow float on the McKenzie might want to consider a pon-

Lava blankets the ground near McKenzie Pass. Mount Washington is in the background.

toon float with **Helfrich Outfitters** (541/741-1905 or 800/507-9889, www.helfrichoutfitter.com, $75 full-day trip with lunch). These large crafts, which are like catamarans without the sail, offer a smoother ride than rafts. Helfrich also offers three- and four-day raft trips as well as fishing and hunting trips.

Oregon Whitewater Adventures (39620 Deerhorn Rd., Springfield, 541/746-5422 or 800/820-7238, www.oregonwhitewater.com) offers guided half-day trips (no lunch) for $50, full-day trips for $75, and a two-day overnighter for $215. All necessary gear and transportation back to your car are included. Group discounts are also available.

FISHING

Sure it's crowded, but scenic beauty and the chance to bag a five-trout limit lines 'em up on one of the state's best trout streams. Unless you can get a driftboat, access is limited. On weekends, driftboats and rafters vie for space. You can cast worms or spinners, though you're better off using flies when you're fishing off a boat for rainbows April–October. Consult the **Oregon Guides and Packers Directory** for guides (531 S.W. 13th St., Bend 97702, 541/617-2876 or 800/747-9552, www.ogpa.org). The best pools tend to be west of Blue River, but it's harder to get to them because of private landholdings. Be sure to check for rules and regulations before you go fishing; the Department of Fish and Wildlife (503/947-6000, www.dfw.state.or.us) can give you the information you need.

CAMPING

The following campgrounds are under the jurisdiction of the Willamette National Forest, McKenzie Ranger District (info 541/822-3381, www.fs.fed.us/r6/willamette; reservations 877/444-6777, www.reserveusa.com). Many are along the beautiful McKenzie River National Recreation Trail. Its prime location halfway between Eugene and Bend also helps make the area a popular vacation spot during the summer, so advance reservations should be made at least five days in advance. Sites at most of these campgrounds run $12–14 per night; those without piped-in water tend to be free.

A half-mile west of McKenzie Bridge on Route 126 is the 20-site riverside **McKenzie Bridge Campground.** Piped well water, vault toilets, and a boat launch are provided. East of McKenzie Bridge about three miles on Route 126 is **Paradise Campground.** Although there are 64 tent/RV (up to 40 feet) campsites, flush and vault toilets, and piped water, only half of the sites are in premium riverside locations. The summer trout fishing here can be very good, and the fireplace grills and wooden tables make it easy to cook and eat a fresh-caught meal. Welcome to paradise!

Olallie Campground is 11 miles outside of McKenzie Bridge on Route 126 and has 17 sites. Olallie is situated on the banks of the McKenzie River; boating, fishing, and hiking are some of the nearby attractions. Piped water, vault toilets, and picnic tables are provided. A couple miles past Olallie on Route 126 is **Trailbridge Campground** (located on the north shore of Trailbridge Reservoir). Piped water, vault and flush toilets, and picnic tables are provided at this 26-site campground. Boat docks are close by, and the reservoir is noted for its good trout fishing. This campground is first-come, first-served (and not on the reservation system); open June–October.

Another ideal campground for boating enthusiasts is **Lake's End** on nearby Smith Reservoir. One of the few boat-in campgrounds in Oregon, this park can only be reached via a two-mile sail across the lake. To get here, take Route 126 for 12 miles northeast of McKenzie Bridge and turn left and follow Forest Service Road 730 to two miles to the south end of the reservoir. Boat across to the north shore for camping. Be sure to take along plenty of water, because the campground does not provide any. You will, however, find picnic tables, vault toilets, and plenty of peace and quiet away from the cars and traffic of the other mainstream parks. Open May–September; no fee or reservations. Vault toilets.

On the south shore of Clear Lake, 19 miles northeast of McKenzie Bridge on Route 126, is **Coldwater Cove Campground.** Piped water, vault toilets, and picnic tables are provided at this 35-site park, open mid-May–mid-October. **Clearlake Resort** (541/258-3729 message line, www.clearlakeresort-oregon.org) is adjacent to the campground and has a store, a summer-only café, and cabins ($45 and up), as well as boat docks, launches, and rentals. Small electric fishing-boat motors are the only mechanical means of propulsion allowed here by the Forest Service. The road to the resort closes at the end of September; guests can hike in to rustic cabins during the winter.

A handful of campgrounds dot Route 242, the old McKenzie Pass road, but only **Alder Springs** (four miles east of McKenzie Bridge then another nine miles east on Rte. 242) has piped water. This remote campground has six tent sites with tables and fire rings; no drinking water. First-come, first-served; open May–end of September. In the same area, RVers should take note of privately owned **Camp Yale** (58980 Rte. 242, McKenzie Bridge, 541/822-3961). Open all year; 14 full hookups (water, sewer line, and electricity) for $20; no tent sites. Modern restrooms with hot water showers are on-site. Camp Yale also offers the only public dump station between Springfield and Sisters.

OTHER ACTIVITIES
Golf
If you like to play golf, you should plan your vacation around a visit to **Tokatee Golf Club** (54947 Rte. 126, Blue River, 541/822-3220 or 800/452-6376, www.tokatee.com, Feb.–mid-Nov., $22 for nine holes, $40 for 18 holes). Consistently rated among the top 25 courses in America by *Golf Digest,* Tokatee is a marriage of golf and wilderness beauty that creates a unique and satisfying experience. Good for all levels of experience; every hole has its own challenge. No houses are on the fairways to obstruct the knockout views of the forested mountains and the Three Sisters Wilderness.

Mountain Biking
In the upper sections of the McKenzie, most of the usable trails gain elevation rapidly due to the steep terrain and make for very challenging biking. The most popular route is the **McKenzie River Trail.** Contact the McKenzie River Ranger District (503/822-3381) for detailed information.

ACCOMMODATIONS
Although the **Sleepy Hollow Motel** (54791 Rte. 126, Blue River, 541/822-3805, $50–70) may not be as charming as some of the other lodgings along the McKenzie, it is located within walking distance of one of the finest public golf courses in the country, Tokatee. Because of this, it's quite popular—reserve in advance.

The **Cedarwood Lodge** (56535 McKenzie Hwy./Rte. 126, McKenzie Bridge, 541/822-3351, www.cedarwoodlodge.com, Mar.–Nov., $95–145) is tucked away in a grove of old cedars just outside the town of McKenzie Bridge. The lodge has nine vacation housekeeping cottages that feature fully equipped kitchens, bathrooms (with showers), fireplaces (wood provided), and portable barbecues. This is our favorite place here, particularly those units with decks on the river.

Unfortunately, fire claimed the historic lodge at the **Log Cabin Inn** (Rte. 126, McKenzie Bridge, 541/822-3432 or 800/355-3432, www.logcabininn.com, $110 summer rates) in spring of 2006. The beautiful 100-year-old lodge had hosted President Hoover, Clark Gable, and the Duke of Windsor and a host of Oregon families over the years. Fortunately, six of the guest cottages, each one boasting a fireplace, a porch, and a view of the McKenzie River, were not damaged by the fire. The inn is located at Mile Marker 51 near the intersection of Route 126 and Route 242.

Belknap Lodge and Hot Springs (P.O. Box 1, McKenzie Bridge, 541/822-3512, www.belknaphotsprings.com) offers lodge rooms, cabins, camping, and access to two hot springs pools. The lodge rooms range $85–185 per couple; bathtubs are plumbed with hot springs water. The five cabins range $55–400. Campsites are $19. The main attraction on the property is Belknap Springs. The water (which contains 26 different minerals) is gently filtered piping hot into a swimming pool on the south bank of the McKenzie. The property is clean, the scenery is beautiful, and the price is right. For $4.50, drop-in visitors can use the lower pool for an hour; a day pass is $8.50, and just what the doctor ordered to ease the aching muscles from that killer hike or the ski marathon. But don't wait too long to fill this prescription—the pool closes at 9 P.M. If you forget your towel, you can rent one.

Both **Heaven's Gate Cottages** (50055 Rte. 126, Vida, 541/822-3214) and **Woodland Cottages** (52560 Rte. 126, Blue River, 541/822-3597) offer housekeeping cabins right on the McKenzie. Though the cabins at either place are sandwiched between the highway and the river, the unspoiled riverside view more than compensates for the traffic (which drops off considerably by nightfall). One Heaven's Gate cabin, Blue Moon, is right over a good fishing hole and nightlights illuminate the rapids for your contemplation. A fireplace adds an additional romantic touch. Woodland Cottages also feature large sun decks on each cabin that are ideal for appreciating the tranquility of the river. Their cabins accommodate two to four occupants, and one unit will sleep six. Both establishments' cabins may be old, small, and semi-rustic, but their riverside location helps overcome a multitude of sins. Rates run $65–90.

You know when you cross over the McKenzie on the 165-foot-long Goodpasture Covered Bridge (circa 1938), the most photographed bridge in Oregon, that you're headed for someplace interesting. A great place for families, including pets, and those who want to get away from the noise of the McKenzie highway is the **Wayfarer Resort** (46725 Goodpasture Rd., Vida, 541/896-3613 www.wayfarerresort.com, $95–280), featuring over a dozen cabins on the McKenzie and glacier-fed Marten Creek. Accommodating 1–6 people, the cabins have porches with barbecues overlooking the water, full kitchens, and lots of wood paneling. Two larger units can sleep eight and are equipped with all the amenities. Children can enjoy fishing privileges in the resort's private trout pond, while the folks play on the resort's tennis court. All guests are welcome to supplement their menus with pickin's from the Wayfarer's organic gardens and berry patch. In the summer, advance reservations are a must for this popular retreat.

FOOD

When the restaurant at the Log Cabin Inn burned down, the area lost its most noteworthy restaurant. Restaurants aren't exactly a big deal out here—most overnight visitors are camping or renting cabins with cooking facilities. Near McKenzie Bridge the **Rustic Skillet** (54771 Rte. 126, 541/822-3400, all meals daily) can be likened to a fancy truck stop—just good ol' American food. Lest this sound like damning with faint praise we should add the menu is diverse for its genre. Kids (young and old alike) will enjoy a complimentary round of miniature golf with their meal.

INFORMATION

Additional information on attractions and services can be acquired from the **McKenzie River Chamber of Commerce** (44643 Rte. 126, Leaburg, 541/896-3330, www.members.aol.com/mcrvcofc), located at the old fish hatchery. Wilderness permits, camping, hiking, and mountain biking information are available the **McKenzie River Ranger District** (57600 McKenzie Hwy., McKenzie Bridge, 541/822-3381, www.fs.fed.us/r6/willamette).

GETTING THERE

Amazingly, travelers without cars can get to the McKenzie National Recreation Trail from Eugene via **Lane Transit District** (541/687-5555, www.ltd.org). Their route 91 bus starts at downtown Eugene and heads up the McKenzie River Highway, making a three-hour round-trip for only $2.50. The bus is equipped to carry a couple of mountain bikes. The terminus point is the McKenzie River Ranger Station at McKenzie Bridge. On weekdays the bus makes two round-trips in the morning and two in the afternoon; on Saturday and Sunday there's one morning and one afternoon trip.

Oakridge and the Upper Willamette River

Halfway between Eugene and the Cascades' summit on Route 58 lies the town of Oakridge. Lumber, secondary wood products (furniture, toys, etc.), recreation, and tourism support this small community (pop. 4,000) tucked away in a foothill valley of the Cascades. The surrounding Willamette National Forest turns out billions of board feet of lumber each year, but it still retains some of the finest wilderness areas in Oregon.

There are over 100 lakes and streams near here, waiting for just about any nimrod to pull out his or her quota of rainbow, German brown, cutthroat, and Dolly Varden trout from the cool waters. A short drive southeast from town, near Willamette Pass, are several Central Oregon gems: Waldo Lake, the Diamond Peak Wilderness Area, and Odell Lake. Winter-sports enthusiasts can find excellent downhill skiing at Willamette Pass, which features 18 runs, four chairlifts, a rope tow, and a day lodge. There are plenty of beautiful trails available for Nordic skiers too. If you like to fish, hike, camp, sail, ski, mountain bike, or just hang out in the woods, it's all only minutes away from Oakridge.

SIGHTS
Westfir Covered Bridge
A short distance out of Oakridge on the paved Aufderheide National Scenic Byway is the Westfir Covered Bridge. This bright red span has the distinction of being the longest covered bridge in Oregon (180 feet) as well as the tallest covered bridge west of the Mississippi. Furthermore, it is likely that it is also the heaviest span of any wood construction bridge due to its Howe trusses, extension rods, and cords. You can see what remains of the Hines Company mill on the opposite side of the bridge; in its heyday it employed 750 people and operated around the clock. You can get a good picture of the bridge from the road as you approach the nearby town of Westfir.

Salt Creek Falls
About 20 miles southeast of Oakridge, just west of Willamette Pass on the way to Odell Lake on Route 58, is Oregon's second-highest waterfall, Salt Creek Falls, which forms the headwaters of the Willamette River. You'll find the pullout on the south side of the highway. The short walk to the viewing area of the 286-foot-high cascade provides a great photo opportunity. Trails access both the top and the bottom of the falls for those interested in taking a closer look at this raw display of hydropower.

Hot Springs
McCredie Hot Springs is found 10 miles southeast of Oakridge on Route 58 near Mile Marker 45. A short walk down to Salt Creek brings you to a small hot spring adjacent to the river. This location allows you to enjoy the rush of simultaneously hot and cold water. Depending on how you position yourself, you can take a bath at any temperature you choose. Because it's so close to the road, this place is often busy; many bathe nude here.

Another primitive hot springs in the area is **Meditation Pool** (Wall Creek). It's really more like a warm spring, as the water ranges from about 90–104°F, depending upon weather conditions. It's a short easy hike in, and the soak is worth the effort. To get there, turn north onto Rose Street from Route 58 in Oakridge. Turn right onto 1st Street, proceed east, and 1st Street will eventually become Forest Service Road 24 paralleling Salmon Creek. About 10 miles out of Oakridge, look for Forest Service Road 1934 on the left (north) side of the road. Approximately a half-mile down Forest Service Road 1934 you'll see a trailhead sign (the kind with no name, only two figures hiking) on the west (left) side of the road. Follow the path along Wall Creek about a third of a mile up to the creekside pool. East of Oakridge on Route 58 on the south side of the highway is Greenwater rest area, a beautiful place to take in the laid-back charm of the upper Willamette River.

HIKING AND CAMPING
Fall Creek National Recreation Trail

The 14-mile-long Fall Creek National Recreation Trail, about 30 miles southeast of Eugene, is ideal for short day hikes or longer expeditions; several national forest entry/exit points crop up along the way. Another plus is the low elevation of the trail, which makes it accessible year-round. Strolling through the wilderness, you will pass many deep pools, white-water rapids, and over a dozen small streams. Giant Douglas firs, bigleaf maples, vine maples, dogwoods, and red alders are some of the predominant vegetation you'll see along the way. In the spring, visitors are treated to shooting stars, trillium, bleeding heart, and other vibrant wildflowers.

To get there, take Route 58 about 15 miles to Lowell, then go north for two miles to the covered bridge at Unity Junction. Take a right onto Forest Service Road 18 (Fall Creek Road), and stay to the left of the reservoir. Follow the road for 11 miles to Dolly Varden Campground, where the trail starts. There are five campgrounds en route and three other spur trails that merge into the Fall Creek Trail. **Bedrock Campground** is a particularly popular spot for swimming.

Larison Creek Trail

The Larison Creek Trail (Trail 3646) is less than 10 minutes from Oakridge. Multicolored mosses cover the valley floor, and its walls simulate a brush-stroked backdrop to stands of old-growth fir. Further contrast is supplied by waterfalls and swimming holes. The mild grade and low elevation of this trail make it accessible year-round. To get here, take Route 58 to Oakridge. Turn onto Kitson Springs County Road and proceed for 0.5 mile. Turn right on Forest Service Road 21 and follow it three miles to the trailhead, which you'll find on the right side of the road. Note that this trail is shared with mountain bikers.

Tufti Creek Trail

Another good hike close to Oakridge is the Tufti Creek Trail (Trail 3624). This easy 0.5-mile trail

winds through large Douglas firs and cedars and overlooks Hills Creek Gorge. There are many small waterfalls and deep swimming holes along the way. This trail is also accessible year-round.

To get here, take Route 58 to Oakridge. Turn onto Kitson Springs County Road and proceed for about a mile. Turn left onto Forest Service Road 23 and follow it for six miles. This will take you along the northeast bank of Hills Creek Lake and on past Kitson Hot Springs (which is also worthy of investigation). Look for the trailhead sign on the right, about a mile past the hot springs.

◖ OAKRIDGE MOUNTAIN BIKING

Mountain biking has become incredibly popular in the Oakridge area, which is not surprising, given that there are an estimated 350 miles of single-track within an hour's drive of town. Find a map of the local trails at www .oregonfattire.com.

Novice bikers and families can start with the **Salmon Creek Trail,** which starts in town and heads along generally flat terrain to Salmon Creek Falls.

Also just outside town, starting at Greenwaters Park near the fish hatchery, **Larison Rock** is a thrilling, technical five-mile downhill ride. Then, unless you've arranged a car shuttle, it's a bit of a slog back to the start. (An easier, though longer route back follows Forest Road 2102.)

The nearly 30-mile-long **Middle Fork River Trail** is a good bet for more experienced mountain bikers who want to test their stamina. It starts at the Sand Prairie campground south of town, and heads south and east along the Middle Fork of the Willamette from there.

Oakridge hosts a couple of mountain-bike events. In late July, the **Fat Tire Festival** (541/782-4146, www.oakridgefattire.com) features races, guided mountain-bike tours, live entertainment, and a barbecue dinner. **Mountain Bike Oregon** (503/459-4508, www. mtbikeoregon.com, mid-August, $150–250) is a three-to-five-day exploration of the area's trails, including meals and camping.

THE WILLAMETTE VALLEY

Road cyclists needn't avoid Oakridge; the Aufderheide Scenic Byway is an excellent low-traffic paved road along the North Fork of the Willamette.

ACCOMMODATIONS

There are some reasonable lodging options in the area. The **Cascade Motel** (47487 Rte. 58, 541/782-2489, $38 and up) is a small, simple motel with microwaves, refrigerators, and wireless Internet access in all rooms; some kitchenettes are also available. The plush place to stay in these parts is the **Best Western Oakridge Inn** (47433 Rte. 58, 541/782-2212 or 800/528-1234, about $70), which has 30 spacious rooms and a pool, hot tub, and HBO.

In the former office building of Hines Lumber Company in Westfir across the street from the covered bridge is the **Westfir Lodge** (47365 1st St., Westfir, 541/782-3103, www.westfir lodge.com, $60–90). The building has been tastefully converted into seven guestrooms with English-style bathrooms (each room has its own private bath, but it's across the hall from the bedroom). The house is full of curious Asian antiques, and the pantry used to be the company vault. A full breakfast (try the English bangers) is included in the rate.

FOOD

Sandwiched in between the roller rink (where the tri-state competition is annually held) and the bowling alley is **Village Cafe** (47961 Rte. 58, 541/782-4550). Standard American cuisine is the order of the day. Nothing terribly fancy, but nothing that terrible either. Open daily for breakfast, lunch, and dinner.

Latecomers or early risers should remember that the **Sportsman Cafe** (48127 Rte. 58, 541/782-2051) is open daily at 7:30 A.M. and closes any time between 9:30 P.M. and 2:30 A.M. This is where you can hear many a fish story about the day's catch or the big one that got away. If the fish weren't biting, you can still find something good on the menu to get your hooks into. Dinners come with salad, fries, and toast. If you're in the mood for a home-cooked meal, try **Manning's Cafe** (47460 Rte. 58, 541/782-4520), the local coffee shop with prototypical coffee-shop fare that's open daily for breakfast, lunch, and dinner.

If you like Mexican food, take in **Mazatlan** (47720 School St., Oakridge, 541/782-5589, lunch and dinner daily) after exploring the Willamette National Forest.

INFORMATION

The **chamber of commerce** (44284 Rte. 58, 541/782-4146, www.oakridgechamber.com) offers a wide assortment of information on the area.

Additional information on biking, hiking, camping, and the Aufderheide National Scenic Byway can be obtained from the **Middle Fork Ranger Station** (46375 Rte. 58, Westfir, 541/782-2291, www.fs.fed.us/r6/willamette).

NORTHERN OREGON COAST

For most Oregon visitors who travel west of the Coast Range, life's a beach. Despite Pacific temperatures cold enough to render swimming an at-your-own-risk activity, the cliffside ocean vistas, wildlife, beachcombing, and other attractions make the coast the state's number-one regional destination.

Though parts of a seamless whole, sharing a common shoreline and linked by an unbroken scenic highway, each section of the coast possesses a distinct regional flavor and allure that has attracted visitors for centuries—to explore, to exploit, to enjoy, to escape. In the north, journey's end for Lewis and Clark, steep headlands break up wide, sandy beaches, extending to the state's far northwestern tip at the mouth of the Columbia River. As the coast stretches southward, craggy head-lands—actually volcanic mountains fronting onto the pounding surf—are separated by immense sandy beaches and the mouths of mighty rivers. Towns here and there break to solitude to offer friendly hospitality.

With rare exceptions, all beaches in Oregon below mean high tide are owned by the public. This is thanks, largely, to Governor Oswald West, who in 1913 pushed through far-sighted legislation defining Oregon's ocean beaches as public highways (which they in fact were before real roads were built) and thus off-limits to private encroachment. Later, Oregon's Beach Bills of 1967 and 1972 were written to further guarantee public access to the state's gem of a coastline. In recent years, however, certain sections of this "publicly owned" paradise have increasingly become exclusive bailiwicks of the

HIGHLIGHTS

◖◖ Columbia River Maritime Museum: One of Oregon's top museums tell the story of seafaring on the Columbia River (page 233).

◖◖ Flavel House Museum: An astounding mansion from Astoria's Victorian heyday filled with antiques and amazing woodwork (page 235).

◖◖ Fort Clatsop National Memorial: This replica of Lewis and Clark's 1805-1806 winter camp is a fascinating glimpse into frontier life (page 235).

◖◖ Haystack Rock: The highlight of Cannon Beach, this soaring sea stack is home to thousands of seabirds (page 252).

◖◖ Saddle Mountain State Park: This knobby mountain rises high above the northern coast, with a hiking trail leading through unusual plantlife on the way to a eye-popping vista (page 253).

◖◖ Oswald West State Park: Hike to a mountaintop or to the edge of a craggy headland, or surf, or camp, all courtesy of one of Oregon's top state parks (page 259).

◖◖ Oregon Coast Aquarium: Explore the life of Oregon's shores and oceans at excellent aquarium (page 285).

◖◖ Yaquina Head Outstanding Natural Area: A soaring lighthouse stands above a tidepool-studded inlet at this small park, the quintessence of the Oregon coast (page 288).

◖◖ Whale-Watching: Thar she blows! Newport is a great departure point for grey whale watching tours (page 290).

◖◖ Cape Perpetua: One of the most dramatic natural areas along the Oregon coast, the mountains here edge out to directly front the Pacific. A top spot for hiking and exploring tidepools (page 298).

LOOK FOR ◖◖ TO FIND RECOMMENDED SIGHTS, ACTIVITIES, DINING, AND LODGING.

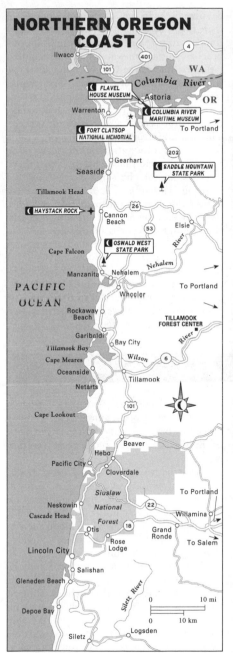

NORTHERN OREGON COAST

NORTHERN OREGON COAST (CONTINUED)

wealthy with gated communities cutting off access to certain beaches.

PLANNING YOUR TIME

In general, the northern Oregon coast is a destination for two types of trips: those that focus on coastal towns with the beach a backdrop to relaxed dining, shopping, golfing, museum visiting, and simply hanging-out, or those that celebrate outdoorsy recreation such as camping, hiking, boating, biking, and fishing. Of course, these aren't either/or choices, and many people combine a coastal hike with a bit of gallery hopping and boutique shopping. However, it's good to keep in mind when planning a trip to the Oregon coast that state parks and national forests offer many opportunities for outdoor adventure—even in rain and winter you can enjoy a hike or explore tidepools.

As for weather, coastal Oregon has a well-deserved reputation for winter rains and inclement weather throughout the year. In general, count on good traveling weather mid-April through mid-October, with a preponderance of daytime highs in the 70s. Within this period, there might be enough cloudy days to dismay travelers accustomed to simmering California beaches, but storm-watching is an acquired taste that makes the Oregon coast attractive when the weather turns nasty. An added plus is that when summertime inversions drive temperatures above 100°F east of the Coast Range, the heat draws cooler maritime air to the shore. The mountains often lock in these welcome fronts, though they also can cause coastal fog and overcast conditions to linger. Nonetheless, respite from the characteristic morning fog banks in summer is often only minutes away upriver along one of the many tidal estuaries. As a general rule, September is the most reliable month for clear coastal weather.

At any time of year, the icy temperatures of the coastal waters (as low as 40–45°F) make the beaches more valued for beachcombing than for swimming. Even in the hottest days of summer, water temperature doesn't exceed 62°F, and hypothermia is an ever-present danger.

Astoria and Vicinity

At the mouth of the Columbia River, with an abundance of natural resources, Astoria was long a traditional meeting place for the Native American tribes of this region. These features continue to lure travelers seeking prime recreational opportunities to this historic seaport town.

Astoria is the oldest permanent U.S. settlement west of the Rockies and its glory days are preserved by museums, historical exhibits, and pastel-colored Victorian homes weathered by the sea air. The city's well-preserved pioneer past softens the rough edges of a once-bustling port that has seen better days, but not enough to let anyone mistake blue-collar Astoria for an ersatz tourist town. The decommissioning of the U.S. Naval station after World War II, the decline in the logging and fishing industries, and the closure of several dozen canneries on the waterfront have had lasting effects on this town of 10,000 people. Empty storefronts here tell the story of a resource-based economy bruised by progress, but there's plenty of pluck left in this old dowager, and her best years may be yet to come.

Astoria hath many charms: Historic buildings downtown are undergoing restoration, cruise ships are calling, fine restaurants are multiplying, a lively music and arts scene is thriving, and there's new life along the waterfront, anchored by the excellent Columbia River Maritime Museum.

The waters surrounding Astoria define the town as much as the steep hills it's built on. Along its northern side, the mighty Columbia, four miles wide, is a mega-highway carrying a steady flow of traffic, from small pleasure boats to massive cargo ships a quarter mile long. Soaring high over the river is an engi-

River pilots guide huge freighters across the Columbia River bar and upstream past Astoria.

neering marvel that's impossible to miss from most locations in town. At just over four miles long, the Astoria-Megler Bridge, completed in 1966, is the longest bridge in Oregon and the longest bridge of its type (cantilever through-truss) in the world. On Astoria's south side, the Young's River, flowing down from the Coast Range, broadens into Young's Bay, separating Astoria from its neighbor Warrenton (pop. 4,000) to the west.

A few miles to the northwest, the Columbia River finally meets the Pacific, 1,243 miles from its headwaters in British Columbia. Where the tremendous outflow (average 118 million gallons per minute) of the River of the West encounters the ocean tides, conditions can be treacherous, and the sometimes monstrous waves around the bar have claimed more than 2,000 vessels over the years. This river-mouth could well be the biggest widow-maker on the high seas, earning it the title Graveyard of the Pacific. Lewis and Clark referred to it as "that seven-shouldered horror" in a journal entry from the winter of 1805–1806.

SIGHTS

Astoria Column

The best introduction to Astoria and environs is undoubtedly the 360-degree panorama from atop the 125-foot-tall Astoria Column on Coxcomb Hill, the highest point in town. Patterned after Trajan's Column in Rome, the reinforced-concrete tower was built in 1926 as a joint project of the Great Northern Railroad and the descendants of John Jacob Astor to commemorate the westward sweep of discovery and migration. The sgraffito frieze spiraling up the exterior illustrates Robert Gray's 1792 discovery of the Columbia River, the establishment of American claims to the Northwest Territory, the arrival of the Great Northern Railway, and other scenes of Northwest history. The vista from the surrounding hilltop park is impressive enough, but for the ultimate experience, the climb up 164 steps to the tower's top is worth the effort.

Before ascending, get oriented with the annotated bronze relief map in front of the column, which notes the distances and directions to such landmarks near and far. From this vantage point, you can see across the rooftops of the town, the Astoria Bridge, giant freighters gliding up and down the Columbia, and a long sweep of the Washington shore. To the northwest are the Columbia Bar and Cape Disappointment. On clear days, look northeast to Mount St. Helens and to Mount Hood on the far eastern horizon. Looking over Young's Bay south and west of Astoria, the Clatsop Plains extend to Tillamook Head and Saddleback Mountain.

Get to the Astoria Column from downtown by following 16th Street south (uphill) to Jerome Avenue. Turn west (right) one block and continue up 15th Street to the park entrance on Coxcomb Drive. Open daily dawn–dusk; call 503/325-2963 for further info. A $1 parking fee is requested at the visitors center.

On the Waterfront

While most of Astoria's waterfront is lined with warehouses, industry, and docks, the **6th Street Riverpark** and River Walk will get you front-row views of the river. The park is a local favorite from which to watch ships from the sheltered observation platform and to fish for Columbia River salmon. Placards around the park display information about the Lewis and Clark Expedition and the area's Chinook natives.

Walk east from Pier 6, past the fish-packing plants, for an interesting if malodorous and noisy (thanks to the sea lions) perspective on what is still a working commercial fishing port. The 11th Street Pier has been developed with a restaurant and shops, and the 14th Street Pier and 17th Street Dock are two other convenient access points for watching cargo ships, sea lions, and fishing boats.

The **River Walk** provides riverside passage for pedestrians and cyclists along a three-mile stretch between the Port of Astoria and the community of Alderbrook. Eventually, the path will extend another two miles eastward to Tongue Point, and west past the Port of Astoria to Smith Point.

An excellent way to cover some of the same ground, accompanied by color commentary on sights and local history, is by taking a 40-minute ride on Old Number 300, the **Astoria Riverfront Trolley** (503/325-6311), which runs on Astoria's original train tracks alongside the River Walk as far east as the East Mooring Basin. The lovingly restored 1913 trolley originally served San Antonio, and later ran between Portland and Lake Oswego in the 1980s. Old Number 300 runs daily during the summer 3 P.M.–9 P.M. weekdays, noon–9 P.M. Friday–Sunday. Off-season, it operates weekends only, until dark. During heavy rains, the antique trolley may stay put in its newly constructed barn. It costs $1 to ride the trolley as

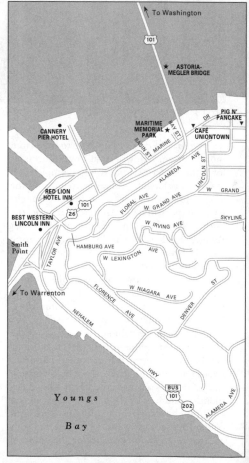

long as you stay on board; the $2 All-Day Fare lets you get on and off as often as you like.

Columbia River Maritime Museum

On the waterfront a few blocks east of downtown Astoria, the Columbia River Maritime Museum (1792 Marine Dr., 503/325-2323, www.crmm.org, open 9:30 A.M.–5 P.M. daily (closed Thanksgiving and Christmas), $8 adults, $7 seniors, $4 ages 6–17, and free for children five and under) is hard to miss. The roof of the 44,000-square-foot museum simu-

lates the curvature of cresting waves, and the gigantic 25,000-pound anchor out front is also hard to ignore. What's inside more than matches this eye-catching facade. The museum's recent $5 million expansion features an award-winning film about the region's maritime history and includes displays on the Coast Guard, salmon fishing, tugboats, and canneries of Astoria. Floor-to-ceiling windows in the Great Hall allow visitors to watch the river traffic in comfort. The most dramatic exhibit is of a 44-foot U.S. Coast Guard motor lifeboat, poised precariously on a wave in a

© AVALON TRAVEL PUBLISHING, INC.

life-size re-creation of a rescue on the Columbia River Bar.

Your ticket also lets you board the 128-foot Lightship *Columbia,* now permanently berthed alongside the museum building. This vessel served as a floating lighthouse, marking the entrance to the mouth of the river and helping many ships navigate the dangerous waters. After almost three decades of service it was replaced in 1979 by an unstaffed 42-foot-high navigational buoy.

The gift shop has a great collection of books on Astoria's history as well as other maritime topics.

Heritage Museum and Research Library

The Clatsop County Historical Society op-
erates the Heritage Museum (1618 Exchange St., 503/325-2203, open 10 A.M.–5 P.M. daily May–Sept., $4 adults, $2.50 seniors, $2 children 6–12). Housed in the handsome neo-classical building that was originally Astoria's city hall, it has several galleries filled with antiquities, tools, vintage photographs, and archives chronicling various aspects of life in Clatsop County. The museum's new centerpiece exhibit concentrates on the culture of the local Clatsop and Chinook tribes, from before European contact to the present day. Other exhibits highlight the natural history, geology, early immigrants and settlers in the region, the development of commerce in such enterprises as fishing, fish packing, logging, and lumber. The research library has recently expanded and is open to the public.

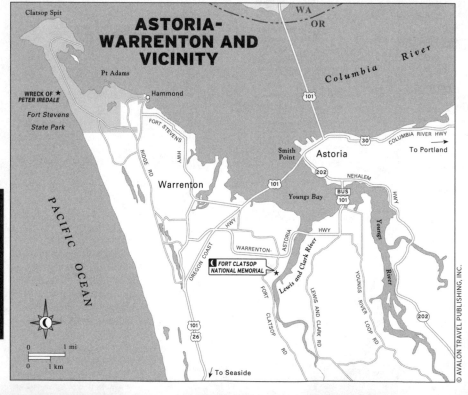

Flavel House Museum

Captain George Flavel, Astoria's first millionaire, amassed a fortune in the mid-19th century through his Columbia Bar piloting monopoly, and later expanded his empire through shipping, banking, and real estate. Between 1884 and 1886, he had a home built in the center of Astoria, now the Flavel House Museum (441 8th St., 503/325-2203, 10 A.M.– 5 P.M. daily May–Sept., 11 A.M.–4 P.M. Oct.–April, $5 adults, $4 seniors/ students, $2 ages 6–17, free for children five and younger) overlooking the Columbia River, where he retired with his wife and two daughters. From its fourth-story cupola, Flavel could watch the comings and goings of his sailing fleet. Although the captain died in 1893, members of the family lived in the house until 1933. The amazing story of the Flavel family was depicted in colorful detail by Calvin Trillin in a February 1993 issue of the *New Yorker.*

The splendidly extravagant Queen Anne mansion reflects the rich style and elegance of the late Victorian era and the lives of Astoria's most prominent family. Known locally as "the house with the red roof," it has withstood more than a century of storms off the Columbia River estuary. This landmark for incoming ships is now the foremost monument to Astoria's golden age as the leading port in the Northwest.

The property encompasses a full city block. With its intricate woodwork inside and out, period furnishings, and art, along with its extravagantly rendered gables, cornices, and porches, the Flavel House ranks with the Carson Mansion in Eureka, California, as a Victorian showplace. The 14-foot ceilings, Persian rugs, and an array of imported tiles are upstaged only by the fireplaces framed in exotic hardwoods in every room. The recently restored Carriage House is now an orientation center for visitors, with exhibits, an interpretive video, and museum store.

Twilight Creek Eagle Sanctuary/Lewis and Clark National Wildlife Refuge

Six miles east of Astoria in the Burnside area is the Twilight Creek Eagle Sanctuary. To get there, drive east on U.S. 30 and turn left at Burnside. Another left 0.5 mile later takes you to the viewing platform, which overlooks the 35,000 acres of mudflats, tidal marshes, and islands (which Lewis and Clark called "Seal Islands") of the Lewis and Clark National Wildlife Refuge. Bald eagles live here year-round, with 30–35 active nest sites. The area provides wintering and resting habitat for waterfowl (including an estimated 1,000 tundra swans in winter), shorebirds, and songbirds. Beavers, raccoons, weasels, mink, muskrats, and river otters live on the islands; harbor seals and California sea lions feed in the rich estuary waters and use the sandbars and mudflats as haul-out sites at low tides.

Fort Clatsop National Memorial

On November 7, 1805, after a journey of nearly 19 months and 4,000 miles, the Lewis and Clark expedition thought they had at last reached their destination, the Pacific Ocean. "Ocian in View! O! the joy," wrote William Clark in his journal. Alas, they were close, but from the Washington side of the Columbia River they had mistaken its broad mouth for the sea itself. Hindered by waves and foul weather, it would take nearly another week before they actually beheld the Pacific. They explored farther west, to Cape Disappointment, and spent 10 uncomfortable days exposed to the elements on the north shore of the Columbia, then decided to move south for a more suitable location to pass the coming winter.

They chose a thickly forested rise alongside the Netul River (now the Lewis and Clark River), a few miles south of present-day Astoria, for their campsite. There the Corps of Discovery quickly set about felling trees and building two parallel rows of cabins, joined by a gated palisade. The finished compound measured about 50 feet square. The party of 33 people moved into the seven small rooms on Christmas Eve, and named their stockade Fort Clatsop for the nearby tribe.

The winter of 1805–1806 was one of the worst on record—cold, wet, rainy, and generally miserable. Of the 106 days spent at the site, it rained on all but 12. The January 18, 1806,

LEWIS AND CLARK NATIONAL PARK

On November 2, 2004 President George W. Bush signed a bill into law to create the 59th national park in the United States. The **Lewis and Clark National and State Historical Parks** honor explorers Meriwether Lewis and William Clark, whose journey in 1804-1806 paved the way for the American settlement of the West. The park focuses on the sites at the mouth of the Columbia River, where the Corps of Discovery spent the famously wet winter of 1805-1806.

The park is somewhat unusual in that it is essentially a rebranding of current National Park facilities and a federalization of current state parks. The new park includes a dozen sites linked to Lewis and Clark exploration, campsites, and lore. One of these, **Fort Clatsop National Memorial** south of Astoria and where the Corps actually spent the winter, was already operated by the National Park Service, while other parks, such as **Cape Disappointment State Park** (formerly Fort Canby State Park) on the Washington side of the Columbia, remains a Washington state park but will be managed by the national park entity.

Besides these two existing facilities, units of the new national park include the **Fort to Sea Trail,** a path linking Fort Clatsop to the Pacific, **Clarks Dismal Nitch,** a notoriously wet campsite near the Washington base of the Astoria-Mengler Bridge, **Station Camp,** another improvident campsite for the Corps, the **Salt Works** in Seaside, where the Corps boiled seawater to make salt, **Netal Landing,** the canoe launch area used by Lewis and Clark near Fort Clatsop, and a **memorial to Thomas Jefferson** yet to be constructed on the grounds of Cape Disappointment State Park.

The new national park also encompasses the existing **Fort Columbia State Park** in Washington, which preserves a turn-of-the-20th-century military encampment, and **Fort Stevens, Sunset Beach,** and **Ecola State Parks** in Oregon.

The national park designation changes little for these once disparate sites, at least in the near future. Fort Clatsop has been expanded to 1,500 acres, and the **Lewis and Clark Interpretive Center** at Fort Disappointment State Park was revamped. Visitors will mostly notice new and consistent signage throughout the park units, and a lot more docents. Living history re-enactors promise to bring to life the famous, often very wet events that took place here more than 200 years ago.

journal entry of expedition member Private Joseph Whitehouse was typical of the comments recorded during the stay: "It rained hard all last night, & still continued the same this morning. It continued Raining during the whole of this day."

While at Fort Clatsop, the men stored up meat and other supplies, sewed moccasins and new garments, and traded with local tribes, all the while coping with the constant damp, illness and injuries, and merciless plagues of fleas. As soon as the weather permitted, on March 23, 1806, they finally departed on their homeward journey to St. Louis.

Within a few years, the elements had erased all traces of Fort Clatsop, and its exact location was lost. In 1955, local history buffs took their best guess and built a replica of the fort, based on the notes and sketches of Captain Clark. In 1999, an anthropologist discovered a 148-year-old map identifying the location of Lewis and Clark's winter encampment, and as it turns out the reproduction is sited very close to the original. In 2005, this replica of Fort Clatsop burned, and a new replica, built mostly by volunteers using period tools, was reopened in 2006. This new Fort Clatsop is more authentic than the previous replica to the actual fort that housed the intrepid Corps of Discovery.

Today, in addition to the log replica of the fort, a well-equipped visitors center, museum, and other attractions make Fort Clatsop National Memorial a must stop for anyone interested in this pivotal chapter of American history. The expedition's story is nicely narrated here with displays, artifacts, slides, and films, but the summertime "living history" reenactments are the main reason to come. Paths lead through the grove of old-growth Sitka spruce, with interpretive placards identifying native plants. A short walk from the fort leads to the riverside, where dugout canoes are modeled on those used by the corps while in this area.

The winter of 1805–1806 put a premium on wilderness survival skills, some of which are exhibited here by rangers in costume. You can see the tanning of hides, making of buckskin clothing and moccasins, and the molding of tallow candles and lead bullets. In addition, visitors may occasionally participate in the construction of a dugout canoe or try their luck at starting a fire by striking flint on steel. For a taste of what Lewis and Clark and their party experienced here, a visit on a cold, wet, wintry day, when every branch and leaf is dripping with rain, is an opportunity to better appreciate their fortitude.

This 125-acre park sits six miles southwest of Astoria and three miles east of U.S. 101 on the Lewis and Clark River. To get there from Astoria, take Marine Drive and head west across Young's Bay to Warrenton. On the other side of the bay look for signs for the Fort Clatsop turnoff. Then turn left off the Coast Highway and follow the direction markers to Fort Clatsop National Memorial (92343 Fort Clatsop Rd., Astoria, 503/861-2471, www.nps.gov/focl, daily 9 A.M.–6 P.M. mid-June–Labor Day, till 5 P.M. the rest of the year, $5 adults, $2.50 ages 16 and under, off-season discounts).

Fort Stevens State Park

Ten miles west of Astoria, at the far northwest corner of the state, this Civil War–era outpost was one of three military installations (the others were Forts Canby and Columbia in Washington) built to safeguard the mouth of the Columbia River. Established shortly before the Confederates surrendered on April 9, 1865, Fort Stevens served for 84 years, until just after the end of World War II. Today, the remaining fortifications and other buildings are preserved along with 3,700 acres of woodland, lakes, wetlands, miles of sand beaches, and three miles of Columbia River frontage.

The fort's creation was not the only outgrowth of the Civil War on the West Coast. The year before, Lincoln had founded the city of Port Angeles, Washington, for "lighthouse purposes." Given the subsequent creation of Fort Stevens shortly thereafter, it's a logical assumption that "lighthouse purposes" also meant watching out for Confederate ships and the British, whom the Union feared would ally with the South.

Though Fort Stevens did not see action in the Civil War, it sustained an attack in a later conflict. On June 21, 1942, a Japanese submarine fired 17 shells on the gun emplacements at Battery Russell, making it the only U.S. fortification in the 48 states to be bombed by a foreign power since the War of 1812. No damage was incurred, and the Army didn't return fire. Shortly after World War II, the fort was deactivated and the armaments were removed.

Today, the site features a memorial rose garden, a Military Museum with old photos, weapons exhibits, and maps, as well as seven different batteries (fortifications) and other structures left over from almost a century of service. Climbing to the commander's station for a scenic view of the Columbia River and South Jetty are popular visitor activities. The massive gun batteries, built of weathered gray concrete and rusting iron, eerily silent amid the thick woodlands, also invite exploration; small children should be closely supervised, as there are steep stairways, high ledges, and other hazards.

During the summer months, guided tours of the underground Battery Mishler ($2) and a narrated tour of the fort's 37 acres on a two-ton U.S. Army truck ($2.50) are also available. The summer programs include Civil War reenactments and archaeological digs; consult the visitors center for schedules.

Nine miles of bike trails and six miles of hiking trails link the historic area to the rest of the park and provide access to Battery Russell and the 1906 wreck of the British schooner *Peter*

BURIED IN THE SAND

exploring the wreck of the *Peter Iredale*, Fort Stevens State Park

Of the hundreds of ships wrecked on the Oregon coast over the centuries, one of the best known is the British schooner *Peter Iredale*. This 278-foot four-master, fashioned of steel plates on an iron frame, was built in Liverpool in 1890. She came to her untimely end on the beach south of Clatsop Spit on October 25, 1906. En route from Mexico to pick up a load of wheat on the Columbia River, the vessel ran aground during high seas and a northwesterly squall. All hands were rescued and, with little damage to the hull, hopes initially ran high that the ship could be towed back to sea and salvaged. That effort proved fruitless, and eventually the ship was written off as a total loss. Today, a century later, the remains of her rusting skeleton protruding from the sands of Fort Stevens State Park are a familiar sight to many who travel the north coast. Signs within Fort Stevens State Park lead the way to the parking area close to the wreck.

Iredale (see *Buried in the Sand* sidebar). You can also bike to the campground one mile south of the Military Museum.

Parking is available at four lots about a mile apart from one another at the foot of the dunes. The beach runs north to the Columbia River, where excellent surf fishing, bird-watching, and a view of the mouth of the river await. South of the campground (east of the *Peter Iredale*) there's a self-guided nature trail around part of the two-mile shoreline of **Coffenbury Lake.** The lake also has two swimming beaches with bathhouses and fishing for trout and perch.

To get there from U.S. 101, drive west on Harbor Street through Warrenton on Route 104 (Fort Stevens Highway) to the suburb of Hammond, and follow the signs to Fort Stevens Historic Area and Military Museum (503/861-1671 or 800/551-6949). The fort's hours are 10 A.M.–6 P.M. daily Memorial Day–Labor Day, and 10 A.M.–4 P.M. Wed.–Sun. the rest of the year. Except for the tours, museum admission is free. There is a $3 parking fee within the park, which is covered by the Oregon Coast Annual Pass and Oregon Coast 5-Day Pass.

SPORTS AND RECREATION
Fishing Charters

More than any other industry, commercial fishing has dominated Astoria throughout its history. Salmon canneries lined the waterfront at the turn of the century. Albacore and long-line shark fishing put dinner on the table in the 1930s and 1940s. In the modern era, commercial fishing has turned to sole, rockfish, flounder, and other bottom fish. If it's not enough to watch these commercial operations from the dock, try joining a charter.

Tiki Charters (503/325-7818, www.tikicharters.com) will take you out for salmon and sturgeon. Trips depart from the West Mooring Basin in Astoria. River tours are also available. Given the retail price of fresh salmon, you could theoretically pay for a charter trip by landing a single fish. **Gale Force Guides** (Warrenton, 503/861-1494), takes sport anglers fishing for salmon in either salt- or freshwater, depending on the season. On your own, go after trout, bass, catfish, steelhead, and sturgeon in freshwater lakes, streams, and rivers. Lingcod, rockfish, surfperch, or other bottom fish can be pursued at sea, off jetties, or along ocean beaches.

Hiking

An in-town hike that's not too strenuous begins at 28th Street and Irving, meandering up the hill to the Astoria Column. If you drive to the trailhead, park along 28th. It's about a one-mile walk to the top. En route is the **Cathedral Tree,** an old-growth fir with a sort of Gothic arch formed at its roots.

The **Oregon Coast Trail** starts (or ends) at Clatsop Spit, at the north end of Fort Stevens State Park. The most northerly stretch extends south along the beach for 14 miles to Gearhart. It's a flat, easy walk, and your journey could well be highlighted by a sighting of the endangered silver-spot butterfly. The species frequents just six sites, including four in Oregon; Clatsop County is one of them. The endangered status of the creature protects it by law, and has stopped developers from building resorts on coastal meadows and dunes north of Gearhart.

Look for a small orange butterfly with silvery spots on the undersides of its wings.

Fort Stevens State Park has nine miles of hiking trails, through woods, wetlands, and dunes. One popular hike here is the two-mile loop around **Coffenbury Lake.**

Camping

Families flock to **Fort Stevens State Park** (800/452-5687 or www.reserveamerica.com for reservations). With 253 tent sites, 343 RV sites, and a special area for walk-in campers and bicyclists, the campground is the largest in the state park system and is the perfect base camp from which to take advantage of the region. Just be sure to avoid spring break (around March 23–29) if you wish to be spared the rites of spring enacted here by Oregon teenagers. Rates are $18–22. Yurts can be had here for $30, hiker-biker sites for $4. The park is open year-round.

Across the road, **Astoria Warrenton Seaside KOA** (1100 N.W. Ridge Rd., Hammond, 503/861-2606 or 800/562-8506) has 310 sites, with 54 cabins. Summer rates (April–Sept.) are $32 for basic tent sites; up to $43–49.95 for deluxe RV sites with all hookups; $51–55.95 for one-room cabins (sleep five); $62–65.95 for two-room cabins (sleep six). Prices drop about 10 percent the rest of the year. Amenities include indoor pool and hot tub, game room, mini golf, and bike rentals.

ENTERTAINMENT

For the lowdown on all the happenings in and around Astoria, get your hands on a copy of *Hipfish,* Astoria's spirited monthly tabloid distributed free all over town.

Astor Street Opry Company

Astoria's long-running *Shanghaied in Astoria,* which is based on the town's dubious distinction as a notorious shanghai port during the late 1800s, is a good old-fashioned melodrama. Chase scenes, bar fights, and a liberal sprinkling of Scandinavian jokes will have you laughing, in between applauding the hero and booing the villain. Performed with gusto by

NORTHERN OREGON COAST

the Astor Street Opry Company, the show has been going on for two decades. Shows Thurs.–Sat. evenings mid-July–mid-Sept., in the converted Old Finnish Meat Market building (279 W. Marine Dr., 503/325-6104). Tickets are $12–16 adults, with discounts for seniors and students.

Liberty Theater

The handsome Liberty Theater (503/325-5922, www.liberty-theater.org), whose colonnaded facades along Commercial and 12th Streets converge at the corner box office, is a vibrant symbol of Astoria's ongoing rejuvenation. The ornate Mediterranean-style building in the heart of downtown began its life in 1925 as a venue for silent films, vaudeville acts, and lectures. The theater continued as a first-run movie house, but after decades of neglect this grande dame was showing her age badly, and it looked as though the Liberty would eventually meet the sad wrecking ball fate of so many fine old movie palaces. Happily, though, a nonprofit organization undertook efforts to restore the theater to its original elegance and equip it to be a state-of-the-art performing arts center. Work is ongoing, but the Liberty currently hosts concerts, recitals, theater, and other events; check the website for scheduled concerts and programs.

River Theater

This local cultural treasure is located underneath the Astoria Bridge. Every May since 1998, the nonprofit River Theater (230 W. Marine Dr., 503/325-7487, www.rivertheater.com) stages a new edition of its original "Simple Salmon" sketch comedy series. Part writing competition, part theatrical production, the cast acts out sketches submitted by the public, and the audience votes for their favorites. Open mic readings, dinner theater, live community-radio (KMUN) broadcasts, and plays from Shakespeare to Ionesco fill out the changing bill of fare. In addition, the River hosts an impressively eclectic lineup of local and touring musicians, covering most of the bases with Celtic, bluegrass, folk, blues, and jazz, with pop, punk, rock, and gospel tossed in for good measure. Check their website or *Hipfish* for scheduled events.

Bookstores

Several bookstores in town invite serious browsing, buying, and intellectual stimulation. **Kneedeep in Books** (1052 Commercial St., 503/325-9722) specializes in used books and remainders, as well as new books. On the next block, **Godfather's Books and Espresso** (1108 Commercial, 503/325-8143) sells a mix of new and used books, and has a case full of excellent antique maps and prints depicting the Columbia River and north coast. The espresso bar is a good place to dry out on a rainy afternoon and catch up on local gossip. **Lucy's Books** (348 12th St., 503/325-4210) is a small but big-hearted locally owned bookshop with an emphasis on Northwest regional subjects. Owner Laura Snyder hosts readings by local and visiting writers, and publishes an entertaining quarterly newsletter and book reviews.

EVENTS

Modeled after Elko, Nevada's popular Cowboy Poets Gathering, the **Fisher Poets Gathering** provides a forum in which men and women involved in the fishing and other maritime industries share their poems, stories, songs, and artwork in a convivial seaport setting. Inaugurated in 1998, the annual February event draws writers and artists from up and down the Pacific coast and farther afield for readings, art shows, concerts, book-signings, workshops, films, silent auction, and other activities at pubs, galleries, theaters, and other venues around town. Participation isn't limited to fisherfolk, but extends to anyone with a connection to maritime activity, and themes range from the rigors (and humor) of life on the water to environmental issues. Admission is by donation ($5), at the ticket booth of the Columbian Theater (11th and Marine Dr.). For more details and full schedule, check the Clatsop Community College website (www.clatsopcollege.com/fisherpoets).

The **Astoria-Warrenton Crab and Seafood**

Festival (503/325-6311 or 800/875-6807), held the last weekend in April at the Clatsop County Fairgrounds, is a hugely popular event that brings in crowds from miles around. Scores of booths feature a cornucopia of seafood and other eats, regional beers and Oregon wines, and arts and crafts. Activities include continuous entertainment, crab races, a petting zoo, and kids' activities. A traditional crab dinner caps off the evening. Admission is $5–7 for adults, $3 for those over 62 and $1 for kids 12 and under. Hours are 4–9 P.M. Friday, 10 A.M.–8 P.M. Saturday, and 11 A.M.–4 P.M. Sunday. To get to the fairgrounds from Astoria, take Route 202 4.5 miles to Walluski Loop Road and watch for signs. Parking is limited at the fairgrounds. Frequent shuttle service takes folks between the fairgrounds, Park & Ride lots, the Port of Astoria, and local hotels and campgrounds.

The legacy of the thousands of Scandinavians who arrived to work in area mills and canneries in the late 19th and early 20th centuries is still strong in Astoria, with public steam baths, *lutefisk, smorrebrod* platters, and church services in Finnish. Today, the biggest event in town is the **Scandinavian Midsummer Festival** (P.O. Box 7, Astoria 97103, 503/325-6311, www.astoriascanfest.com), which usually takes place the third weekend of June, Friday through Sunday. Local Danes, Finns, Icelanders, Norwegians, and Swedes come together to celebrate their heritage. Costumed participants dance around a flowered midsummer pole (a fertility rite), burn a bonfire to destroy evil spirits, and have tugs-of-war pitting Scandinavian nationalities against each other. Food, dancing, crafts, and a parade bring the whole town out to the Clatsop County Fairgrounds on Walluski Loop Road just off Highway 202. Admission is $6 for adults and $2 for children over six.

A tradition since 1894, **Astoria Regatta Week** is considered the Pacific Northwest's longest-running festival. Held on the waterfront in early August, the five-day event kicks off with the regatta queen's coronation and reception. Attractions include live entertainment, a grand land parade, historic home tours, ship tours and boat rides, sailboat and dragon boat races, a classic car show, a salmon barbecue, arts and crafts, food booths, a beer garden, and a twilight boat parade. For details and schedule, contact the Astoria Regatta Association (P.O. Box 24, Astoria 97103, www.astoriaregatta.org).

ACCOMMODATIONS

With its wealth of large, elegant Victorians, it's not surprising that Astoria has more B&Bs than any other town on the Oregon coast. The historic former homes of merchants, politicians, sea captains, and salmon canners number among them.

You'll also find about a dozen motels to choose from in and around Astoria, most of them located along U.S. 30, otherwise known as Marine Drive, in the northwest section of town. Most are fairly similar, and don't have the charm that the town's B&Bs offer, but they're generally a bit less expensive and are reasonably close to downtown.

The prices noted in the text are for high season summer season. Rates fall by as much as half off-season.

$50-100

On the eastern edge of Astoria, the **Crest Motel** (5366 Leif Erickson Dr./U.S. 30, 503/325-3141 or 800/421-3141, doubles from $62–84, depending on views) offers cliffside river views, a coin-operated laundry, and a whirlpool set in a gazebo overlooking the river. Discounts are available for AAA members and seniors. Built as a private Georgian-style residence in 1902, then converted to use as a convent in the 1950s, the elegant **Rosebriar Hotel** (636 14th St., 503/325-7427 or 800/482-0224, www.rosebriar.net, doubles $75–275) was renovated into a small, comfortable hotel in the early 1990s. Set on a quiet neighborhood street a few blocks uphill from the Maritime Museum, the large bowfront windows of the parlor/lobby and many of the upstairs rooms command a sweeping view of the town and river below. Original woodwork, tastefully understated decor and furnishings, private bathrooms, and cordial service make a stay here quite pleasant. Discounts offered for three-night stays; call or check the website for packages and other specials. A full breakfast is also included. The recently opened Captain's Suite includes a kitchenette, large master bath, soaking tub overlooking the Columbia, and a sitting room with fireplace. The 1885 carriage-house cottage adjacent to the main hotel has its own kitchen, plus fireplace, whirlpool tub, and private patio. The Rosebriar is one of Astoria's most popular lodgings, so it's a good idea to reserve at least a week and a half in advance during summer.

A block east of the Rosebriar Hotel, the **Rose River Inn B&B** (1510 Franklin Ave., 503/325-7175, www.roseriverinn.com, doubles from $90), offers two river-view suites and two guestrooms in a large, cheerfully painted Victorian, decorated with European antiques and art and surrounded by a neatly tended garden. Each room includes a clawfoot tub, and the River Suite also has a Finnish sauna.

Franklin Street Bed and Breakfast (1140 Franklin St., 503/325-4314, www.franklin-st-station-bb.com, doubles from $80) is a grand, four-story Victorian built in 1900. Six rooms and suites, five with private bath, and queen beds accommodate up to 14 guests. The view from the fourth-floor Starlight Suite is unmatched, and there's even a telescope for up-close ship spotting. The Hide-Away Suite has its own kitchen, dining area, living room, and private entry. Rich woodwork and local art are appreciated extras. It's within easy walking distance of downtown. A minimum two-night stay is required on weekends, and 10-day advance reservations have become necessary due to the popularity of this place.

Clementine's Bed and Breakfast (847 Exchange St., 800/521-6801, www.clementines-bb.com, doubles from $90), a handsome two-story home built in the Italianate style in 1888, stands in good company across the street from the Flavel House, and is itself on Astoria's Historic Homes Walking Tour. From the gardens around the house come the fresh flowers that accent the guestrooms and common areas, as do the herbs that spice the delicious gourmet breakfasts. There are five rooms in the main house, all with featherbeds and private baths; upper-story rooms have private balconies with river views.

In addition to these guest rooms, two spacious, sunny suites are available in the Moose Temple Lodge, adjacent to the main house, for $150–155. Built in 1850, this is the oldest extant building in Astoria; it was the Moose Temple from 1900 to 1940 and later served as a Mormon church. Renovated with skylights, wood floors, and fireplaces, small kitchens, and several beds, these are ideal for families or groups. Pets are welcome. September–May, Clementine's offers packages combining cooking classes with one- or two-night stays. Courses include bread- and pastry-making and theme classes such as "A Weekend in Provence." Clementine's requires a two-night minimum stay on weekends mid-May–mid-October and on holiday weekends. Single-night stays are fine the rest of the year, and discounts are available off-season.

$100-150

Comfort Suites (3420 Leif Erickson Dr./U.S. 30, 503/325-2000, doubles from $119) has river-view rooms with microwave, fridge, and free HBO; continental breakfast is served 6–10 A.M. Facilities include a heated pool, spa, sauna, exercise room, and laundry.

The sprawling **Red Lion Inn** (400 Industry, 503/325-7373 or 800/733-5466, doubles from $115) is located right at the Mooring Basin Marina, just off Marina Drive. Motel units seem a bit worse for wear, but it's right on the river, and view rooms have a front-row seat on the passing ship traffic.

$150-200

At the west end of town, the **Best Western Lincoln Inn** (555 Hamburg St., 503/325-2205 or 800/621-0641, doubles from $157) has 73 rooms in a five-story structure overlooking Young's Bay. Facilities include indoor pool, sauna, hot tubs, and laundry.

After a $4.3 million, two-year renovation, the ◖ **Hotel Elliott** (357 12th St., 877/378-1924, www.hotelelliott.com, doubles from $169) reinvented itself in 2003 as a tiny boutique hotel in the heart of downtown Astoria. The Elliott first opened in 1924, and its current incarnation preserved much of the original charm of its Craftsman-era details, including the mahogany-clad lobby, hand-crafted cabinetry, wood and marble fireplaces and stone floors in all bathrooms, plus such 21st-century mod-cons as high-speed Internet access and big-screen TVs. The Elliott has five lovely suites (from $275 nightly) plus the five-room Presidential Suite ($650) with access to a rooftop garden. An original banner painted across the hotel's north side proudly proclaims: Hotel Elliott—Wonderful Beds. The new Elliott has made a point of living up to this claim, with goose-down pillows, luxurious 440-count Egyptian-cotton sheets, featherbeds, and top-of-the-line mattresses to ensure a memorable slumber.

◖ Cannery Pier Hotel (10 Basin St., 503/325-4996 or 888/325-4996, www.cannery pierhotel.com, doubles from $159) is a newly built luxury hotel on the former site of a historic cannery, jutting 600 feet out into the Columbia below the Astoria-Megler bridge. The opulently furnished rooms have dramatic views, even from the shower, all rooms have balconies, fireplaces, and beautiful hardwood floors. Complimentary continental breakfast is included in the rates, as are hors d'oeuvres and wine in the afternoon. There's also a day spa in the hotel, plus a Finnish sauna, fitness room, and hot tub.

FOOD

Over the past several years, Astoria has developed a reputation for excellent dining at fair prices, with a number of restaurants standing out for their creative and consistently delicious fare. Espresso fans will also be pleased to know that there are no fewer than 20 outlets in town, with hole-in-the-wall cafés seemingly down every side street. Part of the fun is finding them.

From Mother's Day to early October, follow local tradition and stroll leisurely up and down 12th Street, between Marine Drive and Duane Street, where vendors offer farm-fresh produce, crafts, and specialty foods. **Astoria's Sunday Market** is held 10 A.M.–3 P.M. each Sunday.

For do-it-yourselfers, visit **Josephson's Smokehouse** (106 Marine Dr., 503/325-2190, www.josephsons.com). Established in 1920 and set in a false-front clapboard building near the waterfront, Oregon's most esteemed purveyor of gourmet smoked fish produces Scandinavian cold-smoked salmon without dyes or preservatives. Josephson's caters to mail-order clientele and fine restaurants. You can buy direct here at a cheaper (but not cheap) price than the mail-order rates. Pickled salmon, salmon jerky, sturgeon caviar, crab, oysters, and a variety of alder-smoked and canned fish are also sold here. On typically foggy days here in midwinter, there's nothing finer than a cup of very thick Josephson's clam chowder.

Casual Fare

As widely appreciated as it is small, the **◖ Columbian Cafe** (1114 Marine Dr., 503/325-2233, breakfast and lunch daily, dinner Wed.–Sat., main courses $11–24) is where the meatless '60s meet cutting-edge Northwest cuisine. The good selection of pasta entrées, crepes, and fresh catch of the day specials are all expertly prepared and moderately priced. The chef here is also famous for Uriah's St. Diablo jelly, which comes in garlic, jalapeno, and red-pepper flavors. These jellies are available here and sold throughout the state. You may also enjoy the free-flowing political repartee with the staff and regulars in this cramped (several booths and a lunch counter) but friendly place. Breakfast is a highlight here.

Adjacent are the Columbian Theatre, which shows second-run flicks which you can enjoy with beer, wine, and pizza, and the VooDoo Room, one of Astoria's most active live music clubs.

A state travel magazine has named the **Ship Inn** (1 Second St., 503/325-0033, main courses $6–14) the best pub in Oregon, and another regional publication gave it a thumbs-up for its seafood and business lunches. Despite its unprepossessing exterior, the Ship is popular with locals and visitors who appreciate good fish-n-chips, cheese plates, Cornish pasties, and other

English specialties such as steak-and-kidney pie and bangers and mash, and imported brews. A welcoming fire, great waterfront views, and live music, including jazz and bluegrass, also provide conviviality here.

"Eat well, laugh often, and love much" is the motto that neatly sums up the vibe at the easygoing **T. Paul's Urban Cafe** (1119 Commercial St., 503/338-5133, lunch and dinner Mon.–Sat., main courses $7–14). The menu of hip diner food with fresh Northwest twists includes towering turkey sandwiches, bay shrimp ceviche, Caribbean jerk quesadilla, prawn pasta, and clam chowder. Coffee drinks, beer, and wine are served.

Astoria's first brewpub, the **Wet Dog Cafe** (144 11th St., 503/325-6975, open lunch and dinner Mon.–Sat., main courses $6–$13), is home to the Pacific Rim Brewery, maker of eight handcrafted microbrews, ranging from the golden Pacific Pale Ale to the full-bodied Sow Your Wild Oatmeal Stout. There's also a full bar and live music Thursday through Saturday nights. The café is housed in a cavernous remodeled former waterfront warehouse, with good views out the big windows. Food is basic pub grub: fish-n-chips, burgers, pizzas, sandwiches, and salads, with all-you-can-eat ribs on Fridays.

A good choice for families with kids, the Astoria outlet of **Pig 'N Pancake** (146 W. Bond St., 503/325-3144, open for three meals daily, main courses $7–17) of this small north-coast chain (others are in Seaside and Cannon Beach) excels at big, filling breakfasts at reasonable prices. Their specialty is homemade pancakes and waffles, available in a dozen variations, including potato pancakes, Swedish (thin, crispy pancakes with lingonberries), pecan-filled, and of course pigs in a blanket. Lunch relies mainly on sandwiches (with some seafood twists such as Dungeness crab on an English muffin, topped with melted cheese), chowder, and salads, while dinners branch out with pasta, stir-fry, prime rib, and halibut and salmon served grilled, broiled, or steamed.

Northwest Cuisine

In the days when transportation here was mostly by water, Astoria's neighborhoods developed unique personalities. One of these was Union-town, located west of the present downtown, where Scandinavian fishermen and longshore-men hung out near the fish-processing plants. Underneath the Astoria Bridge in this waterfront district, **Cafe Uniontown** (218 W. Marine Dr., 503/323-8708, dinner Tues.–Sun., main courses $12–22) boasts an upscale menu with such seasonal offerings as raspberry hazelnut chicken breast; oven-roasted lobster tail; portobello, ricotta, and garlic ravioli; and bacon-wrapped filet mignon. Live music on Tuesday through Saturday nights. Check out the 1907-vintage bar in the restaurant's lounge.

For one of Astoria's more upscale restaurants, try **Silver Salmon Grille** (1185 Commercial St., 503/338-6640, lunch and dinner daily, main courses $15–24) for fine dining in an atmosphere that's somewhat formal but not starchy. Attractive murals of the eponymous fish adorn the walls inside and out, and salmon takes pride of place on the dinner menu as well, in a variety of preparations that are fresh and cooked to a T. Additional seafood items such as razor clams, several beef choices such as London broil, pork and chicken, and pasta dishes fill out the extensive menu. A selection of Northwest microbrews and a wine list favoring Oregon and French vintages nicely complements the main courses.

In a century-old converted cannery building on Pier 6, **Gunderson's Cannery Cafe** (1 Sixth St., 503/325-8642, lunch and dinner Mon.–Sat., brunch Sun., main courses $9.50–25) seats you as close to the waterfront as you can get without a boat. This 13-table restaurant serves up an innovative bill of fare that's popular with locals and knowledgeable out-of-towners. Whether you have crabcakes in red pepper pesto or pecan-crusted halibut, leave room for the desserts you'll pass in the display case at the entrance. The lunch menu features a halibut burger, generous Caesar salads, pizzas on homemade focaccia crust, and what many consider to be Astoria's best clam chowder.

At the end of 12th Street, overlooking the Columbia, **Baked Alaska** (1 12th St., 503/325-

7414, lunch and dinner daily, main courses $18–24) is a spacious restaurant featuring local seafood in Northwest cuisine preparations. Featured dishes include Alaska-style campfire wild salmon with amber ale barbecue sauce, coffee-dusted albacore tuna with balsamic-ginger glaze, and a selection of hand-cut steaks and baby back ribs. Views rival the food, particularly in summer when there's deck seating.

Located across from Hotel Elliott, and just behind the renovated Liberty Theater the **Schooner and Twelfth Street Bistro** (360 12th St., 503/325-7882, lunch and dinner daily, main courses $11–23) is in the space of a former tavern (the cool neon is about all that's left). The urban swank dining room is a good spot for steak, pasta, and seafood. The adjacent bar has a hip martini-sipping crowd at night, and offers live music on Friday and Saturday nights.

For Astoria's top Italian food, go to **Fulio's Pastaria** (1149 Commercial St., 503/325-9001, lunch and dinner daily, main courses $8–17) with excellent pasta plus Tuscan-style steaks in a lively and convivial dining room. Good wine list.

INFORMATION

The **Astoria Chamber of Commerce** (111 W. Marine Dr., 503/325-6311 or 800/875-6807, www.oldoregon.com) operates the Oregon Welcome Center at its offices, providing a plethora of brochures and maps for visitors to Astoria and other destinations on the northern Oregon coast and southwest Washington. They will send you a free guidebook with plenty of handy info (write to P.O. Box 176, Astoria 97103, or order online; open 8 A.M.–6 P.M. daily May Nov., 9 A.M. 5 P.M. Mon. Fri. Oct.–Apr.).

GETTING THERE AND AROUND

Amtrak Thruway Motorcoach Service runs daily between the north coast and Portland Union Station. Board the coach In Astoria at the Welcome Center (111 W. Marine Dr.). Departure from Astoria is at 8 A.M.; arrival in Portland, 10:15 A.M. Depart Portland at 6 P.M.; arrive in Astoria at 8:15 P.M. The bus stops upon request at Seaside, Warrenton, and Gearhart. For information and reservations, call 800/872-7245 or check the Amtrak website (www.amtrak.com).

For visitors willing to let go of their cars for a while, the Sunset Empire Transportation District, better known as **The Bus** (503/861-7433 or 800/776-6406, www.ride thebus.org), provides reasonably frequent transportation around Astoria, and along the coast from Warrenton (including Fort Stevens State Park and Fort Clatsop) to Cannon Beach. Most routes are served every 40–60 minutes, Monday–Saturday.

Seaside and Gearhart

Seaside is Oregon's quintessential, and oldest, family beach resort. The beach is long and flat, sheltered by a scenic headland, with lifeguards on duty during the summer months, beachside playground equipment, and the West Coast's only boardwalk north of Santa Cruz, California. Ice cream parlors, game arcades, eateries, and gift shops crowd shoulder to shoulder along the main drag, Broadway. The aroma of cotton candy and french fries lend a heady incense to the salt air, and the clatter of bumper cars and other amusements can induce sensory overload. Atlantic City it's not, thank goodness, but on a crowded summer day the resort evokes the feeling of a carnival midway by the sea. During spring break, when Northwest high school and college students arrive, the town's population of 6,200 can quadruple almost overnight.

South of town, the presence of clammers and waders in the shallows, and surfers negotiating the swells, also recalls the liveliness of a southern California or Atlantic shore-front instead of the remote peaceful-ness of many Oregon beaches. East Coast visitors often liken Cannon Beach to Provincetown, and Seaside to Coney Island—prior to their de-clines as destination resorts. Neigh-boring Gearhart, a mainly residential community (pop. 995) just to the north, has a few lodgings away from the bustle of Seaside, as well as a ven-erable 18-hole golf course.

Located along the Necanicum River, in the shadow of majestic Til-lamook Head, Seaside has attracted tourists since the early 1870s, when transportation magnate Ben Holla-day sensed the potential of a resort hotel near the water. But better trans-portation was needed to get custom-ers to the place. At that time, the way to get to Seaside was first by boat from Portland down the Columbia River to Skipanon (now Warrenton), and from there by carriage south to Seaside. To speed the connection, Holladay constructed a railroad line from Skipanon to Seaside.

To escape Portland's summer heat, families would make the boat and railroad journey to spend their sum-mer in Seaside. Most men would go back to Portland to work during the week, returning to the coast on Fri-day to visit the family. Every week-end the families would gather at the railroad station to greet him, then see him off again for his trip back to Portland. It wasn't long before the train became known as the "Daddy Train." As roads between Portland and the coast were constructed, the car took over, and the railroad car-ried its last dad in 1939.

Prior to becoming the state's first coastal resort, Seaside's fame as the end of the Lewis and Clark Trail made it a national landmark. In re-

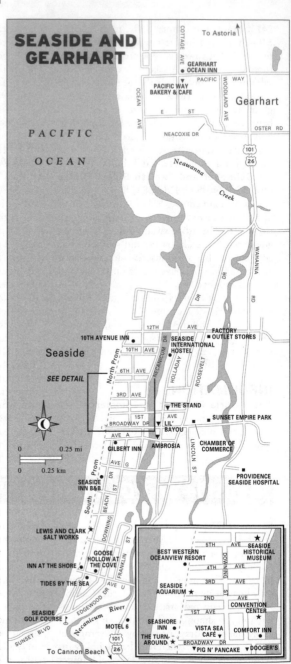

© AVALON TRAVEL PUBLISHING, INC.

cent years, the town has become more than just a retreat for Portland families. Oregon's apostle of haute cuisine, the late James Beard, used to hold a celebrated cooking class here each summer. This opened the door for writers' retreats, art classes, and business conventions. If these occasions or a family outing should bring you to Seaside, you'll enjoy the spirit of fun if you don't mind plenty of company on summer weekends.

SIGHTS
The Prom and Broadway
Sightseeing in Seaside means hustling up and down Broadway and strolling leisurely along the Prom. This two-mile-long boardwalk, extending from Avenue U north to 12th Avenue, was constructed in 1921 to replace the rotten planks from a wooden walkway built in 1908 and to protect ocean properties from the waves. A pleasant walk alongside the beach, it offers good vantages from which to contemplate the sand, surf, and massive contours of 1,200-foot-high Tillamook Head to the south.

Midway along the Prom is the **Turnaround,** a concrete and brick traffic circle that is the west end of Broadway. A bronze statue of Lewis and Clark gazing ever seaward proclaims this point the end of the trail for their expedition, though in fact they explored a bit farther south, beyond Tillamook Head (see *Following Lewis and Clark* under *Recreation*). Eight blocks south of the Turnaround, between Beach Drive and the Prom is a replica of the Lewis and Clark salt cairn (see *Lewis and Clark Salt Works,*).

Running east from the Turnaround, Broadway runs 0.5 mile to Roosevelt Avenue (U.S. 101) through a dizzy gamut of tourist attractions. Along Broadway, in a four-block area running west of U.S. 101 and bordered by the Necanicum River and 1st Avenue, and Avenue A, you'll find some fancy Victorian frame houses, some of the few old buildings that survived the 1912 fire that destroyed much of the town.

Today, the most notable sight along the Turnaround is the enormous $73.3 million TrendWest time-share condo development.

This eight-story structure has 283 one-, two-, and three-bedroom oceanview vacation condominiums. The condos aren't available for rent directly from TrendWest, but you can do an Internet search to fine property management companies who are able to sublet them.

Seaside Historical Museum
If you tire of having a good time on Broadway and the beach, make your way to the Seaside Historical Museum (570 Necanicum Dr., 503/738-7065, 10 A.M.–4 P.M. Mon.–Sat. late Mar.–Oct., noon–3 P.M. Mon.–Sat. the rest of the year, noon 3 P.M. Sun. year-round, $2 adults, $1 children), six blocks north of Broadway, where Clatsop artifacts and exhibits on early tourism in Seaside will impart more of a sense of history than anything else in town.

Seaside Aquarium
Right on the Prom north of the Turnaround is the Seaside Aquarium (200 N. Prom, 503/738-6211, open 9 A.M.–5 P.M. daily Mar.–Oct., 9 A.M.–5 P.M. Wed.–Sun. in winter, $6 ages 14 and up, $3 ages 6–13). It's not quite the Oregon Coast Aquarium in Newport, but if you're not going to make it that far south it's an okay introduction to sea life for young children. Back in the era of the Daddy Train, this place served as a natatorium, but was converted to its current use in 1937. Today the pool is filled with the raucously barking results of one of the best captive-breeding programs for seals in the world. In addition, 100 species of marine life here include 20-ray sea stars, crabs, ferocious-looking wolf eels and moray eels, and octopi.

Lewis and Clark Salt Works
Near the south end of the Prom are the reconstructed salt works of Lewis and Clark. While camped at Fort Clatsop during the winter of 1805–1806, the captains sent a detachment south to find a place suitable for rendering salt from seawater. Their supply was nearly exhausted, and the precious commodity was a necessity for preserving and seasoning their food on the expedition's return journey. At the south end of present-day Seaside, five men built

ROUTES TO THE NORTHERN OREGON COAST

From the I-5 corridor, where most of the state's population is concentrated, 10 main routes will get you to the coast. Most are two-lane state highways for all or part of the journey through rural hinterlands and the coastal mountains.

From Portland, **U.S. 30** runs north through St. Helen's and follows the bottomlands along the south bank of the Columbia River to Astoria, 98 miles to the northwest. If you're coming down from the north on I-5, cross the Columbia from Longview, Washington, to Rainier, Oregon, and continue west on U.S. 30 from there.

Busy **U.S. 26** runs west, then angles northwest, from Portland, through agricultural Washington County and then into the woods of the Clatsop State Forest before joining U.S. 101 between Cannon Beach and Seaside. About 25 miles west of Portland, **Route 6** branches off from U.S. 26 and follows a roller-coaster course alongside the Wilson River to Tillamook.

A third route from Portland starts with Route 99W and a dozen maddening stop-and-go miles through the strip development of Tigard. After Newburg you emerge into a lovely countryside of vineyards and hazelnut orchards around Dundee. Pick up **Route 18** for the second half of the trip, which runs past Oregon's number one attraction, the Spirit Mountain Casino in Grande Ronde, before you hit the Coast Highway just north of Lincoln City and another Indian-owned casino, Chinook Winds. Note that the casinos attract more than three million visitors a year, which helps make Route 18 one of the most dangerous roads to drive in the state.

From Salem, **Route 22** runs 26 miles to the west and connects with Route 18 about midway to the coast.

Farther south, **U.S. 20** curves down from Albany through Corvallis and on to Philomath. From there you can continue 46 miles to Newport, or veer southwest on **Route 34** for a winding 59 miles through a remote section of the Siuslaw National Forest to Waldport.

a cairn-like stone oven near a settlement of the Clatsop and Killamox tribes, and set about boiling seawater nonstop for seven weeks to produce three and a half bushels (about 112 quarts) of salt for the trip back east.

Tillamook Head

From the south end of Seaside you can walk in the footsteps of Lewis and Clark on an exhilarating hike over Tillamook Head. In January 1806, neighboring Native Americans told of a beached whale lying several miles south of their encampment. William Clark and a few companions, including Sacajawea, set off in an attempt to find it and trade for blubber and whale oil, which fueled the expedition's lanterns. Climbing Tillamook Head from the north, the party crested the promontory. Clark was moved enough by the view to later write about it in his journal:

I beheld the grandest and most pleasing prospect which my eyes ever surveyed. Immediately in front of us is the ocean breaking in fury. To this boisterous scene the Columbia with its tributaries and studded on both sides with the Chinook and Clatsop villages forms a charming contrast, while beneath our feet are stretched the rich prairies.

They eventually found the whale, south of Tillamook Head. Ecola Point and State Park here are named for it, after the Chinook word for "whale," *ecola* or *ekkoli*. By the time Clark arrived, however, the whale had been reduced to little more than a skeleton by the industrious Tillamooks, who used every part of the beast they could harvest. Clark measured the leviathan at 105 feet, which, if accurate, could only mean it was blue whale, the largest animal on earth and an extraordinary windfall for the Native Americans. He found the Tillamooks busily engaged in boiling the blubber in a large wooden trough by means of hot stones. The oil, when extracted, was stored in bladders. He had to bargain hard for a share, and wrote this of the negotiations:

> The Tillamooks, although they possessed large quantities of this blubber and oil, were so penurious that they disposed of it with great reluctance, and in small quantities only; insomuch that my utmost exertions, aided by the party, with the small stock of merchandise I had taken with me, were not able to procure more blubber than about 300 pounds and a few gallons of oil. Small as this stock is, I prize it highly; and thank Providence for directing the whale to us; and think Him much more kind to us than He was to Jonah having sent this monster to be swallowed by us, instead of swallowing of us, as Jonah's did.

Today, you can experience the view that so impressed Clark on the **Tillamook Head National Recreation Trail,** which runs seven miles through Ecola State Park. Prior to setting out, you could arrange to have a friend drive south to **Indian Beach** to pick you up at the end of this three- to five-hour trek. Or you can be picked up another mile south at the Ecola Point parking lot. To get to the trailhead from Seaside, drive south, following Avenue U past the golf course to Edgewood Street and turn left; continue until you reach the parking lot at the end of the road.

Nearby is an area known as **the cove,** frequented by surfers (prevailing winds favor winter surfing rather than summer) and anglers. As you head up the forested trail on the north side of Tillamook Head, you can look back over the Seaside townsite. In about 20 minutes, you'll be gazing down at the ocean from cliffs 1,000 feet above. A few hours later, you'll hike down onto Indian Beach.

SPORTS AND RECREATION
Water Sports
Despite the lifeguard on duty in summer, swimming at Seaside's beach isn't the most comfortable unless you're used to the North Sea.

Gearhart boasts a quieter beach than Seaside's, though the water's every bit as cool. Warm-blooded swimmers can head to the pool and spa at **Sunset Empire Park** (1140 E. Broadway, Seaside, 503/738-3311, open daily). At Quatat Park, beside the Necanicum River in downtown Seaside, you can rent kayaks, canoes, and pedal boats for exploring the waterway.

The surfing venues north of Tillamook Head, Indian Basin, near Short Sands Beach in Oswald West State Park and in Manzanita can be enjoyed with surfboard and equipment rentals from **Cleanline Surf Shop** (719 1st Ave., Seaside, 503/738 7888). The shop rents boogie boards and surfboards, as well as wetsuits, boots, and flippers.

Golf
Golfers can escape to public courses south of Seaside and north in the small town of Gearhart. At **Seaside Golf Course** (451 Ave. U, 503/738-5261), green fees are $9–10 for nine holes. The British links–style course at **Gearhart Golf Links** (Marion St., 503/738-3538) was established in 1882, making it one of the oldest on the West Coast and Oregon's oldest. Green fees are $45 in summer for the 18-hole course. The **Highlands at Gearhart** (1 Highland Rd., Gearhart, 503/738-5248) is another public nine-hole course, with ocean views from most holes; $21 for 18 holes.

ACCOMMODATIONS
Whatever your price range, you'll have to reserve ahead for a room in Seaside during the summer, weekends, and holidays (especially spring break). If you do, chances are you'll be able to find the specs you're looking for, given the area's array of lodgings (more than three dozen motels, a few B&Bs, and many vacation rentals); if you don't, come prepared to camp. The Seaside Visitors Bureau's helpful website (www.seasideor.com) provides comprehensive listings. A good option for families and groups might be one of the several dozen vacation rentals. Check with the Seaside Visitors Bureau, or contact one of the rental agencies: **Oceanside Vacation Rental** (503/738-7767

or 800/840-7764); **D. B. Rentals** (503/717-9516 or 800/203-1681); or **Northwind Property Management** (503/738-5532 or 800/488-3301).

The cheapest place in town is the **Seaside International Hostel** (930 N. Holladay, 503/738-7911 or 800/909-4776, dorm-style rooms $22, private rooms $41–57 per person, add $3 for non-members). There's an espresso bar, and the Necanicum River runs through the backyard. Close by is the Necanicum Estuary Park. To get there from U.S. 101, make a left at the city center sign, turn on Holladay, and continue north. When you get to 9th Avenue look for the hostel on the left. There's no curfew here and unlike other hostels, it doesn't close down during the day.

Motel 6 (2369 S. Roosevelt, 503/738-6269, doubles $75), on U.S. 101 about a half mile south of Broadway, isn't near the beach, but does offer reasonable priced rooms. There's a clutch of motels south of the Broadway/Boardwalk axis that offer easy beach access at fair prices - and a much quieter beachfront experience. The **Inn at the Shore** 2275 S Prom, 503/738-3113 or 800/713-9914, www.innattheshore.com, doubles from $129) has nicely appointed rooms each with gas fireplace, balcony, wet bar, microwave, coffeemaker, refrigerator, TV and VCR plus balcony. Another good value in this same area is **The Tides by the Sea**, (2316 Beach Drive, 503/738-6317 or 800/548-2846, www.thetidesbythesea.com, doubles from $82) an older motel that's converted its large rooms and cottages into condos. About a quarter of the units face onto the boardwalk, but those that don't are just seconds away from the beach anyway. If you can live without an ocean view, you'll save a bundle here with cottages and condo rooms less than a block from the beach. Each of the units is different but most have kitchens and fireplaces.

Another good value are the rooms at **Seashore Inn** (60 North Promenade (503/738-6368 or 888/738-6368, www.seashoreinnor.com, doubles from $69) right in the thick of it along the Promenade. Half the rooms face the beach, but half don't. These rooms are just

steps from the beach, but are a fraction of the cost of rooms on the other side of the building. All rooms have microwaves & mini-refrigerators, and some have full kitchens. There's also an indoor pool in case the weather turns foul.

Gearhart offers a respite from the bustle of Seaside. The **Gearhart Ocean Inn** (67 N. Cottage St., 503/738-7373, www.gearhartoceaninn.com, doubles from $105) offers a choice of 12 New England–style wooden cottages with comforters, wicker chairs, throw rugs, and a location close to the beach. The two-story deluxe units have kitchens and hardwood floors. Pets are allowed in some units. This spruced-up old motor court is one of the best values on the North Coast.

Best Western Oceanview Resort (414 N. Prom, 503/738-3264 or 800/234-8439, www.oceanviewresort.com, doubles from $129) is another large hotel/motel right on the beach. Amenities include on-site restaurant and lounge, heated pool and spa; the majority of rooms face the ocean. Non-ocean-view rooms are about one-third less than view rooms.

The **Comfort Inn** (545 Broadway Ave., Seaside, 503/738-3011, doubles from $159), is right on the Necanicum River. Rooms feature fireplaces, spa baths, microwave, fridge, and balconies overlooking the river.

Bed-and-Breakfasts

While motels dominate the lodging scene in Seaside, a few B&Bs offer an alternative. Our top award for creativity goes to the **Seaside Inn B&B** (581 S. Prom, 503/319-3300 or 800/772-7766, www.theseasideinn.com, doubles from $95). This four-story, shingle-sided structure stands right on the beach, with its north gable skewered by a clock tower. Each of the 15 guestrooms is decorated in a unique theme. The queen bed in the '50–'60s Rock & Roll Room ($115–195), for example, is incorporated into the tail end of a '59 Oldsmobile. Other themes include the Bubble Room ($120–199), and the Clock Tower Suite ($160–325). Most have a spectacular ocean view.

The **Gilbert Inn** (341 Beach Dr., 503/738-9770 or 800/410-9770, www.gilbertinn.com, doubles from $110) is a well-preserved 1892

Queen Anne, located just a block south of Broadway and a block from the beach. Period furnishings adorn the 10 guestrooms, which all have private bath, down comforters, and other nice touches. The third-floor "Garret" sleeps up to four in a queen and two twin beds, with ocean views from the dormer window.

North of Broadway, the **10th Avenue Inn** (125 10th Ave., 503/738-0643 or 800/745-2378, www.10aveinn.com, doubles from $99) is a comfortable 1900 home built just a few steps from the beach. In the parlor, a baby grand piano, guitar, and other instruments are available for musically inclined guests. The three guestrooms have king-sized beds, attached baths, TVs, and small refrigerators. Next door and operated by the same folks is the **Doll House** (www.summerhouse-seaside. com), a sweet two-bedroom cottage (ideal for four adults plus two or three children) with full kitchen and a deck with barbecue grill. It goes for $850/week in summer (minimum week's rental), $160 per night off-season (two-night minimum).

FOOD

While a stroll down Broadway might have you thinking that cotton candy, corn dogs, and saltwater taffy are the staples of Seaside cuisine, several eateries here can satisfy taste and nutrition as well as the broad-based clientele of this beach town.

For breakfast, the Swedish pancakes and crab-and-cheese omelettes at **Pig 'N Pancake** (323 Broadway, 503/738-7243, main courses $7–17) are tops. If you're seriously hungry try the Frisbee-sized cinnamon rolls. At last count, you could choose from 33 different breakfast variations at this place. You can count on this local chain (with additional outlets in Astoria and Cannon Beach) for three solid meals every day of the week.

The Stand (109 N. Holladay, 503/738-6592, main courses $5–12) features the satisfying and inexpensive Mexican fare that you'd find on the streetcart *loncherias* of Guadalajara. The carnitas taco is a mouthful of seasoned pork only exceeded perhaps by its beefy counterpart, the carne asada taco. The chili verde burrito as well as enchiladas, tamales,

and other specialties can be enjoyed in the tiled confines of the restaurant.

The **Vista Sea Cafe** (150 Broadway, 503/738-8108, lunch and dinner daily, main courses $7–17) is known for pizza with ingredients such as artichokes, feta, chorizo, and pesto, plus top-notch clam chowder with homemade beer bread. Its location one block from the Turnaround makes it especially convenient.

Dooger's (505 Broadway, 503/738 3773, lunch and dinner daily, main courses $8–19), which also has an outlet in Cannon Beach, has won acclaim for its clam chowder. Local clams and oysters, fresh Dungeness crab legs, sautéed shrimp, and marionberry cobbler are also the basis of Dooger's do-good reputation.

A rarity in these parts, **Lil' Bayou** (20 N. Holladay Dr., 503/717-0624, open lunch and dinner daily, main courses from $12–21) dishes up authentic muffulettas, jambalaya, blackened catfish, gumbo, and a host of other Cajun and Creole standards, right down to side dishes of collard greens, at reasonable prices. Finish off with a slice of sweet potato pecan pie or Aunt B's cheesecake. Ooo weeee.

Just looking for a pub with local microbrews and good sandwiches? Your destination should be **Goose Hollow at the Cove,** (220 Ave. U, 503/717-1940, lunch and dinner daily, main courses $7–13). There's nice deck seating plus 14 beers on tap; smoke-free. The reuben sandwiches here are locally famed.

Should the ambience of Seaside on a holiday weekend pall, try the **Pacific Way Bakery and Cafe** in Gearhart (601 Pacific Way, 503/738-0245, three meals daily, main courses $14–22). Gearhart is the area where famed food writer James Beard was raised. Beard himself would probably give Pacific Way's croissants five stars, so flaky and buttery are these breakfast mainstays. They take center stage again at lunch, providing the foundations for delectable sandwich fillings. Particularly recommended are the smoked salmon and cream cheese with thin-sliced red onion on croissant, the cioppino, and Caesar salad. Pasta, crusty pizzas, and seafood dishes (including thick seafood stew) as well as crepes also pop up at lunch and dinnertime. Rib-eye steak and local razor clams are other frequent dinnertime highlights in the surprisingly urbane little café hidden behind a rustic old storefront.

INFORMATION

The **Seaside Chamber of Commerce and Visitors Bureau** (7 N. Roosevelt St., Seaside 97138, 503/738-6391 or 800/444-6740, www.seasidechamber.com) is open 8 A.M.–5 P.M. daily.

GETTING THERE AND AROUND

Seaside is very walkable, but for $2 you can ride around town on the brightly painted **Seaside Street Car,** which runs hourly. Sunset Empire Transportation District also operates **The Bus,** which serves Cannon Beach, Seaside, Astoria-Warrenton, and points in between. For schedule and fare info, call 503/861-7433.

Cannon Beach and Vicinity

In 1846, the USS *Shark* met its end on the Columbia River Bar. The ship broke apart, and a section of deck bearing a small cannon and an iron capstan drifted south, finally washing ashore south of the current city limits at Arch Cape. And so this town got its name, which it adopted in 1922. Replicas of the hardware now stand near that spot, while the originals are preserved at the Cannon Beach Historical Society Museum.

In 1873, stagecoach and railroad tycoon Ben Holladay helped create Oregon's first coastal tourist mecca, Seaside, while ignoring its attractive neighbor in the shadow of Haystack Rock. In the 20th century, Cannon Beach evolved into a bohemian alternative to the hustle and bustle of the family-oriented resort scene to the north. Before the recent era of development, this place was a quaint backwater attracting laid-back artists, summer-home residents, and the overflow from pricier digs in Seaside.

Nonetheless, the broad, three-mile stretch of beach dominated by the impressive monolith of Haystack Rock still provides a contemplative experience—although you might have to walk a half mile from your parking place to get to it. And if you're patient and resourceful enough to find a space for your wheels, the finest gallery-hopping, crafts, and shopping on the coast await. The city is small enough for strolling, only 1.3 miles long, and its location removed from U.S. 101 spares it the kind of blight seen on the main drags of other coastal tourist towns.

SIGHTS

◖ Haystack Rock

As you get closer to town, Haystack Rock looms larger. This is the third-highest sea stack in the world, measuring 235 feet high. As part of the Oregon Islands National Wildlife Refuge, it has wilderness status, and is off-limits to climbing. Puffins and other seabirds nest on its steep faces, and intertidal organisms thrive in the tidepools around the base. The surrounding tidepools, within a radius of 300 yards from the base of the monolith, are designated a "marine garden"; it's open to exploration, but with strict no-collecting (of anything) and no-harassment (of any living organisms) protections in effect. Flanking the mountain are two rock formations known as the Needles. These spires had two other counterparts at the turn of the 20th century that have gradually been leveled by weathering and erosion. Old-timers will tell you that a trail to the top of Haystack was dynamited by the government in 1968 to keep people off this bird rookery. It also reduced the number of intrepid hikers trapped on the rock at high tide.

The **Haystack Rock Awareness Program** (503/436-1581, www.haystackrock.org) sponsors free interpretive programs June– August. While these talks are interesting and informative, the beach also speaks to you with its own distinctive voices. You can't miss the cacophony of seabirds at sunset and, if you listen closely, the winter phenomenon of "singing sands" created by wind blowing over the beach.

Ecola State Park

Ecola State Park is just north of the Cannon Beach townsite. Thick conifer forests line the access road to Ecola Point. This forested cliff has many trails leading down to the water. The view south takes in Haystack Rock and the overlapping peaks of the Coast Range extending to Neahkahnie Mountain. This is one of the most photographed views on the coast. Out to sea, the sight of sea lions basking on surf-drenched rocks (mid-April–July) or migrating gray whales (December and March) and orcas (May) are seasonal highlights.

From Ecola Point, trails lead north to horseshoe-shaped **Indian Beach,** a favorite with surfers. Some prefer to drive there as a prelude to hiking up Tillamook Head, considered by Lewis and Clark to be the region's most beautiful viewpoint.

The name Ecola means "whale" in Chinook and was first used as a place-name by William Clark, referring to a creek in the area. Lewis and Clark journals note a 105-foot beached whale found somewhere within present-day Ecola Park's southern border, Crescent Beach. This area represents the southernmost extent of Lewis and Clark's coastal Oregon travels.

There is a $3 day-use fee at the park. The Oregon Coast Annual Pass and Oregon Coast 5-Day Pass are also honored.

Cannon Beach History Center

Permanent exhibits at the small Cannon Beach History Center (1387 South Spruce St., 503/436-9301, 1–5 P.M. Wed.–Sat., free) chronicle the town's timeline, from prehistory to the modern expansion of tourism and recreation. The original, eponymous cannon from the ill-fated *Shark* is also on display here.

◖ Saddle Mountain State Park

Another reason to head east from Cannon Beach is the hike up 3,283-foot Saddle Mountain. To get to the trailhead, take U.S. 26 from its junction with U.S. 101 for 10 miles and turn left on the prominently indicated Saddle Mountain Road. Although it's paved, this road is not suitable for RVs or wide-bodied vehicles. After seven

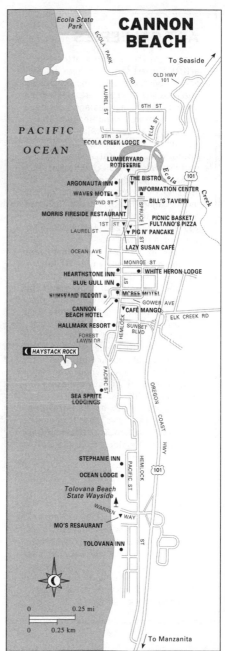

ART GALLERIES

Cannon Beach has long attracted artists and artisans, and here art lovers and purchasers will find nearly two dozen outlets for their work. Most of the Cannon Beach galleries and boutiques are concentrated along Hemlock Street, where you can hardly swing a Winsor & Newton No. 12 hogbristle brush without hitting one. Not surprisingly, the seashore itself is the subject and inspiration of many works you'll see here, with Haystack Rock frequently depicted in various media. Cannon Beach Information Center has a guide to all the galleries in town, or you can just stroll and discover them for yourself. A few we like:

At the north end of town, **Northwest by Northwest Gallery** (232 N. Spruce, 503/436-2428) has a new location to showcase its works of photography by Christopher Burkett and leading glass artists such as Duane Dahl. **White Bird Gallery** (251 N. Hemlock, 503/436-2681), founded in 1971 and one of Cannon Beach's oldest galleries, casts a wide net with paintings, sculpture, prints, photography, glass, ceramics, and jewelry. Nearby, the **Artists Gallerie** (224 N. Hemlock St., 503/436-0336) is a working studio showing the works of 12 painters whose styles range from realist to pure abstraction. The **Uffelman Gallery** (271 N. Hemlock, 503/436-2404) showcases the strikingly modern still lifes of Jeff Uffelman, which transform such mundane ingredients as a handful of peapods or peeled cucumbers into mesmerizing images.

DragonFire Gallery (123 S. Hemlock, 503/436-1533) is a teaching studio, offering weekend classes on various media. Throughout the summer, everyone is invited to come and express his or her creativity, tipple some wine, and listen to live music at the Saturday-night "Paint Party," hosted by local artists 6–10 P.M.

twisting miles, you'll come to the trailhead of the highest peak in this part of the Coast Range. The trail itself is steep and gains more than 1,600 feet in 2.5 miles. Wet conditions can make the going difficult (allow four hours round-trip) and the scenery en route is not always exceptional, but the view from the top is worth it.

On a clear day, hikers can see some 50 miles of the Oregon and Washington coastlines, including the Columbia River. Also possible are spectacular views of Mounts Rainier, St. Helens, and Hood, and, unfortunately, miles of clear-cuts. If you go May–August you'll be treated to a wildflower display that'll surprise you. On the upper part of the trail, plant species that pushed south from Alaska and Canada during the last Ice Age thrive. The cool, moist climate here keeps them from dying out as they did at lower elevations. Some early blooms include pink coast fawn lily, monkeyflower, wild rose, wood violet, bleeding heart, oxalis, Indian paintbrush, and trillium. Cable handrails provide safety on the narrow final 0.25-mile trail to the summit.

RECREATION
Horseback Riding
Sea Ranch Stables (415 Old U.S. 101, 503/436-2815), at the north entrance to Cannon Beach off U.S. 101, rents horses 9 A.M.– 5 P.M. for beach rides mid-May–Labor Day. Horses are allowed on the beach anywhere along the coast using public access points. Sea Ranch offers a number of one- to two-hour guided rides, starting at $45 per hour, including night rides on the beach.

Mountain Biking
Mike's Bike Shop, (248 N. Spruce St., 503/436-1266), has rentals for $3–6 per hour. Mike's specializes in mountain bikes, which can also be returned at a Warrenton outlet. You'll also find three-wheel beach-cycles for rent at the north end of town. These are fun for zipping up and down the hard-packed sand when the tide is out.

Camping
For easier access to Cannon Beach's natural

© BILL MCRAE

low tide at Cannon Beach

wonders, camping offers nature at a bargain price. Although camping is not permitted on the beach or in Cannon Beach city parks, there are plenty of options for RV, tent, and outdoor enthusiasts.

The **Sea Ranch RV Park** (415 Old U.S. 101, 503/436-2815, www.cannon-beach.net/searanch) has grassy sites nestled among the trees, also home to horses, ducks, rabbits, and raccoons. Open year-round with both full and partial hookups for RVs, campsites include a picnic table and fire ring (firewood sold on the premises), access to restrooms with hot showers—all just three blocks from the beach and downtown. Sites run $23–27. Cabins are also available for $70. Pets are welcome, but must be on a leash. Reservations recommended.

For a more pampered experience, check out the **RV Resort at Cannon Beach** (345 Elk Creek Rd., 503/436-2231 or 800/847-2231, www.cbrvresort.com). Open year-round, with 100 full hookups, indoor pool and spa, free cable TV, on-site convenience store, laundry, restrooms, and meeting room. This resort fea-

tures a Saturday night weenie roast during the summer months. Call for rates.

The family-run **Wright's for Camping** (334 Reservoir Rd., 503/436-2347, www.wrightsforcamping.com) has quite a history. During the 1930s, the Wrights came from Portland to camp in this area. Then in 1946, Pop Wright bought 10 acres in Cannon Beach from a friend. After running a successful construction company in town, Wright and his wife turned their 10-acre site into a campground. Choose from 19 sites with picnic tables, restrooms, laundry, and fire rings. Wheelchair accessible; leashed pets okay. Rates run $20 and up.

ENTERTAINMENT AND EVENTS

Going strong for over 30 years, the **Coaster Theatre Playhouse** (108 N. Hemlock, Cannon Beach, 503/436-1242, http://coastertheatre.com) stages a varied bill of musicals, dramas, mysteries, comedies, concerts, and other productions. It's open year-round, in a building that

NORTHERN OREGON COAST

started in the 1920s as a skating rink cum silent-movie house. Tickets run $12–18.

The **Puffin Kite Festival,** one of several kite events held on the coast, takes advantage of late April's blustery winds. Individuals and teams demonstrate flying techniques and compete for prizes, and for kids there's a treasure hunt, sandcastle building, and face painting. The festival is held just north of Haystack Rock, in front of the Surfsand Resort, which sponsors the event.

The half dozen or so other sand-sculpting contests that take place on the Oregon coast pale in comparison to Cannon Beach's annual **Sandcastle Day** (503/436-2623), which usually coincides with the lowest-tide Saturday in June. In 1964, a tsunami washed out a bridge, and the isolated residents of Cannon Beach organized the first contest as a way to amuse their children. Now in its fifth decade, this is the state's oldest and most prestigious competition of its kind. Tens of thousands of spectators show up to watch 1,000-plus competitors fashion their sculptures with the aid of buckets, shovels, squirt guns, and any natural material found on the beach. The resulting sculptures are often amazingly complex and inventive. Recent winners included Egyptian pyramids and a gigantic sea turtle. Building begins in the early morning; winners are announced at noon. The American Legion serves up a big breakfast buffet at 1216 S. Hemlock, open to all. The event is free to spectators, but entrants pay a fee.

Beginning in July, the city park (Spruce and 2nd Sts.) hosts **Concerts in the Park,** a series of jazz, rhythm and blues, and popular music, Sunday afternoons at the bandstand 2–4 P.M.

In July and August, the well-regarded **Haystack Summer Program in the Arts** (503/464-4812, www.haystack.pdx.edu) offers classes and workshops in painting, music, gardening, and writing, including the annual Pacific Northwest Children's Book Conference. In addition, evening readings, art exhibits, and lectures are open to the public.

ACCOMMODATIONS

Several local property management companies offer a large selection of furnished rentals ranging from grand oceanfront homes to quaint secluded cottages. **Cannon Beach Property Management** (3188 S. Hemlock, 503/436-2021 or 877/386-3402) allows visitors to virtually tour its list of homes (www.cbpm.com), as does **Cannon Beach Vacation Rentals** (P.O. Box 723, 866/436-0940, www.visitcb.com). Rates for both range $65–400.

About a one-minute walk to the beach, with friendly management and a great vibe, the **Blue Gull Inn** (632 S. Hemlock, 503/436-2714 or 800/507-2714, www.bluegullinn.net, doubles from $99) offers a choice between a beach house or less expensive motel units which come with housekeeping facilities. The modern cottages have in-room whirlpool tubs, fireplaces, and full kitchens. Cottages for larger groups are also available. On-site are a sauna and laundry room. Blue Gull Inn is one of four relatively inexpensive properties managed by Haystack Lodgings, which can be reached through the Blue Gull Inn website.

There aren't many inexpensive lodging options in Cannon Beach but the **McBee Motel** (888 S. Hemlock, 503/ 436-0247, www.mcbeecottages.com, $45–130) is clean and perfectly comfortable. Nothing fancy and certainly not expansive, the McBee nonetheless is a favorite of those who like it simple and inexpensive. And it's just a minute from the beach and within walking distance of downtown. McBee accepts pets in its homey cottages.

For a homey atmosphere, try the **Argonauta Inn** or the **The Waves Motel** (both located at 188 W. 2nd St., 503/436-2205 or 800/822-2468, www.thewavesmotel.com, doubles from $109). The Argonauta is made up of four houses in the middle of downtown, and has five furnished units just 150 feet from the beach. A cluster of six buildings makes up The Waves, with units to fit the needs of families, couples, or larger groups. These are not cookie-cutter units but the kind of individual lodgings you'd expect in Oregon.

For a family-oriented beachfront lodgings try **Sea Sprite Guest Lodgings** (280 S. Nebesna, 503/436-2266 or 866/828-1050, www.seasprite.com), just south of Haystack Rock, with six cottages with kitchens, TV, and spectacular views, which hold up to two, six, or eight. These family-style beach cottages are a throwback to the Oregon coast of an earlier era. Inside you'll find such homey touches as fireplaces, games, books, periodicals, and rockers.

The **Cannon Beach Hotel** (1116 Hemlock, 503/436-1392, doubles from $120) is a converted 1910 loggers' boardinghouse with 30 rooms and a small café and restaurant on the premises. The most expensive rooms have fireplaces, whirlpools, and partial ocean views. Meals are available in the restaurant adjacent to the lobby.

The **Surfsand Resort** (148 W. Gower, 503/436-2274 or 800/547-6100, www.surfsand.com, doubles from $239) offers a great combination of location and amenities in Cannon Beach. There are a number of room types, but most are spacious rooms with kitchens, fireplaces, and spas (in addition to use of the Cannon Beach Athletic Club and an indoor pool and spa)

Just a few minutes' walk from downtown, **Ecola Creek Lodge** (208 E. 5th St., 503/436-2776 or 800/873-2749, www.cannonbeachlodge.com, doubles from $125) is a Cape Cod–style inn with 22 unique units set within four buildings. Accommodations range from simple queen-bed studios to two-bedroom suites. Special features include stained glass, lawns, fountains, flower gardens, and a lily pond. Les Shirley Park and Ecola Creek separate the lodge from the beach.

The oceanfront **Hallmark Resort** (1400 S. Hemlock, 503/436-1566 or 888/448-4449, www.hallmarkinns.com) boasts romantic views of Haystock Rock. With convention and meeting facilities, a pool and on-site massage available, this is a service-oriented resort geared to accommodate couples, families, and large groups. In-room fireplaces add a romantic touch. Rates run $59–349.

For a more private experience and just steps from the ocean, the **White Heron Lodge** (356 N. Spruce, 503/436-2205 or 800/822-2468, doubles from $279) comprises two fully furnished oceanfront Victorian-style homes,

both of which sleep up to four. Each of the suites looks directly out to the Pacific. Wide sandy beaches and spacious front lawns make it a great location for families, especially those with small children. Located on a residential dead-end street, the lodge is only one block from the village.

The enormous **Tolovana Inn** hotel complex (3400 South Hemlock, 503/436-2211 or 800/333-8890, www.tolovanainn.com, doubles from $75) sits at the southern end of the Cannon Beach sprawl. Tolovana Inn has a number of room types, ranging from studios to one- and two bedroom condos, all with full kitchens, balconies, and fireplaces. In exchange for the rather identikit design and furnishings, you'll get a swimming pool, spa and sauna, a number of restaurants sharing the same parking lots, and the beach right out the front door. The least expensive rooms have "mountain views" while oceanfront rooms are roughly $100 more per night.

Two new top-end hotels offer beach front lodging and luxury. The [**Stephanie Inn** (2740 Pacific St., 503/436-3466 or 800/633-3466, www.stephanie-inn.com, doubles from $199) offers attentive, B&B-style service and attention to detail plus luxury-level rooms. All guestrooms have balconies, fireplaces, wet bars, hot tubs, fine linens and all the extras you'd expect in an upscale resort hotel—including a fine dining restaurant. Every room has outstanding views of the beach and Haystack Rock.

The **Ocean Lodge** (2864 S. Pacific, 503/436-2241 or 888/777-4047, doubles from $269) feels like a long-established beach getaway, though in fact it's recently built. The high-end furnishings also give a clue that despite its venerable design this rambling lodge isn't soaked in tradition. Rooms all have oceanfront views, balconies, DVD players, fireplaces, microwaves, and fridges.

FOOD

If you're on a budget, keep dining prices down at the **Mariner Market** (139 N. Hemlock, 503/436-2442), an antique-filled grocery that's fully stocked with fresh meat, fruit, and vegetables. They carry organic produce and natural food products as well as a deli with fast-food takeout items. Open 9 A.M.–9 P.M. In the fishing business for more than 25 years, **Ecola Seafoods** (208 N. Spruce, 503/436-9130) features fresh-catch Dungeness crab and bay shrimp cocktails, as well as a decent clam chowder. Or sample their smoked salmon and fish-n-chips. You'll find it across from the public parking lots and information center.

Bill's Tavern (188 N. Hemlock St., 503/436-2202, lunch and dinner, main courses $7–14), once a legendary watering hole, is now a more traditional remodeled brewpub. Sweet thick onion rings, good fries, one-third-pound burgers, sautéed prawns, and grilled oysters are the bill of fare.

Try the wood-paneled, skylit **Lazy Susan Cafe** (126 N. Hemlock, 503/436-2816, three meals daily, main courses $8–15) for anytime breakfast (eggs with a side of bread pudding), lunch (sandwiches and salads), and light dinner (hot seafood salad). There's also the fresh fish catch of the day and pizza. Head up the street to the **Lazy Susan Grill & Scoop** (156 N. Hemlock) to wash it all down with espresso or a soda fountain concoction at this spacious family-friendly establishment. Open till 5 P.M. (8 P.M. on weekends).

Cafe Mango (1235 S. Hemlock, 503/436-2393, breakfast and lunch daily, main courses $5–13) is another mainstay, locally famous for such dishes as Amish oatcake waffles, blueberry cornmeal pancakes, frittatas, bagels and lox, and creative omelettes. Such Mexican dishes as pozole soup, chilaquiles, and a breakfast burrito stuffed with homemade refried beans and eggs are also winners in this homey restaurant. Fresh fruit smoothies, homemade ketchup and jam, as well as extensive vegetarian options with organic ingredients also explain Mango's cult status.

Morris' Fireside Restaurant (207 N. Hemlock, 503/436-2917, three meals daily, main courses $8–19) is an attractive log building where pot roasts, steak, and seafood are featured along with "logger" breakfasts. Portions are large, and prices are moderate.

The local **Pig 'N Pancake** (223 S. Hemlock, 503/436-2851, main courses $5–12) has large picture windows overlooking a leafy ravine. Open daily for breakfast and lunch, offering 35 varieties of breakfast (including homemade pancakes) served anytime. For lunch, try the soups, chowder, or halibut fish-n-chips.

Fultano's Pizza (200 N. Hemlock, 503/436-9717, pizzas from $11, pasta from $8) sits unobtrusively near the corner of 2nd and Hemlock on your way to the beach. If you're hungry, aromas of fresh cheese, garlic, and fresh-baked dough will draw you inside this brick enclave.

Hankering for some authentic West Coast chowder? Head to **Dooger's Seafood and Grill** (1371 S. Hemlock, 503/436-2225, three meals daily, main courses $11–14) for award-winning seafood. **Mo's at Tolovana** (195 Warren Way, 503/436-1111, main courses $4–17), next to Tolovana Park, boasts a restaurant site once selected by *Pacific Northwest* magazine as having "the most romantic view on the Oregon coast." Add this to Mo's reliable formula of fresh fish and rich clam chowder at very reasonable prices in a family-friendly atmosphere and you can't miss.

Whether or not you're staying at the **Stephanie Inn** (2740 S. Pacific, 503/436-2221 or 800/633-3466, main courses $16–$27), you are welcome to join guests in the dining room for a four-course prix-fixe dinner featuring innovative Northwest cuisine. The atmosphere boasts mountain views, open wood beams, and a river-rock fireplace. Due to "cozy" seating, reserve well ahead of time.

The **Lumberyard Rotisserie and Grill** (264 3rd St., 503/436-0285, lunch and dinner daily, main courses $10–19) is a block away from busy downtown Cannon Beach, but this spacious newer restaurant offers high quality food at good prices. The specialty is rotisserie cook meats, including turkey, chicken and prime rib, but the pizza here is also good.

Cozy and refined, **The Bistro** (263 N Hemlock St., 503/436-2661, dinner Wed.–Mon, main courses $14–25), is tucked back in a maze of shops and gardens in downtown Cannon Beach. The atmosphere is quintessential

French country inn, and the menu brings a taste of Provence to traditional fish and seafood dishes—the seafood stew is a wonderful blend of Northwest fish and shellfish prepared with Mediterranean zest. The dining room is truly tiny, and the food superlative, so reservations are mandatory.

Half restaurant, half European-style charcuterie and deli, the **Gower Street Bistro** (1116 S. Hemlock St., 503/436-2729, brunch Mon., Wed., Fri.–Sun., dinner nightly, main courses $10–22) offers lots of goodies for impromptu picnics by day, then by night shifts gear and turns into a casual but well-honed dining room with a cocktail bar ambience. The salads are fantastic, and the garlicky, roast 40-Clove Chicken is delicious. Located in the Cannon Beach Hotel.

INFORMATION

The chamber of commerce operates the **Cannon Beach Information Center** (201 E. 2nd, Cannon Beach, 503/436-2623, www. cannonbeach.org, 11 A.M.–5 P.M. Mon.–Sat., 10 A.M.–4 P.M. Sun.) This facility is near the public restrooms (2nd and Spruce) and basketball and tennis courts.

GETTING THERE AND GETTING AROUND

From U.S. 101, there's a choice of four entrances to the beach loop (also known as U.S. 101 Alternate, a section of the old Oregon Coast Highway) to take you into town. As you wade into the town's shops, galleries, and restaurants, the beach loop becomes Hemlock Street, the main drag.

Sunset Empire Transportation District operates **The Bus,** which serves Cannon Beach, Seaside, Astoria-Warrenton, and points in between. For schedule and fare info, call 503/861-7433. The free **Cannon Beach Shuttle** runs every half-hour on a 6.5-mile loop, from Les Shirley Park on the north end of town to Tolovana Park. It operates 10 A.M.–6 P.M. daily, with extended summer hours.

Parking can be hard to come by, especially on weekends, but you'll find public lots south of town at Tolovana Park, and in town at Hemlock at 1st Street and on 2nd Street.

Cannon Beach to Tillamook

South of Cannon Beach along U.S. 101 are more excellent beaches, sharing Cannon Beach's beauty without its crowds. **Hug Point State Recreation Area** is a nice picnic area with access to a quiet beach. Hug Point is a rocky cape that protrudes far out into the beach. Before U.S. 101 was built in the 1930s, horse-drawn wagons and early automobiles used the beach as a road surface, and only at low tide could they "hug" passed this rocky outcrop. The old tracks—plus two sea caves—are still visible in the headland at low tide.

Just north of Manzanita, **Neahkahnie Mountain** towers nearly 1,700 feet up from the edge of the sea. U.S. 101 climbs up and over its shoulders, to an elevation of 700 feet, and the vistas from a half-dozen pullouts (highest along the Oregon coast) are spectacular—but do try to keep your eyes on the snaking road until you've parked your car. This stretch of the highway, built by the WPA in the 1930s, was constructed by blasting a roadbed from the rock face and buttressing it with stonework walls on the precarious cliffs. Soaring a thousand feet above, on the east side of the highway, is the peak named for the Tillamook tribe's fire spirit, Neah-Kah-Nie. The faint-hearted or acrophobic certainly couldn't have lasted long on this job. The handiwork of these road builders and masons can be admired at several pullouts, along with the breathtaking vista of Manzanita Beach, Nehalem Spit, and some 17 miles south to Cape Meares.

◀ OSWALD WEST STATE PARK

Most of Neahkahnie Mountain the mountain and the prominent headlands of Cape Falcon

NORTHERN OREGON COAST

© JUDY JEWELL

Pitch your tent in a coastal old-growth forest at Oswald West State Park, south of Cannon Beach.

ascent. Allow about 45 minutes to get to the top. The summit view south to Cape Meares and east to the Nehalem Valley ranks as one of the finest on the coast.

To camp at Oswald West State Park (800/551-6949), you walk 0.3 mile from the campers' parking lot to 30 primitive campsites in a grove of old-growth conifers surrounded by high cliffs. You can use the wheelbarrows at the parking lot and campground to cart your gear back and forth. Campsites are $14. There are flush toilets, but no electrical hookups.

MANZANITA AND VICINITY

Huddled along an expansive curve of beach at the foot of Neahkahnie Mountain, quiet Manzanita (pop. 785) makes a pleasant stop for lunch or for the weekend. As one of the few towns along the northern Oregon coast that's not located directly on U.S. 101, Manzanita seems to feel more peaceful and secluded than most others. When adjacent coastal areas are fogbound, the seven-mile-long Manzanita Beach usually enjoys sunshine because of the shelter of Neahkahnie Mountain. It also has good surfing and windsurfing.

are encompassed within the 2,500-acre gem of Oswald West State Park. Several hiking trails weave through the park, including the 13 miles of the Oregon Coast Trail linking Arch Cape to the north with Manzanita. From the main parking lot on the east side of U.S. 101, a 0.5-mile trail follows Short Sand Creek to **Short Sand Beach.** From Short Sand Beach, you can pick up the three-mile old-growth–lined Cape Falcon Trail to the highway, or you might want just to linger at Smuggler's Cove, which is a popular spot for surfers year-round. Rainforests of hemlock, cedar, and gigantic Sitka spruce crowd the secluded, boulder-strewn shoreline. At daybreak or dusk, keep an eye out for Roosevelt elk.

A mile south of the main parking lot is the access road to the **Neahkahnie Mountain Summit Trail** on the east side of the highway. It's not well marked; look for a subdivision on the golf course to the west. Drive the gravel road up a quarter mile to the trailhead parking lot and begin a moderately difficult 1.5-mile

Nehalem Bay State Park

Just south of Manzanita, and occupying the entire sandy appendage of Nehalem Spit, is scenic, sprawling Nehalem Bay State Park (503/368-5943 information, 800/452-5687 or www.reserveamerica.com for reservations, open year-round), a favorite with beginning windsurfers, bikers, beachcombers, and anglers. Sandwiched between the bay and a four-mile beach stretching from Manzanita to the mouth of the Nehalem River is a vast campground (rates are $20) with flush toilets and hot showers. There are 18 yurts for $27. A $3 daily day-use fee applies to non-campers. Park amenities include evening programs, flush toilets, and piped water. As big as this park is, it does fill up in summer, so reservations are recommended (particularly during July and August). To get there, turn south at Bayshore Junction just before U.S. 101 heads east into the town of Nehalem.

© JUDY JEWELL

Public art or beach shelter? driftwood sculpture at Nehalem Bay State Park, Manzanita

Accommodations

Overnighters can choose from a variety of tasteful vacation cottages, B&Bs, and other lodgings in Manzanita. Advance reservations at most are a must, especially in summer, and many require two- to three-night stays during the high season and on some holidays. A good alternative to motels for families here are the rentals available from the several property management agencies in town. Among these is **Ribbon Investment Firm** (430 Laneda Ave., Manzanita 97130, 888/503-6009, www .ribbonvacationrentals.com), with more than 40 fully furnished homes to let, running $110–225 per night (most require weekly rentals July and August).

If you're looking for an upscale retreat, the cedar-clad **Inn at Manzanita** (67 Laneda Ave., Manzanita 97130, 503/368-6754, www.innat manzanita.com, doubles from $120), set in a Japanese-accented garden just a short walk from the beach, promises guests (no children) the three Rs: recreation, relaxation, romance.

Each of its 13 wood-paneled rooms features a gas fireplace and two-person spa; most rooms have a balcony, offering glimpses through the evergreens of the nearby beach. Fresh flowers daily, robes, and other amenities help you feel pampered. Despite being in the middle of town near restaurants and the beach, a feeling of luxurious seclusion prevails. A two-night minimum stay is required on weekends and July 1–Labor Day, and discounts are available.

Six blocks from the beach, the five spacious and airy cabins of **Coast Cabins** (635 Laneda Ave., 503/368-7113, www.coastcabins.com, doubles from $125) comfortably sleep one or two (two-story Cabin 5 is designed for up to four persons) and offer kitchenettes or full kitchens, satellite TV, and goose-down pillows and comforters. Two-night minimum for advance reservations in summer and weekends all year. Pets are allowed in some cabins for a $20 nightly fee.

The Arbors Bed-and-Breakfast (78 Idaho Ave., 503/368-7566 or 888/664-9587, $105–115), one block from the beach, offers two cozy rooms with private bath in a handsome, Craftsman-style cottage built in the early 1920s.

Food

Left Coast Siesta (288 Laneda Ave., 503/368-7997, closed Mon.–Tues.) specializes in design-your-own-burritos, the perfect takeout for a filling lunch or dinner. Options include spicy beef, spicy chicken, tequila-lime chicken, or black beans to put into a selection of flavored tortillas. They also have tacos and enchiladas. Budget diners can eat well here for less than $6. And even though they advertise "fast, healthy, and fresh," Left Coast doesn't sacrifice flavor. And if you like *caliente*, this is the place for you: Left Coast Siesta stocks a hot sauce bar with 200-plus different types of the hot stuff.

Even closer to the water, **Marzano's** (60 Laneda Ave., 503/368-5593) serves the coast's best slices of gourmet pizza, with prices to match—$15–24 for large-size whole pies. The roasted vegetable pizza is recommended, and the smoked prosciutto with aged Montegrappa cheese is another winner. The understated

NORTHERN OREGON COAST

decor here is dominated by reproductions of French advertising posters. If you're looking for a brew and a burger, the **San Dune Tavern** (127 Laneda Ave., 503/368-5080) is a friendly spot to hole up; it's smoke-free, too.

Up near U.S. 101, **Terra Cotta Cafe** (725 Manzanita Ave., 503/368-3700, dinner Wed.–Sun., main courses $9–28) offers French-influenced dining in a charmingly low-key ambience. Parchment-poached salmon is served with apples and blue cheese, while lamb chops are served with cranberry-jalapeno sauce.

Three miles east of Manzanita, the **[Nehalem River Inn** (34910 Route 53, 503/368-7708, www.nehalemriverinn.com, dinner Fri.–Mon., main courses $18–29) is one of the best places on the coast to experience fresh and inventive Northwest cuisine. The inn's sophisticated menu blends Northwest seafood, game, locally grown organic produce, wild mushrooms, and other ingredients to create dishes that will turn the heads of even the most discriminating diners—such as Muscovy duck breast served with black truffle potato gnocchi. Complement your meal with a bottle from a well-selected wine list favoring Oregon wineries, including its own private-label wines. Reservations are recommended.

GARIBALDI

Tillamook Bay's commercial fishing fleet is concentrated in this little port town (pop. 970) near the north end of the bay. Garibaldi, named in 1879 by the local postmaster for the Italian patriot, is a fish-processing center: Crab, shrimp, fresh salmon, lingcod, and bottom fish (halibut, cabezon, rockfish, and sea perch) are the specialties here. At the marina, **Bayocean Seafood** (608 Commercial Dr., 503/322-3316) gets it right off the boats, so the selection is both low-priced and fresh. Likewise the crab,

fish, and other seafood available next door at **Oregon Gourmet** (606 Commercial Dr., 503/322-2544). If you want it fresher, you'll have to catch it yourself.

The **Fisherman's Korner Restaurant** (306 Mooring Basin, 503/322-2033, breakfast and lunch) is right on the wharf and offers absolutely fresh fish-n-chips and excellent clam chowder. Breakfasts here are massive—meant for hungry sailors.

The town's fishing and crabbing piers *do* attract hordes who want to catch their own. Rent crab traps, kayaks, and other gear at the **Garibaldi Marina** (302 Mooring Basin Rd., 503/322-3312). In addition to dock fishing, guide and charter services offer salmon and halibut fishing, bird-watching, and whale-watching excursions. North of Garibaldi on U.S. 101, the bay entrance is a good place to see brown pelicans, harlequin ducks, oystercatchers, and guillemots. The Miami River marsh, south of town, is a bird-watching paradise at low tide, when ducks and shorebirds hunt for food.

Fishing

The **Miami River** and **Kilchis River,** which empty into Tillamook Bay south of Garibaldi, get the state's only two significant runs of chum salmon, a species that is much more common from Washington northward. There's a catch-and-release season for them mid-September to mid-November. Both rivers also get the runs of spring chinook and are open for steelhead most of the year.

Several charter companies have offices at the marina. **Garibaldi Charters** (607 Garibaldi Ave., 503/322-0007, www.garibaldicharters. com) offers fishing excursions ($100 for a full day of salmon fishing) and wildlife-viewing or whale-watching trips ($20 per person).

Tillamook and the Tillamook Bay Area

Without much sun or surf, what could possibly draw enough visitors to the town of Tillamook (pop. 4,270) to make it one of Oregon's top three tourism attractions? Superficially speaking, tours of a cheese factory and a World War II blimp hangar, in a town flanked by mudflats and rain-soaked dairy country, shouldn't pull in more than a million tourists a year. But they do. As anyone who has driven to Tillamook via the scenic Three Capes Loop or past Neahkahnie Mountain on U.S. 101 can attest, those tasty morsels of jack and cheddar provide the perfect complement to the surrounding region's scenic beauty.

Tillamook County is home to more than 26,000 cows, which easily outnumber the county's human population. They're the foundation of the Tillamook County Creamery Association's famous cheddar cheese and other dairy products, which generate about $85 million in annual sales. Other important contributors to the local economy are fishing and oyster farming.

In 1933, a wildfire devastated forests in the Coast Range east of town in what was the worst natural disaster in the state's history. The Tillamook Burn raged for four weeks, reducing massive acreage of old growth to rows of charred stumps. The fire pushed a cloud of ash 40,000 feet into the air. Ashfall was recorded 500 miles out to sea and as far east as Yellowstone National Park in Wyoming, while Oregon's upper left edge lived in semidarkness for weeks. Fires in 1939 and 1945 further ravaged the area, leaving a total of 355,000 acres destroyed by the three blazes. More than 72 million seedlings planted by a community reforestation effort in the years that followed have produced an impressive stand of trees in these forests today.

In 1940–1942, partially in response to a Japanese submarine firing on Fort Stevens in Astoria, the U.S. Navy built two blimp hangars south of town, the two largest wooden structures ever built, according to *Guinness*. Of the five naval air stations on the Pacific coast, the Tillamook blimp guard patrolled the waters from Northern California to the San Juan Islands and escorted ships into Puget Sound. While all kinds of blimp stories abound in Tillamook bars, only one wartime encounter has been documented. Recently declassified records confirm that blimps were involved in the sinking of what was believed to be two Japanese submarines off Cape Meares. In late May 1943, two of the high-flying craft, assisted by U.S. Navy subchasers and destroyers, dropped several depth charges on the submarines, which are still lying on the ocean floor.

SIGHTS
Tillamook Cheese Factory

With over a million visitors a year, the Tillamook Cheese Factory (4175 U.S. 101 N., Tillamook, 503/842-4481, open 8 A.M.–8 P.M. daily in summer and 8 A.M.–6 P.M. daily Labor Day–mid June, free admission) is far and away the county's biggest drawing card. The plant welcomes visitors with a reproduction of the *Morningstar,* the schooner that transported locally made butter and cheese in the late 1800s and now adorns the label of every Tillamook product. The quaint vessel symbolizing Tillamook cheesemaking's humble beginnings stands in stark contrast to the technology and sophistication that go into making this world-famous gourmet product today.

In the early 1900s, the Tillamook County Creamery Association absorbed smaller operations and opened the modern plant in 1949. Today, Tillamook produces tens of millions of pounds of cheese annually, including Monterey jack, Swiss, and multiple variations of their award-winning white cheddar.

Inside the plant, a self-guided tour follows the movement of curds and whey to the "cheddaring table." Come for the tour, but stay for the tastings. Tillamook ice cream has been touted by the *New York Times* as superior to Häagen-Dazs, and their extra premium aged sharp white cheddar was rated by the National Milk Producers in 1997 as the country's best cheese. Pepperoni, butter, cheese soup, milk, and other products are also available. There's a gift shop (more Holstein-themed tchochkes than you've probably dreamed of) and a full-service restaurant, but the big attraction is the ice cream counter. Have a double-scoop chocolate peanut butter cone—worth every penny.

Blue Heron French Cheese Company

A quarter-million people a year visit Tillamook County's *second*-most-popular attraction, Blue Heron French Cheese Company (2001 Blue Heron Dr., 503/842-8282, open daily 8 A.M.–8 P.M. in summer and 8 A.M.–6 P.M. Labor Day–mid-June, free admission), located a mile south of the Tillamook Cheese Factory. Housed in a large white barn, Blue Heron is famous for its Brie, though the cheese is no longer produced on site. In addition to cheeses and other gourmet foods, the shop sells gift baskets, and over 90 varieties of Oregon

wines are available in their wine-tasting room. A deli serves lunches of homemade soups and salads. For kids, there's a petting farm with the usual barnyard suspects.

Tillamook Air Museum

South of town off U.S. 101 you can't possibly miss the enormous Quonset hut–like building east of the highway. The world-class aircraft collection of the Tillamook Air Museum (6030 Hangar Rd., Tillamook, 503/842-1130, www.tillamookair.com, open 10 A.M.–5 P.M. daily, $11 adults, $10 seniors, $6 ages 6–17) is housed in and around Hangar B of the decommissioned Tillamook Naval Air Station. At 1,072 feet long, 206 feet wide, and 192 feet high, it's the largest wooden structure in the world. During World War II, this and another gargantuan hangar on the site (which burned down in 1992) sheltered eight K-class blimps, each 242 feet long.

Inside the seven-acre structure, you can learn about the role the big blimps played during wartime as well as how they are used today.

Blue Heron Cheese farm, Tillamook

In addition, there's a large collection of World War II fighter planes (many one-of-a-kind models) as well as photos and artifacts from the naval air station days. Be sure to check out the cyclo-crane, a combination blimp/plane/helicopter. This was devised in the 1980s to aid in remote logging operations; it ended up an $8 million bust.

If possible, bring binoculars here to see the interesting latticework of rafters and Navy-uniformed mannequins on the catwalks 20 stories up. To get there from downtown, take U.S. 101 south two miles, make a left at the flashing yellow light, and follow the signs.

Tillamook County Pioneer Museum

East of the highway in the heart of downtown, Tillamook County Pioneer Museum (2106 2nd St., Tillamook, 503/842-4553, open 9 A.M.–5 P.M. Mon.–Sat., 11 A.M.–5 P.M. Sun., $3 general admission, $2.50 for seniors) is famous for its taxidermy exhibits as well as memorabilia from pioneer households. Particularly intriguing are hunks of ancient beeswax with odd inscriptions recovered from near Neahkahnie Mountain. Old photos are also worth the admission price. The old courtroom on the second floor has one of the best displays of natural history in the state. There are many beautiful dioramas, plus shells, insects, and nests. The Beals Memorial Room houses a famous rock and mineral collection along with fossils.

The main floor and the basement highlight human history with antique kitchen tools, old-time logging equipment, Native American artifacts and basketry, historic modes of conveyance (from stagecoaches to cars), and simulated pioneer households.

Oregon Coast Explorer Trains

The Port of Tillamook Bay (503/842-8206, www.potb.org/oregoncoastexplorer.htm) operate a number of rail excursions between the fishing village of Garibaldi (eight miles north of Tillamook) to points north along the coast and west to Banks, on the other side of the Coast Range. The selection of trips and the schedule are both complex, so it's a good idea to check the website or call the office to find out what is on the calendar during your visit. The least expensive option is the 1.5 hour round-trip between Garibaldi and Rockaway Beach, which operates on Saturdays and Sundays from Memorial Day weekend to mid-September, and Fridays from July 4 through August, plus Memorial Day, July 4, and Labor Day. This train is pulled by a 1910 Heisler Locomotive Works engine. Tickets for this run are $13 adults, and $7 for children 3–10. Check the online schedule for periodically scheduled dinner and brunch trips between other destinations.

Munson Creek Falls

Seven miles south of Tillamook, a 1.5-mile access road turns east from U.S. 101, leading to the highest waterfall in the Oregon Coast Range. Munson Creek Falls drops 266 feet over mossy cliffs surrounded by an old-growth forest. The very narrow, bumpy dirt road then takes you to the parking lot. A quarter-mile trail leads to the base of the falls, while another, slightly longer trail leads to a higher viewpoint; wooden walkways clinging to the cliff lead to a small viewing platform. This is a spectacle in all seasons, but come in winter when the falls pour down with greater fury. Note that motor homes and trailers cannot get into the park; the lot is too small.

Tillamook State Forest

A series of intense forest fires in the 1930s and '40s burned vast amounts of land in the northern Coast Range. Most of this land was owned by private timber companies, who walked away from the seemingly worthless "Tillamook Burn," leaving property rights to revert to the counties, who then handed the land over to the state. A massive replanting effort ensued, and in 1973, the Tillamook Burn became the Tillamook State Forest. In 2006, the Tillamook Forest Visitor Center opened in a soaring timbered building in the middle of the once-burned, now-lush forest. Be sure to stop in to see the short movie about the area's history; the vivid fire scenes are a bit frightening,

A footbridge connects the Tillamook Forest Visitor Center with hiking trails.

© PAUL LEVY

a sensation that's enhanced when the smell of smoke is released into the auditorium. Don't leave without walking out through the center's back door, crossing the footbridge, and taking at least a short hike, where you'll see an assortment of native wildflowers, shrubs, and trees. If you head west from the bridge, Wilson Falls is about two miles away.

If a short hike outside the Forest Center leaves you hankering for more, head east along Route 6 to the Kings Mountain trailhead. On a clear day (ha!) there are good views from the top. Several more trails start at the summit of the Coast Range. The campgrounds along Route 6, including **Jones Creek,** which is right next to the Tillamook Forest Center, are popular with off-road-vehicle drivers, who have their own trail network back in the hills.

SPORTS AND RECREATION
Golf

Golfers choose between two public courses in Tillamook. About two miles north of town, east of U.S. 101, **Bay Breeze Golf Course** (2325 Latimer Rd., Tillamook, 503/842-1166) charges $10 for nine holes on weekends. Another two miles north, **Alderbrook Golf Course** (7300 Alderbrook Rd., Tillamook, 503/842-6413) charges $52 on weekends for 18 holes.

Hiking

Two challenging trails off Route 6, **King Mountain,** 25 miles east of Tillamook, and **Elk Mountain,** 28 miles east of Tillamook, climb through lands affected by the Tillamook Burn, but with scenic views throughout. Thanks to salvage logging in the wake of the disaster and subsequent replanting, myriad trails crisscross forests of Douglas and noble fir, hemlock, and red alder. Pick up the helpful pamphlet *Tillamook Forest Trails* put out by the Oregon Department of Forestry, Tillamook District (4907 E. 3rd St., Tillamook 97141, 503/842-2543).

ACCOMMODATIONS

Most travelers seem to pass through Tillamook on their way to someplace else, but a good local choice is **Best Western Inn & Suites** (1722 N. Makinster Rd., Tillamook, 503/842-7599 or 800/299-4817, doubles from $129), which is close to everything. Rooms have dataports, refrigerator, microwave, iron and ironing board, coffeemaker, and cable TV. Amenities include indoor pool, sauna, and hot tub, plus complimentary continental breakfast.

FOOD

Tillamook restaurant fare draws on the local bounty from the sea and surrounding farm country. Dungeness crab, bay shrimp, clams, and oysters are indigenous to the area, and a burgeoning number of wine and gourmet outlets throughout Tillamook County can make for a surprisingly interesting taste tour. But the best food is found in the county's smaller towns—Oceanside, Manzanita, Nehalem, and Pacific City. To sample the county's freshest produce, visit the **Tillamook Farmers Market** in downtown Tillamook. It runs every Saturday, late June–early October, on Laurel Avenue.

The **Farmhouse Cafe** at the Tillamook Cheese Factory serves breakfast and lunch; open daily at 8 A.M. The **deli** at the Blue Heron French Cheese Company fixes sandwiches, soups, and salads daily. On the west side of U.S. 101, between the two cheese meccas, lunchtime do-it-yourselfers might check the locally raised and cured meat and smoked salmon at **Debbie D's Sausage Factory** (503/842-2622).

Casual passersby wouldn't figure tiny Bay City, five miles north of Tillamook, as a key stop on a Tillamook County gourmet tour, but those in the know hit the brakes here for excellent seafood, especially oysters. Motoring through Bay City, you'll notice piles of oyster shells on the roadside, destined to be ground into chicken feed. Predictably, local menu entrées with grilled Tillamook Bay oysters are a good bet.

You can't find oysters much fresher than those at **Pacific Seafood** (5150 Oyster Bay Dr., 503/377-2323, lunch and dinner daily, main courses $8–14), where you can enjoy just-off-the-boat bivalves grilled oysters, smoked, cocktail style, or on the half-shell. Crabcakes, halibut burgers, and clam chowder are also highlights in an extensive menu of fresh seafood. Takeout lunches can be enjoyed outside on the jetty close by interpretive placards that explain this environment.

Downie's Cafe (9320 5th St., Bay City, 503/377-2220) is a greasy-spoon favorite among anglers. Whether it's homemade buttermilk pancakes for breakfast or the famous oysterburger ($6.50) for lunch, you'll leave full and satisfied. Finish off with a slice of homemade pie, especially pumpkin with Tillamook ice cream. To get to Downie's, look for the muraled facade of Artspace Cafe on the east side of U.S. 101 opposite Tillamook Bay. Turn at Artspace onto 5th Street and drive two blocks to its intersection with C Street.

INFORMATION

The **Tillamook Chamber of Commerce** (3705 U.S. 101 N., Tillamook 97191, 503/842-7525, www.tillamookchamber.org) is located across the parking lot from the cheese factory. It's open 9 A.M.–5 P.M. Monday–Friday, 10 A.M.–3 P.M. Saturday, 10 A.M.–2 P.M. Sunday mid-June–September.

Three Capes Scenic Loop

The Three Capes Scenic Loop, a 35-mile byway off U.S. 101 between Tillamook and Pacific City, is considered by many to be the preeminent scenic area on the north coast. While the beauty of Capes Kiwanda, Lookout, and Meares certainly justifies leaving the main highway, it would be an overstatement to portray this drive as a thrill-a-minute detour on the order of the south coast's Boardman Park or the central coast's Otter Crest Loop. Instead of fronting the ocean, the road connecting the capes winds mostly through dairy country, small beach towns, and second-growth forest. What's special here are the three capes themselves, and unless you get out of the car and walk on the trails, you'll miss the aesthetic appeal and distinctiveness of each headland's ecosystem. The wave-battered bluffs of Cape Kiwanda, the precipitous overlooks along the Cape Lookout Highway, and the curious Octopus Tree at Cape Meares are the perfect antidotes to the inland towns along U.S. 101. The majority of the Three Capes lodging and dining options are clustered in Pacific City and at the other end in Netarts and Oceanside. In between, it's mostly sand dunes, isolated beaches, rainforest, and pasture. To reach the Three Capes Scenic Loop from the north, turn west at Tillamook and follow signs to Cape Meares. From the south, follow signs north of Neskowin to Pacific City.

CAPE MEARES SCENIC VIEWPOINT

With stunning views, picnic tables, a newly restored lighthouse, and a uniquely contorted tree a short walk from the parking lot, Cape Meares Scenic Viewpoint is the user-friendliest site on the Three Capes Loop. The park was named for English navigator John Meares, who mapped many points along this coast in a 1788 voyage. The famed **Octopus Tree** is less than a quarter mile up a forested hill. The tentacle-like extensions of this Sitka spruce have also

been compared to the arms of a candelabra. Another writer likened this tree to a gargantuan spider in a near-fetal position.

The 10-foot diameter of its base supports five-foot-thick trunks, each of which by itself is large enough to be a single tree. Scientists have propounded several theories for the cause of its unusual shape, including everything from wind and weather to insects damaging the spruce when it was young. A Native American legend about the spruce contends that it was shaped this way so that the branches could hold the canoes of a chief's dead family. Supposedly, the bodies were buried near the tree. This was a traditional practice among the tribes of the area, who referred to species formed thusly as "council trees."

Beyond the tree you can look back at Oceanside and Three Arch Rocks Refuge. The sweep of Pacific shore and offshore monoliths makes a fitting beginning (or finale, if you're driving from the south) to your sojourn along the Three Capes Loop, but be sure to also stroll the short paved trail down to the lighthouse, which begins at the parking lot and provides dramatic views of an offshore wildlife refuge, Cape Meares Rocks. Bring binoculars to see tufted puffins, pelagic cormorants, seals, and sea lions. The landward portion of the refuge protects rare old-growth evergreens.

The restored interior of **Cape Meares Lighthouse,** built in 1890, is open 11 A.M.–4 P.M. daily May–September. This beacon was replaced as a functioning light in 1963 by the automated facility located behind it, and it now houses a gift shop. A free tour is occasionally staffed by volunteers who might tell you about how the lighthouse was built here by mistake, and perhaps offer a peek into the prismatic Fresnel lenses.

OCEANSIDE

The road between Cape Meares and Netarts heads into the beach-house community of Oceanside (pop. about 250). Many of the homes are built into the cliff overlooking the ocean, Sausalito style. This motif reaches its apex atop Maxwell Point. You can peer several hundred feet down at **Three Arch Rocks Wildlife Refuge,** part-time home to one of the continent's largest and most varied collections of shorebirds. A herd of sea lions also populates this trio of sea stacks from time to time.

While low prices and a window on the water can be found at **Ocean Front Cabins** (1610 Pacific Ave., Oceanside, 503/842-6081 or 888/845-8470, www.oceanfrontcabins.com), the older, smallish rooms here might at first give some travelers pause. Nonetheless, for as little as $60 (a sleeping unit without a kitchenette) or two-bed rooms with full kitchens for $90 you'll find yourself literally within a stone's throw of Oceanside's beachcombing and dining highlights.

The aptly named **House on the Hill** (1816 Maxwell Mountain Rd., Oceanside, 503/842-6030, www.houseonthehillmotel.com, doubles from $95), also called the Clifftop Inn, is perched on a bluff at Maxwell Point, with both seclusion and cliffside ocean grandeur of this headland. Most of the 16 units here are not especially elaborate, but the sweeping view is easily worth whatever you pay for the room. The office maintains a little museum with sea specimens and newspaper articles about the area as well as a telescope focused on the offshore Three Arch Rocks bird refuge.

Another good lodging option is **Bender Vacation Rental Properties** (503/233-4363), boasting six units with cliffside ocean views, large private decks, and full kitchens (except for one unit). Other amenities include fireplaces, TVs, VCRs, and microwaves. Pets are welcome at most locations. For $90–225 per night on a two-night minimum, this is a great deal.

A popular draw for hungry Three Capes travelers, **[Roseanna's Oceanside Cafe** (1490 Pacific Ave. N.W., Oceanside, 503/842-7351, main courses $14–22) garners high marks from just about everyone. At first, the weather-beaten cedar-shake exterior might lead you to expect an old general store, as indeed it was decades ago. Once you're inside, however, the ornate decor leaves little doubt that this place takes its new identity seriously. From an elevated perch above the breakers, you'll be treated to expertly prepared local oysters and fresh salmon. The menu is surprisingly extensive, as is the wine list. Be sure to save room for blackberry cobbler; order it warm so the Tillamook Vanilla Bean ice cream on top melts down the sides, and watch the waves over a long cup of coffee.

The **Anchor Tavern** (1495 Pacific Ave., Oceanside, 503/842-2041) is a nearby alternative for food by the beach. Along with microbrews, specialties are smoked meats, BBQ ribs, clam chowder, pizza, and burgers. Hanging above the bar is a wide-angle photo of Hartford, Connecticut. The four-foot-long picture depicts the kind of urban sprawl that will make you glad you're here.

NETARTS

Tiny Netarts (pop. about 200) has an enviable location overlooking the bay and the Pacific beyond. Along with nearby Oceanside, it's the closest coastal settlement from Tillamook, and makes for a fine quiet getaway. Netarts Bay and seven-mile-long Netarts Spit are popular with clamdiggers and crabbers, who can launch boats from Netarts Landing, at the northeast corner of the bay. **Netarts Bay RV Park and Marina** (2260 Bilyeu, Netarts, 503/842-7774) and **Big Spruce RV Park** (4850 Netarts Hwy. W., 503/842-7443) rent motorboats and crabbing supplies.

The **Terimore** (5105 Crab Ave., Netarts, 503/842-4623 or 800/635-1821, motel rooms from $55, cabins from $68) is situated a short walk from the water at the north end of Netarts Bay. Other than some units with fireplaces and kitchens, there are few frills here, but for fair rates you'll find yourself close by the water and within easy driving distance of the Cape Lookout trail and a beach walk away from Roseanna's, the best restaurant on the Capes Loop.

You'll find several lunch and dinner spots to choose from. The view of Cape Lookout is tops at **The Schooner** (2065 Netarts Bay Rd., 503/842-4988), which serves breakfast (starting at 8 A.M.), lunch, and dinner (seafood and steak) daily.

CAPE LOOKOUT STATE PARK

On the north side of the cape is the campground and beach extension of expansive Cape Lookout State Park (13000 Whiskey Creek Rd. W., Tillamook, 503/842-4981 information, 800/452-5687 or www.reserve america.com for reservations), which also encompasses the entire cape and the seven-mile-long Netarts Spit within its boundaries. The park has 176 tent sites ($16) and 38 full-hookup sites ($20), as well as 10 yurts ($27), three cabins (with bathrooms, kitchen, TV/VCR, $66), and a hiker/biker camp ($4); discounts apply October–April. Amenities include showers, flush toilets, a laundry, and evening programs. Reservations and deposit are required at this popular campground.

Eight miles of hiking trails include a trail heading north through a variety of estuarine habitats along a sand spit separating Netarts Bay from the Pacific, a popular site for agate hunters, clammers, and crabbers. The most popular trail, though, is to land's end at Cape Lookout. The 2.5-mile-long, one-mile-wide cape juts out from the coast so that hikers feel like they're on the prow of a giant ship suspended 500 feet above the ocean on all sides. Here, more than anywhere else on the Oregon coast, you get the sense of being on the edge of the continent. Giant spruce, western red cedars, and hemlocks surround the gently hilly trail to the tip of the cape. In March, Cape Lookout is a popular vantage

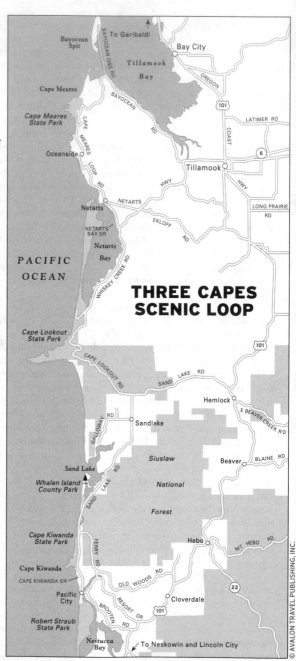

THREE CAPES SCENIC LOOP

point for whale-watching. June through August, a bevy of wildflowers and birds further enhances the rolling terrain en route to the tip of this headland, and in late summer red huckleberries line the path.

Halfway to the overlook, there are views north to Cape Meares over the Netarts sand spit. Even if you settle for a mere 15-minute stroll down the trail, you can look southward to Cascade Head. Right about where the trees open up, look for a bronze plaque commemorating the crash of a World War II plane (with nearly a dozen casualties) embedded into the rock wall bordering the right-hand (north) side of the trail at eye-level. If you're unable to take this hike, there are two unmarked turnouts along the highway between the sand dunes and Cape Lookout parking lot that let you survey the terrain south to Cape Kiwanda. There is a $3 day-use fee, which is covered by the Coast Passport.

PACIFIC CITY

As you approach the shore in Pacific City, the sight of **Haystack Rock** will immediately grab your attention. At 327 feet, this sea stack is nearly 100 feet taller than the like-named rock in Cannon Beach. Standing a mile offshore, this monolith has a brooding, enigmatic quality that constantly draws the eye to it. Look closely, and you'll understand why some folks called it Teacup Rock.

The small town of Pacific City, with about 1,000 citizens, is at the base of **Cape Kiwanda** and it attracts growing numbers of vacationers and retirees, but remains true to its 19th-century origins as a working fishing village. In addition to the knockout seascapes and recreation, if you come here at the right times of day you may be treated to a unique spectacle—the launch or return of the **dory fleet.**

It's a tradition dating back to the 1920s, when gillnetting was banned on the Nestucca River to protect the dwindling salmon runs. To retain their livelihood, commercial fishermen began to haul flat-bottomed, double-ended dories down to the beach on horse-drawn wagons, then rowing out through the surf to fish.

These days, trucks and trailers get the boats to and from the beach, and outboard motors have replaced oar power, enabling the dories to get 50 miles out to sea. If you come here around 6 A.M., you can watch them taking off. The fleet's late afternoon return attracts a crowd that comes to see the dory operators skidding their crafts as far as possible up the beach to the waiting boat trailers. Others meet the dories to buy salmon and tuna direct.

In late July, the **Dory Festival** celebrates the area's fleet. The three-day fete includes craft and food booths, a pancake breakfast, a fishing derby, and other activities. Visitors also have the opportunity to ride out through the surf in a dory, for about $10 per person. For more information, call the chamber of commerce (503/965-6161). If you want to join the fishermen other times of year, contact the **Haystack Fishing Club** (888/965-7555), across from the beach near the Inn at Cape Kiwanda.

In addition, the Pacific City area is besieged by surfers, who enjoy some of the longest waves on the Oregon coast. **Robert Straub State Park,** just south of town, offers access to Nestucca Bay and to the dunes and a long uninterrupted stretch of beach.

ACCOMMODATIONS

The nicest motel on the Three Capes Loop is the **Inn at Cape Kiwanda** (33105 Cape Kiwanda Dr., Pacific City, 503/965-6366 and 888/965-7001, www.innatcapekiwanda.com, doubles from $179). All rooms face a beautiful beach and Cape Kiwanda's giant sand dune. If it's too rainy to go outside, fireplaces and spacious well-appointed rooms make for great storm-watching. Whirlpool tub rooms are available here and pets are permitted in some rooms.

Five blocks from the beach, the **Inn at Pacific City** (35215 Brooten Rd., Pacific City, 503/965-6366 or 888/722-2489, www.innatpacificcity.com, doubles from $89) is a low-slung, shingle-clad compound. Across the street is the **Pacific City Inn** (35280 Brooten Rd., 503/965-6464 or 866/567-3466, www.pacificcityinn.com, doubles from $95).

NORTHERN OREGON COAST

FOOD

Los Caporales (35025 Brooten Rd., 503/965-6999, open 11 A.M. Wed.–Sun., main courses $7–10) serves up bountiful plates of Mexican food and seafood; the combination plates could feed several people. The restaurant's name refers to foremen at a cattle ranch, perhaps explaining portions fit for wrangler-sized appetites.

If hanging plants, a piano, and Nestucca River frontage don't make you feel at home, the apple pie and other wholesome fare at the **Riverhouse** (34450 Brooten Rd., Pacific City, 503/965-6722, www.riverhousefoods.com, lunch and dinner daily, main courses $8–27) probably will. The burgers and open-face sandwich combinations are the perfect pick-me-ups after a morning of fishing or beachcombing along the Nestucca River estuary. Dinners focus on steak, pasta, burgers fish and shellfish. Steamer clams simmered in vermouth make a hearty starter. Or try a salad with the sweet blue cheese dressing, which has enough of a following throughout western Oregon that it's sold in regional supermarkets. Come early, as seating is limited in this 11-table restaurant.

Close by, at the **Grateful Bread Bakery** (34085 Brooten Rd., 503/965-7337, 8 A.M.– 8:30 P.M. Thurs.–Mon., main courses $10–20) the challah, carrot cake, marionberry strudel, and other homemade baked goods deserve special mention. The full breakfast menu offers a range of tasty omelettes, served with oven-roasted spuds at great prices. Lunch here might include thin crust New York–style pizza paying homage to the owners' East Coast roots, Tillamook cheese chowder, or dilled shrimp salad sandwich. Dinners feature dory-caught cod prepared breaded and grilled or blackened, plus salmon, chicken, and steak.

A popular and well-known Pacific City hangout is the **Pelican Pub and Brewery** (33180 Cape Kiwanda Dr., Pacific City, 503/965-7007, www.pelicanbrewery.com, three meals daily, main courses $11–20). Set in a most enviable spot right on the beach opposite Cape Kiwanda and Haystack Rock, this place boasts the best coastal view of any brewpub in Oregon. Halibut fish-n-chips, gourmet pizzas, steamed clams, BBQ pork ribs, and hazelnut-crusted salmon are some of the standouts. The pub's brews, including Tsunami Stout, Doryman's Dark Ale, India Pelican Ale, and MacPelican's Scottish Style Ale, have garnered stacks of awards.

Lincoln City

Back in 1964, five burgs that straddled seven miles of beachfront between Siletz Bay and the Salmon River came together and incorporated as Lincoln City. In commemoration, a 14-foot bronze statue of Abraham Lincoln was donated to the city by an Illinois sculptor. *The Lank Lawyer Reading in His Saddle While His Horse Grazes* originally occupied a city park; Governor Mark Hatfield and actor Raymond Massey, who had portrayed Honest Abe in a 1940 film, attended the dedication. Today the statue stands in a nondescript lot at N.E. 22nd and Quay Avenue. Look for the sign on U.S. 101 near the Dairy Queen pointing the way.

In the following decades, what were discrete towns have grown and melded into an unin-terrupted conurbation with a population of about 6,800 (which can balloon to 30,000 on a busy weekend). While the resulting sprawl and "zoned commercial" signs can be maddening at times, the most visited town on the coast must be doing something right. Perhaps it's the proximity to Portland and Salem, or the area's two tribal-run casinos. Perhaps it's the long, broad sandy beach, or the superlative wildlife viewing around Siletz Bay. Or maybe it's the attraction of Devils Lake State Park, a gem without equal among coastal freshwater playgrounds. Add prime kite-flying, some of the coast's better restaurants, and bibliophilic and antiquing haunts, and it's clear that there's more to the area than the pull of saltwater taffy and outlet malls.

SIGHTS
The Beach

Lincoln City boasts seven uninterrupted miles of sandy beach. From Siletz Bay north to Road's End State Recreation Area, there are more than a dozen access points. You can head west from U.S. 101 on just about any side street to get there. High coastal bluffs lining the north-central portion of town, though, may mean a climb down (and back up) long flights of stairs cut into the cliff. For something approaching solitude on a crowded day, follow Logan Road west from the highway near the north end of town to **Road's End State Recreation Area;** tidepools and a secluded cove add to the allure. This stretch is also popular with sailboarders.

Tidepool explorers should also check out the rock formations at S.W. 11th Street (Canyon Drive Park), N.W. 15th Street, and S.W. 32nd Street.

The **D River Wayside,** a small park on the beach in more or less the middle of town, is a state park property where you can watch what locals claim is the "world's shortest river" empty into the ocean. Flowing just 120 feet from its source, Devils Lake, to its mouth at the Pacific, it's short, all right, and despite its unspectacular appearance, was a cause celebre when *Guinness* withdrew the D's claim to fame in favor of a Montana waterway, the Roe. Local schoolkids rallied to the D's defense with an amended measurement, but the Roe, at a mere 53 feet long, carries the *Guinness* imprimatur as the most diminutive stream. In addition to seeing D River flow from "D" Lake into "D" ocean, you can fly a kite on the beach here. It's one of the easier beach-access points, between stretches of high, motel-topped bluffs, so it can get a little crowded here.

Another convenient beach-access point is off S.W. 51st Street at the south end of town, just before **Siletz Bay.** A large parking area here in what's known as the Taft District stands beside the driftwood-strewn shore of the bay, where you can often see a group of harbor seals chasing their dinner or coming in for a closer look at you. It's a short walk to the ocean.

Time was when it was common for storms

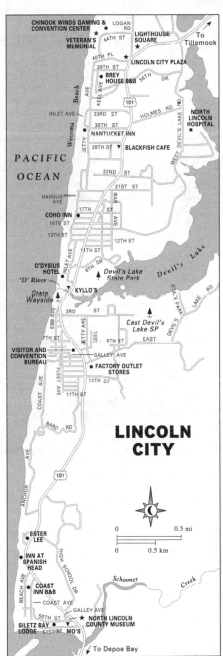

NORTHERN OREGON COAST

CASCADE HEAD SCENIC RESEARCH AREA

About 10 miles north of Lincoln City, the 11,890-acre Cascade Head Experimental Forest was set aside in 1934 for scientific study of typical coastal Sitka spruce and western hemlock forests found along the Oregon coast. In 1974, Congress established the 9,670-acre Cascade Head Scenic Research Area, which includes the western half of the forest, several prairie headlands, and the Salmon River estuary. In 1980, the entire area was designated a Biosphere Reserve as part of the United Nations Biosphere Reserve system.

The headlands, reaching as high as 1,800 feet, are unusual for their extensive prairies still dominated by native grasses: red fescue, wild rye, and Pacific reedgrass. The people of the Nechesney tribe, who inhabited the area as long as 12,000 years ago, purposely burned forest tracts around Cascade Head to provide browse for deer and to reduce the possibility of larger, uncontrollable blazes. In contrast to these grasslands, the northern part of the headland is the domain of giant spruces and firs because it catches the brunt of the heavy rainfalls and lingering fogs. Wildflowers include coastal paintbrush, goldenrod, streambank lupine, rare hairy checkermallow, and blue violet, a plant critical to the survival of the Oregon silverspot butterfly, a threatened species found in only six locations. Deer, elk, coyote, snowshoe hare, and the Pacific giant salamander find refuge here, while bald eagles, great horned owls, and peregrine falcons may be seen hunting above the grassy slopes.

On the north side of the Salmon River, turn west from U.S. 101 onto **Three Rocks Road** for a scenic driving detour on the south side of Cascade Head. The paved road curves about 2.5 miles above the wetlands and widening channel of the Salmon River estuary, passes Savage Road, and ends at a parking area and boat launch at Knight County Park. From the park, the road turns to gravel and narrows (not suitable for RVs or trailers) and continues another 0.5 mile to its end at a spectacular overlook across the estuary.

Not surprisingly, the area is a mecca for some 6,000 hikers annually and for anglers who target the salmon and steelhead runs on the Salmon River. The **Cascade Head Trail** runs six miles roughly parallel to the highway, with a south trailhead near the intersection of Three Rocks Road and U.S. 101 and a north trailhead at Falls Creek, on U.S. 101 about a mile south of Neskowin. It passes through old-growth forest and offers coastal views near its north end.

A short but brisk hike to the top of the headland on a **Nature Conservancy trail** begins near Knight County Park. Leave your car at the park and walk about a half mile up Savage Road to the trailhead. It's 1.7 miles one-way, with a 1,100-foot elevation gain. No dogs or bicycles allowed on the trail.

About three miles north of Three Rocks Road, gravel Cascade Head Road (Forest Service Road 1861), leads four miles west of U.S. 101 to the **Hart's Cove trailhead.** The first part of the trail runs through arching red alder treetops and 250-year-old Sitka spruces with five-foot diameters. The understory of mosses and ferns is nourished by 100-inch rainfalls. Next, the trail emerges into open grasslands. The hilly, five-mile round-trip hike finally leads to an oceanfront meadow overlooking Hart's Cove, where the barking of sea lions might greet you. This trail can be muddy, so boots are recommended to tromp through the rainforest. Note: The trail is closed January 15–July 15.

and currents to wash up that ultimate beach-comber's prize—glass fishing floats—on the Oregon coast. Lincoln City improves the beachcomber's odds by distributing over 2,000 glass floats along its beaches October–Memorial Day. Handcrafted by Northwest glass artists, each of the colorful floats is signed and numbered, and placed by volunteers on the beaches above the high-tide line. If you find one, you can call or stop in at the visitors center for a certificate and information about the artist who created it.

Devils Lake

Devils Lake, just east of town, is the recreation center of Lincoln City. In addition to windsurfing and hydroplaning, eight species of fish can be caught here, including catfish, yellow perch, crappie, largemouth bass, and trout. Chinese grass carp were introduced to the lake to help control the rampant aquatic weeds. There's also good bird-watching on and around this shallow, 678-acre lake, which attracts flocks of migratory geese, ducks, and other waterfowl. Species to look for include canvasbacks, Canada geese, widgeons, gadwalls, grebes, and mallards. Bald eagles and ospreys also nest in the trees bordering the lake.

The lake takes its name from a local Native American legend. The story tells that when Siletz warriors paddled a canoe across the lake one moonlit night, a tentacled beast erupted from the still water and pulled the men under. It's said that boaters today who cross the moon's reflection in the middle of the lake tempt the same fate, but the lake's devil has remained silent for years.

Of the five access points, East Devils Lake Road off U.S. 101 northeast of town offers a scenic route around the lake's east side before rejoining U.S. 101 near the day-use portion of the state park at the south end of the lake. To reach the camping area of **Devils Lake State Recreation Area,** take N.E. 6th Drive east from U.S. 101, about a quarter mile north of the D River. The day-use area has a boat ramp, while there's a moorage dock across the lake adjacent to the campground.

Mountain bikes, canoes, and paddleboats can be rented at the **Blue Heron Landing** (4006 W. Devils Lake Rd., Lincoln City, 541/994-4708).

SPORTS AND RECREATION

Casinos

One of the biggest draws in town is the **Chinook Winds Casino** (1777 N.W. 44th St., Lincoln City, 541/996-5825 or 888/244-6665, www.chinookwindscasino.com), near the north end of town, operated by the Confederated Tribes of Siletz Indians. In addition to slots, blackjack, poker, keno, bingo, craps, and roulette, the casino has two on-site restaurants and a busy schedule of big-name (or formerly big-name) entertainment. Recent shows, for example, have included David Cassidy, Dionne Warwick, and Don McLean. Open daily, 24 hours.

About 25 miles east of Lincoln City is the state's number-one visitor attraction, **Spirit Mountain Casino** (P.O. Box 39, Grand Ronde 97347, 800/760-7977, http://spiritmountain.com), operated by the Confederated Tribes of Grand Ronde. Games include slots, craps, blackjack, poker, keno, and bingo. It's open daily, 24 hours.

Camping

Several wilderness retreats are worth noting in the Lincoln City area. One remote escape is at **Van Duzer Wayside,** about 12 miles east of town on Route 18, which offers a dozen primitive (and free) hiker/biker sites in a beautiful forest near the Salmon River.

More free rustic sites can be found about eight miles north of town and just south of Neskowin. To get there, look for the "Scenic Drive" sign east of U.S. 101 and follow County Road 12 for four miles. From there, travel about 100 yards west on Forest Service Road 12131 and you'll see the campground set along **Neskowin Creek.** To find out about the trails in the surrounding rainforest, contact the Siuslaw National Forest in Hebo (541/392-3161). The campground is open mid-April–mid-October. Bring your own water or water-purification kit. The nearby scenic drive continues up

SALISHAN LODGE

When asked to choose *the* place to stay on the Oregon coast, most Oregonians would recommend the Salishan Lodge (7760 N. U.S. 101, Gleneden Beach, 541/764-2371 or 800/452-2300, www.salishan.com). Named for a widespread native dialect in the Oregon Territory, this resort a couple of miles south of Lincoln City is one of a dozen properties in the nation that consistently receives a four-star as well as a five-diamond rating. Almost every year, *Condé Nast Traveler* rates Salishan one of the country's top resorts.

While there are distant Siletz Bay views, Salishan isn't a beach-front resort, and most folks quickly learn to appreciate the peace of the forest and golf course here. This paradigm shift is facilitated by art and landscape architecture that convey the vision of John Gray, who built Salishan and such other Northwest properties as Skamania Lodge (on the Washington side of the Columbia Gorge) and Sunriver (south of Bend) from native materials with respect for the surrounding environment.

Even if you don't stay here, the grounds and facilities are worth a look. The art gallery is free and features works by top Oregon artists (also check out master woodcarver Leroy Setziol's bas-relief panels in the dining room). The forested trails behind the golf course (rated among the top 75 in the United States) showcase the rainforested foothills of the Coast Range and the waterfowl near Siletz Bay. Across the street, the Salishan Marketplace features first-rate galleries and a good bookstore, Allegory Books.

In high season, rooms at Salishan start at $159, attracting well-heeled nature lovers, corporate expense-account clientele, folks enjoying a special occasion, and serious golfers. You'll also find everyday folks and seminar attendees on winter weekend specials at half the summertime rates. Ask about multiday packages for big savings on your room rate.

In addition to the recreational and aesthetic appeal of the resort, the Dining Room contributes to Salishan's lofty reputation.

---

into an area of huge trees captioned by forest service placards explaining the ecology.

More elaborate camping is available at **Devils Lake State Park** (1452 N.E. 6th St., Lincoln City, information 541/994-2002, reservations 800/452-5687 or www.reserve america.com) with 68 tent sites and 32 RV sites with full hookups. Amenities include showers, a café, and a laundry. The fee is $17–22 per night, $29 for yurts, $4 for hiker/biker spaces, mid-April–late October. This campground is just off U.S. 101 at the northeast end of town, between the ocean and Devils Lake.

Devils Lake RV Park (4041 N.E. West Devils Lake Rd., 541/994-3400), near Lakeside Golf, has 80 paved sites with full hookups ($19–25); no tent camping.

Golf and Tennis
At the north end of town, 18-hole **Lakeside Golf Club** (3245 N.E. 50th St., 541/994-8442) charges $45 for a full day, $25 for nine holes.

Serious devotees can head seven miles south to **Salishan Spa and Golf Resort** (U.S. 101, Gleneden Beach, 541/764-3632 or 800/890-8037) to play the award-winning 18-hole course set in the foothills of the Coast Range and bordered by Siletz Bay and the sea. The green fees for 18 holes are $99 in summer. Keep in mind that this is a Scottish-links course, where the roughs are really rough.

ENTERTAINMENT AND EVENTS
Eden Hall
Housed within the renovated Gleneden Brick and Tile Factory, five miles south of Lincoln City in Gleneden Beach, Eden Hall (6645 Gleneden Beach Loop Rd., 541/764-3826 for performance info, 541/764-3825 for restaurant, www.edenhall.com) stages live theater and hosts an impressively eclectic roster of regional and touring musicians. This spacious, airy warehouse has an excellent sound

system and is a wonderful place to take in a concert, with an emphasis on jazz, folk, and blues. Enjoy dinner at the adjacent Side Door Café (see *Food*).

Festivals

Lincoln City calls itself the kite capital of the world, pointing to its position midway between the pole and the equator, which gives the area predictable wind patterns. The town holds not one but two kite fiestas at the D River Wayside each year. The spring **Kite Festival** takes place the first weekend in May; the fall festival is held the third weekend in September (541/994-3070 or 800/452-2151, in Oregon). The event is famous for giant spin socks, some as long as 150 feet.

The **Cascade Head Chamber Music Festival** (P.O. Box 605, Lincoln City 97367, 541/994-5333 or 877/994-5333, www.cascade headmusic.org) is another Oregon kulturfest that brings together world-class artists in an informal setting. Events are hosted at St. Peter the Fisherman Lutheran Church (1226 S.W. 13th St., 541/994-2007), under the direction of Sergiu Luca, a famed violinist who draws on decades of international experience and the friendship of virtuosi who fly in from all corners of the globe to make music on the Oregon coast. Old World artists such as Beethoven and Brahms as well as contemporary composers are featured in a series of June concerts (usually two a week over several weeks). To order tickets, contact the festival ticket office (541/994-5333), or get them at the gallery in Salishan or the Lincoln City Visitor and Convention Bureau. Tickets run around $15 and may not always be available at the door.

Lincoln City's popular **Sandcastle Building Contest** happens the first Saturday in August, off S.W. 51st, in the historic Taft District alongside Siletz Bay. Call 541/996-3800 for details.

ACCOMMODATIONS

Of the cheek-by-jowl selection of lodgings in Lincoln City, we're partial to the hotels at the south end of town and near Siletz Bay. While the views are not always expansive, the beach-front isn't as crowded here as it is from the D River north, and you're far from casino traffic. If you want something closer to the gaming tables, there are more than 1,000 other rooms in this town.

The **Ester Lee** (3803 S.W. U.S. 101, 541/996-3606 or 888/996-3606, www.ester lee.com, doubles from $85) is a decades-old family motel complex along with some cottages on a bluff above miles of beachfront. All rooms have ocean views and fireplaces and some have kitchens and Jacuzzis. Pets are allowed. It's nothing fancy, but it's just fine and a good value for the money.

Another pet-friendly place, the **Coho Inn** (1635 N.W. Harbor, 541/994-3684 or 800/848-7006, www.thecohoinn.com, doubles from $69) has 50 oceanfront units with fireplaces, kitchens, and continental breakfast.

If you've been fantasizing about rolling out of bed, slipping on your robe—coffee in hand—and walking out onto a semi-private stretch of beach, then the **Inn at Spanish Head** (4009 S.W. U.S. 101, 541/996-2161 or 800/452-8127, www.spanishhead.com, doubles from $185) may be your best bet. Oregon's only resort hotel right on the beach, the inn takes its place—large and looming—against the backdrop of rugged cliffs. Whether in a suite, studio, or bedroom unit, every room has an ocean view. On-site amenities include Fathoms, the 10th-floor restaurant/bar (see *Food*), a fireplace lounge, meeting rooms, heated outdoor pool, saunas, spa, and exercise room.

With five newer units, the **Nantucket Inn** (3135 N.W. Inlet Ave., 541/996-9300, www. thenantucketinn.com, doubles from $99) provides guests with oceanfront accommodations just steps from the beach; some rooms come equipped with kitchens, hot tubs, and fireplaces. Continental breakfast is served.

For a small oceanfront luxury hotel, the **O'dysius Hotel** (120 N.W. Inlet Ct., 541/994-4121 or 800/869-8069, www.odysius.com, doubles from $155) offers 30 units furnished with period antiques. Guests meet in the lobby every afternoon to sample Oregon wine. The hotel accepts pets, and provides concierge, massage, and a continental breakfast. Wheelchair accessible.

The **Siletz Bay Lodge** (1012 S.W. 51st St., 541/996-6111 or 888/430-2100, www.siletz baylodge.com, doubles from $118), on the north end of Siletz Bay on a driftwood-strewn beach, is a family-friendly and wheelchair-accessible (with elevators) lodging in a location ideal for bird-watching and viewing seals. About half of the standard rooms have balconies, with delightful views of the bay and the sun going down over Salishan Spit. Spa rooms and spa suites are also available. In-room amenities include microwaves, refrigerators, and coffeemakers, and a continental breakfast is provided).

Bed-and-Breakfasts

Close to the beach, **Brey House B&B** (3725 N.W. Keel Ave., 541/994-7123, www.brey house.com, doubles from $103) is one of the oldest B&Bs on the Oregon coast, a 1940-built three-story Cape Cod–style home with four bedrooms (all private baths and entrances). You'll love the excellent breakfast, which is served in a light-filled room overlooking the ocean. Not appropriate for children.

The light and bright **Coast Inn B&B** (4507 S.W. Coast Ave., 541/994-7932 or 888/994-7932, www.oregoncoastinn.com, doubles from $99) offers nonsmoking guestrooms and a hot breakfast in a sprawling Craftsman-style home located in historic Taft heights, south of Spanish Head. Siletz Bay is a short walk away, as is public beach access. Entirely remodeled in 2001, this home features comfortable new furnishings and homey decor.

To rent vacation homes throughout Lincoln County, contact the **Lincoln City Visitor and Convention Bureau** (800/452-2151). Or, try **Pacific Retreats** (3126-A N.E. U.S. 101, 800/473-4833, www.pacificretreats.com), which features a selection of vacation home rentals.

FOOD

Lincoln City offers many affordable and palate-pleasing dining options. Some of the best are located near the north end of town. South of the D River (city center), there's a cluster of gourmet eateries that merit special consideration.

Cafe Roma Bookstore and Coffeehouse (1437 N.W. U.S. 101, 541/994-6616) brings an air of refinement to Lincoln City. Fresh homebaked pastries and desserts, fresh-roasted gourmet coffees and espresso drinks, as well as a collection of interesting books make this a wonderful retreat on a cold and drizzly day.

The **Lighthouse Brewpub** (4157 U.S. 101 N., 541/994-7238, lunch and dinner daily, main courses $6–11) is a welcome rehash of the McMenamins formula so successful in the Willamette Valley. Just look for a lighthouse replica in a parking lot on the northwest side of 101 across from McDonald's. Pizza bread, burgers, sandwiches, and chili can be washed down by McMenamin's own ales or some other quality brew, as well as hard cider and wine. Live music at night is an added plus. **Figaro's Pizza** (4095 N.W. Logan Rd., 541/994-4443, lunch and dinner daily) offers family dining options such as pizza, lasagna, and salad.

If coastal restaurants are eating a hole in your wallet, there's always tried-and-true **Mo's** (860 S.W. 51st St., 541/996-2535, open daily for lunch and dinner, main courses $8–18). As usual, count on good clam chowder and full fish dinners as well as superlative views of the water.

Heading north, **Dory Cove Restaurant** (5819 Logan Rd., 541/994-5180, lunch and dinner daily, $8–22), near Road's End State Park, has prices that are a little higher than Mo's, but the range of deep-fried and sautéed seafood main courses (halibut fish-n-chips recommended) is impressive, as is the fact that in a place so clearly dominated by seafood, so many people come here for steaks and burgers. Save room for the home-made pies.

The ☾ **Blackfish Cafe** (2733 N.W. U.S. 101, 541/996-1007, www.blackfishcafe.com, lunch and dinner Wed.–Mon., main courses $13–18) is a great find. Presided over by former Salishan Resort executive chef Rob Pounding, who has long-standing relationships with local farmers, fishermen, and mushroom foragers, the Blackfish Cafe is dedicated to fairly priced and delicious regional cooking. The emphasis is on what's fresh, homegrown, and creative—Willamette Valley pork medallions in huckleberry compote and troll-caught chinook salmon with Oregon blue cheese mashed potatoes. In addition to the emphasis on there is no shortage of humbler fare such as the self-proclaimed "best" clam chowder on the coast and halibut fish-n-chips.

If you're en route to the wine country or the Willamette Valley or just want a respite from resort traffic, a place that appeals to everybody is **Ⓒ Otis Cafe** (1259 Salmon River Hwy., 541/994-9560, three meals daily, main courses $7–14), at the Otis Junction on Route 18 two miles east of U.S. 101. Here, innovative variations on American road food have been warmly embraced by everyone from local loggers to yuppies (and *New York Times* food critics) stopping off on the drive between Portland and the coast. In September, salmon-fishing devotees can be seen lining up here at 6:30 A.M. Breakfast in this unpretentious café, five miles northeast of Lincoln City, is such an institution that long waits on the porch are the rule on weekend mornings. The reasons why include the thick-crusted molasses bread that comes with many orders, buttermilk waffles, and their legendary hash browns under a crust of melted Rogue Valley white cheddar. Large portions, low prices, and a culinary touch that turns pork chops and rhubarb pie into epicurean delights are in full evidence at lunch and dinner.

Kyllo's (1110 N.W. 1st Ct., 541/994-3179, lunch and dinner daily, main courses $16–20) specializes in broiled, sautéed, and baked seafood, plus excellent homemade desserts. The former can be washed down by Oregon microbrews and wines. The restaurant is visible from U.S. 101 as you drive by the D River Wayside. With views of the water on all sides, this restaurant is a good place to linger, though waits can be long in the evening as no reservations are taken.

Some of coastal Oregon's top dining experiences are found just south of Lincoln City. The reasonable prices at the Salishan Lodge's **Sun Room Restaurant** (541/764-2371, main courses $10–25) are a welcome surprise. This casual restaurant (see *Salishan Lodge* sidebar) might be less elaborate and half the price of Salishan's five-star Dining Room, but its Northwest cuisine comes from the same kitchen. Complete breakfasts won't lighten the wallet too much. For a few pennies more, the hot smoked chinook salmon hash is a highlight. Affordable lunch-time specialties include oyster stew and Northwest chicken salad, with hazelnuts and banana bread. At dinner, main courses range from chicken pot-pie to pasta to steaks.

At the Salishan's **Dining Room** (800/452-2300, dinner nightly, main courses $25–58) special emphasis is placed on seasonal seafood, game, and other regional delicacies. The elegance of the setting, expansive wine list, and creative dishes have long made this a coastal dining destination. Dishes may include salmon with wild mushrooms and blue cheese soufflé or duck breast with pecan and pear bread pudding. For decades the Dining Room has been the top-rated restaurant in Oregon, famed for its creative interpretations of seasonal Northwest delicacies and a 12,000-bottle wine cellar (noted for the world's largest collection of Oregon pinot noir).

A half mile south of Salishan (five miles equidistant from Depoe Bay and Lincoln City) are two other Gleneden Beach eateries with considerable appeal. The **Side Door Cafe** (6675 Gleneden Beach Loop, 541/764-3825, www.edenhall.com, main courses $17–31) combines a gourmet restaurant with a musical venue. The airy yet cozy-feeling dining room features a menu where peach barbecue glazed salmon and chanterelle mushroom hazelnut lasagna exemplify the menu offerings. The adjoining state-of-the-art Eden Hall theater might feature a Northwest artist with a national reputation, such as jazz singer Nancy King or Portland-based Delta blues artist Kelly Joe Phelps.

The **Bay House** (5911 S.W. U.S. 101, 541/996-3222, www.bayhouserestaurant.com, main courses $26–49) combines oceanfront views with exquisite Northwest cuisine. Alaskan Halibut is Parmesan-crusted and served with sorrel velouté and the signature crab cakes come with lemon aioli. Oenophiles will want to look at the wine list praised by *Wine Spectator*. Dinner here with a bottle of Oregon pinot noir can easily set you back $75 a person, but for a special occasion the setting and the food can't be beat.

INFORMATION

A little south of the D River, the helpful **Lincoln City Visitor and Convention Bureau** (801 S.W. U.S. 101, 541/994-8378 or 800/452-2151) is open 9 A.M.–5 P.M. Monday–Friday, 9 A.M.–5 P.M. Saturday, and 10 A.M.–4 P.M.

Sunday. **Driftwood Public Library** (541/996-2277) is in the same municipal complex.

The **Central Oregon Coast Association** (541/265-2064 or 800/767-2064, www.coast visitor.com) maintains a useful website with details on Lincoln City and the rest of coastal Lincoln County.

GETTING THERE

Lincoln County Transit (541/265-4900, www.co.lincoln.or.us/transit) buses stop in town. The latter line goes as far south as Yachats; weekday service only, closed major holidays.

Depoe Bay

Depoe Bay is in the heart of the so-called Twenty Miracle Miles, describing the attractive stretch of rockbound coast from the broad beaches of Lincoln City south past Depoe Bay north. Regardless of what you think of the short commercial strip along the highway here, the scenic appeal of Depoe's location is impossible to ignore. The rocky outer bay, flanked by headlands to the north and south, is pierced by a narrow channel through the basalt cliffs leading to the inner harbor. It's home to an active sport-fishing fleet as well as the whale-watching charters that have earned Depoe Bay its distinction as whale-watching capital of the state.

For all intents and purposes, Depot Bay didn't really exist until the completion of the Roosevelt Highway (U.S. 101) in 1927, which opened the area up to car travelers. Prior to that time, the area had been occupied mainly by a few members of the Siletz Reservation. One of the group, who worked at the U.S. Army depot, called himself Charlie Depot. The town was named after him, eventually taking on the current spelling.

SIGHTS
The Bayfront and Harbor

Depoe Bay is situated along a truly beautiful coastline that cannot be fully appreciated from the highway. A 0.25-mile-long seawall

and promenade invite a stroll. For a panorama of the harbor, continue along the sidewalks across the gracefully arching concrete bridge, designed by Conde McCullough and built in 1927. Other nice perspectives are offered from residential streets west of U.S. 101; try Ellingson Street, south of the bridge, and Sunset Street at the north end of the bay.

Perhaps the most all-encompassing overlook is offered by the glass-enclosed rooftop lookout (open to the public) on top of the **Oregon Coast Aquarium Store,** located right at the harbor entrance. Two "spouting horns," natural blowholes in the rocks north of the harbor entrance, can send plumes of spray 60 feet into the air when the tide and waves are right.

East of the bridge is Depoe Bay's claim to international fame, the world's smallest navigable natural harbor. This distinction is announced by a sign citing its recognition by the *Guinness Book of World Records.* This boat basin is also exceptional because it's a harbor within a harbor. This topography is the result of wave action cutting into the basalt over eons until a 50-foot passageway leading to a six-acre inland lagoon was created. In addition to whale-watching, folks congregate on the bridge between the ocean and the harbor to watch boats maneuver into the enclosure.

DRAKE'S LOST HARBOR?

In 1996, the media exploded with stories raising the possibility that the tiny hamlet of Whale Cove, two miles south of Depoe Bay, could supplant Plymouth Rock as the birthplace of a nation. Rotting timbers from what is theorized to have been a stockade built by Sir Francis Drake in 1579 were unearthed in an area where stories have long circulated that the English privateer made landfall.

Over the years, these notions have been fueled by a number of tantalizing pieces of evidence: an unsigned ship log from Drake's voyage in a museum in England that identified 44 degrees north latitude – the same as Whale Cove – as a landing site; an English shilling dating from 1560 found on the central Oregon coast in 1982; a photo from the 1930s showing a local resident with a distinctly English sword he unearthed; and a ship's cutlass found in Newport in the early 19th century bearing the markings of a 16th-century English arsenal. Moreover, excavations of a nearby Native American village thought to have been buried in the year 1600 turned up brass items, blades, and Venetian beads.

An amateur British historian, Bob Ward, makes a compelling case for Whale Cove as the place where Drake spent five weeks in the summer of 1579. In his flagship *Golden Hynde*, the only one of his five-ship fleet to survive the stormy straits around Cape Horn, Drake harassed Spanish settlements throughout Latin America and plundered Spanish ships wherever he met them. Sailing west from Mexico on its return to England via the Cape of Good Hope, the treasure-laden *Golden Hynde* was beset by storms, and Drake had to retreat to

land to make repairs. Conventional history has held that he made landfall around San Francisco, most likely on the Marin County coast.

Ward, however, believes that Drake continued his voyage farther north, and sailed into the Strait of Juan de Fuca, thinking he had found the fabled Northwest Passage. Turning around before he realized his mistake, Drake then headed south down the Washington and Oregon coasts, where he found a sandy cove in which to drop anchor and make repairs before the long journey home.

On Drake's return to England after four years at sea, news of his exploits was suppressed. Queen Elizabeth confiscated the logs and charts, and it would be 10 years before an official account of the voyage would be published. In it New Albion, Drake's fabled lost settlement, was described as being around 38 degrees north latitude (in what is now Northern California), in an attempt, Ward believes, to fool the Spanish into thinking the Northwest Passage was much farther south.

After Elizabeth's death in 1603, however, new charts began to appear which placed the landing site much farther north, and early 17th-century charts show a small, shallow bay labeled "Novus Albionis" (New Albion) that is an uncannily accurate depiction of Whale Cove.

Since the initial blizzard of publicity, there has been no final word from the archaeologists and historians involved in corroborating these claims. As most history books have placed New Albion near San Francisco, researchers will not be too quick to claim otherwise without definitive research.

Depoe Bay's Harbor was scenic enough to be selected as the sight from which Jack Nicholson commandeered a yacht for his mental patient crew in *One Flew Over the Cuckoo's Nest*.

Boiler Bay State Scenic Viewpoint

A half mile north of town is Boiler Bay, so named because of the boiler left from the 1910

wreck of the *J. Marhoffer*. The ship caught fire three miles offshore and drifted into the bay. The remains of the boiler are visible at low tide. This rock-rimmed bay is a favorite spot for rock fishing, birding, and whale-watching. A trail leads down to some excellent tidepools.

Whale Cove

Half a mile south of Depoe Bay, a picturesque

bay has been scooped out of the sandstone bluffs. The tranquility of this calendar-photo-come-to-life is deceptive. There's considerable evidence to suggest that this tiny embayment—and not California's Marin County—was the site of Francis Drake's 1579 landing (see *Drake's Lost Harbor?* sidebar), but the jury is still out. During Prohibition, bootleggers used the protected cove as a clandestine port. In the 1980s, a court decision allowing property owners to restrict access to Whale Cove set a precedent undermining public ownership of other Oregon beaches. (More recently, however, this trend was counteracted by another high court decision that prevented a Cannon Beach innkeeper from building on a public beach.)

Rocky Creek State Scenic Viewpoint overlooks Whale Cove. There are picnic tables, and it's a good spot for whale-watching, but there's no access down to the beach.

Otter Crest Loop

The rocky bluffs of this coastal stretch take on an even more dramatic aspect as you leave the highway at the Otter Crest Loop, a winding three-mile section of the old Coast Highway, two miles south of Depoe Bay.

From atop **Cape Foulweather,** the visibility can extend 40 miles on a clear day. The view south to Yaquina Head and its lighthouse is a photographer's fantasy of headlands, coves, and offshore monoliths. Bronze plaques in the parking lot tell of Captain Cook naming the 500-foot-high headland during a bout with storm- tossed seas on March 7, 1778. Comic relief from the coast's parade of historical plaques comes with another tablet bearing the inscription, "On this site in 1897, nothing happened."

The Lookout gift shop on the north side of the promontory is a good place to buy Japanese fishing floats for a few bucks. The million-dollar view from inside the shop is easily one of the most spectacular windows on the ocean to be found anywhere.

Another mile south, in the hamlet of Otter Rock, you'll find another of the Oregon coast's several diabolically named natural features, the **Devil's Punchbowl.** The urn-like sandstone formation, filled with swirling water, has been sculpted by centuries of waves flooding into what had been a cave until its roof collapsed. The inexorable process continues today, thanks to the ebb and flow of the Pacific through two openings in the cauldron wall. A state park viewpoint gives you a ringside seat on this frothy confrontation between rock and tide. When the water recedes, you can see purple sea urchins and starfish in the tidepools of the **Marine Gardens** 100 feet to the north.

To the south of the Punchbowl vantage point are picnic tables and a wooden walkway down to the beach. Close by, in the Otter Rock **Mo's** restaurant, a seat occupied by "The Boss" himself, Bruce Springsteen, on June 11, 1987, is enshrined. Also in Otter Rock, the **Flying Dutchman Winery** (541/765-2553) makes limited batches of hand-crafted wines. It is open 11 A.M.–6 P.M. daily for tastings and tours.

Back on U.S. 101, a mile's drive south brings you to Beverly Beach State Park.

FISHING AND WHALE-WATCHING CHARTERS

With the ocean minutes from Depoe Bay's port, catching a salmon or seeing a whale is possible as soon as you leave the harbor. Most charter operators here offer both fishing and whale-watching excursions. Bottom-fishing trips average around $55 for a five-hour run, salmon fishing about $100 for a seven- or eight-hour day; whale-watching excursions run $15–25 per person per hour.

Dockside Charters (541/765-2545 or 800/733-8915, www.docksidedepoebay.com) offers 1.5 hour whale-watching trips aboard their 50-foot excursion boat for $20/adult and on 25-foot rigid-hull inflatables for $25/adult. **Tradewinds Charters** (541/765-2345 or 800/445-8730, www.tradewindscharters.com) hosts one- and two-hour trips December–February and March–May. Rates run $15–45 on their fleet of 30- to 52-foot boats and 18-foot Zodiac. A 12-hour tuna charter costs $160.

© BILL MCRAE

Whale-watchers depart Depoe Bay.

EVENTS

The **Depoe Bay Salmon Bake** takes place on the third Saturday of September, 10 A.M.– 5 P.M., at Depoe Bay City Park, flanking the rear of the boat basin. Some 3,000 pounds of fresh ocean fish are caught and cooked Native American–style on alder stakes over an open fire and served with all the trimmings, to be savored to the accompaniment of live entertainment. Cost is $14 per adults, $8 children. It always seems to rain on the day of this event, but that's life on the Oregon coast.

ACCOMMODATIONS

Lodgings in popular Depoe Bay require advance reservations on most weekends and holidays.

The **Surfrider Resort** (3115 N.W. U.S. 101, 541/764-2311 or 800/662-2378, www. surfriderresort.com, doubles from $114) is a few miles north of town on picturesque Fogarty Creek's rockbound coast. While it's been around for a while and is not too elaborate, its setting and other appeals mandate a men-

tion. Oceanfront suites and rooms have decks; some feature whirlpool tubs, kitchens, and fireplaces. A good restaurant, an indoor pool, and midweek specials are also noteworthy.

The **Inn at Arch Rock** (70 N.W. Sunset St., 800/767-1835, www.innatarchrock.com, doubles from $79) comprises a cluster of white clapboard buildings that overlook the bay from their clifftop perch at the north end of town. In addition to 13 oceanfront rooms, there are three two-bedroom condo units next door that sleep six, for $239.

Located about three miles south of Depoe Bay, at one of the most scenic spots on the central coast), is the **Inn at Otter Crest** (301 Otter Crest Loop, Otter Rock, 541/765-2111 or 800/452-2101, www.innatottercrest.com, hotel rooms from $129, studios from $139, suites from $199), a condo resort perched close to the edge of the sandstone bluffs at the ocean's edge. Hotel rooms have two queen-size beds, refrigerator, coffeemaker, and private deck with picture windows, while studios have a queen Murphy bed, full kitchen, fireplace, and dining area. Suites have one to two-bedrooms, plus full kitchens and balconies.

Harbor Lights Inn (235 S.E. Bay View Ave., 541/765-2322 or 800/228-0448, www. gracieslanding.com, doubles $89–135), a small inn overlooking the harbor, affords views of sea otters, ducks, and geese while the whale-watching and fishing boats come and go. All rooms have a harbor view; rates include a hot breakfast. Pets allowed.

The ❸ **Channel House** (35 Ellingson St., 541/765-2140 or 800/447-2140, www.channel house.com, rooms from $100, suites from $235) features three rooms and nine spacious suites boasting expansive dramatic views of the ocean, private decks with outdoor whirlpool tubs (in the majority of rooms), fireplaces, plush robes, and other amenities. This blufftop B&B (there isn't a beach below, just miles of ocean and surrounding cliffs) may not look prepossessing from the outside, but inside the place is all windows and angles. Imagine *Architectural Digest* in a nautical theme. This is the best place on the Oregon coast to commune with whales, passing boats, winter storms, and the setting sun. A continental breakfast with tasty baked goods in an oceanside dining area is included in the rates.

FOOD

Head to the locally popular **Harbor Lights Inn** (58 U.S. 101, 541/765-2734, dinner daily, main courses $11–25). Their seafood hors d'oeuvres (fried whitefish, scallops, oysters, smoked tuna, and boiled baby shrimp) give ample testimony to their claim that it's "seafood so fresh the ocean hasn't missed it yet." Another popular dish is salmon stuffed with crab and shrimp, baked in wine and herb butter. A lavish salad bar, a Friday night all-you-can-eat seafood buffet, and a recipe for clam chowder feted by the *New York Times* has also generated local praise.

Tidal Raves (279 N.W. U.S. 101, 541/765-2995, lunch and dinner daily, main courses $10–18) boasts the best views in town and a casual ambience. In addition to fresh fish and other seafood dishes such as Thai prawns and oyster spinach bisque, the restaurant's pasta specialties are uniformly excellent. The Pasta Rave features crab, shrimp, lingcod, snapper, and more on a bed of linguine with pesto. The Dungeness crab casserole is also note-worthy. For dessert don't miss warm chocolate chunk cookie with Tillamook Vanilla Bean ice cream.

Oceanus (177 Highway 101, 541/765-4553, lunch and dinner Thurs.–Tues., main courses $11–22) is a real gem of a seafood restaurant. The windows overlook the bay but the real action is on your plate. Eclectic preparations, including fish tacos, Thai prawns, Cajun shrimp, and cioppino fish stew, borrow from many cuisines—though the traditional clam chowder is excellent also. The key lime pie is locally renowned.

INFORMATION

On the east side of the highway, opposite the seawall, the **Depoe Bay Chamber of Commerce** (70 N.E. U.S. 101, Depoe Bay 97341, 541/765-2889 or 877/485-8348, www.depoebaychamber.org) offers literature about the town and the central coast in general. Open 11 A.M.–3 P.M. weekdays, 9 A.M.–4 P.M. weekends.

GETTING THERE

On weekdays, **Lincoln County Transit** (541/265-4900, www.co.lincoln.or.us/transit) runs buses four times daily, north to Lincoln City and south to Yachats.

Newport

In January 1852, a storm grounded the schooner *Juliet* near Yaquina (pronounced yah-KWIN-nah) Bay, where her captain and crew were stranded for two months. When they finally made their way inland to the Willamette Valley, they reported their discovery of an abundance of tiny, sweet-tasting oysters in the bay. Within a decade, commercial oyster farms were established here, the first major impetus to growth and settlement in Newport. The tasty morsels that delighted diners in San Francisco and at New York's Waldorf-Astoria Hotel are almost gone now, but the oyster industry continues by harvesting introduced species.

The port bustles with the activity of Oregon's largest commercial fishing fleet and second-largest recreational fleet. New factories to process *surimi* (a fish paste popular in Japan) and whiting have provided hundreds of jobs here, and a state-of-the-art aquarium that once housed Keiko the whale (from *Free Willy*) also brings in the tourist dollar. In this vein, new wildlife observation facilities and improved access to tidalpools north of town at Yaquina Head make this park a highlight of the coast. The shops, galleries, and restaurants along Newport's historic Bayfront, together with the Performing Arts Center and quieter charm of

© BILL MCRAE

seals loafing in Newport harbor

Nye Beach, keep up a tourism tradition that goes back to when this town was the "honeymoon capital of Oregon."

SIGHTS
Oregon Coast Aquarium

There are 6,000 miles of water between the Oregon coast and Japan—the largest stretch of open ocean on earth. You can hear *our* side of the story at the Oregon Coast Aquarium (2820 S.E. Ferry Slip Rd., Newport, 541/867-3474, www.aquarium.org, open daily year-round (except Christmas Day), 9 A.M.–6 P.M. Memorial Day weekend–Labor Day weekend, 10 A.M.–5 P.M. the rest of the year. $12 adults, $10 seniors, $7 for ages 4–13), one of the state's most popular attractions.

The aquarium initially featured 40,000 square feet of galleries devoted to wetland communities, near-shore and marine ecosystems, and an environmental center. While it was respected as a top-notch educational facility, it lacked "star power" until the 1996 arrival of Keiko, a 7,720-pound, 32-foot-long orca who

starred in *Free Willy.* Understandably, his presence overshadowed four acres of sea lions, sea otters, tidepools, and undersea caves, as well as the largest walk-in seabird aviary in the Americas. Keiko was subsequently moved to Iceland for re-entry into the wild, where he died in 2003. Keiko or no, there are still many attractions at the Oregon Aquarium to hold your interest.

One of the gems of the aquarium is "Passages of the Deep," a 200-foot-long acrylic tunnel offering 360-degree underwater views in three diverse habitats, from "Orford Reef" to "Halibut Flats" to "Open Sea," where you're surrounded by free-swimming sharks. The "Jewels of the Sea" exhibit showcases several dozen kinds of jellyfish in an almost psychedelic display.

"At the Jetty" is the aquarium's largest permanent indoor exhibit to date. Visitors look through a window into a 35,000-gallon tank to watch white sturgeon and coho and chinook salmon swimming among large basalt boulders that simulate a coastal jetty, such as these anadromous fish in the wild might pass through on their upriver journey to their spawning grounds.

Of the several hundred species of Pacific Northwest fish, birds, and mammals on display in the rest of the facility, don't miss the sea otters, wolf eel, leopard sharks, lion's mane jellyfish, and tufted puffins. The younger set will enjoy the sea cave with simulated wave action, which houses a resident octopus.

Indigenous simulated ecosystems help articulate the region's biology. The centerpiece of the Wetland's Gallery, for example, is a cross section of the salt marsh subject to the periodic ebb and flow of tides. Another ecological niche is illustrated by a 4,730-gallon tank in the Sandy Shores exhibit. Here, you can see smelt, perch, and leopard sharks navigate amid human-made rocks and piers. The Rock Shores Gallery adds another dimension to the experience with an open tidal pool that allows visitors to handle starfish, sea anemones, and the like. In the outside aviary and sea mammal pools, latex molds of rocky outcroppings provide perches for birds, otters, and sea lions

NORTHERN OREGON COAST

(some of these animals were rescued from such debacles as the *Exxon-Valdez* oil spill).

In addition to gaining a heightened understanding of the coast biome, you might also come away with something from the museum shop's first-rate collection of regional books and oceanographic tomes or perhaps a crystal or gemstone. The on-site Mermaid Cafe emphasizes such Oregon fare as Tillamook dairy products, seasonal fruits, and seafood. Outside in the summer, enjoy barbecued burgers and hot dogs and teriyaki shish-kebabs.

Advance tickets are recommended on weekends, major holidays, and during the summer. To get there from U.S. 101, turn east on OSU Drive or 32nd Street, south of the Yaquina Bay Bridge, and follow Ferry Slip Road to the parking lot.

Oregon State University Hatfield Marine Science Center

Just south of the Yaquina Bay Bridge, head east on the road that parallels the bay to the OSU Hatfield Marine Science Center (Marine Science Drive, Newport, 541/867-0100, http://hmsc.oregonstate.edu, open 10 A.M.–5 P.M. daily in summer and 10 A.M.–4 P.M. Thurs.–Mon. the rest of the year, suggested donation of $3 adult). This research and education facility is a low-key but still interesting complement to the very popular Oregon Coast Aquarium, located half a mile south. In addition to a "hands-on" area where you can experience the feel of starfish, anemones, and other sea creatures, the center has educational dioramas and a theater shows marine-science films throughout the day. Beyond the walls of the museum,

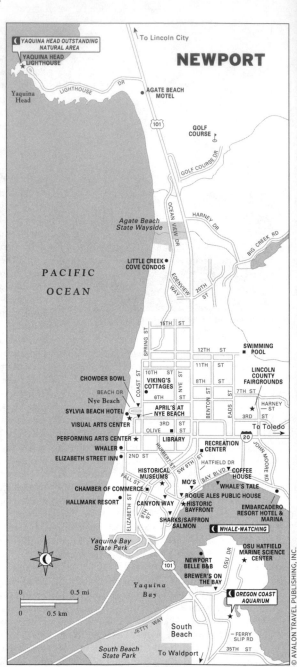

guided field trips (fee charged) explore estuary, beach, and coastal forest habitats at various times of the year (check with the front desk or the website for details). The bookstore has a good selection of nature books, posters, games, and gifts.

Oregon Coast History Center

For a glimpse into the rich past of Lincoln County, stop at the Oregon Coast History Center (545 S.W. 9th St., Newport, 541/265-7509, www.oregoncoast.history.museum, open 10 A.M.–5 P.M. Tues.–Sun. June–Sept., 11 A.M.–4 P.M. Tues.–Sun. Oct.–May, free admission), which incorporates the Log Cabin Museum and the adjacent Queen Anne–style Burrows House, a former boardinghouse built in 1895. It's located a half block east of the chamber of commerce on U.S. 101. The logging, farming, pioneer life, and maritime exhibits (particularly Newport shipwrecks) are interesting, but the Siletz baskets and other Native American artifacts steal the show.

Here you can learn the heartbreaking story of the hardships—forced displacement, inadequate housing, insufficient food, and poor medical facilities—that plagued the diverse tribes that made up the Confederated Tribes of Siletz Indians.

The Bayfront

Newport's Old Town Bayfront District can be easy to miss if you're not alert. At the north end of the Yaquina Bay Bridge, look for the signs pointing off U.S. 101, which lead you down the hill to Bay Boulevard, the Bayfront's main drag. Alternatively, turn southeast off the highway a few blocks north onto Hurbert Street; this runs into Canyon Way, which ends at Bay. On summer weekends, forget about parking anywhere here unless you arrive early. Spots close by the boulevard can often be found, however, along Canyon Way, the hillside access route to downtown.

Until 1936, ferries shuttled people and vehicles to and from Newport's waterfront. With the completion of the Yaquina Bay Bridge that year, however, traffic bypassed the old town area. Commerce and development moved to the highway corridor, and the Bayfront faded in importance. Within the last couple of decades, the pendulum has swung back, and the Bayfront District is now one of Newport's prime attractions, with some of its best restaurants and watering holes, shopping, and tourist facilities.

One of the first things that'll strike you about the Bayfront today is that it's still a working neighborhood, not a sanitized re-creation of a real seaport. Chowderhouses, galleries, and shops stand shoulder to shoulder with fish-processing plants and canneries, and the air is filled with the cries of fishmongers purveying wharfside walkaway cocktails and the harmonious discord of sea lions and harbor seals. On the waterfront, sport anglers step off charter boats with their catches, and vessels laden with everything from wood products to whale-watchers ply the bay. Unfortunately, the severe catch limits and cost of equipment make this less of a working port every year. In deference to the Oregon commercial fisherman and other endangered species, wall murals memorialize fishing boats and whales here on the Bayfront.

Also in the Bayfront District, Mariner Square (250 S.W. Bay Blvd., 541/265-2206) is a complex of three attractions that mostly appeal to kids: **Ripley's Believe It or Not!, The Waxworks,** and the **Undersea Gardens.** Admission per attraction is $9.95 for adults, $5.95 for children; discounts are offered to hardy souls who want to take in all three.

Yaquina Bay State Park

In 1871, a lighthouse was built here on a bluff overlooking the mouth of Yaquina Bay, and the lighthouse keeper, his wife, and seven children moved into the two-story wood-frame structure. It soon became apparent, however, that the location was not ideal, as the light could not be seen by ships approaching the harbor from the north. The station was abandoned after just three years, once the nearby light at Yaquina Head was completed. The building was slated for demolition in 1934, when local residents formed the Lincoln County Historical Society to preserve it. In 1997, the government decided to turn Yaquina Bay's beacon back on.

Today, the handsome restored structure and surrounding grounds make up Yaquina Bay State Park (541/574-3129 or 800/-551-6949), in a beautiful location at the north end of the Yaquina Bay Bridge. The oldest building in Newport, it's the last wooden lighthouse on the Oregon coast. The living quarters, replete with period furnishings, are open noon–4 P.M. daily. Admission is free. Be sure to ask the volunteers about the resident ghost here.

From the parking area, you have an excellent photo-op of the bay and the bridge. The park is a good place to have a picnic, or you can descend the trails to the beach and dig for razor clams or hunt for agates and petrified wood.

Nye Beach

The 1890s-era tourism boom that came to Newport's Bayfront spilled over into Nye Beach. In 1891, the city built a wooden sidewalk connecting the two neighborhoods and soon "summer people" were filling the cedar cottages here. In the next century, thanks to an improved river-and-land route from Corvallis, health faddists (who came for hot seawater baths in the sanatorium) and honeymooners soon joined the mix.

Located a mile north from the Bayfront, to the west of U.S. 101 (look for signs on the highway), this one-time favorite retreat for wealthy Portlanders has undergone a revival in recent years. Rough times and rougher weather had reduced luxurious beach houses here to a cluster of weather-beaten shacks until a performing arts center went up two decades ago. On the heels of the development of this first-rate cultural facility, came the conversion of vintage hotels and plenty of new construction. Culture vultures, beach lovers, and people-watchers now flock to Nye Beach.

◖ Yaquina Head Outstanding Natural Area

Five miles north of Newport, rocky Yaquina Head juts out to sea. Tools dating back 5,000

years have been unearthed at Yaquina Head. Many were made from elk and deer antler and bone as well as stone. Clam and mussel shells from middens in the area evidence a diet rich in shellfish for the area's ancient inhabitants.

Today, much of the headland is encompassed in the Yaquina Head Outstanding Natural Area (P.O. Box 936, Newport 97365, 541/574-3100, admission $5 per vehicle), managed by the BLM. "Outstanding" is indeed the word for this place; a visitor could easily spend several hours exploring all the site has to offer.

At its outer tip stands **Yaquina Head Lighthouse,** the coast's tallest beacon. In the early 1870s, materials intended for construction of a lighthouse several miles north at Otter Crest were mistakenly delivered here. The 93-foot tower began operation in 1873, replacing the poorly located lighthouse south of here at the mouth of Newport's harbor. Walk up the 114 cast-iron steps for a spectacular panorama

The recently renovated Yaquina Head Lighthouse is in a beautiful natural setting. Take some time to explore the surrounding headland.

of the headland and surrounding coast. The lighthouse is open daily, weather permitting.

Below, an observation deck provides views of seals, sea lions, gray whales, and seabirds. Of the half dozen varieties of pelagic birds that cluster on Colony Rock—a large monolith in the shallows 200 yards offshore—the tufted puffin is the most colorful. It's sometimes called a sea parrot because of its large yellow-orange bill. Puffins arrive here in April and are most visible early in the day on the rock's grassy patches. The most ubiquitous species here are common murres, pigeon guillemots, and cormorants. The murres' white breasts and bellies contrast with their darker bills and elongated backs. The guillemots resemble pigeons with white wing patches and bright red webbed feet. The cormorants look like prehistoric pelicans.

East of the lighthouse, the large Interpretive Center (541/574-3116, open daily 10 A.M.–5 P.M. in summer, till 4 P.M. the rest of the year) features exhibits on local ecosystems, Native American culture, and historical artifacts such as a 19th-century lighthouse keeper's journal. Other highlights include a life-size replica of the Fresnel lens that shines from the top of the nearby lighthouse, a sea cave simulation with a life-size mural of a California gray whale (accompanied by an exhibit detailing its migratory pattern), as well as statues of birds and harbor seals, and information on tidepool inhabitants.

Close by, wheelchair-friendly paths give access to tidal pools, augmented by the hand of man, in an abandoned basalt quarry on the south side of the headland. Enjoy sea stars, purple urchins, anemones, and hermit crabs at low tide.

Beaches

North of town, **Agate Beach** is a broad swath of coastline famed for its agate-hunting opportunities and its views of nearby Yaquina Head. In addition to the semiprecious stones, the contemplative appeal of Agate Beach inspired no less a figure than Ernest Bloch, the noted Swiss composer, who lived here from 1940 until his death in 1959. Famed violinist Yehudi Menuhin spoke of Bloch and the locale thusly: "Agate Beach is a wild forlorn stretch of coastline looking down upon waves coming in all the way from Asia to break on the shore, a place which suited the grandeur and intensity of Bloch's character." Each summer, the Ernest Bloch Music Festival (see *Entertainment and Events*) pays tribute to the spirit and music of this man.

Moolack Beach, two miles north of Yaquina Head, is a favorite with kite flyers and agate hunters. Another 1.5 miles north, at **Beverly Beach,** 20-million-year old fossils have been found in the sandstone cliffs above the shore. Beverly Beach also attracts waders, unique for Oregon's chilly waters. Offshore sandbars temper the waves and the weather so it's not as rough or as cold as many coastal locales. This long stretch of sand (panoramic photos are best taken in from Yaquina Head Lighthouse looking north) is rated among America's 50 best beaches in a list that considers both scenic and recreational appeals.

The beach at **Yaquina Bay State Park,** accessible via a trail from the bluff-top parking area, is a popular spot for clam-digging and agate hunting. Two miles south of the Yaquina Bay Bridge, **South Beach State Park** draws beachcombers, anglers, and picnickers to its miles of broad, sandy beach. The large campground here is the closest available to Newport (see *Camping*).

Toledo

Aficionados of antiquities can head east of Newport six miles up the Yaquina River on U.S. 20 to Toledo, where "junque" shops abound. This small town's fortunes have risen and fallen with the timber cut. At one time, the world's largest spruce mill was here, but in the era of big timber's swan song, dealers of collectibles have sprouted up to take advantage of coast-bound traffic from the Willamette Valley. Most of the antique shops are located on Main Street. Timber has enjoyed a resurgence here with the mill getting old-growth logs submerged in Yaquina Bay during World War II.

SPORTS AND RECREATION
Fishing
Newport is one of the top spots on the coast for charter fishing, and opportunities abound here at the home port of Oregon's second-largest recreational fleet. Bottom fishing (year-round), tuna fishing (Aug.–Oct.), crabbing (year-round), and salmon and halibut fishing (seasonal) are all possible. Typical rates here are $65 for a half day of bottom fishing, $100 for a full day; $110 for an eight-hour salmon outing; $190 for 12 hours of tuna fishing; and $165 for a 12-hour halibut charter.

Newport Marina Store and Charters (2212 OSU Dr., South Beach, 541/867-4470 or 877/867-4470, www.newportmarinacharters.com) offers a combination crabbing/fishing trip ($90 for six hours). Two-hour whale watching trips are $25. Two other local operators are **Newport Tradewinds** (653 S.W. Bay Blvd., 541/265-2101 or 800/676-7819, www.newport tradewinds.com); and **Sea Gull Charters, Inc.** (343 S.W. Bay Blvd., 541/265-7441 or 800/865-7441, www.seagullcharters.com).

For those who prefer to take matters into their own hands, the clamming and Dungeness crabbing are superlative in Yaquina Bay. If you haven't done this before, local tackle shops, such as the Newport Marina Store in South Beach, rent crab pots or rings and offer instruction. The best time to dig clams is at an extremely low tide. At that time, look for clammers grabbing up cockles in the shallows of the bay. Tide tables are available from the chamber of commerce and many local businesses.

(Whale-Watching
In addition to the fishing charter companies noted above, which all offer whale-watching tours, the best company on the coast in terms of state-of-the-art equipment and natural history interpretation is **Marine Discovery Tours** (345 S.W. Bay Blvd., 800/903-2628, www.marinediscovery.com). Whale-, seal-, and bird-watching, an oyster-bed tour, estuary and ocean exploration, and a harbor tour, narrated by naturalist guides, exemplify their offerings. Their 65-foot *Discovery* features videocameras

that magnify the fascinating interplay between smaller life forms, but the real attractions can be appreciated by the naked eye. Landlubbers will especially relish the full crab pots pulled up from the deep and the resident pod of whales often visible north of Yaquina Bay off Yaquina Head. The two-hour SeaLife tour costs $30 for adults, $28 seniors, $15 for ages 4–13.

During the prime whale-watching weeks of late December and late March, volunteers from Whale Watching Spoken Here staff the **Don A. Davis City Kiosk** in Nye Beach, to answer questions and help you spot whales.

Camping
The campgrounds at Beverly Beach State Park and South Beach State Park could well be the most popular places of their kind on the Oregon coast. Their proximity to Newport, the absence of other camping in the area, and the special features of each explain their appeal.

Beverly Beach State Park (information 541/265-9278 or 800/452-5687, reservations 800/452-5687 or www.reserveamerica.com) offers 152 tent sites and 127 RV spaces (both $17–21), as well as yurts, set seven miles north of Newport on the east side of the highway in a mossy glade. Across the road is a tunnel leading to a beach. **Devil's Punchbowl** and **Otter Crest** are one and two miles up the highway, respectively. Fees include all amenities; on-site café. Campground is open year-round.

South Beach State Park (information 541/867-4715 or 800/551-6949, reservations 800/452-5687 or www.reserveamerica.com) located just south of the Yaquina Bay Bridge, occupies a long beach with opportunities for fishing, agate hunting, windsurfing (for experts), horseback riding, and hiking. It has the full range of creature comforts, including a laundry. It's open mid-April–late October at $17–21 per night (hiker and biker spaces $5).

ENTERTAINMENT AND EVENTS
Overlooking the sea in Nye Beach, the **Newport Performing Arts Center** (777 W. Olive, 541/265-2787, www.coastarts.org/

pac), the coast's largest performance venue, hosts local and national entertainment in the 400-seat Alice Silverman Theatre and the smaller Studio Theatre. At the same address is the **Oregon Coast Council for the Arts,** (541/265-9231 or 888/701-7123, www.coast arts.org), which puts out a free monthly newsletter and has ticket information on the PAC venues. It also has updates on the **Newport Visual Arts Center** (777 N.W. Beach Dr., 541/265-6540), located right above the beach two blocks north at the Nye Beach turnaround. The two floors and two galleries here offer art-education programs and exhibition space for paintings, sculpture, and other works, often with a maritime theme. Runyan Gallery is open 11 A.M.–6 P.M. Tues.–Sun.; Upstairs Gallery is open noon–4 P.M. Tues.–Sat. All exhibits are free.

In addition to its impressive schedule of music, dance, drama, and other arts, the Performing Arts Center screens a series of imported and art films—the ones you probably won't find at the multiplex **Newport Cinema** (5836 North Coast Hwy., 541/265-2111).

The biggest bash here (and one of the largest events of its kind in the country) is late February's **Newport Seafood and Wine Festival** (541/265-8801 or 800/262-7844, www.sea foodandwine.com), which features dozens of food booths and scores of Oregon wineries serving up these palate pleasers, along with music and crafts, at the South Beach Marina (across Yaquina Bay from the Bayfront). A huge tent joins the exhibition hall wherein festival-goers wash down delights from the deep with Oregon vintages. Admission runs $6–12, and the event is open only to the 21-and-over crowd.

The second event of note is **Loyalty Days and Sea Fair** (541/265-8801 or 800/262-7844) in early May, featuring sailboat races, a chicken feed, and a parade. What began during the Depression as the Crab Festival, intended to stimulate the market for Dungeness crab, was recast during the depths of the Red Scare of the 1950s as a public expression of patriotism. Although that aspect still undergirds the

events, as evidenced by visiting naval vessels, it's really just a big community party stretching over four days, with carnival rides, boat tours, yacht races, bed races, a car show, a parade, and the coronation of the Crab Queen. Admission fee charged.

Each summer, the lectures, recitals, and concerts of the **Ernest Bloch Music Festival** (information 541/574-0614, tickets 541/265-2787, www.baymusic.org) are eagerly anticipated by classical music lovers. The festival usually takes place late June–mid-July, at the Newport Performing Arts Center (777 W. Olive St.), with related performances at other central-coast locales. Along with Bloch's compositions, works by Schubert, Ravel, Saint-Saëns, and other icons of classical music are performed by top musicians in this acoustically superior hall. Ticket prices range from free to $25.

"Suds & Surf" is the theme of the annual mid October **Newport Microbrew Festival** (541/265-8801 or 800/262-7844), held at the Rogue Ales Brewery (2320 OSU Dr., Newport, 541/867-3660), at South Beach Marina, just south of the bridge. This event, Oregon's second-largest microbrew festival, brings together 30 of the Northwest's finest craft breweries, complemented by musical entertainment and a variety of food and arts and crafts booths. The festival also features commercial and home-brew competitions. Admission is $6, 21 and over only.

ACCOMMODATIONS

Viking's Cottages (729 N.W. Coast St., 541/265-2477 or 800/480-2477, www.vikings oregoncoast.com, rooms up to $165, condos $115–195) has until recently offered simple beachfront Cape Cod–style cottages originally built in the 1920s. However, time and the weather have been harsh to these venerable structures and in 2007 they were replaced with a series of modern shake-sided fourplex units with kitchens. These spacious rooms still offer great beach access and most have ocean views. In addition, Viking's offers oceanfront condos with full kitchens and access to an indoor pool.

Built in the 1940s, the recently refurbished **Agate Beach Motel** (175 N.W. Gilbert Way, 541/265-8746 or 800/755-5674, www.agate beachmotel.com, doubles $125–145) has 10 simple but charming beachfront units overlooking Agate Beach, each with a private bedroom, kitchen, living room, and sundeck. Drop-ins are welcome, but reservations are recommended.

Elizabeth Street Inn (232 S.W. Elizabeth St., 541/265-9400 or 877/265-9400, www .elizabethstreetinn.com, doubles from $169) sits on a bluff overlooking the ocean. All of the rooms in this newer property face the ocean and have private balconies. They come fully equipped with fireplaces, refrigerators, microwaves, and coffeemakers. Guests also get a complimentary continental breakfast and have use of the indoor pool, spa, and fitness room.

For comfort, you can't beat the **The Whaler** (155 S.W. Elizabeth St., 541/265-9261 or 800/433-9444, www.whalernewport.com, doubles from $105). With 73 rooms—each with a view and some with fireplaces, wetbars, and private balconies—guests are treated to fresh-popped popcorn, pool facilities, and continental breakfast.

The **Hallmark Resort** (744 S.W. Elizabeth St., 541/265-2600 or 888/448-4449, www.hall markinns.com, doubles from $139) is a large hotel complex sitting atop the Newport bluffs, looking westward over the Pacific and miles of sandy beach. Of the many modern hotels that share this vista, the Hallmark has the largest rooms and is the best maintained. Facilities include an indoor pool, spa, and restaurant.

The ever-popular **Embarcadero Resort Hotel & Marina** (1000 S.E. Bay Blvd., 541/265-8521 or 800/547-4779, www.embarcadero-resort.com, studio suites from $149, one-bedroom suites from $179), is bayfront, but not beachfront, as it overlooks Yaquina Bay and the soaring bay bridge, arguably one of the best views in Oregon. The Embarcadero has an assortment of suites and townhouses with full kitchen and fireplaces. Facilities include an indoor pool, sauna and two outdoor Jacuzzis, restaurant and bar, private dock and boat rentals. If you want to get away from it all, **Little**

Creek Cove Condominiums (3641 NW Oceanview Dr., 541/265-8587 or 800/294-8025, www.littlecreekcove.com, studios from $129, one-bedroom units from $169) is a small condo resort that might be what you're looking for. Little Creek Cove resort is two miles north of Newport, perched above an isolated stretch of beach. You have a choice of studio, one- and two-bedroom units, each with private deck, full kitchen, and fireplace.

Bed-and-Breakfasts

You may not find any riverboat gamblers aboard the **Newport Belle Bed & Breakfast** (H Dock, Newport Marina, 541/867-6290 or 800/348-1922, www.newportbelle.com, doubles $125–145), a recently constructed sternwheeler designed as a floating inn, but this 97-foot-long B&B evokes the ambience of the sternwheeler heyday. Choose from five generous staterooms, each with its own personality and private bath. Three of the rooms have queen beds, one has a king, and the family room has a full and a twin. Most have fabulous vistas of the bustling marina and bridge area. In the evening, guests either retire to their staterooms, enjoy the open afterdeck, or socialize in the main salon, where a gourmet breakfast is served every morning. No pets, children, or smoking allowed. Soft-soled shoes required.

The **Sylvia Beach Hotel** (267 N.W. Cliff, 541/265-5428, www.sylviabeachhotel.com) combines the camaraderie of a hostel with the intimate charm of a bed-and-breakfast. Built in the era when the Corvallis-to-Yaquina Bay train and seven-seater Studebaker touring cars from Portland ferried the summer folks to Nye Beach, its National Historic Landmark designation and literary theme have attracted an enthusiastic following. The 20 guestrooms, named after different authors, are furnished with decor evocative of each respective literary legacy. The Edgar Allen Poe Room, for instance, has a pendulum guillotine blade and stuffed ravens, while the Agatha Christie Room drops such clues as shoes underneath the curtains and capsules marked "poison" in the medicine cabinet.

Most of the rooms ("bestsellers") run $131, with several oceanfront suites ("classics") featuring a fireplace and deck going for $183. "Novels" go for $94. All rates include a full breakfast and reflect double occupancy. At breakfast, you have a choice of entrées and share a table with eight other guests, so misanthropes beware! The fact that no smoking, pets, or radios are allowed on the premises should also be mentioned. Small children are discouraged. If you're looking for a budget room, Sylvia Beach features dormitory bunk beds for $25 per night.

To get there, turn off U.S. 101 onto N.W. 3rd and follow it down to the beach, where N.W. 3rd and Cliff Streets meet. Then look for a large four-story dark green vintage wooden structure with a red roof on a bluff above the surf.

FOOD

This is a town for serious diners—folks who know good food and don't mind paying a tad more for it. It's also the kind of place where wharfside vendors do it on the cheap. June through October, you can pick up the freshest garden produce the area has to offer, plus baked goods, honey, and other delectables, at the Lincoln County Small Farmers' Association's **Saturday Farmers Market,** held in the parking area of the Newport Armory (41 S.W. U.S. 101, 541/574-4040), on the east side of the highway just behind City Hall. It kicks off at 9 A.M.

About seven miles east of the Bayfront, **Oregon Oyster Farms** (6878 Yaquina Bay Rd., Newport, 541/265-5078) is the only remaining commercial outlet for Yaquina Bay oysters, on sale 9 A.M.–5 P.M. daily. Visitors are welcome to observe the farming and processing of these succulent shellfish. Try oysters on the half-shell, or sample the smoked oysters on a stick. To get there, follow Bay Boulevard east six miles from the Embarcadero Resort.

Because you'll probably be spending most of your time at either Nye Beach or the Bayfront, eateries in those neighborhoods predominate in this section. The Newport Bayfront is where Mohava Niemi first opened the original **Mo's** (622 S.W. Bay Blvd., 541/265-2979, www.mos chowder.com) several decades ago. When word got out about the good food and low prices, Mo's small homey place soon had more busi-

ness than it could handle. In response to the overflow, **Mo's Annex** (541/265-7512) was created across the street. While both establishments feature such favorites as oyster stew and peanut butter cream pie, the Annex bay windows have the best view. Both are open daily for lunch and dinner.

Another solid choice for those who crave fresh seafood is the **Whale's Tale** (452 S.W. Bay Blvd., 541/265-8660, lunch and dinner daily, main courses $22). A Newport institution, the Whale's Tale is a venerable and friendly seafood restaurant that perfectly captures a moment of early 1970s charm, when even loggers and fishermen wanted to be hippies. The woodsy maritime decor creates a gastronomic time capsule that's well suited to a plate of grilled local oysters or a piece of grilled halibut. Excellent food and a fun atmosphere.

Chowder Bowl at Nye Beach (728 N.W. Beach Dr., 541/265-7477, lunch and dinner daily, main courses $5–18) is perfect after a long beach walk. A first-rate salad bar, garlic bread, and award-winning chowder make an excellent lunch.

April's at Nye Beach (749 N.W. 3rd St., 541/265-6855, dinner Wed.–Sun., main courses $12–25) is a small, stylish café with big Mediterranean flavors close to the Sylvia Beach Hotel. Fish soup and portobello mushrooms in cheese-laden cannelloni are standouts here in a creative menu. House-made bruschetta and steamed Manila clams are excellent appetizers. For dessert have an eclair dipped in chocolate ganache and topped with slivered almonds. Affordable wines by the glass (around $5) add to one of Newport's best dining experiences.

Right on the bayfront, with windows overlooking the active fishing port, **Saffron Salmon** (859 SW Bay Blvd, 541/265-8921, lunch and dinner Wed.–Mon., main courses $16–26) is one of Newport's finest choices for expertly prepared seafood with up-to-date preparations. The restaurant's namesake dish is pan-seared chinook salmon with saffron cream sauce, while calamari are sautéed with olive oil and red cabbage. There's also a selection of organically produced steaks and rack of lamb.

Also in the old town harbor area, **Sharks Seafood Bar & Steamer Co.** (852 S.W. Bay Blvd., 541/574-0590, www.sharksseafoodbar. com, dinner Fri.–Wed., $12–26) provides a tasty antidote to the heavy breaded and fried seafood omnipresent in most Oregon coast restaurants. All Sharks' main courses are sautéed, steamed, or braised, with the result that not only are the dishes more delicate tasting, they are also better for you. But don't worry—this isn't tasteless health food. The Catalina Bouillabaisse packs a wallop—1.5 pounds of seafood in every spice-filled bowl. You'll also find a savory seafood gumbo, oyster stew, and a mix of stewed and sautéed fish called a pan roast. Fresh fish gets the steam treatment—in season, try halibut, salmon, and rockfish steamed and served with the chef's special sauces.

Georgie's Beachside Grill (744 S.W. Elizabeth St., 541/265-9800, three meals daily, main courses $12–22) in Nye Beach's Hallmark Resort has the best ocean view in town as well as good food. The salmon hash and smoked seafood pasta are highlights. The restaurant also features Cajun (try the catfish or shrimp creole) and Jamaican seafood specials.

C Canyon Way Bookstore and Restaurant (1216 S.W. Canyon Way, 541/265-8319, lunch and dinner Tues.–Sat., lunch only Mon., main courses $12 –25) has been a mainstay of Newport's culinary and cultural scenes since 1971. A combination restaurant, art gallery, clothing boutique, and 20,000-title bookstore, it offers something for everybody. Stay for haute cuisine or carry out homemade quiche, croissants, and espresso. Early-dinner prices halve the later ones, which average $20, for the same order. Menu highlights include prawns Provençale, Yaquina Bay oysters, crabcakes, plus local lamb and beef, and a good Oregon-centered wine list. You'll also appreciate extras such as outdoor patio dining and works by local artists adorning the walls.

You don't have to be a guest to have a meal at the **Tables of Content** (267 N.W. Cliff, 541/265-5428, www.sylviabeachhotel.com, dinner nightly, four-course prix fixe meals for $19), the excellent restaurant at the Sylvia Beach Hotel. There's a nice view of the breakers, good company, and it's a good dollar value for creatively prepared Northwest cuisine. Each night features several entrée selections with an appetizer, salad, bread, beverages (alcohol extra), and dessert. Diners share tables and are encouraged to break the ice with a game called Two Truths and a Lie, in which they regale each other with several stories, the object being to distinguish which one is true. Reservations mandatory.

Rogue Ales Public House (748 S.W. Bay Blvd., 541/265-3188, lunch and dinner daily, main courses $11–16) is along the Bay in Old Town, serving seafood salads, shrimp melt sandwiches, pizza, fish-n-chips, and seasonal fish dishes. A new dinner menu and expanded dining area offer a more upscale though still casual dining experience. In addition to washing down all the above with renowned Rogue ales, there's Keiko draft root beer, a creamy concoction laced with honey and vanilla. Rogue Ales brewery, called **Brewers on the Bay** (320 OSU Dr., 541/867-3660), is across Yaquina Bay near the Oregon Aquarium and offers a brewpub experience and light dining.

Down along the Bay Front is a wonderful breakfast haunt, the **Coffee House** (156 S.W. Bay Blvd., 541/265-6263, breakfast and lunch daily). Gourmet pastry and such creative brunch fare as a wild mushroom omelette, crabcakes Florentine, various crepes, and oysters lightly breaded with Japanese panko breadcrumbs are complemented by the best espresso drinks in Newport. In fair weather, the outside deck is a relaxing spot for soaking in some rays while you gaze out on the harbor.

Lighthouse Deli (640 U.S. 101 in South Beach, 541/867-6800, 8 A.M.–8 P.M. daily, $8–12) has fish-n-chips in a batter that's light enough not to obscure the flavor of fresh salmon, halibut, or cod. If you're looking for a family stop after visiting the Aquarium (just south of the Aquarium turnoff), this is it.

INFORMATION

The **Greater Newport Chamber of Commerce** (555 S.W. U.S. 101, Newport 97365, 541/265-

8801 or 800/541/262-7844, www.newport chamber.org) has lots of literature and helpful staff. The office is open 8:30 A.M.–5 P.M. Monday–Friday year-round; it's also open weekends 10 A.M.–4 P.M. June–September.

The **Central Oregon Coast Association** (541/265-2064 or 800/767-2064, www.coast visitor.com) maintains a useful website with details on Newport and the rest of Lincoln County. The City of Newport operates another informative website, **Get to Know Newport** (www.discovernewport.com).

GETTING THERE

Newport is one of the few places on the Oregon coast that's reached by public transportation. **Valley Retriever** (541/265-2253) buses connect Newport with Corvallis Monday–Saturday. On weekdays, **Lincoln County Transit** (541/265-4900, www.co.lincoln.or.us/transit) runs buses four times daily, north to Lincoln City and south to Yachats, with numerous stops en route through Newport. A brochure with schedules and fare info is available in commercial establishments all over town.

Waldport

Originally a stronghold of the Alsea tribe, Waldport also has had incarnations as a gold rush town, salmon-canning center, and lumber port. This town of about 2,000, whose name in German means "Forest Port," is pretty quiet today. The chamber of commerce touts Waldport's livability, suggesting that the town's "relative obscurity" has spared it the fate of more crowded tourist hot spots. This may also be explained by a nondescript main drag that gives no hint of surrounding beaches and prime fishing and crabbing spots. A recent influx of retirees has spurred new home building, but this place is still decidedly low-key. For those passing through, Waldport provides a low-cost alternative to the big-name destinations; in Waldport you won't have to fight for a parking spot or make reservations months in advance.

SIGHTS

Alsea Bay Bridge Historical Interpretive Center

This small museum cum visitors center (541/563-2002, open 9 A.M.–5 P.M. daily in summer, 9 A.M.–4 P.M. Tues.–Sat. the rest of the year, free admission), operated by the Oregon Parks and Recreation Department and Waldport Chamber of Commerce, stands along the highway on the south side of the river. Exhibits here tell the story of how the sleek 1991 bridge replaced the aging Conde McCullough span across the bay, which has since been demolished. Displays about transportation methods along the central coast since the 1800s, information on the Alsea tribe, and a telescope trained on the seals and waterfowl on the bay are worth a quick stop. In addition, Oregon Parks and Recreation guides lead bridge tours and give clamming and crabbing demonstrations during the summer.

Seal Rock State Recreation Site

Four miles north of town, this park attracts beachcombers and agate-hunters as well as folks who come to explore the tidepools and observe the seals on offshore rocks. The park's name derives from a seal-shaped rock in the cluster of interesting formations in the tidewater. The picnic area is set in a shady area behind the sandy beach. During Christmas and spring breaks, the volunteers of Whale Watching Spoken Here are on hand to help visitors spot passing grays 10 A.M.–1 P.M. The park is open for day use only; call 800/551-6949 for information.

Ona Beach State Park

A couple of miles north of Seal Rock, this beguiling park on the west side of the highway includes a forested picnic area with a quarter-mile trail and a footbridge over Beaver Creek leading to a fine stretch of beach. Day use only; call 800/551-6949 for information.

Drift Creek Wilderness

Seven miles east of Waldport are the nearly 5,800 acres of the Drift Creek Wilderness, which protects the Coast Range's largest remaining stands of old-growth rainforest. Here you can see giant Sitka spruce and western hemlock hundreds of years old, nourished by up to 120 inches of rain per year. These trees are the "climax forest" in the Douglas fir ecosystem. They seldom reach old-growth status because the timber industry tends to replant only fir seedlings after logging operations. The largest population of spotted owls in the state is also here, along with bald eagles, Roosevelt elk, and black bear. Drift Creek sustains wild runs of chinook, steelhead, and coho, which come up the Alsea River.

Steep ridges and their drainages as well as small meadows make up the topography, which is accessed via a couple of hiking trails. The trailhead closest to Waldport is the **Harris Ranch Trail,** which descends 1,200 feet in two miles to a meadow near Drift Creek. The local access to Harris Ranch and Horse Creek trails leaves Route 34 at the Alsea River crossing seven miles east of Waldport. Here, pick up Risely Creek Road (Forest Service Road 3446) and Forest Service Road Road 346. The wilderness is administered by the Siuslaw National Forest–Waldport Ranger Station (541/563-3211) which can supply specific directions to the different trailheads into this increasingly rare ecosystem.

SPORTS AND RECREATION

Fishing

Waldport's recreational raison d'être is fishing. World-class clamming and Dungeness crabbing in Alsea Bay and the Alsea River's famous salmon, steelhead, and cutthroat trout runs account for a high percentage of visits to the area. Before commercial fishing on the river was shut down in 1957, as much as 137,000 pounds of chinook were netted in a season. The wild fall chinook run remains healthy, and starts up in

late August. Catch-and-release for sea-run cutthroats starts in mid-August, while steelhead are in the river December–March. Crabbers without boats can take advantage of the Port of Waldport docks.

Dock of the Bay Marina (1245 N.E. Mill, 541/563-2003) and **Kozy Kove Marina** (9646 Alsea Hwy.) rent and sell crabbing and fishing supplies, and can guide you to the best spots.

Camping

Two excellent campgrounds sit about four miles south of Waldport on U.S. 101 along the beach. **Beachside State Park** (information 541/563-3220 or 800/551-6949, reservations 800/452-5687 or www.reserveamerica.com) is located near a half mile of beach not far from Alsea Bay and Alsea River. This is a paradise for rock fishing, surfcasting, clamming, and crabbing. For $17–21 a night mid-April–mid-October, there are 50 tent sites, 32 sites for RVs up to 30 feet long, and some hiker/biker sites. Beachside fills up fast, with such amenities as a laundry and hot showers, so reserve early for space Memorial Day–Labor Day.

A half mile down U.S. 101, the Forest Service operates **Tillicum Beach** (reservations 877/444-6777 or www.reserveusa.com). Set right along the ocean, the campground is open all year but requires reservations. For $20 a night you have flush toilets plus ranger campfire programs in summer. Forest service roads from here access Coast Range fishing streams, which are detailed in a forest service map. You'll also appreciate the strip of vegetation blocking the cool evening winds that whip up off the ocean here.

Should Beachside and Tillicum be filled to overflowing, you might want to set up a base camp in the Coast Range along Route 34—especially if you have fishing or hiking in the Drift Creek Wilderness in mind. Just go east of Waldport 17 miles on Route 34 to the Siuslaw National Forest's **Blackberry Campground** (reservations 877/444-6777 or www.reserve usa.com). The 33 sites ($15/night) are open year-round for tents and RVs, most of them on the river. A boat ramp, flush toilets, and piped water are on site.

ACCOMMODATIONS

"Cottage" is a word often used to describe accommodations between Yachats and Waldport. It may be a duplex or self-contained cabin, generally by a beach.

The **Terry-a-While Motel** (7160 S.W. U.S. 101, 541/563-3377, www.terry-a-while.com, doubles $50–110) has well-appointed rooms that range in style, from modern to vintage, and size (the newer fourplex is ideal for families).

The vintage **Cape Cod Cottages** (4150 S.W. U.S. 101, 541/563-2106, www.dream water.com, doubles $70–100.) offer one- and two-bedroom oceanfront units with complete kitchens, cozy fireplaces, cable television, spectacular views and private decks. Three night minimum stay in summer.

At the **Howard Johnson Inn Waldport** (902 N.W. Bayshore Dr., 541/563-7700 or 877/327-6500, doubles from $81) half of the 84 rooms enjoy sweeping views of the bay, bridge, and town, and all are equipped with either one or two queen beds and the usual amenities. There's also a dining room and cocktail lounge, with occasional entertainment, and a fitness room.

The historic **Cliff House** (1450 Adahi Rd., 541/563-2506, www.cliffhouseoregon.com, doubles $110–225) may appear to be rustic, but in fact this is a beautifully restored historic home, and the location can't be beat to set a romantic mood. Four rooms, some with whirlpools, are decorated with antiques; even the woodstoves are period. (No pets allowed, and children are best left home with grandma or the sitter.)

FOOD

Grand Central Pizza (245 S.W. Arrow, 541/563-3232, lunch and dinner daily, main courses $7–14) is a favorite with the locals, across the street from the 76 gas station—you can't miss it. *Oregon Coast* magazine

voted this the best pie on the coast. In addition to spaghetti dinners, lasagna, and pizza, the homemade garlic rolls, selection of microbrews, fish-n-chips, and grinder sandwiches are also noteworthy.

For a hearty breakfast and other meal specials served in a sport-lovers' atmosphere replete with big-screen TV, the **Flounder Inn Tavern** (U.S. 101, 541/563-2266, three meals daily, main courses $7–15) offers customers lots of pub grub choices, including fish-n-chips and a popular roasted chicken dinner.

Yuzen (U.S. 101, Seal Rock, 541/563-4766, lunch and dinner Tues.–Sun., main courses $8–16), five miles north of Waldport, is a Japanese restaurant with an oddly Bavarian facade. In addition to sushi and miso soup, less well-known fare such as fish noodle soup, *yuza* (rock shrimp with vegetables in a dumpling), and *syo-yaki* (a small whole fish roast in a salt crust) leave room for new discoveries. *Shabu shabu,* paper-thin beef, fresh vegetables, and tofu simmered in a pot and served with three gourmet sauces, is another favorite.

INFORMATION

The Walport Chamber of Commerce operates the **visitors center** (P.O. Box 669, Waldport 97394, 541/563-2133, www.waldport-chamber.com) in the Alsea Bay Bridge Historical Interpretive Center, just south of the river. Open 9 A.M.–5 P.M. daily in summer, 9 A.M.–4 P.M. Tuesday–Saturday the rest of the year.

The **Siuslaw National Forest-Waldport Ranger Station** (1094 S.W. U.S. 101, Waldport 97394, 541/563-3211), can provide information on area camping and hiking, including the trails in the Drift Creek Wilderness.

GETTING THERE

The Lincoln County buses run four times a day, Monday–Saturday, between Yachats and Newport.

NORTHERN OREGON COAST

Yachats and Cape Perpetua

Yachats (pronounced "YAH-hots") is derived from an Alsea word meaning "dark waters at the foot of the mountain." The phrase aptly describes the location of this picturesque resort village of 635 people, clustered on the hillsides and coastal shelf beside the Yachats River mouth in the shadow of Cape Perpetua. Word of mouth has helped to spread the popularity of Yachats as a place for a quiet getaway and a base for enjoying the 2,700-acre Cape Perpetua Scenic Area and nearby beaches.

SIGHTS
◖ Cape Perpetua

The most notable sight near Yachats, indeed on the whole central coast, is the view from 803-foot-high Cape Perpetua. The name derives from Captain Cook's sighting of the promontory on March 7, 1778, St. Perpetua's Day. It's too bad the British explorer didn't make landfall here to enjoy one of the world's preeminent coastal panoramas. Oregon's highest paved public road this close to the shoreline affords 150 miles of north-to-south visibility from the top of the headland. On a clear day, you can also see 39 miles out to sea.

Prior to hiking the 23 miles of foot trails or driving to the top of the cape, stop off at the **Cape Perpetua Visitor Center** (541/547-3289), three miles south of Yachats on the east side of the highway. A picture window framing a bird's-eye view of rockbound coast, along with exhibits on forestry and marine life, begin your introduction to the region. Cataclysms such as the forest fire of 1846, the monsoons and 138 mph winds unleashed by the 1962 Columbus Day Storm, and 1964 Hurricane Frieda are artfully explained by exhibits. An excellent 15-minute film about Oregon's intertidal biome will also hold your interest.

Personnel at the desk have maps and pamphlets about such trails as Cook's Ridge, Riggin' Slinger, and Giant Spruce, as well as directions for the auto tour to the summit. In addition, they can point the way to tidepools

and berry patches. Two naturalist-guided hikes a day are offered to coastal rainforest and tidepools. The center is open 9 A.M.–5 P.M. early May–October, and opens during peak whale-watching weeks from Christmas to New Year's and in late March. Admission is $5 per car. The Pacific Coast Passport, Northwest Forest Pass, and Golden Passports are honored here.

The awe-inspiring 1.5 mile **Saint Perpetua Trail** (from the visitors center) to the cape's summit is of moderate difficulty, gaining 600 feet in elevation. En route, placards explain the role of wind, erosion, and fire in forest succession in this mixed-conifer ecosystem.

At the crest of Cape Perpetua the **Trail of the Whispering Spruce** begins, a 0.25-mile loop through the grounds of a former World War II Coast Guard lookout built by the Civilian Conservation Corps in 1933. The southern views from the crest take in the highway and headlands as far as Coos Bay. Halfway along the path, you'll come to a WPA-built rock hut called the West Shelter that makes a lofty perch for whale-watching, one of the best spots on the entire coast. Beyond this ridge-top aerie the curtain of trees parts to reveal fantastic views of the shoreline between Yachats and Cape Foulweather.

The two-mile drive up the cape (where the Whispering Spruce Trailhead can be accessed) is complicated by a not-so-prominent sign on U.S. 101 (Mile Marker 188.5) indicating the turnoff onto Forest Service Road 55. To begin your auto ascent, drive 100 yards north on U.S. 101 from the visitors center and look for the steep winding spur road on the right. As you climb, you'll notice large Sitka spruce trees abutting the road. Halfway up, you'll come to a Y in the road. Take a hard left and follow the road another mile to the top of Cape Perpetua. If you miss the left turn and go straight ahead, you'll soon find yourself on a 22-mile loop through the Coast Range to Yachats. Along the way, 18 placards annotate forest ecology. Another hike from the visitors center goes down to a geological blowhole (called a "spouting horn"), where sea water is funneled between rocks and explodes into spray. This is the **Captain Cook Trail,** which goes six miles through a dense wind-carved forest and the remains of an old CCC camp under U.S. 101 to an ancient lava deposit on the shore. Given enough wave action, water bubbles up through fissures in the basalt. There are also Native American shell middens built up 300–2,000 years ago in the area.

Just north of the turnoff for the top of Cape Perpetua (Forest Service Road 55) and U.S. 101 is the turnout for **Devil's Churn,** on the west side of the highway. Here, the tides have cut a deep fissure in a basalt embankment on the shore. You can observe the action from a vertigo-inducing overlook high above, or take the easy, switchbacking trail down to the water's edge. While watching the white-water torrents in this foaming cistern, beware of "sneaker waves," particularly if you venture beyond the boundaries of the **Trail of the Restless Waters.** The highlights here are the spouting horns and acres of tidepools. All along this stretch of the coast, many trees appear to be leaning away from the ocean as if bent by storms. This illusion is caused by salt-laden westerlies drying out and killing the buds on the exposed side of the tree, leaving growth only on the leeward branches.

A mile south, **Neptune State Park** has a beautiful beach and is near the 9,300-acre **Cummin's Creek Wilderness** east of U.S. 101. Just north of Neptune Park, Forest Service Road 1050 leads east to the Cummins Creek Trailhead. A half-mile south, gravelly Forest Service Road 1051 can take you to a point where a moderately difficult 2.5-mile hike leads to Cummin's Ridge Trailhead. This pathway has some of the last remaining coastal old-growth Sitka spruce stands. Get maps and detailed directions for these and other area trails at the Cape Perpetua Visitor Center.

Close by, there's a chance to explore tidepools and sometimes observe harbor seals at **Strawberry Hill.** Scenic shorelines can also be found in the next few miles farther south at **Stonesfield Beach State Recreation Site** and

Muriel O. Ponsler State Scenic Viewpoint, before you arrive at Carl G. Washburne Memorial State Park (see *Florence and Vicinity,* in the *Southern Oregon Coast* chapter).

State Parks, Coastal Waysides

In this part of the coast, state parks and viewpoints abound with attractions. There's so much to see here that keeping your eyes on the road in this heavily traveled section is a challenge.

A mile north of town, **Smelt Sands State Recreation Site** gives access to tidepools and the 0.75-mile 804 Trail, which follows the rocky shore to a broad, sandy beach to the north. In Yachats, turn west onto 2nd Street to loop around wave-battered **Yachats State Recreation Area,** overlooking Yachats Bay. The route heads north along the ocean, where it becomes Marine Drive. After going through a residential community, it eventually takes an easterly turn to reconnect with U.S. 101.

On the south bank of the Yachats River is a short but beautiful beach loop off U.S. 101 (going south, look for the sign that says "Beach Access"). The road runs between the landscaped grounds of beach houses and resorts on one side and the foamy sea on the other. A wide beach, tidepools, and blowholes on the bank by the river's mouth are a special treat.

SPORTS AND RECREATION
Camping

Set along Cape Creek in the Cape Perpetua Scenic Area, the Forest Service's **Cape Perpetua Campground** (reservations 877/444-6777 or www.reserveusa.com) has 38 sites for tent and trailers or motor homes up to 22 feet long. Picnic tables and fire grills are provided. Flush toilets, piped water, and sanitary services are available. The $20 fee applies May–October, when they're open. Reservations are necessary for groups. The Forest Service rangers put on slide-illustrated campfire talks here and at Tillicum Beach during summer months.

EVENTS

Spring brings two art and crafts festivals to the Yachats Commons (U.S. 101 and W. 4th St.):

In late March, the chamber-sponsored **Original Yachats Arts and Crafts Fair** (541/547-3530 or 800/929-0477) exhibits the work of some 75 Pacific Northwest artists and artisans. Admission is free. If you miss that one, come back in late May for **Crafts on the Coast** (541/547-4738 or 541/547-4664).

During the Yachats **Smelt Fry,** held the second Saturday of July, up to 750 pounds of this sardinelike fish are served on the grounds of Yachats Commons on 4th Street (just follow the signs to this refurbished schoolhouse). Yachats used to be one of the few places in the world blessed with a run of oceangoing smelt but they have declined drastically due to changing ocean conditions. Nonetheless, the town's traditional "welcome to summer" event has continued thanks to imported Northern California smelt, which augment the local catch. For $8 you get all the deep-fried, delicately flavored smelt (or a sausage plate for $5) you can eat ($3 for children 12 and younger) with side dishes and a beverage. What you're really paying for is a classic small-town festival where you get to rub elbows with a spirited community. More info is available from the chamber of commerce.

The same weekend, the **Yachats Music Festival** takes place several blocks north at the Presbyterian Church (360 W. 7th St., 541/547-3141 or 510/601-6184). Admission is $15 for each performance. The line-up features classical virtuosi and vocalists from the San Francisco Bay Area for evening concerts and a Sunday matinee performance.

A relatively new but popular event here is the **Yachats Village Mushroom Fest** (541/547-3530 or 800/929-0477), held the third weekend in October. Native mushrooms abound in the temperate rainforests of the Cape Perpetua region, and fall is the season to harvest them. The Yachats event was started by Chef John Ullman, who was inspired by similar festivals in Italy. Activities over the weekend include the Friday-night Yachats Rainforest Fungi Feast, mushroom-cooking demonstrations, guided mushroom walks at Cape Perpetua Visitors Center, and the last farmers market of the season.

ACCOMMODATIONS

If you're planning a long stay, check out **Yachats Village Rentals** (541/547-3501, www.97498.com), which offers a varied stable of vacation homes ($110–215) for rent.

At the beginning of the beach loop (on the south bank of the Yachats River and west of U.S. 101) are the **Shamrock Lodgettes** (105 U.S. 101 S., 541/547-3312 or 800/845-5028, www.shamrocklodgettes.com, cabins $79–179, motel and one-bedroom units $79–149). Shamrock's beautiful parklike landscape frames a selection of individual log cabins plus redwood motel rooms and one and two-bedroom units. Stone fireplaces, in-room movies, and ocean or bay views all contribute to a relaxed get-away-from-it-all feeling. The sauna and whirlpool tub on the premises also enhance the "mellowing-out" process. The on-site health spa features a redwood hot tub and sauna. Ask about midwinter specials. Kids okay; pets are allowed in some units.

A short drive farther south, the **Yachats Inn** (331 U.S. 101, 541/547-3456 or 888/270-3456, www.yachatsinn.com, doubles from $80) is a great place for group retreats or families, with spacious units that are more like well-furnished apartments, all just steps from the beach. The landscaped grounds include an indoor pool, sauna, and teahouse (for large groups, meetings or parties). There are a number of different room types available, all nicely furnished and maintained; check the website for details.

For those looking for a budget place close to the center of town, try **Rock Park Cottages** (431 W. 2nd, 541/547-3214 or 541/343-4382, www.trillian.com/rockpark, doubles fror $65), adjacent to Yachats State Recreation Area. Consisting of five rustic cottages arranged around a courtyard, Rock Park has to be considered one of the better bargains on the coast. The kitchens are well equipped and the vintage cottages couldn't be better located.

The **Dublin House Motel** (U.S. 101 and 7th St., 866/922-4287, www.dublinhouse motel.com, doubles from $69) offers large guest rooms and ocean views, each with microwaves, refrigerators, coffeemakers, and cable

TV; some kitchen units are also available. The indoor heated pool is especially nice in the winter months.

A little north of the town center, the imposing **Adobe Resort** (155 U.S. 101 N., 541/547-3141 or 800/522-3623, doubles from $104) overlooks Smelt Sands Beach. If you appreciate all services in one compound, from dining room to gift shop, the Adobe gets the nod. All units have refrigerators, microwaves, satellite TV and DVD players, and phone with voicemail. Pets accepted in some rooms. Brand-new two-bedroom Jacuzzi suites have 1,400 square feet and have all the comforts of a small home.

A mile north of Yachats, above a thrust of wave-pounded tide pools, **Overleaf Lodge,** (280 Overleaf Lodge Ln., 541/547-4880 or 800/338-0507, www.overleaflodge.com, doubles from $159) offers the newest and nicest rooms in the Yachats area. Most rooms have balconies, Jacuzzi tubs, and fireplaces, and all have fantastic views. Rates include a breakfast buffet, plus access to an indoor pool and fitness area. New in 2007 is a 3,000-square-foot spa with treatment rooms, steam rooms and saunas, plus oceanview hot tubs. Adjacent to the lodge are six newly built cottages (actually small homes) tucked into the forest. Ranging from two- to four bedrooms, these charming units, designed with Craftsman-style decor, have full kitchens and everything that a family or small group will need for a great beach vacation.

The aptly named **SeeVue** (95590 U.S. 101, 541/547-3227, www.seevue.com, doubles from $75) has long been a favorite window on the Pacific for storm- and whale-watchers. This 10-room complex thrives today thanks to an eminently affordable combination of comfort and location, just six miles south of Yachats and three miles south of Cape Perpetua. Assuming you can pull yourself away from watching the waves, there's also prime beachcombing and wildlife-viewing close by. All units here boast Pacific perspectives and the decor follows an individual theme that's funky and charming in equal measures. There are nonsmoking rooms as well as some housekeeping units. Pets allowed.

For the ultimate in seclusion, the **Oregon House** (94288 U.S. 101, 541/547-3329, www.oregonhouse.com, doubles from $95), eight miles south of Yachats, overlooks the Pacific from a bluff and offers guests a reflective phone-free, TV-less atmosphere. Twelve apartments (housed in five different buildings, including a carriage house and gate house) with baths and kitchens, some with fireplaces and whirlpool tubs, are perfect for groups. In fact, they specialize in groups, but also rent the apartments to individuals. No pets; quiet children okay. Stroll the three acres of gardens or head down the private path to the beach.

Bed-and-Breakfasts

Some outstanding bed-and-breakfasts south of Yachats rate a mention for those willing to spend a little more for comfort, location, and privacy. Look for this inn seven miles south of Yachats near Mile Marker 171 at Ten Mile Creek.

Perched above the pounding surf, the **Sea Quest Inn** (95354 U.S. 101, 541/547-3782 or 800/341-4878, www.seaq.com, doubles from $170) is an antique-filled but contemporary inn of cedar and glass, with private entrances and a location adjacent to Ten Mile Creek. The "Tis Sweete" is a 1,000-square-foot suite with a king-size canopy bed, a woodburning fireplace, 25-foot-high windows, and wraparound deck all located on a private wing ($375/night, two people). From the fine cognac and wines in the evening, the fruit, scones, and popcorn in the commons, to the chocolates and bottled water in your room, the inn is well stocked with quality goodies catering to your whim and pleasure. Breakfasts are delicacy-laden presentations superior to many hotel dining rooms. The wraparound deck affords superlative views of the beach, and telescopes and binoculars are always on hand for spotting whales and other marine life. Many guests return each year, so be sure to book well in advance. Not appropriate for pets or children under 12 years of age.

FOOD

Right off U.S. 101 is **La Serre** (2nd and Beach, 541/547-3420, dinner Wed.–Mon., main courses $12–22), a bright skylit restaurant with lots of plants (La Serre means "the greenhouse") that creates a relaxing setting for well-prepared Northwest cuisine. The salmon, crabcakes, oven-roasted marinated free-range chicken, Manhattan clam chowder, bouillabaisse, and clam-puffs appetizer are all welcome choices after a day of hiking or exploring tidepools. For dessert, try the flourless chocolate cake.

On a bluff overlooking Smelt Sands Beach is the glass-enclosed **Adobe Resort** (1555 U.S. 101, 541/547-3141, three meals daily). Two side-by-side semicircular dining rooms, with windows on the crashing surf, are a great place to start the day for breakfast or end it with a romantic evening repast, with such favorites as pan-fried oysters, salmon, and steaks. Ask about the loft, where elevated coastal views provide photo-ops; this is the perfect place to nurse a drink. A Sunday champagne brunch is served 9 A.M.–1 P.M.

The carefully restored but fun-loving **(** **Drift Inn Pub** (U.S. 101, 541/457-4477, lunch and dinner daily) offers seafood dishes, crunchy salads, fish-n-chips, and other well-prepared pub grub in a casual atmosphere.

There's often really good live music here, making this a lively spot whether you're here to eat or to quaff a pint or two.

INFORMATION

The **Yachats Area Chamber of Commerce** (241 U.S. 101, P.O. Box 728, Yachats 97498, 541/547-3530 or 800/929-0477, www.yachats .org) has a central location on the highway (next to Clark's Market) and a loquacious staff. Ask them about fishing, rockhounding, bird-watching, and beachcombing in the area. Open 10 A.M.–4 P.M. daily March–September, Thursday–Sunday the rest of the year.

The **Central Oregon Coast Association** (541/265-2064 or 800/767-2064, www.coast visitor.com) maintains a useful website with details on Yachats and the rest of coastal Lincoln County.

GETTING THERE

The bus stop is also in the parking lot of the Clark's Market complex (U.S. 101 and W. 2nd). Here you can catch **Lincoln County Transit** buses (541/265-4900), which run four times a day, Monday–Saturday, between Yachats and Newport, with a link to Lincoln City.

SOUTHERN OREGON COAST

Along the southern Oregon coast, the towns are mostly small and scattered, and the beaches are spectacular. Amazingly, as you drive down U.S. 101, these spectacular beaches just keep coming. And, with more than 30 state parks along this stretch of road, beach access is excellent.

For the most part, travelers come here for the beaches, the fishing, and/or the hiking, and don't expect opulence. However, since the arrival of the luxurious Bandon Dunes Golf Resort, it's become easier to find good restaurants and chic accommodations, if campgrounds and clam chowder don't float your boat.

PLANNING YOUR TIME

At the northern end of the region, **Florence** is known for its charming (but not too faked-up) Old Town. South of Florence, the **Oregon Dunes National Recreation Area** is home to massive sand dunes, which can be explored either on foot or in a dune buggy. These 32,000 acres of shimmering white dunes are the largest oceanfront collection in North America and the highest in the world. Some hills top out at over 500 feet high. Oregon's Sahara is located along a 40-mile stretch between Coos Bay and Florence. Buffeted by winds, the dunes are continually on the move; in some places, highways are in danger of being engulfed by the shifting sands.

Coos Bay is the only real city along the southern coast and, like Tillamook to the north, it's a gateway to some spectacular areas, but pretty workaday itself. Be sure to head west and south from town to explore the coastal estuary at **South Slough National Estuarine Research Reserve,** south of Coos Bay.

© JUDY JEWELL

HIGHLIGHTS

◖ **Sea Lion Caves:** Here you'll take an elevator ride down to the cave at cliff's bottom to get a close look at the Steller sea lion rookery. During the spring and summer, the animals are outside, and you can get a good look from the roadside (page 307).

◖ **South Slough Estuarine Research Reserve:** Here, where freshwater meets salt, is a nutrient-rich environment that supports many wildlife species. Hike or paddle; either way, pay attention to the tides (page 320).

◖ **Bandon Dunes Golf Resort:** There are actually three golf courses here now, each expertly designed in a setting that's strikingly gorgeous, even for the Oregon coast (page 330).

◖ **Humbug Mountain:** The three-mile trail to the top of Humbug Mountain passes a spectacular array of native plants. Even if the promised mountaintop view is shrouded in fog, it's a great hike (page 333).

◖ **Rogue River Jet-Boat Cruise:** Even die-hard paddlers won't regret succumbing to a jet-boats tour up the Rogue River. Boaters often get to see ospreys and eagles fishing along this stretch of river (page 337).

◖ **Samuel H. Boardman State Scenic Corridor:** North of Brookings, the roadbed winds hundreds of feet above the surf, allowing you to peer down at one of the most dramatic meetings of rock and tide in the world. Trails lead down to secluded, often nearly deserted, beaches (page 345).

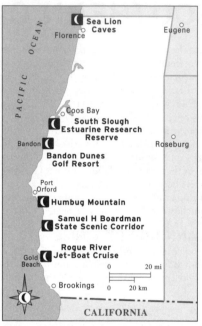

LOOK FOR ◖ TO FIND RECOMMENDED SIGHTS, ACTIVITIES, DINING, AND LODGING.

Bandon Marsh National Wildlife Refuge protects the largest remaining tract of salt marsh within the Coquille River estuary. Major habitats include undisturbed saltmarsh, mudflat, and Sitka spruce and alder riparian communities, which provide resting and feeding areas for migratory waterfowl, shore and wading birds, and raptors.

Although, Bandon is now best known for its world-class **Bandon Dunes Golf Resort,** but there's also a real community here. Bandon's beachfront, along with the Coos Bay sand spit, the beaches on the western side of Humbug Mountain, and the isolated shorelines of Boardman State Park are choice beachcombing spots.

Port Orford is often overlooked, but it's one of our favorite spots, with great ocean vistas from town, and lots of hiking at nearby Humbug Mountain. It also doesn't hurt that there's good eating here.

Jet-boat tours start in Gold Beach and head up the Rogue River, offering those with just a morning to spare the chance to explore this lush river. Between Gold Beach and Brookings, save some serious time to explore beaches sequestered between steep cliffs and pounding surf at the 11-mile-long Boardman State Park.

Florence and Vicinity

"Location, location, and location." This tenet of business success also explains the growing appeal of Florence (pop. 8,100) for retirees and vacationers. Many people who could afford to live almost anywhere choose to do so here between the Oregon Dunes National Recreation Area and some of the most beautiful headlands on U.S. 101. The fact that Florence is also situated halfway up Oregon's coastal route and little more than an hour's drive from shopping and culture in Eugene has made it a major beachhead of vacation-home development in the region.

Florence began shortly after the California gold rush of 1849 put a premium on the lumber and produce shipped out via the Siuslaw River estuary here. Several decades later, the town's name was inspired by a remnant from a French shipwreck that floated ashore, bearing the ship's name, *Florence*. The townspeople either recognized an omen when they saw it or just figured they couldn't come up with anything better.

SIGHTS

If first and last impressions are enduring, Florence is truly blessed. Just before you enter city limits from the north, U.S. 101 climbs to dizzying heights above the ocean. As you leave the city to the south, a graceful bridge over the Siuslaw ushers you away.

The Siuslaw River Bridge is perhaps the most impressive of Conde McCullough's WPA-built spans. The Egyptian obelisks and art deco styling characteristic of other McCullough designs are complemented by the views to the west of the coruscating sand dunes. To the east, the riverside panorama of Florence's Old Town beckons further investigation.

Old Town itself is a tasteful restoration, with all manner of shops and restaurants and an inviting boardwalk along the river. The relative

© JUDY JEWELL

The Heceta Head Lighthouse is one of the most photographed sites in Oregon.

absence of car traffic is conducive to a pleasant walk after lunch there. Easy access to beach and dunes is offered by South Jetty Road just south of the Siuslaw River Bridge.

Siuslaw Pioneer Museum

To fill yourself in on the early history of Florence and the Siuslaw River valley, and get some notion of Native American and pioneer life, spend an hour or so at the Siuslaw Pioneer Museum (85294 U.S. 101, Florence, 541/997-7884, noon– 4 P.M. Tues.–Sun. year-round, $3 adults). You'll find it on the south side of the Siuslaw River on the west side of the highway in a converted church. Along with exhibits on early logging and farming, read an account of how the U.S. government double-crossed the Siuslaw tribespeople, who sold their land to the feds and never received the promised recompense.

Heceta Head State Scenic Viewpoint and Devil's Elbow

About 11 miles north of Florence, Heceta Head State Scenic Viewpoint is located in a lovely cove at the mouth of Cape Creek, at the base of thousand-foot-high Heceta Head. From here you can get a good look at the graceful arc of Conde McCullough's Cape Creek Bridge, spanning the chasm more than 200 feet above you. Across the cove, **Heceta Head Lighthouse** (541/547-3416, tours 11 A.M.–5 P.M. daily May–Sept., 11 A.M.–3 P.M. daily Mar., Apr., and Oct., $3 day-use fee), completed in 1894, beams the strongest light on the Oregon coast, from a shelf 205 feet up the rocky headland. An easy 0.5-mile trail leads up from the park's picnic and parking area to the tower. A little below the lighthouse is **Heceta House,** where the lighthouse keepers used to live. Today, it's a B&B.

Heceta Head is said to be the most photographed lighthouse in the country; that may be difficult to verify, but it's impossible to quibble with the magnificent sight of the gleaming white tower and outbuildings on the headland, particularly when viewed from a set of highway pullouts just south of the bridge. The vistas from the lighthouse and network of trails on the headland are no less dramatic: see murres,

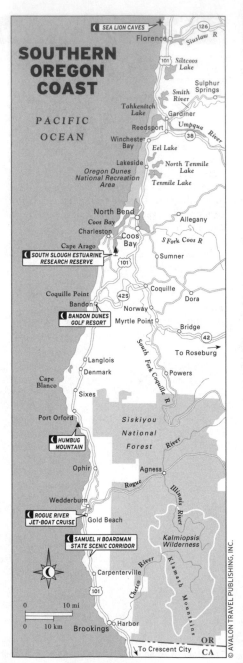

© AVALON TRAVEL PUBLISHING, INC.

tufted puffins, and other seabirds as well as sea lions on the rock islands below, bald eagles soaring overhead, and, in spring, northbound female gray whales and their calves as they pass close to shore. A trail leading to the north side of Heceta Head offers views to Cape Perpetua, 10 miles to the north.

Just south of Heceta Head is a trail down to the beach at adjoining **Devil's Elbow State Park.** Be conscious of tides here if you climb along the rocks adjoining the beach.

◖ Sea Lion Caves

Ten miles north of Florence, you can descend into the world's largest sea cave to observe the only mainland rookery of Steller sea lions (*Eumetopias jubatus*) in the Lower 48. Sea Lion Caves (91560 U.S. 101, 541/547-3111, 9 A.M.–7 P.M. daily summer, 9 A.M.–4 P.M. daily winter, closed Christmas, $8 adults, $4.50 ages 6–15, free for five and under) is home to a herd that averages 200 individuals, though the numbers change from season to season. These animals occupy the cave during the fall

and winter, which are thus the prime visitation times. The Steller sea lions you'll see at those times are cows, yearlings, and immature bulls. In spring and summer, they breed and raise their young on the rock ledges just outside the cave. In addition, California sea lions (*Zalophus californianus*), common all along the Pacific coast, are found at Sea Lion Caves from late fall to early spring.

Enter Sea Lion Caves through the gift shop on U.S. 101. A steep downhill walk reveals stunning perspectives of the coastal cliffs as well as several kinds of gulls and cormorants that nest here. The final 208 feet of the descent is via an elevator. After your eyes adjust to the cave's gloomy subterranean light, you'll see the sea lions on the rock shelves amid the surging water. Flash photography is forbidden, so learn to adjust the settings on your camera if you wish to take pictures inside. You have a better chance of seeing these animals inside during fall and winter. A stairway here leads up to a view of Heceta Head Lighthouse through an opening in the cave.

© BILL MCRAE

For a close-up view of sea lions, ride the elevator down to Sea Lion Caves.

Steller sea lions were referred to as *lobos marinos* (sea wolves) in early Spanish mariners' accounts of their 16th-century West Coast voyages, and their doglike yelps might explain why. You'll notice several shades of color in the herd, which has to do with the progressive lightening of their coats with age. Males sometimes weigh over a ton and dominate the scene here with macho posturings to scare off rivals for harems of as many as two dozen cows. Their protection as an endangered species enrages many fishermen, who claim that the sea lions take a significant bite out of fishing revenues by preying on salmon. In any case, the sight of these huge sea mammals close-up in the cavernous enclaves of their natural habitat should not be missed... despite an odor that can be likened to sweat-soaked sneakers.

If you can't observe the animals to your satisfaction in the cave, go 0.25 mile north of the concession entrance to the "rockwork" turnout, where the herd sometimes populates the rocky ledges several hundred feet below. It's also a good place to snap a shot of the picturesque Heceta Head Lighthouse across the cove to the north from the turnout.

© BILL MCRAE

Darlingtonia, a carnivorous plant, thrives at a state wayside outside Florence.

Darlingtonia Botanical Wayside

Three miles north of Florence, in an area noted for dune access and freshwater lakes, is the Darlingtonia Wayside. In a sylvan grove of spruce and alder are a series of wooden platforms that guide you through a bog where carnivorous *Darlingtonia californica* plants thrive. Shaped like a serpent head, the Darlingtonia is variously referred to as the cobra orchid, cobra lily, or pitcher plant. The sweet smell the plant produces invites insects to crawl through an opening into a chamber.

Inside, thin transparent "windows" allow light to shine inside the chamber, confusing the bug as to where the exit is. As the insect crawls around in search of an escape, downward-pointing hairs within the enclosure inhibit its movement to freedom. Eventually, the weary bug falls to the bottom of the stem, where it is digested. The plant needs the nutrients from the trapped insects to compensate for the lack of sustenance supplied by its small root system. If you still have an appetite after witnessing this carnage, you might want to enjoy lunch at one of the shaded picnic tables here.

Jessie M. Honeyman Memorial State Park

Honeyman State Park ($3 day use fee), three miles south of Florence, has a spectacular dunescape and then some. Come here in May when the rhododendrons bloom along the short, sinuous road heading to the parking lot. A short walk west of the lot brings you to a 150-foot-high dune overlooking Cleawox Lake. From the top of this dune, look westward across the expanse of sand, marsh, and remnants of forest at the blue Pacific, some two miles away. For details on camping at this huge state park, see *Camping* later in this section.

RECREATION
Horseback Riding

Riding across the dunes into the sunset on a trusty steed sounds like a fantasy, but you can do it, thanks to **C&M Stables** (90241 U.S. 101, Florence, 541/997-7540). Rates range $35–55 per person for trips of 1–2 hours (with discounts for larger parties). The stables are open daily. With beach rides, dune trail excursions, and sunset trips, there's something for everybody. Call for specific times and reservations.

Dune Rides

Another option for those who fear to tread is **Sand Dunes Frontier** (83960 U.S. 101, Florence, 541/997-3544). This company rents vehicles for travel in specially designated areas within the Dunes NRA. Odysseys, small one-person dune buggies, go for $45 per hour and a $100 deposit. You must be strapped in, with a helmet, stay within the marked territory, and be especially careful going uphill. If you lose power on an incline, it's possible to roll over when turning around to go back down. The 20-person dune buggy rides cost $12 for adults, $10 for children 4–11 years old. Protective goggles are provided, along with a driver. Go in the morning when the sand tends to blow around less.

Sandboarding

Dude, it's a natural! Wax up a board, strap it onto your bare feet, and carve your way down the dunes. Rent a board and try out the rails and jumps at **Sand Master Park** (87541 U.S. 101, 541/997-6006, www.sandmasterpark. com, 9 A.M.–7 P.M. daily June–Aug., 10 A.M.– 5 P.M. Thurs.–Tues., Sept.–May, board rentals from $16 includes admission).

Siltcoos Lake

Oregon's largest coastal lake, 3,100-acre Siltcoos Lake offers excellent fishing and other recreation six miles south of Florence. Rainbows are stocked in the spring, and steelhead, salmon (closed to coho fishing), and sea-run cutthroat trout move from the ocean into the lake via the short Siltcoos River in late summer and fall. But the real excitement here is the fishing for warmwater species, which is some of the best in the Northwest. Bluegill, crappie, yellow perch, and brown bullhead action

is good through the summer, while fishing for largemouth bass can be good year-round. Access points include several public and private boat ramps on the lake, as well as a wheelchair-accessible fishing pier at Westlake Resort.

In addition, kayakers and canoeists can explore the **Siltcoos River** between the lake and the sea. Meandering two miles through dunes, forest, and estuary, the Siltcoos is a gentle paddle with no white water or rapids, though there is a small dam midway that must be portaged. Local wildlife includes mink, raccoons, otters, beaver, and even bears. In the estuary, sea lions and harbor seals are common.

For more information on the Siltcoos area, contact the **Oregon Dunes National Recreation Area Visitor Center** (541/271-3611) in Reedsport.

SPORTS AND RECREATION
Camping and Hiking

Camping here offers recreational opportunities comparable to those at the Oregon Dunes NRA, with more varied scenery.

Carl G. Washburne Memorial State Park (93111 U.S. 101 N., Florence, 541/547-3416 for information, 800/452-5687 for reservations) is popular with Oregonians due to its proximity to beaches, tidepools, Sea Lion Caves, and elk. The seven walk-in tent sites and 58 RV sites have such modern conveniences as showers, a laundry, electricity, and piped water. They also have two yurts, which can also be reserved. It's 14 miles north of Florence on U.S. 101 (several miles past Sea Lion Caves), then one mile west on a park road. The fee is $17–22, $4 for hiker and biker spaces, and it's open all year.

In addition, there are nearby forest pathways such as the **Hobbit Trail,** named after the furry-footed characters in J. R. R. Tolkien's works. You'll probably feel like a hobbit when peering up at the high walls woven of roots, peat, and sand that loom above the trail cut deep into the forest floor here. The path winds through dense forest thickets of pine, fir, and rhododendrons down to the beach. Look for the turnout on the right side of the road just over the hill north of the Heceta Head curves on U.S. 101.

Ask the park personnel about this and China Creek Trail. Yet another starts trail right near the Hobbit Trail and runs three-quarters of a mile uphill to the Heceta Head Lighthouse.

Three miles south of Florence's McCullough Bridge and on both sides of U.S. 101 is **Honeyman State Park** (84505 U.S. 101 S., 541/997-3641, reservations 800/452-5687). This exceedingly popular campground gets very crowded in the summer—reservations are a must—but it empties out enough during spring and autumn to make a stay here worthwhile. There are 240 tent sites with the basics, a large number of RV spaces with all the amenities, and many hiker/biker spots as well (more than 400 sites in total). Rates are $13–22 depending on the season and type of site. Ask about canoe rentals here to savor the serenity of Cleawox Lake. Fishing, swimming, hiking, and dune buggies are available nearby. In spring, pink rhodies line the highway and park roads. Advance reservations are accepted Memorial Day–Labor Day.

An ideal place to escape from the summertime coastal crowds is the **North Fork of the Siuslaw** campground. Chances are you'll see mostly locals here—if anybody. From Florence follow Route 126 about 15 miles to Mapleton and the junction with Route 36. The latter road takes you 13 miles to County Route 5070. Then it's a short drive to the riverside campsite (or you can drive the North Fork Siuslaw River Road from Florence for 14.5 miles). The fee is $4 July–early September. Picnic tables, fire pits, and crawdads are other reasons to come. Contact the Siuslaw National Forest Ranger Station (4480 U.S. 101 N., Florence, 541/902-8526, www.fs.fed.us/r6/siuslaw/) for more information.

Close by is the **Pawn Old Growth Trail,** a 0.5-mile pathway through several-hundred-year-old 100-inch-in-diameter, 275-feet-tall Douglas fir and hemlock. The trailhead, located at the confluence of the North Fork of the Siuslaw and Taylor's Creek, is a good place to see salmon spawning in the fall and observe water ouzels (also called "dippers"). It follows the creek and offers interpretive placards along the way. At one point in the trail visitors walk through fallen Douglas fir logs 260 inches in diameter. Placards explain the science of tree rings. From Florence, take Route 126 one mile to Forest Road 5070, then go 12 miles to Forest Road 5084; stay right and go five miles to the trailhead.

Nearby Route 36 makes an interesting access road back to the Willamette Valley if you're not in a hurry. Its circuitous route passes through Deadwood and ends up in the Junction City area.

Golf

Ocean Dunes Golf Links (3345 Munsel Lake Rd., 541/997-3232) lets you tee off with sand dunes (some more than 60 feet tall) as a backdrop. The manicured 18-hole course has a driving range, a full pro shop, and equipment rentals on-site. For the ultimate in golfing by the dunes, however, try **Sandpines Golf Course** (1050 35th St., 541/997-1940), voted *Golf Digest*'s number-one new public course in 1993. To get there, go west off U.S. 101 on 35th Street. In May and June rhododendrons line this drive, which heads into dune country as you move toward the sea. Follow the signs until you see a water tower not far from the pro shop. Sandpines' layout features fairways lined with Douglas fir and beach grass on gently undulating terrain. Coastal winds that kick up in the morning can figure prominently in your shot selection. Summertime green fees are $80 weekdays, $95 weekends, carts $30.

ENTERTAINMENT AND EVENTS

Art shows, classical concerts by acclaimed virtuosi (including performances as part of the Ernest Bloch Music Festival—see Newport *Entertainment and Events,* in the *Northern Oregon Coast* chapter), ballet, theater, and community events can be enjoyed within the warm, welcoming, and spacious **Florence Events Center** (715 Quince St., 541/997-1994 or 888/968-4086, www.eventcenter.org). A gallery on-site displays the works of local artists.

During the third weekend of May, Florence

celebrates the **Rhododendron Festival,** coinciding with the bloom of these flowers that proliferate in the area. It's a tradition that goes back to 1908, when the festival was started as a way to draw attention and commerce to the area. A parade, a carnival, a flower show, a 5K and 10K"Rhody Run," and the crowning of Queen Rhododendra are highlights of the festivities. Today, the event attracts more than 15,000 visitors each year. Contact the chamber of commerce (541/997-3128) for more information.

Independence Day celebrations include live outdoor music and a barbecue in Old Town, and a fireworks display over the river.

Chowder, Brews, and Blues (541/997-1994) in late September is a three-day event honoring several things the community relishes. A coast-wide clam chowder contest here is a highlight, along with live music and microbrew tasting at the Florence Events Center. Admission is $6–10.

ACCOMMODATIONS

As just about everywhere else, there are budget motels on the main drag here, but to experience the coast fully, try one of the romantic getaways between Florence and Yachats. Romantic B&Bs abound north of town, covered under *Yachats and Vicinity* in the *Northern Oregon Coast* chapter.

One of the best bargains in town is the **Lighthouse Inn** (155 U.S. 101, 541/997-3221 or 866/997-3221, $55 and up), a Cape Cod–style two-story motel on the highway close to the bridge and convenient to Old Town. With neatly kept rooms in an untouched 1938 lodging, decorated with bric-a-brac and other homey touches, it may remind you of your grandmother's house. No in-room kitchens, but a common refrigerator and microwave are available for guest use. Most rooms have a queen or king bed; some are considered suites, with two rooms and a connecting bath, which sleep up to five.

One block north of Old Town, just across the highway from the Lighthouse Inn, the pet-friendly **Old Town Inn** (170 U.S. 101 N., 541/997-7131 or 800/570-8738, www.old-town-inn.com, $71 and up) provides guests with spacious rooms a short walk away from the river and Old Town.

For a river experience, try the **River House Motel** (1202 Bay St., 541/997-3933 or 888/824-2750, www.riverhousemotel.com, $89 and up, $109 and up for riverfront). It's worth paying extra for a riverfront balcony.

On the south bank of the river, the recently renovated **Best Western Pier Point Inn** (85625 U.S. 101, 541/997-7191, $135 and up) offers spacious rooms, bay views, sand-dune hiking across the street, and a good restaurant on-site (Lovejoy's fish-n-chips and selection of English ales and microbrews are worth a stop). There is also a beach house for rent along the Siuslaw River that sleeps six. Rates at this large luxury motel drop by about half in the off-season.

Bed-and-Breakfasts

The **Edwin K B&B** (1155 Bay St., 541/997-8360 or 800/8-EDWINK, www.edwink.com, $130–150) has six units with private bath two blocks from Old Town near the Siuslaw River and an cottage. River views, period antiques, and multicourse breakfasts featuring locally famous soufflés and home-baked breads on fine china have established this gracious 1914 home as Florence's preeminent B&B. Add private baths and whirlpool tubs in some units and a private courtyard and waterfall in back and you'll understand the need to reserve well in advance.

About three miles east of town, the **Blue Heron Inn** (6563 Rte. 126, Florence, 541/997-4091 or 800/997-7780, www.blue-heroninn.com, $100–140) is a good choice for amateur ornithologists. River frontage highlighted by a spotting scope might reveal cormorants, herons, bald eagles, and every so often, a tundra swan. Whirlpool tubs, antiques, and a charming home rich in nooks and crannies make the rates a good value. A full breakfast enthusiastically praised by guests is included. A newer media room downstairs entertains guests with rented or in-house videos.

Nine miles north of Florence, and just a short walk from Heceta Head Lighthouse, is **Heceta Light Station B&B** (92072 U.S. 101, 541/547-

3696, www.hecetalighthouse.com, $157–251), built in 1893, where the lighthouse keepers used to live. Today, it's a B&B with antique furnishings and vintage photos, which help re-create the lives of the keepers of the flame. Among the bedrooms, the two Mariners' rooms command the finest view have private baths (two of the other rooms share a bathroom down the hall). The current caretakers maintain a flock of chickens on the grounds as did the actual lighthouse keepers of yesteryear. Your current hosts keep them as a source of fresh eggs to be used in the included seven-course breakfast, a several-hours affair replete with such dishes as d'Anjou pear with chèvre and Oregon honey and vol-au-vent stuffed with chived eggs and asparagus.

FOOD

A famous Zen master once said, "If you can make a cup of tea right, you can do anything." The same aphorism seems to apply to clam chowder in coastal restaurants, if Florence's eateries are any indication.

In Old Town, the local **Mo's** (1436 Bay St., 541/997-2185) is the largest outlet of this famed Oregon chowderhouse, and its fresh fish, fast service, fair prices, and Siuslaw River frontage make it this neighborhood's most popular restaurant. Lunch with a cup of chowder might run $6 and bouillabaisse is the most expensive item on the menu. Even if you don't eat here, you might want to stock up on Mo's clam chowder base packaged to go.

The **Bridgewater Seafood Restaurant and Oyster Bar** (129 Bay St., Old Town, 541/997-9405, breakfast, lunch, and dinner daily, $10–20) features exotic clam chowder with Indonesian clams, in keeping with a Banana Republic decor, and the only "fine dining" in Old Town. Of course, this also means the highest prices on the waterfront and more tourists than locals. But it's still a pretty good bet. The Bridgewater was the recipient of a People's Choice Award for the best clam chowder in town for several years. Fresh fish, often with a Cajun flair, is the star of the menu. Winter through early spring, Wednesdays feature an all-you-can-eat seafood dinner buffet.

Traveler's Cove (1362 Bay St., 541/997-

6845, 9 A.M.–9 P.M., daily, $8–15) manages to combine an import shop and gourmet café under the same roof. The café serves good lunches and is worth a stop for the homemade clam chowder and interesting salads and sandwiches. Fresh Dungeness crab makes an appearance here with crab quiche, crab enchiladas, and "crabby" Caesar salad. Best of all, the patio out back provides river views to enjoy along with your meal. A full bar with flavored margaritas might also enhance your appreciation of the river frontage.

The **International C-Food Market** (1498 Bay St., 541/997-9646, lunch and dinner daily) gets good word of mouth from locals. This combination restaurant and retail market offers seafood right off the boat. Not only is the freshness of the fish exceptional, but prices are low.

Sick of clam chowder? **Thai Talay** (2515 U.S. 101, 541/997-7227, lunch and dinner daily, $8–19) might come as a welcome change, especially if you go for the spicy mango-and-broccoli stir fry. If you can't be away from seafood for too long, try one of the seafood specialties here.

North of town, the **Windward Inn** (3757 U.S. 101, 541/997-8243, open daily for breakfast, lunch, and dinner; dinner entrees $9–25) rates a special mention. Long a mainstay of the coastal dining scene, the fresh-cut flowers, skylights, and wood-paneled interior have set the stage for memorable repasts for more than half a century. Dinner entrées are typified by such creations as fresh mussels broiled on the half shell with Oregon hazelnuts, Oregon peppered bacon, and Tillamook cheddar cheese.

INFORMATION

The **Florence Area Chamber of Commerce** (270 U.S. 101, Florence 97439, 541/997-3128, www.florencechamber.com), is three blocks north of the Siuslaw River Bridge; open 9 A.M.–5 P.M.

The **Siuslaw National Forest Ranger Station** (4480 U.S. 101 N., Florence, 541/902-8526) is located near the BiMart on Florence's main drag.

Tune into radio station **KCST,** at 106.9 FM

or 1250 AM, for coastal news, weather, and a whole lotta Paul Harvey.

GETTING THERE

Greyhound (www.greyhound.com) still runs to Florence, but its service is limited (don't count on checking luggage). The bus stop, at the 37th Street Laundry (1857-1 37th St., 541/997-5111), sees twice-daily service. **Porter Stage Lines** (541/269-7183) runs along the southern Oregon coast, then turns inland at Florence and goes to Eugene, Bend, and Ontario.

Reedsport and Winchester Bay

If you're going fishing or are coming back from a dunes hike, you'll appreciate a hot meal and a clean, low-priced motel room in Reedsport. Otherwise, this town of 5,000 people might seem like a strange mirage of cut-rate motels, taverns, and burger joints in the midst of the Oregon Dunes NRA.

Jedediah Smith explored this country in 1828, after the Hudson's Bay Company's Peter Skene Ogden theorized that the Umpqua River—the largest river between San Francisco Bay and the Columbia—might be the fabled Northwest Passage. It wasn't, of course, but this river is still one of the great fishing streams of the state. Zane Grey avoided writing about it, lavishing the publicity instead upon the Rogue to divert people from his favorite steelhead spots here.

Cargo ships from Scottsburg, a hamlet some 17 miles upriver from Reedsport, supplied San Francisco markets with meat, milk, and produce between 1856 and the early 20th century. In its 1850s heyday, Scottsburg was larger than Portland, with some 5,000 residents, before an 1861 flood destroyed much of the town.

Two miles north of Reedsport, the little burg of Gardiner was created in the wake of a shipwreck. The *Bostonian* (owned by a Mr. Gardiner) was dashed against the rocks at the mouth of the Umpqua in 1856 and from its remnants the first wood-frame structure in this area was built. It was soon joined by other white-painted homes and facilities for a port on the Umpqua. While this "white city by the sea" declined in importance when the highway elevated Reedsport to regional hub status, the homes still bear the same color scheme from the earlier era.

Three miles southwest of Reedsport, Salmon Harbor Marina in Winchester Bay (pop. 1,000), a busy port for commercial sport fishing at the mouth of the Umpqua, has given the whole area new life in recent years, following hard times precipitated by the decline in timber revenues.

SIGHTS

Umpqua Discovery Center

In Reedsport's Old Town on the south bank of the river, the Umpqua Discovery Center (409 Riverfront Way, 541/271-4816, 9 A.M.–5 P.M. daily June–Sept., 10 A.M.–4 P.M. daily Oct.–May $8 adults, $4 children) interprets the regional human and natural history of this area through multimedia programs, dioramas, scale models, and helpful staff. The boardwalk and observation tower give a good view of the broad lower reaches of the Umpqua. The center is the site of the September Tsalila festival.

Dean Creek Elk Viewing Area

Three miles east of Reedsport, and stretching three miles along the south side of Route 38, the Dean Creek Elk Viewing Area provides parking areas and viewing platforms for observing the herd of some 120 wild Roosevelt elk that roam this 1,100-acre preserve. The elk move out of the forest to graze the preserve's marshy pastures, sometimes coming quite close to the highway. Oregon's largest land mammal can reach 1,100 pounds at maturity, and the majestic rack on a fully grown bull can spread three feet across. Early mornings and just before dusk are the most promising times to look for them; during hot weather and storms the elk tend to stay within the cover of the woods.

Umpqua Lighthouse State Park

Less than a mile south of Winchester Bay is Umpqua Lighthouse State Park (460 Lighthouse Rd., Winchester Bay, 541/271-4118). Tour the red-capped 1894 lighthouse (541/271-4631, 10 A.M.–4 P.M. daily May–Sept., $2) or admire it from the roadside. Adjacent, in a former Coast Guard building, the **visitors center and museum** (541/271-4631, 10 A.M.–5 P.M. Wed.–Sat., 1–5 P.M. Sun. May–Sept.) has marine and timber exhibits. Directly opposite the lighthouse, overlooking the mouth of the Umpqua and oceanfront dunes, is a whale-watching platform.

Lake Marie, just south near the camping area, has a swimming beach and is stocked with rainbow trout. A one-mile forest trail around the lake makes for an easy hike. A trail from the campground leads to the highest dunes in the United States (elevation 545 feet), west of Clear Lake.

SPORTS AND RECREATION
Fishing

Winchester Bay and the tidewater reaches of the lower Umpqua River comprise Oregon's top coastal sturgeon fishery, and one of the best areas for striped bass, particularly near the mouth of the Smith River, which enters the Umpqua just east of Reedsport. The best action for the Umpqua's spring chinook tends to be inland, below Scottsburg. Fall chinook enter the bay July–September. Other notable fisheries here are the huge runs of shad, which peak May–June, and smallmouth bass, which offer action upstream from Reedsport. Crabbing and clamming are also popular and productive pastimes in Winchester Bay and the lower reaches of the river. August–mid-September, tagged crabs are released into the water in and around Winchester Bay, one of them worth a cash prize of $5,000 to whoever catches it.

Charter services operating in the area include: **Reel Fishing Trips** (541/271-3850); **Strike Zone Charters** (541/271-9706 or 800/230-5350, www.strikezonecharters.com); **River's End Guide Service** (541/271-3125, www.umpquafishing.com); and **Jerry Jarmain** (541/271-5583 or 800/653-5583, www.umpqua-river-guide.com).

Dune Access

Some of the most spectacular dunes landscape can be found nine miles south of Reedsport at **Umpqua Dunes,** at North Eel Campground near Lakeside. After you emerge from a quarter-mile hike through coastal evergreen forest, you'll be greeted by dunes 300–400 feet high. It's said that dunes near here can approach 500 feet high and a mile long after a windblown buildup.

Because a regular trail through the dunes is impossible to maintain, you should only expect to find wooden posts spaced at irregular intervals west of the dunes to guide you to the beach. This trail can also be accessed from the Middle Eel Creek Campground. Look for gray posts about 10 feet high with a blue band at the top marking the trail to the beach, a fairly strenuous five-mile round-trip mostly over soft sand. A shorter and easier one-mile loop trail leads through woodlands to the dunes for a quick introduction to this landscape.

Lakeside Area

Ten miles south of Reedsport, the sleepy resort town of Lakeside hosted visits from Bob Hope, Bing Crosby, and the Ink Spots, among other luminaries, back in its 1930s and '40s heyday. Today, it's still a popular destination, primarily for its proximity to the sprawling, many-armed Tenmile and North Tenmile Lakes. These large, shallow lakes offer water-skiing and excellent fishing for stocked rainbow trout and warmwater species, including crappie, yellow perch, bluegill, and lunker largemouth bass up to 10 pounds. A quarter-mile channel connects the two lakes, and a county park on Tenmile Lake has a paved boat ramp, fishing docks, sandy swimming beach, and picnic area.

Camping

Choices abound in this recreation-rich area.

Just south of Winchester Bay is **Umpqua Lighthouse State Park** (460 Lighthouse Rd., Winchester Bay, information 541/271-4118, reservations 800/452-5687). The campground alongside Lake Marie has firewood, flush toilets, showers, picnic tables, electricity, and piped water. The 20 RV sites go for $20, 24 tent sites for $16, two basic yurts for $27, six deluxe yurts (with shower, small kitchen, refrigerator, microwave, TV/VCR) for $66, and two rustic cabins for $35. The lake offers fishing, boating, and swimming. Trails from here lead to the highest dunes in the United States (elevation 545 feet), west of Clear Lake.

William A. Tugman State Park (information 541/759-3604, reservations 800/452-5687) is eight miles south of Reedsport, in the heart of dune country. This larger campground, with 115 sites, offers a similar range of creature comforts, prices, and recreation opportunities. It sits on the west shore of Eel Lake, east of U.S. 101 across from where the dunes reach their widest extent, two miles to the sea.

Windy Cove Campground (541/271-4138) is a county park with 24 full-hookup sites and four other sites with electricity only. Located on the south side of Salmon Harbor Drive, across from the Winchester Bay marina, it has restrooms, picnic tables, grass, and paved site pads. No reservations taken. It is legal to drive your OHV from this campground directly to the dunes, but it is a couple of miles on the pavement.

About nine miles south of Reedsport, set along Eel Creek near Eel Lake and Tenmile Lake, is **Eel Creek Campground,** a Siuslaw National Forest facility with 51 basic tent and RV sites. Open mid-May–September, reservations (877/444-6777, www.reserve usa.com) are advised. Sites are $17 nightly. The Umpqua Dunes Trail offers access to the dunes and beach.

Eight miles north of Reedsport, the **Tahkenitch Campground** (reservations 877/444-6777, www.reserveusa.com) is another Forest Service facility, set among ancient Douglas firs and conveniently located near Tahkenitch and other lakes, dunes, and ocean beaches. Open mid-May–September, sites are $17 nightly. A network of trails branches out from here through the dunes, along Tahkenitch, and to the beach.

Winchester Bay's **Discovery Point Resort** (242 Discovery Point Lane, 541/271-3443, www.discoverypointresort.com) offers dunes enthusiasts dune access and ATV rentals, while providing one- to three-bedroom cabins (sleep up to six) and 60 RV spaces. To get there from Reedsport, head two miles south on U.S. 101 to Winchester Bay; turn right at Pelican Market onto Salmon Harbor Drive. Go one mile, and you'll see Discovery Point Resort on the left. Reservations are highly recommended. RV sites are $18; cabins range $68–98.

EVENTS

Every June, over Father's Day weekend, chainsaw sculptors compete for prize money as they transform pieces of raw western red cedar into grizzly bears, giant salmon, and other rustic works of art during the **Chainsaw Sculpture Championships** (800/247-2155). The event happens at the Rainbow Plaza Old Town Reedsport.

An interesting annual event is **Tsalila** (pronounced sa-LEE-la). Based on the Coos word for "river," this festival (800/247-2155) held the second weekend in September features music, interpretive tours of the Umpqua, alder-baked salmon with squash and corn-on-the-cob dinners, and a traditional tribal village centered around the waterfront at the Umpqua Discovery Center. There's no charge except for dinner.

ACCOMMODATIONS

Of the half dozen motels that sit along U.S. 101 in Reedsport, the **Fir Grove Motel** (2178 Winchester Ave., 541/271-4848, $44 and up) is slightly less expensive but comparable in comfort (i.e., clean with no frills) to its counterparts.

Anchor Bay Inn (1821 Winchester Ave., 541/271-2149 or 800/767-1821, $57 and up, ask for discounts) also has clean rooms with one, two, or three beds, family suite, and kitchenettes, and an outdoor pool that's just big enough to satisfy the kids.

If you're interested in this area's ultimate get-away-from-it-all alternative, try the **Salbasgeon Inn of the Umpqua** (45209 Route 38, Reedsport, 541/271-2025, $80–145) with nicely appointed rooms on the Umpqua and a romantic location near the elk preserve. They also have an upscale motel unit with an indoor pool managed by **Best Western** (541/271-4831 or 800/528-1234, $100 and up) in downtown Reedsport, on U.S. 101. Both places permit pets. By the way, the name was inspired by the region's most popular sport-fishing species: *sal*mon, *bass*, and stur*geon*.

The pet-friendly **Winchester Bay Inn** (390 Broadway, Winchester Bay, 541/271-4871 or 800/246-1462, $72 and up) puts you next to the water with all the comfort bases covered. Reserve ahead of time in fishing season.

A few miles north of Reedsport in Gardiner is another lodging with more character than those along motel row for not significantly more money. The **Gardiner Guest House** (401 Front St., 541/271-4005, $55–75) is located in a cute, tranquil, former paper-mill town that sits close by the confluence of the Smith and Umpqua Rivers. The 1883 home was built by local bigwig and State Senator Albert Reed, for whom Reedsport was named. The recently remodeled home still has the Victorian feel, without lacking in modern conveniences. Choose between a room with the facility down the hall and a view room with private bath. A large home-cooked breakfast is included in the rate.

FOOD

There is no shortage of basic but decent places to eat in Reedsport. An example is **Don's Main Street Restaurant** (U.S. 101, 541/271-2032, open daily for breakfast, lunch, and dinner, lunch from $5–8), whose burgers and soup are good enough to get you to Florence. After a bite of Umpqua ice cream, however, touted by many to be the best in the state, you might stick around till you're hungry again.

The **Schooner Cafe** (423 Riverfront Way, 541/271-3945, 10 A.M.–3 P.M. daily, lunch around $10), on the boardwalk next door to the Umpqua Discovery Center, has a pleasant riverside patio with a casual atmosphere for a burger, salad, or sandwich.

The friendly staff at the **Sportsmen's Cannery and Smokehouse** (Bayfront Loop, Winchester Bay, 541/271-3293, shop open 9 A.M.–5 P.M. daily, seafood barbeque Sat. and Sun. afternoon and evening, $12–17) hosts a seafood barbecue smorgasbord that features the catch of the day, oysters, prawns, and all the trimmings. You can also purchase smoked or canned fish; they'll even smoke your catch for you.

INFORMATION

The **Oregon Dunes NRA Visitor Information Center** (885 U.S. 101, Reedsport 97467, 541/271-3611, www.fs.fed.us/r6/siuslaw) and **Reedsport Chamber of Commerce** (541/271-3495 or 800/247-2155, www.reedsportcc.org) share a building at the junction of U.S. 101 and Route 38. Mid-May–mid-September, it's open 8 A.M.–4:30 P.M. weekdays, 10 A.M.–4 P.M. weekends; weekdays only the rest of the year.

Coos Bay and North Bend

The towns around the harbor of Coos Bay refer to themselves collectively as "the Bay Area." In contrast to its namesake in California, the Oregon version is not exactly the Athens of the coast. Nonetheless, the visitor will be impressed by the area's beautiful beaches and three wonderfully scenic and historic state parks. Because much of this natural beauty is on the periphery of the industrialized core of the Bay Area, away from U.S. 101, it's easy to miss. All that many motorists see upon entering Coos Bay/North Bend on the Coast Highway are the dockside lumber mills and foreign vessels anchored at the one-time site of the world's largest (and currently, Oregon's second-busiest) lumber port.

The little town of Charleston (pop. 700) to the southwest makes few pretensions of being anything other than what it really is—a commercial fishing port. Processing plants here can or cold-pack tuna, salmon, crab, oysters, shrimp, and other kinds of seafood. The town might occasionally smell of fish, but the few restaurants and lodgings here are good values. Moreover, a post office, a laundry, and a visitors center are all conveniently crammed together on the main street, the Cape Arago Highway (County Road 240), and the town is the gateway to a trio of extraordinary state parks: Sunset Bay, Shore Acres, and Cape Arago.

To reach Charleston from points south, or to head south from town, take the interesting **Seven Devils Road,** which has its southern terminus about three miles north of Bandon. This route runs 13 miles alongside beaches, state parks, and an estuarine preserve.

SIGHTS
Coos Art Museum
Located in downtown Coos Bay, the Coos Art Museum (235 Anderson Ave., Coos Bay, 541/267-3901, www.coosart.org, 10 A.M.–4 P.M. Tues.–Fri., 1 P.M.–4 P.M. Sat., $2), the Oregon coast's only art museum, features primarily 20th-century and contemporary works by American artists, including pieces by Robert Rauschenberg and Larry Rivers. Etchings, woodcuts, serigraphs, and other prints make up a large part of the permanent collection, which includes several of Janet Turner's richly detailed depictions of birds in natural settings. Other highlights include Kirk Lybecker's photo-realistic watercolors. Don't miss the Prefontaine Room on the second floor of the museum. Photos, trophies, medals, and other memorabilia of this native-son world-class runner illustrate his credo: "I want to make something beautiful when I run."

In addition to the permanent collection, recurring events worth detouring for are the May–June juried show of artists from the western states, and the Maritime Art Exhibit, August–mid-September.

Coos County Historical Museum
The Coos County Historical Museum (1220 Sherman Ave., North Bend, 541/756-6320, www.cooshistory.org, 10 A.M.–4 P.M. Tues.–Sat., $2) is located near the south end of the Conde McCullough Bridge, one of several distinctive Depression-era high-wire acts by Oregon's master bridgebuilder. The museum houses more than the usual bric-a-brac from earlier eras, thanks largely to the region's heritage as a shipping center. An early 20th century Regina music box, a piano shipped around the Horn, miniature boat models, and a jade Chinese plaque, as well as Coos tribe beadwork and other artifacts make this collection especially memorable. Outside, old-time logging equipment and a 1920s steam train are also worth a look.

Sunset Bay State Park
The Cape Arago Highway west of Charleston leads to some of the most dramatic beaches and interesting state parks on the coast. Among the several beaches on the road to Cape Arago, the strand at Sunset Bay State Park (13030 Cape Arago Hwy., Coos Bay, information 541/888-4902, reservations 800/452-5687) is the big

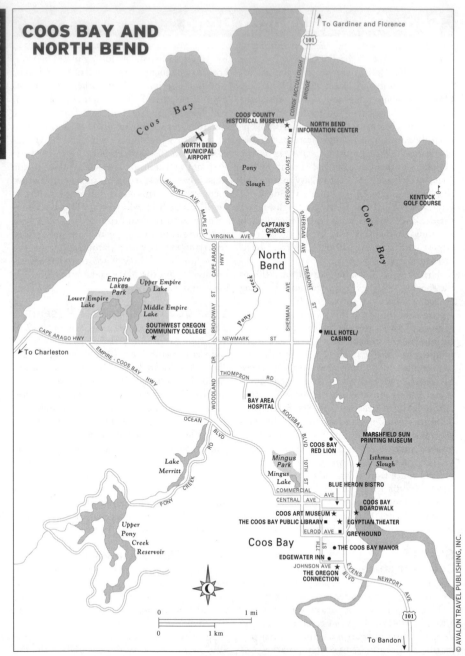

COOS BAY AND NORTH BEND

To Gardiner and Florence

101

CONDE McCULLOUGH BRIDGE

Coos Bay

COOS COUNTY
HISTORICAL MUSEUM

NORTH BEND
INFORMATION CENTER

NORTH BEND
MUNICIPAL
AIRPORT

Pony
Slough

OREGON COAST HWY

SHERIDAN AVE

Coos Bay

KENTUCK
GOLF COURSE

CAPTAIN'S
CHOICE

AIRPORT AVE

MAPLE ST

VIRGINIA   AVE

North
Bend

Pony Creek

TREMONT ST

Empire
Lakes
Park

Upper Empire
Lake

Lower Empire
Lake

Middle Empire
Lake

SOUTHWEST OREGON
COMMUNITY COLLEGE

CAPE ARAGO HWY

BROADWAY ST

SHERMAN AVE

NEWMARK   ST

MILL HOTEL/
CASINO

To Charleston

EMPIRE - COOS BAY   HWY

WOODLAND DR

THOMPSON   RD

OCEAN

BLVD

BAY AREA
HOSPITAL

KOOSBAY BLVD

Lake
Merritt

PONY CREEK RD

Mingus
Park

Mingus
Lake

COMMERCIAL

CENTRAL   AVE

COOS BAY
RED LION

MARSHFIELD SUN
PRINTING MUSEUM

Isthmus
Slough

BLUE HERON BISTRO

10TH ST

COOS BAY
BOARDWALK

Upper
Pony
Creek
Reservoir

COOS ART MUSEUM
THE COOS BAY PUBLIC LIBRARY

ELROD   AVE

EGYPTIAN THEATER

GREYHOUND

THE COOS BAY MANOR

Coos Bay

7TH ST

EDGEWATER INN

JOHNSON AVE
THE OREGON
CONNECTION

EVENS BLVD

NEWPORT AVE

0   1 mi

0   1 km

101

To Bandon

attraction. This is because its sheltered shallow cove, encircled by sandstone bluffs, is warm and calm enough for swimming, a rarity in the Pacific north of Santa Barbara, California. In addition to swimmers, divers, surfers, kayakers, and boaters, many people come here to watch the sunset. Local legend tells that pirates hid out in this well-protected cove.

A four-mile cliffside segment of the Oregon Coast Trail from Sunset Beach south is the best way to appreciate the sea stacks and islands between here and Cape Arago. Good views of Cape Arago Lighthouse across the water can be had along this route. Listen for its unique foghorn. For a shorter hike, follow the signs from the mouth of Big Creek to the viewpoint overlooking Sunset Bay.

Shore Acres State Park

Less than a mile south of Sunset Bay at Shore Acres State Park (541/888-3732, 8 A.M.–sunset year-round, $3 per vehicle), the grandeur of nature is complemented by the hand of man. The park is set on the grounds of lumber magnate and entrepreneur Louis J. Simpson's mansion, which began as a summer home in 1906 and grew into a three-story mansion complete with an indoor heated swimming pool and large ballroom.

Originally a Christmas present to his wife, Shore Acres became the showplace of the Oregon coast, with formal and Japanese gardens eventually added to the 743-acre estate. Over the years the building fell into disrepair, and it and the grounds were ceded to the state in 1942. Because of the high cost of upkeep, the mansion had to be razed, but the gardens have been lovingly maintained.

The gardens here are themselves compelling attractions, but the headland's rim is more dramatic. Perched near the edge of the bluff, on the site formerly occupied the mansion, there now stands a glass-enclosed observation shelter that makes a perfect vantage point from which to watch for whales, or marvel at the crashing waves. When there's a storm, particularly, the waves really slam into the sandstone reefs

and cliffs, hurling up tremendous fountains of spray.

Thanksgiving–New Year's, during the annual **Holiday Lights and Open House,** the gardens are decorated with 250,000 colored lights and other holiday touches, daily 4–10 P.M. The gardener's cottage opens and serves free refreshments during this time.

If you bear right and follow the pond's contours toward the ocean, you'll come to a trail. Follow it north for cliffside views of the rock-studded shallows below. Southward, the trail goes downhill to a scene of exceptional beauty. From the vantage point of a small beach, you can watch waves crash into rocks with such force that the white spray appears to hang suspended in the air. Exploring tidepools and caves, as well as springtime swimming in a cove formed by winter storms on the south side of the beach, are pursuits for the active traveler here. In summer, thimbleberries growing along the trail down to the beach can provide sustenance for these activities.

Cape Arago State Park

Located 1.25 miles south of Shore Acres, Cape Arago State Park (800/551-6949) lies at the end of the Cape Arago Highway. Locals have made much of the fact that this was a possible landing site of the English explorer Sir Francis Drake in 1579, and have put a plaque here commemorating him.

Beachcombers can make their own discoveries in the numerous tidepools, some of the best on the coast. The south cove trail runs down to a sandy beach and the better tidepools, while the north cove trail leads to more tidepools, good spots for fishing, and views of the colonies of seals and sea lions at Shell Island, including the most northerly breeding colony of enormous elephant seals. Their huge pups, when just a month old, may already weigh 300–400 pounds. Note that the north trail closes March–June to protect seal pups. The picnic tables on the headlands command beautiful ocean panoramas, and are superbly placed for whale-watching. The park is free, and open for day use only year-round.

C South Slough Estuarine Research Reserve

Estuaries, where fresh and salt water interface, form some of the richest ecosystems on earth, capable of producing five times more plant material than a cornfield of comparable size, while supporting great numbers of fish, birds, and other wildlife. The South Slough of Coos Bay is the largest estuary on the Oregon coast. The staff at the South Slough Estuarine Reserve Interpretive Center (541/888-5558, www.south sloughestuary.org, 8:30 A.M.–4:30 P.M. daily June–Aug., 8:30 A.M.–4:30 P.M. Mon.–Sat. Sept.–May, free), on Seven Devils Road, four miles south of Charleston, will help you coordinate a canoe trip through the estuary and offers guided hikes as well.

The center looks out over several estuarine arms of Coos Bay, the largest harbor between San Francisco Bay and the Columbia River. These vital wetlands nurture a vast web of life, which is detailed by the placards captioning the center's exhibits.

Coastal salt marshes, occurring in the upper intertidal zones of coastal bays and estuaries, have been dramatically reduced due to land "reclamation" projects such as drainage, diking, and other human disturbances. The halophytes (salt-loving plants) that thrive in this specialized environment include pickleweed, saltgrass, fleshy jaumea, salt marsh dodder, arrow-grass, sand spurrey, and seaside plantain.

The coastal ecosystem is presented by the "10-minute trail" in back of the interpretive center. Branch trails lead down toward the water for an up-close view of the estuary itself. Down by the slough, you may see elk grazing in marshy meadows and bald eagles circling above, while *Homo sapiens* harvest oysters and shrimp.

Beginning near the visitors center is the easy, three-mile **estuary study trail,** which follows Hidden Creek from the wooded uplands down the valley to a boardwalk that winds through fresh- and saltwater marshes and leads to several wildlife-observations points.

Myrtlewood

To see an Oregon coast folk art in the making, visit the **Oregon Connection** (1125 S. 1st St., Coos Bay, 541/267-7804), just off U.S. 101 at the south end of Coos Bay. The myrtlewood factory tour shows you how a myrtlewood log gets fashioned into bowls, clocks, tables, and other utensils. No admission is charged for this 25-minute guided run through a working factory. After you're done, the store itself is a delight, with Oregon gourmet foods and crafts supplementing the quality woodwork.

In 1869, the golden spike marking the completion of the nation's first transcontinental railroad was driven into a highly polished myrtlewood tie. Novelist Jack London was so taken by the beauty of the wood's swirling grain that he ordered an entire suite of furniture. Hudson's Bay trappers used myrtlewood leaves to brew tea as a remedy for chills.

During the Depression years, the city of North Bend issued myrtlewood coins after the only bank in town failed. The coins ranged from 50 cents to $10 and are still redeemable—though they are worth far more as collector's items.

Five miles north of North Bend, the **Real Oregon Gift** (68794 Hauser Depot Rd. at U.S. 101, 541/756-2220) is another large myrtlewood factory and showroom.

SPORTS AND RECREATION
Fishing

Spring chinook salmon, which sometimes exceed 30 pounds and are renowned as an unrivaled dining treat, offer prime fishing in Coos Bay. However, their population levels, and fishing rules, vary from year to year. Fall chinook and hatchery-reared coho salmon runs have had generally healthy runs in recent years. Mid-August–November, Isthmus Slough sees a good return of fin-clipped cohos. In saltwater, chinook and coho are found in good numbers within a one- to two-mile radius of the mouth of Coos Bay May through September, though the legal season varies; carefully check the regulations. Remnant striped bass are still occasionally caught in Coos Bay's sloughs and upper tidewater, but their numbers are diminishing.

Coos Bay is also one of the premier areas for

crabbing and clamming. The Charleston Fishing Pier is a productive spot for crabs, while the best clamming spots are found along the bay side of the North Spit.

Fishing charters, bay cruises, whale-watching, and the like can be arranged through a number of charter outfits based at the Charleston Boat Basin. **Betty Kay Charters** (541/888-9021 or 800/752-6303, www.betty kaycharters.com) charges typical per-person prices: $62 for five hours of rock fishing, $82 for five hours of salmon fishin, $170 for 12 hours of tuna fishing or 12 hours of halibut fishing; $30 for bay cruises, whale-watching, or eco-tours. **Bob's Sportfishing** (541/888-4241 or 800/628-9633, www.bobssport fishing.com) is another charter operator.

Camping

Bastendorff Beach County Park (63379 Bastendorff Beach Rd., Charleston, 541/888-5353) is a conveniently and beautifully located park two miles west of Charleston just off the Cape Arago Highway. It's open for camping year-round, with RV and tent sites for $16–20 (less off-season), as well as cabins ($30) and some hiker/biker sites. Campsites have access to drinking water, woodstoves, flush toilets, and coin-operated showers. Fishing, hiking, surfing, and a nice stretch of beach are the recreational attractions, plus there's a good playground for toddlers.

Even though the crowds at **Sunset Bay State Park** (13030 Cape Arago Hwy., Coos Bay, 541/888-4902, reservations 800/452-5687) can make it seem like a trailer park in midsummer, the proximity of Oregon's only major swimming beach on the ocean keeps occupants of the 66 tent sites ($16) and 65 trailer sites ($20) here happy. The eight yurts go for $27, and primitive hiker/biker sites are $4. Facilities include a laundry and showers, and a boat launch at the north end of the beach. This site, located three miles southwest of Charleston, is popular with anglers, who can cast into the rocky intertidal area for cabezon and sea bass.

Northwest of the Bay Area—2.5 miles north of the McCullough Bridge—is the Trans-Pacific Parkway, a causeway west across the water leading to Coos Bay's North Spit and the south end of the Oregon Dunes National Recreation Area (NRA), with four Siuslaw National Forest campgrounds and expansive dunes that draw off-road vehicle enthusiasts. The main **Horsfall Campground** is popular with crowds of noisy all-terrain vehicles and RVs; it is the only campground in the area with showers. For more quiet and privacy, continue another mile on Horsfall Beach Road to **Bluebill Lake.** The 18 tent/RV sites are equipped with picnic tables and bathrooms, and the campground is open all year. Ask the campground hosts about area trails and the nearby oyster farm for the ultimate in campfire fare. Close by, **Horsfall Beach Campground** is located in the dunes next to the beach. OHV access and beachcombing are popular activities. Half a mile away, **Wild Mare Horse Camp** has beach and dune access and a dozen primitive campsites, each with a single or double horse corral. Each of these Siuslaw National Forest campgrounds charges $20 nightly, year-round. Only Horsfall Campground takes reservations (877/444-6777, www.reserveusa.com), May–September.

Golf

There are two inexpensive public golf courses in the Bay Area: **Sunset Bay Golf Course** (11001 Cape Arago Hwy., Charleston, 541/888-9301), a nine-holer close to Sunset Bay State Park, and the 18-hole **Kentuck Golf Course,** (675 Golf Course Ln., North Bend, 541/756-4464), across the bay from North Bend along the Kentuck Inlet. Neither can hold a candle to the lush (and quite expensive) courses just to the south at Bandon Dunes.

Mill Casino

Occupying the former bayside site of the Weyerhaeuser mill alongside U.S. 101 in North Bend, the Mill Casino (3201 Tremont Ave., North Bend, 541/756-8800 or 800/953-4800, www.themillcasino.com) is operated by the Coquille tribe. Open 24 hours a day, the casino offers blackjack, slots, poker, and bingo. A large hotel, lounge, and several restaurants are on-site. Nightly entertainment includes jazz and R&B, while headliners lean toward country performers such as Wynonna and Kenny Rogers.

ENTERTAINMENT AND EVENTS

The **Egyptian Theater** (229 S. Broadway, Coos Bay, 541/267-3456), is a movie house with a pharaonic motif that goes back to the 1920s, when many small towns took to emulating the opulence and foreign intrigue of such big-city movie houses as Graumann's Chinese Theater in Hollywood. Four first-run movies are usually showing here. Across the street, the players of the **On Broadway Theater** (226 S. Broadway, 541/269-2501) stage a changing program of live theater throughout the year, ranging from current Broadway hits to relatively unknown scripts to children's entertainments.

The **Dune Mushers Mail Run** (541/677-8393, http://webpages.charter.net/arago/odm/) is an annual noncompetitive endurance dogsled run held the first weekend of March. This is the world's longest organized dry-land run for dogsled teams. Small teams of 3–5 dogs, and larger teams of 5–10 dogs, haul mushers on wheeled buggies over 70 miles of dunes from North Bend to Florence. The smaller teams start off from Horsfall Beach on Friday, while the larger teams leave the next morning. En route, spectators have opportunities to watch the teams as they pass through Spinreel Park, Winchester Bay, Gardiner, and Florence's South Jetty area, to finish up with a parade through Old Town Florence on Sunday. The "mail" carried by the dog teams are commemorative envelopes, which are sold as souvenirs to support the event.

The first event of note in summer is the **Oregon Coast Music Festival** (P.O. Box 663, Coos Bay 97420, 541/267-0938 or 877/897-9350, www.oregoncoastmusic.com), which runs for two weeks in mid-July and has been going for over 25 years. Coos Bay is the central venue for these south coast classical, jazz,

pop, and world music concerts but Bandon, North Bend, Charleston, and other neighboring burgs host some performances as well. Tickets range $5–18.

In late August, the ubiquitous blackberry is celebrated with the **Blackberry Arts Festival** (541/888-1095 or 541/888-6572). Food and wine-tasting booths, a juried arts and crafts show, and entertainers fill the Coos Bay Mall, Central Avenue, in downtown Coos Bay.

ACCOMMODATIONS
Charleston

Captain John's Motel (63360 Kingfisher Dr., 541/888-4041, www.captjohnsmotel.com, $50 and up) is within walking distance of fishing, charter boats, clamming, and dock crabbing. Close by is a special fish/shellfish-cleaning station and, with any luck, your dinner. Staying in Charleston also puts you close to state parks and within easy reach of laundry and postal services, as well as offering temperatures that are warmer than Coos Bay in winter and cooler in summer. Reserve well in advance for July and August. Pets okay.

If you'd rather catch your own dinner, the **Plainview Motel** (91904 Cape Arago Hwy., 541/888-5166 or 800/962-2815, $59 and up) provides guests with crab rings and fishing gear. This motel has 12 pet-friendly units, some with kitchens.

Coos Bay

A spendier alternative is the **Coos Bay Red Lion** (1313 N. Bayshore Dr., 541/267-4141 or 800/733-5466, $100 and up). Large rooms have immense beds, thick pile carpet, and everything else in the way of little extras. This hotel is also distinguished by its restaurant, one of the best in town.

The **Coos Bay Manor** (955 5th St., 800/269-1224, $135, full breakfast included) is the kind of place where a fluffy terry robe and bubble bath sustain the first impressions made by the grand, high-ceilinged colonial-style home and eye-popping river views from the B&B's open-air second-floor breakfast balcony. The five spacious rooms here have their own distinct decor; two of the rooms can become a suite for families.

The bayfront **Edgewater Inn** (275 E. Johnson, 541/267-0423 or 800/233-0423, $120–130) has loads of perks. With 82 units, many with views and kitchens, guests can take advantage of the fitness and tanning rooms, indoor pool, spa and sauna, and meeting room. A shuttle is also provided.

North Bend

The **Mill Casino Hotel** (3201 Tremont Ave., 541/756-8800 or 800/953-4800, www.the millcasino.com, $109 and up, discounts often available) is located just south of the Mill Casino along the waterfront in a building that once housed a plywood mill. But rather than a milltown ambience this economic development project of the Coquille tribe expresses its owners' patrimony. The exterior of this three-story hotel is the same cedar that tribe members used to build their plank houses, and the fireplace in the lobby is made of Coquille River rocks. The canoe displayed behind the front desk was carved by tribal members and is part of an interpretive display that tells the story of the Coquilles. The well-appointed rooms feature Internet access and views of oceangoing ships.

Also popular with the casino crowd is the **Comfort Inn** (1503 Virginia Ave., 541/756-3191, $86 and up), just five blocks from U.S. 101. With 96 units and the standard chain hotel amenities, this hotel provides a quiet escape.

FOOD
Charleston

The hot restaurant of the moment in the Bay Area is casual but upscale **◖ Oyster Cove Grill** (63346 Boat Basin Rd., 541/888-0703, dinner Tues.–Sun., main courses $18–35), with seafood every bit as fresh as it should be, and tastier than you'll generally find it. The simple preparations of wild salmon or Alaskan halibut are delicious, and the chef also has a way with Cajun spices—a crab-stuffed halibut loaded with cheese and topped with spicy sauce ($27) is a worthy splurge. Steaks are also taken seriously here.

The **Sea Basket** (63502 Kingfisher Rd., 541/888-5711, breakfast, lunch, and dinner daily, main courses $8–13) typifies the good seafood, fast service, and relatively low prices in these parts. Oysters are especially tasty in this restaurant, with noted breeding farms close by. They are also famous for their Bigman burgers. The fluorescent glare above the cafeteria-style tables frequented by fishermen in work-blackened denims may not count much for atmosphere, but you'll leave satisfied.

Close by, the somewhat classier **Portside** (63383 Kingfisher Rd., Charleston Boat Basin, 541/888-5544, lunch and dinner daily, main courses $13–34) offers the chance to select your own lobsters and crabs out of a tank as the fleet unloads other dinners just outside the door. Reserve ahead for the Friday night all-you-can-eat seafood buffet at a reasonable price. Beware of the karaoke.

Just before the Charleston Bridge, the **Fisherman's Grotto** (91149 Cape Arago Hwy., 541/888-3251, lunch and dinner daily, main courses $8–20) is a good place for fish and chips or standard seafood dinners. If you're an oyster lover, you'll certainly want to visit **Qualman's** (4898 Crown Point Rd., 541/888-3145). Just look for the signs on the north side of the Charleston Bridge on the east side of the highway. Open 10 A.M.–5:30 P.M., it sells fresh high-quality oysters. Several other oyster purveyors make this delicacy available at other Bay Area outlets.

Coos Bay

Even though the **◖ Blue Heron Bistro** (110 W. Commercial, 541/267-3933, lunch and dinner Mon.–Sat., dinner Sun.) is located in the heart of downtown Coos Bay, it evokes dining experiences in San Francisco or Portland. The tile floors, newspapers on library-style posts, and international posters adorning the walls are in keeping with a European-influenced bill of fare. The extensive menu's eclectic array ranges from Greek salad to Cajun-style blackened fish and emphasizes fresh ingredients and creative interpretations. An impressive list of microbrews and imports as well as Oregon, California, and

European wines will complement whatever dish you order. Best of all, for not much more than you'd pay at Denny's, you can enjoy an oasis of refinement in "Timbertown, U.S.A."

Brickstones, the dining room at the Coos Bay Red Lion (1313 N. Bayshore Dr., 541/267-4141, ext. 305, main courses $12–26), offers extra-thick cuts of prime rib and flambé items prepared tableside that are as much a treat to look at as to taste. This restaurant is popular, so make reservations. We recommend the smoked prime rib.

For a "Logging Camp Breakfast" locals recommend the **Timber Inn Restaurant** (1001 N. Bayshore Dr., 541/267-4622), where it's served all day long.

For old-school Italian food, try **Benetti's** (290 S. Broadway, 541/267-6066, $9–19). Here the spaghetti can be tailored to satisfy the pickiest eater, and the less fussy can enjoy both the warm atmosphere (hang around long enough and you'll learn that Joe Benetti is the mayor of Coos Bay) and the lasagna.

North Bend

A prime rib special is usually on the menu at the **Mill Casino** (800/953-4800, open 24 hours) on the east side of U.S. 101 in North Bend. The restaurant's windows on the bay make the bargain meal of prime rib, salad, vegetables, dessert, and beverage taste even better. The Friday seafood buffet and other buffets throughout the week offer good food in unlimited quantities for less than $12.

For sit-down or takeout seafood, the **Captain's Choice** (1210 Virginia, 541/756-0125, main courses $10–12) serves enormous pots of clam chowder and oyster stew, but has plenty of "steak and (insert favorite seafood here)" selections for about $10.

If you've had enough of the standard coastal fare, try **Cafe Mediterranean** (1860 Union St., 541/756-2299, 11 A.M.–9 P.M. Mon.–Fri., 3 P.M. to 9 P.M. Sat., $4–12) for Middle Eastern–style Mediterranean food, including a locally loved lentil soup, in a family-style setting.

Natural food fans converge at **Coos Head Natural Foods** (1960 Sherman, 541/756-7264), with the largest selection of certified organic produce on the south coast.

INFORMATION

The **Coos Bay Visitor Information Center** (50 E. Central, Coos Bay, 541/269-0215 or 800/824-8486, www.oregonsbayareachamber. com, 9 A.M.– 5 P.M. Mon.–Fri., 10 A.M.–4 P.M. Sat., noon–4 P.M. Sun.) is five blocks west of U.S. 101 off Commercial Avenue. Inquire here about tours of the *New Carissa* shipwreck site north of town near Horsfall Dunes.

The *Coos Bay World* is the largest daily paper on the south coast. In May and August, catch their "Let's Go" section on area getaways.

GETTING THERE AND AROUND

It's possible to get to and from Roseburg, 87 miles from Coos Bay, on Route 42 in under two hours. Motorists should be aware that this thoroughfare carries more truck traffic than any other interior-to-coast road in Oregon, but weekenders will usually encounter few trucks and light traffic.

Coastal Express buses (800/921-2871) run up and down the south coast weekdays only between North Bend and the California border. **Porter Stage Lines** (541/269-7183) also runs along the southern Oregon coast, then turns inland at Florence and goes to Eugene, Bend, and Ontario. If the bus doesn't fit into your plans (or your style), consider the North Bend Airport at the north end of town. Horizon Air (800/547-9308) flies between the Bay Area and Portland daily. To get to the airport, follow the signs on the road between Charleston and North Bend.

Public transportation in the Bay Area is limited. The one bus line makes a loop in Coos Bay and North Bend, and **Dial-A-Ride** (541/267-7111) operates on-call 8:30 A.M.–4:30 P.M. daily.

Bandon

Bandon-by-the-Sea (pop. 2,900) is characterized by the style and grace of an earlier era, especially in Old Town, a picturesque collection of shops, galleries, restaurants, and historical memorabilia. It's at Bandon that the coast highway finally re encounters the coast, after long inland stretches of pastureland and forests to the south and north.

While logging, fishing, dairy products, and the harvest of cranberries have been the traditional mainstays of the local economy, in the early part of the 20th century Bandon also enjoyed its first tourism boom. In addition to being a summer retreat from the heat of the Willamette Valley, it was a port of call for thousands of San Francisco–to–Seattle steamship passengers. This era inspired such touristic venues as the Silver Spray dance hall and a natatorium with a saltwater swimming pool. The golden age that began with the advent of large-scale steamship traffic in 1900 came to an abrupt end following a devastating fire in 1936, which destroyed most of the town. The blaze was started by the easily ignitable gorse weed, imported from Ireland (as was the town's name) in the mid-1800s; townspeople fought the flames with their backs to the sea earned the incident a citation as one of the top-10 news stories of the year.

Decades after the fire, Old Town was given a facelift, and tourists began to return. Today, Bandon is a curious mixture of provincial backwater, destination resort, and new-age artist colony. Travelers from all over the world flock to this town because of its beaches and its world-class golf course. They coexist happily with the large population of retirees, artisans, and locals who seem to have cornered the market on late-model pickups with gun racks.

SIGHTS

One of the appealing things about Bandon is that many of its attractions are within walking distance of each other. In addition, on the periphery of town is a varied array of things to see and do.

Old Town

Bandon's Old Town, much of which dates from after the 1936 fire, is a half dozen blocks of shops, cafés, and galleries squeezed in between the harbor and the highway. The renovated waterfront invites relaxed strolling, and crabbers and anglers pull in catches right off the city docks. The small commercial fleet based here pursues salmon and tuna offshore.

Throughout Old Town are artists and artisans. **Second Street Gallery** (210 2nd St., 541/347-4133) has a little of everything, from functional and art pottery to blown glass to paintings to sculptures. **Winter River Books and Gallery** (170 2nd St., 541/347-4111) has crystals, objets d'art, and a wide-ranging assortment of travel titles, photo essays, fiction, and tapes that makes this the best bookstore on the south coast.

Close by, the **Bandon Driftwood Museum**

© STEFANO BONI
beach in Bandon

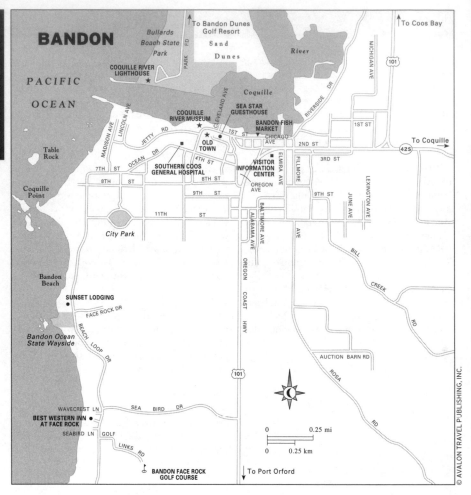

© AVALON TRAVEL PUBLISHING, INC.

and Art Gallery (130 Baltimore, 541/347-3719) shows off an interesting collection of natural sculptures, from gnarly root balls to whole tree trunks. It's housed at the Big Wheel General Store, where you'll also find the Fudge Factory (24 flavors of homemade ice cream and butter fudges).

Bandon Historical Society Museum

This museum, at the corner of U.S. 101 and Fillmore Street (270 Fillmore, 541/347-2164, 10 A.M.–4 P.M. Mon.–Sat., $2 adults) in Bandon's former city hall, traces the history of the Coquille tribe (pronounced ko-KWELL in native dialect) and its forebears. The chronology continues with the steamers and the railroads that brought in white settlers. One room is devoted to Bandon's unofficial standing as the Cranberry Capital of Oregon. Black-and-white blowups showing women stooping over in the bogs to harvest the ripe berries are captioned with such quips as this politically incorrect classic from an overseer: "I had 25 women picking for me, and I knew every one by her fanny." Color photos spanning five decades of Cranberry Festival princesses also adorn the walls.

Another room depicts "Bandon's Resort Years, 1900–1931," when the town was called the Playground of the Pacific. The most compelling exhibits in the museum deal with shipwrecks and the fires of 1914 and 1936.

The Beach Loop

U.S. 101 follows an inland path for more than 50 miles between Coos Bay and Port Orford, but you can leave the highway in Bandon and take the four-mile Beach Loop for a lovely seaside detour south of town. Several access roads lead west from the highway to Beach Loop Drive (County Road 29), each about a quarter mile from each other. Most people begin the drive by heading west from Old Town on 1st Street along the Coquille. Another popular approach is from 11th Street, which leads to Coquille Point. The south end of the drive runs through the northern portion of **Bandon State Natural Area,** providing parking, beach access, and picnic tables.

Along the fine stretch of beach are rock formations with such evocative names as Table Rock, Elephant Rock, Garden of the Gods, and Cat and Kittens Rocks. The whole grouping of sea stacks, included within the Oregon Islands National Wildlife Refuge, looks like a surrealist chess set cast upon the waters. The most eye-catching of all is **Face Rock,** a basalt monolith that resembles the face of a woman gazing skyward. A Native American legend says that she was a princess frozen by an evil sea spirit. Look for the Face Rock turnout 0.25 mile south of Coquille Point on the Beach Loop.

Despite their scenic and recreational attractions, the beaches south of town can be surprisingly deserted. Perhaps this is due to the long, steep trails up from the water along some parts of the beach. In any case, this dearth of people can make for great beachcombing. Agates, driftwood, and tidepools full of starfish and anemones are commonly encountered here, along with bird-watching opportunities galore. Elephant Rock has a reputation as the Parthenon of puffins, while murres, oystercatchers, and other species proliferate on the other offshore formations.

Bullards Beach State Park

Two miles north of Bandon, bordering the Coquille River estuary and over four miles of beachfront, Bullards Beach State Park (P.O. Box 25, Bandon 97411, information 541/347-2209 or 800/551-6949, reservations 800/452-5687) is a great place to fish, crab, bike, fly a kite, windsurf, picnic, or overnight in the large, sheltered campground. The beach and lighthouse are reached via a scenic three-mile drive paralleling the Coquille River. Look for jasper and agates amidst the heaps of driftwood on the shore. Equestrian trails and horse camping facilities make this a popular destination for riders. The boat ramp gives fishermen, kayakers, and canoeists access to the lower Coquille River and Bandon Marsh National Wildlife Refuge.

Just north of Bandon, Bullards Beach State Park is home to a campground and the Coquille River Lighthouse.

The riverside road going out to the Coquille's north jetty takes you through the dunes to the picturesque **Coquille River Lighthouse,** a squat tower with adjacent octagonal quarters. The last lighthouse built on the Oregon coast, it was completed in 1896, then was abandoned in 1939 when the Coast Guard installed an automated light across the river. After years of neglect, the structure was restored in the late 1970s, and is now open throughout the year. Etchings of ships that made it across Bandon's treacherous bar, and some that didn't, greet you as you enter. Volunteers are on duty to staff the gift shop and show you around April–October.

For details on camping at Bullards Beach State Park, see *Camping,* later in this section.

Bandon Marsh National Wildlife Refuge

Bird-watchers flock to the Bandon Marsh National Wildlife Refuge (541/347-3683), especially in the fall, to take in what may be the prime birding site on the coast. The extensive mudflats, especially, attract flocks of shorebirds, including red phalaropes, black-bellied plovers, long-billed curlews, and dunlins, as well as such strays from Asia as Mongolian plovers.

Bandon Marsh lies a short paddle across the river from the state park, or via Riverside Drive, which runs from Bandon to U.S. 101 on the south side of the Coquille River bridge. The refuge protects over 700 precious acres of the Coquille estuary's remaining salt marsh habitat, along the southeastern side of the river. Migrating birds, waterfowl, bald eagles, California brown pelicans, and other species feast on the rich food sources here.

The refuge and its elevated observation deck are open sunrise–sunset daily.

West Coast Game Park

Seven miles south of Bandon is the West Coast Game Park (46914 U.S. 101 S., Bandon, 541/347-3106, 9 A.M.–7 P.M. daily June 15–Aug., 9 A.M.–5 P.M. spring and early fall, call for late fall and winter hours, $13 ages 13 and up, $8.50 ages 7–12, $5.50 ages 2–6, $12 seniors), the self-proclaimed largest wild-animal petting park in the country. There are 450 animals representing 75 different species, including tiger cubs, chimps, camels, zebras, bison, and snow leopards. Along with these exotics you'll also encounter such indigenous species as elk, bears, raccoons, and cougars. Visitors may be surprised to see a lion and tiger caged together, or a fox and a raccoon sharing the same nursery. The park tries raising different species together and often finds that animals can live harmoniously with their natural enemies. Free-roaming animals include deer, peacock, pygmy goats, and llamas. An elk refuge is another popular area of the park.

Even if you're not with a child, the opportunity to pet a pup, a cub, or a kit can bring out the kid in you.

EVENTS

The annual **Wine and Seafood Festival** happens every Memorial Day weekend, at the Community Center in City Park off 11th Street West in Bandon. The free event includes live music, horse-drawn buggy rides, arts and crafts booths, and wine-tasting. The same weekend, competitors in the **Sandcastle Contest** create amazing sculptures out of sand, water, and imagination. This takes place on the beach off Beach Loop Drive at Seabird Lane. Construction starts at 9 A.M.; judging is at 1 P.M. Contact the chamber of commerce (541/347-9619) for details on both events.

A fish fry, kayak and driftboat races, parade, and classic car and motorcycle show are highlights of Bandon's **Fourth of July** celebration; at dusk, fireworks are launched across the Coquille to burst above the river.

The biggest weekend of the year for Bandonians comes the second weekend in September, when the **Cranberry Festival** (541/347-9616) brings everyone together in Old Town for a parade, crafts fair, tours of a cranberry farm, and the Bandon High Cranberry Bowl, when the local football team takes on traditional rival Coquille High.

During the holiday season, the merchants of Old Town and fisherfolk deck their stores and boats with twinkling lights in the traditional

Festival of Lights. Particularly striking is the Coquille River Lighthouse, lit up across the water like a Christmas tree.

SPORTS AND RECREATION
Fishing
The Coquille River runs 30 miles from its Siskiyou headwaters before meandering leisurely through Bandon. The north and south jetties are popular spots for perch and rockfish, while the city docks right in Old Town yield catches of perch and crab April–October and smelt July–September. The spring chinook run pales in comparison to those in the Rogue and Chetco to the south, but the fall runs of chinook (beginning Sept.–Oct.) and coho (Oct.–Nov.) are strong and productive. Steelhead usually arrive in November, and the run gathers steam January–February. A boat is necessary for the best steelhead and salmon water, but bank anglers can fish the mouth of Ferry Creek, just off Riverside Drive in Bandon. Fishing guides and gear can be arranged through the **Bandon Bait Shop** (1st and Alabama, 541/347-3905), across from the boat basin. The shop also rents crab rings and other gear, and can point you to productive spots for catching Dungeness crab.

Just off the south end of Beach Loop Drive, 30-acre **Bradley Lake,** protected from ocean winds by high dunes, offers good trout fishing and a boat ramp. Trophy rainbows averaging five pounds, reared at the Bandon Fish Hatchery east of town, are stocked here each spring.

Camping
Bullards Beach State Park (P.O. Box 25, Bandon 97411, information 541/347-2209 or 800/551-6949, reservations 800/452-5687) is a wonderful state park in a great location, between the Coquille River and four miles of beach. The park has 190 campsites, 13 yurts, eight horse-camping sites, and hiker/biker spaces. To get there, drive north of town on U.S. 101 for about a mile; just past the bridge on the west side of the highway is the park entrance. The beach itself is reached via a scenic two-mile drive paralleling the Coquille River.

© JUDY JEWELL

Most Oregon state park campgrounds have yurts for rent.

Electricity, picnic tables, and fire grills are provided. You'll also find a store, a café, a laundry, horse riding/camping facilities, an inviting sandy beach, summer evening campfire talks Tuesday– Saturday, and hiking trails. The fee for camping at Bullards Beach along the Coquille is $16–20 a night. Yurts go for $27.

📘 Bandon Dunes Golf Resort

Dubbed "Pebble Beach North," Bandon Dunes Golf Resort (57744 Round Lake Dr., Bandon, 541/347-4380 or 888/345-6008, www.bandondunesgolf.com) was hailed by *Golf Digest* as the number one new course in 1999 and named the third-best course in the United States by *Golf* magazine, due to its seven holes by the Pacific and unobstructed ocean views from all 18. Two other 18-hole courses, **Pacific Dunes,** and **Bandon Trails** give golfers a chance stay for a few days and keep encountering new territory.

To preserve the natural surroundings along the ocean bluffs, these Scottish links courses don't allow carts, so you'll have to hire a caddy or schlep your own bag. A luxurious resort (see *Accommodations* later in this section) with Pacific views from a sand dune and a restaurant are also here for those who come to worship in the south coast's Sistine Chapel of golf. It's a mile north of the Coquille River. Green fees for either course, June–September, are $185 for hotel guests, $240 for nonguests; during the rest of the year, rates run $75–130. Caddie fee is $50 per bag.

Bandon Face Rock Golf Course

Duffers and other mortals may choose instead to tread the equally scenic seaside links two miles south of town at Bandon Face Rock Golf Course (3235 Beach Loop Rd., 541/347-3818), where nine holes will set you back just $10, 18 holes for $16.

Other Activities

On the waterfront in Old Town, **Adventure Kayak** (315 1st St., 541/347-3480), rents kayaks (from $30 for 2 hours) and teaches classes on a variety of kayak techniques. Open 10 A.M.–5 P.M. daily in summer.

Bandon Beach Riding Stables (2640 Beach Loop, 541/347-3423) is four miles south of Face Rock on the Beach Loop. Several beach rides are offered daily, plus sunset rides in the summer. Riders of all abilities are welcomed, including those with handicaps. Prices range $30–40 for a 1.5- to two-hour ride. Reservations are advised. Open year-round.

ACCOMMODATIONS

Bandon bills itself as America's Storm-Watching Capital, and special packages are often available October–March.

The 📘 **Sea Star Guesthouse** (370 1st St., 541/347-9632 or 888/732-7871, www.seastar bandon.com, $75–150) has a room and four suites with skylights, a wood-beam ceilings, and views onto the harbor. Suites sleep 2–6 people and have cooking facilities. Sea Star also has hostel rooms facing onto a courtyard, including two rooms with bunkbeds and a shared bath ($19 per person), a room with a private bath ($39), and a family with kitchenette ($75). All units are nonsmoking, and no pets are permitted.

A favorite place to stay is the older-but-refurbished **Windermere Motel** (3250 Beach Loop, 541/347-3710, www.windermerebythesea.com, $105–170), where baby boomers can relive their childhood beach getaways in cedarwood efficiencies or two-story condolike units, situated on a bluff above a windswept beach. Housekeeping facilities and proximity to restaurants (Lord Bennett's) and West Coast Game Park also make this an idea family vacation spot.

Not far away is **Sunset Lodging** (1865 Beach Loop, 541/347-2453 or 800/842-2407, www.sunsetmotel.com, $60–150). With some units built right into the cliff above a scenic beach, the view here is hard to beat, although new construction has obstructed the view of some units. Whether you're looking for rooms with a kitchen, rooms that accommodate pets, or rooms with a fireplace, there's something here for you. A hot tub, indoor pool, on-site laundry, and Lord Bennett's restaurant across the street also recommend this place. Nonetheless, the steep steps down to the 80-foot-high bluff to the beach, the popularity of the place, and the rusticity of the least expensive rooms might not be to everyone's liking.

The "sleeper" property on the beach loop is the **Best Western Inn at Face Rock** (3225 Beach Loop, 541/347-9441 or 800/638-3092, $120 and up). Part of this status has to do with the motel's location set back from the road near the end of the beach loop across the street from Bandon's coastline and near the nine-hole golf course. Many of the modern, well-appointed rooms have magnificent ocean views. An indoor pool, fitness room, whirlpool, and restaurant also make this an especially good choice for active travelers. Some suites have fireplaces, kitchenettes, and private patios. There's an on-site restaurant and a short path to the beach.

For avid golfers, the **Lodge at Bandon Dunes** (57744 Round Lake Dr., 888/345-6008, www.bandondunesgolf.com, $180 and up) is a deluxe resort at what is considered one of the country's finest courses. This is one of the most luxurious places on the Oregon coast. Lodging is in several different locations around the resort and includes single lodge rooms in various sizes, two- or four-bedroom suites, and cottages. View options vary from golf course and ocean views to dune and surrounding woods. Bandon Dunes is five minutes from Bandon, a mile north of the Coquille, and 30 minutes from the North Bend Airport, which is served by daily flights from Portland.

FOOD

The most elegant restaurant in Bandon is two miles north of town in main lodge of the Bandon Dunes Golf Resort. Here, the **Gallery** (Round Lake Rd., 541/347-4380, three meals daily, dinner $17–36) is a good place to eat an excellent steak, and the meatloaf is also a favorite. If you're not staying at the resort, lunch is an interesting time to get a feel for the place and to enjoy the views out onto the Bandon Dunes course, all for the price of a hefty $8 burger.

Budget diners and smoked-fish connoisseurs will appreciate the **Bandon Fish Market** (at the boat basin near the intersection of 1st and Chicago, 541/347-4282, lunch and early dinner daily, lunch around $8). Heartier appetites call

for the market's excellent fish-n-chips; takeout only. A picnic table outside by the harbor is the place to enjoy it all with a trip across the street to Cranberry Sweets for dessert.

Wheelhouse Seafood Grill (1st and Chicago, 541/347-9331, lunch and dinner daily, dinner with salad and sides, about $20) deep-fries the fish (they also grill and broil) with a beer batter that doesn't mask the taste of the food. Their homemade soup is a specialty (as is the sirloin steak with prawns), especially the Cioppino Rick, using diverse shellfish and bottomfish in a marinara base.

South of downtown, **Lord Bennett's** (1695 Beach Loop Dr., 541/347-3663, lunch and dinner daily, dinner $15–20) cliffside aerie looks out over the breakers toward Bandon's most dramatic restaurant view. Elegantly rendered seafood dishes do justice to the surroundings. Recommended are the bouillabaisse, crab cakes, and blackened ahi. Jazz on selected evenings in the lounge is another nice touch.

Five miles south of Bandon, on the east side of U.S. 101, hit the brakes at **Misty Meadows Jams** (48053 U.S. 101 S., 541/347-2575) for first-rate jams and jellies, including a variety of products incorporating Bandon cranberries. This family-owned and -operated business has been making delicious concoctions from Oregon-grown fruits since 1970. In addition to preserves, the shop sells olives and fruit-based barbecue sauces, syrups, honey, and salsas. Usually open 9 A.M.–5 P.M.

INFORMATION

The **Bandon Chamber of Commerce** (300 2nd St., Bandon 97411, 541/347-9616, www. bandon.com), in Old Town, distributes a comprehensive guide and a large annotated pictographic map of the town. Ask them about what they call "the best river fishing and crabbing docks on the coast."

GETTING THERE

North- and southbound **Coastal Express** buses (800/921-2871) run three times daily, weekdays only, between North Bend and Brookings, stopping near the north end of Bandon at Ray's Food Place supermarket.

Port Orford and Vicinity

In 1850, the U.S. Congress passed the Oregon Donation Land Act, allowing white settlers to file claims on Native American land in western Oregon. This was news, of course, to the tribal nations of the region, who had not been consulted on the decision. William Tichenor, captain of the steamship *Gull,* hoping to exploit the new act, had ambitions to establish an outpost on the coast at what's now Port Orford. When Tichenor observed the hostility of the Quatomah band of the Tututni tribe in the tidewater, he put nine men ashore on an immense rock promontory fronting the beach, due to its suitability as a defensive position. The Native Americans besieged the rock for two weeks, before the whites escaped under cover of night. Tichenor returned with a well-armed party of 70 men, and succeeded in founding his settlement.

From this inauspicious beginning, "Awferd," as the locals call it, established itself as the first townsite on the south coast. Shortly thereafter, the town became the site of the first fort established on the coast during the Rogue River Wars.

Besides the tragic tribal conflicts, Port Orford has other claims to fame. It is the most westerly incorporated city in the contiguous United States. The outskirts of Port Orford host such diverse undertakings as an escargot farm, llama and sheep ranches, a goat-milk dairy, and commercial berry growers, as well as plots of land devoted to Christmas trees and exotic herbs. Offshore, divers harvest kelp for use as a food supplement and sea urchins to supply the Japanese with a popular aphrodisiac and seafood delicacy. In town, the stunning scenery and low rents probably have played a role in the development of a passel of galleries here, supporting a nascent artist colony.

SIGHTS

Port Orford has an ocean view from downtown that is arguably the most scenic of any city's on the coast. A waterfront stroll lets you appreciate the cliffs and offshore sea stacks as well as the unusual sight of commercial fishing boats being hoisted by large cranes into and out of the harbor. With only a short jetty on its north side, Port Orford's harbor, the only open-water port in Oregon, is unprotected from southerly swells, so boats can't be safely moored on the water. When not in use, the fleet rests on wheeled, trailer-like dollies near the foot of the pier.

Battle Rock Park

As you come into town on U.S. 101, it's hard to ignore enormous Battle Rock on the shoreline, the site of the 1851 conflict between the local tribes and the first landing party of white settlers. If you can make your way through driftwood and blackberry bushes surrounding its base, you can climb the short trail to the top for a heightened perspective on the rockbound coast that parallels the town. You'll also notice

misty spring weather near Port Orford

© JUDY JEWELL

the east-west orientation of the harbor. Once you get to the top of the rock, don't think that the battle is necessarily over. Bracing winds often chill you, and high tides can sometimes render this huge coastal extension an island.

Port Orford Heads State Park

Another shoreline scene worth taking in, featuring a striking panorama from north to south, is located up West 9th Street at what the locals call "The Heads," Port Orford Heads State Park. If you go down the cement trail to the tip of the blustery headland, you look south to the mouth of Port Orford's harbor. To the north, many small rocks fill the water, along with boats trolling for salmon or checking crab pots. On clear days visibility extends from Cape Blanco to Humbug Mountain.

Also located here is the historic **Port Orford Lifeboat Station** (541/332-0521, 10 A.M.–3:30 P.M. Thurs.–Mon. Apr.–Oct., free), built by the Coast Guard in 1934 to provide rescue service to the southern Oregon coast. After it was decommissioned in 1970, the officer's quarters, the pleasingly proportioned crew barracks, and other outbuildings were converted to a museum depicting the work of the station. A trail leads down to Nellie's Cove, site of the former boathouse and launch ramp.

◖ Humbug Mountain

Some people will tell you that 1,756-foot-high Humbug Mountain, six miles south of Port Orford on U.S. 101, is the highest mountain rising directly off the Oregon shoreline. Because the criteria for such a distinction varies as much as the tides, let's just say it's a special place.

There's more than one version of how the peak, formerly called Sugarloaf Mountain, got its name. According to one version, gold miners who were drawn here in the 1850s by tales of gold in the black sands nearby soon discovered that the rumored riches proved to be just "humbug."

Once the site of Native American vision-quests, today Humbug Mountain's shadow falls upon an Edenlike state park campground surrounded by myrtles, alders, and maples. Just

north is a breezy black-sand beach. A three-mile trail to the top of Humbug rewards hardy hikers with impressive vistas to the south of Nesika Beach and a chance to see wild rhododendrons 20–25 feet high. Rising above the rhodies and giant ferns are bigleaf maple, Port Orford cedar, and Douglas and grand firs. Access the trail from the campground, or from a trailhead parking area off the highway near the south end of the park. In addition, the **Oregon Coast Trail**, which follows the beach south from Battle Rock, traverses the mountain and leads down its south side to the beach at Rocky Point.

Prehistoric Gardens

What can we say about this one-of-a-kind roadside attraction, featuring a 25-foot-tall, Formica-green *Tyrannosaurus rex* standing beside the parking lot? Is it kitsch, or is it educational? You decide. In any case, if you've got children in the car, unless they're sleeping or blindfolded, you're probably going to have to pull over. Prehistoric Gardens (36848 U.S. 101, 541/332-4463, 9 A.M.–dusk daily spring–fall; call for winter hours, $7 adults, $6 ages 11–17 and 65-plus, $5 children 3–10), about 10 miles south of Port Orford, is the creation of E. V. Nelson, a sculptor and self-taught paleontologist who began fabricating life-size dinosaurs here back in 1953, and placing them amidst the lush rainforest on the backside of Humbug Mountain. Paths lead through the ferns, trees, and undergrowth to a towering brontosaurus, triceratops, and 20 other ferro-concrete replicas, painted in a dazzling palette of Fiestaware colors.

Cape Blanco State Park, Hughes House

Four miles north of Port Orford, west of U.S. 101, is Cape Blanco, whose remote appendages give you the feeling of being at the edge of the continent—as indeed you are, here at the westernmost point in Oregon. From the vantage of Cape Blanco, dark mountains rise behind you and the eaves of the forest overhang tidewater. Below, driftwood and 100-foot-long bull kelp on slivers of black-sand beach fan out from both sides of this earthy red bluff. Somehow, the Spaniards who sailed past it in 1603 viewed the cape as being *blanco*, white. It's been theorized that perhaps they were referring to the fossilized shells on the front of the cliff.

With its exposed location, Cape Blanco really takes it on the chin from Pacific storms. The vegetation along the five-mile state park road down to the beach attests to the severity of winter storms in the area. Gales of 100 mph (record winds were clocked at 184 mph) and horizontal sheets of rain have given some of the usually massive Sitka spruces the appearance of bonsai trees. An understory of salmonberry and bracken fern evokes the look of a southeast Alaska forest.

Atop the weathered headland is Oregon's oldest, most westerly, and highest lighthouse in continuous use. Built in 1870, the beacon stands 256 feet above sea level and can be seen some 23 nautical miles out at sea. **Cape Blanco Lighthouse** (541/332-6774, 10 A.M.–3:30 P.M. Tues.–Sun. Apr.–Oct., $2 adults, $1 children under 12) also holds the distinction of having Oregon's first female lighthouse keeper, Mabel E. Bretherton, who assumed her duties in 1903. Tours of the facility include the chance to climb the 64 spiraling steps to the top; this is the only operational lighthouse in the state that allows visitors into the lantern room, to view the working Fresnel lens.

Over the years a number of shipwrecks have occurred on the reefs near Cape Blanco, including the *J. A. Chanslor,* an oil tanker that collided with the offshore rocks in 1919, with a loss of 36 lives.

Near Cape Blanco on a side road along the Sixes River is the **Hughes House** (541/332 0248, 10 A.M.–3:30 P.M. Tues.–Sun. Apr.–Oct.), a restored Victorian home built in 1898 for rancher and county commissioner Patrick Hughes. Owned and operated today by the state of Oregon, the house serves as a museum and repository of antique furnishings. The house opens during the winter holiday season, when punch and cookies are often served the weekend before Christmas.

SPORTS AND RECREATION
Fishing and Water Sports

Beachcombing for agates and fishing floats on nearby beaches and searching for the lost Port Orford meteorite in the surrounding foothills typify the adventures available in the area. The meteorite was found in the 1860s by a government geologist, who estimated its weight at 22,000 tons. Unfortunately, he was unable to relocate the meteorite when he returned for another look.

In the northwest of town, drive west of the highway on 14th or 18th Streets to 90-acre **Garrison Lake** for boating, waterskiing, and fishing for stocked rainbow and cutthroat trout. **Buffington Memorial City Park,** at the end of 14th Street, has a dock for fishing or swimming, plus playing fields, tennis courts, picnic areas, hiking trails, and a horse arena. A half mile north of the lake, look for agates on **Paradise Point Beach.**

The **Elk River,** which empties on the south side of Cape Blanco, and the **Sixes River,** which meets the sea north of the cape, are two popular streams for salmon and steelhead fishing. Chinook and steelhead begin to enter both rivers after the first good rains of fall arrive, usually in November. Private lands limit bank access, with the exception of a good stretch of the Sixes that runs through Cape Blanco State Park. The salmon season runs to the end of the year, steelhead through the following March. **Lamm's Guide Service** (541/440-0558, www.umpqua fishingguide.com) runs trips on both rivers.

Between Port Orford and Bandon (just south of Langlois) is **Floras Lake,** a popular coastal windsurfing and kiteboarding spot. For more information, contact Floras Lake Windsurfing School (541/348-9912, www.floraslake.com). It's 11 miles north of Port Orford, about four miles west of the highway on Floras Lake Loop Road. On the lake is **Boice Cope County Park,** which has basic tent and RV sites, and a boat ramp. From Floras Lake north to Bandon, the most desolate beachfront on the coast can be found—ideal for beachcombing. Grasses, dunes, and shore pine usher you the third of a mile back to Bandon and chances are good you won't see a soul.

Camping

Cape Blanco State Park (39745 S. U.S. 101, 541/332-6774 info, 800/452-5687 for cabin reservations) can be reached by driving four miles north of Port Orford on U.S. 101, then heading northwest on the park road that continues five miles beyond to the campground. It features 54 sites (first-come, first-served) for tents ($16), four cabins ($35), trailers and motor homes ($16), a horse camp ($14), and hiker/biker sites ($4); picnic tables, water, and showers are available. For horseback riders, there's a seven-mile trail and a huge open riding area; horses are also allowed on the beach.

Humbug Mountain State Park (541/332-6774 or 800/551-6949, reservations not accepted), six miles south of Port Orford, features 80 tent sites and 30 sites for trailers and motor homes, and wind-protected sites reserved for hikers and bikers. Flush toilets, showers, picnic tables, water, and firewood are available. The regular campsites are $14–16; rates fall by $4 off season. Hiker/biker sites go for $4 year-round.

Arizona Beach Campground (P.O. Box 621, Gold Beach 97444, 541/332-6491, www.arizona beachrv.com, reservations not accepted) is a 70-acre campground 15 miles north of Gold Beach on U.S. 101, close to a beach with lots of driftwood. It has 31 tent sites and almost a hundred RV spaces. You can camp on the beach, in an adjoining meadow, or back in the woods by a tiny stream for $20–30. All the amenities are here, but the closely spaced sites lack privacy. Nonetheless, there are few better places for kids, due to the creek running though the site and the proximity of the Prehistoric Gardens. It's open all year.

ACCOMMODATIONS

With one notable exception, Port Orford is the kind of place where a room with a view will not break your budget.

That exception is **❰ Wildspring Guest Habitat** (www.wildspring.com, $199–249, including continental breakfast), a beautifully tranquil getaway. The small (five-cabin) resort is in a forested setting with views of the ocean. The cabins are meticulously designed and furnished (including a refrigerator, massage table, and Wi-Fi access

in each cabin, but no telephones or TVs). Bikes, backpacks, and hiking trail maps are available to all guests, and the slate-lined hot tub is available for all to use. Guests may participate in guided meditation, drumming, and tai chi, all of which are offered one or two times a month (check website or call to inquire). This is a good place to go either for a romantic retreat or for a quiet solo getaway.

Back in the real world of budgets, the **Shoreline Motel** (206 6th St., 541/332-2903, $40–60), across the highway from Battle Rock, has an outstanding view, offers clean rooms, and accommodates pets.

The **Seacrest Motel** (44 U.S. 101 S., 541/332-3040, $57–79) features views of coastal cliffs and a garden from a quiet hillside on the east side of the highway. Pets are welcome at this older motel.

Castaway-by-the-Sea (545 W. 5th St., 541/332-4502) features ocean/harbor views from high on a bluff, fireplaces, and housekeeping units, and allows pets; rates are $65–135. The rates on the upper-end lodgings go down significantly in the off-season. It's said that Jack London once stayed in an earlier incarnation of this place.

Home-by-the-Sea (444 Jackson St., 541/332-2855 or 800/480-2144, www.home bythesea.com) includes a full breakfast at rates of $105–115 a night for two. The dramatic hillside view of Battle Rock seascape makes for excellent storm-watching here. Wireless Internet access is available.

FOOD

Port Orford doesn't have a lot of restaurants, but there are a few very good places to eat.

Vegetarian soup and sandwiches can be enjoyed at **Seaweed Natural Food and Grocery** (832 Oregon St., 541/332-3640). More elaborate fare can be had across the street from Battle Rock at **Paula's Bistro** (236 6th St., 541/332-9378, dinner Tues.–Sat., $13–18), whose menu of pasta, barbecue, and seafood specials and wild decor show ambition and creativity. The other really memorable place to eat in town is **❰ Port Orford Breadworks** (190 6th St., 541/332-4022, lunch and dinner Wed.–Sat., dinner Sun., $8–23, dinner reservations recommended) with great trattoria-style Italian food, good bread, and gourmet sandwiches.

INFORMATION

Begin your travels here at **Battle Rock Information Center,** open daily on the west side of U.S. 101 (541/332-8055, www.port orfordoregon.com).

The **library** (555 W. 20th St.) is open 8 A.M.–5 P.M. weekdays.

GETTING THERE

Curry County's **Coastal Express** buses (in Port Orford, call 800/921-2871) run up and down the south coast weekdays only between North Bend and the California border, including local service in Port Orford.

Gold Beach and Vicinity

Despite the name Gold Beach, the real riches here are silver, and they swim up the Rogue River in great numbers every year. This town is one part of the coast where the action is definitely away from the ocean. Although the gold-laden black sands that were mined in the 1850s and 1860s gave Gold Beach its name, the arrival of Robert Hume, later known as the Salmon King of the Rogue, had greater historical significance. By the turn of the 20th century, Hume's canneries were shipping some 16,000 cases of salmon a year, and established the river's image as a leading salmon and steelhead stream, a reputation that was later enhanced by outdoorsman Zane Grey in his *Rogue River Feud* and other writings. Over the years, Herbert Hoover, Winston Churchill, Ginger Rogers (who had a home on the Rogue), Clark Gable, Jack London, George Bush, and Jimmy Carter, among other notables, have come here to try their luck. During the last several decades, white-water rafting and jet-boat tours focusing on the abundant wildlife, scenic beauty, and fascinating lore of the region have hooked other sectors of the traveling public.

Today, Gold Beach is a town of about 2,100 and the Curry County seat. Besides serving as the south coast tourism hub, a pulp mill and commercial ocean-fishing industry make up the local economy here. The seasonal nature of many local businesses creates serious wintertime unemployment. This fact, combined with torrential rains, drastically reduces the population of Gold Beach from Thanksgiving until spring. Thereafter, the wildflowers and warm weather transform this town into a vacation mecca.

At the north end of town, just before the road gives way to Conde McCullough's elegant Patterson Bridge, the harbor comes into view on the left, full of salmon trawlers, jet boats, pelicans, and seals bobbing up and down. Across the bridge is **Wedderburn,** a baby sister to Gold Beach. Named for the Scottish birthplace of Robert Hume, its major claim to fame is as the home port of the Mailboat, which has been the mail carrier to upriver residents on the Rogue since 1895.

SIGHTS

Curry Historical Museum

At the Curry Historical Museum (920 S. Ellensburg, 541/247-6113, 10 A.M.–4 P.M. Tues.–Sat., closed Jan., $2), the local historical society has assembled a small collection of exhibits on Native American and pioneer life, mining in the region's golden age, logging, fishing, and agriculture. It's located at the county fairgrounds at the south edge of town. Particularly interesting are a realistic reconstruction of a miner's cabin, vintage photos, and Native American petroglyphs.

Rogue River Museum

In the harbor area on the west side of U.S. 101, Jerry's Jetboats has assembled the best regional museum on the south coast, the Rogue

River Museum (541/247-4571, 8 A.M.–9 P.M. summer, 8 A.M.– 6 P.M. in other seasons, free). Centuries of natural and human history are depicted here. In addition to geologic history, photos of pioneer families, arrowheads and other native artifacts, and a taxidermic collage of local critters will round out your introduction to the Rogue Valley. Jerry's river tour clientele will find that perspectives from the museum on the local salmon industry in the 1920s and on early river travel are expanded upon in their jet-boat guide's commentary, Museum photos of early river runs, hauling freight, passengers, and mail, also can impart a sense of history to your trip upriver or up the road.

Cape Sebastian

Seven miles south of Gold Beach is Cape Sebastian. This spectacular windswept headland was named by Sebastián Vizcaíno, who plied offshore waters here for Spain in 1602 along with Manuel d'Alguilar. At least 700 feet above the sea, Cape Sebastian is the highest south coast overlook reachable by paved public road. On a clear day, visibility extends 43 miles north to Humbug Mountain, and 50 miles south to California. This is one of the best perches along the south coast for whale-watching. A trail zigzags through beautiful springtime wildflowers down the south side of the cape for about two miles until it reaches the sea. In April and May, Pacific paintbrush, Douglas iris, orchids, and snow queen usher you along. In addition, Cape Sebastian supports a population of large-headed goldfields, a summer-blooming daisylike yellow flower found only in coastal Curry County.

In 1942, a caretaker here heard Japanese voices drifting across the water through the fog. When the mist lifted he looked down from Cape Sebastian trail to see a surfaced submarine. This sighting, together with the Japanese bombing at Brookings and the incendiary balloon spotted over Cape Blanco, sent shock waves up the south coast. But the potential threat remained just that, and local anxiety eventually subsided.

Beaches

The driftwood-strewn strand of **South Beach,** just south of Gold Beach's harbor, is convenient but only so-so. You'll find more exciting stretches both north and south of town. Tidepoolers might want to stop at the visitors center before heading out and ask for the "Tidepools Are Alive" brochure, with tips and species descriptions. Two miles south, there's easy access to a nice beach and some tidepooling at tiny **Buena Vista State Park,** at the mouth of Hunter Creek. Seven miles south of Gold Beach, there's more tidepooling amid the camera-friendly basalt sea stacks at beautiful **Myers Beach,** part of Pistol River State Park south of Cape Sebastian. The south side of Cape Sebastian and **Pistol River State Park,** a couple of miles farther south, are the only places on the Oregon coast where sailboarders can enjoy wave sailing. The beaches around Pistol River are also productive areas for finding razor clams.

Bailey Beach, north of town between the Rogue River jetty and Otter Point, is another popular spot for razor clamming, and **Nesika Beach,** seven miles from Gold Beach, is another good tidepooling destination.

SPORTS AND RECREATION
Ⓒ Rogue River Jet-Boat Cruise

The best way to take in the mighty Rogue is on a jet-boat ride from Gold Beach harbor. Several different companies run this trip, and they all provide comparable service and prices. It's an exciting and interesting look at the varied flora and fauna along the estuary as well as the changing moods of the river. Most of the estimated 50,000 people per year who "do" the Rogue in this way take the 64-mile round-trip cruise. This and the more adventurous 104-mile cruise include a stop for a sumptuous lunch at one of several secluded fishing lodges upriver. The pilots/commentators usually have grown up on the river, and their evocations of the diverse ecosystems and Native American and gold-mining history add greatly to your enjoyment. Bears, otters, seals, and beavers may be sighted en route, and anglers may hold up a big keeper to show off. Ospreys, snowy egrets, eagles, mergansers, and kingfishers are also seen with regularity in this stopover for migratory waterfowl.

In the first part of the journey, idyllic riverside retreats dot the hillsides, breaking up stands of fir and hemlock. Myrtle, madrone, and impressive springtime wildflower groupings also vary the landscape. Both the 64- and 104-mile trips focus on the section of the Rogue protected by the government as a Wild and Scenic River. Only the longer trips take you into the pristine Rogue Wilderness, an area that motor launches from Grants Pass do not reach either. The 13 miles of this wilderness you see from the boat have canyon walls rising 1,500 feet above you. Geologists say that this part of the Klamaths is composed of ancient islands and sea floor that collided with North America. To deal with the rapids upstream, smaller, faster boats are used that skim over the boulders with just six inches of water between hull and rock surface.

The season runs May–October 15. Remember that chill and fog near the mouth of the estuary usually give way to much warmer conditions upstream. These tour outfits have wool blankets available on cold days as well as complimentary hot beverages. Also keep in mind that the upriver lodges can be booked for overnight stays and your trip may be resumed the following day. The following suppliers offer 64- and 104-mile trips; meals are included in the cost of the 104-mile trip (rates range $42–84 for adults, $16–37 for children).

Just south of the Rogue River Bridge, west of U.S. 101 on Harbor Way, is **Jerry's Rogue River Jetboats** (P.O. Box 1011, Gold Beach, 541/247-4571 or 800/451-3645, www.rogue-jets.com). This heavily patronized company runs trips May–October. Jerry's is noted for personable, well-informed guides. If you forgot a hat to buffer the winds at the mouth of the Rogue, stop in at Jerry's gift shop. While you're there, check out the local jams and critically acclaimed fish prints of local artist Don Jensen.

Rogue River Mailboats (P.O. Box 1165, Gold Beach, 541/247-7033 or 800/458-3511, www.mailboat.com) is located a quarter mile upstream from the north end of the Rogue River bridge. Besides human cargo, this boat also carries sacks of U.S. mail, ensuring a warm welcome in upriver locations.

Fishing

Fishing is a mighty big deal in Gold Beach, which has one of the highest concentrations of professional guides in the state. There's something to fish for just about year-round, but salmon and steelhead are the top quarry. When the spring chinook pour in, April–June, anglers will need to book guided trips well in advance to get a shot at them. Catches peak in May. Summer steelhead and fall-run chinook usually arrive July–September, then it's hatchery coho September–November (sometimes as early as August). In December, the first of the winter steelhead make their appearance and continue into March.

The **Rogue Outdoor Store** (560 N. Ellensburg, Gold Beach, 541/247-7142) is well stocked with fishing, camping, and other gear, and can advise on where, when, and what to fish. Typical rates for guided salmon trips here are $150–200 per person. Contact the Gold Beach Visitor Center ((29279 Ellensburg, 541/247-7526 or 800/525-2334, www.gold-beach.org)) or the Curry Guide Association (800/775-0886) for a list of over two dozen licensed guides.

Some well-established **guides** include: Darrell Allen (541/247-2082); Denny Hughson (541/247-2684, www.hughsons-rogue river.com); Steve Beyerlin (541/247-4138 or 800/348-4138, www.fishoregon.com), for both conventional and fly-fishing; Shaun Carpenter (541/247-2049, www.end oftherogue.com), conventional and fly-fishing; Helen Burns (541/247-2441 or 541/290-8402, www.helensguideservice.com), one of the few women in a male-dominated club; Ron Smith (541/247-6046 or 800/501-6391, www.sportfishingoregon.com); and John Ward (541/247-2866).

Hiking and Horseback Riding

The 40-mile **Rogue River Trail** offers lodge-to-lodge hiking, which means you need little more in your pack than the essentials. The lodges here are comfortably rustic, serve home-style food in copious portions, and run $150–200 for a double room. They are also comfortably spaced, so extended hiking is seldom a necessity.

Before you go, check with the Gold Beach Ranger Station on trail conditions and directions to the trailhead. Pick up the western end of the trail 35 miles east of Gold Beach, about one-half mile from Foster Bar, a popular boat landing. Park there and walk east and north on the paved road until you see signs on the left marking the Rogue River Trail. Go in spring before the hot weather and enjoy yellow Siskiyou iris and fragrant wild azaleas. The trail ends at Graves Creek, 27 miles northwest of Grants Pass. Be careful of rattlesnakes on the trail.

Hawk's Rest Ranch at Siskiyou West Day Lodge (94667 N. Bank Pistol River Rd., Pistol River, 541/247-6423, www.siskiyouwest. com) offers horseback riding on the beach near the scenic Pistol River, riding lessons, a petting zoo, and other family-oriented attractions.

Camping

Campsites east of town along the Rogue and off U.S. 101 en route to Port Orford provide wonderful spots to bed down for the night. Those driving the road along the Rogue should be alert for oncoming log trucks, raft transport vehicles, and other wide-body vehicles.

Foster Bar Campground (Siskiyou National Forest, Gold Beach Ranger Station, 1225 S. Ellensburg, 541/247-6651, www. fs.fed.us/r6/rogue-siskiyou, year-round, $5, no reservations) is located 30 miles east of Gold Beach on the south bank of the Rogue. Take Jerry's Flat Road east for 30 miles to the turn-off for Agness. Turn right on Illahe Agness Road and drive three miles to camp. The campground has drinking water, toilets, accessible facilities, picnic tables, fire rings, and a boat ramp. This is a popular spot from which

to embark on an eight-mile inner tube ride to Agness. It's also where rafters pull out, so the parking lot may be jam-packed. The rapids are dangerous, so wear a life jacket. You are also within walking distance of the trailhead of the Rogue River Trail.

Lobster Creek Campground (541/247-3600, www.fs.fed.us/r6/rogue-siskiyou, year-round, $5) is a small campground nine miles east of Gold Beach via Forest Service Road 33. The nearby Schrader old-growth trail is a gentle one-mile walk through a rare and majestic ecosystem.

Honeybear Campground and RV Resort (P.O. Box 97, 34161 Ophir Rd., Ophir 97464, 541/247-2765 or 800/822-4444, www.honey bearrv.com, year-round, $16–27) is nine miles north of Gold Beach on U.S. 101, then two miles north on Ophir Road, but could just as well be in the Black Forest. The owners have built a large rathskeller with a dance floor. Six nights a week during the summer, there are dances here with traditional German music. Check out their version of Octoberfest. Locals praise the Honeybear's on-site delicatessen for its homemade German sausage. There are 20 tent and RV sites, picnic tables, flush toilets, hot showers, firewood, a laundry, and ocean views.

Golf

Cedar Bend Golf Course (P.O. Box 1234, Gold Beach, 541/247-6911) is located in nearby Ophir. Eleven miles north of Gold Beach, pick up Ophir Road off U.S. 101. Follow it to Squaw Valley Road, turn right at the Old Ophir Store, and continue until you see the links. Woods line the fairways, and a winding creek offers a challenge on each of the nine holes. Green fees are $20 for 18 holes, $15 for nine.

EVENTS

The **Wild Rivers Coast Seafood, Art, and Wine Festival** is a two-day event that celebrates wine, fine dining, and arts and crafts of the southern Oregon coast, in mid-May at the Event Center on the Beach (29392 Ellensburg, 541/247-4541).

People line the river for the annual **jet-boat races,** which take place in mid-June. Contact Jot's Resort (800/367-5687) or the chamber of commerce for further information

The **Pistol River Wave Bash National Windsurfing Competition** bring four days of competitive riding to Pistol River State Park each June. For details, contact the Gold Beach Visitor Center (541/247-0923 or 800/525-2334).

In late July or early August, the **Curry County Fair and Rodeo** (541/247-4541) takes place at the Event Center on the Beach. Highlights include Oregon's largest flower show and a lamb barbecue.

ACCOMMODATIONS

As in most coastal towns, there is no shortage of places to stay along the main drag, Ellensburg Street (a.k.a. U.S. 101). In fact, Gold Beach offers the largest number and widest range of accommodations on the south coast, with intimate lodges overlooking the Rogue as popular as the oceanfront motels. A discount of 20 percent or more on rooms is usually available during the winter, when 80–90 inches of rain can fall here.

If you're looking for a simple place to spend a night or two and don't really care about frills, the **Azalea Lodge** (29481 Ellensburg Ave., 541/247-6635 or 866/381-6635, double $86) is a good bet, with friendly owners and clean rooms. No pets are allowed; all rooms are nonsmoking and have refrigerators.

Ireland's Rustic Lodge (29330 Ellensburg, 541/247-7718, www.irelendsrusticlodges.com, $95–150) was started by two women who used to bring meals to the cabins. While this is no longer the case, the touch of home has not been lost. Many of the rooms have fireplaces, knottypine interiors, and distinctive decor. Best of all, the grounds are lovingly landscaped with pine trees, flowers, and ocean views. A sandy beach is a short stroll to the west. There are 33 motel lodge units (some with kitchens), seven old but well-kept log cabins (recommended) that sleep up to five, and houses that sleep as many as 11. Ireland's also has an RV park close by the lodge.

Located on the Rogue River's north bank, the sprawling **Jot's Resort** (94360 Wedderburn Loop, Wedderburn, 541/247-6676 or 800/367-5687, www.jotsresort.com, $75–300) is a sprawling motel complex with a nice view. The rooms here are at a premium in summer when the motorcoach tours come through, leaving other travelers with the less-desirable rooms and a sense that the motel staff's priorities are elsewhere.

◖ **Tu Tu Tun Resort** (96550 N. Bank, 541/247-6664 or 800/864-6357, www.tutu tun.com, $195 and up) emphasizes the tranquility reinforced by the absence of TV in the rooms (except in the suites and houses). The lodge is located seven miles up the Rogue River from Gold Beach. While there is a TV in the cedar-planked lodge, most guests prefer to take in the view of the river through the floor-to-ceiling windows or enjoy a good book from the lodge's library in front of the massive river rock fireplace. Other appeals include a heated pool and other recreational facilities, beautifully appointed interiors, and delicious meals (served on an inclusive Modified American Plan for about $53 per person May–October; in the off-season, guests are served a continental breakfast only).

For vacation house rentals, check out the offerings at **Rogue Reef Vacation Rentals** (www.roguereefvacationrentals.com). A variety of condos and houses are available, starting at about $150 per day.

Upriver Lodges

Several lodges on the Rogue, some accessible only by boat or via hiking trails, lure visitors deep into the interior. Jet-boat trips can drop you off for an overnight or longer stay. Advance reservations are essential.

Accessible by road or jet boat 32 miles inland from the coast, the **Cougar Lane Lodge** (04219 Agness Rd., 541/247-7233, $45–65) was established in 1949 on the east shore of the Rogue. Spend the night in one of the simple lodge rooms or come for the day to fish (licenses and tackle available at the Cougar Lane store). Dine at the lodge restaurant, overlooking the

Rogue, which serves standard American breakfast, lunch, and dinner every day. From here, hike the Rogue or Illinois trails. The Agness RV Park is nearby, for overnight camping.

Also accessible by road and boat, the **Lucas Pioneer Ranch & Fishing Lodge** (03904 Cougar Lane, 541/247-7443, $45–80) is also 32 miles east of Gold Beach. Cabins here come equipped with cooking and noncooking options. Lunch and dinner are served daily in the lodge—chicken, biscuits, and garden vegetables are standard fare. Reservations are required.

The more remote **Half Moon Bar Lodge** (Box 455, Gold Beach 97444, 541/247-6968 or 888/291-8268, www.halfmoonbarlodge.com, $150 adults, $65 children, includes three meals) is located in the wild and secluded piece of wilderness, once the site of Native American encampments. Choose from three private cabins or stay in the rustic lodge, which houses a sauna, dining room, and bar. Meals are served family-style and include fresh seasonal garden veggies and fruits. Tour boats take visitors 52 miles upriver; raft down with a white-water guide or fish for steelhead. To get there, hike in 11 miles from Foster Bar along the Rogue River Trail or five miles from Bear Camp near Agness. The lodge can also accommodate small planes on its private airstrip. Call to make arrangements.

Only accessible by helicopter, jet boat, or foot, the **Paradise Lodge** (541/247-6504 or 800/525-2161, www.go-oregon.com, $150 adults, $65 children, includes three meals) attracts nature enthusiasts interested in the "wildest" experience. Only the meals are scheduled here, where you can take an eco tour, enjoy a sauna, raft or jet boat the rapids, or check out some of the old mining sites in the vicinity. A huge on-site garden provides ingredients for home-cooked meals. Jet-boat round-trip rates are $95.

FOOD

You can't eat scenery, but Gold Beach restaurants charge you for it anyway. Still, this is one place where the oceanfront and riverside views are often worth the price. Then, too, there's always the option of cheaper restaurants away from port. Spring chinook salmon, blackberry pie, and other indigenous specialties taste good anywhere.

One of the best places to eat in Curry County is **Rollin 'n Dough** (94257 North Bank Rogue, Wedderburn, 541/247-4438, lunch, dinner, and Sunday brunch, dinner entrées $12–28), a deli and bistro with imported cheeses, high-quality deli meats, and excellent baked goods.

Grant's Pancake House (29790 U.S. 101, 541/247-7208, breakfast and lunch daily, breakfast $5–9) is the breakfast place of choice from the Rogue estuary to California. Filling omelettes, pancakes, waffles, and corned beef hash often make lunch (in the same price range) an afterthought. Nonetheless, locals consider the Thursday clam steak lunch special (breaded East Coast sea clams in a spicy homemade sauce) one of the town's culinary highlights.

Stop by **Biscuits Café** (29707 Ellensburg, 541/247-2495) in Gold Beach Books for coffee and pastries. Be sure to take a look in the rare-book room after you finish eating.

The Nor'Wester (10 Harbor Way, 541/247-2333, dinner daily) is located at the port of Gold Beach, so sometimes you can watch boats unloading your dinner. Not surprisingly, the menu is dominated by seafood, though the wait staff tout the New Zealand lamb chops. What is surprising are such occasional culinary flourishes as chinook salmon broiled under a flame, then covered with a glaze of sake, cayenne, ginger, and soy. Dinner prices top out above $40 for steak and lobster but most entrées are in the $18–20 range. There are also light (less expensive) dinner options.

A very good dinner house with ocean views (and the corresponding prices) is **Spinner's Seafood, Steak, and Chop House** (29430 Ellensburg Ave., 541/247-51160, dinner nightly, main courses $20–30). The menu is wide ranging and the dining room extremely pleasant. Look for fresh seafood, pasta, prime rib, and chops.

Locals recommend the **Port Hole Cafe** (29975 Harbor Way, 541/247-7411, 6 A.M.– 9 P.M. daily, dinner $9–18), in the Cannery building at the port with bay and river views, for hearty portions of fish-n-chips, chowder, and homemade pies at decent prices.

Pick up some fresh seafood or the best canned tuna you'll ever taste at **Fishermen Direct Seafoods** (29975 Harbor Way, 541/247-9494).

INFORMATION

The **Gold Beach Visitor Center** (29279 Ellensburg, 541/247-7526 or 800/525-2334, www.goldbeach.org) is open 9 A.M.–5 P.M. Monday– Friday and 10 A.M.–4 P.M. Saturday and Sunday.

Their website is excellent and informative, and they'll send you a good, comprehensive information folder upon request. An independently run website, www.goldbeach.net, is also packed with detailed tourist information.

The **Gold Beach Ranger District** (29279 Ellensburg, 541/247-3600), offers a free packet on camping and recreation in the district. It's open 7:30 A.M.–5 P.M. Monday–Friday.

GETTING THERE

Curry County's **Coastal Express** buses (in Gold Beach, call 800/921-2871) run up and down the south coast weekdays only between North Bend and the California border, including local service in Gold Beach.

Brookings-Harbor

There are people who don't like Brookings, and if you form your judgment by simply driving down U.S. 101, it's easy to join that crowd. But something as simple as turning off into Harris Beach State Park can begin to change your view. To really fall for the area, it may take a drive up the Chetco River. A couple of miles inland, the fog that frequently drenches the coastline here during the summer months burns away. There are ample hiking opportunities upriver, most especially in the Kalmiopsis Wilderness Area.

During winter Brookings (pop. 5,725) and its unincorporated bigger neighbor, Harbor (pop. 8,775) enjoy mild temperatures. Enough 60–70°F days occur during January and February in this south coast "banana belt" town that more than 50 species of flowering plants thrive here—along with retirees, sports enthusiasts, and beachcombers. With two gorgeous state parks virtually part of the city and world-class salmon and steelhead fishing nearby, only the lavish winter rainfall that averages over 73 inches a year can cool the ardor of local outdoor enthusiasts. In the springtime, the area south of town is lush with lilies—it's the Easter lily capital of the world.

Brookings and Harbor sit on a coastal plain overlooking the Pacific six miles north of the California border, split by U.S. 101 (Chetco Avenue) and the Chetco River. Flowing out of the Klamath Mountains east of town, the Chetco drains part of the nearby Siskiyou National Forest and the Kalmiopsis Wilderness, extensive tracts encompassing some of the wildest country in the Lower 48 and renowned for their rare flowers and trees. This area enjoys strict federal protection, safeguarding the northernmost stand of giant redwoods as well as the coveted Port Orford cedar (whose strong but pliable lumber can fetch $10,000 and up for a single tree). The Kalmiopsis Wilderness is named for a unique shrub, the *Kalmiopsis leachiana,* one of the oldest members of the heath family (Ericaceae) that grows nowhere else on earth.

But you don't have to trek miles into the backcountry to enjoy the natural beauty of Brookings and vicinity. Just make your way past the somewhat drab main drag to Samuel Boardman State Park north of town, where 11 of the most scenic miles of the Oregon coast await you. Or head down to the harbor to embark on a boating expedition, amid some of the

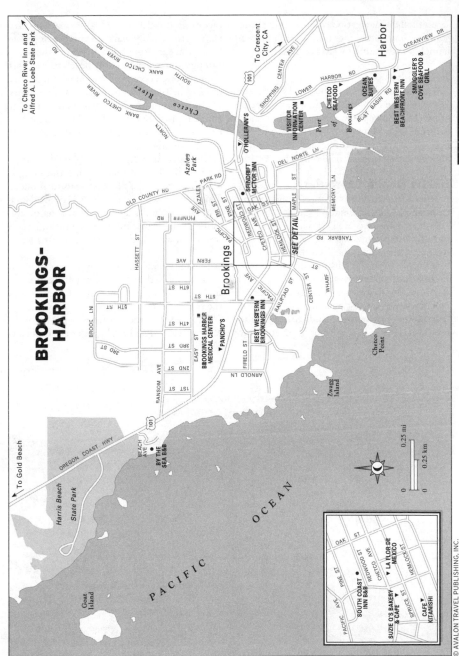

BROOKINGS-HARBOR

To Chetco River Inn and
Alfred A. Loeb State Park

To Crescent
City, CA

To Gold Beach

SOUTH BANK CHETCO RIVER RD

NORTH BANK CHETCO RIVER RD

Chetco River

Azalea Park

OLD COUNTY RD

PARK RD

AZALEA AVE

PIONEER RD

HASSETT ST

FERN AVE

BROOK LN

5TH ST

5TH ST

4TH ST

6TH ST

3RD ST

3RD ST

2ND ST

1ST ST

RANSOM AVE

EASY ST

FIFIELD ST

ARNOLD LN

OREGON COAST HWY

BEACH AVE

Harris Beach
State Park

Goat
Island

Zwagg
Island

Chetco
Point

PACIFIC OCEAN

SHOPPING CENTER AVE

LOWER HARBOR RD

OCEANVIEW DR

Harbor

Port of Brookings

BOAT BASIN RD

DEL NORTE LN

OAK ST

MAPLE ST

MEMORY LN

TANBARK RD

REDWOOD ST

CHETCO AVE

HEMLOCK ST

PINE ST

PACIFIC AVE

FIR ST

WHARF ST

CENTER ST

PACIFIC AVE

RAILROAD ST

Brookings

O'HOLLERAN'S

VISITOR INFORMATION CENTER

CHETCO SEAFOOD

OCEAN SUITES

BEST WESTERN BEACHFRONT INN

SMUGGLER'S COVE SEAFOOD & GRILL

SPINDRIFT MOTOR INN

BEST WESTERN BROOKINGS INN

BROOKINGS HARBOR MEDICAL CENTER

PANCHO'S

BY THE SEA B&B

SEE DETAIL

0.25 mi

0.25 km

0

0

Detail inset:

OAK ST

PINE ST

REDWOOD ST

CHETCO AVE

SPRUCE ST

HEMLOCK ST

PACIFIC AVE

SOUTH COAST INN B&B

LA FLOR DE MEXICO

SUZIE Q'S BAKERY & CAFE

CAFE KITANISHI

safest offshore navigation conditions in the region. In short, Brookings is the perfect place to launch an adventure by land or by sea.

SIGHTS

Camellias bloom at Christmas and the flowering plums add color the next month. Daffodils, grown commercially on the coastal plain south of Brookings, bloom in late January and into February. Magnolia shrubs, some early azaleas, and rhododendrons also bloom in late winter.

Harris Beach State Park

At the northern limits of Brookings, across from the State Information Center on U.S. 101, Harris Beach State Park makes up for all the ugly architecture that you'll find on Chetco Avenue. One look at the 24 miles of rock and tide visible from the parking-lot promontory should quell any misgivings.

Harris Beach was named after the Scottish pioneer George Harris, who settled here in the late 1880s to raise sheep and cattle. Besides stunning views, this state park offers many incoming travelers from California their first chance to actually walk on the beach in Oregon. You can begin directly west of the park's campground, where a sandy beach strewn with boulders often becomes flooded with intertidal life and driftwood. The early morning hours, as the waves crash through a small tunnel in a massive rock onto the shoreline, are the best time to look for sponges, umbrella crabs, solitary corals, and starfish.

Offshore, Bird Island (also called Goat Island) is the largest island along the Oregon coast and the state's largest seabird rookery. This outpost of Oregon Islands National Wildlife Sanctuary dispatches squadrons of cormorants, pelicans, tufted puffins, and other waterfowl who divebomb the incoming waves for food.

In addition to beachcombing, you can picnic at tables above the parking lot, loll about in the shallow waters of nearby Harris Creek, or cast the surf for perch.

Mill Beach is the southernmost part of the Harris Beach area. Locals prefer the beach ac-

The Brookings-Harbor area is an active fishing port.

© BILL MCRAE

cess from downtown, which is easy to miss. To get there, drive toward the ocean on Center Street in downtown Brookings, make a right at the plywood mill, and stop next to a small ballpark. An unimproved road leads to a hillock from which trails take you down to a beach full of driftwood. Residents say that Japanese fishing floats occasionally roll up onto the beach after a storm.

Chetco Valley
Historical Society Museum

Located in the red-and-white Blake House, the Chetco Valley Museum (5461 Museum Rd., Brookings, 541/469-6651, 1– 5 p.m. Fri.– Sun. Memorial Day–Labor Day, $3 donation suggested) sits on a hill overlooking U.S. 101 two miles south of the Chetco River. Built in 1857, the structure was used as a stagecoach way station and trading post before Lincoln was president.

Even if you are not one for museums, several exhibits here stand apart from the traditional collections of pioneer wedding dresses, Native American baskets, and spinning wheels. These include a small trunk that came around Cape Horn in 1706 and a Native American dugout canoe. Should these fail to inspire, a mysterious iron casting of a woman's face might do the trick—especially in light of the speculation that this relic was left by an early undocumented landing on the Oregon coast, perhaps by Sir Francis Drake. Drake has been commonly suggested because of the mask's likeness to Queen Elizabeth.

Oregon's largest Monterey cypress tree is located on the hill near the museum. The 130-foot-tall tree has a trunk circumference of more than 27 feet and has been home to a pair of owls for years.

◖ Samuel H. Boardman
State Scenic Corridor

The stretch of highway from Brookings to Port Orford is known as the "fabulous 50 miles." Some consider the section of coastline just north of Brookings to be the most scenic in Oregon—and one of the most dramatic meetings of rock and tide in the world. The offshore rock formations and winding roadbed hundreds of feet above the surf invite comparison to Europe's Amalfi Drive. This sobriquet is perhaps most apt in the first dozen miles north of Brookings, encompassed by Samuel Boardman State Scenic Corridor. You'll want to have a camera at the ready and a loose schedule when you make this drive, because you'll find it hard not to pull over again and again, as each photo opportunity seems to out-dazzle the last. Of the 11 named viewpoints that have been cut into the highway's shoulder here, the following are especially recommended (all viewpoints are marked by signs on the west side of U.S. 101 and are listed from north to south).

Near the north end of Boardman Park a short walk down the hillside trail leads you to the **Arch Rocks** viewpoint, where an immense boomerang-shaped basalt archway juts out of the water about a quarter mile offshore. This site has picnic tables within view of the monolith.

A few miles to the south, the sign for **Natural Bridges Cove** seems to front just a forested parking lot. However, the paved walkway at the south end of the lot leads to a spectacular overlook. Below, several rock archways frame an azure cove. This feature was created by the collapse of the entrance and exit of a sea cave. A steep, winding trail through giant ferns and towering Sitka spruce and Douglas fir takes you down for a closer look. Thimbleberry (a sweet but seedy raspberry) is plentiful in late spring. Here as in similar forests on the south coast, it's important to stay on the trail. The rainforest-like biome is exceptionally fragile, and the soil erodes easily when the delicate vegetation is damaged.

Thomas Creek Bridge, the highest bridge in Oregon (345 feet above the water) as well as the highest north of San Francisco, has been used as a silent star in many TV commercials. A parking lot at the south end of the bridge marks a trailhead down. Do not take the path you see closest to the bridge; it's too steep. At the south end of the lot, the true trail eventually leads down to a view of the bridge on one side and miles of coast on the other. The offshore rock formations here are especially interesting.

From here hikers can access the Indian Sands Trail, ending up in pine-rimmed dunes and a sandstone bluff high above the sea.

House Rock was the site of a World War II air-raid sentry tower that sits hundreds of feet above whitecaps pounding the rock-strewn beaches. To the north, you'll see one of the highest cliffs on the coast, Cape Sebastian. A steep, circuitous trail lined with salal goes down to the water. The path begins behind the Samuel Boardman monument on the west end of the parking lot. The sign to the highest viewpoint in Boardman Park is easy to miss, but look for the turnout that precedes House Rock, called Cape Ferrelo (for Cabrillo's navigator, who sailed up much of the West Coast in 1543).

Alfred A. Loeb State Park

Eight miles northeast of Brookings on North Bank Chetco River Road along the Chetco River, Loeb State Park preserves 320 acres of old-growth myrtlewood, the state's largest grove. Many of the aromatic trees here are well over 200 years old.

The 0.25-mile Riverview Trail passes numerous big trees to connect Loeb Park with the **Redwood Nature Trail.** This trail winds 1.2 miles through the northernmost stands of naturally occurring *Sequoia sempervirens.* This is the northernmost redwood grove in the United States, and contains Oregon's largest specimens. Within the grove are a number of trees more than 500 years old, measuring 5–8 feet in diameter, towering more than 300 feet above the forest floor. One tree here has a 33-foot girth and is estimated to exceed 800 years in age. When the south coast is foggy and cold on summer mornings, it's often warm and dry in upriver locations such as this one.

Bombsite Trail

Brookings takes a peculiar pride in having been bombed by the Japanese during World War II. In 1942, two incendiary bombs were dropped about 16 miles east of town on the slopes of Mount Emily. Although they were intended to start a fire, conditions were wet and the small

fire that resulted was easily controlled. A sort of mutual respect eventually developed between the Japanese pilot who dropped the bomb and the town of Brookings. The pilot was a guest of honor at one Azalea Festival, and his family later presented the town with his samurai sword, which he wore during the bombing and throughout the war. The sword is on exhibit at the local library (420 Alder St.).

The Mount Emily Bombsite Trail commemorates the bombing. It's a two-mile stretch with redwoods near the beginning and fire-dependent species such as knobcone pine and manzanita along the way. To reach the trail, head eight miles east up South Bank Road and turn right onto Mount Emily Road. At the fork, turn onto Wheeler Creek Road and follow the signs.

The Kalmiopsis Wilderness

The lure of untrammeled wilderness attracts intrepid hikers to the Kalmiopsis, despite summer's blazing heat and winter's torrential rains. In addition to enjoying the isolation of Oregon's largest (179,655 acres) wilderness area, they come to take in the pink rhododendron-like blooms of *Kalmiopsis leachiana* (in June) and other rare flowers. The area is also home to such economically valued species as Port Orford cedar and marijuana. The illicit weed is a major cash crop in the area, and its vigilant protection by growers should inspire extra care for those hiking here during the late-fall harvest season. The potential for violence associated with the mushroom harvest here also mandates a measure of caution.

In any case, the Forest Service prohibits plant collection *of any kind* to preserve the region's special botanical populations. These include the insect-eating Darlingtonia plant and the Brewer's weeping spruce. The forest canopy is composed largely of the more common Douglas fir, canyon live oak, madrone, and chinquapin. Stark peaks top this red-rock forest, whose understory is choked with blueberry, manzanita, and dense chaparral.

Many of the rare species in this wilderness survived the glacial epoch because the glaciers from that era left the area untouched. This, combined with the fact that the area was an ancient offshore island, has enabled the region's singular ecosystem to maintain its integrity through the millennia. You'd think that federal protection, remoteness, and climatic extremes would ensure a sanguine outlook for this ice-age forest, but an active debate still rages over the validity of some logging claims.

In the summer of 2002, the **Biscuit Fire** raged out of control for weeks, ravaging nearly half a million acres of southwestern Oregon, engulfing most of the Siskiyou National Forest and virtually all of the Kalmiopsis Wilderness. This inferno, the nation's largest wildfire of 2002 and the biggest in Oregon for well over a century, destroyed extensive habitat of the endangered northern spotted owl, whose population National Forest Service biologists predict may drop by 20 percent. It will likely be decades before the forest returns to normal. The good news, however, is that flora of the region is well adapted to periodic fires; many of the old-growth trees survived the blaze, and within a few months green sprouts and new growth of many species were reappearing amidst the ashes.

SPORTS AND RECREATION
Fishing
Fishing on the Chetco was once one of southern Oregon's best-kept secrets, but the word has gotten out about the river's October run of huge chinook as well as a superlative influx of winter steelhead. And should river traffic become too heavy, the late-summer ocean salmon season out of Brookings may be the best in the Northwest. Boatless anglers can try their luck at the public fishing pier at the harbor and on the south jetty at the mouth of the Chetco. Chinook season generally runs mid-May–mid-September, but that's subject to change so check the regulations.

Various fishing trips for salmon ($75 for 5–6 hours), tuna ($125 for 12 hours), and bottom fishing ($60 for 5–6 hours) can be arranged through **Sporthaven Marina** (16374 Lower Harbor Rd., Brookings, 541/469-3301). In addition to fishing charters, **Tidewind Sportfishing** (16368 Lower Harbor Rd.,

541/469-0337) offers **whale-watching** excursions in season.

Camping
Harris Beach State Park (1655 U.S. 101, Brookings, 541/469-2021 or 800/452-5687, $17–21), two miles north of town, is open all year, but reservations are definitely necessary Memorial Day–Labor Day. Of the 155 total sites, 149 are paved (50 electricity only, 36 full hookups), some are shaded, and six are yurts. There is a special camping area for hikers and bicyclists. Picnic tables and fire grills are provided. Flush toilets, electricity, piped-in water, sewer hookups, sanitary service, showers, firewood, laundry, and playground round out the amenities. Whale-watching is particularly good here in January and May, on this piece of beach peppered with basalt outcroppings.

The 320-acre **Alfred A. Loeb State Park** (541/469-2021, camping year-round, $12–16) is nine miles northeast of Brookings on North Bank Chetco River Road. There are 53 sites for trailers/motor homes (50 feet maximum), a special campground for bicyclists and hikers, and some cabins (reservations 800/452-5687, $35). Electricity, piped water, and picnic tables are provided; showers, flush toilets, and firewood are available. The campground is located in a fragrant, secluded myrtlewood grove on the north bank of the Chetco River.

There are also some less-developed campgrounds in the Siskiyou National Forest. Head up the North Bank Road to find the riverside **Little Redwood** (mid-May–Sept., $10).

Golf
All the press about Bandon Dunes has obscured the development of another great course, **Salmon Run Golf and Wilderness Preserve** (99040 South Bank Chetco River Rd., 541/469-4888). This beautiful 18-hole public links not far from the Kalmiopsis Wilderness was designed with environmentally sensitive imperatives so that numerous wildlife sightings can be enjoyed here long into the future. Whether it's the chance to see salmon (usually after the first rains in Nov.) and steelhead spawning (Jan.),

black bears, elk, and wild turkeys, or just the opportunity to play a first-rate course, golfers shouldn't overlook this one. Green fees are $29 for nine holes, $49 for 18, excluding cart. Beginner and intermediate players may find the Executive 9 ideal. This par-34 course within a course is located on the back nine holes, and measures 1,310 yards. Your Oregon coastal golf pilgrimage can include Salmon Run along with Bandon Dunes, Sandpines (Florence), and Salishan (near Lincoln City).

EVENTS

Brookings' big event is the **Azalea Festival,** an unforgettable floral fantasia that takes place each Memorial Day weekend. Among the activities are a parade, flower display, crafts fair, a 10K run, seafood luncheon, and beef barbecue. Much of the activity revolves around Azalea Park. This WPA-built enclave features 20-foot-high azaleas (several hundred years old) and hand-hewn myrtlewood picnic tables. Wild cherry and crabapple blooms, wild strawberry blossoms, and purple and red violets round out the bouquet. Butterflies, bees, and birds all seem to concur with locals that this array smells sweetest around graduation time in mid-June. To get there, take Pacific Avenue east of the highway, and turn onto Azalea Park Road.

Like several other Oregon coast towns, Brookings puts the windy weather to good use, with its annual **Southern Oregon Kite Festival** (541/469-2218), held over two days in mid-July. Individuals and teams display their aerial skills at the port of Brookings-Harbor.

Azalea Park is also home to **Nature's Coastal Holiday Light Show** in December, with more than 75,000 lights. The Brookings-Harbor Garden Club and Chamber of Commerce offer garden tours of this park and other gardens. Call the chamber (541/469-3181) for more information on tours and garden-related events.

ACCOMMODATIONS

For the full oceanfront experience, head south to the town of Harbor. Here, **Best Western Beachfront Inn** (16008 Boat Basin Rd., Harbor, 541/469-7779 or 800/468-4081, $149 and up), is the nicer of the town's two Best Westerns. It's off the main highway, offering a window on a colorful port. All units feature private decks, microwaves, and refrigerators. Kitchenettes as well as suites with ocean-view hot tubs and an indoor pool are available. Pets are permitted on a very limited basis; call the hotel direct to plead your case.

Perhaps the best value in Brookings lodgings is **Ocean Suites** (16045 Lower Harbor Rd., 541/469-4004, www.oceansuitesmotel. com, $99), at the Harbor end of town, which also has weekly rates ($550). These really are suites: each has a full kitchen and living room. No pets allowed.

The highway-side **Best Western Brookings Inn** (1143 U.S. 101, 541/469-2173 or 800/822-9087, $85 and up) may be about a mile from the ocean, but it's family-friendly with a pool and whirlpool tub, a comfy myrtlewood-paneled lounge, and a decent on-site restaurant. No pets allowed.

The **Spindrift Motor Inn** (1215 Chetco Ave., 541/469-5345 or 800/292-1171, $55 and up) is a good dollar value. However, its ambiance is strictly roadside budget, and it is a bit of a walk to the beach.

Bed-and-Breakfasts

Head upstream to find a really great B&B, the [**Chetco River Inn** (21202 High Prairie Rd., 541/251-0087 or 800/327-2688, www.chetco riverinn.com, $125–145), an intimate inn surrounded by water on three sides. Eighteen miles inland from the coast, the half-hour drive to the inn takes you to the periphery of the Kalmiopsis; once there you feel as if you're in your own private forest. Its location near prime fishing river frontage makes this place especially popular during steelhead season. Swimming holes abound close by and the absence of city lights makes for good stargazing. The welcome mat here is laid out in the form of thick oriental carpets on floors of green and black marble. Tasteful antiques also decorate this reasonably priced first-class lodging. The five rooms plus cottage can easily accommodate up to 14 people in separate beds, or six couples. Children are welcome; cottages are suggested for their comfort. Smoking is limited to outdoors only. No pets allowed.

A coastal gem one block north of the highway, the **South Coast Inn B&B** (516 Redwood St., Brookings, 541/469-5557 or 800/525-9273, www.southcoastinn.com, $119–159) is a 1917 Craftsman building and was once the home of lumber baron William Ward. De signed by famed architect Bernard Maybeck and situated in the heart of old Brookings away from the beach, this 4,000-square-foot B&B offers three rooms, a guest cottage with kitchenette, and a one-bedroom apartment. Ask the innkeepers about other Maybeck structures in town.

For a B&B with an ocean view, **By the Sea B&B** (1545 Beach Ave., 541/469-4692 or 877/469-4692, www.brookingsbythesea. com, $150) offers a choice of two rooms, or the lodge room featuring a fishing and hunting decor. A full breakfast is served upstairs in the dining room. Enjoy breakfast and breathtaking ocean views from the stained-glass-topped windows. The house is filled with antiques and the smell of homemade bread. A deluxe continental breakfast is also available, with seasonal fruits and homemade breads, if you prefer to eat in private. On the upper veranda, a spa and a wood-burning fire pot is available for guests' use.

FOOD

Brookings has a profusion of family-friendly, though somewhat mediocre, restaurants that serve large portions at a good dollar value. For slightly more distinctive fare, check out the following places.

Suzie Q's Bakery and Cafe (613 Chetco Ave., 541/412-7444, breakfast and lunch daily, dinner Thurs.–Sat., dinner entreés around $20) is a delightful spot with good morning pastries, artisan bread, and a more romantic bistro-style ambiance at dinner.

At the north end of town, **La Flor de Mexico** (541 Chetco Ave., 541/469-4102, lunch and dinner daily, entreés $8–12) has a lunchtime

buffet and good Mexican dinners. Another longtime Brookings favorite, Rubio's, has reopened in its old location with a new name: **Pancho's** (1136 Chetco Ave., 541/469-4919, entreés $8–13). Look for homemade salsa and chiles rellenos here.

A coastal town is certainly a safe place to eat sushi. In Brookings, find it at **Cafe Kitanishi** (632 Hemlock St., 541/469-7864, lunch Tues.–Sat., dinner Thurs.–Sat., sushi $2–14, dinner entreés $16–18), which also serves bento boxes to go and has an espresso bar with Internet access.

In Harbor, **Chetco Seafood** (16182 Lower Harbor Rd., 541/469-9251, 10 A.M.–8 P.M. daily, main courses $8–23) is the best place in town to buy fish, either to cook yourself or to eat on-site. It's owned by fishermen, and you'll always find the freshest stuff here. The fish and chips in beer batter are as good as any on the coast.

Wild River Pizza (16279 U.S. 101, Harbor, 541/469-7454, lunch and dinner daily, large pizza $13–20) is part of the Wild River Brewing family, with pizzeria-brewpubs in Cave Junction and Grants Pass. The crispy crust pizza is the best you'll find in the area. While the food is good and inexpensive, this large restaurant tends to fill up with families enjoying the video games and pool tables on weekends. In other words, go elsewhere for an intimate Saturday night dinner. Look for it on the east side of the highway about a mile south of the Brookings-Harbor Bridge at the four-way stoplight.

Breakfast is good at **Mattie's Pancake House** (15975 U.S. 101 South, 541/469-7311, breakfast $4–9).

INFORMATION

Pull off the highway and talk to the friendly folks at the **Oregon Welcome Center** just north of town (1650 U.S. 101, Brookings 97415, 541/469-4117, 9 A.M.–5 P.M. Mon.–Sat. Apr.–Oct.). It offers brochures covering the coast and the rest of the state. For additional information pertinent to Brookings and environs, the **Brookings-Harbor Chamber of Commerce**

(16330 Lower Harbor Rd., Brookings 97415, 541/469-3181 or 800/535-9469, www.brookingsor.com) is located down at the harbor.

Recreational information, including forest and trail maps for the Siskiyou National Forest and the Kalmiopsis Wilderness, is available at the **Chetco Ranger Station** (539 Chetco Ave., Brookings 97415, 541/412-6000, 7:30 A.M.– 4:30 P.M. Mon.–Fri.). Inquire here about mushroom picking.

GETTING THERE

It's a little tough to get to Brookings using public transportation. Curry County's **Coastal Express** buses (800/921-2871) run up and down the south coast weekdays only between North Bend and the California border, including local service in Brookings. **Porter Stage Lines** (541/269-7183) also runs along the southern Oregon coast, then turns inland at Florence and goes to Eugene, Bend, and Ontario.

SOUTHERN OREGON

When Oregonians talk about southern Oregon, they usually mean the southwestern corner of the state, including the upper valleys of the Umpqua and Rogue Rivers, the spine of the southern Cascade mountains and east to Klamath Falls. The outstanding features of this region include world-class kulturfests, the biggest chunk of remaining wilderness on the Pacific coast, and California retirees who've come in search of cheaper real estate and more sun than they'll see anywhere else west of the Cascades.

If you think of Oregon as a bastion of progressive politics, then some aspects of southern Oregon may surprise you. From back-to-the-land idealists to hard-core survivalists, southern Oregon attracts settlers of all stripes, many of whom seem united in distrust of government and liberal politics. Added to this eclectic mix are more than 100 high-tech companies (the "Silicon Orchard"), white-water rafters, anglers, and theater lovers who flock to the Oregon Shakespeare Festival in Ashland and the Peter Britt Music Festival in Jacksonville. It's an unlikely mix of populations, but confounding expectations is just part of the mix in southern Oregon.

PLANNING YOUR TIME

Ashland and the Oregon Shakespeare Festival are undeniably the largest tourist draw in southern Oregon, though to make the most of this world-class theater festival you'll need to make plans and reserve seats and lodgings well in advance. If you've waited until the last minute and can't get play tickets, you can sign up for a backstage tour of

HIGHLIGHTS

◖ Oregon Shakespeare Festival: At one of the world's great theatre festivals, you should at least take in a show – or maybe just the backstage tour if you didn't plan ahead for tickets (page 359).

◖ Table Rocks: These mesas just north of Medford contain islands of habitat that make them the most interesting and easily accessible hiking destination along the I-5 corridor (page 367).

◖ Oregon Caves National Monument: Descend deep into an Oregon mountainside to find stalactites and stalagmites, plus outside the cavern the unexpected pleasure of a classic mountain lodge (page 383).

◖ Wildlife Safari: Oregon's only drive-through zoo features 600 animals from around the world, including such African visitors as lions, giraffes, and hippopotami (page 388).

◖ Toketee Falls: Ask any local to list the single most beautiful waterfall in Oregon, and chances are Toketee is at the top of the list (page 393).

◖ Crater Lake National Park: The nation's deepest lake, caused by a catastrophic volcanic eruption 6,600 years ago. You won't believe the color of the water (page 401).

◖ Favell Museum: Spend an afternoon admiring the collection of Native American arti-

facts and the gallery of western art at this fine Klamath Falls museum (page 409).

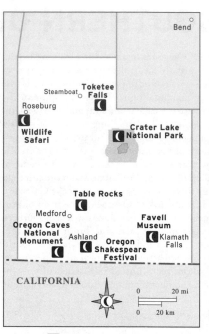

LOOK FOR ◖ TO FIND RECOMMENDED SIGHTS, ACTIVITIES, DINING, AND LODGING.

the festival and enjoy some of Ashland's fine restaurants—but even for these, you'll need to have reservations.

Southern Oregon's other top destination is Crater Lake National Park. Even though a visit to the park itself—which for most travelers involves driving the loop route around the rim of the caldera—can be depressingly unbucolic due to abundant traffic, the approaches to the park along the Rogue or Umpqua river valleys offer excellent opportunities for outdoor recreation. If you're in despair by the crowds at Crater Lake, simply drive to a trailhead in one

of these river valleys and hike into the forest. Soon you'll have waterfalls, river vistas, and fishing holes all to yourself.

The cities of southern Oregon—Medford, Grants Pass, and Roseburg—are mostly charm-free centers with little to delay or seduce the traveler. If you were planning to camp during your Oregon visit, this might be the best time to do so. With the exception of Ashland and a few destination resorts, southern Oregon doesn't offer unforgettable dining and lodging options, so pitch a tent, light a fire, and let the forests and rivers lull you to sleep.

Ashland

With the exceptions of Stratford-upon-Avon and its Shakespeare productions, and Oberammergau, Germany, and its passion play, few towns are as closely identified with theater as is Ashland (population 19,500). Tickets to the renowned Oregon Shakespeare Festival are the coin of the realm here, with contemporary classics and off off Broadway shows joining productions by the Bard. You immediately sense this is not just another timber town from the Tudor-style McDonald's, vintage Victorians, and high property values.

Blessed with a bucolic setting between the Siskiyous and the Cascades, Ashland embodies the spirit of the Chautauqua movement of a century ago, which dedicated itself to bringing culture to the rural hinterlands. Up until the 1930s, however, entertainment in these parts mostly consisted of traveling vaudeville shows that visited the Ashland/Jacksonville area to cheer up the residents of a gold-rush country in decline.

The Southern Oregon University, then Ashland College, started up the Shakespeare Festival under the direction of Professor Angus Bowmer. Such noted thespians as George Peppard, Stacy Keach, and William Hurt graced Ashland's stages early in their careers, and the festival has garnered its share of Tony awards and other accolades. Today, the Oregon Shakespeare Festival is the largest classic repertory theater in the country and enjoys the largest audience of any kind of theater in the United States. Annual attendance generally exceeds 350,000.

Ashland's tourist economy is also sustained by its auspicious location roughly equidistant to Portland and San Francisco. Closer to home, day trips to Crater Lake, Rogue River country, and the southern Oregon coast have joined the tradition of "stay four days, see four plays" as a major part of Ashland's appeal.

SIGHTS
Lithia Park
Ashland's centerpiece is 100-acre Lithia Park. Recognized as a National Historic Site, the park was designed by John McLaren, landscape architect of San Francisco's Golden Gate Park. It's set along Ashland Creek where the Takelmas camped and the region's first flour mill was created. Ashland, Ohio, natives built the mill here in 1854, originally calling it Mill Creek. (Some scholars suggest Ashland was named after the birthplace of Henry Clay, Ashland, Kentucky.) The park was also the site of Ashland's Chautauqua.

The park owes its existence to Jesse Winburne, who made a fortune from New York subway advertising and tried to develop a spa around Ashland's Lithia Springs, which he said rivaled the venerated waters of Saratoga Springs, New York. Although the spa never caught on due to the Depression, Winburne was nevertheless instrumental in landscaping Lithia Park with one of the most varied collections of trees and shrubs of any park in the state. Winburne was also responsible for piping the famous Lithia water to the plaza fountains so all might enjoy its beneficial minerals. While many visitors find this slightly sulfurous, effervescent water a bit hard to swallow, many locals have acquired a taste for Ashland's acerbic answer to Perrier and happily chugalug it down.

A walk along **Winburne Way**'s beautiful tree-shaded trail is a must on any itinerary here. This footpath and a scenic drive through the park start west of the Lithia Fountain. Redwoods, Port Orford cedar, and other species line the drive, which takes you along Ashland Creek to the base of the Siskiyous.

The hub of the park in the summer is the bandshell, where concerts, ballets, and silent movies are shown. Children love to play at the playgrounds or feed the ducks in the ponds. Big kids enjoy tennis, volleyball, horseshoes, or traversing one of the many trails in the park. Every Tuesday on Water Street next to Ashland Creek the **Farmers Market** is held. Rogue Valley farmers, craftspeople, and ranchers sell arts and crafts, fruit and produce, and dried flowers.

Pick up the *Woodland Trail* guide at the plaza's visitors center kiosk. The gentle mile-long loop takes you from the plaza past a beautiful Japanese garden to the upper duck pond where mallards, wood ducks, and the endangered western pond turtle can be seen on the pond's island. A highlight for bird-watchers is in winter when there are 100–200 wood ducks here and ouzels diving below the surface of Ashland Creek for fish.

Museums and Galleries

The **Hanson Howard Gallery** (82 N. Main, 541/488-2562, www.hhgallery.com) features monthly exhibits of contemporary artists in a bright, airy corner shop at the north end of downtown. Closed Monday. The **Foray Gallery** (500 A St., 541/482-2917) is an artist-owned enterprise that features an eclectic collection of sculpture, paintings, fiber arts, printmaking, and jewelry. It's located in a thriving commercial strip by the railroad tracks. Closed Sunday and Monday.

Schneider Museum of Art (Southern Oregon State College campus, 541/482-6245, 11 A.M.–5 P.M. Tues.–Sat.) features contemporary art by national and international artists. Ashland is also home to the **Science Works** (1500 Main St., near Walker St., 541/482-6767, www.scienceworksmuseum.org, 10 A.M.–4 P.M. Wed.–Sat., noon–4 P.M. Sun., $7.50 adults, $5 ages 2–12, under 2 free), a hands-on museum that offers interactive exhibits, live performances, and activities

SPORTS AND RECREATION

Ashland Mountain Supply (31 N. Main St., 541/488-2749, www.ashlandmountainsupply.com) rents outdoor recreation equipment at reasonable rates.

Skiing

Perched high atop the Siskiyou range and straddling the California-Oregon border is 7,523-foot **Mount Ashland** (541/482-2897, www.mtashland.com). To get here, take the Mount Ashland Exit off I-5 and follow the road four miles uphill.

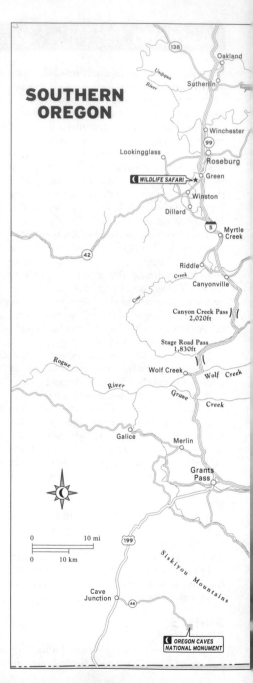

SOUTHERN OREGON

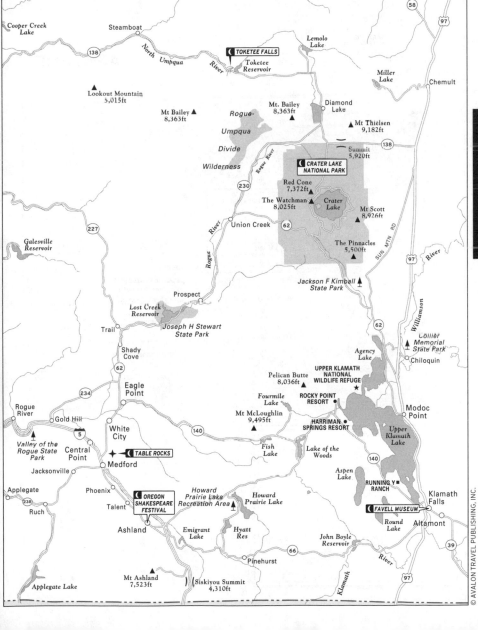

SOUTHERN OREGON

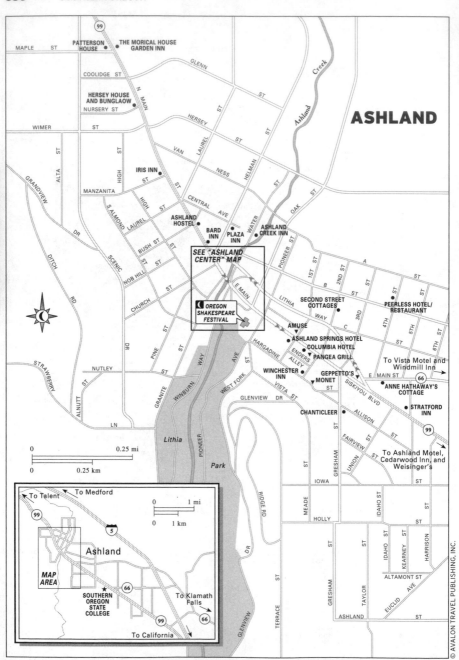

ASHLAND

SEE "ASHLAND CENTER" MAP

OREGON SHAKESPEARE FESTIVAL

PATTERSON HOUSE
THE MORICAL HOUSE GARDEN INN
HERSEY HOUSE AND BUNGLAOW
IRIS INN
ASHLAND HOSTEL
BARD INN
PLAZA INN
ASHLAND CREEK INN
SECOND STREET COTTAGES
PEERLESS HOTEL/ RESTAURANT
AMUSE
ASHLAND SPRINGS HOTEL
COLUMBIA HOTEL
ENDERS ALLEY
PANGEA GRILL
WINCHESTER INN
GEPPETTO'S
MONET
ANNE HATHAWAY'S COTTAGE
STRATFORD INN
CHANTICLEER
To Vista Motel and Windmill Inn
To Ashland Motel, Cedarwood Inn, and Weisinger's
To Klamath Falls
To California
To Talent
To Medford
Ashland
MAP AREA
SOUTHERN OREGON STATE COLLEGE
Lithia Park

0   0.25 mi
0   0.25 km

0   1 mi
0   1 km

© AVALON TRAVEL PUBLISHING, INC.

© JUDY JEWELL

Mount Ashland, just south of town, is home to a wintertime ski area and summertime hiking and camping.

While Mount Ashland is 15 miles from downtown Ashland by road, it's only eight miles away by Nordic ski trail. Skiers of all levels enjoy the 23 different runs, 100 miles of cross-country trails, and breathtaking vistas. The vertical drop here is 1,150 feet. An average of 325 inches of snow falls on the mountain, making it possible to ski Thanksgiving through Easter. Daily lift rates ($17–39) vary depending on the lift; lower rates are available for seniors and youth (ages 9–17); children under eight ski free. Ski at night for $23. Don't forget to purchase your Oregon Sno-Park permit.

Spring and fall are good times to visit Ashland, as accommodation rates are lower than during the peak summer tourist season. Many proprietors include free Mount Ashland lift tickets with the price of the room. Check with the Southern Oregon Reservation Center (110 E. Main St., Ashland 97520, 541/482-3486, www.ashlandchamber.com) about available ski packages. After the snow has melted, the walk to the top of Mount Ashland is an easy one, with good views

of the Siskiyous and 14,162-foot Mount Shasta in California. It's prudent to bring along a sweater even in warm weather, as it can get fairly windy.

Adventure Center

The Adventure Center (40 N. Main St., 541/488-2819 or 800/444-2819, www.raftingtours.com) offers half-day, full-day, and multiday fishing, rafting, and cycle trips for any size party. The cost of the rafting trips includes gear (wetsuits, splash jackets, etc.), guides, and transport from Ashland. Half-day trips ($70) include a snack and run 9 A.M.–1 P.M. or 1–5 P.M. The longer white-water picnic trip ($120) includes lunch and runs 9:30 A.M.–4 P.M. Rated one of the best floats in southern Oregon, the upper Klamath River trip ($135) generally runs 7:30 A.M.–5:30 P.M. and includes all meals.

The **Bear Creek Bike and Nature Trail** crisscrosses through town before going down the valley to Medford along Bear Creek. If you like to ride a bike but are not big on pedaling, contact the Adventure Center for information about their Mount Ashland downhill bike cruise. This half-day morning or picnic-lunch ride descends 4,000 feet on 16 miles of quiet paved roads through the countryside to Emigrant Reservoir. The three-hour morning cruise ($65) departs at 8 A.M. and includes fruit, pastries, and drinks. The four-hour picnic cruise

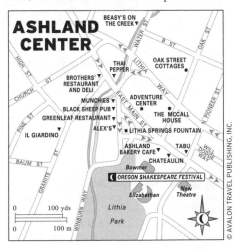

ASHLAND CENTER

© AVALON TRAVEL PUBLISHING, INC.

SOUTHERN OREGON

ELDERHOSTEL IN ASHLAND

Ashland is famous for having one of the most dynamic Elderhostel programs in the country. The program operates February–October (the same as the season at the Oregon Shakespeare Festival) at Southern Oregon University's Cox Hall, which is both the Elderhostel office and dormitory. The program welcomes approximately 2,400 participants to the campus community each year, and is proud to create an intergenerational community on this public, liberal arts campus.

Many of the classes offered deal with Shakespeare and the theater, and usually include theater tours, classes with actors and theater professionals, plus tickets to selected plays. Other classes provide education in natural history and often include field trips to southern Oregon wildlife habitat or geological curiosities. Other courses are recreation-oriented and involve outdoor pursuits such as hiking, rafting, or bird-watching. The Ashland Elderhostel program also offers a few Portland-based courses each year. To find out about current courses, contact Elderhostel (1250 Siskiyou Blvd., Ashland, OR 97520, 541/552-6378 or 800/257-0577, www.sou.edu/siskiyoucenter/elderhostel).

($69) departs at 11 A.M. and includes a great lunch in a beautiful mountain glade. Bicycles, safety equipment, round-trip transfer from Ashland, and an experienced guide are provided. All you have to do is steer! The Adventure Center also rents mountain bikes by the hour or by the day; the fee includes helmet, lock, and maps.

Mountain Biking

One of the more popular local bike rides is the **Lithia Loop Mountain Bike Route.** The 28-mile ride is strenuous, gaining 3,000 feet in elevation the first six miles. Caution is in order the last seven miles of descent. To avoid the steep ups and downs, you can drive up to the top and ride the fairly level 15-mile stretch. The Lithia Loop is mostly within the Ashland watershed, the source of the city's water supply, and it may be closed during midsummer and fall.

The **Siskiyou Crest Mountain Bike Route** begins at the Mount Ashland ski area parking lot. The 31-mile round-trip ranges from moderate to difficult and affords incredible views of Mount Shasta. The route ends at Dutchman Peak, where you'll find one of the few cupola-style fire lookouts left in the Pacific Northwest. This particular lookout was built in 1927. Please note, bicycles are not allowed on the nearby Pacific Crest Trail.

The **Ashland Ranger District** (645 Washington St., 541/482-3333) can provide directions and additional information about these and other mountain bike trails in the area.

Golf

A few miles outside of Ashland on ORE 66 is **Oak Knoll Golf Course** (3070 ORE 66, 541/378-0344, www.golfoakknoll.com). Get into the swing of things before the play; at $15 for nine holes and $24 for 18 holes, even if you triple bogey, you can't miss. For weekend rates, add a dollar or two to the greens fee.

Water Recreation

Jackson Hot Springs (2253 Route 99, 541/482-3776) is two miles north of Ashland on the old highway and has a naturally heated public swimming pool as well as private mineral baths.

Meyer Memorial Pool (Hunter Park, Summit Street, Ashland, 541/488-0313) includes a wading pool for infants and toddlers under age five, as well as a large swimming pool for grown-ups. Open summer season.

Six miles east of Ashland on Highway 66 is **Emigrant Reservoir** (541/776-7001). In addition to waterskiing, sailing, fishing, and swimming, there is a 270-foot twin flume waterslide open 10 A.M.–7 P.M. Monday–Thursday, 10 A.M.–8 P.M. Friday–Sunday.

A half hour east of Ashland on Dead Indian Road is **Howard Prairie Lake Resort** (P.O. Box 4709, Medford 97501, 541/482-1979, www.howardprairieresort.com). Tucked away in the Cascade Mountains at 4,500 feet and surrounded by tall pines and fir trees, this six-mile-long lake peppered with small islands is noted for its runs of rainbow trout. The resort marina offers boat rentals ($35 half day, $45 full day) and everything else you may need (including friendly advice about where the fish are biting) to land some supper. A general store, restaurant, lodging, and 250-acre campground are also found at this retreat.

ENTERTAINMENT AND EVENTS
◖ Oregon Shakespeare Festival

While Lithia Park is the heart of Ashland, Shakespeare is the soul of this community. The festival began when Angus Bowmer, an English professor at Ashland College, decided to celebrate Independence Day weekend in 1935 with a Shakespeare production. The city fathers were so unsure of the reception they asked him to allow boxing matches on the stage during the day prior to the performance. By the time

he retired as artistic director of the festival in 1971, his Fourth of July dream had grown into an internationally acclaimed drama company with three theaters, one named in his honor.

The three festival theaters are located at the southeast end of Lithia Park. Take the Shakespeare steps up the small hill by the Lithia water fountains to get to the Festival Courtyard complex. The **Elizabethan Theatre,** built on the site of Ashland's Chautauqua Dome, was modeled after the Fortune Theatre of London, circa 1600. This outdoor summer-only theater, the largest of the three, is primarily the domain of the Bard. While Shakespeare under the stars is incredibly romantic, it can also get very cold after sunset in the spring and fall. In summer, even on 100°F days, it's not uncommon for it to cool down to the low 60s after intermission. Dress warmly and consider investing a few bucks in the rental lap blankets and pillows for extra comfort. Curtain-times run 8–8:30 P.M. with most shows ending around 11 P.M. This theater closes by mid-October and the festival itself ends October 30.

Downtown Ashland is home to the Oregon Shakespeare Festival.

SOUTHERN OREGON

The second-largest playhouse is the 600-seat **Angus Bowmer.** This indoor complex has excellent acoustics, computerized sound and lighting, and nary a bad seat in the house. The echoes of Shakespeare's immortal poetry fill this hall during the wetter winter months when the outdoor stage is closed. Finally, the 150-seat **New Theatre** is the actors' and directors' theater, where modern works and experimental productions are the norm. This theater is small enough to stage plays that might be overwhelmed by a larger venue.

Getting tickets to the Oregon Shakespeare Festival (15 S. Pioneer St., P.O. Box 158, Ashland 97520, 541/482-4331, www.orshakes.org) is as much a part of the show as the performance. Due to tremendous popularity, seats sell out months in advance, especially for the comedies. All seats are reserved; ticket prices range $17–65. Children under age six are not permitted. Once tickets are purchased, there are no refunds. Call the box office for performance times, dates, and ticket availability. Open 9:30 A.M. through performance time Tuesday–Sunday, 9:30 A.M.–5 P.M. Monday; closed most holidays.

If you are unable to get advance tickets, your best bet is to show up at the Shakespeare Plaza an hour or two before the show with a sign stating what show you want to see. If you are lucky, you will score tickets from someone with extras. Avoid bidding wars with other would-be theater-goers, as ticket scalping is frowned upon here. Otherwise, be at the ticket window at 6 P.M.; any available seats will be released at that time. There are usually standing-room-only tickets ($12) if all else fails. And remember, there is no late seating.

In addition to the plays themselves, two other events are popular with theater-goers. **Backstage Tours** (10 A.M. Tues.–Sun., $11 adults, $8.25 youth 6–17) explore the history, design, and technology of all of the festival's repertory theaters, including the fascinating Elizabethan Stage. Reservations are required. Outside of summer high season, prices are $8.25 adult, $5.50 youth The regular tour is a walking tour and has six flights of stairs; call ahead to schedule a tour without stairs.

Catch the free **Green Show** before the play. It begins at 7:15 P.M. (6:45 P.M. in Sept.) on the plaza outside the Elizabethan Theatre and features elaborately costumed dancers, jugglers, and medieval musicians. Humorous asides, flirtatious Renaissance dancing, magic tricks, and other hijinks help liven things up. The Green Show serves as an appetizer to the main course, often relating directly to the show it precedes in the Elizabethan Theatre. It ends at 7:30 P.M. with a second show at 7:45 P.M. in a small stage to the rear of the Elizabethan Theatre. A 32-page *Guide to the Green Show* sells for about two bucks at the Tudor Guild booth, detailing the historical antecedents of the show's instruments, music, dances, and scripts.

Other Acts in Town

Shakespeare isn't the only act in town. Some of the other local companies include the **Oregon Cabaret Theatre** (1st and Hargadine, 541/488-2902, www.oregoncabaret.com) with musical revues in a club setting; and **Southern Oregon State College** productions. Ashland is also home to the **Ballet Rogue,** Southern Oregon's only professional company, which gives many summer performances. The **Ashland Visitor Information Center** (541/482-3486) has complete information on all the goings-on, as does the Southern Oregon Reservation Center (541/488-1011 or 800/547-8052).

Nightlife

Allann Brothers (1602 Ashland St., 541/488-0700) is a cozy coffeehouse with live music Friday and Saturday nights. Gourmet coffee drinks, soups and sandwiches, and fine desserts are available. **Evo's Java and Tea House** (376 E. Main St., 541/488-3581) occasionally features late-night jazz and blues. **Kat Wok** (62 E. Main St., 541/482-0787), a pan-Asian restaurant, sushi bar, and nightclub, is the only venue where hip hop and funk join R&B and jazz on the dance floor. For cocktails in an intimate setting overlooking the plaza, try **Alex's** (35 N. Main St., 541/482-8818).

Wine-Tasting

The climate of southern Oregon is ideal for

many Bordeaux varietals such as cabernet sauvignon, sauvignon blanc, and merlot. The country cottage tasting room at **Ashland Vineyards** (2275 E. Main St., 541/488-0088, 11 A.M.–5 P.M. daily except Monday, by appointment only Jan.–Feb.) gives you the opportunity to sample the local product.

Nearby is **Weisinger's Vineyard** (3150 Siskiyou Blvd., 541/488-5989 or 800/551-9463, 11 A.M.–5 P.M. daily May–Sept., 11 A.M.–5 P.M. Wed.–Sun. Oct.–Apr.). The vineyard, which has received national and international awards, produces cabernet sauvignon, gewurtztraminer, pinot noir, chardonnay, sauvignon blanc, and Italian varietals. Perched upon a knoll, the view of the valley, vineyard, and surrounding mountains from the tasting room heightens the experience. In addition to wines, visitors may purchase deli foods, soft drinks, and gifts. A beehive displayed in the tasting room is set up so you can see the queen and her subjects hard at work.

Events

The **Ashland Independent Film Fest** (541/488-3823) is five-day affair held in April, during which filmmaker and audience get to know one another. The **Rogue Valley Growers and Crafters Market** (under the Lithia Street/ Siskiyou Boulevard overpass a half-block north of the plaza) takes place 8:30 A.M.–1:30 P.M. Tuesdays May–October.

ACCOMMODATIONS

Quoted rates are for the summer high season. Expect prices to drop around a third outside of the June–September season.

Ashland's high cost of living is reflected in the rack rates of the town's accommodations. Nonetheless, there's generally something to be found to meet the needs of most every budget. A few small ma 'n pa motels still remain offering time-warp rates.

The warm traditions of Britain are represented in Ashland not only by the Oregon Shakespeare Festival but also by the town's numerous bed-and-breakfasts, the most of any locale in the state (as well as the most per capita in the country).

Although they cost a bit more than motel units, you get much more for your money. In addition to such extras as fresh flowers in your room, antique brass beds with down comforters, and complimentary evening aperitifs, hearty morning meals are usually included. Another plus is that most of these inns are within easy walking distance of the theaters. Many B&Bs require a two-night minimum stay during summer.

The **Ashland Bed and Breakfast Network** (800/944-0329, www.bandbashland.com) can help you find quality B&B lodgings in Ashland. For help with B&Bs in Ashland, and around the state, contact the **Oregon Bed and Breakfast Guild** (800/944-6196, www.obbg.org).

Under $50

Offering 35 beds and family rooms, the **Ashland Hostel** (150 N. Main St., 541/482-9217, www.theashlandhostel.com, $25 per person for dorm space, $55 for two people in a private room) is a two-story 1902 house near the Pacific Crest Trail, only three blocks from the Elizabethan Theater and Lithia Park, and two blocks from the Greyhound station. Reservations are essential, especially March–October. The hostel also has a coin-op laundry.

$50-100

A number of older motels offer good value, including **Vista Motel** (535 Clover Ln., 541/482-4423, doubles from $50) and **Ashland Motel** (1145 Siskiyou Blvd., 541/482-2561 or 800/460-8858, www.ashlandmotel.com, doubles from $52).

Moderately priced rooms include **Cedarwood Inn** (1801 Siskiyou Blvd., 541/488-2000 or 800/547-4141, www.ashlandcedarwoodinn. com, doubles from $88); and **Windmill Inn** (2525 Ashland St., 541/482-8310 or 800/547-4747, www.windmillinns.com, doubles from $92). Both of these properties accept pets, have pools, and include a continental breakfast.

A dollar-wise choice in this high-priced town is the **Columbia Hotel** (262 ½ E. Main St., 541/482-3726 or 800/718-2530, www. columbiahotel.com, doubles from $64), in the center of town. This well-kept 1910 hotel with a grand piano in the lobby has 24 rooms. Rooms at their sister property, **The Palm** (1065 Siskiyou Blvd., 877/482-2635, www.palm cottages.com, doubles from $89) are in a well-maintained cottage-style motel in the midst of lovely gardens.

$100-150

A clean and meticulously maintained, privately owned and operated premium motel is the **Stratford Inn** (555 Siskiyou Blvd., 541/488-2151 or 800/547-4741, www.stratfordinn ashland.com, doubles from $140), located just five blocks from the theaters with reserved parking for guests. All rooms have a fridge, and a couple of kitchen suites are available. Free laundry services, free ski lockers during ski season, elaborate continental breakfast, and an indoor pool and whirlpool tub all contribute to the inn's high occupancy rate.

Out at the freeway exit is **La Quinta Inn** (434 Valley View Rd., 541/482-6932 or 800/527-1133, www.hotels-west.com, doubles from $115).

The **Ashland Springs Hotel** (212 E. Main St., 541/488-1700 or 800/325-4000, www.ashland springshotel.com, doubles from $129) on the corner of 1st and Main (a block from the Elizabethan Theater) is a first-class historic hotel. Dating back to 1925, when it was considered a skyscraper showplace, it's the tallest building between San Francisco and Portland. It languished in obscurity for decades until its multimillion-dollar restoration a few years back.

This 70-room, nine-story hotel evokes the grandeur of the past. The lobby boasts an original terrazzo floor and lavish rugs amid copious indoor greenery. Afternoon tea is served on the mezzanine under old-style ceiling fans. A grand ballroom, a bar in which parlor games and musical entertainment may be enjoyed, as well as English gardens add more touches evocative of another era. Luxuriously appointed guestrooms boast oversized windows highlighting nice views.

If you don't want to spend a bundle on lodging but want to stay in the center of Ashland, **Best Western Bard's Inn Motel** (132 N. Main, 541/482-0049 or 800/528-1234, www.bardsinn.com, doubles from $136) is a good choice. Located just across the Main Street bridge from downtown, the Bard's Inn is no more than five minutes from the theaters. There are a number of room types, all nicely furnished and well maintained. Facilities include a stream-side restaurant and bar.

The historic **Peerless Hotel** (243 Fourth St., 541/488-1082 or 800/460-8758, www. peerlesshotel.com, doubles from $145) was established in 1900 when the railroad came to Ashland. It served the needs of railroad travelers for many years before falling into disuse. The old hotel was brought back to life in the 1990s, when it was thoroughly modernized and converted into a boutique B&B-style hotel. One of the most distinctive places to stay in Ashland, the Peerless also offers a fine dining restaurant and a location in the art-gallery-rich Railroad District.

The **Morical House Garden Inn** (668 N. Main St., 541/482-2254 or 800/208-0960, www.garden-inn.com, doubles from $140), is a restored seven-room 1880s farmhouse plus a newer guesthouse with three luxury suites, each with a picture-postcard view of Grizzly Mountain and the Siskiyou foothills. Wooden floors, stained-glass windows, and antiques sustain the "good old days" theme despite no shortage of modern conveniences. The two acres of gardens provide organic produce for breakfast in season, as well as a wide variety of herbs and flowers. Many species of birds and butterflies are attracted to the gardens, which are tastefully accented by a waterfall and stream meandering through the grounds. Given all this, it's sometimes hard to remember that you are only a few blocks away from downtown theaters and shopping.

You'll bathe in naturally occurring hot spring water at the **Lithia Springs Inn** (2165 W. Jackson Rd., 541/482-7128 or 800/482-7128, www. ashlandinn.com, doubles from $129). Located a couple of miles from downtown, the inn is close enough for access to Ashland culture, yet far enough away for some real peace and quiet. Seven acres of working gardens provide fresh food and flowers for breakfasts and decoration. Their 3,000-book library has all kinds of interesting tomes, and a secret bookcase in the living room hides an entrance to another room. Twelve of the 14 rooms have whirlpools fed from the hot springs. There are eight cottage suites, two theme suites, and four regular rooms available for guests to enjoy. Most of the one- and two-room cottages adjacent to the lodge feature a fireplace, refrigerator, wet bar, and double Jacuzzi. Be sure to book well in advance.

$150-200

Plaza Inn and Suites (98 Central Ave., 541/488 8900 or 888/488-0358, www.plazainn ashland.com, doubles from $150), is a large, modern hotel just below downtown and within easy walking distance of the theaters. Many of the rooms look onto a park-like courtyard that fronts onto Ashland Creek. Rooms are very nicely appointed, many have balconies. A breakfast buffet is included in the rates.

(Chanticleer Inn (120 Gresham, www. ashlandbnb.com, 541/482-1919 or 800/898-1950, doubles from $150) rules the roost with five romantic rooms replete with fluffy comforters and private baths. Their gourmet breakfasts are the talk of Ashland. Round-the-clock refrigerator rights, complimentary wines and sherry, and a full cookie jar on the kitchen counter help keep you wined and dined throughout your stay.

Anne Hathaway's Cottage (586 E. Main St., 541/488-1050 or 800/643-4434, www.ashlandbandb.com, doubles from $150), four blocks from the theaters, boasts fresh-cut flowers, down comforters, firm beds, and private baths. This building was once a boarding house; the cottages across the street are now part of this B&B complex.

The **Hersey House B&B** (451 N. Main St., 541/482-4563 or 888/343-7739, www.hersey house.com, rooms from $150, cottage from $195) is an elegantly restored Victorian home with antique furniture and private baths, plus a garden cottage with a fully equipped kitchen, living room, and two bedrooms, making it well-suited for families and groups up to six.

The **Iris Inn** (59 Manzanita, 541/488-2286 or 800/460-7650, www.irisinnbb.com, doubles from $155), is a cheerful Victorian with a fitting decor located four blocks from the theaters. Full breakfast in the morning, cold drinks during the day, and wine and sherry at night add to the classical atmosphere.

The **McCall House** (153 Oak St., 541/482-9296 or 800/808-9749, www.mccallhouse.com, doubles from $170), is a restored Italianate built in 1883 by Ashland pioneer John McCall. A National Historic Landmark, this nine-room inn is a block from restaurants, shops, theaters, and Lithia Park. Delectable fresh baked goodies with juice or tea are served each afternoon. The Carriage House offers two beds, a kitchenette, and a private phone.

Two blocks south of the theaters is the acclaimed **Winchester Country Inn** (35 S. 2nd St., 541/488-1113 or 800/972-4991, www.winchesterinn.com, doubles from $175), offering 19 rooms and suites with private baths and loads of personality. The individual attentiveness of the staff of 35 recalls a traditional English country inn. Bay windows, private balconies, and exquisite English gardens add further distinction. Exotic gourmet delicacies are featured at breakfast, and dinner and Sunday brunch is available in the full-service dining room (see *Fine Dining*, later in this section). Visit the website to check out their changing special packages.

The **Pelton House** bed-and-breakfast (228 B Street, 866/488-7003 or 541/488-7003, www.peltonhouse.com, doubles from $125 including breakfast) is located in a historic Victorian just a few blocks from the Shakespeare festival. Each of its seven rooms is has an earthy theme, and two suites are available for families or groups.

Skiers, hikers, and anyone who wants to savor views of Mounts McLoughlin and Shasta from the snug confines of a three-story cedar lodge will appreciate **(Mt. Ashland Inn** (Box 9444, 550 Mt. Ashland Rd., Ashland 97520, 541/482-8707 or 800/830-8707, www.mtashlandinn.com, doubles from $175). Flourishes such as stained glass, oriental rugs, an ornate fireplace, and Windsor chairs impart a cozy charm.

SOUTHERN OREGON

The Mt. McLoughlin suite affords views of Shasta out one window and McLoughlin out the other. Sky Lakes Suite offers another knockout vista as well as a whirlpool tub for two with a rock waterfall, river rock gas fireplace, microwave, refrigerator, and other luxurious amenities. Paul Bunyan–esque breakfasts emphasizing locally produced foodstuffs fuel hikes and cross-country ski trips on the nearby Pacific Crest Trail. Complimentary cross-country skis, snowshoes, sleds, and mountain bikes are available for hotel guests. In addition, the inn's 7,500-foot elevation makes for excellent stargazing from its comfortable deck. The inn is located 20 minutes south of Ashland on Mt. Ashland Road.

$200 and Up

At the **C Ashland Creek Inn** (70 Water St., 541/482-3315, www.ashlandcreekinn.com, doubles from $220) you won't get any closer to Ashland Creek without getting wet. This small, luxury-level inn is directly adjacent to the stream, with several rooms offering cantilevered decks directly above the rushing water. Each of the seven suites is uniquely decorated according to theme—from the Caribe to the Marrakech to the Edinburgh—and each offers complete kitchens, living rooms, private entrances, and decks. Best of all, all this comfort and style is just moments from downtown shopping and the theaters.

Families and couples traveling together will appreciate the space and privacy of the **Oak Street Cottages** (171 Oak St., 541/488-3778, www.oakstreetcottages.com, $210–280). Located a block from Lithia Park and the theaters, each cottage has a full service kitchen, dining room, and large living room. Enjoy eating outside on your own private patio equipped with a picnic table and barbecue. These units can comfortably accommodate 6–10 people.

FOOD

Ashland's creative talents are not just confined to theatrical pursuits. Some of Oregon's better restaurants can be found around Main Street. Even the humbler fare served in Ashland's unpretentious cafés and burger joints can be memorable. The city has a five percent restaurant tax, a surcharge seen nowhere else in the Beaver State except Lincoln City.

Breakfast and American Cafés

Close to the Lithia Fountain, the **Ashland Bakery Cafe** (38 E. Main St., 503/482-2117, breakfast and lunch daily, dinner Wed.–Sunday, main courses $9–17) is a low-cost alternative to the array of haute cuisine on this block, with high-quality breakfasts, sandwiches, and main courses. Whether it's smoked salmon and cream cheese on a bagel, a tofu scramble, or fresh-baked pastry, you can't go wrong.

The second-floor patio at the **Greenleaf Restaurant** (49 N. Main St., 541/482-2808, three meals daily, main courses $6–18) makes a wonderful spot to enjoy an evening snack. Healthful fare with Mediterranean flair, espresso, and a good selection of desserts pull in the evening crowds, just as the omelettes, frittatas, and fruit smoothies attract devotees of healthy breakfasts.

New York meets the Northwest at **Brothers Restaurant and Deli** (95 N. Main St., 541/482-9671 three meals daily, main courses $6–12), another popular local hangout for breakfast, specializing in gourmet soup and sandwiches.

Eclectic

Alex's (35 N. Main St., 541/482-8818, lunch and dinner daily, main courses $12–20) highlights regional ingredients on a changing menu. For lunch, you can't go wrong with the Dungeness crab quesadilla, chicken pine nut dumplings, or Cajun fish tacos. Dinner favorites include rack of lamb. Arrive early at this temple to elegant but inexpensive cuisine to get one of the three tables on the balcony above the street.

Pangea Grills and Wraps (272 E. Main St., 541/552-1630, lunch and dinner daily, main courses $7–14) is a creative sandwich/salad emporium featuring free-range meats, and organic coffee and produce. Whether it's a Cleopatra salad or a wrap, the preparations are light, flavorful, and reasonably priced. This place is perfect for a quick meal before the show on a hot midsummer night.

Omars (1380 Siskiyou Blvd., 541/482-1281, lunch and dinner Mon.–Fri., dinner only Sat. and Sun., winter hours may vary, main courses $10–30), Ashland's oldest restaurant (mastodon bones were found when excavating for the restaurant in 1946), is noted for its seafood. You'll also be impressed by the restaurant's chicken Dijon, steaks, and moderate prices.

International

The excellent **Thai Pepper** (84 Main St., 541/482-8058, lunch and dinner daily, main courses $7–16) has a lot to offer—not only is the spicy, flavorful Southeast Asian cuisine well prepared and moderately priced, the dining room steps down into the steep gulch of Ashland Creek, offering a cool and quiet haven in the summer heat of Ashland and one of the most pleasant patio dining areas in Ashland.

A fun and exciting place to explore new tastes is **Tabu** (76 N. Pioneer, 541/482-3900 www.taburestaurant.com, lunch and dinner daily, main courses $8–15), a restaurant that takes the zesty foods of Central America and updates them with new flavors and preparations. Choose from entrées like banana-leaf-wrapped fish or select a series of tapas—the sugarcane shrimp is especially delicious. The cocktail bar at Tabu is a favorite late-night haunt of thespians.

One story above Ashland Plaza, the **Black Sheep Pub and Restaurant** (51 N. Main St., 541/482-6414, lunch and dinner daily, main courses $8–24) is a vast Olde English pub with better than average pub fare, plus a wide selection of British and Northwestern ales. This is the place to come for a late night, after-theater supper with frothy pints of beer.

Italian

The food at **Il Giardino** (5 Granite St., 541/488-0816, dinner daily, main courses $9–17) is as Italian as the Vespa scooter parked in the foyer. No American-style spaghetti and meatballs here, just tried-and-true Italian food by a *paesano* chef. The rolled eggplant stuffed with goat cheese is one haymaker of an appetizer and their pasta dishes bring Old World taste back home. A half-dozen seafood entrées come with salad made from fresh organic greens. Daily specials are also always a good bet as is a wine list well suited to all palates and pocketbooks. Seating is limited, so reservations are highly recommended.

Geppetto's (345 E. Main St., 541/482-1138, three meals daily, main courses $8–20) is the place to go for Italian cuisine. Nothing fancy, just real food prepared and served by real people at real prices. This Ashland institution offers some deliciously wild concoctions, such as cheese wontons with homemade salsa.

Health Food

One of the best alternative groceries in southern Oregon is the **Ashland Community Food Co-op** (237 N. 1st, 541/482-2237, open daily); a great variety of organic produce and organic bulk foods can be found here.

Fine Dining

The **Winchester Inn** (35 S. 2nd St., 541/488-1113 or 800/972-4991, dinner nightly and for Sunday brunch, main courses $15–26, brunch $8–13) is not only a renowned B&B but a first-rate dinner-house as well. The Victorian National Historic Landmark dining room may look out on an English garden with a gazebo, but modern sensibilities permeate a menu that changes seasonally. Their *teng-da* beef, an Indochinese filet mignon in a marinade of soy, lemon, horseradish, black pepper, and anise, is a permanent fixture.

As with the Winchester Inn, the **Peerless Restaurant** (265 4th St., 541/488-6067 or 800/460-8758, dinner nightly, $16–30) is set in a picturesque historic hotel (the garden is spectacular, so dine alfresco if possible). The appetizer list on the summer menu trumpets the restaurant's fresh-and-homegrown orientation. The extensive, seasonally rotating entrée menu of Northwest cuisine with global influences might contain braised Oregon rabbit, hot alder-smoked king salmon, and a sashimi dish.

Monet (36 S. 2nd, 541/482-1339, dinner Tues.–Sat., main courses $20–30) is an excellent choice for upscale French cuisine. The French-born and -trained chef/owner imparts an impressionistic flair to the restaurant's culinary delights. Classical music, white tablecloths, and paintings from local artists further enhance the mood. Fresh herbs for dinner come from the garden adjacent to the outdoor patio where patrons can enjoy a memorable meal during the warmer months. Seating is limited, and reservations are recommended.

Beasy's on the Creek (51 Water St., 541/488-5009, dinner nightly, main courses $13–25) brings to Ashland a fusion of Texan and Mediterranean flavors. While the fresh fish and center-cut steaks are the main draw, the pasta dishes are also winners. But whatever the entrée, be sure to ask for some of Bud's Black Seafood Gumbo. A warm interior of brass and mahogany, a good wine list, and organic Mexican coffee with dessert put on the finishing touches to an elegant dinner presentation. Outdoor seating overlooking Ashland Creek is available during the warmer months.

Chateaulin (150 E. Main St., 541/482-2264, www.chateaulin.com, dinner Tues.–Sun., main courses $15–30) looks Parisian, with its dark wooden interior and lighted stained glass behind the bar. Traditional French and nouvelle cuisines are offered from a weekly menu. Chateaulin's bistro menu averages half the cost of their regular offerings. Whether it's crepes stuffed with portobello mushrooms, spinach, goat cheese, and garlic or escargot served with country pâté, the bistro fare here manages to fuse a medley of delicate flavors. If you can't decide, go for the prix-fixe dinner ($35). Beginning nightly at 5:30, this menu offering (which changes weekly) features a three-course dinner and two courses of specially chosen wine. Chateaulin's adjoining gourmet food and wine shop also offers custom picnic lunch baskets (order 24 hours in advance). If you go there after the play for one of their 25 specialty coffee drinks, be careful what you say about the performance—Hamlet or Falstaff may show up wearing blue jeans.

Amuse (15 N. First St., 541/488-9000, www.amuserestaurant.com, dinner nightly, main courses $18–30) is Ashland's top French via Northwest restaurant, with a weekly changing menu that features fresh local fruit, vegetables and mushrooms, with ranch beef and lamb and locally harvested fish. Desserts are especially good here. The small dining room is deceptive—the back patio is shady and expansive.

Just down the road from Ashland is the absolutely unique **New Sammy's Cowboy Diner** (2210 S. Pacific Hwy., 541/535-2779, dinner Thurs.– Sun., main courses $18–28). The chef-owners are Bay Area refugees, who moved to Ashland with retirement in mind, but somehow got talked into cooking for friends, then for the public a few nights a week. The restaurant is inauspiciously located in a former gas station—with no visible signage, first-time diners will need to call ahead for directions. But don't let the humble surroundings fool you—with a 500-bottle wine list, and excellent New American dining, this is the Ashland restaurant you'll tell you friends about. Reservations are a must—there are only six tables!

INFORMATION

Ashland Visitor Information Center (110 E. Main St., Ashland, 541/482-3486, www.ashlandchamber.com) offers brochures, play schedules, and other up-to-date information on happenings. Another excellent source of information is the **Southern Oregon Reservation Center** (P.O. Box 477, Ashland 97520, 541/488-1011 or 800/547-8052, www.sorc.com). This agency specializes in arranging Shakespearean vacation packages with quality lodging, choice seats for performances in all three theaters, and other tour and entertainment extras.

The **Oregon Welcome Center** offers travel information on the whole state. Traveling on I-5, take Exit 14. At the stop sign, turn left onto Ashland Street. Go over the freeway overpass and get into the left-hand turn lane and turn left onto Washington Street. The center is located at the Ashland Ranger District. Watch for "Tourism Information" signs.

GETTING THERE AND AROUND

Greyhound (91 Oak St., 541/482-2516) serves Ashland with a handful of daily north- and southbound departures. Local connections between Medford and Ashland are possible through **Rogue Valley Transportation** (541/779-2877, www.rvtd.org). Pick up a bus schedule at area businesses or libraries, or online. Contact **Ski Ashland** (P.O. Box 220, Ashland 97520, 541/482-2897) for information on the Mount Ashland daily bus to and from Medford and Ashland.

Twenty-four-hour taxi service is available from **Ashland Taxi** (541/890-8080). United Express and Horizon Air fly into Medford-Jackson airport, 15 miles north of town. Amtrak has a station 70 miles east of Klamath Falls and 75 miles south at Dunsmuir, California.

Medford

Today, along with a resource-based economy revolving around agriculture and timber products, Medford is becoming established as a retirement center. Proximity to Ashland's culture, Rogue Valley recreation, and Cascade getaways, as well as rainfall totals half those recorded in the Willamette Valley, are some of the enticements. Unfortunately, if the current population of 63,000 grows much larger, the already poor air quality here will become worse. Already smog alerts brought on by heat and inversions have some folks calling the city "Dreadford."

Call it what you will, but for cost of living, proximity to mountains and coast, and employment opportunities, many folks consider Medford the best place to live in southern Oregon.

SIGHTS
C Table Rocks

About 10 miles northeast of Medford are two eye-catching basaltic buttes, Upper and Lower Table Rock. They are composed of sandstone with erosion-resistant lava caps deposited during a massive Cascade eruption about 4–5 million years ago. Over the years, wind and water have undercut the sandstone. Stripped of their underpinnings, the heavy basalt on top of the eroded sandstone is pulled down by gravity, creating the nearly vertical slabs that we see today.

The Table Rocks were the site of a decisive battle in the first of a series of Rogue Indian wars in the 1850s. Major Philip Kearny, who later went on to distinguish himself as the great one-armed Civil War general, was successful in routing the Native Americans from this seemingly impervious stronghold. A peace treaty was signed here soon afterward by the Rogue (Takelma) tribe and the American government. For a time, this area was also part of the Table Rock Indian Reservation, but the reservation status was terminated shortly thereafter.

The 1,890-acre **Lower Table Rock Preserve** was established in 1979 near the westernmost butte, which towers 800 feet above the surrounding valley floor. The preserve protects an area of special biologic, geologic, historic, and scenic value. Pacific madrone, white oak, manzanita, and ponderosa pine grow on the flank of the mountain; the crown is covered with grasses and wildflowers. Newcomers to the region will be especially taken by the madrone trees. This glossy-leafed evergreen has a "skin" that peels in warm weather to reveal a smooth, coppery orange bark. It's found mostly in the Northwest and was noted by early explorers as fuel for long, slow, hot-burning fires.

Park checklists show that more than 140 kinds of plants reside here, including dwarf meadow foam, which grows no place else on earth. One reason is that water doesn't readily percolate through the lava. Small vernal ponds collect on top of the butte, nurturing the wildflowers that flourish in early spring. The wildflower display reaches its zenith in April. A

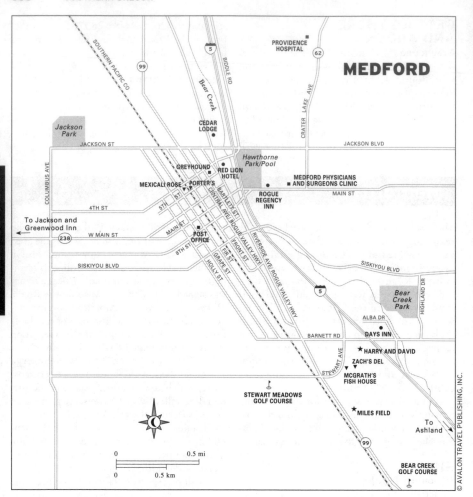

dozen species of flowers cover the rock-strewn flats with bright yellows and vivid purples.

Hikers who take the two-mile trail to the top of horseshoe-shaped Lower Table Rock are in for a treat. Be on the lookout for batches of pale lavender fawn lilies peeking out from underneath the shelter of the scraggly scrub oaks on the way up the mountain. You'll want to walk over to the cliff's edge, which will take you past some of the "mima mounds" or "patterned ground" that distinguishes the surface

of the butte. How the mounds were formed is a matter of scientific debate. Some scientists believe they represent centuries of work by rodents, others think they are accumulated silt deposits, while still others maintain they were created by the action of the wind. However they got there, the mounds are the only soil banks on the mountain that support grasses, which are unable to grow on the lava. Lichens and mosses manage to grow on the lava, however, painting the dull black basalt with luxuri-

JACKSON AND PERKINS

Medford is home not only to fruit megacorporation Harry and David, but also to the world's largest private rose grower. The history of Jackson and Perkins (1310 Center Dr., 800/292-4769) began in 1872 on the East Coast, where the company first began wholesaling nursery stock. Their mail-order business started at the 1939 World's Fair in New York. Many customers who had ordered roses appreciated having them shipped and requested the same service the following year. From this nucleus, the reputation quickly spread, and orders for the company's roses came in from all over the country.

Jackson and Perkins moved to California's San Joaquin Valley in 1966 to take advantage of the 262-day growing season. The roses are now raised in California, then harvested and sent to the Medford plant where they are prepared for nationwide shipment.

The company's annual catalogues offer bulbs, seeds, and plants of all kinds, as well as their award-winning roses. Take a walk down the primrose path of their 43,000-square-foot Test and Display Garden (next to the warehouse on Rte. 99) May–October to enjoy the colorful sights and sweet smells of the floral displays.

ant greens and fluorescent yellows during the wetter months.

The trail up Upper Table Rock is a little over a mile but much steeper than the Lower Table Rock trail. Clay clings to the slopes of Upper Table Rock, making the going both sticky and slippery during the wet season. The trail affords wonderful vistas of the Rogue River and Sams Valley to the north. The trail reaches the top of the butte on the far eastern side. The ponds up here are smaller and fewer than those on Lower Table Rock, but the mima mounds are more clearly defined. Upper Table Rock also shows less wear and tear from human activity, and the flower show is just as spectacular. Long black strips of hexagonal basalt look as though they were formed by tanks marching across the butte while the lava was cooling. This irregular, knobby surface is difficult to walk on, but the colorful mosses and lichens love it. Also look for the tiny bouquets of grass widows, lovely purple flowers that dangle on long, graceful stalks. The odd-looking building off to the west is a navigation device maintained by the Federal Aviation Administration. It's easy to get disoriented out here, with hundreds of acres to explore. The point where the trail heads back down the mountain is marked by two large trees, a ponderosa pine and a Douglas fir, accompanied by a smaller cedar.

To get to the Table Rocks, take Route 62 northeast out of Medford. Take the Central Point Exit (Exit 33) east about one mile to Table Rock Road, and turn north (left). Continue 7.6 miles, passing Tou Velle State Park. Turn east (right) and continue approximately one mile to the signed parking lot, which will be on your left. The trail to the top of Upper Table Rock begins there. The **BLM** (3040 Biddle Rd., 541/770-2200) has additional information on the Table Rocks.

Harry and David

Harry and David (1314 Center Dr., Medford 97501, 541/776-2277, www.harryanddavid. com), the nation's leading purveyor of mail-order fruit, has a store in the south part of Medford. From November till Christmas, no catalogue concern of any kind in the country ships more weekly packages. The fruit-stand section of the large company store offers farm-fresh fruit and vegetables. You can also find rejects from Harry and David's Fruit-of-the-Month Club that are nearly as good as the mail-order fruit but are too small or blemished to meet their high-quality standards. The jams and fruit spreads are also less expensive here.

Harry and David took over their family's Bear Creek Orchards in 1914. Bear Creek Orchards was recognized for the size and quality of its pears, which were shipped to the grand hotels of Europe. But the lucrative export market of this company collapsed during the Depression, so the brothers decided to sell their fruit by mail.

Today, the company is owned by the Japanese behemoth Yamanouchi Pharmaceutical, which has built stores coast-to-coast. While changes abound, Harry and David still grows all its fruit within a 15-mile radius of the Medford store.

Butte Creek Mill

About 15 minutes away from Medford on Route 62 is Oregon's last original water-powered grist mill still in operation, the Butte Creek Mill (402 Royal, Eagle Point, 541/826-3531, 9 A.M.–5 P.M. Mon.–Sat.). To get here, take Route 62 about 10 miles north to Eagle Point and follow the signs to the mill. Built in 1872, the foundation pillars were hand-hewn with an axe, and wooden pegs and square nails hold up the rest of the structure. The two 1,400-pound millstones were quarried in France and assembled in Illinois. From there, they were shipped around the Horn and then transported over the mountains by wagon. Stone-ground products are available in the mill shop, including 12 kinds of flours, four kinds of meal, four cracked grains, six cereals, four mixes (pancake, waffle, cornbread, and biscuit), and other grain products.

Adjacent to the mill is the **Oregon General Store Museum.** This museum is a re-creation of a typical late-1800s general store. Home remedies, giant coffee grinders, pickle barrels, and other common goods of the day are exhibited. Open 11 A.M.–4 P.M. Saturday, donations are eagerly accepted.

Just down the street from the mill is the **Lost Creek Covered Bridge.** The 39-foot-long bridge was built in 1919 and exhibits a queen-post truss design with a shingle roof and flying buttress braces. The rough wooden floor is composed of diagonal planks. Lost Creek was so named because, during its thousand-foot drop in elevation over a distance of two

miles, it disappears beneath a lava flow for a while before resurfacing again. The bridge is closed to vehicular traffic, but you can get a good picture of it by walking across it to the east side of Lost Creek.

SPORTS AND RECREATION
Golf

Near Miles Field is **Bear Creek Golf Course** (2325 South Pacific Hwy., 541/773-1822). This is a compact nine-hole course that's both a challenge and a bargain at $11 a round. If you would rather go for a regulation-sized course, **Cedar Links Golf Course** (3144 Cedar Links Dr., 541/773-4373), in northeastern Medford, has 18 holes waiting for you. To get there, take Route 62 north toward White City. Turn right on Delta Waters Road, right again on Springbrook Road, and then left on Cedar Links Drive. The greens fee is $14 for nine holes and $25 for 18 holes; add a dollar or two more on weekends.

Eagle Point Golf Course (100 Eagle Point Dr., Eagle Point 97524, 541/826-8225, www.eaglepointgolf.com) is arguably the finest course in the Rogue River Valley. Designed by Robert Trent Jones II, this 175-acre collection of golf holes boasts enough character to challenge beginners and experts alike. Impressive views of Mount McLoughlin and Table Rocks add to the experience. Greens fees are $68 to walk and $78 to ride. Carts, clubs, and shoes are available for rent.

Swimming

When the summer mercury heats up into the 90s, it's time to cool off in one of Medford's several public swimming pools. **Jackson Pool** (815 Summit, 541/770-4586, mid-June–early Sept.) is a popular family place. In addition to the 100-foot-long waterslide, a concession stand sells ice cream, soft drinks, and other snacks. An open recreational swim is held 1–3 P.M. Monday–Wednesday and also on Friday. Thursday evening is reserved for family swims, 7:30–9:15 P.M. A small admission is charged. **Hawthorne Pool** (505 E. Main St., 541/770-4586) features an open swim 1–3 P.M. and 3:30–5:30 P.M. Sunday–Friday.

ENTERTAINMENT AND EVENTS

Jackson County Fair

The Jackson County Fair is held at the county fairgrounds just north of town the third weekend of July. Cowboys, ranchers, and farmers all come with their families. Country music dominates the stage, with performers like Ricky Skaggs, Waylon Jennings, and Charley Pride drawling out their tunes. If the kids are going to spend the day at the midway, consider purchasing their ride tickets in advance and saving 50 percent off the regular "one price for all rides" (except Saturday). Check with the **Southern Oregon Reservation Center** (541/488-1011 or 800/547-8052) for pre-sale ticket outlets. Frequent shuttle-bus departures provided by Rogue Valley Transportation relieve you of fighting the crowds for limited parking spaces. The buses leave from downtown Medford, Poplar Square, Crater High School, and other points around town. The trip back from the fair is free, and the shuttles run approximately every 15 minutes.

Pear Blossom Festival

The Pear Blossom Festival takes place the second weekend of April with arts and crafts exhibits, a parade, and a 10K run. The real attraction is the panorama of the orchards in bloom against the backdrop of snowcapped Mount McLoughlin. The parade and run take place downtown, and festivities continue at Alba Park with more than 100 booths of arts and crafts, food, music and children's activities. The fair continues till 4 P.M.

ACCOMMODATIONS

Medford has no shortage of motel rooms, most of them clustered near the interstate exits. Most are national chains so there's no mystery as to what you're checking into. Two budget choices, both with outdoor pools, include **Cedar Lodge** (518 N. Riverside, 541/773-7361 or 800/282-3419, doubles from $60); and **Super 8 Pear Tree Motel** (300 Pear Tree Ln., 541/535-4445 or 800/645-7332, www.peartreemotel.com, doubles from $72).

Red Lion Hotel (200 N. Riverside, 541/779-5811 or 800/833-5466, www.redlion.com, doubles from $129) offers high-speed wireless Internet access, room service, laundry and valet service, plus two outdoor pools, health club, and three dining options. **Rogue Regency Inn** (2345 Rte. 62, 541/770-1234 or 800/535-5805, www.rogueregency.com, doubles from $105) offers newly remodeled rooms, an indoor pool and spa, fitness center, business center, complimentary shuttle to the airport, and high speed Internet access.

A romantic bed-and-breakfast with a park-like ambience is **C Under the Greenwood Tree** (3045 Bellinger Ln., 541/776-0000 or 800/766-8099, www.greenwoodtree.com, doubles from $140). The rooms and suites have private baths and are decorated with antiques, Persian rugs, and fabric art collections. A lavish breakfast and afternoon tea served in the parlor, on the porch, or out in the garden, as well as chocolate truffles on your pillow at night, further enhance the atmosphere. Outside this hand-hewn and -pegged building dating back to the Civil War, you'll find a willow swing in a three-story barn, a hammock suspended between enormous 300-year-old oaks, and a gazebo beneath shady apple trees overlooking the rose garden.

FOOD

Medford is very fond of chain restaurants, which are easily found at the freeway exits. Here are a few locally owned options. "Dagwood-style" sandwiches can be found at **Zach's Deli** (1310 Center Dr., 541/779-8272, open daily, sandwiches from $4–9). If your taste buds are set for border food, **Mexicali Rose** (17 W. 4th St., 541/779-4289, lunch and dinner daily, main courses $5–13) can satisfy your cravings for Mexican food. Large dinners replete with rice and beans (be sure to ask for the special black beans) and Super Nachos are perfect complements to the list of Latin American import beers or giant margaritas on the menu.

You'll find a good selection of seafood at **McGrath's Fish House** (68 E. Stewart Ave.,

541/732-1732, lunch and dinner daily, $9–17), a decent regional chain. There are several good appetizers on the menu here you could make a meal out of, like the crab and artichoke dip, the Sicilian prawn quesadilla, or the combo of sampler baskets. Their seafood, meat, and pasta entrées are all generously portioned, and come with two sides and tangy sourdough bread. Ask for the marionberry cobbler for dessert, served warm with French vanilla ice cream dripping down the sides.

For fine dining in Medford, go downtown to the old rail depot, where **◖ Porters** (147 N. Front St., 541/857-1910, www.porterstrain station.com, dinner nightly, main courses $10– 22) serves pasta and steaks, with plenty of local seafood options as well. Double-cut pork chops are stuffed with local blue cheese and served with pear demi-glace.

INFORMATION
The **Medford Visitors and Convention Bureau** (101 E. 8th St., 541/779-4847 or 800/ 469-6307, www.visitmedford.org, 9 A.M.– 5 P.M. Mon.–Fri.) has all kinds of useful maps, directories, and information for the asking.

GETTING THERE AND AROUND
A half-dozen buses dock daily at the **Greyhound** station (212 Barnett Rd., 541/779-2103). **Rogue Valley Transportation** (3200 Crater Lake Ave., 541/799-2988) provides connections to Jacksonville, Phoenix, White City, Talent, and Ashland. Most buses depart Medford at 6th and Barnett, 8 A.M.–5 P.M. Monday–Friday, 9 A.M.–5 P.M. Saturday, no service Sunday. Linkages to Eagle Point and White City are courtesy of **Cascade Bus Lines** (541/664-4801); the schedule fluctuates. **Courtesy Yellow Cab** (541/772-6288) has 24-hour service in the Medford area. A wheelchair van, senior-citizen discounts, and special rates on airport transfers are all available on request.

Medford/Jackson County Airport (800/882-7488, www.co.jackson.or.us), the air hub for southern Oregon, is served by America West, Skywest, United, Horizon, and other carriers. Three rental-car agencies are at the airport: **Budget** (541/773-0488), **Avis** (541/773-3003 or 800/831-2847), and **Hertz** (541/773-4293 or 800/654-3131).

Jacksonville

Southern Oregon's pioneer past is tastefully preserved in Jacksonville. Located five miles west of Medford and cradled in the foothills of the Siskiyou Mountains, this small town of 2,400 residents retains an atmosphere of tranquil isolation. With more than 100 original wooden and brick buildings dating back to the 1850s, it was the first designated National Historic Landmark District in Oregon and the third of eight such sites in the nation.

Named in honor of President Andrew Jackson and the town's namesake county, Jacksonville was surveyed in September 1851 into 200-foot-square blocks. Then as now, California and Oregon Streets were the hubs of Jacksonville business and social life. But the city's tightly packed wooden structures proved to

be especially prone to fire. Between 1873 and 1884, three major fires reduced most of the original buildings to ash. These harsh experiences prompted merchants to use brick in the construction of a second generation of buildings, and the practice was furthered by an 1878 city ordinance requiring brick construction. Most of the building blocks were made and fired locally. To protect them from the elements and the damp season, the porous bricks were painted; cast-iron window shutters and door frames further reinforced the structures.

Boomtown Jacksonville was the first and largest town in the region and was selected as the county seat. It was even nominated and briefly considered for the state capital. The prominence of Jacksonville was made manifest with the 1883 erection of a 60-foot-high courthouse with 14-inch-thick walls. But like the gold finds that quickly dwindled, Jacksonville's exuberance faded when the Oregon and California Railroad bypassed the town in the early 1880s in favor of nearby Medford. Businesses were quick to move east to greet the coming of the iron horse, and Jacksonville's stature as a trading center diminished. By the time the county seat was moved to Medford in 1925, Jacksonville's heady days had long since vanished.

During the Depression, families with low incomes took up residence in the town's derelict buildings, taking advantage of the cheap rents. Gold mining enjoyed a brief comeback, with residents digging shafts and tunnels in backyards, but it was not enough to revive the derailed economy. However, the following decades saw a gradual resurgence of interest in Jacksonville's gold-rush heritage. The Southern Oregon Historical Society was created after World War II, and individuals began to care for the many unaltered late-1880s buildings and restore them to their former glory. The **Beekman Bank** was one of the first structures to be spruced up, and the prominent **United States Hotel** was rehabilitated in 1964. The restoration movement was rewarded when the National Park Service designated Jacksonville a National Historic Landmark in 1966.

Today, Jacksonville paints a memorable picture of a western town with its historic buildings, excellent museum, and beautiful pioneer cemetery. In addition, a renowned music festival, colorful pageants, and rich local folklore all pay tribute to Jacksonville's golden age.

SIGHTS
Jacksonville Museum of Southern Oregon History

A good place to start your explorations is at the museum (206 N. Fifth St., www.sohs.org, 11 A.M.–4 P.M. Wed.–Sat., $5 adults, $3 seniors and children 3–12). This imposing two-story brick-and-stone Italianate building, completed in 1883, served as the county administration building until 1925, when the county seat was moved to Medford. Nowadays, in addition to pioneer artifacts, a mock-up of pioneer photographer Peter Britt's studio, and interesting old pictures, the museum also has a good walking-tour map of the other historical sites in the city. The stucco building next door to the courthouse used to be the county jail, but serves today as the children's museum. Kids of all ages will enjoy hands-on play with old-fashioned toys. A small bookstore, the History Store, is located here as well, specializing in local and regional historical publications.

An adjunct to the museum, the Historic C. C. Beekman House Living History Program (corner of California and Laurelwood Streets) offers tours by costumed interpreters who introduce you to the friends and family of pioneer banker Cornelius Beekman. The 20-minute guided tours ($4 adults, $3 seniors and children 3–12) charmingly set the time machine in motion. The house is open only on the first weekend of the month, 11 A.M.–4 P.M.

Peter Britt Gardens

Peter Britt came to Jacksonville not long after gold was discovered in Rich Gulch in 1851. After trying his hand at prospecting, he redirected his efforts toward painting and photography. The latter turned out to be his specialty, and for nearly 50 years he photographed the people, places, and events of southern Oregon (Britt was the first person to photograph Crater Lake). He also incorporated new photographic techniques and equipment in his studio as they developed. You'll find his ambrotypes, daguerreotypes, stereographs, and tintypes on display at the Jacksonville Museum of Southern Oregon History.

The Swiss-born Britt was also an accomplished horticulturalist and among the first vintners in southern Oregon. In addition to experimenting with several varieties of fruit and nut trees to see which grew best in the Rogue River Valley, he kept the first weather data records of the region. Another testimonial to his love of plants is the giant redwood tree on the western edge of the Britt Gardens, South 1st and West Pine Streets, which he planted 130 years ago to commemorate the birth of his first child, Emil.

SOUTHERN OREGON

His house was a beautifully detailed Gothic revival home that was built in 1860 and then enlarged in the 1880s. Unfortunately, it was destroyed by fires in 1957 and 1960 and can now be remembered only through photographs. Some of the remaining plantings are part of the original gardens, and many others were lovingly cultivated in 1976 by Robert Lovinger, a landscape architecture professor from the University of Oregon. The Peter Britt Music Festival was held on the grounds of the estate from 1962 until 1978, when the new Britt Pavilion was built just south of Britt's house.

A 0.5-mile hike begins 15 yards uphill from the Emil Britt redwood tree. A fairly level path follows the abandoned irrigation ditch that used to divert water from Jackson Creek to the Britt property. Soon you will notice Jackson Creek below the trail, as well as several overgrown sections of a nearly forgotten logging railroad bed. This is a particularly nice walk in the spring when the wildflowers are in bloom and the mosses and ferns are green.

Wine-Tasting

About eight miles southwest of Jacksonville in the Applegate Valley is **Valley View Winery** (1000 Upper Applegate Rd., 541/899-8468 or 800/781-9463, www.valleyviewwinery.com). While the microclimate and the soil types allow for a great diversity of grape varieties, Valley View concentrates mainly on cabernet sauvignon, merlot, and chardonnay. They must be doing something right, because their Barrel Select bottlings have graced U.S. presidents' tables, and their award-winning wines are found in many restaurants and wine shops throughout Oregon. Call ahead to confirm hours, which change with the season.

With a new tasting room that resembles a French villa, **Troon Vineyard** (1475 Kubli Rd., 541/846-9900) offers zinfandel, cabernet sauvignon, merlot, syrah, and chardonnay, plus a red blend called Druid Fluid. Open daily, except when closed in January.

For a taste of some of the Pacific Northwest's best, head for the **Gary West Tasting Room** (690 N. 5th, 541/899-1829, www.garywest.

com). Here you can sample and buy fine food and wine from a variety of producers. Oregon wines, hickory-smoked meats and jerky, and cheeses are some of the goodies you'll want to take home with you. The tasting room packs special Britt Festival picnic baskets, too.

EVENTS
Peter Britt Music Festival

On a grassy hillside amid majestic ponderosa pines near the Britt homesite, a small classical music festival began in 1962. More than 40 years later, the scope of the Britt Festival (541/773-6077 or 800/882-7488, www.britt fest.org) has broadened into a musical smorgasbord encompassing such diverse styles as jazz, folk, country, bluegrass, rock, and dance, in addition to the original classical repertoire. B. B. King, k. d. lang, the Doobie Brothers, Jean-Pierre Rampal, and Joshua Redman are just a few of the artists who have performed here over the years.

The festival runs from the last week of June through the first week of September; most of the nearly 40 concerts occur in August. Tickets typically range $19–36 for general admission. Reserved seats run $5 more than general admission. Concert-goers often bring along blankets, small lawn chairs (allowed only in designated areas), wine, and a picnic supper to enjoy along with entertainment on balmy summer evenings. Be sure to order your tickets well in advance to avoid having to stand outside. Like the Oregon Shakespeare Festival, the shows sell out months in advance, especially for the well-known performers.

Pioneer Days

The Wild West returns to Jacksonville in mid-June with the annual Pioneer Days. A parade in old-time regalia down the main street of town kicks off the party. Following the parade, a street fair featuring arts, crafts, and food booths is held along California Street for the rest of the day. A street dance follows in the afternoon with live music, as well as an old-time fiddlers' performance. Children's games and activities are also scheduled for the afternoon. One of the most popular is the haystack search, in which tots grub around in the straw for more than $200 in hidden currency. Later in the day another fun annual event called the Ugly Legs Contest takes place. Contestants wear paper sacks over their heads so they are judged solely on how bad their legs look. Mud, sandals, worn-out sneakers, and other cosmetic touches are allowed. Other special events are also planned for seniors, and bingo games are held all day long. Call the chamber of commerce (541/889-8118) for details.

ACCOMMODATIONS

Most of the lodgings in Jacksonville are B&Bs. If this isn't your style, you do have one option. The **Stage Lodge** (830 N. 5th St., 541/899-3953 or 800/253-8254, www.stagelodge.com, doubles from $92) is a comfortable motel whose exterior was designed to resemble historic stage stops along the stage route from Sacramento to Portland.

The **◖ Jacksonville Inn** (175 E. California St., 541/899-1900 or 800/321-9344, www.jacksonvilleinn.com, doubles from $145, breakfast included), lies in the heart of the commercial historic district. In addition to eight air-conditioned rooms furnished with restored antiques and private baths, the inn also offers three deluxe cottages complete with antiques, fireplace, king canopied beds, fruit, and champagne. The inn has an excellent dining room (see *Food*). Use of mountain bikes to explore the area is included in the room rate. Reservations are highly recommended, especially during the summer.

A block down California Street is the **McCully Country House Inn** (240 E. California St., 541/899-1942 or 800/367-1942, www.mccullycountryhouseinn.com, doubles from $135). Built in 1861 in the classical revival style, this mansion has four beautifully decorated bedrooms with private baths. European and American antiques, oriental rugs, delicate lace curtains, and a magnificent square grand piano (tuned a half step lower than today's A-440) add to the historical ambience. A full "country continental" breakfast is included. The **Touvelle House** (455 N. Oregon St.,

541/899-3938 or 800/846-3992, www.touvelle house.com, doubles from $135) offers five rooms and one suite (all with private baths). Each room has its own theme and features touches like antiques, handmade quilts, and tasteful interior decorations. Out back by the carriage house is a heated swimming pool and spa. Common areas include a library and a large living room. A full, three-course breakfast is included, and other goodies like fruit and cookies are available for snacking anytime.

The **Orth House** (105 W. Main St., 541/899-8665 or 800/700-7301, www.orth-bnb.com, $110), was built in 1880 and is listed in the National Register of Historic Homes. Large rooms with claw-foot tubs and period furnishings help to recall a bygone era but with the benefit of modern air-conditioning. Full country breakfast and treats are included.

FOOD

The **Jacksonville Inn** (175 E. California St., 541/899-1900 800/321-9344, www.jackson villeinn.com, dinner daily, lunch Tues.–Sun., main courses $16–32) is consistently rated one of the top restaurants in Oregon. While the gold-rich mortar sparkles in the walls of the dining room and lounge, the menu is what offers real treasures. Steaks, seafood, and specialties of the inn like veal, duck, and prime rib are among the offerings in a Victorian atmosphere of red brick and velvet. Vegetarian dishes are also available. A connoisseur's cellar of over 200 wines further enhances your dining experience. There's also a bistro menu for lighter appetites, and lovely patio seating during the summer.

The **Bella Union Restaurant and Saloon** (170 W. California St., 541/899-1770, lunch and dinner daily, main courses $6–15) is another popular spot. Soups, salads, sandwiches, chicken, steaks, pasta, and pizza are some of the items you'll find on the menu here. Vegetarians have many choices to choose from as well. When the weather is right, the patio behind the restaurant is a pleasant place to eat lunch or enjoy a beer. Picnic baskets are also available, a good choice if going to a Britt festival concert. Be sure to call in your order by 2 P.M.

SOUTHERN OREGON

Mexican food in downtown Jacksonville can be found at **La Fiesta** (150 S. Oregon St., 541/899-4450, lunch and dinner daily, main courses $8–16). Located in the Orth building, built in 1872, this place is noted for its large portions of gourmet south-of-the-border fare and vegetarian selections. Arrive early to claim one of the half dozen or so tables on the balcony.

For the best Thai food in the valley, head for the **Thai House Restaurant** (215 W. California St., 541/899-3585, lunch and dinner Tues.–Fri., dinner only Sat. and Sun., main courses $7–14). The pineapple fried rice with shrimp, chicken, cashews, pineapple, and raisins is a winner.

Farmers Market

The **Jacksonville Farmers Market** (N. 5th and C Streets) takes place 9 A.M.–2 P.M. on Saturday, May–October. Look for local peaches and nectarines in the summer, apples and pears in the fall.

INFORMATION

The **Jacksonville Chamber of Commerce** (P.O. Box 33, 185 N. Oregon St., Jacksonville 97530, 541/899-8118, www.jacksonville oregon.org), open 10 A.M.–5 P.M. daily, has the scoop on events and activities.

Drivers, note that the 25-mph speed limit on the main street through town is strictly enforced.

Grants Pass

The banner across the main thoroughfare in town proudly proclaims: "It's the Climate." But while the 30-inches-a-year precipitation average and 52–F yearly mean temperature might seem desirable, the true allure of Grants Pass is the mighty Rogue River, which flows through the heart of this community. More than 25 outfitters in Grants Pass and the surrounding villages of Rogue River and Merlin specialize in fishing, float, and jet-boat trips. Numerous riverside lodges, accessible by car, river, or footpath, yield remote relaxation in the shadow of the nearby Klamath-Siskiyou Wilderness.

It was the climate that attracted back-to-the-land refugees of the 1960s to nearby Takilma, a planned utopian community. More recently, survivalists, in expectation of nuclear Armageddon, established a network of shelters in the area.

The climate is also responsible for the once-thick forests in the surrounding mountains, a timber source for the numerous mills which in turn provided many jobs. However, decades of over-cutting by the lumber companies has dramatically diminished the supply of sawtimber, resulting in mill shutdowns and high unemployment rates. In response, the economic base gradually shifted away from wood products to concentrate on the area's natural beauty, recreational opportunities, and, of course, benign weather.

It's hard to miss the 18-foot-high statue near the north Grants Pass Exit 58 off of I-5. Sporting a simulated mammoth-skin and a dinosaur bone club, and looking like he just strode in off the set of the *Flintstones,* the Caveman been the official welcome to Grants Pass since 1972. Spawned by a semi-notorious local civic group called the Oregon Cavemen, who also parade around in skins, drink saber-toothed tiger "blood," and eat raw meat during their secret initiation rites, the Caveman cost $18,000 to build. While many locals have lambasted the city's mascot as portraying a backward, redneck image for Grant's Pass, it's worth noting that over a dozen businesses and the local high school have proudly embraced the Caveman symbol.

SIGHTS
Palmerton Arboretum

Six miles down Route 99 in the town of Rogue River is the Palmerton Arboretum. Originally a five-acre nursery, the arboretum features plant specimens from around the globe, including Japanese pines and Mediterranean cedars in addition to redwoods and other trees native to the Northwest. A real treat in the spring, the ornamental arboretum offers over 40 species of mature trees complemented by several kinds of azaleas and rhododendrons. Admission is free. While you're there, be sure to see **Skevington's Crossing,** a 200-foot-high swinging suspension bridge over Evans Creek that connects the arboretum to Anna Classick city park.

Wildlife Images Rehabilitation and Education Center

Originally a rehabilitation station for injured birds of prey, Wildlife Images (11845 Lower River Rd., 541/476-0222, www.wildlifeimages.org) has expanded into an outreach program to aid all kinds of injured or orphaned wildlife as well as to educate the public. Bears, cougars, raccoons, and many other indigenous creatures have been helped by this organization. Once the animals are well enough to survive in the wild, they are released. Guided tours (by reservation only—call to find out tour times) allow groups to view the wildlife currently at the facility. Admission is free, but this nonprofit organization relies upon donations. To get here from 6th Street downtown, head south, turn right onto G Street, continue to Upper River Road, and then onto Lower River Road.

Oregon Vortex

About 10 miles south of Grants Pass on I-5 is the **House of Mystery at the Oregon Vortex** (4303 Sardine Creek Rd., Gold Hill, 541/855-1543, www.oregonvortex.com, daily Mar.–Oct., $8.50 adults, $7.50 seniors, $6.50 children ages 6–11.). Called the "Forbidden Ground" by the Rogue tribe because the place spooked their horses, it is actually a repelling magnetic field where objects tend to move away from their center of alignment and lean in funny directions. For example, a ball at the end of a string does not hang straight up and down, and people seem taller when viewed from one side of the field as opposed to the other. Visitors may bring balls, levels, cameras (but not movie cameras), or any other instrument they wish to test the vortex for themselves.

Big Pine

About an hour outside of Grants Pass is the tallest ponderosa pine in the world. Standing a whopping 246 feet high and sporting a 57-inch diameter, Big Pine lives up to its name with an estimated volume of 12,500 board feet of wood. This 300-year-old giant lives in a grove of large pines, cedars, and Douglas firs at **Big Pine Campground** (Galice Ranger District, 541/471-6500, www.fs.fed.us/r6/siskiyou).

To get here, take the Merlin exit off I-5 just north of Grants Pass if you're traveling south, or Exit 61 if you're traveling north, and proceed toward Galice (this Merlin-Galice Road goes 100 windy miles to Gold Beach on the coast). Just beyond Morrison's Lodge, a luxurious getaway on the Rogue River, turn left onto Taylor Creek Road 25. Big Pine Campground is about 10 miles farther. Another routing option is via U.S. 199. About 20 miles south of Grants Pass on U.S. 199, take Onion Creek Road on the north side of the highway and follow it 20 miles to Big Pine.

The campground features 12 picnic sites and 14 campsites with hand-pumped water. A small playground and primitive softball diamond are incorporated into the grounds. Many trails take hikers to Big Pine and beyond for a short hike or an all-day adventure. A lazy creek meanders through the area, with alders, hazelnuts, and an array of colorful wildflowers growing along its banks. Deer and other wildlife are frequently spotted grazing in the fragrant meadows nearby. Foragers can pick their fill of blackberries in July and August. Cost is $16–22 a night.

SPORTS AND RECREATION
Rafting

There are about as many ways to enjoy the Rogue River as there are critters in and around it. Some people prefer the excitement and challenge of maneuvering their own craft down the treacherous rapids. Oar rafts (which a guide rows for you), paddle rafts (which you paddle yourself), and one-person inflatable kayaks are the most widely used boats for this sort of river exploration. The 40-mile section downstream from Graves Creek is open only to nonmotorized vessels, and river traffic is strictly regulated by the National Forest Service. For more information, stop at the **Rand Visitor Center** (4335 Galice Rd., Merlin, 541/479-3735).

The limited float permits (25 issued daily) are prized by rafters around the world, as the Rogue not only has some of the best white water in America but also guarantees a first-rate wilderness adventure. And yet, it can be a civilized wilderness. Hot showers, comfortable beds, and sumptuous meals at several of the river lodges tucked away in remote quarters of this famous waterway welcome boaters after a day's voyage. Excellent camping facilities are available for those who want to experience nature directly.

Many outfitters can be found off I-5 Exit 61 toward Merlin and Galice just north of Grants Pass. Rafters hit Class III and IV rapids a little before Galice and for 35 miles thereafter, the stiffest whitewater encountered on the Rogue. **Adventure Center** (541/482-5139, www.raftingtours.com) has half-, full-, and multiday trips on oar or paddle rafts. Their adventures range from the mild to the wild. A half-day trip on the Rogue is $69.

Galice Resort and Store Raft Trips (11744 Galice Rd., Merlin, 541/476-3818, www.galice.com) offers full-day raft or inflatable-kayak trips as well as river craft rentals. A half-day float is $55 and a full day on the river is $75, which includes lunch at the resort.

Another river retreat with attractive packages is **Morrison's Rogue River Lodge** (8500 Galice Rd., Merlin, 541/476-3825 or 800/826-1963, www.morrisonslodge.com or www.rogueriverraft.com), located about 16 miles from Grants Pass. Everything from one-day floats and excursions to two- to four-day trips is available; see their excellent website for further details. The longer excursions include either stays at other river lodges or camping along the great green Rogue. Transportation back to Morrison's is included, or your car can be shuttled downriver to meet you at the end of the trip. You can spend extra time at Morrison's before or after your trip with their American

Plan lodging package, which includes breakfast, dinner, and room for $115–185.

Noah's River Adventures (53 N. Main, Ashland, 800/858-2811, www.noahsrafting.com) has been providing quality rafting and fishing trips since 1974. They have half-day and one- to four-day excursions that vary from exciting white-water rafting highs to kinder, gentler floats. From late March–early October, they depart Ashland for the Rogue three times daily, and a round-trip transfer from your lodging is included in the price. See the website for rates and package details.

Orange Torpedo Trips (541/479-5061 or 800/635-2925, www.orangetorpedo.com) has half-day and one- to three-day raft or inflatable-kayak (also affectionately known as "orange torpedoes" because of their color and shape) adventures. They also offer a unique VIP two-day package that combines the best on the river: jet-boat tour, wagon ride, gourmet dining, lodging, wildlife park, and float trip all rolled into one. A full-day trip that covers 14 miles of the Rogue is $79.

River Trips Unlimited, Inc. (4140 Dry Creek Rd., Medford, 541/779-3798 or 800/460-3865, www.raftingtrips.com) has been guiding trips on the Rogue for over 40 years. They have one- to four-day raft trips on the Rogue or summer-run steelhead fishing trips that include meals and overnight stays at some of the river lodges.

Rogue/Klamath River Adventures (541/779-3708 or 800/231-0769, www.rogueklamath.com) has one- to three-day white-water rafting and inflatable-kayak trips that give you the option of camping out under the stars or roughing it in style at a river lodge.

For more information on scenic fishing and white-water rafting trips, contact the previously mentioned Rand Visitor Center, or the **Visitors Information Center** (1995 N.W. Vine St., Grants Pass 97526, 800/547-5927, www.visitgrantspass.org). These information outlets can also supply tips on riverside hiking. The Rogue trails out of Grants Pass aren't as remote as their Gold Beach counterparts, and litter can sometimes mar the route. Nonetheless, the fall color in certain areas along the Rogue, and a profusion of swimming and fishing holes, can add a special dimension to your hike.

Jet-Boating

You don't have to risk life and limb in a fancy inner tube to see the Rogue: several local companies offer jet-boat tours. On a jet boat, powerful engines suck in hundreds of gallons of water a minute and shoot it out the back of the boat through a narrow nozzle, generating the necessary thrust for navigation. With no propeller to hit rocks and other obstacles, these 20-ton machines can carry 40 or more passengers in water only six inches deep. This makes the jet boat an ideal way to enjoy the beauty of the Rogue while keeping your feet dry. Also, many outfitters charter drift boats to secret fishing holes for anglers to try their luck landing supper.

Hellgate Excursions (953 S.E. 7th, Grants Pass, 541/479-7204 or 800/648-4874, www.hellgate.com) is the premier jet-boat operator on this end of the river. Their trips begin at the dock of the Riverside Inn (971 S.E. 6th St., Grants Pass) and proceed downriver through the forested Siskiyou foothills. En route, black-tailed deer, ospreys, and great blue herons are commonly seen. If you're lucky, a bald eagle or black bear might also be sighted. The scenic highlight is the deep-walled Hellgate Canyon, where you'll look upon what are believed to be the oldest rocks in the state. The rugged beauty here provided the backdrop for John Wayne and Katherine Hepburn in *Rooster Cogburn*. Trips including a champagne brunch and a weekday lunch served at a wilderness lodge are two popular offerings ($43 and $40 per adult, respectively). Another option is the whitewater adventure trip that goes beyond Hellgate; adults $55, kids $37 (lunch is available but not included). These excursions run May 1–September 30 and feature commentary by your pilot, who knows every eddy in the river. Be sure to call ahead for reservations, as space on all of their runs books up fast.

Fishing

The upper Rogue River is renowned for one of the world's best late-winter steelhead fisheries. Numerous highways and backroads offer easy access to 155 miles of well-ramped river between Lost Creek Reservoir east of Medford and Galice west of Grants Pass. With fall and spring chinook runs and other forms of river recreation, it's no accident that the Rogue Valley is home to the world's top three aluminum and fiberglass drift-boat manufacturers. Add rafters, kayakers, and plenty of bank anglers, and you can understand why peak salmon or steelhead season is sometimes described as "combat fishing." Contact southern Oregon visitors information outlets for rules, regulations, and leads on outfitters.

Biking

The place to go for mountain bike rentals and information on area bike trails is **BikeKraft** (785 Rogue River Highway, 541/476-4935, www.bikekraft.com). They rent mountain bikes by the day or half-day. If you want to go on an extended trip, for a few days or a week, they can outfit you. Car racks and trailers are also available for rent. A cash deposit is required. Other helpful resources are the **Siskiyou National Forest Service** (P.O. Box 440, 200 N.E. Greenfield Rd., Grants Pass 97526, 541/479-5301) and the **BLM** (P.O. Box 1047, Medford 97501, 541/770-2200).

Camping

Many fine campgrounds are found along the banks of the Rogue River near Grants Pass. The privately owned and operated RV campgrounds tend to be more expensive than their public counterparts but offer more amenities like swimming pools, laundries, and other conveniences. **RiverPark RV Resort** (2956 Rogue River Hwy., Grants Pass, 541/479-0046 or 800/677-8857, www.riverparkrvresort.com, $25) boasts a tennis/basketball court, hot showers, laundry facilities, and 700 feet of Rogue River footage to enjoy. Near Tom Pearce Park and the Rogue River is **Moon Mountain RV Resort** (3298 Pearce Park Rd., Grants Pass, 541/479-1145, www.moonmountainrv.com, $27), another well-maintained property offering 50 RV sites with power and propane hookups. About halfway between Cave Junction and Grants Pass is **Redwood Highway KOA** (13370 U.S. 199, Wilderville, 541/476-6508 or 800/562-7566, www.koakampgrounds.com, $22–35), which has everything you would expect from a KOA.

The four county parks listed below cost $20 for hookup sites, $18 for tent sites. Contact the **Josephine County Parks Department** (Rogue River 97537, 541/474-5285, www.co.josephine.or.us) for reservations and additional information.

Indian Mary Park is the showcase of Josephine County parks. To get here, go about eight miles east of Merlin on the Merlin-Galice Road. Located on the banks of the Rogue River, this campground has 89 sites, several with sewer hookups and utilities, as well as showers, flush toilets, and piped water. A boat ramp, beautiful hiking trails, a playground, and one of the best beaches on the Rogue make this one of the most popular county campgrounds on the river.

Griffen Park is a smaller campground with 24 sites for tents and trailers. To get here, take the Redwood Highway (U.S. 199) to Riverbanks Road, then turn onto Griffen Road and follow it about five miles to where it meets the Rogue. The park has a boat ramp, showers, flush toilets, piped water, and RV dumping facilities.

Schroeder Park is another complete campground near town. Located on Schroeder Lane off Redwood Avenue, the park has 31 sites, some with hookups and utilities. Showers, flush toilets, and a boat ramp make this a favorite spot for fishing enthusiasts. In addition to a picnic area and an excellent swimming hole, a rope tied to a huge cottonwood on the opposite bank of the river near the park is waiting for any swingers who like to make a big splash.

Whitehorse Park, six miles west of Grants Pass on Upper River Road, has 44 campsites, many with hookups and utilities. Showers, piped water, lighting, and good hiking trails are also found here. The river channel shifted away from the park in the wake of the Christ-mas flood of 1964, but it's only about a half-mile walk to a fine beach on the Rogue.

The only state park in the area is the **Valley of the Rogue** (3792 N. River Rd., Gold Hill, 541/582-1118 or 800/452-5687, www.oregon-stateparks.org). Located about halfway between Medford and Grants Pass off I-5, the park is set along the banks of its namesake river. The Rogue supports year-round salmon and spring steelhead runs. There are 98 sites for trailers and motor homes ($20), 21 tent sites ($16), and a few yurts ($27), but this place fills up fast, so reservations are recommended during the warmer months. Hookups, utilities, showers, laundry, and some wheelchair-accessible facilities round out the amenities here.

Golf
About 15 minutes north of Grants Pass is **Red Mountain Golf Course** (324 Mountain Green Ln., 541/479-2297). This small but challenging executive course of 2,245 yards is a bargain to play. Greens fee is $8 for nine holes, $12 for 18, and $15 for all day Monday–Friday; add a dollar for weekends.

ENTERTAINMENT AND EVENTS
Josephine County Fair
The Josephine County Fair normally takes place in mid-August at the fairgrounds in Grants Pass. In addition to the usual fair attractions such as the carnival, concessions, and 4-H livestock, entertainers like Three Dog Night perform for enthusiastic crowds. A popular annual competition held here is the four-wheel tractor pull, in which souped-up farm vehicles attempt to drag a bulldozer (with its blade down) 100 yards as fast as possible.

Rogue River Rooster Crow
The nearby city of Rogue River, southeast of Grants Pass on I-5, has something to crow about. On the last day of June, the Rogue River Rooster Crow is held at the Rogue River Elementary School grounds, beginning with a parade and followed by live music and entertainment. A street fair featuring arts, crafts,

and food is also set up on the premises. But the big event takes place early in the afternoon. Farmers from all over Oregon and northern California bring their roosters to strut their stuff and sing out songs to the enthusiastic crowds. A fowl tradition since 1953, the rooster to crow the most times in his allotted time period wins the prize for his proud owner.

ACCOMMODATIONS

You'll find most motel accommodations clustered around the two Grants Pass I-5 exits. Economy choices include **Rodeway Inn** (1253 N.E. 6th, 541/479-2952, doubles from $75); **Knights' Inn** (104 S.E. 7th, 541/479-5595 or 800/826-6835, doubles from $65); and **Motel 6** (1800 N.E. 7th, 541/474-1331, doubles from $55).

There are plenty of midrange hotel chain choices, and most of them have pools, allow pets, and include breakfast. Several such options are **Comfort Inn** (1889 N.E. 6th, 541/479-8301, doubles from $81); **Best Western Grants Pass** (111 N.E. Agness Ave., 541/476-1117, www.bestwesterninn. com, doubles from $96); **Best Western Inn at the Rogue** (8959 Rogue River Hwy., 541/582-2200 or 800/238-0700, doubles from $90); and **La Quinta Inn** (243 N.E. Morgan Ln., 541/472-1808 or 800/531-5900, www .laquinta.com, doubles form $94).

One of the premium lodgings in town is **Weasku Inn** (5560 Rogue River Hwy., 541/471-8000 or 800/493-2758, www.weasku .com, doubles from $185), a venerable river lodge that was the secret retreat of Clark Gable, Walt Disney, Carole Lombard, and other entertainment figures. Only 17 guestrooms are available, ranging from lodge rooms and suites to an A-frame cabin. All look out on the Rogue River and have genuine rustic-chic decor. A deluxe continental breakfast is served, as is evening wine and cheese.

With 174 rooms on the Rogue, the **Riverside Inn Resort** (971 S.E. 6th, 541/476-6873 or 800/334-4567, www.riverside-inn.com, double rooms from $99) is both right downtown and right on the river. Two swimming pools, two hot tubs, a 24-hour coffee shop, and a day spa provide luxury in a style you can easily get accustomed to. The Hellgate jet-boat excursion boats depart from just below the hotel.

Bed-and-Breakfasts

Situated about 20 minutes outside of Grants Pass and well within the wild and scenic section of the Rogue River is the **Doubletree Ranch** (6000 Abegg Rd., Merlin, 541/476-0120, doubletree-ranch.com,, doubles $85–125). Originally homesteaded 100 years ago, this 160-acre, four-generation working ranch offers cabins with breakfast included.

About 15 minutes north of town a couple of miles off I-5 Exit 66 is **Flery Manor** (2000 Jumpoff Joe Creek Rd., 541/476-3591, www. flerymanor.com, $90–200). Canopied beds, unique furnishings, and a quiet secluded setting give this country manor a genteel air. All rooms have nice little touches like plush robes, fresh flowers, and morning coffee and tea service. The breakfast features a health-conscious menu. With a private balcony, double Jacuzzi, and fireplace, the Moonlight Suite is the right prescription for a romantic hideaway. Reservations are a must.

Tucked away in the quiet ponderosa of the Rogue River Valley about 15 minutes from Grants Pass is the lovely **Pine Meadow Inn** (1000 Crow Rd., Merlin, 541/471-6277 or 800/554-0806, www.pinemeadowinn.com, doubles $95–130). This large country home atop a wooded knoll was designed and built specifically as a B&B. Downstairs, French doors open out to the backyard herb and English cutting gardens landscaped with a koi pond and waterfall. The wraparound porch has inviting wicker chairs to relax in while enjoying morning coffee or evening tea with a book from the extensive library. Beneath the pines a hot tub awaits. After your stay here, you'll understand exactly why Meryl Streep wanted to rent the entire house for the summer when *The River Wild* was being filmed on the Rogue.

Not to be confused with Pine Meadow Inn is the **Ponderosa Pine Inn** (907 Stringer Gap Rd., Grants Pass, 541/474-4933 or 866/299-7463,

the 1883 Wolf Creek Tavern at the Wolf Creek Inn

© BILL McRAE

www.ponderosapineinn.com, doubles from $90). Only two rooms are available in this bright and cheery country retreat, which was completed in 2000. It is located about 15 minutes from downtown Grants Pass; see the inn's website for map and directions.

Approximately 20 miles north of Grants Pass on I-5 in Wolf Creek is the Pacific Northwest's oldest continuously operated hostelry, the **Wolf Creek Inn** (100 Front St., Wolf Creek, 541/866-2474, www.wolfcreekinn.com, doubles from $80). Originally a hotel for the California and Oregon Stagecoach Line, this historic property built in 1883 is now owned by the state and operated as a hotel and restaurant. Legend has it that President Rutherford B. Hayes visited the tavern in the late 1880s and One-Eyed Charlie used to chew the fat in the dining room. You can also view the small room where author Jack London stayed and wrote part of his novel, *The End of the Story.*

Wolf Creek's boardinghouse had its heyday when it was a halfway house on the Portland–Sacramento stagecoach route, but it continues to serve road-weary travelers. The period furniture imparts atmosphere, while the beds and private baths are modern enough to be comfortable. The restaurant, open for three meals a day in high season, serves admirable Northwest cuisine, with veggies from the inn's gardens and home-smoked meats.

FOOD

Although it's not the gourmet capital of Oregon, Grants Pass is a town where many travelers pull in for a bite. Its proximity to Rogue River recreation and fishing, together with a wide range of reasonably priced dining options, explain its popularity.

R-Haus (2140 Rogue River Hwy., 541/474-3335, dinner nightly, main courses $13–20), a local favorite dinner spot, is a formal dining room in an early 20th century house. Basic fare includes steak, seafood, and pasta.

The menu at **China Hut** (1434 N.W. 6th, 541/476-3441, lunch and dinner daily, main courses $6–12) features interesting entrées such as vegetarian *chow yuk,* Mandarin pineapple duck, and *ma po* tofu. You'll need a big appetite to finish their large portions. The **Hong Kong Restaurant** (820 N.W. 6th, 541/476-4244, lunch and dinner Mon.–Sat.) has a takeout family-pack dinner that, at around $15 for two, is one of the best deals in town. **Pongsri's** (202 Redwood Hwy, 541/955-1662, lunch and dinner Mon.–Sat., main courses $6–12) is a Thai restaurant (with some Chinese dishes) hidden away in a nondescript shopping mall near the Visitor Center. You'd never guess it, but you'll find exotic dishes such as *tom ka gai* (a coconut cream soup flavored with ginger-like galangka root) and nearly two dozen vegetarian dishes on the menu here.

Aficionados of the old-time soda fountain will appreciate the **Grants Pass Pharmacy** (414 S.W. 6th St., 541/476-4262). Decent sandwiches ($5) and phosphate drinks for a quarter are featured here. Local old-timers meet here every afternoon, and it's the kids' first stop after school.

The **Wild River Brewing and Pizza Company** (595 N.E. E St., 541/471-7487, lunch and dinner daily, main courses $8–16) features wood-fired pizza ($16–24 for a large), pastas, burgers, and sandwiches as well as microbrewed beers. All breads used for sandwiches are baked on the premises. If you're there for the beer, five brews are offered year-round and are complemented by four seasonal ones. One of the best ways to sample the local product is via the $1.50 taster glasses. Free brewery tours are also offered.

Another place to find a great selection of microbrews on tap is at the **Laughing Clam** (121 S.W. G St., 541/479-1110, lunch and dinner daily, main dishes $7–15). This nonsmoking eatery and alehouse is kid-friendly, and you can bring the family up until 9 P.M. The moderately priced menu offers a wide range of salads, sandwiches, pastas, and burgers. Their appetizers break away from the ordinary pub grub. One example is the onion anemones, sweet Northwest onions dipped in beer batter and deep-fried, accompanied by chili mayonnaise. They look kind of like flowers when you get them, putting ordinary onion rings to shame.

Oregon wines are featured exclusively here, so check out the house wine specials to taste some of the best in the state.

A popular place for a weekday buffet or Sunday brunch is **The Brewery** (509 S.W. G St., 541/479-9850, dinner Tues.–Sun, lunch daily except Mon. and Sat., main courses $12–23). Salads and sandwiches are served at lunch while at dinnertime classic American steaks, seafood, and other standards are well prepared and served with aplomb. Set in a brewery building built in 1886, the place is dripping with historical ambience. A half-dozen quality microbrews are available on draught.

Sunshine Natural Foods (128 S.W. H St., 541/474-5044, Mon.–Sat.) has a café and market catering to those seeking sustenance that's fresh, homegrown, and organic. The soup and salad bar at lunch is always a winner in the $6 range.

Grants Pass has a large farmers market, boasting produce, crafts, prepared foods, and strolling entertainers at 4th and F Streets. For more information, contact **Growers Market** (541/476-5375, www.growersmarket.org). It's open 9 A.M.–1 P.M. Saturday, mid-March–Thanksgiving.

PRACTICALITIES

The **Grants Pass/Josephine County Visitor Information Center/Chamber of Commerce** (1995 N.W. Vine, Grants Pass 97526, 541/476-7717 or 800/547-5927, www.visitgrantspass.com) is open 8 A.M.–5 P.M. daily in summer, weekdays in winter.

Greyhound (460 N.E. Agness Ave., 541/476-4513) offers access to the I-5 corridor.

◖ OREGON CAVES NATIONAL MONUMENT

About 30 miles southwest of Grants Pass is the Oregon Caves National Monument (541/592-3400, www.nps.gov/orca, $8.50 adults, $6 children ages 6–11.). The cave itself—as there is really only one, which opens onto successive caverns—was formed over the eons by the action of water. As rain and snowmelt seeped through cracks and fissures in the rock above the cave and percolated down into the underlying limestone, huge sections of the limestone became saturated and collapsed—much as a sand castle too close to the sea always caves in. When the water table eventually lowered, these pockets were drained of water and the process of cave decoration began.

First, the limestone was dissolved by the water and carried in solution into the cave. When the water evaporated, it left behind a microscopic layer of calcite. This process was repeated countless times, gradually creating the beautiful formations visible today. When the minerals are deposited on the ceiling, a stalactite begins to form. Limestone-laden water that evaporates on the floor might leave behind a stalagmite. When a stalactite and a stalagmite meet, they become a column. Other cave sculptures you'll see include helicites, hell-bent formations that twist and turn in crazy directions; draperies, looking just like their household namesakes but cast in stone instead of cloth; and soda straws, stalactites that are hollow in the center like a straw, carrying mineral-rich drops of moisture to their tips.

Discovered in 1874, the Oregon Caves attract thousands of visitors annually. During the Depression, walkways and turnoffs were built to make the cave more accessible. Unfortunately, tons of waste rock and rubble were stashed into nooks and crannies in the cave, instead of being transported out. This had the ironic effect of obscuring the very formations intended for display. However, the National Park Service started to remove the artificial debris in 1985, exposing the natural formations once again. Little by little, the cave is returning to the way it looked before the "improvements" began.

The River Styx, another victim of Depression-era meddling, is enjoying a similar resurrection. This stream used to run through the cave but was diverted into pipes to aid trail and tunnel construction. The pipes ended up buried beneath tons of pulverized rock, and now the Park Service is hard at work undoing the work of humans to let the stream flow where Nature intended.

Take U.S. 199 to Cave Junction, then wind your way 20 miles up Route 46 (a beautiful old-growth Douglas fir forest lining the road might help divert the faint-of-heart from the nail-biting turns). The last 13 miles of this trip are especially exciting. Remember that there are few turnouts of sufficient size to enable a large vehicle to reverse direction.

Tours of the cave are conducted year-round by National Park Service interpreters. Their presentations are both informative and entertaining, and you will leave the cave with a better understanding of its natural, geologic, and human history. A recent discovery in an unexplored part of the caverns was a grizzly bear fossil believed to be over 40,000 years old. Children younger than six must pass ability requirements (e.g., walking up many stairs for a total vertical climb of 218 feet) and stand a minimum of 42 inches tall to gain entry. The tour (limited to 16 persons) takes a little over an hour and requires some uphill walking. Good walking shoes and warm clothing are recommended. It may be warm and toasty outside, but the cave maintains a fairly consistent year-round temperature of 41°F. Passageways can be narrow, ceilings low, and the footing slippery. During summer you can wait in line up to an hour to go on a tour, and fewer tours are offered October–April. Call ahead for tour times.

Wine-Tasting

You can sample some of the local product at **Foris Vineyards** (654 Kendall Rd., 541/592-3752, www.foriswine.com) and **Bridgeview Vineyards and Winery** (4210 Holland Loop Road, 541/592-4688 or 877/273-4843, www.bridgeviewwine.com). Both wineries offer tastings 11 A.M.–5 P.M. year-round, although their operating hours tend to be reduced in winter.

Camping

Near the Oregon Caves, camping is available at **Grayback** (Illinois Valley Ranger District, 26568 Redwood Hwy., Cave Junction 97523, 541/592-4000, www.fs.fed.us.r6 .siskiyou), 12 miles from Cave Junction on Route

BED-AND-BREAKFAST IN THE TREES

Located in Takilma near Cave Junction, **Out 'n About Treehouse Institute and Treesort** (300 Page Creek Rd., Cave Junction 97523, 541/598-2208 or 800/200-5484, www.tree-houses.com) is a unique lodging option that's worth driving a bit out of your way from the Oregon Caves. After all, how many bed-and-breakfasts do you find in a treehouse?

I his comfortable rural retreat blends the whimsy of the '60s with 21st-century creature comforts. The 10 well-appointed treehouse guest rooms are bolted to hundred-year-old white oaks, some 18 feet above the ground. Should you have misgivings about the structural integrity of these accommodations, be advised that the innkeeper gathered nearly 11,000 pounds of his friends to stand on several units simultaneously – 35 times the weight requirements of the local code. Those desiring a more down-to-earth lodging op-

tion can stay in a peeled-fir cabin with a cozy woodstove. For the deluxe treatment, reserve a 300-square-foot structure built of redwood and Douglas fir that features a sink, tub, fridge, queen-sized futon, loft, and 200-square-foot deck with mountain views. The "treepee," a tepee done up in Out 'n About style, is always popular with the kids.

Horseback trail rides, trips to the best Illinois River swimming holes, and white-water rafting trips can be arranged through the management. Or, swim in the river that runs through the property. Rates range $110-200 (two-night minimum stay) and include a continental breakfast. Your stay here will help you better understand treehouses, treeology, and treeminology, and, like many other guests, you may well leave a "treemusketeer." Tours of Out 'n About run noon-3 P.M. April-October and cost $4 for adults and $2 for children under 13.

SOUTHERN OREGON

---

46. There are 25 tent sites and 16 trailer sites close to Sucker Creek. Electricity and piped water are provided, with a store, laundry, and showers within a mile. Closer to the caves is **Cave Creek** (same address as Grayback); just take Route 46 four miles south of the caves to Forest Service Road 4032. Piped water and pit toilets are provided, and showers are available five miles away. You'll also find a ranger station and informative campfire programs here on summer evenings. Both campgrounds charge $10.

Accommodations

The six-story **Oregon Caves Lodge** (P.O. Box 128, Cave Junction 97523, 541/592-3400, doubles from $80) offers food and accommodations May 1–October 31. Located about 50 miles west of Grants Pass on U.S. 199, the château stands at an elevation of 4,000 feet. Built in 1934, this artistically rustic building blends in with the forest and moss-covered marble ledges. Indigenous wood and stone permeate this building so that you never lose a sense of where you are. The rooms feature

views of Cave Creek canyon, waterfalls, or the Oregon Caves entrance. For a unique experience, we recommend the sixth floor. The rooms might be small, but they have more character and extend out at odd angles from the building. The Pendleton blankets, tall painted chairs, and wooden bed frames add to the historical nuance.

The château has been nicknamed the "Marble Halls of Oregon," and you can see the huge marble fireplace in the fourth-floor lobby for yourself while you thaw out after your spelunking expedition. The food at the château is surprisingly good, and having Cave Creek running through the center of the dining room definitely adds to the unique atmosphere. Downstairs, the old-fashioned 1930s-style soda fountain dishes up the classic American fare of burgers, fries, and shakes. Open daily.

For a nice after-dinner hike, take a walk down the Big Tree Trail, so named for a huge Douglas fir estimated to be more than 1,000 years old. With a circumference of 38 feet, seven inches, it is among the largest standing trees in

Oregon. The three-mile round-trip wends its way through virgin forest that has tan oak, canyon live oak, Pacific madrone, chinquapin, and manzanita, as well as Douglas fir and ponderosa pine. The hike is not that difficult, and the solitude and views of the surrounding mountains are as inspiring as the Big Tree. For a jaunt that's just under a mile, try the Cliff Nature Trail. Placards will help you identify the plant life as you traverse the mossy cliffs, and there are also some good vistas of the Siskiyou Mountains.

Food

In Cave Junction, **Miller's Wild River Deli and Brewery** (249 U.S. 199 N., 541/592-3556, lunch and dinner daily, $6–13) makes pizza dough, sandwich rolls, and croissants from scratch and then tops or stuffs them with fresh ingredients. A salad bar, soup, and Southern-style fried chicken round out the menu. Enjoy their handcrafted European-style beers and ales along with their beer-battered potato chips and onion rings.

Roseburg

Many people passing through the Roseburg area might quickly dismiss it as a rural backwater. A closer look, however, reveals many more interesting layers beneath the mill-town veneer. While about half of the folks here rely upon the woods as a workplace (and this fact is reflected in the no-nonsense cafés and businesses meeting their needs), growing pockets of refinement are found in between the pickup trucks and lumber mills. An award-winning museum, Oregon's only drive-through zoo, and some fine restaurants are a few examples of culture in the hinterland.

And yet, the true allure of Roseburg is not really in town, but in the surrounding countryside. The Mediterranean climate of the Umpqua Valley has proven ideal for producing world-class wines and contributes to wonderful wine-tasting tours. The beautiful North Umpqua River to the east offers rafting, camping, hiking, and fishing. In addition to catching trout, salmon, and bass, anglers come from all over to enjoy one of the world's last rivers with a native run of summer steelhead. Numerous waterfalls along the river and the frothy white water make the Native American word Umpqua ("Thunder Water") an appropriate name.

SIGHTS
Douglas County Museum of History and Natural History
This nationally acclaimed museum (123 Mu-

seum Dr., 541/957-7007, www.co.douglas. or.us/museum, 9 A.M.–5 P.M. Mon.–Fri., 10 A.M.–5 P.M. Sat., noon– 5 P.M. Sun., $3.50 adults, $1 kids.) is located at the Douglas County Fairgrounds (Exit 123 off I-5). Its four wings feature exhibits that range from a million-year-old saber-toothed tiger to 19th-century steam-logging equipment. The museum also hosts children's programming held the second Saturday of each month.

Gardens
The **Lotus Knight Memorial Gardens** are in Riverside Park. Located between Oak and Washington Streets on the banks of the South Umpqua River, these gardens are alight with colorful azaleas and rhododendrons in the spring. Open 5 A.M.–10 P.M. daily.

South of Roseburg about 15 minutes, near the town of Myrtle Creek, is **Beneschoen Gardens,** with a good collection of rhododendrons, azaleas, azalea-dendrons, and other rare and unusual plants. Over 150 varieties of azaleas are featured here. Peak blooms for both parks occur late April–early May.

Winchester Fish Ladder
The Winchester Fish Ladder is just off I-5 at Exit 129 on the north bank of the North Umpqua River. Here visitors can watch salmon and steelhead in their native environment as they swim by the viewing window at

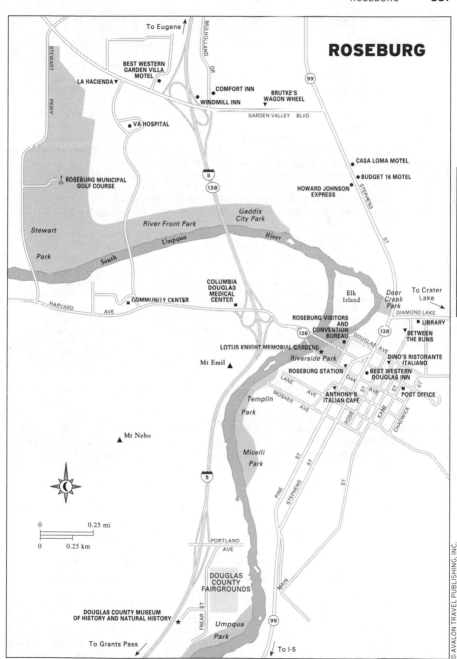

ROSEBURG

To Eugene

STEWART PKWY

MULHOLLAND DR

BEST WESTERN GARDEN VILLA MOTEL

LA HACIENDA ▼

COMFORT INN

BRUTKE'S WAGON WHEEL

WINDMILL INN

99

GARDEN VALLEY BLVD

■ VA HOSPITAL

CASA LOMA MOTEL

● BUDGET 16 MOTEL

HOWARD JOHNSON EXPRESS

STEPHENS ST

5

138

ROSEBURG MUNICIPAL GOLF COURSE

Gaddis City Park

River Front Park

Stewart

Umpqua

River

Park

South

COLUMBIA DOUGLAS MEDICAL CENTER

HARVARD AVE

■ COMMUNITY CENTER

Elk Island

Door Creek Park

To Crater Lake

DIAMOND LAKE

■ LIBRARY

ROSEBURG VISITORS AND CONVENTION BUREAU

138

138

DOUGLAS AVE

▼ BETWEEN THE BUNS

LOTUS KNIGHT MEMORIAL GARDENS

Riverside Park

DINO'S RISTORANTE ITALIANO

Mt Emil ▲

ROSEBURG STATION

BEST WESTERN DOUGLAS INN

LANE

OAK ST

AVE

ST

■ POST OFFICE

MOSHER AVE

ANTHONY'S ITALIAN CAFÉ

ROSE ST

KANE ST

CHADWICK ST

Templin Park

▲ Mt Nebo

Micelli Park

PINE ST

STEPHENS ST

ST

5

0   0.25 mi

0   0.25 km

PORTLAND AVE

DOUGLAS COUNTY FAIRGROUNDS

FREAR ST

MAIN ST

DOUGLAS COUNTY MUSEUM OF HISTORY AND NATURAL HISTORY ★

Umpqua Park

To Grants Pass

99

To I-5

SOUTHERN OREGON

OAKLAND

Many travelers drive by the exit marked Oakland on I-5 joking that maybe they made a wrong turn somewhere and ended up in California. But the curious who venture a few miles off the freeway to explore this National Historic Landmark discover that *this* Oakland is an interesting voyage into Oregon's past. Established in the 1850s, this hamlet today gives little indication of the caprices of fate and fortune it has experienced in its century-and-a half history. Oakland is noteworthy for leftover touches of refinement from its golden age, which seem almost incongruous against its present-day small-town facade.

Oakland was a stopover point for the main stagecoach line linking Portland and Sacramento until the Oregon and California Railroad came to town in 1872. With these two transportation linkages, Oakland thrived as a trading center for outlying hop fields and prune orchards. In the early 1900s, millions of pounds of dried prunes were shipped all over the world from Oakland. In the 1920s and '30s, raising turkeys became the prominent industry in the area, and Oakland became the leading turkey-shipping center in the western United States.

From the '40s through the '60s, the lumber industry dominated the local economy. Today, livestock ranching, farming, and tourism are the economic mainstays.

While not as commercialized as its counterpart farther south in Jacksonville, Oakland still provides a good place to pull off the interstate and reflect on the passage of years in a one-time boomtown turned rural hamlet.

Old Town Oakland is a good place to start your tour, because this is where it all began. An excellent free history and walking-tour pamphlet is available at the city hall (117 3rd St.). The original wooden buildings were destroyed by fires in the 1890s, and most of the brick and stone structures in the historical district date back to this era of reconstruction. The **Oakland Museum** (136 Locust) is worth visiting. The exhibit in the back re-creates Oakland during its boom times. There are many antique stores, art galleries, and curio shops to browse through as well.

Tolly's (115 Locust, 541/459-3796), is a beautifully preserved restaurant and a great place to stop by for lunch or dinner. Be sure to save some room for the homemade desserts.

Winchester Dam. Spring chinook and summer steelhead migrate upriver May–August, and coho, fall chinook, and more summer steelhead swim on by September–November. December–May, winter steelhead is the primary species seen going through the fish ladders and on past the window. The Umpqua River offers the largest variety of game fish in Oregon.

◖ Wildlife Safari

Tucked away in a 600-acre wooded valley is Wildlife Safari (Safari Road, Winston 97496, 541/679-6761 or 800/355-4848, www.wild lifesafari.org, 9 A.M.–5 P.M. (or dusk) every day except Christmas, $17.50 adults, $14.50 seniors, and $11.50 kids ages 4–12), Oregon's drive-through zoo.

Once inside the park gates, the brightly colored birds and exotic game animals transport you to other lands, with an oddly appropriate Oregon backdrop. Be that as it may, every possible step has been taken at Wildlife Safari to re-create African and North American animal-life zones. Lest this conjure the image of lions, tigers, and bears eating Bambi and company for supper before your very eyes, these critters are kept apart from their natural prey. Similar precautions are taken with humans. People must remain inside their vehicles except in designated areas, and windows and sunroofs must be kept closed in the big cats' and bears' areas.

The first loop takes you to see the tigers and cheetahs. These giant felines loll lazily about or catch catnaps in the tall grass. The next link takes you through the heart of "Africa," where the deer and the antelope play. Wildebeests, zebras, and other creatures scamper freely about, seemingly oblivious to the slow parade of cars. Elephants, rhinoceroses, and other African big game are also represented here. Soon you are in "North America." Bears, bighorn sheep, pronghorns, moose, and buffalo are just a few of the animals that live down in the valley. Perhaps the most popular attraction is the petting zoo. When the weather is good, you can take a memorable ride on a camel or elephant.

With 600 animals, including America's largest (and cutest) collection of cheetah cubs, this is one safari that appeals to all ages. Speaking of cheetahs, this is one of the few places where they are successfully bred in captivity. After your "safari," pull into the White Rhino restaurant, serving good food within view of lions, giraffes, and white rhinos.

To get here, take Exit 119 off I-5 and follow Route 42 for four miles. Turn right on Lookingglass Road and right again on Safari Road.

Wineries

Several wineries in the Roseburg vicinity offer tasting rooms and tours. The dry, Mediterranean climate and rich variety of soils in the area are ideal for chardonnay, pinot noir, gewürztraminer, riesling, zinfandel, and cabernet sauvignon varietals. A good wine-tour pamphlet with a fine map showing the location of wineries is available from the Roseburg Visitors and Convention Bureau.

Abacela Vineyards and Winery (12500 Lookingglass Road, 541/679-6642, 11 A.M.–5 P.M. daily) is noted for the large variety of wine grapes grown, from Tempranillo to Malbec to Dolcetto. Even if you came to Oregon seeking pinot noir, you'll find the enthusiasm of these winemakers infectious.

Girardet Wine Cellars (895 Reston Rd., 541/679-7252, www.girardetwine.com, 11–5 P.M. daily Apr.–Oct., 11–4 P.M. Nov.–Mar.) is one of the oldest in the area. Philippe Girardet, from a town at the headwaters of the Rhine River in Switzerland, brings European wine-blending techniques to Oregon. This process produces unique chardonnay, pinot noir, cabernet sauvignon, and riesling wines.

The winery is closed December 20–January 30 and major holidays.

The **Henry Estate Winery** (687 Hubbard Creek Rd., Umpqua 97486, 541/459-5120 or 800/782-2686, www.henryestate.com, 11 A.M.–5 P.M. daily) has produced a string of award-winning varietals from chardonnay, gewürztraminer, and pinot noir grapes. Newcomers to their outstanding lineup include pinot noir blanc and Muller-Thurgau. Lunch at shaded picnic tables near the vineyard and the Umpqua River can heighten your enjoyment of the fruit of the vine. The third weekend in August is the Henry Goes Wine gala, which you won't want to miss if in the region.

SPORTS AND RECREATION
Fishing

The Umpqua River system is home to a dozen species of popular eating fish that range from the big chinook salmon to the tiny silver smelt. Visit the Oregon Department of Fish and Wildlife website (www.dfw.state.or.us) for additional information on the Umpqua.

Spring chinook enter the North Umpqua River March–June, work their way upstream during July and August, and spawn September–October. Fall chinook are mainly found in the warmer South Umpqua River. Their migration starts in midsummer and peaks in September when the rains increase water flow and lower the river's temperature. The best fishing for summer steelhead on the North Umpqua is June–October; the fish spawn January–March. This fish averages only 6–8 pounds, but it will make you think you are trying to reel in a chinook by the way it struggles.

Coho salmon, alias "silvers," are found throughout the Umpqua River system. The coho life cycle lasts about three years. Each spends its first year in freshwater, heads for the ocean to spend one to two years, and then returns to freshwater to spawn. The adults weigh an average of seven pounds each. This fishery has had some lean years recently.

You'll find rainbow trout in nearly all rivers and streams of the Umpqua River system where the water is relatively cool and gravel bars clean. This is the river's most common game fish, mainly because the rivers, lakes, and streams of the Umpqua are routinely seeded with over 100,000 legal-size (eight inches or longer) rainbows. The fishing season opens in April, with the best fishing in early summer when the fish are actively feeding.

Camping

Armacher County Park (541/672-4901), $11–20, is five miles north of town directly beneath I-5 on Exit 129. **Twin Rivers Vacation Park** (433 Rivers Forks Rd., 541/673-3811, $18–25), is six miles out of town (via I-5, take Exit 125), where the north and south forks of the Umpqua converge. Water, electricity, waste disposal, showers, and a coin-op laundry are available at this 85-site park. **Fairgrounds RV Park** (210 Frear St., 541/440-4505, $20–25), has 50 hookups, water, and a drive-through dump station. **U-Haul RV Center** (1182 N.E. Stephens, 541/672-6864) has a dump station for self-contained vehicles.

Golf

Stewart Park Golf Course (1005 Stewart Park Dr., 541/672-4592) charges $16 for nine holes, $26 for 18 holes; add on a few extra dollars on weekends. In addition to power carts, a lighted driving range, and rental golf clubs, a complete pro shop offers lessons and any peripherals you may need.

EVENTS

Roseburg's big event is the **Douglas County Fair,** held annually at the fairgrounds the second week of August. Besides the usual assortment of 4-H prize steers, Mom's marmalade, and Grandma's-secret-recipe apple pie, the bright lights of the midway rides, food booths, and horse and stock-car races add to the festive atmosphere. In the afternoon, big-name singers entertain the crowds with toe-tapping country music. While it's seven days of fun, and well worth seeing if you're in the neighborhood, high temperatures compel an early start. In September, a wine, art, and cheese fest attracts vintners, artisans, and food booths. Contact the Roseburg Visitors and Convention Bureau (800/444-9584) for specifics.

Stewart Park hosts free Tuesday-evening concerts during the summer **Music on the Halfshell** (www.halfshell.org) series, featuring such urbane entertainers as David Grisman and B. B. King. The park's bandstand is located near the banks of the South Umpqua.

ACCOMMODATIONS

There are over 1,000 motel rooms for rent in Roseburg, and this competition keeps rates relatively low. Budget travelers can bunk down at **Budget 16 Motel** (1067 N.E. Stephens, 541/673-5556) or **Casa Loma Motel** (1107 N.E. Stephens, 541/673-5569) for $50–65 per night.

The following chains are all midrange in price ($65–85) and amenities: **Comfort Inn** (1539 Mulholland Dr., 541/957-1100 or 800/228-5160); **Best Western Douglas Inn** (511 S.E. Stephens, 541/673-6625 or 877/368-4466, www.bestwesternoregon.com); **Best Western Garden Villa Motel** (760 N.W. Garden Valley Blvd., 541/672-1601 or 800/547-3446); and **Howard Johnson Express** (978 N.E. Stephens, 541/673-5082, www.hojo.com).

For comfortable accommodations with laundry, restaurant/lounge, and pool, where pets are permitted, head for the **Windmill Inn** (1450 N.W. Mulholland Dr., 541/673-0901 or 800/547-4747, www.windmillinns.com, $85–110).

FOOD

Roseburg is not exactly the fine-dining capital of Oregon. Since there is no shortage of fast-food joints, greasy spoons, and truck-driver restaurants, let's focus instead on a few unique options in town.

The **Douglas County Farmers Market** (541/672-9380) takes place April 12–October 25. Located in the parking lot of Roseburg Valley Mall on Stewart Parkway and Garden Valley Boulevard, it's a great place to sample fresh flavors 9 A.M.–1 P.M. each Saturday.

A highly regarded Tex-Mex establishment is **La Hacienda** (940 N.W. Garden Valley Blvd., 541/672-5330, lunch and dinner daily, main courses $7–15). You'll know the place when you see it. In front of the cream-colored stucco building with green and orange stripes are tall arches of typical Spanish design. The food inside is equally inviting. In addition to the usual assortment of tacos, tostadas, and tamales, you'll find tasty shrimp and chicken fajitas, combination dinners, and seafood dishes. La Hacienda also features a wide selection of Mexican beers to enhance your meal.

You'll find good deli sandwiches at **Between the Buns** (214 S.E. Jackson, 541/672-0342, 10 A.M.–5 P.M. Mon.–Sat.). "Dagwood-style" sandwiches piled way too high with fillings come at a low price that makes them easy to swallow.

Brutke's Wagon Wheel (227 N.W. Garden Valley Blvd., 541/672-7555, lunch and dinner Mon.–Fri., dinner Sat. and Sun., main courses $12–24) is the place to go for prime rib. The chef's prime rib recipe dates back 30 years and accounts for more than a third of the food sales at the restaurant. But if you don't fit the beef-eater's profile, chicken and "heart-smart" entrées are also featured on the menu.

The McMenamins brewery empire has an appealing operation at **Roseburg Station** (700 S.E. Sheridan St., 541/672-1934, lunch and dinner daily, main courses $6–13). The 1912 Southern Pacific Station was purchased and restored while preserving original features like the 16-foot-high ceiling, tongue-and-groove Douglas fir wainscoting, and marble molding. Historical photos and art further recount the depot's storied past. Quality food and microbrews in a setting suitable for family further enhance the appeal.

Some of Roseburg's best dining is Italian-style. (**Dino's Ristorante Italiano** (404 SE Jackson, 541/673-0848, dinner Mon.–Sat., main courses $10–16) is a cozy, family-run spot with a decor that's a sprawl of wine cases, travel guides, and cookbooks. The husband-and-wife cooking team spend part of each year in Italy so the food is about as authentic as you'll find anywhere in southern Oregon. Another local favorite for pasta is **Anthony's Italian Café** (500 S.E. Cass, 541/229-2233, dinner Tues.–Sat., main courses $12–19).

INFORMATION

The **Roseburg Visitors and Convention Bureau** (410 S.E. Spruce St., 541/672-9731 or 800/444-9584, www.visitroseburg.com) has among its brochures a particularly useful drivers' guide to historic places. Although the courteous staff offer decent travel-planning suggestions, they are tight-lipped when it comes to specific recommendations on food and lodging.

GETTING THERE AND AROUND

Buses to/from the **Greyhound** bus depot (835 S.E. Stephens, 541/673-5326) connect Roseburg with other cities along the I-5 corridor.

Roseburg Sunshine Taxi Express (541/ 672-2888) can chauffeur you around the city.

Umpqua Highway

One of the great escapes into the Cascade Mountains is via the Umpqua Highway, Route 138. This road runs along the part of the Umpqua River fished by Zane Grey and Clark Gable as well as legions of less-ballyhooed nimrods during steelhead season. The North Umpqua is a premier fishing river full of trout and salmon, as well as a source of excitement for white-water rafters who shoot the rapids. Numerous waterfalls, including Watson Falls, feed this great waterway and are found close to the road. Tall timbers line the road through the Umpqua National Forest, and many fine campgrounds are situated within its confines. Mountain lakes like Toketee Reservoir, Lemolo Lake, and Diamond Lake offer boating and other recreational opportunities. The Umpqua National Forest also boasts challenging yet accessible mountain trails up the flanks of Mount Bailey (8,363 feet) and Mount

Thielsen (9,182 feet). And when snow carpets the landscape in winter, you can go cross-country skiing, snowmobiling, and Sno-Cat skiing on Mount Bailey free from the crowds at other winter-sports areas.

This place is still so wild primarily because of the rugged terrain. The first road was built in the 1920s, a crude dirt trail that ran from Roseburg to Steamboat. Travelers of the day who wanted to get to the Diamond Lake Lodge spent three days traversing this road by car, then had to journey another 20 miles on horseback to reach their final destination. The North Umpqua Road was expanded to Copeland Creek by the Civilian Conservation Corps during the Depression, but the trips to Diamond and Crater Lakes were still limited to a trailwise few.

It wasn't until the late 1950s, when President Dwight D. Eisenhower pushed for development of the nation's interstate freeways and state highways, that road improvement began in earnest. Douglas County allocated $2.76 million toward federal matching funds to construct the Umpqua Highway. The road was completed in the summer of 1964, opening up the North Umpqua basin to timber interests, sportspeople, and tourists.

SIGHTS
Colliding Rivers

Just off of Route 138 on the west side of the town of **Glide** is the site of this curiosity. The Wild and Umpqua Rivers meet head-on in a bowl of green serpentine. The best times to view this spectacle are after winter storms and when spring runoff is high. If the water is low, check out the high-water mark from the Christmas Flood of 1964. Water levels from that great inundation were lapping at the parking lot, a chilling reminder that *umpqua* means "thundering water" in Chinook.

Waterfalls

Visitors can get an unusual perspective of **Grotto Falls** because there's a trail in back of this 100-foot cascade. If you venture behind the shimmering water, watch your step because the moss-covered rocks are very slippery. To get here, take Route 138 for 18 miles east of Roseburg to Glide. Follow Little River Road to the Coolwater Campground, and you'll find the turnoff to Forest Service Road 2703 nearby. Take it for five miles until you reach the junction of Forest Service Road 2703-150. Proceed down Forest Service Road 2703-150 for another two miles until you reach the trailhead. It's only a short hike in to view Grotto Falls.

About 10 miles west of the town of **Steamboat** is 50-foot-high **Susan Creek Falls** whose trailhead sits off Route 138 near the Susan Creek picnic area. A one-mile trail winds through a rainforest-like setting to the falls. The cascade is bordered on three sides by green mossy rock walls that never see the light of the sun and stay wet 365 days a year. Another 0.25 mile up the trail are the **Indian Mounds.** One of the rites of manhood for Umpqua boys was to fast and pile up stones in hopes of being granted a vision or spiritual powers. Also called the Vision Quest Site, the site still holds stacks of moss-covered stones in an area protected by a fence.

Four miles west of Susan Creek Falls is **Fall Creek Falls.** Look for the trailhead off of Route 138 at Fall Creek. A good walk for families with young children and for older people, the mild one-mile trail goes around and through slabs of bedrock. Halfway up the trail is a lush area called **Job's Garden.** Stay on the Fall Creek Trail and in another half mile you'll come to the falls. It's a double falls with each tier 35–50 feet in height. Back at Job's Garden, you may care to explore the Job's Garden Trail, which leads to the base of columnar basalt outcroppings.

During fish-migration season, it's fun to venture off of Route 138 at Steamboat and go up Steamboat Creek Road 38 to see the fish battle two small waterfalls. The first, **Little Falls,** is a mile up the road. It's always exciting to see the fish miraculously wriggle their way up this 10-foot cascade. Four miles farther down Steamboat Creek Road is **Steamboat Falls.** A viewpoint showcases this 30-foot falls, but not as many fish try to swim up this one because of the fish ladders nearby.

Back on Route 138 about three miles east of Steamboat is **Jack Falls.** Look for the trailhead sign and follow the trail along the brushy bank of Jack Creek to a series of three closely grouped falls ranging 20–70 feet in height.

From Route 138 take Forest Service Road 37 near the east entrance of the Toketee Ranger Station. This road will take you to the trailhead of **Watson Falls,** a 272-foot-high flume of water. A moderate 0.5-mile trail climbs through tall stands of Douglas fir and western hemlock and is complemented by an understory of green salal, Oregon grape, and ferns. A bridge spans the canyon just below the falls, giving outstanding views of this towering cascade. The cool spray that billows up to the bridge always feels good on a hot day after the hike uphill.

Another falls worth a visit is **Lemolo Falls.** *Lemolo* is a Chinook word meaning "wild and untamed," and you'll see that this is the case with this thunderous 100-foot waterfall. To get here, take Lemolo Lake Road off of Route 138, then follow Forest Service Roads 2610 and 2610-600 and look for the trailhead sign. The trail is a gentle one-mile path that drops down into the North Umpqua Canyon and passes several small waterfalls on the way to Lemolo Falls.

◖ Toketee Falls

Two big waterfalls are another 19 miles up Route 138 near the Toketee Ranger Station. To get to Toketee Falls, follow Forest Service Road 34 at the west entrance of the ranger station, cross the first bridge, and turn left. There you'll find the trailhead and a parking area. The 0.5-mile trail ends at a double waterfall with a combined height of over 150 feet. The word *toketee* means "graceful" in the tribal dialect, and after viewing the water plunge over the sheer wall of basalt you'll probably agree it's aptly named.

Umpqua Hot Springs

The Umpqua Hot Springs is mostly unknown

and far enough from civilized haunts not to be overused, yet it's accessible enough for those in the know to enjoy. The springs have been developed with wooden pools and a crude lean-to shelter. It's best to go midweek, as weekends tend to attract more visitors, forcing you to wait your turn for a soak.

To get here, go north from the Toketee Ranger Station and turn right onto County Road 34, just past the Pacific Power and Light buildings. Proceed down 34 past Toketee Lake about six miles. When you cross the bridge over Deer Creek, which is clearly signed, you will be a little less than a half mile from the turnoff. The turnoff is Thorn Prairie Road to the right that goes a mile and ends at a small parking area. Please note that in wet weather this road may be impassable, and it is not recommended for low-slung cars in any season. From the parking area, it's 0.5 mile down the blocked road to the hot springs trailhead and another half mile to the pool.

Of the many waterfalls along the North Umpqua River, Toketee Falls is the most striking.

© JUDY JEWELL

SOUTHERN OREGON

SPORTS AND RECREATION

Hiking

Over 570 miles of trails crisscross the one-million-acre **Umpqua National Forest,** with elevations that range 1,000–9,000 feet. There are hikes to please families and mountain climbers alike. Wildlife and wildflowers, mountain lakes and mountain peaks, old-growth forest and alpine meadows are some of the attractions visitors see along the way.

If you're camping along the North Umpqua River, many pleasant day hikes are possible on the **North Umpqua Trail.** Beginning near the town of Glide, this thoroughfare parallels the North Umpqua River for most of its 79 miles. Divided into 11 segments from over three to just under 16 miles in length, the trail leads high into the Cascades and connects with the Pacific Crest Trail as well as many campgrounds. Route 138 affords many access points to the trail. Check with the Umpqua National Forest Ranger Station, Diamond Lake Ranger District (HC 60, P.O. Box 101, Idleyld Park 97447, 541/498-2531), for a map and brochure to plan your expedition along this beautiful walkway.

One segment of the North Umpqua Trail is the one-mile **Panther Trail.** This gentle hike begins near Steamboat at the parking lot of the former ranger station. Many wildflowers are seen late April–early June on the way up to the old fish hatchery. One flower to look for is the bright red snow plant, *Sarcodes sanguinea,* which grows beneath Douglas firs and sugar pine trees. Also called the carmine snowflower or snow lily, the snow plant is classified as a saprophyte, a plant that contains no chlorophyll and derives nourishment from decayed materials. Growing 8–24 inches in height, the plant has red flowers crowded at the crown of the stem.

A five-mile hike that ranges from easy to moderate is found on the south slope of 8,363-foot **Mount Bailey.** Bring plenty of water and good, sturdy hiking shoes because the last half mile of the ascent is steep, with many sharp rocks. To get to the trailhead, take Route 138 to the north entrance of Diamond Lake. Turn off onto Forest Service Road 4795 and follow it five miles to the junction of Forest Service Road 4795-300. Proceed down 4795-300 another mile until you see the trail marker.

The easy two-mile **Diamond Lake Loop** takes hikers through a mix of lodgepole pine and true fir to Lake Creek, Diamond Lake's only outlet. There are many views of Mount Bailey along the way, as well as some private coves ideal for a swim on hot days. But while the grade is easy, keep in mind that the elevation is nearly a mile high and pace yourself accordingly. To get to the loop, take Forest Service Road 4795 off of Route 138 on the north entrance to Diamond Lake and look for the trailhead sign on the west side of the road.

For those who like to climb mountains for reasons other than just because they are there, the **Mount Thielsen Trail** offers a million-dollar view from the top of the mountain. This four-mile moderate-to-difficult trail winds to the top of Mount Thielsen's spire-pointed 9,182-foot-high volcanic peak.

Bring along water and quick-energy snacks; hiking boots are also recommended due to the sharp volcanic rocks that could easily damage ordinary shoes. Extra care should be taken getting up and down the last 200 feet, since the rocks weaken from ice and erosion during the winter and are prone to crumbling underfoot. If you make it to the top, be sure to enter your name in the climbing register found there. Then take a look at the view, which stretches from Mount Shasta to Mount Hood, and forget all the silly preoccupations that plague us mortals. You'll find the trailhead on the east side of Route 138 one mile north of the junction of Route 230.

Fishing

The North Umpqua has several distinctions. First, it is known as one of the most difficult North American rivers to fish. No boats are permitted from 15 miles in either direction of Steamboat, and no bait or spinners are allowed either. This puts a premium on skillful fly-fishing. You can wade on in and poke around for the best fishing holes on the North Umpqua, one of the few rivers with a summer run of native steelhead—or better yet, hire a guide. **Larry's Guide Service** (12736 N. Umpqua Hwy., Roseburg 97470, 541/673-3099 or 800/763-6277, pin number 8406, www.oregon guides.com) can help you get out on the river year-round to fish for salmon, steelhead, and striped bass. The driftboats are large and heated; bait, tackle, and safety equipment are all provided. Rates are $175 for one person, or $300 for two, on full-day trips; call ahead for reservations and additional information.

Rafting

Over the past few years, the North Umpqua has gained popularity with white-water rafters and kayakers. But fishing and floating are not always compatible, so guidelines for boaters and rafters have been established by the Bureau of Land Management and the Umpqua National Forest.

The area around Steamboat has the most restrictions, mainly because of the heavy fishing in the area that boaters would disturb. Be sure to check with the Forest Service (541/672-6601) prior to setting out, to make sure you are making a legal trip. A good way to get started rafting and avoid the hassle of rules, regulations, and gear is to go along with an experienced white-water guide. These leaders provide the safety equipment, the boats, and the expertise; all you have to do is paddle.

In addition to rafting, inflatable kayak trips are offered by outfitters. Inflatables are easier for the neophyte to handle than the hardshell type, though these craft expose you to more chills and spills. Whatever your mode of floating the river, expect more than a dozen Class III or IV rapids, and plenty of Class IIs, as well as old-growth trees and osprey nests. Best of all, this world-class river is still relatively undiscovered. Spring and summer are the best times to enjoy the North Umpqua, although it's boatable year-round. Boaters are allowed on the river 10 A.M.–6 P.M. only, leaving the morning and evening for fish.

North Umpqua Outfitters (222 Oakview Dr., Roseburg 97470, 541/673-4599, www. nuorafting.com) offers raft, kayak, and driftboat trips. Three-hour raft trips are $105 per person; five-hour raft trips with lunch are $115 per person. This company operates the North Umpqua Kayak School, which gives classes on how to paddle safely, to roll and handle surfing waves, and to survive souse holes. Half- and full-day kayak lessons include all necessary equipment. Half- and full-day drift-boat trips are available for those who like to troll their fishing line in the water on their way downstream. They also rent boats, rafts, kayaks, and the appropriate accoutrements. Other outfitters are the **Adventure Center** (541/482-2897, Ashland) and **Orange Torpedo Trips** (209 Merlin Rd., Merlin 97532, 800/635-2925, www.orangetorpedo.com).

You can combine rafting and mountain biking with **Oregon Ridge and River Excursions** (P.O. Box 495, Glide, 541/496-3333 or 888/454-9696, www.umpquarivers.com). Their popular two- or three-day trips take mountain bikes down the trail along the North Umpqua River and feature white-water paddle rafting, too. They also offer raft and kayak packages as well as guesthouse accommodations. Snacks, great outdoor cooking, and comfortable camping are provided. Call for rates and reservations.

Mount Bailey Cat Skiing

Located 80 miles east of Roseburg off of Route 138 in the central Cascades is Mount Bailey. The experienced skiers at **Cat Ski Mt. Bailey** (800/733-7593, www.catskimtbailey.com) know where the best runs are to be had. Cats transport no more than 12 skiers up the mountain from Diamond Lake Resort to the summit of this 8,363-foot peak. Experienced guides then lead small groups down routes that best suit the abilities of each group. The skiing is challenging and should be attempted only by advanced skiers. Open bowls, steep chutes, and tree-lined glaciers are some of the types of terrain encountered during the 3,000-foot drop in elevation back to the resort.

The prices may also seem steep at up to $250

SOUTHERN OREGON

a day, but it's worth it given the pristine beauty of the area, dearth of crowds, and superlative skiing. Attractive packages include overnight lodging in fireside cabins at Diamond Lake Resort as well as an "alpine lunch" of breads, meats, cheeses, vegetables, homemade pie, and coffee served up on the mountain. Only a limited number of skiers can be booked, so be sure to call ahead for reservations.

Tubing and Snowboarding

If you ski the bunny hill, you might enjoy inner-tubing or snowboarding near Diamond Lake Resort (800/733-7593, www.diamond lake.net). A rope tow takes "tubers" to the top of the hill 9 A.M.–5 P.M. daily for nonstop thrills and spills on the way back down. The hill has a ticket system similar to other ski lifts, with full-day, half-day, and two-hour passes available. The tubing and snowboarding hill is located at the Hilltop Shop. The $10 entry fee includes inner tube, tow rope, and cable clip. Uphill tows are $0.50. You can also buy tow ticket packages: 10 tickets for $5; 20 tickets for $8; and 50 tickets for $20.

Cross-Country Skiing

Over 56 miles of designated Nordic trails are found in the Diamond and Lemolo Lakes area along the upper reaches of Route 138. The trails range in elevation from 4,200 feet to over 8,000 feet at the top of Mount Bailey. Some of the trails are groomed, and all of them are clearly marked by blue trail signs. Contact the **Umpqua National Forest** (Diamond Lake Ranger District, HC 60, P.O. Box 101, Idle-yld Park 97447, 541/498-2531) to request maps and information on these trails.

The **Diamond Lake Resort** (800/733-7593) has equipment, waxes, and rentals, and is open 8 A.M.–5 P.M. daily. It costs $20 per day for a rental package including skis, boots, and poles. Lessons are also available.

Snowmobiling

Approximately 133 miles of designated motorized snow trails are concentrated around the Lemolo and Diamond Lakes area. The trails are usually open in late November, when snow accumulations permit, and range from 4,000 to over 8,000 feet in elevation. Many of these trails are groomed on a regular basis, and all are clearly marked by orange trail signs and diamond-shaped trail blazes pegged up on trees above the snowline. Contact Umpqua National Forest (541/498-2531) for maps and additional information.

One of the more exotic runs is into Crater Lake National Park. Snowmobiles and ATVs (all-terrain vehicles) must register at the north entrance of the park and stay on the road. The trail climbs up about 10 miles from the park gates to the north rim of the lake. Be aware that the mountain weather here can change suddenly, creating dangerous subzero temperatures and whiteout conditions. Also, watch for Nordic skiers and other people sometimes found on motorized-vehicle trails.

If you've ever wanted to ride on one of these motorized snow broncs, then this is the way to go. Each person is furnished with his or her own snowmobile and fuel. A half dozen tours are available ranging from $65 for the 1.5-hour, 17-mile ride around Diamond Lake to $125 for the four-hour trip around Crater Lake. The tour makes a lunch stop at South Shore Plaza.

Little River Camping

If the thought of a campground with good shade trees and a waterfall with a swimming hole sounds idyllic, head for **Cavitt Creek Falls** (Bureau of Land Management, 541/672-4491). To get there, head east of Roseburg on Route 138 to Glide, take Little Creek Road (County Road 17) for seven miles, then continue three miles down Cavitt Creek Road. Ten campsites with picnic tables and fire grills are provided, with piped water, vaulted toilets, and firewood available on the premises. Open May–late October, Cavitt Creek runs $8 per night.

Another campsite five miles up Little River Road is **Wolf Creek** (North Umpqua Ranger District, 541/496-3532), which features eight sites for tents and RVs (30 feet maximum) and three tent-only sites. Picnic tables, fire grills, vault toilets, and piped water are provided.

Open mid-May–late October, the fee is $8 per night.

An easy way to keep your cool is at **Coolwater** (North Umpqua Ranger District, 541/496-3532). Seven tent and RV sites (24 feet maximum) with picnic tables and fire grills are available; vault toilets and well water from a hand pump are also on the grounds. Open mid-May–late October, the campground is $5 per site. To get here, follow Little River Road 15 miles out of Glide. There are many good hiking trails nearby, including **Grotto Falls, Wolf Creek Nature Trail** and **Wolf Creek Falls Trail.**

One of the best deals on the Little River is at **White Creek** (North Umpqua Ranger District, 541/496-3532). Open mid-May–late September, this small four-site campground accommodates tents and RVs for $5 per site. Picnic tables and fire grills are provided, and piped water and vault toilets are available. Situated on the confluence of White Creek and Little River, a good beach and shallow water provide excellent swimming for children. The only catch to this oasis of tranquility is that your stay is limited to two weeks at a time. To get here, take Little Creek Road 17 miles to Red Butte Road and proceed a mile down Red Butte Road to the campground.

Tucked away at an elevation of 3,200 feet on the upper reaches of the Little River is **Lake in the Woods** (North Umpqua Ranger District, 541/496-3532). Here you'll find 11 sites for tents and RVs (16 feet maximum), with picnic tables, fire grills, vault toilets, and hand-pumped water. Open June–late October, the camp charges $8 per night. Set along the shore of four-acre, human-made Little Lake in the Woods, motorized craft are not permitted in this eight-foot-deep pond. Two good hikes nearby are to **Hemlock Falls** and **Yakso Falls.** To get here, head 20 miles up Little River Road to where the pavement ends; proceed another seven miles until you reach the campground.

North Umpqua River Camping

Set along the bank of the North Umpqua River 15 miles east of Roseburg on Route 138 is **Whistler's Bend** (541/673-4863, $12). Picnic tables and fire grills are provided at this county park, as are piped water, flush toilets, and showers. The fishing is good here, and even though it's fairly close to town, it doesn't usually get too crowded.

About 30 miles east of Route 138 is **Susan Creek** (Bureau of Land Management, 541/672-4491, open May–late October, $11). This campground has 31 tent and RV sites (20 feet maximum) with picnic tables and fire grills. Flush toilets, piped water, and firewood are also available. Situated in a grove of old-growth Douglas fir and sugar pine next to the North Umpqua River, the campground is enhanced by the presence of a fine beach and swimming hole as well.

Within easy access to great fishing (fly-angling only), rafting, and hiking, **Bogus Creek** (North Umpqua Ranger District, 541/496-3532, open May 1–Oct. 31, $9) offers you the real thing. Here you'll find five tent sites and 10 tent and RV sites (30 feet maximum) with picnic tables and fire grills. Flush toilets, iodinated water, and gray wastewater sumps are available. As the campground is a major launching point for white-water expeditions and within a few miles of Fall Creek Falls and Job's Garden Geological Area, it's good to get here early to assure a campsite.

About 38 miles east of Roseburg on Route 138 near Steamboat is **Canton Creek** (North Umpqua Ranger District, 541/496-3532, open mid-May–late October, $7). Take Steamboat Creek Road off Route 138 and proceed 400 yards to the campground. This campground features 12 sites for tents and RVs (22 feet maximum) with the standard picnic tables and fire grills, plus piped water, flush toilets, and gray wastewater sumps. Close to good fly-fishing on the North Umpqua, this site gets surprisingly little use.

Horseshoe Bend (North Umpqua Ranger District, 541/496-3532, open mid-May–late September, $11) is 10 miles east of Steamboat. There are 34 sites for tents and RVs (35 feet maximum) with picnic tables and fire grills.

SOUTHERN OREGON

Flush toilets, piped water, gray wastewater sumps, a laundry, and a general store are also available. Located in the middle of a big bend of the North Umpqua covered with old-growth Douglas firs and sugar pines, this is a popular base camp for rafting and fishing enthusiasts.

Diamond Lake Camping

Several campgrounds are in the vicinity of beautiful 5,200-foot-high Diamond Lake; boating, fishing, swimming, bicycling, and hiking are among the popular recreational options here. The trout fishing is particularly good in the early summer, and there are also excellent hikes into the Mount Thielsen Wilderness, Crater Lake National Park, and Mount Bailey areas. While no reservations are technically necessary, these campgrounds can fill up fast, so it's always a good idea to book a space ahead of time. For the campgrounds listed below, contact Diamond Lake Ranger District (HC 60, P.O. Box 101, Idleyld Park 97447, 541/498-2531).

Though Route 138 twists and turns most of the 80 miles from Roseburg to Diamond Lake, many people head straight for **Broken Arrow.** This 142-site campground with standard picnic tables and fire grills has plenty of room for tents and RVs (30 feet maximum); flush toilets, piped water, and gray wastewater sumps are available. Open early May–late September, the fee is $11–24 per night, depending upon the site. Premium lakeshore sites command top dollar. Diamond Lake and Broken Arrow both accept reservations (877/444-6777, www.reserveusa.com).

The next campground bears the name of its raison d'être, **Diamond Lake.** Here you'll find 160 campsites for tents and RVs (22 feet maximum) with picnic tables and fire grills. Piped water, flush toilets, and firewood are also available. Open May 15–October 31, the fee is $18–24 per night. Numerous hiking trails lead from the campground, including the Pacific Crest National Scenic Trail. Boat docks, launching facilities, and rentals are nearby at Diamond Lake Lodge.

On the east shore of Diamond Lake is

Lemolo Lake, with pointy Mount Thielsen in the background

Thielsen View. It features 60 tent and RV sites (30 feet maximum) with picnic tables and fire grills. Piped water, vault toilets, gray wastewater sumps, and a boat ramp are also available. It's open late May–late September, and the fee ranges $11–14 per night, depending upon the site. As the name implies, this campground has picturesque views of Mount Thielsen.

ACCOMMODATIONS

The number of lodgings on the North Umpqua is limited to a few properties that range from rustic quarters to full-service resorts.

About four miles east of Idleyld Park is the **Dogwood Motel** (HC 60, P.O. Box 19, Idleyld Park 97447, 541/496-3403, www.dogwoodmotel.com, doubles from $60). Here you'll find clean modern units with or without kitchenettes located on tidy, well-kept grounds.

Near the summit of the Cascade Mountains about 75 miles east of Roseburg and 13 miles from Diamond Lake is **Lemolo Lake Resort** (2610 Birds Point Rd., Idleyld Park 97447, 541/643-0750). Formed by a Pacific Power and Light dam, Lemolo Lake has good fishing for German brown trout, as well as kokanee salmon, eastern brook trout, and rainbow trout. The lake is sheltered from wind by gently sloping ridges, and there are many coves and sandy beaches along the 8.3 miles of shoreline. Waterskiing is permitted on the lake. Boats and canoes can be rented, and many miles of snowmobiling and cross-country skiing trails are nearby.

The resort itself has cabins, both housekeeping and standard, and rooms available. Each Swiss-chalet housekeeping cabin is equipped with a furnished kitchen, bathroom with shower, and wood-burning stove. They can sleep up to six and they cost $125–175 per night. The Swiss-chalet standard cabins (with bathroom but no kitchen) sleep six in two double and two single beds for $115–130. Large lodge rooms start at $80 double.

Diamond Lake Resort (Diamond Lake, 541/793-3333 or 800/733-7593, www.diamondlake.net) offers lodgings, restaurants, groceries, a service station, a laundry, and showers. Two-bedroom cabins rent for $165–285; lodge and motel rooms start at $80. Lodgings here are popular as base camps for a Crater Lake excursion. This is a rustic mountain resort with enough modern amenities to suit the tenderfoot all four seasons. Mountain bikes, paddle boats, kayaks, canoes, and fishing boats as well as an equestrian center keep you out of the modest accommodations and busy enjoying the spectacular location.

The **(Steamboat Inn** (42705 N. Umpqua Hwy., Steamboat, 541/498-2230 or 800/840-8825, www.thesteamboatinn.com, doubles from $160) is the premier dining and accommodations property on the North Umpqua, situated in the middle of a stretch of 31 miles of premium fly-fishing turf. The inn's rooms and cabins are extremely popular, so reservations are a must. It's an ideal getaway from civilization, near the hiking trails, waterfalls, and fishing holes for which the Umpqua is famous. Lodging is in handsomely furnished riverside cabins, cottages and suites; a number of three-bedroom ranch-style houses are also available. The inn serves breakfast, lunch and dinner to guests; nonguests may also dine (see *Food*). Closed January and February; other winter months, weekends only.

FOOD

Make a reservation at the **Steamboat Inn** (42705 N. Umpqua Hwy., 541/498-2230 or 800/840-8825, www.thesteamboatinn.com) to dine with hotel guests on main dishes of beef, fish, poultry, lamb, or pork, served with fresh vegetables and homemade bread. Choose from a wide selection of Oregon wines. Each meal is topped off with a sweet finish. The chef can also accommodate any food allergies, strong dislikes, and vegetarian diets. The Evening Dinner ($50) and Winemaker's Dinner ($85) are served nightly during the summer and on weekends the rest of the year. Reservations recommended.

SOUTHERN OREGON

Crater Lake

High in the Cascades lies the crown jewel of Oregon, Crater Lake, America's deepest lake (1,943 feet) glimmers like a polished sapphire in a setting created by a volcano that blew its top and collapsed thousands of years ago. Crater Lake's extraordinary hues are produced by the depth and clarity of the water and its ability to absorb all the colors of the spectrum except the shortest light waves, blue and violet, which are scattered skyward. Kodak used to send their apologies along with customers' photographs of Crater Lake—they thought they had goofed on the processing, so unbelievable is the blue of the water.

In addition to a 33-mile rim drive around the crater, the park, established in 1902, also features 210 campsites, dozens of hiking trails, and boat tours on the lake itself. Admission to the park is $10 per vehicle, or $5 per bicycle.

If you're seeing Crater Lake for the first time, drive into the area from the north for the most dramatic perspective. After crossing through a pumice desert you climb up to higher elevations overlooking the lake. In contrast to this subdued approach, the blueness and size of the lake can hit with a suddenness that stops all thought. On a clear day, you can peer south across Crater Lake and discern the snowy eminence of Mount Shasta over 100 miles away in California.

The Land

Geologically speaking, the name Crater Lake is a misnomer. Technically, Crater Lake lies in a caldera, which is produced when the center of a volcano caves in upon itself; in this case, the cataclysm occurred 6,600 years ago with the destruction of formerly 12,000-foot-high Mount Mazama.

Klamath Native American legend has it that Mount Mazama was the home of Llao, King of the Underworld. The chief of the world above was Skell, who sometimes would stand upon Mount Shasta, 100 miles to the south. A fierce battle between these two gods took place, a time marked by great explosions, thunder, and lightning. Burning ash fell from the sky, igniting the forest, and molten rivers of lava gushed 35 miles down the mountainside, burying Native American villages. For a week the night sky was lit by the flames of the great confrontation.

The story climaxes with Skell's destruction of Llao's throne, as the mountain collapsed upon itself and sealed Llao beneath the surface, never again to frighten the Native Americans and destroy their homes. Although the lake became serene and beautiful as the caldera filled with water, the Klamaths believed that only punishment awaited those who foolishly gazed upon the sacred battleground of the gods.

The aftereffects of this great eruption can still be seen. Huge drifts of ash and pumice hundreds of feet deep were deposited over a wide area—up to 80 miles away. The pumice deserts to the north of the lake and the deep, ashen canyons to the south are the most dramatic examples. So thick and widespread is the pumice that water percolates through too rapidly for plants to survive, creating reddish pockets of bleakness in the otherwise green forest. The eerie gray hoodoos in the southern canyons were created by hot gases bubbling up through the ash, hardening it into rocklike towers. These formations have withstood centuries of erosion by water that has long since washed away the loosely packed ash, creating the steep canyons visible today.

Wizard Island, a large cinder cone that rises 760 feet above the surface of the lake, offers evidence of volcanic activity since the caldera's formation. The **Phantom Ship,** located in the southeastern corner, is a much older feature.

The lake is confined by walls of multicolored lava that rise 500–2,000 feet above the water. Although Crater Lake is fed entirely by snow and rain, the lake does contain small amount of saline from surrounding rocks. But the salty water is replaced by pure rain and snow as the saltwater is dissolved away. And yet the level of the lake fluctuates only 1–3 feet a year, as evaporation and seepage keep it remarkably constant.

Another surprise is that while Crater Lake often records the coldest temperatures in the Cascades, the lake itself has only frozen over once since records have been kept. The surface of the lake can warm up to the 60°F mark during the summer. The deeper water stays around 38°F, although scientists have discovered hot spots 1,400 feet below the lake's surface that are 66°F.

Rainbow trout and kokanee (a landlocked salmon) were introduced to the lake many years ago by humans. The rainbow can get up to 25 inches (feeding mainly on the kokanee); the kokanee do not exceed 15 inches. Some types of mosses and green algae grow more than 400 feet below the lake's surface, a world record for these freshwater species. Another distinction is Crater Lake's selection as the purest lake in the world by scientists who, in 1997, determined the water's clarity extended down 142 feet.

At Crater Lake, hoodoos were created from the eruption of Mount Mazama.

© BILL MCRAE

CRATER LAKE NATIONAL PARK

Visitors Center

The visitors center is located below Rim Village near park headquarters and is a good place to start. Open year-round except Christmas day (8:30 A.M.–4:30 P.M.), the center provides information, maps, and publications, as well as backcountry permits and first aid. If the lake is socked in by lousy weather, you can see it anyway: excellent films about Crater Lake are shown in the center's theater every half hour and by special arrangement. For information about weather and activities at Crater Lake, log on to www.nps.gov/crla or call 541/594-3000.

The original visitors center is on the rim. A rock stairway behind the small building leads to Sinnott Memorial and one of the best views of the lake. It is perched on a rock outcropping, where accompanying interpretive placards help you identify the surrounding formations as well as flora and fauna. As you drive north from Rim Village you'll notice brown earth a few miles later, having spread out from the last major eruption.

Boat Tours

There are over 100 miles of hiking trails in the park, yet only one leads down to the lake itself. This is because the 1.1-mile-long **Cleetwood Trail** is the only part of the caldera's steep, avalanche-prone slope safe enough for passage. The trail drops 700 feet in elevation and is recommended only for those in good physical condition. There is no alternative transportation to **Cleetwood Cove dock,** located at the end of the trail, where the Crater Lake boat tours (541/830-8700), begin. These narrated excursions depart on the hour 10 A.M.–4 P.M. early-to-mid-July–mid-September and cost $20 adult and $12 for children 11 and under. Allow one hour from Rim Village to drive 12 miles to Cleetwood trailhead and to hike down to the boat's departure point. Dress warmly because it's cooler on the lake than on terra firma.

In addition to cruising around the lake and giving you a close look at the Phantom Ship and other geologic oddities, the two-hour tour includes a 10-minute stop on Wizard Island.

SOUTHERN OREGON

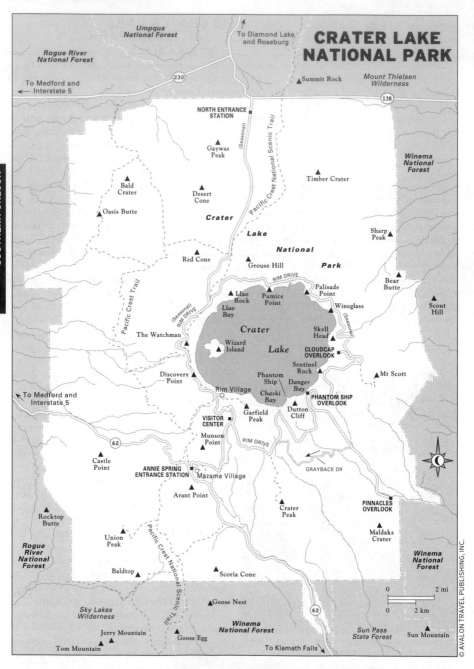

CRATER LAKE
NATIONAL PARK

Umpqua
National Forest

To Diamond Lake
and Roseburg

Rogue River
National Forest

Mount Thielsen
Wilderness

Summit Rock

To Medford and
Interstate 5

230

138

NORTH ENTRANCE
STATION

Winema
National
Forest

Gaywas
Peak

Pacific Crest National Scenic Trail

(Seasonal)

Bald
Crater

Desert
Cone

Timber Crater

Oasis Butte

Crater

Sharp
Peak

Lake

National

Red Cone

Grouse Hill

Park

Bear
Butte

RIM DRIVE

Llao
Rock

Pumice
Point

Palisade
Point

Scout
Hill

Pacific Crest Trail

Llao
Rock

Llao
Bay

Wineglass

(Seasonal)
RIM DRIVE

Crater

Skell
Head

(Seasonal)

The Watchman

Wizard
Island

Lake

CLOUDCAP
OVERLOOK

Discovery
Point

Phantom
Ship

Sentinel
Rock

Danger
Bay

Mt Scott

Rim Village

Chaski
Bay

PHANTOM SHIP
OVERLOOK

Garfield
Peak

Dutton
Cliff

VISITOR
CENTER

Munson
Point

RIM DRIVE

62

Castle
Point

ANNIE SPRING
ENTRANCE STATION

Mazama Village

GRAYBACK DR

Arant Point

PINNACLES
OVERLOOK

Crater
Peak

Rocktop
Butte

Winema
National
Forest

Union
Peak

Maldaks
Crater

Rogue
River
National
Forest

Pacific Crest National Scenic Trail

Baldtop

Scoria Cone

0   2 mi

0   2 km

Sky Lakes
Wilderness

Goose Nest

62

Winema
National Forest

Jerry Mountain

Goose Egg

Sun Pass
State Forest

Sun Mountain

Tom Mountain

To Klamath Falls

Passengers electing to hike the steep, one-mile spiral path to the top of the island volcano can catch a later boat back to the dock. However, keep in mind that boats have limited space, which means your return trip could be as late as 5 P.M., depending upon availability. And while it's a great place for a picnic, please be careful to leave this unique island in an unspoiled condition for future visitors. Allow three hours for the whole experience. It takes one hour to reach the point of embarkation and two hours for the tour itself. Tickets are sold at the dock on a first-come first-served basis.

Hiking

July and August are the most popular months for hiking. Colorful flowers and mild weather greet the summer throngs. One of the best places to view the mid-July flora is on the **Castle Crest Wildflower Trail.** The trailhead to this 0.5-mile loop trail is 0.5 mile from the park headquarters. Stop there for directions to the trailhead as well as a self-guiding trail booklet that will tell you about the ponderosa pine, Shasta red fir, mountain hemlock, lodgepole pine, and rabbit brush along the trail. Wildlife in the area include elk, deer, foxes, pikas, marmots, and a variety of birds. Peak wildflower season is usually around the last two weeks of July.

A suitable challenge of brawn and breath is the **Garfield Peak Trail.** The trailhead to this imposing ridge is just east of Crater Lake Lodge. It is a steep climb up the 1.7-mile-long trail, but the wildflower displays of phlox, Indian paintbrush, and lupine, as well as frequent sightings of eagles and hawks, give ample opportunity for you to stop and catch your breath. The highlight of the hike is atop Garfield Peak, which provides a spectacular view of Crater Lake 1,888 feet below.

When snow buries the area in the wintertime, services and activities are cut to a minimum. However, many cross-country skiers, snowshoe enthusiasts, and winter campers enjoy this solitude. Park rangers lead snowshoe hikes (weather permitting) at 1 P.M. weekends, daily during Christmas week. Ski and snowshoe rentals are available at Rim Village.

Winter trekkers should be aware that there are no groomed cross-country trails. Thus, it's imperative to inquire about trail, avalanche, road, and weather conditions at the visitors center (open 8:30 A.M.–4:30 P.M. daily). Circumnavigating the lake, which is visited by frequent snowstorms, takes two to three days, even in good weather. Only skilled winter hikers should attempt this 33-mile route that requires a compass and maps to traverse unmarked routes and avalanche paths.

Prior to setting out on any extended backcountry journey, pick up a permit and some free advice at the visitors center. You might also inquire about a hike to the top of **Mount Scott** (8,926 feet), the highest peak in the area. Lake views and perspectives on 12 Cascade peaks are potential rewards at the end of the 2.5-mile trek.

There are no overnight accommodations in the area mid-October–June (and you are not allowed to sleep in your vehicle), necessitating a long drive out of the park at night.

Camping

Mazama Campground, seven miles south of the rim, has 200 sites, restrooms with showers, and a dump station. It's open early June–mid-October. Sites are $18 for tents, $21–24 for RVs. **Lost Creek Campground,** located on the eastern section of Rim Drive, has 16 sites, water, and pit toilets. Neither campground has hookups. Lost Creek opens in mid-July and closes mid-September. Contact the park superintendent (541/594-3100) for more information. Foot traffic in the backcountry is light, so you can set up camp wherever you like in the remote areas surrounding Crater Lake.

Accommodations and Food

One of the nicest things about 183,180-acre Crater Lake National Park is that it's not very developed. Lodging and services are concentrated on the southern edge of the lake at **Rim Village;** the exact opening and closing dates for services changes from year to year, depending on snowpack. In general, restaurants and information services are open mid-May–October, with the exception of **The**

Cafeteria, which is open year-round, serving traditional breakfasts, with lunch and dinner offerings including a salad bar, cook-to-order entrées, and deli sandwiches. The **Watchman Deli Lounge** is located upstairs above the Cafeteria and is open noon–11 P.M., mid-June–Labor Day. The menu includes hamburgers, deli sandwiches, pizza, and snacks, as well as microbrews, espresso, wine, and spirits. Service can be slow, but the great view from the second-floor window makes up for it. Even though it's called a lounge, families are always welcome. A small grocery section in the adjoining gift shop sells basic foodstuffs and beverages in case you've run out of peanut butter and beer.

In 1995, the ◖ **Crater Lake Lodge** (P.O. Box 97, Crater Lake 97604, 541/830-8700, www.craterlakelodges.com, open late May–mid-Oct., doubles from $129, lakefront rooms extra) reopened to full capacity—71 rooms—after years of restoration. The lodge is situated on the rim south of the Sinnott Overlook and is hewn of indigenous wood and stone. The massive lobby boasts a picture window on the lake and has decor echoing back to its 1915 origins. The stone fireplace is large enough to walk into and serves as a gathering spot on chilly evenings. Many of the rooms have expansive views of the lake below. Others face out toward upper Klamath Lake and Mount Shasta, 150 miles away in California.

Amid all the amenities of a national park hotel, it's nice to be reminded of the past by such touches as antique wallpaper and old-fashioned bathtubs (rooms 401 and 201 offer views of the lake from claw-foot tubs). This marriage of past and present in such a prime location has proven so popular that it's imperative to reserve many months in advance. The 72-seat dining room, $20–29 for Northwest cuisine in a classic setting, gives preference to reservations made by hotel guests.

Seven miles south of the rim is another cluster of services called Mazama Village. The **Cabins at Mazama Village** (541/830-8700, www.craterlakelodges.com, cabins from $111) are open June–early October. Each room fea-

ROGUE VALLEY MOREL PICKING

Wild-mushroom picking can be a fun pastime and/or a money-making proposition in various parts of Oregon. Here in the Rogue Valley, morels, a cone-shaped fungus with deeply crenulated caps and short hollow stems, are one of several coveted varieties that fare especially well. The fact that they're easily identifiable, fry up great in omelettes, and come out in spring makes them especially popular among residents. Although usually found in forested areas such as the foothill below Mount McLoughlin, morels also can be harvested from backyard orchards in Rogue Valley fruit country.

The combination of night temperatures above freezing, high humidity, and daytime temps of 46-60°F is optimum to bring this fungus to fruit. They often pop up in the wake of forest fires or in landscapes disturbed by logging and road building. If it's warm, these mushrooms can be found in late March. When spring conditions hit the lower slopes of the Cascades in the months to follow, pickers usually aren't far behind, in pursuit of what many consider to be the most savory mushroom of all. If you can't find morels in the wild, you should check a local farmers market where they are generally available from professional mushroom foragers.

tures two queen beds and a bath, and two are designed for wheelchair access. Be sure to call ahead for reservations.

Also in Mazama Village, **Annie Creek Restaurant,** open early June–October for three meals daily, serves pizza, pasta, salads, and soups. Beer and wine are also available.

Getting There

The only year-round access to Crater Lake is from the south via Route 62. To reach Crater Lake from Grants Pass, head for Gold Hill and take Route 234 until it meets Route 62. As you head up Route 62 you might spot roadside snow poles in anticipation of the onset of winter. This highway makes a horseshoe bend through the Cascades, starting at Medford and ending 20 miles north of Klamath Falls. The northern route via Route 138 (Roseburg to U.S. 97, south of Beaver Marsh) is usually closed by snow mid-October–July. The tremendous snowfall also closes 33-mile-long Rim Drive, although portions are opened when conditions permit. Rim Drive is generally opened to motorists around the same time as the northern entrance to the park.

The quickest route from Portland is I-5 to Eugene; Route 58 east across the Cascades to U.S. 97 south. At Chiloquin, take Route 62 through Fort Klamath into the south entrance of the park.

CRATER LAKE HIGHWAY

Many locals who live near the Crater Lake Highway sport bumper stickers on their vehicles that read, "I Survived Highway 62." The challenges of successfully navigating this precipitous and circuitous thoroughfare, with its horrific winter weather and slow-moving summer crowds, help give it a killer reputation. Snow can sometimes get deep enough on the upper reaches that 15-foot high snow poles lining the roadbed are rendered useless in helping the snowplows navigate. In these cases, the crews can only locate the road by means of a radio transmitter, embedded in steel cable, which emits a signal.

Even so, there always seems to be traffic on this winding conduit between Crater Lake and southern Oregon. This isn't surprising when you consider the scenic appeals of the Rogue River and Cascade Mountains. And then there's fishing. The salmon runs on the Rogue River are second in size only to the ones on the Columbia. Nearly three million fish are reared and released into the Rogue from the Cole Rivers Fish Hatchery, located 153 miles from the mouth of the Rogue. With swimming, boating, and rafting opportunities, the Rogue River is indeed tempting and you too will be taking to the hills along Route 62.

The following contacts can help plan your foray into the Rogue River National Forest: **Prospect Ranger Station** (541/498-2531), **Rogue River National Forest Service** (Medford, 541/858-2200), and the **Oregon Tourism Commission** (www.traveloregon.com).

Hiking

Many choice hikes are found along the 50-mile stretch of the Rogue River Trail from Lost Creek Lake to the river's source at Boundary Springs just inside Crater Lake National Park. Tall waterfalls, deep gushing gorges, and a natural bridge are all easily accessible. Those interested in more than just a short walk from the parking lot to the viewpoint can design hikes of 2–18 miles with or without an overnight stay. Travelers with two cars can arrange shuttles to avoid having to double back.

Mill Creek Falls: One of the more scenic recreation spots is owned by Boise Cascade, a timber conglomerate. Boise Cascade has constructed a botanically marked nature trail system through its land to a series of three waterfalls in an impressive, rock-choked section of the Rogue River called the Avenue of the Giant Boulders.

The largest of the three waterfalls is Mill Creek Falls, which plunges 173 feet down into the river. Signs along the highway and Mill Creek Drive (formerly the old Crater Lake Highway), a scenic loop out of the community of Prospect, direct visitors to the trailhead. A large map further details the trail routes. The trail is short but steep. Wear shoes you don't mind getting wet and that have good traction, as you may have to scramble over some of the boulders and wade through some small ponds along the way.

Takelma Gorge: A particularly wild section of the river is found at Takelma Gorge. Located one mile from River Bridge Campground on the upper Rogue River, the trail offers vistas of sharp, foaming bends in the river with logs jammed in at crazy angles on the rocks, and ferns growing in the mist of the waterfalls. Although the river's course is rugged, the grade on the trail is an easy one.

SOUTHERN OREGON

Natural Bridge: Even if you're in a hurry, you should take 15 minutes to get out of your car and stretch your legs at the Natural Bridge. Located 0.25 mile from Natural Bridge Campground, a mile west of Union Creek on Route 62, here the Rogue River drops into a lava tube and disappears from sight, only to emerge later a little way downstream. A short paved path takes you to a human-made bridge that fords this unique section of the river. Several placards along the way explain the formation of the Natural Bridge and other points of interest.

Rogue River Gorge: Just outside of Union Creek on Route 62 is the spectacular Rogue River Gorge. The narrowest point on the river, the action of the water has carved out a deep chasm in the rock. A short trail with several well-placed overlooks follows the rim of the gorge. Green mossy walls, logjams, and a frothy torrent of water are all clearly visible from the trail. Informative placards discuss curiosities like the living stump and the potholes carved in the lava rock by pebbles and the action of the water.

National Creek Falls: Another short hike for hurried motorists is National Creek Falls. An easy 0.5-mile walk down a trail bordered by magnificent Douglas firs leads to this tumultuous cascade. To get here, take Route 230 to Forest Service Road 6530. Follow the road until you reach the trailhead marked by a sign.

Boundary Springs: A two-mile hike down a cool and shady trail takes you to the source of the mighty Rogue River—Boundary Springs. Situated just inside Crater Lake National Park, it's a great place for a picnic. About a mile down the path from the trailhead, hang a left at the fork to get to Boundary Springs. Once at the springs, you'll discover small cataracts rising out of the jumbled volcanic rock that's densely covered with moss and other vegetation. Despite the temptation to get a closer look, the vegetation here is extremely fragile, so please refrain from walking on the moss. To get here, take Route 230 north from Route 62 to the crater rim viewpoint, where parking can be found on the left-hand side of the road.

In the fall, take Route 62 from Medford and turn east onto Route 140 to enjoy the golden hues of larch and aspen. En route, you might stop at Fish Lake or Lake of the Woods resorts. From here you can take scenic Westside Road to Fort Klamath. Crater Lake lies a scant six miles from here.

Rafting

Noah's River Adventures (541/488-2811 or 800/858-2811 www.noahsrafting.com) offers guided trips on the upper Rogue River, but you can also do the mild, 10-mile section of the upper Rogue from the hatchery back to town by yourself. It takes about a half day to float downstream, and many people like to enjoy a picnic along the way. **Rogue Rafting Co.** (7725 Rogue River Dr. in Shady Cove, across from Shady Cove Park, 541/878-2585) can get you set up. Equipment ranging from inflatable kayaks to 12-person rafts is available. Life vests, paddles, and a shuttle service from Shady Cove up to Cole Rivers Fish Hatchery are provided at no extra charge. The outfitter can even provide an ice chest and dry bags to carry your riverbank feast.

Camping

For those who like roughing it in style with all of the amenities in their RVs, a couple of well-maintained trailer parks in the Rogue country can accommodate large vehicles. **Fly-Casters Campground and Trailer Park** (P.O. Box 1170, Shady Cove 97539, 541/878-2749, $18–23) and **Shady Trails RV Park and Campground** (P.O. Box 1299, Shady Cove 97539, 541/878-2206, $18–$24) are both located about 23 miles north of Medford on Route 62. Situated on the banks of the Rogue River, these parks feature hookups and picnic tables. Flush toilets, bottled gas, gray wastewater disposal, and showers are also available. A grocery store and restaurants are in the nearby town of **Shady Cove.** Both of these parks are good home bases for RV owners who like to fish and hike.

Five miles below Lost Creek Lake on ORE 62 at 1,476 feet in elevation is **Rogue Elk County**

Park (Jackson County Parks and Recreation, 541/776-7001). This campground features 37 sites for tents and RVs (28 feet maximum) with picnic tables and fire grills. Piped water, showers, and flush toilets are also on the premises. Open mid-April–mid-October, the camp fee is $16 per night, $18 for sites with electricity and water hookups. The kids will enjoy swimming in Elk Creek, which, in addition to being adjacent to the campground, is warmer and safer than the Rogue. A playground adds to the fun; $3 day use fee per vehicle.

Along the shore of Lost Creek Lake is **Joseph Stewart State Park** (35251 Rte. 62, Trail 97541, 541/560-3334). Here you'll find 50 tent and 151 RV sites (40 feet maximum). Electricity, dump station, fire grills, and picnic tables are provided. Flush toilets, water, gray wastewater disposal services, showers, and firewood are also available. Bike paths, a beach, and barbecue grills make this a family-friendly locale. Boat-launching facilities for Lost Creek Lake are located nearby. Open March–October, the fee is $14–16 per night. Eight miles of hiking trails and bike paths crisscross the park. Lost Creek Lake also has a marina, beach, and boat rentals.

If you want to get away from the highway, head for **Abbott Creek** (Rogue National Forest, Prospect Ranger Station, 541/560-3623). One of the few backwoods camps in the area that has potable water, it's seven miles northeast of the town of Prospect on Route 62 and three miles down Forest Service Road 68. Situated at the confluence of Abbott and Woodruff Creeks and not far from the upper Rogue River, this campground has 25 tent and RV sites (22 feet maximum) with picnic tables and fire grills. Hand-pumped water and vault toilets are also available. Open late May–October, the camp charges $10 per night for the first vehicle and $5 for each thereafter.

Set along the bank of Union Creek where it merges with the upper Rogue River is **Union Creek** (Rogue National Forest, Prospect Ranger Station, 541/560-3623). Located 11 miles northeast of Prospect, you'll find 78 tent and RV sites (16 feet maximum) with picnic tables, fire grills, piped water, and vault toilets. Open late May–October, the fee is $14 per night. Many fine hikes on the Rogue River Trail (see *Hiking,* earlier in this section) are within close proximity of the campground.

A half mile past Union Creek Campground on Route 62 is **Farewell Bend** (Rogue National Forest, Prospect Ranger Station, 541/560-3623). Located near the junction of Route 62 and Route 230, the camp has 61 tent and RV sites (22 feet maximum) with picnic tables and fire grills. Piped water and flush toilets are also within the campground boundaries. Open late May–early September, the fee is $14 per night. This campground is situated along the banks of the upper Rogue near the Rogue River Gorge (see *Hiking,* earlier in this section).

A nice little campground tucked off the highway yet fairly close to the Rogue River and Crater Lake National Park is **Huckleberry Campground** (Rogue National Forest, Prospect Ranger Station, 541/560-3623). To get here, go about 18 miles northeast of Prospect on Route 62 and then four miles down Forest Service Road 60. There you'll find 25 tent and RV sites (21 feet maximum) with picnic tables and fire grills. Water and vault toilets are also available. Open late May–October (weather permitting), the campground is free of charge (14-day maximum stay). This campground is at an elevation of 5,400 feet, so be sure to have the proper gear to ensure a comfortable visit.

Accommodations

The accommodations you'll find on Route 62 are rustic and simple, catering mainly to anglers and lovers of the great outdoors.

Rooms at the **Maple Leaf Motel** (20717 Rte. 62, Shady Cove, 541/878-2169, www.mapleleafmotel.org, doubles from $75) come equipped with microwave, toaster oven, small fridge, cable TV, and a picnic and barbecue area to grill the day's catch or some burgers if the fish weren't biting. The **Royal Coachman Motel** (21906 Rte. 62, Shady Cove, 541/878-2481, www.royalcoachmanmotel.com, doubles from $54) has kitchenettes, cable TV, and

HBO. The more expensive rooms have lovely decks that overlook the river.

The **Prospect Hotel and Motel** (391 Mill Creek Rd., Prospect 97536, 541/560-3664 or 800/944-6490, www.prospecthotel.com, historic hotel rooms from $100, including breakfast, motel rooms from $70) gives you a choice between something old and something new. The hotel, built in 1889 and listed on the National Register of Historic Places, has several small but comfortable rooms with bath. The rooms are named after local residents and famous people who have stayed at the hotel, including Zane Grey, Teddy Roosevelt, and Jack London. Because the hotel is small and old, no children, smoking, or pets are permitted. The adjacent motel features clean, spacious, and modern units, with some kitchenettes available. Pets and children are OK here.

Not far away from Prospect on the Crater Lake Highway is the **Union Creek Resort** (Prospect, 541/560-3565, www.unioncreekoregon.com). Built in the early 1930s, the Union Creek is listed on the National Register of Historic Places. Open year-round, it has rooms available in your choice of the original lodge, simple cabins with bathrooms, or housekeeping cabins with kitchens and bathrooms. The lodge rooms ($40–50), paneled in knotty pine, have washbasins in them; guests share the bathrooms down the hall. The stone fireplace in the lobby is built of opalized wood from Lakeview, Oregon. The sleeping cabins with bath range $80–90. The housekeeping cabins sleep up to 10; they range $90–225. The **Union Creek Country Store,** located at the resort, carries groceries and other essential items. Fishing licenses and Sno-Park permits can also be purchased here.

Food

Route 62 parallels an old stagecoach road between Fort Klamath and the Rogue Valley. While the ruts in the road are gone, the tradition of frontier hospitality lives on in the establishments along this much-traveled mountain pass.

The finest restaurant on this section of the Rogue River is **Bel Dis on the Rogue** (541/878-2010, dinner Tues.–Sun., main courses $12–25). From the cloth napkins to the crystal wineglasses, you're assured a first-class dinner from start to finish, with moderate prices. The dining room is perched on a bluff overlooking the river, further enhancing the visual appeal of the meal presentation. Be sure to call ahead for reservations.

About halfway between Medford and Crater Lake in the vicinity of Prospect are a few eateries worth mention. For moderately priced standard American grub, the **Prospect Cafe and Lounge** (311 Mill Creek Dr., Prospect, 541/560-3641, main courses $12–22) is open daily for breakfast, lunch, and dinner. The dining room at the **Prospect Hotel** (391 Mill Creek Rd., Prospect, 541/560-3664 or 800/944-6490, 5:30 P.M.–8:30 P.M. daily June–Sept. and holidays, Fri.–Sun. May and Oct., main courses $10–23) is also recommended. Here you'll enjoy roasted red pepper chicken or "Shroomed" Chicken ala Karen with Linguine, a delicious mixture of pasta, chicken, mushrooms, and olives, Local huckleberry pie is a wonderful seasonal treat.

Beckie's (Union Creek Resort, 56484 Rte. 62, 541/560-3565 or 866/560-3565, three meals daily most of the year, only lunch Mon.–Fri. in winter, main courses $7–15) is an intimate place to stop for a bite to eat. One half of the building is an old log cabin; the other half is a modern design with plenty of windows. Breakfast comes with all the trimmings. The lunch menu features sandwiches and burgers. Dinners include chicken, pork, and steak entrées.

Klamath Falls

"One person's conservation is another's unemployment." This bromide underscores life in Klamath County, which has endured some of the highest unemployment rates and lowest per-capita incomes in the state, largely due to cutbacks in logging. Similarly, the ongoing tug-of-war between farmers and fish—a drama playing out all over the West—brought the area national notoriety in 2002. In a year of low rainfall, warm temperatures, and an unusually large run of chinook salmon, some 34,000 spawning salmon and other fish died in the Klamath River, due to water diversions to Klamath Basin farms. The diminished river flow forced crowded salmon into warm, sluggish pools, where disease erupted and quickly spread with deadly consequences.

Klamath Falls, or "K Falls" as locals call it, is the county's population hub, with nearly 21,000 people in the city limits and an additional 40,000 population in the surrounding urban growth boundary. It's used to hard times after witnessing the decline of its previous economic base, the railroads. In an attempt to build a viable future, the Salt Caves Dam Project was proposed on the Klamath River.

This hydropower project was cancelled after a decade of legal battles over its alleged negative effects on fish populations. The latter paralleled the restrictions put on the ponderosa pine logging (at one time, Klamath Falls milled the most in the United States). Just when it seemed that Klamath Falls was doomed to economic oblivion, help came from unexpected quarters. High-tech and secondary-wood-product companies relocated here, and the development of Klamath Lake's blue-green algae, a high-protein food source, into a multimillion dollar business gave a boost to sagging spirits and fortunes (see sidebar). The establishment of the Klamath Tribes Casino, 22 miles north of Klamath Falls at U.S. 97 (Route 62 junction), is also viewed as a potential economic impetus.

The biggest hopes for the future here center on K Falls as a place to live. The cost of living here is comparatively low, and the climate is dry, with more than 290 days of sunshine and cold but not damp winters (less cold and rainy than Bend).

In town, three interesting museums shine lights on different aspects of local history and culture. But the real draw of Klamath Falls is out in the surrounding countryside. The native trout of Klamath Lake and the nearby Wood and Williamson Rivers are legendary (averaging 21 inches). There's world-class white-water rafting on the upper Klamath River, with several hair-raising rapids topping Class IV. But most of all it's the Klamath Basin National Wildlife refuges, a complex of six lake and wetland units stretching into California, that draw visitors—and lots of birds—to the area. The refuges host the largest concentration of bald eagles (up to 500 in winter), the most in the United States outside of Alaska, as well as more than 400 other bird species.

SIGHTS

During the summer, a restored 1906 trolley will give you free transportation from the Klamath County Museum to the Favell Museum and the historic Baldwin Hotel.

◖ Favell Museum

A fine collection of Native American artifacts and western art is found at the Favell Museum (125 W. Main St., Klamath Falls 97601, 541/882-9996 or 800/762-9096, www.favell-museum.org, 9:30 A.M.–5:30 P.M. Mon.–Sat., $6 adults, $5 seniors, $3 for ages 6–16, kids under 6 get in free). Here you'll find beautiful displays of tribal stonework, bone and shell-work, beadwork, quilts, basketry, pottery, and Northwest coast carvings as well as a collection of over 60,000 mounted arrowheads. Another attraction is the collection of miniature working firearms, ranging from Gatling guns to inch-long Colt 45s, displayed in the museum's walk-in vault.

SOUTHERN OREGON

If artifacts aren't your bag, you're bound to appreciate one of the best collections of western art in the state. Oils, acrylics, and watercolors are featured, as well as bronzes, dioramas, photography, taxidermy, and woodcarvings. The gift shop and art gallery specialize in limited-edition prints and original western art.

Baldwin Hotel Museum

Travel back in time to the early 1900s thanks to the Baldwin Hotel (31 Main St., 541/883-4207, 10 A.M.–4 P.M. Tues.–Sat., June–Sept., $4 adults, $3 seniors and students, $2 ages 5–12, kids under five are free), adorned with original fixtures and furnishings, the legacy of a talented female photographer whose father—a U.S. Senator—built the place. A video presentation in the lobby complements guided tours of digs once occupied by Presidents Teddy Roosevelt, Taft, and Wilson. Call ahead to check times for tours; shorter tours are sometimes offered.

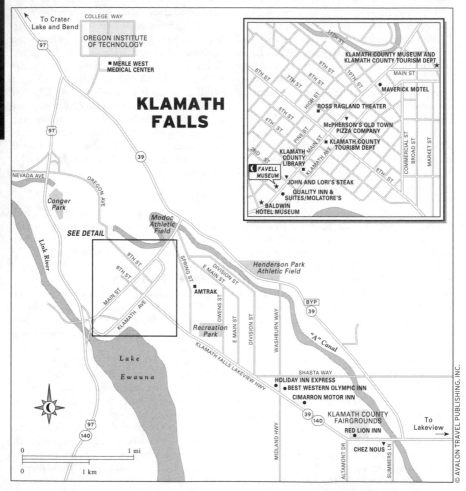

Klamath County Museum

A good background on the region can be gained from a visit to the Klamath County Museum (1451 Main St., 541/883-4208, 9 A.M.–5 P.M. Mon.– Sat., $3 adults, $2 seniors and students, $1 kids ages 5–12), in the old national armory building. The natural-history section has exhibits on fossils, geology, minerals, and indigenous wildlife of the Klamath Basin. The exploration and settlement area depicts the hardships of pioneer life and the events leading to the Modoc Indian War. The general history section takes you through the World Wars and up memory lane to the present.

Those who really want to revel in local history can make an appointment to pore through the museum's research library, which includes one of the largest regional collections of primary sources on Captain Jack and the Modoc Indian War.

Collier Memorial State Park

About 30 miles north of Klamath Falls on U.S. 97 is Collier Memorial State Park (541/783-2471 or 800/551-6949). Donated to the state in 1945 by Alfred and Andrew Collier as a memorial to their parents, this 146-acre park documents the history of logging's technological improvements (there is no charge for these day-use facilities).

The park's Pioneer Village includes a logger's homestead cabin stocked with a wide variety of tools and artifacts, a blacksmith shed, an assortment of logging machinery including log wagons with wheels made of cross-cut sections of logs bound in iron, and chain-drive trucks with hard rubber tires. Also on display are steam-propelled devices including tractors, a narrow-gauge locomotive, and a one-person handcart.

Don't miss the 200+-foot-long, 16-foot-wide **Clatsop Fir,** a fallen tree that was mature when Columbus landed in the New World. The tree could supply enough wood for several four-bedroom homes. For better or worse, it's probably the largest Douglas fir ever cut.

Across from the museum are 18 tent sites and 50 spaces with full hookups. The campground is open April–October 29, with fees at $15–17. A nature trail and fishing spot are nearby.

Bear Valley National Wildlife Refuge

December–February, the Klamath Basin is home to the largest wintering concentration of **bald eagles** in the lower 48 states. The thousands of winter waterfowl that reside here provide a plentiful food source for these raptors. By January, 700–800 eagles from as far north as southeastern Alaska's Chilkat River, Saskatchewan, and the Northwest Territories congregate here.

In addition to a readily available food supply, the eagles require night-roosting areas. The Bear Valley National Wildlife Refuge (between Keno and Worden) has mature stands of timber that can support up to 300 eagles a night. The eagles prefer trees on northeastern slopes that protect them from the cold southwest and westerly winds. However, the eagles *don't* like it when people bother them. Hence, the roosting areas are closed early November–March 30.

The good news is that there are still ample viewing opportunities of our national bird, especially when it is very cold. Contact the Fish and Wildlife office for the latest information on the best eagle-watching locations. A good sighting can be had driving to Bear Valley at sunrise. To get there, drive one mile south of Worden on U.S. 97. Turn right on Keno Worden Road after the grain silos, cross the railroad tracks, and take an immediate left on the gravel road. Travel for about a mile and pull off the road. From here you can sometimes see up to 100 bald eagles soar from their roosts at the top of the ridge to their daytime feeding area on the refuge to the east. Bring binoculars, warm clothing, and a camera with a telephoto lens.

A world-renowned event, the **Winter Wings Festival** (www.winterwingsfest.org) is held in February. The highlight is a pre-dawn field trip to the nearby Bear Valley roost.

Get a free map and bald-eagle brochure by

SOUTHERN OREGON

sending a stamped, self-addressed envelope to: Klamath Basin National Wildlife Refuges, 4009 Hill Rd., Tule Lake, CA 96134 (530/667-2231, www.fws.gov/klamathbasinrefuges). Ask them to include information on local accommodations and restaurants. The nearest motels are in Merrill, Oregon, or Tule Lake and Dorris, both across the border in California.

Klamath Marsh National Wildlife Refuge

March–May is when **waterfowl and shorebirds** stop over in the basin on their way north to their breeding grounds in Alaska and Canada. They rest and fatten up during the spring to build the necessary strength and body fat to carry them through their long migration. May–July is the nesting season for thousands of marsh birds and waterfowl. The Klamath Marsh National Wildlife Refuge (north of Klamath Falls off U.S. 97) is a good place during spring to observe sandhill cranes, shorebirds, waterfowl, and raptors.

The summer months are ideal for taking the self-guided auto tour routes and canoe trails. Descriptive leaflets are available for both attractions from the refuge office. Among the most prolific waterfowl and marsh bird areas in the Northwest, over 25,000 ducks, 2,600 Canada geese, and thousands of marsh and shorebirds are raised here each year. You may also see American white pelicans, *Pelecanus erythrorhynchos,* at the Upper Klamath National Wildlife Refuge during the summer.

Tule Lake and Lower Klamath refuges are open during daylight hours. Overnight camping is not permitted at any of the refuges.

ENTERTAINMENT

The region's cultural hub is the **Ross Ragland Theater** (218 N. 7th, Klamath Falls, 541/884-5483, www.rrtheater.org). In addition to the Klamath Symphony and other community organizations, country stars, internationally acclaimed guest artists, and touring Broadway troupes grace the stage of this 800-seat auditorium. Call the theater or check the daily *Herald & News* to see what's scheduled.

SPORTS AND RECREATION

With all the lakes, rivers, and mountains in the region, there's no shortage of fishing, rafting, golfing, and other recreational opportunities. Here's a short list of some local attractions.

Fishing

Local guides can get you outfitted and on the water angling for the elusive big one. **Lynn Hescock** (Klamath Falls, 541/783-2548, www.hescockfishing.com) and **Darren Roe Guide Service** (4849 Summers Ln., Klamath Falls, 541/884-3825 or 877/943-5700, www.roeoutfitters.com) each offer trips on the Klamath Lakes and the nearby Wood and Willamson Rivers, noted for their runs of wild trout. Rates for both outfitters are roughly the same, charging $175 per person for 2–3 people per day, or $275–350 per single person per day.

Boating

One way to get out onto Oregon's largest lake is to rent a sailboat through **Meridian Sail Center** (Pelican Marina, Dock C, 928 Front St., 541/884-5869, www.meridiansail.com). Sailboat rentals are $40 half day, $70 full day. Sailing instruction is also available. Call ahead for the sailing report and to make reservations. **Klamath Lake Touring Company** (541/883-4622, www.klamathbelle.com) offers paddle-wheeler lake tours, for similiar rates, that emphasize the natural history and geography of the area.

Rafting

Just under an hour west of Klamath Falls is what's known as Hell's Corner of the Upper Klamath River. Jume–September, day-long adventures ($129) through this remote, secluded canyon are offered by **Arrowhead River Adventures** (541/830-3388 or 800/227-7741, www.arrowheadadventures.com) With several Class IV+ rapids, the Upper Klamath provides some of the best spring and summer rafting in the state.

You can also arrange a raft trip in the Upper Klamath River canyons through Ashland's **Adventure Center** (40 N. Main St., Ashland

97520, 800/444-2819, www.raftingtours.com). In addition to a day trip ($135, which includes transportation to/from Ashland), they offer a two-day trip down the river with a night of fully catered riverside camping ($339).

Camping

Most of the campgrounds you'll find in the vicinity of Klamath Falls are privately owned. These facilities cater mostly to RVs with electric, water, and sewer hookups, as well as other creature comforts like swimming pools, laundries, and recreational halls. These properties also tend to be in prime locations, which accounts for rates that are steeper than those of their public counterparts. Fortunately, there are several places to pitch a tent in both types of parks without having to deal with a 40-foot-long mobile home parked right next to your sleeping bag.

On the north end of Upper Klamath Lake adjacent to the Upper Klamath National Wildlife Refuge lies **Harriman Springs Resort and Marina** (Harriman Route, Box 79, Klamath Falls 97601, 541/356-2331). The campground features six tent and 12 RV sites with hookups. Flush toilets, showers, firewood, and a laundry are also available. Tent sites are $14; RV sites are $18. Open year-round. To get there, go 27 miles northwest of Klamath Falls on Route 140W and take a right onto Rocky Point Road. Proceed another two miles and you will see the resort on the right.

Another mile down Rocky Point Road is **Rocky Point Resort** (28121 Rocky Point Rd., Klamath Falls 97601, 541/356-2287, www.rockypointoregon.com), also in close proximity to the Upper Klamath National Wildlife Refuge. This resort has five tent and 28 RV sites with hookups and rustic cabins. Flush toilets, showers, firewood, a laundry, a recreation hall, and other summer-camp trappings are available. Open April–mid-November, the camp charges $18–25 per night. Ask about canoe rentals for trips on the Upper Klamath Canoe Trail. For more information about the trail, contact the **U.S. Fish and Wildlife Service** (Klamath Basin National Wildlife Refuge, P.O. Box 74, Tule Lake, CA 96134, 530/667-2231).

Several other campgrounds are also found on Upper Klamath Lake. Although a fire in 2003 caused minor damage, the best deal around is still **Hagelstein Park** (County Parks Dept., Klamath Falls 97601, 541/883-5371). The park can accommodate five tent campers and five RVs in sites that feature picnic tables and fire grills, with flush toilets and water nearby. In addition to being the only campground on the east shore of the lake, it's the least expensive campground in the area. Open April–late November, reservations are advisable in this small park. To get there, head north of Klamath Falls for 12 miles and look for the signs on the left side of the road.

Approximately seven miles farther north of Mallard Campground on U.S. 97 is **KOA Klamath Falls** (3435 Shasta Way, Klamath Falls 97601, 541/884-4644). Set along the shore of Upper Klamath Lake, the park features 18 tent and 73 RV sites with hookups. In true KOA style, flush toilets, showers, a pool, laundry, recreation hall, and other amenities are available. Open all year, $22–39 per night; $32–48 for cabin accommodations.

Golf

There are several area courses open to the public. **Harbor Links** (601 Harbor Isle Blvd., 541/882-0609) and **Shield Crest** (3151 Shieldcrest Dr., 541/884-1493) both offer 9- and 18-hole courses with greens fees in the $25–45 range. Rental golf clubs are also available at these two establishments for about $10. Smaller 9-hole **Round Lake** (4000 Round Lake Rd., 541/884-2520) is a bargain at $10 for 9 holes, $18 for 18 holes.

ACCOMMODATIONS

Travelers on a budget will appreciate **Maverick Motel** (1220 Main St., 541/882-6688 or 800/404-6690, doubles from $54), and **Cimarron Motor Inn** (3060 S. 6th, 541/882-4601 or 800/742-2648, doubles from $65) for the pool and continental breakfast, and for allowing pets.

Mid-range properties are the domain of the chains. **Best Western Olympic Inn** (2627 S. 6th, 541/882-9665 or 800/600-9665, doubles from $99); **Holiday Inn Express** (2500 S. 6th, 541/884-9999 or 800/465-4329, doubles from $88); **Quality Inn & Suites** (100 Main St., 541/882-4666 or 888/762-2466, doubles from $83); and **Red Lion Inn** (3612 S. 6th, 541/882-8864 or 800/833-5466, doubles from $89), all feature the pool, continental breakfast, and other upgrades expected. The latter two accept pets.

Ten minutes from town on the south shore of Upper Klamath Lake adjacent to 400-acre Moore Park is **Thompson's B&B** (1420 Wild Plum Ct., 541/882-7938, doubles $95–115). Their location on the lake and a huge deck overlooking the water make it an ideal place to spot all manner of wildlife. They've been in the business for over two decades, and know how to take care of people right. From the commons room stocked with goodies (popcorn, candy, drinks), microwave, and refrigerator to the full American breakfast, everything here is geared to please the guests. Payment in cash or check only, $25 deposit required, 48-hour cancellation notice policy.

Right on Klamath Lake, **Rocky Point Resort** (28124 Rocky Point Rd., 541/356-2287, www.rockypointoregon.com, lodge rooms from $75, cabins from $110) offers lodge rooms plus attractive one- and two-bedroom cabins each with fully equipped kitchen, private bath, and outdoor barbecue. The lakefront dining room here serves up good American-style food. You can rent everything from a kayak to a motor boat at their marina to explore the waters of Klamath Lake. This is a popular spot so call ahead for reservations.

The **Running Y Ranch Resort** (5500 Running Y Rd., 541/850-5500 or 888/850-0275, www.runningy.com) offers the total Klamath Basin package experience. This upscale golf resort offers country-club homes to the lucky, while travelers can partake of the deluxe rooms at the ranch lodge. The 83 guest rooms, a mix of comfortable hotel-style rooms and well-appointed one-bedroom suites, overlook the 10th fairway, and are furnished with sofa sleepers and have balconies. Lodge doubles begin at $169; one-bedroom suites begin at $219. Two- and three-bedroom houses are also available. **Schatzie's on the Green** restaurant features Northwest and German cuisine and the resort coffee shop offers hearty breakfasts and lunch with a premium on freshly made items. Lodge guests can use all resort facilities including bike paths, canoes, hiking trails, and stables. Most people come here for the golf, of course: the Y's Arnold Palmer–designed golf course, recently rated by *Golf Digest* as the best new public course in America, is one of Oregon's best.

FOOD

For Italian, try **Fiorella Italian Ristorante** (6139 Summers, 541/882-1878, open Tues.–Sat. for dinner, main courses $12–19). One of the specialties is *pasticcio* (Venetian-style lasagna), though other pastas and main courses featuring seafood, chicken, and beef are also found on the menu, as well as imported beers and wines.

The more upscale **Chez Nous** (3927 S. 6th, 541/883-8719, dinner Tues.–Sat., main courses $12–22) offers continental cuisine, steak, pasta, and seafood, along with an extensive wine list. The food is excellent, the ambience classy. All entrées are served as full-course meals (with soup, salad, potato or rice, vegetables, and bread included).

When it comes to pizza in Klamath Falls, the locals swear by **McPherson's Old Town Pizza Company** (722 Main, 541/884-8858, and 6200 S. 6th, 541/883-2918, 11 A.M.–10 P.M. daily, pizza from $12, main courses from $8). Pizzas come in four sizes, from individual to large, and with three kinds of crusts (thick, thin, or pan), but it is the thin-crust pizza that accounts for over 75 percent of their sales. You'll find one of the best lunch buffet deals in town here; it includes pizza, chicken (regular or barbecue), lasagna, spuds, soups, desserts, and a huge salad bar.

For steak, chicken, and pasta dishes, **John and Lori's Steak Country** (205 Main St., 541/883-3910, open nightly, main courses $11–24) is the local favorite.

INFORMATION

Over 2.2 million acres of Klamath County is publicly owned. The **Klamath Ranger District Office** (1936 California Ave., Klamath Falls, 541/885-3400) can give or send you outdoor recreational information on the Winema National Forest and other surrounding natural areas of interest. The **Bureau of Land Management** (2795 Anderson Ave., #25, Klamath Falls, 541/883-6916) can also be of assistance in this regard.

You'll find the **Oregon Welcome Center** located on U.S. 97 about halfway between Klamath Falls and the California–Oregon border. They have a broad collection of brochures and information about locales all over the state.

The **Klamath County Tourism Department** (507 Main St., Klamath Falls, 541/884-0666 or 800/445-6728), can provide an excellent pamphlet on the self-guided loop tour. Look for this visitors center in Veteran's Park, just off U.S. 97 at the entrance to the city.

GETTING THERE

Amtrak (S. Spring and Oak Sts., 541/884-2822) can connect you with northern and southern destinations via the *Coast Starlight*. **Greyhound** (1200 Klamath Ave., 541/882-4616) can also take you to California and the Willamette Valley. The **Klamath Falls airport** is serviced by **United Express** (800/241-6522) and **Horizon** (541/884-3331).

CENTRAL OREGON

Central Oregon is one of the most magnificent natural playgrounds in this part of the world, with a scenic collage of green forest and black basalt outcroppings topped by extinct volcano cones covered with snow. Plenty of lakes, rivers, and waterfalls provide a sparkling contrast to the earth tones here. It's easy to find ways to explore these natural areas: hiking, biking, and cross-country ski trails abound, as do resorts (both luxurious and rustic), waterways teeming with fish, and, increasingly, good restaurants and shopping.

With respect to everything except rain, the climate is a bit more extreme here that it is on the west side of the Cascades. Expect it to be fairly dry (though perhaps not as constantly sunny as advertised in many tourist publications—that snow on Mount Bachelor has to come from somewhere), cold in the winter, and hot in the summer, with cool to cold evenings year-round.

PLANNING YOUR TIME

Escape from the rainy west side with a week-long tour of central Oregon. If you're starting from Portland, drive U.S. 26 over the hump of Mount Hood and spend your first afternoon and night at **Kah-Nee-Ta,** on the Warm Springs Reservation. Plan to spend plenty of time by the pool—and venture down to the big day use pool for a real swim or a few runs on the water slide. On Day 2, following a morning swim, visit the **Museum at Warm Springs** to learn more about tribal culture. Then drive to Madras and have lunch at **Pepé's.** Continue south on U.S. 97 to Terrebone, where you'll turn off to **Smith Rock State Park.** Hike the trails and watch climb-

© JUDY JEWELL

HIGHLIGHTS

High Desert Museum: Curators at this indoor-outdoor museum have dared to mix it up, creating exhibits focusing on contemporary Native American life, the development of the West, photography, and wildlife. Don't miss the outdoor exhibits (page 422).

Mount Bachelor: Enough snow to cover the stumps, and enough sun to ease the seasonal affective disorder of western Oregon skiers and snowboarders, When the weather permits, be sure to ride the Summit Lift all the way to the top of the mountain (page 425).

Deschutes River Trail: In and around Bend, this trail ushers runners, walkers, and bicyclists along the Deschutes. With a map and a little practice, cyclists can ride from downtown Bend all the way to Benham Falls, with less than a mile on the roadway (page 426).

Metolius River: Visit the headwaters of the Metolius, where the water emerges from hillside springs and immediately gets about the business of being a full-size river. The cool, clear Metolius is a favorite of anglers (page 444).

Smith Rock State Park: Famed for its rock climbing, Smith Rock has just as much to offer hikers. Bring plenty of water and binoculars to search for golden eagles on the cliffs (page 449).

Museum at Warm Springs: Not only does this museum display a wide variety of tribal artifacts, but it also evokes the experience of Warm Springs tribal members through both audio and visual exhibits portraying the cultures of the Paiute, Warm Springs, and Wasco people who make up the Confederated Tribes of Warm Springs (page 456).

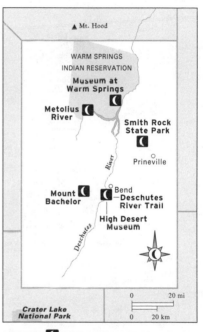

LOOK FOR TO FIND RECOMMENDED SIGHTS, ACTIVITIES, DINING, AND LODGING.

ers scale the rocks, then drive down to Bend and settle into your room at **McMenamins Old St. Francis School.** Day 3 begins with breakfast at the **Victorian Cafe** and a stroll or bike ride along the Deschutes River Trail. Spend part of the day wandering around downtown and the Old Mill District—stop by Pine Mountain Sports or REI to pick up any camping or outdoor gear you might need for the next couple of nights. Day 4 will take you up the Cascade Lakes Highway. Hike, fish, or just hang out on a lakeshore. Camp at a hike-in site at Todd Lake or find a more convenient car-camping site at one of the other lakes along the road. (If you're not camping, several lakeside resorts rent rustic cabins.) Once you've found the perfect camping spot, it seems a shame to leave it, and there are plenty of trails to hike up here. But we recommend that Day 5 be spent driving down to Sunriver on Route 42 (catch it just past Crane Prairie Reservoir), then south a few miles on U.S. 97 to the turnoff for Newberry Volcano. Head up to the caldera, where you can hike the trail through the Big Obsidian Flow and then

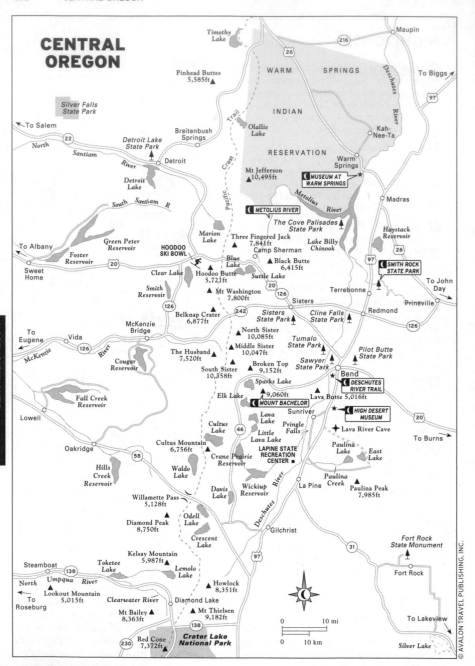

CENTRAL OREGON

find your new campground at either Paulina or East Lake (or a cabin at one of the rustic lakeside resorts). After you break camp the next morning, head back down the volcano and north on U.S. 97. Stop to explore the **Lava River Caves** and the **Lava Lands Visitor Center,** then take the short hike to **Benham Falls.** Continue north and spend the afternoon at the **High Desert Museum** (don't worry, they have a café). After your visit to the museum, you can spend night 6 in either Bend or Sisters. Finish your week with a river trip. Get up early and drive north of Madras to Maupin, where you'll meet your river guide for a day trip on the Deschutes River. Wear sunscreen and quick-dry shorts, and take a swim down the Elevator for us!

RECREATION

The Central Oregon Cascades are a haven for winter sports that range from alpine and Nordic skiing to snowmobiling, snowboarding, and snowshoeing.

If you plan to do a bit of hiking in the national forests, pick up a Northwest Forest Pass, which is required for parking at most trailheads, and which will get you into sites such as the Lava Lands Visitor Center. Passes ($5 one-day, $30 one-year) are sold at ranger stations, visitors centers, most local resorts, and many sporting-goods and outdoors stores.

Central Oregon has gained recognition for world-class golfing. And no wonder. With a dozen courses and six more slated for construction, this region of the state offers just about every kind of golf challenge. The warm, sunny days, cool evenings, and spectacular mountain scenery make every shot a memorable one.

Central Oregon Resorts

There are several premier resorts in Deschutes County that have helped transform it from a primarily agricultural area to the Aspen of the Northwest. Golf, horseback riding, tennis, swimming, biking/jogging/hiking trails, saunas, and hot tubs grace these year-round playgrounds, along with first-rate lodgings and restaurants. Ski packages and other special offers are also available at each establishment. Among the best resorts are Black Butte Ranch near Sisters, Eagle Crest Resort near Redmond, Seventh Mountain Resort on the outskirts of Bend, Sunriver Lodge in Sunriver, and Kah-Nee-Ta on the Warm Springs Reservation.

Tours

A great way to explore central Oregon in depth is through **Wanderlust Tours** (143 S.W. Cleveland Ave., Bend, 541/389-8359 or 800/962-2862, www.wanderlusttours.com), where the focus is on the area's geology, history, flora, fauna, and local issues. Day trips to Crater Lake, the lava lands, the Deschutes River, and the Cascades Lakes Highway are featured. Wanderlust's ecotourism packages have rated special notice in Oregon media, and it's generally thought to be the best tour company east of the Cascades. Canoe lakes in the high Cascades ($47) or take a hike that's selected for your group's interests and abilities (from $420 per group). Snowshoe tours and snow camping ($37 and up) are available in winter, and special moonlight trips can be arranged too. All-day trips include lunch; vegetarian meals available upon request.

Bend

There are two important things to know about Bend. First, it's different than it was last month. Growth is crazy here, with its population of 70,000 mostly housed in expensive new developments (which earned it, in 2006, the ranking of the nation's fifth-most overvalued real estate market). Second, many of the new inhabitants have money to spend on overvalued real estate, expensive restaurant meals, and top-of-the-line recreational toys and cars. And oh yes, there is one other thing about Bend: It's still a fantastic place to visit. The hiking trails, fishing streams, golf courses, white-water runs, and ski slopes are all still here, and all still top notch, and there's still sunshine 250 days a year and a dry climate that makes the average winter low of 27°F feel warmer than 40°F temperatures in the wet Willamette Valley.

Visitors will notice that thanks to the boom (fueled largely by California retirees attracted by the climate), zoning and planning efforts are still playing catch-up. However, after years of traffic jams, there seems to be a sense of controlled mayhem emerging thanks to a massive road-building effort, which has focused on the use of traffic roundabouts rather than stoplights.

The Old Mill District, a huge housing, office, and shopping area just south of downtown, opens up access to the Deschutes River in this part of town. Here, the actual old mill smokestacks now soar above an REI store, and serving as a fitting symbol of Bend's transformation from mill town into recreational hot spot.

SIGHTS
Drake Park

The Deschutes River has a dam and diversion channel just above downtown Bend. It provides valuable irrigation water for the farmers and ranchers of the dry but fertile plateau to the north, and creates a placid stretch of water called Mirror Pond that is home to Canada geese, ducks, and other wildlife. Drake Park is on the east bank of this greenbelt and is a nice place to relax, have a quiet lunch, or maybe toss a Frisbee around.

However, you had better be careful where you step, as the birds leave behind numerous land mines. The folks living in those nice houses on the west bank of Mirror Pond got tired of scraping the guano off of their shoes, but unfortunately for them, they were legally unable to do anything against their fowl neighbors due to the birds' protected status.

They came up with a rather ingenious solution to the geese and their offensive droppings. The residents chipped in $1,500 to buy a pair of swans from Queen Elizabeth's Royal Swannery in England. Since geese and swans do not get along, the citizens reasoned that the blue-blooded swans would chase away the common Canada geese. While the geese are still here, you will notice that they tend to congregate in Drake Park, while the swans have a decided

You'll find Mirror Pond just out the back door of downtown Bend.

© JUDY JEWELL

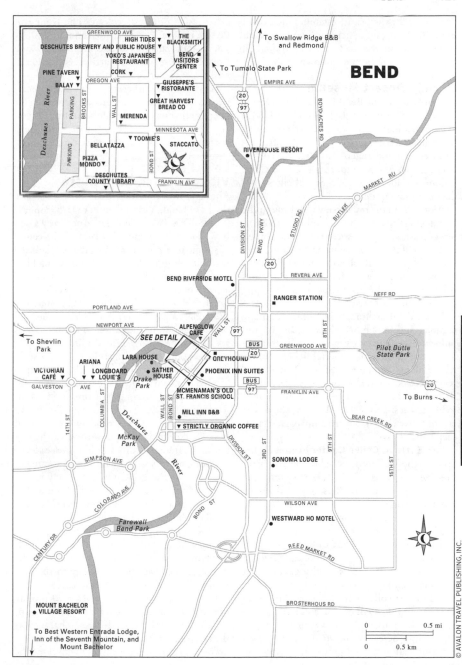

preference for the private estates. This part of Bend has a refreshing neighborhood feel with older homes surrounded by lawns and trees, providing respite from downtown sprawl.

◖ High Desert Museum

Six miles south of Bend is the High Desert Museum (59800 U.S. 97 S., Bend, 541/382-4754, www.highdesert.org, 9 A.M.–5 P.M. daily, $12 adults, $11 seniors, $7 ages 5–12, free for children four and under). Although the admission fee may seem steep, this is an excellent indoor–outdoor museum that will take half a day to explore in detail.

Along the many trails that wind through the 150-acre facility, visitors can observe river otters at play, porcupines sticking it to each other, and birds of prey dispassionately watching over the whole scene. Replicas of a sheepherder's cabin, a settler's cabin, forestry displays, and other historical interpretations are also along the museum walkways.

Inside the museum's main building, unique exhibits, slide and movie shows, galleries, and pioneer history demonstrations are presented. The "desertarium" is a special delight full of native plants and populated by 37 small critters whose nocturnal lifestyles often keep them from view in the wild. Bats, lizards, mice, toads, snakes, and owls reveal that the desert is more alive than its superficially barren landscape might suggest.

The **Earle A. Chiles Center** exhibit on the Spirit of the West features eight "you are there" life-sized dioramas. This walk through time begins 8,000 years ago beside a still marsh and takes you to a fur brigade camp, into the depths of a gold mine, and down Main Street of a boisterous frontier town.

The **Spirit of the West Gallery** has representative arts and artifacts of the early American West, as well as tools, clothing, and other personal belongings from the 19th century. The Bounds collection of Native American artifacts and the Hall of Plateau Heritage balance out the museum's coverage of the peoples of the high desert, while the Changing Forest exhibit addresses old-growth life cycles and other issues of forest ecology. The **Henry J. Casey Hall of Plateau Heritage,** an 8,000-square-foot venue, showcases the Doris Swayze Bounds Native American artifact collection as well as other Native Americana.

As you might gather, the scope and interactive nature of this facility make it appealing for people who don't usually like museums. If you end up staying longer than you expected, stop for lunch or a snack at the museum café.

Lava Lands Visitor Center, Lava Butte

About 11 miles south of Bend on U.S. 97 are the Lava Lands Visitor Center (541/593-2421, 9 A.M.–5 P.M. Wed.–Sun. late Apr.–early Oct., NW Forest Pass) and Lava Butte. The center has some interpretive exhibits that explain the region's volcanic history, as well as a small but good selection of local geology books and an assortment of free pamphlets on local attractions; their bulletin board has the latest activities and goings-on posted. Guided walks that provide a good introduction to the lava lands are offered here during the summer.

After your orientation, cruise on up the steep drive to the top of 500-foot-high Lava Butte, located just behind the visitors center. The observation platform on top of this fire lookout (established in 1928) offers the best viewpoint. Be sure to talk with the resident lookout and have him or her explain how to work the Osborne fire finder. Nearly a mile above sea level, the butte affords a commanding panorama of the Cascade Range. On a clear day you can see most of the major peaks, with Mounts Jefferson and Hood looming prominently on the northern horizon. These snow-capped turrets backdrop a 10-square-mile lava field.

You can venture out into this eerie landscape by taking the trail that starts from the visitors center and makes its way to the Phil Brogan lookout. July and August on Saturday evenings, a park naturalist gives a 90-minute presentation on top of Lava Butte. After sunset, the forest takes on a different character as the creatures of the night make their presences known. As darkness continues to envelope the area and celestial objects come into view, the emphasis shifts to a tour of the constellations and planets. Be sure to call ahead for starting times of this excellent attraction for families.

A short trail circumnavigates the 150-foot-deep crater on Lava Butte and is complemented by informative placards that help you interpret this otherworldly environment. From the trail you can see how the lava flow from the butte changed the course of the Deschutes River. You can also see the *kipukas*, small islands of green trees surrounded by a sea of black lava. Along the trail, look for some of what geologists call splatter. You'll know it when you see it, because it looks exactly like what it sounds like. Pick up a couple of red pumice rocks for the children, who will be fascinated by the way the stones float in the bathtub.

Benham Falls

Four miles down Forest Service Road 9702 from the Lava Lands Visitor Center is Benham Falls. Give other cars a wide berth and plenty of following distance, as the road's pumice and fine dust are hard on paint jobs and engines. The road leads to a small picnic area in a grove of giant ponderosa pines on the bank of the Deschutes River. With tables, pit toilets, fire grills, and plenty of shade, this is a nice place for a picnic. Be sure to tote your own fluids, though, because there is no water.

The hike to the falls is an easy one-mile jaunt downstream. Take the footbridge across the river, and enjoy your stroll past a spectacular section of untamed white water. While the water in the Deschutes is much too cold and dangerous for a swim, it's ideal for soaking your feet a little after you've completed your hike. Benham Falls was created when magma from Lava Butte splashed over the side, flowing five miles to the Deschutes. When the molten rock collided with the icy water, the churning rapids and crashing waterfall were created here.

Lava River Cave

About 12 miles south of Bend on U.S. 97 and one mile south of Lava Butte is Oregon's longest known lava tube, the Lava River Cave

(541/593-2421, mid-May–mid-Oct., NW Forest Pass). The cave is a cool 40°F year-round, so dress warmly. Since the walking surface is uneven, flat shoes are recommended. Bring a flashlight to guide you through this lava tube or rent a propane lantern at the entrance for $3 (lanterns come recommended—no batteries to die out one mile deep in darkness). The trail is an easy 2.4-mile round-trip from the parking lot.

The first chamber you enter is called the Collapsed Corridor. Volcanic rocks that fell from the roof and walls lie in jumbled piles. Freezing water in cracks pries a few rocks loose each winter, which is why the cave is usually closed during the cold months. Stairs take you out of the Collapsed Corridor into a large void called Echo Hall. Here the ceiling reaches 58 feet high and the cave is 50 feet wide. Conversations return from the opposite side of the hall as eerie noises in the dark. The lateral markings you see etched on the walls here show the various levels of past volcanic flows.

At Low Bridge Lane, watch your head because the ceiling dips down to five feet. Look for the "lavacicles" in this and other areas of the cave. (This term comes from a geologist's 1923 publication on the cave called *The Lava River Tunnel*.) Two kinds of them are found here: The hollow cylindrical "soda straws" were formed by escaping gases, and the other cone-shaped formations were created by remelted lava dripping down from the ceiling.

The next curiosity you'll come across is a cave inside the cave, the Two Tube Tunnel. Two tubes running for 95 feet intermittently connect. The smaller tube was formed when the level of the lava flow dropped and the cooling lava created a second roof and tube inside the existing cave.

The terrain changes again in the Sand Gardens. Rain and snowmelt carry volcanic ash down through cracks and openings in the cave and deposit them here. The process continues today with the nearly constant dripping water carving out spires and pinnacles in the sand. These formations take hundreds of years to grow, so please stay behind the fenced-off

CENTRAL OREGON

area. The sand gets thicker and thicker until it completely blocks off the lava tube, forcing an abrupt about-face. The walk back to the light of the sun affords a different perspective on this remarkable natural attraction.

It is important to avoid littering the cave, collecting samples, or doing anything else to mar this national treasure. Don't light flares, paper, or cigarettes, because the fumes kill off insects, a food source for the cave's bat population. Roosting bats should not be disturbed, because waking them from hibernation results in certain death for these winged mammals. Incidentally, bat droppings support this cavernous ecosystem, and others; bat guano is harvested commercially and used for detoxifying wastes, improving detergents, and producing antibiotics. Bats can catch hundreds of mosquitoes within an hour, and are also important pollinators. There are nearly 50 species of bats living in North America, and if left alone, they pose little threat to humans. In short, "leave nothing but footprints, take nothing but pictures, and kill nothing but time."

A couple miles south of Lava River Cave is the **Lava Cast Forest.** Take U.S. 97 and go nine miles on the cinder road (Forest Service Road 9720). From there, follow a self-guided trail through an unreal world created when lava enveloped the trees 6,000 years ago. The lava hardened, leaving behind a mold of the once living trees, much like how the eruption of Pompeii in Italy left casts of residents.

Pilot Butte

On the east side of town is Pilot Butte. A road spirals its way up to the top of this 511-foot-high volcanic remnant. Locals enjoy a fitness regime of following a trail to the top. You can enjoy a sweeping view of nine snowcapped Cascade peaks and their green forests. It is also pretty at night, with the twinkling lights of the city below and the stars above. Full moons are especially awesome, illuminating the ghostly forms of the mountains in icy, light-blue silhouettes. The scent of juniper and sage adds to the visual splendor.

Pine Mountain Observatory

Another peak experience worth investigating is the Pine Mountain Observatory (541/382-8331, http://guernsey.uoregon.edu, $3 donation) located about 40 miles east of Bend on U.S. 20. Take the road out of Millican to the top of 6,395-foot-high Pine Mountain to reach the installation. Three Cassegrain telescopes with 15-, 24-, and 32-inch mirrors are used by University of Oregon professors and students to unlock the secrets of the universe. On this 6,300-foot mountain the friendly astronomers will often allow visitors an intriguing peek at the neighboring stars and planets. Call ahead for information and weather conditions before making the trip. Generally, the public visits after April on Friday and Saturday evenings. Wear warm clothes and take a flashlight.

A Mountain of Glass

Farther down U.S. 20 you ease into the Great Basin desert and such attractions as the Sagehen Nature Trail (see *Burns and Vicinity* in the *Southeastern Oregon* chapter), located 70 miles from the Pine Mountain Observatory turnoff, and the Glass Buttes. Located 36 miles past the observatory, the latter attraction is one of the world's largest obsidian outcroppings, a mountain of volcanic glass, gently rising 2,000 feet above the surrounding countryside. The Bureau of Land Management (3050 N.E. 3rd St., P.O. Box 550, Prineville 97754, 541/416-6700, www.blm.gov) can provide you with additional information. From here the next big town is Burns, 55 miles to the east.

ENTERTAINMENT

Downtown Bend's classic **Tower Theatre** (835 N.W. Wall St., 541/317-0700, www.tower theatre.org) was renovated in 2002 and now hosts music, films, and other performances. This is a good venue to see some relatively big-name acoustic musicians.

Bend's other main music venue, the **Les Schwab Amphitheater** (541/322-9383, www.lsabend.com), is located on the edge of the Old Mill District, on Shevlin-Hixon Drive between Simpson and Columbia. This is the place to see

© JUDY JEWELL

Downtown Bend's Tower Theatre has been renovated and is a great venue for films and performances.

performers such as Fiona Apple, Bonnie Raitt, Jack Johnson, or Nickel Creek. It's also the site of quite a few free concerts, some of which are dog-friendly!

EVENTS

Quintessentially Bend, the **Pole Pedal Paddle** (541/388-0002, www.pole-pedal-paddle.com) is either a relay or, for the exceptionally tough, a single-person event that starts at the top of Mount Bachelor and ends at the Les Schwab Amphitheater in Bend's Old Mill District. Between the two points, participants downhill ski, cross-country ski, bike, run, and canoe or kayak to the finish line. Although some participants take the event quite seriously, most enter in a spirit of fun.

The **Bend Summer Fest** brings out food booths, Oregon wine and microbrews, art exhibits, and live music all in one big block party the second weekend in July. Contact the Bend Visitors Information Bureau (541/382-8048, www.visitbend.com) for more details.

The **Cascade Festival of Music** (541/383-2202 or 888/545-7435, www.cascademusic.org, $15–38) is held in late August through Labor Day weekend on the banks of the Deschutes River in Drake Park. In addition to world-class performances of classical, pop, and jazz in the pavilion tent, children's concerts, music workshops, and strolling minstrels round out the pageant.

SPORTS AND RECREATION
【 Mount Bachelor

The Northwest's largest and most complete ski area is Mount Bachelor (541/382-2607 information, 541/382-7888 hours and snow report, www.mtbachelor.com, $49 adult, $30 child). Located 22 miles southwest of Bend on Century Drive, 12 ski lifts, including five high-speed quads, and trails that range from beginner to expert, make for some of the most popular skiing in the state. This is the winter training grounds for the U.S. Olympic Ski Team.

The lift here takes you right to the top of the mountain, yielding great sunny-day views of the neighboring Cascade peaks. You may also see puffs of steam coming off the slopes, which serve as reminders that Bachelor is a still-kicking volcanic peak. Although central Oregon is known for its clear skies, the truth is that storms do pass through quite regularly. This is a good thing for skiers and snowboarders, who count on the snow piling up deep enough on Bachelor for the ski season to extend into late spring, but it can mean skiing or boarding in high wind and flying snow pellets. Conditions are often best here in late winter and early spring.

Expert skiers and boarders should ride the Northwest Express lift (a high-speed quad) to the mountain's Northwest Territory, where trees and bowls keep skills honed. The Summit lift is a must, both for the views and the trails, which include some blue runs. Another good area is the part of the mountain served by the Outback Express; runs here are mostly blue.

With a top elevation over 9,000 feet and steady northwest air flow, skiing here can run into the early summer. However, avoid skiing

MOUNT BACHELOR SUMMIT CHAIRLIFT

Even when ski season is over, Mount Bachelor Summit Chairlift (541/382-2442 or 800/829-2442, www.mtbachelor.com) and the Sunrise Lodge Lift are in operation. The view from the top of 9,065 foot Mount Bachelor takes in many of the Cascade lakes and peaks. The lift runs 10 A.M.-4 P.M. daily, July 1-Labor Day and costs $15 adults, $9 children ages 6-12. Try to time your journey to the top with the ranger talks offered at 11:30 A.M. and 2:30 P.M. seven days a week. Lunch is served daily in the mid-mountain Pine Marten Lodge 10 A.M.-4 P.M. Mountain bike rentals are available from the Mount Bachelor Ski and Sport shop at West Village. Bikes are allowed on the cross-country trails, but not on the chairlift.

The peak's natural history is conveyed by a three-mile trail where white bark pine and pumice grape-fern grow. The purplish fern is found in only four other alpine plant communities in Oregon, most notably in the pumice desert on the northwest side of Crater Lake. You can get to Sunrise Lodge and Lift via the Cascades Lakes Highway. Many consider the perspective from Mount Bachelor's 9,065-foot summit to be the finest alpine view in the state.

here after 1 P.M. in May and June, when conditions become slushy. If you must ski then, choose the west-side snowfields, which hold up better in the late afternoon light. Finally, while there may not be enough snow in summer to ski, you can still ride the chairlift to the peak of this volcano for an unsurpassed view of the surrounding countryside.

Unlike most ski resorts of its size, Mount Bachelor has no slopeside lodging. The closest lodging is down the hill at the Seventh Mountain Resort. Sunriver is also about a 20-minute drive.

Deschutes River Trail

The best thing about Bend's booming growth is the development of the Deschutes River Trail. The trail, which will ultimately run 19 miles from Tumalo State Park north of town to the Meadow Picnic Area near Widgi Creek Golf Course, offers excellent river access to walkers, runners, and cyclists. Pick up the trail downtown in Drake Park or in the Old Mill District, from either Farewell Bend Park on the east side of the river (on Reed Market Road) or from the Les Schwab Amphitheater on the west. The trail is a bit of a patchwork of paved and unpaved surfaces, so for a ride of any length it's good to have a mountain bike.

If, at the trail's southern terminus, you want to keep going, hop up onto Century Drive and head past the golf course and the Seventh Mountain Resort to the turnoff for Dillon Falls. This road will quickly reconnect you with riverside hiking and mountain biking trails that go all the way to Benham Falls.

The outlying, less urban section of the trail runs 9.1 miles (one-way) through riverside pine forests and lava flows, and is actually a set of three parallel trails—one each dedicated to hikers, bikes, and horseback riders—beginning about seven miles southwest of Bend. To get there, follow Century Drive southwest, then turn south onto Forest Road 41 (Conklin Road), from which there are several access points to the trails, at Lava Island, Big Eddy, Aspen, Dillon, Slough, Benham West, and Benham Falls day-use areas. Traffic in the section closest to Bend can be heavy on weekends. The season is spring to fall, though most of the trails may remain open in winter during years of low snowfall. A Northwest Forest Pass is required for parking, and dogs must be leashed. Four trail sections—at Big Eddy Rapids, Dillon Falls, Benham Falls West, and Benham Falls Picnic Area—are wheelchair accessible. They're surfaced with crushed gravel and are of intermediate difficulty level.

Hiking and Mountain Biking

The area in and around Bend boasts a rich network of hiking and mountain biking trails, ranging from short, barrier-free interpretive walks in town to strenuous wilderness treks. The best hiking is on trails accessed by the Cascade Lakes Highway; see that section for details. Snow can lock up many of these high-elevation trails until as late as June or July, so you'll want to inquire locally before heading out fall through spring. The offices of the **Deschutes National Forest** (1645 U.S. 20 E., Bend, 541/383-5300, www.fs.fed.us/r6/centraloregon) can be worth a visit. Note that parking at most trailheads in the national forests requires a Northwest Forest Pass, available at most outdoor stores and resorts.

For mountain bikers, the **Central Oregon Trail Alliance** (1293 N.W. Wall #72, Bend, www.cotamtb.org) is a good resource. This volunteer group works with the Forest Service, BLM, and other land managers to enhance mountain biking in and around Bend. Their website describes area trails and shows current conditions.

Rent a mountain bike at **Pine Mountain Sports** (255 SW Century Dr., 541/385-8080, $20 for four hours, $25 for 24 hours). Store staff also leads hikes on Friday afternoons during the summer; call for details.

About five miles west of town, **Shevlin Park** lures both hikers and mountain bikers with an easy five-mile loop through the pines along the Tumalo Creek gorge and along a ridge burned in the Awbrey Hall fire of August 1990. It's open year-round, with no parking or access fees. Several picnic areas offer quiet spots for lunch. To get there, follow Greenwood Avenue west from U.S. 97 in Bend; Greenwood changes its name to Newport Avenue after a few blocks, then changes again to Shevlin Road as it angles to the northwest.

Another trail close to town that's very popular with mountain bikers is **Phil's Trail**, an eight-mile segment of a larger network of eponymous bike trails (Kent's, Paul's, Jimmy's, etc.—named for the riders who established or popularized them) among the canyon and butte country just west of Bend. Difficulty is generally easy to moderate, with some steep climbs to challenge your lower gears the farther

west you ride. To get to the trailhead, head 2.5 miles west on Skyliners Road, then turn left on the first paved road to the south and travel 0.5 mile. A little farther west, Roads 4610 and 300 also intersect the network. A Northwest Forest Pass is required for parking.

Farther afield, Mount Bachelor beckons hikers in the summer and fall to walk the four-mile **Mount Bachelor Summit Trail** to the mountain's top. This is one of the easiest and safest routes to the top of any Cascade peak, requiring no climbing skills or equipment. An even easier way to reach the top is via the chairlift (see *Mount Bachelor Summit Chairlift* sidebar), which runs during the off-season.

To get to the trailhead, follow signs for the upper (east) parking lot at the ski area. The trail begins at the western end of the lot, and climbs to a forested ridge on the mountain's northeastern side, to the upper station of the first section of the ski lift. From there, the trail climbs steeply through the timberline area and continues up to a talus ridge leading to the mountain station of the second lift segment. It's a short hike from this lift station to the summit.

Plaques stationed at viewpoints along the way identify lakes and mountains visible from this 9,000-foot elevation, including Diamond Peak to the south, and the Three Sisters, Broken Top, and Mount Jefferson, and sometimes even Mount Hood, 100 miles away, to the north. The hike involves an elevation gain of 2,600 feet; average hikers should allow 2–3 hours one-way. Mountain bikes are not recommended on the trail.

Cross-Country Skiing

Just west of downtown Bend on the road to Mount Bachelor, **Virginia Meissner** and **Swampy Lakes** are excellent cross-country ski areas. The Sno-Park area at Virginia Meissner is about 13 miles west of town; Swampy Lakes is about two miles up the road from Meissner. The two trail systems join up, and together access more than 25 miles of ski trails dotted with strategically placed warming huts. There are also snowshoe trails leading from each Sno-Park. Dogs and motorized vehicles are prohibited at both Virginia Meissner and Swampy Lakes. Sno-Park permits are required. In the summer, these trails are good for mountain biking.

Up the mountain at **Dutchman Flat** Sno-Park, what you gain in elevation and early-season snowpack, you'll lose in peacefulness. This Sno-Park, located almost directly across from the turnoff to Mount Bachelor's Sunrise Lodge, has trails for both skiers and snowmobilers and can be extremely busy on weekends and holidays. Snowmobilers can use this spot to access roughly 150 miles of trails; skiers find about 19 miles of trails, including some fairly challenging ones.

Horseback Riding

Several public stables in the vicinity of Bend offer horseback rides that satisfy everyone from the dude to the experienced equestrian. Whether it be a mild-mannered pony for young children or a lively steed for the wannabe buckaroos, you'll find appropriate mounts and trail rides for all ages and skill levels. One of the best places to saddle up is at the Seventh Mountain Resort (541/382-8711).

Fishing

With over 100 mountain lakes and the Deschutes River within an hour's drive of Bend, your piscatorial pleasures will be satisfied in central Oregon. The high lakes offer rainbow, brown, and brook trout as well as landlocked Atlantic and coho salmon. The Deschutes River is famed for its red-sided rainbow trout and summer steelhead. Not surprisingly, the best fishing is outside of the Bend metropolitan area; see the sections on Sunriver, Cascade Lakes, and Prineville to find details on some of the best fishing areas. You will need appropriate fishing gear like chest waders, rod 'n reel, and fishing license/steelhead tags, and Bend is a good place to supply yourself with these items. Several outfitters are also based in Bend.

A full-service pro shop with everything for the fly fisher is the **Fly Box** (1293 S.E. 3rd St., 541/388-3330). Custom-tied flies and a full se-

lection of fly-tying tools and materials provide you with the goodies to keep the fish biting. Fly-fishing classes, fishing guide services, and equipment sales, rentals, and repairs can also be found here.

Deschutes River Outfitters (61115 U.S. 97 S., 541/388-8191 or 888/315-7272, www.deschutesoutfitters.com) features float trips, lake walk-in trips, and steelhead fishing trips that can be customized into single-day or multiday excursions. They have so many different packages and rates that it's best to refer you to their outstanding website for specifics.

All of these outfitters require completion of a trip application form and a deposit. It's always a good idea to plan your reservations well in advance, especially during the fall fishing season.

Rafting

Around Bend, you're likely to see all manner of vehicle carrying kayaks and rafts. (Our favorite: a motorcycle with a kayak and a bike strapped onto the back.)

The Deschutes River offers some of the finest white water in central Oregon. The numerous lava flows have diverted the river to create tumultuous rapids that attract raft, kayak, and canoe enthusiasts. From short rafting trips to multiday adventures, you'll find many options available to enjoy the exciting Deschutes River. You will need swimwear, footwear, sunblock, and sunglasses for all rafting trips. It's also advisable to have a set of dry clothes handy at the end of the voyage.

The prime spot for day-long trips is actually the Lower Deschutes, out of the town of Maupin (see *Maupin* section), but there are a couple of spots close to Bend that'll satisfy that urge to be in the river on a hot summer day.

Right in town, it's an easy float from either McKay Park (166 SW Shevlin Hixon Dr., on the river's west bank) or Farewell Bend Park (on the east bank along Reed Market Dr.) to Drake Park. This is a do-it-yourself trip, made easier during the summer by a shuttle bus that will take you and your raft or inner tube from the takeout to McKay Park. **Alder Creek Kayaks**

(250 S.W. Industrial Way, 541/317-9407) offers lessons and rentals (from $10 per hour) at their store located right where N.W. Colorado Avenue crosses the Deschutes on S.W. Industrial Way, close to a put-in at McKay Park.

Upstream a few miles, the Big Eddy section of the river is a bit more thrilling. Several outfitters lead trips on this section of the Deschutes: The **Seventh Mountain Resort** (18575 S.W. Century Dr., Bend, 541/389-2722 or 800/452-6810, www.seventhmountain.com) offers a short two-hour raft trip, $40 adults, $35 children, down a three-mile section of the Deschutes that takes in some Class I–IV rapids. With names like Pinball Alley and the Souse Hole, you can be assured of a good ride! Transfer between the inn and the river is included.

Sun Country Tours (531 S.W. 13th St., Bend 97702, 541/382-6277 or 800/770-2161, www.suncountrytours.com) runs a two-hour, three-mile Big Eddy Thriller takes in Class I–IV rapids on the Deschutes River and costs $40 per person.

Camping

With the Three Sisters Wilderness and the Deschutes National Forest flanking Bend, there are many wonderful spots to enjoy camping out under the stars. But for those who want to stay closer to civilization, **Tumalo State Park** (64120 O.B. Riley Rd., Bend, 541/382-3586 or 800/551-6949, www.oregonstateparks.org, open year-round, $13–17 tents, $22 hookups, $29 yurts) is convenient and not overly urbanized. Located five miles northwest of Bend off of U.S. 20 along the banks of the Deschutes River, 54 tent sites and 23 sites for RVs up to 35 feet long are available here. Showers, flush toilets, hookups, utilities, and a laundry are also accessible.

A couple of decent RV parks can be found near Bend. **Crown Villa** (60801 Brosterhous, Bend, 541/388-1131 or 866/500-5300, $30–37) and **Scandia** (61415 S. 3rd St., 541/382-6206, $26–30) offer all of the major amenities.

Golf

Widgi Creek (18707 Century Dr., 541/382-4449, www.widgi.com, $30–75, reservations strongly recommended), just north of the Seventh Mountain Resort, was designed by Robert Muir Graves. The course's strategically placed trees, lakes, and sand traps have already given this place the reputation as the "mean green" golf course of central Oregon. The 18 holes here are mentioned in the same breath as Sunriver's North Course and Black Butte's Glaze Meadows—good company indeed.

Close to town along the Deschutes River, the hillside **River's Edge Golf Course** (3075 N. Business 97, 541/389-2828 or 866/453-4480, $30–76) is a convenient and pretty alternative.

Juniper Aquatic and Fitness Center

One of the finest aquatic and fitness centers east of the Cascades is found at Juniper Aquatic and Fitness Center (800 N.E. 6th St., 541/389-7665, www.bendparksandrec.org/Juniper_Swim_Fitness). Part of the Bend Metro Park and Recreation District, the center is located in 20-acre Juniper Park and features two indoor pools and a large 40-yard outdoor pool providing plenty of space for splashing around. Serious swimmers can enjoy frequent lap swims and adults-only swim times daily. An aerobics room, weight room, group exercise classes, jogging trail, and tennis court offer other exercise options. A sauna and whirlpool tub provide you with yet another way to sweat it out.

ACCOMMODATIONS

Bend has exploded into the largest full-fledged resort town in the state. On holidays or ski weekends, it's hard to find a decent room if you don't have reservations, and it's bound to get worse. Nonetheless, a profusion of cut-rate motels just off the main drag makes it possible to put a roof over your head without putting a dent in your pocketbook. For a comprehensive list of motels, see the www.visitbend.org.

Under $50

Most of the less-expensive motels are along 3rd Street. Although they're in a "less than $50" category, during busy weekends in the middle of the summer, the prices may creep

CENTRAL OREGON

a little bit higher. **Sonoma Lodge** (450 S.E. 3rd, 541/382-4891, www.sonomalodge.com, $39–89) is a personal favorite in this category. The rooms are simple but clean, the staff is friendly, pets are welcome, and there's a small breakfast buffet in the morning. **Westward Ho Motel** (904 S.E. 3rd St., 541/382-2111 or 800/999-8143, www.westwardho.com, $35–65) has a decent-sized indoor pool and a hot tub; pets are welcome here.

In addition to the budget motels, **Mill Inn** has a bunkroom with beds for $30, shared bath. See its listing in the *$50–100* category for details.

$50-100

(McMenamins Old St. Francis School (700 N.W. Bond St., 541/382-5174 or 877/661-4228, www.mcmenamins.com, $94–139) is right downtown, but in its own little world surrounded by gardens with quiet sitting areas. Rooms in this historic 1936 Catholic school are nicely appointed with televisions, telephones, wireless Internet access, hair dryers, private bathrooms (shower only though), and nice bathrobes to wear on the way over to the wonderful Turkish-style soaking pool. Guests also have free admission to movies at the school theatre. In addition to the standard rooms, several cottages are available.

In a pleasant neighborhood near Drake Park is the **Sather House** (7 N.W. Tumalo, Bend, 541/388-1065 or 888/388-1065, www.satherhouse.com, $88–126), an elegantly decorated B&B with cheery quilts and comforters, antiques, afternoon tea, and satisfying breakfasts.

Just south of downtown, on the edge of the Old Mill District, is another distinctive inn. Originally an early 1900s hotel and boarding house, the **Mill Inn B&B** (642 N.W. Colorado, Bend, 541/389-9198 or 877/748-1200, www.millinn.com, $60–100) has been remodeled into a 10-bedroom inn. The least expensive rooms have a shared bath, but many have private baths, and some rooms adjoin to accommodate families (one room has four bunks, a bargain at $30/person). All rates include a full breakfast, and ski and golf packages are available. Add access to a washer/dryer, refrigerator, and hot tub, and you'll understand why advance booking is a necessity here.

Good dollar value is found at **Bend Riverside Motel** (1565 N.W. Hill St., 541/388-4000 or 800/284-2363, $58–139), although the least expensive rooms don't have a riverside view, and none of them are particularly swanky. Rooms vary widely, so it's good to take a look, especially if the view is important to you.

Up the road toward Mount Bachelor, find the **(Entrada Lodge** (19221 Century Dr., 541/382-4080, www.entradalodge.com, $79), a rather standard motel in an exceptionally nice setting. It's nestled in among the ponderosa pines at a nexus of hiking and mountain bike trails that can take you toward town or down to the Deschutes River (about a 20-minute walk). A small pool, a large hot tub, a rather basic breakfast buffet, and in-room microwave and refrigerator are the amenities here. It's a good place to bring your dog… and a pleasure to take dog walks here.

About 15 minutes outside of town on the banks of the Deschutes River near Tumalo is **Swallow Ridge Bed & Breakfast** (65711 Twin Bridges Rd., Bend, 541/389-1913, www.teleport.com/~bluesky, $50–70), where every window affords a view of either mountain or stream along with generous doses of peace and quiet. Instead of breakfast, you're given all the fixings and a kitchen, and the rest is up to you.

Over $100

Just up the road from the Entrada Lodge is the **(Seventh Mountain Resort** (18575 S.W. Century Dr., Bend, 541/382-8711 or 800/452-6810, www.seventhmountain.com, $90 and up, mostly over $100), a great spot for families. It is located five miles outside of Bend on Century Drive in the Deschutes National Forest. Bedroom units, fireside studios, and condos are available in the $90–270 range. Their outstanding recreation department plugs the kids into nonstop fun, leaving the parents free to enjoy grown-up pursuits. Ice-skating, cross-country skiing, and snowmobile trips are available during the winter months, and rafting, swimming, tennis, golf, horseback riding, and more are offered during the summer. Ask about their ski, rafting, or golf packages.

Close to downtown Bend, Drake Park, and Mirror Pond is **Lara House** (640 N.W. Congress, 541/388-4064 or 800/766-4064, www.larahouse.com, $95–150). This large three-story house was built in 1910 and features six large bedrooms with private bath. All rooms are furnished with antiques and reflect individual grace and charm. A delicious homemade breakfast is served in the bright solarium overlooking the colorful gardens and Drake Park. A large hot tub helps loosen aching muscles after a long day skiing, hiking, or other outdoor sports. Call ahead for reservations.

The **Riverhouse Resort** (3075 Business 97 N., 541/389-3111 or 866/453-4479, www.riverhouse.com, $105 and up) is situated along the Deschutes River at the north end of town. Although this hotel features a conference center and other business amenities, it's also a good place for vacationers. The rooms are well kept, and equipped with wireless Internet access, microwave, and refrigerator. Pets are permitted and guests have access to indoor and outdoor pools, an exercise room, and tennis courts. There's also a golf course on-site.

Right downtown, the **Phoenix Inn Suites** (300 N.W. Franklin Ave., 541/317-9292 or 888/291-4764, $99 and up) is a good choice for a business traveler, or for anyone who wants spacious rooms, although some of the "suites" don't exactly fit the usual definition of that term (they don't have separate rooms for sleeping).

Mount Bachelor Village Resort (19717 Mount Bachelor Dr., 541/452-9846 or 800/452-9846, $105 and up) is just out of the downtown area off Century Drive. Some of the units, which include a wide variety of condos and hotel room suites, overlook the Deschutes River. The rooms here are some of the nicest in Bend. It's easy for guests to get onto the Deschutes River Trail, and they can also use the adjacent Athletic Club of Bend, the most upscale gym in town.

Tucked away in a small valley nine miles west of Bend is **Rock Springs Guest Ranch** (64201 Tyler Rd., 541/382-1957 or 800/225-3833, www.rocksprings.com). Summer guests here stay by the week (Sat.–Sat.) on the American Plan, where all meals, lodging, horseback riding, and other ranch activities are included in one flat rate; $2,310 adults (double occupancy), $1,785 ages 6–17, $1,525 ages 3–5. (Stays of less than a week are sometimes permitted—call to inquire.) Only 50 guests are allowed per week, ensuring a high degree of personal service. Food is ample and delicious, and those with special dietary preferences will be accommodated adequately. Cookies, fruit, and beverages are always available for guests in the lodge dining room. Guests get their own cabins that are clean and well furnished.

A proactive recreation program supervised by well-qualified counselors keeps the kids on the go all day long with croquet, badminton, volleyball, basketball, and horseback riding. The horseback riding program is outstanding, and is the forte of the ranch. Riders are matched up with steeds appropriate to their level, and enjoy rides catered to all levels of experience that grow more challenging as the week progresses. After a day in the saddle, it's great to relax in their spa to work out the kinks. If your family likes to horse around, this is the place to do it.

FOOD
Fine Dining

The scenery around Bend feeds the soul, and restaurants here do the rest. While area restaurants run the gamut from fast-food franchises to elegant dinner houses, many travelers also want something in between those extremes. Some alternatives for every budget are listed below.

The Blacksmith (211 N.W. Greenwood Ave., 541/318-0588, dinner nightly, $16–28, reservations recommended), housed in an actual old blacksmith shop, has a brawny atmosphere, with highly polished wood-plank tables and a composite concrete floor. The food is similarly robust: try the steak frites or oven-seared and pan-roasted halibut served over potato purée. Even the veggie lasagna is filled with hearty roasted vegetables. The starters, including a tasty shrimp tostada, are good enough here that it's tempting to make a meal of them.

Set on a corner in the heart of downtown, **Merenda** (900 N.W. Wall St., 541/330-2304, lunch and dinner daily, $10–23, reservations recommended) fairly pulses with energy. In fact, if there were to be any complaint about this place, it would be that it can be a bit noisy, with an almost frenetic feeling. But the food is delicious and happy-hour deals abound. For lunch, the huge Cobb salad requires a rather determined eater, and sandwiches, such as pulled pork, are also filling. The selection of wines by the glass is huge, and they're available as two-ounce tastes as well as standard four-ounce glasses, making it possible to sample some rather special wines. Diners can also choose from a selection of fine cheeses. Wood-fired pizzas or handmade pastas make an inexpensive light dinner, but it's easy to be tempted by grilled hanger steak or sole saltimbocca.

Staccato (5 N.W. Minnesota, 541/312-3100, lunch and dinner daily, $12–29), a lively Italian restaurant located in Bend's first fire station (yes, the firepole is still in place) has a huge wine list and great homemade pasta. Try the wild boar pappardelle (a house-made chickpea pasta with wild boar ragout) or a lively linguine puttanesca with shrimp.

Also in the downtown core, The **Pine Tavern Restaurant** (967 N.W. Brooks St., 541/382-5581, $10–25) has been in business since 1919, so they must be doing something right. The restaurant is located in a garden setting overlooking Mirror Pond, and ponderosa pines coming up through the floor enhance the interior ambience. Fresh mountain trout, prime rib, lamb, and hot sourdough scones with honey butter are among the many specialties. Reservations are recommended. Open daily; dinner only on Sunday.

Just out of the downtown core, in a small bungalow, **Ariana** (1304 N.W. Galveston Ave., 541/330-5539, dinner Tues.–Sat., $18–27, reservations recommended) is one of the most appealing and intimate dinner restaurants in town. The Mediterranean-influenced cuisine is prepared with care, elevating dishes as simple as beet salad to remarkable heights. The oven-roasted halibut here may be served with zucchini "pasta" and lemon sauce, and truffles are used to flavor corn and frites. In the summer, seating expands to a deck.

Another romantic place is **(Cork** (150 N.W. Oregon Ave., 541/382-6881, dinner Tues.–Sat., $20–30, reservations recommended). Stop in for a glass of wine or a full dinner—although somewhat pricey, Cork is often cited as the best restaurant in Bend. The food is seasonal American, with Pacific Rim influences.

Casual Dining

Downtown coffee lovers head to **Bellatazza** (869 N.W. Wall St., 541/318-0606) for brew and a wireless connection. If you'd rather sip coffee or tea in a peaceful setting, try **Balay** (961 N.W. Brooks, 541/389-6464), tucked in beside the Pine Tavern with a back lawn extending down to the river. South of downtown, near the Old Mill District, **Strictly Organic Coffee** (6 S.W. Bond St., 541/383-1570) is a great place for coffee or tea and a snack. They also serve good pre-made sandwiches.

Perhaps the best spot for breakfast in downtown Bend is the **Alpenglow Cafe** (1133 N.W. Wall, 541/383-7676, breakfast and lunch). A summer seasonal favorite is the berry-stuffed French toast, extra-thick slices of the restaurant's own special bread filled with fresh blueberries or raspberries.

Just outside of downtown, breakfasters linger at the **(Victorian Café** (1404 N.W. Galveston Ave., 541/382-6411, breakfast and lunch), one of the few breakfast and lunch joints that has a full bar. Bloody Mary or no, breakfasts here are an extravaganza.

Budget gourmets, including many construction workers who keep busy building the new Bend, hit the **Longboard Louie's** (1254 N.W. Galveston Ave., 541/383-2449, lunch and dinner daily, $4–8), where seafood tacos are excellent (get the halibut if it's in season) and the ambiance easygoing. Sit out on the deck in nice weather.

Giuseppe's Ristorante (932 N.W. Bond St., 541/389-8899) brings the taste of northern Italy to Bend. A clean, family style restaurant that is well-rounded and well-known in Central Oregon. All entrées ($14–20) come with a vegetable, a side of spaghetti on polenta, and choice of soup, salad, or minestrone. Their most popular dish is Sambuca di Gamberi, tiger prawns sautéed with pancetta, mushrooms, spinach, and garlic and glazed with sambuca. A good wine list and full-service bar known for generous portions complement the food.

Bend also boasts central Oregon's first brewery and brewpub, **Deschutes Brewery and Public House** (1044 N.W. Bond St., 541/382-9242, lunch and dinner daily, $8–12). This is the place to come and relax with fresh, handcrafted ales and better-than-average pub food. There are vegetarian burgers, sandwiches, and black bean chili among the offerings. The main brewery is at 901 S.W. Simpson Avenue, where tours and tastings are offered.

Microbreweries are commonplace in Oregon, but microdistilleries are not often seen. Visit the **Bendistillery** tasting room (850 N.W. Brooks St., 541/388-6868), which is essentially a hip bar, for specialty martinis made with small-batch gin. Be forewarned that the drinks here are potent and perhaps best not consumed on an empty stomach. Fortunately, the bar has a pretty good selection of small plates.

High Tides (1045 N.W. Bond, 541/389-5244, lunch Mon.–Fri., dinner Mon.–Sat., $10–20) is the child of restaurant Tidal Raves in Depoe Bay, which brings a renowned legacy of cooking experience to central Oregon. This Bend incarnation features more creative versions of upscale seafood entrées), and the chef will gladly customize gourmet vegetarian dishes to your liking. Wines, microbrews, gourmet sodas, an espresso cart, and not-too-sweet desserts round out the offerings.

The best place for pizza is **Pizza Mondo** (811 N.W. Wall St., 541/330-9093, lunch and dinner daily), with hand-tossed, stone-baked pies. Dynamite calzones and a mean Caesar salad that would give Brutus pause add to their diverse selections. Pizza is also available by the slice.

You can find over 100 Thai dishes at **Toomie's** (119 N.W. Minnesota, 541/388-5590, lunch Mon.–Fri., dinner daily, $7–18), which serves a wide variety of rice, noodle, curry, chicken, seafood, pork, beef, and vegetarian dishes. Be forewarned that when they say "look out!" about hot and spicy dishes, they mean it.

INFORMATION

Bend Visitor and Convention Bureau (917 N.W. Harriman St., 541/382-8048 or 800/949-6086, www.visitbend.com) has an office downtown on N.W. Harriman at Irving Street. The **Central Oregon Visitors Association** (661 S.W. Powerhouse Dr., 800/800-8334, www.covisitors.com) is in the Old Mill District.

The Bend and Fort Rock **Ranger Station** (1230 N.E. 3rd St., 541/383-4000, www.fs.fed.us/r6/centraloregon) is the place to go for permits and information on the vast array of lands in central Oregon managed by the Forest Service. The **library** (507 N.W. Wall St., 541/388-6677) is a good place to get on the Internet; they are a wireless hotspot.

GETTING THERE
By Air

With daily flights to/from Portland, Eugene, Seattle, San Francisco, and Salt Lake City, access to central Oregon has improved dramatically in the last decade. The air hub of this section of the state is Redmond Air Center (Redmond 97756, 541/504-7200), located 16 miles north of Bend and east of U.S. 97. **Alaska/Horizon Airlines** (800/547-9308, www.alaskaair.com), **United Express** (800/241-6522), and **Delta Connection** (800/221-1212) fly into Redmond. Avis, Budget, Hertz, and Enterprise have car-rental offices in the terminal. Taxis, limos, and shuttle buses connect the traveler to Bend at nominal costs. The terminal has interesting displays on central Oregon attractions. Interactive media and audiovisual aids can even teach locals about their home region.

CENTRAL OREGON

By Bus

The **Central Oregon Breeze Shuttle** (541/389-7469 or 800/847-0157, www.cobreeze.com, $45 one-way, $81 round-trip) serves Bend to and from Portland International Airport, with pick-ups and drop-offs at downtown hotels. **Redmond Airport Shuttle** (541/382-1687 or 888/664-8449) offers door-to-door service to and from the Redmond airport and to and from the Chemult Amtrak station. A free **ski shuttle** run by Mount Bachelor (541/382-2442) links Bend (from a park-and-ride lot near McKay Park and the Colorado Ave.–Simpson Ave. traffic roundabout) to West Village on the mountain. **Bend Cab** (541/389-8090) can always haul you around if you need a ride. There is no inner-city bus service.

By Train

The closest you can get to Bend via **Amtrak** (800/872-7245, www.amtrak.com) is Chemult, 60 miles to the south on U.S. 97. Amtrak will assist you in scheduling your transfer to Bend.

By Car

The automobile is still the vehicle of choice for exploring this quadrant of the state. U.S. 97 and 20 converge on Bend, much as the Native American trails and pioneer wagon roads did 150 years ago when this outpost on the Deschutes was called Farewell Bend. Portland is three hours away via U.S. 97 and U.S. 26, Salem is two hours away via U.S. 20 and Route 22, and Eugene is two hours away via U.S. 20 and Route 126. Crater Lake National Park is about two hours south down U.S. 97. There are also many loops worth investigating, like the Cascade Lakes Highway, Newberry Crater, and the Lava Lands, as well as other touring corridors.

The Bend Parkway (a.k.a. U.S. 97) moves traffic fairly smoothly north and south through town. It parallels 3rd Street. On the road up to Bachelor and in some of the newer developments, including the area around the Old Mill District, traffic roundabouts are used instead of stoplights. Your awareness of other vehicles should naturally heighten as you approach a roundabout; traffic slows, but doesn't necessarily stop at these junctions.

You can rent a car for around $40 per day with 50 free miles daily from **Hertz** (2025 N.E. U.S. 20, 541/382-1711, Redmond Airport 541/923-1411) and **Budget** (315 S.E. 3rd St., 541/385-1107).

Sunriver and Vicinity

The seeds of growth were planted in central Oregon in the mid-1960s when a onetime military encampment a dozen miles south of Bend was transformed into the Sunriver Resort community. The resort, with its mix of private houses, rental units, and a lodge, has an increasing number of year-round residents, but it is still largely a hub for families looking to rent a house in central Oregon for a week. And indeed, this is an ideal spot for a family get-together, with miles of bike paths, swimming pools, tennis courts, and the lovely Deschutes River. It's also an easy base for exploring the nearby volcanic landscape and sites along the Cascade Lakes Highway and, in the winter, for skiing Mount Bachelor.

SIGHTS
Newberry Volcano

Newberry Volcano, a vast shield volcano that reached to about 10,000 feet before it blew its top about 1,500 years ago, covers 500 square miles. Its caldera alone is five miles in diameter caldera and contains two alpine lakes, Paulina and East Lakes. A 1981 U.S. Geological Survey probe drilled into the caldera floor found temperatures of 510°F, the highest recorded in an inactive Cascade volcano.

The volcano itself is at the southeastern end of the area designated as the Newberry National Volcanic Monument, which extends in a swath from Newberry Crater, south and east of Sunriver, all the way to Lava Butte, on the highway between Bend and Sunriver, enshrines the obsidian fields, deep mountain lakes, and lava formations left in the wake of a massive series of eruptions. While lacking the visual impact of Crater Lake, this preserve is more accessible and less crowded than its southern Cascade counterpart.

The main focus of interest here are the two lakes in the caldera: **Paulina Lake** and **East Lake.** A 9,500-year-old circular structure called a "wickiup" was excavated at Paulina Lake in 1992—this dates back well before the latest eruptions of the volcano, and indicates that native people used this area though various stages of volcanic activity. Several campgrounds and two resorts are located along the shores of these lakes, which are noted for their excellent trout fishing, said to be best in the fall. In Paulina Lake, fisherfolk can troll for kokanee, a gourmet's delight, as well as brown and rainbow trout. Paulina's twin, East Lake, features a fall run of German brown trout that move out of the depths to spawn in shoreline shallows. The Oregon state record German brown trout was caught here in 1993, weighing in at a hair over 27 pounds.

Be sure to take the four-mile drive (summer only) to the top of 7,985-foot-high **Paulina Peak,** the highest point along the jagged edge of Newberry Crater, on Forest Service Road 500. Towering 1,500 feet over the lakes in Newberry Crater, the peak also allows a perspective on the forest, obsidian fields, and basalt flows in the surrounding area. To the far west, a palisade of snow-clad Cascade peaks runs the length of the horizon.

The other must-see site on the volcano is the **Big Obsidian Flow,** which was formed 1,300 years ago and served as the source of raw material for Native American spearpoints, arrowheads, and hide scrapers. Prized by the original inhabitants of the area, the obsidian tools were also highly valued by other tribal nations and were a medium of exchange for blankets, firearms, and other possessions at the Taos Fair in New Mexico. These tools and other barterings helped to spread Newberry Volcano obsidian

all across the West and into Canada and Mexico. Centuries later, NASA sent astronauts to walk on the volcano's pumice-dusted surface in preparation for landing on the moon. A 0.9-mile trail now crosses the obsidian flow. Find the trailhead on the road between the two lakes.

Newberry National Volcanic Monument is managed by the Deschutes National Forest (1645 U.S. 20 E., Bend 97701, 541/383-5300). Contact the Lava Land Visitor Center (58201 S. U.S. 97, Bend 541/593-2421); or Newberry National Volcanic Monument (Fort Rock Ranger District, Suite A 262, Bend 97701, 541/388-5667, www.fs.fed.us/r6/central oregon) for more information.

To reach Newberry Crater, head south from Sunriver about 12 miles (or 27 miles from Bend) on U.S. 97 to the turnoff to Paulina and East Lakes. The 16-mile paved but ragged County Road 21 twists and turns its way up to the lakes in the caldera of Newberry Crater.

Sunriver Nature Center

Educational programs and interpretive exhibits, including a nature trail and a botanical garden, help orient visitors to the high desert ecology of the area around Sunriver. The nature center (541/593-4394, www.sunriver naturecenter.org) is also home to an observatory, which hosts Friday night "Dinner Under the Stars" events throughout the summer. Classes are held for both kids and adults, and there are also summertime day camps for children; all of these things focus on nature and science.

ENTERTAINMENT AND EVENTS

The **Sunriver Music and Arts Festival,** (541/593-1084 or 541/593-9310, www.sunriver music.org), held in the magnificent log-and-stone structure called the Great Hall at Sunriver Resort, has been pleasing capacity crowds since the festival's inception in 1977. The five-concert series features top performers from around the world. Highlights include the gala pops concert and the gourmet dinner as well as four traditional classical concerts and two children's concerts.

CENTRAL OREGON

SPORTS AND RECREATION
Fishing

Although some people do fish the Upper Deschutes in the area around Sunriver from the bank, most anglers use drift boats. If you don't have a boat, consider fishing the Fall River, off Route 43 (Century Drive) southwest of Sunriver.

You can get equipment, licenses, advice, or a fishing guide at the **Sunriver Fly Shop** (56805 Venture Ln., 541/593-8814), located near the Chevron station in the business park/shopping area across the road from the entrance to Sunriver.

Families are catered to by **Garrison's Fishing Service** (Box 4113, Sunriver 97707, 541/593-8394, www.garrisonguide.com), which features pontoon boats with padded swivel chairs that cruise the lakes and rivers of Central Oregon looking for the big ones.

Golf

Three distinct 18-hole courses are found at **Sunriver Resort** (541/593-4402 or 800/801-8765, www.sunriver-resort.com). The Meadows Course has been renovated (it was formerly the rather flat South Course) and is many golfers' favorite at the moment. The Woodlands Course has water, abundant bunkers, and constricted approaches to the greens, making club selection and shot accuracy very important. The private Crosswater course is touted by the management as the best course north of Pebble Beach. In 2000, it was honored as one of *Golf Digest*'s top 100 courses in the United States. You must be a resort guest or member to play on it. The greens fees are $45–55 and $70–125 for 18 on the Meadows and Woodlands courses, while the exclusive Crosswater course is over $100.

A nearby, more economical championship golf course alternative would be **Quail Run** (541/536-1303 or 800/895-4653), a nine-hole course in La Pine. Sand traps, ponds, and tree-lined fairways challenge golfers of all levels without seriously challenging their pocketbooks. Greens fees are $20 for nine holes, and $35 for 18.

Cycling

For many visitors, a visit to Sunriver is a chance to ride a bike. The gentle off-street bike paths provide the perfect way to get around the resort area. It's also possible to ride along paths and back roads from the edge of Sunriver to Benham Falls, on the Deschutes. Sunriver's Bike Barn (541/593-3721) can set you up with a rented bike.

If you like to bike but would rather have gravity do all of the work, consider the **Paulina Plunge** (541/389-0562 or 800/296-0562, www.paulinaplunge.com, May–Oct., $55), a six-mile downhill mountain bike ride. They provide high-quality mountain bikes, helmets, experienced guides, and the shuttle transfer from Sunriver and back. The action starts at Paulina Lake, where you begin your coast down forested trails alongside Paulina Creek. You'll pass by 50 waterfalls on your 2,500-foot descent, as well as abundant wildlife and varied vegetation. Three short nature hikes are necessary to experience the waterfalls and natural waterslides that make this trip famous. You may bring your own bike, but this will not afford you a discount from the tour price.

Horseback Riding

About 15 miles south of Bend on U.S. 97 at Sunriver Resort is **Saddleback Stables** (22777 Crestview Ln., Bend 97702, 541/593-6995, www.sunriverlodging.com/horseback), offering rides ranging from a 15-minute pony ride to the half-hour Bald Eagle Loop, which goes along the Deschutes River to the two-hour Ramsey Ride, which climbs to a panoramic viewpoint overlooking the resort.

Camping

The nicest campgrounds in the area are in the Newberry Volcano area. The creekside **McKay Crossing** (Deschutes National Forest, 541/383-4000) is about three miles east of U.S. 97 on the road up to Newberry Volcano. **Paulina Lake, Little Crater,** and **East Lake** are the best bets up at the top of the Newberry Volcano.

La Pine State Park (541/536-2071 or 800/452-5687, www.oregonstateparks.org, year-round) is a large campground south of Sunriver. Look for a sign on the west side of the highway marking the three-mile-long entrance road located eight miles north of La Pine off U.S. 97. This area also has one of the taller ponderosa pines in Oregon (191 feet) and close proximity to the Cascade Lakes Highway and an array of volcanic phenomena. If offers such amenities as flush toilets, firewood, showers, and a laundry. Fees run $13–17 for full-hookup sites and $38–70 for cabins.

Bird-Watching

About an hour south of Sunriver near Fort Rock is **Cabin Lake Campground** (Deschutes National Forest, 541/383-5300, www.fs.fed.us/r6/centraloregon) an exceptional spot for viewing a wide variety of birds and wildlife. There is no lake at Cabin Lake and the campground is pretty marginal, but the Forest Service has built two small ponds that blend in with the natural surroundings. Permanent wildlife-viewing blinds made of logs, built and donated by the Portland Audubon Society, are adjacent to this small, 12-site campground, and give close visual access to these ponds. In fact, the blinds are so close that binoculars aren't really needed.

Since there is little water in this 3,000-foot-high meeting of desert and mountain biomes, both mountain and desert birds are regularly attracted, usually in large quantities. The red crossbill, a member of the finch family that is increasingly rare, is a regular visitor to this avian oasis. The pinyon jay is another fairly uncommon bird that can be seen here with frequency. Woodpeckers, including Lewis' woodpecker, the common flicker, the white-headed woodpecker, and the hairy woodpecker are also often sighted here. Park checklists show the California quail, bluebirds, chickadees, flycatchers, sparrows, warblers, and the Western tanager making appearances, too. Best viewing times are in the morning, but birds can usually be seen all day long.

ACCOMMODATIONS

The Northwest's most complete resort, **C Sunriver Lodge** (800/547-3922, www.

sunriver-resort.com), not only has proximity to Mount Bachelor skiing, Deschutes River canoeing/white-water rafting, and hiking/horse trails in the Deschutes National Forest but also boasts golf courses, pools, tennis courts, and 30 miles of biking routes. An on-site astronomical observatory and nature center, which features live animal displays and botanical gardens, together with Sunriver's shopping mall, compound the impression of a recreation mecca with something for everybody.

Larger parties may find the spacious lodge suites to be well worth the $219 and up asking prices. Each of these units features a large fireplace, a fully equipped kitchen, a sleeping loft, and tall picture windows that open onto a patio.

However, it can be a much better deal to rent a condo or a house. Sunriver Resort's website allows you to set your criteria and browse available properties, which start at about $165.

Condo rentals are also available through **Mountain Resort Properties** (541/593-8685 or 800/346-6337, www.mtresort.com). All units have a fully equipped kitchen, linens, washer/dryer, TV, barbecue, and telephone as well as access to swimming and tennis at Sunriver. Since these are privately owned units, other amenities like VCR, hot tub, sauna, and bicycles will vary. Most of these condos do not allow pets or smoking, but there are a couple of exceptions; inquire when making reservations. Other agencies brokering vacation house rentals include **Village Properties** (800/786-7483, www.villageproperties.com) and **Discover Sunriver** (800/544-0300, www.discoversunriver.com). Many houses have hot tubs, and quite a few allow pets.

Paulina Lake Resort (P.O. Box 95, La Pine 97739, 541/536-2240) books up early with a dozen three-bedroom log cabins going for $100–185 a night. Hearty lunches and dinners ($4–15) can be had in the resort's log-paneled dining room. Boat rentals and a general store are also on-site. During winter, the resort is open September–March to cross-country skiers and snowmobilers, giving access to over 330,000 acres of designated snowmobile areas.

CENTRAL OREGON

East Lake Resort (541/536-2230) offers 16 cabins with housekeeping facilities for $55–160 per night. A snack bar, general store, and boat rentals are on-site, and the nearby RV park has a laundry, public showers, and pay phones. Each year, 225,000 trout are planted in East Lake, and in 1990, Atlantic salmon were introduced here. The cold water and abundant freshwater shrimp make for excellent-tasting fish. East Lake Resort is open mid-May–mid-October.

FOOD

Although there are a number of casual eateries in and around Sunriver's main shopping area, as well as a well-stocked grocery store, two local restaurants stand out.

The Meadows, in Sunriver Resort's main lodge (541/593-3740, breakfast, lunch, and dinner daily), is an attractive restaurant with a western theme. Views of Mount Bachelor backdropping the golf course go well with a dinner menu emphasizing game dishes in the $19–34 range. Breakfast and lunch options run half this price.

Trout House (541/596-8880, breakfast, lunch, and dinner daily Apr.–Oct., $17–30), next to the marina in Sunriver, is known for both its food and its lovely views onto the Deschutes River. Not surprisingly, fish is a good bet here.

Cascade Lakes Highway

The Cascades Lakes Highway (a.k.a. Century Drive or Route 46) is an 89-mile drive leading to more than half a dozen lakes in the shadow of the snowcapped Cascades. These lakes feature boating, fishing, and other water sports. Hiking, bird-watching, biking, skiing, and camping also attract people. From downtown Bend, drive south on Franklin, which becomes Galveston, to the traffic circle at Galveston and Century Drive (14th Street, about one mile from downtown). Go three-quarters of the way around the circle, and you'll be headed south on Century Drive. The route is well marked and the road climbs in elevation for a significant portion of the drive.

Although there are many places to stop and explore along the highway, the stretch between Mount Bachelor and Crane Prairie Reservoir is the most spectacular, so if you're just out for an eye-popping drive, you can take the shortened version described in the sidebar.

The area around the Cascade Lakes Highway is part of the Deschutes National Forest (www.fs.fed.us/r6/centraloregon). A Northwest Forest Pass is required to park at most trailheads.

SIGHTS
Todd Lake
Shortly after you pass Mount Bachelor, you'll find the turnoff to the exceptionally beautiful but equally rustic National Forest Service campground at Todd Lake. It's a short walk up the trail from a parking area to the campsites at this 6,200-foot-high alpine lake. While tables, fire grills, and pit toilets are provided, you will need to pack in your own water and supplies, as no vehicles are allowed. It's a good thing, because the drone of a Winnebago generator into the wee hours of the night would definitely detract from the grandeur of this pristine spot. You'll find good swimming and wading on the sandy shoal on the south end of the lake, and you can't miss the captivating views of Broken Top to the north. Hearty explorers can portage a canoe up the trail for a paddle around Todd Lake. Because of the lake's high elevation, it is often socked in by snow until about the 4th of July.

Sparks Lake
Clear, shallow Sparks Lake was a favorite of Oregon photographer Ray Atkeson, and most visitors can't resist trying to capture views of Mount Bachelor, South Sister, and Broken Top reflected in the lake. Broken volcanic rock forms the lakebed, and water slowly drains out during the course of the summer, leaving

A THREE-HOUR TOUR OF THE CASCADE LAKES HIGHWAY

If you just want a gourmet taste of the Cascade Lakes Highway, a shortened version of the loop manages to take in some of the highlights. The following tour can be enjoyed in several hours, even allowing for several stops. By contrast, driving the entire loop necessitates a whole day with only limited time spent out of the car.

Begin by taking U.S. 97 13 miles south of Bend and taking the Sunriver exit. After about 1.5 miles, the turnoff to Sunriver Resort will be on your right; stay on the main road as it curves to the left. Follow this road (Route 40, or Spring River Road) to Cascade Lakes Highway (Route 46) and turn right to reach Little Lava Lake. The Deschutes River begins its 252-mile course to the Columbia from here. Head just down the road to Lava Lake where there's a small rustic resort, camping, and a store, with a grand view of South Sister from the store's porch; in the summer your attention could be diverted by the hummingbirds that flock to a hanging feeder.

Follow the highway north to the shores of Elk Lake, a favorite of windsurfers and sailors. The year-round cabins at **Elk Lake Resort** (541/480 7228) are popular, as is picture-taking from the lake's beach picnic grounds on the southernmost tip of shoreline. Here you have the full length of Elk Lake before you, back-dropped by South Sister and Mount Bachelor. During the snowbound months of winter, access to Elk Lake is by snowmobile, Sno-Cat van, or dogsled (really!) to a world of groomed cross-country ski and snowshoe trails amidst spectacular alpine scenery.

Not far away, the red volcanic cinder highway contrasts with the black lava flows en route to aqua-tinted Devil's Lake. From the northern end of this lake, on the other side of the highway, you'll find Devil's Pile, a conglomeration of lava flows and volcanic glass where *Apollo 11* astronauts reportedly culled a rock to deposit on the lunar surface. The road winds around to the Mount Bachelor Summit ski lifts. From the deck in front of the sport shop/cafeteria complex, you can see the Three Sisters and Broken Top.

You might want to hike the short trail to Todd Lake, canoe Sparks Lake in the shadow of Broken Top and South Sister, or visit the Ray Atkeson Memorial, dedicated to Oregon's "photographer laureate." All are located between Devil's Pile and the ski lifts. From Mount Bachelor it's a 20-minute drive back to Sunriver.

not much more than a marsh by late summer. This is a good place to let go of the idea of a formal trail, and just explore the lakeshore by foot or canoe.

The campground here, **Soda Creek,** is open from about mid-June–October. Bring your own drinking water, or be prepared to filter lake water.

The lake is open to fly-fishing only for the local brook trout and cutthroat trout; use of barbless hooks is encouraged.

Sparks Lake is located about 25 miles west of Bend.

Green Lakes Trailhead

Begin a hike into the **Three Sisters** **Wilderness Area** here. It's about 4.5 miles from the trailhead (27 miles west of Bend) along waterfall-studded Fall Creek, past a big lava flow, to Green Lakes. From here, the trail continues to the pass between Broken Top and South Sister. This trail is extremely popular, and it's best to hike it on a weekday.

Devils Lake

The eerily green Devils Lake (29 miles west of Bend) is home to a very nice campground (no piped water) and an easy lakeside trail. Just across the highway from the lake is a popular trailhead used by South Sister climbers. The climb up 10,358-foot **South Sister** (Oregon's third-highest peak) is challenging,

© JUDY JEWELL

Sparks Lake offers up fine views of South Sister.

but not technical. Many choose to do this 11-mile round-trip as an overnight backpacking trip. Many more hike the trail just as far as the pretty Moraine Lake area (about 3.5 miles), then return along the same route.

Elk Lake

A resort and a marina mean that this is not the quietest lake in the Cascades. Elk Lake is just about the only place along this road that you'll see sailboats, and it's also a good swimming lake, come about August. The cabins at the **Elk Lake Resort** (541/480-7228) make a good base for exploring the local trails if you are not up for camping. The resort is open during the winter for cross-country skiers and snowmobilers. Please note that during spring of 2006 the resort was closed, but was projected to reopen on a limited basis in the winter of 2006.

Hosmer Lake

Just off the highway, Hosmer Lake (39 miles from Bend) is a favorite fishing and canoeing lake. It's the only lake in the West that's stocked with Atlantic salmon, but don't count on eating them. Fishing is limited to catch-and-release fly-fishing with barbless hooks.

Even if you don't fish and don't have a canoe, it's worth visiting Hosmer Lake for its spectacular views of Mount Bachelor, South Sister, and Broken Top. Of the two campgrounds on the lake, **South** has the best views and the best lake access.

Lava Lake

Lava flows formed a dam that created Lava Lake, which is fed largely by underground springs. Rainbow trout, brook trout, whitefish, and illegally introduced tui chub live in the lake, which is 30 feet deep at its deepest point and open to bait fishing as well as flies. A lakeside lodge (541/382-9443) rents boats and operates an RV park; there is also a Forest Service campground near the resort.

Little Lava Lake

Visiting Little Lava Lake is a bit like making a pilgrimage, for this is the headwaters of the Deschutes River. Groundwater from the snowpack percolates down from the Mount Bachelor and Three Sisters area to fill the lake (it's figured that there's a large groundwater reservoir upstream from the lake); the Deschutes exits the lake as a meandering stream, flowing south about 8.4 miles to Crane Prairie Reservoir.

Cultus Lake

Diehard Oregon windsurfers tow their sailboards up into the Cascades to catch a breeze on glacier-formed Cultus Lake. The lake is also popular with campers, swimmers, boaters, water-skiers, and Jet Skiers. Anglers go for the big lake trout, also called mackinaw. An easy hiking trail follows the northern shore of the lake, and then heads north along the Winopee Lake Trail to Teddy Lakes. From the trailhead to Teddy Lakes, it's about four miles.

The **Cultus Lake Resort** (541/389-3230) rents cabins ($79 and up), motorboats, canoes, kayaks, and Jet Skis and operates a restaurant.

Crane Prairie Reservoir

Crane Prairie Reservoir, an artificial lake, is a breeding ground for osprey. These large birds, sometimes known as fish hawks, nest in the snags surrounding the water and fish by plunging headfirst into the water from great heights. Cormorants, terns, bald eagles, and a variety of ducks are also commonly seen here. Humans also like to fish here—the most-prized fish is a "cranebow," a rainbow trout that grows almost freakishly large in this shallow, nutrient-rich reservoir.

A Forest Service campground and the private **Crane Prairie Resort** RV park (541/383-3939) are located here.

Wickiup Reservoir

The area of the Deschutes River around present-day Wickiup Reservoir was a traditional Native American camping area during the fall. When the dam was completed in 1949, these campsites were flooded. Today, the reservoir (about 60 miles from Bend) is known for its relatively warm water and its good fishing, especially for brown trout, which can weigh in at over 20 pounds. Kokanee and coho salmon as well as rainbow trout, brook trout, whitefish, and the nasty invasive tui chub also live here. Campgrounds are at Wickiup Reservoir and across at access road at North and South Twin Lakes, small natural lakes that flank the large reservoir.

From Wickiup Reservoir, Route42 heads east and north along the Fall River toward Sunriver. The Cascade Lakes Highway, Route 46, continues south past Davis Lake.

Davis Lake

It takes a little doing to get to the large, shallow Davis Lake, and many of those who make it here come for fly fishing. It's known for large rainbow trout as well as illegally introduced largemouth bass. Most anglers use boats or float tubes here, because the vegetation along the shoreline and the muddy lake bottom make it difficult to wade.

Davis Lake was formed about 6,000 years ago when a lava flow cut off Odell Creek. A fire in 2003 wiped out the West Davis campground; the East Davis campground, though reduced in size by the fire, still exists. Davis Lake is a good spot for bird watching; expect to see waterfowl, woodpeckers, owls, and osprey.

INFORMATION

For information about sites along the Cascade Lakes Highway, contact the Bend–Fort Rock Ranger Station (1230 N.E. 3rd St., Suite A-262, Bend, 541/383-4000, www.fs.fed.us/r6/centraloregon).

Willamette Pass and Vicinity

In the area around Willamette Pass it's easy to see the shift from the greener, damper, Douglas fir–dominated west side of the Cascades to the dry east side, forested by lodgepole and ponderosa pines. Each of the lakes here has its own partisans—families who have camped in the same spot for decades—and its own personality. Campgrounds are available at Crescent, Odell, and Waldo Lakes.

Pick one place to explore in depth, or hop between lakes—perhaps you'll carve out a new personal tradition.

SIGHTS
Crescent Lake

On the sun-drenched east side of Willamette Pass, Crescent Lake is home to a tremendously popular campground and is often abuzz with power boats and Jet Skis. Large lake trout (including one whopping 30-pounder) are regularly pulled from the lake. Crescent Lake is located about three miles south of Route 58 via Deschutes National Forest Road 60 from Crescent Lake junction.

CENTRAL OREGON

Odell Lake

Odell Lake, 30 miles southeast of Oakridge on Route 58, deserves a special mention. There are two resorts, several summer homes, and five campgrounds around this 3,582-acre lake. Located in a deep glacial trough, the lake probably filled with water about 11,000 years ago when a terminal moraine blocked the drainage of Odell Creek. Due to the depth of the lake and the nearly perpetual west-to-east winds that blow through Willamette Pass, the water averages a cold 39°F. Those breezes, however, help to keep the pesky mosquitoes and other obnoxious insects away and make for some of the best sailing in the Cascades. Odell Lake Lodge (see *Accommodations*) is particularly charming, though somewhat on the rustic side. It has lodge rooms and cabins, and is open during the winter, when it's popular with cross-country skiers.

Willamette Pass Ski Area

Willamette Pass (1899 Willamette St., Ste. 1, Eugene 97401, 800/444-5030, www.willamette pass.com, 9 A.M.–4 P.M. Thurs.–Sun., $36 adult, $20 youth and seniors), 69 miles southeast of Eugene on Route 58, has some of the most challenging runs in the state as well as a multitude of beginner and intermediate trails. You'll find some of the steepest runs here, unlike the open chutes or powder bowls at other ski areas. Since Willamette Pass plows its own parking lot, you will not need a Sno-Park permit here. Night skiing runs Friday and Saturday nights from December until sometime in March. Call 541/345-SNOW (541/345-7669) for the ski report.

For information on cross-country skiing from Sno-Park areas, contact the **Sisters Ranger District** (Deschutes National Forest, Sisters 97759, 541/549-2111) or the **McKenzie Ranger District** (Willamette National Forest, McKenzie Bridge 97413, 541/822-3381).

Waldo Lake

The Waldo Lake Wilderness is a 37,000-acre gem 70 miles southeast of Eugene via Route 58 (take Forest Service Road 5897 before the Willamette Pass turnoff to go 10 miles to the lake). The centerpiece of this alpine paradise is 10-square-mile Waldo Lake (the third largest in Oregon), whose waters were once rated the purest in the country in a nationwide study of 30 lakes. Peer down into the green translucent depths of this 420-foot-deep lake to see rocky reefs and fish 50–100 feet below.

Canoeing, sailing, trout fishing, and windsurfing (no motorized craft allowed) on the lake complement hiking and cross-country skiing to give you different ways to experience the lake and surrounding region. Add wildlife-watching highlighted by the early September rutting season of Roosevelt elk and you'll quickly understand why Waldo Lake is a favorite with Cascades connoisseurs. The 22-mile loop trail around the lake is popular with mountain bikers and backpackers, and day hikes on the south end edify less diehard recreationists.

To best savor it all, visit the area between late August and mid-October to avoid a plague of summer mosquitoes and early winter snowfall. Whenever you go, expect a lack of crowds, views of 8,744-foot Diamond Peak in the distance, as well as first-rate trails and campgrounds. There's even one Forest Service campground, **Rhododendron Island** that is accessed only by boat.

There are two other very nice campgrounds up at Waldo Lake called **Shadow Bay** and **North Waldo.** To get there, take Route 58 for 24 miles southeast of Oakridge. Take a left on Forest Service Road 5897. It is five miles to Forest Service Road 5896, which takes you to Shadow Bay, and 10 miles down Forest Service Road 5897 to North Waldo. Both campgrounds charge $14.

Since there are 150 campsites between the two campgrounds, this usually ensures enough views of this mile-high lake for everyone to enjoy. Open June–late September, the fee is $14 a night. Boat docks and launching facilities are available, plus good sailing and fishing at Waldo. Many trails lead to small backcountry lakes from here; this is a good place to establish a base camp. Contact the Oakridge Ranger District for additional information.

Rigdon Lakes

An ambitious hike is up to Rigdon Lakes (Trails

3590 and 3583). To get there, follow Route 58 for 24 miles southeast of Oakridge. Take a left on Forest Service Road 5897. Follow it 10 miles to North Waldo Campground; the trailhead is to the right of the restrooms. This three-mile walk starts at North Waldo Lake Campground on Trail 3590. The trail is mild and scenic, paralleling the north shore of Waldo Lake for about two miles until the Rigdon Trail junction (Trail 3583). Head north (turn right) at the trail intersection for another mile to get to the first of the three Rigdon lakes, which has several peninsulas that are ideal for a picnic and several small islands that might tempt swimmers who don't mind cold water. A hike afterward to the top of Rigdon Butte is highly recommended. You will have to bushwhack, as there is no clear trail, but it is not a difficult climb if you follow the saddle of the ridge. From this vantage point, you can see all three Rigdon Lakes as well as many other nearby Cascade landmarks. If you want to take a closer look at the two other Rigdon Lakes, they're only another mile or so down Trail 3583 from the first lake.

If you want to get away from the traffic of Route 58 and don't mind bouncing down Forest Service roads for over half an hour, you might consider **Blair Lake Campground** (Willamette National Forest, 46375 Route 58, Westfir 97492, 541/782-2291). To get to Blair Lake, head east out of Oakridge on County Route 149 for one mile. Turn left onto Forest Service Road 24 and go eight miles until you hit Forest Service Road 1934. It's another seven miles down Forest Service Road 1934 to Blair Lake.

On the shore of little Blair Lake, a picturesque setting at 4,800 feet with seven tent sites awaits the determined explorer. Open June–mid-October, the fee is $6 per night, no reservations necessary. Picnic tables and fireplace grills are provided, with piped water, firewood, and pit toilets available. Boat docks are nearby, but no motorized craft are permitted on the lake.

ACCOMMODATIONS
Crescent Lake Lodge and Resort (541/433-2505, www.crescentlakeresort.com, $70–205,

three-night minimum in summer) is an easy place to while away a few days. Crescent Lake is located about three miles south of Route 58 via Deschutes National Forest Road 60 from Crescent Lake junction.

The premier property on Odell Lake is the ◖ **Odell Lake Lodge** (P.O. Box 72, Crescent Lake 97425, 541/433-2540, www.odelllake resort.com, $58–250). To get there, take the East Odell Exit off of Route 58 and follow the road a couple of miles. The hotel rooms range $58–62 a night, with the cabins going for $90–250. Skiers may want to take advantage of large cabin 12, which comfortably houses as many as 16 people for $250 a night. Since the lodge is extremely popular, reservations are strongly recommended, as much as a year in advance for weekends.

Moorages are available for rent, as are canoes, powerboats, and sailboats. The lodge has a complete tackle shop to help outfit you to catch the kokanee and mackinaw that inhabit the icy waters, and rental equipment is also available if you didn't bring your own. The restaurant at the lodge will cook your bounty for you and serve it along with soup or salad, potatoes, vegetables, and bread. The lodge also maintains its own system of trails, which provide good biking in the summer and cross-country skiing in the winter. The owners of the resort have put together an area map to guide you to various waterfalls. Bikes and ski equipment can be rented from the lodge. In addition to these outdoor pursuits, basketball, volleyball, badminton, and horseshoes round out the fun. Tots and toddlers will enjoy the sandbox, the toy library, and the swings.

Across the lake from the lodge is **Shelter Cove Resort** (W. Odell Lake Rd., Cascade Summit, 541/433-2548, www.sheltercoveresort. com), which features eight cabins complete with kitchens, 69 campsites with picnic tables and electricity, and 65 moorages in the marina. The General Store handles everything from groceries, tackle, and boat rentals to Sno-Park permits and fishing/hunting licenses. The September–October displays of Odell Lake's landlocked salmon spawning are unforgettable.

Sisters

Sisters was established in 1888 when nearby Camp Polk, a short-lived military outpost established along Squaw Creek, was dismantled. Following abandonment of the camp, the site was homesteaded in 1870 by Samuel M. Hindman, who subsequently operated a store and post office. Sisters is named after its backdrop to the south, the Three Sisters. These 10,000+-foot-high peaks were the last major obstacle for the pioneers to circumnavigate on their journey to the fertile Willamette Valley. The emigrants named the mountains after some of the virtues that helped propel them through the hardships of the frontier: faith, hope, and charity. Over the years, no one could agree upon exactly which mountain was named what, so the Oregon legislature settled the dispute by labeling the mountains as the North, Middle, and South Sisters respectively.

In any case, while most of the Old Santiam Wagon Road has long since been replaced by asphalt and forest overgrowth, the 19th-century flavor has been preserved in the town of Sisters. Wooden boardwalks, 1880s-style storefronts, and plenty of good old-fashioned western hospitality grace this small town of about 1,000. Some people are quick to lambast the thematic zoning ordinances of Sisters as cheap gimmicks to lure tourists, while others enjoy the lovingly re-created ambience and the abundance of charming, independently owned shops.

As well as being a food, fuel, and lodging stop, Sisters is also a jumping-off point for a wealth of outdoor activities. Skiing at Hoodoo Ski Bowl, fly-fishing and rafting on the Metolius River, and backpacking into the great Three Sisters Wilderness are just a few of the popular local pursuits. Nearby luxury resorts such as Black Butte Ranch, an annual rodeo a nationally famous quilting event, and a large and scenic llama ranch on the outskirts of town add to the appeal of this vintage-1888 village.

SIGHTS
Three Creek Lake and Tam McArthur Rim

Three Creek Lake, tucked under Tam McArthur Rim, is a good place for a summer swim, especially if you have an inflatable raft to prevent full-body immersion in the often quite cold water. A tiny lakeside store rents rowboats; from the center of the lake you'll get a good view of Tam McArthur Rim (named for the original author of the classic and fascinating reference book *Oregon Geographic Names*).

From the lake, trails lead into the Three Sisters Wilderness Area. A trail leads up to the 7,700-foot rim, and from the top the views of the Three Sisters and Broken Top are quite astounding. Snows can be heavy here (the lake itself is at 6,500 feet), so don't count on hiking this trail before July.

A lakeside campground makes this a pleasant place to spend a couple of days in midsummer, but be forewarned that most return campers bring insect repellent.

From Sisters, turn south on Elm Street, which becomes Forest Road 16. Follow Road 16 south about 17 miles to the lake. Be prepared for a couple of miles of fairly rough dirt road. During the winter, Road 16 between the lake and Sisters has a couple of snow-park areas that mark cross-country ski trails.

Black Butte

Hike up to the Black Butte lookout towers for a bird's eye view of the Sisters area. It's about two miles of uphill hiking (often in full sun) to the top of the cinder cone; bring plenty of water. To reach the trailhead, take U.S. 20 west from Sisters. Turn north (right) onto Forest Road 11 (Green Ridge Rd.) and pass Indian Ford campground. Turn left onto Road 1110 and follow it 5.1 miles to the trailhead.

◖ Metolius River

About 10 miles from Sisters is the second-largest tributary of the Deschutes River, the

Metolius. To get here, take the Camp Sherman Highway off of U.S. 20 five miles west of Sisters. This road will take you around Black Butte. On the north face of this steep, evergreen-covered cinder cone lies the source of the Metolius. A 0.25-mile trail takes you to a railing where you can see the water bubbling out of the ground.

Known simply as "the Spring," the water wells up out of the earth at a constant 48°F. The warm, spring-fed waters of the upper Metolius are ideal for insect egg and larval development, which in turn provides an abundant food source for rainbow, brown, brook, and bull trout, kokanee salmon, and whitefish. Consequently, some of the best fly-fishing in the state is found on the upper Metolius. This was no secret to the Native Americans. The name Metolius derives from an Indian word for "floating fish," because of the dead salmon carcasses found in the river after spawning. A beautiful riverside trail follows the Metolius as it meanders through the ponderosa trees past many excellent fishing holes. Drift boats are used to tackle the harder-to-reach places along this 25-mile-long waterway.

Other streams merge with the Metolius, lowering the water temperature to an average of 35°F. While the fishing isn't as good as in the warmer upper reaches, the white-water rafting is actually better downstream. The increased water volume coupled with steeper flow gradients provide plenty of exciting rapids for river-runners to splash around in. The Metolius was designated a National Wild and Scenic River in 1988, creating a 4,600-acre corridor within the unique 86,000-acre Metolius Conservation Area.

Five miles downstream from Camp Sherman (seven miles from the Head of the Metolius Trail) is the Wizard Falls Fish Hatchery. Open every day for visitors. Over 2.5 million fish, including Atlantic salmon, brook and rainbow trout, and kokanee salmon, are raised here annually. This hatchery is the only place in the state that stocks Atlantic salmon, which migrate to Hosmer Lake.

Hoodoo Ski Bowl

A little more than a half hour west of Sisters on Route 126 is one of Oregon's most family-oriented skiing areas, Hoodoo Ski Bowl (541/822-3799 or 541/822-3337 snow phone, www.hoodoo.com, $38 adult, $28 senior or junior). Generally operating from Thanksgiving to Easter (snow conditions permitting), it's open 9 A.M.–4 P.M. Sunday–Tuesday and Thursday; 9 A.M.–9 P.M. Friday and Saturday; closed Wednesday. Hoodoo has five chairlifts and a rope tow. The maximum vertical drop is 1,035 feet, and the runs are fairly evenly divided between advanced, intermediate, and beginner levels of difficulty.

SPORTS AND RECREATION
Horseback Riding
Black Butte Stables (541/595-2061 or 800/452-7455, www.blackbutteranch.com) at Black Butte Ranch has several packages that take you down trails in the shadow of the Three Sisters. The one-hour Big Loop trail ride costs $35; the 90-minute Gobblers Knob ride costs $40; the two-hour Hole-in-the-Wall Gang ride costs $50; and the four-hour Reata Trail ride (for experienced riders only) costs $100. The full-day Black Butte Posse ride costs $150. Given a couple days' advance notice, the proprietors will provide breakfast or a barbecue at the end of the one- and two-hour rides. Reservations are suggested; riding lessons and horse boarding are also available.

Camping
Six miles northwest of Sisters on Route 126, find **Indian Ford Campground,** the closest public campground to town. Farther west on Route 126, find the turnoff to the **Metolius River campgrounds,** a number of very pleasant campgrounds strung along the river both upstream and downstream from the hub of Camp Sherman.

A handful of campgrounds open only in summer are near Sisters on the old McKenzie Highway, Route 242. **Cold Springs Campground** is $12 and just five miles west of town on Route 242. This campground, 3,400 feet in elevation, has 23 sites for tents and small trailers (22 feet maximum). Picnic tables, fire grills, pit toilets, and water are provided. It's a pretty spot, near the source of Trout Creek. Six miles farther down the road is **Whispering Pine Campground.** No fees are charged at this primitive campground with six tent sites, mainly because there is no water available. Another six miles up the pass at 5,200 feet is **Lava Camp Lake Campground.** Two tent sites and 10 RV sites (22 feet maximum) are available at this rustic campground. There is no fee, but there's also no water. The main allure is its close proximity to the Pacific Crest Trail and the Three Sisters Wilderness.

Information about these campgrounds is available from Sisters Ranger Station (541/549-7700, www.fs.fed.us/r6/centraloregon).

Golf

Two well-groomed courses, **Big Meadow** and **Glaze Meadow,** are found at Black Butte Ranch (541/595-1500 or 800/399-2322, www.black butteranch.com). Big Meadow is more open and forgiving, while Glaze Meadow demands precise shots. Both have tall trees and lush fairways from tee to green. This course was recently named by *Golf Digest* as one of Oregon's top 10 golf courses. Greens fees are $25–29 for nine holes and $45–59 for 18 holes. Reservations for weekdays must be made at least one day in advance, while weekend bookings must be made no later than the Monday before.

Located three miles outside of nearby Sisters, **Aspen Lakes** (541/549-4653, www .aspenlakes.com) offers 27 holes in the shadow of the Three Sisters. Bent-grass fairways and distinct volcanic red cinder bunkers add to the stunning mountain vistas. Greens fees are $25–40 for nine holes and $45–70 for 18; reservations are always a good idea.

EVENTS

The annual **Sisters Rodeo** (800/827-7522) opens the second weekend of June. In addition to the normal assortment of calf-roping and bronco-bucking, country dances, a buckaroo breakfast, and a 10K Stampede Run round out

the fun. A **quilters' festival** takes place during the first week of July and can attract over 20,000 during the July 4 weekend. Also noteworthy is the annual **Sisters Folk Festival,** held in early September. This even attracts some of the biggest names in blues and folk. Contact the Sisters Chamber of Commerce (P.O. Box 476, Sisters 97759, 541/549-0251, www.sister schamber.com) for the schedule of events.

ACCOMMODATIONS

Right in the heart of downtown Sisters, upstairs from an antique shop, the ((**Grand Palace Hotel** (101 E. Cascade St., 541/549-2211 or 541/771-7731, www.grandpalacehotel sisters.com, $69–169) has renovated rooms in a historic hotel. Each of the five suites was inspired by one of the owners' children (don't worry—the kids are grown, so there aren't any kiddy themes) and they all offer at least rudimentary cooking facilities. The two-bedroom suites are nice for families or groups of friends traveling together, and a couple of these suites have full kitchens.

((**Sisters Motor Lodge** (600 W. Cascade, 541/549-2551, $79–225) is within easy walking distance of the shops and boutiques of Sisters. Beds are decorated with quilts, and the kitchenettes have charmingly retro appliances and formica tables; pets are allowed in some rooms.

The **Best Western Ponderosa Lodge** (505 U.S. 20, 541/549-1234 or 888/549-4321, $98 and up) is a large ranch-style resort motel set back from the road in the scattered pines. Rooms feature private balconies with views of the mountains and the adjacent Deschutes National Forest. Other amenities include a spa, heated pool, and free continental breakfast.

Located eight miles west of Sisters on U.S. 20, **Black Butte Ranch** (541/595-6211 or 800/452-7455, www.blackbutteranch.com, $100 and up) sits in line with other Cascade peaks in a setting of ponderosa pines, lush meadows, and aspen-lined streams. Over 16 miles of trails thread through the 1,800 acres of forested grounds. Accommodations include deluxe hotel-type bedrooms, one- to three-bedroom condominium suites, and resort homes. A nationally rated golf course, bike trails, tennis courts, and other facilities also explain why this resort has won the *Family Circle* "Resort of the Year" award twice.

A lovely place to enjoy Sisters is at the **Blue Spruce Bed & Breakfast** (444 S. Spruce, 541/549-9644 or 888/328-9644, www.blue sprucebandb.com, $160). Designed and built from the ground up as a B&B, the four rooms here all have their own theme. All bathrooms have a towel warmer, shower, and two-person whirlpool tub. Rooms are clean, bright, big, well apportioned, and all come equipped with a fridge stocked with complimentary water and sodas. Throw in laundry facilities for guests and a great country breakfast, and it's clear this is a good value.

Lake Creek Lodge (541/595-6331 or 800/797-6331, www.lakecreeklodge.com) is located near Camp Sherman in the nearby Metolius Recreation Area. This full-service resort has individual houses and cottages that range $140–375 depending upon the unit and number of people (about $50 less in the off-season). Tennis, swimming, and fishing are some of the many activities available here. Although cabins have kitchenettes, many guests like to eat at least one dinner at the lodge; dinner is served family-style on the deck or in the pine-paneled main lodge and features a different entrée each day, complemented by homemade breads, salads, and desserts ($25 adults, $12–15 kids). The establishment caters especially well to families; pets are allowed in selected cabins.

Another Metolius retreat can be found at **Cold Springs Resort** (Cold Springs Resort Lane, HCR 1270, Camp Sherman 97730, 541/595-6271, www.coldsprings-resort.com, mid-April–mid-October, $154–186) The cabins here feature naturally pure artesian well water. A footbridge across the Metolius connects the resort to Camp Sherman, where groceries, a church, and a café are within easy walking distance. Pets are allowed here for $8 per night but must be kept on a leash at all times and never left unattended.

The cabins at the **C Metolius River Lodge**

(541/595-6290 or 800/595-6290, www.metolius riverlodges.com, $95–265) are tucked in by the Metolius River right near the Camp Sherman store. The most coveted pair have decks extending over the river, and the majority have fireplaces and kitchens.

Wedged in between giant ponderosa pines and the banks of the Metolius are the 12 elegant cabins of the **C Metolius River Resort** (541/595-6281 or 800/818-7688, www.metolius riverresort.com, $180–205). These beautiful wooden structures, built in 1992, are bright and airy with lots of windows. The cabins are two stories high with more than 900 square feet of living space, comfortably sleep 4–6 people, and feature a fully equipped modern kitchen, full bath, river rock fireplace (stocked with all the firewood you'll need), and a river-view deck. Reservations made well in advance are a must if you want to stay here. You'll find the resort behind the Kokanee Cafe.

A few miles west of the Metolius River turnoff on U.S. 20 is the turnoff to Suttle Lake and the elegant new **Suttle Lake Lodge** (13300 U.S. 20, 541/595-2628, www.thelodgeatsuttle lake.com, $75–450), where a Native American theme predominates. The least expensive accommodations are in newly built but rustic (and very clean) cabins that share a central bathhouse; lodge rooms and waterfront cabins are much more posh. Elegant dinners ($40) are offered in the lodge.

FOOD

The **Depot Deli** (250 W. Cascade, 541/549-2572, breakfast, lunch, and dinner daily, $5–7) serves creative, reasonably priced fare in a re-creation of an old train station. Breakfast is highlighted by multi-ingredient omelettes and scrambles and espresso drinks. For lunch, homemade soups, sandwiches, burgers, and salads will fill you up. The outdoor deck is a nice place to escape Sisters's shop-till-you-drop ambience.

The **Gallery Restaurant** (230 W. Cascade, 541/549-2631, breakfast, lunch, and dinner) offers chuckwagon dinners that range $7–16. Surprisingly tasteful paintings on Old West themes, along with flintlocks and other ancient armaments, pay homage to the area's pioneer past. Many eastern Oregonians will tell you that **Papandrea** (325 S.W. Hood and 442 E. Cascade, 541/549-6081, lunch and dinner daily, pizza $12–19) makes the best pizza in the state. While such claims are highly subjective, outlets in Bend and Oregon City attest to this small chain's dedicated following.

There are plenty of pizza joints in town: **Coyote Creek** (497 U.S. 20 W., 541/549-9514, breakfast, lunch, and dinner daily, $10–22) serves standard American fare with pastas, pizzas, and prime rib. **Martoli's Pizza Inc.** (220 W. Cascade, 541/549-8356, lunch and dinner daily, $3.50 slice) makes a great pie and is a good place to grab a quick slice.

The hot spot in town is undoubtedly the **Hotel Sisters and Bronco Billy Saloon** (190 E. Cascade, 541/549-7427, lunch and dinner daily, $5–20). Built in 1912, the upstairs rooms of this historical structure have been refurbished into intimate mini-dining rooms. Barbecued ribs are the specialty of the house, but you can also find fresh seafood, steaks, chicken dishes, and Mexican fare here. In one corner of the building, on the other side of the western-style saloon doors, is Bronco Billy's. This funky watering hole must look much the same as it did 80 years ago. A racy painting that used to grace the local brothel is proudly displayed behind the bar, and cowboy hats on most heads complete the picture of a town whose Old West ambience gets better with age. For the price of a beer, you can get one of the local guys to tell you the inside scoop on where to go and what to do in this neck of the woods.

In nearby Camp Sherman, a special treat awaits at the (**Kokanee Cafe** (541/595-6420, dinner nightly, late Apr.–Dec., $22–32), which is known for its fresh and innovative cuisine served in a small, simply furnished dining room. Their house salad made with loads of organic greens, dried cranberries, and toasted walnuts is alone worth the trip, the fresh rainbow trout is perfectly cooked and seasoned with herbs, and depending on the night, the seared venison may be seasoned with cumin, cinnamon, and garlic. Dinner reservations are crucial during the summer and fishing season, given the small size of the building. During its season, the restaurant rents out two rooms upstairs.

INFORMATION

Detailed information about the geology, natural history, wildlife, wilderness areas, and numerous recreational opportunities in the Metolius Recreation Area can be obtained by calling the **Sisters Ranger Station** (541/549-2111, www.fs.fed.us/r6/centraloregon). More information is available from the **Sisters Chamber of Commerce** (541/549-0251).

Redmond

Sixteen miles north of Bend is Redmond, another rapidly growing central Oregon city. This hub city is centrally located between Madras, Prineville, Bend, and Sisters, so traffic can get congested here.

Redmond got its start when the Deschutes Irrigation and Power Company established irrigation canals here in the early 1900s. The railroad soon came, and realtors shortly followed. Like most central Oregon towns, it was once home to several mills, but now, thanks to its regional airport and nearby resorts, tourism plays a major role in its economy.

SIGHTS
Peter Skene Ogden Scenic Wayside

Stop here to peer into the dramatic Crooked River Gorge, a 300-foot-deep canyon. The old railroad trestle spanning the gorge was built in 1911 and helped to establish Redmond as a transportation hub. The old highway bridge, now open only to foot traffic, was built in 1926; before it was built, travelers had to descend the canyon walls to ford the river. The current highway bridge was built in 2003.

◖ Smith Rock State Park

The majestic spires towering above the Crooked River north of Redmond on U.S. 97 are part of this 623-acre state park. Named after a soldier who fell to his death off of the highest promontory (3,230 feet) in the configuration, the park is a popular retreat for hikers, rock climbers, and casual visitors. Picnic tables, drinking water, and restrooms can be found near the parking area. The more adventurous can camp out in the park's primitive walk-in camping area for $4 a night. It's located near the park entrance about 100 yards from the Rockhard Store, 9297 N.E. Crooked River Drive, Terrebonne. The campground includes showers and sanitary facilities.

Although Smith Rock is known for its rock climbing, many visitors come here to hike.

The Crooked River runs through Smith Rock State Park.

© JUDY JEWELL

Seven miles of well-marked trails follow the Crooked River and wend up the canyon walls to emerge on the ridge tops. Because the area is delicate and extremely sensitive to erosion, it's important not to blaze any trails because they may leave visible scars for years.

Some of the sport-climbing routes at Smith Rock are as difficult and challenging as any you'll find in the United States. Most of the mountain's 17-million-year-old volcanic rock is soft and crumbly, making descents extra challenging. Chocks, nuts, friends, and other clean-climbing equipment and techniques are encouraged to reduce damage to the rock. On certain routes where these methods would prove impractical, permanent anchors have been placed. Climbers should use these fixed bolts (after testing them first for safety, of course) to minimize impact on the rock face. Stop in at the parkside store to pick up a climbing guide to the routes at Smith Rock that do not require mounting of additional fixed protection.

Climbers should never disturb birds of prey and their young in the lofty aeries. Finally, pack plenty of water. The Crooked River is contaminated with chemicals from nearby farmlands and isn't suitable for drinking. **Redpoint Climbing Supply** (800/923-6207), on the corner of U.S. 97 and Smith Rock Way, is a good information and supply stop for climbers. Climbing lessons are offered by **First Ascent** (541/548-5137 or 800/325-5462, www.goclimbing.com).

Petersen's Rock Garden

What began as one man's flight of fancy over the years has metamorphosed into a full-fledged rock fantasy. Petersen, a Danish immigrant farmer, created four acres of intricately detailed miniature castles, towers, and bridges made of agate, jasper, obsidian, malachite, petrified wood, and thunder eggs. There are also the Statue of Liberty, the American flag, and many other compositions hewn out of natural rock.

This rock garden to end all rock gardens, Petersen's (7930 S.W. 77th St., Redmond, 541/382-5574, 9 A.M.–7 P.M. daily or till dusk

© BILL MCRAE

highway bridge over the Crooked River Gorge

CENTRAL OREGON

in winter, $3 adults, $1.50 children). To get here, take Gift Road off of U.S. 97 seven miles south of Redmond and 10 miles north of Bend. Follow the signs; it's only three miles off the highway. There is a funky museum and gift shop in the rear of the complex featuring a jumbled collection of many types of rocks, crystals, fossils, and semiprecious gemstones. In the back of the museum is the Fluorescent Room, where little castles made of zinc, tungsten, uranium, and manganese glow in the dark. Free-roaming peacocks strike poses in front of the sculptures. The staff will help direct rockhounds to promising sites in the vicinity to further their own collections.

Crooked River Dinner Train

The Crooked River Dinner Train (4075 O'Neil Rd., Redmond 97756, 541/548-8630, www.crookedriverrailroad.com, office hours Mon.–Sat.) shows off the broad vistas of central Oregon's high desert as well as local food and wines. The 2.5-hour, 38-mile route through the Ochoco River Valley goes from Redmond

to Prineville, offering Sunday champagne brunches, murder mystery theater, and western theme dinners mid-June–October. Call for prices and schedule updates. This deluxe service can cost up to $79 per person.

SPORTS AND RECREATION

Golf

Eagle Crest Resort (541/923-4653, www.eagle-crest.com) has two 18-hole golf course: Resort and Ridge. The greens fees for registered guests are $36–54 for nine holes and $50–81 for 18 holes. Weekend reservations must be made by Thursday.

Crooked River Ranch (541/923-6343 or 800/833-3197, www.crookedriverranch.com), an 18-hole par-71 course, is wide open with few trees, but that doesn't detract from the challenge or the scenic vistas. Rates are $20–25 for nine holes and $35–40 for 18 holes. Weekend reservations must be made by Thursday.

A true desert course found in Redmond that requires shot accuracy is the **Juniper Golf Club** (1938 S.W. Elkhorn Ave., 541/548-3121, www.junipergolf.com). This is an 18-hole par-72 course that snakes through the juniper and lava of the high desert. The prevailing winds and abundance of rocks off of the fairway challenge the golfer's shot-making abilities. Rates are $30–45 for nine holes, $40–55 for 18.

Horseback Riding

The **Crooked River Stables** (Crooked River Ranch, Terrebone, 541/504-8753) offers horseback rides along the rim of the Crooked River gorge and through the surrounding sagebrush and juniper. The rates are $25 for 35 minutes, $30 for one hour, and $40 for 90-minute rides.

ACCOMMODATIONS

Eagle Crest Resort (P.O. Box 1215, Redmond 97756, 541/923-2453 or 800/682-4786, www.eagle-crest.com, $94–340) is five miles west of Redmond. Though mostly a time-share operation, the resort also offers hotel rooms, two-bedroom suites, and condos. The terrain and vegetation are representative of the high desert, and backdropped by views of eight Cascade peaks. Ask about ski and golf packages. This is a low-key, family-oriented place.

In town, the **Redmond Inn** (1545 S. U.S. 97, 541/548-1091 or 800/833-3259, www.redmond inn.net, $52 and up) is a good value and a nice enough place to spend a night or two, with microwaves and fridges in the rooms, and a pool. Pets are welcome for a small fee.

Rock climbers tend to camp, but when that gets old, the **Hub Motel** (1128 N.W. 6th St., 541/548-2101, $42–52) is inexpensive, close to Smith Rock, allows dogs, and has kitchenettes.

FOOD

Unlike neighboring Bend, a culinary boom has not yet hit Redmond. However, there are a few decent places to stop. On the main drag, stop at **Santiago's Mate** (528 S.W. 6th St., 541/504-8870) for some energizing brew and a wireless connection. Sharing the same address is **Parilla Grill** (541/923-2171), with good wraps.

Just a block off busy 6th Street, find the **Seventh Street Brew House** (855 S.W. 7th St., 541/923-1795, lunch and dinner daily, $8–12), with Cascade Lakes microbrews, pizza, and satisfying pub food.

The (**Terrebone Depot** (400 N.W. Smith Rock Way, Terrebonne, 541/548-5030, lunch and dinner Wed.–Mon., $8–25), located on the road to Smith Rock, offers fresh food, including a good selection of vegetarian options, in the gorgeously renovated historic Terrebonne train depot. Climbers and hikers can also get picnic lunches to go.

The other restaurant of note in Terrebonne is **La Siesta Mexican Restaurant** (8320 U.S. 97, Terrebonne, 541/548-4848, lunch and dinner daily, $6–14, lunch and dinner daily, $5–12). Located on the south side of town in a nondescript crackerbox of a structure, for many years this was *the* culinary hot spot of this stretch of U.S. 97. It's still good, with moderate prices and dishes made from scratch.

Prineville

Prineville (population 9,100), the geographic center of Oregon, is the oldest incorporated town in central Oregon and still feels a bit like the Old West, even as it becomes a bedroom community for those who can't afford Bend's housing prices. The seat of Crook County and home to the corporate headquarters of Les Schwab Tires, Prineville has a population of 8,150, gets a meager 10 inches of rain a year, and relies on tires, agriculture, wood products, and tourism for its economy. The tourist economy is largely fueled by anglers, who come to fish the Crooked River and the two local reservoirs. Rockhounds and antique shoppers should also consider visiting Prineville.

Coming into town from the west, you drop down from tall bluffs into the Crooked River Valley and, nearing the city, cruise through hills dotted with juniper. White-and-black magpies dart in front of your car, and red-winged blackbirds observe your passing from their fenceposts.

Prineville is also known as the Gateway to the Ochocos, a heavily wooded mountain range that runs east–west for 50 miles. One of Oregon's least-known recreational areas, the Ochocos are still ruggedly pristine. Beyond these mountains stretches the long valley of the John Day River.

SIGHTS
A. R. Bowman Museum

A good place to begin your travels in Ochoco country is at the A. R. Bowman Museum (246 N. Main St., Prineville 97754, 541/447-3715, www.bowmanmuseum.org, 10 A.M.–5 P.M. Mon.–Fri., 11 P.M.–4 P.M. Sat.) This museum's two floors of exhibits and displays are a notch above most small-town historical museums. Fans of the Old West will enjoy the tack room with saddles, halters, and woolly chaps.

CENTRAL OREGON

WILLOWS, WAGON TRAINS, AND RANGE WARS: A BRIEF HISTORY OF THE OCHOCO COUNTRY

The Ochoco country, named after a Paiute word for willows, was heavily populated by natives who lived off a bounty of deer, elk, fish, and camas roots. The first significant passage of Europeans other than trappers through the area was the Lost Wagon Train of 1845. Led by Stephen Meek, brother of the Oregon Territory spokesman Joe Meek, the pioneers were seeking a route to the Willamette Valley easier than the arduous trek over the Blue Mountains.

Instead, they found hardship, starvation, thirst, and death on a tortuous journey through the deserts of Malheur and Harney Counties and along the rugged ridges of the Ochoco Mountains. Their hardships finally ended when they found the Crooked River and followed it north to The Dalles. Somewhere during the trek, members of the party scooped up gold nuggets and kept them in a blue bucket. Though the legend of the Blue Bucket Mine has since captivated Oregon history buffs, its actual site has never been found.

In 1860, Major Enoch Steen led an expedition through the region, which resulted in a number of geographic features being named after him, including Steens Mountain and Stein's Pillar. Eight years later, Barney Prine built a blacksmith shop, a store, and a saloon near the bank of Ochoco Creek; the outpost grew into the city of Prineville, the only town in 10,000 square miles. It was settled by the sons of the pioneers who had come west on wagon trains. It was their turn to carve out a life from the wilds.

At the turn of the century, cinnabar, the raw ore in which mercury is found, was discovered in the Ochocos, resulting in an influx of miners. About the same time, a range war broke out between the cattlemen and sheepherders. Groups like the Ezee Sheep Shooters and the Crook County Sheep Shooters Association bragged that they had slaughtered 8,000-10,000 sheep in 1905 alone. Incensed by this lawlessness, the citizens of Oregon moved to stop the killing; still, troubles continued for cattle and sheep ranchers and farmers. Harsh winters took their toll on livestock, and the hope that the plains would be receptive to wheat farming was unrealized.

During World War I, many homesteaders gave up and moved to the cities to work for the war effort. In 1917, Prineville made a decision that wound up boosting the local economy. The town built a railroad to Redmond, linking its line with the Union Pacific. Used primarily to haul ponderosa pine logs, the railroad remains the only city-owned railroad still in operation in the United States. In the 1950s a new industry was added to the mainstays of logging, ranching, and farming. Gemstones of high quality were discovered in the Ochocos, prompting a rockhound/tourism boom that continues to this day.

Rockhounds will be delighted with the displays of Blue Mountain picture jasper, thunder eggs, and fossils. Other classic displays include a moonshine still, a country store, an upstairs parlor of the early 1900s, and a campfire setup with a graniteware coffee pot and a pound of Bull Durham tobacco.

SPORTS AND RECREATION
Hiking
Stein's Pillar is a distinctive rock outcropping in the Ochoco National Forest about 15 miles northeast of Prineville. A four-mile round-trip hike passes through meadows and old-growth forest with some lovely panoramic views and a final steep, challenging stretch of trail before reaching the rock. From town, head east on U.S. 26 for nine miles and turn north onto Mill Creek Road. Continue for 6.5 miles to the turnoff for the trailhead.

Farther up the Mill Creek Road, find Wildcat Campground and a trailhead for the **Mill Creek-Twin Pillars** trail. From the campground, the trail follows Mill Creek into the Mill Creek Wilderness Area. This wet area supports lots of wildflowers and also a few cattle.

Stein's Pillar, a volcanic plug in the Ochoco Mountains, is a good hiking destination.

© EMILY ROTH

If you go the full 8.3 miles to the Twin Pillars, a pair of 200-foot-tall volcanic plugs, it's necessary to ford the river a number of times, which can be difficult early in the season.

Another worthwhile place to visit is the **Lookout Mountain Special Management Area** (541/416-6500). Located in the Ochocos, it's a unique biosphere with 28 plant communities, one of the finest stands of ponderosa pines in the state, lots of elk and deer, a wild mustang herd, and creeks full of rainbow and brook trout. A seven-mile trail starts near the Ochoco Ranger Station 22 miles east of Prineville on Forest Service Road 22 at the campground picnic area, and ends at the summit of Lookout Mountain, from which 11 major peaks are visible. June is the time to see one of the best wildflower displays in the state. Friends of Lookout, a coalition of environmental and recreational groups, invites you to visit the area and lend your support to efforts to secure legislation protecting this unique habitat. To get there, drive 15.3 miles east from Prineville on U.S. 26, and bear right at the sign for the ranger station.

Fishing

The 310-acre **Prineville Reservoir,** 17 miles south of Prineville on Route 27, was built for irrigation and flood control. A popular year-round boating and fishing lake, it is famous for its huge bass and is also stocked with rainbow trout.

Just downstream from the reservoir dam is a winding stretch of the **Crooked River** that offers some of the best fly-fishing in the state, in an incredibly scenic atmosphere beneath basalt rimrock cliffs. This section of the river is also dotted with a series of campgrounds, all of which are good places to camp and to fish. This is a good place to learn to fly fish; it's easy to wade into the water away from streamside brush. Non-anglers can climb the short trail up Chimney Rock (from the Chimney Rock campground) to the top of the rimrock. From there, it's possible to walk along the ridge all afternoon.

Ochoco Reservoir, six miles east of Prineville on U.S. 26, is a favorite recreational spot for locals, with year-round fishing, boating, and camping.

Camping

For good campsites in the Ochocos, take Ochoco Creek Road approximately 10 miles east of Ochoco Lake. Choices include **Ochoco Camp, Walton Lake,** where you can fish, boat, or hike the trail to Round Mountain, **Wildwood,** and **Ochoco Divide.** Open mid-April–late October, these campgrounds charge $10 per night. While on this loop, stop at the mining ghost town of **Mayflower.** Founded in 1873, the community was active until 1925. A stamp mill is still visible.

Camp alongside the Crooked River at any of the nine campgrounds on Route 27 about 15–20 miles south of Prineville. Be sure to bring water or be prepared to filter river water. Contact the BLM's Prineville office (541/416-6700) for more information on the area.

EVENTS

A popular Prineville get-together is the **Annual Prineville Rockhound Show and Powwow**

(P.O. Box 671, Prineville 97754, 541/447-6304), held in mid–late June. The powwow attracts prospectors and rockhounds from all over the country.

The end of July is the time and Prineville is the site for the **Crooked River Roundup,** with pari-mutuel horse racing. Check with the **Prineville-Crook County Chamber of Commerce** (390 N. Fairview St., 541/447-6304, www.visitprineville.com) for details on it and other area attractions.

ACCOMMODATIONS

The **Rustlers Inn Motel** (960 W. 3rd, Prineville 97754, 541/447-4185, $40 and up) was designed in the Old West style. Art by local artists and antique furniture grace the rooms.

A budget motel that's popular with anglers is **Executive Inn** (1050 E. 3rd, Prineville, 541/447-4152, www.executiveinnonline.com, $45 and up), east of downtown. The large multiroom family unit is recommended as a base for a family weekend visit to the Painted Hills as motel accommodations in Mitchell are limited.

More upscale accommodations are available at the **Stafford Inn** (1773 N.E. 3rd St., 541/447-7100 or 877/744-7100, $75 and up), near the east end of town next door to the Club Pioneer.

The **Prineville Reservoir Resort** (541/447-7468) is on the shoreline of Prineville Reservoir, 17 miles southeast of Prineville on the Paulina Highway (Rte. 27). This resort offers motel accommodations with kitchenettes starting at $75 for a double. Camping units go for $19. The resort also rents fishing boats, paddleboats, and motors.

FOOD

If you get hungry while in Prineville, try the folksy and inexpensive **Barr's Cafe** (887 N.

Main, 541/447-5897, breakfast $4–9). It's open 5 A.M.–10 P.M., with breakfast served all day. Another small-town classic with good breakfasts and large portions is **Dad's Place** (229 Main St., 541/447-7059, 5 A.M.–2 P.M. Tues–Fri., 7 A.M.–1 P.M. most Saturdays, breakfast $4–8).

For lunch, the **Sandwich Factory** (277 N.E. Court St., 541/447-4429, lunch Mon-Sat, most sandwiches $6–7), just west of the courthouse, has a huge menu of really good sandwiches. It's also a good place to people-watch at lunch—most of downtown Prineville seems to eat here.

Behind an uninviting exterior lies the most popular steak house in town: **Club Pioneer** (1851 E. 3rd St., 541/447-6177, dinner nightly, $14–21). The competition, downtown's **Barney Prine's Steakhouse and Saloon** (380 N. Main St., 541/447-3333, dinner nightly, $18–22), is a bit more stylish, with beechwood floors salvaged from a Jim Beam distillery and a good wine list.

Next door to Barney Prine's is the **Vineyard** (386 N. Main St., 541/447-1980, lunch and dinner Tues.–Sun., $10–22), a cheery Italian restaurant with homemade pasta and good salads and desserts. **Ranchero** (964 N.W. 3rd St., 541/316-0103, lunch and dinner daily, $6–15), next to the Rustler's Inn, has a great selection of south-of-the-border specialties, in the moderate price range.

INFORMATION

The **Prineville-Crook County Chamber of Commerce** (390 N. Fairview St., 541/447-6304, www.visitprineville.com) has a helpful staff and lots of information to dispense. The **Ochoco National Forest** (3160 N.E. 3rd St., Prineville 97754, 541/416-6500, www.fs.fed.us/r6/centraloregon) can offer details on hiking in the Ochocos; the website is an excellent resource of trail information, including maps.

Warm Springs and Lower Deschutes River

North of the Bend-Redmond area, the juniper-and-sage-lined roadsides and the fields of mint and wheat stand in welcome contrast to the malled-over main drags of central Oregon's biggest urban complex.

MADRAS

Madras (population 5,600) is mostly known as a supply town for the surrounding agricultural area, which in places comes right up to downtown's doorstep. West of town, the Crooked River, the Metolius, and the Deschutes join up and are impounded by Round Butte Dam to form Lake Billy Chinook. The main access to the lake is via Cove Palisades State Park. Downstream from the lake, the Deschutes River continues on its path to the Columbia. The most popular place for rafting the Deschutes is the area around Maupin, 47 miles north of Madras.

Madras is one of the region's most culturally diverse towns: just over 16 percent of the residents are Native American, and just under 15 percent are Latino.

Lake Billy Chinook

Heading north from Bend, outdoor recreationists needn't put away their gear. Just outside of Madras is a park that offers hiking, boating, fishing, waterskiing, and bird-watching. **Cove Palisades State Park** (541/546-3412 or 800/551-6949, www.oregonstateparks.org) is located 14 miles southwest of Madras, off U.S. 97. Towering cliffs, Cascade vistas, gnarled junipers, and Lake Billy Chinook with its 72-mile shoreline create a stunning backdrop for outdoor activities. The lake was created when Round Butte Dam backed up the waters of the Deschutes, Metolius, and Crooked Rivers. For the best views of how these rivers come together, hike up the Tam-a-lau Trail to the top of The Peninsula (a quick 600-foot elevation gain), a plateau of land between the backed-up Crooked and Deschutes rivers. At the top, the trail makes a loop around The Peninsula,

with good views onto the Cascades and the river canyons. In total, it's a six-mile round-trip, best done in the springtime when it's not too hot, and when the balsamroot and lupine are in bloom.

Two overnight campgrounds offer all the amenities: Deschutes Camp has 82 full-hookup sites and 92 tent sites (May–Sept.); the year-round Crooked River camp, perched right on the canyon rim, has 93 sites with electricity and water. Campsites cost $17–22; reserve sites through Oregon State Parks (800/452-5687); this is an extremely popular campground.

Richardson's Recreational Ranch

If you're a rockhound, you'll want to visit Richardson's Recreational Ranch, (541/475-2680 or 800/433-2680, www.richardsonrockranch.com, 7 A.M.–5 P.M. daily Apr.–Oct., $0.75 cents per pound). This family-owned and -operated enterprise has extensive rock beds loaded with thunder eggs, moss agates, jaspers, jasper agate, Oregon sunset, and rainbow agates and it is a huge hit with most kids. If you want to chip agates out of one of the many exposed ledges on the ranch, you will need to bring chisels, wedges, and other necessary hard-rock mining tools. Once you've completed your dig, you drop your rocks off at the office and pay for them by the pound. And if you don't care for dirt under your fingernails, you can always find rocks for sale from all over the world in the ranch's rock shop. To get there, take U.S. 97 north of Madras for 11 miles and turn right at the sign near Mile Marker 81. Follow the road for three miles to the ranch office. Free camping is available here for dedicated rockhounds.

Shaniko

A half hour northeast of Madras is the ghost town of Shaniko (www.shaniko.com). In its day, Shaniko was the largest wool-shipping center in the United States. The Columbia Southern railroad transported wool, sheep, cattle, gold, and people deep into the remote

Oregon outback, and the city at the terminus prospered. Boomtown Shaniko had 13 saloons, stores, hotels, a schoolhouse, and a city hall. But when the railroad's main line was diverted to the Deschutes River, Shaniko's prominence quickly faded.

Today you can still see many old buildings in Shaniko. The water tower provides a remarkable display of the jerry-rigged but nonetheless efficient water-distribution system. The three-room Shaniko schoolhouse (built in 1901) and City Hall, featuring the Constable's office and the jail, are also still standing. If you'd like to overnight here, the moderately priced **Shaniko Historic Hotel** (541/489-3441 or 800/483-3441) has been restored and combines the ambience of the past with modern comforts.

Accommodations and Food

Sonny's Motel (1539 S.W. U.S. 97, 541/475-7217 or 800/624-6137, $55 and up), on the south end of town is a good deal and allows pets. For more amenities, the **Best Western Madras Inn** (12 S.W. 4th St., 541/475-6141, $84) offers comfortable rooms and a small outdoor pool (quite nice on a hot afternoon in Madras).

A friend who spent a summer working in Madras claims to have eaten every meal at **Pepe's Mexican Bakery** (221 S.E. 5th Street, 541/475-3286, breakfast, lunch, and dinner daily, $5–10), which is not just a bakery, but a good all-around Mexican restaurant. Other folks swear by the tamales at **Martina's Market** (839 S.W. U.S. 97, 541/475-4469), which are available to go, if you want to stock up for your trip.

WARM SPRINGS INDIAN RESERVATION

The past lives on as more than a memory at the Warm Springs Indian Reservation (www.warmsprings.com), which straddles U.S. 26. Within this 600,000-acre bailiwick, you can see the age-old practice of dip-net fishing on the Deschutes, as well as the richest collection of tribal artifacts in the country at a 27,000-square-foot museum. Along with these touches of tradition, the reservation is the embodiment of the modern-day American dream, successfully operating a dam, a resort hotel, and a lumber mill. It's interesting to note that the employees of these enterprises are the descendants of the same Native Americans who greeted Lewis and Clark on the Columbia in 1805, as well as such Deschutes explorers as Peter Skene Ogden (in 1826), John Fremont, and Kit Carson (both in 1843).

(Museum at Warm Springs

You'll find an impressive display of tribal wealth at the Museum at Warm Springs (541/553-3331, 9 A.M.–5 P.M. daily, $6 adults, $5 seniors, $4.50 students and Native Americans with tribal ID, $3 children), located just east of the town of Warm Springs below the viewpoint at the bottom of the Deschutes River Canyon. Audiovisual displays, old photos, and tapes of traditional chants of the Paiute, Warm Springs, and Wasco peoples (the three tribes that live on the Warm Springs Reservation) are aesthetically arrayed here. Each tribe's distinct culture, along with the thriving social and economic community they collectively formed, constitutes the major themes of this museum.

Replicas of a Paiute mat lodge, a Warm Springs tepee, and a Wasco plank house, along with recordings of each tribe's language, underscore the cultural richness and diversity of the area's original inhabitants. The exhibits, culled from a collection of more than 20,000 artifacts, range from primitive prehistoric hand tools to a high-tech push-button-activated Wasco wedding scene. Tribal foodstuffs and art are on sale in the bookstore.

Kah-Nee-Ta

A good place to bring the family is **Kah-Nee-Ta Resort** (541/553-1112 or 800/554-4786, www.kah-nee-taresort.com). Located at the bottom of a canyon about a dozen miles off U.S. 26 from the town of Warm Springs, Kah-Nee-Ta basks in 300 days of sunshine a year. The 1,000-foot elevation and 12-inch annual rainfall enable golfers to play its championship course year-round. It's even snow-free in February. Owned by the Confederated Tribes of Warm Springs, this arrow-shaped hotel is the centerpiece of the 600,000-acre reservation, which includes a working ranch and wild horses.

Lodging possibilities include authentic te-pees from $73; hotel rooms, suites, and cottages range $140–250. The hot mineral baths and spring-fed Olympic-sized swimming pool are among the highlights here. There are also bike rentals, tennis, horseback riding, and hiking. There is a gaming resort on-site as well. Day visitors can take advantage of Kah-Nee-Ta's venerated hot spring pool and baths (included in overnight room rate) for $8. The kids are sure to enjoy the 140-foot water slide ($2).

The resort has two restaurants; the Chinook Room, (breakfast, lunch, and dinner daily year-round, $5–30) and the **Juniper Room** (open for dinner Memorial Day-Labor Day, main courses $20–30), which is the more elegant of the two, and worth the splurge for such native-inspired dishes as bird-in-clay (a game hen stewing in its own juices inside a clay mold). The summertime Saturday-night **salmon bake** ($26) featuring salmon cooked outside on cedar sticks over an alder fire is also a good bet.

MAUPIN

The riverside town of Maupin becomes a bit of a zoo on summer weekends, when river rafters descend on it. Most of the time, though, it's a pretty quiet place, catering mostly to anglers who come to fly-fish for the native Deschutes redside trout.

Sherar's Falls

Downstream from the Sandy Beach raft take-out is Sherar's Falls, a cascade that demands a portage if you're rafting to the Columbia. A bridge crosses the Deschutes just downstream from the falls. At the bottom of the falls is a traditional Native American fishing area, still used by Warm Springs tribal members. You'll see the rather rickety-looking fishing platforms perched over the river and you may also see people dip-netting from the platforms. If you're in the mood for tooling around, cross the bridge to the west side of the Deschutes and follow Route 216 a few miles to **White River Falls State Park,** a day-use park with another excellent waterfall and a short trail to the remains of an old hydroelectric power plant.

Rafting

Just about every tour company operating in central Oregon runs raft trips down the 13-mile "splash and giggle" stretch of the Deschutes, from Harpham Flat Campground to Sandy Beach, just above Sherar's Falls. Wapinita, Box Car, Oak Springs, White River, and Elevator rapids are the highlights of this trip; look also for the resident ospreys as you pass the Maupin bridge.

Sun Country Tours (531 S.W. 13th St., Bend, 541/382-6277 or 800/770-2161, www.suncountrytours.com) runs a full-day trip ($105 adults, $95 children) along the Harpham Flat–Sandy Beach stretch of the river. A hearty barbecued chicken lunch is included. Transportation from Bend or Sunriver to Maupin is also part of the day-trip packages.

Rapid River Rafters (1151 Centennial Ct., #5, Bend 97702, 541/382-1514 or 800/962-3327, www.rapidriverrafters.com) offers a series of full- and multiday packages on the Deschutes River. The one-day trip ($85) takes in 17 miles of the river from Harpham Flat to Lone Pine. A hearty lunch is included. The two-day trip ($275) floats 44 miles of exciting white water from Trout Creek to Sandy Beach. The three-day trip ($400) runs 55 miles from Warm Springs to Sandy Beach. On all of the multiday trips, the camping and meal preparations at pleasant riverside locations are taken care of by your veteran guides. Season runs late April–early October, and camping equipment is available for rent if you don't have your own.

Ouzel Outfitters (1441 S.W. Chandler, Bend, 541/385-5947 or 800/788-7238, www.oregonrafting.com) offers a full-day trip ($100) on the Lower Deschutes out of Maupin.

CENTRAL OREGON

Experienced rafters can rent a boat from **Allstar Rafting** (405 Deschutes Ave., 541/395-2201, from $80 per day for a raft, $30 per day for an inflatable kayak) or **River Trails Deschutes** (301 Bakeoven Rd., 541/395-2545 or 888/324-8837). Both of these Maupin outfitters also offer guided trips. Currently no permits are needed to run the river. There is a $2 per day per person fee collected by the Oregon State Parks at the Harpham Flat put-in site. Call **Affordable Deschutes Shuttle** (541/395-2809) if you need someone to take your car from put-in to take-out ($30 for Harpham Flat to Sandy Beach).

Fishing

Downstream from Maupin, anglers fish the Deschutes year-round for trout; August–November, steelhead are in the river. Part of the reason to fish here, especially in the spring and fall, is the beautiful canyon.

Deschutes Canyon Fly Shop (599 S. U.S. 197, 541/395-2565 or 866/647-4721) sells supplies and can advise you on the hatches and other conditions. They can also set you up with a guide (about $400 per day). John, the shop's owner, is very helpful, and really encourages female anglers. Maupin's other fly shop, the **Deschutes Angler Fly Shop** (504 Deschutes Ave., 877/395-0995), is also worth a visit for both gear and information. The owners of this shop are experts on Spey casting, a two-handed technique, and they hold regular casting clinics. The **Oasis Resort** (609 S. U.S. 197, 541/395-2611) also runs a guide service.

Camping

Right in town, the **Maupin City Park** (Bakeoven Rd., just downstream from the bridge, 541/395-2252) is on a grassy riverbank lot. Unlike almost all of the BLM campgrounds along the Deschutes, the city park has water and showers.

Both upstream and downstream from Maupin are a number of riverside BLM campgrounds. Bring water, or be prepared to filter it from the river. **Harpham Flat Campground** is the main launching spot for day trips on the Deschutes, and this place can be a little wilder than the neighboring campgrounds. The nicest spots are actually a ways downstream from Maupin, at **Beavertail** and **Macks Canyon,** 21 and 29 miles north of Maupin, respectively.

Accommodations and Food

If you don't want to camp, stay in a cabin at the **Oasis Resort** (609 S. U.S. 197, 541/395-2611, $35–75). The **Deschutes Motel** (616 Mill St., 541/395-2626, www.deschutesmotel.com, $61) is above the river near Maupin's main downtown area. The fanciest place in Maupin is the **Imperial River Company** (304 Bakeoven Rd., 541/395-2404, www.deschutesriver.com, $75 and up), which has a riverside lodge. Some rooms have balconies overlooking the river and all are nicely decorated and quite comfortable.

Eat a hearty pre-float breakfast at the **Oasis**—it's also a good place for a burger or casual dinner. **Imperial River Company** also serves breakfast, lunch, and dinner, featuring steaks from the family cattle. However, the eatery that is most attractive to rafters coming off a hot day on the river is the ice cream shop by the bridge.

NORTHEASTERN OREGON

Oregon's northeastern corner offers plenty of places to escape from the modern urban world—nearly all of them highly scenic and filled with fascinating history. Stretching over 200 miles east to west, from the canyon-trenching Snake River the fossil-rich John Day River country, this part of Oregon is part of the larger Columbia Basin, a vast lava plateau that encompasses much of eastern Washington and Oregon. Two features characterize this epic landscape: mountains and canyons. Imagine a sea of molten lava, with mountain ranges rising like islands above the steaming, cooling basalt, and you have a snapshot of the region's geologic history. Rivers have cut mighty canyons through the banded layers of basalt, creating awe-inspiring clefts that, among other things, expose the fossil remains of ancient life.

For jaw-dropping scenic grandeur and outdoor recreation, the area is hard to top. The magnificent Wallowa Mountains easily invoke comparisons to the Swiss Alps, and are topped by 10,004-foot Matterhorn and 9,933-foot Sacajawea Peak. Hells Canyon, carved by the Snake River, is one the deepest river-carved gorges in the world, averaging 6,600 feet in depth. Inside the canyon, a 67-mile stretch of the Snake is now one of the nation's protected Wild and Scenic Rivers. West of the Wallowas rise the Blue Mountains. The high country of the Blue Mountains was often filled with snow by September, when Oregon Trail pioneers crossed these mountain passes. With its headwaters in the Blue Mountains, the John Day River cuts one of Oregon's most dramatic canyons, with fascinating fossil beds and a new

© JUDY JEWELL

HIGHLIGHTS

(**John Day Fossil Beds National Monument:** At these three separate fossil bed units in the canyons of the John Day River, you'll learn about saber-toothed tigers and wind through one of eastern Oregon's top road trips, linking remote outposts of Miocene-era life (page 463).

(**Kam Wah Chung and Company Museum:** This is a fascinating remnant of a forgotten history, when Chinese laborers outnumbered white settlers in gold camps of the West (page 466).

(**Pendleton Underground Tours:** Service tunnels formed their own network of businesses in 1880s Pendleton, and these tours explore everything from Chinese jail to brothel, the true underground of frontier life (page 471).

(**Hot Lake Mineral Hot Springs:** Beside one of the world's largest hot springs,

a bronze foundry revives a century-old resort (page 476).

(**Eagle Cap Excursion Train:** Explore the canyons and meadows of the Wallowa Valley on this vintage tour train (page 479).

(**Wallowa Lake Tramway:** Hitch a ride on a gondola and whiz to the top of Mount Howard, with views over the Wallowa Mountains and nearby Hells Canyon (page 484).

(**Hells Canyon National Recreation Area:** The world's deepest river gorge is trenched by the Snake River, and the best way to see this otherwise almost inaccessible canyon is by raft or jet boat (page 489).

(**National Historic Oregon Trail Interpretive Center:** This excellent museum tells the story of the Oregon Trail pioneers and their treacherous traversal of the West (page 492).

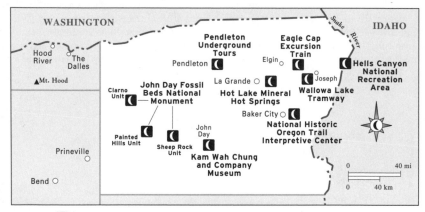

LOOK FOR (TO FIND RECOMMENDED SIGHTS, ACTIVITIES, DINING, AND LODGING.

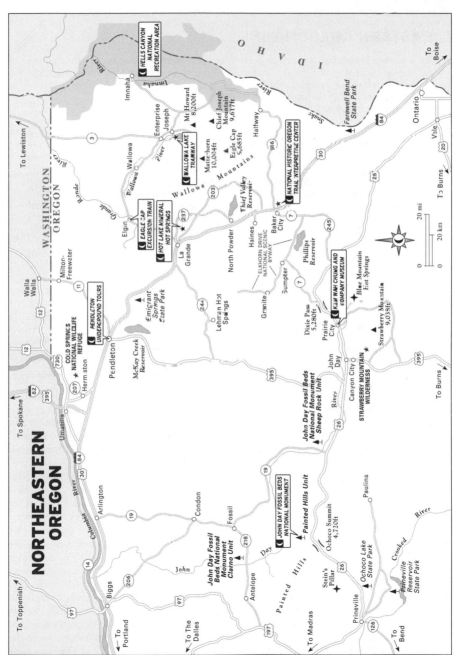

© AVALON TRAVEL PUBLISHING, INC.

EASTERN OREGON WINE

While eastern Oregon doesn't offer an abundance of wineries, a number of wine-makers have pioneered wine production amid the region's sagebrush and wheat fields. Near John Day, in the little town of Mt. Vernon, **David Hamilton Winery** (541/932-4567, davidhamiltonwinery.com) makes a large variety of fruit wines, including wines made apples, apricots, huckleberries, and elderberries. While these wines aren't particularly made to accompany meals, they are delicious to sip on their own, tasting like "summer in a bottle." The winery also makes unusual wines, such as those made from wild rose petals and pomegranates. The tasting room (150 Mountain Blvd., Mt. Vernon) is open noon–5 P.M. Friday–Sunday year-round.

Out on the flanks of the Wallowa Mountains is **Gilstrap Brothers Vineyard & Winery** (69789 Antles Ln., Cove, 541/568-4646, www.gilstrapbrothers.com), which makes high-quality merlot, syrah, and other red wines. One particularly good choice is CSM, a red blend. Another interesting variety is Kuhlman Foch, a little-known French hybrid grape that thrives

in the robust winters of eastern Oregon. The Gilstrap Brothers don't have regular tasting-room hours but are happy to schedule tasting appointments when you call.

Up north of Pendleton, straddling the Oregon/Washington border is the Walla Walla wine country, one of the most exciting wine regions in the Pacific Northwest, if not in the country. The long hot growing season favors the grapes of the Bordeaux region of France, and the cabernet sauvignon and merlot wines made here rival those of Napa and Sonoma Valleys, according to wine enthusiasts. What many wine lovers don't realize is that a third of the sanctioned Walla Walla AVA (American Viticultural Area) is in Oregon. While there are many vineyards in this part of Oregon, there's only one Oregon winery operating in this AVA. **Zerba Cellars** (85530 Hwy. 11, Milton-Freewater, 541/938-9463, www.zerbacellars.com) offers a number of Bordeaux-style wines, including a cabernet franc, and chardonnay as well as an intriguing syrah ice wine. The log-cabin tasting room is open noon–5 P.M. Monday–Saturday and noon–4 P.M. Sunday.

interpretive center to help make sense of the region's long-buried natural history.

Just as the fossil beds provide a cross section of the earth's history, a trip through northeastern Oregon will give you a feel for the leather-tough people who settled here. In country towns and larger cities like Baker City, La Grande, and Pendleton, history is not very old. What may seem like the Old West is still a way of life here. And while it remains primarily rural ranch country, the area is becoming an increasingly popular haven for artists, sculptors, and writers.

PLANNING YOUR TIME

For many travelers on a road trip, northeastern Oregon will either be the first or the last part of Oregon they will encounter. If the Willamette Valley or the Oregon coast is the focus of your Oregon vacation you might find it tempting to

hurtle right through this corner of the state on I-84. However, plan to devote at least a day or two here to explore the area's rich history and astoundingly dramatic scenery. Don't forget: The world's deepest river gorge is here, as are some of its richest fossil beds.

Our first piece of advice? Get off the freeway. Yes, of course I-84 is the fastest way across northeastern Oregon but there are many other routes that don't take much more time (if your destination is western Oregon) and offer a lot in return. From Ontario, consider crossing the state on either U.S 20 or U.S 26. Although these routes parallel each other across the state, they offer quite different aspects. U.S. 20 edges along the northern boundary of the Great Basin desert (and is covered more completely in this book's *Southeastern Oregon* chapter) while U.S. 26 travels through pine-clad mountains to the John Day River Valley, one of Oregon's most scenic. The river trenches through a layer cake of dramatic geologic formations to expose the **John Day Fossil Beds National Monument.** Even if you stay closer to the freeway, consider branching off and making a loop around the **Wallowa Mountains,** a soaring piece of real estate that contains 17 individual peaks over 9,000 feet high. This side road also takes you to the brink of **Hells Canyon,** where the Snake River carves a gorge beneath 6,500-foot cliffs.

If you do stick to I-84 and the fast track, at least realize that this route parallels the original Oregon Trail, the wagon route that brought in upwards of 50,000 pioneers to the Northwest 1843–1860. Stop at the **National Historic Oregon Trail Visitor Center** near Baker City to learn more about this great human migration. Then pull off the freeway at Pendleton to experience the city's colorful past on **Pendleton Underground Tours,** which explores an subterranean business district and a brothel from the turn of the 20th century.

John Day Fossil Beds and Vicinity

The canyon-cutting John Day River drains the western slopes of the Blue Mountains, trenching through north-central Oregon before spilling into the Columbia River. The John Day River valley also offers some of Oregon's most tantalizing history plus fascinating glimpses into the region's prehistory. In the 1860s, self-taught geologist Thomas Condon discovered what is now known as the John Day Fossil Beds. These archives of stone provide a paleontological record of 40-plus million years of ancient life.

◖ JOHN DAY FOSSIL BEDS NATIONAL MONUMENT

The 14,000-acre John Day Fossil Beds National Monument is divided into three areas: the Sheep Rock Unit, located about 40 miles west of John Day, with a new visitors center; the Painted Hills Unit, another 45 miles farther west; and the Clarno Unit, located northwest of the other units, about 20 miles from the town of Fossil. For further information, contact John Day Fossil Beds National Monument (32651 Highway 19, Kimberly, OR 97848-9701 or 541/987-2333, www.nps.gov/joda). Admission is free to all units of the monument.

The days of 50-ton brontosaurs and 50-foot-long crocodiles, as well as delicate ferns and flowers, are captured in the rock formations of the three beds, easily visited in a day's road trip. This is the richest concentration of pre-historic early mammal and plant fossils in the world. More than 120 species have been identified here, documenting a period dating from the extinction of the dinosaurs to the beginning of the last great ice age.

Accommodations are in short supply in this remote part of Oregon. The small towns near the monument's individual units have motels, though the town of John Day has the largest selection.

The Painted Hills

The highly photogenic Painted Hills are a series of low slung hills banded with highly differentiated colors, formed when a series of volcanic eruptions around 30 million years ago deposited red, yellow, ochre, grey, and black-hued ash into drifts hundreds of feet deep. Erosion has cut through the multi-colored layers and sculpted the hills into soft mounds. While many tourists are satisfied with snapping photos from the monument's parking lot, easy hiking trails lead to more interesting vistas.

The 0.5-mile **Painted Hills Overlook Trail** provides a view of mineral-bearing clays exposed by erosion. Near the junction with the road and the preceding trail is the 1.5-mile **Carroll Rim Trail,** with a spectacular all-encompassing view of the Painted Hills. The **High Desert Trail** is a three-mile loop into the desert for those seeking the quiet and the solitude of the big empty. Enjoy deep yellows,

NORTHEASTERN OREGON

browns, and reds thanks to the multihued volcanic debris that piled up centuries ago.

But the most vivid colors of all are found at the **Painted Cove Trail.** Viewing the red mounds up close is a highlight. A printed trail guide is available at the trailhead. Close by, the **Leaf Hill Trail** will lead you to remnants of a 30-million-year-old hardwood forest. Walking on the hill itself is prohibited, but take a look at the exhibit describing how our knowledge of Oregon's most ancient forests emanated from studies of this area. It's common knowledge among wildflower buffs that the springtime display here is exceptional.

To reach the Painted Hills drive three miles west of Mitchell on U.S. 26 and turn left at the sign and travel six miles along Bridge Creek to the site. Stop first at the visitors center to get oriented and fill your canteen. Although the view from the road is impressive, you really have to get out and hike the trails to literally get the picture.

Mitchell is the closest town to the Painted Hills, offering lodging in the basic **Sky Hook Motel** (101 U.S. 26, 541/462-3569, doubles from $50) and the historic **Oregon Hotel** (104 E. Main, 541/462-3027, doubles from $65), which offers continental breakfast and pleasantly vintage guest rooms. Several hotels have been on this site since the 1800s, with the current incarnation dating back to 1938. The historic photos in the lobby recount three catastrophic floods that have hit this town. Choose between distinctively decorated rooms (some with shared bath) and a set of duplexes in back. The **Bridge Creek Café** (218 U.S. 26, 541/462-3434) is Mitchell's family restaurant, open for three meals daily.

The Clarno Unit

Right on the John Day River, the Clarno Formations are the monument's oldest and most remote. The 40-million-year-old Clarno Unit exposes mudflows that washed over an Eocene-era forest. The Clarno Unit's petrified mudslides is one of the few places in the world where stems of ancient plants, as well as their leaves, seeds, and nuts, are preserved in the

© BILL MCRAE

Ancient muds form the Clarno Unit of the John Day Fossil Beds National Monument.

same location. Fossilized imprints of palm, gingko, and magnolia leaves culled from volcanic mudflows point to a subtropical forest capable of supporting flowering trees. The formations eroded into distinctive, chalky-white cliffs topped with spires and turrets of stone. The **Clarno Arch Trail** leads you into the formations where boulder-sized fossils containing logs, seeds, and other remains of an ancient forest await. Picnic facilities, drinking water, and restrooms are available at the monument.

The Clarno Formations are 18 miles west of the small and aptly named town of **Fossil** on Route 218. When traveling in the John Day country, Fossil makes an intriguing and perhaps necessary stop—in this remote area, chances are you'll need to gas up or get a bite to eat, and the Old West town of Fossil has a full range of services for travelers. Fossil also offers fossils: When the townspeople began digging into a hillside to build a football field, they exposed an ancient lakebed rich with fossil leaf prints and petrified wood. The site (just behind the high school) is open to amateur fossil hunters for a $3 fee.

The closest facilities to the Clarno Unit are in Fossil. The **Bridge Creek Flora Inn** and the **Fossil Lodge** (828 Main St, 541/763-2355, www.fossilinn.com, doubles from $65) are adjacent historic homes under the same ownership, and are both now comfortable B&Bs that invite you to "sleep in a fossil bed." These inns are near the public fossil-digging beds, feature rooms with private as well as shared baths, and are definitely the best lodging in this town of 400 people. The **Big Timber Family Restaurant** (540 First St., 541/763-4328) offers tasty American fare and is open for three meals daily. Twenty miles north of Fossil is the town of **Condon,** where the town's landmark 1920s hotel has been completely refurbished, updated, and reopened as (**Hotel Condon** (202 S. Main St., 541/384-4624 or 800/201-6706, www.hotelcondon.com, doubles from $70). With a fireplace-dominated dining room, cozy bar, and comfortable guest rooms, Hotel Condon is one of the swankest lodging choices in this part of Oregon.

Sheep Rock Unit

The Sheep Rock Unit is the largest of the monument's three divisions, and offers the most visitor facilities. The new **Thomas Condon Paleontology Center** (eight miles northwest of Dayville, 541/987-2333, www.nps.gov/joda, 8:30 A.M.–4:30 P.M. daily, free admission) serves as the monument's visitors center. It features a fossil museum with exceptional discoveries from local digs, a maze-like series of dioramas, and displays telling the geological and biological history of the fossil beds—plus short films that help explain the area's prehistory and current research. **The Cant Ranch House,** formerly the park visitors center, is a handsome 1917 ranch house across the highway from the new paleontology center that now houses a museum on the human history of the ranch and area. A former bunkhouse and a small log cabin behind the ranch house contain additional exhibits on fossil history. The tree-shaded grounds surrounding the ranch house are perfect for picnicking and short trails lead to the fast-flowing John Day River.

North of the visitors centers on Route 19 are two fossil viewing areas. Two miles north is the parking area for **Blue Basin,** with several hiking trails leading into fossil-rich formations. The mile-long **Island in Time Trail** climbs into a badlands basin of highly eroded, uncannily green sediments. Along the trail are displays that reveal fossils protruding from the soil. The trail dead-ends at a natural box canyon; high around are barren, castellated walls rich in 25-million-year-old life forms. The **Overlook Trail** offers a longer three-mile loop to the rim of Blue Basin with views over the fossil beds and the layer-cake topography of the John Day Valley.

Two miles further north, at the day-use **Foree Picnic Area** are more hiking trails that explore green mud-stone formations capped with basalt from ancient lava flows.

The drive between the junction of Route 19 and U.S. 26 and the small community of Spray is highly scenic, interesting geology and spectacular scenery don't always occur together but they form an amazing team here. Along this route you'll see **Sheep Rock,** a steep-sided mesa rising hundreds of feet to a small rock cap, and **Cathedral Rock,** where erosion has stripped away a hillside to reveal highly colored sediments beneath a thick overlay of basalt. Most astonishing of all is **Picture Gorge,** where the John Day River rips through an immense 1,500-foot-high lava flow and begins trenching its canyon to the Columbia River. The gorge, wide enough only for the river and the road, is named for the pictographs drawn there by early Indians; look for them near Mile Marker 125, on the west side of the road.

The Sheep Rock Unit of the John Day Fossil Beds is eight miles northwest of Dayville, and 40 miles from John Day.

The closest lodgings to the Sheep Rock Unit are in the tiny community of Dayville, where the **Fish House Inn** (110 Franklin, 541/987-2124 or 888/286-3474, www.fishhouseinn.com, doubles from $50) offers B&B accommodation in a vintage Craftsman home. These pleasant digs are decorated with antique farm tools and fishing gear, hence the inn's name.

RV and tent camping sites are also available. The inn is in the process of opening a steak house and also offers barbecue facilities to its guests, with dinner-makings available from a historical grocery, the century-old Dayville Mercantile on U.S. 26. More dining options are available in John Day, 30 miles east.

The most comfortable campground in the area is **Clyde Holliday State Park** (seven miles west of John Day, 33 miles east of the Sheep Rock Unit, 541/923-4453). In addition to shaded hookups for $17 and hiker/biker sites for $5 near the John Day River, the park offers showers and interpretive events on the nearby fossil beds. The park is located off U.S. 26 between the towns of John Day and Mt. Vernon.

JOHN DAY AND ENVIRONS

The early history of John Day and nearby Canyon City centers around the discovery of gold in 1862. According to most estimates, $26 million in gold was taken out of the steams and mines in the Strawberry Mountains. At the peak of the gold rush, Whiskey Flat, later called Canyon City, was populated by 5,000 miners, which made it larger than Portland at the time. Thousands of Chinese immigrated to the area to work the tailings, or leftovers, from the mines. Their fascinating history is vividly retold at the Kam Wah Chung and Company Museum in John Day.

One of the more colorful denizens of Canyon City was the celebrated poet Joaquin Miller, who served as the first elected judge in Grant County. Known as the "Byron of Oregon," this dashing figure dressed like Buffalo Bill and recited his florid sonnets to a baffled audience of miners.

Today John Day is principally a market town for local farmers and ranchers, with adequate facilities for travelers passing through to visit nearby fossil beds or hike in the lovely Strawberry Mountains.

(Kam Wah Chung and Company Museum

A must-stop in the town of John Day, the Kam Wah Chung and Company Museum

WHO WAS JOHN DAY?

John Day is such a common name in this part of Oregon (it is affixed to a river, two towns, a dam, a series of fossil beds, a valley and several parks) that you might assume the original John Day had been a early pioneer settler. In fact, the eponymous John Day never visited any of the places that now carry his name. A hunter from Virginia, Day was hired to provide meat for the Pacific Fur Company expedition led by Wilson Price Hunt in 1812. Thirty miles east of The Dalles, near what was then known as the Mau Hau River, Day and another mountain man were ambushed by Native Americans, who robbed them and left them naked and injured. The two survived the ordeal and eventually made their way to Fort Astoria. The Mau Hau River soon became known as Day's River; mapmakers later changed it to the John Day River and the name spread like wildfire. Even at Astoria, John Day's place-naming achievement continued: A *second* John Day River flows into the Columbia just east of Astoria.

(250 N.W. Canton, 541/575-2800, www.oregon.gov/oprd/parks, 9 A.M.–5 P.M. daily May–Oct., free admission) was the center of Chinese life in the John Day area, serving as a general store and pharmacy with over 500 herbs. People came from hundreds of miles away for the herbal remedies of Doc Hay, who lived here. The building also served in more limited capacities as an assay office, fortune-teller's studio, and Taoist shrine.

It began as a trading post on The Dalles Military Road in 1866. With the influx of Chinese to the area during the gold rush, the outpost was purchased in 1887 by two Chinese apothecaries and evolved into a center for Asian medicine, trade, and spirituality. It remained a gathering place for the Chinese community in eastern Oregon until the early 1940s. While it admirably fulfilled this role, the opium-blackened walls, bootleg whiskey, and gambling paraphernalia here evidence the less salutary aspects of the Kam Wah Chung lifestyle. At the time of the 1879 census, eastern Oregon had 960 East Coast emigrants and 2,468 Chinese, proof that the current museum is not an arcane exhibit but rather a significant window on the past. In fact, in 1983, scholars from China came to categorize the herbs and religious objects here.

It's the little touches in the faithfully restored building that stay with you. First your eye will be drawn to the metal shutters and outside wooden staircase on this rough stone edifice. Inside, there's a locked and barred herb cage where Ing Hay prepared medicine and where gold dust was weighed. A Taoist shrine graces the room where groceries and opium were dispensed. In addition to the herbal remedies arrayed in cigar boxes labeled with Chinese calligraphy, there are vintage photos, old tools, furnishings, and other artifacts. Even the labels on the old canned goods are fascinating. Finally, the meat cleaver by Doc Hay's bed bespeaks the fear and despair of Chinese life here near the turn of the century.

Grant County Historical Museum

Another repository of local history, the Grant County Historical Museum (541/575-0509, 9 A.M.–4:30 P.M. Mon.–Sat, May 15–Sept. 30, $4 adult, $3.50 seniors, $2 children 6–17, free for children five and under) in is Canyon City, a couple of miles south of John Day on U.S. 395. Centered in the heart of Oregon's mining and ranching country, the facility's wealth of memorabilia depicts the early days of Grant County and includes an extensive rock collection plus Chinese and Native American items. The main focus of the museum is the 1860s gold rush, with displays of vintage mine equipment and household items. Miners' cabins and a jail building stand in the courtyard.

'62 Days Celebration

If you're in Canyon City in mid-June, plan to attend the '62 Days Celebration, which commemorates the local discovery of gold in 1862

with a parade, country music dance, medicine-wagon show, street fair, period costumes, and a reenactment of the opening of historic Sel's Brewery. Contact the Grant County Chamber (541/575-0547) for more information.

Accommodations

The **Best Western John Day Inn** (315 W. Main St., 541/932-4451 or 800/668-8919, doubles from $60) is the top lodging choice in John Day, with comfortable rooms, fitness center, indoor pool, and free high-speed Internet access. A family restaurant is adjacent. The **Dreamers Lodge** (144 N. Canyon St., 541/575-0526 or 800/654-2849, doubles from $50), a classic, well-maintained motor court motel, is close to town center but on a quiet side street.

Food

The popular **Outpost Pizza, Pub and Grill** (201 W. Main, 541/575-0250, three meals daily) offers a broad menu of American-style favorites, with pasta dishes at $11 and steaks starting at $15. The **Grubsteak Mining Co.** (149 E. Main St., 541/575-1970, three meals daily, $13–21) is John Day's long-established steak house, but you can also order pizza from the same worthy kitchen at the adjacent Dirty Shame Tavern.

Information

For information on John Day and vicinity, contact the **Grant County Chamber of Commerce** (281 W. Main St., John Day, OR 97845, 541/757-0547 or 800/769-5664, www.grantcounty.cc). The Malheur National Forest and the BLM share an office at 431 Paterson Bridge Road, 541/575-3000.

STRAWBERRY MOUNTAINS AND VICINITY

Thirteen miles east of John Day, the landscape becomes more mountainous and forests begin to encroach on the ranchland. **Prairie City** is an attractive small town in this lovely locale. The **Dewitt Museum** (Bridge Street, 541/820-3598, www.grantcounty.cc, 10 A.M.–3 P.M.

© JUDY JEWELL

Strawberry Lake, south of Prairie City, is a short hike up the trail.

Thurs.–Sat., May 15–Oct. 15) is housed in the Sumpter Valley Railroad's old depot, which operated between Baker City and Prairie City from 1909 until 1947. The building was restored in 1979 and today has 10 rooms full of artifacts from Grant County's early days.

Just south of Prairie City are the Strawberry Mountains, a pocket mountain range that offers a good system of trails, seven lakes, volcanic rock formations, and, if you're lucky, glimpses of bighorn sheep. Set up your base camp at **Strawberry Campground,** 11 miles south of Prairie City on County Route 60, then two miles west on Forest Service Road 6001. Open June–mid-October, Strawberry's fees are $7 per night. The campground is next to Strawberry Creek and is the trailhead for jaunts to Strawberry Lake, Strawberry Falls, and Strawberry Mountain. As you might guess, chances are good that you'll find some wild berries along the way!

For information on Strawberry Mountain hiking, contact the Prairie City Ranger District at the Malheur National Forest office (P.O. Box 337, Prairie City 97869, 541/820-3311). Ask about the 11-mile loop circumnavigating 9,000-foot Strawberry Mountain.

Accommodations and Food

Prairie City's most pleasant place to stay is the **Strawberry Mountain Inn B&B** (710 N.E. Front St., 541/820-4522 or 800/545-6913, www.strawberrymountaininn.com, doubles from $85), with five guest rooms in a turn-of-the-20th-century Craftsman home. A full breakfast is included in the rates. **Depot Park,** which surrounds the DeWitt Museum, also offers both RV and tent camping (541/820-3605). If you're hungry, try **Chuck's Little Diner** (142 Front St., 541/820-4353, three meals daily) for down-home cooking and reasonable prices.

Pendleton

For a lot of people in the West, Pendleton is synonymous with rodeo and woolens, both pointing to the city's intriguing history as a frontier trade settlement. Pendleton still has Western spirit to spare, but proximity to the highly successful wineries in Washington's Walla Walla Valley is bringing change to this bastion of Cowboy Country. With ranchers planting their cattle pastures to cabernet, can wine bistros and boutique hotels be far behind?

Pendleton is in the midst of a fascinating evolution, an authentic Western community on the fast track to reinvention as a 21st-century lifestyle destination.

With a population of 17,000, Pendleton is the largest city in eastern Oregon. It's an economic force thanks to vast wheat fields (Umatilla County ranks fifth in the nation in wheat production), rows of green peas, its famous woolen mills, and tourism from the Pendleton

NORTHEASTERN OREGON

PENDLETON

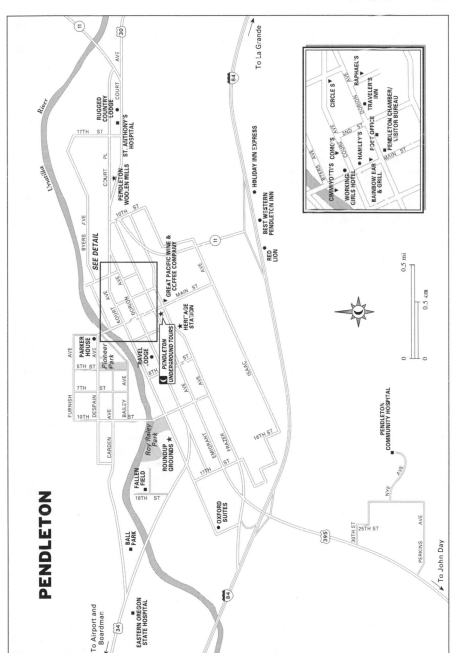

NORTHEASTERN OREGON

© AVALON TRAVEL PUBLISHING, INC.

TAMASTSLIKT CULTURAL INSTITUTE

The Confederated Tribes of the Umatilla Indian Reservation – which include the Walla Walla, Umatilla, and Cayuse nations – had little reason to celebrate the 150th anniversary of the Oregon Trail, which was marked by celebrations in other parts of the West. For these eastern Oregon tribes, the Oregon Trail led to war and to a huge loss of land and people. The tribes felt that it was important for their view of the Oregon Trail story to be told, and built the $18 million **Tamastslikt Cultural Institute,** (72789 Highway 331, 541/966-9748 or 800/654-9453, 9 a.m.-5 p.m. daily Apr.-Oct., closed Sun. Nov.-Mar., $6 adult, $4 senior and student, $12 family) which opened in 1998. Comprising 45,000 square feet, this cultural center describes the effects that European-American settlement have had on the region's original inhabitants. Exhibits depict tribal life prior to the pioneers' arrival; the impact of the horse (brought to North America by Europeans) on native peoples; and an Oregon Trail retrospective from the point of view of the Cayuse, Umatilla, and Walla Walla tribes.

The trail, which passed through the current reservation site, created such long-term environmental problems as diminished salmon runs and deforestation in the Blue Mountains. White settlement also brought chicken pox, tobacco, alcohol, syphilis, tuberculosis, and measles to native communities. Today, nuclear wastes are transported along I-84, paralleling the ruts where prairie schooners once traveled.

The interpretive center adds a living encampment, interpretive trails, and an outdoor amphitheater. Sharing this 640-acre site at the base of the Blue Mountains is a casino, golf course, RV park, motel, and restaurant.

The institute is six miles east of Pendleton on I-84, and one mile north of Exit 216.

Round-Up, the September rodeo and weeklong party that brings in cowboys, cowgirls, and the crowds that love them. The climate is mild and dry, with an average temperature of 51°F and annual rainfall of 13 inches (Locals joke that this is where summer spends the winter). Fall is usually long and sunny, making this an excellent climate for raising wine grapes. It's a little-noted fact that over a third of the Walla Walla Valley American Viticultural Area (AVA) is in Oregon, just north of Pendleton.

Located on I-84 equidistant from Portland, Seattle, Spokane, and Boise (a little over 200 miles from each), Pendleton sits pretty much by itself in the midst of wide-open spaces, beneath the lumpy peaks of the Blue Mountains. Residents—and an increasing flow of visitors—seem to like it that way.

HISTORY

Pendleton, originally called Goodwin's Station, is situated two miles downriver from the Oregon Trail's crossing at Emigrant Springs State Park. The ancient homeland of the Umatilla tribe, the area was visited by Lewis and Clark in 1805 and John Jacob Astor's American Fur Company in 1812. No Europeans established roots until 1843, when Methodist missionaries led by Dr. Marcus Whitman brought 1,000 settlers and 1,300 cattle to the region.

The town itself, named after Senator George Hunt Pendleton, was founded in 1868 and incorporated in 1880. At that time, Pendleton consisted of a hotel and five houses. But it grew through the late 1880s into a rip-snorting cattle and farming center with 18 houses of negotiable affection and 32 saloons. It quickly gained the reputation of being the town that couldn't be tamed. The feistiness of the citizens was demonstrated by the theft of the county seal and records from Umatilla Landing, thus making Pendleton the county seat.

SIGHTS
Pendleton Woolen Mills

Next to the Pendleton Round-Up, the town is best known for the Pendleton Woolen Mills (1307 S.E. Court Pl., 541/276-6911), where they make those immortal plaid shirts. After shearing, the wool goes to a scouring mill near Portland where it's graded, sorted, and washed. Then the dried wool returns to the Pendleton mill for dyeing, carding, spinning, rewinding, and weaving.

The business began over in the Willamette Valley in Brownsville when Thomas Kay, a Yorkshire man whose family was in the woolen business in England, started a weaving mill. His descendant, Clarence Bishop, founded the Pendleton facility. Production began here in 1909 with Native American–style blankets, which are still going strong, along with men's and women's sportswear.

Pendleton produces several different labels. The all-wool "Pendleton" blankets are the most extensively marketed to the public. The "Beaver State" blankets are made with a pure fleece wool filling and are heavier, with more intricate designs than the Pendletons; they're also more expensive. The "Cayuse Blanket" is a lower-priced version of the "Beaver State." Pendleton carved its lucrative niche by copying traditional designs for blankets used by Native Americans in Arizona and New Mexico. It introduced Western-style woolen shirts in the 1920s.

Tours run Monday–Saturday, March–October; exact tour times vary. Large groups are asked to make an appointment. To get to the mills, take Exit 207 and follow Dorion Street through Pendleton. Do not cross the viaduct, but turn left and proceed four blocks.

Heritage Station: The Umatilla County Historical Society Museum

In 1881 the Oregon–Washington Railway and Navigation Company, a subsidiary of the Union Pacific Railroad, constructed the northern branch of its transcontinental railroad through northeastern Oregon, and Pendleton served as an important stop on the route. By 1910, Pendleton had become the second-largest city in eastern Oregon, meriting a new railroad depot.

The building (108 S.W. Frazer, Pendleton 97801, 541/276-0012, www.umatillahistory.

org, 10 A.M.–4 P.M. Tues.–Sat,), an adaptation of the California Mission style, boasts multipaneled windows, decorative brickwork, and wide, flaring eaves. The depot no longer serves railroad passengers but instead houses the Umatilla County Historical Society's collection of Oregon Trail pioneer and Native American artifacts. Gold miners, sheep ranchers, and moonshiners are also given attention here in well-designed displays.

◖ Pendleton Underground Tours

One of the area's liveliest attractions is Pendleton Underground Tours (37 S.W. Emigrant Ave., 541/276-0730 or 800/226-6398, www.pendletonundergroundtours.com). This visit to the wild and woolly days of the Old West takes you through the tunnels underneath the downtown historic district. At one time a series of 90 passageways, originally dug as freight tunnels by Chinese workers who weren't allowed to walk above ground, crisscrossed beneath the downtown area. During the Prohibition era, bootleggers, gamblers, opium dealers, and Chinese railroad laborers frequented the businesses that developed here.

The tour starts at S.W. 1st and Emigrant and continues to the old Shamrock Cardroom, filled with the bouncy sounds of honky-tonk music, where bartenders were once paid with gold dust. From there, it's on to Hop Sing's laundry and bathhouse (a Prohibition speakeasy with secret escapes and a dank opium den), and the Empire Meat Company, complete with mannequins. The tour finishes in the well-preserved Cozy Rooms Bordello. After this tour you'll understand how the old town of 3,000 once supported 32 saloons and 18 bordellos.

Open 9:30 A.M.–3 P.M., Monday–Saturday, March–October. Exact tour times vary according to demand, so stop by or call to find out when tours are scheduled. Tours continue in winter, though by reservation, so call ahead to schedule. Admission is $10. Tours run 90 minutes; reservations are recommended. To get here from I-84, take Exit 209 and turn north into Pendleton. Continue up Emigrant Avenue to S.W. 1st Street.

EVENTS

Pendleton Round-Up

In 1910, Pendleton farmers and ranchers got together to celebrate the end of the wheat harvest. This was the first year of the Pendleton Round-Up (P.O. Box 609, Pendleton 97801, 541/276-2553, www.pendletonroundup.com). The annual event now draws 45,000 rodeo fans in the grand tradition started by legendary rodeo stars like Jackson Sundown and Yakima Canutt.

Held in mid-September, this high spirited week-long celebration includes a lot more than just a rodeo. On Friday, the **Westward Ho Historical Parade** brings together covered wagons, mule teams, buggies, and hundreds of Native Americans in full regalia. Wednesday–Saturday evenings at the Round-Up grounds (at Raley Park west of downtown), the **Happy Canyon Pageant** depicts the opening of the West in a series of vignettes, complete with strutting cowboys and traditional Umatilla dancing. The pageant is an object of much love and some contention; its old-fashioned script is rife with stereotypes. During Round-Up week, Pendleton's Main Street is converted into a street fair, with food booths, arts and crafts stalls, live music, carnival rides and other entertainment. The **tepee encampment** on the Round-Up grounds and the **cowboy breakfast** of ham, eggs, flapjacks, and coffee served Wednesday–Saturday at 6 A.M. in Stillman Park exemplify the traditions here that take the Old West beyond the rodeo ring.

Of course, the Round-Up is also a rodeo—in fact, one of the largest and richest in the United States. Cowboys and cowgirls come from across North American to compete for $530,000 in prize money in such classic rodeo events as bulldogging, calf-roping, barrel racing, and wild-horse races. The rodeo events are held Wednesday–Saturday at 1:15 P.M. Tickets for each day run $11–20, depending on seat location. Tickets are available by calling the Round-Up office and also through Ticketmaster (www.ticketmaster.com).

The **Round-Up Hall of Fame** (13th and S.W. Court Ave., 10 A.M.–5 P.M. daily during the summer), can be found under the south grandstand area at the Round-Up Stadium. The history of America's biggest rodeo is depicted in photos of past champions and famous bucking broncos along with displays of artifacts. The star of the show is a stuffed horse named War Paint. Admission is free and guided tours are available.

Hotel rooms in Pendleton are totally booked up months in advance during the Round-Up, so call to make room reservations as early as possible.

SHOPPING

If you're starting to like the look of pearl snap shirts, Wrangler jeans, and cowboy boots, then make your way to **Hamley's** (30 S.E. Court Ave., 541/278-1100, 9 A.M.–6 P.M. Mon.–Sat.) a classic Western clothing and tack store, complete with saddlemakers in the back. Hamley's also has an impressive collection of Western art on the mezzanine level of the store. A good place to learn more about the local scene is **Armchair Books** (39 S.W. Dorion, 541/276-7323, 9:30 A.M.–5:30 P.M. Mon.–Sat.), which specializes in regional titles and authors. The store offers a good selection of titles concerning Native Americans.

SPORTS AND RECREATION

Lots of sun is conducive to such outdoor activities as golf at **Pendleton Country Club** (seven miles south of town on U.S. 395, 541/278-1739), and boating and water-skiing on **McKay Reservoir** (541/922-3232), near the country club. In a little over an hour, fishing enthusiasts can head north and arrive at the Columbia River for salmon, steelhead, and bass, or try the area's reservoirs for bluegills, bass, and catfish. The **River Parkway**, a paved strip paralleling the Umatilla River through much of downtown Pendleton, is recommended for walkers and bikers.

During the winter months, skiing is on tap up at **Spout Springs** (40 miles northeast of Pendleton, 541/566-0320, www.skispout springs.com), one of the oldest ski resorts in the Northwest. To get here, drive north on Route

11 to Weston, turn east on Route 204, and travel a few miles past Tollgate to the ski area. Spout Springs usually holds on to its dry powder longer than other ski areas in the state.

ACCOMMODATIONS

Pendleton lodging is concentrated in two areas. A number of new chain motels are found along the I-84 exits south of town. Older but well-maintained motor courts are located close to downtown and within walking distance of Pendleton's famed nightlife. Plus, rooms at these older motels are usually cheaper than those on the outskirts of town.

But first, a word about lodging at Round-Up time. If you show up at Pendleton in mid-September without a reservation or unprepared to pay double the usual room rate, you might be out of luck. The town—and all those within easy driving distance—is completely booked to the rafters. The chamber of commerce has a list of private homes that rent for a little less than a motel room, but they are also normally booked well in advance. If you bring a tent, camping is usually available in schoolyards and other special sites set up for the Round-Up crowds.

The **Rugged Country Lodge** (1807 S.E. Court Ave., 541/966-6800 or 877/778-4433, www.ruggedcountrylodge.com, doubles from $68) is quite a find. Just west of downtown, this 1950s vintage motel has been lovingly refurbished into a "bed-and-breakfast motel"— each of the rooms was renovated in 2004, and have been charmingly decorated with fine furniture, fresh flowers, and art, and the grounds are nicely landscaped. Plus, there's the convivial welcome and hospitality of a home-away-from-home B&B, and a hearty continental breakfast. This is a great alternative to build-'em-by-the-dozen chain motels.

A bit closer to downtown, within walking distance of downtown shopping, dining, and entertainment, the **Traveler's Inn** (310 S.E. Dorion Ave., 541/276-6231, www.travelers-inn.net, doubles from $55) offers an outdoor pool and hot tub, and the newly renovated rooms each have a microwave, coffeemaker, and refrigerator. The **Travelodge** (411 S.W.

Dorion Ave., 541/276-7531, www.travelodge.com, doubles from $52) is another good deal, with free continental breakfast, high-speed Internet access, and movie channels. The rooms are basic, but clean and newly remodeled.

For something uniquely Pendleton, consider a night at the **Working Girls Hotel** (17 S.W. Emigrant, 800/226-6398, www.pendletonundergroundtours.org, doubles from $50). An offshoot of the popular Pendleton Underground Tours, this five-bedroom downtown hotel once served as a brothel in the Pendleton's rowdy heyday. The rooms have been modernized but the hardwood floors, 18-foot ceilings, and exposed brick walls point to the hotel's 1890s' birthright.

Equally historic but from the other end of the economic ladder, the **❰ Parker House Bed and Breakfast** (311 N. Main, 800/700-8581, www.parkerhousebnb.com, doubles from $85) is a fantastic 1917 mansion, with five guest rooms and 6,000 square feet of period luxury. Filled with antiques, oriental rugs, and original silk wall coverings, the Parker House even boasts a formal ballroom. A comfy porch, a backyard garden, and a fire blazing in the dining room while you enjoy creative breakfast fare evoke blissful thoughts of the good old days. Highly recommended.

At I-84 Exit 209, the recently opened **Oxford Suites** (2400 S.W. Court Pl. 541/276-6000 or 877/545-7848, www.oxfordsuitespendleton.com, doubles from $89), offers a complimentary breakfast buffet and evening appetizers, plus an indoor pool and hot tub. All rooms have microwaves, refrigerators, coffeemakers, and high-speed Internet.

There's a large cluster of motels at I-84 Exit 210. If you want to call ahead, consider these choices. The **Best Western Pendleton Inn** (400 S.E. Nye Ave., 541/276-2135 or 800/528-1234, doubles from $72) features an outdoor pool, plus fitness room and hot tub. Standard rooms come with coffeemaker plus iron and board. **Holiday Inn Express** (600 S.E. Nye, 541/966-6520 or 800/465-4329, www.hiexpress.com, doubles from $72) offers free continental breakfast, indoor pool, and hot tub.

Rooms come with coffeemaker and high-speed Internet access. **Red Lion Hotel** (304 S.E. Nye Ave., 541/276-6111 or 800/733-5466, www. redlion.com, doubles from $69) is a full-service hotel and small convention center, with two restaurants, lounge, room service, outdoor pool, plus free wireless Internet access. Rooms come with a microwave, refrigerator, and private balcony.

Further from Pendleton, the **Wildhorse Resort Hotel and Casino** (72779 Rte. 331, 541/278-2274 or 800/654-9453, www.wildhorseresort.com, doubles from $70), with 100 guest rooms, is six miles east of town. Facilities include an indoor pool, restaurant, and, of course, 24-hour gaming.

A tonic to modern life is a stay at the **Bar M Ranch** (58440 Bar M Ln., Adams, 541/566-3381 or 888/824-3381, www.barmranch.com), 31 miles northeast of Pendleton on Route 11. Built on the site of the historic Bingham Springs Resort, the ranch lies at the base of the Blue Mountains in the Umatilla National Forest. A stable of 50 horses, a natural warm springs, a recreation barn, and eight rooms in hand-hewn log houses let you rough it in style. During the summer high season, three-day minimum stays are required, starting at $753 per adult, which includes trail rides, meals, and all amenities.

FOOD

The **Rainbow Bar and Grill** (209 S. Main, 541/276-4120, daily 6 A.M.–2 A.M., no credit cards) is a famous saloon/restaurant for rodeo fans and local buckaroos. The Rainbow serves passable American diner food, which you shouldn't pass up, if only for local color. It's a favorite for breakfast, or for a late-night burger.

Main Street Diner (349 S. Main St., 541/278-1952, 7 A.M.–3 P.M. Mon.–Fri., 7 A.M.–2 P.M. Sat. and Sun.) is styled after a 1950s burger joint, with hearty breakfasts and excellent burgers ($7) and milkshakes. Pasta, salads, and pizza are a great value at **Como's Italian Eatery** (39 S.E. Court Ave., 541/278-9142, 11 A.M.–7 P.M. Mon.–Fri., 11 A.M.–3 P.M. Sat.). Ostensibly an espresso and ice cream

shop, the main-course offerings are tasty and almost nothing costs more then $10. Splurge on a bottle of local wine—the markup is minuscule. The **Great Pacific Wine and Coffee Co.** (403 S. Main, 541/276-1350) features imported cheeses, desserts, croissant sandwiches ($5–8), microbrews, the area's largest wine selection, an espresso bar, and gourmet products. Live music is presented on weekends. **Health Nuts** (1728 S.W. Court Pl., 541/276-2251, 8:30 A.M.–8 P.M. Mon.–Sat.) is an oasis of natural foods with a complete selection of whole grains, nuts, yogurt, and organic vegetables in season.

Cimmiyotti's (137 Main, 541/276-4314, open 4–10 P.M. daily) is a dark, cozy spot that's been around for decades, but recently reopened under new ownership as a Basque-style supperclub. All main courses come with bread, salad, Basque cabbage soup, and your choice from a small menu of steaks, prime rib, chicken and a daily fish special—quite a deal for $20. Cimmiyotti's also has a good selection of wines from the nearby Walla Walla Valley.

In an elegant older home across from City Hall, enjoy upscale Northwest cuisine at **Raphael's** (233 S.E. 4th, 541/276-8500, www.raphaelsrestaurant.com, 5–9 P.M. Tues.–Sat.). As you savor marionberry barbecued elk chops, crab stuffed salmon, venison marsala, or smoked prime rib, a visual feast of Native American art will further engage your senses. Main courses here can top $20.

INFORMATION

The **Pendleton Chamber of Commerce Visitor and Convention Bureau** (501 S. Main, Pendleton 97801, 541/276-7411 or 800/547-8911) can steer you to local sights and special events. A self-guided walking-tour map of the historic downtown district is helpful. The tour starts at the corner of Main and Frazer and takes in many historic buildings.

GETTING THERE AND AROUND

Pendleton Airport (2016 Airport Rd., 541/567-3694), located 3.5 miles west of town center, is served by **Horizon Air** (800/547-9308), which offers multiple flights daily to/from Portland and Pasco, Washington. **Greyhound** (320 Court Ave., 541/276-1551) offers two buses daily each way on the I-84 corridor between Portland and Boise.

Be aware that the stretch of I-84 above Pendleton known as Cabbage Hill is treacherous to drive during icy winters. In addition to the slickness of the surface, sudden blizzards and high winds can result in whiteout conditions.

La Grande and Vicinity

La Grande is located in the Grande Ronde Valley, which the indigenous peoples called Copi Copi ("Valley of Peace"). The broad valley is completely ringed by mountains and gives the impression of being circular, hence the valley's French name, which translates as the Big Circle. The Nez Perce once gathered for their summer encampments until the Oregon Trail cut through their territory. At La Grande, the Oregon Trail pioneers rested and prepared to traverse the Blue Mountains, a substantial challenge as the passes were often snow-filled by the time the wagon trains reached eastern Oregon. In downtown La Grande, Birnie Park, located on B Avenue and Bekeler, is one of the areas where the wagon trains rested, and it contains an abstract pioneer art memorial and a life-size wrought-iron pioneer play wagon.

More than a few of the pioneers were impressed with the agricultural possibilities of the Grande Ronde country, and they stayed to build a town that became the market center for a broad stretch of wheat and grass-seed farms. The city itself was established in 1864; a tavern on the south bank of the Grande Ronde River was the catalyst for the town's early growth. Lumber from the Blue Mountains and livestock fattened on lush fields of tall grass also propelled the community's early growth. Now home of Eastern Oregon University, La Grande (population 12,500) enjoys a brisk economy based on beef ranching, wheat farming, and timber. In addition to serving as gateway to Wallowa Lake and the northern flank of the Wallowa Range, La Grande is a pleasant destination in itself, with a historic downtown and several good restaurants to intrigue the travel-

ing gourmet. A drive through the valley reveals small towns with noteworthy museums and other curiosities.

SIGHTS
Union County Museum
Located in the town of Union, 11 miles southeast of La Grande, the Union County Museum (333 S. Main St., 541/562-6003, 10 A.M.–4 P.M. Mon.–Sat. and 1–4 P.M. Sun., $4 adults, $3 seniors and students) preserves the history of early settlement in the Grande Ronde Valley. Housed in a century-old red brick former bank, the museum has an interesting collection of vintage farm, household, and mining tools and equipment, but the highlight is the **Cowboys Then and Now** collection. Formerly housed in Portland, the collection is from the Oregon Cattleman's Heritage Foundation, and tells the story of the American cowboy starting from the arrival of cattle aboard Columbus' ships to the rise of modern agribusiness. Exhibits on the Hollywood Western and the history of rodeos are also intriguing.

The collection could not have found a more suitable setting for its new home. Union is a lovely town with a very well-preserved town center of late Victorian homes and storefronts. In fact, nearly the entire town is protected as a National Historic District. You can't miss the grand **Union Hotel,** built in 1920 as one of eastern Oregon's landmark lodgings, and now a comfortable B&B. Rates range from $59 double for an "original" bedroom with bathroom down the hall, to $119 for a suite that includes a kitchenette, bathroom with clawfoot tub, and sleeps up to six. The majority of rooms do have private bathrooms and cost around $85 for a double.

Eastern Oregon Fire Museum

La Grande's former fire hall, built in 1899, is now a museum of antique fire engines (102 Elm St., 541/963-8588, 10 A.M.–3 P.M. Mon.–Fri., plus Sat. during summer). Six beautifully restored fire trucks are on display, including a restored 1939 Seagrave ladder truck and a 1925 Stutz engine that's one of only nine such models ever built. Visitors are welcome to climb aboard and ring the bells.

The Oregon Trail Interpretive Park at Blue Mountain Crossing

This park commemorates the crossing of the Blue Mountains by the Oregon Trail pioneers. Paved, easily accessible trails follow some of the best-preserved and most scenic traces of the Oregon Trail. Sign panels describe the pioneers' struggle through the thick forests and over the rugged mountain passes. Living history interpretive events are offered weekends during the summer. The park includes a picnic area, restrooms, and drinking water. Open May–October. To reach the park, take Spring Creek Exit off I-84 12 miles west of La Grande.

(Hot Lake Mineral Hot Springs

Hot Lake Mineral Hot Springs was considered "Big Medicine" by the western tribes that camped near its healing waters. Here, a steady flow of super-heated water reaches the surface at nearly the boiling point and pours into a large pond, reportedly the world's largest natural hot spring. In 1810, Astor Pacific Fur Company trappers described elk crowding around this spring. Thereafter, the lake, located five miles east of La Grande on Route 203, became a popular spot for explorers and emigrants. In 1864, Samuel Newhart built a hotel and bathhouse here. A hospital was added in 1906, and the facility soon became known as the Mayo Clinic of the West. During that era, the healing waters were thought to give relief from arthritis and rheumatism, and the medical team here was noted for their success with treating tuberculo-

sis. With a ballroom and library, the sanatorium was also a fashionable place to have a spa vacation. After the hospital closed in the 1930s, the building was used variously as a resort, a hotel, a boarding house, a restaurant, and a nursing home. Then, for many years, the resort sat vacant, and was frequently vandalized.

In 2004, David Manuel, a nationally renowned artist and sculptor who owned a bronze foundry and gallery in the nearby town of Joseph, and his wife Lee bought the crumbling resort and embarked on a very ambitious remodel and revival of the historic structure. Still under renovation, the Hot Lake Resort is being redeveloped as an arts and art education center plus bed-and-breakfast spa. Plans for the new resort are quite ambitious and include a school for glassblowers and a bronze arts school where students will learn about bronze casting. The bronze foundry and studio are currently open for tours at 10 A.M. and 2 P.M. ($9 adults, $8 seniors, $5 children); the coffee shop and gift store is also open daily. The resort will also feature a fine dining restaurant and a bed-and-breakfast inn, with some rooms upgraded to executive suites, all scheduled to open in 2007. The hot mineral waters will be put to use in a full-service spa (scheduled for opening in late 2007) offering mineral baths, mud baths, body wraps, and massages. Guests will also enjoy saunas and foot soaks in the property's renovated spring house. To check on the progress of this long-time landmark, check the website at www.hotlakesprings.com, call 541/963-4685, or just stop by during the week.

SPORTS AND RECREATION
Golf

The **Buffalo Peak Golf Course** (1224 E. Fulton St., Union, 541/562-5527 or 866/202-5950) is an 18-hole, Par-72 links-style course set in the Grande Ronde Valley. The course offers a variety of landscapes, with native vegetation and natural terrain, such as patches of native prairie, streams and lakes incorporated into the play. The course, which plays 5,000–6,500 yards with four sets of tees per hole, has $29 greens fees.

Camping

A number of La Grande area campgrounds share history with the Oregon Trail. Between La Grande and Pendleton in the midst of the Blue Mountains, **Emigrant Springs State Park** (541/983-2277 or 800/551-6949), is a large facility with flush toilets, showers, a laundry, and a playground, right off I-84. The fee is $14 per night for a tent site, $20 for a cabin. The park has a display on local Oregon Trail history. There are 33 tent sites and 18 fuel hookups in a wooded area. To reserve Emigrant Springs campsites online, go to www.reserveamerica.com.

Hilgard Junction State Park is on the Grande Ronde River, at the foot of the Blue Mountains. Fees for this 18-site (no hookups) campground are $8 per night. To get here drive eight miles west of La Grande to I-84 Exit 252 at the junction with Route 244, or Starkey Road. This campground is on the original route of the Oregon Trail. Information placards detail how their wagons maneuvered over this precipitous terrain. The campground is convenient to the freeway, which also means that it's noisy and not particularly private. Consider driving eight miles up Route 244 to **Red Bridge State Park** for more appealing campsites ($8).

Another option off Route 244 is **Sherwood Forest Campground,** a small site on the banks of the Grande Ronde River. There is no fee for this campground, which is open late May–late November. From I-84 Exit 252 drove 13 miles southwest on Route 244 as it meanders along the river and its valley, where ponderosa pine and aspen are broken up by meadows and farmland. From there, drive six miles south on Forest Service Road 51.

After camping, you might want to follow Route 244 up to **Lehman Hot Springs** (541/427-3015, www.lehmanhotsprings.com). Each of the three chambers in Lehman's giant swimming pool is calibrated to an increasing degree of hotness, with the hottest level being scorching. Pool fees are $7, and the pool is usually closed on Mondays and Tuesdays for cleaning. The resort also offers campsites ($12 for tents, $20 for RVs) and cabins and lodge rooms for $95.

ACCOMMODATIONS

Out at I-84 Exit 261, **Best Western Rama Inn and Suites** (1711 21st St., 541/963-3100 or 800/528-1234, doubles from $84) offers complimentary continental breakfast, plus indoor pool, steam room, hot tub, and exercise facility. Rooms feature cable TV, high-speed Internet access, coffeemaker, refrigerator, microwave, and iron. Adjacent, **Best Value Sandman Inn** (2410 East R Ave., 541/963-3707 or 888/315-2378, doubles from $74) has an indoor pool and spa, free continental breakfast, and bright clean rooms. Downtown, the **La Grande Royal Motor Inn**, (1510 Adams Ave., 541/963-4154 or 800/990-7575, doubles from $50) offers basic but just fine rooms within walking distance of good restaurants and bars.

At different level of comfort, the **Stange Manor** (1612 Walnut, 541/963-2400 or 888/286-9463, www.stangemanor.com, doubles from $98) is a Georgian colonial mansion built in the 1920s by a timber baron. Period furniture and stunning woodwork, large individually decorated guestrooms, and views of the mountains evoke the good life in the heyday of La Grande. Each of the four rooms has a bath. Other appreciated features are the cozy dining room fireplace, bikes available to guests, and home-cooked delicacies for breakfast. Not appropriate for children under age 10.

Eleven miles southeast of La Grande on Route 203, the nine-unit ◖ **Union Hotel** (326 N. Main, Union 97883, 541/562-6135, www.theunionhotel.com) will take you back to 1920s when this imposing hotel was built to satisfy the needs of sophisticated travelers between Portland and Boise. The hotel has been beautifully renovated keeping its high style intact, with theme-decorated rooms, all with private baths. This three-story brick hotel—with beautiful tile floors, an Old West lobby, and a Ladies Parlor—is one of the most charming and unusual hotels in eastern Oregon. Forget the chain motels along the freeway and stay in a historic landmark.

FOOD

A lot of people will tell you that the state's best fast food is available at **Nells In 'n' Out** (1704

Adams Ave., 541/963-5733). Creative variations on shakes and floats, hand-curled french fries, and a full array of burgers are highlights. **Mamacita's International Grill** (2003 4th St., 541/963-6223, lunch Mon.–Fri., dinner Tues.–Sun.) serves tasty and affordable Mexican food. At $8, the Guadalajara tostada and *arroz con pollo* are particularly good values. An excellent spot for morning coffee and pastries is **Joe and Sugar's** (1119 Adams Ave., 541/975-5282), a tiny bakery right downtown that also turns out excellent breakfast burritos and omelets.

La Grande has two of eastern Oregon's most refined restaurants. **Ten Depot Street** (10 Depot St., 541/963-8766, Mon.–Sat for dinner) offers an up-to-date menu that might include grilled local lamb chops, fresh Northwest salmon and perfectly prepared prime rib (the house specialty). Salads are particularly delicious, a rarity out here in meat country. The restaurant's classy structure was once a Masonic hall, and the saloon is as popular as the restaurant—it's a great place to indulge in a succulent half-pound burger. Weeknights there's usually an easy-on-the-wallet Blue Plate Special under $10; otherwise expect to spend $20 for a main course.

Foley Station (1114 Adams Ave, 541/963-7473, www.foleystation.com,

10:30 A.M.–10 P.M. Mon.–Sat., 7 A.M.–10 P.M. Sun.) is also housed in a beautiful historic building, but the cooking is more rarified, borrowing from French and Italian haute cuisine while employing local seasonal produce and meats. The menu is prodigious and you'll have to choose between full-on gourmet delights—the tournedos Henri IV translates as beef tenderloins, artichoke hearts. and Béarnaise sauce—or such traditional favorites as roast beef and Yorkshire pudding. Desserts are a marvel. Who knew you would find macadamia meringues and hibiscus cake in La Grande? Expect to pay $17–30 for main courses, though the ample small plates menu provides less-expensive options.

INFORMATION

For information on La Grande and Union County, contact Union County Tourism (102 Elm St., 541/963-8588 or 800/848-9969, www.visitlagrande.com). The La Grande Ranger Station of the Wallowa-Whitman Forest Service is at 3502 Route 30 (541/963-7186).

GETTING THERE

Two buses daily travel each day between Portland and Boise with stops in La Grande. The station is at 63276 Route 203, 541/963-5165. The closest scheduled air service is in Pendleton.

The Wallowas

Ask most Oregonians who have been there and they will tell you that the Wallowa Range is one place in Oregon "you gotta see—you just gotta." Come now, before the word gets out about this scenic paradise where snowcapped, Teton-like spires soar 5,000 feet above Wallowa County farmlands and six-mile-long Wallowa Lake.

The **Eagle Cap Wilderness Area**—with 17 of the state's 29 mountains over 9,000 feet and 50 glacial lakes sprinkled throughout 300,000 acres—is a recreational area that should figure prominently in your travel plans. Campers

and cross-country skiers are regularly treated to glimpses of bighorn sheep, mountain goats, elk, and mule deer, as well as snow-streaked granite and limestone peaks rising above meadows dotted with an artist's palette of wildflowers. But you don't have to go far into the backcountry to get away from it all here.

The Wallowa Valley is formed by the drainages of the Wallowa, Minam, and Grande Ronde Rivers. It is backdropped by the half moon–shaped Wallowa range, 80 miles long and 25 miles at its widest. The traditional eastern Oregon triad of timber, farming, and cattle ranching fuels the area's economy, with tourism rapidly increasing. Nineteenth-century farmhouses dot the landscape, and cowboy-hatted ranchers and farmers mix freely with local merchants and a cluster of renowned artists who have settled here.

After a visit to this larger-than-life countryside, it is easy to see how it sustained the proud and indomitable Nez Perce, the native people who once roamed its river canyons, glacial basins, and grassy hills. The air here has a soft sweetness, and a surprising degree of epicurean refinement awaits the discerning visitor. Locals will tell you to come in September when pleasant weather and smaller crowds showcase the region at its best.

There are several choices of home base when it comes to exploring the Wallowas. The town of Enterprise is the commercial center of it all, while Joseph is the hub of a growing arts community and the gateway to Wallowa Lake, a recreational haven at the end of the road. And then there's camping: The Wallowas have many Forest Service and state park campgrounds where you can roll out the tent and get even closer to nature.

The Wallowas are the wettest place east of the Cascades. The higher reaches of the range may get 60 inches of precipitation annually. These upper elevations crest in the Eagle Cap Wilderness Area and descend gradually to the south toward Baker City. This is why you sometimes hear Eagle Cap's peaks referred to as the hub of the range and the various ridges, spokes splaying outward in a wagonwheel pattern. Seashells in limestone and greenstone outcroppings attest to the range's age, some 200 million years.

It's theorized that these mountains were once part of a tropical island chain in the mid-Pacific. As North America drifted, the island range bumped into the continent and attached itself to the ancient coastline. Curiously, the Austrian Alps contain similar fossilized corals, mollusks, algae, and sponges, suggesting a shared birthright lost to the mists of prehistory.

HISTORY

The Wallowa Valley, set apart by deep river canyons and mountain ranges, is the ancestral home of the Nez Perce, a tribe known for its horse-training skills and fierce independence. These proud people, astride their spotted Appaloosas, first encountered Europeans when mountain men wandered onto their land. Lewis and Clark believed that the tribe's generosity with food saved their lives. The tribe's willingness to feed and care for the Bonneville Party, which had struggled up out of the Snake River Canyon in 1834, reinforced their reputation for honor and largesse. Later, however, when a dry spell in the Grande Ronde Valley to the south prompted homesteaders to farm the Wallowas, native and white cultures clashed.

One source of tension was the settlers' permitting their hogs to trample the camas fields where the natives came to gather food. The U.S. government attempted to resolve the situation by creating a seven-million-acre reservation in 1855, but reneged on the land treaty five years later when gold was discovered in the Wallowas. This breach initiated an era of bad feelings during which various drafts of different treaties generated confusion and distrust.

The settlers later successfully lobbied the government to evict the natives, which led to the Nez Perce War of 1877. Chief Joseph and his people fought a running battle that covered 1,700 miles and ended with their surrender in the Bear's Paw Mountains, 50 miles from the Montana–Canada border. The Nez Perce Reservation is in central Idaho.

◖ EAGLE CAP EXCURSION TRAIN

Trains arrived in La Grande in 1884, but didn't reach the remote canyon country of Wallowas until 1908. Passenger service fizzled in the 1920s after decent roads and bridges allowed easy vehicle access to Wallowa farms and towns, and finally in the 1990s freight service stopped along this lonely rail line that passes through stunning mountain meadows and deep river gorges. Citizens in Wallowa and Union County banded together to purchase the track and today the system operates both freight and excursion services between Elgin and Joseph. The Eagle Cap Excursion Train is run by a volunteer organization called the Friends of the Joseph Branch.

The excursion train offers a variety of trips along this route, ranging from a 2.5-hour trip between the town of Wallowa and Joseph (with a return via motorcoach, adult tickets are $45, including box lunch or dessert buffet) to a 7.5-hour trip down into the canyons of the Grande Ronde and Wallowa Rivers starting from either Elgin or Wallowa ($80 adult, includes lunch). The specifics of the excursions, and the schedule, is rather confusing and you should check out the website or call for information. In general, the excursion train operates on Saturdays late May–late October, with additional runs on the second Thursday of the month. Only one trip is made per day, so check the schedule before setting your heart on one excursion or another. For more information on the schedule, contact the visitor information center for Union County (800/848-9969) or Wallowa County (800/585-4121) or check www.eagle captrain.com. For tickets, call Alegre Travel at 541/963-9000 or 800/323-7330.

Enterprise is a traditional Western town at the gateway to the Wallowa Mountains.

ENTERPRISE

Enterprise is the larger of the two towns that dominate the Wallowa Valley, with a population of around 2,000, and unlike Joseph, it has the feel of an authentic Western town. Much of the original downtown, built in the 1890s, is still here and functions as the mercantile center. Enterprise is a friendly town, and you should stop to explore and enjoy the town's shops and handsome locale. Stop by the chamber of commerce booth in the Enterprise Mall and pick up the **walking tour** brochure prepared by the Wallowa County Centennial Committee. It has descriptions and locations of many of the historic buildings in the area, such as the Wallowa County Courthouse, the Enterprise Hotel, the Oddfellows Hall, and a number of private homes. After an hour of edification and exercise, take a break at the **Bookloft-Skylight Gallery** (107 E. Main, 541/426-3351), just across the street from the county courthouse. Open every day except Sunday, this gathering spot for artists and community activists sells best-sellers and local-history books and offers monthly shows of guest artists, as well as freshly brewed coffee and home-baked cookies.

Given that two-thirds of the county hereabouts is federal land contained in the Eagle Cap Wilderness, the Wallowa-Whitman National Forest, and the Hells Canyon National Recreation Area, it's a good idea to start your visit the federal public lands-sponsored **Wallowa Mountains Visitor Center** (88401 Hwy. 82, 541/426-4978, 8 A.M.–5 P.M. Mon.–Sat. in the summer months, with shorter winter hours), a half-mile west of Enterprise. There are exhibits highlighting forests, geology, and wildlife, as well as an observation deck with views of meadows, farms, and mountains.

Wildlife-Watching

Two wildlife-viewing areas await you as you sweep down into the Wallowa Valley. The **Spring Branch Wildlife Area,** a woodland marsh, is two miles east of Wallowa on Route 82, on the north side where the road leaves the

Wallowa River. The eight-acre viewing area, managed by the Oregon Department of Fish and Wildlife, has beaver dams and lots of waterfowl, including the black tern, an insect-eating bird found in eastern Oregon marshes. The **Enterprise Wildlife Area** is two miles west of Enterprise off Route 82. To get there, turn south on Fish Hatchery Road to this 32-acre site located just before the fish hatchery. Walk down the dike that goes through a grove of trees to view marsh wrens, snipe, mink, beavers, and muskrats.

Entertainment and Events

The **Wallowa County Fiddlers' Contest** brings non-professional fiddlers from throughout the Northwest to mix it up with music, good grub, and the spirit of the pioneer days. Held in Enterprise in mid-June, the contest is a treat for both the performers and their appreciative audiences.

Hells Canyon Mule Days (www.hellscanyonmuledays.com), held the weekend after Labor Day at the Enterprise Fairgrounds, is where pack-animal fanciers can get their kicks. The action includes mule races, a parade, a speed mule-shoeing contest, and endurance competitions.

Accommodations

Lodging in Enterprise can be less expensive than other Wallowa area options—and not booked up months in advance, like the lodges at Wallowa Lake. A couple of standard motels are noteworthy for being clean, well priced, and friendly. The **Ponderosa Motel** (102 S.E. Greenwood, 541/426-3186, doubles from $55) is south of downtown, with some newly remodeled rooms. **Wilderness Inn** (301 W. North, 541/426-4535, doubles from $55) has everything you need for a comfortable night in Enterprise. The modern **Best Western Rama Inn** (1200 Highland Ave., 541/426-2000 or 888/726-2466, www.enterpriseramainn.com, doubles from $99) is one of the newer lodgings in the area, with an indoor heated pool, hot tub, exercise room, sauna, guest laundry; all rooms have a coffeemaker, microwave, and refrigerator. **1910 Historic Enterprise House B&B** (508 First South St., 541/426-4238 or 888/448-8825, www.enterprisehousebnb.com, doubles from $110) is a very large, rambling farmhouse from the turn of the 20th century that's now a stylish B&B. Each of the five guest rooms has a private bath, and the massive third-floor room can sleep up to 10. The entire house is beautifully refurbished, furnished with antiques and offers lovely mountain and garden views.

Food

The **Cloud 9 Bakery** (105 S.E. 1st St., 541/426-3790, 6 A.M.–4 P.M. Mon.–Fri.) is a great place to know about—its pastries, donuts, and coffee are great for morning fueling and soups, sandwiches, and light meals are available until late afternoon. Cloud 9 is a lively spot—one of the hubs for the Wallowas' youthful subculture. For a good family restaurant with well prepared standard American fare, go to **Lee's High Country Dining** (215 W. Main St., 541/426-9378, lunch and dinner daily). **Lear's Main Street Pub and Grill** (111 West Main St., 541/426-3300, three meals daily) combines many excellent virtues, among them a selection of regional microbrews, a vintage bar atmosphere that's smoke-free, and really good food that's prepared on-site and from scratch—nothing is frozen or comes out of cans. Local organic produce is used when available, the beef is also local and all natural, and even the bacon and ham are cured in the restaurant. Main courses like pan-seared porcini-dusted halibut, smoked pork loin with rosemary cream sauce, and the trademark 16-ounce "Big Ass" rib steak are $16–24, though burgers, oyster po' boys, and barbecued brisket sandwiches are available for around $8.

❰ Terminal Gravity Brewing (803 School St., 541/426-0158, www.terminalgravitybrewing.com, 3–9 P.M. Tues.–Sat.) serves as the region's brewpub and multi-ethnic restaurant. Located in an idyllic poplar grove by a creek, it has also become a hub for frontier vaudeville and offbeat entertainment. The menu is basic but the nightly special can feature Italian,

Moroccan, Mexican, or Middle Eastern food, averaging $12 for dinner.

For the region's fine-dining option, you'll need to drive 30 miles north of Enterprise on Highway 3 to the tiny town of Flora, where the (**Rimrock Inn** (83471 Lewiston Hwy., 541/828-7769, www.rimrockrestaurant.com, lunch and dinner Tues.–Sat., late May–Nov., main courses $20 and up) awaits. This one-of-a-kind restaurant began as a 1940s road-house before being transformed in 2004 into a very stylish dining room that blends historic authenticity with chic decor. And the views? As its name suggests, the Rimrock Inn sits above a staggering view of Joseph Canyon as it trenches its way toward Hells Canyon, the world's deepest river gorge. The kitchen produces some of best food for hundreds of miles, focusing on well-prepared steaks but also offering refined dishes otherwise uncommon in eastern Oregon: grilled salmon with capers and *Jaeger*-sauced spaetzle, mandarin and caramelized almond salad, and Dungeness crab cakes with firecracker dipping sauce. To prolong the

Rimrock Inn experience, consider settling into one of three luxury tepees at the canyon's edge ($36 per tent, for 1–6 people). Just bring a sleeping bag; everything else—pine furniture, leather armchairs, indoor and outdoor fireplaces—is provided.

Information

The **Wallowa County Chamber of Commerce** (P.O. Box 427A, 107 S.W. 1st St., Enterprise 97828, 541/426-4622 or 800/585-4121, www.wallowacountychamber.com) has a booth in the Enterprise Mall with a full complement of brochures, maps, and other information on the area.

JOSEPH

At the base of the Wallowa Mountains is Joseph (elev. 4,150 ft.), a lively community of 1,200 that's named after the famous Nez Perce chief. The old-timey charm of Joseph's false-fronted buildings with the snow-capped Wallowas for a backdrop make it seem more than 335 miles away from Portland. Joseph is noted

© BILL MCRAE

The streets of Joseph preserve their Old West facades.

across the West as an arts town. The colorful main street is lined with galleries and open-air sculpture, and many of the residents (including a high percentage of transplants from more urban areas) are themselves artists.

Joseph lost one star in its artistic firmament when one of its most famous artists, bronze sculptor David Manuel, left town. Manuel has moved his gallery and foundry to Hot Lake, near La Grande. However, there are still plenty of galleries and arts-related shops to visit, and **Valley Bronze** (18 Main St., 541/432-7445), Joseph's original bronze-casting operation—and the second-largest in the nation—displays works and offers daily tours ($15) of their Alder Street foundry. Call ahead for the tour schedule. For more information on Joseph, check www.josephoregon.com.

Wallowa County Museum

A must-stop for history buffs is the Wallowa County Museum (110 Main St., 541/432-6095, 10 A.M.–5 P.M. daily, late May–late Sept., donations requested). Built in 1888, the museum building has served as a newspaper office, a private hospital, a meeting hall, and a bank (one of the crooks who robbed the bank later became its president). Its current incarnation as a museum started in 1960. The theme of the museum is Wallowa history, including displays of pioneer life and the Nez Perce and the museum is crammed with interesting curiosities and curios.

Entertainment and Events

Most of the local celebrations here revolve around cowboys, Native Americans, and the arts community. The **Wallowa Valley Festival of the Arts** (www.wallowavalleyarts.org) is held at the Joseph Civic Center on the first weekend of June. Along with awards for Northwest artists, there are wine-tasting parties, a silent auction, and a quick-draw competition.

Held the last week of July, **Chief Joseph Days** (541/432-1015, www.chiefjosephdays.com) is a weeklong festival in Joseph that features dances, a carnival, a Grand Parade, a ranch-style breakfast, and a three-day rodeo,

one of the largest in the Northwest. Also in Joseph, **Bronze, Blues, and Brews** (800/585-4121) takes place in mid-August, featuring big-name musical talent, gallery and foundry open houses, and locally brewed beer.

At various times throughout the year, Joseph hosts a low-key but talent-laden literary gathering known as **Fishtrap** (P.O. Box 38, Enterprise 97828, 541/426-3623, www.fishtrap.org) in an old Methodist meetinghouse. Authors writing in different genres attend; past participants have included William Kittredge, Ursula LeGuin, Ivan Doig, Sandra Scofield, and Terry Tempest Williams. Writers of all levels come to read their works and discuss social issues. Fishtrap also offers workshops in mid-September and October, such as an all-day seminar on writing and illustrating children's books and an intensive memoir workshop. Check the website for fees and registration forms.

Accommodations

For clean, basic rooms with fair prices and such little touches as flower baskets and decorative prints, try the **Indian Lodge Motel** (201 S. Main St., 541/432-2651 or 888/286-5484, doubles from $56). Joseph also has a number of excellent B&Bs. **Bronze Antler Bed & Breakfast** (309 S. Main St., 541/432-0230 or 866/520-9769, www.bronzeantler.com, doubles from $120) is a friendly B&B in a 1925 bungalow originally built by a local sawmill supervisor who filled the arts-and-crafts home with custom millwork and beautiful wood floors. The three guest rooms have private baths and luxurious linens and towels—the room appointments rival those at upscale hotels. The living and dining rooms are warmly decorated with antiques and quality furniture, adding to the comfortable atmosphere of Rocky Mountain Chic. **Belle Pepper's Bed & Breakfast** (101 S. Mill St., 541/432-0490 or 866/432-0490, www.bellepeppersbnb.com, doubles from $90), is in a 1912 mansion built by one of Joseph's early leading citizens. The three guestrooms, all with private baths, are handsomely decorated, but without the usual B&B clutter, and the living and dining room share a gracious formality.

Food

Joseph is the place for mountainous breakfasts; for evening fine dining the best options are in Enterprise or at the south end of Wallowa Lake. **Wildflour Bakery** (600 N. Main St., 541/432-7225, breakfast and lunch, closed Tues.) offers home-made organic soups, sandwiches and meals in addition to great baked goods. The log-sided **Old Town Café** (8 S. Main St., 541/432-9898, Tues.–Sun for breakfast and lunch) looks the part of a vintage frontier town eatery—it's a great spot for onion-y hash brown potatoes topped with cheese, bacon, and home-made salsa. The **Mountain Air Cafe** (4 S. Main St., 541/432-0233, breakfast and lunch daily) is the kind of classic rural American restaurant where all the bread, cinnamon rolls, and pies are homemade, and breakfast is served all day. The mountain berry cobbler is the house specialty. **Outlaw Restaurant & Saloon** (108 N. Main, 541/432-4321, open Open Mon.–Sat. for lunch and dinner) offers standard American fare, but in summer there's ample outdoor seating. **Embers Brewhouse** (204 N. Main St., 541/432-2739, lunch and dinner daily) offers 17 regional microbrews on tap plus pizza and deli sandwiches.

WALLOWA LAKE

The brightest gem in the Wallowas is Wallowa Lake, which at 5,000 feet in elevation is the highest large body of water in eastern Oregon. This classic moraine-held glacial lake begins a mile south of Joseph on Route 82 at the east end of the Wallowa Valley, though most development is at the south end of the lake, about six miles from Joseph. The lake is ringed with lodges, amusement rides, a large state park with a campground, pack-horse corrals, boat launches, and marinas. It is also home to the **Wallowa Lake Monster,** a creature with a gentle disposition and a length varying 30–100 feet, depending on the sighting. Reports of the critter go back several centuries to Native American tales.

The lake is bordered on one side by peaks of the Eagle Cap Wilderness and on the other by rolling farmland that novelist Ethan Canin says "might have given Monet the inspiration for his palette." Be that as it may, exercise caution before you dive in for a swim. Invitingly clear, the lake waters here are extremely cold and should not be experienced until August (and not much thereafter). The beach in the county park at the northern end of the lake is a good spot to test the waters.

Wallowa State Park

One of the most popular in the Oregon state park system, Wallowa State Park (Wallowa Lake, Rte. 1, Box 323, Joseph 97846, reservations 800/452-5687, information 541/432-4185, www.oregonstateparks.org), is set lakeside amid big, old ponderosa pines. It's a beautiful spot and the perfect place for an outdoorsy family vacation. The lake is popular for fishing, boating, and summer splashing, and the park is moments from wilderness hiking trails, horseback riding, bumper boats, canoeing, and miniature golf.

The campground accepts reservations (800/452-5687, www.reserveamerica.com). For high season, reserve seven months in advance or you may be outta luck. Lake views, large campsites (89 tent, two yurts, one cabin, and 121 RV sites), clean bathhouses, and covered kitchen shelters make it worth the $17–21 nightly camping fee (yurts are $29 and the cabins $80). A marina, picnic area, and a sports field are other pleasing features. As one of six outstanding Far West parks chosen by *National Geographic,* this site is not what you'd call a secret hideaway. But if you're looking for a campground surrounded on three sides by 9,000-foot-high snow-capped peaks and a large, clear lake, this is the park for you.

◖ Wallowa Lake Tramway

This gondola up Mount Howard (544/432-5331, www.wallowalaketramway.com, 10 A.M.–5 P.M. in summer) is the steepest and longest in North America—lifting passengers up 3,700 feet, from the edge of Wallowa Lake to the 8,200-foot summit of Mount Howard. As the lift floats upward, the pastureland and wheatfield views near Wallowa Lake give way to for-

CHIEF JOSEPH

Known by his people as In-mut-too-yah-lat-lat ("Thunder coming up over the land from the water"), Chief Joseph was best known for his brave resistance to the government's attempts to force his tribe onto a reservation. A nation that spread from Idaho to northern Washington, the Nez Perce had peacefully coexisted with European Americans after the Lewis and Clark expedition; indeed, the tribe had given the newcomers much-needed horses. Joseph had spent much of his early childhood at a mission maintained by Christian missionaries.

But with the incursion of miners and settlers, and because of misunderstandings surrounding the annexation of Native American land through a series of treaties never signed by Chief Joseph, tension increased to the breaking point. White disregard of native property spurred some rash young Nez Perce to retaliate. The ensuing 11-week conflict, during which the Nez Perce engaged 10 separate U.S. military commands in 13 battles (the majority of which the Nez Perce won), guaranteed Chief Joseph's fame as a brilliant military tactician. However, after many hardships including starvation and many lost lives, Chief Joseph surrendered to Generals Miles and Howard on October 5, 1877, only 50 miles from the sanctuary of the Canadian border.

In 1879, Chief Joseph spoke to the Department of Indian Affairs in Washington, D.C., detailing the broken promises of the government, the suffering of his people, and the unjust treatment of the Native Americans by white society saying:

I have heard talk and talk, but nothing is done. Good words do not last long unless they amount to something. Words do not pay for my dead people. They do not pay for my country, now overrun by white men. They do not protect my father's grave. They do not pay for all my horses and cattle. Good words will not give me back my children. I only ask of the government to be treated as all other men are treated.

Chief Joseph appealed repeatedly to the federal authorities to return the Nez Perce to the land of their ancestors, but to no avail. In 1885, he and many of his band were sent to a reservation in Washington, where, as the presiding doctor was heard to have said, he died of a broken heart.

---

ests of lodgepole pine, tamarack, and quaking aspen. On top, stay on the trails through the fragile alpine tundra so as not to damage the tiny and rare plants here.

The 15-minute ride ends at the Summit Grill and Alpine Patio, with drinks and meals at the top of the peak. But forget about the snacks, knickknacks, and trinkets; the best reason for taking the trip is the view of 26 mountain peaks, including the Wallowa Range, Snake River country, and Idaho's Seven Devils area. The eight peaks of Eagle Cap Wilderness are mirrored in the lake below, and the gorges of the Snake and Imnaha Rivers stretch to the east.

The ride in closed, four-person gondola cars costs $20 for adults, $17 for youths 12–17, and $13 for children 4–11. It operates daily from June–first three weeks of September; it also operates weekends in the latter half of May (plus Memorial Day), late September and early October. The gondola also operates on some winter weekends; call for information.

Events

Alpenfest (800/585-4121) is a three-day festival held the third weekend after Labor Day in Edelweiss Hall next to the tramway at Wallowa Lake. This gala is a return to the old country and all that's Bavarian, sending echoes into the mountains with music, alpenhorn blowing, and yodeling competitions. Dancing, sailboat racing, and a bounty of Northern European cuisine are also featured.

Accommodations

The following lodgings on Wallowa Lake reflect the special woodsy flavor of this outback locality. These accommodations are all at the south end of the lake, adjacent to the state park, which offers campsites.

The **Flying Arrow Resort** (59782 Wallowa Lake Hwy., Joseph 97846, 541/432-2951, www.flyarrowresort.com, double-occupancy cabins $75–180), offers lodging in 24 cabins, ranging from one-bedroom cabins to four-bedroom houses that can sleep 14. All have kitchens, fireplaces, and bathrooms, but otherwise they are all unique, so get on the website to find out which cabin matches your needs. The resort also features a swimming pool, hot tub, chocolate shop, bookstore, and market. The Flying Arrow is kid- and pet-friendly.

The **Eagle Cap Chalets** (59879 Wallowa Lake Hwy., 541/432-4704, http://eaglecapchalets.com) is tucked into the pines near the base of the gondola. This cluster of motel-style chalet rooms, cabins, and condos—plus an indoor pool, snack shack, and miniature golf course—has all you need for a pleasant stay at Wallowa Lake. In high season, chalet room doubles and double-occupancy cabins start at $80, and condos start at $115. There are also many multi-bedroom units designed for families and groups.

The **Wallowa Lake Lodge** (P.O. Box 1, Joseph 97846, 541/432-9821, www.wallowalakelodge.com) is a renovated 1923 hunting lodge on the lakefront that fairly drips with vintage atmosphere. In addition to an excellent restaurant, the lodge itself has 22 bedrooms in a variety of sizes and layouts. While some rooms are quite small, others have two bedrooms; all have private bathrooms. In addition, the lodge offers lodging in eight charming cabins scattered around the eight-acre property. The cabins were built in the 1950s and feature knotty pine cabinets, stone fireplaces, and fully modern kitchens and bathrooms; most have lake views. It's hard to imagine a more enchanting setting. A great deal of care is taken to preserve the historic atmosphere of the lodge and the cabins, though comfort is not sacrificed. Lodge room doubles begin at $89, double-occupancy cabins range $125–190.

In keeping with the notion that the Wallowas are the Switzerland of America, **Matterhorn Swiss Village** (59950 Wallowa Lake Hwy., 541/432-4071 or 800/891-2551, www.matterhornswissvillage.com) has six "Swiss" cottages with names like the Alpenhof and Berghof. Rates range from $60–90 for double-occupancy self-catering cabins, though most units are set up for larger families.

On the quieter western side of the lake, **Trouthaven Resort** (61841 Lakeshore Dr., 541/432-2221, www.trouthavencabins.com) is another venerable cabin resort. The cabins come in two sizes, have knotty pine paneling and a covered porch with outdoor dining table. The Trouthaven also has a half-mile of Wallowa Lake frontage, with a couple of docks; boats and fishing gear is available for rent. The rustic cabins begin at $76 for double occupancy; the larger cabins can sleep up to six. These cabins and this location are perfect ingredients for a family vacation. Open May 1–September 14.

Wallowa Lake Resort (84681 Ponderosa Ln., 541/432-2391, www.wallowalakeresort.com) rents 31 different properties in the Lake Wallowa area, from small cabins perfect for a couple (starting at $80) to large homes that will sleep up to 11. No two are alike so get on the website and make your selection.

If you aren't into the traditional cabin scene, then check out the comfortable guest rooms at the **Tamarack Pines B&B** (60093 Wallowa Lake Hwy., 541/432-2920 or 866/200-8804, www.tamarackpines.com, doubles from $120), a quiet spot with a private trout pond. Three of the guest rooms are in the rambling ranch-style house, while the fourth is in the owner's RV.

Food

Most of the cabins along Lake Wallowa have kitchens, so even though this is a major tourist destinations, there's not a vast selection of restaurants. Nonetheless, there are a couple notable places to eat. **Vali's Alpine Delicatessen** (541/432-5691) features a different dinner menu each day featuring German and Hungarian specialties. Seatings are at 6 and 8 P.M.; reservations are recommended. Dinners are in the $15 range. Open Tuesday.–Sunday in summer, weekends only in winter. The dining room at the 1920s-era **《 Wallowa Lake Lodge** (60060 Wallowa Lake Hwy., 541/432-9821) is beautifully preserved, though the food here—steaks, pasta, fresh seafood—is very up-to-date. Main courses such as grilled halibut with marionberry glaze range from $18–28. For standard American fare and a more moderate price point, go to **Russell's at the Lake** (59984 Wallowa Lake Hwy., 541/432- 0591, three meals daily).

THE WALLOWA MOUNTAINS HIGH COUNTRY

The Wallowa Mountains are some of Oregon's most rugged, beautiful, and least visited: 715 square miles of this craggy backcountry is preserved as the **Eagle Cap Wilderness Area.** Glacier-torn valleys, high mountain lakes, and marble peaks are some of the rewards that long-distance hikers find on overnight treks. A few hiking trails offer recreation to day hikers. In addition, there's good fishing in streams and lakes, and in winter the heavy snowfalls attract both downhill and Nordic skiers. Forest Service campgrounds serve as base for Wallowa Mountains exploration. For more information on recreation and camping in the Wallowas, contact the Wallowa-Whitman National Forest (88401 Hwy. 82 in Enterprise, 541/426-4978, www.fs.fed.us/r6/w-w).

Hiking and Camping

Most Eagle Cap Wilderness Area trails are long and steep, and most alpine lakes are at least five miles from a trailhead, so opportunities for easy day hikes into the wilderness are limited. Camping is the best way to enjoy the area. Before heading out, pick up the Eagle Cap map from a Forest Service office or at local sporting goods stores. Higher elevations are usually free from snow by July 1.

Camping out in the Wallowa Valley and the Eagle Cap Wilderness can be as easy as pull-

The Wallowa Mountains rise above farmland in the Wallowa Valley.

ing off Route 82 just 15 miles east of Elgin and pitching your tent at **Minam State Recreation Area** ($5–8), or as rigorous as using one of the following three campsites as a jumping-off point for backpacking into the high country.

Boundary Campsite is five miles south of Wallowa on County Route 515, then two miles south on Forest Service Road 163. There's no fee for this site set along the banks of Bear Creek, but there's also no water. A trailhead provides access to the dazzling grandeur of the Eagle Cap basin.

The next campsite/trailhead is **Two Pan,** one of the most popular gateways into the Wallowas. To get here, head south from Lostine on County Route 551 for seven miles and down Forest Service Road 5202 for 11 miles. This is a rough and rocky washboard grade, so take your time. Firewood and vault toilets are available; there are no fees or water. Trails leave Two Pan for the Lostine River Valley and the glacial lakes at the base of Eagle Cap.

The third campsite is **Hurricane Creek,** three miles southwest of Joseph on Forest

NORTHEASTERN OREGON

Service Road 8205. There's no charge for overnight camping, and piped water and firewood are available. The Hurricane Creek trailhead leads to a hike along the east slope of the Hurricane Divide past Sacajawea Peak and the Matterhorn to the glacial lakes basin. An ambitious trek would start at Two Pan and end at Hurricane Creek. The lake basin area south of Joseph can get crowded, especially on July and August weekends.

If your budget allows for a guided adventure into the Wallowa wilds, here are two excellent services. The **Eagle Cap Wilderness Pack Station** (Rte. 1, Box 416, Joseph, 541/432-4145, www.eaglecapwildernesspackstation. com) has rides that cost as little as $25 per hour for short trips to lakes and streams in the Eagle Cap high country. However, the primary focus of this operation is outfitting backcountry expeditions into the Eagle Cap backcountry. For $225 per person per day, the outfitters will furnish your complete camp, including riding horses, pack stock, guide, wranglers, cook, and food. You furnish only your personal gear, such as clothing, sleeping bag, sleeping pad, and all other personal necessities. These outfitters also offer "drop" trips, where horses and mules carry people and supplies to a lake, then leave and return at an appointed time to pack you and your gear out. This service costs $295–325 per person.

Wallowa Llamas (Route 1, Box 84, Halfway 97834, 541/742-2661, www.wallowa llamas.com) offers a unique way to venture into the wilderness. One surefooted, even-tempered llama will carry 20 pounds of your gear; you carry the rest. The outfit offers three- to seven-day trips to Hells Canyon, Imnaha Falls, Eagle Meadows, and across the rugged Wallowas. The expeditions are designed for those with some backpacking experience or anyone in reasonably good shape. The outfitters provide provides tents, eating utensils, and all meals—and of course llamas. All you'll need is a sleeping bag and pad and personal effects. Three-day excursions begin at $395.

Skiing

The recreational delights of the Wallowas are not reserved for summer only. The skiing in this alpine wonderland can be excellent. **Ferguson Ridge Ski Area** (541/426-3493) is a small and laidback downhill facility with a rope tow and T-bar that climb from a 5,100-foot base to 5,800-foot-high Ferguson Ridge. The light eastern Oregon powder, when there's enough of it, makes for good skiing. Lift tickets are $12 a day; children under 13 pay $8. It's open 10 A.M.–4 P.M. weekends and holidays, and during the week when snow conditions are optimal. To get there, drive east from Joseph about five miles on the Wallowa Loop Highway, then follow signs south on Tucker Down Road.

For cross-country skiers, the **Sacajawea Park Cross-Country Ski Trail** challenges the ambitious. Take Hurricane Creek Road west from Joseph to the Hurricane Creek trailhead. This cross-country ski route will take you up into a basin on the northeast side of Sacajawea Peak. After two steep miles through the forest, the trail opens up into a clear area with a view of the surrounding glacial peaks.

Another popular spot is **Salt Creek Summit,** about 20 miles southeast of Joseph on Wallowa Loop Highway. The facility has five miles of marked but ungroomed ski trails and a plowed snow park. Backcountry ski mountaineering is the focus of **Wallowa Alpine Huts** (P.O. Box 762, Joseph 97846, 541/426-4887 or 800/545-5537, www.wallowahuts.com), which offers three- to five-day trips to 7,500-foot McCully Basin within the Eagle Cap Wilderness. Ski seven miles in to a yurt base camp, and spend the days exploring the high country on backcountry snowboards, telemark or randonee skis, then return to cooked meals, warm yurts, and even a sauna. Three-day trips begin at $425 and include all backcountry meals, accommodations, bedding, and guides.

Hells Canyon

❿ HELLS CANYON NATIONAL RECREATION AREA

In 1975, Congress established the Hells Canyon National Recreation Area (P.O. Box 490, Enterprise 97828, 541/426-5546, www.fs.fed. us/hellscanyon), which straddles a 71-mile portion of the Snake River (the river canyon itself is preserved in the 215,223-acre Hells Canyon Wilderness Area). Most of the terrain is made up of precipitous rock walls and steep, slot-like side valleys, which, along with the wilderness designation, means that just about the only way to experience this epic landscape is on foot, horseback, or—most excitingly—by boat.

The mighty Hells Canyon is the deepest river gorge in North America. It's also one of the wildest and most remote pieces of real estate in the Lower 48. For a distance of 106 miles, no bridge crosses the river, and few paved roads come even near the canyon. Between Hells Canyon Dam and Lewiston, Idaho, the Snake drops 1,300 feet in elevation in just 70 miles (in comparison, the Mississippi has an elevation change of 840 feet between Minneapolis and the Gulf of Mexico). At its deepest point, the gorge walls rise nearly 8,000 feet, deep enough to hold 47 Niagara Falls, stacked atop each other.

This isolation helps to preserve some the area's greatly varied plant and animal life. From Idaho's Seven Devils Wilderness to the Snake River in Hells Canyon and back up to Oregon's Wallowa Mountains, you'll find areas that replicate most of North America's ecological zones. Cheatgrass, primroses, sunflowers, and prickly pear cactus are included in the canyon's varied botany. Bear, elk, mule deer, bighorn sheep, eagles, otters, and chukhar partridges are frequently seen here. Several outfitters can steer you to the canyon's pictographs, which some sources place at 10,000 years of age. In addition to Chief Joseph and his Nez Perce tribe, miners and pioneers also occupied Hells Canyon, as many turn-of-the-century log cabins and shacks attest.

Seeing Hells Canyon by Vehicle

There are several ways to get to Hells Canyon from Oregon. From Baker City take Route 86 for 50 miles east to **Halfway.** Stop here to stock up on groceries and gas, continue on Route 86 another 16 miles to Oxbow Dam, and then downstream 20 miles on the Idaho side of the Snake River to **Hells Canyon Dam.** A visitors center is adjacent to where rafts put in on the Snake River at the beginning of the river's Wild and Scenic stretch. This site affords a spectacular view of the canyon. Another approach is via Route 82 through the Wallowa Valley to Enterprise, Joseph, and Imnaha. From Imnaha, one of the most isolated towns in America, take a rough, albeit recently improved road for 24 miles to **Hat Point Lookout.** The first five miles of ascent is not for the faint of heart—the guardrail-free dirt road is vertigo-inducing.

© BILL MCRAE

Hells Canyon is the deepest river canyon in the world.

NORTHEASTERN OREGON

However, once on ridge-top, the road edges to Hat Point and a view into Hells Canyon and the Snake River, a dizzying 7,000 feet below.

An altogether simpler way to glimpse the canyon is from the Wallowa Mountain Loop Road (a.k.a. Forest Road 39), which runs between Joseph and Halfway. The **Hells Canyon Lookout,** the only paved viewpoint into Hells Canyon, is 31 miles north of Halfway. The vista looks into the canyon (no glimpses of the river, however) with interpretive displays, picnic tables, and toilets.

Hiking

More than 900 miles of trails await hikers and backpackers in the Hells Canyon Recreation Area, and hiking is just about the only way to get to some of the canyon's more remote areas. However, it's not a hiking destination for novices. Before strapping on you hiking boots, consider that summer temperatures soar above 100°F, rattlesnakes abound, and potable water can be hard to find. Ticks and poison oak can be problems here, too. Black widow and brown recluse spiders can constitute the biggest danger, however. Major trails are maintained but others are difficult to follow. It's a good idea to talk to rangers before setting out, as this is extremely remote and challenging wilderness. You'll also want a recent map and a trail guide.

There are long-distance, riverside trails on both the Oregon and Idaho shores of the Snake River, but reaching them is a challenge. The rugged cliffs along the Hell's Canyon Dam are too steep for hiking trails, although a short, mile-long trail from the jet-boat launch area does pick its way down the Oregon side before ending precipitously. For longer hikes, you will need to start from trailheads along the ridges, and hike down to the river. Hat Point is a good place to drop onto the **Oregon Snake River Trail,** on the river's western edge. The most comfortable long-distance trail on the Oregon side is the **Western Rim Trail.** There are comparatively few steep ups and downs and daytime temperatures are much less oppressive than within the canyon. There is also plenty of shade among the rim's evergreen forests. On the other hand, the rim route has fewer water sources, so camping choices are limited.

Boating

Outfitters arrange Snake River float trips on rafts, dories, or kayaks, providing high adventure as the river bounces though 34 named rapids rated Class II–IV in the most commonly floated part of the canyon, the two- to three-day passage between Hells Canyon Dam and Pittsburgh Landing in Idaho (longer trips are available). For travelers with less time, turbine-powered jet-boat tours are also available—a less idyllic but equally exciting way to see the canyon in as little as a day. These turbine-powered, flat-bottomed boats are able to maneuver shallow water and rapids, though they are also very noisy and annoying if you aren't among the passengers. The recreation area website provides a list of outfitters licensed to guide trips on the Snake River. Be sure to check the offerings available, as they are abundant. The brief selection below is just taste of what's available and is intended to provide a guideline to prices and trips.

From the landing just below Hells Canyon Dam, **Hells Canyon Adventures, Inc.** (541/785-3352 or 800/422-3568, www.hells canyonadventures.com) offers a variety of jet-boat tours daily March–mid-October. The briefest and least expensive excursion is a two-hour afternoon jet-boat trip into the deepest part of the canyon, costing $35. A six-hour, $127 tour leaves at 9 A.M. and runs all the principal rapids of the canyon, and includes lunch and a stop at the Kirkwood Ranch Museum, a frontier ranch at the base of the canyon. For most tours, children under 12 are half price. Hells Canyon Excursion offers other tours, including float trips and fishing charters. Reservations are required.

Another local outfitter that specializes in white-water raft trips is **Hells Canyon Whitewater** (P.O. Box 566, Joseph, 97846, 541/432-0747 or 877/426-7238, www.hells canyonwhitewater.com) Three- to six-day trips are offered mid-June–mid-August, and include guide services, tent accommodations, transport to/from Joseph, and food. A three-day trip from Hells Canyon Dam to Pittsburg Landing in Idaho starts at $850 for adults, and $680 for youths.

If you plan to shoot the Class III and IV rapids of the Snake River on your own, you'll need a permit from the Hells Canyon Recreation Area office in Enterprise.

Fishing

Fishing for trout, catfish, smallmouth bass, and, if you're lucky, 100-year-old sturgeon can add to the pleasure of a raft trip. **Canyon Outfitters** (P.O. Box 893, Halfway 97834, 541/742-7238 or 877/742-7270, www.canyon outfitters.com) offers four-day drift boat fishing trips through Hells Canyon for $1,600 per person. Canyon Outfitters also offers summer white-water float trips with ample time for fishing (four days for $1,100).

Camping

Of the 12 campgrounds on the Oregon side of the national recreation area, we recommend the following three. **Lake Fork Campground,** 18 miles northeast of Halfway on Forest Service Road 39, has 10 sites with drinking water, and the fishing is good at nearby Fish Lake. **Indian Crossing,** located 45 miles southeast of Joseph on Forest Service Road 3960, has drinking water as well as a trailhead for backpacking into the Eagle Cap Wilderness. On the northern end of the recreational area, **Buckhorn Springs** is 43 miles northeast of Enterprise and features a great view, spring water, and berry-picking in season.

Accommodations

The town of Halfway (pop. 345), 17 miles from the Oxbow Dam on the Snake River, is a popular way station for Hells Canyon–bound travelers. The **(Pine Valley Lodge** (163 N. Main St., Halfway 97834, 541/742-2027, www.pv lodge.com, doubles from $75) is an unexpected pleasure in the rugged Hells Canyon country. You can't get much more Old-West-meets-Western-chic than this! Eight guest rooms have been created in three different vintage log and wood structures in downtown Halfway, and each is filled with amazing cowboy decor that's part history and part whimsy. Staying here is like settling into a really charming, upscale bunkhouse. Rates include a deluxe continental breakfast.

Reasonably priced standard rooms can be had at the **Halfway Motel** (170 S. Main, Halfway 97834, 541/742-5722, doubles from $55). Some have kitchenettes; all are close to gas, food, and shops.

Food

Restaurants are few and far between in this country, and it would be prudent to pack a few picnic items. In Halfway, **Wild Bill's and Co.** (157 Main St., 541/742-5833) is a bar and restaurant that serves three meals a day. Down at Oxbow, near the Snake River on Highway 86, is the **Hells Canyon Inn** (541/785-3383), a family restaurant that serves breakfast, lunch, and dinner.

Baker City

Baker City, set in a valley between the Wallowas and the Blue Mountains, is the quintessential Western ranch town, with a handsome downtown area filled with classic stone and red brick storefronts. Ranchers hereabout still drive their herds down the highways here, and folks wave howdy to passersby. Baker City a friendly place that has held on to its pioneer spirit. There's lots of history here—highlighted by the nation's foremost Oregon Trail interpretive center—and with its abundant and high quality facilities, Baker City is a good jumping-off spot for Hells Canyon, the deepest gorge in the world.

HISTORY

Baker City was named after Colonel Edward Baker, Oregon's first senator, Union general in

© BILL MCRAE

Baker City is home to the tallest building in Oregon east of the Cascades.

the Civil War, and a one-time law partner of Abraham Lincoln. In 1861, it became the hub of the eastern Oregon gold rush and its population swelled to 6,600, making it bigger than Boise. Baker City got its charter in 1874 and soon became known as the "Queen City," for all roads led to this commercial center. Stop by the U.S. National Bank here and check out the 80.4-ounce **Armstrong gold nugget,** found in 1913. It's a remnant from the days when this wealthy, raucous frontier boomtown was the biggest and most important in the region. It boasted the finest hotel between Salt Lake City and Portland—now reopened and polished to a fine patina—and even had a high school, the second in the Pacific Northwest.

East of town, along Route 7 and its offshoots leading into the Elkhorn and Blue Mountains, ghost towns like Granite, McEwen, and Sumpter are remnants of the gold rush days of the 1860s. The route, which follows the twisty contours of the Powder River, is particularly pretty when the deciduous trees take on fall hues.

SIGHTS
◖ National Historic Oregon Trail Interpretive Center

Six miles east of Baker City is the 23,000-square-foot National Historic Oregon Trail Interpretive Center (P.O. Box 854, Baker City 97814, 541/523-6391, www.blm.gov/or/oregontrail 9 A.M.–6 P.M. Apr.–Oct., 9 A.M.–4 P.M. Nov.–Mar., $5 adult, $3.50 for seniors and children). The museum is perched atop Flagstaff Hill overlooking a picturesque section of this famous frontier thoroughfare. The exhibit halls are arranged to simulate the route and experiences of pioneers on the 547-mile section of the trail within Oregon borders. While there are impressive artifacts as well as thought-provoking historic photos and video presentations, don't think of this as another passive viewing experience. The life-sized dioramas of Oregon Trail scenes, accompanied by taped renditions of immigrant voices and wagon wheels, make you feel like part of the great migration.

Theatrical entertainment, living-history exhibits, paintings, and aptly chosen pioneer diary entries recount the crossing of the Blue Mountains and the Cascades, or rafting down the Columbia into the Willamette Valley. The museum's interpretive loop articulates the immigrant's state of mind—whether it's awe giving way to boredom across the Oregon prairie, emotional duress on a perilous river crossing, or relief while adjusting to settlement at journey's end. Attention is given also to the pioneers' effect on Native American lands and cultures.

Outside the museum, your historical reverie is sustained by living-history exhibits and the chance to stand in the actual ruts left behind by pioneer wagons at **Virtue Flat,** a two-mile walk from the center. Here, surrounded by the 10,000-foot Elkhorn Mountains to the west, the Blues to the south, and the craggy Eagle Cap to the northeast, the "land at Eden's gate" becomes more than just another florid phrase from a pioneer diary.

Prior to departing the Oregon Trail Interpretive Center, check out the raised relief map of northeastern Oregon. Besides getting the lay of the land, you can call up information on area attractions by pushing a button.

Oregon Trail Regional Museum

Housed in a showcase natatorium built in 1920, the Oregon Trail Regional Museum (2490 Grove St., 541/523-9308, 9 A.M.–4 P.M. daily Mar.–Oct, admission by donation), houses an extensive collection of furniture, vehicles, and machinery from Baker City's frontier days as well as exhibits depicting the great migration. An extensive collection of rocks, minerals, and stones—including a display of florescent rocks—will be of interest to more than rockhounds. The museum is located across from Geiser Pollman Park, which has picnic tables and playgrounds.

Eastern Oregon Museum

Ten miles northwest of Baker City in the town of Haines is the Eastern Oregon Museum (3rd and School Sts., 541/856-3233, 9 A.M.–5 P.M. Thurs.–Mon., May 15–Sept. 15). One of the largest historical museums in this part of the state, it boasts over 10,000 artifacts. It has an outstanding collection of vintage farming equipment, mining tools and paraphernalia, and pioneer relics. The museum also has a fascinating collection of antique toys and dolls, and the grounds include a one-room school and the 1880s train depot.

SPORTS AND RECREATION
Skiing
Anthony Lakes Ski Area (541/856-3277, www. anthonylakes.com) is 18 miles west of Haines on the Elkhorn Scenic Byway. Generally open daily Thanksgiving–mid-April, this ski resort offers a triple chairlift, Nordic trail system, day lodge, ski shop, and ski lessons. All-day lift tickets are $32 adults, $28 children under 13 and seniors, $19 ages 7–12. This is Oregon's first and highest (7,000 feet) ski area. It offers pristine dry powder and a family-oriented environment. The 1,100 acres of slopes offer plenty of challenge—80 percent of the runs are intermediate or expert.

Camping

The area's best camping is up in the Elkhorn Range near Anthony Lakes. **Anthony Lakes Campground** (541/523-6391, www.fs.fed. us/r6/w-w) is right at the base of the Anthony Lakes Ski Area, with campsites tucked among huge boulders a short walk from the lake. About a mile farther east along Forest Road 73, find **Grande Ronde Lake Campground,** a pretty spot located at the headwaters of the Grande Ronde River.

ACCOMMODATIONS

Baker City's pre-eminent lodging choice is the **C Geiser Grand Hotel** (1996 Main St., 541/523-1899 or 888/434-7374, www.geiser grand.com, doubles from $99), a showplace of period grandeur and refinement. Built in 1889 as the finest hotel between Portland and Salt Lake City, the Geiser Grand was totally updated and refurbished in the 1990s, and again sparkles with old-fashioned charm and modern comforts. Amid Viennese chandeliers, mahogany columns, and a stained-glass skylight 40 feet above the dining room, you'll feel like you've traveled back in time to a more gracious time. For a hotel of this vintage, the standard rooms are large but for just $10 more you can step up to a suite—particularly one on a corner or perhaps in the copula—and have lots of room and 10-foot-high windows on two sides to drink in the Blue Mountain views. Add in reasonably priced, nicely prepare meals, and you might want to extend your stay.

The **Best Western Sunridge Inn** (1 Sunridge Ln., 97814, 541/523-6444, www.best western.com, doubles from $86), is a large

© BILL MCRAE

The Geiser Grand is eastern Oregon's most elegant hotel.

motel complex with the feel of a small resort. Five motel blocks surround a nicely landscaped central garden, pool and fitness area, which is also linked to the motel's two restaurants. Rooms have private patios, coffeemakers, and high-speed Internet access. A less costly choice is the **El Dorado Inn** (695 Campbell St., 541/523-6494 or 800/537-5756, www.eldoradoinn.net, doubles from $45), which offers clean comfortable rooms and an indoor pool.

Baer House Bed & Breakfast (2333 Main St., 541/523-1055 or 800/709-7637), is a handsome Italianate Victorian home built in 1882 that's been lovely transformed into a B&B. There are three guest rooms, one of which is a two-bedroom suite with private bath. The hosts are friendly and welcoming, and it is just a few minutes walk from Baker City's historic downtown.

FOOD

Along Baker City's Main Street, watch for Luigi, the life-size plaster cast of an Italian waiter who stands in front of the **Baker City**

Café (1840 Main St., 541/523-6099, 10 A.M.–3 P.M. Mon.–Sat.), a friendly little spot with huge portions of pasta, pizza, salads,, and sandwiches. ❰ **Barley Brown's Brew Pub** (2190 Main St., 541/523-4266) serves some of the best brews in the country—in fact, the pub won eight medals, including two golds at the 2006 North American Brewers Association beer competition. The beer is only available at the pub, so make a pilgrimage for a pint and enjoy well-prepared food as well. The menu goes far beyond pub grub, including steak, seafood, and pasta. Most main courses are $8–18.

The **Geiser Grill** in the Geiser Grand Hotel (1996 Main St., 541/523-1899, lunch and dinner daily, also for breakfast Sat. and Sun.) is easily the classiest places to eat in Baker City, if not in all of eastern Oregon. The setting is splendid—a soaring stained-glass ceiling surmounts a wood-paneled dining room sparkling with linen, crystal, and candles. The food's tasty, too—great steak and prime rib plus fresh salmon and seafood from the Pacific, all prepared with the kind of verve you'd expect in Portland or San Francisco. Main courses range $18–25.

Ten miles north of Baker City is the beloved **Haines Steakhouse** (Rte. 30, 541/856-3639, dinner Wed.–Mon.), where the tab will run $20–25 per person, but it's worth it. Antiques and cowboy Americana decorate the restaurant, enhancing what may be described as first-rate chuckwagon fare.

INFORMATION

Contact the **Baker County Chamber and Visitor Center** (490 Campbell St., Baker City 97814, 541/523-3356 or 800/523-1235, www.visitbaker.com) for more information.

The *Baker City Herald* (P.O. Box 807, Baker City 97814) publishes a good annual travel guide to the local area. It's available free at area museums and tourist facilities.

GETTING THERE

Greyhound buses serve Baker City on runs between Portland and Boise. There are two buses daily in each direction, and the terminal is at 515 Campbell (541/523-5011).

Sumpter and Vicinity

In the Elkhorn Mountains west of Baker City, Sumpter is a former gold-mining town, one of many small communities in this area that hovers between ghost-town and tourist-town status. The first settlers here were five Southerners who in 1862 found gold in Cracker Creek. They built a stone cabin and christened it Fort Sumter after the South Carolina garrison that was shelled in April of 1861, signaling the start of the Civil War. In 1883, the U.S. Post Office rejected the name, so locals changed it by dropping the "Fort" and adding a "p." The heyday of gold mining in the area was 1900–1905, when over 3,000 miners worked the hard-rock mines and dredged the Powder River. By 1905, most of the easily accessed gold was gone, but dredging continued until 1954. Today, Sumpter has around 150 year-round residents—almost, but not quite, a ghost town—and the old storefronts are now antique shops and art galleries. A few vintage watering holes still provide food and drink to locals and travelers alike. Sumpter is 30 miles west of Baker City and 57 miles east of John Day.

SIGHTS
Sumpter Valley Dredge State Heritage Area

This state-parks-managed site right in Sumpter (541/894-2486 or 800/551-6949) preserves one of three gold dredges that scooped up and sifted gold-rich Powder River gravels. With a hull 125 feet long and 52 feet wide, this is the longest and most accessible gold dredge in the country, in its day capable of chewing up 225 cubic feet (8.33 cubic yards) per minute, or an average of 100 acres of riverbed per year. Sticking out from the dredge's hull is a massive boom bearing 72 one-ton buckets. The buckets, moving like the chain of a chainsaw, would bore into the riverbank and carry the loose rock back into the dredge interior. Once inside, the rock passed through a series of steel cylinders that separated the material by size, sending the smaller material deeper into the

dredge. Using water and sluices, the gold was separated from the sediment, which along with the gravel and larger rocks passed through the back of the dredge and was deposited as mine tailings. In its lifetime this dredge alone made $4.5 million when gold prices were a mere $35 per troy ounce. The dredge passed to Oregon state parks in 1995, which has restored the dredge and in summer offers interpretive displays and tours. Access to the park is free, with trails leading out into wildlife viewing areas—the orderly piles of mine tailings along the Powder River have become an unlikely wetlands habitat.

Sumpter Valley Railroad

Another piece of local history is the Sumpter Valley Railroad (P.O. Box 389, Baker City 97814, 866/894-2268 or 541/894-2268, http://svry.com), a rebuilt narrow-gauge excursion train pulled by steam engines. The railway originally ran between Baker City and Prairie City from 1890 to 1961, transporting logs and ore in addition to passengers. Today, passengers ride the five miles between McEwen Station and Sumpter in two vintage observation cars; a restored 1890 caboose is also part of the train. Ticket are $12.50 round-trip for adults ($9 one-way), $11.50 round-trip for seniors ($8 one-way) $8 round-trip for children 6–16 ($5 one-way), and $30 round-trip per family ($20 one-way). The railroad is open on weekends from Memorial Day weekend to the last weekend in September with three runs daily at 10 A.M., 12:39 P.M., and 3 P.M.

Ghost Towns and Backroads

The Sumpter area is rich in abandoned gold-rush towns. While not an official tourist site, the ghost town of **Whitney,** located 12 miles up Route 7 from its junction with U.S. 26 (about 15 miles east of Prairie City), has a story to tell to those who visit its ruins. Whitney was the terminus for stage lines to the mining and

NORTHEASTERN OREGON

NORTHEASTERN OREGON SCENIC BYWAYS

© BILL MCRAE

Jet boats depart from below Hells Canyon Dam on the Snake River.

Northeastern Oregon is road trip country. To underscore this contention, several roads in this region are designated as scenic byways.

The **Wallowa Mountain Loop Road** is a scenic, 54-mile drive through Hells Canyon Country. The route begins with the Joseph-Imnaha Highway through farms and canyons. Turn south on Wallowa Mountain Loop Road to the Imnaha River, then ascend into alpine forests along Dry Creek Road to Halfway. You'll come out on the south flank of the Wallowas where *Paint Your Wagon* was filmed in the '60s and Disney's *Homeward Bound* was shot in the early '90s. Turn east for a shoreline view of Snake River Canyon and Hells Canyon at Oxbow (Hells Canyon and Brownlee Dams). This fully paved route can serve as a shortcut to Baker City and Boise in summer.

Explore the high country behind Sumpter by driving the **Elkhorn Drive National Scenic Byway,** which takes you northwest from Sumpter through the gold-mining territory to Granite, across the north fork of the John Day, past Anthony Lake, and on to Baker City. Because much of this road is above 5,000 feet in elevation, the loop is open only a few months of the year. The portion south of Anthony Lakes and north of Granite is closed by snow from early November through June or early July. The Elkhorn Byway climbs higher than any other paved road in Oregon (7,392 feet), after passing North Fork John Day Campground and the junction with Blue Mountains Scenic Byway. The craggy granite peaks of the northern Elkhorns – several higher than 8,000 feet – are near this area.

The longest of eastern Oregon's scenic byways is the **Journey Through Time Scenic Byway.** Departing from (or ending at) Biggs, on I-5 and the Columbia Gorge, this highly scenic route takes the back roads through the canyon-cut Columbia Plateau, extending to Baker City. The highlight of this tour is the John Day River canyon, where millennia of erosion have sculpted a dramatic gorge through layers of volcanic formations, in the process unveiling the fossil remains of ancient life.

cattle towns of Unity, Bridgeport, and Malheur City. Now abandoned buildings are all that remain of this bustling community of the early 1900s. An interpretive sign just off Route 7 explains the local history.

Back-road and ghost-town connoisseurs will want to stop and take a gander at the remains of **Granite** (population 22), Oregon's smallest incorporated town. With its false-fronted buildings of unpainted, splintered boards, Granite is a true "ghost town." Hard as it is to believe, this place once had four saloons, a 50-room hotel, several smaller hotels, a boardinghouse, a church, and a wooden jail. Founded in 1862, its mining legacy sustained the town through the 1930s. The need for miners in World War II defense industries at that time compelled President Franklin Delano Roosevelt to shut down the mines. Today, people are moving back despite the lack of modern conveniences (phone service didn't arrive in Granite until 2000). Community ties are maintained by regular visits to the Granite store where miners, retirees, and other residents meet up to keep the ghost alive.

EVENTS

On Memorial Day, July 4, and Labor Day weekend, folks head to the fairgrounds for the **Sumpter Flea Market.** Collectibles, crafts, and food are arrayed in a beautiful mountain setting. This event is legendary among Oregon's bargain hunters.

ACCOMMODATIONS AND FOOD

The **Sumpter Stockade Hostel** (129 E. Austin, 541/894-2253, www.sumpterstockade.com, $15 per bed in bunk accommodations, $5 tent) offers dorm-style accommodations, plus two- and three-bed rooms in a newly built structure designed to resemble a Old West military fort, complete with pole stockade. Tent campers can set up on the lawn inside the stockade. Facilities include a kitchen, barbecue, and a saloon. Sumpter's original 1900 hospital is back in business as **Sumpter Bed and Breakfast** (344 N.E. Columbia St., 541/894-0048 or 800/287-5234, www.sumpterbb.com, doubles from $80), with six antique-filled guestrooms and a hearty breakfast that may, if you're lucky, include the inn's delectable huckleberry pancakes. **The Depot Inn** (179 Mill St., 541/894-2522 or 800/390-2522, doubles from $65) is a log-sided motel with basic rooms right at the center of town. For food, the **Elkhorn Saloon** (open daily for lunch and dinner, main courses $6–17) offers pizza and standard American fare, plus live music on weekend evenings. **Borello's** (175 S. Mill, 541/894-2480, open daily for lunch and dinner in summer; call ahead for winter hour, main courses $9–15) is rather a surprise in this near ghost town, offering tasty pasta and pizza that would pass muster in a far larger town. **Sumpter Nugget & Gold Room Steak House,** (200 N. Mill St., 541/894-2366, lunch and dinner, main courses $8–17) is the local steakhouse.

Ontario

Located midway between Portland and Salt Lake City in Oregon's far east, Ontario is where "Oregon's day begins." It's the biggest city in Malheur County, with a population of 10,000. Ontario ships over 5 percent of the nation's onions and provides a good portion of the sweet russet potatoes used for french fries in national fast food chains. Other local crops include sugar beets, peppermint, grains, and ornamental flowers. This abundance derives from a location on the fertile plains at the Snake and Malheur Rivers confluence.

HISTORY

Ontario, the town at the beginning of the Oregon section of the Oregon Trail, began as a cattle-shipping depot. The 1883 completion of the Oregon Short Line Railroad connected it to the Union Pacific and markets in the east. In 1939, reservoirs on the Snake River provided

THE OREGON TRAIL

The pioneer trek along the Oregon Trail, a tide of migration starting in 1841 and lasting over 20 years, is one of this country's great epochs, celebrated in novels, films, books, and songs. It is among the largest voluntary human migrations ever recorded.

The wagon trains started in Independence, Missouri, as soon as the spring grass was green. Then the race was on to get across the far mountains before the winter snows. The route – which usually required six months to complete – followed the North Platte River to South Pass in Wyoming, then crossed the Snake River Plalin in Idaho, then across the Snake River and up and over the Blue Mountains in eastern Oregon to The Dalles. Here, the pioneers faced a decision: Either they put themselves and all their belongings onto rafts to float the rapids of the otherwise impassive Columbia Gorge, or they struggled up the flanks of Mount Hood, descending into the Willamette Valley via the precipitous Barlow Trail.

In 1843, some 900 immigrants traveled the Oregon Trail, a number that swelled to 17,500 just 10 years later. When it was all over, about 50,000 pioneers followed the trail to the end and settled in Oregon Country – present-day Oregon, Washington, and Idaho. But these numbers tell only part of the story.

Although the first few hundred miles were easy traveling across the plains, the hardships were not long in coming. Contrary to the stereotype of hostile Native Americans being a major cause of casualties, cholera was by far the leading cause of death on the 2,000-mile journey that became known as "The Longest Graveyard." Some historians estimate at least 30,000 immigrants had died on the Oregon Trail by 1859. This would amount to an average of one unmarked grave for every 100 yards between Independence and Oregon City.

At Fort Hall in eastern Idaho, there was a fork in the trail and a sign that read "To Oregon." It was here that the pioneers had to make a key decision. They could head south to California and the gold fields shining with the promise of instant wealth, or they could continue west to Oregon, where the fertile Willamette Valley offered its own allure as a New Jerusalem for serious farmers and homesteaders. Some Oregonians like to tell a more pointed version of the story, which claims that the sign for the California road was marked by a pile of gold-painted rocks, in contrast to the "To Oregon" sign. The implication was that people who could read – or who were more interested in domestic pursuits than adventure – would head to Oregon. While this intepretation is not seriously accepted by historians, it remains a source of good-natured humor between the two states.

irrigation water to the otherwise parched valley, turning it into a rich agricultural region.

In 1942, President Franklin D. Roosevelt issued Executive Order 9066, which ordered the removal of 120,000 Japanese Americans from the West Coast to 10 inland concentration camps located in isolated areas of seven states. About 5,000 Japanese Americans were moved to an internment camp near Ontario. Under the leadership of Ontario mayor Elmo Smith, the southeastern Oregon farming community invited internees to help fill service and farm jobs. By the end of the war, 1,000 Japanese Americans had settled in the Ontario area, giving Malheur County the largest percentage of Japanese Americans in Oregon. As a result, Japanese surnames grace many a ranch or farmstead in eastern Oregon. An influx of migrant workers from Latin America who came to work the crops in the 1950s and '60s also stayed to start new lives, adding yet another ethnic flavor to a cultural stew that already contained Paiutes and Basques. All of the above is celebrated in the **Four Rivers Cultural Center** (888/211-1222) at Treasure Valley Community College, at the junction of I-84 (Route 20, U.S. 26, and U.S. 95), featuring a museum, theater, convention center, and formal Japanese garden.

SIGHTS
Vale

Remnants of the Oregon Trail still cross this remote corner of Oregon. Museums, historic markers, and wagon rut memorials stud the area. South of Ontario, between Nyssa and Adrian along Route 201, a roadside monument commemorates the trail's **Snake River Crossing** into Oregon. Directly across the Snake from this point was Fort Boise, a Hudson's Bay Company fur-trading fort that doubled as a landmark and trade center for often-desperate pioneers. The fort was swept away by floods years ago; the site is now part of a wildlife refuge.

Follow the Oregon Trail from Nyssa to Vale to find several other historic sites. Take Enterprise Ave just west of Nyssa and turn right on Lytle Boulevard. From here, the paved road closely follows the tracks of the Oregon Trail to Vale.

Keeney Pass Oregon Trail Historic Site

The Keeney Pass Oregon Trail Historic Site, four miles south of Vale, has a display of the deep ruts cut into the earth by ironclad wagon wheels. This exhibit marks the most-used route of the wagon trains as they passed through the Snake River Valley on their way to Baker Valley to the north. From the top of this pass you can see the route of a whole day's journey on the trail to Oregon, 150 years ago. Ponder the fact that one pioneer in 10 died on this arduous transcontinental trek. In June and July, Indian paintbrush and penstemon add a dash of color to the sagebrush and rabbitbrush that surround the ruts in the trail.

Vale, the seat of Malheur County, is located on the Malheur River at the spot where Oregon Trail wagon trains crossed the Malheur River, 28 miles west of Ontario on U.S. 20/26. If you're intrigued by the drama of the pioneers, this little town offers an abundance of historical insight as well as evocative murals of historical scenes. On your visit to Vale, look north to **Malheur Butte** at Mile Marker 254. This long-extinct volcano was used as a lookout point by Native Americans watching for the wagon trains. At **Malheur Crossing,** on the east edge of Vale, the pioneers stopped to take advantage of natural hot water from underground thermal springs to bathe and do their laundry. On cool days, steam rises off the hot springs, which flow into the river between the two highway bridges. Another site of interest in Vale is the **Stone House,** one block east of the Courthouse on Main Street. Built in 1872, it replaced a mud hut way station on the trail.

Farewell Bend

Twenty-two miles north of Ontario on I-84 is Farewell Bend, where travelers along the old Oregon Trail left the valley of the Snake River, which they had more or less followed since central Idaho, and climbed up into the desert uplands of eastern Oregon.

Before undertaking the strenuous journey through desert landscapes to the imposing Blue Mountains, Oregon Trail travelers usually rested at Farewell Bend, grazing livestock, gathering wood and otherwise preparing themselves for the arduous trip ahead. Today **Farewell Bend State Park,** commemorates this placid pioneer wayside with a picnic and play area, boat launch and large campground.

EVENTS

The **Vale Rodeo** is a four-day fete that takes place over the July 1–4 holiday. It's highlighted by the **Suicide Race,** an event held at nearby Vale Butte in which cowboys race their horses off a steep slope into an arena.

The **Obon Odori Festival** celebrating Ontario's Japanese heritage is held the third week in July at Ontario's Buddhist temple (286 S.E. 4th St., 541/889-8562). On the schedule are tours of the temple, a dinner featuring Asian cuisine, arts-and-crafts displays, and an evening of dancing with audience participation.

SPORTS AND RECREATION

Ontario-Shadow Butte Golf Course (541/889-9022) is an 18-hole municipal course with pro shop and lounge, two miles west of Ontario.

ACCOMMODATIONS AND FOOD

There is a cluster of motels at I-84 Exit 376. If you want to call ahead, the **Holiday Motor Inn** (615 E. Idaho Ave., 541/889-9188, doubles from $48) is a good value and has a restaurant and outdoor pool. The **Best Western Inn** (251 Goodfellow St., 541/889-2600 or 800/828-0364, doubles from $74), has an indoor pool, exercise room, guest laundry, plus a free continental breakfast. Some rooms have microwaves and refrigerators.

Start the day with lattes and muffins at **Coyote Coffee and Deli** (146 S.W. 4th Ave. 541/889-4695). For a traditional breakfast, try the **Fourth Avenue Diner** (1281 S.W. 4th Ave., 541/889-4052) or wait until lunch to try great Mexican food as some of the Ontario's best food takes you south of the border, befitting a city with a large Mexican population. **Fiesta Guadalajara,** (336 S. Oregon St., 541/889-8064, open Mon.–Sat. for lunch and dinner) is downtown's liveliest Mexican restaurant. Between the interstate and downtown is **Casa Jaramillo** (157 S.E. 2nd Ave., 541/889-9258, open Mon.–Sat. for lunch and dinner), an Ontario institution. At both of these restaurants expect high quality Mexican fare with most main courses $8–12. At **Cheyenne's Social Club Steakhouse** (111 S.W. 1st Ave., 541/889-3777, open nightly for dinner, main courses $11–24) you'll find a supper-club atmosphere and the city's best steaks and prime rib.

INFORMATION

Contact the **Malheur County Chamber of Commerce** (676 S.W. 5th Ave., Ontario 97914, 541/889-8012, www.ontariochamber.com) for more information on the area.

GETTING THERE

Greyhound buses pass through Ontario on twice-daily trips in each direction between Portland and Boise. The terminal is at 653 East Idaho Avenue (541/823-2567).

SOUTHEASTERN OREGON

Southeastern Oregon is a place where travelers shed their notions of what Oregon is supposed to be like. It's dry, but with huge wetland areas. It's a little bit backcountry, but also surprisingly sophisticated. It's out in the middle of nowhere, but has a couple of the state's most charming hotels. And it does deliver on what most travelers seek: wildlife galore. Malheur National Wildlife Refuge is one of the Northwest's top birding areas, especially during the spring and fall migrations, when it's easy to spot well over 50 species in a day. Hart Mountain has a refuge for pronghorn antelope, which can be seen across all of southeastern Oregon, and there are even wild mustangs living on Steens Mountain.

Although it's handy to come to southeastern Oregon prepared to camp, there are enough lodgings, mostly simple, to make your trip a little less rugged.

The area between La Pine and Lakeview has some of the most intriguing geological formations in the Northwest. Evidence of the cataclysmic forces that shaped the Columbia Plateau and the Great Basin are on display in this starkly beautiful part of the state. Fractures in the ground and wave patterns left by ancient lakes on the flanks of mountains are some of the fingerprints left here by the hand of nature.

The sparsely populated sagebrush, rimrock, and grassy plains around Malheur Wildlife Refuge and Steens Mountain is home to cattle ranches, a large wildlife refuge, a usually dry alkaline lakebed, and some hot springs. The tiny town of Crane has one of the few public boarding schools in the United States. Students

HIGHLIGHTS

◖ Summer Lake: You could say that this is the middle of nowhere, but you're actually surrounded by geological curiosities such as Crack-in-the-Ground and Hole-in-the-Ground; birds, including grebes, pintails, and cinnamon teals; and minimally developed hot springs (page 508).

◖ Hart Mountain National Antelope Refuge: Antelope they're not, but you will find pronghorn here, along with much more wildlife and, once again, hot springs (page 511).

◖ Crystal Crane Hot Springs: Southeastern Oregon is awash in hot water... you can actually swim in the big hot springs-fed pond here (page 514).

◖ Malheur National Wildlife Refuge: This wet spot in the desert supports a huge variety of bird life, especially during the spring and fall migrations. Early-rising springtime birders may get to witness the sage grouse courtship ritual (page 516).

◖ Steens Mountain: Drive up the gradually sloping west face of this fault-block mountain; when you get to the top, it drops straight off to the Alvord Desert. Take your time, hike the trails, and bring binoculars – you may catch a glimpse of the local wild mustangs (page 519).

◖ Alvord Desert: It's hard to believe that this dry, blindingly white alkaline playa, or lakebed, is in the same state as the lush forests of western Oregon. But here, once again, you'll find hot springs (page 522).

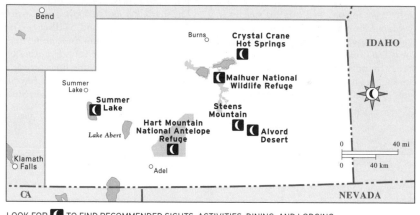

LOOK FOR ◖ TO FIND RECOMMENDED SIGHTS, ACTIVITIES, DINING, AND LODGING.

reside in dorms on campus because most come from ranches located many miles from town.

In the very southeast corner of the state, the area carved out by the Owyhee River is wild and beautiful, with only a handful of very small settlements.

PLANNING YOUR TIME

If you're looking to explore the open spaces and wildlife of southeastern Oregon, be pre-pared to take your time. Once you settle into the rhythm of driving, poking around, and pausing to look at a kingfisher or some prong-horn, you may find that the rest of the world seems very far away. You'll get the most out of this tour if you combine motel/hotel lodgings with camping.

Start this pilgrimage south of Bend in La Pine. From the La Pine State Park, head southeast on Route 31, with detours to visit

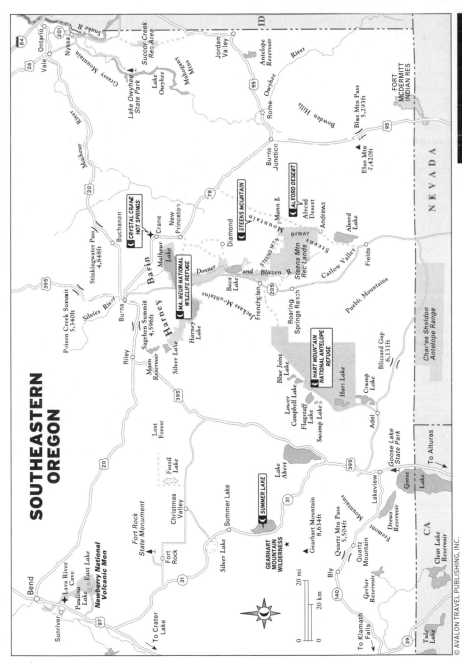

SOUTHEASTERN OREGON

© AVALON TRAVEL PUBLISHING, INC.

Hole-in-the-Ground, Fort Rock, and Crack-in-the-Ground. Spend the first night at **Summer Lake,** with a drive over to the Cowboy Dinner Tree for a steak or chicken dinner (reservations required). The next morning, take an early walk to look at birds and stop to soak in the pool at Summer Lake Hot Springs.

Continue down the highway to Paisley and, if you're prepared to fish, head up the Chewaucan River to see what's biting. Otherwise, keep going to Lakeview, where it's a good idea to stock up on groceries and gas. In Lakeview, stop to take a look at Old Perpetual, a geyser in the front yard of Hunter's Hot Springs, then head east to **Hart Mountain.** From tiny Plush, it's almost straight up the west side of the fault-block mountain to a gently eastward-sloping plateau. This is where you'll find your second night's lodging, the campground. The big reason to stay the night here, besides having a chance to explore the trails on foot or mountain bike, is a soak in the hot springs. But if camping is not in the picture, push on east to Frenchglen. Day 3 begins with a soak in the hot springs before breaking camp and driving east along the 50-mile gravel road to Route 205 and Frenchglen. Take your time along this stretch of road—it's a good place to watch for wildlife. Once in Frenchglen, either check in at the rustic Frenchglen Hotel or find a campsite at Page Springs Campground. Spend some time wandering around P Ranch, admiring the old barn and watching birds. (Even complete novices will be able to find the turkey vultures perching on the fire tower!)

It will take all of the next day to explore **Steens Mountain.** Be sure to take your time

and get out of the car from time to time. After the long drive, treat yourself to dinner and the company of fellow travelers at the Frenchglen Hotel, and head to bed early, because Day 5 will be devoted to bird-watching, and everybody knows that birds are most active around dawn. In fact, early morning at Page Springs offers the chance to see many birds, especially if you hike upriver from the campground. Devote the rest of the day to driving (or mountain biking) slowly up the Central Patrol Road, then making your way to the **Malheur Wildlife Refuge's** headquarters. Return south on Route 205, with a stop at the Buena Vista Ponds, then head east to your night's dinner and lodging at the Hotel Diamond.

Day 6 begins by exploring Peter French's Round Barn and the nearby Diamond Craters. Then, get ready for a long drive south along Route 205 to Fields for lunch and a milkshake. From Fields, turn north and head up to the Alvord Desert, located under the eastern face of Steens Mountain. If it's not scorching hot outside, pay a visit to the roadside hot springs.

From here, if you need to get back to civilization, continue on north. Spend the night either in Burns or at a tiny cabin at **Crystal Crane Hot Springs,** just west of the town of Crane.

But if you can spend an extra day or two on the road, turn southeast on Route 78, and at Burns Junction head east on U.S. 95. Stop and camp along the Owyhee River in Rome and, the next day, continue on to Jordan Valley and north to Leslie Gulch and Succor Creek State Park. Camp at the state park and wind up your tour by going north to Vale or Ontario, where you'll find a highway that leads toward home.

Lake County

One of Oregon's three largest counties, Lake County is home to just 7,500 people—and about 120,000 head of cattle. In other words, there's lots of elbow room, with the population density working out to about one person per square mile. This land of open spaces and geologic marvels spawns a hardy breed that clings to Old West traditions. Cowboys herd cattle on horseback, itinerant prospectors dig for color in the Quartz Mountains, and homesteaders tend to their farms in the remote outback. The county is called the Gem of Oregon not only because the region is the best place to find Oregon's official gemstone, the suntone or "Plush diamond," a semi-precious stone found in the area north of Plush. The moniker also pays homage to the gemlike beauty of the county's wide vistas beneath skies of pastel blue.

Visitors can climb the ancient citadel of Fort Rock, camp along a high mountain stream in Fremont National Forest, soak their bones in the soothing mineral waters of Hunter's Hot Springs, or enjoy wildlife viewing at Hart Mountain National Antelope Refuge. Because of the varied vertical topography and wind drafts, hang gliding has drawn a fair number of visitors to the cliffs around Lakeview.

The semi-arid climate here is generally cool, with 250 days of sunshine a year. Summer temperatures stay in the mid-80s; winter temperatures drop to the low 30s. Precipitation averages about 16 inches a year. At higher elevations in Lake County, there are as few as 20 frost-free days a year. This area can be a harsh land with little tolerance for the foolish, so take sensible precautions like toting extra water and gas. Despite a low density of creature comforts, you'll enjoy exploring this high desert country loaded to its sandy brim with wonders found nowhere else.

HISTORY

The history of human occupation here and in the Pacific Northwest has been dated back 13,200 years through carbon-dating of grass sandals found in Fort Rock Cave. Early desert dwellers who roamed the Great Basin in search of game and food witnessed the eruption of Mount Mazama 6,000–8,000 years ago. Their descendants, the Northern Paiutes, were also hunter-gatherers. This Lake County tribe was known as the Groundhog Eaters. These indigenous peoples left more petroglyphs and pictographs in Lake County than in all the rest of Oregon and Washington.

The first Europeans to venture into the area were French-Canadian trappers working for the Hudson's Bay Company in the early 1800s, who were eventually joined by American mountain men. In 1825 that Peter Skene Ogden, chief trader for the Hudson's Bay Company, made an "official" tour of the area when he sensed the threat of an American incursion. John Frémont and a party guided by Kit Carson marched through here in 1843, naming Summer and Abert Lakes.

The journals kept during these expeditions noted broad valleys with grasses "belly-high to a horse." This information attracted a new cast of players: the cattle and sheep barons. With the passage of the Homestead Act in 1862, homesteaders moved in and started up more modest spreads. The white influx resulted in frequent tensions with the original occupants, which often culminated in bloodletting on both sides. But after the Bannock-Paiute uprising in 1878, the local natives were herded up and banished to a reservation.

In the growth spurt that followed, the town of Lakeview was chartered, in 1889; it burned to the ground in 1900 and was rebuilt with brick and corrugated-iron roofs. Other hopeful hamlets with names like Arrow, Buffalo, and Loma Vista sprang up around the county, thanks to a reactivated Federal Homestead Act in 1909 that sanctioned 320 free acres per settler. Many of these tiny burgs dried up and blew away after the 1918–1920 drought. However, larger communities like Lakeview, Paisley, and Summer Lake held

SOUTHEASTERN OREGON

CRACKS AND CAVES

© BILL MCRAE

Crack-in-the-Ground is one of the many geological oddities you'll see on the road from La Pine to Lakeview.

Southeast of La Pine, off Route 31, lies a concentration of interesting geological features,. One of the more unusual of these oddities is **Hole-in-the-Ground.** Although this 300-foot-deep indentation looks like a meteor crater, scientists believe molten lava came into contact with water here, causing a massive explosion that quarried out a 7.5-mile-diameter crater, or maar. We estimate the total area to be about 280 acres. Astronauts came here in 1966 to experience the lunarlike terrain.

To find this unusual and awesome sight from U.S. 97, drive 22 miles southeast on Route 31; turn left at the Hole-in-the-Ground sign. Drive 3.1 miles to the next sign. Turn right and go 1.1 mile to the final sign. Turn left and go 0.2 miles to the rim of the Hole.

About five miles farther down Route 31 from the turnoff to Hole-in-the-Ground is **Fort Rock Cave** (a.k.a. Sandal Cave, www.fortrockmuseum.com/cave), a formation that was carved by wave action against what was once

on. With the advent of refrigerated railroad cars, big ranchers prospered. Local farmers figured out how to irrigate and cultivate this ornery land, and those tough enough to survive eventually came to terms with life on the dry side.

ALONG ROUTE 31: LA PINE TO LAKEVIEW

Starting at the junction of U.S. 97 and Route 31 at La Pine, many sites described in the following itinerary are annotated in the BLM's "Christmas Valley" publication, available from the BLM Lakeview office (1301 S. G St., Lakeview 97630, 541/947-2177), and in a Forest Service brochure available from the Fort Rock Ranger District (1230 N.E. 3rd, Ste. A-262, Bend 97701, 541/383-4700, www.fs.fed.us/r6/centraloregon).

A vehicle with a bit of clearance is indispensable in this region if you value your oil pan (a Subaru wagon made it to all the places described). Stock up on provisions in Bend or La Pine.

a basalt island in an immense lake. In 1938 anthropologist Luther Cressman discovered over 70 ancient sandals woven from sagebrush in the 50-foot-deep cave. Dated at almost 10,000 years old, the sandals are the oldest human artifacts found in the Northwest and the oldest known surviving footwear on earth.

A mile east of the cave is **Fort Rock State Park** (800/551-6949, www.oregonstateparks.org/park_40.php), which towers 400 feet above the sagebrush plains. At the base of this tuff ring is an area of wave erosion cut by a long-disappeared lake. Fall and winter here offer wildlife-viewing par excellence; large herds of mule deer can be seen mid-November–mid-April, and pronghorn range over the alfalfa fields year-round. Many birds nest in the rocks, and golden eagles, hawks, kestrels, and peregrine falcons soar overhead. The state park offers trails and amenities for climbers and sightseers.

The nearby town of Fort Rock has an old-time flavor that has been accentuated by the recent restoration of homestead cabins in a pioneer village at the **Fort Rock Valley Historical Homestead Museum** (541/576-2251, www.fortrockmuseum.com, 10 A.M.–4 P.M. Fri.–Sun.).

An interesting journey down into the bowels of the earth is offered at **Derrick Cave,** located 22 miles north of Fort Rock. This large lava tube is 0.5-mile long, with rooms up to 40 feet wide and 60 feet high. During the Cuban missile crisis of 1962, the cave was turned into a fallout shelter. Metal doors were installed and provisions for 1,000 people were stockpiled. The supplies were later plundered by vandals and the cave's civil-defense status was eventually dropped.

If you drive eight dusty miles (the last mile a teeth-chattering ride) north of Christmas Valley on a rough BLM road that begins one mile east of town, you'll come to another break in terra firma that'll pique your imagination. **Crack-in-the-Ground** (www.fortrockmuseum.com/crack1.htm) is about two miles long, 10–15 feet wide, and up to 70 feet deep. On hot days, it's nice and cool within this chasm. In fact, the crack is so deep that cold winter air sometimes gets trapped within and ice is preserved into summer. According to geologists, this dramatic fissure has been open for at least 1,000 years; the opening was once larger but lava from nearby volcanoes filled it in to its present dimensions. A BLM picnic area is at one end of this curious landmark.

Five miles northwest of Crack-in-the-Ground (on rough BLM Road 6109C) is **Green Mountain Campground** and fire lookout, which sits high above the Derrick Cave site. This primitive campground (large enough for three cars, but without water or toilets) sits atop a small cinder cone overlooking hundreds of square miles of high desert, lava beds, and forest from 5,190 feet above sea level. In addition to Christmas Valley and Fort Rock Valley, you'll see snow-capped Diamond Peak 70 miles to the west and Wagontire Mountain 50 miles east.

La Pine State Park

Located in Deschutes County, this huge state park lies just a few miles off of U.S. 97. Visitors come to the 2,333-acre park to picnic, camp, mountain bike, and fish the Fall River; it is so vast visitors rarely see one another. The 15 miles of single-track mountain biking trails are, for the most part, flat and perfect for beginners. Bikes can be rented at Bend and Sunriver cycle shops (see the *Central Oregon* chapter for listings). The park's 137 campsites ($17) and five cabins ($38) can be reserved (800/551-6949).

Visit www.oregonstateparks.org for more information about this wonderful area.

Christmas Valley and Vicinity

Christmas Valley, a rather nondescript alfalfa-farming town got its picturesque name by accident. Southeast of here, John C. Frémont spent Christmas at a lake during one of his mid-19th-century treks and called it Christmas Lake. A turn-of-the-century mapmaker mistakenly affixed this name to a lake adjacent to the present-day town site, which also took on the merry moniker. Although the expanse of sagebrush dotted with mobile homes is not immediately appealing, there are some fascinating areas nearby.

Fossil Lake is two miles east of town. During wetter times thousands of years ago, this was a watering hole for camels, enormous beavers, flamingos, mammoths, and miniature horses. It was once part of a much larger body of water in the Fort Rock basin that was perhaps 40 miles wide and 200 feet deep. The water and animals disappeared when the climate changed, but their fossilized remains are still unearthed by paleontologists on sanctioned digs. Be aware that it is illegal to remove *any* fossils from the beds without proper authorization. Unfortunately, unscrupulous profiteers have been looting these timeless treasures from the lake and other fossil-rich sites in eastern Oregon. Be sure to notify the authorities immediately if you see any suspicious characters pilfering these valuable relics.

Lost Forest, an unusual sight in this area, is located 10 miles northeast of Christmas Valley on a rough but passable BLM road. A 9,000-acre stand of ponderosa pines intermixed with the largest juniper trees in Oregon is all that is left of an grove that dates back thousands of years. Surprisingly, studies of tree rings show that this area has received only nine inches of rain a year for the last 600 years, half the amount normally needed to sustain growth of ponderosa pines. But here, a layer of pumicelike soil beneath the surface traps and retains enough moisture to allow the trees to draw water up through shorter-than-usual root systems.

This island of green is 40 miles away from the nearest forest, accentuating the isolation and solitude of these stately sentinels. Many of the junipers here are over 1,000 years old. On hot summer days, this place is a welcome source of shade. Any time of year, the sound of the desert wind through the trees can stir contemplation. The final three-mile stretch of the approach to Lost Forest requires high vehicle clearance. To reach the area, drive eight miles east of the Christmas Valley post office, go eight miles north, and then eight miles east.

The forest borders the largest inland sand dunes in the state. During warm months, check yourself for ticks before leaving here.

Although accommodations are generally more appealing at Summer Lake, Christmas Valley has a couple of motels: the **Desert Inn** (541/576-2262) and the **Lakeside Terrace Motel** (541/576-2309), both of which offer basic, inexpensive accommodations. Twelve miles east of town, get a feel for life in this remote area at the **Outback B&B** (92946 Christmas Valley Hwy., 541/420-5229, $85 includes breakfast).

ℂ Summer Lake

Summer Lake lies on Route 32 about halfway between La Pine and Lakeview and is a good place to stop for a night or two while you explore the area. Just north of Summer Lake on Route 31, pull into **Picture Rock Turnout.** Take the trail 80 feet to the southeast. Behind the tallest rock is a pictograph. In the town of Summer Lake, the old **Harris School** is worth a picture. This classic one-room schoolhouse, complete with bell tower, is straight out of *Little House on the Prairie.*

The highway also passes through the **Summer Lake Wildlife Area** (541/943-3152, www.dfw.state.or.us), home to 170 species of migratory birds. Spring is the best time to see snow geese, avocets, black-necked stilts, and snowy plovers. An eight-mile wildlife-viewing trail around the lake is a recommended diversion at Mile Marker 70. Pick up a bird checklist from the Oregon Department of Fish and Wildlife.

The region surrounding Summer Lake (541/943-3931) sits at the interface of desert and mixed conifer forest. Abundant wildlife, geological wonders, Native American sites, and historic structures beckon further investigation. The 20-mile-long and 10-mile-wide lake is surrounded by the mountains of the Fremont National Forest and Winter Ridge.

Anglers should head due west of Summer Lake to the **Thompson Valley Reservoir,** which has been known to yield large rainbow trout. It's most easily reached by driving south from Silver Lake on County Road 4–12.

Wildlife Refuge Campground is on the Ana River just north of Summer Lake on Route 31. Bird-watchers like to camp here and walk the dikes of Summer Lake looking for waterfowl and swamp mammals.

Summer Lake Hot Springs (541/943-3931, www.summerlakehotsprings.com), six miles north of Paisley on the southern tip of Summer Lake, is a private operation open 8 A.M.– 9 P.M. daily. A dip in the 30-foot-long pool, housed in a rustic shed, and originally built in 1927 as a bathhouse for local cowboys, costs $5 for people ages six and over, free to children under six and overnight guests. This hot-spring resort has campsites on a bluff above the lake, a couple of small cabins ($60), and cottages ($100–125) for rent.

Another good base for exploration is the **Summer Lake Inn** (31501 Rte. 31, 541/943-3983 or 800/261-2778, www.summerlakeinn.com). Situated along the shore of the lake, this reconstructed pioneer homestead is paneled with a variety of wood. The feeling of warmth is enhanced by innkeeper Darrell Seven, whose flair for interior decorating, gourmet cooking, and local storytelling compels a stay here as much as the beautiful outdoor environment does. Guestroom views of the lake and the surrounding 8,000-foot mountains will stimulate dreams of your next day's activities. Amenities include a sauna, hot tub, and activities such as world-class bird-watching, cross-country skiing, fly-fishing, rock-hounding, and candlelight dining. The inn is 110 miles from Bend and 65 miles north of Lakeview. Rates are $115–235. Dogs are permitted with a $10 fee. The more expensive rates are for self-contained cabins with Jacuzzis and skylights. Gourmet breakfasts and dinners (Wed.– Sat., $9 breakfast, $16–30 dinner) are available; give advance notice if you're not a steak-eater.

The 1940s-era accommodations of the **Lodge at Summer Lake** (53460 Highway 31, 541/943-3994, www.thelodgeatsummerlake.com) feature seven motel units ($56–76) and cabin and house rentals ($50–100) that sleep up to six. Rates are lower in the winter.

There is an on-site restaurant and a private bass pond.

The one local eatery that's gained a statewide reputation is the ❰❰ **Cowboy Dinner Tree Steakhouse** (County Road 4–12, Forest Service Road 28, 541/576-2426, $21, reservations required), located in a remote rustic shack four miles south of Hager Mountain Road in Silver Lake. Here you must specify when you make your reservations whether you'd like the nearly 30-ounce top sirloin steak or the chicken (and we do mean "the chicken"—an order is an entire chicken). Sides include soup, salad, beans, a baked potato, dessert, and nonalcoholic beverages served in mason jars. If you're too stuffed to drive after the meal, bunk down in a cabin here ($95 for two people includes dinner).

Paisley

A few miles south of Summer Lake is the town of Paisley (pop. 240). The **Paisley Ranger Compound** features several structures built by the Civilian Conservation Corps during the Depression. Check out the pine dugout canoe carved by CCC workers for Forest Service personnel. Trout fishing on the Chewaucan River west of town and deer hunting also draw folks here. Paisley's is home to the ZX Ranch, the nation's largest at over 1.3 million acres. The ranch property is 137 miles long and 64 miles wide. Its other main claim to fame is its annual Mosquito Festival, held the last full weekend of July.

If you need to stay over, the **Sage Rooms** (541/943-3145) offer comfortable accommodations and a couple of restaurants, including the historic **Pioneer Saloon** offer a taste of the West. Campers should head west out of downtown, up the Chewaucan River; **Marster Spring** campground is about six miles from town on Forest Road 33.

Plan ahead to rent the historic and quite scenic **Bald Butte Lookout** (541/943-3114 information, 877/444-6667 reservations, www.fs.fed.us/r6/recreation/rentals, mid-June–mid-Oct., $30), located in the Fremont National Forest near the Gearhart Mountain Wilderness.

LAKEVIEW AND VICINITY

The "big city" in this part of the world is Lakeview (pop. 2,420), located 142 miles south of La Pine on Route 31, 96 miles east of Klamath Falls on Route 140 and 139 miles to Burns on Route 395. Lakeview, the county hub, bills itself as the highest town in Oregon, at 4,800 feet in elevation.

Most of what's appealing about Lakeview lies outside the main downtown area. But if you're spending time in town, the **Schminck Memorial Museum** (128 S. E St. 541/947-3134, 1–5 P.M. Tues.–Sat.) has antiques and Native American artifacts assembled by the Oregon chapter of the Daughters of the American Revolution.

Look for hang gliders coming off 2,000-foot Black Cap Hill above the east side of Lakeview May–October. This town's fault blocks and winds have made Lakeview a center for this activity among enthusiasts.

Be sure to pay a visit to the local geyser, Old Perpetual, which is in the front yard of **Hunter's Hot Springs Resort** (P.O. Box 268, Lakeview 97630, 541/947-4242 or 800/858-8266, www.huntersresort.com), on U.S. 395 north of town. There's also a hot springs–fed swimming pool at the resort, which drop-in visitors can use for a few bucks.

Abert Rim

Fifteen miles north of Lakeview on U.S. 395 is the Abert Rim, the highest fault escarpment in the United States. The rim rises 2,000 feet above Lake Abert. This unusual body of water has no outlet and is rich in brine shrimp, which attract countless waterfowl and shorebirds. As at Summer Lake, fall is prime bird-watching season; expect thousands of plovers and other shorebirds. Due to its high alkalinity, it is hazardous to swim in the lake.

Below Abert Rim along the east shore of Lake Abert, the slope is covered with boulders, some of which sport petroglyphs. Several are located right off the highway near the geological marker. Forest Service roads lead through the North Warner Mountains to BLM trails up the back side of Abert Rim; obtain rout-

© JUDY JEWELL

The Tall Man welcomes visitors to Lakeview, Oregon's highest-elevation town.

ing information on these obscure byways from the Lakeview Ranger Station (U.S. 395 N., 541/947-3334). Though reaching the rim requires an arduous journey down bumpy back roads and a steep hike up the mountain, the view from the top is spectacular. Just watch for rattlesnakes in the rocks.

Gearhart Mountain Wilderness Area

About 40 miles west of Lakeview off of Route 140 is the 22,000-acre roadless Gearhart Mountain Wilderness Area. Accessible only on foot or horseback, two major trails take adventurers into a challenging outdoor environment.

Gearhart Trail (#100) incorporates 12 of the area's 16 miles of improved trails. This trail runs from **Lookout Rock** in the southeast corner of the wilderness, up over the mountain, down to **Blue Lake,** and to a trailhead on North Creek. The **Boulder Springs Trail** (#100A) runs from the west side of the wilderness to a junction with the other trail a half mile from the mountain summit. For maps and more information, contact the Forest Service ranger stations in Lakeview, Paisley, or Silver Lake (U.S. 395 N., Lakeview 97360, 541/947-3334).

While you're in the neighborhood, you might want to visit the **Mitchell Monument,** on Route 140 between the wilderness area and Bly, which commemorates a tragedy that occurred on May 5, 1945. Reverend Archie Mitchell and his wife were escorting five children on a picnic near Corral Creek when one of the kids discovered a bomb dropped by an incendiary balloon. Unfortunately, the child triggered the bomb, and all but the good reverend were killed. This is the only recorded incident of World War II fatalities in the 48 contiguous states. Balloon bombs came down all over the western states, but only Oregon recorded civilian deaths due to their detonation. The balloons were released in hopes of setting fire to Oregon forests.

More recently, the town of Bly was in the news when members of Al-Qaeda allegedly attempted to set up a training camp on a nearby ranch.

◖ Hart Mountain National Antelope Refuge

North and east of Lakeview, Hart Mountain National Antelope Refuge stretches across a high plateau rising above Warner Lakes. From U.S. 395 just north of Lakeview, head east on Route 140 15 miles to the Plush Cut-Off Road, go northeast 19 miles to Plush and take the road up the steep west face of Hart Mountain to the refuge headquarters. The U.S. Fish and Wildlife Service office in Lakeview (18 S. G St., 541/947-3315) has information.

In summer, hundreds of the agile tan-and-white pronghorn occasionally gather at sunset along the dirt road south of the refuge. The refuge is also home to bighorn sheep, mule deer, 213 species of birds, and many small mammals. The campground, a few miles south of the refuge headquarters, features a hot springs surrounded by a cinder-block privacy wall; a dunk in the hot springs is highly recommended to loosen the stiffness from bouncing down the dirt roads to get here. The refuge is also a popular place for rockhounds searching for agates, fire opals, crystals, and sunstones. Check with the chamber of commerce (126 N. E St., Lakeview 97630, 541/947-6040, www.lakecountychamber.org) or the ranger at Hart Mountain for more information.

Despite the name of the preserve, you won't find any antelope here. In fact, there are no wild antelope in North America—only pronghorn. Because these animals shed the outer sheaths of their horns each year, they differ from their Asian and African counterparts, which have permanent horns. Male pronghorn have prongs, protrusions extending from their sheaths, to further distinguish them from antelope. The lingering misnomer was bestowed on these Oregon animals by Lewis and Clark. At any rate, many scientists believe that pronghorn could be the world's fastest land mammals over a long distance, barely edging out the cheetah on distances exceeding 1,000 yards. It's said they can cruise at more than 35 miles per hour, maintain 60 mph for half a mile, and reach 70 mph in short bursts.

Fishing

With a name like Lake County, you'd be right to think that fishing holes are plentiful here. Known for excellent trout fishing in the mountainous areas, the region is also gaining a reputation for bass, crappie, catfish, and other warm-water fishing. **Crump, Flagstaff, Anderson,** and **Campbell Lakes** in eastern Lake County provide the hottest action for crappie.

Friday Reservoir, located between Adel and Plush, is stocked with Lahontan cutthroat trout, and **Rock Creek,** which flows out of the Hart Mountain National Antelope Refuge, has red-banded trout. Off U.S. 395 in western Lake County, **Goose Lake,** a few miles south of Lakeview, and half in California, half in Oregon, is also home to the native red-banded trout, but it's hard to fish for this unique subspecies in the lake's shallow water. **Drews Reservoir,** 25 miles west of Lakeview on Route 140, offers excellent fishing for channel catfish—some as large as 10 pounds. In the northern section of the county, the **Chewaucan River,** which flows into Abert Lake, is heavily stocked with trout.

Skiing

Warner Canyon Ski Area (541/947-5001, www.lakecountychamber.org/skihill.html, $22), seven miles east of Lakeview on Route 140, is a small area with 14 runs, one chairlift (but no lines), and three miles of cross-country trails. Thanks to a mile-high base elevation and the dry southeastern Oregon climate, excellent dry powder conditions are common. The area has a day lodge near the base of the hill with a snack bar that serves breakfast and lunch. The season may start as early as mid-December and run through the end of March. Rent skis at **M&D Ski** (118 N. L St., 541/947-4862). Note that at the authors' last visit, the future of this ski area was uncertain because of steep increases in insurance costs. Please call before planning a trip here.

Rockhounding

Rockhounding is a popular hobby in Lake County. Best known for its abundance of sun-stones (also known as aventurine or Plush diamonds), the area has jasper, agates, petrified wood, fire opal, wonder stones, thunder eggs, and obsidian as well. To get to the sunstone-hunting grounds, go east on Route 140 to the Plush junction and turn north. Another spot for rockhounding can be reached by taking Hogback Road just north of the upper section of the Abert Rim; the Hogback junction is about 50 miles north of Lakeview on U.S. 395. For more information visit the **High Desert Rock Shop** (244 N. M St., 541/947-3237).

Camping

Junipers Reservoir RV Resort (541/947-2050, www.junipersrv.com) is 10 miles west of Lakeview on Route 140. This private reservoir with campgrounds (including some tent sites) is situated on a working cattle ranch that's open May 1–Oct. 15, depending on the weather. Designated as one of six private wildlife-viewing areas in the state, a visit to this spread offers an excellent chance to view longhorn cattle, deer, eagles, ospreys, and coyotes.

Goose Lake State Park (541/947-3111 or 800/551-6949, www.oregonstateparks.org, mid-Apr.–early Oct., $16) is a big spread 15 miles south of Lakeview on U.S. 395. The campground has tent sites, RV hookups, and a boat launch on the shore of the huge lake. **Corral Creek Campground** is a good headquarters for an exploration of the Gearhart Mountain Wilderness, an area of high meadows, cliffs, and worn-down volcanoes. To get to the campsite turn off Route 140 at Quartz Mountain, 24 miles west of Lakeview, and drive north on Forest Service Road 3600.

Entertainment and Events

Many of the earliest pioneers in Lake County were Irish immigrants who worked as sheepherders, some of whom turned to cattle ranching. To celebrate St. Patrick's Day, the Lakeview Chamber holds **Irish Days** with a parade led by the Grand Leprechaun, usually the town's oldest Irishman. Other popular events are the potato stick races and the cow-chip fling.

During the last weekend in June, the **Lake**

County Junior Rodeo is held at the Lake County Fairgrounds in Lakeview. Finally, the fall **Lake County Round-Up** and fair held Labor Day weekend at the county fairgrounds includes a carnival, a parade, a barbecue, a buckaroo breakfast, and the annual rodeo. Call the Christmas Valley Chamber (541/576-2166) for more information.

Lakeview's **Festival of Free Flight** takes place around July 4 each year. This large event features recreational pilots, barbecues, fireworks, and biking and running races.

Accommodations and Food

In Lakeview, the **Best Western Skyline Motor Lodge** (414 N. G St., 541/947-2194) has a pool and hot tub as well as large rooms. Rates run $48–68. Just north of Lakeview, **Hunter's Hot Springs Resort** (U.S. 395, 541/947-4282) has basic motel rooms for $55–65 as well as an RV park and restaurant. It's worth staying here if you want to soak in the hot springs pool.

Lakeview isn't known for its cuisine. However, the **Eagles Nest** (117 N. E St., 541/947-4824, dinner Mon.–Sat., main courses $10–25) serves a varied menu in a warm, welcoming atmosphere. The reasonably priced prime rib here is testimony to the quality of Oregon beef. The local Mexican restaurant, **El Aguila Real** (406 N. G St., 541/947-5655, lunch and dinner daily, main courses $6–12) is a good bet if you don't want to eat steak. Just north of town, **Geyser Grill** at Hunter's Hot Springs Resort (U.S. 395) has traditionally been a good place to eat pizza; however, it was closed for renovations in the spring of 2006 and it does have a history of closing for long stretches of time.

Information

Stop by the **Lakeview Welcome Center** at the Lake County Chamber of Commerce (126 N. E St., 541/947-6040) for maps and brochures.

Getting There

Buses depart twice a day from the **Red Ball Stage Lines Depot** (619 Center St., 541/884-6460) and travel to transportation to Klamath Falls to connect with Amtrak and the K Falls airport. **Goose Lake Aviation** (541/947-4222 or 541/947-3592) provides air taxi service and an air ambulance at the Lakeview airfield.

Steens Mountain Country

If you judge this part of southeastern Oregon by a drive-through on U.S. 20, you probably won't find it too memorable. But off the main thoroughfares are recreational retreats worthy of closer investigation. The Malheur Wildlife Refuge is nationally recognized as one of the best bird-watching sites in the country, and Steens Mountain is famous for its stunning scenery.

HISTORY

Oregon's high desert county was first inhabited by the Bannock, Northern Paiute, and Shoshone tribes. When French-Canadian trappers arrived in the area, they were promptly ripped off by the natives. After losing horses and supplies, the trappers named the nearby river "Malheur" ("Unhappiness" or "Misfortune"). The surrounding region's alkali flats and parched hills also suggest this moniker.

Explorer Peter Skene Ogden scouted the area in 1826 while leading a fur brigade for the Hudson's Bay Company. He wasn't impressed with the region as a place for settlers, but the Idaho gold rush of 1860 brought prospectors through the area on their way to the gold fields, and they told stories of rich grasslands, plentiful water, and broad forests.

Pony soldiers under the command of General William Harney explored the region in 1848 and again in 1858, opening up southeastern Oregon to settlement. The most noted military adventure was the construction of a wagon road built between Harney County and

Eugene. The leader of this work party, Enoch Steen, gave his name to Steens Mountain.

In 1878, 2,000 Bannocks, fed up with their loss of territory and poor treatment, took to the warpath. Troops from forts all over the West were sent to fight the natives in a war that dragged on until 1880.

BURNS

The town of Burns, named after the Scottish poet Robert Burns, was founded in 1884. By 1889 it had a population of 250, which has since grown to over 3,000. A significant boost to the town's economy came in 1924 when a rail line reached Burns. Its sister city, **Hines,** was incorporated in 1930. Named after Chicago lumberman Edward Hines, this town of 1,400 residents is primarily a bedroom community for Burns.

Sagehen Hill Nature Trail

The Sagehen Hill Nature Trail is 16 miles west of Burns at the Sagehen rest stop on U.S. 20. This 0.5-mile nature trail has 11 stations on a route that takes you around Sagehen Hill through sagebrush, bitterbrush, and western juniper. Other plants found along the way include lupine, larkspur, owl clover, and yellowbell. The lucky early-morning visitor in March or April might also catch the sage grouse courtship ritual. The male will display his plumage and make clucking noises to attract the attention of the females. The puffed-up necks and bobbing heads of these feathered philanderers are something to see. If these creatures are not visible, the views of Steens Mountain (elevation 9,733 feet) to the southeast will make the hike worthwhile.

Harney County Museum

The Harney County Museum (18 W. D St., Burns 97720, 541/573-5618, www.burnsmuseum.com, 10 A.M.–4 P.M. Tues.–Fri., 10 A.M.–3 P.M. Sat., Apr.–Sept., $4 adults, $6 for a family, and $1 for children) started its career as a brewery and then became a laundry and a wrecking yard. Local pioneer families have donated quilts, furniture, a complete

kitchen, a wagon shed, and machinery to the museum. Of special interest are artifacts from Pete French's ranch.

🄲 Crystal Crane Hot Springs

Spend an idyllic couple of hours at Crystal Crane Hot Springs (59315 Rte. 78, 541/493-2312, www.cranehotsprings.com, $3), 25 miles southeast of Burns, just west of the town of Crane. Here, the local hot springs feed a large pond, big enough to swim in if you have the energy. But it's more likely that you'll lounge at the pond's edge and watch the coots and shovelers paddling around in the adjacent cool pond. For visitors who prefer private soaking tubs ($5 per person per hour), several bathhouses have cattle troughs filled with the hot water. Rustic cabins ($35, shared bathhouse a bit of a walk away) and a camping area make it possible to spend the night here and greet the morning with a dip in the pond.

Oard's Free Museum and Store

Oard's Free Museum (541/493-2535, 7 A.M.–8 P.M. daily) is located 23 miles east of Burns on U.S. 20 in Buchanan. The museum has antique guns, clocks, barbed wire, spinning wheels, and dolls as well as native artifacts, including a Yakama chief's regalia. In addition to the permanent collection, Oard's has a sales gallery full of Native American jewelry collected on regular buying trips to the Southwest.

Paiute Reservation

If you want a livelier encounter with Native American culture, visit the Burns Paiute Reservation. The only real attraction here is the tribal casino (2205 W. Monroe, 541/573-1500), located just outside downtown Burns. Contact the tribal headquarters first for information (100 Pa' Si' Go St., 541/573-2088, www.burnspaiute-nsn.gov).

Rockhounding

Southeastern Oregon is rockhound country. Each year, thousands of enthusiasts flock to this far-flung corner of the state to collect fossils, agates, jasper, obsidian, and thunder eggs.

The **Stinking Water Mountains,** 30 miles east of Burns, are a good source of gemstones and petrified wood. Thunder eggs can be dug up four miles south of Oard's Museum on U.S. 20 after getting permission from the Don Robbins family. Contact them through the museum (541/493-2535).

Warm Springs Reservoir, just east of the Stinking Water Mountains, is popular with agate hunters. **Charlie Creek** and **Radar,** west and north of Burns, respectively, produce black, banded, and brown obsidians. Be sure to collect only your limit—be a rockhound, not a rockhog. Also keep in mind that it is illegal to take arrowheads and other artifacts from public lands.

Camping

A couple of campgrounds to the north of Burns up in the Malheur National Forest are **Idlewild** and **Yellowjacket** (541/573-4300, www.fs.fed.us/r6/Malheur, $7) Idlewild is right off U.S. 395 about 17 miles north of Burns in a pretty setting. The more remote Yellowjacket is on the shore of Yellowjacket Lake, 37 miles northwest of Burns on Forest Service Road 3745. From Burns, take County Road 127 out of town, then take Forest Road 47 to 37 and follow signs to the campground. Be sure to keep your food under wraps, especially meats, if you want to avoid being visited by the namesake hosts of the lake. Yellowjacket Lake is stocked with trout.

Entertainment and Events

In mid-April, the **John Scharff Migratory Waterfowl Conference** (541/573-2636, www.migratorybirdfestival.com) held in Burns celebrates the spring return of waterbirds to the region with lectures, movies, slides, a high-quality art show, and guided bird-watching tours, including early morning visits to the sage grouse leks, or strutting grounds. This is an excellent opportunity to learn more about birds, and it attracts some really knowledgeable and interesting people.

Burns is also the site of **Obsidian Days,** a rock and gem show, during the second week-

end of June. During the first week of September, Burns hosts the **Harney County Fair** (541/573-6166), an old-fashioned county fair featuring a rodeo, 4-H competitions, and exhibits on canning, wine- and beer-making, and leatherworking. At 4,140 feet in elevation, Burns is sometimes dusted with snow during the fair.

Accommodations

If you're seeking shelter in Burns, you'll find that the properties here are generally inexpensive, have air-conditioning to help you beat the heat, and allow you to bring the family dog along, too.

The pet-friendly **Silver Spur Motel** (789 N. Broadway, 541/573-2077 or 800/400-2077, about $45) is a pretty nice place on the north edge of downtown, with refrigerators and microwaves in the rooms. Guests can get passes to use the local health club, located a couple of blocks away.

On the main drag through town, the **Best Inn** (999 Oregon Ave., 541/573-1700, www.bestinn.com, $45–65) is another comfortable, though not fancy, motel. It has a small indoor pool

By far, the nicest place to stay in Burns is the 🄲 **Sage Country Inn** (351 ½ W. Monroe St., 541/573-7243, www.sagecountryinn.com, $85). This lovely, spacious house is set back just far enough from the main drag to make it quiet, but still easy to walk to restaurants in the downtown area.

Food

Although Burns isn't known as a culinary mecca, there are a few decent places to eat in town, especially if you're hankering after a steak dinner. The **Meat Hook** (673 W. Monroe St., 541/573-7698, open daily for lunch and dinner spring–fall, closed Sun. in winter, main courses $8–27) serves meals family-style, with the focus on local grass-fed beef. Vegetarians can dine on side dishes without the meat for $8. For lunch or a snack, try the **Broadway Deli** (530 N. Broadway, 541/573-7020), with tasty sandwiches, pie, and baked goods. An adjacent wine shop, **90+ Wines,** has a well-chosen selection of reasonably priced wines as well as a small selection of flies hand-tied by the shop's owner.

Information and Services

For general information on the region, contact the **Harney County Chamber of Commerce** (76 E. Washington St., 541/573-2636, www.harneycounty.com). For information on recreation, stop by the **Bureau of Land Management** office (12533 U.S. 20 W., Hines 97738, 541/573-5241). The **Emigrant Creek Ranger District** is also nearby (265 U.S. 20, Hines 97738, 541/573-4300).

◖ MALHEUR NATIONAL WILDLIFE REFUGE

Malheur and Harney Lakes, fed by the mountain snow runoff filling the Blitzen and Silvies Rivers, have been major avian nesting and migration stopovers since prehistoric times. The contrast between the stark, dry basin land, with its red sandstone monoliths and mesas, and the lush green marshes is startling. These vast marshes (the longest freshwater marsh in the western United States), meadows, and riparian areas surrounded by the eastern Oregon desert attract thousands of birds and hundreds of bird-watchers. The Malheur National Wildlife Refuge (36391 Sodhouse Ln., Princeton, 541/493-2612, www.fws.gov/malheur) is dominated by three fluctuating lakes—Malheur, Mud, and Harney. These are nourished by a scant eight inches of rain a year.

Refuge officials say that 250 species have been counted within its boundaries. Prime bird-watching times are spring and fall, when migratory flocks pass through. Late spring is an especially good time to visit, before summer's scorching heat. In March, the first Malheur arrivals include Canada and snow geese, and in the vast Malheur Marsh, swans, mallards, and other ducks. Also look for sandhill cranes in the wet meadows. Great horned owls and golden eagles are two other early arrivals. Shorebirds are followed by warblers, sparrows, and other songbirds in spring. Red-tailed hawks can be seen swooping over the sage-covered prairies throughout spring, summer, and fall. In the late spring, ponds and canals at Malheur occasionally host the trumpeter swan, a majestic bird with a seven-foot wingspan. This is one of the few places where you can observe this endangered species nesting. Flocks of pelicans are a summertime spectacle worth catching. See them before they head south to Mexico in the fall.

August–October is another prime time, when birders might see 100 species. At this time, lucky visitors might see the magnificent snow goose. Another fall arrival is the wood thrush, graced with one of the most beautiful songs in the bird kingdom. Another September–October highlight is the concentration of greater sandhill cranes, Canada geese, and mallard ducks foraging on Blitzen Valley grain fields. The first two weeks of September are particularly nice because hunting season has yet to begin and the aspens have turned golden.

Be sure to visit the refuge headquarters, located in a grove of cottonwoods looking out over the huge expanse of Malheur Lake. Here you can pick up maps for the self-guided auto tour of the refuge. A short distance downhill is a small museum where more than 250 bird specimens are beautifully arrayed. Also of interest is the charming park on the edge of the lake.

While the absolute numbers of birds at Malheur are not as great as they are at the Klamath Lakes or along the Oregon coast, the variety here is unsurpassed anywhere in the area. Among birders, however, it is the "accidental list" of 55 infrequently sighted species that makes this preserve special. Many of these "exotics" are sighted nowhere else in the region. A total of 312 different species has been sighted here over the last century.

In the late 1800s, settlers enjoyed unrestricted hunting here, and at the turn of the 20th century, hunters killed thousands of swans, egrets, herons, and grebes for feathers for the millinery trade. In 1908, President Theodore Roosevelt put a stop to the slaughter by protecting the area as a bird sanctuary. The Blitzen Valley and P Ranch were added

© JUDY JEWELL

Malheur's Buena Vista Ponds are a scenic stop, even for non-birders.

to the refuge in 1935. Today, 185,000 acres are protected.

Not everybody comes to Malheur just to watch birds—some folks come to fish. Krumbo Reservoir is a good bet for trout or largemouth bass.

To get to the refuge drive 25 miles south from Burns on Route 205 and then nine miles east on the county road to Princeton. The Buena Vista Ponds are an excellent place to stop along the way.

Accommodations

A convenient, though bare-bones place to stay on the refuge is the **Malheur Field Station** (541/493-2629, www.malhearfieldstation.org, $18–60), where you can bunk in dorm rooms or trailers. Guests should bring bedding and towels; dorm-dwellers should be prepared to share a restroom. Although most accommodations have kitchen facilities, during the peak season, meals are available here. Note that the trailers are the most coveted accommodations here... they're often full during spring and fall birding seasons. Reserve a room in advance to avoid driving 35 miles to Burns for bed and board.

Frenchglen

Named for famous rancher Pete French and his wealthy father in law, Dr. Hugh Glenn, the town of Frenchglen was originally known as P Station and was part of the nearby P Ranch. Today, this historic community with its hotel, store, corral, and post office remains essentially the same as it was 50 years ago. To get here, drive about 60 miles south on Route 205 from Burns.

In Frenchglen, the (**Frenchglen Hotel** (541/493-2825, www.oregonstateparks.org/park_3.php, mid-March–mid-November, $68–85), 60 miles south of Burns on Route 205, is an excellent place to stay while visiting Steens Mountain or Malheur Wildlife Refuge. Built in 1914 as a stage stopover, the hotel has eight smallish rooms (with shared bath down the hall) and a few more modern rooms in a separate unit behind the main hotel. Ranch cooks prepare delicious family-style dinners (about $20), served at 6:30 P.M. sharp; breakfast and lunch are also available. Watching thunderstorms sweep across Steens Mountain from the hotel's screened-in porch while you chat with birders from

© JUDY JEWELL

The Frenchglen Hotel is a favorite among bird-watchers.

all over the West can provide after-dinner entertainment.

DIAMOND AND VICINITY
Diamond Craters

Diamond Craters have been described by scientists as the most diverse basaltic volcanic features in the United States. To tour these unique formations, drive 55 miles south of Burns on Route 205 until you reach the Diamond junction. Turn left and begin a 40-mile route ending at New Princeton on Route 78. On the way you'll see why this area is called "Oregon's Geologic Gem." There are craters, domes, lava flows, and pits that give an outstanding visual lesson on volcanism. To aid your self-guided tour, pick up the "Diamond Craters" brochure at the BLM office in Hines.

Round Barn

While in the Diamond Craters area, stop at the Round Barn, a historic structure built in the 1870s or '80s by rancher Pete French as a place to spend the winter breaking his saddle horses. Located 20 miles north of Diamond, the barn is 100 feet in diameter with a 60-foot circular lava-rock corral inside. Twelve tall juniper poles support a roof covered with 50,000 shingles. Hundreds of cowpokes have carved their initials in the posts of this famous corral.

Just up the road from the barn, the privately owned **Round Barn Visitors Center** (541/493-2070 or 888/493-2420, www.round barn.net, 9 A.M.–5 P.M. daily, free), which is a combination of a gift shop, cold-drink vendor, and historical museum, is worth a stop. Its architecture mirrors that of the historic barn, and the genial proprietor, a third-generation Diamond Valley rancher, leads day-long tours of the area (**Jenkins Historical Tours,** $100 adult), with stops in some rather remote areas, focusing on the area's colorful history.

Diamond

Tall Lombardy poplars mark the tiny hamlet of Diamond, which is a cluster of buildings tucked in at the bottom of a hill. The focal

© JUDY JEWELL

The Hotel Diamond is one of the best places to stay in this part of the state. The meals are especially noteworthy.

point of the town is the **❰ Hotel Diamond** (541/493-1898, www.central-oregon.com/hoteldiamond, $68–90), a wonderfully and unpretentiously restored hotel dating from the late 1800s. Don't worry about where to eat when you book a stay here: breakfast, lunch, and family-style dinners ($16–19) are quite good. Reserve a seat at the table at least a day in advance so there will be plenty of food to go around.

❰ STEENS MOUNTAIN

Steens Mountain, named after Major Enoch Steen, an Army officer assigned the task of building a military road through Harney County, is one of the great scenic wonders of Oregon. A 30-mile fault block, the eastern flank of the mountain rises straight up from the Alvord Desert to a row of glacial peaks. On the western side, huge gorges carved out by glaciers a million years ago descend to a gentle slope drained by the Donner and Blitzen River, which flows into Malheur Lake.

Steens Mountain has five vegetation zones ranging from tall sage to alpine tundra. The best way to see the transition is to drive the **Steens Mountain Byway** out of Frenchglen to the top of Steens Mountain. This is the highest road in Oregon, rising 9,000 feet in elevation. The first 15 miles of the road are gravel and the last nine miles are dirt. The latter portion is not recommended for low-slung passenger cars. Expect to spend the entire day traveling this 59-mile byway.

Starting and ending at Frenchglen, the route up Steens Mountain, sans significant tree cover save for some beautiful aspens, evokes Alaskan alpine tundra. Multicolored low-to-the-ground wildflowers and a vast spaciousness give the feeling of being on top of the world. This impression is accentuated by standing in snow while you look 5,000 feet straight down into the sun-scorched Alvord Desert, which records just seven inches of rain annually.

The first four miles of the trek lead across the Malheur Wildlife Refuge and up to the foothills of Steens Mountain. **Page Springs,** the first campground on the route, is a popular spot

THE CATTLE KINGS OF EASTERN OREGON

Cattle barons, those early-day entrepreneurs who ran the huge livestock operations of the 19th century, have typically been portrayed as imperious characters in old Westerns. A look at the lives of three eastern Oregon cattle kings – John Devine, Pete French, and Bill Brown – paints a fuller picture.

John Devine came to Oregon in 1868 and started snapping up land by the simple method of squatting on it. He grabbed U.S. government land, tribal territory, and acreage ostensibly owned by road companies, which he quickly covered with vast herds of cattle. Part of his holding included the Alvord and the White-horse Ranches on the east side of the Steens. After the devastating winter of 1889–1890, during which he lost 75 percent of his stock, Devine's fortunes plummeted. He was bought out by another cattle baron, Henry Miller, and held on to only the Whitehorse Ranch until his death in 1901 at the age of 62.

Another rancher whose fate is still debated in this arid country is Pete French, an arrogant, forceful man with a bushy mustache that gave him the appearance of Wyatt Earp. Born in Red Bluff, California, in 1849, French moved to Oregon in 1873 to manage the stock ranch of Dr. Hugh Glenn in the Donner and Blitzen Valley. French married the boss's daughter, and after Glenn was murdered by his bookkeeper, French built the French-Glenn Livestock Company into one of the largest spreads in the West. At its peak, the ranch had 100,000 acres on which roamed 30,000 head of cattle and 3,000 horses. Five hundred miles of barbed wire defined this empire stretching from Donner and Blitzen River to Harney Lake.

While he was developing the P Ranch, French earned the enmity of hundreds of local home-steaders, many of whom were evicted from their squatters' shacks. One of his enemies, homesteader Ed Oliver, rode up to French one day and shot him dead. Oliver was arrested but later acquitted by a jury of settlers.

Bill Brown was a more popular and certainly more eccentric rancher than Pete French. His Gap Ranch, headquartered a few miles east of Hampton, halfway between Brothers and Riley, was at its largest 38,000 acres spread throughout four counties. Bill Brown didn't start out rich and he died penniless. In between he earned and lost a number of fortunes.

His first enterprise was running a flock of 400 sheep. During that era he was so hard up he had only one sock, which he switched from one foot to the other every day. Brown added horses to his holdings with such zeal that by World War I he owned 25,000 head, many of which he sold to the U.S. Cavalry. After the war, and with the advent of mass production of au-tomobiles, Brown lost his shirt and his land.

Many stories have been told about this balding six-footer with a square jaw and a mild manner. He never cussed, drank, or gambled, unless his faith in his store customers could be considered gambling. The operator of a shop, Brown was seldom behind the counter, relying instead on the honesty of his customers, who were asked to toss their cash in a cigar box. Another quirk was Brown's legendary habit of writing checks on anything available, from tomato-can labels to wooden slats. Local bank-ers had no problem cashing the "checks" for Brown's hired help or suppliers.

---

offering campsites along the bank of the Donner and Blitzen River. Approximately 13 miles beyond Page Springs is **Lily Lake,** a good place for a picnic. This shallow lake has an abundance of water lilies, frogs, songbirds, and waterfowl.

After Lily Lake, you really start to climb up the mountain to **Fish Lake, Jackman Park** (both with campsites), and viewpoints of Kiger Gorge and the East Rim. **Kiger Gorge**

is a spectacular example of a wide, U-shaped path left by a glacier. Blanketed in meadow grasses, quaking aspen, cottonwood, and mountain mahogany at lower elevations, tiny tundra-like flowers proliferate on the 8,000-foot viewpoint.

The **East Rim** is a dramatic example of earth-shifting in prehistoric epochs. The lava layers that cap the mountain are thousands of feet thick, formed 15 million years ago when lava erupted from cracks in the ground. Several million years later, the Steens Mountain fault block began to lift along a fault below the east rim. The fault block tilted to the west, forming the gentler slope that stretches to the Malheur Lake Basin. At the summit (9,670 feet) you can see the corners of four states on a clear day—California, Nevada, Oregon, and Idaho.

From the summit, it's about a mile and 1,300 feet down the slopes of Wildhorse Canyon to **Wildhorse Lake.** Expect the hike back uphill to be tough—after all, you're climbing to 9,670 feet!

A good time to visit is August–mid-September—Indian summer. Nights are cold but daytime temperatures are more pleasant than those of summertime scorchers. Later in the fall, red bushes and yellow aspens attract photographers. Some of the aspens are located at Whorehouse Meadow and are indirectly responsible for its name. Lonely shepherds would scratch love notes and erotica in the tree bark, pining away for a visit from the horse-drawn bordellos that serviced these parts. Wildlife-viewing highlights include bighorn sheep, seen around the East Rim viewpoint in summer; hummingbirds, often observed at high elevations; and hawks, which can be spotted anywhere, anytime here, especially from the ridge above Fish Lake.

The area has off-highway vehicle restrictions to protect the environment. Five gates controlling access to the Steens are located at various elevations and are opened as road and weather conditions permit. Normally, the Steens Byway is not open until early July and is closed by snow in October or November. Gas is available only in Burns, Frenchglen, and Fields. Take reasonable precautions when driving the loop: sudden storms, lightning, flash floods, and extreme road conditions can be hazardous to travelers. The loop returns to Route 205 about 10 miles south of Frenchglen.

Visit the Steens the first Saturday of August for the **Chris Miller Memorial Steens Mountain Rim Run** (541/573-2636), a 10K run or walk along the east rim of Steens Mountain that starts at an elevation of 7,835 feet and finishes at above 9,700 feet.

Blitzen

Four miles south of the southern terminus of the Steens Mountain Loop Road, turn west off Route 205 to take a side trip to the ghost town of Blitzen. This eight-mile jaunt will take you to the ruins of a little town (a half-dozen dilapidated buildings) founded in the late 1800s. Blitzen was named after the Donner and Blitzen River, which flows nearby. *Donner und Blitzen* is German for "thunder and lightning," the label given this stream by Captain George Curry, who tried to cross it during a fierce thunderstorm.

Also of interest is **Roaring Springs Ranch,** located near the turnoff to Blitzen. Originally homesteaded by Tom Wall, the ranch was sold to Pete French and subsequently developed into the largest cattle operation in the country. The dramatic backdrop, well-kept classic ranch building, and the surrounding meadows make Roaring Springs Ranch an ideal Western movie set.

Camping

There are three high-elevation campgrounds along the Steens Mountain Loop Road. No reservations are accepted and sites are $8 per vehicle per night. For more info, contact the BLM (541/573-4400). As for summertime Steens weather, the 100°F temperatures in the high desert give way to 50–80°F daytime temperatures atop the mountain. Nonetheless, be aware that the summit can see severe thunderstorms and lightning, and at night, the mercury can drop below freezing, even on days with high noontime temperatures.

Page Springs, four miles southeast of Frenchglen, is open all year. Close to the Malheur Wildlife Refuge, the campground is a good headquarters for bird-watching, fishing, hiking, and sightseeing. **Fish Lake** is 17 miles east of Frenchglen and open July 1–Nov. 15. The namesake lake is stocked with eastern brook, cutthroat, and rainbow trout. Aspens surround the campsites, which have toilets, well water, and firepits; firewood is included in the campsite fee. Climb up on the ridge above the canpground to watch hawks here. **Jackman Park,** three miles east of Fish Lake, is particularly popular with backpackers, who use it as a takeoff point. It has six sites with toilets and potable water.

Another alternative is the **Steens Mountain Resort** (North Loop Road, Frenchglen, 541/493-2415 or 800/542-3765, www.steens mountainresort.com), just before you get to the Page Springs campground. Views of the surrounding gorges are spectacular and there are more amenities than at the BLM facility, including showers, a small store, laundry, dumping facilities, and a public phone. Reservations are recommended and fees are $15–23 for the 99 sites accommodating RVs, trailers, and tents. There are also cabins and trailers that rent for $70–85.

ALVORD DESERT AND VICINITY
Fields

Fields, the largest community on the east side of Steens, was established as a supply station in 1881. And a supply station it still is. Fields now has a gas station, store, café, a motel, and a B&B. All but the B&B are part of the same business, **Fields Station** (541/495-2275). The accommodations here, though very simple, are perfectly sufficient and very reasonably priced; there are a couple of one-bedroom units ($45) and an old hotel that'll sleep up to 10 people ($90). The other place to stay, the **Alvord Inn B&B** (541/495-2441, $55–65) is very comfortable and nicely decorated. The café at Fields Station serves great milkshakes. Be sure to take a few minutes to knock around Fields; find the remains of the original Mr. Field's stone cabin across the road from the gas pumps, and if you walk back a little ways, you may find a great horned owl perching in a tree.

◀ Alvord Desert

About 20 miles north of Fields, the vast hardpan playa of the Alvord Desert comes into view. This usually dry and stark white alkali lakebed

© JUDY JEWELL

The steep eastern face of Steens Mountain drops off to the Alvord Desert.

(or "playa") gets about six inches of rain a year, which quickly evaporates. It's possible to drive down to, and even on, the playa (unless it's wet, in which case it's quite slick). The best way down is about 1.5 miles north of the southern edge of the playa. But rather than driving, get out of the car and walk. One popular activity here is land-sailing, which is done in a "boat" that's sort of like a go-cart with a sail.

There is a small informal camping area nestled under the east face of Steens Mountain along Pike Creek. Look for a spur road leading off the west about two miles north of Alvord Hot Springs—you may also be able to spot the outhouse (voted "world's most disgusting" by one seasoned traveler). Some folks also camp on the edge of the playa.

Alvord Hot Springs

North of Fields, look for Alvord Hot Springs, a rustic spa recognizable by its corrugated-steel shack on the east side of the road. Two pools of hot mineral water piped in from spring runoff will cook your bones and soak away your aches and pains at no charge. The view from the hot springs up onto the east face of Steens Mountain is magnificent.

Mickey Hot Springs

Here at the remote northern edge of the Alvord Desert is a little thermal basin. Don't plan to soak here—the water is way too hot for that—but it's a good place to tromp around and inspect the pools and the mud flats. A little six- to eight-foot jet of 200°F water on the north end of an ancient dry lakebed is often visible in the spring in the Alvord Desert. Also quite amazing is a 30-foot-deep hot pool. To get to Mickey Hot Springs, head about 10 miles north from Alvord Hot Springs, pass the Alvord Ranch, and go through a series of two sharp turns. At the second turn (a sharp left), turn onto the rough but drivable side road and head east and south. Stay to the left at the fork in the road; it's about 6.5 miles from the main road to the hot springs parking area.

Mann Lake

North of the Alvord Desert, just west of the road, Mann Lake is a popular fishing destination. Early spring trout fishing is especially good here, and the lake is the repository for the breeding stock of Lahontan cutthroat trout, a subspecies that's adapted to alkaline water. Although the lakeshore is pretty sagebrushy and unshaded, there is a campground here.

OWYHEE RIVER COUNTRY

It's a long way from just about anywhere to the far southeastern corner of Oregon, but the canyons of the Owyhee are, for those visitors who don't mind roughing it, enchanting. If you aren't prepared to camp, you can stay in one of the two very basic motels in Jordan Valley, or come down from the north, where Ontario (see *Northeastern Oregon* chapter) has more services.

Jordan Valley

This town, located almost on the Idaho border where U.S. 95 takes a sharp bend north, is mostly visited by long-haul truckers. But it's also known for its Basque heritage, which is

© BILL MCRAE

Bighorn sheep near Succor Creek

not exactly obvious, but celebrated to some small degree at the **Old Basque Inn** (541/586-2800), where, as in most American Basque restaurants, dinners are served family style. If you're not hopping right back into the car, you may dare to try the inn's traditional Basque Picon punch, whose main ingredient is a bitter orange cordial liqueur.

After a few sips of Picon, you'll be ready to check into a motel. Big surprise—they're not fancy. Both the **Sahara Motel** (607 Main St., 541/586-2810), which is part of the Chevron station, and the **Basque Station Motel** (801 Main St., 541/586-2244) have rooms for about $40.

Owyhee River Trips

The big treat for a visitor to this area is a four- to six-day raft trip down the Owyhee River. The river can be run only for a few weeks in the spring, and during drought years it can't be run at all. Trips start in the tiny town of Rome, east of Jordan Valley, and end at the southern edge of the Owyhee Reservoir, at the base of Leslie Gulch. Expect to pay $800–1,300, depending on the length of the trip. Float (with an occasional run through hair-raising rapids) through deep, rugged canyons past tall rock pillars, petroglyphs, many species of birds, and

a number of hot springs. The following outfitters offer Owyhee River trips: Ouzel Outfitters (541/385-5947 or 800/788-7238, www.oregonrafting.com), Oregon Whitewater Adventures (800/820-7238, www.oregonwhitewater.com), ROW Adventures (208/765-0841 or 800/451-6034, www.rowadventures.com), and Destination Wilderness (541/549-1336, www.wildernesstrips.com).

Succor Creek and Leslie Gulch

From Jordan Valley, head north on U.S. 95, then turn left onto Succor Creek Road and follow it to the turnoff for Leslie Gulch. Turn left to head down the relatively rough, steep 13-mile-long road through the remarkably colorful and steep-walled Leslie Gulch canyon. Along the way are a couple of trails leading up beautiful side canyons. The road ends on the shores of the Owyhee Reservoir, where there's a boat ramp and a hardscrabble camping area.

Farther north, there's a campground in a pretty area along Succor Creek. Bring your own water (and toilet paper). From the campground, wander upstream to explore the geology and wildflowers, but be sure to watch out for rattlesnakes.

BACKGROUND

The Land

GEOGRAPHY

If Oregon were part of a jigsaw puzzle of the United States, it would be a squarish piece with a divot carved out of the center top. To the west is the Pacific Ocean, and some 370 miles of beaches, dunes, and headlands; to the east are the Snake River and Idaho. Up north, much of the boundary between Oregon and Washington is defined by the mighty Columbia River, while southern Oregon lies atop the upper borders of California and Nevada.

Broad rows of mountains divide the coast from the inland valleys, and western Oregon from the central and eastern parts of the state.

East of the highest central range the Columbia Plateau predominates, broken up in the northeast where mountainous features reassert themselves. In the southeast, scattered lakes dot the landscape and fault-block mountains gently ascend on one slope, then drop sharply off. The Great Basin desert—characterized by rivers that evaporate, peter out, or disappear into underground aquifers—makes up the bottom corner of eastern Oregon. Here, the seven-inch annual rainfall of the Alvord Desert seems as if it would be more at home in southeastern California and Nevada than in a state known for blustery rainstorms and lush greenery.

© BILL MCRAE

WHAT'S IN A NAME?

One rather peculiar theory of how Oregon got its name derives from a reputed encounter between native peoples and the Spanish mariners who plied West Coast waters in the 17th and 18th centuries. Upon seeing the abalone shell earrings of the coastal Salish, the European sailors are said to have exclaimed, *"Orejon!"* ("What big ears!") – later anglicized to "Oregon." Others point out the similarity between the name of the state and the Spanish locales Aragon and Obregon (in Mexico). Additionally, the word "Oregon" belonged to a Wisconsin tribe who purportedly traded with Columbia River natives during salmon season.

A less fanciful explanation has it that the state's name was inspired by the English word "origin," conjuring the image of the forest primeval. The French word *ouragan* ("hurricane") has also been suggested as the source of the state's name, courtesy of French Canadian fur trappers who became the first permanent white settlers in the region during the early 19th century. In this vein, the reference to the Columbia River as the "Oregan" by some French Canadian voyageurs who came here with the "beaver brigades" of the Northwest and Hudson Bay Companies is another possible etymological ancestor.

It was recently noted that "Oregonon" and "Orenogonia," two Greek words pertaining to mountainous locales, were seen on old navigators' maps marking the area between Northern California and British Columbia. Given that the famous Pacific Northwest explorer Juan de Fuca was actually Greek (born Valerianos) and that many navigators were schooled in Greece, perhaps Oregon's name originated in the Mediterranean.

Highs and Lows

Moving west to east, the major mountain systems start with the Klamath Mountains and the Coast Range. The Klamaths form the lower quarter of the state's western barrier to the Pacific; the eastern flank of this range is generally referred to as the Siskiyous. To the north, the Oregon Coast Range, a younger volcanic range, replaces the Klamaths. The highest peaks in each of these cordilleras barely top 4,000 feet and stand in between narrow coastal plateaus on the west side and the rich agricultural lands of the Willamette and Rogue valleys on the other. Running up the west-central portion of the state is the Cascade Range, which extends from Northern California up to Canada. Five of the dormant volcanoes within Oregon top 10,000 feet above sea level, with Mount Hood the state's highest peak, at 11,239 feet.

Beyond the Cascades' eastern slope, semi-arid high-desert conditions contrast with the Coast Range rainforests and the mild, wet maritime climate that characterizes much of western Oregon. In the northeast, the 10,000-foot crests of the snowcapped Wallowas rise less than 50 miles distant from the hot, arid floor of Hells Canyon, itself about 1,300 feet above sea level.

In addition to Hells Canyon, America's biggest hole in the ground (7,900 feet maximum depth), Oregon also boasts the continent's deepest lake: Crater Lake, with a depth of 1,958 feet.

Last of the Red-Hot Lavas

Each part of the state contains other well-known remnants of Oregon's cataclysmic past. Offshore waters here feature 1,477 islands and islets, the eroded remains of ancient volcanic flows. Lava fields dot the approaches to the High Cascades. East of the range a volcanic plateau supports cinder cones, lava caves, and lava-cast forests in the most varied array of these phenomena outside of Hawaii.

The imposing volcanic cones of the Cascades and the inundated caldera that is Crater Lake, formed by the implosion of Mount Mazama some 6,600 years ago, are some of the most dramatic reminders of Oregon's volcanic origins. More fascinating evidence can be seen up-close at Newberry National Volcanic Monument, an extensive area south of Bend that encompasses obsidian fields and lava formations left by massive eruptions. (Incidentally, geologists have cited Newberry on their list of volcanoes in the continental United States most likely to erupt again.) Not far from the Lava Lands Visitor Center in the national monument are the Lava River Cave and Lava Cast Forest—created when lava enveloped living trees 6,000 years ago.

Earthquakes and Tsunamis

Scientists exploring Tillamook County in 1990 unearthed discontinuities in both rock strata and tree rings indicating that the north Oregon coast has experienced major **earthquakes** every several hundred years. They estimate that the next one could come within our lifetimes and be of significant magnitude. In this vein, Japanese scientists maintain that a 9.0 quake struck the Northwest coast in 1700, based on tsunami records indicating that six- to nine-foot-high tidal waves hit Japan's coastline. This date is also consistent with Northwest Native American oral histories and geologic evidence.

These coastal quakes are caused by subduction, which occurs when one of the giant plates that make up the earth's crust slides under another as they collide. In Pacific Northwest coastal regions, this takes place when the Juan de Fuca plate's marine layer is pushed under the continental North American plate. With virtually every part of the state possessing seismic potential that hasn't been released in many years, the pressure along the fault lines is increasing.

In coastal areas, one of the greatest dangers associated with earthquakes is the possibility of **tsunamis.** The waves are produced by an offshore quake—even one centered thousands of miles distant. As a tsunami draws closer to the shore, driven by the force of the quake, it takes in preceding waters and builds into a series of waves traveling as fast as 500 miles per hour

and reaching as high as 100 feet. Ever since a tsunami unleashed by Alaska's 1964 quake (measured at 14.2 feet high at the mouth of the Umpqua River) resulted in four casualties in Beverly Beach and over $1 million in damage, local authorities have made seismic preparedness a priority, with a system of warning sirens and evacuation signs pointing the way to higher ground.

The Great Meltdown

However pervasive the effects of seismic activity and volcanism here, they must still share top billing with the last Ice Age in the grand epic of Oregon's topography.

At the height of the most recent major glaciation, the world's oceans were lower by 300–500 feet, North America and Asia were connected by a land bridge across the Bering Strait, and the Oregon coast was miles west of where it is today. The Columbia Gorge extended out past present-day Astoria. As the glaciers melted, the sea rose.

When that glacial epoch's final meltdown 12,000 years ago unleashed water dammed up by thousands of feet of ice, great rivers were spawned and existing channels were enlarged. A particularly large inundation was the Missoula Flood, which began with an ice dam breaking up in what's now northern Idaho. Floodwaters carved out the contours of what are now the Columbia River Gorge and the Willamette Valley. Other glacial floodwaters found their outlet westward to the sea, digging out silt-ridden estuaries in the process. Pacific wave action washed this debris back up onto the land, helping to create dunes and beaches.

CLIMATE
The Rain Shadow

Oregon's location equidistant from the equator and the North Pole subjects it to weather from both tropical and polar air flows. This makes for a pattern of changeability in which calm often alternates with storm, and extreme heat and extreme cold seldom last long.

Oregon's weather system is best understood as a series of valley climates separated from each other by mountain ranges that draw precipitation from the eastbound weather systems. Moving west to east, each of these valley zones records progressively lower rainfall levels until one encounters a desert on the eastern side of the state.

Moisture-laden westerlies off the Pacific slam into the Coast and Klamath Ranges. As the mountains push the clouds higher, they drop their moisture in the form of rain or snow. That's because rising air cools 3°F for every 1,000 feet of altitude gain, and cooler air can't hold as much moisture as warm air. As a consequence, rainfall at the coast often exceeds 80 inches a year. In parts of the coastal ranges, yearly totals of well over 100 inches aren't uncommon.

By contrast, the Willamette and other inland valleys on the east side of the mountains usually record half that total.

The rain shadow effect is repeated when the Cascades catch precipitation from eastward-moving cloud masses, wringing the moisture out of the storms; consequently, the eastern side of this range often records annual rainfall totals below 10 inches.

The Coast

Wet but mild, average rainfall on the coast ranges from a low of 64 inches per year in the Coos Bay area to nearly 100 inches around Lincoln City. The Pacific Ocean moderates coastal weather year-round, softening the extremes. Spring, summer, and fall generally don't get very hot, with highs generally in the 60s and 70s, and seldom topping 90°F. Winter temperatures only drop to the 40s and 50s, and freezes and snowfall are quite rare occurrences.

Western Oregon

If there is one constant in western Oregon, it is cloudiness. Portland and the Willamette Valley receive only about 45 percent of maximum potential sunshine; more than 200 days of the year are cloudy and rain falls an average of 150 days. While this might sound bleak, consider that the cloud cover helps moderate the climate by trapping and reflecting the earth's heat. On average, fewer than 30 days of the year record temperatures below freezing. Thus, the region, despite being on a more northerly latitude than parts of Canada, has a milder climate. Except in mountainous areas, snow usually isn't a force to be reckoned with here. Another surprise is that Portland's average annual rainfall of 40 inches is usually less than totals recorded in New York, Miami, or Chicago.

The southern end of the Willamette Valley can be affected by temperature inversions. In winter, for example, warm air above the valley walls holds in the colder air below, resulting in fog. In the southern valleys, fog helps to counterbalance the region's long dry season: Ashland and Medford sometimes record only half the yearly precipitation of their neighbors to the north, as well as higher winter and summer temperatures. At the same time, these inversions can cause unwelcome pollution to linger.

While it's difficult to predict daily weather patterns in western Oregon, there are definite seasonal climatic shifts here. In winter, arctic and tropical air masses collide over the Pacific, producing much of the state's rain. During the summer the clashes are less frequent. At that time, Oregon weather is more affected by Pacific Ocean temperatures and air pressure differences between inland and coastal areas.

Eastern Oregon

By contrast, the scorching deserts of eastern Oregon can give way to cold temperatures at night. This is because clear skies and a dearth of vegetation facilitate the escape of heat. Consider that on May 2, 1968, the difference between the high and low temperatures at Juniper Lake, north of the Alvord Desert in southeastern Oregon, was 81 degrees.

Mountain areas also experience extreme diurnal temperature fluctuations. Thin mountain air does not filter out ultraviolet radiation as effectively as the denser air at lower elevations, so the sun's force is accentuated at higher elevations. At night, chill spreads quickly through this thin air.

Flora and Fauna

FLORA

With 4,400 known species and varieties, Oregon ranks fourth among U.S. states for plant diversity, including dozens of species found nowhere else.

Trees

The mixed-conifer ecosystem of western Oregon—dense, far-reaching forests of Douglas fir, Sitka spruce, western hemlock, interspersed with bigleaf maple, vine maple, alder—is among the most productive woodlands in the world.

In southern Oregon, find redwood groves and rare myrtle trees (prized by woodworkers and for its distinctive coloring and grain); huge ponderosa pines are a hallmark of central Oregon. A particularly striking natural display along the McKenzie River mixes red vine maple and sumacs with golden oaks and alders against an evergreen backdrop.

Eastern Oregon's desert is largely rabbitbrush, cheatgrass, sagebrush, and juniper. In the John Day backcountry of eastern Oregon, you can find even hedgehog cactus.

Just in case all the tree identification becomes overwhelming, remember a mnemonic taught to Oregon schoolchildren: The needles of a fir are flat, flexible, and friendly. Spruce needles are square, stiff, and will stick you. Hemlock needles have a hammocklike configuration, and the crown of the tree is curved as though it's tipping its hat. Finally, the ponderosa pine's platelike bark is a distinctive feature.

Coastal Plant Life

While giant conifers and a profuse understory of greenery predominate coastal forests, this ecosystem represents only the most visible part of the Oregon coast's bountiful botany. Many coastal travelers will notice **European beachgrass** (*Ammophila arenaria*) covering the sand wherever they go. Originally planted in the 1930s to inhibit dune growth, the thick, rapidly spreading grass worked too well, solidifying into a ridge behind the shoreline, blocking the windblown sand from replenishing the rest of the beach and suppressing native plants. Populations of formerly common natives such as beach morning-glory, yellow abronia, gray beach pea, and American dune-grass are now much diminished. The now-endangered pink sand verbena, once abundant along the coast from British Columbia to northern California, is restricted to a few locations along central and southern Oregon coast. Herbicides, burning, and tilling have been employed in recent years to remove European beachgrass and restore the dune ecosystem to a more natural state, but progress against the pernicious weed is slow and difficult.

Freshwater wetlands and bogs, created where water is trapped by the sprawling sand dunes along the central coast, provide habitats for some unusual species. Best known among

Wood violets grow in wet areas of the Oregon coast.

these is the **cobra lily** *(Darlingtonia californica)*, which can be viewed up close at the just north of Florence. Also called pitcher plant, this carnivorous bog dweller survives on hapless insects lured into a specialized chamber, where they are trapped and digested.

Coastal salt marshes, occurring in the upper intertidal zones of coastal bays and estuaries, have been dramatically reduced due to land "reclamation" projects such as drainage, diking, and other human disturbances. The halophytes (salt-loving plants) that thrive in this specialized environment include pickleweed, saltgrass, fleshy jaumea, salt marsh dodder, arrow-grass, sand spurrey, and seaside plantain. Coastal forests include Sitka spruce and alder riparian communities, which provide resting and feeding areas for migratory waterfowl, shore and wading birds, and raptors.

Old-Growth Forests

Of the 19 million acres of old growth that once proliferated Oregon and Washington, only 10 percent survive, and portions are always under threat of further destruction by logging. Naturalists describe an old-growth forest as a mixture of trees, some of which must be at least 200 years old, and a supply of snags or standing dead trees, nurse logs, and streams with downed logs.

Throughout this book, references are made to old-growth groves that are noteworthy for size, age, beauty, ecological significance, or ease of access. Of all the old-growth forests mentioned in this volume, **Opal Creek** (see *The Willamette Valley* chapter) most spectacularly embodies all of the above characteristics.

Flowers and Fruits

While not as visually arresting as the evergreens of western Oregon, the state's several varieties of **berries** are no less pervasive. Found mostly from the coast to the mid-Cascades, blackberries favor clearings, burned-over areas, and people's gardens. They also take root in the woods alongside wild strawberries, salmonberries, thimbleberries, currants, and salal. Within this edible realm, wild-food connois-

© JUDY JEWELL

Trillium flowers are a sure sign of spring in western Oregon.

seurs especially seek out the thin-leafed huckleberry found in the Wallowa, Blue, Cascade, and Klamath Ranges. Prime snacking season for all these berries ranges from midsummer to midfall.

No less prized are the rare plant communities of the Columbia River Gorge and the Klamath/Siskiyou region. A quarter of Oregon's rare and endangered plants are found in the latter area, a portion of which is in the valley of the Illinois River, a designated Wild and Scenic tributary of the Rogue. *Kalmiopsis leachiana,* a rare member of the heath family endemic to southwestern Oregon, even has a wilderness area named after it.

Motorists will treasure such springtime floral fantasias (both wild and domesticated) as the dahlias and irises near Canby off I-5; tulips near Woodburn; irises off Route 213 outside Salem; the Easter lilies along U.S. 101 near Brookings; blue lupines alongside U.S. 97 in central Oregon; apple blossoms in the Hood River Valley near the Columbia Gorge; pear blossoms in the Bear Creek Valley near

Salal flourishes along the Oregon coast. The flowers are followed by purple berries.

Medford; beargrass, columbines, and Indian paintbrush on Cascades thoroughfares; and rhododendrons and fireweed along the coast.

East of the Cascades, the undergrowth is often more varied than the ground cover in the damp forests on the west side of the mountains. This is because sunny openings in the forest permit room for more species and for plants of different heights. And, in contrast to the white flowers that predominate in the shady forests in western Oregon, "dry-side" wildflowers generally have brighter colors. These blossoms attract color-sensitive pollinators such as bees and butterflies. On the opposite flank of the range, the commonly seen white trillium relies on beetles and ants for propagation, lessening the need for eye-catching pigments.

Mushrooms

Autumn is the season for those who covet wild chanterelle, matsutake, and morel mushrooms. The Coast Range from September through November is the prime picking area for chanterelles—a fluted orange or yellow mushroom

in the tall second-growth Douglas fir forests. Of course, you should be absolutely certain of what you have before you eat wild mushrooms, or any other wild food.

FAUNA

Oregon's creatures great and small comprise an excitingly diverse group. Oregon's low population density, abundance of wildlife refuges and nature preserves, and biomes running the gamut from rainforest to desert explain this variety. Throughout the state, numerous refuges, such as the **South Slough National Estuarine Research Reserve,** the **Malheur Bird/Wildlife Refuge,** the **Jewell Preserve for Roosevelt Elk,** and the **Finley Bird and Wildlife Preserve** provide safe havens for both feathered and furry friends.

Life in Tidepools

For most visitors, the most fascinating coastal ecosystems in Oregon are the rocky tidepools. These Technicolor windows offer an up-close look at one of the richest—and harshest—environments, the intertidal zone, where pummeling surf, unflinching sun, predators, and the cycle of tides demand tenacity and special adaptation of its inhabitants.

The natural zone where surf meets shore is divided into three main habitat layers, based on their position relative to tide levels. The **high intertidal zone,** inundated only during the highest tides, is home to creatures that can either move, such as crabs, or are well adapted to tolerate daily desiccation, such as acorn barnacles and finger limpets, chitons, green algae, and limpets. The turbulent **mid-intertidal zone** is covered and uncovered by the tides, usually twice each day. In the upper portion of this zone, California mussels and goose barnacles may thickly blanket the rocks, while ochre sea stars and green sea anemones are common lower down, along with sea lettuce, sea palms, snails, sponges, and whelks. Below that, the **low intertidal zone** is exposed only during the lowest tides. Because it is covered by water most of the time, this zone has the greatest diversity of organisms in the tidal area. Residents

© BILL MCRAE

Inspecting tidepools is a favorite activity on the Oregon coast.

include many of the organisms found in the higher zones, as well as sculpins, abalone, and purple sea urchins.

Standout destinations for exploring tidepools include Cape Arago, Cape Perpetua, the Marine Gardens at Devil's Punchbowl, and beaches south and north of Gold Beach—among many other spots. Tidepool explorers should be mindful that, despite the fact that the plants and animals in the tidepools are well adapted to withstand the elements, they and their ecosystem are actually quite fragile, and they're very sensitive to human interference. Avoid stepping on mussels, anemones, and barnacles, and take nothing from the tidepools. In the Oregon Islands National Wildlife Refuge and other specially protected areas, removal or harassment of any living organism may be treated as a misdemeanor punishable by fines.

Seals, Sea Lions, and Otters
Pacific harbor seals, California sea lions, and Steller sea lions are frequently sighted in Oregon waters. California sea lions are the animals

you might have seen in circuses. These 1,000-pound mammals are characterized by their large size and small earflaps, which seals lack. Unlike seals, they can point their rear flippers forward to give them better mobility on land. Lacking the dense underfur that covers seals, sea lions tend to prefer warmer waters.

Steller sea lions can be seen at the Sea Lion Caves (covered under *Florence and Vicinity*, in the *Southern Oregon Coast* chapter). They also breed on reefs off Gold Beach and Port Orford. The largest sea lion species, males can weigh more than a ton. Their coats tend to be gray rather than black like California sea lions'. They also differ from their California counterparts in that they are comfortable in colder water.

Look for Pacific harbor seals in bays and estuaries up and down the coast, sometimes miles inland. They're nonmigratory, have no earflaps, and can be distinguished from sea lions because they're much smaller (150–300 pounds) and have mottled fur that ranges in color from pale cream to rusty brown.

Gray Whales
Few sights along the Oregon coast elicit more excitement than that of a surfacing whale. The most common large whale seen from shore along the west coast of North America is the gray whale *(Eschrichtius robustus)*. These behemoths can reach 45 feet in length and 35 tons in weight. The sight of a mammal as big as a Greyhound bus erupting from the sea has a way of emptying the mind of mundane concerns. Wreathed in seaweed and sporting barnacles and other parasites on its back, a California gray whale might look more like the hull of an old ship were it not for its expressive eyes.

Some gray whales are found off the Oregon coast all year, including an estimated 200–400 during the summer, though they're most visible and numerous when migrating populations pass through Oregon waters on their way south December–February and northward early March–April. This annual journey from the rich feeding grounds of the Bering and Chukchi Seas of Alaska to the calving

sea lions on the coast, a frequent sight during the summer months

grounds of Mexico amounts to some 10,000 miles, the longest migration of any mammal. Their numbers peak usually during the first week of January, when as many as 30 per hour may pass a given point. By mid-February, most of the whales will have moved on toward their breeding and calving lagoons on the west coast of Baja California.

Early March–April, the juveniles, adult males, and females without calves begin returning northward past the Oregon coast. Mothers and their new calves are the last to leave Mexico and move more slowly, passing Oregon late April–June. During the spring migration, the whales may pass within just a few hundred yards of coastal headlands, making this a particularly exciting time for whale-watching from any number of vantage points along the coast. Researchers speculate that gray whales stay close to shore as a way to help them navigate.

Small Mammals

Many of the most frequently sighted animals in Oregon are small scavengers. Even in the most urban parts of the state, it's possible to see raccoons, skunks, chipmunks, squirrels, and opossums.

West of the Cascades, the dark-colored Townsend's chipmunks are among the most commonly encountered mammals; east of the Cascades, lighter-colored pine chipmunks and golden mantled ground squirrels proliferate in drier interior forests. The latter two look almost alike, but the stripes on the side of the chipmunk's head distinguish them from each other. Expect to see the dark brown, cinnamon-bellied Douglas squirrel on both sides of the Cascades.

Beavers

Beavers *(Castor canadensis)*, North America's largest rodents, are widespread throughout the Beaver State, though they're most commonly sighted in second-growth forests near marshes after sunset. Fall is a good time to spot beavers as they gather food for winter. The beaver has long been Oregon's mascot, and for good reason: It was the beaver that drew brigades of fur trappers and spurred the initial exploration and settlement of the state. The beaver also merits a special mention for being important to Oregon's forest ecosystem. Contrary to popular conception, the abilities of Mother Nature's carpenter extend far beyond the mere destruction of trees to dam a waterway. In fact, the activities associated with lodge construction actually serve to maintain the food chain and the health of the forest.

The beaver's lodge, together with its pond, fosters a fertile web of life. Aged trees killed by the intrusion of a pond into a forest become homes for millions of insects, which provide food for woodpeckers and other birds. Fish, turtles, frogs, and snakes soon inhabit the pond and its surrounding environment, and herons, muskrats, otters, and raccoons arrive later as part of the newly emerging ecosystem. Bears, birds of prey, and deer may come to the shore to drink or feed on smaller animals. Fish may feed on mosquito larvae in the still waters. After the beavers have exhausted the nearby food supply and have moved on, the pond may eventually drain and become a fertile meadow and home to yet other creatures.

The presence of beavers has other positive implications for the nearby human population. In early times, pioneers coveted the fertile soil left from a drained beaver pond. Floods and droughts are tempered in the long run by beaver activities; control of soil erosion and reduced numbers of forest fires are other positive byproducts.

Deer, Elk, and Pronghorn

Sportspeople and wildlife enthusiasts alike appreciate Oregon's big-game herds. Big-game habitats differ dramatically from one side of the Cascades to the other, with Roosevelt elk and blacktail deer in the west and Rocky Mountain elk and mule deer east of the Cascades. The Columbian whitetail deer is a seldom-seen, endangered species that populates western Oregon. Pronghorns reside in the high desert country of southeastern Oregon. The continent's fastest mammal, it is able to sprint at over 60 miles per hour in short bursts. The low brush of the open country east of the Cascades suits the pronghorns' excellent vision, which enables them to spot predators.

Desert Critters

Because 99 percent of desert animals are nocturnal, it's difficult to see many of them. Nonetheless, their variety and exotic presences should be noted. Horned lizards, kangaroo rats, red-and-black ground snakes, kit foxes, and four-inch-long greenish-yellow hairy scorpions are some of the more interesting denizens of the desert east of the Cascade Mountains. Marine fossils dating back 225 million years have been found in eastern Oregon creekbeds in an area that is now home to pronghorns and wild mustangs.

Bears

Black bears *(Ursus americanus)* proliferate in remote mountain forests of Oregon. Adults average 200–500 pounds and have dark coats. Black bears shy away from people except when provoked by the scent of food,

---

BANANA SLUGS

You won't go far in the Oregon coast woodlands or underbrush before you encounter the state's best-known invertebrates – and lots of them. There are few places on earth where these snails-out-of-shells grow as large (3–10 inches long) or as numerous. The reason is western Oregon's climate: moister than mist but drier than drizzle. This balance, combined with calcium-poor soil, enables the native banana slug and the more common European black slug to thrive.

The bane of Oregon gardeners, the eight species of nonnative slugs that have established themselves in the Northwest prey on crops and gardens. Native species generally confine themselves to forests, where they feast on indigenous plants. When these critters are not eating vegetation, you'll see them moseying along at a snail's pace on sidewalks or forest trails.

---

when cornered or surprised, or upon human intrusion into territory near their cubs. Female bears tend to have a very strong maternal instinct that may construe any alien presence as an attack upon their young. Authorities counsel hikers to act aggressively and defend themselves with whatever means possible if a bear is in attack mode or shows signs that it considers a hiker prey. Jump up and down, shout, and wave your arms. It may help to raise your jacket or pack to make yourself appear larger. Bears can run much faster than humans, and their retractable claws enable black bears to scramble up trees. Furthermore, bears tend to give chase when they see something running.

If you see a bear at a distance, try to stay downwind of it and back away slowly. Bears have a strong sense of smell, and some studies suggest that our body scent is abhorrent to them. Our food, however, can be quite appealing. Campers should place all food in a sack tied to a rope and suspend it 20 feet or more from the ground.

Other Land Animals

The state is also home to cougars, also known as mountain lions. As human development encroaches on their territory, sightings of these large cats become more common. Although they tend to shy away from big people, they've been known to attack children and small adults. For this reason, if no other, keep your kids close to adults when hiking.

Wild "Kiger" mustangs, descendants of horses that the Spanish conquistadores brought to America centuries ago, live on Steens Mountain and are identified by their hooked ears, thin dorsal stripes, two-toned manes, and faint zebra stripes on their legs. Narrow trunks and a short back are other distinguishing physical characteristics. They sometimes can be identified from a distance by the herding instinct bred into them by the Spanish. The kigers constitute a small percentage of the 2,000 wild mustangs in the state.

Birds

The Pacific Flyway is an important migratory route that passes through Oregon, and the state's varied ecosystems provide habitats for a variety of species, ranging from shorebirds to raptors to songbirds. The U.S. Fish and Wildlife Service has established viewpoints for wildlife- and bird-watching at 12 Oregon national wildlife refuges, which are detailed in the destination chapters.

In the winter the outskirts of Klamath Falls become inundated with bald eagles. Along the lower Columbia east of Astoria and on Sauvie Island, just outside Portland, are other bald-eagle wintering spots. (Visitors to Sauvie Island near Portland will be treated to an amazing variety of birds. More than 200 bird species come through here on the Pacific Flyway, feeding in grassy clearings. Look for eagles here on the island's northwest side. Herons, ducks of all sorts, and geese also live on the island.)

Other birds of prey, or raptors, abound all over the state. Northeast of Enterprise, near Zumwalt, is one of the best places to see hawks. Species commonly sighted include the ferruginous, red-tailed, and Swainson's hawks. Rafters in Hells Canyon might see golden eagles' and peregrine falcons' nests. Portlanders driving the Fremont Bridge over the Willamette River also might get to see peregrine falcons. Along I-5 in the Willamette Valley, look for red-tailed hawks on fenceposts, and American kestrels, North America's smallest falcons, sitting on phone wires.

Turkey vultures circle the dry areas during the warmer months. Vultures are commonly sighted above the Rogue River. In central Oregon, osprey are frequently sighted off the Cascades Lakes Highway south of Bend, nesting atop hollowed-out snags near water (especially Crane Prairie Reservoir).

In terms of sheer numbers and variety, the coast's mudflats at low tide and the tidal estuaries are among the best birding environments. Numerous locations along the coast—including Bandon Marsh, Three Arch Rock near Cape Meares, and South Slough Estuarine Research Reserve near Coos Bay—offer outstanding opportunities for spotting such pelagic species as pelicans, cormorants, guillemots, and puffins, as well as waders such as curlews, sandpipers, and plovers, plus various ducks and geese. Rare species such as tufted puffins and the snowy plover enjoy special protection here, along with other types of migratory birds. The **Oregon Islands National Wildlife Refuge,** which comprises all the 1,400-plus offshore islands, reefs, and rocks from Tillamook Head to the California border, is a haven for the largest concentration of nesting seabirds along the West Coast, thanks to the abundance of protected nesting habitat.

Malheur Wildlife Refuge, in the southeast portion of the state, is Oregon's premier bird and birder retreat and stopover point for large groups of sandhill cranes, Canada and snow geese, whistling swans, and pintail ducks.

In the mountains, look for Clark's nutcracker and the large Steller's jay, whose grating voice and dazzling blue plumage often command the most attention. Mountain hikers are bound to share part of their picnic lunch with these birds. At high elevations, the quieter Clark's nutcracker will more likely be your guest.

Unfortunately, the western meadowlark, the state bird, has nearly vanished from western Oregon due to loss of habitat, but thanks to natural pasture east of the Cascades you can still hear its distinctive song. The meadowlark is distinguished by a yellow underside with a black crescent pattern across the breast and white outer tail feathers.

Salmon and Steelhead

In recent decades, dwindling Pacific salmon and steelhead stocks have prompted restrictions on commercial and recreational fishing in order to restore threatened and endangered species throughout the Northwest. Runs are highly variable from year to year; for more information about fish populations and fishing restrictions, see Oregon Department of Fish and Wildlife's website, www.dfw.state.or.us.

The salmon's life cycle begins and ends in a freshwater stream. After an upriver journey from the sea of sometimes hundreds of miles, the spawning female deposits 3,000–7,000 eggs in hollows (called redds) she has scooped out of the coarse sand or gravel, where the male fertilizes them. These adult salmon die soon after mating, and their bodies then deteriorate to become part of the food chain for young fish.

Within 3–4 months, the eggs hatch into alevin, tiny immature fish with their yolk sac still attached. As the alevin exhaust the nutrients in the sac, they enter the fry stage, and begin to resemble very small salmon. The length they remain as fry differs among various species. Chinook fry, for example, immediately start heading for saltwater, whereas coho or silver salmon will remain in their home stream for one to three years before moving downstream.

The salmon are in the smolt stage when they start to enter saltwater. The five- to seven-inch smolts will spend some time in the estuary area of the river or stream, while they feed and adjust to the saltwater.

When it finally enters the ocean, the salmon is considered an adult. Each species varies in the number of years it remains away from its natal stream, foraging sometimes thousands of miles throughout the Pacific. Chinook can spend as many as seven years away from its nesting (and ultimately its resting) place; most other species remain in the salt for 2–4 years. Spring and fall mark the main upstream runs of the Pacific salmon. It is suspected that young salmon imprint the odor of their birth stream, enabling them to find their way home years later.

SALMON OR STEELHEAD?

Touted as the best-tasting salmon, king or chinook salmon are also the largest species, sometimes weighing in at over 80 pounds. Coho or silver salmon are known among anglers as fiercely fighting fish, despite a weight of just 10-20 pounds. In 1994, the El Niño warming current inhibited coho reproduction enough to bring about a total ban on harvesting this species. That turned around after 2000, when a cautious sport-fishing season reopened in Oregon.

Chum salmon (known derogatorily as "dog salmon" because Canadian and Alaskan native people thought them worthy only of being fed to their dog teams) are found only in the Miami and Kilchis Rivers, near Tillamook.

Sockeye and pink (or humpback) salmon, two other species, are not caught south of Washington waters, but you may see them sold in Oregon stores.

Steelhead are sea-run rainbow trout averaging 5-20 pounds whose life-cycle generally resembles that of salmon – save for the fact that steelhead generally survive after spawning and may live to spawn multiple times. Runs of steelhead, often heavily supplemented by hatchery-raised fish, are found in rivers and streams up and down the coast. They provide great – if challenging – sport angling, but are not fished for commercially (though you will find farm-raised steelhead in the grocery store).

The salmon's traditional predators such as the sea lion, northern pikeminnow, harbor seal, black bear, Caspian tern, and herring gull pale in comparison to the threats posed by modern civilization. Everything from pesticides to sewage to nuclear waste has polluted Oregon waters, and until mitigation efforts were enacted, dams and hydroelectric turbines threatened to block Oregon's all-important Columbia River spawning route.

History

NATIVE PEOPLES
Early Days

Long before Europeans came to this hemisphere, native peoples thrived for thousands of years in the region of present-day Oregon. A leading theory concerning their origins maintains that their ancestors came over from Asia on a land/ice bridge spanning what is now the Bering Strait. Along with archaeological evidence, shipwrecks of Asian craft on the Pacific coast also support the theory that Native Americans had Eastern Hemisphere contact. This contention has been further substantiated by facial features and dental patterns common to both peoples, as well as isolated correspondences in ritual, music, and dialect.

Despite common ancestry, the tribes on the rain-soaked coast and in the Willamette Valley lived quite differently from those on the drier eastern flank of the Cascade Mountains. Tribes west of the Cascades enjoyed abundant salmon, shellfish, berries, and game. Broad rivers facilitated travel, and thick stands of the finest softwood timber in the world ensured that there was never a dearth of building materials. A mild climate with plentiful food and resources allowed the wet-siders the leisure time to evolve a complex culture rich with artistic endeavors, theatrical pursuits, and such ceremonial gatherings as the traditional potlatch, where the divesting of one's material wealth was seen as a status symbol. Dentalium and abalone shells, woodpecker feathers, obsidian blades, and hides were especially coveted. Later on, Hudson's Bay blankets were added to this list.

After contact with traders, Chinook, an amalgam of Native American tongues with some French and English thrown in, was the common argot among the diverse tribes that gathered in the Columbia Gorge each year. It was at these gatherings that the coast and valley dwellers would come into contact with tribes from east of the Cascades. These drysiders led a seminomadic existence, following the game and avoiding the climatic extremes of winter and summer in their region. In the southeast desert of the Great Basin, seeds and roots added protein to their diet.

The introduction of horses in the mid-1700s made hunting, especially for large bison, much easier. In contrast to their west-of-the-Cascade counterparts, who lived in 100- by 40-foot longhouses, extended families in the eastern tribes inhabited pit houses when not hunting. The demands of chasing migratory game necessitated caves or crude rock shelters.

Twelve separate nations populated Oregon. Although these were further divided into 80 tribes, the primary allegiance was to the village. The "nation" status referred to language groupings such as Salish and Athabascan. Tribal names such as Alsea or Shasta Costa were usually derived from a word in the local argot for "The People," or from what a neighboring tribe called "Them." On occasion, European explorers bestowed a name upon the particular native grouping. An example of this was the "Rogue" Native American appellation. Across the region, many Native Americans were united in their worship of Spilyai, the coyote demigod. Spilyai, as well as many other figures animal and human, formed the subject of a large body of folk tales that explain the origins of the land in ways that are both entertaining and insightful.

Conflicts with White Settlers

The coming of white settlers meant the usurpation of tribal homelands, exposure to European diseases such as smallpox and diphtheria, and the passing of ancient ways of life. Violent conflicts ensued on a large scale with the influx of settlers seeking missionary work and government land giveaways in the 1830s and '40s. In the 1850s, mining activity in southern Oregon and on the coast incited the Rogue River Indian Wars, adding to the strife brought on by annexation to the United States.

All these events compelled the federal government to send in troops and to eventually set up treaties with Oregon's first inhabitants. The attempts at arbitration in the 1850s added insult to injury. Tribes of different—indeed, often incompatible—backgrounds were rounded up and grouped together haphazardly on reservations, often far from their homelands. In the century that followed, the evils of modern civilization destroyed much of the ecosystem upon which these cultures were based. An especially regrettable result of settlement was the decline of the Columbia River salmon runs due to overfishing, loss of habitat, and pollution. This not only weakened the food chain but treated this spiritual totem of the many tribes along the Columbia as an expendable resource.

For a while, there was an attempt to restore the balance. In 1924, the government accorded citizenship to Native Americans. Ten years later, the Indian Reorganization Act provided tribal management of reservation lands. A decade later a court of treaty claims was established. In the 1960s, however, the government, acting on the premise that the Native Americans needed to assimilate into white society, terminated several reservations.

Recent government reparations have accorded many native peoples preferential hunting and fishing rights, monetary/land grants, and the restoration of tribal status to certain disenfranchised groups. In Oregon, there are now nine federally recognized tribes and six reservations: Warm Springs, Umatilla, Burns Paiute, Siletz, Grand Ronde, and Coquille. Against all odds, tribal culture is still a vital part of Oregon; the 2000 census estimated that over 45,000 Oregonians are Native American. Native American gaming came to Oregon in the mid-1990s, and Native Oregonians now operate eight lucrative casinos in the state; the Confederated Tribes of the Grand Ronde, owners of the phenomenally popular Spirit Mountain Casino, are among the state's biggest philanthropists.

Archaeological Perspectives

Archaeologists have unearthed all manner of native artifacts. One that has evoked considerable controversy is a site found at Fort Rock, east of the Cascades near Bend. Charcoals from a hearth there are thought to be more than 13,000 years old, exceeding earlier estimates of the period of human presence in the region by about 3,500 years. A sandal found at the same site dated at around 10,000 years old had been the previous standard-bearer.

Another significant find is a gallery of 5,000-year-old petroglyphs on the walls of a cave in the foothills just east of the Willamette Valley. Relics excavated from the site of the Oregon Country Fair near Eugene have been dated at 8,000–10,000 years of age.

Other finds include coastal and Rogue Valley digs where 9,000-year-old artifacts have been unearthed. Obsidian flaked in the Clovis style indicates that Ice Age people roamed the Rogue Valley as long as 11,000 years ago. The distinctive grooves in the obsidian mark it as a product of the Clovis big-game hunter culture. Researchers excavating a site at Indian Sands, in Samuel H. Boardman State Park north of Brookings, which yielded artifacts dating back more 12,000 years, making it the oldest known site of human activity yet found on the coast.

In 1999, the oldest house in Oregon, and possibly the United States, was discovered on the shoreline of Paulina Lake. The archaeological significance of this 9,500-year-old site might eventually be rivaled by finds in several Woodburn city parks, 35 miles south of Portland. In the summer of 2000, a human hair was found in 12,000-year-old soils of an ancient wetland, along with animal bones thousands of years old.

EXPLORATION, SETTLEMENT, AND GROWTH

In the 17th and 18th centuries, Spanish, English, and Russian vessels came to offshore waters here in search of a sea route connecting the Atlantic with the Pacific. Accounts differ, but the first sightings of the Oregon coast have been credited to either Juan Cabrillo (in 1543) or the English explorer Sir Francis Drake (in 1579). Other voyagers of note included Spain's Vizcaíno and de Alguilar (in 1603) and Don Bruno de Heceta (in 1775), and England's James Cook and John Meares during the late 1770s, as well as George Vancouver (in 1792). Robert Gray's 1792 voyage 10 miles up the Columbia River estuary was the first American incursion into the area.

In 1996, a front-page story in the *London Times* proclaimed Sir Francis Drake the first European to set foot on the coast (previously Heceta was credited with the first landing) on the basis of an archaeological find in Little Whale Cove south of Depoe Bay. Timbers from a stockade left by Drake, who is known to have beached for repairs, were purportedly found, leading to this speculation. (See *Drake's Lost Harbor?* sidebar in the *Northern Oregon Coast* chapter.)

Sea otter and beaver pelts added impetus to the search for a trade route connecting the Atlantic and Pacific oceans. While the Northwest Passage turned out to be a myth, the fur trade became a basis of commerce and contention between European, Asian, and eventually American governments.

American Expansion in Oregon

The Americans entered the area when Robert Gray sailed up the Columbia River in 1792. The first American overland excursion into Oregon was made by the Corps of Discovery in 1804–1806. Dispatched by Thomas Jefferson to explore the lands of the Louisiana Purchase and beyond, Captains Meriwether Lewis and William Clark and their party of 30 men and one woman, Sacajawea, trekked across the continent to the mouth of the Columbia, camped south of present-day Astoria during the winter of 1805–1806, and then returned to St. Louis. Lewis and Clark's exploration and mapping of Oregon threw down the gauntlet for future settlement and eventual annexation of the Oregon Territory by the United States. The expedition also initially secured good relations with the Native Americans in the West, thus establishing the preconditions to trade and the missionary influx.

Following Lewis and Clark's journey, there were years of wrangling over America's right to settle in the new territory. The mere threat of British gunboats on the Columbia caused the quick departure of American John Jacob Astor's Pacific Fur Company during the War of 1812. It wasn't until the Convention of 1818 that the country west of the Rockies, south of Russian America, and north of Spanish America was open for use by American citizens as well as British subjects.

During the 1820s, the Hudson's Bay Company continued to hold sway over Oregon country by means of Fort Vancouver, on the north shore of the Columbia. More than 500 people settled here under the charismatic leadership of John McLoughlin, who oversaw the planting of crops and the raising of livestock. Despite the establishment of almost half a dozen Hudson's Bay outposts, several factors presaged the inevitable demise of British influence in Oregon. Most obvious was the decline of the fur trade as well as England's difficulty in maintaining her far-flung empire. Less apparent but equally influential was the lack of white females in a land populated predominantly by white trappers and explorers. If the Americans could attract settlers of both genders, they'd be in a position to create an expanding population base that could dominate the region.

The first step in this process was the arrival of missionaries. In 1834, Methodist soul-seekers led by Jason Lee settled near the Willamette River. Four years later, another mission was started in the eastern Columbia River Gorge. In 1843, Marcus and Narcissa Whitman's missions started up on the upper Columbia in present-day Walla Walla, Washington (until

THE CORPS OF DISCOVERY

For nearly two decades at the end of the 18th century, Thomas Jefferson dreamed of mounting an expedition to explore the virtually unknown North American continent west of the Mississippi River. Like others of his era, Jefferson believed in the existence of the Northwest Passage, a navigable route between the northern Pacific and Atlantic Oceans, the discovery of which could revolutionize trade between the United States and the Orient, and speed the growth (and increase the wealth) of the young republic. In January 1803, President Jefferson finally succeeded in securing funding from Congress to outfit such an ambitious undertaking. Congress granted $2,500, though the eventual cost would top $38,000.

Jefferson invited his secretary, 28-year-old Meriwether Lewis, to lead the expedition, which the president named the Corps of Discovery. Its stated goals would be "to make friends and allies of the far Western Indians while at the same time diverting valuable pelts from the rugged northern routes used by [Great Britain]... and bringing the harvest down the Missouri to the Mississippi and thence eastward by a variety of routes." Furthermore, Lewis would be charged with mapping the territory and chronicling the peoples, plants, and animals encountered along the way. Lewis, in turn, asked a former Army comrade, William Clark, to co-captain the expedition with him.

Just two months after Congress approved the request, Jefferson consummated the Louisiana Purchase, an agreement that ceded New Orleans and 820,000 square miles of France's North American territories to the United States, for $15 million dollars – about three cents an acre. Overnight, the area of the United States doubled, and Lewis and Clark's mission assumed even greater importance.

In May 1804, after months of preparation and recruitment, the Corps set off in a large keelboat and two pirogues up the Missouri River, from a base near St. Louis, then the western edge of white civilization. Over the next two years, their route would take them north and west, up the drainages of the Missouri River, across the Rockies, and into the Columbia River system and finally to the Pacific Ocean. The Corps, consisting of 32 men and one woman, the Shoshone Sacajawea, would spend October 1805 to May 1806 in what today are Oregon and Washington, including four wet, miserable months at Fort Clatsop, near Astoria (see *Astoria and Vicinity* in the *Northern Oregon Coast* chapter).

Along the way, Lewis and Clark charted some 8,000 miles of territory hitherto unexplored by European Americans and documented 300 species of flora and fauna previously unknown to Western science. Journals kept by Lewis, Clark, and three of their sergeants chronicle their experiences with such vividness they still captivate readers today. The effect their journey had in accelerating westward expansion of the United States across the continent can hardly be overstated.

1853, the Washington area was considered a single entity with Oregon). The missionaries brought alien ways and diseases for which the Native Americans had no immunity. As if this weren't enough to provoke a violent reaction, the Native Americans would soon have their homelands inundated by thousands of settlers lured by government land giveaways.

The Oregon Trail

The march across the frontier was fueled by the 640 free acres that each adult white male could claim in the mid-1840s. The westward expansion that Americans regarded as their "manifest destiny" seemed a ready solution to the problems of the 1830s, when the country was in a deep depression, with land panics, droughts, and an unstable currency. Despite ignorance of western geography and the hardships it held, the Oregon Trail, a 2,000-mile frontier thoroughfare, was viewed with covetous eyes, especially in increasingly populous Missouri. Around Independence, Missouri, the trees thinned, the settlements ended, and the Oregon Trail began.

More than 53,000 people traversed the trail between 1840 and 1850 en route to western Oregon. In 1850, the Donation Land Act cut in half the allotted free acreage, reflecting the diminishing availability of real estate. But although a single pioneer man was now entitled to only 320 acres, and single women were excluded from land ownership, as part of a couple they could claim an additional 320 free acres. This promoted marriage and, in turn, families on the western frontier, and helped to fulfill Secretary of State John C. Calhoun's prediction that American families could outbreed the Hudson's Bay Company's bachelor trappers, thus winning the battle of the West in the bedroom.

The Donation Land Act also stipulated that nonwhites could not own any part of the Oregon Territory, enabling the pioneers to seize native people's lands with impunity. The act impeded the growth of towns and industries, too, as large parcels of land were given away to relatively small numbers of people, which kept the population geographically distant from one another. This was one reason why urbanization was slow in coming to the Northwest.

The Applegate Trail

Another route west was the Applegate Trail, pioneered by brothers Lindsay and Jesse Applegate in the mid-1840s. Each had lost sons several years before to drowning on the Columbia River. The treacherous rapids here had initially been the last leg of a journey to the Willamette Valley.

On their return journey to the region, the brothers departed from the established trail when they reached Fort Hall, Idaho. Veering south from the Oregon Trail across northern Nevada's Black Rock Desert, they traversed the northeast top of California to enter Oregon near present-day Klamath Falls. A southern Oregon gold rush in the 1850s drew thousands across this route.

Early Government and Statehood

There was enough unity among American settlers to organize a provisional government in 1843. Then, in 1848, the federal government decided to accord Oregon territorial status. With migration increasing exponentially from 1843 on, there was little doubt in Congress about Oregon's viability. Still, it took frontiersman Joe Meek to coalesce popular opinion. He had first performed this role in Champoeg, at the northern end of the Willamette Valley, in 1843, when he boomed out the rallying cry for regional confederation, "Who's for a divide?", in order to force a vote on the question of whether to challenge the British claim of sovereignty in the region. Two Canadians, F. X. Matthieu and Etienne Lucier, crossed the line and won the day for the Americans. In equally dramatic fashion, Meek strode into the halls of Congress fresh from the trail in mountain-man regalia to forcefully argue the case for territoriality. Congress granted the petition and Meek accompanied newly appointed territorial governor Joseph Lane to Oregon in the spring of 1849.

The Oregon Territory got off to a rousing start thanks to the California gold rush of 1849. The rush occasioned a housing boom in San Francisco and a need for lumber, and the dramatic population influx created instant markets for the agriculture of the Willamette Valley. Portland was located at the north end of the valley and 110 miles upriver from the Pacific on the Columbia, near the world's largest supply of accessible softwood timber. The young city was in a perfect position to channel goods from the interior to coastal ports. So great was the need in California for food that wheat from eastern Oregon was declared legal tender. The exchange rate started around $1 a bushel and went as high as $6. The economic benefits from the gold rush notwithstanding, Oregon lost two-thirds of its adult male population to gold fever. Many of the emigrants returned when the news of gold discoveries in southwestern Oregon came out between 1850 and 1860. The resulting influx helped establish the Rogue Valley and coastal population centers.

However, strategic importance and population growth alone do not explain Oregon's becoming the 33rd state in the Union. Shortly before statehood, the Dred Scott decision had become law in 1857. This had the effect of opening the territory to slavery. While slavery didn't lack for adherents in Oregon, the prevailing sentiment was that it was neither necessary nor desirable. Because territorial status would be a potential liability to a Union on the mend, the congressional majority saw an especially compelling reason to open its doors to this new member. When nonslavery status was assured, Oregon entered the Union on Valentine's Day, 1859.

Economic Growing Pains

During the years of the Civil War and its aftermath, internal conflicts were the order of the day within the state. By 1861, good Willamette Valley land was becoming scarce, so many farmers moved east of the Cascades to farm wheat. They ran into violent confrontations with Native Americans over land. Between 1862 and 1934, the Homestead Act land giveaways helped fuel these fires of resentment. Miners encroaching on Native American territory around the southern coast eventually flared into the bloody Rogue River Wars, which would lead to the destruction of most of the native peoples of the coast.

In the 1870s, cattlemen came to eastern Oregon, followed by sheep ranchers, and the two groups fought for dominance of the range. Just when it appeared that eastern Oregon land was ripe for agricultural promoters and community planners, the bottom fell out. Overproduction of wheat, uncertain markets, and two severe winters were the culprits. In the early 20th century a population influx created further problems by draining the water table. Thus, the glory that was gold, grass, and grain east of the Cascades was short-lived. Many eastern Oregon towns grew up and flourished for a decade, only to fall back into desert, leaving no trace of their existence.

Unlike the downturn east of the Cascades, boom times were ahead for the rest of the state as the 20th century approached. In the 1860s and '70s, Jacksonville to the south became the commercial counterpart to Portland, owing to its proximity to the Rogue Valley and south coast goldfields as well as the California border. During this period, transportation links began to consolidate, in part due to the efforts of stagecoach magnate Ben Holladay. The first stagecoach, steamship, and rail lines moved south from the Columbia River into the Willamette Valley; by the 1880s, Portland was joined to San Francisco and to the east by railroad. Henry Villard was the prime mover in this effort, eventually dominating all commerce in the Northwest by channeling freight and passengers through Portland and along the Columbia. In 1900, Union Pacific magnate James J. Hill picked up where Villard left off. By selling 900,000 acres of timberland to lumber baron Frederic Weyerhaeuser at $6 an acre (with the stipulation that Weyerhaeuser build his mills close by Union Pacific tracks), he hitched the destinies of the region to the iron horse.

Progressive Politics

In the modern era, Oregon blazed trails in the thicket of governmental legislation and reform. The so-called Oregon system of initiative, referendum, and recall was first conceived in the 1890s, coming to fruition in the first decade of the 1900s. The system has since become an integral part of the democratic process.

In like measure, Oregon's extension of suffrage to women in 1912, a 1921 compulsory education law, and the first large-scale union activity in the country during the 1920s were red-letter events in American history.

The 1930s were exciting years in the Northwest. Despite widespread poverty, the foundations of future prosperity were laid during this decade. New Deal programs such as the Works Projects Administration and the Civilian Conservation Corps undertook many projects around the state. Building roads and hydroelectric dams created jobs and improved the quality of life in Oregon, in addition to bolstering the country's defense during wartime. Hydroelectric power from the Bonneville Dam, completed in 1938, enabled Portland's shipyards and aluminum plants to thrive. Low utility rates encouraged more employment and settlement, while the Columbia's irrigation water enhanced agriculture.

World War II

Thanks to Henry Kaiser's mass-production techniques, 10,000 workers were employed in the Portland shipyards. But in addition to laying the foundations for future growth, the war years in Oregon and their immediate aftermath were full of trials for state residents. Vanport— a city of, at one time, 45,000—that grew up in the shadow of Kaiser aluminum plants and the shipyards north of Portland, was washed off the map in 1948 by a Columbia River flood. Tillamook County forests, which supplied Sitka spruce for airplanes, endured several massive fires that destroyed 500 square miles of trees. Along with these natural disasters, Oregon was the only state among the contiguous 48 to have a military installation (Fort Stevens, near Astoria) shelled by a Japanese submarine, to endure a Japanese bombing mission on the mainland (on Mount Emily, near Brookings), and to suffer civilian casualties when a balloon bomb exploded (near the Gearhart Mountain Wilderness Area in Lake County).

The Modern Era

With the perfection of the chainsaw in the 1940s, the timber industry could take advantage of the postwar housing boom. During that decade, the population increased by nearly 50 percent, growing to over 1.5 million. During the 1950s and 1960s, the Army Corps of Engineers carried out a massive program of new dam projects, resulting in construction of The Dalles, John Day, and McNary dams on the main stem of the Columbia and the Oxbow and Brownlee dams on the Snake River. In addition, the flooding on the Willamette was tamed through a series of dams on its major tributary watersheds, the Santiam, the Middle Fork of the Willamette, and the McKenzie.

Politically, the late 1960s and '70s brought environmentally groundbreaking measures spearheaded by Governor Tom McCall. The bottle bill, land-use statutes, and the cleanup of the Willamette River were part of this legacy.

The 1990s saw the Oregon economy flourish, fueled by the growth of computer hardware and software industries here as well as a real estate market favorable to California retirees. The latter has had sociological ripple effects with many longtime state residents feeling displaced by the transformed economy and living standards. The legalization of gambling and drastic cuts in education have provoked controversy on all sides of the political spectrum. While a retreat from longstanding legislative commitments reflects the demographics of Oregon's new arrivals as well as its changing economic climate, Oregon's physician-assisted suicide bill, extensive vote-by-mail procedures, medical marijuana initiative, and low-cost health insurance program for low-income Oregonians have sustained its maverick image.

Today's Economy

Until recently, logging and wood products have been the most important industries to Oregon in terms of jobs provided and revenue produced. Despite recent declines, many workers are still

wheat fields north of Enterprise

© BILL MCRAE

employed in logging, sawmills, and paper production. Fishing, although it has its ups and downs, is another traditional part of the economy that has persisted.

Oregon's economy has traditionally followed a boom-bust cycle, but has in recent decades diversified away from its earlier dependence on resource-based industries, forest products in particular. The state's major manufacturing industries today also include high tech, primary and fabricated metals, transportation equipment, and agricultural crops and processing. Important non-manufacturing sectors, which account for five out of seven jobs in the state, include wholesale and retail trade, education, health, and social services, high-tech non-manufacturing jobs (such as software development), and tourism.

In agriculture, organic produce, often sold in farmers markets, and specialty products have helped many small farmers to survive. These products include nursery crops (Monrovia is the nation's largest nursery and Oregon is the number one Christmas tree state); wine grapes; berries, cherries, apples, and pears; herbs and organic produce; gourmet mushrooms; and goat cheese. Oregon wineries, most small operations, turn out increasingly good wine, and for some this is actually a viable way to make a living. Large-scale agribusiness is also thriving with the booming food-processing and -packing industries proliferating in the lower Willamette Valley and eastern Oregon.

But it must be said that Intel is the state's largest employer, and Nike, Adidas America, Columbia, and other sportswear companies have headquarters here, employing a substantial number of people in the Portland area.

Sports and Recreation

BICYCLING

While not for everybody, biking all or part of the Oregon coast is the surest way to get on intimate terms with this spectacular region. Before going, get a free copy of the **Oregon Coast Bike Route Map** from the Oregon Department of Transportation (355 Capitol St. N.E., Salem 97310, www.oregon.gov/ODOT/HWY/BIKEPED/) or from coastal information centers and chambers of commerce. This brochure features strip maps of the route, noting services from Astoria to the California border. With information on campsites, hostels, bike-repair facilities, elevation changes, temperatures, and wind speed, this pamphlet does everything but map the ruts in the road.

Because the prevailing winds in summer are from the northwest, most people cycle south on U.S. 101 to take advantage of a steady tailwind. You'll also be riding on the ocean side of the road with better views and easier access to turnouts, and generally wider bike lanes and shoulders. The entire 370-mile trip (or 380-mile if you include the Three Capes Loop) involves nearly 16,000 feet of elevation change. Most cyclists cover the distance in 6–8 days, pedaling an average of 50–65 miles daily.

A number of companies offer pre-planned group bicycle trips, with everything from the bicycle to the meals and lodging included. For example, **Bicycle Adventures** (206/786-0989 or 800/443-6060, www.bicycleadventures. com) offers several coast packages, including a six-day fully supported tour from Astoria to Newport for $2,066. **Cycle Oregon** (503/287-0405 or 800/292-5367, www.cycleoregon.org) sponsors an annual week-long supported tour of rural Oregon in September. Considered one of the best bike tours in America, Cycle Oregon tours cover around 500 miles and attract up to 2,000 riders each year. Fees, which include all meals, showers, support, and entertainment, are around $800 per person.

HIKING

While every corner of Oregon features hiking trails, one trail deserves special notice. For 362 miles, from the Columbia River to the Cali-

TOP FIVE HIKES IN OREGON

WILDWOOD TRAIL

Who would imagine that one of the state's top trails is only 10 minutes from downtown Portland? Thanks to 5,000-acre Forest Park, it's true. One close-in access point onto the 30+-mile-long leafy haven of the Wildwood Trail is via the shorter but quite scenic Lower Macleay Trail. Reach it at the end of N.W. Upshur Street (the equivalent of N.W. 29 Ave. and Upshur). (See the *Portland* chapter.)

EAGLE CREEK TRAIL

This classic Columbia River Gorge trail starts near Bonneville Dam and follows Eagle Creek up past waterfalls and a profusion of springtime wildflowers. Your face will be misted with spray, and in places you'll need to grab hold of cables bolted into the basalt cliffs as the trail narrows. The Eagle Creek Trail is 41 miles east of Portland on I-84. There are two common destinations: Punchbowl Falls is two miles in; Tunnel Falls is six miles from the trailhead. Hike back the way you came. (See the *Columbia River Gorge and Mount Hood* chapter.)

OSWALD WEST STATE PARK

Most of the mountain, and the prominent headlands of Cape Falcon, are encompassed within the 2,500-acre gem of Oswald West State Park. Several hiking trails weave through the park, including the 13 miles of the Oregon Coast Trail linking Arch Cape to the north with Manzanita. To get there head 10 miles south on U.S. 101 from Cannon Beach to the Cape Falcon Trail parking lot. Start there and head south on Cape Falcon Trail, where you can continue south to Neahanie Mountain or north to Cape Falcon. Excellent coastal views the entire way. (See the *Northern Oregon Coast* chapter.)

SILVER FALLS STATE PARK

Ten waterfalls cascade off canyon walls in a forest filled with gargantuan Douglas fir, ferns, and bigleaf and vine maple at this park. The best time to come is during fall foliage season when there are few visitors, just before icy roads and trail closures inhibit travel. To get there, drive 15 miles southeast of Silverton on Route 214 to get to the park. At the parking area near the South Fork of Silver Creek, start the 7.5-mile Trail of Ten Falls loop through Silver Canyon. (See *The Willamette Valley* chapter.)

SMITH ROCK STATE PARK

Majestic spires tower above the Crooked River at this 623-acre state park. Seven miles of well-marked trails follow the Crooked River and wend up the canyon walls to emerge on the ridge tops. Please stay on well-worn paths. To get there, drive nine miles north from Redmond to N.W. Crooked River Drive and head north to the park entrance about 100 yards from the Rockhard Store. Begin your hike here, starting a five-mile loop over Misery Ridge. (See the *Central Oregon* chapter.)

---

fornia border, the **Oregon Coast Trail** hugs the beaches and headlands, leading hikers into intimate contact with some of the most beautiful landscapes anywhere. Most of the trail runs through public lands, though some portions traverse easements on private parcels and the trail follows the highway and city streets in a number of places. The only coastal long-distance treks separated from U.S. 101 are the 30 miles between Seaside and Manzanita and Bandon and Port Orford. A free trail map and directory are available from the Oregon State Parks information center (800/551-6949, www.

oregonstateparks.org). This pamphlet makes it clear where this trail crosses open beaches, forested headlands, the shoulder of the Coast Highway, and even city streets in some towns. Be sure to bring water, particularly on northerly sections of the trail, as much of the trek here is on beachfront away from a potable supply.

USER FEES AND PASSES

In recent years, numerous state and federal parks, national recreation areas, trails, picnic areas, and other facilities have begun charging day-use fees, which are separate from overnight camping fees (the exception to this is camping at rustic campsites in national forests, which is covered by the Northwest Forest Pass). At sites that charge fees, the day-use fee is currently $3 per vehicle at state parks, $5 per vehicle at federal sites. Visitors can pay for day use at individual sites or purchase one of the annual passes described below.

Oregon Pacific Coast Passport

The best deal if you plan to visit many parks along the Oregon coast, this pass covers entrance, day-use, and vehicle parking fees at all state and federal fee sites along the entire Oregon portion of U.S. 101. It does not cover the cost of camping at state parks, which is a separate fee.

Two basic Passports are available depending, on customer needs and preferences. An **Annual Passport,** valid for the calendar year, is $35. A **Five-Day Passport** is $10. Passports may be purchased at welcome centers, ranger stations, national forest headquarters, national memorials, and state park offices. Call 800/551-6949 to purchase an annual pass by credit card or for directions to a convenient location near you.

State Park Passes

Another option, valid for day-use fees at Oregon's state parks that levy fees, is to buy a one-year ($25) or two-year ($40) State Park Pass. It's available from state park offices, by phone (800/551-6949), and from G.I. Joe's stores and other vendors. See the Oregon State Parks website (www.oregonstateparks.org/dayuse_permit.shtml) for more details and a complete list of vendors.

Northwest Forest Pass

In response to major reductions in timber harvests and cutbacks in federal money, a revenue shortfall has made it hard to keep up trails and campgrounds at a time when the region's population has put more demand on these facilities. The Northwest Forest Pass ($5 for one day, $30 for one year) is a vehicle-parking pass for the use of many improved trailheads, picnic areas, boat launches, and interpretive sites in the national forests of Oregon and Washington. Funds generated from pass sales go directly to maintaining and improving the trails, land, and facilities. You will see "Northwest Forest Pass Required" signs posted at participating sites. Fees are collected at kiosks or dispensed by machine. Passes are also available at many local vendors (such as G.I. Joe's, park stores, and chambers of commerce) as well as by phone (800/270-7504). You can also order them online at www.fs.fed.us/r6/passespermits. You can also check this website to find out if a pass is required before you head out.

These passes are good all over the Northwest, eliminating the necessity to purchase a separate pass with each entrance to another national forest. This pass covers most National Park Service and Forest Service sites in Oregon and Washington but is not valid for campground fees (with the exception of rustic campsites), concessionaire-operated sites, or Sno-Parks.

Golden Passport Program

Most National Park Service sites, such as national parks and monuments, charge a fee for use. You can pay an entrance fee at each site or park you visit, or you can participate in the Golden Passport Program, which offers three distinct passports. The annual **Golden Eagle Passport** ($65) allows the owner to use all Forest Service, Park Service, BLM, and U.S. Fish and Wildlife sites, as well as developed day-use sites and recreation areas. The $10 **Golden Age Passport** is a lifetime pass covering entrance fees for U.S. citizens over the age of 62 (proof of age required). Passport holders also get a 50 percent discount at campgrounds, boat launches, and swimming areas. The third pass, the free **Golden Access Passport,** is available only to those who are blind or permanently disabled (check with the forest service for eligibility requirements). It offers the same benefits as the Golden Eagle Pass.

For more details or to purchase a pass, contact the National Forest Foundation (877/465-2727, www.natlforests.org).

CAMPING

Oregon has more state parks than almost any other state, as well as a natural environment suited to all manner of recreational activities.

Camping in State Parks

From May 1 to October 30, camping prices are about the following: electrical hookup sites $20; tent sites $16; primitive/overflow sites $9; hiker/biker sites $4–6; yurts $27–42. During the discounted "Discovery Season," October 1–April 30, electrical hookup sites are $16; tent sites are $12; and hiker-biker site and yurt fees remain the same. The extra-vehicle charge during either season is $7.

Most state park campgrounds have at least a couple of yurts—canvas-walled, wood-floored shelters equipped with fold-up beds, heaters, and lamps; they sleep five.

Many state park campgrounds accept campsite reservations, and reservations are accepted for all special facilities such as cabins, yurts, and tepees. The state park system has a central information hotline (800/551-6949) and a website (www.oregonstateparks.org) where you can get park maps, campground layouts, rates, and other information.

Reservations for state parks can be made by phone via Reservations Northwest (503/731-3411 in Portland metro area, 800/452-5687 elsewhere). Business hours are 8 A.M.–7 P.M. Monday–Friday. Online reservations, with a Visa or MasterCard, are handled by a private vendor, ReserveAmerica (www.reserveamerica.com). Reservations may be made from two days up to nine months in advance. In addition to the campsite fee, a $6 processing fee is charged.

If you need to **cancel your reservation** three days or more before your scheduled arrival, call Reservations Northwest at the numbers above. Two or fewer days before your trip, call the park directly to cancel your reservation. Phone numbers for all parks are found on each individual park's web page (www.oregonstateparks.org). Cancellation service fees and requirements for special facilities, such as yurts and cabins, may vary. Your $6 reservation fee is nonrefundable, and a $3 cancellation fee will be charged if you cancel in the last two days.

Camping in National Forests

The U.S. Forest Service maintains hundreds of campsites, trails, and day-use areas. Refer to the Forest Service website (www.fs.fed.us/r6/rec.htm) or one of the specific destination chapters in this guide, for listings.

National forest campsites are usually much less developed than those at state parks, electric hookups are not available, although most campgrounds have water and vault or flush toilets. Most overnight sites charge a user fee. Fees are $10–15 for campsites, $5–7 for an extra vehicle. Campsites can be reserved online with a Visa or MasterCard through ReserveAmerica (www.reserveamerica.com).

FISHING AND HUNTING

Oregon takes a back seat to few other places when it comes to sport fishing and hunting opportunities, with varied shooting and angling possible all over the state. Rules and bag limits for both are subject to frequent change, so get a copy of the **Oregon Department of Fish and Wildlife**'s hunting and fishing regulations, available at the agency office or online (2501 S.W. 1st Ave., Portland, 503/872-5268, www.dfw.state.or.us), as well as at sporting goods stores, some grocery stores (such as Fred Meyer), and other outlets.

Fishing

Fishing for trout, both wild native cutthroat and rainbows as well as planted hatchery fish, is popular all across the state. Standout areas include the Deschutes River, a blue-ribbon stream noted for its large "redband" rainbow trout, as well as excellent steelhead fishing. Other notable steelhead streams include the coastal Rogue and Umpqua Rivers, as well as the Sandy and Clackamas Rivers, right in Portland's backyard. Smallmouth bass provide excellent sport on the John Day and Umpqua Rivers, and largemouth bass draw anglers to warm-water lakes across the state.

© JUDY JEWELL

The Metolius River is limited to fly fishing only.

The returns of salmon and steelhead, though aided by such efforts as habitat protection, improvements to dams that make them more fish-friendly, and other conservation efforts, as well as by cyclical changes in ocean currents and nutrient levels, remain uneven.

Sturgeon is another extremely popular game fish, weighing into the hundreds of pounds, in the larger rivers, particularly the Columbia and the Umpqua. Off the coast, bottom fishing for rockfish and other species is a year-round activity, depending on the weather. Warm ocean currents bring albacore tuna in August and September, and halibut are usually available in summer, though the season is variable and is set yearly by the Pacific Fisheries Management Council.

About 1,000 fishing guides are licensed in Oregon. Fishing opportunities on your own are almost limitless, but hiring a guide can be money well spent if you're exploring unfamiliar waters or you lack a boat. Major **charter-fishing** centers on the coast include Astoria, Hammond, Warrenton, Garibaldi, Depoe Bay, Newport, Winchester Bay, Charleston, Gold Beach, Bandon, and Brookings. Charter rates vary a bit, but typical prices up and down the coast are as follows: $55–60 for a half day (5–6 hours) of bottom fishing, $100 for a full day; $100 for an eight-hour salmon outing; $175 for 12 hours of tuna fishing; $150 for a 12-hour halibut charter. Inland, expect to pay at least $150–250 per person per day for guided trips for salmon, steelhead, sturgeon, and other species. Guide and charter services are listed in each destination chapter. Chambers of commerce in each town can also provide extensive listings.

Fishing licenses cost $12 (for one day), $22.50 (two days), $33 (three days), $43.50 (four days), $43.75 (seven days), or $61.50 (full year for non-residents; $24.75 for Oregonians). Nonresident licenses include Combined Angling Tags (allowing the taking of salmon, sturgeon, steelhead, and halibut).

Hunting

Hunters, too, enjoy a broad range of opportunities throughout Oregon. Shooting for upland game birds—chukar, Hungarian partridge, pheasant, grouse, and quail—can be good to excellent in eastern and central Oregon, the Cascades, and the coastal ranges. The eastern half of the state, as well as the Willamette Valley, Columbia River basin, and coastal areas, offer waterfowl hunting. Wild turkeys, introduced successfully on the eastern side of Mount Hood, have proliferated and are now hunted in almost every county of the state. Bigger game include elk, black bears, cougars, blacktail deer in western Oregon and mule deer in the east. A limited number of special tags are issued also for pronghorn, bighorn sheep, and mountain goats.

The rules governing hunting in the state are more complex and variable than those for fishing. Check the regulations carefully for seasons, restrictions, and bag limits, and, again, consult the Department of Fish and Wildlife's website (www.dfw.state.or.us) for the latest information.

WINDSURFING AND KITEBOARDING

Windsurfing conditions near the town of Hood River have made the Columbia River Gorge world famous. In recent years, kiteboarding has become almost as popular. Other than the San Francisco Bay Area, no other place in the continental United States boasts summertime air flows as consistently strong as those in the Gorge. Championship events and top competitors have coalesced on the shores of the river here, 60 miles east of Portland. The Columbia River runs in the opposite direction of the westerly air flows, which can cause large waves to stack up and allow sailboarders to maintain their positions relative to the shore. In short, the area offers the perfect marriage of optimal conditions and scenic beauty.

Some coastal waters, too, are gaining popularity for sailboarders. Floras Lake, near Port Orford, and Pistol River State Park, near Gold Beach, are top destinations. The latter hosts the Pistol River Wave Bash National Windsurfing Competition, each June.

WHITE-WATER ACTIVITIES

With 90,000 river miles in the state and hundreds of outfitters to choose from, however, neophyte rafters have an embarrassment of riches. To help navigate the tricky currents of brochure jargon and select the experience that's right for you, here's a list of rivers to run and questions to ask before going.

Raft the famous **Rogue River** from June to September to avoid the rainy season and be spared current fluctuations due to dams upstream. This run is characterized by gentle stretches broken up by abrupt and occasionally severe drop-offs as well as swift currents. In fact, Blossom Bar is often cited as one of the state's consummate tests of skill for rafters. The Rogue is ideal for half- and full-day rafting trips, with most outfitters putting in near the town of Merlin and continuing downstream as far as Foster Bar. Water turbulence on the Rogue is often intensified by constricted channels created by huge boulders. Depending on the season, rafters can expect Class II, III, and IV rapids, interspersed by deep pools and cascading waterfalls. At day's end, superlative campsites offer repose and the chance to savor your adventures.

Despite the dryness and isolation of Oregon's southeast corner, the **Owyhee River** has become a prime springtime destination for whitewater enthusiasts. The 53 miles from Rome to the Owyhee Reservoir have two sections of exceptionally heavy rapids, but the many pools of short, intense white water alternating with easy drifts make for a well-paced trip. The best times to come are during May and early June. Before going, check conditions with the Vale BLM District office (541/473-3144, www.or.blm.gov/vale), because the Owyhee can only be run in high snowmelt years. Access to rafting take-out points in this part of the state is greatly facilitated by a four-wheel-drive vehicle.

The **John Day River** in northeastern Oregon offers an even-flowing current as it winds 175 miles through unpopulated rangeland and scenic rock formations. This is the longest free-flowing river in the United States. Below Clarno, the grade gets steep, creating the most treacherous part of the state's longest river (275 miles) within Oregon. The 157-mile section of the John Day that rafters, canoeists, and kayakers come to experience also has falls near the mouth that require a portage. The special charm of this Columbia tributary is the dearth of company you'll have here even during the river-running season of late March through May and then again in November. Just watch out for rattlesnakes along the bank and remember that the siltload in this undammed river reduces it to an unboatable trickle in summer months. Contact the Prineville BLM office (541/416-6700) for more information.

Unlike the John Day and the Owyhee Rivers, the **Deschutes River** rapids aren't totally dependent on snowmelt and it is the busiest vacation waterway in the state. The 44 miles between Maupin and the Columbia River contain sage-covered grasslands and wild rocky canyons where you might see bald eagles, pronghorns, and other wildlife. If there's a good run of salmon or steelhead, you might also encounter plenty of fishing boats. This area averages 310 days of sunshine annually, so weather is seldom a problem except for excessively hot summer days.

Typical rafting outfitter services include

meals, wetsuits or rain gear, and inflatable rafts and kayaks. Guided raft trips begin at about $50 for a half-day trip and increase to $200 (and up) a day for longer trips. Groups can get volume discounts. To ensure an intimate wilderness experience, ask about the number of people in a raft and how many rafts on the river at one time. Are there any hidden costs such as camping gear rental or added transfer charges? What is the cancellation policy? Another consideration is the training and experience of the guides. Can he or she be expected to give commentary about history, geology, and local color? You might also want to check about the company's willingness to customize its trips to special interests such as photography, bird-watching, or hiking.

SNOW SPORTS

One of the silver linings to Oregon's legendary precipitation is that so much of it falls in the form of snow in the mountains. Mount Hood, for example, has been buried by as much as 100 feet of snow in a single year. That makes a lot of people happy here from late fall through spring and even into summer, as Oregon snowpacks support the longest ski season in the country (at Timberline on Mount Hood), as well as snowboarding, snowmobiling, and snowshoeing.

In addition to hundreds of miles of groomed and backcountry cross-country ski routes, alpine resorts are concentrated in the northern and central Cascades and in the state's northeast corner. Portlanders have their choice of five developed ski resorts—Mount Hood Ski Bowl, Cooper Spur, Mount Hood Meadows, Timberline, and tiny Summit (the Northwest's oldest ski resort, dating to 1927)—just an hour's drive away on **Mount Hood.** In the central Cascades, there's family-friendly **Hoodoo Ski Bowl** southeast of Salem, **Willamette Pass** southeast of Eugene, and **Mount Bachelor,** the Northwest's largest and most developed ski area, southwest of Bend. At **Mount Bailey,** near Diamond Lake in the southern Cascades, downhillers can experience Sno-Cat skiing, a more affordable alternative to being dropped off on inaccessible slopes by helicopter. The area also offers extensive cross-country, skating, sledding, and snowmobiling terrain. Near the California border, **Mount Ashland** offers downhill action in southern Oregon, in addition to 100 miles of cross-country trails.

In the northeast, skiers have their choice of **Anthony Lakes Ski Area,** between Baker City and La Grande, and **Ferguson Ridge Ski Area** and **Salt Creek Summit,** both east of Joseph.

For details on all the above ski areas, see individual destination chapters. For snow reports and other updated information throughout the season, a good source is OnTheSnow .com (www.onthesnow.com/OR/).

Sno-Park Permits

Between November 15 and April 30, note that for winter sports in many areas, you'll need to purchase a Sno-Park permit to park your vehicle in posted winter recreation areas. Sporting goods stores, ski shops, and resorts near the slopes sell them for $15/season, $3/day.

Entertainment and Events

The majority of large crowd-drawing events take place June–September, but there are plenty of cool-weather and ongoing activities to keep you entertained throughout the year. The free weekly local magazines are a great source for events and entertainment listings and can be found in most of the larger burgs and college towns.

Oregon loves to celebrate its heritage, as well as its artistic and gastronomic bounty. The following seasonal sampler highlights some of the festivals and celebrations throughout the state.

In spring, two coastal gourmet affairs of note are the **Newport Seafood and Wine Festival** and the **Astoria Crab Feed and Seafood Festival.** Also around this time,

Florence's **Rhododendron Festival** and Brookings's **Azalea Festival,** both on the coast, attract blossom connoisseurs.

If you have kids in tow, take advantage in June of the parades, carnival rides, air shows, and floral splendor of Portland's **Rose Festival** or the Cannon Beach **Sandcastle Festival.** You could fill up July and August with such varied musical talents as the new vaudeville acts of the **Oregon Country Fair,** the gold-record performers at Jacksonville's **Peter Britt Music Festival,** not to mention the blues icons who appear at the **Waterfront Blues Festival** in Portland, the West Coast's largest.

During August, festival goers can toast their appreciation of Oregon at Portland's **Oregon Brewers Festival,** where more than 60 microbreweries are showcased, and the **Annual International Pinot Noir Festival** in McMinnville, attracting master vintners from around the world. Summer festival-hoppers might also want to take in **Da Vinci Days** in Corvallis, uniting the community's scientific and artistic elements, and Portland's **Bite,** featuring the best in food.

In the fall and winter, the leading events west of the Cascades include Mount Angel's **Oktoberfest,** the **Eugene Celebration,** the **Corvallis Fall Festival,** and Thanksgiving open houses in the wine country. At Christmastime the leading events are Albany's **Victorian Parlor tours,** Portland's **Christmas Ships,** and light displays all over the state.

While most of Oregon's celebrations take place west of the Cascades, there are notable exceptions to the rule. Bird-watchers relish the Klamath Basin **Bald Eagle Conference** in February and the springtime **John Scharff Migratory Waterfowl Conference** in Burns. Highbrows can take in the summertime literary festival at **Fishtrap** in the Wallowas or rock out at the **Bend Summer Fest** in central Oregon. Rockhounds flock to summer mineral shows in the central Oregon hamlets of Madras and Prineville. Rodeo fans can whoop and holler at the venerable **Pendleton Roundup** in September.

Such celebrations of ethnicity as Portland's **Cinco de Mayo** (one of the largest celebrations of this kind in the nation) and **Scandanavian festivals** in Astoria and Junction City express the state's diversity.

ESSENTIALS

Accommodations and Food

ACCOMMODATIONS

For extremely popular destinations, such as Cannon Beach and other coastal towns, plan to reserve well in advance during peak times, such as summer weekends and holidays. "Off-season" specials are a way to beat the crowds and the costs. For example, before Memorial Day and Labor Day room rates on the coast can drop by 25 percent or so, and in winter, even by 50 percent.

While there's no sales tax in Oregon, note that a local lodging tax—ranging 6–12 percent, depending on the locale—will be added to your bill. In addition, a recently implemented one percent statewide "transient lodging" tax, dedicated to tourism-promotion efforts, also applies.

OREGON CUISINE

Oregon has become known for its excellent restaurants, the most notable of which focus on using locally grown, raised, or gathered foods. Oregon's abundance of fresh produce, seafood, and other indigenous ingredients prompted America's apostle of haute cuisine, James Beard, to extol the restaurants and cooking of his home state. In his autobiography, *Delights and Prejudices,* he implies that Oregon strawberries, Seaside peas, Dungeness crab, and other local fare are the standards by which he judges culinary staples around the

© BILL MCRAE

world. This cornucopia is the basis of a regional cuisine emphasizing fresh natural foods cooked lightly to preserve flavor, color, and texture.

As for humbler fare, jo-jos (refried baked potato spears encased in spices, found mostly at truck stops), the patented Gardenburger (Portland's own version of the vegetarian hamburger), and marionberry jams, jellies, and pies are foodstuffs most likely to confound out-of-staters.

The marionberry is a purple berry whose tarter-than-blackberry taste and small seeds make it ideal for dessert fare, especially marionberry ice cream. Higher up on the food chain, world-class Oregon lamb and the seasonally available excellent fresh sturgeon, venison, and game birds are other little-known taste treasures here. Oregon specialties can be complemented with a world-class pinot noir, gourmet coffee, or microbrew.

Nonetheless, it is possible to have a bad meal in this state. In fact, the quality of the cuisine in some remote Oregon towns is a source of self-deprecating humor for the locals. And as many Yankees will tell you, there is no shortage of bland New England–style clam chowder on the Oregon coast.

LIQUOR AND MICROBREWERIES

Note Oregon's liquor laws: Liquor is sold by the bottle in state-sanctioned liquor stores only, open Monday–Saturday. Beer and wine are also sold in grocery stores and retail outlets. Liquor is sold by the drink in licensed establishments 7 A.M.–2:30 A.M. The minimum drinking age is 21.

Throughout the Northwest one encounters the popular phenomenon of microbreweries and pubs serving their own beers. Oregon has over 70 craft breweries, a third of them located in Portland, making beer without preservatives or chemical additives to enhance head or color. Instead of the rice or corn used by the big outfits, the micros just use barley, malt, hops, yeast, and water. The end result is a more full-bodied, tastier brew with a distinct personality.

The reason Oregon is awash in gourmet suds owes much to the availability of topnotch ingredients—hops, barley, and clear water. Almost a third of the world's hops are produced here in the Northwest. The Willamette Valley alone cultivates more than a dozen varieties. Add Cascade mountain water, malted barley from the Klamath basin, and Hood River–grown yeast cultures and you can see why there are more breweries and brewpubs per capita in Oregon than anywhere else in the United States.

One of the best opportunities to sample at least some of these fine brews is at the Oregon Brewers Festival, held in Portland in August.

Getting There and Around

BY CAR

For the vast majority of visitors (and residents), the automobile is the vehicle of choice for exploring the state. Speed limits top out at 65 mph on sections of I-5 and I-84; the rest of the roads in the state have a 55 mph maximum speed limit.

Many Oregon roads are strikingly beautiful. The magnificent scenery prompted the construction of the first paved public road in the state with the Columbia River Highway, constructed 1913–1915. Now known as the Historic Columbia River Gorge Highway, it is rated by AAA among the country's top 10 most scenic roads. The Oregon Coast Scenic Highway, U.S. 101 along the entire Oregon coast, is another internationally renowned drive. Entirely different in character, but equally stunning, is the Cascade Lakes Highway out of Bend.

Although the roads are beautiful, motorists must be sensitive to the weather and pavement conditions. Cloudbursts can cause cars to hydroplane, thick palls of fog that hang over the Willamette Valley can cause multicar pileups, and the icy mountain roads of the Cascades and eastern Oregon also claim their share of victims.

The Oregon Department of Transportation advises on **road conditions** by phone (503/588-2941 in Oregon, 800/977-6368 out of state) and via the TripCheck website (www.tripcheck.com).

Gas is readily available on the main routes, but finding it can be a little trickier in remote eastern Oregon, especially after 5 P.M. Fill up before you leave the city. Another thing to remember is that Oregon is one of the few states that does not have self-service gasoline outlets.

Winter Driving

The first rule to follow when rain, snow, or hail make pavement slick or fog reduces visibility is to slow down. From late fall to early spring, expect snow on the Cascade passes and I-5 through the Siskiyous; snow tires and/or chains are often required.

A **Sno-Park permit** is required to park at most ski areas and plowed parking lots leading to cross-country ski trails. Without the daily sticker or season pass in your left-hand window, a car left in a Sno-Park area can receive a $30 ticket. This permit is essentially a duty levied by the state to pay for the upkeep of parking and rest areas and for snowplowing in the mountains. Pick these up at a Department of Motor Vehicles office, ski shops, sporting goods stores, and other commercial establishments: $3/day, $7/three consecutive days, and $15/season. They apply to travel November 15–April 15.

BY AIR

It is a simple enough matter getting to and getting around Oregon by air. If there is a break in the weather, the views are breathtaking. (Get a window seat on the left side of the plane on a west-bound flight for close-up views of Mount Hood.) The main point of entry is Portland International Airport (PDX), which is serviced by over a dozen airlines.

Horizon Air (800/547-9308, www.horizon air.com), the commuter-league farm club of Alaska Airlines, connects Portland and a half-

dozen small airfields in the state (Bend/Redmond, Eugene/Springfield, Medford, Klamath Falls, North Bend/Coos Bay, and Pendleton) as well as numerous other cities around the western states. Horizon operates commuter prop planes with 10–40 seats. If you are sensitive to loud noises and pressure change, bring earplugs.

BY TRAIN

Thanks to **Amtrak**'s (800/872-7245, www.amtrak.com) high-speed Spanish-made Talgo trains, the stretch from Eugene to Vancouver, B.C. enjoys an efficient and scenic mass-transit link. Three *Cascades* trains make daily round-trips between Portland and Seattle, supplemented by another train from Seattle to Vancouver, B.C. Two trains go from Portland south to Eugene daily. The *Coast Starlight* runs between L.A. and Seattle with stops in Oregon at Klamath Falls, Chemult, Oakridge, Eugene, Salem, and Portland.

Note that getting a sleeper on the extremely popular *Coast Starlight* requires reservations 5–11 months in advance any time of the year. Those who take this route northbound from California will see why when the train crosses into Oregon. After riding all night from the San Francisco Bay Area, passengers wake up to sunrise over alpine lakes and the snowcapped Cascades. From the Cascade summit, you head down into Eugene along the beautiful Upper Willamette River.

The *Empire Builder,* which connects Portland with Chicago, shows off the Columbia River Gorge to good advantage in modern Superliner coaches. Trains run on the Washington side of the Columbia, giving a distant perspective on the waterfalls and mountains across the river. In summer, this train stops in Glacier Park, Montana.

Amtrak also runs bus service in such corridors as Portland to Eugene and Chemult to Bend. The latter service makes Bend accessible to *Coast Starlight* passengers who disembark in Chemult.

BY BUS

Greyhound (800/229-9424, www.greyhound.com) has cut most of its service to Oregon and now travels only along the freeway corridors of I-5 and I-84, but many smaller companies have picked up the slack. Pierce Pacific Stages, Porter, Valley Retriever, Gray Line, and other smaller companies operate on former Greyhound routes. Check www.tripcheck.com to find details on bus service to Oregon's cities and towns.

BY BICYCLE

Oregon is user-friendly to bicyclists. In the 1970s, the Oregon legislature allocated one percent of the state highways budget to develop bike lanes and encourage energy-saving bicyclists. In addition to establishing routes throughout the state with these funds, many special parks were developed with bicycle and foot access specifically in mind. For example, Eugene's Willamette River Greenway bikepath system winds through a string of parks. A decent biker can easily beat a car across town during rush hour using the bicycle network.

The Oregon Department of Transportation (503/986-3556, www.odot.state.or.us/techserv/bikewalk) produces some useful and free resources for cyclists, which can be ordered by phone or online. *The Oregon Bicycling Guide* includes statewide maps of bike trails and routing suggestions as well as listings for rental/repair shops and bike touring groups. Other publications include the *Oregon Coast Bike Route Map* and *Oregon Bicyclist Manual*.

Tips for Travelers

ENTRY REQUIREMENTS

Entry requirements are subject to change. For current information, see the U.S. Department of State's Bureau of Consular Affairs website (www.travel.state.gov). With the exception of Canadian citizens, all visitors from abroad must be in possession of a valid passport in order to enter the United States. Canadians need only present proof of citizenship, though a passport is recommended. Also required in most cases is a round-trip or return ticket, or proof of sufficient funds during a visit and to afford a return ticket. Visitors from most countries must also have a valid visa for entry. (See the State Department website, www.state.gov, for a current list of countries for which the visa requirement is waived.) Applicants for visitor visas should generally apply at the American embassy or consulate with jurisdiction over their place of permanent residence. Although visa applicants may apply at any U.S. consular office abroad, it may be more difficult to qualify for the visa outside the country of permanent residence.

TRAVELING WITH CHILDREN

Oregon is a great place to travel with kids, with plenty of attractions and activities to keep them interested. One of the first things travelers by car will notice is the ample number of rest stops, with one every 30–60 miles or so on most major routes. In most towns and cities, public parks offer play structures and open spaces where kids can burn off some energy. Many Oregon state parks offer excellent recreational opportunities for families such as guided hikes, nature programs, and campfire presentations.

Many B&Bs discourage children. Where possible, we've indicated policies (for and against) in accommodations listings, but it's always a good idea when making a reservation to inquire as to whether the lodging is appropriate for children.

TRAVELERS WITH DISABILITIES

Oregon is generally proactive with regard to providing accessible facilities for persons with disabilities, though there's always room for improvement. The great outdoors and some older buildings (lighthouses, for example), of course, can pose some insurmountable challenges, but many parks and recreation areas work to accommodate visitors with mobility issues. **Access-Able Travel Source** (303/232-2979, www.access-able.com) is a good resource for information on accessible travel.

The **Golden Access Passport,** which allows free entry to designated federal recreation areas such as national parks and monuments, BLM lands, and U.S. Fish and Wildlife sites, is available to those who are blind or permanently disabled. The pass is free to qualified applicants. Get details from the National Forest Foundation (877/465-2727, www.natlforests.org).

SENIORS

Elderhostel (877/426-8056, www.elderhostel. org) is a nonprofit organization that offers travelers aged 55 and over a full spectrum of affordable recreational and cultural experiences all over the world. Dozens of opportunities are usually available in Oregon at any given time, and may include such experiences as natural history courses on the coast, theater tours and performances at the Ashland Shakespeare Festival, train excursions, field trips to the desert, Columbia River cruises, and much more.

GAY AND LESBIAN TRAVELERS

In Portland, college towns such as Eugene and Corvallis, and most touristed areas, gay and lesbian visitors can expect to find progressive attitudes. In these places there are venues that specifically cater to same-sex couples. Outside of these places, one may find the attitude considerably less open and accepting; in more rural parts of the state, the attitude may be downright hostile. On the other hand, gays and lesbians live all over the state, and the relationships that these folks have built with their neighbors and co-workers often paves the way for acceptance of gay and lesbian travelers. In Portland, a free monthly magazine, *Just Out* (www.justout. com), is a useful resource, providing entertainment and events listings in the area as well as addressing political and social issues. Another useful resource, with some destination and travel-planning information for Oregon (as well as the rest of the world), is Gay .com's travel pages (www.gay.com/travel).

Health and Safety

EMERGENCY SERVICES

Throughout Oregon, dial 911 for medical, police, or fire emergencies. Most hospitals offer a 24-hour emergency room. Oregon's larger cities maintain switchboard referral services as well as hospital-sponsored free advice lines. Remember that medical costs are high here, as in the rest of the U.S. and emergency rooms are the most expensive for medical care; for non-emergency situations, look for urgency clinics. Also, several Rite-Aid drugstores in Portland have nurse practitioners on staff to deal with minor medical problems.

HEALTH HAZARDS
Hypothermia

In this part of the country, anyone who participates in outdoor recreation should be alerted to problems with hypothermia—when your body

loses more heat than can be recovered and shock ensues. The damp chill of the Northwest climate poses more of a hypothermia threat than do colder climes with low humidity. In other words, it doesn't have to be freezing in order for death from hypothermia to occur; wind and wetness often turn out to be greater risk factors. Remember that a wet human body loses heat 23 times faster than a dry one.

One of the first signs of hypothermia is a diminished ability to think and act rationally. Speech can become slurred, and uncontrollable shivering usually takes place. Stumbling, memory lapses, and drowsiness also tend to characterize the afflicted. Unless the body temperature can be raised several degrees by a knowledgeable helper, cardiac arrhythmia and/or arrest may occur. Getting out of the wind and rain into a dry, warm environment is essential for survival. This might mean placing the victim into a sleeping bag with another person. Ideally, a groundcloth should be used to insulate the sleeping bag from cold surface temperatures. Internal heat can be generated by feeding the victim high-carbohydrate snacks and hot liquids. Placing wrapped heated objects against the victim's body is also a good way to restore body heat. Be careful not to raise body heat too quickly, which could also cause cardiac problems.

Measures you can take to prevent hypothermia include eating a nutritious diet, avoiding overexertion followed by exposure to wet and cold, and dressing warmly in layers of wool and polypropylene. Wool insulates even when wet, and because polypropylene tends to wick moisture away from your skin, it makes a good first layer. Gore-Tex and other waterproof breathable fabrics make for more comfortable rain gear than nylon because they don't become cumbersome and hot in a steady rain. Finally, wear a hat: More radiated heat leaves from the head than from any other part of the body.

Frostbite

Frostbite is not generally a major problem until the combined air and wind-chill temperature falls below 20°F. Outer appendages such as fingers and toes are the most susceptible, with the ears and nose running a close second. Frostbite occurs when blood is redirected out of the limbs to warm vital organs in cold weather, and the exposed parts of the face and peripherals cool very rapidly. Mild frostbite is characterized by extremely pale skin with random splotchiness; in more severe cases, the skin will take on a gray, ashen look and feel numb. At the first signs of suspected frostbite, you should gently warm the afflicted area. In more aggravated cases, immerse hands and feet in warm water. Do not massage or you risk further skin damage. Warming frostbitten areas against the skin of another person is suitable for less serious frostbite. The warmth of a campfire cannot help once the skin is discolored. As with hypothermia, it's important to avoid exposing the hands and feet to wind and wetness by dressing properly.

Poison Oak

Neither the best intentions nor knowledge from a lifetime in the woods can spare the western Oregon hiker at least one brush with poison oak. Major infestations of the plant are seldom encountered in the Coast Range, but are prevalent in the Columbia Gorge. In the fall, the leaves are tinged with red. Even when the plant is totally denuded in winter, the toxicity of its irritating sap still remains a threat.

When hiking in hardwood forests, it's a good idea to wear long pants, shirts, and other covering. When you know you've been exposed, try to get your clothes off before the resin permeates your garments. Follow up as soon as possible by washing with Tecnu, a type of soap that seems to help remove the poison oak oil from skin. It's available at REI and at many drugstores. If you get the rash, cortisone cream is effective at temporarily quelling the intense itching.

Giardia

Medically known as giardiasis, but colloquially called "beaver fever," this syndrome afflicts those who drink water contaminated by *Giardia lamblia* parasites. Even water from cold, clear streams can be infested by this microorganism, which is spread throughout the backcountry by beavers, muskrats, livestock, and other hikers. Boiling water for 20 minutes or applying five drops of chlorine, or preferably iodine, to every quart of water and let it sit for a half hour are simple ways to kill the giardia spores. Backpackers should use water pumps that filter out giardia and other organisms.

Mosquitoes

Mosquitoes can be a problem particularly in the Cascades, the Willamette Valley, and parts of the Columbia River Gorge. Cutter's is a popular brand of repellent. Citronella-based products and other natural repellents are not toxic, and they work for a few hours before reapplication is necessary. When mosquitoes are present, it's a good idea to wear long pants and shirts to reduce the chance of getting bitten. Otherwise, you may want to stay indoors during prime mosquito time, around dusk.

Ticks

Of approximately 20 species of hard ticks found in Oregon, only four species are commonly found on humans. Of these, the western black-legged tick (also known as the Pacific tick and deer tick) is the only known carrier in the western United States of the bacterium that causes Lyme disease, a debilitating condition you do not want to catch.

The first sign of Lyme disease is a circular rash that appears within 3–30 days at the site of the bite, and gradually enlarges to several inches in diameter, clearing up at the center while staying red around the edges. The rash may be accompanied by flu-like symptoms, and it spreads all over the body in one out of two cases.

The second stage of the illness affects only about 15 percent of those infected, but the consequences can be severe. Inflammation of the nerves and covering tissues of the spinal cord and brain can often result in headaches, as well as memory loss and concentration problems. The heart can also be affected, resulting in decreased heart function and fainting spells. The last stage, characterized by aching joints, occurs weeks to years after the bite.

The disease can usually be cured with a 10-day dosage of antibiotics, if caught early. Delay in treatment can lead to serious complications. If you see the telltale red rash days or weeks after your romp in grassy, brushy, or wooded areas, see a doctor.

A prescription for prevention would be to lay the insect repellent on thickly before venturing into potentially infested areas. Also, be sure to check your body and clothing frequently during and after possible exposure. Ticks often may be found attached in the underarms, the groin, behind the knees, and at the nape of the neck.

If you find an attached tick, remove it promptly by grasping it with tweezers, as close to the skin as possible, and pulling it straight out, steadily and firmly. Don't twist, as this increases the chance of breaking off mouth parts and leaving them embedded in your skin. Afterward, wash up with soap and water, and apply an antiseptic to the bite area. The same routine applies to pets.

Information and Services

TRAVEL INFORMATION

The Oregon Tourism Commission (775 Summer St. N.E., Salem, 800/547-7842, www.traveloregon.com) is an outstanding resource for visitors and residents alike. The state-run organization maintains an exceptionally informative website and produces a number of useful free maps and publications, with extensive listings of lodgings and activities, suggested itineraries, events, and more.

Nine "welcome centers," located near the borders along major routes into the state, are a good first stop for newly arriving visitors. They stock literature and maps on the entire state, though their regional offerings tend to be best represented.

Other useful contacts are the Oregon Parks and Recreation Department (1115 Commercial St. N.E., Salem, 503/378-6305 or 800/551-6949, www.prd.state.or.us); the Bureau of Land Management (333 S.W. 1st Ave., Portland, 503/808-6002, www.or.blm.gov); and the National Forest Service (333 S.W. 1st Ave., Portland, 503/808-2971, www.fs.fed.us/r6/). All offer free information and maps on the specific recreation areas and preserves under their respective auspices.

For members only, AAA Oregon/Idaho (600 S.W. Market St., Portland, 503/222-6734 or 800/452-1643, www.aaaorid.com) provides free tour guides and high quality, detailed maps of the state, counties, and major towns.

In addition, several regional tourism authorities offer similar information and services for their corner of Oregon; see *Internet Resources* at the back of this book for a complete listing. Finally, the best sources for local information are the many chambers of commerce and visitor info centers operating in communities across the state. These are listed in the destination chapters.

MAPS

The visitor information offices noted above are all good sources for free state, regional, and town maps. Some of the best road and city maps available are those produced by AAA for their members.

Particularly useful for outdoor recreation is *Oregon Road & Recreation Atlas,* a large-format book of beautiful shaded-relief maps of the entire state, published by Benchmark Maps (800/237-0798, www.benchmarkmaps.com). The atlas is available in bookstores and sporting goods shops and directly from the publisher.

Trail Maps

Accurate trail and topo maps are worth their weight in gold for hikers, mountain bikers, anglers, and other outdoorspersons. Oregon maps published by the U.S. Geological Survey can be purchased at Powell's Technical Store in Portland for $7 each. If you plan to use many of these maps, consider buying them on a computer CD. DeLorme makes a good product called TopoUSA; its package for the western states retails for about $50 and is available at REI and other outdoor stores.

Another good series of paper maps is put out by Green Trails. Unlike USGS maps, these maps show trail mileage and campsites. Look for them at outdoor stores and ranger stations.

An excellent resource for trail and specialty maps and other outdoor information is **Nature of the Northwest** (800 N.E. Oregon St., Suite 177, Portland, 503/872-2750, www.naturenw.org).

MEDIA

The state's two largest-circulation dailies, the *Oregonian* and the *Eugene Register Guard,* come out of the most populous cities, Portland and Eugene. The *Oregonian* is distributed statewide, while the *Register Guard* is carried in newspaper dispensers as far away as the southern coast of Oregon.

Alternatives to the big dailies are found in a number of excellent tabloids, including Portland's *Willamette Week,* the *Eugene Weekly,* Astoria's monthly *Hipfish,* and others.

Portland and Eugene also dominate the broadcast media, serving far-flung rural communities by means of electronic translators. Oregon Public Broadcasting (www.opb.org) is also a statewide presence, both on TV and radio. Some standout TV programs of interest to visitors include the long-running "Oregon Field Guide," which explores natural history, outdoor recreation, travel, and environmental issues; and "Oregon Art Beat," which profiles local artists, craftspersons, and performers of all stripes.

Warm Springs Indian Reservation's KWSO 91.9 FM is a progressive country radio station spiced with elders chanting in the morning and topical discussions of native issues by younger tribe members. Other local stations of interest are listed in individual destination chapters.

Even though regional monthlies such as *Northwest Travel* and *Sunset* do not have a strictly Oregon focus, there are usually several destination pieces about the state in each edition of these magazines. *Oregon Coast* magazine confines its coverage to subjects closer to home. All these periodicals can be obtained at newsstands throughout the state.

TELEPHONES

Oregon has two area codes. **503** is in use for the greater Portland metropolitan area including Mount Hood and the westerly portion of the Columbia River Gorge, as well as Astoria to Lincoln City on the coast, and Portland to Salem in the Willamette Valley. It's **541** for the rest of the state. Refer to the area code map at the beginning of phone books if you are not sure of the long-distance prefix. Note that in Oregon you must dial the area code, even for local calls. For long-distance calls within the state, dial 1 before the correct area code and then the seven-digit telephone number. For directory assistance dial 1, the appropriate area code for the locale you are searching, and then 555-1212.

Cell phone users should be aware that service in some parts of Oregon—including mountainous regions, the southern coast, and the state's eastern areas—can be spotty to nonexistent. You may have to hunt around for that increasingly rare species, the phone booth, to make your call in those cases.

WEBSITES AND INTERNET ACCESS

Most hotels, visitor attractions, government agencies, and even restaurants have websites. We've included those websites that can help with planning or that enhance the travel experience.

Many hotels and motels offer rooms with Internet access, as do most libraries. Internet cafés, providing access by the hour, have largely been supplanted by cafés with wireless connectivity.

RESOURCES

Suggested Reading

In addition to the titles cited in the text, Oregon-bound travelers would do well to acquaint themselves with these books. We advise readers to search for out-of-print books at www.powells.com.

ATLASES

Benchmark Maps. *Oregon Road and Recreation Atlas.* Medford, OR: Benchmark Maps, 2005. Use this atlas to help plan your trip or as a travel companion. Lots of detail and shaded relief.

Loy, William G. *Atlas of Oregon.* Eugene: University of Oregon Press, 2001. Find graphic details on economy, climate, geology, and historic trails in this detailed, gorgeous reference atlas.

MacArthur, Lewis. *Oregon Geographic Names.* Portland: Oregon Historical Society, 2003. This text might be physically weighty, but its alphabetic historical rundown of place names makes for light and informative reading.

COASTAL OREGON

Gibbs, James A. *Shipwrecks of the Pacific Coast.* Portland: Binford and Mort, 1989. Endlessly fascinating and frequently heartbreaking reading from a master of Northwest maritime lore. Covers all known shipwrecks off the coasts of Oregon, Washington, and California.

Morris, Elizabeth and Mark. *Moon Coastal Oregon.* Emeryville: Avalon Travel Publishing, 2007. An expanded and more detailed version of the coastal Oregon chapters in this book.

O'Donnell, Terence. *Cannon Beach: A Place by the Sea.* Portland: Oregon Historical Society, 1996. A highly personal historical evocation of life in Cannon Beach and environs.

Ostertag, Rhonda, and George Ostertag. *75 Hikes in Oregon's Coast Range.* Seattle: Mountaineers Books, 2003. A well-chosen selection of hikes along the length of the coastal ranges covers a broad variety of terrain and difficulty levels. Detailed trail descriptions and maps make this guide particularly useful.

Sullivan, William L. *100 Hikes Travel Guide: Oregon Coast and Coast Range.* Eugene: Navillus Press, 2002. William Sullivan puts out the most carefully researched hiking guides in the business—we'd follow him down any trail!

EASTERN OREGON

Jackman, E. R., and R. A. Long. *The Oregon Desert.* Caldwell, ID: Caxton Press, 2003.

Jackman, E. R., John Scharff, and Charles Conkling (photographer). *Steens Mountain in Oregon's High Desert Country.* Caldwell, ID: Caxton Press, 2003. These two works are the classics for eastern Oregon. Within the volumes, history and local color fill in the east side of the state's wide-open spaces.

Kerr, Andy. *Oregon Desert Guide: 70 Hikes.* Seattle: The Mountaineers, 2000. Kerr, a well-known Oregon environmental activist, focuses on wilderness areas and those that deserve protection.

Sullivan, William L. *100 Hikes Travel Guide: Eastern Oregon.* Eugene: Navillus Press, 2001. Along with his usual well-researched hikes and detailed hand-drawn maps, Sullivan offers up a bit of history and a few travel recommendations.

FICTION

Davis, H. L. *Honey in the Horn.* Moscow, ID: University of Idaho Press, 2004. This reprint edition of a 1935 Pulitzer Prize-winning novel about rowdy southern Oregon settlers makes the pioneer days seem quite real.

Kesey, Ken. *The Last Go Round.* New York: Viking, 1994. The original prankster's latest Oregon-oriented effort is recommended reading for anyone seeking a little texture about the Pendleton Round-Up. Old photos and background information impart a sense of history, and the tensions among a white, a black, and a Nez Perce contestant during the 1911 rodeo will hold your interest.

Kesey, Ken. *Sometimes a Great Notion.* New York: Viking, 1964. This book is a fictional portrayal of what Mark Twain called the "westering spirit."

Lesley, Craig. *Winterkill.* New York: Picador, 1996. Native American characters make their way in the modern world.

GENERAL INTEREST

Adams, Melvin. *Netting the Sun.* Pullman, WA: Washington State University Press, 2001. Born and raised in eastern Oregon, Adams's passion for Oregon's high desert informs this collection of haunting and beautifully written essays.

Douglas, William O. *Of Men and Mountains.* San Francisco: Chronicle Books, 1985. The final chapters of the late Supreme Court Justice's autobiography provide some redolent descriptions of life in Oregon. Particularly evocative are his descriptions of the Wallowas.

Egan, Timothy. *The Good Rain.* New York: Alfred A. Knopf, 1990. Egan brings the practiced eye of a *New York Times* correspondent to towns along the Columbia and other parts of Oregon and Washington caught in the transition from a resource-based economy. The historical perspectives of a 19th-century diarist's entries underscore his descriptions of local color and contemporary issues.

Hadlow, Robert W. *Elegant Arches, Soaring Spans: C. B. McCullough, Oregon's Master Bridge Builder.* Corvallis, OR: Oregon State University Press, 2003. Covers the beautiful dozen bridges designed by McCullough between the two World Wars, which he called "jeweled clasps in a wonderful string of pearls."

Jewell, Judy. *Oregon.* New York: Fodor's Compass American Guides, 2005. Read this guide before traveling to the state to complement *Moon Oregon* as your on-the-road reference. Beautiful color photos and insightful travel tips liven up this literary rendition of Oregon's greatest hits.

Tisdale, Sallie. *Stepping Westward.* New York: Holt and Co., 1991. The award-winning essayist deftly blends fact and fancy. In her treatment of the past, present, and future of the Northwest, the Portland author emphasizes a native worldview.

GUIDEBOOKS

Barringer, Jody, and Ruth Berkowitz. *Kidding Around the Gorge.* Hood River, OR: Gorgebooks, 2003. A kid-tested list of activities for and places to take children in the Columbia River Gorge, with easy-to-follow driving directions.

Fanselow, Julie. *Traveling the Lewis and Clark Trail.* Helena, MT: Falcon Publishing, 2003. This guidebook for the modern-day explorer acquaints readers with what to see and do along Lewis and Clark's celebrated route from Illinois to Oregon.

Fanselow, Julie. *Traveling the Oregon Trail.* Guilford, CT: Globe Pequot Press, 2001. The adventures continue with Fanselow's scenic and informative guide to the present-day Oregon Trail.

Foster, Laura O. *Portland Hill Walks: Twenty Explorations in Parks and Neighborhoods.* Portland: Timber Press, 2005. Great walking guide will colorful commentary that will take you through Portland's neighborhoods.

Friedman, Ralph. *Oregon for the Curious.* Caldwell, ID: Caxton Ltd., 1972. Friedman is Oregon's King of the Road. Of his half-dozen books, this one is the most recommended. It still is the best mile-by-mile description of the state ever done.

Garren, John. *Oregon River Tours.* Portland: Garren Publishing, 1991. Detailed maps and charts make this an indispensable tool for anyone braving Oregon's white water.

Nix, Nell. *Out and About: Portland with Kids.* Portland: Sasquatch Books, 2002. A must-have for those exploring Portland with children.

HISTORY

Ambrose, Stephen. *Undaunted Courage.* New York, Touchstone Press: 1996. A classic book on the country's seminal voyage of discovery, the Lewis and Clark expedition. It gives a historical context to the explorers' journals in an entertaining, enlightening way. Read this before taking on *The Journals of Lewis and Clark* themselves. The latter work is available through many different publishers, but the antiquated grammar and archaic English make it difficult reading.

Beckham, Steven Dow, and Robert M. Reynolds (photographer). *Lewis & Clark from the Rockies to the Pacific.* Portland: Graphic Arts Center Publishing Co., 2002. Focusing on the second half of the expedition's outward-bound journey, this gorgeously illustrated and insightful book covers Lewis and Clark's trying months spent camped in the rainy woodlands of the northern Oregon coast.

Del Mar, David Peterson. *Oregon's Promise: An Interpretive History.* Corvallis: Oregon State University Press, 2003. Something of an alternative to more traditional histories of the state, this one focuses on the diversity of the people, and their varied experiences.

Federal Writers' Project (editor). *WPA Guide to Oregon.* The granddaddy of them all, this 1941 guide is the primary inspiration for *Moon Oregon.* The product of dozens of authors working in the Federal Writers' Project, this post-Depression guidebook still sets the standard for thorough coverage and vivid description. Although much of the information is dated, its rundown of pioneer history and glimpses of early 20th-century Oregon make it a valuable tool for any modern traveler. Available in many public libraries.

Friedman, Ralph. *In Search of Western Oregon.* Caldwell, ID: Caxton Press, 1991. A fascinating read, packed with anecdotes, folklore, historical details, and more, all told in Friedman's engaging style.

O'Donnell, Terrence. *Portland: An Informal History and Guide.* Portland: Oregon Historical Society, 1964. This book is widely available used, and makes for entertaining reading.

Oregon Secretary of State (editor). *Oregon Blue Book.* Salem, OR: State of Oregon, 2005. Published biannually by the state of Oregon, this volume provides the best concise history of Oregon and a wide assortment of facts about the state. Much of the text is available at http://bluebook.state.or.us.

Robbins, William G. *Landscapes of Promise: The Oregon Story 1800–1940.* Seattle: University of Washington Press, 1999. In this fascinating environmental history of Oregon, Robbins examines ways that Oregonians have interacted with the land; he shows that Native Americans altered the landscape in a number of ways, and that the landscape encountered by early white settlers was, in some areas, highly managed.

Smith, Landon. *The Essential Lewis and Clark.* New York: Ecco Press, 2000. Covers information similar to the dynamic duo's journals, yet provides a much easier read.

NATURAL HISTORY

Alt, David, and Donald W. Hyndman. *Roadside Geology of Oregon.* Missoula, MT: Mountain Press Publishing Company, 2003. This book's mile-by-mile approach makes it a good book to have in the car to answer your questions about Oregon's geology.

Bishop, Ellen Morris. *In Search of Ancient Oregon: A Geological and Natural History.* Portland: Timber Press, 2003. If you enjoy reading about geology, this is the book for you. Even if you are not so sure about your commitment to geological study, it's a good read, with lots of illustrative photos.

Evanich, Joseph E., Jr. *Birders Guide to Oregon.* Portland: Audubon Society of Portland, June 2003. A good all-around guide to the state's birdlife, with a useful breakdown of specific coastal locations and details on what species to watch for and when.

Jolley, Russ. *Wildflowers of the Columbia Gorge.* Portland: Oregon Historical Society Press, 1988. An exhaustive study of the gorge's plant species, with excellent color photos identifying 744 of the Columbia Gorge's more than 800 species of flowering shrubs and wildflowers.

Laskin, David. *Rains All the Time.* Seattle: Sasquatch Press, 1998. A fascinating inquiry into the region's rainforest-to-desert diversity.

Littlefield, Caroll D. *Birds of Malheur Refuge.* Corvallis, OR: Oregon State University Press, 1990. Recommended for serious birders.

Paulson, Dennis. *Shorebirds of the Pacific Northwest.* Seattle: University of Washington Press, 1998. For the specialist rather than the generalist, there is no better book than this richly detailed guide for distinguishing an avocet from a stilt, a plover from a curlew, and identifying any of the dozens of other species found near the water's edge. Unless you're a collector, borrow this out-of-print gem from the library.

Pojar, Jim, and Andy MacKinnon (editors). *Plants of the Pacific Northwest Coast: Washington, Oregon, British Columbia, and Alaska.* Edmonton, AB: Lone Pine Publishing, 2003. A highly regarded guide to the flora of the entire Northwest region, illustrated with excellent photos.

Sept, J. Duane. *The Beachcomber's Guide to Seashore Life in the Pacific Northwest.* Vancouver, BC: Harbour Publishing Company Limited, 1999. This ideal guide for the casual and curious observer aids in understanding the intertidal zone and in identifying more than 270 species encountered there, including crabs, clams and other mollusks, seaweeds, sea stars, sea anemones, and more.

Wallace, David Rains. *The Klamath Knot.* San Francisco: Sierra Club Books, 1984. An excellent book on the natural history of southern Oregon.

OUTDOOR RECREATION

Giordano, Pete. *The Soggy Sneakers Guide to Oregon Rivers.* Seattle: Mountaineers Books, 2004. An indispensable guide to Oregon's rivers, replete with maps, class ratings, gradient listings, river lengths, and best seasons to visit.

McMorris, Megan. *Foghorn Outdoors Oregon Hiking.* Emeryville, CA: Avalon Travel Publishing, 2004. Details more than 280 hikes throughout Oregon, including hiking tips and top ten lists of Oregon's best trails.

Stienstra, Tom. *Moon Oregon Camping.* Emeryville, CA: Avalon Travel Publishing, 2006. Details nearly 700 campgrounds across the state, with an excellent selection on the coast. Rich with tips on gear, safety, and other topics.

Sullivan, William L. *100 Hikes in Northwest Oregon and Southwest Washington.* Eugene: Navillus Press, 2006. Sullivan's excellent hiking guides also include 100 Hikes books for the Central Oregon Cascades, Southern Oregon, Eastern Oregon, and the Oregon Coast and Coast Range.

Internet Resources

Statewide Information and Services

All Oregon
www.all-oregon.com
A directory with links to over 5,000 Oregon websites including real estate, wineries, and the Oregon Trail.

Travel Oregon
www.traveloregon.com
A useful website with information about lodging, recreation opportunities, and a statewide calendar of events.

Regional Information and Services

Central Oregon Coast Association
www.orcoast.com
P.O. Box 2094
313 S.W. 2nd Street, Suite B
Newport, OR 97365
541/265-2064 or 800/767-2064

Central Oregon Visitors Association
www.covisitors.com
63085 N. Hwy. 97, Suite 107
Bend, OR 97701
541/389-8799 or 800/800-8334

Clackamas County Tourism Development Council
www.clackamas-oregon.com
P.O. Box 182
621 High Street
Oregon City, OR 97045
503/655-5511 or 800/647-3843

Columbia River Gorge Visitor's Association
www.crgva.org
404 W. 2nd Street
The Dalles, OR 97058
541/296-2231 or 800/98GORGE (800/984-6743)

Convention & Visitors Association of Lane County
www.visitlanecounty.org
P.O. Box 10286
115 W. 8th, Suite 190
Eugene, OR 97440
541/484-5307 or 800/547-5445

Convention & Visitors Bureau of Washington County
www.wcva.org
5075 S.W. Griffith Drive, #120
Beaverton, OR 97005
503/644-5555 or 800/537-3149

Eastern Oregon Visitors Association
www.eova.com
P.O. Box 1087
Baker City, OR 97814
541/523-9200 or 800/332-1843

Oregon Coast Visitors Association
www.VisitTheOregonCoast.com
P.O. Box 74
313 S.W. 2nd Street, Suite B
Newport, OR 97365
541/574-2679 or 888/628-2101

Oregon's Mt. Hood Territory
www.MtHoodTerritory.com
619 High Street
Oregon City, OR 97045
503/655-5511 or 888/622-4822

Portland Oregon Visitors Association
www.travelportland.com
701 S.W. Sixth Avenue, Suite 1
Portland, OR 97204
503/275-8355 or 877/678-5263

Southern Oregon Visitors Association
www.sova.org
P.O. Box 1645
Medford, OR 97504
541/779-4691 or 800/448-4856

Willamette Valley Visitors Association
www.oregonwinecountry.org
P.O. Box 965
300 2nd Avenue S.W.
Albany, OR 97321
541/928-0911 or 800/526-2256

Accommodations and Food

Oregon Bed and Breakfast Guild
www.obbg.org
Lists links to Oregon bed-and-breakfasts by region.

Oregon Lodging
www.oregon.com
All-Oregon lodging and travel guide.

Oregon Restaurants Network
www.oregonrestaurants.net
A comprehensive guide to Oregon's restaurants and culinary events.

Events and Entertainment

Oregon Arts Commission
www.oregonartscommission.org
A guide to public art, events, and galleries throughout the state.

Oregon Beer
www.oregonbeer.org
Proffers merchandise and features a calendar of statewide beer-related events and an extremely useful map of Oregon's microbreweries.

Oregon Endowment for the Humanities
www.oregonhum.org
Includes an amazingly thorough calendar of talks and lectures throughout the state.

Oregon Wine
www.oregonwine.org
Everything you ever wanted to know about Oregon wines, wineries, and events.

Wines Northwest
www.winesnw.com
A guide to the world of wine in the great Pacific Northwest (and a useful link to guides and driving services).

History

Haunted Places
www.ghostsandcritters.com
An eerie look into Oregon's underworld. Offers advice for novice ghost hunters and info about haunted places in the state.

Oregon Historical Society
www.ohs.org
A resource for Oregon history.

Outdoor Recreation and Camping

GORP
www.gorp.com
An online magazine focusing on outdoor recreational pursuits in Oregon.

Hiking and Backbacking
www.hikingandbackpacking.com/oregon.html
An online magazine about hiking and backpacking in the state.

Oregon Cycling Magazine Online
www.efn.org/ percent7Ecat/ ocycling/index.php
Useful information for Oregon cyclists including events, trails, safety tips, and more.

Oregon Department of Fish and Wildlife
www.dfw.state.or.us
Information on fishing and wildlife in Oregon.

Oregon Hiking
www.oregonhiking.com
Information on outdoor adventures such as hiking, snowshoeing, rafting, and climbing.

Oregon Road Runners Club
www.orrc.net
A community resource for runners and walkers listing info about events, training opportunities, and courses.

Ski Resorts
web.pdx.edu/~cyjh/orresorts.html
Administered by Portland State University, this comprehensive website lists links to all major ski areas in the state.

State Parks
www.oregonstateparks.org
Find a state park or a campsite, make a reservation, or download brochures.

U.S. Forest Service
www.fs.fed.us/r6
Links to national forests, camping information and reservation, ranger station contact info, maps and brochures, fees, passes, and permit info.

Windsor Nature Discovery, LLC
www.nature-discovery.com
An Oregon company specializing in marine life identification charts and posters of all the wildlife you will see on your trip to the coast.

Transportation

Amtrak
www.amtrak.com
Train schedules, fares, and booking information.

Greyhound
www.greyhound.com
Schedules, fares, and booking information.

Oregon Department of Transportation
www.tripcheck.com
Great site with webcams, road conditions, public transportation, and mileage calculator.

Portland International Airport
www.flypdx.com
Portland International Airport's website provides a list of carriers, ground transport, and other useful information on the area.

Weather

Oregon Climate Service
www.ocs.orst.edu
Weather information including forecasts, road conditions, ski conditions and reports, marine conditions, watches and warnings.

Index

FISHING

HIKING

MUSEUMS

STATE PARKS

XYZ

www.moon.com

For helpful advice on planning a trip, visit www.moon.com
for the **TRAVEL PLANNER** and get access to useful travel
strategies and valuable information about great places to
visit. When you travel with Moon, expect an experience that is
uncommon and truly unique.

HANDBOOKS | METRO | OUTDOORS | LIVING ABROAD